ESSAYS IN HONOR OF PETER C. B. PHILLIPS

ADVANCES IN ECONOMETRICS

Series Editors: Thomas B. Fomby, R. Carter Hill, Ivan Jeliazkov, Juan Carlos Escanciano, Eric Hillebrand, Daniel L. Millimet, Rodney Strachan and David Jacho-Chávez

Recent Volumes:

Volume 24: Measurement Error: Consequences, Applications and Solutions – Edited by Jane Binner, David Edgerton and Thomas Elger

Volume 25: Nonparametric Econometric Methods – Edited by Qi Li and Jeffrey S. Racine

Volume 26: Maximum Simulated Likelihood Methods and Applications – Edited by R. Carter Hill and William Greene

Volume 27A: Missing Data Methods: Cross-Sectional Methods and Applications – Edited by David M. Drukker

Volume 27B: Missing Data Methods: Time-Series Methods and Applications – Edited by David M. Drukker

Volume 28: DSGE Models in Macroeconomics: Estimation, Evaluation and New Developments – Edited by Nathan Balke, Fabio Canova, Fabio Milani and Mark Wynne

Volume 29: Essays in Honor of Jerry Hausman – Edited by Badi H. Baltagi, Whitney Newey, Hal White and R. Carter Hill

Volume 30: 30th Anniversary Edition – Edited by Dek Terrell and Daniel Millmet

Volume 31: Structural Econometric Models – Edited by Eugene Choo and Matthew Shum

Volume 32: VAR Models in Macroeconomics – New Developments and Applications: Essays in Honor of Christopher A. Sims – Edited by Thomas B. Fomby, Lutz Kilian and Anthony Murphy

ADVANCES IN ECONOMETRICS VOLUME 33

ESSAYS IN HONOR OF PETER C. B. PHILLIPS

EDITED BY

YOOSOON CHANG
Department of Economics, Indiana University Bloomington, Bloomington, IN, USA

THOMAS B. FOMBY
Department of Economics, Southern Methodist University, Dallas, TX, USA

JOON Y. PARK
Department of Economics, Indiana University Bloomington, Bloomington, IN, USA

United Kingdom – North America – Japan
India – Malaysia – China

Emerald Group Publishing Limited
Howard House, Wagon Lane, Bingley BD16 1WA, UK

First edition 2014

British Library Cataloguing in Publication Data
A catalogue record for this book is available from the British Library

ISBN: 978-1-78441-183-1
ISSN: 0731-9053 (Series)

ISOQAR
REGISTERED
Certificate Number 1985
ISO 14001

ISOQAR certified Management System, awarded to Emerald for adherence to Environmental standard ISO 14001:2004.

INVESTOR IN PEOPLE

CONTENTS

DEDICATION

This 33rd volume of *Advances in Econometrics* is dedicated to Professor Peter C. B. Phillips, one of the most respected scholars and teachers of econometrics in our time. Professor Phillips stands out universally in his scholarly work in terms of quality, quantity, and breadth. It is not an exaggeration to say that he has done foundational research in virtually all areas of econometrics including continuous time models, finite sample distributions, stationary and nonstationary time series, panel data models, Bayesian methods, and various issues in financial econometrics. In particular, his research has laid foundations for many important topics in the econometrics of time series and panel models. For example, the extensive existing literature on the asymptotic theory of time series and panel models with variables involving stochastic trends is all built upon his innovative theoretical contributions on the topics of unit roots and cointegrated models in one way or another. The editors of this volume are pleased to dedicate this volume to Professor Phillips in honor of the unprecedented contributions and everlasting intellectual impact of his research on our profession.

The majority of the research articles contained in this volume were presented at the 14th *Advances in Econometrics* Conference held at Southern Methodist University in Dallas, Texas, November 1–3, 2013. On Saturday, November 2, the conference honored Professor Phillips with a special recognition dinner in the beautiful Jones Great Hall in the Meadows Museum of Art on the SMU campus. The first picture below is of Professor Phillips giving an after dinner speech on his research and reflections on his students and his various professional pursuits. The second picture is of Professor Thomas Fomby, Senior Co-editor of the *Advances in Econometrics* series awarding Professor Phillips the *Advances in Econometrics* Lifetime Achievement Award given to him by the Editorial Board of *Advances in Econometrics* and Emerald Publishing Limited, the publisher of the *Advances in Econometrics* series. A facsimile of the inscription on Professor Phillips' *Advances in Econometrics* Lifetime Achievement Award is in the third frame below. The videos of Professor Phillips' dinner speech and an informal interview of Professor Phillips during the conference are available online at the Richard B. Johnson Center for Economics Studies website at http://www.smu.edu/Dedman/Academics/InstitutesCenters/RBJCenter under "Recent Multimedia."

Yoosoon Chang, Thomas B. Fomby, and Joon Y. Park
Editors

Emerald
Advances in Econometrics
Research Annual
Emerald Publishing, Ltd.
In Appreciation of
Peter C. B. Phillips
For Outstanding Research
in Econometrics and
Founding and Sustaining the
Econometric Theory Journal.
Awarded
November 2, 2013
Southern Methodist University
Dallas, Texas

LIST OF CONTRIBUTORS

Badi H. Baltagi	Department of Economics and Center for Policy Research, Syracuse University, Syracuse, NY, USA; Department of Economics, Leicester University, Leicester, UK
Yong Bao	Department of Economics, Purdue University, West Lafayette, IN, USA
Brendan K. Beare	Department of Economics, University of California – San Diego, La Jolla, CA, USA
Yoosoon Chang	Department of Economics, Indiana University, Bloomington, IN, USA
John Chao	Department of Economics, University of Maryland, College Park, MD, USA
Jin Seo Cho	School of Economics, Yonsei University, Seoul, South Korea
Thomas B. Fomby	Department of Economics and Richard B. Johnson Center for Economic Studies, Southern Methodist University, Dallas, TX, USA
Jiti Gao	Department of Econometrics and Business Statistics, Monash University, Melbourne, Australia
Eric Ghysels	Department of Economics and Department of Finance, University of North Carolina – Chapel Hill, Chapel Hill, NC, USA
Ryan Greenaway-McGrevy	Department of Economics, University of Auckland, Auckland, New Zealand

Chirok Han	Department of Economics, Korea University, Seoul, South Korea
Bruce E. Hansen	Department of Economics, University of Wisconsin, Madison, WI, USA
Javier Hidalgo	Department of Economics, London School of Economics, London, UK
Cheng Hsiao	Department of Economics, University of Southern California, Los Angeles, CA, USA; WISE, Xiamen University, Xiamen, China; Department of Quantitative Finance, National Tsinghua University, Hsinchu
Liang Hu	Department of Economics, Wayne State University, Detroit, MI, USA
Chihwa Kao	Department of Economics, Center for Policy Research, Syracuse University, Syracuse, NY, USA
Myungsup Kim	Department of Economics, University of North Texas, Denton, TX, USA
Maxwell King	Department of Econometrics and Business Statistics, Monash University, Melbourne, Australia
Jan F. Kiviet	Division of Economics, Nanyang Technological University, Singapore; Republic of Singapore and University of Amsterdam, Amsterdam, The Netherlands
Yong Li	Hanqing Advanced Institute of Economics and Finance, Renmin University of China, Beijing, China
Long Liu	Department of Economics, College of Business, University of Texas at San Antonio, San Antonio, TX, USA
Jungyoon Lee	Department of Economics, New College of the Humanities, London, UK

Esfandiar Maasoumi	Department of Economics, Emory University, Atlanta, GA, USA
Alex Maynard	Department of Economics, University of Guelph, Guelph, Canada
J. Isaac Miller	Department of Economics, University of Missouri, Columbia, MO, USA
Jerzy Niemczyk	European Central Bank, Frankfurt, Germany
Joon Y. Park	Department of Economics, Indiana University, Bloomington, IN, USA
Melinda Pitts	Federal Reserve Bank of Atlanta, Atlanta, GA, USA
Dongmeng Ren	Department of Economics, University of Guelph, Guelph, Canada
Yongcheol Shin	Department of Economics and Related Studies, University of York, York, UK
Kyungchul Song	Vancouver School of Economics, University of British Columbia, Vancouver, Canada
Donggyu Sul	Department of Economics, University of Texas at Dallas, Richardson, TX, USA
Yixiao Sun	Department of Economics, University of California – San Diego, La Jolla, CA, USA
Purevdorj Tuvaandorj	Department of Economics, McGill University, CIREQ, CIRANO, Montreal, Canada
Aman Ullah	Department of Economics, University of California – Riverside, Riverside, CA, USA
Igor Vaynman	Department of Economics, University of California – San Diego, La Jolla, CA, USA
Chi Wan	Department of Accounting and Finance, University of Massachusetts, Boston, MA, USA

Halbert White	Department of Economics, University of California – San Diego, La Jolla, CA, USA
Ke Wu	Department of Economics, Emory University, Atlanta, GA, USA
Zhijie Xiao	Department of Economics, Boston College, Chestnut Hill, MA, USA
Jun Yu	School of Economics and Lee Kong Chian School of Business, Singapore Management University, Singapore, Republic of Singapore
Tao Zeng	Economics and Management School, Wuhan University, Wuhan, China
Ru Zhang	Department of Economics, University of California – Riverside, Riverside, CA, USA
Victoria Zinde-Walsh	Department of Economics, McGill University, CIREQ, CIRANO, Montreal, Canada

INTRODUCTION

This 33rd volume of *Advances in Econometrics* in honor of Peter C. B. Phillips is a collection of 20 articles contributed by his students, former colleagues and academic friends on various issues in econometrics covering a wide range of subfields in econometrics. The volume is divided into four parts and each part presents contributed articles that are more closely related with each other in terms of topics. The four parts consist of Part I: Persistence and Trend, Part II: Panel Data Models, Part III: Issues in Econometric Theory, and Part IV: Theory and Application of Time Series.

Part I contains the articles on the subject of persistence and trend, and starts with Bruce E. Hansen's contribution, "Asymptotic Moments of Autoregressive Estimators with a Near Unit Root and Minimax Risk." He provides a method of obtaining the moments of the asymptotic distribution of the least-squares estimator of the local-to-unity autoregressive model by computationally simple integration, and finds that the required size of simulation sample to achieve a preset level of accuracy increases sharply as the autoregressive coefficient becomes closer to unity. The article also studies the minimax efficiency of autoregressive coefficient and computationally shows that simple Stein shrinkage estimation uniformly outperforms least squares even for the one-dimensional case.

Yixiao Sun's contribution, "Fixed-smoothing Asymptotics and Asymptotic F and t Tests in the Presence of Strong Autocorrelation," derives a fixed-smoothing asymptotic theory for the Wald and t statistics in models with near unit root and weak unit root processes, which nicely extends the conventional stationary fixed-smoothing asymptotics. In particular, the article shows that the new fixed-smoothing asymptotic distribution changes smoothly from the unit-root fixed-smoothing asymptotic distribution to the stationary fixed-smoothing asymptotics as the locality parameter increases from zero to infinity. The new asymptotic theory also provides asymptotic approximations for the Wald and t tests that are shown to be more accurate than the usual fixed-smoothing approximations.

Yong Bao, Aman Ullah, and Ru Zhang contribute the article "Moment Approximation for Least-Squares Estimator in First-Order Regression Models with Unit Root and Nonnormal Errors." It considers moments of the least-squares estimator in the first-order autoregressive model with a unit root and nonnormal errors. The article extends the existing results for stationary autoregressive models and models with normal errors. The authors obtain new analytical approximations for the first two moments in terms of model parameters and the distribution parameters. It is shown that, unless the noise-to-signal ratio is too high, the new approximation formula works quite well in small samples across many different error distributions.

Eric Ghysels and J. Issac Miller present the article "On the Size Distortion from Linearly Interpolating Low-frequency Series for Cointegration Tests." It analyzes the effect of linear interpolation of low-frequency observations on cointegration tests under a mixed-frequency setup. The article obtains the limit distributions of standard cointegration tests when they are applied to data subject to linear interpolation, and shows that linear interpolation introduces additional terms in the limit distributions of standard cointegration tests. Upon finding that the presence of additional terms results in substantial size distortions, the authors propose modifications to the standard cointegration tests to effectively eliminate size distortions.

Liang Hu and Yongcheol Shin are authors the article "Testing for Cointegration in Markov Switching Error Correction Models." This article follows a commonly used approach and considers testing for cointegration in the error correction model, rejecting the null hypothesis of no cointegration in favor of cointegration when the error correction term of the model is significant. However, the authors consider a more plausible alternative hypothesis – cointegration given by error correction with markov switching – and propose an optimal test to increase the power of the test. In fact, they show that the proposed test displays superior power compared to the usual test against the linear error correction model. In an application to price-dividend relationships, the test reveals cointegration that the usual tests fail to find.

Jiti Gao and Maxwell King's contribution, "Specification Testing in Parametric Trending Models with Unknown Errors," deals with the specification test for error process in the standard linear regression model. The dynamics of the error process is specified as the parametric nonlinear first-order autoregressive process, which accommodates many interesting models including nonstationary unit root process. Such a specification can be very useful, for instance, to estimate the form of the errors and test for stationarity and non-stationarity simultaneously. The article develops the asymptotic distribution of the proposed test and provides both simulations and real-data examples to show the usefulness of the test.

Part II presents the articles on the topic of panel data models and begins with Cheng Hsiao's work, "Panel Macroeconometric Modeling." His article provides a survey of the panel macroeconometric techniques that are useful to control unobserved heterogeneities across individuals and over time and obtain valid inferences on the common structures invariably existing across individuals and over time. Various issues including the estimation of vector autoregressive models, testing for unit root and cointegration, statistical inference in dynamic simultaneous equations models, and aggregation and prediction are considered in the article.

John Chao, Myungsup Kim, and Donggyu Sul present the article "Mean Average Estimation of Dynamic Panel Models with Nonstationary Initial Condition." It proposes a new class of estimators for the autoregressive coefficient of a dynamic panel data model with a random individual effect and a general form of nonstationary initial condition. The proposed estimators are weighted averages of the first difference GMM/IV estimator and the pooled ordinary least squares estimator, utilizing the differing advantages of the two estimators: the former is known to perform well when the autoregressive coefficient is away from unity, while the latter has a faster rate of convergence when the autoregressive coefficient is unity. The proposed class of estimators average the two estimators in an appropriate way so that they behave nicely for both stationary and unit root cases.

Ryan Greenaway-McGrevy, Chirok Han, and Donggyu Sul contribute the paper "Efficient Estimation and Inference for Difference-in-Difference Regressions with Persistent Errors" which is concerned with estimation of and testing for difference-in-differences in panels with possibly persistent and trending errors. The authors rely on the X-differencing transformation to estimate the autoregressive dynamics of the error process in the first stage, and then use the estimated autoregressive structure of error dynamics to do inference on the underlying panel regressions more efficiently. The proposed approach is simple and more flexible compared with other existing methods.

Javier Hidalgo and Jungyoon Lee, in their article "A CUSUM Test for Common Trends in Large Heterogeneous Panels," examine a class of nonparametric CUSUM-type tests for common trends in large panel data sets with individual fixed effects. The tests are based on the partial sum processes constructed from cross-sectionally demeaned panel observations, which are expected to have discriminatory power between the models with common trends and those with trends that vary cross-sectionally. The tests do not involve local smoothing that requires the choice of a bandwidth parameter. The authors show that their test statistics converge to the functionals of Gaussian processes.

In their article "Test of Hypotheses in a Time Trend Panel Data Model with Serially Correlated Error Component Disturbances" Badi H. Baltagi, Chihwa Kao, and Long Liu study testing for the time coefficient in the panel regression model with linear time trend and first-order autoregressive errors. In particular, they consider the test based on the fixed effects feasible generalized least squares estimator, which uses a bias corrected estimator for the autoregressive parameter of the error process. Assuming both cross-sectional and time dimensions go to infinity, they show that their test statistic has the standard normal limiting distribution when the error process has a unit root as well as when they are stationary.

Part III consists of the articles dealing with various issues in econometric theory and starts with the contribution by Purevdorj Tuvaandorj and Victoria Zinde-Walsh, "Limit Theory and Inference about Conditional Distributions." Their article explores the asymptotics based on generalized functions, and regards conditional distribution and conditional density as elements in the space of generalized functions that is formally defined as the dual space of well-behaved test functions. Using such asymptotics, in particular, the authors obtain the limit of the kernel estimators for weakly dependent data without differentiability of the distribution function, and the limit Gaussian process is characterized as a stochastic random generalized function.

Jan F. Kiviet and Jerzy Niemczyk contribute the article "On the Limiting and Empirical Distributions of IV Estimators When Some of the Instruments Are Actually Endogenous." It investigates the effect of invalid instruments especially in comparison with that of weak instruments. The authors analyze the limit distribution of inconsistent IV and examine normal first-order asymptotic approximations to its density in finite samples. They find that, with respect to the accuracy of large sample approximations, instrument weakness is much more detrimental than instrument invalidity. Moreover, IV estimators using invalid but strong instruments are usually much closer to the true parameter values than those obtained from valid but weak instruments.

Jin Seo Cho and Halbert White provide the article "Testing the Equality of Two Positive-Definite Matrices with Application to Information Matrix Testing." They introduce a new characterization of the equality of two positive-definite matrices, and use it to construct simple and convenient tests for the equality of two unknown positive-definite matrices. Their tests are applied to the information matrix equality hypothesis in a variety of models including linear regression, exponential duration, probit and Tobit models. The authors find that the critical values obtained by a parametric bootstrap are quite precise even in very small samples, and the tests implemented with the bootstrap critical values generally perform very well.

In his article "Minimax Estimation of Nonregular Parameters and Discontinuity in Minimax Risk," Kyungchul Song considers the situation where a parameter of interest is non-differentiable in probability so that the existing theory of semiparametric efficient estimation is not applicable, and develops a useful minimax estimation theory that is more widely applicable. The article extends the existing local asymptotic minimax theory to allow for a wider class of parameters that are nonregular, and investigates the discontinuity of local asymptotic minimax risk and the local robustification of risk.

Esfandiar Maasoumi, Melinda Pitts, and Ke Wu present the article "The Gap between the Conditional Wage Distributions of Incumbents and the Newly Hired Employees: Decomposition and Uniform Ordering." They analyze the gap between the conditional wage distributions of incumbents and the newly hired employees. By identifying counterfactual distributions and comparing them with observed conditional distributions using a metric entropy measure and stochastic dominance, the authors find interesting facts on the wage differentials between the incumbents and the newly hired employees.

Part IV includes the articles on the theory and application of time series and begins with the article of Tao Zeng, Yong Li, and Jun Yu, "Deviance Information Criterion for Comparing VAR Models." To determine the best candidate model among alternative Bayesian VAR models estimated by MCMC methods, the article employs a robust version of deviance information criterion (RDIC) that is known to perform better than the widely used deviance information criterion (DIC) in cases where candidate models involve latent variables. It is demonstrated that, for VAR models fitted using US data, the optimal model selected by RDIC can be different from that chosen by DIC.

In their article "Stable Limit Theory for the Variance Targeting Estimator," Igor Vaynman and Brendan K. Beare propose the variance targeting estimator as an alternative to the QMLE for GARCH processes. The new estimator is computationally simpler and robust to model misspecification. The authors study the asymptotic properties of the estimator and establish a stable limit distribution theory when the stationary distribution of the GARCH process has infinite fourth moment. The rate of convergence of the new estimator is determined by the tails of the distribution and is slower than that achieved by the QMLE. Moreover, its limit distribution is non-degenerate but singular.

Alex Maynard and Dongmeng Ren present the article "Assessing the Power of Long-Horizon Predictive Tests in Models of Bull and Bear Markets." They consider the test for predictability in short and long horizons based on the regression involving regime switching between bull and bear markets with time varying transition probabilities, and compares its finite sample power with that of the test based on the usual linear predictive regression model without regime switching. The authors cannot find a desirable level of power for any long horizon test in the linear or nonlinear regime switching models.

Last in the volume but certainly not least is Chi Wan and Zhijie Xiao's article "Idiosyncratic Volatility, Expected Windfall, and the Cross-Section of Stock Returns." They investigate the role of idiosyncratic risk in determining cross-sectional returns, on which the existing literature provides undecided and even conflicting evidences. The authors analyze the effect of skewness in stock returns on the seemingly contradicting observed relationships between idiosyncratic risk and cross-sectional returns. In particular, by employing a new estimator for idiosyncratic risk that is more robust against nonnormal innovations and using the notion of the expected windfall as an alternative measure of return skewness, they manage to solve a major piece of the idiosyncratic volatility puzzle.

Yoosoon Chang
Thomas B. Fomby
Joon Y. Park
Editors

PART I
PERSISTENCE AND TREND

ASYMPTOTIC MOMENTS OF AUTOREGRESSIVE ESTIMATORS WITH A NEAR UNIT ROOT AND MINIMAX RISK

Bruce E. Hansen

Department of Economics, University of Wisconsin, Madison, Wisconsin, USA

ABSTRACT

These moments of the asymptotic distribution of the least-squares estimator of the local-to-unity autoregressive model are computed using computationally simple integration. These calculations show that conventional simulation estimation of moments can be substantially inaccurate unless the simulation sample size is very large. We also explore the minimax efficiency of autoregressive coefficient estimation, and numerically show that a simple Stein shrinkage estimator has minimax risk which is uniformly better than least squares, even though the estimation dimension is just one.

Keywords: Minimax; efficiency; unit root; autoregression; shrinkage; moments

JEL classification: C22

Essays in Honor of Peter C. B. Phillips
Advances in Econometrics, Volume 33, 3–21

ISSN: 0731-9053/doi:10.1108/S0731-905320140000033001

1. INTRODUCTION

In a series of seminal contributions, Phillips (1987a, 1987b) and Phillips and Perron (1988) developed an asymptotic theory of inference for unit roots in autoregressive models. A core component of this theory is the near-unit-root model which is parameterized by a localizing parameter c. This model has been the foundation for nearly all subsequent work in nonstationary time series econometric theory.

A key feature of this theory is that it yields simple expression for asymptotic distributions as functions of continuous-time Brownian motions and diffusion processes indexed by c. An inconvenience is that analytic expressions for the distributions are not available. The standard view is that this is not a problem, as the distributions can always be simulated. And indeed numerical calculation of nonstationary asymptotic distributions by simulation is the standard approach. Important examples include MacKinnon (1994)'s calculation of asymptotic critical values and Stock (1991)'s calculation of quantiles for confidence interval construction. A recent example is of Phillips (2014) who examines confidence interval construction.

Following Nabeya (1999), we show that moments of the asymptotic distribution can be calculated by direct integration. This is computationally much simpler (a matter of minutes) and more accurate. As a by-product of our calculations, we find that simulation estimation of near-unit-root distributions for large values of c requires very large sample sizes, much larger than those used in conventional practice.

We also explore the issue of efficient estimation in the near-unit-root model. Ploberger and Phillips (2012) have recently argued that while the OLS estimator is non standard, it is minimax efficient in a certain sense. We argue that their argument is incomplete, that it ignores the unbounded nature of estimation variance in the local-to-unit model. We show numerically that a standard Stein shrinkage estimator uniformly dominates the OLS estimator and can be viewed as dominating OLS in a minimax sense. This result suggests that efficiency is an open question ready to be explored.

This paper is organized as follows. Section 2 introduces the local-to-unit model, its asymptotic moments, and the main theoretical contribution of the paper, which is an expression for the moments in terms of a simple integral. Section 3 presents numerical computation of the moments by both integration and simulation. Section 4 presents a discussion of minimax efficiency. Section 5 introduces the Stein-type shrinkage estimator and contrasts its asymptotic risk versus OLS by numerical simulation. Section 6 is a conclusion, and Section 7 contains the proof of Theorem 1.

A Gauss program which creates the numerical work reported in this paper is available on the author's webpage http://www.ssc.wisc.edu/~bhansen/

2. MOMENTS OF THE ASYMPTOTIC DISTRIBUTION

Take the classic AR(1) with a near unit root

$$y_t = \alpha_n y_{t-1} + e_t \tag{1}$$

$$\alpha_n = 1 + c/n \tag{2}$$

with e_t zero mean white noise and $y_0 = 0$. Let $\hat{\alpha}_n$ denote the OLS estimator of α. As shown by Chan and Wei (1987) and Phillips (1987b)

$$n(\hat{\alpha}_n - \alpha_n) \to_d \frac{U_c}{V_c} \tag{3}$$

as $n \to \infty$, where $U_c = \int_0^1 W_c \mathrm{d}W$ and $V_c = \int_0^1 W_c^2$. In this expression, $W(r)$ denotes a standard Brownian motion, and $\mathrm{d}W_c(r) = cW_c(r)\mathrm{d}r + \mathrm{d}W(r)$ is a standard diffusion process.

Define the rth moment of the asymptotic distribution (3):

$$\mu_r(c) = E\left(\frac{U_c}{V_c}\right)^r \tag{4}$$

The main theoretical contribution of the paper is a convenient expression for $\mu_r(c)$ as a simple integral.

Theorem 1. For any integer $r \geq 1$ and $c \leq 0$,

$$\mu_r(c) = \sum_{j=0}^{r} \binom{r}{j} (-c)^{r-j} \int_0^1 g_j(x, c)\mathrm{d}x \tag{5}$$

where

$$g_j(x,c) = \frac{2^{3/2-2j}\lambda(x,c)(\lambda(x,c)^2 - c^2)^{j-1}}{(j-1)!(1-x)^2 e^{x/(2-2x)}(1+e^{-2\lambda(x,c)})^{1/2}} \times \sum_{\ell=0}^{j} \binom{j}{\ell} \frac{(-1)^{j-\ell}(2\ell-1)!!\psi(\lambda(x,c))^{\ell}}{(1-c\psi(\lambda(x,c)))^{1/2+\ell}}$$

with $\lambda(x,c) = x/(1-x) - c$ and $\psi(u) = \tan h\,(u)/u$ with $\psi(0) = 1$. The notation $a!!$ is the double factorial defined as $a!! = 1 \cdot 3 \cdots a$ with the convention $a!! = 1$ for $a < 0$. ■

Theorem 1 restricts the near-unity parameter c to be nonpositive, and thus does not cover the locally explosive case. The technical reason for this restriction is due to one of the change of variables used in obtaining Eq. (5); it could be avoided by alternative manipulations. The representation Eq. (5) is particularly convenient, however, as the functions $g_j(x,c)$ (with $c \leq 0$) are free of poles on [0, 1] and thus numerical integration is well behaved.

Theorem 1 gives an integral representation for the exact moments of the local-to-unity asymptotic distribution. This extends Nabeya (1999) who provided an integral representation for the exact moments in the case $c = 0$.

There is a long history of papers investigating asymptotic expansions for asymptotic bias and variance of $\hat{\alpha}_n$, including White (1961), Shenton and Johnson (1965), and Shenton and Vinod (1995). Most recently, Phillips (2012, Theorem 3) provides an integral representation of the finite sample bias of $\hat{\alpha}_n$, and Phillips (2012, Theorem 4) provides asymptotic expansions for the bias. Theorem 1 above is complementary to these results, as it provides an exact integral representation for the asymptotic local-to-unity model.

3. CALCULATION OF ASYMPTOTIC MOMENTS

We calculated the integrals in Eq. (5) by numerical integration.[1] We divided the interval [0, 1] into 100 intervals of length 1/100, and over each interval numerically integrated using Gauss–Legendre quadrature with 40 grid-points in each interval. We calculated the first four moments, and then transformed into conventional cummulants, including the mean $\mu_1(c)$, variance

$$\sigma^2(c) = \mu_2(c) - \mu_1(c)^2$$

skewness

$$\text{skew}(c) = \frac{\mu_3(c) - 3\mu_2(c)\mu_1(c) + 2\mu_1(c)^3}{\sigma^{3/2}(c)}$$

and kurtosis

$$\text{kurtosis}(c) = \frac{\mu_4(c) - 4\mu_3(c)\mu_1(c) + 6\mu_2(c)\mu_1(c)^2 - 3\mu_1(c)^4}{\sigma^4(c)}$$

These four cummulants are reported in Table 1 (for $c=0$ to $c=-20$ in steps of 1) and in Table 2 (for $c=-40$ to $c=-400$ in steps of 20). The values for $c=0$ are identical to those reported in Nabeya (1999).

Table 1. Asymptotic Cummulants: $c=0$ to -20.

	Mean	Variance	Skewness	Kurtosis
$c=0$	−1.781	10.11	−2.270	11.37
$c=-1$	−1.882	11.76	−2.068	9.971
$c=-2$	−1.930	13.54	−1.901	8.887
$c=-3$	−1.954	15.41	−1.759	8.043
$c=-4$	−1.968	17.33	−1.640	7.385
$c=-5$	−1.976	19.27	−1.539	6.886
$c=-6$	−1.981	21.23	−1.453	6.451
$c=-7$	−1.985	23.20	−1.379	6.112
$c=-8$	−1.988	25.18	−1.315	5.831
$c=-9$	−1.990	27.16	−1.258	5.596
$c=-10$	−1.991	29.15	−1.208	5.395
$c=-11$	−1.992	31.13	−1.163	5.223
$c=-12$	−1.993	33.12	−1.123	5.073
$c=-13$	−1.994	35.11	−1.086	4.942
$c=-14$	−1.995	37.11	−1.053	4.826
$c=-15$	−1.995	39.10	−1.023	4.723
$c=-16$	−1.996	41.09	−0.9947	4.631
$c=-17$	−1.996	43.09	−0.9689	4.548
$c=-18$	−1.997	45.08	−0.9449	4.473
$c=-19$	−1.997	47.08	−0.9226	4.405
$c=-20$	−1.997	48.07	−0.9018	4.343

Table 2. Asymptotic Cummulants: $c=-40$ to -400.

	Mean	Variance	Skewness	Kurtosis
$c=-40$	−1.997	89	−0.6546	3.711
$c=-60$	−1.999	129	−0.5390	3.483
$c=-80$	−2.000	169	−0.4687	3.365
$c=-100$	−2.000	209	−0.4203	3.294
$c=-120$	−2.000	249	−0.3843	3.246
$c=-140$	−2.000	289	−0.3562	3.211
$c=-160$	−2.000	329	−0.3335	3.185
$c=-180$	−2.000	369	−0.3146	3.165
$c=-200$	−2.000	409	−0.2986	3.148
$c=-220$	−2.000	449	−0.2848	3.135
$c=-240$	−2.000	489	−0.2728	3.124
$c=-260$	−2.000	529	−0.2622	3.114
$c=-280$	−2.000	569	−0.2527	3.106
$c=-300$	−2.000	609	−0.2442	3.099
$c=-320$	−2.000	649	−0.2365	3.093
$c=-340$	−2.000	689	−0.2295	3.088
$c=-360$	−2.000	729	−0.2230	3.083
$c=-380$	−2.000	769	−0.2171	3.079
$c=-400$	−2.000	809	−0.2116	3.075

The exact moments can be compared to estimated moments from simulations. The rth finite sample moment approximation to the asymptotic distribution is

$$\mu_r(c,n)=E\left(\frac{\frac{1}{2}\left(\frac{1}{n}y_n^2-1\right)}{\frac{1}{n^2}\sum_{t=1}^{n-1}y_{t-1}^2}\right)^r$$

which approaches $\mu_r(c)$ as $n\to\infty$. (This yields a better approximation to the asymptotic distribution than using, say, $E(n(\hat{\alpha}_n-\alpha_n))^r$, and thus is the standard method for simulation estimation of the asymptotic distribution.)

Unit root distributions are typically calculated by simulation with large values of n, including $n=500$ in early papers and $n=1,000$ in later papers. We calculated the same moments (and cummulants) by simulation using 1,000,000 simulation replications and $n=500$, $n=1,000$, $n=10,000$, and $n=100,000$. The results are presened graphically in Fig. 1 (for c ranging from −20 to 0) and in Fig. 2 (for c ranging from −400 to 0).

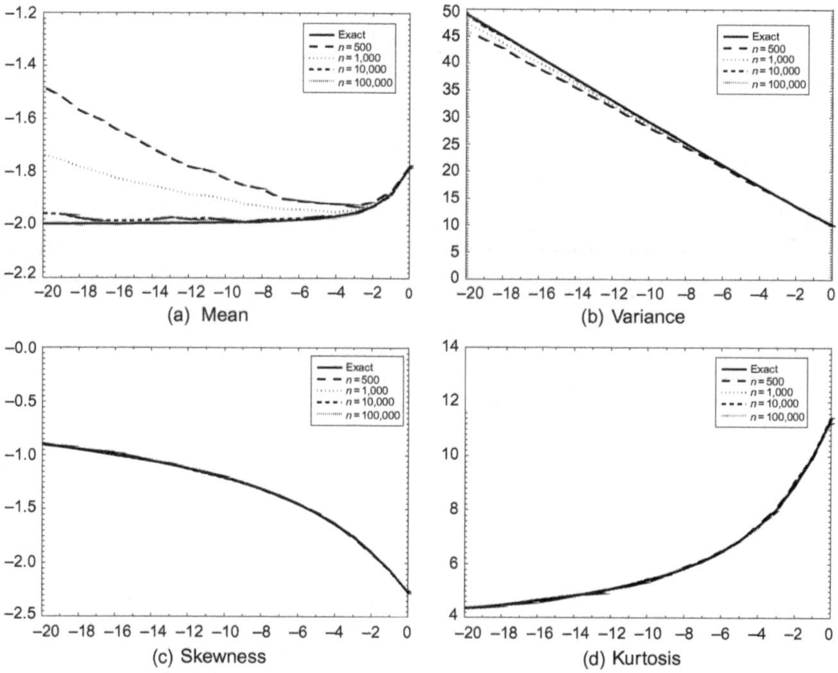

Fig. 1. Numerical Integration versus Numerical Simulation, $-20 \leq c \leq 0$.

Examining the figures, we can see that the simulation moment estimates can be quite poor unless n is very large. The discrepancy is worst for the low order moments. In particular, the simulation estimate of the mean with $n = 500$ and $n = 1{,}000$ is far from accurate even for small values of c. The simulation estimates of the variance are reasonably accurate for small c, but are quite inaccurate for large c, unless n is very large. The simulation estimates of skewness and kurtosis, however, are excellent even for small n.

The errors displayed in the figures show that for reasonable accuracy (except for very small c), the simulation estimate requires setting $n = 100{,}000$. This is surprisingly large, and much larger than the values used in existing studies. For example, Stock (1991) used $n = 500$ to calculate the distributions for c as large as $c = -38$. Phillips (2014) used $n = 10{,}000$ to calculate distributions for c as large as $c = -450$. Our calculations suggest that these values of n are much too small.

As an additional advantage, numerical integration is less computationally time-consuming than simulation. All the results reported in this paper

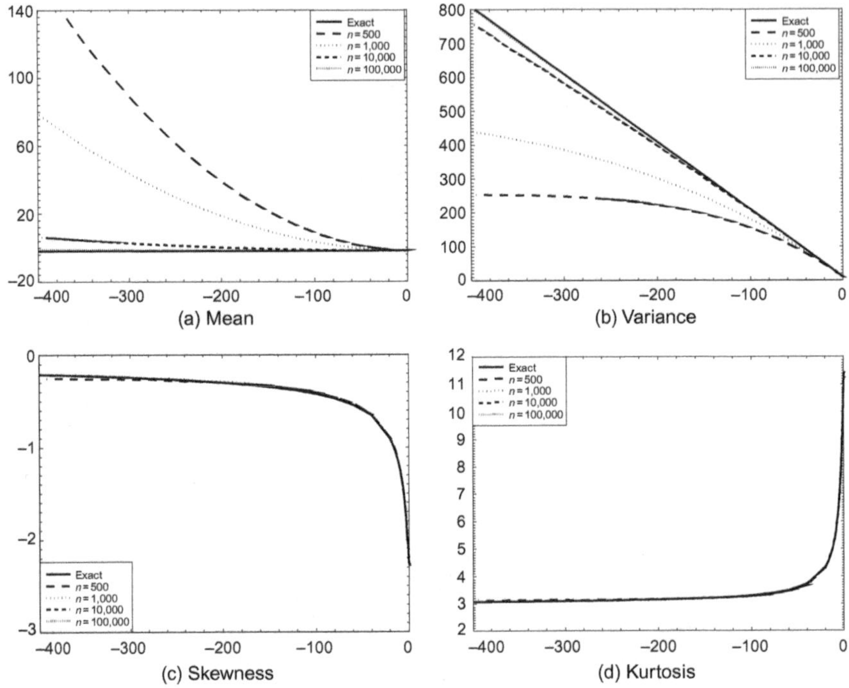

Fig. 2. Numerical Integration versus Numerical Simulation, $-400 \leq c \leq 0$.

were computed in just a few minutes on an office PC. In contrast, the simulation results took six days to compute, though a referee has suggested that more efficient programming can reduce the computation to a matter of hours.

4. MINIMAX EFFICIENCY

Is the OLS estimator $\hat{\alpha}_n$ efficient for α_n? Ploberger and Phillips (2012) argue that it is in a certain sense. We re-investigate this question.

We start by reviewing the classic theory of estimation efficiency developed by Hájek (1970, 1972), Le Cam (1982), and van der Vaart (1998) in the locally asymptotic normality (LAN) case. For concreteness and simplicity let's consider a LAN model $f(x, \theta)$ with $\theta \in \Theta \subset \mathbb{R}^k$. If $\hat{\theta}_n$ denotes the MLE from a sample of size n, then

$$\sqrt{n}(\hat{\theta}_n - \theta) \to_d Z \sim N(0, J(\theta))$$

where $J(\theta)$ is the inverse of the Fisher information matrix. For any bowl-shaped loss function $\ell(u)$, the asymptotic risk of this estimator is

$$\rho(\hat{\theta}, \theta) = \lim_{n\to\infty} E_\theta \ell\left(\sqrt{n}(\hat{\theta}_n - \theta)\right) = E_\theta \ell(Z)$$

where E_θ means expectation with respect to the model $f(x, \theta)$. For example, with quadratic risk $\ell(u) = u'u$, then $\rho(\hat{\theta}, \theta) = \text{tr}\, J(\theta)$.

In this setting, we might ask if there is an alternative estimator $\tilde{\theta}_n$ with smaller risk. This is a treacherous question. Consider the estimator $\tilde{\theta}_n = \theta$. Then $\rho(\hat{\theta}, \theta) = \rho(\theta, \theta)$ is minimized and $\tilde{\theta}_n$ has smaller risk than the MLE. This seems disingenuous, as we have constructed an estimator which uses knowledge of the true value of the parameter. But it points to the need to be more careful about what we mean by "smaller risk."

A classic solution to this problem is the minimax criterion: we say an estimator is minimax efficient if it minimizes the maximum risk over (a region of) the parameter space. For $\Gamma \subset \Theta$, we define the maximum asymptotic risk of an estimator $\tilde{\theta}_n$ as

$$\sup_{\theta\in\Gamma} \rho(\hat{\theta}, \theta) = \sup_{\theta\in\Gamma} \lim_{n\to\infty} E_\theta \ell(\sqrt{n}(\tilde{\theta}_n - \theta))$$

This definition escapes the superefficiency paradox. So long as Γ is not a singleton (contains more than one value of θ) then we cannot artificially set the maximum risk to zero. Essentially, the minimax criterion requires efficient estimators to have uniformly low risk.

There is another difficulty, however. This maximum risk can easily be infinite. For example, suppose $X \sim N(\mu, \sigma^2)$ so that $\theta = (\mu, \sigma^2)$ and $\Theta = \mathbb{R} \times \mathbb{R}^+$, and consider quadratic loss on μ, $\ell(\tilde{\theta} - \theta) = (\tilde{\mu} - \mu)^2$. Then $\rho(\hat{\theta}, \theta) = \sigma^2$ and $\sup_{\theta\in\Theta} \rho(\hat{\theta}, \theta) = \sup_{\sigma^2>0} \sigma^2 = \infty$. The problem is that the "worst-case" risk is dominated by the extreme parameter values, and cannot be compensated by good estimation methods.

The solution to this difficulty is to define the maximal risk over a local neighborhood of a parameter value θ. An elegant formulation (see van der Vaart (1998), Chapter 8) reparameterizes using a local parameter space. Define the parameter sequence

$$\theta_n = \theta + n^{-1/2} h$$

where $\theta \in \Theta$ and $h \in \mathbb{R}^k$. We then consider the sequence of probability models indexed by θ_n. In this local reparameterization, for any $h \in \mathbb{R}^k$ the MLE satisfies

$$\sqrt{n}(\hat{\theta}_n - \theta_n) \to_d Z \sim N(0, J(\theta))$$

and the asymptotic risk equals

$$\rho(\hat{\theta}, \theta) = \lim_{n\to\infty} E_{\theta_n} \ell(\sqrt{n}(\hat{\theta}_n - \theta_n)) = E_\theta \ell(Z)$$

Since the limit is independent of h, the maximal (local) risk of the MLE is thus

$$\sup_{h\in\mathbb{R}^k} \lim_{n\to\infty} E_{\theta_n} \ell(\sqrt{n}(\hat{\theta}_n - \theta_n)) = E_\theta \ell(Z)$$

Furthermore, the famous minimax theorem due to Hájek (see van der Vaart (1998), Theorem 8.11) shows that $E_\theta l(Z)$ is a lower bound on the maximal risk for any estimator sequence, showing that the MLE is minimax efficient.

Now let's apply this theory to the local-to-unity model (1)–(2) which is parameterized in terms of the local-to-unity parameter $c \leq 0$ and is local to $\alpha = 1$. The asymptotic risk of the OLS estimator is

$$\begin{aligned}\rho(\hat{\alpha}, \alpha) &= \lim\nolimits_{n\to\infty} E_{\alpha_n} \ell(n(\hat{\alpha}_n - \alpha_n)) \\ &= E_c \ell\left(\frac{U_c}{V_c}\right) \\ &= \mu_2(c)\end{aligned}$$

the final equality in the case of quadratic risk, and $\mu_2(c)$ is the second moment defined in Eq. (4). It follows that the maximal risk of the OLS estimator is

$$\sup_{c\leq 0} \lim_{n\to\infty} E_{\alpha_n} \ell(n(\hat{\alpha}_n - \alpha_n)) = \sup_{c\leq 0} \mu_2(c)$$

But this is infinite! The second moment $\mu_2(c)$ is larger than the variance of U_c/V_c, which as shown in panel (b) of Figs. 1 and 2, diverges to infinity as

$c \to -\infty$. Since the maximal risk is unbounded, it is not possible to define efficiency in terms of minimizing the maximal risk.

The solution pursued by Ploberger and Phillips (2012) is to restrict the loss function $\ell(u)$ to be bounded, in which case the maximal risk is necessarily finite. However, the fact that the risk is increasing as $c \to -\infty$ means that the maximal risk will be determined by the extreme values of c. In other words, efficiency improvements for small c will not be captured by a theory that computes maximal risk over unbounded c.

A solution to this dilemma was proposed by Hansen (2013) in the context of LAN models. Instead of defining the maximal risk over all values of c, it can be defined over bounded sets, creating a maximal risk function. Specifically, define the maximal risk function of a sequence of estimators $\tilde{\alpha}_n$ as

$$\rho(C, \tilde{\alpha}, \alpha) = \sup_{C \leq c \leq 0} \lim_{n \to \infty} E_{\alpha_n} \ell(n(\tilde{\alpha}_n - \alpha_n))$$

The maximal risk function of the OLS estimator is

$$\rho(C, \hat{\alpha}, \alpha) = \sup_{C \leq c \leq 0} \mu_2(c) = \mu_2(C)$$

the second equality since $\mu_2(c)$ is monotonic in c. (As shown in Figs. 1 and 2, both the squared mean and variance are monotonically increasing as c decreases.)

The maximal risk function $\rho(C, \tilde{\alpha}, \alpha)$ can be used to rank the efficiency of estimators. If we have two estimators $\tilde{\alpha}_1$ and $\tilde{\alpha}_2$ and we can show that $\rho(C, \tilde{\alpha}_1, \alpha) < \rho(C, \tilde{\alpha}_2, \alpha)$, this means that the maximum risk of $\tilde{\alpha}_1$ is less than that of $\tilde{\alpha}_2$ for $-C \leq c \leq 0$. If this holds for all C then clearly $\tilde{\alpha}_1$ is more efficient than $\tilde{\alpha}_2$.

Furthermore, we can define an estimator $\tilde{\alpha}_n$ of α_n as minimax efficient if its maximal risk function $\rho(C, \tilde{\alpha}, \alpha)$ is the smallest possible for all values of C. Unfortunately this lower bound is unknown, and it is unknown if such an estimator exists.

5. STEIN-TYPE SHRINKAGE ESTIMATOR

In LAN models, Stein-type estimators can achieve efficiency improvements relative to MLE when the estimation dimension is three or greater

(Stein, 1956, 1981; James & Stein, 1961). The local-to-unity model (1)–(2) only has one parameter and is not LAN, so we should not expect such improvements to hold, but it is intriguing to see what happens.

A Stein-type estimator that shrinks the MLE toward unity is

$$\hat{\alpha}_n^* = 1 + (\hat{\alpha}_n - 1)\left(1 - \frac{s(\hat{\alpha}_n)^2}{(\hat{\alpha}_n - 1)^2}\right)_+ = \begin{cases} 1 & \text{if } \left|\frac{\hat{\alpha}_n - 1}{s(\hat{\alpha}_n)}\right| \leq 1 \\ \hat{\alpha}_n - \frac{s(\hat{\alpha}_n)^2}{(\hat{\alpha}_n - 1)} & \text{if } \left|\frac{\hat{\alpha}_n - 1}{s(\hat{\alpha}_n)}\right| > 1 \end{cases}$$

where

$$s(\hat{\alpha}_n) = \left(\frac{\frac{1}{n}\sum_{t=1}^{n}(y_t - \hat{\alpha}_n y_{t-1})^2}{\sum_{t=1}^{n} y_{t-1}^2}\right)^{1/2}$$

is the conventional standard error for $\hat{\alpha}_n$. The notation $(a)_+ = 1(a \geq 0)$ is the positive-part operator, so that the estimator $\hat{\alpha}_n^*$ takes the "positive-part" form introduced by Baranchick (1964).

The asymptotic distribution of $\hat{\alpha}_n^*$ in the local-to-unity model (1)–(2) is simple to calculate from Eq. (3). The maximal risk function is then a function of the asymptotic distribution.

Proposition 1.

$$n(\hat{\alpha}_n^* - \alpha_n) \rightarrow_d \left(\frac{U_c}{V_c} + c\right)\left(1 - \frac{V_c}{(U_c + cV_c)^2}\right)_+ - c$$

$$\rho(C, \hat{\alpha}^*, \alpha) = \sup_{C \leq c \leq 0} E\left(\left(\frac{U_c}{V_c} + c\right)\left(1 - \frac{V_c}{(U_c + cV_c)^2}\right)_+ - c\right)^2$$

■

The asymptotic risk is not a simple function of the moments of (U_c, V_c), so it cannot be calculated by the exact methods of Theorem 1. Instead, we calculate it by simulation. The results of Section 3 suggest that to obtain accurate results we need to use samples of size $n = 100,000$, and as before, we used 1,000,000 simulation replications.

As we are interested in the relative performance of the Stein estimator relative to OLS, we define the relative maximal risk

$$\rho^*(C, \hat{\alpha}^*, \alpha) = \frac{\rho(C, \hat{\alpha}^*, \alpha)}{\rho(C, \hat{\alpha}, \alpha)}$$

Values less than one indicate improved risk relative to OLS, values over one indicate higher risk than OLS.

The results are presented graphically in Fig. 3. The panel on left is shown for C ranging from −20 to 0 and the right panel for C ranging from −400 to 0. As can be seen, the Stein estimator has uniformly decreased risk relative to OLS. The risk reduction is greatest at $C = 0$. (At $c = 0$, the risk of the Stein estimator is 51% of that of the OLS estimator). The risk reduction remains quite substantial for small C (20% at $C = -4$ and 10% at $C = -10$), but asymptotes to zero. The fact that the relative risk function lies strictly below one for all C below −400 means that there is no value of c for which the Stein estimator does not have lower risk than OLS. Uniformly in the local-to-unity model, the Stein estimator dominates OLS.

This finding is quite surprising given that this is a one-dimensional problem and classic Stein theory only applies when the dimension is three or higher. It may not be that surprising, however, given that Ploberger (2008) shows that OLS-based unit root tests are not admissible.

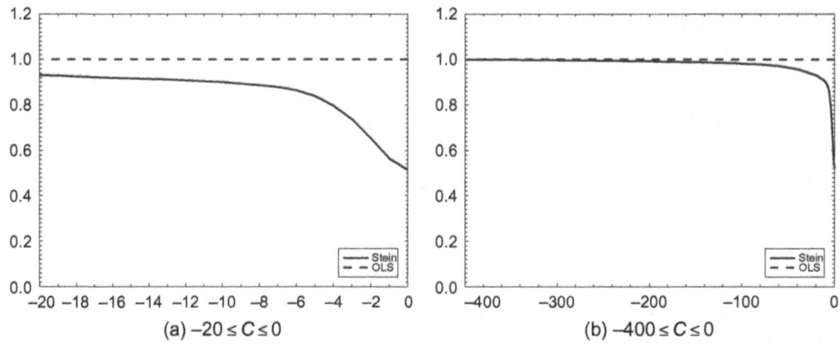

Fig. 3. Relative Asymptotic Risk of Stein Estimator.

It should be emphasized that our finding is numerical; we do not have a formal proof. Given the large number of simulation replications (1 million) and the large range of the local-to-unity parameter explored, the finding appears quite robust. However, based on the numerical evidence alone we cannot exclude the possibility that the relationship will invert for values of C below −400. Such a numerical exercise does not appear to be fruitful. First, the sample size n would likely need to be increased. We set $n = 100,000$ based on our earlier calculations which showed that this value was needed to obtain good approximations for the mean and variance of the OLS estimator for local-to-unity parameters up to −400. For values beyond this point this numerical comparison would need to be repeated.

It also should be emphasized that our results concern the asymptotic local-to-unity model; the Stein estimator dominates the OLS estimator in the asymptotic limit, not in finite samples for values of α which are not close to 1.

The results of this section are meant to be suggestive, and not guidance for empirical work. We have shown intriguing evidence that a simple shrinkage adjustment can provide major reductions in estimation risk when the local-to-unity parameter is small. This suggests that further research into optimal shrinkage methods could prove fruitful.

6. CONCLUSION

Many papers have been written about the AR(1) model, and many have used the local-to-unity framework of Chan and Wei (1987) and Phillips (1987b). Implementation of the theory typically requires numerical evaluation, and most of the latter uses simulation methods. We have extended earlier work on the exact moments of the unit root model to the local-to-unity framework, and have shown that the moments of the distribution can be easily calculated by numerical integration. Comparing these exact moments with moments from simulated distributions, we have shown that conventional sample sizes are far too small to provide good approximations. For large local-to-unity parameters, we suggest $n = 100,000$.

We have also explored the theory of efficient estimation in the context of the local-to-unity model. We suggest that the minimax risk should be evaluated locally, as a function of the localizing parameter, and have introduced a simple Stein shrinkage estimator that has lower (numerical) minimax risk than the OLS estimator. This suggests that improvements over OLS are potentially important and feasible.

7. PROOF OF THEOREM 1

The method of proof is a straightforward generalization of the method introduced by Nabeya (1999). It will be useful to start by defining the random variables $(U, V) = \left(\int_0^1 W\,\mathrm{d}W,\ \int_0^1 W^2\right)$, and let $f(u, v)$ denote their joint density function. White (1958) showed that their moment generating function equals

$$\begin{aligned}\phi(s,t) &= E\exp(sU + tV) = \int \exp(su+tv) f(u,v)\ \mathrm{d}u\mathrm{d}v \\ &= \mathrm{e}^{-s/2}\left(\cos\sqrt{2t} - s\frac{\sin\sqrt{2t}}{\sqrt{2t}}\right)^{-1/2}\end{aligned}$$

Making the substitutions

$$\begin{aligned}\sqrt{2t} &= i\sqrt{-2t}, \\ \cos\sqrt{2t} &= \cos(i\sqrt{-2t}) = \cosh\sqrt{-2t}\end{aligned}$$

and

$$\frac{\tan\sqrt{2t}}{\sqrt{2t}} = \frac{\tan(i\sqrt{-2t})}{i\sqrt{-2t}} = \frac{-i\tan(i\sqrt{-2t})}{\sqrt{-2t}} = \frac{\tanh(\sqrt{-2t})}{\sqrt{-2t}} = \psi(\sqrt{-2t})$$

we find the alternative expression

$$\phi(s,t) = \mathrm{e}^{-s/2}(\cosh\sqrt{-2t})^{-1/2}(1 - s\psi(\sqrt{-2t}))^{-1/2} \qquad (6)$$

Define $U_c^* = \int_0^1 W_c \mathrm{d}W_c = U_c + cV_c$. Crump (2008) showed the joint density of (U_c^*, V_c) equals $f_c(u,v) = \exp(cu - c^2 v/2)\ f(u,v)$. It follows that their moment generating function equals

$$
\begin{aligned}
\phi_c(s,t) &= \int \exp(su+tv) f_c(u,v)\, du\, dv \\
&= \int \exp\left((s+c)u + \left(t - \frac{c^2}{2} \right) v \right) f(u,v)\, du\, dv \\
&= \phi\left(s+c, t - \frac{c^2}{2} \right)
\end{aligned} \tag{7}
$$

Eq. (7) can alternatively be derived from the moment generating function for (U_c, V_c) derived by Phillips (1987b). See also Proposition A.1 of Phillips, Magdalinos, and Giraitis (2010). It turns out that the form of expression (7) is convenient for our calculations.

By the binomial expansion

$$
E\left(\frac{U_c}{V_c}\right)^r = E\left(\frac{U_c^*}{V_c} - c\right)^r = \sum_{j=0}^{r} \binom{r}{j} (-c)^{r-j} E\left(\frac{U_c^*}{V_c}\right)^j \tag{8}
$$

Following Nabeya (1999) and Sawa (1972), the moments in Eq. (8) can be expressed as

$$
E\left(\frac{U_c^*}{V_c}\right)^j = \frac{1}{(j-1)!} \int_0^\infty t^{j-1} \frac{\partial^j}{\partial s^j} \phi_c(s, -t) \Big|_{s=0} \, dt \tag{9}
$$

Using Eq. (7) and then making the change of variables $t = ((z-c)^2 - c^2)/2$ we find that Eq. (9) equals

$$
\begin{aligned}
&\frac{1}{(j-1)!} \int_0^\infty t^{j-1} \frac{\partial^j}{\partial s^j} \phi\left(s+c, -t - \frac{c^2}{2} \right) \Big|_{s=0} \, dt \\
&= \frac{1}{(j-1)! 2^{j-1}} \int_0^\infty (z-c)((z-c)^2 - c^2)^{j-1} \\
&\quad \times \frac{\partial^j}{\partial s^j} \phi\left(s+c, -\frac{(z-c)^2}{2} \right) \Big|_{s=0} \, dz
\end{aligned} \tag{10}
$$

Note that this change of variables is appropriate when $c \leq 0$ for the transformation is invertible for $t \geq 0$, but it would not be invertible for $c > 0$.

Using Eq. (6) and

$$(\cosh(z-c))^{-1/2} = \sqrt{2}e^{(c-z)/2}(1+e^{-2(z-c)})^{-1/2}$$

we can see that

$$\phi\left(s+c, -\frac{(z-c)^2}{2}\right) = e^{-(s+c)/2}(\cosh\ (z-c))^{-1/2}(1-(s+c)\psi(z-c))^{-1/2}$$

$$= \frac{\sqrt{2}}{e^{z/2}(1+e^{-2(z-c)})^{1/2}} e^{-s/2}(1-(s+c)\psi(z-c))^{-1/2}$$

Therefore

$$\frac{\partial^j}{\partial s^j}\phi\left(s+c, -\frac{(z-c)^2}{2}\right)\bigg|_{s=0} = \frac{\sqrt{2}}{e^{z/2}(1+e^{-2(z-c)})^{1/2}} \times \frac{\partial^j}{\partial s^j}\left\{e^{-s/2}(1-(s+c)\psi(z-c))^{-1/2}\right\}\bigg|_{s=0}$$

$$= \frac{2^{1/2-j}}{e^{z/2}(1+e^{-2(z-c)})^{1/2}} \times \sum_{\ell=0}^{j}\binom{j}{\ell}\frac{(-1)^{j-\ell}(2\ell-1)!!\psi(z-c)^{\ell}}{(1-c\psi\ (z-c))^{1/2+\ell}}$$

Substituted into Eq. (10), and then making the change of variables $z = x/(1-x)$, we obtain

$$E\left(\frac{U_c^*}{V_c}\right)^j = \frac{2^{3/2-2j}}{(j-1)!}\int_0^{\infty}\frac{(z-c)((z-c)^2-c^2)^{j-1}}{e^{z/2}(1+e^{-2(z-c)})^{1/2}} \times \sum_{\ell=0}^{j}\binom{j}{\ell}\frac{(-1)^{j-\ell}(2\ell-1)!!\psi(z-c)^{\ell}}{(1-c\psi(z-c))^{1/2+\ell}}\ dz$$

$$= \frac{2^{3/2-2j}}{(j-1)!}\int_0^{1}\frac{\lambda(x,c)(\lambda(x,c)^2-c^2)^{j-1}}{(1-x)^2 e^{x/(2-2x)}(1+e^{-2\lambda(x,c)})^{1/2}} \times \sum_{\ell=0}^{j}\binom{j}{\ell}\frac{(-1)^{j-\ell}(2\ell-1)!!\psi(\lambda(x,c))^{\ell}}{(1-c\psi(\lambda(x,c)))^{1/2+\ell}}\ dx$$

$$= \int_0^1 g_j(x,c)\ dx$$

Substituted into Eq. (8) we obtain Eq. (5). ■

NOTE

1. The computation was done in Gauss using the intquad1 command.

ACKNOWLEDGEMENT

Research supported by the National Science Foundation. I thank a referee for helpful comments.

REFERENCES

Baranchick, A. (1964). Multiple regression and estimation of the mean of a multivariate normal distribution. Technical Report No. 51, Department of Statistics, Stanford University, CA.

Chan, N. H., & Wei, C. Z. (1987). Asymptotic inference for nearly nonstationary AR(1) processes. *Annals of Statistics*, *15*, 1050–1063.

Crump, R. K. (2008). *Optimal conditional inference in nearly-integrated autoregressive processes*. Working Paper. Federal Reserve Bank of New York, NY.

Hájek, J. (1970). A characterization of limiting distributions of regular estimates. *Zeitschrift für Wahrscheinlichkeitstheorie und Verwandte Gebiete*, *14*, 323–330.

Hájek, J. (1972). Local asymptotic minimax and admissibility in estimation. *Proceedings of the Sixth Berkeley Symposium on Mathematical Statistics and Probability*, *1*, 175–194.

Hansen, B. E. (2013). *Efficient shrinkage in parametric models*. Madison, WI: University of Wisconsin.

James, W., & Stein, C. M. (1961). Estimation with quadratic loss. *Proceedings of the Fourth Berkeley Symposium on Mathematical Statistics and Probability*, *1*, 361–380.

Le Cam, L. (1982). *Asymptotic methods in statistical decision theory*. New York, NY: Springer-Verlag.

MacKinnon, J. G. (1994). Approximate asymptotic distribution functions for unit-root and cointegration tests. *Journal of Business and Economic Statistics*, *12*, 167–176.

Nabeya, S. (1999). Asymptotic moments of some unit root test statistics in the null case. *Econometric Theory*, *15*, 139–149.

Phillips, P. C. B. (1987a). Time series regression with a unit root. *Econometrica*, *55*, 277–302.

Phillips, P. C. B. (1987b). Towards a unified asymptotic theory for autoregression. *Biometrika*, *74*, 535–547.

Phillips, P. C. B. (2012). Fokelore theorems, implicit maps, and indirect inference. *Econometrica*, *80*, 425–454.

Phillips, P. C. B. (2014). On confidence intervals for autoregressive roots and predictive regression. *Econometrica*, *82*, 1177–1195.

Phillips, P. C. B., Magdalinos, T., & Giraitis, L. (2010). Smoothing local-to-moderate unit root theory. *Journal of Econometrics*, *158*, 274–279.

Phillips, P. C. B., & Perron, P. (1988). Testing for a unit root in time series regression. *Biometrika*, *75*, 335–346.

Ploberger, W. (2008). Admissible and non-admissible tests in unit-root-like situations. *Econometric Theory*, *24*, 15–42.

Ploberger, W., & Phillips, P. C. B. (2012). Optimal estimation under nonstandard conditions. *Journal of Econometrics*, *169*, 258–265.

Sawa, T. (1972). Finite sample properties of k-class estimators. *Econometrica*, *40*, 653–680.

Shenton, L. R., & Johnson, W. L. (1965). Moments of a serial correlation coefficient. *Journal of the Royal Statistical Society, Series B*, *27*, 308–320.

Shenton, L. R., & Vinod, H. D. (1995). Closed forms for asymptotic bias and variance in autoregressive models with unit roots. *Journal of Computational and Applied Mathematics*, *61*, 231–243.

Stein, C. M. (1956). Inadmissibility of the usual estimator for the mean of a multivariate normal distribution. *Proceedings of the Third Berkeley Symposium on Mathematical Statistics and Probability*, *1*, 197–206.

Stein, C. M. (1981). Estimation of the mean of a multivariate normal distribution. *Annals of Statistics*, *9*, 1135–1151.

Stock, J. H. (1991). Confidence intervals for the largest autoregressive root in U.S. macroeconomic time series. *Journal of Monetary Economics*, *28*, 435–459.

van der Vaart, A. W. (1998). *Asymptotic statistics*. New York, NY: Cambridge University Press.

White, J. S. (1958). The limiting distribution of the serial correlation coefficient in the explosive case. *Annals of Mathematical Statistics*, *29*, 1188–1197.

White, J. S. (1961). Asymptotic expansions for the mean and variance of the serial correlation coefficient. *Biometrika*, *48*, 85–94.

FIXED-SMOOTHING ASYMPTOTICS AND ASYMPTOTIC *F* AND *t* TESTS IN THE PRESENCE OF STRONG AUTOCORRELATION

Yixiao Sun

Department of Economics, University of California – San Diego, La Jolla, California, USA

ABSTRACT

New asymptotic approximations are established for the Wald and t statistics in the presence of unknown but strong autocorrelation. The asymptotic theory extends the usual fixed-smoothing asymptotics under weak dependence to allow for near-unit-root and weak-unit-root processes. As the locality parameter that characterizes the neighborhood of the autoregressive root increases from zero to infinity, the new fixed-smoothing asymptotic distribution changes smoothly from the unit-root fixed-smoothing asymptotics to the usual fixed-smoothing asymptotics

Essays in Honor of Peter C. B. Phillips
Advances in Econometrics, Volume 33, 23–63

ISSN: 0731-9053/doi:10.1108/S0731-905320140000033002

under weak dependence. Simulations show that the new approximation is more accurate than the usual fixed-smoothing approximation.

Keywords: Autocorrelation robust test; fixed-smoothing asymptotics; local-to-unity; strong autocorrelation; weak unit root

JEL classifications: C13; C14; C32; C51

1. INTRODUCTION

In order to robustify statistical inferences to heteroskedasticity and autocorrelation, it is now a standard practice to make use of heteroskedasticity and autocorrelation robust (HAR) standard errors in time series analysis. The last decade of research on this topic has been largely focused on more accurate approximations to the test statistics constructed on the basis of HAR standard errors and variances. There are now two types of asymptotic approximations: the conventional increasing-smoothing asymptotic approximation and the relatively new fixed-smoothing asymptotic approximation. For kernel HAR inference, the fixed-smoothing asymptotics is the so-called fixed-b asymptotics of Kiefer, Vogelsang and Bunzel (2000; KVB hereafter) and Kiefer and Vogelsang (2002a, 2002b, 2005; KV hereafter). For series HAR inference, the fixed-smoothing asymptotics is the so-called fixed-K asymptotics of Sun (2011, 2013). While the fixed-smoothing asymptotic approximation is more accurate than the conventional increasing-smoothing asymptotic approximation, that is, the chi-square approximation (Jansson, 2004; Sun, Phillips, & Jin, 2008), the quality of the fixed-smoothing approximation is not completely satisfactory when the underlying time series has strong autocorrelation. To confront with this problem, the paper develops a new fixed-smoothing asymptotic that accommodates strong autocorrelation.

We start by considering a multivariate time series whose mean value is the parameter of interest. Each component of the time series follows an autoregressive process with the autoregressive parameter ρ changing with the sample size T. More specifically, $\rho = 1 - c_m/T$ for some positive sequence c_m. Depending on the limiting thought experiments employed, c_m may be held fixed as the sample size $T \to \infty$ or grow with the sample size. The former case is the conventional local-to-unit-root specification and the latter case specifies a moderate deviation from the unit root. Park (2003) refers to these two cases as "near unit root" and "weak unit root," respectively. For more discussions, see Giraitis and Phillips (2006), Phillips and Magdalinos (2007), and Phillips, Magdalinos, and Giraitis (2010).

We establish the fixed-smoothing asymptotics for the Wald and t statistics when c_m is held fixed. This leads to our pivotal near-unit-root fixed-smoothing asymptotics. As $c_m \to \infty$, we show that the near-unit-root fixed-smoothing asymptotics converges to the fixed-smoothing asymptotics under weak dependence. Depending on the value of c_m, the near-unit-root fixed-smoothing asymptotics thus provides a smooth transition from the usual stationary fixed-smoothing asymptotics to the unit-root fixed-smoothing asymptotics.

The near-unit-root fixed-smoothing asymptotic distribution is nonstandard but can be simulated. The critical values from this distribution are larger than the corresponding ones from the usual fixed-smoothing asymptotic distribution, which in turn are larger than those from the conventional chi-square distribution. A direct implication is that statistical inference based on the chi-square approximation and stationary fixed-smoothing approximation may lead to the finding of statistical significance that does not actually exist.

In the case of series variance estimation, we can judiciously design a set of basis functions such that the near-unit-root fixed-smoothing asymptotic distribution becomes a standard F or t distribution. The designing process involves projection and orthogonalization. The F and t approximations are very handy in empirical applications, as the F and t critical values are readily available from statistical programs and software packages. There is no need to simulate nonstandard critical values. The possibility of deriving a standard approximation under the fixed-smoothing asymptotics is an advantage of using series variance estimators. For this type of estimators, we have the complete freedom in choosing the basis functions. This is in contrast with the kernel variance estimators where the basis functions are implicitly given and cannot be changed.

Monte Carlo simulations show that the chi-square tests have the largest size distortion, the tests based on the near-unit-root fixed-smoothing asymptotics have the smallest size distortion, and the tests based on the usual fixed-smoothing asymptotics are in the middle. The near-unit-root fixed-smoothing tests, which include tests based on F and t approximation, achieve triple robustness in the following sense: it is asymptotically valid regardless of whether autocorrelation is present or not, whether the autocorrelation is strong or not, and whether the level of smoothing is held fixed or is allowed to increase with the sample size.

The rest of this paper is organized as follows. Section 2 describes the basic setting and the problem at hand. Section 3 develops the fixed-smoothing asymptotics in the presence of near unit roots. This section also establishes the behavior of the near-unit-root fixed-smoothing asymptotic distribution as $c_m \to \infty$. Section 4 presents the F and t approximations based on a set of judiciously designed basis functions. Section 5 discusses the applicability of our fixed-smoothing approximation for location models to more general models. The subsequent section reports simulation evidence, and the last section provides some concluding discussions. Proofs of the main results are given in the appendix.

2. THE BASIC SETTING AND THE PROBLEM

Assume that p-dimensional time series y_t follows the process:

$$y_t = \theta + e_t, \quad t = 1, 2, \ldots, T \tag{1}$$

where $y_t = (y_{1t}, \ldots, y_{pt})'$, $\theta = (\theta_1, \ldots, \theta_p)'$, and $e_t = (e_{1t}, \ldots, e_{pt})'$ are a zero mean process. The location model, as simple as it is, is empirically relevant in a number of situations. For example, the data might consist of a multivariate time series of forecasting loss that are produced by different forecasting methods. We can test equal predictive accuracy of these forecasting methods by examining whether the loss differential series has mean zero. There is also a large and active literature on inference for the mean of simulated time series. See, for example, Alexopoulos (2006, 2007) and references therein. More importantly, our points can be made more clearly in the simple location model.

We are interested in testing the null $H_0 : \theta = \theta_0$ against the alternative $H_1 : \theta \neq \theta_0$. The OLS estimator of θ is the average of $\{y_t\}$, that is, $\hat{\theta} = \bar{y} := T^{-1} \sum_{t=1}^{T} y_t$. The F test version of the Wald statistic based on the OLS estimator is then given by

$$F_T = D_T(\hat{\theta} - \theta_0)'\hat{\Omega}^{-1} D_T(\hat{\theta} - \theta_0)/p = D_T^2(\hat{\theta} - \theta_0)'\hat{\Omega}^{-1}(\hat{\theta} - \theta_0)/p$$

where D_T is a real-valued scaling factor that characterizes the rate of convergence of $\hat{\theta}$ to θ_0, and $\hat{\Omega}$ is an estimator of the asymptotic variance of $D_T(\hat{\theta} - \theta_0)$. Usually $D_T = \sqrt{T}$ but the exact magnitude of D_T is not important in practice, as it will be canceled out. When $p = 1$, we can construct the t statistic as follows:

$$t_T = \frac{D_T(\hat{\theta} - \theta_0)}{\sqrt{\hat{\Omega}}}$$

Many nonparametric estimators of the asymptotic variance matrix are available in the literature. In this paper, we consider a class of quadratic variance estimators, which includes the conventional kernel variance estimators of Andrews (1991), Newey and West (1987), Politis (2011), and the series variance estimators of Phillips (2005), Müller (2007), and Sun (2006, 2011, 2013) as special cases. The quadratic variance estimators take the following form:

$$\hat{\Omega}=\frac{D_T^2}{T^2}\sum_{t=1}^{T}\sum_{s=1}^{T}Q_h\left(\frac{t}{T},\frac{s}{T}\right)\hat{e}_t\hat{e}_s' \tag{2}$$

where $\hat{e}_t=y_t-\hat{\theta}=e_t-\bar{e}$ for $\bar{e}=T^{-1}\sum_{t=1}^{T}e_t$ and $Q_h(r,s)$ is a weighting function that depends on the smoothing parameter h. A reasonable choice of $Q_h(r,s)$ should satisfy: (i) $Q_h\left(\frac{t}{T},\frac{s}{T}\right)$ decays to zero as $|t-s|/T$ approaches 1; (ii) $Q_h\left(\frac{t}{T},\frac{s}{T}\right)$ increases to 1 as $|t-s|/T$ approaches 0. The speed of change is controlled by h. For conventional kernel variance estimators, $Q_h(r,s)=k((r-s)/b)$ and we take $h=1/b$, where $k(\cdot)$ is a kernel function. For the series variance estimators, $Q_h(r,s)=K^{-1}\sum_{j=1}^{K}\boldsymbol{\phi}_j(r)\,\boldsymbol{\phi}_j(s)$ and we take $h=K$, where $\{\boldsymbol{\phi}_j(r)\}$ are basis functions on $\mathbb{L}^2[0,1]$ satisfying $\int_0^1\boldsymbol{\phi}_j(r)\,\mathrm{d}r=0$. We parameterize h in such a way that h indicates the level or amount of smoothing in both cases.

Define

$$Q_{T,h}^{*}(r,s)=Q_h(r,s)-\frac{1}{T}\sum_{\tau_1=1}^{T}Q_h\left(\frac{\tau_1}{T},s\right)-\frac{1}{T}\sum_{\tau_2=1}^{T}Q_h\left(r,\frac{\tau_2}{T}\right)+\frac{1}{T}\sum_{\tau_1=1}^{T}\sum_{\tau_2=1}^{T}Q_h\left(\frac{\tau_1}{T},\frac{\tau_2}{T}\right)$$

then

$$\hat{\Omega}=\frac{D_T^2}{T^2}\sum_{t=1}^{T}\sum_{s=1}^{T}Q_{T,h}^{*}\left(\frac{t}{T},\frac{s}{T}\right)e_te_s' \tag{3}$$

where the demeaning operation on e_t and e_s has been moved to the weighting function. The Wald statistic is then equal to

$$F_T=\left(\sum_{t=1}^{T}e_t\right)'\left[\sum_{t=1}^{T}\sum_{s=1}^{T}Q_{Th}^{*}\left(\frac{t}{T},\frac{s}{T}\right)e_te_s'\right]^{-1}\left(\sum_{t=1}^{T}e_t\right)\Big/p$$

Similarly, the t statistic becomes

$$t_T = \frac{\sum_{t=1}^{T} e_t}{\left[\sum_{t=1}^{T}\sum_{s=1}^{T} Q_{Th}^{*}\left(\frac{t}{T},\frac{s}{T}\right)e_t e_s\right]^{1/2}}$$

Note that the scaling factor D_T has been canceled out in both F_T and t_T.

The question is how to approximate the sampling distributions of F_T and t_T. If $T^{-1/2}\sum_{t=1}^{[Tr]} e_t$ converges weakly to a Brownian motion process, then under some conditions on Q_h, it can be shown that for a fixed h

$$F_T \to^d F_\infty := W_p(1)'\left[\int_0^1\int_0^1 Q_h^{*}(r,s)\,\mathrm{d}W_p(r)\,\mathrm{d}W_p'(s)\right]^{-1} W_p(1)/p \quad (4)$$

$$t_T \to^d t_\infty := \frac{W_p(1)}{\sqrt{\int_0^1\int_0^1 Q_h^{*}(r,s)\,\mathrm{d}W_p(r)\,\mathrm{d}W_p'(s)}} \quad (5)$$

where $W_p(r)$ is a $p\times 1$ vector of standard Wiener processes and

$$Q_h^{*}(r,s) = Q_h(r,s) - \int_0^1 Q_h(\tau_1,s)\,\mathrm{d}\tau_1 - \int_0^1 Q_h(r,\tau_2)\,\mathrm{d}\tau_2 + \int_0^1\int_0^1 Q_h(\tau_1,\tau_2)\,\mathrm{d}\tau_1\mathrm{d}\tau_2$$

is the "continuous" version of $Q_{T,h}^{*}(r,s)$. See, for example, Kiefer and Vogelsang (2005) for the kernel case and Sun (2013) for the series case.

For both variance estimators, $W_p(1)$ is independent of $\int_0^1\int_0^1 Q_h^{*}(r,s)\,\mathrm{d}W_p(r)\,\mathrm{d}W_p'(s)$. So F_∞ resembles an F distribution in the sense that both can be written as a quadratic form in standard normals with an independent weighting matrix. Similarly, t_∞ resembles a t distribution in the sense that both can be written as a standard normal scaled by an independent random variable.

The asymptotic approximation obtained under a fixed h as $T\to\infty$ is the fixed-smoothing asymptotic approximation. This approximation improves the traditional chi-square or normal approximation, which is obtained under the increasing-smoothing asymptotics where h increases with T but at a slower rate. However, the fixed-smoothing asymptotic approximation is still not satisfactory when the underlying process has strong autocorrelation. Our goal is to establish a further improved approximation when e_t may be strongly autocorrelated.

3. FIXED-SMOOTHING ASYMPTOTICS UNDER THE LOCAL-TO-UNITY SPECIFICATION

To model strong autocorrelation, we maintain the following assumption on $\{e_t\}$.

Assumption 1.

(i) For some positive sequence $\{c_m\}$

$$e_t = \rho_{T,m} e_{t-1} + u_t \text{ where } e_0 = O_p(1) \text{ and } \rho_{T,m} = 1 - \frac{c_m}{T}$$

(ii) $T^{-1} \sum_{t=1}^{T} \sum_{s=1}^{T} \|Eu_t u_s'\|$ is bounded uniformly in T;

(iii) $\{u_t\}$ satisfies a FCLT:

$$\frac{1}{\sqrt{T}} \sum_{t=1}^{[Tr]} u_t \rightarrow^d \Lambda W_p(r), \text{ as } T \rightarrow \infty \tag{6}$$

where $W_p(r)$ is a $p \times 1$ vector of standard Wiener processes and $\Lambda = \Omega^{1/2}$ is the matrix square root of the long-run variance matrix Ω of u_t:

$$\Omega = \Lambda \Lambda' = \sum_{j=-\infty}^{\infty} Eu_t u_{t-j}'$$

The data generating process in Assumption 1 is similar to that used in Phillips et al. (2010), which establishes a smooth transition between the conventional unit root distribution and the standard norm distribution. When c_m is fixed, each component of $\{e_t\}$ has a local-to-unity root in the conventional sense (Phillips, 1987). When $c_m \rightarrow \infty$ as $T \rightarrow \infty$, each

component of $\{e_t\}$ has a moderate unit root in the sense that the root belongs to a larger neighborhood of unity than the conventional local-to-unity roots. We could allow for different c_m's for different components of $\{e_t\}$. For notational simplicity, we assume that all components have the same local-to-moderate unit root. The FCLT assumption holds for serially correlated and heterogeneously distributed data that satisfy certain regularity conditions on moments and the dependence structure over time. These primitive regularity conditions can be found in Phillips and Durlauf (1986), Phillips and Solo (1992), and Davidson (1994), among others.
Under Assumption 1, we have

$$\frac{1}{\sqrt{T}} e_{[Tr]} \to \Lambda J_{c_m}(r)$$

for each fixed c_m, where $J_{c_m}(r)$ is the Ornstein–Uhlenbeck (OU) process defined by

$$\mathrm{d}J_{c_m}(r) = -c_m J_{c_m}(r)\,\mathrm{d}r + \mathrm{d}W_p(r)$$

with $J_{c_m}(0)=0$ or $J_{c_m}(r)=\int_0^r e^{-c_m(r-s)}\,\mathrm{d}W_p(s)$.

Assumption 2. (i) For kernel variance estimators, the kernel function $k(\cdot)$ satisfies: for any $b \in (0,1]$, $k_b(x) := k(x/b)$ is symmetric, continuous, piecewise monotonic, and piecewise continuously differentiable on $[-1,1]$. (ii) For the series variance estimator, $\{\boldsymbol{\phi}_j(\cdot)\}$ are piecewise monotonic, continuously differentiable, and orthonormal in $\mathbb{L}^2[0,1]$ and $\int_0^1 \boldsymbol{\phi}_j(x)\,\mathrm{d}x = 0$ for each j.

Assumption 2 is similar to Assumption 1 in Sun (forthcoming). Under this assumption, we can replace $Q^*_{Th}(r,s)$ in Eq. (3) by $Q^*_h(r,s)$ and all our asymptotic results continue to hold. For our theoretical development, we can assume that such a replacement has been made. Furthermore, under Assumption 2, $Q^*_h(r,s)$ has the following unified representation for both types of variance estimators we consider:

$$Q^*_h(r,s) = \sum_{j=1}^{\infty} \lambda_j \Phi_j(r)\,\Phi_j(s) \tag{7}$$

where $\{\Phi_j(r)\}$ is a sequence of continuously differentiable functions satisfying $\int_0^1 \Phi_j(r)\,\mathrm{d}r = 0$. The right-hand side of Eq. (7) converges absolutely and uniformly over $(r,s) \in [0,1] \times [0,1]$.

The representation holds trivially for the case of series variance estimation as

$$Q_h^*(r,s) = Q_h(r,s) = \frac{1}{K}\sum_{j=1}^{K} \boldsymbol{\phi}_j(r)\,\boldsymbol{\phi}_j(s)$$

and so we can take $\{\lambda_j\} = \{K^{-1}, \ldots, K^{-1}, 0, \ldots, 0, \ldots\}$ and $\Phi_j = \boldsymbol{\phi}_j$. For the case of kernel variance estimation, Sun (forthcoming) proves that the representation holds with the following choices of Φ_j and λ_j:

$$\Phi_j(r) = \begin{cases} \cos\left(\frac{1}{2}\pi j r\right), & j \text{ is even} \\ \sin\left(\frac{1}{2}\pi(j+1)r\right) - \int_0^1 \sin\left(\frac{1}{2}\pi(j+1)\tau\right)\mathrm{d}\tau, & j \text{ is odd} \end{cases} \tag{8}$$

and

$$\lambda_j = \begin{cases} \tilde{\lambda}_{j/2}, & j \text{ is even} \\ \tilde{\lambda}_{(j+1)/2}, & j \text{ is odd} \end{cases}$$

where $\{\tilde{\lambda}_j\}$ are the Fourier transforms of $k_b(\cdot)$, that is, $\tilde{\lambda}_j = \int_0^1 k(x/b)\cos(j\pi x)\,\mathrm{d}x$. For easy reference, we define $\Phi_0(r) \equiv 1$.

Theorem 1. Let Assumptions 1 and 2 hold. Then for fixed c_m and h,

$$\begin{aligned} F_T \rightarrow^d F_\infty(c_m) := &\left[\int_0^1 J_{c_m}(r)\,\mathrm{d}r\right]' \\ &\times \left[\int_0^1\int_0^1 Q_h^*(r,s)\,J_{c_m}(r)\,J'_{c_m}(s)\,\mathrm{d}r\mathrm{d}s\right]^{-1} \\ &\times \left[\int_0^1 J_{c_m}(r)\,\mathrm{d}r\right]\Big/ p \end{aligned}$$

If we further assume that $Q_h(r,s)$ is positive definite, then

$$t_T \rightarrow^d t_\infty(c_m) := \frac{\int_0^1 J_{c_m}(r)\,\mathrm{d}r}{\left[\int_0^1\int_0^1 Q_h^*(r,s)\,J_{c_m}(r)\,J'_{c_m}(s)\,\mathrm{d}r\mathrm{d}s\right]^{1/2}}$$

Since

$$cov\ (J_{c_m}(r),\ J_{c_m}(s)) = \frac{1}{2c_m}\{\exp[-c_m|r-s|] - \exp[-c_m(r+s)]\}I_p$$

where I_p is the $p \times p$ identity matrix, we have

$$cov\left(\int_0^1 \Phi_{j_1}(r)\, J_{c_m}(r)\, \mathrm{d}r,\ \int_0^1 \Phi_{j_2}(r)\, J_{c_m}(r)\, \mathrm{d}r\right)$$
$$= \frac{1}{2c_m}\int_0^1 \int_0^1 \Phi_{j_1}(r)\, \Phi_{j_2}(s)\{\exp[-c_m|r-s|] - \exp[-c_m(r+s)]\}\ \mathrm{d}r\mathrm{d}s \times I_p$$

for all $j_1 \geq 0$ and $j_2 \geq 0$. In general, the covariance matrix is not zero. A direct implication is that the weighting matrix $\int_0^1 \int_0^1 Q_h^*(r,s)\, J_{c_m}(r)\, J'_{c_m}(s)\,\mathrm{d}r\mathrm{d}s$ is not independent of $\int_0^1 J_{c_m}(r)\,\mathrm{d}r$. Hence the limiting distribution $F_\infty(c_m)$ cannot be written as a quadratic form in standard normals with an independent random weighting matrix. This is in contrast with F_∞ which takes such a form.

The limiting distribution depends not only on the kernel/basis functions, the smoothing parameter h, the number of joint hypotheses p but also on the local-to-unit-root parameter c_m. In the extreme case when $c_m = 0$, e_t has unit roots and $F_\infty(c_m)$ becomes

$$F_\infty(0) := \left[\int_0^1 W_p(r)\mathrm{d}r\right]' \left[\int_0^1 \int_0^1 Q_h^*(r,s)\, W_p(r)\, W_p'(s)\mathrm{d}r\mathrm{d}s\right]^{-1} \left[\int_0^1 W_p(r)\mathrm{d}r\right] \Big/ p$$

This case seems to be of only theoretical interest. The empirically more relevant case is when c_m is large. The theorem below characterizes the behaviors of $F_\infty(c_m)$ and $t_\infty(c_m)$ as $c_m \to \infty$.

Theorem 2. As $c_m \to \infty$ for a fixed h, we have

$$F_\infty(c_m) = F_\infty(\infty) + o_p(1) \ \text{ and } \ t_\infty(c_m) = t_\infty(\infty) + o_p(1)$$

where $F_\infty(\infty) := F_\infty$ and $t_\infty(\infty) := t_\infty$ as defined in Eqs. (4) and (5) respectively.

Theorem 2 shows that the sequential limits when $T \to \infty$ followed by $c_m \to \infty$ lead to the usual fixed-smoothing asymptotics under weak dependence. Depending on the value of c_m, the limiting distributions $F_\infty(c_m)$ and $t_\infty(c_m)$ provide a smooth transition from the usual fixed-smoothing asymptotics to the unit-root fixed-smoothing asymptotics.

Figs. 1–3 present the 5% critical values from $F_\infty(c_m)$ with $p = 1$ for two kernel variance estimators and one series variance estimator. For the series variance estimator, we take K to be even and use $\phi_{2j-1}(x) = \sqrt{2}\cos(2j\pi x)$, $\phi_{2j}(x) = \sqrt{2}\sin(2j\pi x)$, $j = 1, \ldots, K/2$ as the basis functions. In these figures, "$c = \infty$" corresponds to the usual fixed-smoothing asymptotics, and the solid line indicates the critical value from the χ_1^2 distribution. For any given variance estimator, the critical values increase monotonically as c_m approaches zero. That is, the more persistent the underlying processes are, the higher the critical values will be. While the critical values from the usual fixed-smoothing asymptotic distribution are larger than those from the chi-square distribution, they are still not large enough when the process is highly autocorrelated. Figs. 1–3 also demonstrate the smooth transition from the near-unit-root fixed-smoothing asymptotics to the usual fixed-smoothing asymptotics.

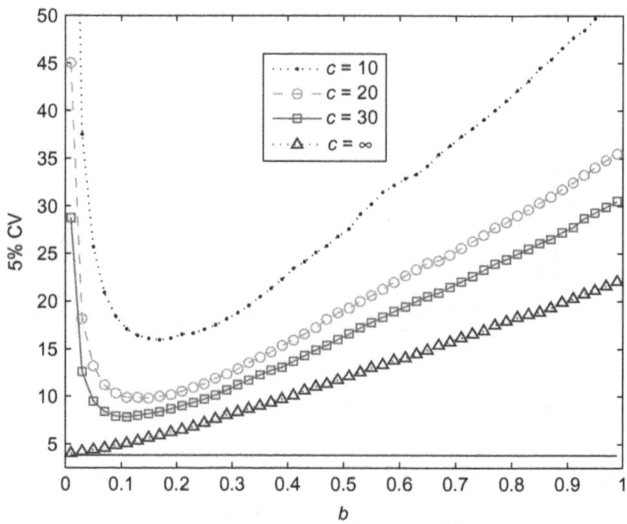

Fig. 1. Critical values from $F_\infty(c)$ with $p = 1$ and the Bartlett kernel.

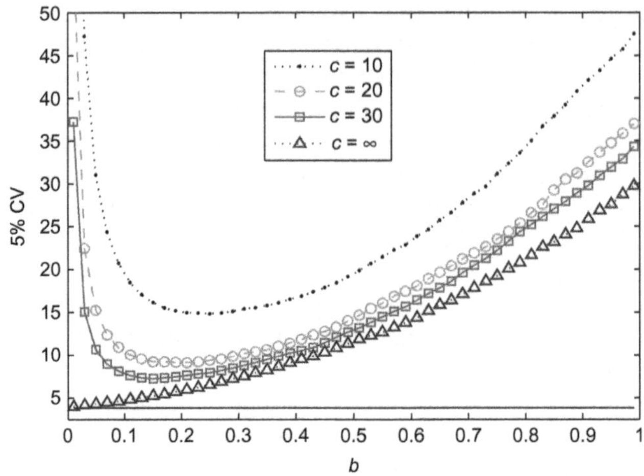

Fig. 2. Critical Values from $F_\infty(c)$ with $p = 1$ and the Parzen Kernel.

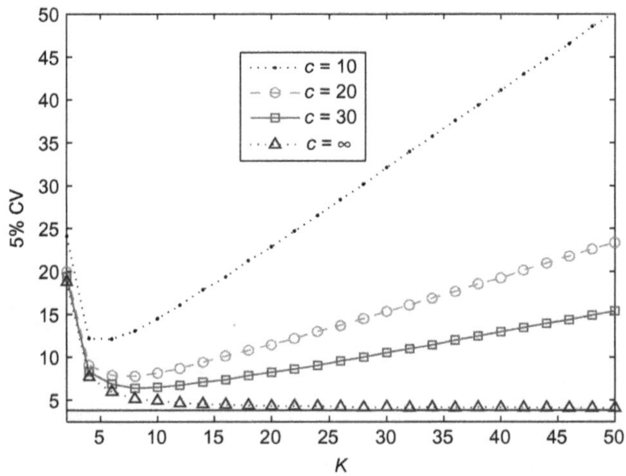

Fig. 3. Critical Values from $F_\infty(c)$ with $p = 1$ and the Series LRV Estimator.

4. *F* APPROXIMATION IN THE CASE OF SERIES VARIANCE ESTIMATION

In this section, we consider the series variance estimation and show that $F_\infty(c_m)$ can be approximated by an F distribution for some (transformed) basis functions.

In the case of series variance estimation, we have

$$pF_{\infty}(c_m) = \left[\int_0^1 \boldsymbol{\phi}_0(r) J_{c_m}(r) \mathrm{d}r\right]' \times \left\{\frac{1}{K}\sum_{\ell=1}^{K}\left[\int_0^1 \boldsymbol{\phi}_\ell(r) J_{c_m}(r) \mathrm{d}r\right]\left[\int_0^1 \boldsymbol{\phi}_\ell(r) J_{c_m}(r) \mathrm{d}r\right]'\right\}^{-1} \times \left[\int_0^1 \boldsymbol{\phi}_0(r) J_{c_m}(r) \mathrm{d}r\right] \Big/ p$$

for $\boldsymbol{\phi}_0(r) \equiv 1$. We want to select the basis functions such that $\int_0^1 \boldsymbol{\phi}_\ell(r) J_{c_m}(r)\,\mathrm{d}r \sim \text{i.i.d.} N(0, I_p)$ across $\ell = 0, 1, \ldots, K$. Note that $\int_0^1 \boldsymbol{\phi}_\ell(r)\, J_{c_m}(r)\,\mathrm{d}r$ for $\ell = 0, 1, \ldots, K$ are jointly normal, it suffices to select $\{\boldsymbol{\phi}_\ell(r), \ell = 1, \ldots, K\}$ such that $\left\{\int_0^1 \boldsymbol{\phi}_\ell(r)\, J_{c_m}(r)\,\mathrm{d}r, \ell = 0, 1, \ldots, K\right\}$ are not correlated with each other. But

$$cov\left(\int_0^1 \boldsymbol{\phi}_{\ell_1}(r)\, J_{c_m}(r)\,\mathrm{d}r, \int_0^1 \boldsymbol{\phi}_{\ell_2}(r)\, J_{c_m}(r)\,\mathrm{d}r\right) = \int_0^1 \int_0^1 \boldsymbol{\phi}_{\ell_1}(r)\, \boldsymbol{\phi}_{\ell_2}(s)\, \kappa_{c_m}(r,s)\,\mathrm{d}r\,\mathrm{d}s \times I_p$$

where

$$\kappa_{c_m}(r,s) := \left\{\exp[-c_m|r-s|] - \exp[-c_m(r+s)]\right\}/(2c_m)$$

is the covariance kernel of $J_{c_m}(\cdot)$. When $c_m = 0$, we define

$$\kappa_{c_m}(r,s)|_{c_m=0} = \lim_{c_m \to 0} \kappa_{c_m}(r,s) = \min(r,s)$$

which is the covariance kernel of the standard Brownian motion. So it suffices to select the basis functions to satisfy

$$\int_0^1 \int_0^1 \boldsymbol{\phi}_{\ell_1}(r)\, \boldsymbol{\phi}_{\ell_2}(s)\, \kappa_{c_m}(r,s)\,\mathrm{d}r\,\mathrm{d}s = \delta_{\ell_1 \ell_2} \quad \text{for all} \quad \ell_1, \ell_2 = 1, \ldots, K \tag{9}$$

$$\int_0^1 \int_0^1 \boldsymbol{\phi}_\ell \kappa_{c_m}(r,s)\,\mathrm{d}r\,\mathrm{d}s = 0 \quad \text{for all} \quad \ell = 1, 2, \ldots, K \tag{10}$$

$$\int_0^1 \boldsymbol{\phi}_\ell(r)\,\mathrm{d}r = 0 \quad \text{for all} \quad \ell = 1, 2, \ldots, K \tag{11}$$

The last set of equations maintains the "zero mean" conditions.

Instead of directly searching for the appropriate basis functions, for computational reasons we consider the discrete analogue of Eqs. (9)–(11). Let $A=(a_{ij})$ be the $T\times T$ matrix with elements $a_{ij}=\kappa_{c_m}(i/T,j/T)$. By definition, A is a positive definite symmetric matrix. For any two vectors $\ell_1,\ell_2\in\mathbb{R}^T$, we define the inner product

$$\langle\ell_1,\ell_2\rangle=\ell_1' A\ell_2/T^2 \tag{12}$$

Then $\mathbb{R}^T$ is a Hilbert space with the above weighted inner product. Let

$$\boldsymbol{\phi}_\ell=[\boldsymbol{\phi}_\ell(1/T),\boldsymbol{\phi}_\ell(2/T),\ \ldots,\ \boldsymbol{\phi}_\ell(T/T)]'$$

be the basis vector associated with the basis function $\boldsymbol{\phi}_\ell(\cdot)$ for $\ell=0,1,\ldots,K$. The finite sample versions of Eqs. (9)–(11) are

$$\langle\boldsymbol{\phi}_{\ell_1},\boldsymbol{\phi}_{\ell_2}\rangle=\delta_{\ell_1\ell_2}\quad\text{for all}\quad\ell_1,\ell_2=1,\ldots,K \tag{13}$$

$$\boldsymbol{\phi}_\ell' A\boldsymbol{\phi}_0=0\quad\text{for all}\quad\ell=1,2,\ldots,K \tag{14}$$

$$\boldsymbol{\phi}_\ell'\boldsymbol{\phi}_0=0\quad\text{for all}\quad\ell=1,2,\ldots,K \tag{15}$$

Note that Eq. (13) is different from the usual orthonormality in the Euclidian sense. In general, the basis vectors $\{\boldsymbol{\phi}_\ell\}$ do not satisfy Eq. (13) even if the basis functions $\{\boldsymbol{\phi}_\ell\}$ are orthonormal in $\mathbb{L}^2[0,1]$. However, given any candidate basis functions or vectors, we can make them satisfy the above conditions via transformation and orthogonalization. We follow the steps below:

(i) Let $V_T=[\boldsymbol{\phi}_0,A\boldsymbol{\phi}_0]$ be a $T\times 2$ matrix and compute

$$\tilde{\boldsymbol{\phi}}_\ell=[I_T-V_T(V_T'V_T)^{-1}V_T']\boldsymbol{\phi}_\ell$$

for $\ell=1,\ldots,K$.

(ii) Employ the Gram–Schmidt scheme to orthogonalize the vectors $\{\tilde{\boldsymbol{\phi}}_\ell\}_{\ell=1}^K$ under the inner product $\langle\cdot,\cdot\rangle$. More specifically, we let

$$\tilde{q}_1 = \tilde{\boldsymbol{\phi}}_1$$

$$\tilde{q}_2 = \tilde{\boldsymbol{\phi}}_2 - \frac{\langle\tilde{\boldsymbol{\phi}}_2, \tilde{q}_1\rangle}{\langle\tilde{q}_1, \tilde{q}_1\rangle}\tilde{q}_1 \qquad \cdots$$

$$\tilde{q}_K = \tilde{\boldsymbol{\phi}}_K - \frac{\langle\tilde{\boldsymbol{\phi}}_K, \tilde{q}_{K-1}\rangle}{\langle\tilde{q}_{K-1}, \tilde{q}_{K-1}\rangle}\tilde{q}_{K-1} - \cdots - \frac{\langle\tilde{\boldsymbol{\phi}}_K, \tilde{q}_1\rangle}{\langle\tilde{q}_1, \tilde{q}_1\rangle}\bar{q}_1$$

Note that $\tilde{\boldsymbol{\phi}}_\ell$ is the projection of $\boldsymbol{\phi}_\ell$ onto the orthogonal complement of the space spanned by $\boldsymbol{\phi}_0$ and $A\boldsymbol{\phi}_0$. By construction $\tilde{\boldsymbol{\phi}}'_\ell A\boldsymbol{\phi}_0 = 0$ and $\tilde{\boldsymbol{\phi}}'_\ell\boldsymbol{\phi}_0 = 0$. Since $\tilde{q}_\ell$ is a linear combination of $\tilde{\boldsymbol{\phi}}_\ell$, we have $\tilde{q}'_\ell A\boldsymbol{\phi}_0 = 0$ and $\tilde{q}'_\ell\boldsymbol{\phi}_0 = 0$. Also by construction, $\langle\tilde{q}_{\ell_1}, \tilde{q}_{\ell_2}\rangle = 0$ for $\ell_1 \neq \ell_2$. Let $q_\ell = \tilde{q}_\ell/\sqrt{\langle\tilde{q}_\ell, \tilde{q}_\ell\rangle}$, then $\{q_1, \ldots, q_K\}$ is a set of bases in $\mathbb{R}^T$ that satisfies the conditions in Eqs. (13)–(15).

Let $\tilde{\Phi} := (\tilde{\boldsymbol{\phi}}_1, \tilde{\boldsymbol{\phi}}_2, \ldots, \tilde{\boldsymbol{\phi}}_K)$ and $\tilde{Q} := (\tilde{q}_1, \tilde{q}_2, \ldots, \tilde{q}_K)$. Then $\tilde{\Phi} = \tilde{Q}\tilde{R}$ where R is the upper triangular matrix given by

$$\tilde{R} = \begin{bmatrix} 1 & \frac{\langle\tilde{\boldsymbol{\phi}}_2, \tilde{q}_1\rangle}{\langle\tilde{q}_1, \tilde{q}_1\rangle} & \cdots & \frac{\langle\tilde{\boldsymbol{\phi}}_K, \tilde{q}_1\rangle}{\langle\tilde{q}_1, \tilde{q}_1\rangle} \\ 0 & 1 & \cdots & \cdots \\ \cdots & \cdots & \ddots & \frac{\langle\tilde{\boldsymbol{\phi}}_K, \tilde{q}_{K-1}\rangle}{\langle\tilde{q}_{K-1}, \tilde{q}_{K-1}\rangle} \\ 0 & \cdots & 0 & 1 \end{bmatrix}$$

To represent $\tilde{\Phi}$ in terms of $Q := (q_1, q_2, \ldots, q_K)$, we let $\mathcal{D} = diag(\langle\tilde{q}_1, \tilde{q}_1\rangle^{1/2}, \ldots, \langle\tilde{q}_K, \tilde{q}_K\rangle^{1/2})$ be a $K \times K$ diagonal matrix. Then $\tilde{Q} = Q\mathcal{D}$ and

$$\tilde{\Phi} = QR$$

where $R = \mathcal{D}\tilde{R}$. The above decomposition is related to the QR decomposition but the columns of Q are not orthonormal in the usual Euclidean sense but instead they are orthonormal under the inner product defined in Eq. (12).

In a matrix programming environment, we can compute Q easily. Let R^* be the upper triangular factor of the Cholesky decomposition of $\tilde{\Phi}' A\tilde{\Phi}/T^2$, that is, $\tilde{\Phi}' A\tilde{\Phi}/T^2 = (R^*)'R^*$. Then we can let $Q = \tilde{\Phi}(R^*)^{-1}$, which satisfies

$$Q'AQ/T^2 = (R^{*\prime})^{-1}\tilde{\Phi}' A\tilde{\Phi}(R^*)^{-1}/T^2 = (R^{*\prime})^{-1}(R^*)'R^*(R^*)^{-1} = I_K$$

as desired.

Using the basis vectors $\{\boldsymbol{q}_1, \ldots, \boldsymbol{q}_K\}$, we can construct the variance estimator:

$$\begin{aligned}\hat{\Omega}_q &= \frac{D_T^2}{T^2}\frac{1}{K}\sum_{\ell=1}^{K}\left(\sum_{t=1}^{T} q_{\ell t}\hat{e}_t\right)\left(\sum_{s=1}^{T} q_{\ell s}\hat{e}_s\right)' \\ &= \frac{D_T^2}{T^2}\frac{1}{K}\sum_{\ell=1}^{K}\left(\sum_{t=1}^{T} q_{\ell t}e_t\right)\left(\sum_{s=1}^{T} q_{\ell s}e_s\right)'\end{aligned}$$

where $q_{\ell t}$ is an element of $\boldsymbol{q}_\ell$ so that $\boldsymbol{q}_\ell = (q_{\ell 1}, \ldots, q_{\ell T})'$ and the second equality holds because $\sum_{t=1}^{T} q_{\ell t} = \boldsymbol{q}_\ell'\boldsymbol{\phi}_0 = 0$. The associated F_T statistic is

$$\begin{aligned}F_{T,q} &= D_T(\hat{\theta}-\theta_0)'\hat{\Omega}_q^{-1} D_T(\hat{\theta}-\theta_0)/p \\ &= \left(\frac{1}{T}\sum_{t=1}^{T}\frac{e_t}{\sqrt{T}}\right)'\left[\frac{1}{K}\sum_{j=1}^{K}\left(\frac{1}{T}\sum_{t=1}^{T} q_{\ell t}\frac{e_t}{\sqrt{T}}\right)\left(\frac{1}{T}\sum_{s=1}^{T} q_{\ell s}\frac{e_s}{\sqrt{T}}\right)'\right]^{-1}\left(\frac{1}{T}\sum_{t=1}^{T}\frac{e_t}{\sqrt{T}}\right)\Big/p\end{aligned}$$

and the t_T statistic is

$$t_{T,q} = \frac{D_T(\hat{\theta}-\theta_0)}{\sqrt{\hat{\Omega}_q}} = \left[\frac{1}{T}\sum_{t=1}^{T}\frac{e_t}{\sqrt{T}}\right]\left[\frac{1}{K}\sum_{j=1}^{K}\left(\frac{1}{T}\sum_{t=1}^{T} q_{\ell t}\frac{e_t}{\sqrt{T}}\right)^2\right]^{-1/2}$$

As $T \to \infty$ for a fixed c_m and h, we have

$$\left(\frac{1}{\sqrt{\langle\boldsymbol{\phi}_0, \boldsymbol{\phi}_0\rangle}}\frac{1}{T}\sum_{t=1}^{T}\frac{e_t}{\sqrt{T}}, \frac{1}{T}\sum_{t=1}^{T} q_{1t}\frac{e_t}{\sqrt{T}}, \ldots, \frac{1}{T}\sum_{t=1}^{T} q_{Kt}\frac{e_t}{\sqrt{T}}\right) \to^d \Lambda\,(\eta_0, \eta_1, \ldots, \eta_K)$$

where $(\eta_0, \eta_1, \ldots, \eta_K)$ are jointly normal. Since $\langle \boldsymbol{q}_\ell, \boldsymbol{\phi}_0 \rangle = 0$ for $\ell = 1, \ldots, K$ and $\langle \boldsymbol{q}_{\ell_1}, \boldsymbol{q}_{\ell_2} \rangle = \delta_{\ell_1, \ell_2}$, we know that $\eta_\ell \sim \text{i.i.d.} N(0, I_p)$ for $\ell = 0, 1, \ldots, K$. Hence

$$\langle \boldsymbol{\phi}_0, \boldsymbol{\phi}_0 \rangle^{-1} F_{T,q} \to^d F_\infty(c_m) = \eta_0' \left\{ \frac{1}{K} \sum_{\ell=1}^{K} \eta_\ell \eta_\ell' \right\}^{-1} \eta_0 / p$$

Note that $pF_\infty(c_m)$ follows Hotelling's $T^2_{p,K}$ distribution. Using the relationship between the T^2 distribution and the F distribution, we have

$$\begin{aligned} F^*_{T,q} &:= \frac{K - p + 1}{K} \langle \boldsymbol{\phi}_0, \boldsymbol{\phi}_0 \rangle^{-1} F_{T,q} \\ &\to^d \frac{K - p + 1}{K} F_\infty(c_m) =^d \frac{K - p + 1}{Kp} T^2_{p,K} =^d F_{p, K - p + 1} \end{aligned} \tag{16}$$

where $F_{p,\, K-p+1}$ is the F distribution with degrees of freedom $(p,\; K - p + 1)$. Similarly

$$t^*_{T,q} := \langle \boldsymbol{\phi}_0, \boldsymbol{\phi}_0 \rangle^{-1} t_{T,q} \to^d t_K \tag{17}$$

where t_K is the t distribution with degrees of freedom K.

Note that

$$\begin{aligned} \langle \boldsymbol{\phi}_0,\, \boldsymbol{\phi}_0 \rangle &= \frac{1}{T^2} \sum_{t=1}^{T} \sum_{s=1}^{T} \kappa_{c_m} \left(\frac{t}{T}, \frac{s}{T} \right) \\ &\to \int_0^1 \int_0^1 \kappa_{c_m}(r, s)\, \mathrm{d}r\, \mathrm{d}s = \frac{1}{c_m^2} - \frac{1}{2c_m^3} (e^{-2c_m} - 4e^{-c_m} + 3) \end{aligned}$$

as $T \to \infty$, we can replace $\langle \boldsymbol{\phi}_0,\, \boldsymbol{\phi}_0 \rangle$ by the above limit in the definitions of $F^*_{T,q}$ and $t^*_{T,q}$ and still get the same limit distributions.

Our asymptotic development justifies the use of standard F and t approximations in hypothesis testing, even if the underlying process has strong autocorrelation. More specifically, we can employ the modified test statistic $\tilde{F}_T$ and a standard F distribution as the reference distribution to test joint hypotheses. When there is a single hypothesis, we can employ the modified t statistic and the standard t distribution. This leads to our asymptotic F test and t test.

The limiting distributions $F_{p,K-p+1}$ and t_K are exactly the same as what Sun (2013) obtained in the absence of strong autocorrelation. More specifically, when ρ is a fixed constant less than 1 in absolute value, Sun (2013) employs orthonormal basis functions, say $\{\boldsymbol{\phi}_{o\ell}(\cdot)\}$, in $\mathbb{L}^2[0,1]$ with $\int_0^1 \boldsymbol{\phi}_{o\ell}(r)\,\mathrm{d}r = 0$ to construct the series variance estimator, and establishes the following weak convergence results for the associated F and t statistics:

$$F_T \rightarrow^d F_\infty(\infty) \text{ and } t_T \rightarrow^d t_\infty(\infty)$$

where

$$\frac{K-p+1}{K} F_\infty(\infty) =^d F_{p,K-p+1} \text{ and } t_\infty(\infty) =^d t_K$$

That is

$$\frac{K-p+1}{K} F_T \rightarrow^d F_{p,K-p+1} \text{ and } t_T \rightarrow^d t_K$$

To relate the above approximations to those in Eqs. (16) and (17), we consider the case when c_m is large. As $c_m \rightarrow \infty$, we have

$$\int_0^1 \int_0^1 \boldsymbol{\phi}_{o\ell_1}(r)\, \boldsymbol{\phi}_{o\ell_2}(s)\, c_m^2 \kappa_{c_m}(r,s)\, \mathrm{d}r\mathrm{d}s = \int_0^1 \boldsymbol{\phi}_{o\ell_1}(r)\, \boldsymbol{\phi}_{o\ell_2}(r)\, \mathrm{d}r + o(1)$$

$$\int_0^1 \int_0^1 \boldsymbol{\phi}_{o\ell_1}(r)\, c_m^2 \kappa_{c_m}(r,s)\, \mathrm{d}r\mathrm{d}s = \int_0^1 \boldsymbol{\phi}_{o\ell_1}(r)\, \mathrm{d}r + o(1)$$

So if $\{\boldsymbol{\phi}_{o\ell}(\cdot)\}$ is a set of orthonormal basis functions in $\mathbb{L}^2[0,1]$ with $\int_0^1 \boldsymbol{\phi}_{o\ell}(r)\,\mathrm{d}r = 0$, then $\{c_m \boldsymbol{\phi}_{o\ell}(r)\}$ will satisfy Eqs. (9)–(11) approximately. That is, as $c_m \rightarrow \infty$, the effects of transformation and orthogonalization on $\{c_m \boldsymbol{\phi}_{o\ell}(\cdot)\}$ becomes negligible. We can just use $\{\boldsymbol{\phi}_{o\ell}(\cdot)\}$ as the basis functions to construct the series variance estimator, leading to the modified F statistic $F^*_{T,\boldsymbol{\phi}_o}$. We have

$$F^*_{T,\boldsymbol{\phi}_o} := \frac{K-p+1}{K} \langle \boldsymbol{\phi}_0, \boldsymbol{\phi}_0 \rangle^{-1} F_{T,\boldsymbol{\phi}_o} \rightarrow^d \frac{K-p+1}{K} F_\infty^{\boldsymbol{\phi}_o}(c_m)$$

where

$$
\begin{aligned}
F_{\infty}^{\phi_o}(c_m) &= \left[\int_0^1 J_{c_m}(r)\,\mathrm{d}r\right]' \left\{\frac{1}{K}\sum_{\ell=1}^{K}\left[\int_0^1 \phi_{o\ell}(r)\,J_{c_m}(r)\,\mathrm{d}r\right]\right. \\
&\quad \times \left.\left[\int_0^1 \phi_{o\ell}(r)\,J_{c_m}(r)\,\mathrm{d}r\right]'\right\}^{-1}\left[\int_0^1 J_{c_m}(r)\,\mathrm{d}r\right]\Big/ p \\
&= \left[\int_0^1\int_0^1 c_m^2\kappa_{c_m}(r,s)\,\mathrm{d}r\,\mathrm{d}s\right]\left[\frac{\int_0^1 c_m J_{c_m}(r)\,\mathrm{d}r}{\sqrt{\int_0^1\int_0^1 c_m^2\kappa_{c_m}(r,s)\,\mathrm{d}r\,\mathrm{d}s}}\right]' \\
&\quad \times \left\{\frac{1}{K}\sum_{\ell=1}^{K}\left[\int_0^1 \phi_{o\ell}(r)\,c_m J_{c_m}(r)\,\mathrm{d}r\right]\left[\int_0^1 \phi_{o\ell}(r)\,c_m J_{c_m}(r)\,\mathrm{d}r\right]'\right\}^{-1} \\
&\quad \times \left[\frac{\int_0^1 c_m J_{c_m}(r)\,\mathrm{d}r}{\sqrt{\int_0^1\int_0^1 c_m^2\kappa_{c_m}(r,s)\,\mathrm{d}r\,\mathrm{d}s}}\right]\Big/ p \\
&\to^d \eta_0'\left\{\frac{1}{K}\sum_{\ell=1}^{K}\eta_\ell\eta_\ell'\right\}^{-1}\eta_0/p =^d F_\infty(\infty)
\end{aligned}
$$

as $c_m \to \infty$, where we have used $\lim_{c_m\to\infty}\int_0^1\int_0^1 c_m^2\kappa_{c_m}(r,s)\,\mathrm{d}r\,\mathrm{d}s = 1$. So F_{T,ϕ_o}^* converges weakly to $F_{p,K-p+1}$ under the sequential limits. This is consistent with Theorem 2.

5. EXTENSION TO A GENERAL SETTING

In the previous section, we use the simple multivariate location model to highlight the effect of strong autocorrelation on distributional approximations. Hypothesis testing in location models, as simple as it seems, includes more general testing problems as special cases.

Consider an M estimator, $\hat{\theta}_T$, of a $n\times 1$ parameter vector θ_0 that satisfies

$$\hat{\theta}_T=\arg\min_{\theta\in\Theta} Q_T(\theta)=\arg\min_{\theta\in\Theta} \frac{1}{T}\sum_{t=1}^{T}\rho(\theta,Z_t)$$

where Θ is a compact parameter space, and $\rho(\theta,Z_t)$ is the criterion function based on observation Z_t. M estimators are a broad class of estimators and include, for example, the maximum likelihood estimator (MLE), ordinary least squares (OLS) estimator, quantile regression estimator as special cases.

Suppose we want to test the null hypothesis that $H_0:\theta=\theta_0$ against $H_1:\theta\neq\theta_0$. Then by the usual identification assumption for the M estimator, under the null hypothesis and additional regularity assumptions, $\theta=\theta_0$ is the unique minimizer of

$$Q(\theta)=E\rho(\theta,Z_t)$$

That is

$$Es_t(\theta)=0 \text{ where } s_t(\theta)=\frac{\partial\rho(\theta,\ Z_t)}{\partial\theta}$$

if and only if $\theta=\theta_0$. So the null hypothesis $H_0:\theta=\theta_0$ is equivalent to the hypothesis that the multivariate process $s_t(\theta_0)$ has mean zero. We have just converted a general testing problem into testing for zero mean of a multivariate process. The latter problem is exactly the testing problem we consider in the previous sections. All results there remain valid if the multivariate process $s_t(\theta_0)$ satisfies the assumptions imposed on y_t.

The above extension applies to hypothesis testing that involves the whole parameter vector θ. Suppose we are only interested in some linear combinations of θ such that the null hypothesis is $H_0:R\theta=r$ and the alternative hypothesis is $H_1:R\theta\neq r$, where R is a $p\times n$ matrix. Under the usual regularity conditions, we have

$$\sqrt{T}(R\hat{\theta}_T-r)=-\frac{1}{\sqrt{T}}\sum_{t=1}^{T}RH_T(\bar{\theta}_T)^{-1}s_t(\theta_0) \text{ for } H_T(\theta)=\frac{1}{T}\sum_{t=1}^{T}\frac{\partial s_t(\theta)}{\partial\theta'}$$

and some value $\bar{\theta}_T$ between θ_0 and $\hat{\theta}_T$. Let $\tilde{s}_t(\theta_1,\theta_2)=-RH_T(\theta_1)^{-1}s_t(\theta_2)$ be the transformed score process, then the F-test version of the Wald statistic is

$$\tilde{F}_T=T\left(R\hat{\theta}_T-r\right)'\tilde{\Omega}^{-1}\left(R\hat{\theta}_T-r\right)/p \tag{18}$$

where

$$\tilde{\Omega} = \frac{1}{T}\sum_{t=1}^{T}\sum_{\tau=1}^{T} Q_{Th}^{*}\left(\frac{t}{T},\frac{\tau}{T}\right)\tilde{s}_t\left(\hat{\theta}_T,\hat{\theta}_T\right)\tilde{s}_\tau'\left(\hat{\theta}_T,\hat{\theta}_T\right)$$

Under the assumptions given in KV (2005) and Sun (2013), $\tilde{F}_T$ is asymptotically equivalent to

$$F_T = \left[\frac{1}{\sqrt{T}}\sum_{t=1}^{T} e_t\right]' \hat{\Omega}^{-1} \left[\frac{1}{\sqrt{T}}\sum_{t=1}^{T} e_t\right] \Big/ p \tag{19}$$

where $e_t = -RH^{-1}(\theta_0)\, s_t\,(\theta_0)$, $H(\theta_0) = p\lim_{T\to\infty} H_T(\overline{\theta}_T)$, and

$$\hat{\Omega} = \frac{1}{T}\sum_{t=1}^{T}\sum_{s=1}^{T} Q_{Th}^{*}\left(\frac{t}{T},\frac{s}{T}\right)(e_t - \overline{e})(e_s - \overline{e})'$$

It follows that the F_T statistic can be viewed as a Wald statistic for testing whether the mean of the multivariate process e_t is zero. So the asymptotic approximation in Theorem 1 applies to the Wald statistic. The same observation remains valid for the t statistic.

More generally, consider a standard GMM framework with the moment conditions

$$Ef(Z_t,\ \theta_0) = 0, \quad t = 1, 2, \ldots, T$$

where $\theta_0 \in \Theta \subseteq \mathbb{R}^n$ and $f(\cdot)$ is an $m \times 1$ vector of twice continuously differentiable functions with $m \geq n$ and rank $E[\partial f(Z_t, \theta_0)/\partial\theta'] = n$. The GMM estimator of θ_0 is then given by

$$\hat{\theta}_T = \arg\min_{\theta\in\Theta} \left(\frac{1}{T}\sum_{t=1}^{T} f(Z_t,\theta)\right)' \mathcal{W}_T \left(\frac{1}{T}\sum_{t=1}^{T} f(Z_t,\theta)\right)$$

where $\mathcal{W}_T$ is an $m \times m$ positive semidefinite weighting matrix and $p\lim_{T\to\infty}\mathcal{W}_T = \mathcal{W}_\infty$.

Suppose we test $H_0 : R\theta = r$ against the alternative $H_1 : R\theta \neq r$. Let $G_T(\theta) = \mathrm{plim}_{T\to\infty}\left[\frac{1}{T}\sum_{t=1}^{T} \partial f(Z_t,\theta)/\partial\theta'\right]$. Then under the usual regularity conditions for GMM estimation, we have

$$\sqrt{T}(R\hat{\theta}_T - r) = -\frac{1}{\sqrt{T}}\sum_{t=1}^{T} R\left[G_T(\hat{\theta}_T)'\mathcal{W}_T G_T(\hat{\theta}_T)\right]^{-1} G_T(\hat{\theta}_T)'\mathcal{W}_T f(Z_t, \theta_0) + o_p(1) \tag{20}$$

As before, we let $\tilde{s}_t(\theta_1, \theta_2) = R[G_T(\theta_1)'\mathcal{W}_T G_T(\theta_1)]^{-1} G_T(\theta_1)'\mathcal{W}_T f(Z_t, \theta_2)$. Then the Wald statistic can be computed in the same way as in Eq. (18), which is asymptotically equivalent to F_T in Eq. (18) with

$$e_t = -R(G_0'\mathcal{W}_\infty G_0)^{-1} G_0'\mathcal{W}_\infty f(Z_t, \theta_0)$$

With this new definition of e_t, the asymptotic approximations in the previous sections are applicable to both the Wald statistic and t statistic.

6. IMPLEMENTATION AND SIMULATION

6.1. Implementation

The near-unit-root fixed-smoothing asymptotic approximations $F_\infty(c_m)$ and $t_\infty(c_m)$ depend on the near-unit-root parameter c_m, which cannot be consistently estimated. There are many ways to gauge the value of c_m in the literature on optimal unit root testing. Sun (forthcoming) constructs confidence intervals for c_m and uses the method of Bonferroni bound to obtain tests with good size properties. Here for simplicity we use the OLS estimator:

$$\hat{\rho}_i = \frac{\sum_{t=2}^{T} \hat{e}_{it}\hat{e}_{i,t-1}}{\sum_{t=2}^{T} \hat{e}_{i,t-1}^2}$$

where for the location model, we let $\hat{e}_{it} = y_{it} - \bar{y}_{i,\cdot}$, for the model estimated by the M estimator, we let $\hat{e}_{it}$ be the i-th component of $RH_T^{-1}(\hat{\theta}_T)s_t(\hat{\theta}_T)$, for the model estimated by the GMM estimator, we let $\hat{e}_{it}$ be the i-th component of $R[\hat{G}_T'\mathcal{W}_T\hat{G}_T]^{-1}\hat{G}_T\mathcal{W}_T f(Z_t, \hat{\theta}_T)$ with $\hat{G}_T = G_T(\hat{\theta}_T)$. Given the average of the estimated autoregressive parameters: $\hat{\rho} = p^{-1}\sum_{i=1}^{p}\hat{\rho}_i$, we take c_m to satisfy $1 - \hat{c}_m/T = \hat{\rho}$, that is, $\hat{c}_m = T(1-\hat{\rho})$. To reduce the randomness of $\hat{\rho}$ and hence $\hat{c}_m$, we can discretize the interval $[-1,1]$ and use the grid point that is closest to $\hat{\rho}$ as the autoregressive parameter. Let $\tilde{\rho}$ be this grid point, we can let $\hat{c}_m = T(1-\tilde{\rho})$.

It is important to point out that while we propose using $F_\infty(c_m)$ or $t_\infty(c_m)$ as the reference distributions to perform hypothesis testing, it does not mean that we literally treat c_m as fixed. Whether we hold c_m fixed or let it increase with the sample size can be viewed as different asymptotic specifications to obtain approximations to the finite sample distribution. The near-unit-root fixed-smoothing asymptotic does not require that we fix the value of c_m in finite samples. In fact, if e_t is stationary with a fixed autoregressive coefficient, then with probability approaching one, $\hat{c}_m$ will increase with the sample size. This will not cause any problem, as we have shown that as c_m increases $F_\infty(c_m)$ will become very close to $F_\infty(\infty)$, the fixed-smoothing asymptotic distribution under weak dependence. So the near-unit-root fixed-smoothing approximation is asymptotically valid under weak dependence. To some extent, $F_\infty(c_m)$ is a more robust approximation than $F_\infty(\infty)$.

6.2. Simulations

For the Monte Carlo experiments, we first consider a simple multivariate location model with four time series:

$$y_t = \theta + u_t \tag{21}$$

where the error u_t follows either a VAR(1) or VMA(1) process:

$$u_t = Au_{t-1} + \varepsilon_t \quad \text{or} \quad u_t = A\varepsilon_{t-1} + \varepsilon_t$$

where $A = \rho\mathbb{I}_4$, $\varepsilon_t = (v_{1t} + \mu f_t, v_{2t} + \mu f_t, \ldots, v_{nt} + \mu f_t)'/\sqrt{1+\mu^2}$ and $(v_t, f_t)'$ is a multivariate Gaussian white noise process with unit variance. In the case of VAR(1), we set $u_0 \sim N(0, \mathbb{I}_4)$. Under this specification, the four time series all follow the same VAR(1) or VMA(1) process with $\varepsilon_t \sim \text{i.i.d}N(0, \Sigma)$ for

$$\Sigma = \frac{1}{1+\mu^2}\mathbb{I}_4 + \frac{\mu^2}{1+\mu^2}\mathbb{J}_4$$

where $\mathbb{J}_4$ is a 4×4 matrix of ones. The parameter μ determines the degree of dependence among the time series considered. When $\mu = 0$, the four series are uncorrelated with each other. The large μ is, the larger the correlation.

For the model parameters, we take $\rho = -0.5, 0, 0.1, 0.3, 0.5, 0.7, 0.9$, and 0.95 and set $\mu = 0$ and 1. We set the intercepts to zero as the tests we consider are invariant to them. For each test, we consider two significance levels $\alpha = 5\%$ and $\alpha = 10\%$ and two different sample sizes $T = 200$ and 400.

We consider the following null hypotheses:

$$
\begin{aligned}
H_{01} &: \theta_1 = 0 \\
H_{02} &: \theta_1 = \theta_2 = 0 \\
H_{03} &: \theta_1 = \theta_2 = \theta_3 = 0 \\
H_{04} &: \theta_1 = \theta_2 = \theta_3 = \theta_4 = 0
\end{aligned}
$$

where $p = 1, 2, 3, 4$, respectively. The corresponding matrix R is the first p rows of the identity matrix $\mathbb{I}_4$.

We examine the finite sample performance of three different groups of tests. The first group of tests consists of the standard fixed-smoothing Wald tests of KVB (2000) and Sun (2013). The KVB test employs the Bartlett kernel variance estimator based with $b = 1$, and the test in Sun (2013) employs the series variance estimator with $K = 6$, 12, and 24. The basis functions used are $\phi_{2j-1}(x) = \sqrt{2}\cos(2j\pi x)$, $\phi_{2j}(x) = \sqrt{2}\sin(2j\pi x)$, $j = 1, \ldots, K/2$. For both the KVB test and the test in Sun (2013), we use standard fixed-smoothing critical values, which are obtained from simulations (the KVB test) or directly from the standard F distributions (the test in Sun (2013)). The second group of tests is similar to the first group but uses critical values from the near-unit-root fixed-smoothing asymptotic distributions developed in Section 3. The critical values are obtained via simulations with 999 simulation replications. The third group of tests is based on the F approximation in Section 4. The basis functions/vectors are transformed and orthogonalized version of $\phi_{2j-1}(x) = \sqrt{2}\cos(2j\pi x)$, $\phi_{2j}(x) = \sqrt{2}\sin(2j\pi x)$, $j = 1, \ldots, K/2$. These three groups of tests will be referred to as the "Stationary Fixed-Smoothing Tests", "Near-Unity Fixed-Smoothing Tests", and "Near-Unity F Tests." We could add the conventional chi-square tests but a large literature has already shown that the chi-square tests have much larger size distortion than the corresponding fixed-smoothing tests.

Table 1 reports the empirical null rejection probability of the three groups of tests for VAR(1) error. The sample size is 200 and the number of simulation replications is 10,000. A few observations can be drawn from the table. First, it is clear that the stationary fixed-smoothing asymptotic

Table 1. Empirical Size of 5% Fixed-Smoothing Asymptotic Tests with $T=200$ Under VAR(1) Errors.

ρ	Stationary Fixed-Smoothing				Near-Unity Fixed-Smoothing				Near-Unity F Tests		
	K6	K12	K24	KVB	K6	K12	K24	KVB	K6*	K12*	K24*
						$p=1$					
−0.5	0.048	0.051	0.050	0.043	0.039	0.045	0.043	0.044	0.048	0.050	0.049
0.0	0.049	0.051	0.052	0.048	0.039	0.045	0.042	0.045	0.049	0.050	0.047
0.1	0.049	0.051	0.052	0.049	0.039	0.044	0.042	0.045	0.048	0.050	0.046
0.3	0.049	0.052	0.054	0.050	0.040	0.044	0.043	0.045	0.048	0.050	0.045
0.5	0.049	0.055	0.062	0.053	0.040	0.046	0.044	0.047	0.048	0.050	0.044
0.7	0.051	0.063	0.087	0.060	0.041	0.049	0.050	0.047	0.048	0.051	0.047
0.9	0.076	0.138	0.254	0.094	0.053	0.066	0.071	0.055	0.059	0.076	0.088
0.95	0.143	0.264	0.415	0.136	0.083	0.103	0.111	0.073	0.091	0.124	0.146
						$p=2$					
−0.5	0.051	0.050	0.050	0.041	0.052	0.043	0.044	0.044	0.052	0.047	0.046
0.0	0.052	0.050	0.051	0.049	0.053	0.043	0.043	0.046	0.052	0.048	0.045
0.1	0.052	0.050	0.052	0.051	0.053	0.043	0.043	0.045	0.051	0.048	0.045
0.3	0.053	0.051	0.056	0.056	0.053	0.044	0.043	0.044	0.051	0.049	0.044
0.5	0.053	0.053	0.067	0.062	0.054	0.044	0.043	0.045	0.050	0.049	0.043
0.7	0.055	0.064	0.101	0.074	0.051	0.045	0.047	0.048	0.050	0.049	0.046
0.9	0.083	0.169	0.353	0.137	0.059	0.073	0.086	0.063	0.062	0.078	0.095
0.95	0.157	0.359	0.590	0.229	0.085	0.120	0.142	0.085	0.096	0.142	0.184
						$p=3$					
−0.5	0.050	0.050	0.048	0.036	0.047	0.050	0.048	0.043	0.050	0.051	0.044
0.0	0.051	0.051	0.049	0.050	0.046	0.050	0.048	0.044	0.051	0.050	0.043
0.1	0.051	0.052	0.050	0.052	0.046	0.050	0.049	0.045	0.051	0.049	0.043
0.3	0.051	0.053	0.054	0.058	0.044	0.051	0.049	0.046	0.052	0.049	0.042

Table 1. *(Continued)*

ρ	Stationary Fixed-Smoothing				Near-Unity Fixed-Smoothing				Near-Unity *F* Tests		
	K6	K12	K24	KVB	K6	K12	K24	KVB	K6*	K12*	K24*
0.5	0.052	0.055	0.065	0.069	0.042	0.051	0.050	0.046	0.053	0.049	0.040
0.7	0.053	0.066	0.110	0.090	0.045	0.055	0.059	0.048	0.052	0.050	0.043
0.9	0.079	0.189	0.428	0.201	0.063	0.085	0.100	0.062	0.058	0.079	0.098
0.95	0.152	0.427	0.710	0.354	0.090	0.150	0.172	0.088	0.089	0.150	0.205
						$p=4$					
−0.5	0.051	0.050	0.048	0.033	0.047	0.050	0.043	0.051	0.052	0.051	0.044
0.0	0.051	0.051	0.050	0.051	0.046	0.052	0.042	0.052	0.051	0.050	0.043
0.1	0.050	0.051	0.051	0.054	0.047	0.052	0.043	0.052	0.050	0.050	0.042
0.3	0.050	0.052	0.055	0.062	0.048	0.051	0.044	0.051	0.050	0.048	0.041
0.5	0.050	0.055	0.066	0.075	0.049	0.052	0.046	0.051	0.049	0.048	0.041
0.7	0.052	0.065	0.117	0.108	0.049	0.052	0.053	0.053	0.050	0.048	0.043
0.9	0.072	0.202	0.493	0.275	0.065	0.083	0.096	0.078	0.057	0.074	0.102
0.95	0.129	0.473	0.795	0.488	0.081	0.154	0.188	0.130	0.081	0.155	0.229

approximation works very well when the processes are not strongly autocorrelated. When the processes become more autocorrelated, the size distortion starts to increase. This is especially true when the number of joint hypotheses is more than one. The size distortion of the stationary fixed-smoothing tests can be as high as 0.795. This happens when $K = 24$ and $p = 4$. Even for the KVB test with $b = 1$, the size distortion is 0.488 when $p = 4$. Second, the near-unity fixed-smoothing asymptotic tests outperform the stationary fixed-smoothing tests in terms of size accuracy. When the processes are not strongly autocorrelated, the near-unity fixed-smoothing asymptotic tests have more or less the same size properties as the stationary fixed-smoothing asymptotic tests. However, when the processes approach unit root nonstationarity, the near-unity fixed-smoothing asymptotic tests succeed in reducing the size distortion. Comparing the tests in the second group, the series test with $K = 6$ and the KVB test have the most accurate size. Third, the near-unity asymptotic F tests are also more accurate than the stationary fixed-smoothing tests, which in the case of series variance estimation use also the F critical values. When K is relatively small, the near-unity asymptotic F test is as accurate as the test based on nonstandard simulated critical values. However, when K is large, the near-unity asymptotic F test has somewhat larger size distortion.

Table 2 is the same as Table 1 except that the sample size is $T = 400$. The qualitative observations we make for Table 1 apply to Table 2. As expected, all tests become more accurate. We omit the tables for the VMA (1) cases as all three groups of tests have similar good size properties for both sample sizes $T = 200$ and 400. There is no adverse effect of using the near-unity fixed-smoothing asymptotic distribution when the underlying processes are not strongly persistent. This is consistent with our theoretical findings.

Fig. 4 is a representative figure for size-adjusted power curves. The sample size is 200 and the number of joint hypotheses is 2. Of course, size adjustment is not feasible in practice, and this is exactly the reason we want to develop an asymptotically valid test that has accurate size in finite samples. Since tests based on the same statistic have the same size-adjusted power, a test in the first group has the same power as the corresponding test in the second group. So it suffices to report the power curves of the tests in the first and second groups. In Fig. 4, "K6", "K12", "K24", and "KVB" are the tests in the first group while "K6*", "K12*", and "K24*" are the tests in the second group. It is clear from the figure that the power of the series test increases with K, as shown in Sun (2013). What is new here is that the power of the fixed-smoothing nonstandard test is close to

Table 2. Empirical Size of 5% Fixed-Smoothing Asymptotic Tests with $T=400$ Under VAR(1) Errors.

ρ	Stationary Fixed-Smoothing				Near-Unity Fixed-Smoothing				Near-Unity F Tests		
	K6	K12	K24	KVB	K6	K12	K24	KVB	K6*	K12*	K24*
						$p=1$					
−0.5	0.051	0.047	0.047	0.048	0.049	0.039	0.042	0.037	0.049	0.047	0.046
0.0	0.051	0.048	0.046	0.050	0.044	0.040	0.044	0.035	0.049	0.046	0.045
0.1	0.050	0.048	0.046	0.051	0.044	0.040	0.045	0.035	0.049	0.046	0.045
0.3	0.050	0.048	0.047	0.052	0.044	0.040	0.045	0.036	0.049	0.046	0.044
0.5	0.050	0.049	0.049	0.054	0.045	0.041	0.044	0.037	0.049	0.046	0.044
0.7	0.051	0.050	0.057	0.056	0.046	0.041	0.044	0.037	0.049	0.046	0.044
0.9	0.058	0.076	0.134	0.072	0.047	0.051	0.058	0.043	0.051	0.053	0.059
0.95	0.080	0.138	0.252	0.090	0.056	0.071	0.086	0.050	0.062	0.079	0.095
						$p=2$					
−0.5	0.049	0.047	0.047	0.043	0.057	0.048	0.045	0.045	0.050	0.046	0.047
0.0	0.048	0.047	0.047	0.048	0.059	0.046	0.045	0.046	0.050	0.046	0.046
0.1	0.048	0.047	0.047	0.048	0.060	0.047	0.046	0.045	0.050	0.047	0.045
0.3	0.048	0.047	0.048	0.050	0.062	0.046	0.047	0.046	0.049	0.046	0.045
0.5	0.049	0.048	0.050	0.053	0.062	0.046	0.048	0.044	0.050	0.045	0.045
0.7	0.050	0.050	0.058	0.058	0.059	0.047	0.048	0.047	0.048	0.045	0.044
0.9	0.058	0.081	0.166	0.088	0.062	0.053	0.062	0.058	0.051	0.054	0.059
0.95	0.081	0.171	0.355	0.134	0.071	0.077	0.095	0.072	0.061	0.080	0.104
						$p=3$					
−0.5	0.049	0.047	0.048	0.042	0.043	0.039	0.043	0.044	0.050	0.047	0.047
0.0	0.048	0.048	0.048	0.047	0.041	0.038	0.044	0.042	0.050	0.047	0.046
0.1	0.048	0.048	0.049	0.049	0.041	0.038	0.044	0.043	0.050	0.047	0.046
0.3	0.048	0.048	0.050	0.052	0.042	0.038	0.043	0.045	0.050	0.048	0.046
0.5	0.049	0.049	0.052	0.057	0.044	0.037	0.040	0.045	0.051	0.047	0.045

Table 2. *(Continued)*

ρ	Stationary Fixed-Smoothing				Near-Unity Fixed-Smoothing				Near-Unity F Tests		
	K6	K12	K24	KVB	K6	K12	K24	KVB	K6*	K12*	K24*
0.7	0.051	0.051	0.062	0.067	0.046	0.037	0.039	0.048	0.049	0.048	0.045
0.9	0.058	0.084	0.192	0.119	0.048	0.042	0.059	0.058	0.051	0.054	0.063
0.95	0.082	0.188	0.438	0.200	0.060	0.063	0.087	0.071	0.061	0.081	0.112
						$p=4$					
−0.5	0.049	0.048	0.048	0.040	0.058	0.043	0.048	0.045	0.051	0.047	0.047
0.0	0.050	0.049	0.049	0.049	0.051	0.044	0.047	0.048	0.052	0.048	0.048
0.1	0.050	0.049	0.049	0.051	0.053	0.044	0.047	0.049	0.052	0.048	0.047
0.3	0.050	0.049	0.050	0.055	0.051	0.045	0.046	0.048	0.052	0.048	0.046
0.5	0.051	0.049	0.052	0.061	0.046	0.044	0.045	0.049	0.051	0.047	0.045
0.7	0.050	0.051	0.063	0.076	0.044	0.044	0.047	0.044	0.049	0.046	0.045
0.9	0.055	0.088	0.216	0.154	0.049	0.051	0.060	0.052	0.051	0.053	0.063
0.95	0.072	0.206	0.505	0.285	0.057	0.081	0.102	0.078	0.058	0.083	0.120

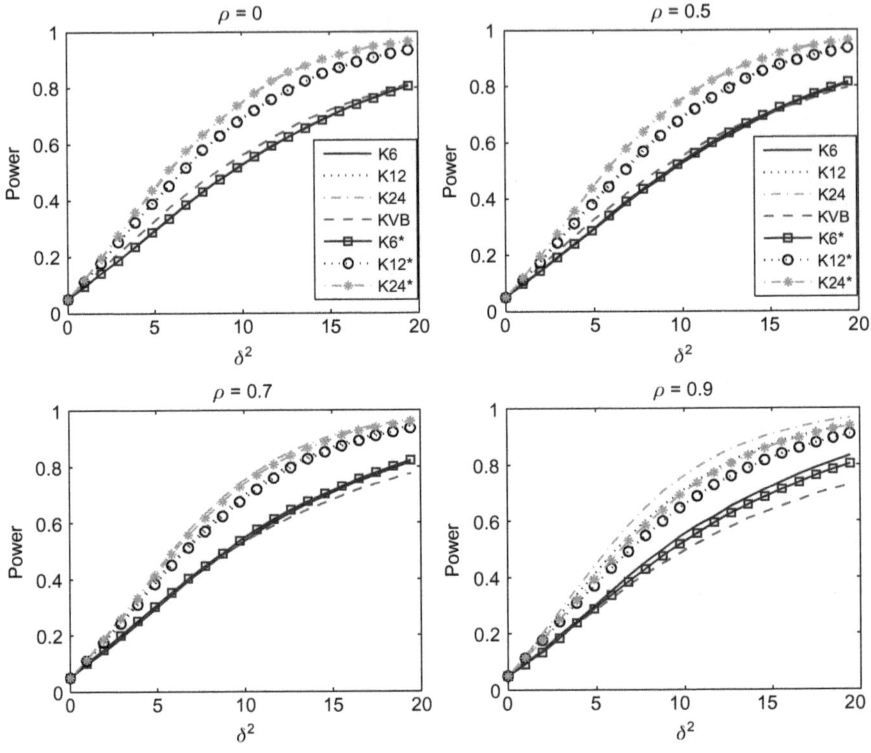

Fig. 4. Size-Adjusted Power of Different Testing Procedures for VAR(1) Error with Sample Size $T = 200$ and the Number of Joint Hypotheses $p = 2$. ("K6", "K12", "K24", and "KVB" Are the Near-Unity Fixed-Smoothing Tests While "K6*", "K12*", and "K24*" are the Near-Unity F Tests.)

that of the fixed-smoothing F test. Transformation and orthogonalization underlying the F test do not lead to power loss.

7. CONCLUSIONS

The paper develops a new fixed-smoothing asymptotic theory that accommodates strongly autocorrelated time series while also working very well in the absence of strong autocorrelation. Our proposed near-unity fixed-smoothing tests achieve triple robustness in the following sense: they are asymptotically valid regardless of whether the amount of smoothing is fixed or increases with the sample size, whether there is temporal dependence of unknown form or not, and whether the temporal dependence is strong or not when presented.

The near-unity fixed-smoothing asymptotic distribution is nonstandard. By choosing the basis functions appropriately, the nonstandard distribution can be reduced to a standard F approximation. See Sun and Kim (forthcoming) for an implementation of this idea in a different setting. An alternative way to characterize the strong autocorrelation is to model the moment process as a fractional process. In this case, we can follow Sun (2004) to develop a new asymptotic approximation. Our testing procedures can be combined with prewhitening. This may lead to a test with potentially very accurate size, even if the underlying processes are highly autocorrelated. We leave all these to future research.

ACKNOWLEDGMENTS

The ideas in the paper were first presented in my discussion of Müller (2014) at the 2013 ASSA meeting in San Diego, CA. For helpful comments, the author thanks Yoosoon Chang, Joon Park, Peter Phillips, an anonymous referee, and the participants of the 14th Advances in Econometrics Conference at Southern Methodist University in 2013.

REFERENCES

Alexopoulos, C. (2006). A comprehensive reviews of methods for simulation output analysis. *Proceedings of the 2006 Winter Simulation Conference*. Monterey, California, USA.

Alexopoulos, C. (2007). Statistical analysis of simulation output: State of the art. *Proceedings of the 2007 Winter Simulation Conference*. Washington, DC, USA.

Andrews, D. W. K. (1991). Heteroskedasticity and autocorrelation consistent covariance matrix estimation. *Econometrica 59*, 817–854.

Davidson, J. (1994). *Stochastic limit theory: An introduction for econometricicans*. New York, NY, USA: Oxford University Press.

Giraitis, L., & Phillips, P. C. B. (2006). Uniform limit theory for stationary autoregression. *Journal of Time Series Analysis*, *27*, 51–60.

Jansson, M. (2004). On the error of rejection probability in simple autocorrelation robust tests. *Econometrica*, *72*, 937–946.

Kiefer, N. M., & Vogelsang, T. J. (2002a). Heteroskedasticity-autocorrelation robust testing using bandwidth equal to sample size. *Econometric Theory*, *18*, 1350–1366.

Kiefer, N. M., & Vogelsang, T. J. (2002b). Heteroskedasticity-autocorrelation robust standard errors using the Bartlett kernel without truncation. *Econometrica*, *70*, 2093–2095.

Kiefer, N. M., & Vogelsang, T. J. (2005). A new asymptotic theory for heteroskedasticity-autocorrelation robust tests. *Econometric Theory*, *21*, 1130–1164.

Kiefer, N. M., Vogelsang, T. J., & Bunzel, H. (2000). Simple robust testing of regression hypotheses. *Econometrica*, *68*, 695–714.

Müller, U. K. (2007). A theory of robust long-run variance estimation. *Journal of Econometrics*, *141*, 1331–1352.

Müller, U. K. (2014). HAC corrections for strongly autocorrelated time series. *Journal of Business & Economic Statistics*, *32*(3), 311–322.

Newey, W. K., & West, K. D. (1987). A simple, positive semidefinite, heteroskedasticity and autocorrelation consistent covariance matrix. *Econometrica*, *55*, 703–708.

Park, J. (2003). *Weak unit roots*. Working Paper. Department of Economics, Indiana University.

Phillips, P. C. B. (1987). Towards a unified asymptotic theory for autoregression. *Biometrika*, *74*, 535–547.

Phillips, P. C. B. (2005). HAC estimation by automated regression. *Econometric Theory*, *21*, 116–142.

Phillips, P. C. B., & Durlauf, S. N. (1986). Multiple regression with integrated processes. *Review of Economic Studies*, *53*, 473–496.

Phillips, P. C. B., & Magdalinos, T. (2007). Limit theory for moderate deviations from a unit root. *Journal of Econometrics*, *136*, 115–130.

Phillips, P. C. B., Magdalinos, T., & Giraitis, L. (2010). Smoothing local-to-moderate unit root theory. *Journal of Econometrics*, *158*, 274–279.

Phillips, P. C. B., & Solo, V. (1992). Asymptotics for linear processes. *Annals of Statistics*, *20*(2), 971–1001.

Politis, D. (2011). Higher-order accurate, positive semi-definite estimation of large-sample covariance and spectral density matrices. *Econometric Theory*, *27*, 703–744.

Sun, Y. (2004). A convergent *t*-statistic in spurious regressions. *Econometric Theory*, *20*, 943–962.

Sun, Y. (2011). Robust trend inference with series variance estimator and testing-optimal smoothing parameter. *Journal of Econometrics*, *164*(2), 345–366.

Sun, Y. (2013). A heteroskedasticity and autocorrelation robust *F* test using orthonormal series variance estimator. *Econometrics Journal*, *16*, 1–26.

Sun, Y. (2014). Comment on "HAC corrections for strongly autocorrelated time series" by U.K. Müller. *Journal of Business & Economic Statistics*, *32*(3), 330–334.

Sun, Y. (forthcoming). Fixed-smoothing asymptotics in a two-step GMM framework. *Econometrica*.

Sun, Y., & Kim, M. S. (forthcoming). Asymptotic F test in a GMM framework with cross sectional dependence. *Review of Economics and Statistics*.

Sun, Y., Phillips, P. C. B., & Jin, S. (2008). Optimal bandwidth selection in heteroskedasticity-autocorrelation robust testing. *Econometrica*, *76*, 175–194.

APPENDIX

The following lemma will be used in our proofs. It is a slight modification of Lemma A.3 in Sun (forthcoming) and can be proved in the same way. The details are omitted here.

Lemma 1. Suppose $\omega_T = \xi_{T,M} + \eta_{T,M}$ and ω_T does not depend on M. Assume that there exist $\xi^*_{\infty,M}$ and $\xi^*_{\infty,\infty}$ such that

(i) $P(\xi_{T,M} < \xi) - P(\xi^*_{\infty,M} < \xi) = o(1)$ for each fixed M and each $\xi \in \mathbb{R}$ as $T \to \infty$,
(ii) $P(\xi^*_{\infty,M} < \xi) - P(\xi^*_{\infty,\infty} < \xi) = o(1)$ for each $\xi \in \mathbb{R}$ as $M \to \infty$,
(iii) the CDF of $\xi^*_{\infty,\infty}$ is continuous on $\mathbb{R}$,
(iv) For every $\delta > 0$, $\sup_T P(|\eta_{T,M}| > \delta) \overset{p}{\to} 0$ as $M \to \infty$. Then

$$P(\omega_T < \xi) = P(\xi^*_{\infty,\infty} < \xi) + o(1) \text{ for each } \xi \in \mathbb{R} \text{ as } T \to \infty.$$

Proof of Theorem 1. Under the null hypothesis, we have

$$\frac{1}{T}\sum_{t=1}^{T}\frac{y_t}{\sqrt{T}} = \frac{1}{T}\sum_{t=1}^{T}\frac{e_t}{\sqrt{T}} \to^d \int_0^1 J_c(r)\,\mathrm{d}r \tag{A.1}$$

by the continuous mapping theorem. Under Assumption 2, it is not hard to show that

$$\frac{1}{T^3}\sum_{t=1}^{T}\sum_{s=1}^{T} Q^*_{Th}\left(\frac{t}{T},\frac{s}{T}\right)(y_t-\bar{y})(y_s-\bar{y})' = \frac{1}{T^3}\sum_{t=1}^{T}\sum_{s=1}^{T} Q^*_h\left(\frac{t}{T},\frac{s}{T}\right)(y_t-\bar{y})(y_s-\bar{y})' + o_p(1)$$

It remains to show that

$$\frac{1}{T^3}\sum_{t=1}^{T}\sum_{s=1}^{T} Q^*_h\left(\frac{t}{T},\frac{s}{T}\right)(y_t-\bar{y})(y_s-\bar{y})' \to^d \int_0^1\int_0^1 Q^*_h(r,s)J_{c_m}(r)J'_{c_m}(s)\,\mathrm{d}r\mathrm{d}s \tag{A.2}$$

jointly with Eq. (A.1) and $\int_0^1\int_0^1 Q_h^*(r,s)\, J_{c_m}(r)\, J_{c_m}'(s)\, dr ds$ is nonsingular with probability one. We focus on proving the marginal convergence in Eq. (A.2), as the joint convergence results can be proved using the Cramer–Wold device and the nonsingularity of the limiting matrix can be proved easily.

Note that Eq. (A.2) is equivalent to

$$\frac{1}{T^3}\sum_{t=1}^{T}\sum_{s=1}^{T} Q_h^*\left(\frac{t}{T},\frac{s}{T}\right)(e_t-\bar{e})'A(e_s-\bar{e}) \to^d \int_0^1\int_0^1 Q_h^*(r,s)\, J_{c_m}'(r)\, AJ_{c_m}(s)\, dr ds \tag{A.3}$$

for all $p\times p$ symmetric matrix A. In view of the spectral decomposition of $A=\sum \mu_\ell a_\ell a_\ell'$, the above holds if

$$\frac{1}{T^3}\sum_{t=1}^{T}\sum_{s=1}^{T} Q_h^*\left(\frac{t}{T},\frac{s}{T}\right)(e_t-\bar{e})'aa'(e_s-\bar{e}) \to^d \int_0^1\int_0^1 Q_h^*(r,s)\, J_{c_m}'(r)\, aa'J_{c_m}(s)\, dr ds \tag{A.4}$$

for all $p\times 1$ vector a. But

$$\begin{aligned}
&\frac{1}{T^3}\sum_{t=1}^{T}\sum_{s=1}^{T} Q_h^*\left(\frac{t}{T},\frac{s}{T}\right)(e_t-\bar{e})'aa'(e_s-\bar{e}) \\
&= \frac{1}{T^3}\sum_{t=1}^{T}\sum_{s=1}^{T}\left[Q_h^*\left(\frac{t}{T},\frac{s}{T}\right)-\bar{Q}_h^*\left(\cdot,\frac{s}{T}\right)-\bar{Q}_h^*\left(\frac{t}{T},\cdot\right)+\bar{Q}_h^*(\cdot,\cdot)\right]e_t'aa'e_s \\
&= \frac{1}{T^3}\sum_{t=1}^{T}\sum_{s=1}^{T} Q_h^*\left(\frac{t}{T},\frac{s}{T}\right)e_t'aa'e_s + O\left(\frac{1}{T}\right)\frac{1}{T^3}\sum_{t=1}^{T}\sum_{s=1}^{T}\left|e_t'aa'e_s\right| \\
&= \frac{1}{T^3}\sum_{t=1}^{T}\sum_{s=1}^{T} Q_h^*\left(\frac{t}{T},\frac{s}{T}\right)e_t'aa'e_s + O\left(\frac{1}{T}\right)\left(\frac{1}{T}\sum_{t=1}^{T}\frac{1}{\sqrt{T}}\|e_t\|\right)^2\|a\|^2 \\
&= \frac{1}{T^3}\sum_{t=1}^{T}\sum_{s=1}^{T} Q_h^*\left(\frac{t}{T},\frac{s}{T}\right)e_t'aa'e_s + O_p\left(\frac{1}{T}\right).
\end{aligned}$$

So it suffices to show that

$$\omega_T := \frac{1}{T^3}\sum_{t=1}^{T}\sum_{s=1}^{T} Q_h^*\left(\frac{t}{T},\frac{s}{T}\right)e_t'aa'e_s \to^d \int_0^1\int_0^1 Q_h^*(r,s)\, J_{c_m}'(r)\, aa' J_{c_m}(s)\, \mathrm{d}r\mathrm{d}s$$

for all $p\times 1$ vector a.

Given that $\sum_j \lambda_j \Phi_j(r)\,\Phi_j(s)$ converges uniformly over $(r,s)\in[0,1]^2$ to $Q_h^*(r,s)$, for any $\varepsilon>0$, there exists an $M>0$ such that

$$\left|Q_h^*\left(\frac{t}{T},\frac{s}{T}\right) - \sum_{j=1}^{M}\lambda_j\Phi_j\left(\frac{t}{T}\right)\Phi_j\left(\frac{s}{T}\right)\right| \leq \varepsilon$$

for all $1\leq t,\ \ s\leq T$, and all T. Now

$$\begin{aligned}
\omega_T &= \frac{1}{T^3}\sum_{t=1}^{T}\sum_{s=1}^{T} Q_h^*\left(\frac{t}{T},\frac{s}{T}\right)e_t'aa'e_s \\
&= \frac{1}{T^3}\sum_{t=1}^{T}\sum_{s=1}^{T}\left[\sum_{j=1}^{M}\lambda_j\Phi_j\left(\frac{t}{T}\right)\Phi_j\left(\frac{s}{T}\right)\right]e_t'aa'e_s \\
&+ \frac{1}{T^3}\sum_{t=1}^{T}\sum_{s=1}^{T}\left[Q_h^*\left(\frac{t}{T},\frac{s}{T}\right) - \sum_{j=1}^{M}\lambda_j\Phi_j\left(\frac{t}{T}\right)\Phi_j\left(\frac{s}{T}\right)\right]e_t'aa'e_s \\
&:= \xi_{T,M} + \eta_{T,M}
\end{aligned}$$

We use Lemma 1 to complete the proof. Condition (i) of Lemma 1 holds because for each fixed M, we have

$$\begin{aligned}
\xi_{T,M} &= \sum_{j=1}^{M}\lambda_j\left[\frac{1}{T}\sum_{t=1}^{T}\Phi_j\left(\frac{t}{T}\right)\frac{e_t'}{\sqrt{T}}a\right]\left[\frac{1}{T}\sum_{s=1}^{T}\Phi_j\left(\frac{s}{T}\right)\frac{e_s'}{\sqrt{T}}a\right] \\
&\to^d \sum_{j=1}^{M}\lambda_j\left[\int_0^1 \Phi_j(r)\, J_{c_m}'(r)a\, \mathrm{d}r\right]\left[\int_0^1 \Phi_j(s)\, J_{c_m}'(s)\, a'\, \mathrm{d}s\right] \\
&= \textstyle\int_0^1\int_0^1 \displaystyle\sum_{j=1}^{M}\lambda_j\Phi_j(r)\,\Phi_j(s)\, J_{c_m}'(r)\, aa' J_{c_m}(s)\, \mathrm{d}s := \xi_{\infty,M}^*
\end{aligned}$$

To verify condition (ii) of Lemma 1, we let

$$\xi^*_{\infty,\infty} = \int_0^1 \int_0^1 \left[\sum_{j=1}^{\infty} \lambda_j \Phi_j(r)\, \Phi_j(s)\right] J'_{c_m}(r)\, aa' J_{c_m}(s)\, \mathrm{d}s$$

$$= \int_0^1 \int_0^1 Q_h^*(r,s)\, J'_{c_m}(r)\, aa' J_{c_m}(s)\, \mathrm{d}s$$

Then

$$\xi^*_{\infty,M} - \xi^*_{\infty,\infty} = \int_0^1 \int_0^1 \left[\sum_{j=M+1}^{\infty} \lambda_j \Phi_j(r)\, \Phi_j(s)\right] J'_{c_m}(r)\, aa' J_{c_m}(s)\, \mathrm{d}r\mathrm{d}s$$

Since $\sum_{j=1}^{M} \lambda_j \Phi_j(r)\, \Phi_j(s)$ converges to $Q_h^*(r,s)$ uniformly in (r,s) as $M \to \infty$, for any $\varepsilon > 0$, there exist $M^* > 0$ such that $\left|\sum_{j=M+1}^{\infty} \lambda_j \Phi_j(r)\, \Phi_j(s)\right| < \varepsilon$ for all $M > M^*$. So when M is large enough

$$\left|\xi^*_{\infty,M} - \xi^*_{\infty,\infty}\right| \le \varepsilon \int_0^1 \int_0^1 \left|J'_{c_m}(r)\, aa' J_{c_m}(s)\right| \mathrm{d}r\mathrm{d}s$$

$$\le \varepsilon \left(\int_0^1 \left|J'_{c_m}(r) a\right| \mathrm{d}r\right)^2 \le \varepsilon \left(\int_0^1 \|J_{c_m}(r)\| \mathrm{d}r\right)^2 \|a\|^2$$

$$\le \varepsilon \left(\int_0^1 \|J_{c_m}(r)\|^2\, \mathrm{d}r\right) \|a\| = \varepsilon O_p(1)$$

Since ε is arbitrary, we have $\xi^*_{\infty,M} - \xi^*_{\infty,\infty} = o_p(1)$ as $M \to \infty$. Hence condition (ii) of Lemma 1 holds. It is easy to see that condition (iii) of Lemma 1 also holds. It remains to verify the last condition in Lemma 1. We have

$$E\left|\eta_{T,M}\right| \le \frac{\varepsilon}{T^3} \sum_{t=1}^{T} \sum_{s=1}^{T} E\left|e'_t aa' e_s\right| \le \frac{\varepsilon}{T^3} \sum_{t=1}^{T} \sum_{s=1}^{T} \left[E(e'_t a)^2\right]^{1/2} \left[E(a' e_s)^2\right]^{1/2}$$

$$= \frac{\varepsilon}{T^3} \left\{\sum_{t=1}^{T} \left[E(e'_t a)^2\right]^{1/2}\right\}^2$$

In view of

$$\frac{e'_t a}{\sqrt{T}} = \frac{1}{\sqrt{T}} \sum_{j=0}^{t-1} \rho^j_{T,m} u'_{t-j} a + \frac{1}{\sqrt{T}} \rho^t_{T,m} e'_0 a$$

and defining $\Gamma_u(j_1 - j_2) := Eu_{t-j_1}u'_{t-j_2}$, we have

$$
\begin{aligned}
var\left(\frac{e_t'a}{\sqrt{T}}\right) &\leq 2\,var\left(\frac{1}{\sqrt{T}}\sum_{j=0}^{t-1}\rho_{T,m}^{j}u'_{t-j}a\right) + \frac{2}{T}\,var\,(e_0)\\
&= \frac{2}{T}\sum_{j_1=0}^{t-1}\sum_{j_2=0}^{t-1}\rho_{T,m}^{j_1}\rho_{T,m}^{j_2}a'u_{t-j_1}u'_{t-j_2}a + O\left(\frac{1}{T}\right)\\
&\leq \frac{2}{T}\sum_{j_1=0}^{t-1}\sum_{j_2=0}^{t-1}\left|a'\Gamma_u(j_1-j_2)a\right| + O\left(\frac{1}{T}\right)\\
&\leq \frac{2}{T}\sum_{j_1=0}^{t-1}\sum_{j_2=0}^{t-1}\|\Gamma_u(j_1-j_2)\|\|a\|^2 + O\left(\frac{1}{T}\right) = O(1)
\end{aligned}
$$

uniformly in T. Hence

$$
E\left|\eta_{T,M}\right| \leq C\frac{\varepsilon}{T^3}\left\{\sum_{t=1}^{T}T^{1/2}\right\}^2 \leq C\varepsilon
$$

for some constant C that does not depend on T. This implies that, for every $\delta > 0$, $\sup_T P(\left|\eta_{T,M}\right| > \delta) \xrightarrow{p} 0$ as $M \to \infty$.

Given that all conditions in Lemma 1 hold, we have

$$
\omega_T := \frac{1}{T^3}\sum_{t=1}^{T}\sum_{s=1}^{T}Q_h^*\left(\frac{t}{T},\frac{s}{T}\right)e_t'aa'e_s \to^d \xi^*_{\infty,\infty} := \int_0^1\int_0^1 Q_h^*(r,s)\,J'_{c_m}(r)\,aa'J_{c_m}(s)\,\mathrm{d}s
$$

Consequently

$$
\begin{aligned}
F_T &= \left(\frac{1}{T}\sum_{t=1}^{T}\frac{y_t}{\sqrt{T}}\right)'\left[\frac{1}{T}\sum_{t=1}^{T}\sum_{s=1}^{T}Q_h^*\left(\frac{t}{T},\frac{s}{T}\right)(y_t-\bar{y})(y_s-\bar{y})'\right]^{-1}\left(\frac{1}{T}\sum_{t=1}^{T}\frac{y_t}{\sqrt{T}}\right)\Big/p\\
&\to^d \left(\int_0^1 J_c(r)\,\mathrm{d}r\right)'\left(\int_0^1\int_0^1 Q_h^*(t,s)\,J_c(r)\,J_c(s)\,\mathrm{d}r\mathrm{d}s\right)^{-1}\left(\int_0^1 J_c(r)\,\mathrm{d}r\right)\Big/p
\end{aligned}
$$

as desired.

The proof for t statistic t_T is similar and is omitted here. ■

Proof of Theorem 2. In view of $J_{c_m}(t)=\int_0^t e^{-c_m(t-s)}\,dW_p(s)$, we have

$$c_m\int_0^1 \Phi_j(r)\,J_{c_m}(r)\,dr = \int_0^1\left[c_m\int_0^r \Phi_j(r)e^{-c_m(r-s)}\,dW_p(s)\right]dr$$
$$= \int_0^1\left[c_m\int_s^1 \Phi_j(r)e^{-c_m(r-s)}\,dr\right]dW_p(s)$$

But

$$c_m\int_s^1 \Phi_j(r)e^{-c_m(r-s)}\,dr = -\int_s^1 \Phi_j(r)d[e^{-c_m(r-s)}]$$
$$= -\Phi_j(r)e^{-c_m(r-s)}\Big|_s^1 + \int_s^1 e^{-c_m(r-s)}\Phi_j'(r)\,dr$$
$$=\Phi_j(s)-\Phi_j(1)e^{-c_m(1-s)}+\int_s^1 e^{-c_m(r-s)}\Phi_j'(r)\,dr$$

and so

$$c_m\int_0^1 \Phi_j(r)\,J_{c_m}(r)\,dr = \int_0^1 \Phi_j(s)\,dW_p(s)-\Phi_j(1)\int_0^1 e^{-c_m(1-s)}\,dW_p(s)$$
$$+\int_0^1\left(\int_s^1 e^{-c_m(r-s)}\Phi_j'(r)\,dr\right)dW_p(s)$$

We now show that the last two terms in the above expression are $o_p(1)$. First, since $E\int_0^1 e^{-c_m(1-s)}\,dW_p(s)=0$ and

$$var\left[\int_0^1 e^{-c_m(1-s)}\,dW_p(s)\right] = \int_0^1 e^{-2c_m(1-s)}ds=\frac{1}{2c_m}(1-e^{-2c_m})\to 0 \text{ as } c_m\to\infty$$

we have

$$\Phi_j(1)\int_0^1 e^{-c_m(1-s)}\,dW_p(s)=\Phi_j(1)\,o_p(1)$$

uniformly over $j=0,1,\ldots$

Second, $E\int_0^1\left(\int_s^1 e^{-c_m(r-s)}\,\Phi_j'(r)\,dr\right)dW_p(s)=0$ and

$$
\begin{aligned}
&var\left[\int_0^1\left(\int_s^1 e^{-c_m(r-s)}\Phi_j'(r)\,\mathrm{d}r\right)\mathrm{d}W_p(s)\right]\\
&\qquad=\int_0^1\left(\int_s^1 e^{-c_m(r-s)}\Phi_j'(r)\,\mathrm{d}r\right)^2\mathrm{d}s\\
&\qquad\leq\int_0^1\left(\int_s^1 e^{-2c_m(r-s)}\,\mathrm{d}r\right)\left(\int_s^1\left[\Phi_j'(r)\right]^2\mathrm{d}r\right)\mathrm{d}s\\
&\qquad\leq\left[\int_0^1\left(\int_s^1 e^{-2c_m(r-s)}\,\mathrm{d}r\right)\mathrm{d}s\right]\left(\int_0^1\left[\Phi_j'(r)\right]^2\mathrm{d}r\right)\\
&\qquad=\left[\frac{1}{2c_m}\int_0^1\left(1-e^{-2c_m(1-s)}\right)\mathrm{d}s\right]\left(\int_0^1\left[\Phi_j'(r)\right]^2\mathrm{d}r\right)\\
&\qquad\leq\frac{1}{2c_m}\left(\int_0^1\left[\Phi_j'(r)\right]^2\mathrm{d}r\right)
\end{aligned}
$$

This implies that

$$\int_0^1\left(\int_s^1 e^{-c_m(r-s)}\,\Phi_j'(r)\,\mathrm{d}r\right)\mathrm{d}W_p(s)=\|\Phi_j'(r)\|_2 o_p(1)$$

When $\Phi_j'(r)\neq 0$ for large enough j as in the kernel case, we need to strengthen the above result. In this case

$$\Phi_j'(r)=\begin{cases}-\dfrac{1}{2}\pi j\sin\dfrac{1}{2}\pi jr, & j\text{ is even}\\[2ex] \dfrac{1}{2}\pi(j+1)\cos\dfrac{1}{2}\pi r(j+1), & j\text{ is odd}\end{cases}$$

When $\Phi_j'(r)=-\pi\ell\sin\pi\ell r$ for $j=2\ell$, we have

$$
\begin{aligned}
&\left|\int_s^1 e^{-c_m(r-s)}(\sin(\pi\ell r))\,\mathrm{d}r\right|\\
&\qquad\leq\left|\frac{1}{c_m^2+\pi^2\ell^2}\left[c_m e^{-c_m(1-s)}\sin\pi\ell+\pi\ell e^{-c_m(1-s)}\cos\pi\ell\right]\right|\\
&\qquad\quad+\left|\frac{1}{c_m^2+\pi^2\ell^2}\left[c_m\sin\pi\ell s+\pi\ell\cos\pi\ell s\right]\right|\\
&\qquad\leq\frac{2(c_m+\pi\ell)}{c_m^2+\pi^2\ell^2}
\end{aligned}
$$

and

$$\int_0^1 \left(\int_s^1 e^{-c_m(r-s)} \sin(\pi k r)\, \mathrm{d}r \right)^2 \mathrm{d}s \leq \frac{4(c_m + \pi \ell)^2}{(c_m^2 + \pi^2 \ell^2)^2} \leq \frac{8}{c_m^2 + \pi^2 \ell^2}$$

Hence

$$\int_0^1 \left(\int_s^1 e^{-c_m(r-s)} \Phi_j'(r)\, \mathrm{d}r \right)^2 \mathrm{d}s \leq \frac{8\pi^2 \ell^2}{c_m^2 + \pi^2 \ell^2} = \frac{2\pi^2 j^2}{\pi^2 j^2 + 4c_m^2} \tag{A.5}$$

Similarly, when $\Phi_j'(r) = \pi \ell \cos \pi r \ell$ for $j = 2\ell - 1$, we have

$$\begin{aligned} \left| \int_s^1 e^{-c_m(r-s)} (\cos \pi r \ell)\, \mathrm{d}r \right| & \\ \leq & \left| \frac{c_m(\cos \pi \ell) e^{-c_m(1-s)} - \pi \ell (\sin \pi \ell) e^{-c_m(1-s)}}{c_m^2 + \pi^2 \ell^2} \right| \\ & + \left| \frac{c_m(\cos \pi s \ell) - \pi \ell (\sin \pi s \ell)}{c_m^2 + \pi^2 \ell^2} \right| \\ \leq & \frac{2(c_m + \pi \ell)}{c_m^2 + \pi^2 \ell^2} \end{aligned}$$

Therefore

$$\int_0^1 \left(\int_s^1 e^{-c_m(r-s)}\, \Phi_j'(r)\, \mathrm{d}r \right)^2 \mathrm{d}s \leq \frac{2\pi (j+1)^2}{\pi^2 (j+1)^2 + 4c_m^2} \tag{A.6}$$

Combining Eq. (A.5) with Eq. (A.6), we have

$$\int_0^1 \left(\int_s^1 e^{-c_m(r-s)} \Phi_j'(r)\, \mathrm{d}r \right) \mathrm{d}W_p(s) = O_p\left(\sqrt{\frac{\pi^2 j^2}{\pi^2 j^2 + 4c_m^2}} \right)$$

To sum up, we have proved the following:

$$c_m \int_0^1 \Phi_j(r)\, J_{c_m}(r)\, \mathrm{d}r = \int_0^1 \Phi_j(s)\, \mathrm{d}W_p(s) + \left[|\Phi_j(1)| + \|\Phi_j'(r)\|_2^2 \right] o_p(1)$$

which holds for both the series case and the kernel case. In the kernel case, we have proved

$$c_m \int_0^1 \Phi_j(r)\, J_{c_m}(r)\, \mathrm{d}r = \int_0^1 \Phi_j(s)\, \mathrm{d}W_p(s) + |\Phi_j(1)| o_p(1) + O_p\left(\sqrt{\frac{\pi^2 j^2}{\pi^2 j^2 + 4c_m^2}}\right)$$

Both results hold uniformly over $j = 1, 2, \ldots$.

It follows that

$$c_m \int_0^1 \Phi_j(r)\, J_{c_m}(r)\, \mathrm{d}r = \int_0^1 \Phi_j(s)\, \mathrm{d}W_p(s) + o_p(1) \quad \text{as} \quad c_m \to \infty$$

uniformly over $j = 0, 1, \ldots$ for both the series case and the kernel case. Therefore

$$\begin{aligned}
&\int_0^1 \int_0^1 Q_h^*(r,s)\, c_m J_{c_m}(r)\, c_m J_{c_m}'(s)\, \mathrm{d}r\mathrm{d}s \\
&= \int_0^1 \int_0^1 \sum_{j=1}^{\infty} \lambda_j \Phi_j(r)\, \Phi_j(s)\, c_m J_{c_m}(r)\, c_m J_{c_m}'(s)\, \mathrm{d}r\mathrm{d}s \\
&= \sum_{j=1}^{\infty} \lambda_j \left[c_m \int_0^1 \Phi_j(r)\, J_{c_m}(r)\, \mathrm{d}r \right] \left[c_m \int_0^1 \Phi_j(s)\, J_{c_m}(s)\, \mathrm{d}s \right]' \\
&= \sum_{j=1}^{\infty} \lambda_j \left[\int_0^1 \Phi_j(r)\, \mathrm{d}W_p(r) \right] \left[\int_0^1 \Phi_j(s)\, \mathrm{d}W_p(s) \right]' + \left[\sum_{j=1}^{\infty} |\lambda_j| \right] o_p(1) \\
&= \int_0^1 \int_0^1 \left[\sum_{j=1}^{\infty} \lambda_j \Phi_j(r)\, \Phi_j(s) \right] \mathrm{d}W_p(r)\, \mathrm{d}W_p'(s) + o_p(1) \\
&= \int_0^1 \int_0^1 Q_h(r,s)\, \mathrm{d}W_p(r)\, \mathrm{d}W_p'(s) + o_p(1)
\end{aligned}$$

As a consequence

$$\begin{aligned}
F_\infty(c_m) = &\left[\int_0^1 \Phi_0(s)\, \mathrm{d}W_p(s) + o_p(1) \right]' \times \left[\int_0^1 \int_0^1 Q_h(r,s)\, \mathrm{d}W_p(r)\, \mathrm{d}W_p'(s) + o_p(1) \right]^{-1} \\
&\times \left[\int_0^1 \Phi_0(s)\, \mathrm{d}W_p(s) + o_p(1) \right] / p \\
= &F_\infty(\infty) + o_p(1) \quad \text{as} \quad c_m \to \infty
\end{aligned}$$

The proof for $t_\infty(c_m)$ is similar and is omitted here. ■

MOMENT APPROXIMATION FOR LEAST-SQUARES ESTIMATOR IN FIRST-ORDER REGRESSION MODELS WITH UNIT ROOT AND NONNORMAL ERRORS

Yong Bao[a], Aman Ullah[b] and Ru Zhang[b]

[a]*Department of Economics, Purdue University, West Lafayette, Indiana, USA*

[b]*Department of Economics, University of California – Riverside, Riverside, California, USA*

ABSTRACT

An extensive literature in econometrics focuses on finding the exact and approximate first and second moments of the least-squares estimator in the stable first-order linear autoregressive model with normally distributed errors. Recently, Kiviet and Phillips (2005) developed approximate moments for the linear autoregressive model with a unit root and normally distributed errors. An objective of this paper is to analyze moments of the estimator in the first-order autoregressive model with a unit root and nonnormal errors. In particular, we develop new analytical

Essays in Honor of Peter C. B. Phillips
Advances in Econometrics, Volume 33, 65–92

ISSN: 0731-9053/doi:10.1108/S0731-905320140000033003

approximations for the first two moments in terms of model parameters and the distribution parameters. Through Monte Carlo simulations, we find that our approximate formula perform quite well across different distribution specifications in small samples. However, when the noise to signal ratio is huge, bias distortion can be quite substantial, and our approximations do not fare well.

Keywords: Unit root; nonnormal; moment approximation

JEL Classifications: C22; C20; C13

1. INTRODUCTION

The autoregressive (AR) model has been a workhorse model in time series econometrics and applied macroeconomics. There has been a huge literature in studying properties of the least-squares (LS) estimator. Hurwicz (1950) was the first to investigate the finite-sample bias issue. Sawa (1978) proposed using the moment generating function approach to numerically evaluating the exact moments; also see Nankervis and Savin (1988) and Hoque and Peters (1986). However, while these papers provided useful numerical results, they did not provide explicit analytical expressions for moments that may lead to further analysis. An alternative procedure to obtaining the moments is to find explicit expressions, for example, by higher-order asymptotic approximations. These have the advantage that they may provide theoretical analysis and suggest corrected estimators. Following this procedure, approximate moments of the LS estimator were developed by Grubb and Symons (1987), Kiviet and Phillips (1993, 1994), and Bao and Ullah (2007), among others. The results in all these papers are under normality, with the exception that it is relaxed in Bao and Ullah (2007) and Bao (2007).

We note that works referred above are all in stable models. Thus, not much attention has been paid to the *analytical* moment approximations of the LS estimator in AR models with a unit root, though numerically, under normality, the moments can be evaluated via the techniques of Sawa (1978). The exceptions are Abadir (1993) and Kiviet and Phillips (2005), in which analytical approximations to the moments of the LS estimator for nonstationary AR models were developed with the normality assumption. Our aim here is to develop new results without assuming normality.

In this paper, we analyze the moments of the LS estimator in the first-order AR model with an arbitrary number of exogenous regressors (ARX(1)) when the true coefficient of the lagged-dependent variable is unity. We do not make any distribution assumption except the existence of moments of the errors up to order 4. We also discuss the case when the exogenous regressors may be nonstationary. Our main achievements are as follows: (i) derive the approximate bias of the estimated autoregressive coefficient up to order T^{-3} in terms of model parameters and the skewness coefficient of the error distribution; (ii) derive the approximate MSE up to order T^{-4} of this estimator also in terms of model parameters and the skewness coefficient; (iii) obtain approximations to the first two moments of the estimated full coefficient vector for AR models with a unit root that may contain an arbitrary number of exogenous and possibly nonstationary regressors; (iv) for the random walk with drift model, present very neat bias and MSE formulae; (v) provide numerical illustrations of the accuracy of our moment approximations in finite samples.

Our paper proceeds as follows. In the next section, we focus on the moment approximations for the LS estimator of the AR coefficient, and discuss also the special case of random walk with drift. Section 3 presents the results for the full coefficient vector estimator. Section 4 investigates the accuracy of the analytical results developed by comparing the calculated moment approximations with those from simulations under several symmetric and skewed distributions. Section 5 concludes. The appendixes contain detailed derivation of the main results in the paper.

2. THE BIAS AND MSE OF THE AUTOREGRESSIVE COEFFICIENT ESTIMATOR

In this section, we discuss the approximate moments of the LS estimator of the AR coefficient when an arbitrary number of exogenous variables, with at least a constant term, are included. Throughout, I is the $T \times T$ identity matrix, ι is a $T \times 1$ vector of ones, and J as a $T \times T$ strict lower triangular matrix with all the elements below the main diagonal being 1.

We follow Kiviet and Phillips (2005) to consider the following model:

$$y = \lambda y_{-1} + X\beta + \sigma\varepsilon \tag{1}$$

where $y=(y_1,\cdots,y_T)'$ contains a $T\times 1$ vector of observations on the dependent variable, $y_{-1}=(y_0,\cdots,y_{T-1})$ contains the lagged values of the dependent variable, X is a $T\times k$ matrix containing all exogenous regressors that include at least an intercept term, and $\varepsilon=(\varepsilon_1,\cdots,\varepsilon_T)'$ is the $T\times 1$ vector of i.i.d. disturbances.

Assumptions. In model (1), the scalar λ and the vector β are unknown coefficients and further: (i) $\lambda=1$; (ii) all elements of β are finite and $\beta\neq 0$; (iii) X is stationary and $X'X=O(T)$; (iv) $Z=(y_{-1},X)$ has rank $k+1$ with probability one; (v) X is strongly exogenous, that is, X and ε are independent, and it contains at least a constant term; (vi) σ is positive and finite, and the disturbances ε_i are i.i.d., with mean zero, variance 1, and skewness and excess kurtosis coefficients γ_1 and γ_2, respectively; (vii) the start-up value is y_0, either fixed or random, and when y_0 is random, it is independent of ε.

Note that we impose stationarity on X in Assumption (iii), but later this will be relaxed. Regarding the error term ε, we do not make distributional assumption, except the existence of its first four moments.

The LS estimator of λ, which is also the quasi maximum likelihood estimator under nonnormality, is

$$\hat{\lambda}=\frac{y'_{-1}My}{y'_{-1}My_{-1}}=\lambda+\sigma\frac{y'_{-1}M\varepsilon}{y'_{-1}My_{-1}} \tag{2}$$

where $M=I-X(X'X)^{-1}X'$. We may write $y_{-1}=y_0\iota+JX\beta+\sigma J\varepsilon$. Then if X contains a constant term, it is obvious that $My_{-1}=MJX\beta+\sigma MJ\varepsilon$, so the properties of $\hat{\lambda}$ do not depend on the initial value y_0.

By plugging $My_{-1}=MJX\beta+\sigma MJ\varepsilon$, we have

$$\hat{\lambda}-1=\frac{\sigma\varepsilon'MJX\beta+\sigma^2\varepsilon'MJ\varepsilon}{\beta'X'J'MJX\beta+2\sigma\varepsilon'J'MJX\beta+\sigma^2\varepsilon'J'MJ\varepsilon} \tag{3}$$

Before we implement an expansion of $\hat{\lambda}-1$, let's examine the various terms on the right-hand side of Eq. (3). First observe that since we assume the regressors are stationary and $X'X=O(T)$, then immediately, $X(X'X)^{-1}X'=o(1)$ and $X(X'X)^{-1}X'J=O(1)$. Also, $X'J'MJX=X'J'JX-X'J'X(X'X)^{-1}X'JX=O(X'J'JX)=O(T^3)$, and $\beta'X'J'MJX\beta=O(T^3)$. This gives $\varepsilon'MJX\beta=O_P(T^{3/2})$. Similarly, we can verify that $\varepsilon'MJ\varepsilon=O_P(T)$, $\varepsilon'J'MJ\varepsilon=O_P(T^2)$, $\varepsilon'J'MJX\beta=O_P(T^{5/2})$. Thus, the dominating term in our expansion is $\beta'X'J'MJX\beta$. For notational convenience, denote $\mu:=(\beta'X'J'MJX\beta)^{-1}=O(T^{-3})$. Thus

$$\hat{\lambda}-1=\frac{\overbrace{\mu\sigma\varepsilon' MJX\beta}^{O_P(T^{-3/2})}+\overbrace{\mu\sigma^2\varepsilon' MJ\varepsilon}^{O_P(T^{-2})}}{1+\underbrace{2\mu\sigma\varepsilon' J' MJX\beta}_{O_P(T^{-1/2})}+\underbrace{\mu\sigma^2\varepsilon' J' MJ\varepsilon}_{O_P(T^{-1})}}$$

$$=(\mu\sigma\varepsilon' MJX\beta+\mu\sigma^2\varepsilon' MJ\varepsilon)\times[1-2\mu\sigma\varepsilon' J' MJX\beta-\mu\sigma^2\varepsilon' J' MJ\varepsilon$$

$$+4\mu^2\sigma^2(\varepsilon' J' MJX\beta)^2+4\mu^2\sigma^3(\varepsilon' J' MJX\beta)(\varepsilon' J' MJ\varepsilon)-8\mu^3\sigma^3(\varepsilon' J' MJX\beta)^3]+o_P(T^{-3})$$

$$=(\mu\sigma\varepsilon' MJX\beta+\mu\sigma^2\varepsilon' MJ\varepsilon)[1-2\mu\sigma\varepsilon' J' MJX\beta-\mu\sigma^2\varepsilon' J' MJ\varepsilon+4\mu^2\sigma^2(\varepsilon' J' MJX\beta)^2]$$

$$+4\mu^3\sigma^4(\varepsilon' MJX\beta)(\varepsilon' J' MJX\beta)(\varepsilon' J' MJ\varepsilon)-8\mu^4\sigma^4\varepsilon' MJX\beta(\varepsilon' J' MJX\beta)^3+o_P(T^{-3})$$

$$=\underbrace{\mu\sigma\varepsilon' MJX\beta}_{O_P(T^{-3/2})}+\underbrace{\mu\sigma^2\varepsilon' MJ\varepsilon-2\mu^2\sigma^2\varepsilon' MJX\beta\beta' X' J' MJ\varepsilon}_{O_P(T^{-2})}$$

$$+\underbrace{4\mu^3\sigma^3\beta' X' J' M\varepsilon\varepsilon' J' MJX\beta\beta' X' J' MJ\varepsilon-\mu^2\sigma^3\beta' X' J' M\varepsilon\varepsilon' J' MJ\varepsilon-2\mu^2\sigma^3\beta' X' J' MJ\varepsilon\varepsilon' MJ\varepsilon}_{O_P(T^{-5/2})}$$

$$+\underbrace{4\mu^3\sigma^4\varepsilon' J' MJ\varepsilon\varepsilon' MJX\beta\beta' X' J' MJ\varepsilon-8\mu^4\sigma^4\varepsilon' MJX\beta\beta' X' J' MJ\varepsilon\varepsilon' J' MJX\beta\beta' X' J' MJ\varepsilon}_{O_P(T^{-3})}$$

$$+\underbrace{4\mu^3\sigma^4\varepsilon' MJ\varepsilon\varepsilon' J' MJX\beta\beta' X' J' MJ\varepsilon-\mu^2\sigma^4\varepsilon' MJ\varepsilon\varepsilon' J' MJ\varepsilon}_{O_P(T^{-3})}+o_P(T^{-3}) \tag{4}$$

Then taking expectations term by term in Eq. (4), collected in Appendix A, and upon substitution, we have the following bias result under nonnormality.

Theorem 1. Under Assumptions (i)–(vii), the bias, to the order of T^{-3}, of the least-squares estimator of λ in model (1) is given by

$$\mathrm{E}(\hat{\lambda}-1)=\sigma^2\mu[1+\mathrm{tr}(MJ)]$$
$$+\sigma^3\mu^2\gamma_1\beta' X' J' M[4\mu(I\odot J' MJX\beta\beta' X' J' MJ)-(I\odot J' MJ)-2J(I\odot MJ)]\iota$$
$$-\sigma^4\mu^2\mathrm{tr}(MJ)[\mathrm{tr}(J' MJ)-4\mu\beta' X' J' MJJ' MJX\beta]+o(T^{-3}) \tag{5}$$

We see that $\hat{\lambda}$ is unbiased up to $O(T^{-3/2})$, in line with the well-known result that $\hat{\lambda}$ is super-consistent with a convergence rate of $T^{3/2}$. It is also unbiased up to $O(\sigma)$. The leading bias term is of order $O(T^{-2})$, given by

$$\mathrm{E}(\hat{\lambda}-1)=-\sigma^2\mu\,\mathrm{tr}((X' X)^{-1}X' JX)+o(T^{-2}) \tag{6}$$

which is robust to nonnormality. The distribution effect of the disturbance term on the approximate bias comes through its skewness coefficient γ_1, and it is of order T^{-3}. This stands in contrast to the stationary AR model, where the LS estimator is $\sqrt{T}$-consistent and the "second-order" bias, up to $O(T^{-2})$, is robust to nonnormality, as shown in Bao and Ullah (2007).

For the special case of $X=\iota$, we observe that $MJX = J\iota - T^{-1}\iota'J\iota$ with the t-th element $t-1-0.5(T-1)$, $J'MJX = J'J\iota - T^{-1}\iota'J\iota J'\iota$ with the t-th element $0.5[T(T-1)-t(t-1)-(T-1)(T-t)]$, $MJ = J - T^{-1}\iota\iota'J$ with the t-th diagonal $-T^{-1}(T-t)$, and $J'MJ = J'J - T^{-1}J'\iota\iota'J$ with the t-th diagonal $T-t-T^{-1}(T-t)^2$. Upon simplification (see Appendix B), the bias result reduces to the following.

Corollary 1. If in the model of Theorem 1 we have $X=\iota$, then the bias simplifies to

$$\mathrm{E}(\hat{\lambda}-1) = -6\left(\frac{\sigma}{\beta}\right)^2\frac{1}{T^2} + 18\left(\frac{\sigma}{\beta}\right)^2\frac{1}{T^3} + 6\gamma_1\left(\frac{\sigma}{\beta}\right)^3\frac{1}{T^3} - \frac{84}{5}\left(\frac{\sigma}{\beta}\right)^4\frac{1}{T^3} + o(T^{-3}) \tag{7}$$

From this, we observe that up to T^{-2}, for the random walk with drift model, the bias of the unit root estimator is negative, and this bias is proportional to the squared noise to signal ratio σ/β. One might immediately predict that in the case of extreme values of σ/β, this bias expression may give poor approximation to the true bias. We might also predict that when the disturbance term is positively skewed, it tends to pull down the magnitude of the bias. (Keep in mind that the leading bias term is negative.)

To approximate the MSE of $\hat{\lambda}$ up to order $O(T^{-4})$, we can directly utilize the expansion of $\hat{\lambda}-1$, and put

$$\begin{aligned}
(\hat{\lambda}-1)^2 =& (\mu\sigma\varepsilon'MJX\beta)^2 + 2(\mu\sigma\varepsilon'MJX\beta)(\mu\sigma^2\varepsilon'MJ\varepsilon - 2\mu^2\sigma^2\varepsilon'MJX\beta\beta'X'J'MJ\varepsilon)\\
&+(\mu\sigma^2\varepsilon'MJ\varepsilon - 2\mu^2\sigma^2\varepsilon'MJX\beta\beta'X'J'MJ\varepsilon)^2\\
&+2(\mu\sigma\varepsilon'MJX\beta)[4\mu^3\sigma^3\beta'X'J'M\varepsilon\varepsilon'J'MJX\beta\beta'X'J'MJ\varepsilon\\
&-\mu^2\sigma^3\beta'X'J'M\varepsilon\varepsilon'J'MJ\varepsilon - 2\mu^2\sigma^3\beta'X'J'MJ\varepsilon\varepsilon'MJ\varepsilon] + o_P(T^{-4})\\
=&\underbrace{\sigma^2\mu^2\varepsilon'MJX\beta\beta'X'J'M\varepsilon}_{O_P(T^{-3})} + \underbrace{2\sigma^3\mu^2\beta'X'J'M\varepsilon\varepsilon'MJ\varepsilon - 4\mu^3\sigma^3\beta'X'J'M\varepsilon\varepsilon'MJX\beta\beta'X'J'MJ\varepsilon}_{O_P(T^{-7/2})}\\
&+\underbrace{\sigma^4\mu^2(\varepsilon'MJ\varepsilon)^2 - 8\sigma^4\mu^3\varepsilon'MJ\varepsilon\varepsilon'MJX\beta\beta'X'J'MJ\varepsilon - 2\sigma^4\mu^3\varepsilon'J'MJ\varepsilon\varepsilon'MJX\beta\beta'X'J'M\varepsilon}_{O_P(T^{-4})}\\
&+\underbrace{12\sigma^4\mu^4(\varepsilon'MJX\beta\beta'X'J'MJ\varepsilon)^2}_{O_P(T^{-4})} + o_P(T^{-4})
\end{aligned} \tag{8}$$

So by substituting the expectations (see Appendix A) and ignoring terms of smaller orders, we obtain the following result.

Theorem 2. In the model of Theorem 1, the MSE of the least-squares estimator of λ to the order of T^{-4} is given by

$$\begin{aligned}\mathrm{E}[(\hat{\lambda}-1)^2] =& \sigma^2\mu+\sigma^4\mu^2\{[\mathrm{tr}(MJ)]^2+\mathrm{tr}(MJMJ)-\mathrm{tr}(J'MJ)\}\\ &+4\sigma^4\mu^3(\beta'X'J'MJJ'MJX\beta-\beta'X'J'MJMJMJX\beta)\\ &+2\sigma^3\mu^2\gamma_1\beta'X'J'M[(I\odot MJ)-2\mu(I\odot MJX\beta\beta'X'J'MJ)]\iota+o(T^{-4})\end{aligned} \tag{9}$$

We see that the leading term of the MSE is of order T^{-3}. The skewness coefficient contributes to the approximate MSE at order T^{-3}. If further $X=\iota$, we have the following result.

Corollary 2. If $X=\iota$ in the model of Theorem 2, then the MSE and the variance simplify to

$$\mathrm{E}\left[(\hat{\lambda}-1)^2\right]=12\left(\frac{\sigma}{\beta}\right)^2\frac{1}{T^3}+\frac{48}{5}\gamma_1\left(\frac{\sigma}{\beta}\right)^3\frac{1}{T^3}+\frac{336}{5}\left(\frac{\sigma}{\beta}\right)^4\frac{1}{T^4}+o(T^{-4}) \tag{10}$$

and

$$\mathrm{Var}(\hat{\lambda})=12\left(\frac{\sigma}{\beta}\right)^2\frac{1}{T^3}+\frac{48}{5}\gamma_1\left(\frac{\sigma}{\beta}\right)^3\frac{1}{T^3}+\frac{156}{5}\left(\frac{\sigma}{\beta}\right)^4\frac{1}{T^4}+o(T^{-4}) \tag{11}$$

From this corollary, we see that the leading term $12T^{-3}(\sigma/\beta)^2$ gives the asymptotic variance of $T^{3/2}(\hat{\lambda}-1)$. Apparently, it suggests again that for the random walk with drift model, the approximate moments of $\hat{\lambda}$ depend crucially on σ/β. For a given sample size T, the quality of the approximation will go down as $|\sigma/\beta|$ goes up. The distribution affects the approximate MSE through its skewness coefficient γ_1. In Bao (2007), it is found that for the stationary AR model with an intercept, the second-order MSE depends on not only the skewness but also the kurtosis of the disturbance distribution.

3. THE FULL COEFFICIENT VECTOR ESTIMATOR

Now we consider the full coefficient vector $\alpha := (\lambda, \beta')'$. Define $Z := (y_{-1}, X)$ and the LS estimator is $\hat{\alpha} = (Z'Z)^{-1}Z'y$. We relax Assumption (iii) so that X may contain a linear trend. As $\hat{\lambda}$ and $\hat{\beta}$ might have different convergence rates, we follow Kiviet and Phillips (2005) to define a nonstochastic diagonal matrix $D = \text{diag}\,(T^{\delta_i}, \cdots, T^{\delta_{k+1}})$, where $\delta_i \leq 0$, $i = 1, \cdots, k+1$, such that $DZ'ZD = O_P(T)$.

Let $\overline{Z} = \text{E}(Z)$, $\tilde{Z} = Z - \overline{Z}$, $W = ZD$, $\overline{W} = \text{E}(W) = \overline{Z}D$, $\tilde{W} = W - \overline{W} = \tilde{Z}D$. Conditional on X and y_0, we can write $y_{-1} - E(y_{-1}) = \sigma J \varepsilon$ and thus $\tilde{Z} = \sigma J \varepsilon e_1'$, where $e_1 = (1, 0, \cdots, 0)'$ is $(k+1) \times 1$. Then $\tilde{W} = \tilde{Z}D = \sigma J \varepsilon e_1' D$. One can verify that $\overline{W}'\overline{W} = O(T)$, $\overline{W}'\tilde{W} = O_P(T^{1/2})$, $\tilde{W}'\tilde{W} = O_P(1)$, $\overline{W}'\varepsilon = O_P(T^{1/2})$, and $\tilde{W}'\varepsilon = O_P(1)$.

The rescaled estimation error may be written as

$$\begin{aligned} D^{-1}(\hat{\alpha} - \alpha) &= \sigma(DZ'ZD)^{-1}DZ'\varepsilon \\ &= \sigma(\overline{W}'\overline{W} + \overline{W}'\tilde{W} + \tilde{W}'\overline{W} + \tilde{W}'\tilde{W})^{-1}(\overline{W} + \tilde{W})'\varepsilon \\ &= \sigma R(I + P + S)^{-1}(\overline{W} + \tilde{W})'\varepsilon \end{aligned}$$

where $R = (\overline{W}'\overline{W})^{-1} = O(T^{-1})$, $P = \overline{W}'\tilde{W}R + \tilde{W}'\overline{W}R = O_P(T^{-1/2})$, $S = \tilde{W}'\tilde{W}R = O_P(T^{-1})$. Thus, for the rescaled estimator, up to order $O_P(T^{-1})$, we have the following expansion:

$$\begin{aligned} D^{-1}(\hat{\alpha} - \alpha) &= \sigma R(I - P)(\overline{W} + \tilde{W})'\varepsilon \\ &= \underbrace{\sigma R\overline{W}'\varepsilon}_{O_P(T^{-1/2})} + \underbrace{\sigma R\tilde{W}'\varepsilon - \sigma RP\overline{W}'\varepsilon}_{O_P(T^{-1})} + O_P(T^{-1}) \end{aligned} \tag{12}$$

Obviously, by substituting $\tilde{W} = \sigma J \varepsilon e_1' D$, we have $\tilde{W}'\varepsilon = \sigma D' e_1 \varepsilon' J' \varepsilon$ and $P\overline{W}'\varepsilon = (\overline{W}'\tilde{W} + \tilde{W}'\overline{W})R\overline{W}'\varepsilon = \sigma \overline{W}' J \varepsilon e_1' D R \overline{W}'\varepsilon + \sigma D' e_1 \varepsilon' J' \overline{W} R \overline{W}'\varepsilon$, where the random terms have expectations $\text{E}(\varepsilon' J' \varepsilon) = 0$, $\text{E}(\varepsilon e_1' D R \overline{W}'\varepsilon) = \overline{W} R D e_1$, and $\text{E}(\varepsilon' J' \overline{W} R \overline{W}'\varepsilon) = \text{tr}(J' \overline{W} R \overline{W}')$, regardless of the distribution of ε_t. Thus, Theorem 3 of Kiviet and Phillips (2005) regarding the bias of $\hat{\alpha}$, up to order $O(T^{-1+\delta_i})$, is robust to nonnormality. For completeness, we reproduce here.

Theorem 3. In the first-order dynamic regression model, where the coefficient of the lagged dependent variable λ is equal to unity, the regressor matrix $Z = (y_{-1}, X)$, and the scaling matrix $D = \text{diag}\,(T^{\delta_1}, \cdots, T^{\delta_{k+1}})$ such that conditional on X and y_0, $DZ'ZD = O_P(T)$, the bias of the the least-squares estimator of the coefficient vector $\alpha = (\lambda, \beta')'$, conditional on X and y_0, can be approximated, provided that $\overline{Z} = (y_0\iota + JX\beta, X)$ has full column rank and β is finite and non-zero, as follows:

$$\mathrm{E}(\hat{\beta}_i - \beta) = -\sigma^2 e'_{i+1}\left[(\overline{Z}'\overline{Z})^{-1}\overline{Z}'J\overline{Z} + \frac{1}{2}(T-k-1)I\right](\overline{Z}'\overline{Z})^{-1}e_1 + o(T^{-1+\delta_{i+1}}) \tag{13}$$

and

$$\mathrm{E}(\hat{\lambda} - 1) = -\frac{1}{2}(T-k)\sigma^2 e'_1(\overline{Z}'\overline{Z})^{-1}e_1 + o(T^{-1+\delta_1}) \tag{14}$$

One can check immediately that $\mathrm{E}(\hat{\lambda}-1)$ in Eq. (14) corresponds to Eq. (6). To approximate the MSE of $\hat{\alpha}$, we further expand

$$\begin{aligned} D^{-1}(\hat{\alpha}-\alpha) &= \sigma R(I-P-S+PP)\overline{W}'\varepsilon + \sigma R(I-P)\tilde{W}'\varepsilon + o_P(T^{-3/2}) \\ &= \underbrace{\sigma R\overline{W}'\varepsilon}_{O_P(T^{-1/2})} + \underbrace{\sigma R\tilde{W}'\varepsilon - \sigma RP\overline{W}'\varepsilon}_{O_P(T^{-1})} + \underbrace{\sigma R(PP-S)\overline{W}'\varepsilon - \sigma RP\tilde{W}'\varepsilon}_{O_P(T^{-3/2})} + o_P(T^{-3/2}) \end{aligned} \tag{15}$$

So the MSE of $D^{-1}(\hat{\alpha}-\alpha)$, up to $O(T^{-2})$, may be written as

$$\begin{aligned} \mathrm{E}[D^{-1}(\hat{\alpha}-\alpha)(\hat{\alpha}-\alpha)'D^{-1}] &= \sigma^2 R + \sigma^2 R\mathrm{E}[(\tilde{W}'\varepsilon - P\overline{W}'\varepsilon)(\tilde{W}'\varepsilon - P\tilde{W}'\varepsilon)']R \\ &\quad + \sigma^2 R\overline{W}'\mathrm{E}[\varepsilon(\tilde{W}'\varepsilon - P\overline{W}'\varepsilon)']R + \sigma^2 R\mathrm{E}[(\tilde{W}'\varepsilon - P\overline{W}'\varepsilon)\varepsilon']\overline{W}R \\ &\quad + \sigma^2 R\overline{W}'\varepsilon[R(PP-S)\overline{W}'\varepsilon - \sigma RP\tilde{W}'\varepsilon]' \\ &\quad + \sigma^2[R(PP-S)\overline{W}'\varepsilon - \sigma RP\tilde{W}'\varepsilon]\varepsilon'\overline{W}R + o(T^{-2}) \\ &= \sigma^2 R + \sigma^2 R\mathrm{E}[\tilde{W}'\varepsilon\varepsilon'\tilde{W} + P\overline{W}'\varepsilon\varepsilon'\overline{W}P' - P\overline{W}'\varepsilon\varepsilon'\tilde{W} - \tilde{W}'\varepsilon\varepsilon'\overline{W}P' \\ &\quad + \overline{W}'\varepsilon\varepsilon'\tilde{W} - \overline{W}'\varepsilon\varepsilon'\overline{W}P' + \tilde{W}'\varepsilon\varepsilon'\overline{W} - P\overline{W}'\varepsilon\varepsilon'\overline{W} \\ &\quad + \overline{W}'\varepsilon\varepsilon'\overline{W}P'P' - \overline{W}'\varepsilon\varepsilon'\overline{W}S' - \overline{W}'\varepsilon\varepsilon'\tilde{W}P' \\ &\quad + PP\overline{W}'\varepsilon\varepsilon'\overline{W} - S\overline{W}'\varepsilon\varepsilon'\overline{W} - P\tilde{W}'\varepsilon\varepsilon'\overline{W}]R + o(T^{-2}) \end{aligned} \tag{16}$$

By substitution, simplification, and omission of terms of smaller orders (see Appendix A), we obtain

$$\begin{aligned}
\mathrm{E}[D^{-1}(\hat{\alpha}-\alpha)(\hat{\alpha}-\alpha)'D^{-1}] = {} & \sigma^2 R + \sigma^4 R\{[-\mathrm{tr}(J'J) + \mathrm{tr}^2(\overline{W}R\overline{W}'J) + \mathrm{tr}(\overline{W}'JJ'\overline{W}R) \\
& + \mathrm{tr}(\overline{W}R\overline{W}'J\overline{W}R\overline{W}'J) - 2\mathrm{tr}(\overline{W}R\overline{W}'J'J')]De_1e_1'D \\
& + \overline{W}'(JJ' - J'J' - J'J)\overline{W}RDe_1e_1'D \\
& + De_1e_1'DR\overline{W}'(JJ' - J'J' - J'J)\overline{W} \\
& + e_1'DRDe_1\overline{W}'(JJ' - J'J' - J'J)\overline{W} \\
& + e_1'DRDe_1(\overline{W}'J\overline{W}R\overline{W}'J\overline{W} + \overline{W}'J'\overline{W}R\overline{W}'J'\overline{W}) \\
& + [e_1'DR\overline{W}'J\overline{W}RDe_1 + \mathrm{tr}(\overline{W}R\overline{W}'J)e_1'DRDe_1]\overline{W}'(J+J')\overline{W}\}R \\
& - \sigma^3\gamma_1 R[\overline{W}'(\overline{W}RDe_1\iota'\odot I)J'\overline{W} + \overline{W}'J(\overline{W}RDe_1\iota'\odot I)\overline{W}]R + o(T^{-2})
\end{aligned}$$

which leads to the following theorem.

Theorem 4. In the model of Theorem 3, the elements of the $MSE(\hat{\alpha})$ matrix, that is, $\mathrm{E}[(\hat{\alpha}_i - \alpha_i)(\hat{\alpha}_j - \alpha_j)]$, $i,j = 1,\cdots,k+1$, are given by

$$\begin{aligned}
& \sigma^2 e_i'Qe_j + \sigma^4[\mathrm{tr}(Q\overline{Z}'JJ'\overline{Z}) - 2\mathrm{tr}(Q\overline{Z}'JJ\overline{Z}) - \mathrm{tr}(J'J) \\
& + \mathrm{tr}(Q\overline{Z}'J\overline{Z}Q\overline{Z}'J\overline{Z}) + \mathrm{tr}^2(Q\overline{Z}'J\overline{Z})]e_i'De_1e_1'De_j \\
& + \sigma^4 e_1'Qe_1e_i'Q\overline{Z}'[JJ' - J'J' - J'J + J\overline{Z}Q\overline{Z}'J + J'\overline{Z}Q\overline{Z}'J']\overline{Z}Qe_j \\
& + \sigma^4 e_1'De_je_i'Q\overline{Z}'(JJ' - J'J' - J'J)\overline{Z}Qe_1 \\
& + \sigma^4 e_1'Qe_ie_1'Q\overline{Z}'(JJ' - J'J' - J'J)\overline{Z}Qe_j \\
& + \sigma^4[e_1'Q\overline{Z}'J\overline{Z}Qe_1 + \mathrm{tr}(Q\overline{Z}'J\overline{Z})e_1'Qe_1]e_i'Q\overline{Z}'(J+J')\overline{Z}Qe_j \\
& - \sigma^3\gamma_1 e_i'Q\overline{Z}'[(\overline{Z}Qe_1\iota'\odot I)J' + J(\overline{Z}Qe_1\iota'\odot I)]\overline{Z}Qe_j + o(T^{-2+\delta_i+\delta_j})
\end{aligned} \tag{17}$$

where $Q = (\overline{Z}'\overline{Z})^{-1}$, $\overline{Z} = \mathrm{E}(Z)$, and e_i is the i-th unit vector.

From this theorem we can obtain, for example, when $k=2$ with the first column of X being the constant and the second being a linear trend, the approximate MSE of $\hat{\beta}_1$ up to $O(T^{-2})$, that of $\hat{\beta}_2$ up to $O(T^{-4})$, and that of $\hat{\lambda}$ up to $O(T^{-6})$ (if $\beta_2 \neq 0$, and up to $O(T^{-4})$ otherwise). For a model with stationary X, the orders of approximations to the MSE of $\hat{\lambda}$ and β_j, $j=1,\cdots,k$, are $O(T^{-4})$ and $O(T^{-2})$, respectively. Compared with Kiviet and Phillips (2005), we see that in Eq. (17) the approximate MSE has an additional term that involves the skewness coefficient γ_1.

4. APPROXIMATION ACCURACY

In this section, we investigate how our moment approximations fare under different distributions, sample sizes, and the noise to signal ratios. We focus on the random walk with drift model $y_t^* = \lambda y_{t-1}^* + \beta^* + \varepsilon_t$, where $y_0^* = 0$, $\lambda = 1$, $\beta^* = \beta/\sigma \neq 0$. Recall that the approximate moments are invariant to the starting value. Since the approximate moments are related to the ratio β/σ, but not to β and σ separately, we rescale the model so that the error term has unit variance. We consider five nonnormal distributions for ε, including both symmetric and asymmetric cases. These five nonnormal distributions are uniform on [0, 1], exponential distribution exp(1), student-t distribution with 5 degrees of freedom, mixture of two normals of N(−3, 1) and N(3,1), with probability equal to 0.2 and 0.8 respectively, and log normal distribution ln N(0,1). The corresponding skewness coefficients are 0, 2, 0, −1.1798, and 8.1073, respectively. For comparison purpose, we also include the results under a standard normal distribution. Our estimates of the true bias, MSE, and variance are based on 10,000,000 simulations and we also provide the estimated standard errors of our Monte Carlo estimates, denoted by MCSE.

We experiment with $T = 10, 15, 20, 40, 80$, $\beta^* = 10, 5, 2, 1, 0.5, 0.2, 0.1$. As indicated in the previous sections, for small values of β^* (equivalently, large values of the noise to signal ratio), the accuracy of our approximations is expected to deteriorate. Similar to Kiviet and Phillips (2005), we may employ an expansion in the orders of β^* and the approximate bias may be defined as

$$E(\hat{\lambda} - 1) = g_0(T) - g_{1/2}(T)\beta^* - g_1(T)\beta^{*2} + o(\beta^{*2}) \tag{18}$$

where

$$g_0(T) = E\left(\frac{\varepsilon' J' A\varepsilon}{\varepsilon' J' AJ\varepsilon}\right), \qquad g_{1/2}(T) = 2E\left[\frac{\iota' J' AJ\varepsilon\varepsilon' J' A\varepsilon}{(\varepsilon' J' AJ\varepsilon)^2}\right]$$

$$g_1(T) = E\left[\frac{\iota' J' AJ\iota\varepsilon' J' A\varepsilon + 2\varepsilon' AJ\iota\iota' J' AJ\varepsilon}{(\varepsilon' J' AJ\varepsilon)^2} - \frac{4\varepsilon' J' A\varepsilon\varepsilon' J' AJ\iota\iota' J' AJ\varepsilon}{(\varepsilon' J' AJ\varepsilon)^3}\right]$$

in which $A = I - T^{-1}\iota\iota'$. Under normality, $g_0(T)$, $g_{1/2}(T)$, and $g_1(T)$ might be numerically calculated via the moment generating function approach of

Sawa (1978). With a general nonnormal distribution, neither analytical nor numerical approach can be straightforwardly applied. So we follow Kiviet and Phillips (2005) to obtain them by simulations.

To save space, we report only the results pertaining to $\beta^* = 5, 1, 0.2$, presented in Tables 1–6, whereas the results under other values of β^* are available upon request from the first author. In each table, we first report the true bias, defined as the averaged $\hat{\lambda} - 1$ across 10,000,000 simulations, together with the MCSE, the approximate biases of $\hat{\lambda}$ up to $O(T^{-2})$ $(-6/(\beta^{*2}T^2))$, $O(\sigma^2)$ $(-6/(\beta^{*2}T^2) + 18/(\beta^{*2}T^3))$, $O(T^{-3})$ (expression (7)), $O(\sigma^3)$ $(-6/(\beta^{*2}T^2) + 18/(\beta^{*2}T^3) + 6\gamma_1/(\beta^{*3}T^3))$, and $O(\beta^{*2})$ (expression (18), when $\beta^* = 0.2$). They are followed by the true variance/MSE and the approximate variance/MSE of $\hat{\lambda}$ up to $O(T^{-4})$ (expressions (11)/(10)). We report next the true bias (together with MCSE)/variance/MSE and approximate bias (up to $O(T^{-1})$, expression (13))/variance (up to $O(T^{-2})$, defined as the $O(T^{-2})$ MSE minus the squared $O(T^{-1})$ bias)/MSE (up to $O(T^{-2})$, expression (17)) of (normalized) $\hat{\beta}$.

We observe that in general our analytical formulae capture well the true moments of the LS estimator for large and moderate β/σ, across different distributions. However, on occasions where there is substantial bias, and these are the cases when the signal to noise ratio is small (0.2), our formulae approximate poorly the true moments, and sometimes the order T^{-3} bias approximations are even worse than the order T^{-2} approximations. For large values of β/σ, the higher-order approximations are typically better. The difference between $O(\sigma^2)$ $(O(\sigma^3))$ and $O(T^{-2})$ $(O(T^{-3}))$ bias approximations is in general small. Under small T and small β^*, the bias in $\hat{\lambda}$ can be quite substantial, and only the $O(\beta^{*2})$ approximation captures the bias well.

The bias of the estimated intercept increases when the intercept decreases and it is very substantial when β/σ is small, and it seems to decrease with T not as quickly as the bias of $\hat{\lambda}$. When β/σ is not small, even for a small $T = 10$, our analytical formulae perform reasonably well in approximating the true moments of $\hat{\lambda}$ and $\hat{\beta}$, regardless of the disturbance distribution.

Note that the effect of nonnormality on the finite-sample moments of the LS estimator is not as strong as other aspects of the model, especially the value of β/σ. In particular, the bias, variance, and MSE approximations developed under normality seem quite robust to the distributions we have experimented with, though we see more variations in those for $\hat{\beta}$. Of course, a more comprehensive conclusion regarding the effects of

Table 1. Moments of the LS Estimator with $\beta^* = 5$ and $T = 10, 20$.

	$T = 10$						$T = 20$					
	Normal	Uniform	Exp(1)	t_5	Mixture	log N	Normal	Uniform	Exp(1)	t_5	Mixture	log N
Bias($\hat{\lambda}$)	−0.00170	−0.00170	−0.00156	−0.00172	−0.00183	−0.00133	−0.00051	−0.00051	−0.00049	−0.00051	−0.00053	−0.00046
(MCSE)	0.00001	0.00001	0.00001	0.00001	0.00001	0.00001	0.00000	0.00000	0.00000	0.00000	0.00000	0.00000
$O(T^{-2})$	−0.00240	−0.00240	−0.00240	−0.00240	−0.00240	−0.00240	−0.00060	−0.00060	−0.00060	−0.00060	−0.00060	−0.00060
$O(\sigma^2)$	−0.00168	−0.00168	−0.00168	−0.00168	−0.00168	−0.00168	−0.00051	−0.00051	−0.00051	−0.00051	−0.00051	−0.00051
$O(T^{-3})$	−0.00170	−0.00170	−0.00161	−0.00170	−0.00176	−0.00131	−0.00051	−0.00051	−0.00050	−0.00051	−0.00052	−0.00046
$O(\sigma^3)$	−0.00168	−0.00168	−0.00158	−0.00168	−0.00173	−0.00129	−0.00051	−0.00051	−0.00049	−0.00051	−0.00051	−0.00046
Var($\hat{\lambda}$)	0.00049	0.00049	0.00048	0.00049	0.00050	0.00046	0.00006	0.00006	0.00006	0.00006	0.00006	0.00006
$O(T^{-4})$	0.00049	0.00049	0.00064	0.00049	0.00039	0.00111	0.00006	0.00006	0.00008	0.00006	0.00005	0.00014
MSE($\hat{\lambda}$)	0.00049	0.00049	0.00048	0.00050	0.00050	0.00047	0.00006	0.00006	0.00006	0.00006	0.00006	0.00006
$O(T^{-4})$	0.00049	0.00049	0.00064	0.00049	0.00040	0.00111	0.00006	0.00006	0.00008	0.00006	0.00005	0.00014
Bias($\hat{\beta}/\sigma$)	0.05815	0.05810	0.05605	0.05829	0.06004	0.05190	0.03448	0.03431	0.03361	0.03412	0.03489	0.03279
(MCSE)	0.00019	0.00019	0.00020	0.00019	0.00018	0.00021	0.00014	0.00014	0.00014	0.00014	0.00013	0.00015
$O(T^{-1})$	0.05818	0.05818	0.05818	0.05818	0.05818	0.05818	0.03429	0.03429	0.03429	0.03429	0.03429	0.03429
Var($\hat{\beta}/\sigma$)	0.34412	0.34371	0.38275	0.34533	0.32115	0.45897	0.18557	0.18540	0.19686	0.18578	0.17894	0.22183
$O(T^{-2})$	0.34119	0.34119	0.35462	0.34119	0.33326	0.39565	0.18454	0.18454	0.18841	0.18454	0.18226	0.20022
MSE($\hat{\beta}/\sigma$)	0.34750	0.34708	0.38590	0.34872	0.32476	0.46166	0.18676	0.18658	0.19799	0.18695	0.18015	0.22290
$O(T^{-2})$	0.34457	0.34457	0.35801	0.34457	0.33665	0.39903	0.18571	0.18571	0.18958	0.18571	0.18343	0.20140

Table 2. Moments of the LS Estimator with $\beta^* = 5$ and $T = 40, 80$.

	$T=40$						$T=80$					
	Normal	Uniform	Exp(1)	t_5	Mixture	log N	Normal	Uniform	Exp(1)	t_5	Mixture	log N
Bias($\hat{\lambda}$)	−0.00014	−0.00014	−0.00013	−0.00014	−0.00014	−0.00013	−0.00003	−0.00003	−0.00003	−0.00003	−0.00003	−0.00003
(MCSE)	0.00000	0.00000	0.00000	0.00000	0.00000	0.00000	0.00000	0.00000	0.00000	0.00000	0.00000	0.00000
$O(T^{-2})$	−0.00015	−0.00015	−0.00015	−0.00015	−0.00015	−0.00015	−0.00003	−0.00003	−0.00003	−0.00003	−0.00003	−0.00003
$O(\sigma^2)$	−0.00013	−0.00013	−0.00013	−0.00013	−0.00013	−0.00013	−0.00003	−0.00003	−0.00003	−0.00003	−0.00003	−0.00003
$O(T^{-3})$	−0.00013	−0.00013	−0.00013	−0.00013	−0.00014	−0.00013	−0.00003	−0.00003	−0.00003	−0.00003	−0.00003	−0.00003
$O(\sigma^3)$	−0.00013	−0.00013	−0.00013	−0.00013	−0.00014	−0.00013	−0.00003	−0.00003	−0.00003	−0.00003	−0.00003	−0.00003
Var($\hat{\lambda}$)	0.00001	0.00001	0.00001	0.00001	0.00001	0.00001	0.00000	0.00000	0.00000	0.00000	0.00000	0.00000
$O(T^{-4})$	0.00001	0.00001	0.00001	0.00001	0.00001	0.00002	0.00000	0.00000	0.00000	0.00000	0.00000	0.00000
MSE($\hat{\lambda}$)	0.00001	0.00001	0.00001	0.00001	0.00001	0.00001	0.00000	0.00000	0.00000	0.00000	0.00000	0.00000
$O(T^{-4})$	0.00001	0.00001	0.00001	0.00001	0.00001	0.00002	0.00000	0.00000	0.00000	0.00000	0.00000	0.00000
Bias($\hat{\beta}/\sigma$)	0.01860	0.01858	0.01832	0.01861	0.01872	0.01811	0.00964	0.00961	0.00958	0.00950	0.00960	0.00951
(MCSE)	0.00010	0.00010	0.00010	0.00010	0.00010	0.00010	0.00007	0.00007	0.00007	0.00007	0.00007	0.00007
$O(T^{-1})$	0.01854	0.01854	0.01854	0.01854	0.01854	0.01854	0.00963	0.00963	0.00963	0.00963	0.00963	0.00963
Var($\hat{\beta}/\sigma$)	0.09631	0.09637	0.09942	0.09642	0.09450	0.10620	0.04906	0.04909	0.04989	0.04909	0.04863	0.05156
$O(T^{-2})$	0.09603	0.09603	0.09706	0.09603	0.09542	0.10022	0.04899	0.04899	0.04926	0.04899	0.04884	0.05008
MSE($\hat{\beta}/\sigma$)	0.09666	0.09671	0.09976	0.09676	0.09486	0.10652	0.04915	0.04918	0.04998	0.04918	0.04872	0.05165
$O(T^{-2})$	0.09637	0.09637	0.09741	0.09637	0.09577	0.10056	0.04909	0.04909	0.04935	0.04909	0.04893	0.05017

Table 3. Moments of the LS Estimator with $\beta^* = 1$ and $T = 10, 20$.

	$T=10$						$T=20$					
	Normal	Uniform	Exp(1)	t_5	Mixture	log N	Normal	Uniform	Exp(1)	t_5	Mixture	log N
Bias($\hat{\lambda}$)	−0.06075	−0.05969	−0.03486	−0.05957	−0.07699	−0.02257	−0.01516	−0.01496	−0.01183	−0.01543	−0.01757	−0.00912
(MCSE)	0.00004	0.00004	0.00004	0.00005	0.00005	0.00003	0.00001	0.00001	0.00001	0.00001	0.00001	0.00001
$O(T^{-2})$	−0.06000	−0.06000	−0.06000	−0.06000	−0.06000	−0.06000	−0.01500	−0.01500	−0.01500	−0.01500	−0.01500	−0.01500
$O(\sigma^2)$	−0.04200	−0.04200	−0.04200	−0.04200	−0.04200	−0.04200	−0.01275	−0.01275	−0.01275	−0.01275	−0.01275	−0.01275
$O(T^{-3})$	−0.05880	−0.05880	−0.04680	−0.05880	−0.06587	−0.01015	−0.01485	−0.01485	−0.01335	−0.01485	−0.01573	−0.00876
$O(\sigma^3)$	−0.04200	−0.04200	−0.03000	−0.04200	−0.04907	0.00664	−0.01275	−0.01275	−0.01125	−0.01275	−0.01363	−0.00666
Var($\hat{\lambda}$)	0.01908	0.01827	0.01399	0.01981	0.02344	0.01120	0.00183	0.00179	0.00164	0.00197	0.00207	0.00149
$O(T^{-4})$	0.01512	0.01512	0.03432	0.01512	0.00379	0.09295	0.00170	0.00170	0.00410	0.00170	0.00028	0.01142
MSE($\hat{\lambda}$)	0.02277	0.02184	0.01521	0.02336	0.02937	0.01171	0.00206	0.00202	0.00178	0.00221	0.00238	0.00158
$O(T^{-4})$	0.01872	0.01872	0.03792	0.01872	0.00739	0.09655	0.00192	0.00192	0.00432	0.00192	0.00050	0.01165
Bias($\hat{\beta}/\sigma$)	0.29577	0.30054	0.25253	0.28036	0.31061	0.20131	0.17667	0.17650	0.16167	0.17480	0.18503	0.14240
(MCSE)	0.00018	0.00018	0.00022	0.00019	0.00016	0.00027	0.00014	0.00013	0.00016	0.00014	0.00012	0.00019
$O(T^{-1})$	0.29091	0.29091	0.29091	0.29091	0.29091	0.29091	0.17143	0.17143	0.17143	0.17143	0.17143	0.17143
Var($\hat{\beta}/\sigma$)	0.32393	0.31068	0.50238	0.35720	0.24459	0.73438	0.18121	0.17884	0.24081	0.18924	0.15136	0.36687
$O(T^{-2})$	0.23874	0.23874	0.30592	0.23874	0.19912	0.51104	0.15629	0.15629	0.17563	0.15629	0.14487	0.23471
MSE($\hat{\beta}/\sigma$)	0.41141	0.40100	0.56615	0.43580	0.34107	0.77491	0.21242	0.20999	0.26695	0.21979	0.18560	0.38715
$O(T^{-2})$	0.32337	0.32337	0.39055	0.32337	0.28375	0.59567	0.18567	0.18567	0.20502	0.18567	0.17426	0.26410

Table 4. Moments of the LS Estimator with $\beta^* = 1$ and $T = 40, 80$.

	$T=40$						$T=80$					
	Normal	Uniform	Exp(1)	t_5	Mixture	log N	Normal	Uniform	Exp(1)	t_5	Mixture	log N
Bias($\hat{\lambda}$)	−0.00375	−0.00373	−0.00335	−0.00378	−0.00401	−0.00287	−0.00093	−0.00093	−0.00088	−0.00093	−0.00096	−0.00081
(MCSE)	0.00001	0.00000	0.00000	0.00001	0.00001	0.00000	0.00000	0.00000	0.00000	0.00000	0.00000	0.00000
$O(T^{-2})$	−0.00375	−0.00375	−0.00375	−0.00375	−0.00375	−0.00375	−0.00093	−0.00093	−0.00093	−0.00093	−0.00093	−0.00093
$O(\sigma^2)$	−0.00346	−0.00346	−0.00346	−0.00346	−0.00346	−0.00346	−0.00090	−0.00090	−0.00090	−0.00090	−0.00090	−0.00090
$O(T^{-3})$	−0.00373	−0.00373	−0.00354	−0.00373	−0.00384	−0.00297	−0.00093	−0.00093	−0.00091	−0.00093	−0.00094	−0.00084
$O(\sigma^3)$	−0.00346	−0.00346	−0.00328	−0.00346	−0.00357	−0.00270	−0.00090	−0.00090	−0.00087	−0.00090	−0.00091	−0.00080
Var($\hat{\lambda}$)	0.00020	0.00020	0.00020	0.00021	0.00021	0.00019	0.00002	0.00002	0.00002	0.00002	0.00003	0.00002
$O(T^{-4})$	0.00020	0.00020	0.00050	0.00020	0.00002	0.00142	0.00002	0.00002	0.00006	0.00002	0.00000	0.00018
MSE($\hat{\lambda}$)	0.00022	0.00022	0.00021	0.00022	0.00023	0.00020	0.00003	0.00003	0.00003	0.00003	0.00003	0.00002
$O(T^{-4})$	0.00021	0.00021	0.00051	0.00021	0.00004	0.00143	0.00003	0.00003	0.00006	0.00003	0.00000	0.00018
Bias($\hat{\beta}/\sigma$)	0.09429	0.09425	0.09029	0.09435	0.09669	0.08423	0.04857	0.04853	0.04756	0.04846	0.04911	0.04582
(MCSE)	0.00010	0.00010	0.00011	0.00010	0.00009	0.00012	0.00007	0.00007	0.00007	0.00007	0.00007	0.00008
$O(T^{-1})$	0.09268	0.09268	0.09268	0.09268	0.09268	0.09268	0.04815	0.04815	0.04815	0.04815	0.04815	0.04815
Var($\hat{\beta}/\sigma$)	0.09539	0.09514	0.11139	0.09689	0.08679	0.15184	0.04885	0.04884	0.05292	0.04906	0.04662	0.06291
$O(T^{-2})$	0.08857	0.08857	0.09373	0.08857	0.08552	0.10951	0.04707	0.04707	0.04841	0.04707	0.04629	0.05248
MSE($\hat{\beta}/\sigma$)	0.10428	0.10402	0.11954	0.10579	0.09613	0.15894	0.05121	0.05120	0.05518	0.05141	0.04903	0.06501
$O(T^{-2})$	0.09716	0.09716	0.10232	0.09716	0.09411	0.11810	0.04939	0.04939	0.05072	0.04939	0.04861	0.05480

Table 5. Moments of the LS Estimator with $\beta^* = 0.2$ and $T = 10, 20$.

	$T=10$						$T=20$					
	Normal	Uniform	Exp(1)	t_5	Mixture	log N	Normal	Uniform	Exp(1)	t_5	Mixture	log N
Bias($\hat{\lambda}$)	−0.37197	−0.38119	−0.37504	−0.36073	−0.35895	−0.36407	−0.19126	−0.19404	−0.19358	−0.18593	−0.18634	−0.18528
(MCSE)	0.00010	0.00010	0.00010	0.00010	0.00010	0.00011	0.00006	0.00006	0.00006	0.00006	0.00006	0.00006
$O(T^{-2})$	−1.50000	−1.50000	−1.50000	−1.50000	−1.50000	−1.50000	−0.37500	−0.37500	−0.37500	−0.37500	−0.37500	−0.37500
$O(\sigma^2)$	−1.05000	−1.05000	−1.05000	−1.05000	−1.05000	−1.05000	−0.31875	−0.31875	−0.31875	−0.31875	−0.31875	−0.31875
$O(T^{-3})$	−11.55000	−11.55000	−10.05000	−11.55000	−12.43480	−5.46949	−1.63125	−1.63125	−1.44375	−1.63125	−1.74185	−0.87118
$O(\sigma^3)$	−1.05000	−1.05000	0.45000	−1.05000	−1.93484	5.03050	−0.31875	−0.31875	−0.13125	−0.31875	−0.42935	0.44131
$O(\beta^{*2})$	−0.36943	−0.37915	−0.38799	−0.35698	−0.34991	−0.40050	−0.18589	−0.18911	−0.19981	−0.17944	−0.17666	−0.20976
Var($\hat{\lambda}$)	0.09672	0.09693	0.09775	0.09821	0.09538	0.12419	0.03112	0.03138	0.03049	0.03085	0.03093	0.03308
$O(T^{-4})$	2.25000	2.25000	4.65000	2.25000	0.83425	11.97880	0.15938	0.15938	0.45938	0.15938	−0.01759	1.37548
MSE($\hat{\lambda}$)	0.23508	0.24224	0.23840	0.22833	0.22423	0.25674	0.06770	0.06903	0.06797	0.06542	0.06566	0.06741
$O(T^{-4})$	4.50000	4.50000	6.90000	4.50000	3.08425	14.22880	0.30000	0.30000	0.60000	0.30000	0.12303	1.51610
Bias$\hat{\beta}/\sigma$	0.21413	0.22174	0.29437	0.20451	0.14695	0.30957	0.23955	0.24344	0.29650	0.23174	0.20067	0.31889
(MCSE)	0.00026	0.00026	0.00028	0.00028	0.00026	0.00032	0.00020	0.00020	0.00022	0.00021	0.00019	0.00027
$O(T^{-1})$	1.45455	1.45455	1.45455	1.45455	1.45455	1.45455	0.85714	0.85714	0.85714	0.85714	0.85714	0.85714
Var($\hat{\beta}/\sigma$)	0.69958	0.67149	0.80646	0.75682	0.66138	1.03012	0.39989	0.38790	0.47785	0.43303	0.37780	0.71659
$O(T^{-2})$	−2.32231	−2.32231	−1.98644	−2.32231	−2.52044	−0.96081	−0.55000	−0.55000	−0.45326	−0.55000	−0.60706	−0.15787
MSE($\hat{\beta}/\sigma$)	0.74543	0.72066	0.89312	0.79864	0.68297	1.12596	0.45727	0.44716	0.56577	0.48673	0.41806	0.81828
$O(T^{-2})$	−0.20661	−0.20661	0.12926	−0.20661	−0.40473	1.15489	0.18469	0.18469	0.28143	0.18469	0.12763	0.57682

Table 6. Moments of the LS Estimator with $\beta^* = 0.2$ and $T = 40, 80$.

	$T = 10$						$T = 20$					
	Normal	Uniform	Exp(1)	t_5	Mixture	log N	Normal	Uniform	Exp(1)	t_5	Mixture	log N
Bias($\hat{\lambda}$)	−0.08464	−0.08536	−0.08498	−0.08267	−0.08353	−0.07894	−0.03075	−0.03092	−0.02993	−0.03025	−0.03097	−0.02625
(MCSE)	0.00003	0.00003	0.00003	0.00003	0.00003	0.00003	0.00001	0.00001	0.00001	0.00001	0.00001	0.00001
$O(T^{-2})$	−0.09375	−0.09375	−0.09375	−0.09375	−0.09375	−0.09375	−0.02343	−0.02343	−0.02343	−0.02343	−0.02343	−0.02343
$O(\sigma^2)$	−0.08671	−0.08671	−0.08671	−0.08671	−0.08671	−0.08671	−0.02255	−0.02255	−0.02255	−0.02255	−0.02255	−0.02255
$O(T^{-3})$	−0.25078	−0.25078	−0.22734	−0.25078	−0.26460	−0.15577	−0.04306	−0.04306	−0.04013	−0.04306	−0.04479	−0.03119
$O(\sigma^3)$	−0.08671	−0.08671	−0.06328	−0.08671	−0.10054	0.00829	−0.02255	−0.02255	−0.01962	−0.02255	−0.02428	−0.01068
$O(\beta^{*2})$	−0.07417	−0.07497	−0.08428	−0.07092	−0.06951	−0.09295	−0.01215	−0.01244	−0.01795	−0.01033	−0.00969	−0.02475
Var($\hat{\lambda}$)	0.00815	0.00819	0.00806	0.00805	0.00813	0.00832	0.00158	0.00159	0.00153	0.00157	0.00161	0.00144
$O(T^{-4})$	0.01231	0.01231	0.04981	0.01231	−0.00981	0.16432	0.00106	0.00106	0.00575	0.00106	−0.00170	0.02006
MSE($\hat{\lambda}$)	0.01531	0.01547	0.01528	0.01489	0.01511	0.01455	0.00253	0.00255	0.00243	0.00248	0.00257	0.00213
$O(T^{-4})$	0.02109	0.02109	0.05859	0.02109	−0.00102	0.17311	0.00161	0.00161	0.00630	0.00161	−0.00115	0.02061
Bias$\hat{\beta}/\sigma$	0.22779	0.22969	0.25950	0.22264	0.20793	0.27512	0.18287	0.18366	0.19444	0.18003	0.17538	0.19670
(MCSE)	0.00014	0.00014	0.00015	0.00014	0.00013	0.00020	0.00009	0.00009	0.00009	0.00009	0.00009	0.00013
$O(T^{-1})$	0.46342	0.46342	0.46342	0.46342	0.46342	0.46342	0.24074	0.24074	0.24074	0.24074	0.24074	0.24074
Var($\hat{\beta}/\sigma$)	0.18814	0.18448	0.22553	0.20138	0.17759	0.38902	0.07590	0.07506	0.08909	0.07951	0.07159	0.15671
$O(T^{-2})$	−0.09802	−0.09802	−0.07220	−0.09802	−0.11326	0.00666	−0.00095	−0.00095	0.00571	−0.00095	−0.00488	0.02606
MSE($\hat{\beta}/\sigma$)	0.24003	0.23724	0.29287	0.25095	0.22083	0.46472	0.10934	0.10879	0.12689	0.11193	0.10235	0.19540
$O(T^{-2})$	0.11672	0.11672	0.14255	0.11672	0.10149	0.22142	0.05700	0.05700	0.06367	0.05700	0.05307	0.08402

nonnormality has yet to be drawn, given that in reality there are countless possibilities of nonnormal distributions.

5. CONCLUDING REMARKS

We have derived analytical moment approximation for the LS estimator in ARX(1) with a unit root, where an arbitrary number of possibly nonstationary exogenous regressors may be included. In this framework, no distribution assumption is made except that we assume the existence of moments of the errors up to order 4. In the special case of random walk with drift, very neat bias and MSE formulae are presented. Numerical illustrations of the accuracy of our moment approximations in finite samples are also provided.

Note that we have restrained ourselves from deriving moment approximation for the random walk model $y=\lambda y_{-1}+\sigma\varepsilon$, $\lambda=1$. One can show that $\hat{\lambda}-1=\sigma(y_0\iota'\varepsilon+\sigma\varepsilon'J\varepsilon)/(y_0^2T+2\sigma y_0\iota'J\varepsilon+\sigma^2\varepsilon'J'J\varepsilon)$, where $y_0\iota'\varepsilon=O_P(T^{1/2})$, $\varepsilon'J\varepsilon=O_P(T)$, $\iota'J\varepsilon=O_P(T^{3/2})$, and $\varepsilon'J'J\varepsilon=O_P(T^2)$. Thus, a possible expansion may be as follows:

$$\begin{aligned}
\hat{\lambda}-1 &= \left(\underbrace{\frac{\sigma y_0\iota'\varepsilon}{\sigma^2\varepsilon'J'J\varepsilon}}_{O_P(T^{-3/2})}+\underbrace{\frac{\sigma^2\varepsilon'J\varepsilon}{\sigma^2\varepsilon'J'J\varepsilon}}_{O_P(T^{-1})}\right)\left(1+\underbrace{\frac{2\sigma y_0\iota'J\varepsilon}{\sigma^2\varepsilon'J'J\varepsilon}}_{O_P(T^{-1/2})}+\underbrace{\frac{y_0^2T}{\sigma^2\varepsilon'J'J\varepsilon}}_{O_P(T^{-1})}\right)^{-1}\\
&=\left(\frac{\varepsilon'J\varepsilon}{\varepsilon'J'J\varepsilon}+\frac{y_0\iota'\varepsilon}{\sigma\varepsilon'J'J\varepsilon}\right)\left[1-\frac{2_0\iota'J\varepsilon}{\sigma\varepsilon'J'J\varepsilon}-\frac{y_0^2T}{\sigma^2\varepsilon'J'J\varepsilon}+\left(\frac{2y_0\iota'J\varepsilon}{\sigma\varepsilon'J'J\varepsilon}+\frac{y_0^2T}{\sigma^2\varepsilon'J'J\varepsilon}\right)^2+o_P(T^{-1})\right]\\
&=\underbrace{\frac{\varepsilon'J\varepsilon}{\varepsilon'J'J\varepsilon}}_{O_P(T^{-1})}+\underbrace{\frac{y_0}{\sigma}\frac{\iota'\varepsilon}{\varepsilon'J'J\varepsilon}-2\frac{y_0}{\sigma}\frac{\iota'J\varepsilon\varepsilon'J\varepsilon}{(\varepsilon'J'J\varepsilon)^2}}_{O_P(T^{-3/2})}\\
&\quad\underbrace{+4\left(\frac{y_0}{\sigma}\right)^2\frac{\varepsilon'J\varepsilon\varepsilon'J'\iota\iota'J\varepsilon}{(\varepsilon'J'J\varepsilon)^3}-\left(\frac{y_0}{\sigma}\right)^2\frac{T\varepsilon'J\varepsilon}{(\varepsilon'J'J\varepsilon)^2}-2\left(\frac{y_0}{\sigma}\right)^2\frac{\varepsilon'\iota\iota'J\varepsilon}{(\varepsilon'J'J\varepsilon)^2}}_{O_P(T^{-2})}+o_P(T^{-2})
\end{aligned}$$

Under nonnormality, it is not obvious how to evaluate directly the above expectations of ratios. We may attempt to implement further expansions for the random ratios. But unfortunately

$$\frac{\varepsilon' J \varepsilon}{\varepsilon' J' J \varepsilon} = \frac{\varepsilon' J \varepsilon}{E(\varepsilon' J' J \varepsilon)} \left[1 + \frac{\varepsilon' J' J \varepsilon - E(\varepsilon' J' J \varepsilon)}{E(\varepsilon' J' J \varepsilon)} \right]^{-1}$$

is not going to work, as $\mathrm{E}(\varepsilon' J' J \varepsilon) = O(T^2)$ and $\varepsilon' J' J \varepsilon - \mathrm{E}(\varepsilon' J' J \varepsilon) = O(T^2)$, and we are not aware of straightforward expansions that allow us to calculate analytically the moments under nonnormality, although Phillips (2012) derived bias expansions under normality with the help of moment generation function of ratio of normal quadratic forms.

One area of future research is to develop Edgeworth-type approximation to the finite-sample distribution of the LS estimator when the model has a unit root and errors are nonnormal. This could be done by following the seminal paper of Phillips (1977) for the case of stable model with normal errors.

Another area of future research is to explore the finite-sample properties of predictive regressions, where the lagged regressor follows a unit-root process. Phillips (2014) considered the asymptotic results when the regressor has local-to-unit behavior and Phillips and Lee (2013) generalized this to the multivariate framework.

Given the analytical results developed in this paper, one can easily write a bias corrected estimator, namely, the LS estimator minus the estimated bias which is obtained by replacing the unknown parameters in the analytical bias with their consistent estimates. One may also follow Phillips (2012) to consider the indirect inference estimator and Abadir (1995) to consider the minimum MSE estimator. We leave these for our future research.

ACKNOWLEDGMENTS

We thank an anonymous referee and Tom Fomby for their helpful comments.

REFERENCES

Abadir, K. M. (1993). OLS bias in a nonstationary regression. *Econometric Theory*, *9*, 81–93.

Abadir, K. M. (1995). Unbiased estimation as a solution to testing for random walks. *Economics Letters*, *47*, 263–268.

Bao, Y. (2007). The approximate moments of the least squares estimator for the stationary autoregressive model under a general error distribution. *Econometric Theory*, *23*, 1013–1021.

Bao, Y., & Ullah, A. (2007). The second-order bias and mean squared error of estimators in time series models. *Journal of Econometrics, 140*, 650–669.

Grubb, D., & Symons, J. (1987). Bias in regressions with a lagged-dependent variable. *Econometric Theory, 3*, 371–386.

Hoque, A., & Peters, T. (1986). Finite sample analysis of the ARMAX models. *Sankhyā: The Indian Journal of Statistics, Series B, 48*, 266–283.

Hurwicz, L. (1950). Least-squares bias in time series. In T. C., Koopmans (Ed.) *Statistical inference in dynamic economic models* (pp. 365–383). New York, NY: Wiley.

Kiviet, J. F., & Phillips, G. D. A. (1993). Alternative bias approximations in regressions with a lagged dependent variable. *Econometric Theory, 9*, 62–80.

Kiviet, J. F., & Phillips, G. D. A. (1994). Bias assessment and reduction in linear error-correction models. *Journal of Econometrics, 63*, 215–243.

Kiviet, J. F., & Phillips, G. D. A. (2005). Moment approximation for least-squares estimators in dynamic regression models with a unit root. *Econometrics Journal, 8*, 115–142.

Nankervis, J. S., & Savin, N. E. (1988). The student's *t* approximation in a stationary first-order autoregressive model. *Econometrica, 56*, 119–145.

Phillips, P. C. B. (1977). Approximations to some finite sample distributions associated with a first order stochastic difference equation. *Econometrica, 45*, 463–485.

Phillips, P. C. B. (2012). Folklore theorems, implicit maps, and indirect inference. *Econometrica, 80*, 425–454.

Phillips, P. C. B., & Lee, J. H. (2013). Predictive regression under various degrees of persistence and robust long-horizon regression. *Journal of Econometrics, 177*, 250–264.

Phillips, P. C. B. (2014). On confidence intervals for autoregressive roots and predictive regression. *Econometrica, 82*, 1177–1195.

Sawa, T. (1978). The exact moments of the least-squares estimator for the autoregressive model. *Journal of Econometrics, 8*, 159–172.

Ullah, A. (2004). *Finite sample econometrics*. New York, NY: Oxford University Press.

APPENDIX A: EXPECTATIONS OF QUADRATIC FORMS

To evaluate the expectations of quadratic forms under nonnormality, we can use the following results (see, e.g., Ullah (2004)):

$$\begin{aligned}\mathrm{E}(\varepsilon\varepsilon' A\varepsilon)=\gamma_1(I\odot A)\iota,\quad \mathrm{E}(\varepsilon' A_1\varepsilon\varepsilon' A_2\varepsilon)&=\mathrm{tr}(A_1)\mathrm{tr}(A_2)+\mathrm{tr}(A_1A_2)\\&\quad+\mathrm{tr}(A_1A_2')+\gamma_2\mathrm{tr}(A_1\odot A_2)\end{aligned} \tag{A.1}$$

In addition

$$\mathrm{E}(\varepsilon\varepsilon' A\varepsilon\varepsilon')=[\mathrm{tr}(A)I+A+A'+\gamma_2(A\odot I)] \tag{A.2}$$

Based on Eqs. (A.1) and (A.2), and observing that $MJ=O(1)$, $JJ'=O(T)$, $MJX=O(T)$, $J'MJ=O(T)$, $J'MJX=O(T^2)$, and $J+J'=0.5(\iota\iota'-I)$, we can derive the following:

$$\mathrm{E}(\varepsilon' MJ\varepsilon)=\mathrm{tr}(MJ)=0.5\mathrm{tr}(M(J+J'))=0.5\mathrm{tr}(M(\iota\iota'-I))=-0.5(T-k)=O(T)$$

$$\mathrm{E}(\varepsilon' MJX\beta\beta' X' J' MJ\varepsilon)=\beta' X' J' MJMJX\beta=-0.5\beta' X' J' MJX\beta=-0.5\mu^{-1}=O(T^3)$$

$$\beta' X' J' M\mathrm{E}(\varepsilon\varepsilon' J' MJX\beta\beta' X' J' MJ\varepsilon)=\gamma_1\beta' X' J' M(I\odot J' MJX\beta\beta' X' J' MJ)\iota=O(T^6)$$

$$\beta' X' J' M\mathrm{E}(\varepsilon\varepsilon' J' MJ\varepsilon)=\gamma_1\beta' X' J' M(I\odot J' MJ)\iota=O(T^3)$$

$$\beta' X' J' MJ\mathrm{E}(\varepsilon\varepsilon' MJ\varepsilon)=\gamma_1\beta' X' J' MJ(I\odot MJ)\iota=O(T^3)$$

$$\begin{aligned}\mathrm{E}(\varepsilon' J' MJ\varepsilon\varepsilon' MJX\beta\beta' X' J' MJ\varepsilon)&=\mathrm{tr}(J' MJ)\mathrm{tr}(MJX\beta\beta' X' J' MJ)+2\mathrm{tr}(J' MJMJX\beta\beta' X' J' MJ)\\&\quad+\gamma_2\mathrm{tr}(J' MJ\odot MJX\beta\beta' X' J' MJ)\\&=\mathrm{tr}(J' MJ)\beta' X' J' MJMJX\beta+2\beta' X' J' MJJ' MJMJX\beta\\&\quad+\gamma_2\mathrm{tr}(J' MJ\odot MJX\beta\beta' X' J' MJ)\\&=O(T^5)\end{aligned}$$

$$\begin{aligned}
E(\varepsilon' MJX\beta\beta' X' J' MJ\varepsilon\varepsilon' J' MJX\beta\beta' X' J' MJ\varepsilon) = & \operatorname{tr}(MJX\beta\beta' X' J' MJ)\operatorname{tr}(J' MJX\beta\beta' X' J' MJ) \\
& + 2\operatorname{tr}(MJX\beta\beta' X' J' MJJ' MJX\beta\beta' X' J' MJ) \\
& + \gamma_2 \operatorname{tr}(MJX\beta\beta' X' J' MJ \odot J' MJX\beta\beta' X' J' MJ) \\
= & 3\beta' X' J' MJMJX\beta\beta' X' J' MJJ' MJX\beta \\
& + \gamma_2 \operatorname{tr}(MJX\beta\beta' X' J' MJ \odot J' MJX\beta\beta' X' J' MJ) \\
= & -1.5\beta' X' J' MJX\beta\beta' X' J' MJJ' MJX\beta \\
& + \gamma_2 \operatorname{tr}(MJX\beta\beta' X' J' MJ \odot J' MJX\beta\beta' X' J' MJ) \\
= & O(T^8)
\end{aligned}$$

$$\begin{aligned}
E(\varepsilon' MJ\varepsilon\varepsilon' J' MJX\beta\beta' X' J' MJ\varepsilon) = & \operatorname{tr}(MJ)\operatorname{tr}(J' MJX\beta\beta' X' J' MJ) \\
& + 2\operatorname{tr}(MJJ' MJX\beta\beta' X' J' MJ) \\
& + \gamma_2 \operatorname{tr}(MJ \odot J' MJX\beta\beta' X' J' MJ) \\
= & \operatorname{tr}(MJ)\beta' X' J' MJJ' MJX\beta + 2\beta' X' J' MJMJJ' MJX\beta \\
& + \gamma_2 \operatorname{tr}(MJ \odot J' MJX\beta\beta' X' J' MJ) \\
= & \operatorname{tr}(MJ)\beta' X' J' MJJ' MJX\beta + o(T^6)
\end{aligned}$$

$$\begin{aligned}
E(\varepsilon' MJ\varepsilon\varepsilon' J' MJ\varepsilon) & = \operatorname{tr}(MJ)\operatorname{tr}(JMJ) + 2\operatorname{tr}(MJJ' MJ) + \gamma_2 \operatorname{tr}(MJ \odot J' MJ) \\
& = \operatorname{tr}(MJ)\operatorname{tr}(J' MJ) - \operatorname{tr}(J' MJ) + \gamma_2 \operatorname{tr}(MJ \odot J' MJ) \\
& = \operatorname{tr}(MJ)\operatorname{tr}(J' MJ) + o(T^3)
\end{aligned}$$

$$E(\varepsilon' MJX\beta\beta' X' J' M\varepsilon) = \beta' X' J' MJX\beta = \mu^{-1} = O(T^3)$$

$$\beta' X' J' M E(\varepsilon\varepsilon' MJ\varepsilon) = \gamma_1 \beta' X' J' M(I \odot MJ)\iota = O(T^2)$$

$$\beta' X' J' M E(\varepsilon\varepsilon' MJX\beta\beta' X' J' MJ\varepsilon) = \gamma_1 \beta' X' J' M(I \odot MJX\beta\beta' X' J' MJ)\iota = O(T^5)$$

$$\begin{aligned}
E[(\varepsilon' MJ\varepsilon)^2] & = [\operatorname{tr}(MJ)]^2 + \operatorname{tr}(MJMJ) + \operatorname{tr}(J' MJ) + \gamma_2 \operatorname{tr}(MJ \odot MJ) \\
& = [\operatorname{tr}(MJ)]^2 + \operatorname{tr}(MJMJ) + \operatorname{tr}(J' MJ) + o(T^2)
\end{aligned}$$

$$\begin{aligned}
E(\varepsilon' MJ\varepsilon\varepsilon' MJX\beta\beta' X' J' MJ\varepsilon) = & \operatorname{tr}(MJ)\beta' X' J' MJMJX\beta + \operatorname{tr}(MJMJX\beta\beta' X' J' MJ) \\
& + \operatorname{tr}(J' MJX\beta\beta' X' J' MJ) + \gamma_2 \operatorname{tr}(MJ \odot MJX\beta\beta' X' J' MJ) \\
= & -0.5\mu^{-1}\operatorname{tr}(MJ) + \beta' X' J' MJMJMJX\beta \\
& + \beta' X' J' MJJ' MJX\beta + \gamma_2 \operatorname{tr}(MJ \odot MJX\beta\beta' X' J' MJ) \\
= & \beta' X' J' M(JMJ + JJ')MJX\beta + o(T^5)
\end{aligned}$$

$$\begin{aligned}\mathrm{E}(\varepsilon' J' MJ\varepsilon\varepsilon' MJX\beta\beta' X' J' M\varepsilon) &= \mu^{-1}\mathrm{tr}(J'MJ) + 2\beta' X' J' MJ' MJMJX\beta \\ &\quad + \gamma_2 \mathrm{tr}(J'MJ \odot MJX\beta\beta' X' J' M) \\ &= \mu^{-1}\mathrm{tr}(J'MJ) + 2\beta' X' J' MJ' MJMJX\beta + o(T^5)\end{aligned}$$

$$\begin{aligned}\mathrm{E}[(\varepsilon' MJX\beta\beta' X' J' MJ\varepsilon)^2] &= (\beta' X' J' MJMJX\beta)^2 + \mathrm{tr}(MJX\beta\beta' X' J' MJMJX\beta\beta' X' J' MJ) \\ &\quad + \mathrm{tr}(MJX\beta\beta' X' J' MJJ' MJX\beta\beta' X' J' M) \\ &\quad + \gamma_2 \mathrm{tr}(MJX\beta\beta' X' J' MJ \odot MJX\beta\beta' X' J' MJ) \\ &= 2(\beta' X' J' MJMJX\beta)^2 + \beta' X' J' MJJ' MJX\beta\beta' X' J' MJX\beta \\ &\quad + \gamma_2 \mathrm{tr}(MJX\beta\beta' X' J' MJ \odot MJX\beta\beta' X' J' MJ) \\ &= 0.5\mu^{-2} + \mu^{-1}\beta' X' J' MJJ' MJX\beta \\ &\quad + \gamma_2 \mathrm{tr}(MJX\beta\beta' X' J' MJ \odot MJX\beta\beta' X' J' MJ) \\ &= \mu^{-1}\beta' X' J' MJJ' MJX\beta + o(T^8)\end{aligned}$$

$$\mathrm{E}(\tilde{W}'\varepsilon\varepsilon'\tilde{W}) = \sigma^2 D' e_1 \mathrm{E}(\varepsilon' J'\varepsilon\varepsilon' J\varepsilon) e_1' D = \sigma^2 \mathrm{tr}(J'J) D e_1 e_1' D$$

$$\begin{aligned}\mathrm{E}(P\overline{W}'\varepsilon\varepsilon'\overline{W}P') &= \sigma^2 \overline{W}' J \mathrm{E}(\varepsilon e_1' DR\overline{W}'\varepsilon\varepsilon'\overline{W}RDe_1\varepsilon') J'\overline{W} \\ &\quad + \sigma^2 De_1 \mathrm{E}(\varepsilon' J'\overline{W}R\overline{W}'\varepsilon\varepsilon'\overline{W}RDe_1\varepsilon') J'\overline{W} \\ &\quad + \sigma^2 \overline{W}' J \mathrm{E}(\varepsilon e_1' DR\overline{W}'\varepsilon\varepsilon'\overline{W}R\overline{W}' J\varepsilon) e_1' D \\ &\quad + \sigma^2 De_1 \mathrm{E}(\varepsilon' J'\overline{W}R\overline{W}'\varepsilon\varepsilon'\overline{W}R\overline{W}' J\varepsilon) e_1' D \\ &= \sigma^2 \overline{W}' J \mathrm{E}(\varepsilon\varepsilon'\overline{W}RDe_1 e_1' DR\overline{W}'\varepsilon\varepsilon') J'\overline{W} + \sigma^2 De_1 e_1' DR\overline{W}' \mathrm{E}(\varepsilon\varepsilon' J'\overline{W}R\overline{W}'\varepsilon\varepsilon') J'\overline{W} \\ &\quad + \sigma^2 \overline{W}' J \mathrm{E}(\varepsilon\varepsilon'\overline{W}R\overline{W}' J\varepsilon\varepsilon')\overline{W}RDe_1 e_1' D + \sigma^2 \mathrm{E}(\varepsilon' J'\overline{W}R\overline{W}'\varepsilon\varepsilon'\overline{W}R\overline{W}' J\varepsilon) De_1 e_1' D \\ &= \sigma^2 e_1' DRDe_1 \overline{W}' JJ'\overline{W} + 2\sigma^2 \overline{W}' J\overline{W}RDe_1 e_1' DR\overline{W}' J'\overline{W} \\ &\quad + \sigma^2\gamma_2 \overline{W}' J(\overline{W}RDe_1 e_1' DR\overline{W}' \odot I) J'\overline{W} + \sigma^2 \mathrm{tr}(\overline{W}R\overline{W}' J) De_1 e_1' DR\overline{W}' J'\overline{W} \\ &\quad + \sigma^2 De_1 e_1' DR\overline{W}' J'\overline{W}R\overline{W}' J'\overline{W} + \sigma^2 De_1 e_1' DR\overline{W}' JJ'\overline{W} \\ &\quad + \sigma^2\gamma_2 De_1 e_1' DR\overline{W}'(\overline{W}R\overline{W}' J \odot I) J'\overline{W} + \sigma^2 \mathrm{tr}(\overline{W}R\overline{W}' J)\overline{W}' J\overline{W}RDe_1 e_1' D \\ &\quad + \sigma^2 \overline{W}' J\overline{W}R\overline{W}' J\overline{W}RDe_1 e_1' D + \sigma^2 \overline{W}' JJ'\overline{W}RDe_1 e_1' D \\ &\quad + \sigma^2\gamma_2 \overline{W}' J(\overline{W}R\overline{W}' J \odot I)\overline{W}RDe_1 e_1' D + \sigma^2 \mathrm{tr}^2(\overline{W}R\overline{W}' J) De_1 e_1' D \\ &\quad + \sigma^2 \mathrm{tr}(\overline{W}R\overline{W}' J\overline{W}R\overline{W}' J) De_1 e_1' D + \sigma^2 \mathrm{tr}(\overline{W}' JJ'\overline{W}R) De_1 e_1' D \\ &\quad + \sigma^2\gamma_2 \mathrm{tr}(\overline{W}R\overline{W}' J \odot \overline{W}R\overline{W}' J) De_1 e_1' D\end{aligned}$$

$$\begin{aligned}
\mathrm{E}(P\overline{W}'\varepsilon\varepsilon'\tilde{W}) &= \sigma^2\overline{W}'J\mathrm{E}(\varepsilon e_1'DR\overline{W}'\varepsilon\varepsilon'J\varepsilon)e_1'D + \sigma^2De_1\mathrm{E}(\varepsilon'J'\overline{W}R\overline{W}'\varepsilon\varepsilon'J\varepsilon)e_1'D \\
&= \sigma^2\overline{W}'J\mathrm{E}(\varepsilon\varepsilon'J\varepsilon\varepsilon')\overline{W}RDe_1e_1'D + \sigma^2\mathrm{E}(\varepsilon'J'\overline{W}R\overline{W}'\varepsilon\varepsilon'J\varepsilon)De_1e_1'D \\
&= \sigma^2\overline{W}'J(J+J')\overline{W}RDe_1e_1'D + \sigma^2\mathrm{tr}(J'\overline{W}R\overline{W}'(J+J'))De_1e_1'D
\end{aligned}$$

$$\mathrm{E}(\overline{W}'\varepsilon\varepsilon'\tilde{W}) = \sigma\overline{W}'\mathrm{E}(\varepsilon\varepsilon'J\varepsilon)e_1'D = 0$$

$$\begin{aligned}
\mathrm{E}(\overline{W}'\varepsilon\varepsilon'\overline{W}P') &= \sigma\overline{W}'\mathrm{E}(\varepsilon\varepsilon'\overline{W}R\overline{W}'J\varepsilon)e_1'D + \sigma\overline{W}'\mathrm{E}(\varepsilon\varepsilon'\overline{W}RDe_1\varepsilon')J'\overline{W} \\
&= \sigma\gamma_1\overline{W}'(I\odot\overline{W}R\overline{W}'J)\iota e_1'D + \sigma\gamma_1\overline{W}'(\overline{W}RDe_1\iota'\odot I)J'\overline{W}
\end{aligned}$$

$$\begin{aligned}
\mathrm{E}(P\tilde{W}'\varepsilon\varepsilon'\overline{W}) &= \sigma^2\overline{W}'J\mathrm{E}(\varepsilon e_1'DRDe_1\varepsilon'J'\varepsilon\varepsilon')\overline{W} + \sigma^2De_1\mathrm{E}(\varepsilon'J'\overline{W}RDe_1\varepsilon'J'\varepsilon\varepsilon')\overline{W} \\
&= \sigma^2e_1'DRDe_1\overline{W}'J\mathrm{E}(\varepsilon\varepsilon'J'\varepsilon\varepsilon')\overline{W} + \sigma^2De_1e_1'DR\overline{W}'J\mathrm{E}(\varepsilon\varepsilon'J'\varepsilon\varepsilon')\overline{W} \\
&= \sigma^2e_1'DRDe_1\overline{W}'J(J+J')\overline{W} + \sigma^2De_1e_1'DR\overline{W}'J(J+J')\overline{W}
\end{aligned}$$

$$\begin{aligned}
\mathrm{E}(PP\overline{W}'\varepsilon\varepsilon'\overline{W}) &= \sigma^2\overline{W}'J\mathrm{E}(\varepsilon e_1'DR\overline{W}'J\varepsilon e_1'DR\overline{W}'\varepsilon\varepsilon')\overline{W} + \sigma^2De_1\mathrm{E}(\varepsilon'J'\overline{W}R\overline{W}'J\varepsilon e_1'DR\overline{W}'\varepsilon\varepsilon')\overline{W} \\
&\quad + \sigma^2\overline{W}'J\mathrm{E}(\varepsilon e_1'DRDe_1\varepsilon'J'\overline{W}R\overline{W}'\varepsilon\varepsilon')\overline{W} + \sigma^2De_1E(\varepsilon'J'\overline{W}RDe_1\varepsilon'J'\overline{W}R\overline{W}'\varepsilon\varepsilon')\overline{W} \\
&= \sigma^2\overline{W}'J\mathrm{E}(\varepsilon\varepsilon'J'\overline{W}RDe_1e_1'DR\overline{W}'\varepsilon\varepsilon')\overline{W} + \sigma^2De_1e_1'DR\overline{W}\mathrm{E}(\varepsilon\varepsilon'J'\overline{W}R\overline{W}'J\varepsilon\varepsilon')\overline{W} \\
&\quad + \sigma^2e_1'DRDe_1\overline{W}'J\mathrm{E}(\varepsilon\varepsilon'J'\overline{W}R\overline{W}'\varepsilon\varepsilon')\overline{W} + \sigma^2De_1e_1'DR\overline{W}'J\mathrm{E}(\varepsilon\varepsilon'J'\overline{W}R\overline{W}'\varepsilon\varepsilon')\overline{W} \\
&= \sigma^2e_1'DR\overline{W}'J\overline{W}RDe_1\overline{W}'J\overline{W} + \sigma^2\overline{W}'JJ'\overline{W}RDe_1e_1'D + \sigma^2\overline{W}'J\overline{W}RDe_1e_1'DR\overline{W}'J\overline{W} \\
&\quad + \sigma^2\gamma_2\overline{W}'J(J'\overline{W}RDe_1e_1'DR\overline{W}'\odot I)\overline{W} + \sigma^2\mathrm{tr}(\overline{W}R\overline{W}'JJ')De_1e_1'D \\
&\quad + 2\sigma^2De_1e_1'DR\overline{W}'J'\overline{W}R\overline{W}'J\overline{W} + \sigma^2\gamma_2De_1e_1'DR\overline{W}'(J'\overline{W}R\overline{W}'J\odot I)\overline{W} \\
&\quad + \sigma^2\mathrm{tr}(\overline{W}R\overline{W}'J)e_1'DRDe_1\overline{W}'J\overline{W} + \sigma^2e_1'DRDe_1\overline{W}'JJ'\overline{W} \\
&\quad + \sigma^2e_1'DRDe_1\overline{W}'J\overline{W}R\overline{W}'J\overline{W} + \sigma^2\gamma_2e_1'DRDe_1\overline{W}'J(\overline{W}R\overline{W}'J\odot I)\overline{W} \\
&\quad + \sigma^2\mathrm{tr}(\overline{W}R\overline{W}'J)De_1e_1'DR\overline{W}'J\overline{W} + \sigma^2De_1e_1'DR\overline{W}'JJ'\overline{W} \\
&\quad + \sigma^2De_1e_1'DR\overline{W}'J\overline{W}R\overline{W}'J\overline{W} + \sigma^2\gamma_2De_1e_1'DR\overline{W}'J(\overline{W}R\overline{W}'J\odot I)\overline{W}
\end{aligned}$$

$$\begin{aligned}
\mathrm{E}(\overline{W}'\varepsilon\varepsilon'\overline{W}S') &= \sigma^2\overline{W}'\mathrm{E}(\varepsilon\varepsilon'\overline{W}RDe_1\varepsilon'J'J\varepsilon)e_1'D = \sigma^2\overline{W}'\mathrm{E}(\varepsilon\varepsilon'J'J\varepsilon\varepsilon')\overline{W}RDe_1e_1'D \\
&= \sigma^2\mathrm{tr}(J'J)De_1e_1'D + 2\sigma^2\overline{W}'J'J\overline{W}RDe_1e_1'D + \sigma^2\gamma_2\overline{W}'(J'J\odot I)\overline{W}RDe_1e_1'D
\end{aligned}$$

Note that since $\overline{W} = \overline{Z}D$ contains a constant term, then $\overline{W}'(\overline{W}'\overline{W})^{-1}\overline{W}'\iota = \iota$. Also, ι is the second column of $\overline{W}$, so $(\overline{W}'\overline{W})^{-1}\overline{W}'\iota = e_2$, where

$e_2 = (0, 1, 0, \cdots, 0)'$ is $(k+1) \times 1$. We can verify that $De_1e_1'D = O(T^{2\delta_1}) = O(T^{-2})$, $e_1'DRDe_1 = O(T^{-1+2\delta_1}) = O(T^{-3})$, $\overline{W}'J = O(T)$, $\overline{W}R = O(T^{-1})$, $\overline{W}'J'\overline{W} = O(T^2)$, $\overline{W}'JJ' = O(T^2)$, $\overline{W}'JJ'\overline{W} = O(T^3)$, $\overline{W}'J'J\overline{W} = O(T^3)$, $\overline{W}'J\overline{W}R = O(T)$, $\overline{W}R\overline{W}'J = O(1)$, $\overline{W}'JJ'\overline{W}R = O(T^2)$, $\mathrm{tr}(\overline{W}R\overline{W}'J) = O(T)$, $\mathrm{tr}(\overline{W}R\overline{W}'J\overline{W}R\overline{W}'J) = O(T^2)$, and $\mathrm{tr}(\overline{W}'JJ'\overline{W}R) = O(T^2)$. We further observe that $\sigma^2\gamma_2\overline{W}'J(\overline{W}RDe_1e_1'DR\overline{W}'\odot I)J'\overline{W}$, $\sigma^2\gamma_2De_1e_1'DR\overline{W}'(\overline{W}R\overline{W}'J\odot I)J'\overline{W}$, $\sigma^2\gamma_2\overline{W}'J(\overline{W}R\overline{W}'J\odot I)\overline{W}RDe_1e_1'D$, $\sigma^2\gamma_2\mathrm{tr}(\overline{W}R\overline{W}'J\odot\overline{W}R\overline{W}'J)De_1e_1'D$, $\sigma\gamma_1\overline{W}'(I\odot\overline{W}R\overline{W}'J)\iota e_1'D$, $\sigma^2\gamma_2\overline{W}'J(J'\overline{W}RDe_1e_1'DR\overline{W}'\odot I)\overline{W}$, $\sigma^2\gamma_2De_1e_1'DR\overline{W}'(J'\overline{W}R\overline{W}'J\odot I)\overline{W}$, $\sigma^2\gamma_2e_1'DRDe_1\overline{W}'J(\overline{W}R\overline{W}'J\odot I)\overline{W}$, $\sigma^2\gamma_2De_1e_1'DR\overline{W}'J(\overline{W}R\overline{W}'J\odot I)\overline{W}$, and $\sigma^2\gamma_2\overline{W}'(J'J\odot I)\overline{W}RDe_1e_1'D$ are all of order $o(1)$.

APPENDIX B: SPECIAL CASE OF $X = \iota$

When $X = \iota$, we collect the following results:

$$\begin{aligned}
&\beta' X' J' M(I \odot J' M J X \beta \beta' X' J' M J)\iota \\
&= \beta^3 \sum_{t=1}^{T} [t-1-0.5(T-1)]\{0.5[T(T-1)-t(t-1)-(T-1)(T-t)]\}^2 \\
&= -\frac{\beta^3}{240}(T^5 - T)
\end{aligned}$$

$$\beta' X' J' M(I \odot J' M J)\iota = \beta \sum_{t=1}^{T} [t-1-0.5(T-1)][T-t-T^{-1}(T-t)^2] = -\frac{\beta}{12}(T^2-1)$$

$$\begin{aligned}
\beta' X' J' M J(I \odot M J)\iota &= \beta \sum_{t=1}^{T} 0.5[T(T-1)-t(t-1)-(T-1)(T-t)][-T^{-1}(T-t)] \\
&= -\frac{\beta}{24}(T^3 - T)
\end{aligned}$$

$$\beta' X' J' M J X \beta = \beta^2 \sum_{t=1}^{T} [t-1-0.5(T-1)]^2 = \frac{\beta^2}{12} T(T^2-1)$$

$$\mathrm{tr}(MJ) = -T^{-1} \sum_{t=1}^{T} (T-t) = -\frac{1}{2}(T-1)$$

$$\mathrm{tr}(J' M J) = \sum_{t=1}^{T} [T-t-T^{-1}(T-t)^2] = \frac{1}{6}(T^2-1)$$

$$\beta' X' J' M J J' M J X \beta = \beta^2 \sum_{t=1}^{T} \{0.5[T(T-1)-t(t-1)-(T-1)(T-t)]\}^2 = \frac{\beta^2}{120}(T^5 - T)$$

$$\begin{aligned}
\mathrm{tr}(MJMJ) = \mathrm{tr}(JJ) - \frac{2}{T}\iota' J J \iota + \frac{1}{T^2}(\iota' J \iota)^2 &= -\frac{1}{T}\sum_{t=1}^{T}(t-1)(t-2) + \frac{1}{T^2}\sum_{t=1}^{T}(t-1) \\
&= -\frac{1}{12}T^2 + \frac{1}{2}T - \frac{5}{12}
\end{aligned}$$

$$\beta' X' J' M(I \odot MJ)\iota = \beta \sum_{t=1}^{T} [t - 1 - 0.5(T-1)][-T^{-1}(T-t)] = \frac{\beta}{12}(T^2 - 1)$$

$$\beta' X' J' M(I \odot MJX\beta\beta' X' J' MJ)\iota = \beta^3 \sum_{t=1}^{T} [t - 1 - 0.5(T-1)]^2 \{0.5[T(T-1) - t(t-1) - (T-1)(T-t)]\} = \frac{\beta^3}{240}(T^5 - T)$$

$$\begin{aligned}
\beta' X' J' MJMJMJX\beta &= \beta^2 \Big[\iota' J' JJJ\iota - \frac{1}{T}\iota' J' J\iota\iota' JJ\iota - \frac{1}{T}\iota' J\iota\iota' JJJ\iota - \frac{1}{T}\iota' J\iota\iota' J' JJ\iota \\
&\quad + \frac{2}{T^2}(\iota' J\iota)^2(\iota' JJ\iota) + \frac{1}{T^2}(\iota' J\iota)^2(\iota' J' J\iota) - \frac{1}{T^3}(\iota' J\iota)^4\Big] \\
&= \beta^2 \Big[\frac{1}{2}\sum_{t=1}^{T}(t-1)(t-2)(t-1)(T-\frac{t}{2}) - \frac{1}{2T}\sum_{t=1}^{T}(t-1)^2\sum_{t=1}^{T}(t-1)(t-2) \\
&\quad - \frac{1}{2T}\sum_{t=1}^{T}(t-1)\sum_{t=1}^{T}(T-t)(t-1)(t-2) - \frac{1}{2T}\sum_{t=1}^{T}(t-1)\sum_{t=1}^{T}(t-1)^2(t-2) \\
&\quad + \frac{1}{T^2}\left(\sum_{t=1}^{T}(t-1)\right)^2\sum_{t=1}^{T}(t-1)(t-2) + \frac{1}{T^2}\left(\sum_{t=1}^{T}(t-1)\right)^2\sum_{t=1}^{T}(t-1)(T-t) \\
&\quad - \frac{1}{T^3}\left(\sum_{t=1}^{T}(t-1)\right)^4\Big] \\
&= -\frac{\beta^2}{720}(T^5 + 10T^3 - 11T)
\end{aligned}$$

ON THE SIZE DISTORTION FROM LINEARLY INTERPOLATING LOW-FREQUENCY SERIES FOR COINTEGRATION TESTS

Eric Ghysels[a] and J. Isaac Miller[b]

[a]Department of Economics and Department of Finance, University of North Carolina – Chapel Hill, Chapel Hill, North Carolina, USA
[b]Department of Economics, University of Missouri, Columbia, Missouri, USA

ABSTRACT

We analyze the sizes of standard cointegration tests applied to data subject to linear interpolation, discovering evidence of substantial size distortions induced by the interpolation. We propose modifications to these tests to effectively eliminate size distortions from such tests conducted on data interpolated from end-of-period sampled low-frequency series. Our results generally do not support linear interpolation when alternatives such as aggregation or mixed-frequency-modified tests are possible.

Keywords: Linear interpolation; cointegration; trace test; residual-based cointegration tests

JEL Classifications: C12; C32

Essays in Honor of Peter C. B. Phillips
Advances in Econometrics, Volume 33, 93–122

ISSN: 0731-9053/doi:10.1108/S0731-905320140000033004

1. INTRODUCTION

Bergstrom (1976) edited a volume on statistical inference in continuous time economic models. The contributors were Bergstrom himself, Phillips, Robinson, Sargan, and Wymer. Chapters 5 through 8 were written by Peter Phillips, and cover a variety of topics ranging from structural estimation of continuous time models to identification issues. Last but not least, Chapter 8, which is based on Chapter 6 of his dissertation, provides a number of empirical applications.

In Chapter 8, Peter Phillips used a discrete time VARX model corresponding to a linear stochastic differential equation with exogenous input variables. The chapter deals with temporal aggregation and in more subtle ways also mixed-frequency data issues. In particular, the discrete time VARX model involves a weighted integral of the exogenous variables and that integral is approximated using higher-frequency data. This work was a precursor to later work by Zadrozny (1988), who studied Gaussian MLE of continuous time ARMAX models when data are stocks and flows at different frequencies.

The topic of mixed frequency data, along with temporal aggregation and linear interpolation, is being researched again more intensely in recent years, and it is therefore quite appropriate to remind ourselves of the pioneering work in the area done by Peter Phillips. While the broad topic of this paper relates to the early work of Peter Phillips, the more narrowly defined topic does as well. Namely, we examine the effects of linear interpolation on the size of standard tests for cointegration and develop modified test statistics to correct for size distortions induced by linear interpolation between the last high-frequency observations of low-frequency intervals. Generally speaking, data transforms, including interpolation, will likely affect finite sample distributions and in some cases asymptotics. The case considered in the aforementioned 1976 chapter by Peter Phillips (and the corresponding 1974 Phillips paper on estimation and inference) involves transforms that are nonlinear functions of the model parameters in a stationary continuous time setting. In such a case he worked out the bias effects as an order of the sampling interval.

The topic of this paper also extends research on cointegration under the assumptions of temporal aggregation or mixed sampling frequencies. In particular, Stock (1987), Granger (1990), and Phillips (1991) were among the first to analyze cointegration under temporal aggregation, and important contributions have been made by Marcellino (1999) and Chambers

(2003, 2011), with simulation studies on the properties of cointegration tests conducted by Hooker (1993), Hu (1996), and Haug (2002). In the setting of cointegrated series observed at different frequencies, a number of recent contributions have been made by Miller (2011, 2014), Götz, Hecq, and Urbain (2012, 2013), and Seong, Ahn, and Zadrozny (2013).

More specifically, the research in this paper extends the recent work by the authors (Ghysels & Miller, 2013) on the effects of temporal aggregation and mixed sampling frequencies on the size of such tests. The latter show that, even though aggregation does not change the cointegrating vector, aggregation can cause size distortion in cointegration tests and thus in tests using either low-frequency or mixed-frequency series when the data are generated at a higher frequency. Ghysels and Miller (2013) – henceforth GM – consider Johansen's (1988) likelihood-based trace test (when in general multiple cointegrating relationships are allowed) and Engle and Granger's (1987) residual-based tests, or the modified tests of Phillips and Ouliaris (1990) (when at most one cointegrating relationship is allowed).

GM show that when all series are skip sampled in the *same* way – e.g., when all series are observed only in December or January of each year – then there will be no size distortions. Considering a second case, where possibly cointegrated series are average sampled (or cumulated, as flows would be), GM show that size distortions are expected but are of an acceptable magnitude. Average sampling characterizes an upper bound on size distortion resulting from sampling or aggregating all series in the same way. Moreover, consider testing for cointegration between stock and flow variables, where the series are aggregated or sampled differently. In such cases, GM show that size distortion can be quite severe. The most severe size distortions that they find appear to be in the case in which series are skip sampled *differently* – e.g., when one series is sampled only in December but another only in January.

GM go beyond characterizing size distortions. They also propose novel ways to solve the size distortion problems. Often series are actually available at different frequencies: e.g., prices are recorded monthly and GDP quarterly. One can take advantage of mixed sampling frequencies to address size distortions. Namely, instead of running a low-frequency (henceforth LF) trace test, GM propose to keep the high frequency (henceforth HF) and run a mixed-frequency (henceforth MF) trace test. Generally, the smallest size distortions possible using the latter MF approach will be smaller than those using the former LF approach.

How do we run MF tests to minimize distortion? GM rely on MF vector autoregressive models modified in a straightforward way for the trace test. If feasible, this trace test suffers from size distortion only from the LF series already aggregated by a statistical agency. In the case of the residual-based tests, size distortion is unavoidable and may be quite severe with a MF regression, because the weights assigned to the HF regressors cannot be estimated consistently using OLS under the null. Instead, GM propose a nonlinear MIDAS scheme based on an exponential Almon lag function that is estimated using NLS. The purpose of the exponential Almon function is simply to restrict the weights to the unit interval in order to limit variation of the inconsistent estimates. The residual-based tests are the standard Dickey–Fuller or Phillips–Perron tests run on NLS residuals rather than on OLS residuals.

In the present paper, we examine a different setting, in which high-frequency series are constructed or available from linear interpolation of the LF data. Our research and findings closely complement those of GM in the sense that an econometrician faced with a MF problem – i.e., series observed at different frequencies – may choose either (a) to aggregate the HF series to the lowest frequency (considered by GM), (b) to modify the tests to take into account the different frequencies (considered by GM), or (c) to impute the LF series to the highest frequency. The common imputation method of linear interpolation is considered here.

Because of the interpolation, although the tests are implemented with HF series, these series are not all genuinely observed. We thus offer critical insights into size distortions of cointegration tests conducted on data that are already subject to interpolation or are deliberately interpolated by the econometrician. Further, since HF series may be imputed using some other (perhaps unknown) method, the size distortions that we obtain using linear interpolation are suggestive of those that might be obtained using an alternative imputation method.

Further, we propose modifications to the three cointegration tests to effectively eliminate size distortions resulting from using the standard critical values with linearly interpolated series. These modified tests are tailored specifically to commonly employed end-of-period (EOP) interpolation – i.e., interpolation that assumes the LF data are sampled at the end of each LF period, as opposed to, say, the beginning. These modifications may not be robust to alternative types of imputation, or to EOP interpolation conducted on data that were not EOP sampled.

Overall, our findings in this analysis and in that of GM suggest that the MF approaches advocated in GM are most desirable, and particularly so in cases in which the econometrician does not know how the LF series at hand were aggregated. Conducting tests using *unmodified* test statistics on linearly interpolated HF data is *never* advisable, because the size distortion appears to be severe in every case that we consider. Using *modified* test statistics *may* alleviate the problem, but the size distortion is only eliminated in the possibly unrealistic case that we know that the series were EOP interpolated from EOP sampled LF data.

The rest of the paper is structured as follows. We lay out our basic modeling assumptions, discuss interpolation, and present the theoretical analysis in the following section. In Section 3, we present Monte Carlo simulations to illustrate the asymptotic results using a finite sample and to numerically compare the size distortions obtained with those of GM. We apply linear interpolation and the modified test statistics to stock prices and dividends in Section 4, and Section 5 concludes with some practical recommendations encompassing all three approaches (LF, MF, and HF) to cointegration testing considered by GM and in this paper. An appendix contains proofs of the main analytical results.

We make use of the following notational conventions throughout the paper. $C \otimes D$ is the usual Kronecker product and $C \odot D$ denotes the element-by-element (Hadamard) product. We use ι to denote a unit vector of length given by the context in which it is used.

2. OBSERVATION FREQUENCY AND INTERPOLATION

In order to introduce linear interpolation, suppose an I(1) series $(y_{L,\,t-i/m})$ of random $p_L \times 1$ vectors is generated at a high frequency but observed only at the *end* of a low-frequency period. Here $t = 1, \ldots, T$ indexes the low-frequency and $i = 0, \ldots, m-1$ for $m < \infty$ indexes the high-frequency vectors within each LF period, and we let the total number of vectors equal $M = mT$.[1,2] Specifically, the data-generating process (DGP) involves $(y_{L,\,t-i/m})$ for $t = 1, \ldots, T$ and $i = 0, \ldots, m-1$, but only $(y_{L,\,t})$ for $t = 1, \ldots, T$ and $i = 0$ is observed.

Stocks, such as interest rates, exchange rates, stock market prices, and other prices, are typically sampled at the end of a particular period even though they evolve at a much higher frequency. EOP sampling of this type is a special but important case of skip sampling – i.e., sampling the HF series every m periods to create a LF series. GM considered yet more general aggregation schemes, but found that skip sampling is the only type of aggregation scheme that does not result in any asymptotic size distortion of these tests. Furthermore, among skip sampling schemes, EOP sampling generates the least number of asymptotically negligible terms in the distributions, providing the best outlook for avoiding size distortion in finite samples.

Let $(y^L_{L,t-i/m})$ denote a series of linearly interpolated values of $(y_{L,t})$. That is, the subscript L denotes that the series is observed only at the LF, but the superscript L denotes that the LF series has been linearly interpolated to the HF. Specifically, the linearly interpolated series may be written as either $y^L_{L,\,t-i/m}=y_{Lt}-m^{-1}i\Delta y_{Lt}$ or $y^L_{L,\,t-i/m}=y_{L,t-1}+m^{-1}(m-i)\Delta y_{Lt}$. The latter will generally be more convenient for analysis, since the first and second terms are uncorrelated when increments of $(y_{L,\,t-i/m})$ are uncorrelated. Note that $\Delta=1-L$ denotes a LF difference, while we use $\Delta^{(1/m)}=1-L^{1/m}$ with a HF lag $L^{1/m}$ to denote a HF difference. Linear interpolation multiplies the number of observations by m, but adds no marginal information at HF increments.

The full HF DGP that we consider may also involve an additional I(1) series $(y_{H,\,t-i/m})$ of $p_H \times 1$ vectors observed directly at the HF, so that

$$y_{t-i/m}=(y'_{L,t-i/m}, y'_{H,t-i/m})' \tag{1}$$

is a $p\times 1$ vector with $p=p_L+p_H$. In other words, the series consisting of each of the p elements of $y_{t-i/m}$ are all I(1), but p_L are observed only at the end of each LF period and p_H are observed directly at the HF. With almost no loss of generality, we assume that the vector $y_{t-i/m}$ is sorted with a LF series first.[3]

We assume an invariance principle of the form $M^{-1/2}\sum_{j=1}^{[rM]}\Delta^{(1/m)}y_{j/m}\to_d B(r)$ as $M\to\infty$, where B is a vector Brownian motion with variance Σ. Thus, $B=\Sigma^{1/2}W$, where W is a vector of independent standard Brownian motions and $\Sigma=\Sigma^{1/2}\Sigma^{1/2\prime}$ is the usual lower triangular Cholesky decomposition. We assume that the increments $\Delta^{(1/m)}y_{t-i/m}$ of the DGP have no serial correlation, in order to demonstrate the size distortion from linear interpolation in its most basic form. Thus, Σ represents both the long-run and contemporaneous variances of $\Delta^{(1/m)}y_{t-i/m}$.

To account for serial correlation in $(\Delta^{(1/m)}y_{t-i/m})$, researchers typically include additional lagged differences or else use a semiparametric test along the lines of Phillips and Ouliaris (1990) that takes into account missing lagged differences. Lagged differences of linearly interpolated data take the form $\Delta^{(1/m)}y^L_{L,t-i/m}=m^{-1}\Delta y_{Lt}$ instead of $\Delta^{(1/m)}y_{L,t-i/m}$, and we speculate that including these terms in the model would exacerbate rather than ameliorate size distortion. Because our main aim is to show size distortion in even the most basic case and because our conclusions even in this case suggest *avoiding* linear interpolation, we do not explicitly consider linear interpolation in the more complicated case.

2.1. Cointegration Tests

It is natural to conduct cointegration tests on the linearly interpolated data as if they were the actual HF data. Unlike with MF data, there is no obvious obstacle to the implementation of such tests. Using otherwise familiar notation from the cointegration literature, we define

$$r_{0,t-i/m}=(\Delta^{(1/m)}y^{L\prime}_{L,t-i/m},\Delta^{(1/m)}y'_{H,t-i/m})'$$

and

$$r_{1,t-i/m}=(y^{L\prime}_{L,t-(i+1)/m},y'_{H,t-(i+1)/m})'$$

which result from interpolating the observed LF series to the HF. We may then define the four sample moments $R_{jk}=M^{-1}\sum_t\sum_{i=0}^{m-1}r_{j,t-i/m}r'_{k,t-i/m}$ for $j,k=0,1$.[4]

Like GM and previous authors, we analyze the trace test only under the null hypothesis of no cointegrating vectors – i.e., p linearly independent stochastic trends. In this sense, the nulls of no cointegration are the same across the three tests, even though the alternatives are different. The usual trace test statistic conducted on the observed and interpolated HF data may be written as

$$\hat{\psi}_M=M\ \mathrm{tr}(R_{11}^{-1}R_{10}R_{00}^{-1}R_{01})$$

up to an asymptotically negligible term (see Johansen (1995) for a more detailed explanation).

Consider the benchmark case in which *all* data are observed at the HF – i.e., in which there is no MF problem and no linear interpolation is involved or needed. In that case, the test statistic has the well-known limiting distribution of

$$\hat{\psi}_M \to_d \mathrm{tr}\left\{\left(\int W\, \mathrm{d}W'\right)'\left(\int WW'\right)^{-1}\int W\, \mathrm{d}W'\right\} = \psi$$

where the only nuisance parameter is the number of stochastic trends under the null hypothesis.

To introduce the residual-based cointegration test statistics in this context, denote the first series in $r_{1,t-i/m}$ by $r_{11,t-i/m}$ and the vector of remaining series by $r_{21,t-i/m}$, so that $r_{1,t-i/m} = (r_{11,t-i/m}, r'_{21,t-i/m})'$. Let $\hat{\alpha} = (1, -\hat{\beta}')'$, where $\hat{\beta}$ is the least squares estimator of the coefficient vector of the regression of $r_{11,t-i/m}$ on $r_{21,t-i/m}$. The residual-based Dickey–Fuller tests may be written as

$$\hat{\rho}_M = (\hat{\alpha}' M^{-1} R_{11}\hat{\alpha})^{-1}\hat{\alpha}' R_{10}\hat{\alpha} \qquad \text{and} \qquad \hat{\tau}_M = (\hat{\alpha}' R_{00}\hat{\alpha}\hat{\alpha}' M^{-1} R_{11}\hat{\alpha})^{-1/2}\hat{\alpha}' R_{10}\hat{\alpha}$$

using this notation.

Similar to Phillips and Ouliaris (1990), we define $\kappa = (1, \kappa_2')'$ with $\kappa_2 = -\left(\int W_2 W_2'\right)^{-1} \int W_2 W_1$ and $Q(r) = W_1(r) - \int W_1 W_2'\left(\int W_2 W_2'\right)^{-1} W_2(r) = \kappa' W(r)$ with $W = (W_1, W_2')'$ partitioned identically to $(r_{11,t-i/m}, r'_{21,t-i/m})'$. The distributions of the test statistics are given by

$$\hat{\rho}_M \to_d \left(\int Q^2\right)^{-1}\int Q\, \mathrm{d}Q = \rho \qquad \text{and} \qquad \hat{\tau}_M \to_d \left(\kappa'\kappa\int Q^2\right)^{-1/2}\int Q\, \mathrm{d}Q = \tau$$

in the benchmark case in which all data are observed at the HF.

2.2. *Limits with Linearly Interpolated Series*

The limits of the three test statistics $\hat{\psi}_M$, $\hat{\rho}_M$, and $\hat{\tau}_M$ very clearly depend on the limits of $M^{-1}R_{11}$, R_{00}, and R_{10}, which we present in the following lemma for the more general case in which some series are subject to linear interpolation. To write these limits, define

$$C_m = \begin{bmatrix} m^{-1}\iota' & m^{-1}\iota' \\ m^{-1}\iota' & \iota' \end{bmatrix} \qquad \text{and} \qquad D_m = \frac{m-1}{2m}\begin{bmatrix} \iota' & \iota' \\ \iota' & 0 \end{bmatrix}$$

to be matrices with rows partitioned identically to those of $y_{t-i/m}$ in Eq. (1) and columns partitioned identically to those of its transpose. Note that the dimension of the unit vector ι is contextual: the matrix $\iota\iota'$ is $p_L \times p_L$ in the upper left block, $p_H \times p_L$ in the lower left block, $p_L \times p_H$ in the upper right block, and $p_H \times p_H$ in the lower right block.

Lemma 1. Sample moments R_{11}, R_{00}, and R_{10} using some linearly interpolated and some observed HF series have limits given by

[a] $M^{-1}R_{11} \rightarrow_d \int BB'$,
[b] $R_{00} \rightarrow_p C_m \odot \Sigma$, and
[c] $R_{10} \rightarrow_d \int BdB' + (D_m \odot \Sigma)$

as $T \rightarrow \infty$.

The result in part [a] is the same as in the benchmark case, which is as expected. As pointed out by Miller (2010), although linear interpolation adds nonlinearity (in time) and nonstationarity through the term $m^{-1}(m-i)\Delta y_{Lt}$, the nonstationarity of this term is only mild and the term is still dominated by the I(1) term $y_{L,t-1}$. More fundamentally, continuous functions created by linearly interpolating discrete functions representing discrete time series have been used to prove invariance principles of the type we assume here – specifically, Donsker's theorem. Additional linear interpolation is redundant as the discrete intervals vanish in the limit.

The limits of parts [b] and [c] in the HF benchmark case are respectively Σ and $\int B\,\mathrm{d}B'$. Deviations from these benchmark limits are driven by the fact that the I(1) term $y_{L,t-1}$ of the linearly interpolated series is observed only at the LF and is completely eliminated by the HF difference. The difference of the second term $m^{-1}\Delta y_{Lt}$ remains, and the limits reflect the structure of that term. The matrix $m^{-1}\iota\iota'$ in the upper left corner of C_m that reflects only the linearly interpolated series can be interpreted intuitively: repeating the same information m times through interpolation decreases the limiting variance by a factor of m. Note that the benchmark results correspond to $C_m = \iota\iota'$ and $D_m = 0$. In other words, the benchmark results are obtained for [b] and [c] only when no interpolation is needed – which is indeed the benchmark case.

To present the limiting distributions of the three tests, the lower block-triangular decomposition $\Sigma = L'L$ employed by Phillips and Ouliaris (1990) is particularly convenient. This decomposition is distinct from the usual lower triangular Cholesky decomposition defined above. We may write $B = L'W$ or $B = \Sigma^{1/2}W$, but note that $L' \neq \Sigma^{1/2}$. (See the proof of Theorem 1 in the appendix for the explicit form of L.) Using the inverse of the matrix L, define $C_m^+ = L^{-1\prime}(C_m \odot \Sigma)L^{-1}$ and $D_m^+ = L^{-1\prime}(D_m \odot \Sigma)L^{-1}$.

Theorem 1. The three test statistics $\hat{\psi}_M$, $\hat{\rho}_M$, and $\hat{\tau}_M$ for tests conducted on mixtures of HF and linearly interpolated series have limiting distributions given by

[a] $\hat{\psi}_M \to_d \mathrm{tr}\{(\int W dW' + D_m^+)'(\int WW')^{-1}(\int W dW' + D_m^+)(C_m^+)^{-1}\}$,
[b] $\hat{\rho}_M \to_d (\int Q^2)^{-1}(\int Q dQ + \kappa' D_m^+ \kappa)$, and
[c] $\hat{\tau}_M \to_d (\kappa' C_m^+ \kappa \int Q^2)^{-1/2}(\int Q dQ + \kappa' D_m^+ \kappa)$

as $T \to \infty$.

As expected, the benchmark results are obtained only when $C_m = \iota\iota'$ so that $C_m^+ = I$ and $D_m = 0$ so that $D_m^+ = 0$. On the other hand, these simplify to

$$C_m^+ = L^{-1\prime}(m^{-1}\iota\iota' \odot \Sigma)L^{-1} = m^{-1}I$$

$$D_m^+ = L^{-1\prime}((m-1)/(2m)\iota\iota' \odot \Sigma)L^{-1} = (m-1)/(2m)I$$

if *all* series have been linearly interpolated. A case in which all series have been linearly interpolated might be one in which the econometrician observes one or more high-frequency series *known* to be interpolated and then interpolates any remaining LF series. Such a situation seems unusual, and this case has limited practical relevance.

Of much more practical relevance is the case in which some series are interpolated, but not others. In particular, the econometrician starts from a MF situation and simply interpolates only the series observed at the LF. Size distortion is evident from Theorem 1 in any case involving linear interpolation.

Because this specific type of interpolation under this specific sampling assumption – i.e., EOP interpolation applied to EOP sampled series – entails a specific and relatively simple multiplicative structure involving C_m and D_m in Lemma 1, size corrections that avoid simulations to generate new critical values are possible. Specifically, the test statistics may be modified so that the rather complicated limits in Theorem 1 reduce to the standard benchmark limits ψ, ρ, and τ.

To this end, define

$$\tilde{C}_m = \begin{bmatrix} m\iota\iota' & m\iota\iota' \\ m\iota\iota' & \iota\iota' \end{bmatrix}$$

so that $\tilde{C}_m \odot C_m = \iota\iota'$. Clearly from Lemma 1, $R_{00}^{(m)} = \tilde{C}_m \odot R_{00}$ provides a consistent estimator of Σ, which is the limit of R_{00} in the HF benchmark case. Likewise, to eliminate the nuisance term from the limit of R_{10}, we may define $R_{10}^{(m)} = R_{10} - D_m \odot \tilde{C}_m \odot R_{00}$. Since $R_{10}^{(m)} = R_{10} - D_m \odot R_{00}^{(m)}$, it clearly has a limiting distribution given by $\int BdB'$, the limit of R_{10} in the HF benchmark case.

Corollary 1. Modified test statistics with limits given respectively by ψ, ρ, and τ are

[a] $\hat{\psi}_M^{(m)} = M \ \mathrm{tr}\left(R_{11}^{-1} R_{10}^{(m)} \left(R_{00}^{(m)}\right)^{-1} R_{01}^{(m)}\right)$,

[b] $\hat{\rho}_M^{(m)} = (\hat{\alpha}' M^{-1} R_{11} \hat{\alpha})^{-1} \hat{\alpha}' R_{10}^{(m)} \hat{\alpha}$, and

[c] $\hat{\tau}_M^{(m)} = (\hat{\alpha}' R_{00}^{(m)} \hat{\alpha} \hat{\alpha}' M^{-1} R_{11} \hat{\alpha})^{-1/2} \hat{\alpha}' R_{10}^{(m)} \hat{\alpha}$.

Appropriately modified test statistics thus have the standard limiting distributions. Consequently, critical values based on these distributions are asymptotically valid. Such test statistics, applied correctly and to large samples, and compared to these critical values, will not exhibit any size distortion.

3. FINITE-SAMPLE COMPARISONS

We conduct Monte Carlo simulations in order to illustrate the magnitudes of the size distortions evident from Theorem 1 and in order to illustrate the reductions in these distortions offered by the modified test statistics of Corollary 1. The basic setup is similar to that of GM and previous authors. We use a bivariate DGP given by

$$\Delta^{(1/m)} y_{t-i/m} \sim \mathbf{iidN}(0, \Sigma) \qquad \text{with} \qquad \Sigma = \begin{bmatrix} 1 & \sigma_{21} \\ \sigma_{21} & 1 \end{bmatrix}$$

under the null. We let $m = 12$ and $T = 200$, generating 2,400 high-frequency observations, as would be the case with 200 years of monthly data. We conduct 1,000 simulations of each model and calculate critical values based on those that gave a size of 0.05 for the HF DGP, so that we can eliminate any size distortion from the random seeds used in the simulations.

Tables 1 and 2 show the results of the Monte Carlo simulations for $\sigma_{21} = 0$ and $\sigma_{21} = 0.9$ respectively. In these tables, *EOP* denotes that end-of-period sampling is used for aggregation, *BOP* denotes that

Table 1. Empirical Sizes for $\sigma_{21} = 0$ with a Nominal Size of 0.05.

Case	Test	EOP	BOP	Flat	Seas
Low-freq	$\hat{\psi}_T$	**0.057***	**0.056***	0.078	0.077
	$\hat{\rho}_T$	**0.047***	**0.046***	0.006	0.006
	$\hat{\tau}_T$	**0.045***	**0.045***	0.009	0.010
Mixed-freq	$\hat{\psi}_T^*$	**0.056***	**0.062***	0.072	0.071
	$\hat{\rho}_T^*$	0.461	0.472	0.362	0.366
	$\hat{\tau}_T^*$	0.462	0.466	0.358	0.366
HF: 2 series LI	$\hat{\psi}_M$	0.789	0.785	0.852	0.853
(Unmodified)	$\hat{\rho}_M$	0.000	0.000	0.000	0.000
	$\hat{\tau}_M$	0.000	0.000	0.000	0.000
HF: 1 series LI	$\hat{\psi}_M$	0.559	0.554	0.654	0.654
(Unmodified)	$\hat{\rho}_M$	0.006	0.006	0.006	0.006
	$\hat{\tau}_M$	0.006	0.006	0.006	0.006
HF: 2 series LI	$\hat{\psi}_M^{(m)}$	**0.054***	**0.054**	0.074	0.073
(Modified)	$\hat{\rho}_M^{(m)}$	**0.049***	**0.049**	0.009	0.010
	$\hat{\tau}_M^{(m)}$	**0.051***	**0.050**	0.011	0.013
HF: 1 series LI	$\hat{\psi}_M^{(m)}$	**0.050***	**0.054**	**0.063**	**0.063**
(Modified)	$\hat{\rho}_M^{(m)}$	**0.051***	**0.053**	0.020	0.021
	$\hat{\tau}_M^{(m)}$	**0.049***	**0.053**	0.020	0.021

Results from 1,000 simulations with $m = 12$ and $T = 200$. *EOP*, any aggregated series aggregated using end-of-period sampling; *BOP*, beginning-of-period sampling; *Flat*, flat sampling; *Seas*, a seasonal sampling scheme. *Low-freq*, both series aggregated; *Mixed-freq*, one series aggregated; *2 series LI*, both series aggregated and then linearly interpolated; *1 series LI*, one series aggregated and then linearly interpolated. *Modified*, test statistics of Corollary 1.
Superscript * denote results corresponding to asymptotically correctly sized tests.
Values in bold denote $|\text{size} - 0.05| < 0.02$.

beginning-of-period sampling is used, and *Flat* denotes that flat sampling (average sampling – i.e., equal weights) is used. A seasonal weighting scheme – also used by GM, denoted by *Seas*, and given by $(1, 3, 9, 1, 3, 9, 1, 3, 9, 1, 3, 9)/52$ – mimics an annual series constructed from, say, quarterly surveys in response to which economic activity from the last month of each quarter is more heavily weighted.

The first three rows of Tables 1 and 2 show the sizes of tests with statistics $\hat{\psi}_T$, $\hat{\rho}_T$, and $\hat{\tau}_T$ using series completely aggregated to the lowest frequency. The next three rows show the sizes from the GM test statistics $\hat{\psi}_T^*$, $\hat{\rho}_T^*$, and $\hat{\tau}_T^*$ adapted to use series at different frequencies directly. To reiterate the findings of GM, the sizes when all series have been aggregated identically are not excessive. The maximum appears to be 0.078 for the case of flat sampling, which indeed GM show yields the maximum size distortion when all series are aggregated in the same way. The fact that the sizes from

Table 2. Empirical Sizes for $\sigma_{21} = 0.9$ with a Nominal Size of 0.05.

Case	Test	EOP	BOP	Flat	Seas
Low-freq	$\hat{\psi}_T$	**0.057***	**0.056***	0.078	0.077
	$\hat{\rho}_T$	**0.048***	**0.050***	0.011	0.011
	$\hat{\tau}_T$	**0.049***	**0.046***	0.012	0.012
Mixed-freq	$\hat{\psi}_T^*$	**0.052***	**0.051***	**0.068**	**0.069**
	$\hat{\rho}_T^*$	0.508	0.519	0.410	0.415
	$\hat{\tau}_T^*$	0.470	0.478	0.378	0.381
HF: 2 series LI	$\hat{\psi}_M$	0.789	0.785	0.852	0.853
(Unmodified)	$\hat{\rho}_M$	0.000	0.000	0.000	0.000
	$\hat{\tau}_M$	0.000	0.000	0.000	0.000
HF: 1 series LI	$\hat{\psi}_M$	0.739	0.947	0.904	0.916
(Unmodified)	$\hat{\rho}_M$	0.467	0.492	0.478	0.480
	$\hat{\tau}_M$	0.447	0.471	0.460	0.461
HF: 2 series LI	$\hat{\psi}_M^{(m)}$	**0.054***	**0.054**	0.074	0.073
(Modified)	$\hat{\rho}_M^{(m)}$	**0.055***	**0.055**	0.012	0.012
	$\hat{\tau}_M^{(m)}$	**0.052***	**0.051**	0.013	0.013
HF: 1 series LI	$\hat{\psi}_M^{(m)}$	0.095*	0.858	0.601	0.657
(Modified)	$\hat{\rho}_M^{(m)}$	**0.067***	0.734	0.403	0.455
	$\hat{\tau}_M^{(m)}$	**0.063***	0.722	0.380	0.440

Results from 1,000 simulations with $m = 12$ and $T = 200$. *EOP*, any aggregated series aggregated using end-of-period sampling; *BOP*, beginning-of-period sampling; *Flat*, flat sampling; *Seas*, a seasonal sampling scheme. *Low-freq*, both series aggregated; *Mixed-freq*, one series aggregated; *2 series LI*, both series aggregated and then linearly interpolated; *1 series LI*, one series aggregated and then linearly interpolated. *Modified*, test statistics of Corollary 1. Superscript * denotes results corresponding to asymptotically correctly sized tests.
Values in bold denote $|\text{size} - 0.05| < 0.02$.

EOP and BOP sampling are not exactly equal to the 0.05 nominal size for all three tests is simply due to small-sample bias.

Further, as GM discuss, the MF trace test works very well – the MF strategy dominates the LF strategy in almost every case. However, the MF residual-based tests using OLS yield very substantial size distortion due to inconsistent weight estimation under the null, which is quite evident for both of these test statistics in both tables under any aggregation scheme.

The seventh through twelfth rows of Tables 1 and 2 show sizes from the usual (unmodified) test statistics $\hat{\psi}_M$, $\hat{\rho}_M$, and $\hat{\tau}_M$ conducted on HF data subject to linear interpolation. Specifically, the first three of these show size from tests with both series subject to the type of aggregation denoted in the respective column and then interpolated using EOP linear interpolation – i.e., annual data are treated as December data regardless of how the annual data were actually aggregated. The second three show similar results when only one series is subject to aggregation and interpolation, but the other is observed at the original HF. The latter case is of more practical value: such would be the case if a researcher encounters MF series, where the underlying aggregation scheme of the LF may be unknown, and interpolates the LF series to the HF.

All of the unmodified tests in both tables with one or more linearly interpolated series exhibit unacceptably large size distortions. Although some size distortion is expected from the analytical results above, the large magnitudes may be somewhat surprising. The trace tests are all extremely oversized. The residual-based tests are either extremely oversized or undersized. Specifically, when both series are subject to linear interpolation, these tests are undersized regardless of σ_{21}. When only one series is subject to linear interpolation, the tests are undersized for $\sigma_{21}=0$ but oversized for $\sigma_{21}=0.9$. There may be a value of σ_{21} for which the tests are approximately correctly sized, but of course σ_{21} is determined by the data in practice.

The last six rows of Tables 1 and 2 show sizes from the same two cases as above, but with test statistics $\hat{\psi}_M^{(m)}$, $\hat{\rho}_M^{(m)}$, and $\hat{\tau}_M^{(m)}$ modified as in Corollary 1. Note that only the first column is "correct" (asymptotically valid) in the sense that one or both series are subject to EOP sampling, then linearly interpolated as if EOP sampled, and then the test statistics are modified to take into account EOP sampling. Indeed, the size distortions are not very large for any of the modified test statistics in the first column.[5]

The remaining columns show size when one or both LF series are subject to a type of aggregation/sampling *other* than EOP but linearly interpolated as if EOP sampled with statistics modified for EOP sampling. The size distortion associated with these improperly modified test statistics depends very much on the aggregation scheme and cross-sectional correlation σ_{21} of the error. When both series are linearly interpolated, BOP works well even though the modified tests are designed for EOP. Indeed, the modified tests eliminate the effects of interpolation as they are intended, so that the results are almost identical to those of the uninterpolated LF series.

When only one series is interpolated, BOP only works well when $\sigma_{21}=0$ – i.e., in the somewhat unrealistic case in which the error variance matrix is diagonal. Otherwise, size distortion with BOP is quite large when $\sigma_{21}=0.9$. The other two aggregation schemes generally lead to unacceptable size distortions, except the modified trace statistic seems to work reasonably well in the case in which σ_{21} happens to be zero. The only difference to note is that, similar to the unmodified tests, the sign of the size distortion of the residual-based tests depends on σ_{21} when only one series is interpolated, with the size increasing in σ_{21}.

To synthesize the results in Tables 1 and 2, suppose that we have series observed at different frequencies and we *know* that the LF series was EOP sampled. The first column of each table shows us that we may either EOP sample the remaining HF series or linearly interpolate the LF series with appropriately modified test statistics. Both of these approaches yield approximately correct sizes, and we only go wrong by using linear interpolation without modifying the test statistics. A MF approach to the trace test along the lines of GM is sensible, but not a MF approach to residual-based tests using OLS.

Instead, suppose that we know that the LF series was sampled by some *other* method. Aggregating all of the series in the same way does not generate very much size distortion for any of the three tests, so this approach is reasonable. Using linear interpolation and tests modified under the incorrect EOP assumption may generate severe size distortion. The best cases using interpolated data seem to yield about the same size as using aggregated data, so linear interpolation is *not* recommended in this case.

Finally, suppose that the way in which the LF series was aggregated is *unknown*. Again, the MF approach dominates other approaches to the trace test, but the choice is less obvious for the residual-based tests. GM show that size distortion is excessive when the data are subject to *different* aggregation schemes, which would be the case if the remaining HF series is aggregated incorrectly. Thus, all three options (aggregation, MF, interpolation) may severely distort the size of residual-based cointegration tests.

To ameliorate the size distortion, GM propose a MF approach using a nonlinear MIDAS approximation, and they show that size distortion may be more acceptable using residual-based tests on residuals from a model with an exponential Almon lag function with parameters estimated using NLS. Since that approach dominates simple aggregation, we also recommend it over linear interpolation in this case. The reader is referred to GM for more details on how this test is constructed.

Overall, our simulations do not yield any convincing reason to use linearly interpolated data if there is a choice not to do so. The modified test statistics work well in the situation for which they were designed, but may be deeply flawed otherwise. In the most optimistic situations, the performance of tests using linearly interpolated series equals that using series aggregated in the same way. Thus, the recommendations made by GM of using MF approaches over LF approaches also hold over the HF approaches considered here.

4. APPLICATION TO STOCK PRICES AND DIVIDENDS

As do GM, we consider the problem of testing for cointegration between log stock prices and log dividends. The data from Robert Shiller's website[6] pertaining to his book *Irrational Exuberance* are essentially available at different frequencies, since prices are available monthly, while dividends are available annually. In order to put these series in the context of our theoretical framework, we are assuming that both series are generated at a monthly frequency – or possibly more often. Annual aggregation of dividends is a process that is upstream of our analysis in the sense that we do not have disaggregated dividend data.

Faced with a MF problem, Shiller made both series available at both frequencies. Shiller (1989) first created annual prices from sampling monthly prices only in January (a BOP scheme), and then he created monthly dividends by linearly interpolating annual dividends (Shiller, 2000). GM studied leaving the data at different frequencies (MF approach) and aggregating monthly prices (LF approach), and we focus on interpolation (HF approach) here.

Both series run from 1871 through 2012, so that $T = 142$. Because prices are monthly, clearly $m = 12$ so that $M = mT = 1{,}704$.[7] We let P and D denote the log of nominal prices and nominal dividends. Fig. 1 plots the log price-dividend ratio. Another way of looking at this ratio is that it is the residual from imposing a cointegrating vector of $(1, -1)'$ on the two series. It seems clear from the figure that $(1, -1)'$ does not cointegrate log prices and log

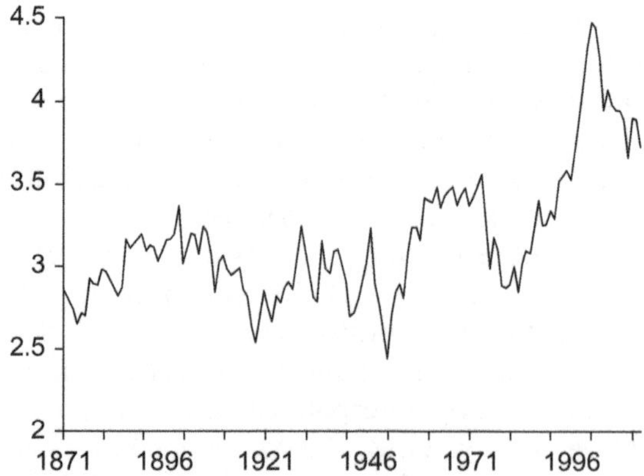

Fig. 1. S&P Annual Log Price-Dividend Ratio.

dividends. Moreover, Phillips, Shi, and Yu (2013) find evidence in support of explosive roots in this ratio over a similar period of time.

The lack of cointegration could reflect a bubble or a structural break of some sort – e.g., an increase in market capitalization of tech firms that do not pay dividends. Our goal here is simply to illustrate how radically the test results vary according to how a researcher handles the practical obstacle posed by different sampling frequencies. We do not impose the cointegrating vector $(1, -1)'$, in order to be as generous as possible in favor of the cointegration result that we do not expect to hold.

As in GM, we consider the following hypotheses and tests:

- Trace test:
  - $H_0(0)$: No cointegrating vector (2 distinct stochastic trends) versus $H_A(2)$: 2 cointegrating vectors (all series stationary)
  - $H_0(1)$: 1 cointegrating vector (1 distinct stochastic trend) versus $H_A(2)$: 2 cointegrating vectors (all series stationary)
- Coefficient and *t*-tests:
  - $H_0(0)$: No cointegrating vector (2 distinct stochastic trends) versus $H_A(1)$: 1 cointegrating vector (1 distinct stochastic trend)

Unit root tests (not shown) support stochastic trends in the individual series. In fact, Phillips, Wu, and Yu (2011) focus on distinguishing explosive roots from unit roots in stock prices and dividends over a different time period, so nonstationarity of the individual series does not seem controversial and we should not find evidence for $H_A(2)$ using the trace tests. Specifically, we should fail to reject either $H_0(0)$ or $H_0(1)$ against $H_A(2)$. The price-dividend ratio plotted in Fig. 1 and our beliefs about the possibility of structural breaks or bubbles suggest that $H_0(1)$ should not hold, either. Thus, we should also fail to reject $H_0(0)$ against $H_0(1)$ using the residual-based tests.

Our empirical results appear in Table 3. We implement the cointegration tests on demeaned and detrended series P and D: a trend is allowed in the cointegrating relationship and a drift is allowed in differences. Since we do not expect any rejection of any of the nulls by a correctly sized test, a rejection by any of the tests or aggregation/sampling/interpolation schemes is indicative of size distortion.

The LF and MF results in the first four rows are reproduced from GM. *Annual-EOP* uses annual D with December P (EOP sampled), *Annual-BOP* uses annual D with January P (BOP sampled), and *Annual-Flat* uses annual D with average P (flat sampled). *MF* denotes the MF VECM for the trace

Table 3. Cointegration Tests.

	Trace Test		Coefficient Test	t-test
	$H_0(1)/H_A(2)$	$H_0(0)/H_A(2)$	$H_0(0)/H_A(1)$	$H_0(0)/H_A(1)$
Annual-EOP	3.58	**35.34**	**−38.39**	**−4.40**
Annual-BOP	3.70	14.27	−19.47	−3.17
Annual-Flat	3.31	17.20	−22.66	−3.40
MF	4.23	15.29	−24.45	−3.53
BOP-Lerp	3.55	**62.29**	−16.10	−2.86
EOP-Lerp	3.57	**93.64**	−14.42	−2.72
EOP-Lerp-M	3.51	**35.38**	**−33.94**	**−4.14**
Critical values	12.25	25.32	−29.73	−3.98

Annual-EOP, annual D with December P; *Annual-BOP*, annual D with January P; *Annual-Flat*, annual D with average P. *MF*, mixed-frequency VECM or residual-based tests using OLS; *BOP-Lerp*, Shiller (2000) monthly dividend data; *EOP-Lerp*, December-December linear interpolation of D; *EOP-Lerp-M*, December-December linear interpolation with modified test statistics.

Values in bold denote rejection at 0.05 significance level using critical values from Osterwald-Lenum (1992, Case 2*) for the trace test and Phillips and Ouliaris (1990) for the residual-based tests.

test and residual-based tests using an unrestricted MF regression estimated using OLS.

The most sensible LF results in this case are obtained using either BOP or flat sampling of log price, since both schemes yield results similar to the MF results for the trace test. The latter results should not exhibit any size distortion other than the unavoidable size distortion from observing log dividends at the LF already. EOP sampling appears to be the worst of the three LF schemes.

We cannot expect to do any better than these cases using linear interpolation, but we can do much worse. The remaining rows of Table 3 use some type of linear interpolation. *BOP-Lerp* denotes the Shiller (2000) monthly dividend data, constructed as the log of January-January linearly interpolated dividends (interpolation *before* taking logs). *EOP-Lerp* denotes the much more common type of linear interpolation discussed above (December-December), but note that we interpolate *after* taking logs, and *EOP-Lerp-M* denotes tests modified to take into account this type of interpolation as in Corollary 1.

Relative to the case of BOP sampling of prices with annual dividends, the case of BOP sampling with linear interpolation shows a serious outlier: the trace test of $H_0(0)$, the null of no cointegrating vectors (two distinct stochastic trends), is strongly rejected against the null of two cointegrating vectors. Such a strong rejection due to size distortion is expected. That the residual-based test values are similar to those of the BOP case is likely a coincidence. Recall from the simulations that the direction of the size distortions in cases of one series linear interpolated with unmodified test statistics depends on the unknown parameter σ_{21}. We get the expected conclusion that there are two distinct stochastic trends from these two tests, but note that is the opposite of the conclusion from the trace test.

The more common EOP-Lerp scheme seems to exacerbate the size distortion of the trace test of the null $H_0(0)$, but does not change the other statistics very much. We draw the same conflicting conclusions with either BOP-Lerp or EOP-Lerp.

The modified test statistics do not give us the desired conclusions either, but we do get a consistent rejection of $H_0(0)$ using all three tests with that null. This would argue *for* cointegration, rather than against it. Is this correct? No. The test statistic values are similar to the case of annual dividends and EOP sampled prices. We know from GM that aggregation generally leads to size distortion, that its magnitude depends on the type of aggregation, and that its sign cannot be negative for the trace test of the null of $H_0(0)$. Since EOP sampling of prices gives the highest value of the trace test of $H_0(0)$, the sizes of *all three* tests must be distorted by that sampling scheme. Since we get very similar values for the modified tests using HF prices and EOP sampled dividends, the tests evidently exhibit size distortion in this case too.

Linear interpolation does not seem very sensible in this application, since dividends represent a flow rather than a stock. Annual dividends are cumulated from monthly dividends. The constant factor from cumulating rather than averaging should not pose a problem for the tests, because we do not restrict the cointegrating vector, but assigning the annual dividend to December and interpolating does. Even when we correctly apply the EOP modification to tests using an EOP interpolated series, the mismatch of the assumption that the annual dividends are subject to EOP sampling with the actual aggregation/sampling scheme of dividends causes size distortions of the type in the last three rows of Table 2, which may indeed be substantial.

5. CONCLUDING REMARKS

Both our large-sample analysis and small-sample simulations suggest that testing for cointegration using trace or residual-based test statistics on linearly interpolated data leads to massive size distortions, even though the interpolation does not affect the long-run properties being tested. We propose convenient and easily implemented size corrections to these three tests for the most common type of linear interpolation (December-December or EOP). Although we demonstrate the effectiveness of the proposed size corrections in large and small samples, we note their lack of robustness to realistic violations of the EOP assumption. That is, if the LF series are subject to a different type of sampling/aggregation, the proposed modifications may not eliminate the size distortion.[8]

Our application of the unmodified and modified tests to stock price and dividend data demonstrates the wide variation in the conclusions that may be drawn under alternative approaches to MF data. A subset of the LF and MF approaches yields test results consistent with our expectations about these data, while none of the interpolation-based HF approaches yield sensible conclusions. The failure of the modified test statistics in this application is likely due to the fact that dividends data are subject to a different type of aggregation than that assumed by the modifications.

Our practical recommendations for implementing these tests on series available at different frequencies mirror those of GM. Specifically, GM suggest that a MF approach to the trace test dominates an aggregation-based LF approach, and we further find that both dominate an interpolation-based HF approach. Even in the case of a correctly modified trace test statistic as in Corollary 1, interpolation does no better than the MF approach. In other cases, it may do worse.

GM find the two residual-based tests to be more complicated in the sense that size distortions may be unavoidable – especially if the underlying aggregation scheme of the LF series is unknown to the econometrician. In this light, the size distortions using linearly interpolated HF data are not particularly surprising. However, we do not find any evidence that linear interpolation dominates the other approaches, and we mirror their recommendation to use a nonlinear approximation to limit the magnitudes of the unavoidable size distortions.

NOTES TO THE APPENDIX

1. If instead the total number of HF observations is not divisible by m, the remaining HF observations after that last LF observation may be extrapolated rather than interpolated. As long as $m<\infty$, handling these should make no difference in the asymptotic analysis.

2. Chambers (2011) analyzes cointegrating regressions with $m \to \infty$. Our main results, starting with Lemma 1, would not hold without modification, since the limiting expressions rely explicitly on m.

3. The only loss of generality is that a reordering would entail redefining C_m and D_m accordingly in Lemma 1 and subsequently. Otherwise, the trace test is implemented by re-sorting eigenvalues, so that the test statistic is invariant with respect to the order of the series. The asymptotic invariance of the residual-based tests with respect to the order is less obvious, because this ordering implies a regression of an interpolated series on a HF series rather than the reverse. Under the null, however, the limiting distribution of the least squares estimator of the regression coefficient is invariant with respect to interpolation, as elucidated in footnote 2 in the proof of Lemma A.2.

4. Note that $r_{1,\,t-i/m}$ is actually observed one HF period earlier, at time $t-(i+1)/m$, which reflects the notation typically used in the cointegration literature, where r_{1t} is observed at time $t-1$. This way, $(r_{0,t-i/m})$ is contemporaneously uncorrelated with increments of $(r_{1,t-i/m})$.

5. The trace test exhibits more size distortion when $\sigma_{21}=0.9$. However, further simulations (not shown) suggest that the size distortion decreases to zero as the sample size increases, consistent with limiting result of Corollary 1[a].

6. http://www.econ.yale.edu/~shiller/data.htm

7. For tests using HF and linearly interpolated data, we drop data from 1871 and use December 1871 only for interpolation of dividends, so that $M=1{,}692$. We retain all 142 years for tests using LF and MF data.

8. Even though both approaches yield the same asymptotic size, we speculate that there might be some small-sample power advantage to using the EOP-sampled LF data instead of interpolating the EOP-sampled data and employing the proposed correction. Although it nominally increases the sample size, interpolation does not increase the amount of new information and therefore should not increase power. The requirement to estimate Σ to implement the correction may in fact decrease power.

ACKNOWLEDGMENTS

The authors are grateful to Peter Phillips, an anonymous referee, and other participants of the 2013 Advances in Econometrics Conference in Honor of Peter Phillips for useful comments. The first author acknowledges support of a Marie Curie FP7-PEOPLE-2010-IIF grant.

REFERENCES

Bergstrom, A. R. (1976). *Statistical inference in continuous time economic models.* New York, NY: American Elsevier Pub Co.

Chambers, M. J. (2003). The asymptotic efficiency of cointegration estimators under temporal aggregation. *Econometric Theory*, *19*, 49–77.

Chambers, M. J. (2011). Cointegration and sampling frequency. *Econometrics Journal*, *14*, 156–185.

Engle, R. F., & Granger, C. W. J. (1987). Co-integration and error correction: Representation, estimation, and testing. *Econometrica*, *55*, 251–276.

Ghysels, E., & Miller, J. I. (2013). *Testing for cointegration with temporally aggregated and mixed-frequency time series.* Working Paper 13–07. Department of Economics, University of Missouri, Columbia, MO.

Götz, T. B., Hecq, A., & Urbain, J.-P. (2012). *Forecasting mixed frequency time series with ECM-MIDAS models.* Department of Quantitative Economics, Maastricht University, mimeo, Maastricht.

Götz, T. B., Hecq, A., & Urbain, J.-P. (2013). Testing for common cycles in non-stationary VARs with varied frequency data. *Advances in Econometrics*, *31*, 361–393.

Granger, C. W. J. (1990). Aggregation of time-series variables: A survey. In T. Barker & M. H. Pesaran (Eds.), *Disaggregation in econometric modelling* (pp. 17–34). New York, NY: Routledge.

Haug, A. A. (2002). Temporal aggregation and the power of cointegration tests: A Monte Carlo study. *Oxford Bulletin of Economics and Statistics*, *64*, 399–411.

Hooker, M. A. (1993). Testing for cointegration: Power versus frequency of observation. *Economics Letters*, *41*, 359–362.

Hu, W. (1996). Time aggregation and skip sampling in cointegration tests. *Statistical Papers*, *37*, 225–234.

Johansen, S. (1988). Statistical analysis of cointegration vectors. *Journal of Economic Dynamics and Control*, *12*, 231–254.

Johansen, S. (1995). *Likelihood-based inference in cointegrated vector autoregressive models.* Oxford, UK: Oxford University Press.

Marcellino, M. (1999). Some consequences of temporal aggregation in empirical analysis. *Journal of Business and Economic Statistics*, *17*, 129–136.

Miller, J. I. (2010). Cointegrating regressions with messy regressors and an application to mixed-frequency series. *Journal of Time Series Analysis*, *31*, 255–277.

Miller, J. I. (2011). *Conditionally efficient estimation of long-run relationships using mixed-frequency time series.* Working Paper 11–03. Department of Economics, University of Missouri, Columbia, MO.

Miller, J. I. (2014). Mixed-frequency cointegrating regressions with parsimonious distributed lag structures. *Journal of Financial Econometrics*, *12*, 584–615.

Osterwald-Lenum, M. (1992). A note with quantiles of the asymptotic distribution of the maximum likelihood cointegration rank test statistics. *Oxford Bulletin of Economics and Statistics*, *54*, 461–472.

Phillips, P. C. B. (1974). The estimation of some continuous time models. *Econometrica*, *42*, 803–823.

Phillips, P. C. B. (1976). Some computations based on observed data series of the exogenous variable component in continuous systems. In A. R. Bergstrom (Ed.), *Statistical inference in continuous time economic models*. New York, NY: American Elsevier Pub Co.

Phillips, P. C. B. (1991). Error correction and long-run equilibrium in continuous time. *Econometrica*, *59*, 967–980.

Phillips, P. C. B., & Ouliaris, S. (1990). Asymptotic properties of residual-based tests for cointegration. *Econometrica*, *58*, 165–193.

Phillips, P. C. B., Shi, S.-P., & Yu, J. (2013). *Testing for multiple bubbles 1: Historical episodes of exuberance and collapse in the S&P 500*. Cowles Foundation Discussion Paper 1914, Yale University, New Haven, CT.

Phillips, P. C. B., Wu, Y., & Yu, J. (2011). Explosive behavior in the 1990s Nasdaq: When did exuberance escalate asset values? *International Economic Review*, *52*, 201–226.

Seong, B., Ahn, S. K., & Zadrozny, P. A. (2013). Cointegration analysis with mixed-frequency data. *Journal of Time Series Analysis*, *34*, 194–205.

Shiller, R. J. (1989). *Market volatility*. Cambridge, MA: MIT Press.

Shiller, R. J. (2000). *Irrational exuberance*. Princeton, NJ: Princeton University Press.

Stock, J. H. (1987). Temporal aggregation and structural inference in macroeconomics – A comment. *Carnegie-Rochester Conference Series of Public Policy*, *26*, 131–139.

Zadrozny, P. A. (1988). Gaussian likelihood of continuous-time ARMAX models when data are stocks and flows at different frequencies. *Econometric Theory*, *4*, 108–124.

APPENDIX: PROOFS OF THE THEORETICAL RESULTS

Proofs of the main results are simplified using the results of the following two lemmas. Some additional notation will ease the presentation of these results. Define the partition $B=(B_L', B_H')'$ identically to that of $y_{t-i/m}$ in Eq. (1). We may partition R_{jk} and Σ as

$$R_{jk} = \begin{bmatrix} R_{jk}^{LL} & R_{jk}^{LH} \\ R_{jk}^{HL} & R_{jk}^{HH} \end{bmatrix} \quad \text{and} \quad \Sigma = \begin{bmatrix} \Sigma_{LL} & \Sigma_{LH} \\ \Sigma_{HL} & \Sigma_{LL} \end{bmatrix}$$

along the lines of C_m and D_m discussed preceding Lemma 1.

Lemma A.1. The blocks of R_{jk} have the following limits as $T \to \infty$.

[a] $R_{00}^{HH} \to_p \Sigma_{HH}$
[b] $R_{00}^{LL} \to_p m^{-1}\Sigma_{LL}$
[c] $R_{00}^{LH} \to_p m^{-1}\Sigma_{LH}$ and $R_{00}^{HL} \to_p m^{-1}\Sigma_{HL}$
[d] $R_{10}^{HH} \to_d \int B_H(r)\mathrm{d}B_H'(r)$
[e] $R_{10}^{LL} \to_d \int B_L(r)\mathrm{d}B_L'(r) + \frac{m-1}{2m}\Sigma_{LL}$
[f] $R_{10}^{LH} \to_d \int B_L(r)\mathrm{d}B_H'(r) + \frac{m-1}{2m}\Sigma_{LH}$
[g] $R_{10}^{HL} \to_d \int B_H(r)\mathrm{d}B_L'(r) + \frac{m-1}{2m}\Sigma_{HL}$
[h] $M^{-1}R_{11} \to_d \int B(r)B'(r)\mathrm{d}r$

Proof of Lemma A.1. Throughout the proof, summations without an index denote summations across t. Recall that $y_{L,t-i/m}^L = y_{L,t-1} + m^{-1}(m-i)\Delta y_{Lt}$. It is straightforward to show that

$$y_{L,t-(i+1)/m}^L = y_{L,t-1} + m^{-1}(m-(i+1))\Delta y_{Lt} \tag{A.1}$$

and

$$\Delta^{(1/m)} y_{L,t-i/m}^L = m^{-1}\Delta y_{Lt} \tag{A.2}$$

which will be useful below.

Recall that we assume a HF invariance principle of the form

$$M^{-1/2}y_{[rM]}=M^{-1/2}\sum_{j=1}^{[rM]}\Delta^{(1/m)}y_{j/m}=M^{-1/2}\sum_{t=1}^{[rT]}\sum_{i=0}^{m-1}\Delta^{(1/m)}y_{t-i/m}\rightarrow_d B(r)$$

where $B(r)=BM(\Sigma)$.[1] As in GM, it will be useful to note the LF invariance principle implied by this HF invariance principle. Specifically

$$T^{-1/2}y_{[rT]}=T^{-1/2}\sum_{t=1}^{[rT]}\Delta y_t\rightarrow_d \tilde{B}(r)=BM(m\Sigma)$$

where $m\Sigma$ is simply the long-run variance of the LF difference series (Δy_t), so that $\tilde{B}(r)=m^{1/2}B(r)$.

[a] $R_{00}^{HH}=M^{-1}\sum\sum_{i=0}^{m-1}\Delta^{(1/m)}y_{H,t-i/m}\Delta^{(1/m)}y'_{H,t-i/m}$, and the stated result follows immediately from a law of large numbers (an LLN) for variance matrices.

[b] $R_{00}^{LL}=m^{-2}[T^{-1}\sum\Delta y_{Lt}\Delta y'_{Lt}]$ follows from substituting Eq. (A.2) and noting that the summands of the summation across i are constant with respect to i. An LLN yields the limit $m\Sigma_{LL}$ of the square-bracketed factor, and the stated result immediately follows.

[c] $R_{00}^{LH}=m^{-2}\left[T^{-1}\sum\Delta y_{Lt}\Delta y'_{Ht}\right]$ follows from substituting Eq. (A.2) and noting that $\sum_{i=0}^{m-1}\Delta^{(1/m)}y'_{H,t-i/m}=\Delta y'_{Ht}$. The two stated results then follow exactly as in part [b] and by noting that $R_{00}^{HL}=R_{00}^{LH\prime}$.

[d] The stated result follows in the usual way from the convergence implied by the HF invariance principle.

[e] Write

$$R_{10}^{LL}=\frac{1}{m}\left[\frac{1}{T}\sum y_{L,t-1}\Delta y'_{Lt}\right]+\frac{1}{m}\left[\frac{1}{T}\sum\Delta y_{Lt}\Delta y'_{Lt}\right]\sum_{i=0}^{m-1}\frac{m-(i+1)}{m^2}$$

by substituting Eq. (A.1), pulling out terms that are invariant with respect to i from the summations across i, and cancelling that summation in the first term. The LF invariance principle and lack of serial correlation in (Δy_t) allow $T^{-1}\sum y_{L,t-1}\Delta y'_{Lt} \rightarrow_d \int \tilde{B}_L(r)\,\mathrm{d}\tilde{B}'_L(r)$, so that, because $\tilde{B}(r) = m^{1/2}B(r)$, the limit of the first term coincides with $\int B_L(r)\,\mathrm{d}B'_L(r)$. Looking at the second term, the square-bracketed expression has a limit given by $m\Sigma_{LL}$ by part [b]. The result follows from cancellation and simplification of $m^{-2}\sum_{i=0}^{m-1}(m-(i+1)) = (m-1)/(2m)$.

[f] Write

$$R_{10}^{LH} = \frac{1}{m}\left[\frac{1}{T}\sum y_{L,t-1}\Delta y'_{Ht}\right] + \sum_{i=0}^{m-1}\frac{m-(i+1)}{m^2}$$
$$\left[\frac{1}{T}\sum\sum_{k=0}^{m-1}\Delta^{(1/m)}y_{L,t-k/m}\Delta^{(1/m)}y'_{H,t-i/m}\right]$$

by noting that $\Sigma_{i=0}^{m-1}\Delta^{(1/m)}y_{H,t-i/m} = \Delta y_{Ht}$ in the first term and $\Delta y_{Lt} = \Sigma_{k=0}^{m-1}\ \Delta^{(1/m)}y_{L,t-k/m}$ in the second. The distribution of the first term follows as in part [e]. The more complicated second term may be simplified by noting that the square-bracketed expression is asymptotically $o_p(1)$ when $k \neq i$ due to serially uncorrelated increments, but converges to Σ_{LH} when $k = i$. Since this limit does not depend on i, simplifying $m^{-2}\Sigma_{i=0}^{m-1}(m-(i+1)) = (m-1)/(2m)$ yields the stated result.

[g] Write

$$R_{10}^{HL} = \frac{1}{m}\left[\frac{1}{T}\sum y_{H,t-1}\Delta y'_{Lt}\right] + \frac{1}{m^2 T}\sum\sum_{i=0}^{m-1}(y_{H,t-(i+1)/m} - y_{H,t-1})$$
$$\sum_{k=0}^{m-1}\Delta^{(1/m)}y'_{L,t-k/m} \tag{A.3}$$

and the limiting distribution of the first term of Eq. (A.3) follows as in parts [e] and [f]. Note that

$$\sum_{i=0}^{m-1}(y_{H,t-(i+1)/m} - y_{H,t-1}) = \sum_{i=1}^{m-1}\sum_{j=i}^{m-1}\Delta^{(1/m)}y_{H,t-j/m} = \sum_{i=1}^{m-1} i\Delta^{(1/m)}y_{H,t-i/m}$$

and that $\Delta^{(1/m)}y_{H,t-i/m}$ and $\Delta^{(1/m)}y_{L,t-k/m}$ are correlated only when $k=i$. We may therefore rewrite the second term of Eq. (A.3) as $\Sigma_{HL}m^{-2}\sum_{i=1}^{m-1} i+o_p(1)$ and the result follows from simplification.

[h] As above, we look at each of the four submatrices of $M^{-1}R_{11}$. The stated result then follows from joint convergence.

(1) $M^{-1}R_{11}^{HH}\to_d \int B_H(r)B_H'(r)\mathrm{d}r$ follows in the usual way by applying the continuous mapping theorem (CMT) on top of the HF invariance principle.

(2) Using Eq. (A.1), we may write $M^{-1}R_{11}^{LL}$ as

$$M^{-2}\sum\sum_{i=0}^{m-1}\left(y_{L,t-1}+\frac{m-(i+1)}{m}\Delta y_{Lt}\right)\left(y_{L,t-1}+\frac{m-(i+1)}{m}\Delta y_{Lt}\right)'$$

$$=M^{-1}\left(T^{-1}\sum y_{L,t-1}y_{L,t-1}'\right)+o_p(1)$$

where the equality follows from an expansion of the outer product in the preceding expression. The negligibility of the remaining terms of this expansion is due to the stationarity of (Δy_{Lt}), with rates derived along the lines of parts [b] and [e] of this lemma, since $m-(i+1)<m<\infty$. Rewrite the first term as

$$m^{-1}\left[T^{-1}\sum(T^{-1/2}y_{L,t-1})(T^{-1/2}y_{L,t-1}')\right]\to_d m^{-1}\int \tilde{B}_L(r)\tilde{B}_L'(r)\mathrm{d}r$$

which coincides with $\int B_L(r)B_L'(r)\,\mathrm{d}r$ by the definition of $\tilde{B}(r)$.

(3) Using Eq. (A.1), we may write $M^{-1}R_{11}^{LH}$ as

$$M^{-1}R_{11}^{LH}=M^{-2}\sum\sum_{i=0}^{m-1}\left(y_{L,t-1}+\frac{m-(i+1)}{m}\Delta y_{Lt}\right)y_{H,t-1}'$$

$$=M^{-1}\left(T^{-1}\sum y_{L,t-1}y_{H,t-1}'\right)+o_p(1)$$

and both the limit of the first term and the negligibility of the second term of the expansion follow by the same logic as in part [h](2).

(4) Finally, note that $R_{11}^{HL} = R_{11}^{LH\prime}$ to complete the proof. ■

Lemma A.2. Let $\hat{\beta}$ be the least squares estimator of the regression coefficient vector of the regression of $r_{11,t-i/m}$ on $r_{21,t-i/m}$. Its limiting distribution under the null of no cointegration as $T \to \infty$ is given by $\hat{\beta} \to_d (\int B_2 B_2')^{-1} \int B_2 B_1$, where $B = (B_1, B_2')'$ is partitioned identically to $(W_1, W_2')'$ and $(r_{11,t-i/m}, r_{21,t-i/m}')'$.[2]

Proof of Lemma A.2. Let e_1' select only the first row of the vector or matrix it precedes, while E_2' selects all but the first row. The least squares estimator $\hat{\beta}$ may be written as

$$\hat{\beta} = (E_2' R_{11} E_2)^{-1} E_2' R_{11} e_1$$

using these definitions. The results then follow directly from Lemma A.1[h]. ■

Proof of Lemma 1. The results follow from joint convergence of the blocks in Lemma A.1.

Proof of Theorem 1. The proof of part [a] follows by substituting the results of Lemma 1 into the trace statistic and using the decomposition $\Sigma = L'L$ to standardize the limits.

The two statistics in parts [b] and [c] of the theorem have in common three moments: $\hat{\alpha}' M^{-1} R_{11} \hat{\alpha}$, $\hat{\alpha}' R_{00} \hat{\alpha}$, and $\hat{\alpha}' R_{10} \hat{\alpha}$. The limits of $M^{-1} R_{11}$, R_{00}, and R_{10} are given by Lemma 1. Define a generic matrix Ξ such that $L' \Xi L$ denotes one of those three limits. Specifically, $\Xi = \int WW'$ corresponds to $M^{-1} R_{11}$, $\Xi = C_m^+$ corresponds to R_{00}, and $\Xi = \int W dW' + D_m^+$ corresponds to R_{10}.

We now more explicitly consider the decomposition $\Sigma = L'L$ of Phillips and Ouliaris (1990). The matrix L may be written as

$$L = \begin{bmatrix} l_{11} & 0 \\ l_{21} & L_{22} \end{bmatrix} = \begin{bmatrix} \sqrt{\sigma_{11} - \sigma_{12} \Sigma_{22}^{-1} \sigma_{21}} & 0 \\ \Sigma_{22}^{-1/2} \sigma_{21} & \Sigma_{22}^{1/2\prime} \end{bmatrix}$$

and allows expressions of B_1 and B_2 explicitly in terms of W_1 and W_2: $B_1 = W_1 l_{11} + W_2' l_{21}$ and $B_2 = L_{22}' W_2 = \Sigma_{22}^{1/2} W_2$.

Define the limit of $\hat{\alpha}$ to be η. By Lemma A.2 and using κ_2 defined in Section 2.1

$$\hat{\beta} \rightarrow_d L_{22}^{-1} \left(\int W_2 W_2' \right)^{-1} \int W_2 (W_1 l_{11} + W_2' l_{21}) = -L_{22}^{-1} (l_{11} \kappa_2 - l_{21})$$

so that $\eta = (1, (l_{11}\kappa_2 - l_{21})' L_{22}^{-1\prime})'$. We are interested in the generic limit given by $\eta' L' \Xi L \eta$. For convenience, we may write $Le_1 = (l_{11}, l_{21}')'$ and $LE_2 = (0, L_{22}')'$, with e_1 and E_2 defined as in the proof of Lemma A.2, and note that

$$Le_1 + LE_2 L_{22}^{-1} (l_{11}\kappa_2 - l_{21}) = l_{11}\kappa \tag{A.4}$$

holds. Generically

$$\begin{aligned} \eta' L' \Xi L \eta &= \begin{bmatrix} 1 \\ L_{22}^{-1}(l_{11}\kappa_2 - l_{21}) \end{bmatrix}' \begin{bmatrix} e_1' L' \Xi L e_1 & e_1' L' \Xi L E_2 \\ E_2' L' \Xi L e_1 & E_2' L' \Xi L E_2 \end{bmatrix} \begin{bmatrix} 1 \\ L_{22}^{-1}(l_{11}\kappa_2 - l_{21}) \end{bmatrix} \\ &= (Le_1 + LE_2 L_{22}^{-1}(l_{11}\kappa_2 - l_{21}))' \Xi (Le_1 + LE_2 L_{22}^{-1}(l_{11}\kappa_2 - l_{21})) \end{aligned}$$

which simplifies to $l_{11}^2 \kappa' \Xi \kappa$ using Eq. (A.4). The generic mechanism of this proof up to this point follows that of GM.

Now, substituting in $\int WW'$ from Lemma 1[a], we get $\hat{\alpha}' M^{-1} R_{11} \hat{\alpha} \rightarrow_d l_{11}^2 \kappa' \int WW' \kappa = l_{11}^2 \int Q^2$. Substituting in C_m^+ from Lemma 1[b], we get $\hat{\alpha}' R_{00} \hat{\alpha} \rightarrow_p l_{11}^2 \kappa' C_m^+ \kappa$. And, substituting in $\int W dW' + D_m^+$ from Lemma 1[c], we get $\hat{\alpha}' R_{10} \hat{\alpha} \rightarrow_d l_{11}^2 \kappa' (\int W dW' + D_m^+) \kappa = l_{11}^2 (\int Q dQ + \kappa' D_m^+ \kappa)$. The stated results follow directly from these.

Proof of Corollary 1. Using the same mechanism as in the preceding proof, $\hat{\alpha}' R_{00}^{(m)} \hat{\alpha} \rightarrow_p l_{11}^2 \kappa' \kappa$ and $\hat{\alpha}' R_{10}^{(m)} \hat{\alpha} \rightarrow_d l_{11}^2 \kappa' \int W \, dW' \kappa = l_{11}^2 \int Q \, dQ$. Substituting these into the test statistics in place of $\hat{\alpha}' R_{00} \hat{\alpha}$ and $\hat{\alpha}' R_{10} \hat{\alpha}$ in the proof of Theorem 1 yields the stated result. ■

NOTES TO THE APPENDIX

1. Since we assume that M is divisible by m, $[rM]=m[rT]$ and the equality in the above expression holds. Otherwise, there is an additional remainder term that is asymptotically negligible, so that the limiting distribution holds.

2. Because this is the well-known distribution of a spurious regression upon which the standard residual-based results of Phillips and Ouliaris (1990) are based, the same limiting distribution is obtained regardless of whether or not the data have been linearly interpolated. Because of the invariance of this limiting distribution, the order of the elements of the vector $y_{t-i/m}$ does not matter in the limit except in the definition of C_m and D_m, as discussed above.

TESTING FOR COINTEGRATION IN MARKOV SWITCHING ERROR CORRECTION MODELS

Liang Hu[*] and Yongcheol Shin[†]

[*]*Department of Economics, Wayne State University, Detroit, Michigan, USA*

[†]*Department of Economics and Related Studies, University of York, York, UK*

ABSTRACT

This paper proposes an efficient test designed to have power against alternatives where the error correction term follows a Markov switching dynamics. The adjustment to long run equilibrium is different in different regimes characterised by the hidden state Markov chain process. Using a general nonlinear MS-ECM framework, we propose an optimal test for the null of no cointegration against an alternative of a globally stationary MS cointegration. The Monte Carlo studies demonstrate that our proposed tests display superior powers compared to the linear tests. In an application to price-dividend relationships,

Essays in Honor of Peter C. B. Phillips
Advances in Econometrics, Volume 33, 123–150

ISSN: 0731-9053/doi:10.1108/S0731-905320140000033005

our test is able to find cointegration while linear based tests fail to do so.

Keywords: Markov switching error correction models; optimal tests; Monte Carlo simulations; price and dividend

JEL classifications: C12; C13; C32

1. INTRODUCTION

Estimation of nonlinear error correction models subject to regime-switching dynamics has recently assumed great significance in the literature, though most attention has fallen almost exclusively on the three types. Balke and Fomby (1997) popularise the three-regime threshold error correction model (ECM), the case where an error correction process may follow a unit root in a middle regime while at the same time being globally geometrically ergodic in outer regimes. Another popular nonlinear schemes being applied are based on the smooth transition regression ECM (e.g. Michael, Nobay, & Peel, 1997), which makes the threshold ECM as a special case by allowing the transition from one regime to another as a smooth function. Psaradakis, Sola, and Spagnolo (2004) consider Markov switching ECM (hereafter, MS-ECM) in which deviations from the long-run equilibrium follow a process which is nonstationary in one regime and mean-reverting in the other and the nature of the regime is governed by the hidden state Markov chain. All these studies demonstrate that the assumption of linear adjustment is likely to be too limited in various economic situations particularly where transaction costs, policy interventions and so on are present.

However, most studies applying these regime-switching ECMs have routinely adopted the two-step testing approach popularised by Balke and Fomby (1997). The first step estimates the cointegrating parameters using the linear models, and the second step tests for the presence of a particular form of nonlinear asymmetry. Once the null of no cointegration is rejected, then they move on to estimate the associated nonlinear ECMs. Although such tests will have power against nonlinear alternatives, it seems far more sensible to develop the test that is designed to be more powerful against the alternative in hand.

Two main issues arise. First, the nuisance parameters characterising the nonlinearity are not identified under the null hypothesis, which renders the testing problem nonstandard (Davies, 1987). Second, we should carefully address the fact the data generating process (DGP) under the null hypothesis is nonstationary. In this regard, a number of studies have proposed the more efficient testing procedure in nonlinear cointegration frameworks. Hansen and Seo (2002) propose the *sup*-based test statistics for testing the null of the linear vector error correction model (VECM) against the alternative of the two-regime threshold VECM, and suggest to employ the bootstrap for constructing critical values or the p-values of the test. Alternatively, Kapetanios, Shin, and Snell (2006) propose the t and F statistics testing for the smooth transition ECM by applying the Taylor series expansion of the transition function.

However, studies that directly address this important issue in MS-ECMs are almost nonexistent despite the empirical popularity of these models. For example, Psaradakis et al. (2004) simply apply the linear tests of cointegration, and then estimate asymmetric or nonlinear dynamics under the Markov switching alternative. See also Krolzig, Marcellino, and Mizon (2002), Sarno and Valente (2005) and Chaudhuri and Kumary (2006), who follow the similar approach. This surprising absence may be due to a more complex nature associated with the hidden Markov chain. Unlike the other two aforementioned models, an MS-ECM model would be more complicated to estimate as the sample path grows exponentially with time, and one needs to estimate the regime probabilities at each time period.

In this paper we propose the equilibrium model that allows the associated error correction adjustments to be different in different regimes, which are assumed to be characterised by the hidden Markov chain process. Therefore, we focus on the case in which the error correction term follows a globally stationary process under the MS-ECM alternative. In this regard we are able to allow for the empirically plausible case where the deviations from the long-run equilibrium may be allowed to be nonstationary locally in the state in which the cointegrating residuals are too small or irrelevant for the mean reversion behaviour to take place. In particular, our approach is motivated by the implication of economic theory applied to asset arbitrage under noise trading and transaction costs (e.g. Campbell & Kyle, 1993).

Using a general nonlinear MS-ECM framework, we propose testing directly the null hypothesis of no cointegration against the alternative of a globally stationary Markov switching cointegration. The testing procedure involves investigating the higher order Taylor expansion of the likelihood ratio and we obtain an LM-type test which is locally asymptotically equivalent to the LR test, therefore maintaining optimality. This requires the model estimation only under the null and therefore facilitates the computation of the test statistics. Our test is similar to the parameter constancy test for random coefficient models proposed by Carrasco, Hu, and Ploberger (2014, CHP thereafter). However, CHP only deal with the stationary DGP under the null, which does not cover the MS-ECM models.

The small sample performance of the suggested tests is compared to that of the linear cointegration tests via Monte Carlo experiments. We find that our proposed nonlinear tests have superior power properties compared to the linear tests. In particular, our proposed tests are superior to both linear or nonlinear Engle–Granger (EG) tests (Engle & Granger, 1987) when the regressors are weakly exogenous in a cointegrating regression. This supports similar findings made in linear models by Kremers, Ericsson, and Dolado (1992), Hansen (1995) and Arranz and Escribano (2000).

We provide an application to investigating the presence of cointegration of prices and dividends for eleven country stock indices (Germany, Belgium, Canada, Denmark, France, Ireland, Italy, Japan, the Netherlands, the United Kingdom, and the United States), allowing for nonlinear adjustment to equilibrium driven by a hidden Markov chain. Interestingly, our new test is able to reject the null of no cointegration in majority of cases, whereas the linear EG test rejects only once.

The plan of this paper is as follows: Section 2 derives the nonlinear MS-ECM models and discuss the assumptions and the stationarity conditions. Section 3 develops the proposed test statistics, and derives the limiting distributions. We then propose how to implement the bootstrap-based inference. Section 4 evaluates the small sample performance of the proposed tests. Section 5 presents an empirical illustration. Section 6 contains some concluding remarks. Mathematical proofs are collected in the appendix.

2. THE MODEL

We begin with the following general nonlinear VECM model for the $m \times 1$ vector of I(1) stochastic processes, $\mathbf{z}_t$:

$$\Delta \mathbf{z}_t = \boldsymbol{\alpha}\boldsymbol{\beta}'\mathbf{z}_{t-1} + g(\boldsymbol{\beta}'\mathbf{z}_{t-1}) + \sum_{i=1}^{p} \boldsymbol{\Gamma}_i \Delta \mathbf{z}_{t-i} + \boldsymbol{\varepsilon}_t, \quad t = 1, 2, \ldots, T \tag{1}$$

where $\boldsymbol{\alpha}(m \times r)$, $\boldsymbol{\beta}(m \times r)$ and $\boldsymbol{\Gamma}_i$ $(m \times m)$ are parameter matrices with $\boldsymbol{\alpha}$ and $\boldsymbol{\beta}$ of full column rank, and $g : \mathbb{R}^r \rightarrow \mathbb{R}^m$ is a nonlinear function.

We follow Saikkonen (2005) and assume as follows.

Assumption 1. (i) The errors, $\boldsymbol{\varepsilon}_t$ in Eq. (1) are i.i.d. (0, Σ), with Σ being an $m \times m$ positive definite matrix and $E|\boldsymbol{\varepsilon}_t|^{\ell} < \infty$ for some $\ell > 6$. (ii) The distribution of $\boldsymbol{\varepsilon}_t$ is absolutely continuous with respect to the Lebesgue measure and has a density that is bounded away from zero on compact subsets of $\mathbb{R}^m$. (iii) The initial observations $\mathbf{Z}_0 \equiv (\mathbf{z}_{-p}, \ldots, \mathbf{z}_0)$ are given. (iv) Let $A(z) = (1-z)\mathbf{I}_n - \boldsymbol{\alpha}\boldsymbol{\beta}' z - \sum_{i=1}^{p} \boldsymbol{\Gamma}_i (1-z) z^i$. If $\det A(z) = 0$, then $|z| > 1$ or $z = 1$, where the number of unit roots is equal to $m - r$. (v) $g(\mathbf{x})$ is asymptotically no greater than a linear function of $\mathbf{x}$.

Assumptions 1(i)–(iv) are standard in linear cointegration literature. Together with 1(v), Saikkonen (2005, Theorem 2) shows that there exist the initial values, $\mathbf{z}_{-p}, \ldots, \mathbf{z}_0$ such that $\Delta\mathbf{z}_t$ and $\beta'\mathbf{z}_{t-1}$ are strictly stationary.

In this paper we aim to analyse at most one long-run cointegrating relationship among $\mathbf{z}_t$, i.e. $r = 1$. Accordingly, we decompose $\mathbf{z}_t = (y_t, \mathbf{x}_t')'$ and focus on the conditional modelling of the scalar variable y_t given the k-vector $\mathbf{x}_t$ with $k = m - 1$. Then, following the literature, we assume that $\mathbf{x}_t$ is weakly exogenous and that there is no cointegration among the k-vector of I(1) variables in $\mathbf{x}_t$. Next, we partition $\boldsymbol{\varepsilon}_t = (\boldsymbol{\varepsilon}_{yt}, \boldsymbol{\varepsilon}_{xt}')'$ conformably with $\mathbf{z}_t$ and its variance matrix as

$$\boldsymbol{\Sigma} = \begin{pmatrix} \sigma_{yy} & \boldsymbol{\sigma}_{yx} \\ \boldsymbol{\sigma}_{xy} & \boldsymbol{\Sigma}_{xx} \end{pmatrix}$$

Then, by projection, it is straightforward to derive

$$\boldsymbol{\varepsilon}_{yt} = \boldsymbol{\sigma}_{yx} \boldsymbol{\Sigma}_{xx}^{-1} \boldsymbol{\varepsilon}_{xt} + e_t$$

where $e_t \sim$ i.i.d. $(0, \sigma_e^2)$, $\sigma_e^2 = \sigma_{yy} - \boldsymbol{\sigma}_{yx} \boldsymbol{\Sigma}_{xx}^{-1} \boldsymbol{\sigma}_{xy}$, and e_t is uncorrelated with $\boldsymbol{\varepsilon}_{xt}$ by construction. Hence, we can reparametrise Eq. (1), and obtain the following conditional ECM for Δy_t and the marginal VAR model for $\Delta\mathbf{x}_t$ (e.g. Kapetanios et al., 2006):[1]

$$\Delta y_t = \phi u_{t-1} + g_u(u_{t-1}) + \boldsymbol{\omega}' \Delta\mathbf{x}_t + \sum_{i=1}^{p} \boldsymbol{\psi}_i' \Delta\mathbf{z}_{t-i} + e_t \tag{2}$$

$$\Delta\mathbf{x}_t = \sum_{i=1}^{p} \boldsymbol{\Gamma}_{xi} \Delta\mathbf{z}_{t-i} + \boldsymbol{\varepsilon}_{xt}$$

where $u_{t-1} = y_{t-1} - \boldsymbol{\beta}_x' \mathbf{x}_{t-1}$ and $\boldsymbol{\beta}_x$ is the $k \times 1$ vector of the cointegrating parameters, $\boldsymbol{\omega} = \boldsymbol{\Sigma}_{xx}^{-1} \boldsymbol{\sigma}_{xy}$ and $\boldsymbol{\psi}_i' = \boldsymbol{\gamma}_{yi} - \boldsymbol{\omega}' \boldsymbol{\Gamma}_{xi}$ with $\boldsymbol{\Gamma}_i = (\boldsymbol{\gamma}_{yi}, \boldsymbol{\Gamma}_{xi}')'$ partitioned conformably with $\mathbf{z}_t = (y_t, \mathbf{x}_t')'$.

Notice that $g_u : \mathbb{R} \to \mathbb{R}$ is the nonlinear function, which allows the speed of the adjustments associated with the error correction term u_t to be nonlinear or regime-dependent. The general specification in Eq. (2) includes all the existing nonlinear ECM models in the literature including the threshold ECM popularised by Balke and Fomby (1997) and the smooth transition ECM by Kapetanios et al. (2006). See also Saikkonen (2005) for further discussions. We follow Psaradakis et al. (2004), and focus on another popular MS-ECM model, where the regime is determined by the hidden Markov chain.

Assumption 2. We assume that the conditional model for Δy_t follows:

$$\Delta y_t = \phi_{s_t} u_{t-1} + \boldsymbol{\omega}' \Delta \mathbf{x}_t + \sum_{i=1}^{p} \boldsymbol{\psi}_i' \Delta \mathbf{z}_{t-i} + e_t \tag{3}$$

where s_t is a scalar geometric ergodic Markov chain with an n-dimensional state space, and s_t has the transition probability, $p_{ij} = \Pr(s_t = j | s_{t-1} = i)$ for $i, j = 1, \ldots, n$. We also assume that $\mathbf{x}_t$ is weakly exogenous and that there is no cointegration among the k-vector of I(1) variables in $\mathbf{x}_t$.

Notice that the model considered by Psaradakis et al. (2004) is a special case of (3), where s_t is a two-state Markov chain. In this case ϕ_{s_t} can be written simply as

$$\phi_{s_t} = \phi_0 + (\phi_1 - \phi_0) s_t, \quad \phi_0 \leq 0, \quad \phi_1 < 0 \tag{4}$$

Thus, cointegration may break under regime 0 whereas the long-run mean reversion occurs at the speed $|\phi_1|$ under regime 1.

Francq and Zakoïan (2001) have derived the condition for strict stationarity of MS-ECM models by adopting the similar theoretical framework in Bougerol and Picard (1992). Following this approach, we rewrite model (3) as a canonical VAR(1) process as follows:

$$\begin{aligned}\begin{bmatrix} y_t \\ \mathbf{x}_t \end{bmatrix} &= \begin{bmatrix} (1 + \phi_{s_t}) & -\boldsymbol{\beta}_x' \phi_{s_t} \\ \mathbf{0} & \mathbf{I}_k \end{bmatrix} \begin{bmatrix} y_{t-1} \\ \mathbf{x}_{t-1} \end{bmatrix} + \begin{bmatrix} \boldsymbol{\omega}' \Delta \mathbf{x}_t + \sum_{i=1}^{p} \boldsymbol{\Gamma}_i \Delta \mathbf{z}_{t-i} \\ 0 \end{bmatrix} + \begin{bmatrix} e_t \\ \boldsymbol{\varepsilon}_{xt} \end{bmatrix} \\ &= \boldsymbol{\Phi}_{s_t} \begin{bmatrix} y_{t-1} \\ \mathbf{x}_{t-1} \end{bmatrix} + \sum_{i=1}^{p} \boldsymbol{\Gamma}_i \Delta \mathbf{z}_{t-i} + \begin{bmatrix} e_t \\ \boldsymbol{\varepsilon}_{xt} \end{bmatrix} \end{aligned} \tag{5}$$

Then, strict stationarity follows if the top Lyapunov exponent associated with VAR coefficients is strictly negative. The top Lyapunov exponent, denoted γ, for (5) is simply derived by

$$\gamma = \inf E\frac{1}{t}\log \|\mathbf{\Phi}_{s_t}\mathbf{\Phi}_{s_{t-1}}\ldots\mathbf{\Phi}_{s_0}\| = \inf E\frac{1}{t}\log \left|(1+\phi_{s_t})(1+\phi_{s_{t-1}})\ldots(1+\phi_{s_1})\right|$$
$$= E\log\left|1+\phi_{s_t}\right|$$

Since ϕ_{s_t} is a discrete random variable, taking values $\{\phi_1, \ldots, \phi_n\}$, the sufficient condition for strict stationarity becomes

$$\gamma = E\log\left|1+\phi_{s_t}\right| = \sum_{i=1}^{n}\pi_i \log\left|1+\phi_i\right| < 0 \tag{6}$$

where π_i denotes the ergodic probability for regime i, i.e. $\pi_i = \Pr(s_t = i)$. For example, consider the two-regime model in (4) with $\phi_0 = 0$ in which case strict stationarity condition is given by $\pi_1 \log\left|1+\phi_1\right| < 0$, under which the MS-ECM is a (globally) strictly stationary process, though it is locally non-stationary in regime 0.

We now turn to the weaker second-order stationarity condition, which has also been addressed in the literature (e.g. Yao & Attali, 2000). We also follow Francq and Zakoïan (2001), and find that the (global) stationarity condition for (3) is given by

$$\rho(\mathbf{M}) < 1 \tag{7}$$

where

$$\mathrm{M} = \begin{bmatrix} p_{11}(1+\phi_1)^2 & p_{21}(1+\phi_1)^2 & \cdots & p_{n1}(1+\phi_1)^2 \\ p_{12}(1+\phi_2)^2 & p_{22}(1+\phi_2)^2 & \cdots & p_{n2}(1+\phi_2)^2 \\ \vdots & \vdots & & \vdots \\ p_{1n}(1+\phi_n)^2 & p_{2n}(1+\phi_n)^2 & \cdots & p_{nn}(1+\phi_n)^2 \end{bmatrix}$$

and $\rho(\mathbf{M})$ refers to the spectral radius of $\mathbf{M}$.[2]

In this paper, we maintain the assumption that the second-order stationarity condition in Eq. (7) holds for the MS-ECM model (3). To illustrate, consider the two-regime MS-ECM in Eq. (4). In this case, the condition $\rho(M) < 1$ can be expressed by

$$p_{00}(1+\phi_0)^2 + p_{11}(1+\phi_1)^2 < 2 \tag{8}$$

$$p_{00}(1+\phi_0)^2 + p_{11}(1+\phi_1)^2 + (1-p_{00}-p_{11})(1+\phi_0)^2(1+\phi_1)^2 < 1 \tag{9}$$

With $\phi_0 = 0$, the condition $|1+\phi_1| < 1$ is again the sufficient condition for both Eqs. (8) and (9) to hold.

3. THE TEST

In testing the null hypothesis of no cointegration under the MS-ECM framework, we should deal with the two main issues associated with nonstationary data and unidentified nuisance parameters under the null. The most popular testing procedure follows the two-step approach proposed by Balke and Fomby (1997). First, one applies the standard linear cointegration tests and establish the presence of the (linear) long-run cointegrating relationship. Then, in the second step, tests of nonlinearity or parameter constancy are applied to the regime-dependent ECM coefficients. Though this approach can be asymptotically valid under certain regularity conditions, it tends to be substantially inefficient in practice. Furthermore, the number of parameters grows exponentially with T under MS-ECM, as we estimate the regime probability at each time period. Here, we develop the direct procedure testing for the null of no cointegration against the alternative of MS-ECM by adopting an optimal testing procedure advanced recently by CHP.[3] As will be clear, the main advantages of our proposed tests lie in that (i) it is an LM-type test, which does not require us to estimate the model under the alternative and (ii) it is shown to be asymptotically equivalent to an LR test, and thus most efficient.

We now set the null and the alternative hypotheses respectively as

$$H_0 : \phi_{s_t} = 0 \text{ vs } H_1 : \phi_{s_t} = \eta_t \tag{10}$$

where η_t is the random coefficient under the alternative. Further, we let

$$\eta_t = c \times \nu_t$$

where ν_t is normalised to have unit variance and c is a scalar specifying the amplitude of the switching with $c^2 = Var(\eta_t)$. Moreover, using the fact that $Corr(\nu_t, \nu_s) = \rho^{|t-s|}$, where ρ denotes the autocorrelation coefficient with $-1 < \underline{\rho} \leq \rho \leq \overline{\rho} < 1$, we have $Cov(\eta_t, \eta_s) = c^2 \rho^{|t-s|}$.

We thus define the vector of nuisance parameters by $\boldsymbol{\lambda} = (c, \rho)'$ and assume as follows.

Assumption 3. (i) $\boldsymbol{\lambda}$ belongs to a compact set Λ. (ii) The stationarity conditions of MS-ECM (Eqs. (6) and (7)) hold under the alternative hypothesis.

Since the parameters of interest are the ECM ones, ϕ_{s_t}, it is more convenient to work directly with the concentrated log likelihood function of Eq. (3) under H_0. For example, under normal assumption, it is given by

$$\ell_T(\boldsymbol{\theta}) \propto -\frac{T}{2}\ln(2\pi\sigma_e^2) - \frac{1}{2\sigma_e^2}(\Delta\mathbf{y} - \phi\mathbf{u}_{-1})'\mathbf{M}_T(\Delta\mathbf{y} - \phi\mathbf{u}_{-1}) \qquad (11)$$

where $\Delta\mathbf{y} = (\Delta y_1, \ldots, \Delta y_T)'$, $\mathbf{u}_{-1} = (u_0, \ldots, u_{T-1})'$, $\mathbf{M}_T = \mathbf{I}_T - \mathbf{W}(\mathbf{W}'\mathbf{W})^{-1}\mathbf{W}'$, $\mathbf{W} = (\mathbf{w}_1, \ldots, \mathbf{w}_t)$, $\mathbf{w}_t = (\Delta\mathbf{x}_t, \Delta\mathbf{z}_{t-1}, \ldots, \Delta\mathbf{z}_{t-p})$ and $\boldsymbol{\theta} = (\phi, \sigma_e^2)'$ with $\phi_{s_t} = \phi = 0$ under H_0. Then, our proposed test statistic can be derived as

$$S_T(\boldsymbol{\lambda}) = S_T(\boldsymbol{\lambda}, \hat{\boldsymbol{\theta}}) = \frac{1}{2\sqrt{T^3}}\sum_{t=1}^{T}\mu_t(\boldsymbol{\lambda}, \hat{\boldsymbol{\theta}}) - \frac{1}{8T^2}\sum_{t=1}^{T}\mu_t^2(\boldsymbol{\lambda}, \hat{\boldsymbol{\theta}}) \qquad (12)$$

where

$$\mu_t(\boldsymbol{\lambda}, \hat{\boldsymbol{\theta}}) = (\ell_{t(2)} + \ell_{t(1)}^2)Var(\eta_t) + 2\sum_{s=1}^{t-1}\rho^{t-s}\ell_{t(1)}\ell_{s(1)}Cov(\eta_t, \eta_s) \qquad (13)$$

$\ell_{t(1)}$ and $\ell_{t(2)}$ are the first and second derivatives of $\ell_t(\boldsymbol{\theta})$ with respect to $\boldsymbol{\theta}$, and $\hat{\boldsymbol{\theta}}$ is the maximum likelihood estimator of $\boldsymbol{\theta}$ obtained under H_0.

Notice that the above testing procedure will suffer from the Davies (1987) problem since $\boldsymbol{\lambda}$ is unidentified under H_0. Thus, we may consider the exponential average (Andrews & Ploberger, 1994) and the supremum (Hansen, 1996) of the statistic defined respectively by

$$S_{\exp} = \int_{\overline{\Lambda}} \exp(S_T(\boldsymbol{\lambda}))\, \mathrm{d}J(\boldsymbol{\lambda}) \quad \text{and} \quad S_{\sup} = \sup_{\boldsymbol{\lambda}\in\overline{\Lambda}} S_T(\boldsymbol{\lambda}) \qquad (14)$$

where $J(\boldsymbol{\lambda})$ is a certain prior distribution for $\boldsymbol{\lambda}$ with support $\overline{\Lambda}$ on a compact subset of $\Lambda = \{c^2, \rho : c^2 > 0, \underline{\rho} < \rho < \overline{\rho}\}$ with $-1 < \underline{\rho} < \overline{\rho} < 1$.[4]

Theorem 1. Let Assumptions 1–3 hold. Then, $S_{\sup}$ and $S_{\exp}$ statistics defined by Eq. (14) are admissible.

The proof is provided in the appendix, but some remarks are in order. The information matrix is singular under H_0, as the score function in this case is identically zero. As a result, the general random coefficients theory does not apply here. To deal with this issue, our proof is based on the approximation of the the log likelihood ratio. A close look at Eq. (13) displays that the test statistic $S_T(\boldsymbol{\lambda})$ contains the common term in the information matrix test $(\ell_{t(2)} + \ell_{t(1)}^2)\ Var(\eta_t)$ and an extra term $\sum_{s<t} \rho^{t-s} \ell_{t(1)} \ell_{s(1)}$ $Cov(\eta_t, \eta_s)$. Recall that Chesher (1984) and Davidson and McKinnon (1991) derive the information matrix type tests, where the random parameters are assumed to be independent. However, the Markov chain is serially correlated. The role of this extra term is to capture the correlations between the conditional scores at different time periods. Finally, the last term $1/8T^2 \sum_{t=1}^{T} \mu_t^2(\boldsymbol{\lambda}, \hat{\phi})$ in Eq. (12) is called the 'compensation term' necessary in deriving the local approximation of the likelihood ratio. This renders the proposed LM-type test asymptotically equivalent to the LR test. Therefore, it is admissible.[5]

Our test extends the CHP test, which can only be applied to the stationary data under H_0 to the case with nonstationary regressors. When testing for Markov switching in stationary processes, the right asymptotic order under the local alternative is given by $T^{-1/4}$, implying that the likelihood ratio in the $T^{-1/4}$ neighborhood will provide its nondegenerate distribution under the alternative (see CHP). For the MS-ECM process, however, its order becomes $T^{-3/4}$, and the sequence of the local alternatives is now given by $\phi_{s_t} = \frac{1}{\sqrt[4]{T^3}} \eta_t$.[6] Furthermore, as $S_T(\boldsymbol{\lambda})$ depends only on the score and its derivative under H_0, our proposed test is indeed an LM-type test, which does not require us to estimate the model under the alternative.

3.1. Asymptotic Distribution

We now describe in detail the proposed testing procedure using the model (3) with normal error $e_t \sim$ i.i.d. $N(0, \sigma_e^2)$.

To this end we consider the following concentrated regression:

$$\Delta\tilde{y}_t = \phi_{s_t}\tilde{u}_{t-1} + \tilde{e}_t \tag{15}$$

where $\Delta\tilde{y}_t$ and $\tilde{u}_{t-1}$ are the least square residuals obtained from the regression of Δy_t and $\hat{u}_{t-1}$ on $(\Delta\mathbf{x}_t, \Delta\mathbf{z}_{t-1}, \ldots, \Delta\mathbf{z}_{t-p})$ respectively. The first and the second derivatives of (concentrated) log likelihood function with respect to $\phi_{s_t} = \phi$ under the null are derived as follows:

$$\ell_{t(1)} = \frac{1}{\tilde{\sigma}_e^2}\tilde{u}_{t-1}\tilde{e}_t; \quad \ell_{t(2)} = -\frac{1}{\tilde{\sigma}_e^2}\tilde{u}_{t-1}^2$$

where $\tilde{\sigma}_e^2$ is the ML estimator of σ_e^2 obtained under H_0. Then, we have $\mu_t = (c^2/\tilde{\sigma}_e^2)\tilde{\mu}_t$, where

$$\tilde{\mu}_t = \frac{1}{\tilde{\sigma}_e^2}(\tilde{e}_t^2 - \tilde{\sigma}_e^2)\tilde{u}_{t-1}^2 + 2\sum_{s=1}^{t-1}\rho^{t-s}\frac{\tilde{e}_t}{\tilde{\sigma}_e}\frac{\tilde{e}_s}{\tilde{\sigma}_e}\tilde{u}_{t-1}\tilde{u}_{s-1}$$

We now express the test statistic $S_T(\lambda)$ in Eq. (12) as

$$S_T(\boldsymbol{\lambda}) = \frac{c^2/\tilde{\sigma}_e^2}{2\sqrt{T^3}}\sum_{t=1}^{T}\tilde{\mu}_t - \frac{c^4/\tilde{\sigma}_e^4}{8T^2}\sum_{t=1}^{T}\tilde{\mu}_t^2$$

We then propose the S_{sup} statistic, and find an analytic solution when maximising $S_T(\boldsymbol{\lambda})$ with respect to c^2 as follows:

$$S_{\text{sup}} = \sup_{\{\rho:\underline{\rho}<\rho<\overline{\rho}\}}\frac{1}{2}\left(\max\left(\frac{\sum_{t=1}^{T}\tilde{\mu}_t}{\sqrt{\sum_{t=1}^{T}\tilde{\mu}_t^2}}, 0\right)\right)^2 \tag{16}$$

The S_{sup} statistic can be easily evaluated using the grid search over the set $\{\rho : \underline{\rho}<\rho<\overline{\rho}\}$.

Furthermore, we could derive the limiting distribution for S_{sup}.

Theorem 2. Let Assumptions 1–3 hold and assume $e_t \sim$ i.i.d. $N(0, \sigma_e^2)$. Under the null hypothesis of no cointegration, the S_{sup} statistic in Eq. (16), has the following asymptotic distribution:

$$S_{\text{sup}} \Rightarrow \sup_{\{\rho:\underline{\rho}<\rho<\overline{\rho}\}} \frac{1}{2}\left[\max\left(\frac{\sqrt{2}\int_0^1 B(a)^2 \mathrm{d}W_0(a) + 2\sum_{i=0}^{\infty}\rho^i \int_0^1 B(a)^2 \mathrm{d}W_i(a)}{\sqrt{\left(2+\frac{4}{1-\rho^2}\right)\int_0^1 B(a)^4 \mathrm{d}a}}, 0\right)\right]^2 \tag{17}$$

where '$\Rightarrow$' denotes a weak convergence. $W(a)$, $W_i(a)$, $i=0,1,\ldots$, are the scalar standard Brownian motion defined on $a \in [0, 1]$, $B(a) = W(a) - \mathbf{W}_x(a)'\left(\int_0^1 \mathbf{W}_x(a)\mathbf{W}_x(a)'\mathrm{d}a\right)^{-1} \times \int_0^1 \mathbf{W}_x(a)W(a)\,\mathrm{d}a$, and $\mathbf{W}_x(a)$ are the k-vector standard Brownian motions independent of $W(a)$.

To accommodate deterministic components in the cointegrating regression, we extend to consider the regression with an intercept

$$y_t = a_0 + \boldsymbol{\beta}'\mathbf{x}_t + u_t \tag{18}$$

and the regression with an intercept and a linear deterministic time trend

$$y_t = a_0 + a_1 t + \boldsymbol{\beta}'\mathbf{x}_t + u_t \tag{19}$$

The respective test statistics are then obtained as follows: first, the appropriate residuals are obtained from Eq. (18) or (19), and then the corresponding MS-ECM regressions are constructed by

$$\Delta y_t^* = \phi_{s_t}\hat{u}_{t-1}^* + \boldsymbol{\omega}'\Delta\mathbf{x}_t^* + \sum_{i=1}^{p-1}\boldsymbol{\psi}_i'\Delta\mathbf{z}_{t-i}^* + error \tag{20}$$

$$\Delta y_t^+ = \phi_{s_t}\hat{u}_{t-1}^+ + \boldsymbol{\omega}'\Delta\mathbf{x}_t^+ + \sum_{i=1}^{p-1}\boldsymbol{\psi}_i'\Delta\mathbf{z}_{t-i}^+ + error \tag{21}$$

where $\hat{u}_t^* = y_t^* - \boldsymbol{\beta}'\mathbf{x}_t^*$, and $\hat{u}_t^+ = y_t^+ - \boldsymbol{\beta}'\mathbf{x}_t^+$ and superscripts '$*$' and '$+$' indicate the demeaned data and the demeaned and detrended data respectively. The appropriate S_{sup} statistics are then obtained from Eq. (20) or (21) respectively following exactly the same procedure described above.

We have so far considered the conditional model for Δy_t in Eq. (3), in which the regime-switching of this model is only confined to the ECM coefficients ϕ_t. Notice that this type of restriction has been routinely applied in the aforementioned existing studies, namely the threshold ECM by Balke and Fomby (1997) and the smooth transition ECM by Kapetanios et al. (2006). But, in the MS-ECM framework, we can allow for all of the short-run dynamics including the error variances to be heterogenous across different regimes without affecting the main distributional results derived above. Thus, we consider the following generalised version of (3):

$$\Delta y_t = \phi_{s_t} u_{t-1} + \boldsymbol{\omega}'_{s_t} \Delta \mathbf{x}_t + \sum_{i=1}^{p} \boldsymbol{\psi}'_{i,s_t} \Delta \mathbf{z}_{t-i} + \eta_{s_t} \varepsilon_t \tag{22}$$

where $\varepsilon_t \sim$ i.i.d. (0, 1). In what follows, we show that the limiting distribution of the test statistic $S_T(\boldsymbol{\lambda})$ in Eq. (12), derived from Eq. (22), is equal to that from Eq. (3).[7] Consider the basis of $S_T(\lambda)$ given by $\sum_t \partial \ell_t^2 / \partial \phi^2 + (\partial \ell_t / \partial \phi)^2$, and it is easily seen that it has the probability order of $\sqrt{T^3}$ under the null of no cointegration. On the other hand, it is clear that the derivatives of ℓ_t with respect to the other short-run dynamic parameters $\boldsymbol{\omega}$ and $\boldsymbol{\psi}$ are of order $\sqrt{T}$ under the null. As a result, our proposed test statistic for ϕ_{s_t} has the same pivotal distribution in Theorem 2, irrespective of whether other short-run dynamic parameters $\boldsymbol{\omega}$ and $\boldsymbol{\psi}$ are subject to Markov regime switching or not. This is an interesting and pleasing finding in practice, and its validity will be investigated in the Monte Carlo section.

3.2. Bootstrap-Based Inference

The limiting distribution derived in Theorem 2 is pivotal for model (3) with normal error. But, we follow Hansen (1996) and CHP, and propose to implement a general bootstrap procedure for tabulating the critical values and/or reporting the p-values, which is expected to produce more reliable inference in small samples. The bootstrap implementation of our test statistics is quite straightforward because our test does not require us to estimate the model under the alternative. In order to evaluate the critical values c_α and the p-values of the S_{sup} statistics, we follow:

1. Using all the observations, estimate $\boldsymbol{\theta}_0$ by MLE under H_0, denoted by $\hat{\boldsymbol{\theta}}$. Then, compute the sup-test statistic S_{sup}.

2. Given $\hat{\boldsymbol{\theta}}$, generate the independent sample, N times under H_0, using non-parametric random draws from the sample residuals. Thus, we obtain the bootstrap sample $\{y_1^i, \ldots y_T^i\}_{i=1,\ldots,N}$.
3. Using each of the bootstrapped samples, $\{y_1^i, \ldots y_T^i\}$, estimate $\boldsymbol{\theta}$ by MLE under H_0, denoted by $\hat{\boldsymbol{\theta}}^i$. Then, compute the sup-test statistic using $\hat{\boldsymbol{\theta}}^i$, denoted by S_{sup}^i, $i=1,2, \ldots, N$.
4. Define $c_{\alpha,S}$ as the critical value using the empirical distribution of S_{sup}^i, $i=1,2,\ldots, N$, i.e. $c_{\alpha,S}$ is constructed as the $(1-\alpha)$ quantile of S_{sup}^i. Moreover, the bootstrapped p-value is obtained by $\frac{1}{N}\sum_{i=1}^{N} I(S_{\text{sup}}^i > S_{\text{sup}})$.

CHP show that the above bootstrap procedure is consistent and thus provides a valid inference. Hence, we recommend the practitioners to employ the bootstrap method in applications.

4. MONTE CARLO STUDIES

We undertake a small-scale Monte Carlo experiments and investigate the small sample size and power performance of our proposed sup-test version of the statistics in conjunction with the linear cointegration tests of Engle and Granger, denoted S_{sup} and t_{EG} respectively. To this end we consider experiments based on a bivariate ECM similar to Arranz and Escribano (2000) and Kapetanios et al. (2006), and generate the data generating DGP as follows:

$$\Delta y_t = \phi_{s_t} u_{t-1} + \lambda \Delta x_t + e_t$$

$$\Delta x_t = v_t$$

$$u_t = y_t - \beta_x x_t$$

$$\begin{bmatrix} e_t \\ v_t \end{bmatrix} \sim \text{i.i.d.}\, N\left(\mathbf{0}, \begin{bmatrix} \sigma_1^2 & 0 \\ 0 & \sigma_2^2 \end{bmatrix}\right)$$

Here we fix $\beta_x = 1$, $\sigma_1^2 = 1$ and $\sigma_2^2 = 4$. We also wish to investigate the impact of the common factor (COMFAC) restriction, $\lambda = 1$ (e.g. Kremers et al., 1992) and consider the different values for $\lambda = \{0.5, 1\}$. Under the null, $\phi_{s_t} = \phi = 0$. To compute the S_{sup} test statistic, we need to construct the grid set $\{\rho : \underline{\rho} < \rho < \overline{\rho}\}$ as described in Section 3, and we use 40 draws for ρ from an equi-spaced grid over the interval $(\underline{\rho}, \overline{\rho}) = (0, 0.98)$.[8] We set the sample size to 100, and use 1,000 replications to present the empirical (size-corrected) power of the tests.

We consider the two experiments under the alternative. Experiment 1 considers the case with two regimes in which we let the Markov chain, s_t, take binary values with transition probabilities given by $p_{ii} = \Pr(s_t = i | s_{t-1} = i)$, $i = 0, 1$. For convenience $s_t = 0$ corresponds to the null regime with $\phi_0 = 0$, but $s_t = 1$ corresponds to the other regime with $\phi_1 < 0$. We consider the different values for $(\phi_0, \phi_1) = \{(0, -0.1), (0, -0.2), (0, -0.4)\}$. In each case we consider the different transition probabilities as $(p_{00}, p_{11}) = \{(0.98, 0.98), (0.9, 0.9), (0.9, 0.98), (0.98, 0.9)\}$. Expecting that our proposed test statistic will be more powerful against the alternative of two stationary Markov switching regimes we also consider $(\phi_0, \phi_1) = (-0.1, -0.3)$.

Table 1 summarises the simulation results for Experiment 1 including the three different cases: (i) with no intercept and no trend, (ii) the demeaned case and (iii) the demeaned and detrended case. Similar to the findings in the linear cointegration test literature, the power of the tests deteriorates as we include more deterministic components, but the overall performance comparison between $S_{\sup}$ and t_{EG} tests are qualitatively similar. So we focus on the demeaned case in Panel B. A close look tells that the powers of both tests depend on the size of ECM parameters as well as the transition probabilities. Not surprisingly, the power increases monotonically as $|\phi_1|$ rises. Also, as expected, the EG test performs quite well when the common factor restriction holds with $\lambda = 1$, a finding consistent with the linear case as documented in Kremers et al. (1992), who also highlight that this condition is most likely to be violated in practice. In a more general case with $\lambda = 0.5$, however, we find that our proposed $S_{\sup}$ test is more powerful than the EG test in all the cases considered.

In Experiment 2, we allow all the parameters to be subject to the Markov switching mechanism. So, we modify the DGP as follows:

$$\Delta y_t = \phi_{s_t} u_{t-1} + \lambda_{s_t} \Delta x_t + e_{s_t} \tag{23}$$

$$\begin{bmatrix} e_{s_t} \\ v_t \end{bmatrix} \sim \text{i.i.d.}\, N\left(\mathbf{0}, \begin{bmatrix} \sigma_{s_t}^2 & 0 \\ 0 & \sigma_v^2 \end{bmatrix}\right) \tag{24}$$

Here, we fix $\beta_x = 1$ and $\sigma_v^2 = 4$. Under H_0, we set $\phi_{s_t} = \phi = 0$, $\lambda_{s_t} = \lambda = 0.5$ and $\sigma_{s_t}^2 = \sigma^2 = 1$. Under H_1, regime 0 ($s_t = 0$) corresponds to no cointegration with relatively large error variance while regime 1 ($s_t = 1$) corresponds to

Table 1. Power of Alternative Tests for Experiment 1 with $T = 100$.

Panel A: The Case with No Intercept and No Trend

	$\lambda = 1$							
(p,q)	(0.98, 0.98)		(0.9, 0.9)		(0.98, 0.9)		(0.9, 0.98)	
(ϕ_0, ϕ_1)	S_{sup}	t_{EG}	S_{sup}	t_{EG}	S_{sup}	t_{EG}	S_{sup}	t_{EG}
(0, −0.1)	17.1	15.2	15.8	14.9	8.8	7.6	31.1	28.2
(0, −0.2)	30.9	30	31	29.5	9.7	8.9	63.1	65.7
(0, −0.4)	40.5	39.6	51.1	49.9	11.5	10.7	86.2	85.2
(−0.1, −0.5)	78.9	79.6	88.2	90.7	57.4	60.3	98.7	98.4
	$\lambda = 0.5$							
(p, q)	(0.98, 0.98)		(0.9, 0.9)		(0.98, 0.9)		(0.9, 0.98)	
(ϕ_0, ϕ_1)	S_{sup}	t_{EG}	S_{sup}	t_{EG}	S_{sup}	t_{EG}	S_{sup}	t_{EG}
(0, −0.1)	27.3	12.1	28.4	11.7	10.1	6.7	51.4	24.2
(0, −0.2)	39.8	25.7	49.6	25.8	12.8	8.3	82.4	62.3
(0, −0.4)	43.6	35.7	64.4	48.8	11.1	8.9	90.9	85
(−0.1, −0.5)	91.1	79.8	97	91.8	81.9	56.8	99.6	98.8

Panel B: The Demeaned Case

	$\lambda = 1$							
(p, q)	(0.98, 0.98)		(0.9, 0.9)		(0.98, 0.9)		(0.9, 0.98)	
(ϕ_0, ϕ_1)	S_{sup}	t_{EG}	S_{sup}	t_{EG}	S_{sup}	t_{EG}	S_{sup}	t_{EG}
(0, −0.1)	8.5	8.9	7.6	7.9	3.6	5.1	14.5	16.4
(0, −0.2)	18.7	20.7	15.3	19.7	4.6	5.7	39.3	46.9
(0, −0.4)	30.1	33.5	32.1	38.5	5.8	8	72.6	79.5
(−0.1, −0.5)	63.3	68.8	68.9	79.7	35.7	42.4	91.8	96

	$\lambda=0.5$							
(p, q)	(0.98, 0.98)		(0.9, 0.9)		(0.98, 0.9)		(0.9, 0.98)	
(ϕ_0, ϕ_1)	S_{sup}	t_{EG}	S_{sup}	t_{EG}	S_{sup}	t_{EG}	S_{sup}	t_{EG}
(0, −0.1)	12.2	7.7	9.6	6.4	4.1	4.2	22.4	11.8
(0, −0.2)	25.4	14.7	23.5	11.5	4.6	5.2	58.8	35.6
(0, −0.4)	33.4	29.2	40.5	31.8	4.8	6.7	82.2	75.8
(−0.1, −0.5)	78.6	62.5	86.3	74.9	54.7	30.4	97.8	95

Panel C: The Detrended Case

	$\lambda=1$							
(p, q)	(0.98, 0.98)		(0.9, 0.9)		(0.98, 0.9)		(0.9, 0.98)	
(ϕ_0, ϕ_1)	S_{sup}	t_{EG}	S_{sup}	t_{EG}	S_{sup}	t_{EG}	S_{sup}	t_{EG}
(0, −0.1)	8	8	7.3	8	5.1	5.4	12.2	13.3
(0, −0.2)	14.8	17.9	12.4	12.3	5.6	5.7	32.5	36.8
(0, −0.4)	29.3	32.6	26.2	31.4	6.4	7.3	65.4	76.4
(−0.1, −0.5)	56.6	62.1	59.2	70.7	29.2	32.3	86.8	94

	$\lambda=0.5$							
(p, q)	(0.98, 0.98)		(0.9, 0.9)		(0.98, 0.9)		(0.9, 0.98)	
(ϕ_0, ϕ_1)	S_{sup}	t_{EG}	S_{sup}	t_{EG}	S_{sup}	t_{EG}	S_{sup}	t_{EG}
(0, −0.1)	7.8	4.4	6.6	4.3	4	4.3	14.3	7.6
(0, −0.2)	20.2	10.6	13.6	7.2	4.7	5	45.6	23.1
(0, −0.4)	32.1	26.4	29.3	20.8	5.2	6.6	71.4	66.6
(−0.1, −0.5)	68.9	53.4	75	59.6	39.8	20.3	94.8	90.9

Table 2. Power of Alternative Tests for Experiment 2 with $T = 100$.

All Parameters Switch								
(p, q)	(0.98, 0.98)		(0.9, 0.9)		(0.98, 0.9)		(0.9, 0.98)	
(ϕ_0, ϕ_1)	S_{sup}	t_{EG}	S_{sup}	t_{EG}	S_{sup}	t_{EG}	S_{sup}	t_{EG}
(0, −0.1)	21.3	10.2	24.2	11	13.2	9.9	30.5	29.1
(0, −0.2)	36.3	14	41.1	19.3	20	15.3	70.2	65.7
(0, −0.4)	69.4	29.1	75.8	34.7	27.4	20.1	92.4	88.2
(−0.1, −0.5)	87.3	47.3	88.9	59.7	64.3	49.9	98.6	90.3

cointegration with the smaller variance.[9] We consider the same sets for (ϕ_0, ϕ_1) and (p_{00}, p_{11}) as in Experiment 1.

The simulation results for Experiment 2 are presented in Table 2. To save space we report only for the demeaned case with $\lambda = 0.5$. Clearly, the power gains of our proposed S_{sup} test over the EG test are now more substantial in all cases considered.

5. EMPIRICAL ILLUSTRATION

Campbell and Shiller (1987) investigate the existence of a linear cointegration between aggregate stock prices and dividends in the United States. The null hypothesis of no cointegration was marginally rejected, but the implied estimate of the long-run coefficient was implausible. Imposing a more credible long-run coefficient does not reject the null of no cointegration. Since then, mixed results were found in the literature (e.g. Froot & Obstfeld, 1991). Nonlinear adjustment or cointegration has been raised as the main cause behind the failure of the linear models in capturing such fundamental nonlinear relationship between prices and dividends (e.g. Balke & Fomby, 1997; Kapetanios et al., 2006). Alternatively, the deviation of stock prices from the fundamentals could be explained by the time varying discount factor or intrinsic bubbles. In this regard, Psaradakis et al. (2004) found that the two-state MS-ECM can capture well the regime-specific adjustments towards the long-run equilibrium between prices and dividends in the United States. However, they apply the standard linear testing procedure for cointegration in the first stage before estimating the MS-ECM under the alternative.

Here, we aim to apply our proposed tests in order to explicitly allow for complex nonlinear adjustments to equilibrium under the MS-ECM framework. From Datastream we collect the monthly data on start period nominal prices and dividends from January 1974 to December 2006 for 11 countries: Belgium, Canada, Denmark, France, Germany, Ireland, Italy, Japan, the Netherlands, the United Kingdom and the United States.

Consider the long-run relationship between prices and dividends:

$$p_t = \mu + \beta d_t + u_t \tag{25}$$

where p_t and d_t are the logarithms of prices and dividends respectively. Accordingly, we construct the MS-ECM specification as

$$\Delta p_t = a_{s_t} + \phi_{s_t} \hat{u}_{t-1} + \omega_{s_t} \Delta d_t + \varepsilon_{s_t}$$

where $\hat{u}_{t-1} = p_t - \hat{\beta} d_t$ and $\hat{\beta}$ is the OLS estimator obtained from Eq. (25).

In order to compute the p-value of the test statistic and the critical values, we follow the bootstrap method outlined in Section 3, and use 40 draws for ρ from an equi-spaced grid over the interval [0, 0.98]. The test results are summarised in Table 3. First, the EG test fails to reject the null of no cointegration in almost all cases with the only exception of the United Kingdom at the 5% level. On the other hand, our proposed S_{sup} test is able to reject the null of no cointegration in 7 out of 11 countries at the 5% level and one more at the 10% level. Furthermore, we notice that the p-values of the S_{sup} test are substantially smaller (no higher than 0.19)

Table 3. Contegration Test for Price and Dividends.

Country	t_{EG}	S_{sup}
Belgium	0.937	0.101
Canada	0.864	0.005
Denmark	0.948	0.190
France	0.774	0.167
Germany	0.989	0.012
Ireland	0.534	0.030
Italy	0.988	0.012
Japan	0.389	0.002
Netherlands	0.976	0.170
United Kingdom	0.017	0.004
United States	0.110	0.001

Notes: p-value of two tests are provided. The p-values for S_{sup} test are obtained using the bootstrapped empirical critical values with 1,000 replications.

than those of the EG test (most of them higher than 0.8). These results suggest that ignoring the nonlinear adjustment to equilibrium may lead to a false conclusion of no cointegration between price and dividends.

6. CONCLUDING REMARKS

Empirical analysis of cointegration and the associated error correction model has been an integral part of the modern time series econometrics. Recently, the growing number of studies have addressed the implications of the existence of a particular kind of nonlinear asymmetric dynamics, implicitly or explicitly, under the Markov switching framework. The popularity of this type of models lies in allowing us to draw inferences about the underlying DGP in a manner that is not possible using linear models.

Following this trend, we have contributed to the literature by developing the new cointegration test, which is designed to be more powerful against a stationary MS-ECM process than the linear test, which has been routinely applied in the first stage of the practical two-step approach. As acknowledged in the literature, the development of such a testing procedure was deemed to be complicated due to the estimation complexities under the alternative Markov switching models. We have overcome this complexity and provided a simple operational test by adopting the optimal testing procedure advanced by CHP, which only requires the model estimation under the null. We show that our proposed test is asymptotically equivalent to the LR test. Monte Carlo simulations and an empirical application demonstrate the usefulness of our suggested testing procedure in practice.

NOTES

1. In practice, the different lag orders of Δy_t and $\Delta \mathbf{x}_t$ can be selected in a data-dependent way (e.g. Ng & Perron, 1995).

2. The spectral radius of the matrix $\mathbf{M}$ is defined as $\rho(M) = \max_{\lambda \in E} |\lambda|$, where E is the set of eigenvalues of $\mathbf{M}$.

3. Hu (2012) develops the testing procedure for stochastic unit roots under the MS framework.

4. To avoid the case where the test statistic grows without bound, we need to rule out the case that ρ is on the boundary of the parameter space.

5. Since nuisance parameters are unidentified under H_0, uniformly most powerful tests do not exist. The admissibility implies that the test will become optimal in

the sense that it is asymptotically equivalent to the LR test statistic for a sequence of local alternatives.

6. The limiting distribution of the test statistics in CHP is derived by applying the Central Limit Theorem (CLT) for stationary martingale difference sequences while the limiting distribution of our test statistics is derived by employing the functional CLT.

7. When testing the null of the parameter constancy against the Markov switching for a vector of parameters, CHP (Theorem 4.1) establish the uniform convergence of the likelihood ratio even in the multivariate version of the $S_T(\lambda)$ statistic.

8. Even as the number of draws rises, we find that the results are qualitatively similar.

9. This model setup is motivated by what practitioners often observe when examining the relationship between prices and dividends. Namely, when prices deviate from the fundamentals, it is often accompanied by the large volatility, reflecting that market participants have heterogeneous beliefs about the market.

10. For example, if we assume that the asset price is free of arbitrage, then the quadratic variation associated with the return measures the realised sample-path variation of squared return processes. Proposition (A.1) suggests that we may approximate the quadratic variation by cumulating products of (high-frequency) returns.

ACKNOWLEDGEMENTS

We are grateful to Charlie Cai, Marine Carrasco, Thomas Fomby, Hans-Martin Krolzig, Peter Phillips, Werner Ploberger, Peter Schmidt, seminar participants at University of Kent, University of Leeds, Michigan State University, University of Montreal, Northern Illinois University, Wayne State University, and conference delegates at Advances of Econometrics Meeting in Honor of Peter C.B. Phillips at Southern Methodist University, Dallas, on November 1–3, 2013 for their helpful comments. The usual disclaimer applies.

REFERENCES

Andrews, D. W. K., & Ploberger, W. (1994). Optimal tests when a nuisance parameter is present only under the alternative. *Econometrica*, *62*, 1383–1414.

Andrews, D. W. K., & Ploberger, W. (1996). Testing for serial correlation against an ARMA (1,1) process. *Journal of the American Statistical Association*, *91*, 1331–1342.

Arranz, M. A., & Escribano, A. (2000). Cointegration testing in the presence of structural breaks. *Oxford Bulletin of Economics and Statistics*, *62*, 23–52.

Balke, N. S., & Fomby, T. B. (1997). Threshold cointegration. *International Economic Review, 38*, 627–645.

Bougerol, P., & Picard, N. (1992). Stationarity of GARCH processes and some nonnegative time series. *Journal of Econometrics, 52*, 115–127.

Campbell, J. Y., & Kyle, A. (1993). Smart money, noise trading and stock price behavior. *Review of Economic Studies, 60*, 1–34.

Campbell, J. Y., & Shiller, R. J. (1987). Cointegration and tests of present value models. *Journal of Political Economy, 95*, 1062–1088.

Carrasco, M., Hu, L., & Ploberger, W. (2014). Optimal test for markov switching parameters. *Econometrica, 82*, 765–784.

Chaudhuri, K., & Kumary, A. (2006). *A Markov-switching vector error model of the Indian stock price volume*. mimeo, IGIDR.

Chesher, A. (1984). Testing for neglected heterogeneity. *Econometrica, 52*, 865–872.

Davidson, R., & MacKinnon, J. (1991). Une nouvelle forme du test de la matrice d'information. *Annales d'Economie et de Statistique, 20/21*, 171–192.

Davies, R. B. (1987). Hypothesis testing when a nuisance parameter is present only under the alternatives. *Biometrika, 74*, 33–43.

Engle, R., & Granger, C. W. J. (1987). Cointegration and error correction: Representation, estimation and testing. *Econometrica, 55*, 251–276.

Francq, C., & Zakoïan, J. M. (2001). Stationarity of multivariate Markov-switching ARMA models. *Journal of Econometrics, 102*, 339–364.

Froot, K. A., & Maurice, M. O. (1991). Intrinsic bubbles: The case of stock prices. *American Economic Review, 81*, 1189–1214.

Hall, P., & Heyde, C. C. (1980). *Martingale limit theory and its application*. New York, NY: Academic Press.

Hansen, B. E. (1995). Rethinking the univariate approach to unit root tests: How to use covariates to increase power. *Econometric Theory, 11*, 1148–1171.

Hansen, B. E. (1996). Inference when a nuisance parameter is not identified under the null hypothesis. *Econometrica, 64*, 413–430.

Hansen, B. E., & Seo, B. (2002). Testing for two-regime threshold cointegration in vector error-correction models. *Journal of Econometrics, 110*, 293–318.

Hu, L. (2012). *Optimal test for stochastic unit root with Markov switching*. mimeo, Wayne State University.

Kapetanios, G., Shin, Y., & Snell, A. (2006). Testing for cointegration in nonlinear smooth transition error correction models. *Econometric Theory, 22*, 279–303.

Karatzas, I., & Shreve, S. E. (1991). *Brownian motion and stochastic calculus*. New York, NY: Springer-Verlag.

Kremers, J. J. M., Ericsson, K. R., & Dolado, J. J. (1992). The power of cointegration tests. *Oxford Bulletin of Economics and Statistics, 54*, 325–348.

Krolzig, H. M., Marcellino, M., & Mizon, G. (2002). A Markov-switching vector equilibrium correction model of the UK labour market. *Empirical Economics, 27*, 233–254.

Michael, P., Nobay, R. A., & Peel, D. A. (1997). Transactions costs and nonlinear adjustment in real exchange rates: An empirical investigation. *Journal of Political Economy, 105*, 862–879.

Mikosch, T. (1998). *Elementary stochastic calculus, with finance in view* (Vol. 6). Advanced Series on Statistical Science and Applied Probability. New York, NY: World Scientific Publishing.

Ng, S., & Perron, P. (1995). Unit root tests in ARMA models with data-dependent methods for the selection of the truncation lag. *Journal of the American Statistical Association, 90*, 268–281.

Park, J. Y., & Phillips, P. C. B. (2001). Nonlinear regressions with integrated time series. *Econometrica, 69*, 117–161.

Psaradakis, Z., Sola, M., & Spagnolo, F. (2004). On Markov error-correction models with an application to stock prices and dividends. *Journal of Applied Econometrics, 19*, 69–88.

Saikkonen, P. (2005). Stability results for nonlinear error correction models. *Journal of Econometrics, 127*, 69–81.

Sarno, L., & Valente, G. (2005). Modeling and forecasting stock returns: Exploiting the futures market, regime shifts and international spillovers. *Journal of Applied Econometrics, 20*, 345–376.

Yao, J. F., & Attali, J. G. (2000). On stability of nonlinear AR processes with Markov switching. *Advances in Applied Probability, 32*, 394–407.

APPENDIX: MATHEMATICAL PROOFS

Proof of Theorem 1

We rewrite the null hypothesis and the sequence of local alternatives by

$$H_0 : \phi_t = 0 \text{ vs } H_{1T} : \phi_t = \frac{1}{\sqrt[4]{T^3}} \eta_t$$

Notice that the alternative is of order $T^{-3/4}$, which is different from the usual T^{-1} order used in threshold ECM framework. This is due to the fact that the information matrix is singular under H_0, and we have to estimate the parameters at each regime. Consequently, the rate of convergence is slower.

Now, consider

$$\Gamma_T = \frac{1}{2\sqrt{T^3}} \sum_t \mu_t(\lambda, \hat{\phi})$$

where

$$\mu_t(\lambda, \hat{\theta}) = (\ell_{t(2)} + \ell_{t(1)}^2) \operatorname{Var}(\eta_t) + 2 \sum_{s=1}^{t-1} \rho^{t-s} \ell_{t(1)} \ell_{s(1)} \operatorname{Cov}(\eta_t, \eta_s)$$

Notice that $\mu_t(\lambda, \hat{\theta})$ is a martingale difference sequence and thus $M_t = \sum_{s=1}^{t} \mu_s(\lambda, \hat{\theta})$ is a martingale.

We now derive some preliminary results. First, we define

$$Q_T = \sum_t E(\mu_t(\lambda, \hat{\phi})^2 | \mathcal{F}_{t-1})$$

where $\mathcal{F}_{t-1}$ is the σ-algebra up to time $t-1$. Notice that Q_T is the quadratic variation associated with M_t defined below (e.g. Hall & Heyde, 1980, p. 54). Moreover, the following proposition explicitly provides an important property for martingales (see Karatzas & Shreve, 1991, p. 32).

Proposition A.1. M_t is a continuous and square-integrable martingale. For a sequence of random partitions, Π of $[0,T]$ with $0 = t_0 \leq t_1 \leq \ldots \leq t_m = T$, define the second variation of M over the partition Π to be

$$V_t^2(\Pi) = \sum_{k=1}^{m} \left| M_{t_k} - M_{t_{k-1}} \right|^2$$

Then, we have

$$\underset{\|\Pi\| \to 0}{\text{plim}} \; V_t^2(\Pi) = \langle M \rangle_t$$

where $\langle M \rangle_t$ is the quadratic variation of M_t.

Proposition A.1 implies that summing up squared differences of M_t at every possible spot time then provides a consistent estimator of $\langle M \rangle_t$.[10]

Let Q_T^λ denote the joint distribution of $(\eta_1, \ldots, \eta_T)$, indexed by the unknown parameter λ. Let $P_{\phi,\lambda}$ be the probability measure on $y_1, y_2, \ldots, y_T$ corresponding to H_{1T}, and P_ϕ be the probability measure on $y_1, y_2, \ldots, y_T$ corresponding to H_0. The ratio of the densities under H_0 and H_{1T} is given by

$$\ell_T \equiv \frac{\mathrm{d}P_{\phi,\lambda}}{\mathrm{d}P_\phi} = \int \prod_{t=1}^{T} f_t(\eta_t/T^{3/4}) \mathrm{d}Q_T^\lambda / \prod_{t=1}^{T} f_t(\phi_0)$$

where $f_t(\cdot)$ are the likelihood functions.

By the Neyman–Pearson lemma, the test based on ℓ_T is the best test of a given significance level for testing the simple null hypothesis that $\prod_{t=1}^{T} f_t(\phi_0)$ is the true density against the simple alternative that $\int \prod_{t=1}^{T} f_t(\eta_t/T^{3/4}) \mathrm{d}Q_T^\lambda$ is true. In addition, the test based on ℓ_T has the best weighted average power for the weight function, Q_T^λ of all tests of a given significance level for testing the simple null hypothesis that $\prod_{t=1}^{T} f_t(\phi_0)$ is the true density versus the alternative that $\prod_{t=1}^{T} f_t(\eta_t/T^{3/4})$ is true for some $\lambda \in \Xi$.

In this paper we choose the sup-type test for its simplicity, but this test corresponds to employing a specific weight function, as pointed out by Andrews and Ploberger (1994). In principle, we pick any prior distribution such that the resulting test statistic should have the best weighted-average power for this prior distribution.

We define the likelihood ratio of the simple null $\prod_{t=1}^{T} f_t(\phi_0)$ and the simple alternative $\prod_{t=1}^{T} f_t(\eta_t/T^{3/4})$ for some given $\lambda \in \Xi$

$$L_T^\lambda = \frac{\prod_{t=1}^{T} f_t(\eta_t/T^{3/4})}{\prod_{t=1}^{T} f_t(\phi_0)} = \exp\left(\sum_{t=1}^{T} l_t^\lambda \right)$$

where

$$l_t^{\lambda} = l_t(\eta_t/T^{3/4}) - l_t(\phi_0)$$

is the log likelihood function defined as before.

Now, we establish the optimality of our tests. To this end we need to show our test is asymptotically equivalent to the Neyman–Pearson test, or we could express it in terms of the following expectation:

$$E_{\eta}\left[\exp\left(\sum_{t=1}^{T} l_t^{\lambda} - S_T(\lambda)\right)\right] = 1$$

where E_{η} denotes the conditional expectation with respect to $(\eta_1, \ldots, \eta_T)$ and $S_T(\lambda)$ is our test statistic defined in Eq. (12).

We have the following theorem from Hu (2012).

Theorem 3. We have under H_0

$$L_T^{\lambda}/\exp\left(\frac{1}{2T^{3/2}}\sum_{t=1}^{T}\mu_t - \frac{1}{8T^2}E\left(\mu_t^2|\mathcal{F}_{t-1}\right)\right) \xrightarrow{P} 1 \tag{A.1}$$

where the convergence in probability is uniform over λ. Moreover, we have $P_{\phi,\lambda}$ which is contiguous with respect to P_{ϕ}.

This gives the asymptotic equivalence between the likelihood ratio and the proposed test statistic in Eq. (A.1). Then by Neyman–Pearson lemma, the above statistic is optimal. Notice that our test statistic in Eq. (12) is obtained by plugging in a consistent estimator of $E(\mu_t^2|\mathcal{F}_{t-1})$, which does not affect the asymptotic admissibility of the test. This completes the proof of Theorem 1.

Proof of Theorem 2

To find the limiting distribution of the $S_{\sup}$ statistic, we need to find a limiting behaviour of $\tilde{\mu}_t$ which is a martingale difference sequence indexed by nuisance parameter ρ with values in the space of continuous functions defined on a compact subset. We now consider

$$\frac{1}{\sqrt{T^3}}\sum_{t=1}^{T}\tilde{\mu}_t=\frac{1}{\sqrt{T}}\sum_{t=1}^{T}\left[\frac{1}{\tilde{\sigma}_e^2}(\tilde{e}_t^2-\tilde{\sigma}_e^2)\left(\frac{\tilde{u}_{t-1}}{\sqrt{T}}\right)^2+2\sum_{s<t}\rho^{t-s}\frac{\tilde{e}_t}{\tilde{\sigma}_e}\frac{\tilde{e}_s}{\tilde{\sigma}_e}\frac{\tilde{u}_{t-1}}{\sqrt{T}}\frac{\tilde{u}_{s-1}}{\sqrt{T}}\right] \tag{A.2}$$

Under H_0, $\tilde{\sigma}_e^2=O_p(\sqrt{T})$ and it is easily seen from functional CLT that as $T\to\infty$

$$T^{-1/2}\sum_{t=1}^{[Ta]}\frac{1}{\tilde{\sigma}_e^2}(\tilde{e}_t^2-\tilde{\sigma}_e^2)\Rightarrow\sqrt{2}W(a),\quad a\in[0,1]$$

where $W(a)$ is the scalar standard Brownian motion. Moreover, from Park and Phillips (2001), we have

$$T^{-1/2}\tilde{u}_{t-1}\Rightarrow\sigma_u B(a),\quad a\in[0,1]$$

where $B(a)=W(a)-\mathbf{W}_x(a)'\left(\int_0^1\mathbf{W}_x(a)\mathbf{W}_x(a)'\mathrm{d}a\right)^{-1}\int_0^1\mathbf{W}_x(a)W(a)\mathrm{d}a$ and $\mathbf{W}_x(a)$ are a k-vector standard Brownian motions independent of $W(a)$. Since $\tilde{e}_t$ and $\tilde{u}_{t-1}$ are asymptotically independent, following Park and Phillips (2001) and Kapetanios et al. (2006), we now have under H_0, as $T\to\infty$:

$$\frac{1}{\sqrt{T}}\sum_{t=1}^{T}\left[\frac{1}{\tilde{\sigma}_e^2}(\tilde{e}_t^2-\tilde{\sigma}_e^2)\left(\frac{\tilde{u}_{t-1}}{\sqrt{T}}\right)^2\right]\Rightarrow\sqrt{2}\sigma_u^2\int_0^1 B(a)^2\mathrm{d}W_0(a),\quad a\in[0,1] \tag{A.3}$$

Next, we examine the second part of Eq. (A.2). First, it is straightforward to show (see Theorem 1 in Andrews and Ploberger, 1996) that under H_0, as $T\to\infty$:

$$\frac{1}{\sqrt{T}}\sum_{t=1}^{T}\frac{\tilde{e}_t}{\tilde{\sigma}_e}\sum_{k<t}\rho^{t-k}\frac{\tilde{e}_k}{\tilde{\sigma}_e}\Rightarrow\sum_{i=0}^{\infty}\rho^i\zeta_i$$

where $\zeta_i\sim$ i.i.d. $N(0,\ 1)$.

Second, noting that

$$T^{-1}\tilde{u}_{t-1}\tilde{u}_{s-1}=T^{-1}\tilde{u}_{t-1}^2+o_p(1)\quad\text{for } s<t$$

together with the fact that $\tilde{e}_t$ and $\tilde{u}_{t-1}$ are asymptotically independent, we obtain

$$\frac{1}{\sqrt{T}}\sum_{t=1}^{T}\left[\sum_{s<t}\rho^{t-s}\frac{\tilde{e}_t}{\tilde{\sigma}_e}\frac{\tilde{e}_s}{\tilde{\sigma}_e}\frac{\tilde{u}_{t-1}}{\sqrt{T}}\frac{\tilde{u}_{s-1}}{\sqrt{T}}\right]\Rightarrow\sigma_u^2\sum_{i=0}^{\infty}\rho^i\int_0^1 B(a)^2\mathrm{d}W_i(a),\quad a\in[0,1] \tag{A.4}$$

where $B(a)$ remains the same as defined earlier, $W_i(\cdot)$ are i.i.d. scalar Brownian motions.

Combining Eqs. (A.3) and (A.4), we obtain

$$\frac{1}{\sqrt{T^3}\sigma_u^2}\sum_{t=1}^{T}\tilde{\mu}_t\Rightarrow G(\rho)\equiv\sqrt{2}\int_0^1 B(a)^2\mathrm{d}W(a)+2\sum_{i=0}^{\infty}\rho^i\int_0^1 B(a)^2\mathrm{d}W_i(a),\quad a\in[0,1] \tag{A.5}$$

Here $G(\rho)$ only depends on the correlation coefficient of the Markov chain, ρ, and it is defined on a compact set $-1<\underline{\rho}<\rho<\overline{\rho}<1$.

Next, since we can rewrite

$$\sum_{i=0}^{\infty}\rho^i\int_0^1 B(a)^2\mathrm{d}W_i(a)=\frac{1}{\sqrt{1-\rho^2}}\int_0^1 B(a)^2\mathrm{d}W_a(a)$$

where W_a is a scalar standard Brownian motion. Using the quadratic variation definition (e.g. Mikosch, 1998), we can establish that

$$\frac{1}{T^2}\sum_{t=1}^{T}\tilde{\mu}_t^2\Rightarrow\left(2+\frac{4}{1-\rho^2}\right)\sigma_u^4\int_0^1 B(a)^4\mathrm{d}a,\quad a\in[0,1] \tag{A.6}$$

Combining Eqs. (A.5) and (A.6) and using Continuous Mapping Theorem, we obtain the limiting distribution in Eq. (17), which completes the proof of Theorem 2.

SPECIFICATION TESTING IN PARAMETRIC TRENDING MODELS WITH UNKNOWN ERRORS

Jiti Gao and Maxwell King

Department of Econometrics and Business Statistics, Monash University, Melbourne, Australia

ABSTRACT

This paper considers a class of parametric models with nonparametric autoregressive errors. A new test is established and studied to deal with the parametric specification of the nonparametric autoregressive errors with either stationarity or nonstationarity. Such a test procedure can initially avoid misspecification through the need to parametrically specify the form of the errors. In other words, we estimate the form of the errors and test for stationarity or nonstationarity simultaneously. We establish asymptotic distributions of the proposed test. Both the setting and the results differ from earlier work on testing for unit roots in parametric time series regression. We provide both simulated and real-data examples to show that the proposed nonparametric unit root test works in practice.

Keywords: Autoregressive process; nonlinear time series; nonparametric method; random walk; semiparametric model; unit root test

JEL Classifications: C12; C14; C22

Essays in Honor of Peter C. B. Phillips
Advances in Econometrics, Volume 33, 151–202

ISSN: 0731-9053/doi:10.1108/S0731-905320140000033006

1. INTRODUCTION

Consider a parametric linear model of the form

$$Y_t = X_t^\tau \beta + v_t, \quad t = 1, 2, \cdots, T \tag{1}$$

where T is the sample size of the time series data $\{Y_t\text{: } 1 \leq t \leq T\}$, $\{X_t\}$ is a $p \times 1$ vector of known deterministic functions, $\beta = (\beta_1, \cdots, \beta_p)^\tau$ is a vector of unknown parameters for $p \geq 1$, $\{v_t\}$ is a sequence of time series residuals. Existing studies mainly discuss tests for the case where $\{v_t\}$ satisfies the first-order autoregressive (AR(1)) model of the form $v_t = \rho v_{t-1} + u_t$ with $\{u_t\}$ being a sequence of independent and identically distributed (i.i.d.) errors. Discussion about tests for $|\rho| < 1$ may be found in the survey papers by King (1987), King and Wu (1997) and King (2001).

For the case of $\rho = 1$, there has been much interest in both theoretical and empirical analysis of economic and financial time series with unit roots during the past three decades or so. Various tests for unit roots have been proposed and studied both theoretically and empirically. Models and methods used have been based initially on parametric linear autoregressive moving average representations with or without trend components. Existing studies may be found in the survey paper by Phillips and Xiao (1998). Other studies include Dickey and Fuller (1979, 1981), Evans and Savin (1981, 1984), Phillips (1987), Phillips and Perron (1988), Dufour and King (1991), Kwiatkowski, Phillips, Schmidt, and Shin (1992), Phillips (1997), Lobato and Robinson (1998), and Robinson (2003).

As pointed out in the literature (Vogelsang, 1998; Zheng & Basher, 1999), there are cases where there is no priori knowledge about either the form of the residuals or whether the residuals are I(0) or I(1). This motivates us to consider using a nonparametric autoregressive error model of the form

$$v_t = g(v_{t-1}) + u_t, \quad t = 1, 2, \cdots, T \tag{2}$$

where $g(\cdot)$ is an unknown function defined over $R^1 = (-\infty, \infty)$, $\{u_t\}$ is a sequence of stationary errors with mean zero and finite variance $\sigma_u^2 = E[u_1^2]$, $\{v_t : t \geq 1\}$ is also a sequence of errors with $E[v_t] = 0$, and v_0 is an initial value. Note that v_0 can be either a given initial value or any $O_P(1)$ random variable. We however set $v_0 = 0$ to avoid some unnecessary complications in exposition.

Combining model (2) with model (1) produces a semiparametric time series model of the form

$$Y_t = X_t^\tau \beta + v_t \quad \text{with} \quad v_t = g(v_{t-1}) + u_t \tag{3}$$

Existing studies (see, e.g., Masry & Tjøstheim, 1995) already discuss the case where $\beta \equiv 0$ and $\{v_t\}$ is strictly stationary when certain technical conditions are imposed on the form of $g(\cdot)$. Meanwhile, various existing studies (see, e.g., Gao, 2007; Koul & Stute, 1999 and the references therein) focus on nonparametric estimation and specification testing for the case where $\{v_t\}$ is stationary since the publication of Robinson (1983).

To the best of our knowledge, semiparametric estimation of β and $g(\cdot)$ for the case where $\{v_t\}$ is stationary has only been discussed in Hidalgo (1992). Nonparametric and semiparametric estimation of $g(\cdot)$ for the case where $v_t = v_{t-1} + u_t$ has been done in Phillips and Park (1998), Karlsen and Tjøstheim (2001), Wang and Phillips (2009), Chen, Gao, and Li (2012), and Gao and Phillips (2013).

Model (3) is quite general and covers many important cases. For example, in order to test whether $\{Y_t\}$ follows a nonstationary model of the form

$$Y_t = \sum_{i=0}^{d} \gamma_i t^i + Y_{t-1} + u_t \tag{4}$$

it suffices to test whether $H_0 : v_t = v_{t-1} + u_t$ holds in a $(d+1)$-order polynomial trend model of the form

$$Y_t = \sum_{j=0}^{d+1} \beta_j t^j + v_t \tag{5}$$

This paper is then concerned with testing

$$\mathcal{H}_0 : g(v) = f_0(v, \theta_0) \quad \text{versus} \quad \mathcal{H}_1 : g(v) = f_1(v, \theta_1) \tag{6}$$

for all $v \in R^1$, where $f_0(v, \theta_0)$ is a known parametric function indexed by a vector of unknown parameters θ_0 and $f_1(v, \theta_1)$ is an unknown semiparametric function indexed by a vector of unknown parameters θ_1.

Forms of $f_0(v,\theta_0)$ include the case of $f_0(v,\theta_0)\equiv 0$. In this case, $v_t=u_t$ and thus $\{v_t\}$ is a sequence of stationary errors. When $\theta_0=1$ is chosen such that $f_0(v,\theta_0)=v$, it means that there is a unit root in $\{v_t\}$. Forms of $f_i(v,\theta_i)$ may be chosen suitably to include various existing cases such as a parametric AR(1) model of the form $v_t=\theta_0 v_{t-1}+u_t$ against a partially linear AR(1) model of the form $v_t=\theta_1 v_{t-1}+\psi(v_{t-1})+u_t$, where $\psi(\cdot)$ is an unknown function such that $\min_{\alpha,\beta}E[\psi(v_1)-\alpha-\beta v_1]^2\geq M$ for some positive constant M. This is needed to ensure that both θ_1 and $\psi(\cdot)$ are identifiable and estimable.

In addition, forms of $f_1(v,\theta_1)$ include existing parametric nonlinear functions, such as $f_1(v,\theta_1)=\rho_1 v+\gamma_1 v(1-\exp\{-\eta_1 v^2\})$ as discussed in Kapetanios, Shin, and Snell (2003), where $\theta_1=(\rho_1,\gamma_1,\eta_1)$ is a vector of unknown parameters.

Our discussion in this paper focuses on the following two cases.

Case A: $f_0(v,\theta_0)$ is chosen as $f_0(v,\theta_0)=\theta_0 v$ with $\theta_0=1$. This implies $v_t=\theta_0 v_{t-1}+u_t$ with $\theta_0=1$ under $\mathcal{H}_0$ while the form of $f_1(v,\theta_1)$ is chosen such that $\{v_t\}$ is a sequence of strictly stationary errors under $\mathcal{H}_1$.

Case B: The form of each of $f_i(v,\theta_i)$ for $i=0,1$ is suitably chosen such that $\{v_t\}$ is a sequence of strictly stationary errors under either $\mathcal{H}_0$ or $\mathcal{H}_1$.

This paper then discusses a nonparametric test for $\mathcal{H}_0$ versus $\mathcal{H}_1$. Unlike existing parametric tests, this test has an asymptotically normal distribution even when $\{v_t\}$ is a sequence of random walk errors. The main advantage of the nonparametric unit root test over existing tests in the parametric case is that it can initially avoid misspecification through the need to parametrically specify the form of $\{v_t\}$ as $v_t=\rho v_{t-1}+u_t$ for example. Such a test may be viewed as a nonparametric counterpart of existing parametric tests proposed in the literature.

Theoretical properties for the nonparametric test are established. Our finite sample results show that the conventional Dickey–Fuller (DF) type test is more powerful than the proposed nonparametric unit root test when the alternative model is an AR(1) model of the form $v_t=\rho v_{t-1}+u_t$. When the alternative is a parametric nonlinear autoregressive model, however, the conventional parametric unit root test seems to be inferior to the proposed nonparametric unit root test in the sense that it is less powerful than the proposed nonparametric unit root test.

The rest of the paper is organized as follows. Section 2 establishes a nonparametric test as well as its asymptotic distributional results. A bootstrap simulation procedure is proposed in Section 3. Section 4 presents two examples to show how to implement the proposed test in practice. Section 5 gives some extensions. Mathematical details are relegated to Appendices A and B.

2. A NONPARAMETRIC TEST

In the parametric linear case where $v_t = \rho v_{t-1} + u_t$, existing tests for $\rho = 0$ include various versions of the test proposed in Durbin and Watson (1950, 1951) (named as DW test), as reviewed in King (1987), King and Wu (1997), King (2001) and others. Various extensions of the DF test for $\rho = 1$ proposed in Dickey and Fuller (1979, 1981) have been discussed in Phillips and Xiao (2003) and others.

In order to deal with the nonparametric case where $v_t = g(v_{t-1}) + u_t$, we propose using a nonparametric version of some existing parametric tests. Assuming that $\{v_t\}$ were observable, we would have a parametric autoregressive model of the form

$$v_t = f_0(v_{t-1}, \theta_0) + u_t \tag{7}$$

with $E[u_t|v_{t-1}] = 0$ under $\mathcal{H}_0$. We thus have

$$E[u_t E(u_t|v_{t-1}) p(v_{t-1})] = E[(E^2(u_t|v_{t-1})) p(v_{t-1})] = 0 \tag{8}$$

under $\mathcal{H}_0$, where $p(\cdot)$ is the marginal density function of $\{v_{t-1}\}$.

Note that $p(\cdot)$ may depend on t when $\{v_t\}$ is nonstationary. Note also that the sample analogue of $E[u_t E(u_t|v_{t-1}) p(v_{t-1})]$ is $\frac{1}{T}\sum_{t=1}^{T} u_t E[u_t| v_{t-1}] p(v_{t-1})$. When $E[u_t|v_{t-1}] p(v_{t-1})$ is replaced by a kind of kernel-based sample analogue of the form $\frac{1}{Th}\sum_{s=1}^{n} K_h(v_{s-1} - v_{t-1}) u_s$, a kernel-based sample analogue of (8) is of the form

$$M_T = \frac{1}{T}\sum_{t=1}^{T}\left(\frac{1}{Th}\sum_{s=1}^{T} u_s K_h(v_{s-1} - v_{t-1})\right) u_t \tag{9}$$

where $K_h(\cdot) = K\left(\frac{\cdot}{h}\right)$ with $K(\cdot)$ being a probability kernel function and h a bandwidth parameter. This suggests using a centralized and then normalized kernel-based sample analogue of (8) of the form

$$L_T = L_T(h) = \frac{\sum_{t=1}^{T}\sum_{s=1,\neq t}^{T} u_s K_h(v_{s-1} - v_{t-1}) u_t}{\tilde{\sigma}_T} \tag{10}$$

where $\tilde{\sigma}_T^2 = 2\sum_{t=1}^{T}\sum_{s=1,\neq t}^{T} u_s^2 K_h^2(v_{s-1} - v_{t-1}) u_t^2$. Note that the numerator of L_T uses a leave-one-out version to ensure that its mean is zero.

Note that existing literature (see, e.g., Chapter 3 of Gao, 2007) shows that $L_T \to_D N(0,1)$ and $\frac{\tilde{\sigma}_T^2}{\sigma_T^2} \to_P 1$ as $T \to \infty$ when both v_t and u_t are stationary, where $\sigma_T^2 = E[\tilde{\sigma}_T^2]$. In the case where $\{v_t\}$ is nonstationary, as shown in Theorem 2, we are also able to show that under the null hypothesis, $L_T \to_D N(0,1)$ and $\frac{\tilde{\sigma}_T^2}{\sigma_T^2} \to_D \xi^2$ for some random variable ξ. In summary, the proposed test is asymptotically normal when the errors are either stationary or nonstationary.

The form of $L_T(h)$ may be regarded as a nonparametric counterpart of the DW test for the stationary case (see Eq. (5) of Dufour & King, 1991) and the DF test for the unit-root case (see Eq. (17) of Dufour & King, 1991). For the case where the time series involved is strictly stationary, similar versions have been used for nonparametric testing of serial correlation (Li & Hsiao, 1998) and nonparametric specification of time series (Gao, 2007). Such tests are extensions of existing tests proposed in Zheng (1996), Li and Wang (1998), Li (1999), and Fan and Linton (2003).

In the original working paper, Gao, King, Lu and Tjøstheim (2006) propose using a version similar to Eq. (10) for parametric specification in both the nonparametric autoregression model of the form $X_t = g(X_{t-1}) + u_t$ and the nonparametric time series regression model of the form $Y_t = m(X_t) + e_t$ with $X_t = X_{t-1} + u_t$, where $\{u_t\}$ is assumed to be a sequence of independent and normally distributed errors. In the recent published papers, Gao, King, Lu, Tjøstheim (2009a, 2009b) consider the specification testing problems for the case where $\{u_t\}$ is a sequence of independent and identically distributed errors.

Since $\{v_t\}$ and $\{u_t\}$ are unobservable, $L_T(h)$ will need to be replaced by

$$\hat{L}_T = \hat{L}_T(h) = \frac{\sum_{t=1}^{T} \sum_{s=1,\neq t}^{T} \hat{u}_s K_h(\hat{v}_{s-1} - \hat{v}_{t-1}) \hat{u}_t}{\hat{\tilde{\sigma}}_T} \tag{11}$$

where $\hat{\tilde{\sigma}}_T^2 = 2\sum_{t=1}^{T} \sum_{s=1,\neq t}^{T} \hat{u}_s^2 K_h^2(\hat{v}_{s-1} - \hat{v}_{t-1}) \hat{u}_t^2$ and $\hat{u}_t = \hat{v}_t - f_0(\hat{v}_{t-1}, \hat{\theta}_0)$, in which $\hat{v}_t = Y_t - X_t^\tau \hat{\beta}$, and $\hat{\theta}_0$ and $\hat{\beta}$ are consistent estimators of θ_0 and β under $\mathcal{H}_0$ respectively.

To establish the asymptotic distribution of $\hat{L}_T(h)$, we need to introduce Assumption 1 for Case A.

Assumption 1. (i) Let $\{u_t\}$ be a stationary ergodic sequence of martingale differences satisfying $E[u_t|\mathcal{F}_{t-1}] = 0$ and $E[u_t^4|\mathcal{F}_{t-1}] < \infty$ almost surely, where $\{\mathcal{F}_t\}$ is a sequence of σ-fields generated by $\{u_s: 1 \leq s \leq t\}$. Let $\sigma_u^2 = E[u_1^2]$.

(ii) Suppose that $\{u_t\}$ has a symmetric marginal density function $g(x)$. Let $g^{(i)}(x)$ be the i-th derivative of $g(x)$ and $g^{(i)}(x)$ be continuous at $x \in (-\infty, \infty)$ *for* $i = 1$.

For any $m \geq 2$, let $S_{m,t} = \frac{1}{\sqrt{m}\sigma_u} \sum_{s=t+1}^{t+m} u_s$, $f_{m,t}(x)$ be the marginal density function of $S_{m,t}$ and $f_{m,t}(x|\mathcal{F}_t)$ be the conditional density function of $S_{m,t}$ given $\mathcal{F}_t$. Let $f_{m,t}^{(i)}(x)$ and $f_{m,t}^{(i)}(x|\mathcal{F}_t)$ be the respective i-th derivatives of $f_{m,t}(x)$ and $f_{m,t}(x|\mathcal{F}_t)$ with respect to x and both $f_{m,t}^{(i)}(x)$ and $f_{m,t}^{(i)}(x|\mathcal{F}_t)$ be continuous at $x \in (-\infty, \infty)$. Suppose that for $i = 0, 1$

$$\inf_{\delta>0} \lim_{m\to\infty} \sup_{t\geq 1} \sup_{|x|\leq\delta} f_{m,t}^{(i)}(x) < \infty \quad \text{and} \tag{12}$$

$$\inf_{\delta>0} \lim_{m\to\infty} \sup_{t\geq 1} \sup_{|x|\leq\delta} f_{m,t}^{(i)}(x|\mathcal{F}_t) < \infty \quad \text{with probability one} \tag{13}$$

For Case B, we need the following assumption.

Assumption 2. (i) Let Assumption 1(i) hold. In addition, the marginal density of $\{u_t\}$ is positive and lower-semicontinuous over R^1.

(ii) $f_0(v, \theta_0)$ is bounded on any bounded Borel measurable set of R^1. Suppose that there is some constant $|\theta_0| < 1$ such that $f_0(v, \theta_0) = \theta_0 v + o(|v|)$ *as* $|v| \to \infty$.

Assumption 1(i) assumes that $\{u_t\}$ is a sequence of stationary martingale differences. This is quite general in this kind of problem. Assumption 1(ii) imposes a set of general conditions on the marginal and conditional density functions. Similar conditions have been used by Assumption A4 of Chen, Gao and Li (2007) and Assumption 3(ii) of Wang and Phillips (2009). Since $v_t = \sum_{i=1}^{t} u_i$ is a random walk process under H_0, we need to impose certain conditions on the distributional structure of a normalized version of v_t of the form $S_{m,t} = \frac{1}{\sqrt{m}\sigma_u}(v_{t+m} - v_t) = \frac{1}{\sqrt{m}\sigma_u} \sum_{s=t+1}^{t+m} u_s$. Eqs. (12) and (13) basically require that the density and conditional density functions and their derivatives are bounded uniformly in $t \geq 1$, $m \to \infty$ and $|x| \leq \delta$ for all small $\delta > 0$.

Eqs. (12) and (13) are justifiable. When $\{u_t\}$ is a sequence of independent and identically distributed random variables for example, Eq. (13) reduces to Eq. (12), which follows from as $m \to \infty$

$$\sup_x |\phi_m(x) - \phi(x)| \to 0 \quad \text{and} \quad \sup_x |\phi_m^{(1)}(x) - \phi^{(1)}(x)| \to 0 \tag{14}$$

under the condition $\int_{-\infty}^{\infty} |v||\psi(v)|dv < \infty$, where $\psi(\cdot)$ is the characteristic function of u_1, $\phi_m^{(1)}(x)$ and $\phi^{(1)}(x)$ are the first derivatives of $\phi_m(x)$, which is the density function of $\frac{1}{\sqrt{m}\sigma_u}\sum_{t=1}^{m} u_t$, and $\phi(x) = \frac{1}{\sqrt{2\pi}} e^{-\frac{x^2}{2}}$ is the density function of the standard normal random variable $N(0, 1)$ respectively. The proof of Eq. (14) is quite standard (see, e.g., the proof of Corollary 2.2 of Wang & Phillips, 2009).

Assumption 2 implies that (see, e.g., Lu, 1998; Meitz & Saikkonen, 2008; Tong, 1990) $\{v_t\}$ is strictly stationary and α-mixing with mixing coefficient

$$\alpha(t) = \sup\{|P(A \cap B) - P(A)P(B)| : A \in \Omega_1^s, B \in \Omega_{s+t}^{\infty}\}$$

for all $s, t \geq 1$, where $\{\Omega_i^j\}$ is a sequence of σ-fields generated by $\{v_s : i \leq s \leq j\}$. There exist constants $c_r > 0$ and $r \in [0, 1)$ such that $\alpha(t) \leq c_r r^t$ for $t \geq 1$.

We now establish the following theorem; its proof is given in Appendix A.

Theorem 1. Assume that either Assumptions 1 and A.1–A.3(i) for Case A or Assumptions 2, A.1–A.3(i) and A.4 for Case B hold. Then under $\mathcal{H}_0$

$$\hat{L}_T(h) \rightarrow_D N(0, 1) \quad \text{as} \quad T \rightarrow \infty \tag{15}$$

Theorem 1 shows that the standard normality can still be an asymptotic distribution of the proposed test even when nonstationarity is involved. Moreover, Theorem 1 shows that the same asymptotically normal test can be used to deal with the stationary and nonstationary cases.

It is our experience that in practice the proposed test $\hat{L}_T(h)$ may not have good small sample properties when using a large sample normal distribution to approximate the small sample distribution of the test under consideration. In order to improve the finite sample performance of $\hat{L}_T(h)$, we propose using a bootstrap method in Section 3. Section 3 also studies the power performance of $\hat{L}_T(h)$ under $\mathcal{H}_1$.

3. BOOTSTRAP SIMULATION SCHEME

This section discusses how to simulate a critical value for the implementation of $\hat{L}_T(h)$ in practice. Before we look at how to implement $\hat{L}_T(h)$ in practice, we propose the following simulation scheme.

Simulation Scheme: The exact $\alpha-$level critical value, $l_\alpha(h)$ $(0 < \alpha < 1)$, is the $1-\alpha$ quantile of the exact finite-sample distribution of $\hat{L}_T(h)$. Because $l_\alpha(h)$ may be unknown, it cannot be evaluated in practice. We thus propose choosing a simulated α-level critical value, $l^*_\alpha(h)$, by using the following simulation procedure:

(i) Let $Y^*_0 = y^*_0$ and $X_0 = x_0$ be the initial values. For $t = 1, 2, \cdots, T$, generate $Y^*_t = Y^*_{t-1} + (X_t - X_{t-1})^\tau \hat{\beta} + \hat{\sigma}_u u^*_t$ for Case A, and $Y^*_t = X^\tau_t \hat{\beta} + f_0(Y^*_{t-1} - X^\tau_{t-1} \hat{\beta}, \hat{\theta}_0) + \hat{\sigma}_u u^*_t$ for Case B, where $\hat{\beta}$, $\hat{\theta}_0$ and $\hat{\sigma}^2_u$ are the respective consistent estimators of β, θ_0 and σ^2_u based on the original sample $\mathcal{W}_T = \{(X_1, Y_1), \cdots, (X_T, Y_T)\}$, which acts in the resampling as a fixed design, and $\{u^*_t\}$ is generated independently by an existing parametric or nonparametric bootstrap method such that $E[u^*_t] = 0$, $E[u^{*2}_t] = 1$ and $E[u^{*4}_t] < \infty$.

(ii) Use the data set $\{(X_t, Y^*_t) : t = 1, 2, \ldots, T\}$ to re-estimate β, θ_0 and σ_u. Denote the resulting estimators by $\hat{\beta}^*$, $\hat{\theta}^*_0$ and $\hat{\sigma}^*_u$. Compute $\hat{L}^*_T(h)$ that is the corresponding version of $\hat{L}_T(h)$ by replacing $\{(X_t, Y_t) : t = 1, 2, \cdots, T\}$ and $\hat{\beta}$, $\hat{\theta}_0$ and $\hat{\sigma}_u$ with $\{(X_t, Y^*_t) : t = 1, 2, \cdots, T\}$ and $\hat{\beta}^*$, $\hat{\theta}^*_0$ and $\hat{\sigma}^*_u$. That is

$$\hat{L}^*_T = \hat{L}^*_T(h) = \frac{\sum_{t=1}^T \sum_{s=1,\neq t}^T \hat{u}^*_s K_h(\hat{v}^*_{s-1} - \hat{v}^*_{t-1}) \hat{u}^*_t}{\sqrt{2 \sum_{t=1}^T \sum_{s=1,\neq t}^T \hat{u}^{*2}_s K^2_h(\hat{v}^*_{s-1} - \hat{v}^*_{t-1}) \hat{u}^{*2}_t}} \tag{16}$$

where $\hat{u}^*_t = \hat{v}^*_t - f_0(\hat{v}^*_{t-1}, \hat{\theta}^*_0)$, in which $\hat{v}^*_t = Y^*_t - X^\tau_t \hat{\beta}^*$. The number of replications in the simulation scheme is denoted by *NS*.

(iii) Repeat the above steps M times and produce M versions of $\hat{L}^*_T(h)$ denoted by $\hat{L}^*_{Tm}(h)$ for $m = 1, 2, \ldots, M$. Use the M versions of $\hat{L}^*_{Tm}(h)$ to construct their empirical bootstrap distribution function. The bootstrap distribution of $\hat{L}^*_T(h)$ given the full sample $\mathcal{W}_T$ is defined by $P^*(\hat{L}^*_T(h) \leq x) = P(\hat{L}^*_T(h) \leq x | \mathcal{W}_T)$. Let $l^*_\alpha(h)$ satisfy $P^*(\hat{L}^*_T(h) \geq l^*_\alpha(h)) = \alpha$ and then estimate $l_\alpha(h)$ by $l^*_\alpha(h)$.

Define the size and power functions by

$$\alpha^*(h) = P^*(\hat{L}_T(h) \geq l^*_\alpha(h) | \mathcal{H}_0) \quad \text{and} \quad \beta^*(h) = P^*(\hat{L}_T(h) \geq l^*_\alpha(h) | \mathcal{H}_1) \tag{17}$$

The objective is to choose an optimal bandwidth, $\hat{h}_{test}$, such that the power function $\beta^*(h)$ is maximized at $h = \hat{h}_{test}$ while the size function $\alpha^*(h)$ is under control.

Let $H_T = \{h : \alpha - \varepsilon_0 < \alpha^*(h) < \alpha + \varepsilon_0\}$ for some $0 < \varepsilon_0 < \alpha$. Choose an optimal bandwidth $\hat{h}_{test}$ such that

$$\hat{h}_{test} = \arg \max_{h \in H_T} \beta^*(h) \tag{18}$$

Since $\{v_t\}$ under $\mathcal{H}_1$ is stationary, existing results (Eq. (46) of Gao & Gijbels, 2008) suggest using an approximate version of the form

$$\hat{h}_{test} = \hat{a}^{-\frac{1}{2}}\hat{C}_T^2 \tag{19}$$

where $\hat{C}_T^2 = \frac{\sum_{t=1}^T (\hat{f}_1(\hat{v}_{t-1},\hat{\theta}_1) - f_0(\hat{v}_{t-1},\hat{\theta}_0))^2 \hat{p}(\hat{v}_{t-1})}{\hat{\mu}_2 \sqrt{2\hat{v}_2 \int K^2(v)dv}}$ and $\hat{a} = \frac{\sqrt{2}K^{(3)}(0)}{3\left(\sqrt{\int K^2(u)du}\right)^3} \hat{c}(p)$, in which $\hat{c}(p) = \frac{\frac{1}{T}\sum_{t=1}^T \hat{p}^2(\hat{v}_{t-1})}{\left(\sqrt{\frac{1}{T}\sum_{t=1}^T \hat{p}(\hat{v}_{t-1})}\right)^3}$, $\hat{\mu}_2 = \frac{1}{T}\sum_{t=1}^T (\hat{v}_t - f_0(\hat{v}_{t-1},\hat{\theta}_0))^2$, $\hat{v}_2 = \frac{1}{T}\sum_{t=1}^T \times \hat{p}^2(\hat{v}_{t-1})$, $\hat{f}_1(v,\hat{\theta}_1)$ is a consistent estimate of $f_1(v,\theta_1)$, $\hat{p}(v) = \frac{1}{T\hat{h}_{cv}} \times \sum_{t=1}^T K\left(\frac{\hat{v}_{t-1} - v}{\hat{h}_{cv}}\right)$ with $\hat{h}_{cv}$ being chosen by a conventional cross-validation selection method, and $K^{(3)}(\cdot)$ is the three-time convolution of $K(\cdot)$ with itself.

We then use $l_\alpha^*(\hat{h}_{test})$ in the computation of both the size and power values of $\hat{L}_T(\hat{h}_{test})$ for each case. Note that the above simulation is based on the so-called regression bootstrap simulation procedure discussed in the literature, such as Chen and Gao (2007). We may also use a block bootstrap (see, e.g., Pararoditis & Politis, 2003) to generate a sequence of resamples for $\{u_t^*\}$. Since the combination of the proposed simulation procedure with the power-based bandwidth selection method works well in this paper, we use the proposed bootstrap method for both theoretical studies and practical applications.

Under $\mathcal{H}_1$, model (3) becomes

$$Y_t = X_t^\tau \beta + v_t \quad \text{with} \quad v_t = f_1(v_{t-1},\theta_1) + u_t \tag{20}$$

where $f_1(v,\theta_1)$ can be consistently estimated by $\hat{f}_1(v,\hat{\theta}_1)$, which depends on the specification of $f_1(v,\theta_1)$. For example, when $f_1(v,\theta_1) = g_1(v,\theta_1) + \psi(v)$ with $g_1(v,\theta_1)$ being parametric and $\psi(v)$ being nonparametric, the form of $\hat{f}_1(v,\hat{\theta}_1)$ can be given by

$$\hat{f}_1(v,\hat{\theta}_1) = g_1(v,\hat{\theta}_1) + \hat{\psi}(v) \tag{21}$$

in which

$$\hat{\psi}(v) = \hat{\psi}(v, \theta_1) = \frac{\sum_{s=1}^{T} K_{\hat{h}_{cv}}(\hat{v}_{s-1} - v)(\hat{v}_s - g_1(\hat{v}_{s-1}, \theta_1))}{\sum_{s=1}^{T} K_{\hat{h}_{cv}}(\hat{v}_{s-1} - v)} \quad \text{and} \tag{22}$$

$$\hat{\theta}_1 = \arg\min_{\theta_1} \frac{1}{T} \sum_{t=1}^{T} (\hat{v}_t - g_1(\hat{v}_{t-1}, \theta_1) - \hat{\psi}(\hat{v}_{t-1}, \theta_1))^2 \tag{23}$$

where $\hat{h}_{cv}$ is chosen by a conventional cross-validation selection method.

To study the power properties of $\hat{L}_T(\hat{h}_{test})$, we need to impose certain conditions on $f_1(v, \theta)$ under $\mathcal{H}_1$. Since we are only interested in testing nonstationarity versus stationarity for Case A and stationarity versus stationarity for Case B, assumptions under $\mathcal{H}_1$ are more verifiable than those conditions for the nonstationarity case.

In addition to Assumptions 1 and 2, we need the following assumption.

Assumption 3. (i) Let Assumption 2 hold under $\mathcal{H}_1$.

(ii) Let $\mathcal{H}_1$ be true. Then there are θ_0 and θ_1 such that

$$\int [f_1(v, \theta_1) - f_0(v, \theta_0)]^2 \pi_1^2(v) dv > 0$$

where $\pi_1(v)$ denotes the marginal density of $\{v_t\}$ under $\mathcal{H}_1$.

Assumption 3(i) is a set of quite general conditions and also standard in this kind of stationary case, as assumed in the literature (see, e.g., Li, 1999). Assumption 3(ii) assumes that there is some significant 'distance' between $\mathcal{H}_0$ and $\mathcal{H}_1$ in order for the test to have power. It is obvious that there are various ways of choosing the forms of $f_i(v, \theta_i)$ for $i = 0, 1$. For example, we may consider testing an AR(1) error model against a nonlinear error model of the form (Granger, Inoue, & Morin, 1997; Gao, 2007; Granger & Teräsvirta, 1993; Tong, 1990)

$$\mathcal{H}_0 : v_t = \rho_0 v_{t-1} + u_t \quad \text{versus} \quad \mathcal{H}_1 : v_t = \rho_1 v_{t-1} - \frac{v_{t-1}}{1 + v_{t-1}^2} + u_t \tag{24}$$

where $\{u_t\}$ is a sequence of i.i.d. normal errors with $E[u_t] = 0$ and $E[u_t^2] = \sigma_u^2 < \infty$, and $|\rho_0| \leq 1$ and $|\rho_1| < 1$ are suitable parameters. It is noted that $\{v_t\}$ under $\mathcal{H}_0$ is stationary when $|\rho_0| < 1$ and nonstationary when $\rho_0 = 1$. Assumption 2 implies that $\{v_t\}$ under $\mathcal{H}_1$ is stationary. In this case, Assumption 3(ii) becomes

$$\int [f_1(v,\theta_1)-f_0(v,\theta_0)]^2\pi_1^2(v)\mathrm{d}v=\int \left(2(\rho_0-\rho_1)+\frac{1}{1+v^2}\right)\frac{v^2}{1+v^2}\pi_1^2(v)\mathrm{d}v + \int (\rho_1-\rho_0)^2 v^2\pi_1^2(v)\mathrm{d}v>0 \tag{25}$$

when ρ_1 is chosen such that $\rho_1 \leq \rho_0$. This implies that Assumption 3(ii) is verifiable.

We state the following theorem; its proof is given in Appendix A.

Theorem 2. (i) Assume that either Assumptions 1 and A.1–A.3 for Case A or Assumptions 2 and A.1–A.5(i) for Case B hold. Then under $\mathcal{H}_0$

$$\lim_{T\to\infty} P(\hat{L}_T(h)>l_\alpha^*|\mathcal{W}_T)=\alpha \text{ in probability}$$

(ii) Assume that either Assumptions 1, 3 and A.1–A.3 for Case A or Assumptions 2, 3 and A.1–A.5 for Case B hold. Then under $\mathcal{H}_1$

$$\lim_{T\to\infty} P(\hat{L}_T(h)>l_\alpha^*|\mathcal{W}_T)=1 \text{ in probability}$$

Theorem 2(i) implies that l_α^* is an asymptotically correct α-level critical value under any model in $\mathcal{H}_0$, while Theorem 2(ii) shows that $\hat{L}_T(h)$ is asymptotically consistent.

4. EXAMPLES OF IMPLEMENTATION

Example 1 compares the small- and medium-sample performance of our test with two natural competitors using a simulated example. A real-data application is then given in Example 2.

Example 1. Consider a nonlinear trend model of the form

$$Y_t=X_t\beta+v_t \quad \text{with} \quad v_t=f_i(v_{t-1},\theta_i)+u_t, \quad 1\leq t\leq T \tag{26}$$

where $X_t=\sin\left(\frac{2\pi t}{T}\right)$, $\{u_t\}$ is a sequence of i.i.d. N(0,1), and the forms of $f_i(v,\theta_i)$ for $i=0,1$ are given as follows:

$$f_0(v,\theta_0)=v \quad \text{and} \quad f_1(v,\theta_1)=v+\theta_1 v \quad \text{for Case } A, \text{ or} \tag{27}$$

$$f_0(v,\theta_0)=v \quad \text{and} \quad f_1(v,\theta_1)=v+\theta_1 v+\frac{\theta_1 v}{1+v^2} \quad \text{for Case } A, \text{ or} \tag{28}$$

$$f_0(v,\theta_0)=0 \quad \text{and} \quad f_1(v,\theta_1)=\theta_1 v \quad \text{for Case } B, \text{ or} \tag{29}$$

$$f_0(v,\theta_0)=0.5v \quad \text{and} \quad f_1(v,\theta_1)=0.5v+\theta_1 v+\frac{\theta_1 v}{1+v^2} \quad \text{for Case B} \tag{30}$$

where $\rho_0=1$ for models (27) and (28), $\rho_0=0$ for model (29) and $\rho_0=0.5$ for model (30), $\theta_1=-\sqrt{T^{-1}\log(\log(T))}$ and $\rho_1=\rho_0+\theta_1$. The rate of θ_1 is chosen because it is an optimal rate of testing in this kind of nonparametric kernel testing problem as discussed in Chapter 3 of Gao (2007). The β parameter is estimated by the conventional semiparametric least squares estimation method (see, e.g., Hidalgo, 1992). Eqs. (21)–(23) are used in the estimation of θ_1. We choose $K(x)=\frac{1}{2}I_{[-1,1]}(x)$ and $\varepsilon_0=\frac{\alpha}{10}$ involved in Eq. (18) throughout this section.

To compute the size of $\hat{L}_T(h)$ under $\mathcal{H}_0$ and the power of $\hat{L}_T(h)$ under $\mathcal{H}_1$ for Eqs. (27)–(30), we first propose using $\hat{L}_T(h)$ associated with $\hat{h}_{test}$ of (18). Let

$$L_{1test}=\hat{L}_T(\hat{h}_{test}) \tag{31}$$

For models (27) and (28), we compare our test with the conventional DF (Dickey & Fuller, 1979) test of the form

$$L_{21}=\frac{\sum_{t=2}^{T}(\hat{v}_t-\hat{v}_{t-1})\hat{v}_{t-1}}{\hat{\sigma}_{22}\sqrt{\sum_{t=2}^{T}\hat{v}_{t-1}^2}} \tag{32}$$

where $\hat{\sigma}_{22}^2=\frac{1}{T-1}\sum_{t=2}^{T}(\hat{v}_t-\hat{\rho}_0\hat{v}_{t-1})^2$ with $\hat{\rho}_0=\sum_{t=2}^{T}\hat{v}_t\hat{v}_{t-1}/\sum_{t=2}^{T}\hat{v}_{t-1}^2$.

For models (29) and (30), we also compare our test with the DK test (Dufour & King, 1991) of the form

$$L_{22}=\frac{\sum_{t=1}^{T}\sum_{s=1}^{T}\hat{v}_s\,a_{st}\,\hat{v}_t}{\sum_{t=1}^{T}\sum_{s=1}^{T}\hat{v}_s\,b_{st}\,\hat{v}_t} \tag{33}$$

where $\{a_{st}\}$ is the (s,t)-th element of A_0 given by $A_0 = -2(1-\rho_0) I_T + A_1 - 2\rho_0 C_1$ with I_T being the $T \times T$ identity matrix, A_1 and C_1 being given in Eqs. (6) and (7) of Dufour and King (1991, p. 120), and $\{b_{st}\}$ is the (s,t)-th element of Σ_0^{-1}, in which $\Sigma_0 = \Sigma(\rho_0)$ with $\Sigma(\rho)$ being given above (G1) of Dufour and King (1991, p. 118).

For $i=1,2$, let $l^*_{2i,\alpha}$ be the corresponding simulated critical value of L_{2i}. Each of them is computed in the same way as has been proposed in the Simulation Scheme in Section 3. Let z_α be the $1-\alpha$ quantile of the standard Normal distribution. Note that $z_{0.05} = 1.645$ at the $\alpha = 5\%$ level and $z_{0.10} = 1.285$ at the $\alpha = 10\%$ level.

Let $l^*_{1,\alpha} = l^*_\alpha(h_{test})$ and $L_{1cv} = \hat{L}_T(\hat{h}_{cv})$, where $\hat{h}_{cv}$ is chosen such that

$$\hat{h}_{cv} = \arg\min_{h \in H_{cv}} \frac{1}{T} \sum_{t=1}^{T} (\hat{v}_t - \hat{g}_{-t}(\hat{v}_{t-1}, h))^2 \tag{34}$$

in which $\hat{g}_{-t}(\hat{v}_{t-1}, h) = \frac{\sum_{s=1,\neq t}^{T} K\left(\frac{\hat{v}_{s-1} - \hat{v}_{t-1}}{h}\right)\hat{v}_s}{\sum_{u=1,\neq t}^{T} K\left(\frac{\hat{v}_{u-1} - \hat{v}_{t-1}}{h}\right)}$ and $H_{cv} = [T^{-1}, T^{-(1-\delta_0)}]$, where $0 < \delta_0 < 1$ is chosen such that $\hat{h}_{cv}$ is achievable and unique in each individual case.

We choose $NS = 250$ in the Simulation Scheme and use $M = 1000$ replications to compute the two-sized power and size values of the tests in Tables 1–4. Let f_{test} denote the frequency of $L_{1test} > l^*_{1,\alpha}$, f_{cv} be the frequency of $L_{1cv} > z_\alpha$, and f_{2i} be the frequency of $L_{2i} > l^*_{2i,\alpha}$ for $i=1,2$ and at $\alpha = 5\%$ or 10%.

Table 1. Sizes and Power Values for Models (27) and (28) at the $\alpha = 5\%$ Significance Level.

Observation	Model (27)			Model (28)		
		Null Hypothesis Is True				
T	f_{cv}	f_{test}	f_{21}	f_{cv}	f_{test}	f_{21}
250	0.007	0.045	0.046	0.005	0.048	0.058
500	0.003	0.042	0.051	0.006	0.054	0.049
750	0.005	0.053	0.057	0.003	0.044	0.052
		Null Hypothesis Is False				
T	f_{cv}	f_{test}	f_{21}	f_{cv}	f_{test}	f_{21}
250	0.171	0.302	0.701	0.462	0.521	0.350
500	0.180	0.345	0.734	0.456	0.554	0.376
750	0.192	0.329	0.752	0.474	0.573	0.402

Table 2. Sizes and Power Values for Models (27) and (28) at the $\alpha = 10\%$ Significance Level.

Observation	Model (27)			Model (28)		
		Null Hypothesis Is True				
T	f_{cv}	f_{test}	f_{21}	f_{cv}	f_{test}	f_{21}
250	0.023	0.088	0.107	0.019	0.094	0.096
500	0.038	0.092	0.098	0.035	0.103	0.109
750	0.029	0.103	0.102	0.037	0.089	0.094
		Null Hypothesis Is False				
T	f_{cv}	f_{test}	f_{21}	f_{cv}	f_{test}	f_{21}
250	0.201	0.432	0.821	0.536	0.631	0.473
500	0.199	0.469	0.847	0.547	0.655	0.489
750	0.234	0.487	0.862	0.561	0.649	0.512

Table 3. Sizes and Power Values for Models (29) and (30) at the $\alpha = 5\%$ Significance Level.

Observation	Model (29)			Model (30)		
		Null Hypothesis Is True				
T	f_{cv}	f_{test}	f_{22}	f_{cv}	f_{test}	f_{22}
250	0.005	0.052	0.049	0.003	0.051	0.048
500	0.004	0.048	0.050	0.007	0.047	0.054
750	0.007	0.051	0.047	0.006	0.052	0.051
		Null Hypothesis Is False				
T	f_{cv}	f_{test}	f_{22}	f_{cv}	f_{test}	f_{22}
250	0.112	0.164	0.348	0.349	0.423	0.312
500	0.107	0.182	0.387	0.361	0.456	0.331
750	0.132	0.191	0.372	0.358	0.481	0.342

Table 4. Sizes and Power Values for Models (29) and (30) at the $\alpha = 10\%$ Significance Level.

Observation	Model (29)			Model (30)		
		Null Hypothesis Is True				
T	f_{cv}	f_{test}	f_{22}	f_{cv}	f_{test}	f_{22}
250	0.031	0.110	0.097	0.023	0.089	0.101
500	0.040	0.097	0.102	0.038	0.101	0.097
750	0.033	0.103	0.096	0.033	0.098	0.095
		Null Hypothesis Is False				
T	f_{cv}	f_{test}	f_{22}	f_{cv}	f_{test}	f_{22}
250	0.197	0.271	0.411	0.452	0.552	0.419
500	0.204	0.267	0.431	0.489	0.581	0.441
750	0.226	0.283	0.456	0.516	0.614	0.476

Tables 1 and 2 (columns 2–3 and 5–6) show that the test coupled with a bootstrap critical value (BCV) is more powerful than that associated with the use of an asymptotic critical value (ACV) in each case, in addition to the fact that there is serious size distortion when using ACV rather than BCV. The main reasons are as follows: (a) the rate of convergence of each $\hat{L}_T(h)$ to an asymptotic normal distribution is quite slow in this kind of nonparametric setting, and (b) the use of an optimal bandwidth based on the cross-validation selection criterion may not be optimal for testing purposes. By contrast, there is only small size distortion between using BCV and ACV for L_{21} and L_{22} in each implementation, although the version of the test associated with BCV has more stable size performance and better power property than that based on ACV. We therefore compare our nonparametric tests with both L_{21} and L_{22} based on a BCV in each case.

Moreover, Tables 1 and 2 show that the proposed test is less powerful than the conventional DF test when the true model (27) is linear. When the true model (28) is nonlinear, however, the DF test is still applicable but is less powerful than the proposed test. Tables 3 and 4 also show that the proposed test is more powerful than the DK test when the true model (30) is nonlinear. When the true model (29) is linear, the DK test is more powerful than the proposed test. In summary, Tables 1–4 show that the proposed test is more powerful in the nonlinear case while the sizes are comparable with the two competitors for the parametric linear case. This supports that the proposed test, which is dedicated to the nonlinear case, is needed to deal with testing stationarity in nonlinear time series models.

Example 2. This example examines the seven-day Eurodollar deposit spot rate data given in Fig. 1 sampled daily over the period from June 1, 1973 to February 25, 1995, providing 5,505 observations.

Let $\{Y_t : t = 1, 2, \cdots, 5505$ be the set of the seven-day Eurodollar deposit spot rate data. The data set has been studied extensively in the literature. Recent studies (see, e.g., Bandi, 2002) are concerned with whether $\{Y_t\}$ follows a random walk model of the form

$$Y_t = \mu_0 + \mu_1 t + Y_{t-1} + u_t \tag{35}$$

where $\{u_t\}$ is a sequence of strictly stationary errors.

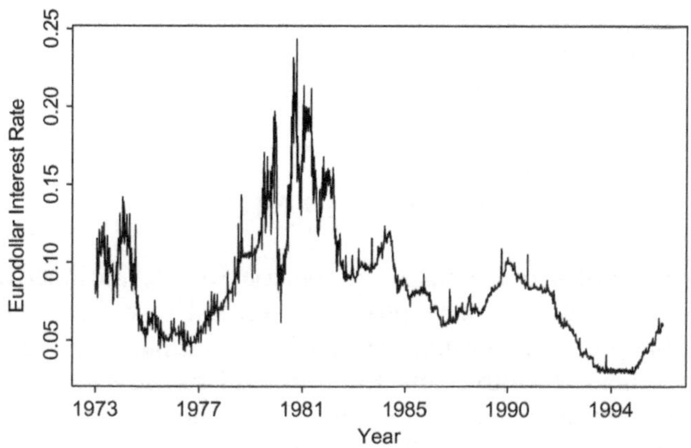

Fig. 1. Plot of the Seven–Day Eurodollar Deposit Spot Rate Data.

We consider a special form of Eq. (3) with $X_t^\tau\beta = \beta_0 + \beta_1 t + \beta_2 t^2$. In this case, in order to apply model (3) to test whether $\{Y_t\}$ follows (35), it suffices to test

$$\mathcal{H}_0 : v_t = v_{t-1} + u_t \quad \text{for} \quad Y_t = \beta_0 + \beta_1 t + \beta_2 t^2 + v_t \tag{36}$$

To apply the test $\hat{L}_T(\hat{h}_{test})$ to determine whether $\{Y_t\}$ follows a random walk model of the form $Y_t = \mu_0 + \mu_1 t + Y_{t-1} + u_t$, we need to propose the following procedure for computing the p-value of $\hat{L}_T(\hat{h}_{test})$:

- For the real data set, compute $\hat{h}_{test}$ and $\hat{L}_T(\hat{h}_{test})$.
- Let $Y_1^* = Y_1$. Generate $Y_t^* = Y_{t-1}^* + (X_t - X_{t-1})^\tau \hat{\beta} + u_t^*$ for $2 \leq t \leq 5505$, where $u_t^* = \hat{u}_t \eta_t$, in which $\hat{u}_t = Y_t - Y_{t-1} - (X_t - X_{t-1})^\tau \hat{\beta}$ and $\{\eta_t\}$ is chosen as a sequence of independent random variables with the following distributional structure: $P\left(\eta_1 = -\frac{\sqrt{5}-1}{2}\right) = \frac{\sqrt{5}+1}{2\sqrt{5}}$ and $P\left(\eta_1 = \frac{\sqrt{5}+1}{2}\right) = \frac{\sqrt{5}-1}{2\sqrt{5}}$. Such two-point distributional structure has been commonly used in the literature (see, e.g., Li & Wang, 1998).
- Compute the corresponding version $\hat{L}_T^*(\hat{h}_{test})$ based on $\{Y_t^*\}$.
- Repeat the above steps M times to find the bootstrap distribution of $\hat{L}_T^*(\hat{h}_{test})$ and then compute the proportion that $\hat{L}_T(\hat{h}_{test}) < \hat{L}_T^*(\hat{h}_{test})$. This proportion is an approximate p-value of $\hat{L}_T(\hat{h}_{test})$.

Our simulation results return the simulated p-values of $\hat{p}_1 = 0.007$ for L_{22} and $\hat{p}_2 = 0.013$ for $\hat{L}_T(\hat{h}_{test})$. While both of the simulated p-values suggest that there is no enough evidence of accepting the unit-root structure at the 5% significance level, there is some evidence of accepting the unit root structure based on $\hat{L}_T(\hat{h}_{test})$ at the 1% significance level. This supports the existing conclusions made in Bandi (2002).

5. CONCLUSION

We have proposed a new nonparametric test for the parametric specification of the residuals. An asymptotically normal distribution of the proposed test has been established. In addition, we have also proposed the Simulation Scheme to implement the proposed test in practice. The small- and medium-sample results show that both the proposed test and the Simulation Scheme are practically applicable and implementable.

This paper has focused on the case where $\{X_t\}$ is a vector of deterministic regressors. The case where $\{X_t\}$ is a vector of stochastic regressors is equally important. Discussion of such a case requires developing new theory and also involves more technicalities. It is therefore left for future research.

ACKNOWLEDGMENTS

The authors thank the editor, Professor Tom Fomby, and a referee for their constructive comments. The first author also acknowledges useful comments from the participants of the the Advances in Econometrics conference held at Southern Methodist University on November 1–3, 2013. Thanks also go to Dr. Jiying Yin for his excellent computing assistance and the Australian Research Council Discovery Grants under Grant Numbers DP0558602 and DP0879088 for the financial support.

REFERENCES

Bandi, F. (2002). Short-term interest rate dynamics: A spatial approach. *Journal of Financial Economics*, *65*, 73–110.

Chen, S. X., & Gao, J. (2007). An adaptive empirical likelihood test for parametric time series regression. *Journal of Econometrics*, *141*, 950–972.

Chen, J., Gao, J., & Li, D. (2012). Estimation in semiparametric regression with nonstationary regressors. *Bernoulli*, *18*, 678–702.

Dickey, D. A., & Fuller, W. A. (1979). Distribution of estimators for autoregressive time series with a unit root. *Journal of the American Statistical Association*, *74*, 427–431.

Dickey, D. A., & Fuller, W. A. (1981). Likelihood ratio statistics for autoregressive time series with a unit root. *Econometrica*, *49*, 1057–1072.

Dufour, J. M., & King, M. L. (1991). Optimal invariant tests for the autocorrelation coefficient in linear regressions with stationary or nonstationary AR(1) errors. *Journal of Econometrics*, *47*, 115–143.

Durbin, J., & Watson, G. S. (1950). Testing for serial correlation in least squares regression I. *Biometrika*, *37*, 409–428.

Durbin, J., & Watson, G. S. (1951). Testing for serial correlation in least squares regression II. *Biometrika*, *38*, 159–178.

Evans, G. B. A., & Savin, N. E. (1981). Testing for unit roots: I. *Econometrica*, *49*, 753–779.

Evans, G. B. A., & Savin, N. E. (1984). Testing for unit roots: II. *Econometrica*, *52*, 1241–1269.

Fan, Y., & Linton, O. (2003). Some higher–theory for a consistent nonparametric model specification test. *Journal of Statistical Planning and Inference*, *109*, 125–154.

Frölich, M. (2008). Parametric and nonparametric regression in the presence of endogenous control variables. *International Statistical Review*, *76*, 214–227.

Gao, J. (2007). *Nonlinear time series: Semiparametric and nonparametric methods*. London: Chapman & Hall.

Gao, J., & Gijbels, I. (2008). Bandwidth selection in nonparametric kernel testing. *Journal of the American Statistical Association*, *484*, 1584–1594.

Gao, J., & King, M. L. (2004). Adaptive testing in continuous–time diffusion models. *Econometric Theory*, *20*, 844–882.

Gao, J., King, M. L., Lu, Z., & Tjøstheim, D. (2006). *Specification testing in nonlinear time series with nonstationarity*. Working Paper. Retrieved from http://www.adelaide.edu.au/directory/jiti.gao

Gao, J., King, M. L., Lu, Z., & Tjøstheim, D. (2009a). Specification testing in nonstationary time series autoregression. *Annals of Statistics*, *37*, 3893–3928.

Gao, J., King, M. L., Lu, Z., & Tjøstheim, D. (2009b). Nonparametric specification testing for nonlinear time series with nonstationarity. *Econometric Theory*, *25*, 1869–1892.

Gao, J., Li, D., & Tjøstheim, D. (2009). *Uniform consistency for nonparametric estimators in null recurrent time series*. Working Paper. Retrieved from http://ideas.repec.org/p/adl/wpaper/2009-26.html

Gao, J., & Phillips, P. C. B. (2013). Semiparametric estimation in triangular system equations with nonstationarity. *Journal of Econometrics*, *176*, 59–79.

Granger, C. W. J., Inoue, T., & Morin, N. (1997). Nonlinear stochastic trends. *Journal of Econometrics*, *81*, 65–92.

Granger, C. W. J., & Teräsvirta, T. (1993). *Modelling nonlinear dynamic relationships*. London: Oxford University Press.

Hall, P., & Heyde, C. (1980). *Martingale limit theory and its applications*. New York, NY: Academic Press.

Hidalgo, F. J. (1992). Adaptive semiparametric estimation in the presence of autocorrelation of unknown form. *Journal of Time Series Analysis*, *13*, 47–78.

Kapetanios, G., Shin, Y., & Snell, A. (2003). Testing for a unit root in the nonlinear STAR framework. *Journal of Econometrics*, *112*, 359–379.

Karlsen, H., & Tjøstheim, D. (2001). Nonparametric estimation in null recurrent time series. *Annals of Statistics*, *29*, 372–416.

King, M. L. (1987). Testing for autocorrelation in linear regression models: A survey. In M. L. King & D. E. A. Giles (Eds.), *Specification analysis in the linear model* (pp. 19–73). London: Routledge and Kegan Paul.

King, M. L. (2001). Serial correlation. In B. H. Baltagi (Ed.), *A companion to theoretical econometrics* (pp. 62–81). London: Blackwell.

King, M. L., & Wu, X. (1997). Locally optimal one-sided tests for multiparameter hypotheses. *Econometric Reviews*, *16*, 131–156.

Koul, H. L., & Stute, W. (1999). Nonparametric model checks for time series. *Annals of Statistics*, *27*, 204–236.

Kwiatkowski, D., Phillips, P. C. B., Schmidt, P., & Shin, Y. (1992). Testing the null hypothesis of stationarity against the alternative of a unit root. *Journal of Econometrics*, *54*, 159–178.

Li, Q. (1999). Consistent model specification tests for time series econometric models. *Journal of Econometrics*, *92*, 101–147.

Li, Q., & Hsiao, C. (1998). Testing serial correlation in semiparametric panel data models. *Journal of Econometrics*, *87*, 207–237.

Li, Q., & Wang, S. (1998). A simple consistent bootstrap tests for a parametric regression functional form. *Journal of Econometrics*, *87*, 145–165.

Lobato, I., & Robinson, P. M. (1998). A nonparametric test for I(0). *Review of Economic Studies*, *65*, 475–495.

Lu, Z. (1998). On the geometric ergodicity of a nonlinear autoregressive model with an autoregressive conditional heteroscedastic term. *Statistica Sinica*, *8*, 1205–1217.

Meitz, M., & Saikkonen, P. (2008). Stability of nonlinear AR–GARCH models. *Journal of Time Series Analysis*, *29*, 453–475.

Paparoditis, E., & Politis, D. N. (2003). Residual–based block bootstrap for unit root testing. *Econometrica*, *71*, 813–856.

Phillips, P. C. B. (1987). Time series regression with a unit root. *Econometrica*, *55*, 277–302.

Phillips, P. C. B. (1997). Unit root tests. In S. Kotz (Ed.), *Encyclopedia of statistical sciences* (Vol. 1, pp. 531–542). Wiley Online Library.

Phillips, P. C. B., & Park, J. (1998). *Nonstationary density estimation and kernel autoregression*. Cowles Foundation Discussion Paper No. 1181, Yale University, New Haven, CT.

Phillips, P. C. B., & Perron, P. (1988). Testing for a unit root in time series regression. *Biometrika*, *75*, 335–346.

Phillips, P. C. B., & Xiao, Z. (1998). A primer on unit root testing. *Journal of Economic Surveys*, *12*, 423–469.

Robinson, P. M. (1983). Nonparametric estimators for time series. *Journal of Time Series Analysis*, *4*, 185–207.

Robinson, P. M. (2003). Efficient tests of nonstationary hypotheses (Vol. 1, pp. 526–543). *Recent developments in time series*. Elgar Reference Collection. Cheltenham, UK: International Library of Critical Writings in Econometrics.

Tong, H. (1990). *Nonlinear time series: A dynamical system approach*. Oxford: Oxford University Press.

Vogelsang, T. J. (1998). Trend function hypothesis testing in the presence of serial correlation. *Econometrica*, *66*, 123–148.

Wang, Q., & Phillips, P. C. B. (2009). Asymptotic theory for local time density estimation and nonparametric cointegrating regression. *Econometric Theory*, *25*, 710–738.

Zheng, J. X. (1996). A consistent test of functional form via nonparametric estimation techniques. *Journal of Econometrics*, *75*, 263–289.

Zheng, X., & Basher, R. E. (1999). Structural time series models and trend detection in global and regional temperature series. *Journal of Climate*, *12*, 2347–2358.

APPENDIX A

In this appendix, we introduce several technical conditions and then give some lemmas for the proofs of Theorems 1 and 2. Assumptions A.1–A.3 are imposed for Case A and Assumptions A.1–A.5 are needed for Case B. To avoid adding some non-essential technicalities, we assume the following initial values $Y_0^* = y_0^* = 0$ and $X_0 = x_0 = 0$, $v_0 = 0$ and $v_0^* = 0$ throughout this appendix.

A.1. ASSUMPTIONS

Assumption A.1. (i) Let $K(\cdot)$ be a symmetric probability density function with compact support $C(K)$. Let also the existence of $K^{(3)}(\cdot)$, the three-time convolution of $K(\cdot)$ with itself. In addition, there is some positive function $M(\cdot)$ such that

$$\left|K(x+y) - K(x)\right| \leq M(x)|y|$$

for all $x \in C(K)$ and any small y, where $M(\cdot) \geq 0$ is assumed to satisfy $\int M^2(u)du < \infty$.

(ii) For Case A, let h satisfy $\lim_{T\to\infty} T^{\frac{3}{10}} h = 0$ and $\limsup_{T\to\infty} T^{\frac{1}{2}-\varepsilon_0} h = \infty$ for any $0 < \varepsilon_0 < \frac{1}{5}$. Let h satisfy $\lim_{T\to\infty} h = 0$ and $\limsup_{T\to\infty} Th = \infty$ for Case B.

Assumption A.2. For $i = 1, 2$, let

$$\lim_{T\to\infty} \frac{h \sum_{t=2}^{T} \sum_{s=1}^{t-1} \frac{||Z_t||^i ||Z_s||^i}{\sqrt{t-s}}}{R_T^{2i} \lambda_T^i} = 0 \tag{A.1}$$

$$\lim_{T\to\infty} \frac{\sum_{t=2}^{T} \sum_{s=1}^{t-1} ||Z_t||^i \frac{||Z_{t-1} - Z_{s-1}||^i}{\sqrt{t-s}} ||Z_s||^i}{R_T^{3i} \lambda_T^i} = 0 \tag{A.2}$$

where $Z_t = X_t - X_{t-1}$ for Case A and $Z_t = X_t$ for Case B, $\lambda_T = T^{\frac{3}{4}}\sqrt{h}$, R_T is chosen such that Assumption A.3 holds, and $||\cdot||$ denotes the Euclidean norm.

Assumption A.3. (i) Let $\mathcal{H}_0$ be true. Then there are some $\hat{\beta}$ and $R_T \to \infty$ such that

$$\lim_{T\to\infty} P(R_T||\hat{\beta}-\beta||>B_0)<\varepsilon_0$$

for any $\varepsilon_0>0$ and some $B_0>0$.

(ii) Let $\mathcal{H}_0$ be true. There is an estimator $\hat{\beta}^*$ such that for some positive constants $B_0^*>0$ and ε_0^* the following inequality

$$\lim_{T\to\infty} P(R_T||\hat{\beta}^*-\hat{\beta}||>B_0^*|\mathcal{W}_T)<\varepsilon_0^*$$

holds with probability one with respect to the distribution of $\mathcal{W}_T$, where $R_T \to \infty$ is the same as in (i).

Assumption A.4. (i) Let $\mathcal{H}_0$ be true. Then there is an estimator $\hat{\theta}_0$ such that

$$\lim_{T\to\infty} P(\sqrt{T}||\hat{\theta}_0-\theta_0||>C_0)<\varepsilon_0$$

for any $\varepsilon_0>0$ and some $C_0>0$

(ii) Let $\pi_0(v)$ denote the marginal density of $\{v_t\}$ under $\mathcal{H}_0$ for Case B. Suppose that $\pi_0(v)$ is continuous and that $f_0(v,\theta)$ is differentiable in both v and θ. In addition

$$0<\int\left[\frac{\partial f_0(v,\theta_0)}{\partial v}\right]^2\pi_0^2(v)dv<\infty \quad \text{and} \quad 0<\int\left|\left|\frac{\partial f_0(v,\theta_0)}{\partial\theta}\right|\right|^2\pi_0^2(v)dv<\infty$$

Assumption A.5. (i) Let $\mathcal{H}_0$ be true. Then there is an estimator $\hat{\theta}_0^*$ such that for some positive constants $C_0^*>0$ and ε_0^* the following inequality

$$\lim_{T\to\infty} P(\sqrt{T}||\hat{\theta}_0^*-\hat{\theta}_0||>C_0^*|\mathcal{W}_T)<\varepsilon_0^*$$

holds with probability one with respect to the distribution of $\mathcal{W}_T$.

(ii) Let $\mathcal{H}_1$ be true. There exists an estimator $\hat{\theta}_1$ such that

$$\lim_{T\to\infty} P(\sqrt{T}||\hat{\theta}_1 - \theta_1|| > C_1) < \varepsilon_1$$

for any $\varepsilon_1 > 0$ and some $C_1 > 0$.

(iii) Let $\pi_1(v)$ denote the marginal density of $\{v_t\}$ under $\mathcal{H}_1$ for either Case A or Case B. Suppose that $\pi_1(v)$ is continuous and that $f_1(v, \theta)$ is differentiable in both v *and* θ. In addition

$$0 < \int \left[\frac{\partial f_1(v,\theta_1)}{\partial v}\right]^2 \pi_1^2(v)dv < \infty \quad \text{and} \quad 0 < \int \left\|\frac{\partial f_1(v,\theta_1)}{\partial \theta}\right\|^2 \pi_1^2(v)dv < \infty$$

Assumption A.1(i) is a mild condition and holds in many cases. For example, Assumption A.1(i) holds when $K(x) = \frac{1}{2}I_{[-1,1]}(x)$. While Assumption A.1(ii) imposes certain conditions, which may look more restrictive than those for the stationary case, they don't look unnatural in the nonstationary case. The corresponding conditions on the bandwidth for nonparametric testing in the stationary case are the same as the minimal conditions $\lim_{T\to\infty} h = 0$ and $\lim_{T\to\infty} Th = \infty$ that are assumed for nonparametric kernel testing for the case where both the regressors and errors are independent (see, e.g. Gao, 2007).

Assumption A.2 imposes some minimal conditions on the trend function such that polynomial trends are included. Considering the case where $X_t = t^2$ for Case A, we have for some $0 < C_1, C_2 < \infty$

$$\sum_{t=2}^{T}\sum_{s=1}^{t-1} |Z_t| \frac{1}{\sqrt{t-s}} |Z_s| \le C_1 \sum_{t=2}^{T}\sum_{s=1}^{t-1} \frac{st}{\sqrt{t-s}} = o\left(T^{\frac{7}{2}}\right)$$

$$R_T^2 = \sum_{t=1}^{T} Z_t^2 = C_2 T^3 \quad \text{and} \quad T^{\frac{3}{2}}(\hat{\beta} - \beta) \to_D N(0, \sigma_1^2)$$

where $Z_t = X_t - X_{t-1}$, $\hat{\beta} = \frac{\sum_{t=1}^{T} Z_t(Y_t - Y_{t-1})}{\sum_{t=1}^{T} Z_t^2}$ is the ordinary least squares estimator of β based on a model of the form $Y_t - Y_{t-1} = (X_t - X_{t-1})\beta + u_t$, and σ_1 is a positive constant.

In this case, Eqs. (A.1) and (A.2) become respectively

$$\frac{h\sum_{t=2}^{T}\sum_{s=1}^{t-1}\frac{|Z_t|\cdot|Z_s|}{\sqrt{t-s}}}{R_T^2\lambda_T}=O\left(\frac{T^{\frac{7}{2}}h}{T^{3+\frac{3}{4}}\sqrt{h}}\right)=O\left(\frac{\sqrt{h}}{T^{\frac{1}{4}}}\right)=o(1)$$

$$\frac{\sum_{t=2}^{T}\sum_{s=1}^{t-1}|Z_t|\frac{|Z_{t-1}-Z_{s-1}|}{\sqrt{t-s}}|Z_s|}{R_T^3\lambda_T}=O\left(\frac{T^{\frac{9}{2}}}{T^{\frac{9}{2}+\frac{3}{4}}\sqrt{h}}\right)=O\left(\frac{1}{T^{\frac{3}{4}}\sqrt{h}}\right)=o(1)$$

Similarly, in the case where $X_t=t^2$ for Case B, we have for some $0<D_1,D_2<\infty$

$$\sum_{t=2}^{T}\sum_{s=1}^{t-1}|X_t|\frac{1}{\sqrt{t-s}}|X_s|\leq D_1\sum_{t=2}^{T}\sum_{s=1}^{t-1}\frac{s^2t^2}{\sqrt{t-s}}=O\left(T^{\frac{11}{2}}\right)$$

$$R_T^2=\sum_{t=1}^{T}X_t^2=D_2T^5 \quad \text{and} \quad T^{\frac{5}{2}}(\hat{\beta}-\beta)\rightarrow_D N(0,\sigma_2^2) \tag{A.3}$$

where $\hat{\beta}=\frac{\sum_{t=1}^{T}X_tY_t}{\sum_{t=1}^{T}X_t^2}$ is the ordinary least squares estimator of β based on a model of the form $Y_t=X_t\beta+v_t$, and σ_2 is a positive constant.

In this case, Eqs. (A.1) and (A.2) become respectively

$$\frac{h\sum_{t=2}^{T}\sum_{s=1}^{t-1}\frac{|X_t|\cdot|X_s|}{\sqrt{t-s}}}{R_T^2\lambda_T}=O\left(\frac{T^{\frac{11}{2}}h}{T^{5+\frac{3}{4}}\sqrt{h}}\right)=O\left(\frac{\sqrt{h}}{T^{\frac{1}{4}}}\right)=o(1)$$

$$\frac{\sum_{t=2}^{T}\sum_{s=1}^{t-1}|X_t|\left|\frac{|X_{t-1}-X_{s-1}|}{\sqrt{t-s}}\right|X_s|}{R_T^3\lambda_T}=O\left(\frac{T^{\frac{15}{2}}}{T^{\frac{15}{2}+\frac{3}{4}}\sqrt{h}}\right)=O\left(\frac{1}{T^{\frac{3}{4}}\sqrt{h}}\right)=o(1)$$

Thus, Eqs. (A.1) and (A.2) hold for $i=1$. Similarly, we can show that the other cases for Eqs. (1) and (2) all hold. In addition, Assumption A.2 is satisfied automatically when the trend functions are all continuous and bounded.

Assumption A.3 requires that the conventional rate of convergence for the parametric case is achievable even when $\{v_t\}$ is nonstationary. When

$X_t = t^2$, it has been shown above that the rate of convergence of $\hat{\beta}$ to β is proportional to $T^{\frac{3}{2}}$ in Case A and $T^{\frac{5}{2}}$ in Case B.

Assumption A.4 imposes the differentiability conditions as well as the moment conditions on $f_0(\cdot, \cdot)$. As $\{v_t\}$ is strictly stationary, it is possible to verify Assumption A.4 in many cases. Assumption A.5(i) is the bootstrap version of Assumption A.4(i). Assumption A.5(ii)(iii) is a kind of corresponding version of Assumption A.4 under H_1. Note that Assumptions A.4(i) and A.5(i)(ii) may also be satisfied even when $\{u_t\}$ is correlated. In this case, an instrumental-variable method may be used to construct a consistent estimator (see, e.g., Frölich, 2008)

A.2. PROOF OF THEOREM 1 IN CASE A

Let $\sigma_u^2 = E[u_1^2] \equiv 1$ throughout the rest of this paper. To avoid notational complication, we introduce

$$a_{st} = K_h\left(\sum_{i=s}^{t-1} u_i\right) \quad \text{and} \quad \eta_t = 2\sum_{s=1}^{t-1} a_{st} u_s$$

Observe that

$$\begin{aligned}
\hat{M}_T &\equiv \sum_{t=1}^{T} \sum_{s=1,\neq t}^{T} \hat{u}_s K_h(\hat{v}_{s-1} - \hat{v}_{t-1})\hat{u}_t \\
&= \sum_{t=1}^{T} \sum_{s=1,\neq t}^{T} u_s K_h(v_{s-1} - v_{t-1})u_t + \sum_{t=1}^{T} \sum_{s=1,\neq t}^{T} \tilde{u}_s K_h(\hat{v}_{s-1} - \hat{v}_{t-1})\tilde{u}_t \\
&\quad + 2\sum_{t=1}^{T} \sum_{s=1,\neq t}^{T} u_s K_h(\hat{v}_{s-1} - \hat{v}_{t-1})\tilde{u}_t + M_{T4} \equiv M_{T1} + M_{T2} + M_{T3} + M_{T4}
\end{aligned} \tag{A.4}$$

$$\begin{aligned}
\hat{\sigma}_T^2 &\equiv 2\sum_{t=1}^{T} \sum_{s=1,\neq t}^{T} \hat{u}_s^2 K_h^2(\hat{v}_{s-1} - \hat{v}_{t-1})\hat{u}_t^2 \\
&= 2\sum_{t=1}^{T} \sum_{s=1,s\neq t}^{T} u_s^2 K_h^2(v_{s-1} - v_{t-1})u_t^2 + 2\sum_{t=1}^{T} \sum_{s=1,\neq t}^{T} \tilde{u}_s^2 K_h^2(\hat{v}_{s-1} - \hat{v}_{t-1})\tilde{u}_t^2 \qquad \text{(A.5)} \\
&\quad + 2\sum_{t=1}^{T} \sum_{s=1,\neq t}^{T} u_s^2 K_h^2(\hat{v}_{s-1} - \hat{v}_{t-1})\tilde{u}_t^2 + \tilde{\sigma}_{T4}^2 \equiv \tilde{\sigma}_{T1}^2 + \tilde{\sigma}_{T2}^2 + \tilde{\sigma}_{T3}^2 + \tilde{\sigma}_{T4}^2
\end{aligned}$$

where for Case A under $\mathcal{H}_0$: $v_t = v_{t-1} + u_t$,

$$\hat{u}_t = \hat{v}_t - \hat{v}_{t-1} = Y_t - X_t^\tau \hat{\beta} - (Y_{t-1} - X_{t-1}^\tau \hat{\beta})$$

$$= (X_t - X_{t-1})^\tau (\beta - \hat{\beta}) + v_t - v_{t-1}$$

$$= u_t + (X_t - X_{t-1})^\tau (\beta - \hat{\beta}) \equiv u_t + \tilde{u}_t$$

$$\tilde{u}_t = (X_t - X_{t-1})^\tau (\beta - \hat{\beta})$$

$$\hat{v}_{s-1} - \hat{v}_{t-1} = v_{s-1} - v_{t-1} + (X_{s-1} - X_{t-1})^\tau (\beta - \hat{\beta})$$

$$M_{T4} = \hat{M}_T - M_{T1} - M_{T2} - M_{T3}$$

$$\tilde{\sigma}_{T4}^2 = \hat{\sigma}_T^2 - \tilde{\sigma}_{T1}^2 - \tilde{\sigma}_{T2}^2 - \tilde{\sigma}_{T3}^2$$

In view of Eqs. (A.4) and (A.5), in order to prove Theorem 1 for Case A, it suffices to show that as $T \to \infty$

$$\frac{M_{T1}}{\tilde{\sigma}_{T1}} \to_D N(0,1) \tag{A.6}$$

$$\frac{M_{Ti}}{\tilde{\sigma}_{T1}} \to_P 0 \quad \text{for} \quad i = 2, 3, 4 \tag{A.7}$$

$$\frac{\tilde{\sigma}_{Tj}}{\tilde{\sigma}_{T1}} \to_P 0 \quad \text{for} \quad j = 2, 3, 4 \tag{A.8}$$

We will return to the proof of Eqs. (A.7) and (A.8) in Lemma A.5 after having proved Eq. (A.6) in Lemmas A.1–A.4. In order to prove Eq. (A.6), we need to apply Lemma B.1.

Before verifying the conditions of Lemma B.1, we introduce the following notation. Let $Y_{Tt} = \frac{\eta_t u_t}{\sigma_{T,1}}$, $\Omega_{T,s} = \sigma\{Y_{Tt}: 1 \le t \le s\}$ be a σ-field generated by $\{Y_{Tt}: 1 \le t \le s\}$, $\mathcal{G}_T = \Omega_{T,M(T)}$ and $\mathcal{G}_{T,s}$ be defined by

$$\mathcal{G}_{T,s} = \begin{cases} \Omega_{T,M(T)}, & 1 \le s \le M(T) \\ \Omega_{T,s}, & M(T)+1 \le s \le T \end{cases} \tag{A.9}$$

where $\sigma_{T,1}^2 = var[\sum_{t=2}^{T} \eta_t u_t]$ and $M(T)$ is chosen such that $M(T) \to \infty$ and $\frac{M(T)}{T} \to 0$ as $T \to \infty$. Let $\tilde{U}_{M(T)}^2 = \frac{\tilde{\sigma}_{M(T),1}^2}{\sigma_{M(T),1}^2}$, where $\sigma_{S,1}^2 = var[\sum_{t=2}^{S} \eta_t u_t]$ for all $1 \leq S \leq T$. We can show that as $T \to \infty$

$$\frac{\tilde{\sigma}_{T1}^2}{\sigma_{T1}^2} - \tilde{U}_{M(T)}^2 \to_P 0 \tag{A.10}$$

Thus, condition (B.2) of Lemma B.1 can be satisfied. The proof of Eq. (A.10) is given in Lemma A.4.

Therefore, in view of Lemma B.1, in order to prove that as $T \to \infty$

$$\frac{M_{T1}}{\tilde{\sigma}_{T1}} = \frac{1}{\tilde{\sigma}_{T1}} \sum_{t=2}^{T} \eta_t u_t \to_D N(0,1) \tag{A.11}$$

it suffices to show that there is an almost surely finite random variable ξ such that for all $\varepsilon > 0$

$$\sum_{t=2}^{T} E[Y_{Tt}^2 I_{\{[|Y_{Tt}| > \varepsilon]\}}(Y_{Tt}) | \Omega_{T,t-1}] \to_P 0 \tag{A.12}$$

$$\sum_{t=2}^{T} E[Y_{Tt}|\mathcal{G}_{T,t-1}] = \sum_{t=2}^{M(T)} Y_{Tt} + \sum_{t=M(T)+1}^{T} E[Y_{Tt}|\Omega_{T,t-1}] = \sum_{t=2}^{M(T)} Y_{Tt} \to_P 0 \tag{A.13}$$

$$\sum_{t=2}^{T} |E[Y_{Tt}|\mathcal{G}_{T,t-1}]|^2 = \sum_{t=2}^{M(T)} Y_{Tt}^2 + \sum_{t=M(T)+1}^{T} |E[Y_{Tt}|\Omega_{T,t-1}]|^2 = \sum_{t=2}^{M(T)} Y_{Tt}^2 \to {}_P 0 \tag{A.14}$$

$$\lim_{\delta \to 0} \lim \inf_{T \to \infty} P\left(\frac{\hat{\sigma}_{T1}}{\sigma_{T1}} > \varepsilon\right) = 1 \tag{A.15}$$

where $I_A(x)$ is the conventional indicator of the form $I_A(x) = 1$ when $x \in A$ and $I_A(x) = 0$ when $x \notin A$. The proof of Eq. (A.12) follows from

Lemma A.2. The proof of Eq. (A.13) is similar to that of Eq. (A.14), which follows from

$$\sum_{t=2}^{M(T)} E\left[Y_{Tt}^2\right] = O\left(\left(\frac{M(T)}{T}\right)^{\frac{3}{2}}\right) \to 0 \tag{A.16}$$

as $T \to \infty$, in which Lemma A.1 is used.

In order to prove Eq. (A.12), it suffices to show that

$$\frac{1}{\sigma_{T1}^4} \sum_{t=2}^{T} E\left[\eta_t^4\right] \to 0 \tag{A.17}$$

which is given in Lemma A.2.

The proof of Eq. (A.15) follows from

$$\frac{\tilde{\sigma}_{T1}^2}{\sigma_{T1}^2} \to_D \xi^2 > 0 \tag{A.18}$$

which is given in Lemma A.3.

Before we establish several lemmas for the proof of Theorem 1, we need to introduce the following notation.

For any $t > s \geq 1$ and $\alpha = \frac{1}{2}$, define $v_{st} = \frac{v_{t-1} - v_{s-1}}{C_\alpha (t-s)^\alpha}$, where $0 < C_\alpha < \infty$ is a normalized constant. We assume without loss of generality that $C_\alpha = 1$ in this appendix. Recall that $g(u)$ is the marginal density of the stationary time series $\{u_t\}$. Let $f_{st}(\cdot)$ be the density function of v_{st} and $g_{st}(\cdot)$ be the density function of $u_{st} = v_{t-1} - v_{s-1}$. Then, the i-th derivative of $g_{st}(v)$ satisfies for $i = 0, 1$

$$g_{st}^{(i)}(v) = \frac{1}{C_\alpha (t-s)^{(1+i)\alpha}} f_{st}^{(i)}\left(\frac{v}{(t-s)^\alpha}\right) \tag{A.19}$$

Similarly, let $f(\cdot|\mathcal{F}_s)$ and $g(\cdot|\mathcal{F}_s)$ be the conditional density functions of v_{st} and u_{st} given $\mathcal{F}_{s-1}$, where $\{\mathcal{F}_s\}$ is a sequence of σ-fields such that $\{v_s\}$ is adapted to $\mathcal{F}_s$. Then

$$g_{st}(v|\mathcal{F}_{s-1}) = \frac{1}{C_\alpha (t-s)^\alpha} f_{st}\left(\frac{v}{(t-s)^\alpha} |\mathcal{F}_{s-1}\right) \tag{A.20}$$

and the first derivatives of $g_{st}(\cdot|\mathcal{F}_{s-1})$ and $f_{st}(\cdot|\mathcal{F}_{s-1})$ satisfy

$$g_{st}^{(1)}(v|\mathcal{F}_{s-1}) = \frac{1}{C_\alpha (t-s)^{2\alpha}} f_{st}^{(1)}\left(\frac{v}{(t-s)^\alpha}|\mathcal{F}_{s-1}\right) \tag{A.21}$$

Assumption 1(ii) then implies the following useful results: as $t-s \to \infty$

$$\sup_{|x| \le \delta} |f_{st}^{(i)}(x)| = O(1) \tag{A.22}$$

$$\sup_{|x| \le \delta} |f_{st}^{(i)}(x|\mathcal{F}_{s-1})| = O_P(1) \tag{A.23}$$

for $i = 0, 1$, where $\delta > 0$ is some small constant. Eqs. (A.22) and (A.23) are used repeatedly in the proofs of Lemmas A.1–A.5.

Lemma A.1. Let Assumptions 1 and A.1 hold. Then for large enough T

$$\sigma_{T1}^2 = var\left[\sum_{t=2}^{T} \eta_t u_t\right] = \frac{16\int K^2(x)dx}{3\sqrt{2\pi}} T^{3/2} h\ (1 + o(1)) \tag{A.24}$$

Proof. It follows from the definition that

$$\begin{aligned}\sigma_{T1}^2 = E\left[\sum_{t=1}^{T} \eta_t u_t\right]^2 &= 2\sum_{t=1}^{T}\sum_{s=1}^{T} E[a_{st}^2 u_s^2 u_t^2] + 4\sum_{t=2}^{T}\sum_{s_1 \neq s_2 = 1}^{t-1} E[a_{s_1 t} a_{s_2 t} u_{s_1} u_{s_2} u_t^2] \\ &= 2\sigma_u^2 \sum_{t=1}^{T}\sum_{s=1}^{T} E[a_{st}^2 u_s^2] + R_{1T}\end{aligned} \tag{A.25}$$

where $R_{1T} = 4\sigma_u^2 \sum_{t=2}^{T} \sum_{s_1 \neq s_2 = 1}^{t-1} E[a_{s_1 t} a_{s_2 t} u_{s_1} u_{s_2}]$.

Let $w_{st} = \sum_{i=s+1}^{t-1} u_i$ and $g_{st}(\cdot,\cdot)$ be the joint density function of w_{st} and u_s. Assumption 1(ii) then implies

$$
\begin{aligned}
E[a_{st}^2u_s^2] &= \int\int K_h^2(w_{st}+u_s)u_s^2 g_{st}(u_{st},u_s)du_s du_{st} \\
&= \int\int K_h^2(u_{st}+u_s)u_s^2 g_{st}(w_{st}|u_s)f(u_s)du_s du_{st} \\
&= \frac{1}{(t-s-1)^\alpha}\int\int K_h^2(w_{st}+u_s)u_s^2 f_{st}\left(\frac{u_{st}}{(t-s-1)^\alpha}|u_s\right)g(u_s)du_s du_{st} \\
&= \frac{h}{(t-s-1)^\alpha}\int\int K^2(x_{st})x^2 f_{st}\left(\frac{x_{st}h}{(t-s-1)^\alpha}|u_s\right)g(x)dxdx_{st} \qquad \text{(A.26)}
\end{aligned}
$$

Choose $m_T \geq 1$ such that $m_T \to \infty$ and $\frac{m_T}{\sqrt{Th}} \to 0$ as $T \to \infty$. Observe that

$$
\sum_{t=2}^{T}\sum_{s=1}^{t-1} E[a_{st}^2u_s^2] = \sum_{s=1}^{T-1}\sum_{t=s+1}^{T} E[a_{st}^2u_s^2] = A_{1T} + A_{2T} \qquad \text{(A.27)}
$$

where $A_{1T} = \sum_{s=1}^{T-1}\sum_{1\leq(t-s)\leq m_T} E[a_{st}^2u_s^2] = O(Tm_T) = o(T^{3/2}h)$ using the fact that $E[a_{st}^2u_s^2] \leq k_0^2 E[u_s^2] = k_0^2$ due to the boundedness of the kernel $K(\cdot)$ by a constant $k_0 > 0$.

Using Assumption 1, it follows from (A.26) that

$$
\begin{aligned}
A_{2T} &= \sum_{s=1}^{T-1}\sum_{m_T+1\leq(t-s)\leq T-1} E[a_{st}^2u_s^2] \\
&= (1+o(1))C_0\sum_{s=1}^{T-1}\sum_{m_T+1\leq(t-s)\leq T-1}\frac{h}{(t-s-1)^\alpha}\int\int K^2(y)x^2 g(x)\mathrm{d}x\mathrm{d}y \\
&= \frac{4\sigma_u^2\int K^2(y)\mathrm{d}y}{3}C_0 T^{3/2}h(1+o(1)) \qquad \text{(A.28)}
\end{aligned}
$$

To deal with R_{1T}, we need to introduce the following notation: for $1 \leq i \leq 2$

$$Z_i = u_{s_i}, \quad Z_{11} = \sum_{i=s_1+1}^{t-1} u_i, \quad Z_{22} = \sum_{j=s_2+1}^{s_1-1} u_j \tag{A.29}$$

ignoring the notational involvement of s, t and others.

Let $g(x_{11}, x_1, x_{22}, x_2)$ be the joint density of $(Z_{11}, Z_1, Z_{22}, Z_2)$, $g_{11}(x_{11}|x_1, x_{22}, x_2)$ be the conditional density function of Z_{11} given (Z_1, Z_{22}, Z_2), $g(x_1|x_{22}, x_2)$ be the conditional density function of Z_1 given (Z_{22}, Z_2), and $g_{22}(x_{22}|x_2)$ be the conditional density function of Z_{22} given Z_2. Similar to Eq. (A.26), we have that for large enough T

$$\begin{aligned}
E[a_{s_1t}a_{s_2t}u_{s_1}u_{s_2}] &= E\left[K_h\left(\sum_{i=s_1}^{t-1} u_i\right)K_h\left(\sum_{j=s_2}^{t-1} u_j\right)u_{s_1}u_{s_2}\right] \\
&= E[Z_1Z_2K_h(Z_2+Z_{22})K_h(Z_1+Z_2+Z_{11}+Z_{22})] \\
&= \int\cdots\int x_1x_2K_h(x_1+x_2+x_{11}+x_{22})K_h(x_2+x_{22}) \\
&\quad \times g(x_{11},x_1,x_{22},x_2)\mathrm{d}x_1\mathrm{d}x_2\mathrm{d}x_{11}\mathrm{d}x_{22} \\
&= \int\cdots\int x_1x_2K_h(x_1+x_2+x_{11}+x_{22})K_h(x_2+x_{22}) \\
&\quad \times g_{11}(x_{11}|x_1,x_{22},x_2)g(x_1|x_{22},x_2)g_{22}(x_{22}|x_2)g(x_2)\mathrm{d}x_1\mathrm{d}x_2\mathrm{d}x_{11}\mathrm{d}x_{22} \\
&\quad \left(\text{using } y_{ii} = \frac{x_i+x_{ii}}{h}\right) \\
&= h^2\int\cdots\int K(y_{22})K(y_{11}+y_{22})x_1x_2 \\
&\quad \times g_{11}(y_{11}h-x_1|x_1,y_{22}h,x_2)g(x_1|hy_{22},x_2)g_{22}(hy_{22}-x_2|x_2)g(x_2) \\
&\quad \times \mathrm{d}x_1\mathrm{d}x_2\mathrm{d}y_{11}\mathrm{d}y_{22} \\
&\quad (\text{using Taylor expansions}) \\
&= h^2(1+o(1))\int\cdots\int K(y_{22})K(y_{11}+y_{22})x_1x_2 \\
&\quad \times g_{11}(-x_1|x_1,0,x_2)g(x_1|0,x_2)g_{22}(-x_2|x_2)g(x_2)\mathrm{d}x_1\mathrm{d}x_2\mathrm{d}y_{11}\mathrm{d}y_{22} \\
&\quad + h^4(1+o(1))\int\cdots\int K(y_{22})K(y_{11}+y_{22})x_1x_2 \\
&\quad \times g'_{11}(-x_1|x_1,0,x_2)g(x_1|0,x_2)g'_{22}(-x_2|x_2)g(x_2)\mathrm{d}x_1\mathrm{d}x_2\mathrm{d}y_{11}\mathrm{d}y_{22} \\
&= h^2(1+o(1))\int\cdots\int K(y_{22})K(y_{11}+y_{22})x_1x_2g(x_1|0,x_2)g(x_2) \\
&\quad \times \frac{1}{(t-s_1-1)^{\alpha}}\frac{1}{(s_1-s_2-1)^{\alpha}}f_{11}\left(\frac{-x_1}{(t-s_1-1)^{\alpha}}\middle| x_1,0,x_2\right)
\end{aligned}$$

$$
\begin{aligned}
&\times f_{22}\left(\frac{-x_2}{(s_1-s_2-1)^{\alpha}}\bigg|x_2\right)\mathrm{d}x_1\mathrm{d}x_2\mathrm{d}y_{11}\mathrm{d}y_{22}\\
&+h^4(1+o(1))\int\cdots\int y_{11}y_{22}K(y_{22})K(y_{11}+y_{22})x_1x_2g(x_1|0,x_2)g(x_2)\\
&\times\frac{1}{(t-s_1-1)^{2\alpha}}\frac{1}{(s_1-s_2-1)^{2\alpha}}f_{11}'\left(\frac{-x_1}{(t-s_1-1)^{\alpha}}\bigg|x_1,0,x_2\right)\\
&\times f_{22}'\left(\frac{-x_2}{(s_1-s_2-1)^{\alpha}}\bigg|x_2\right)\mathrm{d}x_1\mathrm{d}x_2\mathrm{d}y_{11}\mathrm{d}y_{22}
\end{aligned}
\tag{A.30}
$$

Thus, similar to Eqs. (A.27) and (A.28), we can show

$$
\begin{aligned}
&\sum_{t=2}^{T}\sum_{s_1\neq s_2=1}^{t-1}E[a_{s_1t}a_{s_2t}u_{s_1}u_{s_2}]\\
&=2\sum_{t=3}^{T}\sum_{s_1=2}^{t-1}\sum_{s_2=1}^{s_1-1}E[a_{s_1t}a_{s_2t}u_{s_1}u_{s_2}]\\
&=o(T^{3/2}h)+2C_0^2h^2(1+o(1))\sum_{t=3}^{T}\sum_{s_1=2}^{t-1}\sum_{s_2=1}^{s_1-1}\frac{1}{(t-s_1-1)^{\alpha}}\frac{1}{(s_1-s_2-1)^{\alpha}}\\
&\quad\times\int\cdots\int K(y_{22})K(y_{11}+y_{22})x_1x_2g(x_1|0,x_2)g(x_2)\mathrm{d}x_1\mathrm{d}x_2\mathrm{d}y_{11}\mathrm{d}y_{22}\\
&\quad+o(T^{3/2}h)+2h^4(1+o(1))\sum_{t=3}^{T}\sum_{s_1=2}^{t-1}\sum_{s_2=1}^{s_1-1}\frac{1}{(t-s_1-1)^{2\alpha}}\frac{1}{(s_1-s_2-1)^{2\alpha}}\\
&\quad\times\int\cdots\int y_{11}y_{22}K(y_{22})K(y_{11}+y_{22})x_1x_2g(x_1|0,x_2)g(x_2)\mathrm{d}x_1\mathrm{d}x_2\mathrm{d}y_{11}\mathrm{d}y_{22}\\
&=o(T^{3/2}h)
\end{aligned}
\tag{A.31}
$$

using Assumption 1.

Eqs. (A.27), (A.28) and (A.31) show that for large enough T

$$
\sigma_{T1}^2=\frac{16\int K^2(y)\mathrm{d}y}{3\sqrt{2\pi}}T^{3/2}h(1+o(1))
\tag{A.32}
$$

The proof of Lemma A.1 is therefore finished.

Lemma A.2. Let Assumptions 1 and A.1 hold. Then for large enough T

$$\lim_{T\to\infty}\frac{1}{\sigma_{T1}^4}\sum_{t=2}^{T}E\left[\eta_t^4\right]=0 \tag{A.33}$$

Proof. Observe that

$$E[\eta_t^4]=16\sum_{s_1=1}^{t-1}\sum_{s_2=1}^{t-1}\sum_{s_3=1}^{t-1}\sum_{s_4=1}^{t-1}E[a_{s_1t}a_{s_2t}a_{s_3t}a_{s_4t}u_{s_1}u_{s_2}u_{s_3}u_{s_4}] \tag{A.34}$$

We mainly consider the cases of $s_i\neq s_j$ for all $i\neq j$ in the following proof. Since the other terms involve at most triple summations, we may deal with such terms similarly. Without loss of generality, we only look at the case of $1\leq s_4<s_3<s_2<s_1\leq t-1$ in the following evaluation. Let

$$u_{s_1t}=u_{s_1}+\sum_{i=s_1+1}^{t-1}u_i,\quad u_{s_2t}=u_{s_1}+u_{s_2}+\sum_{i=s_2+1}^{s_1-1}u_i+\sum_{j=s_1+1}^{t-1}u_j$$

$$u_{s_3t}=u_{s_1}+u_{s_2}+u_{s_3}+\sum_{k=s_3+1}^{s_2-1}u_k+\sum_{i=s_2+1}^{s_1-1}u_i+\sum_{j=s_1+1}^{t-1}u_j$$

$$u_{s_4t}=u_{s_1}+u_{s_2}+u_{s_3}+u_{s_4}+\sum_{l=s_4+1}^{s_3-1}u_l+\sum_{k=s_3+1}^{s_2-1}u_k+\sum_{i=s_2+1}^{s_1-1}u_i+\sum_{j=s_1+1}^{t-1}u_j$$

Similar to (A.29), let again $Z_i=u_{s_i}$ for $1\leq i\leq 4$,

$$Z_{11}=\sum_{i=s_1+1}^{t-1}u_i,\quad Z_{22}=\sum_{j=s_2+1}^{s_1-1}u_j,\quad Z_{33}=\sum_{k=s_3+1}^{s_2-1}u_k,\quad Z_{44}=\sum_{l=s_4+1}^{s_3-1}u_l$$

Analogous to (A.30), we may have

$$\begin{aligned}E\left[\prod_{i=1}^{4}a_{s_it}u_{s_i}\right]&=E\left[\prod_{j=1}^{4}Z_jK_h\left(\sum_{i=1}^{j}[Z_i+Z_{ii}]\right)\right]\\&=\int\cdots\int g(x_{11},x_1,\cdots,x_{44},x_4)\\&\quad\times\prod_{j=1}^{4}\left(K_h\left(\sum_{i=1}^{j}[x_i+x_{ii}]\right)x_j\mathrm{d}x_{jj}\mathrm{d}x_j\right)\end{aligned}$$

$$= \int \cdots \int g_{11}(x_{11}|x_1, \cdots, x_{44}, x_4) g(x_1|x_{22}, \cdots, x_{44}, x_4)$$
$$\times g_{22}(x_{22}|x_2, \cdots, x_{44}, x_4) g(x_2|x_{33}, \cdots, x_{44}, x_4)$$
$$\times g_{33}(x_{33}|x_3, x_{44}, x_4) g(x_3|x_{44}, x_4) g_{44}(x_{44}|x_4) g(x_4)$$
$$\times \prod_{j=1}^{4} \left(K_h \left(\sum_{i=1}^{j} [x_i + x_{ii}] \right) x_j \mathrm{d}x_{jj} \mathrm{d}x_j \right)$$
$$\left(\text{using } y_{ii} = \frac{x_i + x_{ii}}{h} \text{ and } y_i = x_i\right)$$

$$\begin{aligned} &= h^4 \int \cdots \int g_{11}(y_{11}h - y_1|y_1, \cdots, hy_{44}, y_4) g(y_1|hy_{22}, \cdots, hy_{44}, y_4) \\ &\times g_{22}(hy_{22} - y_2|y_2, \cdots, hy_{44}, y_4) g(y_2|hy_{33}, \cdots, hy_{44}, y_4) \\ &\times g_{33}(hy_{33} - y_3|y_3, hy_{44}, y_4) g(y_3|hy_{44}, y_4) g_{44}(hy_{44} - y_4|y_4) g(y_4) \\ &\times \prod_{j=1}^{4} \left(K \left(\sum_{i=1}^{j} y_{ii} \right) y_j \mathrm{d}y_{jj} \mathrm{d}y_j \right) \\ &= h^4(1 + o(1)) \int \cdots \int g_{11}(-y_1|y_1, \cdots, 0, y_4) g(y_1|0, \cdots, 0, y_4) \\ &\times g_{22}(-y_2|y_2, \cdots, 0, y_4) g(y_2|0, \cdots, 0, y_4) \\ &\times g_{33}(-y_3|y_3, 0, y_4) g(y_3|0, y_4) g_{44}(-y_4|y_4) g(y_4) \\ &\times \prod_{j=1}^{4} \left(K \left(\sum_{i=1}^{j} y_{ii} \right) y_j dy_{jj} dy_j \right) \end{aligned} \tag{A.35}$$

where $C_{22}(K) \equiv \prod_{j=1}^{4} \int y_{jj} K\left(\sum_{i=1}^{j} y_{ii}\right) \mathrm{d}y_{jj} < \infty$ involved in Eq. (A.35).

Hence, similar to Eq. (A.31) we have by Assumption 1

$$\begin{aligned} &\sum_{t=2}^{T} \sum_{1 \le s_4 < s_3 < s_2 < s_1 \le t-1} E[a_{s_1 t} a_{s_2 t} a_{s_3 t} a_{s_4 t} u_{s_1} u_{s_2} u_{s_3} u_{s_4}] \\ &= O(h^4) \sum_{t=2}^{T} \sum_{1 \le s_4 < s_3 < s_2 < s_1 \le t-1} \frac{1}{\sqrt{t - s_1}} \frac{1}{\sqrt{s_1 - s_2}} \frac{1}{\sqrt{s_2 - s_3}} \frac{1}{\sqrt{s_3 - s_4}} \\ &= O(T^3 h^4) = o(T^3 h^2) \end{aligned} \tag{A.36}$$

Analogously, we can deal with the other terms of Eq. (A.34) as follows:

$$\sum_{t=2}^{T} \sum_{1 \le s_2 \ne s_1 \le t-1} E[a_{s_1 t}^2 a_{s_2 t}^2 u_{s_1}^2 u_{s_2}^2] = o(T^3 h^2) \tag{A.37}$$

$$\sum_{t=2}^{T} \sum_{1 \le s_3 \ne s_2 \ne s_1 \le t-1} E[a_{s_1 t}^2 a_{s_2 t} a_{s_3 t} u_{s_1}^2 u_{s_2} u_{s_3}] = o(T^3 h^2) \tag{A.38}$$

$$\sum_{t=2}^{T} \sum_{1 \le s_2 \ne s_1 \le t-1} E[a_{s_1 t}^3 a_{s_2 t} u_{s_1}^3 u_{s_2}] = o(T^3 h^2) \tag{A.39}$$

Thus, the proof of Eq. (A.33) is completed using Eqs. (A.34)–(A.39).

Lemma A.3. Let Assumptions 1 and A.1 hold. Then as $T \to \infty$

$$\frac{\tilde{\sigma}_{T1}^2}{\sigma_{T1}^2} \to_D \xi^2 > 0 \tag{A.40}$$

with $\xi^2 = \frac{\sqrt{\pi}}{2} M_{\frac{1}{2}}(1)$, where $M_{\frac{1}{2}}(\cdot)$ is a special case of the Mittag–Leffer process $M_\beta(\cdot)$ with $\beta = \frac{1}{2}$ as described by Karlsen and Tjøstheim (2001, p. 388).

Proof. To simplify the following proof, ignoring the higher-order term we rewrite

$$\sigma_{T1}^2 = \frac{16\sigma_u^4 J_{02}}{3\sqrt{2\pi}} T^{3/2} h \equiv C_{10} T^{3/2} h \tag{A.41}$$

Let $Q(u) = \frac{K^2(u)}{J_{02}}$ and $T(n)$ be the same as in Karlsen and Tjøstheim (2001). It then follows from Lemma B.2 that as $T \to \infty$

$$\max_{1 \le t \le T} \left| \frac{1}{T(n)h} \sum_{s=2}^{T} Q\left(\frac{v_{s-1} - v_{t-1}}{h}\right) - 1 \right| = o(1) \quad \text{almost surely} \tag{A.42}$$

Meanwhile, Theorem 3.2 of Karlsen and Tjøstheim (2001, p. 389) is applicable to the current case of $v_t = v_{t-1} + u_t$ under H_0 to show that as $T \to \infty$

$$\frac{T(n)}{L_0 \sqrt{T}} \to_D M_{\frac{1}{2}}(1) \tag{A.43}$$

when the slowly varying function in this case is $L_0 = \frac{2\sqrt{2}}{3}$.

Therefore, Eqs. (A.42) and (A.43) imply as $T \to \infty$

$$\begin{aligned}\frac{4}{\sigma_{T1}^2}\sum_{t=1}^{T}\left(\sum_{s=1}^{T}a_{st}^2\right)u_t^2 &= \frac{2}{TC_{10}}\sum_{t=1}^{T}u_t^2\left(\frac{1}{\sqrt{T}h}\sum_{s=1}^{T}a_{st}^2\right)\\ &= \frac{2L_0J_{02}}{C_{10}}\frac{T(n)}{L_0\sqrt{T}}\frac{1}{T}\sum_{t=1}^{T}u_t^2\left(\frac{1}{T(n)h}\sum_{s=1}^{T}Q\left(\frac{v_{s-1}-v_{t-1}}{h}\right)-1\right)\\ &+\frac{2L_0J_{02}}{C_{10}}\frac{T(n)}{L_0\sqrt{T}}\frac{1}{T}\sum_{t=1}^{T}u_t^2 \to_D \frac{2J_{02}L_0}{C_{10}}M_{\frac{1}{2}}(1) = \frac{\sqrt{\pi}}{2}M_{\frac{1}{2}}(1) \equiv \xi^2\end{aligned} \tag{A.44}$$

Therefore, Eq. (A.44) completes the proof of Lemma A.3.

Lemma A.4. Let Assumptions 1 and A.1 hold. Then as $T \to \infty$, $M(T) \to \infty$ and $\frac{M(T)}{T} \to 0$

$$\frac{\tilde{\sigma}_{T1}^2}{\sigma_{T1}^2} - \frac{\tilde{\sigma}_{M(T),1}^2}{\sigma_{M(T),1}^2} \to_P 0 \tag{A.45}$$

Proof. To simplify our proofs, we introduce the following lower case notation: $m=T$, $n=M(T)$, $\sigma_m^2=\sigma_{T1}^2$, $\sigma_n^2=\sigma_{M(T),1}^2$, and for $1 \le i \le n$, $1 \le j \le i-1$

$$e_{ij} = (u_i^2 - E[u_i^2])K_h^2\left(\sum_{l=j}^{i-1}u_l\right)u_j^2 \quad \text{and} \quad W_{mi} = \frac{1}{\sigma_m^2}\sum_{j=1}^{i-1}e_{ij} \tag{A.46}$$

$$w_i^2 = \sum_{j=1}^{i-1}K_h^2\left(\sum_{l=j}^{i-1}u_l\right)u_j^2 = \sum_{j=1}^{i-1}K_h^2\left(\sum_{l=j+1}^{i-1}u_l + u_j\right)u_j^2 \tag{A.47}$$

Note that $W_{mi} = \frac{1}{\sigma_m^2}(u_i^2 - E[u_1^2])w_i^2$.

Observe that

$$\frac{\tilde{\sigma}_{m1}^2}{\sigma_{m1}^2} - \frac{\tilde{\sigma}_{n1}^2}{\sigma_{n1}^2} = \sum_{i=1}^{m} W_{mi} - \sum_{j=1}^{n} W_{nj} + E\left[u_1^2\right]\left(\frac{1}{\sigma_m^2}\sum_{i=1}^{m} w_i^2 - \frac{1}{\sigma_n^2}\sum_{j=1}^{n} w_j^2\right)$$

$$\equiv I_{mn} + E[u_1^2]\ J_{mn} \tag{A.48}$$

In view of Eq. (A.47), in order to prove Eq. (A.45), it suffices to show that as $m,\quad n \to \infty$

$$I_{mn} \to_P 0 \quad \text{and} \quad J_{mn} \to_P 0 \tag{A.49}$$

We start by proving the second part of Eq. (A.49). Observe also that

$$E\left[J_{mn}^2\right] = E\left[\frac{1}{\sigma_m^2}\sum_{i=1}^{m} w_i^2 - \frac{1}{\sigma_n^2}\sum_{j=1}^{n} w_j^2\right]^2 = E\left[\frac{1}{\sigma_m^2}\sum_{i=n+1}^{m} w_i^2 + \frac{\sigma_n^2 - \sigma_m^2}{\sigma_m^2\sigma_n^2}\sum_{j=1}^{n} w_j^2\right]^2$$
$$= \frac{1}{\sigma_m^4}\sum_{i=n+1}^{m}\sum_{k=n+1}^{m} E\left[w_k^2 w_i^2\right] + \frac{(\sigma_n^2 - \sigma_m^2)^2}{\sigma_m^4\sigma_n^4}\sum_{j=1}^{n}\sum_{k=1}^{n} E\left[w_k^2 w_j^2\right]$$
$$- 2\frac{\sigma_m^2 - \sigma_n^2}{\sigma_m^4\sigma_n^2}\sum_{i=n+1}^{m}\sum_{j=1}^{n} E\left[w_i^2 w_j^2\right] \tag{A.50}$$

We first deal with the first term. Recalling $a_{ji} = K_h\left(\sum_{l=j}^{i-1} u_l\right)$, we have

$$E\left(\sum_{i=n+1}^{m} w_i^2\right)^2 = E\left[\sum_{i=n+1}^{m}\sum_{j=n+1}^{m} w_i^2 w_j^2\right] = \sum_{i=n+1}^{m} E[w_i^4] + \sum_{i=n+1}^{m}\sum_{j=n+1, \neq i}^{m} E[w_i^2 w_j^2] \tag{A.51}$$

We now evaluate the orders of $\sum_{i=n+1}^{m} E[w_i^4]$ and $\sum_{i=n+1}^{m} \sum_{j=n+1,\neq i}^{m} E[w_i^2\ w_j^2]$ respectively. To do so, we now consider one of the cases $1 \leq t \leq s-1; 2 \leq s \leq j-1; n+1 \leq j \leq i-1; n+2 \leq i \leq m$ for the following term:

$$E\left[\sum_{i=n+2}^{m}\sum_{j=n+1}^{i-1}\sum_{s=2}^{j-1}\sum_{t=1}^{s-1}a_{si}^2u_s^2a_{tj}^2u_t^2\right]$$
$$=\sum_{i=n+2}^{m}\sum_{j=n+1}^{i-1}\sum_{s=2}^{j-1}\sum_{t=1}^{s-1}E[a_{si}^2u_s^2a_{tj}^2u_t^2]$$
$$=\sum_{i=n+2}^{m}\sum_{j=n+1}^{i-1}\sum_{s=2}^{j-1}\sum_{t=1}^{s-1}E\times\left[K_h^2\left(\sum_{c=s+1}^{j-1}u_c+\sum_{c=j}^{i-1}u_c+u_s\right)u_s^2\right.$$
$$\left.\times K_h^2\left(\sum_{d=t+1}^{s-1}u_d+\sum_{d=s+1}^{j-1}u_d+u_s+u_t\right)u_t^2\right]$$

Other terms may be dealt with similarly. To simplify our calculation, we now introduce the following simplistic symbols:

$$Z_{11}=\sum\nolimits_{d=t+1}^{s-1}u_d,\, Z_{22}=\sum\nolimits_{c=s+1}^{j-1}u_c,\, Z_{33}=\sum\nolimits_{c=j}^{i-1}u_c,\, Z_1=u_t$$

and $Z_2=u_s$.

As in the proof of Lemma A.1, using the same techniques as in Eq. (A.35) we have

$$E\left[K_h^2\left(\sum_{i=1}^{2}(Z_i+Z_{ii})\right)K_h^2(Z_2+Z_{22}+Z_{33})Z_1^2Z_2^2\right]$$
$$=\int\cdots\int K_h^2\left(\sum_{i=1}^{2}(x_i+x_{ii})\right)K_h^2(x_2+x_{22}+x_{33})x_1^2x_2^2$$
$$\times g(x_{33},x_{22},x_2,x_{11},x_1)\mathrm{d}x_{33}\mathrm{d}x_{22}\mathrm{d}x_{11}\mathrm{d}x_1\mathrm{d}x_2$$
$$=\int\cdots\int K_h^2\left(\sum_{i=1}^{2}(x_i+x_{ii})\right)K_h^2(x_2+x_{22}+x_{33})x_1^2x_2^2$$
$$\times g_{33}(x_{33}|x_{22},x_2,x_{11},x_1)g_{22}(x_{22}|x_2,x_{11},x_1)g(x_2|x_{11},x_1)g_{11}(x_{11}|x_1)g(x_1)$$
$$\times \mathrm{d}x_{33}\mathrm{d}x_{22}\mathrm{d}x_{11}\mathrm{d}x_1\mathrm{d}x_2$$
$$\left(\text{using } y_i=x_i \text{ and } y_{ii}=\frac{x_i+x_{ii}}{h} \text{ for } i=1,2 \text{ and } y_{33}=\frac{x_{33}}{h}\right)$$

$$
\begin{aligned}
&= h^3 \int \cdots \int K^2(y_{11}+y_{22})K^2(y_{22}+y_{33})\ y_1^2 y_2^2 \\
&\quad \times g_{33}(y_{33}h|y_{22}h-y_2, y_2, y_{11}h-y_1, y_1) g_{22}(y_{22}h-y_2|y_2, y_{11}h-y_1, y_1) \\
&\quad \times g_{11}(y_{11}h-y_1|y_1) g(y_2|y_{11}h-y_1, y_1) g(y_1) dy_{33}dy_{22}dy_{11}dy_1dy_2 \\
&= h^3(1+o(1)) \int \cdots \int K^2(y_{11}+y_{22})K^2(y_{22}+y_{33}) y_1^2 y_2^2 \\
&\quad \times g_{33}(0|-y_2, y_2, -y_1, y_1) g_{22}(-y_2|y_2, -y_1, y_1) g_{11}(-y_1|y_1) \\
&\quad \times g(y_2|-y_1, y_1) g(y_1) dy_{33}dy_{22}dy_{11}dy_1dy_2 \\
&= h^3(1+o(1)) \int \cdots \int K^2(y_{11}+y_{22})K^2(y_{22}+y_{33}) y_1^2 y_2^2 \\
&\quad \times f_{33}(0|-y_2, y_2, -y_1, y_1) f_{22}\left(\frac{-y_2}{(j-s-1)^\alpha}|y_2, -y_1, y_1\right) \\
&\quad \times f_{11}\left(\frac{-y_1}{(s-t-1)^\alpha}|y_1\right) g(y_2|-y_1, y_1) g(y_1) dy_{33}dy_{22}dy_{11}dy_1dy_2
\end{aligned}
\tag{A.52}
$$

In view of Eqs. (A.51) and (A.52), similar to the calculations of Eqs. (A.26)–(A.28), it can be shown that for large enough m and n

$$
\begin{aligned}
E\left[\sum_{i=n+1}^{m} \sum_{j=n+1,\neq i}^{m} w_i^2 w_j^2\right] &= \sum_{i=n+1}^{m} \sum_{j=n+1,\neq i}^{m} E[w_i^2 w_j^2] \\
&= Ch^3(1+o(1)) \sum_{i=n+2}^{m} \sum_{j=n+1}^{i-1} \sum_{s=2}^{j-1} \sum_{t=1}^{s-1} \frac{1}{(i-j)^\alpha} \frac{1}{(j-s-1)^\alpha} \frac{1}{(s-t-1)^\alpha} \\
&= Ch^3(1+o(1))(m-n)^{\frac{5}{2}}
\end{aligned}
\tag{A.53}
$$

Similar to Eq. (A.53), we may have for sufficiently large m and n

$$
\sum_{i=n+1}^{m} E\left[w_i^4\right] = Ch^2(1+o(1))(m-n)^{\frac{3}{2}} \tag{A.54}
$$

$$
E\left[\sum_{i=n+1}^{m} \sum_{j=1}^{n} w_i^2 w_j^2\right] = o\left(h^3(m-n)^{\frac{5}{2}}\right) \tag{A.55}
$$

$$
E\left[\sum_{i=}^{m} \sum_{j=1}^{n} w_i^2 w_j^2\right] = o\left(h^3(m-n)^{\frac{5}{2}}\right) \tag{A.56}
$$

using $\lim_{m,n\to\infty} \frac{n}{m} = 0$.

Thus, Eqs. (A.50)–(A.56) imply that for large enough m and n

$$\begin{aligned} E[J_{mn}^2] &= E\left[\frac{1}{\sigma_m^2}\sum_{i=1}^{m} w_i^2 - \frac{1}{\sigma_n^2}\sum_{j=1}^{n} w_j^2\right]^2 \\ &= \frac{1}{\sigma_m^4}\sum_{i=n+1}^{m}\sum_{k=n+1}^{m} E\left[w_k^2 w_i^2\right] + \frac{(\sigma_n^2-\sigma_m^2)^2}{\sigma_m^4\sigma_n^4}\sum_{j=1}^{n}\sum_{k=1}^{n} E\left[w_k^2 w_j^2\right] \\ &\quad - 2\frac{\sigma_m^2-\sigma_n^2}{\sigma_m^4\sigma_n^2}\sum_{i=n+1}^{m}\sum_{j=1}^{n} E\left[w_i^2 w_j^2\right] \\ &= Ch\left(1-\frac{n}{m}\right)^{\frac{3}{2}}(1+o(1)) = o(1) \end{aligned} \tag{A.57}$$

using again $\lim_{m,n\to\infty}\frac{n}{m}=0$. We thus complete the second part of Eq. (A.49).

Let $z_i = u_i^2 - E[u_1^2]$. We now come back to prove the first part of Eq. (A.49). Note that for $n+1 \le i \le m$ and $1 \le j \le n$

$$I_{mn} = \frac{1}{\sigma_m^2}\sum_{i=1}^{m}(u_i^2 - E\left[u_1^2\right])w_i^2 - \frac{1}{\sigma_n^2}\sum_{j=1}^{n}(u_j^2 - E\left[u_1^2\right])w_j^2 = \frac{1}{\sigma_m^2}\sum_{i=1}^{m} z_i w_i^2 - \frac{1}{\sigma_n^2}\sum_{j=1}^{n} z_j w_j^2 \tag{A.58}$$

Note that $\{w_i^2\}$ is a function of $\{u_j\colon 1 \le j \le i-1\}$ while $\{z_i\}$ is a function of $\{u_i\}$. Let $g_{zw}(\cdot,\cdot)$ be the joint density function of (z_i, w_i^2), $g_{z|w}(\cdot|\cdot)$ be the conditional density function of z_i given w_i, and $g_w(\cdot)$ be the marginal density function of w_i^2. Obviously, $g_{zw}(z,w) = g_z(z)g_w(w)$ when $\{u_i\}$ is assumed to be a sequence of independent random variables.

Thus, in view of the relationship $g_{zw}(z,w) = g_{z|w}(z|w)g_w(w)$ and the fact that the conditional moments of z_i given w_i do not affect the order of $E\left[I_{mn}^2\right]$, by using the same arguments as in Eqs. (A.50)–(A.57), we can show that for large enough m and n

$$E\left[I_{mn}^2\right] = E\left[\frac{1}{\sigma_m^2}\sum_{i=1}^{m} z_i w_i^2 - \frac{1}{\sigma_n^2}\sum_{j=1}^{n} z_j w_j^2\right]^2$$

$$= \frac{1}{\sigma_m^4}\sum_{i=n+1}^{m}\sum_{k=n+1}^{m} E\left[z_k w_k^2 z_i w_i^2\right] + \frac{(\sigma_n^2 - \sigma_m^2)^2}{\sigma_m^4 \sigma_n^4}\sum_{j=1}^{n}\sum_{k=1}^{n} E\left[z_k w_k^2 z_j w_j^2\right]$$

$$- 2\frac{\sigma_m^2 - \sigma_n^2}{\sigma_m^4 \sigma_n^2}\sum_{i=n+1}^{m}\sum_{j=1}^{n} E\left[z_i w_i^2 z_j w_j^2\right]$$

$$= Ch\left(1 - \frac{n}{m}\right)^{\frac{3}{2}}(1 + o(1)) = o(1) \tag{A.59}$$

We therefore have completed the proof of Lemma A.4.

Lemma A.5. Let the conditions of Theorem 1 hold. Then as $T \to \infty$

$$\frac{M_{Ti}}{\tilde{\sigma}_{T1}} \to_P 0 \quad \text{for} \quad i = 2, 3, 4 \tag{A.60}$$

$$\frac{\tilde{\sigma}_{Tj}}{\tilde{\sigma}_{T1}} \to_P 0 \quad \text{for} \quad j = 2, 3, 4 \tag{A.61}$$

Proof. Since $\frac{\tilde{\sigma}_{T1}^2}{\sigma_{T1}^2} \to_D \xi^2$ as shown in Lemma A.3, in order to prove Eqs. (A.60) and (A.61), it suffices to show that as $T \to \infty$

$$\frac{M_{Ti}}{\sigma_{T1}} \to_P 0 \quad \text{for} \quad i = 2, 3, 4 \tag{A.62}$$

$$\frac{\tilde{\sigma}_{Tj}}{\sigma_{T1}} \to_P 0 \quad \text{for} \quad j = 2, 3, 4 \tag{A.63}$$

Since the details are very similar, we prove only Eq. (A.62) for $i = 2$. Observe that

$$M_{T2}=\sum_{t=1}^{T}\sum_{s=1,\neq t}^{T}\tilde{u}_sK_h(\hat{v}_{s-1}-\hat{v}_{t-1})\tilde{u}_t=\sum_{t=1}^{T}\sum_{s=1,\neq t}^{T}\tilde{u}_sK_h(v_{s-1}-v_{t-1})\tilde{u}_t$$

$$+\sum_{t=1}^{T}\sum_{s=1,\neq t}^{T}\tilde{u}_s(K_h(\hat{v}_{s-1}-\hat{v}_{t-1})-K_h(v_{s-1}-v_{t-1}))\tilde{u}_t$$

$$\equiv M_{T21}+M_{T22} \tag{A.64}$$

For some $B_0>0$, let $\Theta(\beta)=\{\hat{\beta}:||\hat{\beta}-\beta||\leq B_0R_T^{-1}\}$ and $I_{\Theta(\beta)}(\hat{\beta})$ be the conventional indicator function. Thus, for sufficiently large T and any given $\varepsilon>0$

$$P(|M_{T21}I_{\Theta(\beta)}(\hat{\beta})|\geq\varepsilon\sigma_{T1})\leq\frac{E|M_{T21}I_{\Theta(\beta)}(\hat{\beta})|}{\sigma_{T1}\varepsilon}$$

$$\leq\frac{\sum_{t=1}^{T}\sum_{s=1,\neq t}^{T}E[|\tilde{u}_s|K_h(v_{s-1}-v_{t-1})|\tilde{u}_t|I_{\Theta(\beta)}(\hat{\beta})]}{\sigma_{T1}\varepsilon}$$

$$\leq C\frac{\sum_{t=1}^{T}\sum_{s=1,\neq t}^{T}||X_s-X_{s-1}||E[K_h(v_{s-1}-v_{t-1})]||X_t-X_{t-1}||}{R_T^2\sigma_{T1}}$$

$$\leq C\frac{2h\sum_{s=2}^{T}\sum_{t=1}^{s-1}||X_s-X_{s-1}||\frac{1}{\sqrt{s-t}}||X_t-X_{t-1}||}{R_T^2\sigma_{T1}}=o(1) \tag{A.65}$$

using $\tilde{u}_t=(X_t-X_{t-1})^{\tau}(\beta-\hat{\beta})$, recalling the definition of $K_h(\cdot)=K\left(\frac{\cdot}{h}\right)$, the first part of Assumption A.2 and for all $s>t$, $E[K_h(v_{s-1}-v_{t-1})]\leq\frac{Ch}{\sqrt{s-t}}$, which follows from

$$E[K_h(v_{s-1}-v_{t-1})]=E\left[K\left(\frac{v_{s-1}-v_{t-1}}{h}\right)\right]$$

$$=\frac{h}{\sqrt{s-t}}\int K(x)f_{st}\left(\frac{xh}{\sqrt{s-t}}\right)\mathrm{d}x$$

$$\leq C\frac{h}{\sqrt{s-t}}$$

using the same argument as in Eq. (A.26) of the proof of Lemma A.1, where $f_{st}(\cdot)$ is the density of $v_{st} = \frac{v_{s-1} - v_{t-1}}{\sqrt{s-t}}$ and $f_{st}\left(\frac{xh}{\sqrt{s-t}}\right)$ is bounded by Eq. (12) of Assumption 1(i).

Therefore, for sufficiently small $\varepsilon > 0$

$$\begin{aligned} P(|M_{T21}| \geq \varepsilon\sigma_{T1} &= P((|M_{T21}| \geq \varepsilon\sigma_{T1}) \cap (\hat{\beta} \notin \Theta(\beta))) \\ &\quad + P((|M_{T21}| \geq \varepsilon\sigma_{T1}) \cap (\hat{\beta} \in \Theta(\beta))) \\ &\leq P(||\hat{\beta} - \beta|| > B_0 R_T^{-1}) + P(|M_{T21} I_{\Theta(\beta)}(\hat{\beta})| \geq \varepsilon\sigma_{T1}) \\ &\to 0 \text{ as } T \to \infty \end{aligned} \tag{A.66}$$

In view of $\hat{v}_{s-1} - \hat{v}_{t-1} = v_{s-1} - v_{t-1} + (X_{s-1} - X_{t-1})^\tau(\beta - \hat{\beta})$ and using Assumption A.1, we have

$$\begin{aligned} \overline{K}_h(s,t) &\equiv \left| K\left(\frac{v_{s-1} - v_{t-1} + (X_{s-1} - X_{t-1})^\tau(\beta - \hat{\beta})}{h}\right) - K\left(\frac{v_{s-1} - v_{t-1}}{h}\right) \right| \\ &\leq M\left(\frac{v_{s-1} - v_{t-1}}{h}\right) \left| \frac{(X_{s-1} - X_{t-1})^\tau(\beta - \hat{\beta})}{h} \right| \end{aligned}$$

This implies that for large enough T

$$\begin{aligned} P(|M_{T22} I_{\Theta(\beta)}(\hat{\beta})| \geq \varepsilon\sigma_{T1}) &\leq \frac{E|M_{T22} I_{\Theta(\beta)}(\hat{\beta})|}{\sigma_{T1}\varepsilon} \\ &\leq \frac{\sum_{t=1}^{T} \sum_{s=1,\neq t}^{T} E\left[|\tilde{u}_s| M\left(\frac{v_{s-1} - v_{t-1}}{h}\right) \left| \frac{(X_{s-1} - X_{t-1})^\tau(\beta - \hat{\beta}))}{h} \right| |\tilde{u}_t| I_{\Theta(\beta)}(\hat{\beta}) \right]}{\sigma_{T1}\varepsilon} \\ &\leq \varepsilon \frac{\sum_{t=1}^{T} \sum_{s=1,\neq t}^{T} ||X_s - X_{s-1}|| ||X_{s-1} - X_{t-1}|| E\left[M\left(\frac{v_{s-1} - v_{t-1}}{h}\right) \right] ||X_t - X_{t-1}||}{R_T^3 h \sigma_{T1}} \\ &\leq C \frac{\sum_{s=2}^{T} \sum_{t=1}^{s-1} ||X_s - X_{s-1}|| \frac{||X_{s-1} - X_{t-1}||}{\sqrt{s-t}} ||X_t - X_{t-1}||}{R_T^3 \sigma_{T1}} = o(1) \end{aligned} \tag{A.67}$$

using the second part of Assumption A.2.

We thus have that for sufficiently small $\varepsilon > 0$

$$
\begin{aligned}
P(|M_{T22}| \geq \varepsilon\sigma_{T1}) &= P((|M_{T22}| \geq \varepsilon\sigma_{T1}) \cap (\hat{\beta} \notin \Theta(\beta))) \\
&\quad + P((|M_{T22}| \geq \varepsilon\sigma_{T1}) \cap (\hat{\beta} \in \Theta(\beta))) \\
&\leq P(||\hat{\beta} - \beta|| > B_0 R_T^{-1}) + P(|M_{T22} I_{\Theta(\beta)}(\hat{\beta})| \geq \varepsilon\sigma_{T1}) \\
&\to 0 \quad \text{as} \quad T \to \infty
\end{aligned} \tag{A.68}
$$

As the detailed proofs for $i=3,4$ are very similar to those for the case of $i=2$, we need only to mention the proof for the case of $i=2$. Similar to Eq. (A.64), we can have

$$
\begin{aligned}
\tilde{\sigma}_{T2}^2 &= 2\sum_{t=1}^{T} \sum_{s=1,\neq t}^{T} \tilde{u}_s^2 K_h^2(\hat{v}_{s-1} - \hat{v}_{t-1})\tilde{u}_t^2 = 2\sum_{t=1}^{T} \sum_{s=1,\neq t}^{T} \tilde{u}_s^2 K_h^2(v_{s-1} - v_{t-1})\tilde{u}_t^2 \\
&\quad + 2\sum_{t=1}^{T} \sum_{s=1,\neq t}^{T} \tilde{u}_s^2 (K_h^2(\hat{v}_{s-1} - \hat{v}_{t-1}) - K_h^2(v_{s-1} - v_{t-1}))\tilde{u}_t^2
\end{aligned} \tag{A.69}
$$

Analogous to Eqs. (A.66) and (A.68), using Assumption A.2 with $i=2$ we can show that for any given $\varepsilon > 0$

$$
P(\tilde{\sigma}_{T2}^2 \geq \varepsilon\sigma_{T1}^2) \to 0 \quad \text{as} \quad T \to \infty \tag{A.70}
$$

This completes the proof of Lemma A.5 and thus the proof of Theorem 1 for Case A.

A.3. PROOF OF THEOREM 1 IN CASE B

In view of Eqs. (A.4) and (A.5), in order to prove Theorem 1 for Case B, it suffices to show that Eqs. (A.6)–(A.8) hold. These proofs are given in Lemmas A.6 and A.7.

Lemma A.6. Let Assumptions 2 and A.1 hold. Then under $\mathcal{H}_0: \ v_t = f_0(v_{t-1}, \theta_0) + u_t$

$$\frac{\sum_{t=1}^{T}\sum_{s=1,\neq t}^{T} u_s K_h(v_{s-1}-v_{t-1})u_t}{\sqrt{2\sum_{t=1}^{T}\sum_{s=1,\neq t}^{T} u_s^2 K_h^2(v_{s-1}-v_{t-1})u_t^2}} \to_D N(0,1) \quad \text{as} \quad T\to\infty \quad (A.71)$$

Proof. The asymptotic normality in Eq. (A.71) is a standard result for the case where $\{u_t\}$ is a sequence of martingale differences and $\{v_t\}$ is a strictly stationary and α-mixing sequence. The proof follows from Lemma A.1 of Gao and King (2004) or Theorem A.1 of Gao (2007). As the details are very similar to the proof of Theorem 2.1 of Gao and King (2004), they are omitted here.

Lemma A.7. Let Assumptions 2, A.1–A.3(i) and A.4 hold. Then as $T\to\infty$

$$\frac{M_{Ti}}{\sigma_{T1}} \to_P 0 \quad \text{for} \quad i=2,3,4 \quad (A.72)$$

$$\frac{\tilde{\sigma}_{Tj}}{\sigma_{T1}} \to_P 0 \quad \text{for} \quad j=2,3,4 \quad (A.73)$$

Proof. Since $\{u_t\}$ is a sequence of martingale differences and $\{v_t\}$ is a strictly stationary and α-mixing time series in Case B, the proofs of Eqs. (A.60) and (A.61) remain true, but become more standard through using Assumptions 2, A.3(i) and A.4.

A.4. PROOF OF THEOREM 2(i)

Recall the notation introduced in the Simulation Scheme in Section 3 and let

$$\tilde{v}_t^* = Y_t^* - X_t^\tau \hat{\beta} = \tilde{v}_{t-1}^* + \hat{\sigma}_u u_t^*, \quad \text{for Case A}$$

$$\tilde{v}_t^* = Y_t^* - X_t^\tau \hat{\beta} = f_0(\tilde{v}_{t-1}^*, \hat{\theta}_0) + \hat{\sigma}_u u_t^*, \quad \text{for Case B}$$

$$\hat{v}_t^* = Y_t^* - X_t^\tau \hat{\beta}^* = \tilde{v}_t^* + X_t^\tau(\hat{\beta} - \hat{\beta}^*)$$

$$\tilde{u}_t^* = X_t^\tau(\hat{\beta} - \hat{\beta}^*) + f_0(\tilde{v}_{t-1}^*, \hat{\theta}_0) - f_0(\tilde{v}_{t-1}^* + X_{t-1}^\tau(\hat{\beta} - \hat{\beta}^*), \hat{\theta}_0^*)$$

$$\hat{u}_t^* = \hat{v}_t^* - f_0(\hat{v}_{t-1}^*, \hat{\theta}_0^*) = \hat{\sigma}_u u_t^* + \tilde{u}_t^*$$

$$\hat{v}_{s-1}^* - \hat{v}_{t-1}^* = \tilde{v}_{s-1}^* - \tilde{v}_{t-1}^* + (X_{s-1} - X_{t-1})^\tau(\hat{\beta} - \hat{\beta}^*)$$

We thus have

$$\hat{M}_T^* \equiv \sum_{t=1}^{T}\sum_{s=1,\neq t}^{T} \hat{u}_s^* K_h(\hat{v}_{s-1}^* - \hat{v}_{t-1}^*)\hat{u}_t^* = \sum_{t=1}^{T}\sum_{s=1,\neq t}^{T} \hat{\sigma}_u u_s^* K_h(\tilde{v}_{s-1}^* - \tilde{v}_{t-1}^*)\hat{\sigma}_u u_t^*$$

$$+\sum_{t=1}^{T}\sum_{s=1,\neq t}^{T} \tilde{u}_s^* K_h(\hat{v}_{s-1}^* - \hat{v}_{t-1}^*)\tilde{u}_t^* + 2\sum_{t=1}^{T}\sum_{s=1,\neq t}^{T} \hat{\sigma}_u u_s^* K_h(\hat{v}_{s-1}^* - \hat{v}_{t-1}^*)\tilde{u}_t^*$$

$$+ M_{T4}^* \equiv M_{T1}^* + M_{T2}^* + M_{T3}^* + M_{T4}^* \tag{A.74}$$

$$\hat{\sigma}_T^{*2} \equiv 2\sum_{t=1}^{T}\sum_{s=1,\neq t}^{T} \hat{u}_s^{*2} K_h^2(\hat{v}_{s-1}^* - \hat{v}_{t-1}^*)\hat{u}_t^{*2} = 2\sum_{t=1}^{T}\sum_{s=1,s\neq t}^{T} \hat{\sigma}_u^2 u_s^{*2} K_h^2(\hat{v}_{s-1}^* - \hat{v}_{t-1}^*)\hat{\sigma}_u^2 u_t^{*2}$$

$$+2\sum_{t=1}^{T}\sum_{s=1,\neq t}^{T} \tilde{u}_s^{*2} K_h^2(\hat{v}_{s-1}^* - \hat{v}_{t-1}^*)\tilde{u}_t^{*2}$$

$$+2\sum_{t=1}^{T}\sum_{s=1,\neq t}^{T} \hat{\sigma}_u^2 u_s^{*2} K_h^2(\hat{v}_{s-1}^* - \hat{v}_{t-1}^*)\tilde{u}_t^{*2} + \hat{\sigma}_{T4}^{*2} \equiv \sum_{j=1}^{4} \tilde{\sigma}_{Tj}^{*2} \tag{A.75}$$

where $\tilde{\sigma}_{T4}^{*2} = \hat{\sigma}_T^{*2} - \tilde{\sigma}_{T1}^{*2} - \tilde{\sigma}_{T2}^{*2} - \tilde{\sigma}_{T3}^{*2}$ and $M_{T4}^* = \hat{M}_T^* - M_{T1}^* - M_{T2}^* - M_{T3}^*$.

In view of Eqs. (A.74) and (A.75), to prove Theorem 2(i), it suffices to show that as $T \to \infty$

$$\frac{M_{T1}^*}{\hat{\sigma}_{T1}^*} \to_D N(0,1) \tag{A.76}$$

$$\frac{M_{Ti}^*}{\tilde{\sigma}_{T1}^*} \to_P 0 \quad \text{for} \quad i=2,3,4 \tag{A.77}$$

$$\frac{\tilde{\sigma}_{Tj}^*}{\tilde{\sigma}_{T1}^*} \to_P 0 \quad \text{for} \quad j=2,3,4 \tag{A.78}$$

Note that $\tilde{v}_t^* = \tilde{v}_{t-1}^* + \hat{\sigma}_u u_t^* = \tilde{v}_0^* + \hat{\sigma}_u \sum_{s=1}^{t} u_s^* = \hat{\sigma}_u \sum_{s=1}^{t} u_s^*$. Note also that $\hat{\sigma}_u^2 = E[u_1^2] + o_P(1)$. Thus, in order to prove Eqs. (A.76)–(A.78), in view of the fact that $\{u_t^*\}$ is a sequence of independent and identically distributed errors with $E[u_t^*]=0$ and $E[u_t^{*2}]=1$, and also independent of $\{Y_s\}$ for all $s,t \geq 1$, it suffices to complete the proofs of the bootstrapping versions of Lemmas A.1–A.5 by successive conditioning arguments.

As a matter of the fact, the derivations in the proofs of Lemmas A.1–A.5 now become less technical and tedious due to the fact that $\{u_t^*\}$ is a sequence of independent and identically distributed errors. Using the conditions of Theorem 2(i), in view of the notation of $\hat{L}_T^*(h)$ introduced in the Simulation Scheme in Section 3, we thus may show that as $T \to \infty$

$$P^*(\hat{L}_T^*(h) \leq x) \to \Phi(x) \quad \text{for all} \quad x \in (-\infty, \infty) \tag{A.79}$$

holds in probability with respect to the distribution of the original sample $\mathcal{W}_T$.

Let z_α be the $1-\alpha$ quantile of $\Phi(\cdot)$ such that $\Phi(z_\alpha) = 1-\alpha$. Then it follows from Eq. (A.79) that as $T \to \infty$

$$P^*(\hat{L}_T^*(h) \geq z_\alpha) \to 1 - \Phi(z_\alpha) = \alpha \tag{A.80}$$

This, together with $P^*(\hat{L}_T^*(h) \geq l_\alpha^*) = \alpha$ by construction, implies that as $T \to \infty$

$$l_\alpha^* - z_\alpha \to_P 0 \tag{A.81}$$

Using the conclusion of Theorem 1 and Eq. (A.79) again, we have that as $T \to \infty$

$$P^*(\hat{L}_T^*(h) \leq x) - P(\hat{L}_T(h) \leq x) \to_P 0 \quad \text{for all} \quad x \in (-\infty, \infty) \tag{A.82}$$

holds in probability. This, along with the construction that $P^*(\hat{L}_T^*(h) \geq l_\alpha^*) = \alpha$ again, shows that as $T \to \infty$

$$\lim_{T \to \infty} P(\hat{L}_T(h) > l_\alpha^*) = \alpha \tag{A.83}$$

holds in probability. Therefore the conclusion of Theorem 2(i) is proved.

A.5. PROOF OF THEOREM 2(ii)

Note that under $\mathcal{H}_1: \ v_t = f_1(v_{t-1}, \theta_1) + u_t$

$$\begin{aligned}\hat{u}_t &= \hat{v}_t - f_0(\hat{v}_{t-1}, \hat{\theta}_0) = X_t^\tau(\beta - \hat{\beta}) + v_t - f_0(\hat{v}_{t-1}, \hat{\theta}_0) \\ &= u_t + X_t^\tau(\beta - \hat{\beta}) + f_1(v_{t-1}, \theta_1) - f_0(\hat{v}_{t-1}, \hat{\theta}_0) \equiv u_t + \tilde{u}_t\end{aligned}$$

$$\begin{aligned}\tilde{u}_t &= X_t^\tau(\beta-\hat{\beta})+f_1(v_{t-1},\theta_1)-f_0(v_{t-1}+X_t^\tau(\beta-\hat{\beta}),\hat{\theta}_0)\\ &= X_t^\tau(\beta-\hat{\beta})+f_1(v_{t-1},\theta_1)-f_0(v_{t-1},\theta_0)\\ &\quad+f_0(v_{t-1},\theta_0)-f_0(v_{t-1}+X_t^\tau(\beta-\hat{\beta}),\hat{\theta}_0)\end{aligned} \tag{A.84}$$

To complete the proof of Theorem 2(ii), we need the following lemma.

Let

$$\Lambda_{T1} = \sum_{t=1}^{T}\sum_{s=1,\neq t}^{T} \tilde{u}_s K_h(v_{s-1}-v_{t-1})\tilde{u}_t \quad \text{and}$$

$$\Lambda_{T2} = \sum_{t=1}^{T}\sum_{s=1,\neq t}^{T} f_{10}(v_{s-1})K_h(v_{s-1}-v_{t-1})f_{10}(v_{t-1})$$

Then we have the following lemma.

Lemma A.8. Let the conditions of Theorem 2(ii) hold. Then as $T\to\infty$

$$\sigma_{T1}\Lambda_{T1}^{-1}\to_P 0 \tag{A.85}$$

Proof. Let $f_{10}(v)=f_1(v,\theta_1)-f_0(v,\theta_0)$. In view of Eq. (A.84), using Assumptions A.4 and A.5(ii), in order to prove Eq. (A.85), it suffices to show that as $T\to\infty$

$$\sigma_{T1}\Lambda_{T2}^{-1}\to_P 0 \tag{A.86}$$

which follows from $\sigma_{T1}=O(T\sqrt{h})$ and

$$\begin{aligned}&\sum_{t=1}^{T}\sum_{s=1,\neq t}^{T} E[f_{10}(v_{s-1})K_h(v_{s-1}-v_{t-1})f_{10}(v_{t-1})]\\ &\quad= T^2h(1+o(1))\cdot\left(\int f_{10}^2(x)\pi_1^2(x)\mathrm{d}x\right)\left(\int K(y)\mathrm{d}y\right)=O(T^2h)\end{aligned}$$

using Assumption 3, where $\pi_1(v)$ denotes the marginal density of $\{v_t\}$ under $\mathcal{H}_1$. Note that in such cases where $\{v_t\}$ is strictly stationary and α-mixing, existing results for the α-mixing case (such as Lemmas A.1 and A.2 of the Appendix of Gao, 2007) can be used to show that $E[\psi(v_{1+\tau_1},\ldots,v_{1+\tau_l})]$

can be approximated by $E[\psi(z_{1+\tau_1}, \ldots, z_{1+\tau_l})]$ with certain rate of convergence related to the α-mixing coefficient for all $2 \leq l \leq 4$, where $\{z_i\}$ is a sequence of independent random variables having the same marginal density $\pi_1(\cdot)$ as $\{v_i\}$ and each $\psi(x_1, \cdots, x_l)$ is a symmetric function.

Proof of Theorem 2(ii): In view of the definition of $\hat{L}_T(h)$ and the proofs of Lemmas A.6–A.8, it may be shown that as $T \to \infty$

$$\begin{aligned}\hat{L}_T(h) &= \frac{\sum_{t=1}^T \sum_{s=1,\neq t}^T \hat{u}_s K_h(\hat{v}_{s-1} - \hat{v}_{t-1})\hat{u}_t}{\sqrt{2\sum_{t=1}^T \sum_{s=1,\neq t}^T \hat{u}_s^2 K_h^2(\hat{v}_{s-1} - \hat{v}_{t-1})\hat{u}_t^2}} \\ &= (1 + o_P(1))\frac{\sum_{t=1}^T \sum_{s=1,\neq t}^T u_s K_h(v_{s-1} - v_{t-1})u_t}{\sigma_{T1}} \\ &\quad + (1 + o_P(1))\frac{\sum_{t=1}^T \sum_{s=1,\neq t}^T f_{10}(v_{s-1}) K_h(v_{s-1} - v_{t-1}) f_{10}(v_{t-1})}{\sigma_{T1}}\end{aligned}$$

The proof of Theorem 2(ii) then follows from Lemma A.8.

APPENDIX B

In this appendix, we give two secondary lemmas for the proofs in Appendix A.

Lemma B.1. Assume that the probability space $(\Omega_n, \mathcal{F}_n, P_n)$ supports square integrable random variables $S_{n,1}, S_{n,2}, \cdots, S_{n,k_n}$, and that the $S_{n,t}$ are adapted to σ-algebras $\mathcal{F}_{n,t}$, $1 \le t \le k_n$, where

$$\mathcal{F}_{n,1} \subset \mathcal{F}_{n,2} \subset \cdots \subset \mathcal{F}_{n,k_n} \subset \mathcal{F}_n$$

Let $X_{n,t} = S_{n,t} - S_{n,t-1}$, $S_{n,0} = 0$ and $U_{n,t}^2 = \sum_{s=1}^{t} X_{n,s}^2$. If $\mathcal{G}_n$ is a sub-σ-algebra of $\mathcal{F}_n$, let $\mathcal{G}_{n,t} = \mathcal{F}_{n,t} \vee \mathcal{G}_n$ (the σ-algebra generated by $\mathcal{F}_{n,t} \cup \mathcal{G}_n$) and let $\mathcal{G}_{n,0} = \{\Omega_n, \phi\}$ denote the trivial σ-algebra. Moreover, suppose that

$$\sum_{t=1}^{n} E(X_{n,t}^2 I_{\{[|X_{n,t}| > \delta]\}}(X_{n,t}) | \mathcal{G}_{n,t-1}) \to_P 0 \tag{B.1}$$

for some $\delta > 0$, and there exists a $\mathcal{G}_n$-measurable random variable u_n^2, such that

$$U_{n,k_n}^2 - u_n^2 \to_P 0 \tag{B.2}$$

$$\sum_{t=1}^{n} E(X_{n,t} | \mathcal{G}_{n,t-1}) \to_P 0 \tag{B.3}$$

and

$$\sum_{t=1}^{n} |E(X_{n,t} | \mathcal{G}_{n,t-1})|^2 \to_P 0 \tag{B.4}$$

If

$$\lim_{\delta \to 0} \lim_{n \to \infty} \inf P\{U_{n,k_n} > \delta\} = 1 \tag{B.5}$$

then $\frac{S_{n,k_n}}{U_{n,k_n}} \to_D N(0, 1)$ as $n \to \infty$.

Proof. The proof of Lemma B.1 follows from Corollary 3.1 and Theorem 3.4 of Hall and Heyde (1980).

Lemma B.2 is concerned with uniform strong convergence of nonparametric kernel density estimate of a nonstationary time series of the form $v_t = v_{t-1} + u_t$. The proof of Lemma B.2 follows from Gao, Li, and Tjøstheim (2009).

Recall that $N(T)$ is defined in the same way as $T(n)$ in Karlsen and Tjøstheim (2001) and define

$$\hat{f}(v) = \hat{f}_s(v) = \frac{1}{N(T)h} \sum_{l=1}^{T} K\left(\frac{v_{l-1} - v}{h}\right) \quad \text{(B.6)}$$

Lemma B.2. Let Assumptions 1(i) and A.1 hold. Then under $\mathcal{H}_0: \ v_t = v_{t-1} + u_t$ and as $T \to \infty$

$$\max_{1 \le t \le T} |\hat{f}(v_{t-1}) - 1| = o(1) \quad \text{almost surely} \quad \text{(B.7)}$$

Note that in the random walk case, the invariant measure π_s of $\{v_t\}$ is proportional to the Lebesgue measure on R^1, i.e., $d\pi_s(x) = c_s$ dx with c_s being a proportionality factor. Referring to the uniqueness discussion in Remark 3.1 of Karlsen and Tjøstheim (2001), we can choose s such that $c_s = 1$ and $d\pi_s(x) = dx$, the Lebesgue measure. This means that π_s has a constant density $f(x) = f_s(x) \equiv 1$. This choice shows why the limit in Eq. (7) is one.

PART II
PANEL DATA MODELS

PANEL MACROECONOMETRIC MODELING[☆]

Cheng Hsiao

Department of Economics, University of Southern California, Los Angeles, CA, USA; WISE, Xiamen University, Xiamen, China; Department of Quantitative Finance, National Tsinghua University, Hsinchu

ABSTRACT

This paper provides a selective survey of the panel macroeconometric techniques that focus on controlling the impact of "unobserved heterogeneity" across individuals and over time to obtain valid inference for "structures" that are common across individuals and over time. We consider issues of (i) estimating vector autoregressive models; (ii) testing of unit root or cointegration; (iii) statistical inference for dynamic simultaneous equations models; (iv) policy evaluation; and (v) aggregation and prediction.

Keywords: Panel macro-modeling; unit root; cointegration; aggregation; prediction

JEL classifications: C10; C33; C51

[☆]This paper is dedicated to P. C. B. Phillips for his creative and lasting contributions to econometrics.

Essays in Honor of Peter C. B. Phillips
Advances in Econometrics, Volume 33, 205–239

ISSN: 0731-9053/doi:10.1108/S0731-905320140000033007

1. INTRODUCTION

One of the distinct features of macroeconometric modeling is that an economy as a whole is not always predictable from the parts which compose the entire *system*. The progress of macroeconometric modeling is principally fueled by four developments: "The improvement in computational capacity, improvements in the quality and availability of economic data, developments in econometric theory, and the virtuous circle of improvements in macroeconomic theory and the evolution of macroeconometric models" (Bodkin, Klein, & Marwah, 1991, p. 527). However, a model is not a mirror. In order to capture the essential relationships of the real world phenomena, a model must simplify. The details are reduced through suitable *aggregation* and *stochastic modeling*, namely, all the omitted factors that affect the outcomes are put into the error terms, $\underset{\sim}{v}$.

Panel data contain more degrees of freedom and more sample variability than a cross-sectional or time series sample, hence, in principal, can yield more powerful inference (e.g., Hsiao, 2007, 2014). However, panel data, by nature, focus on individual outcomes. Factors affecting individual outcomes are numerous. The conventional "homogeneity" assumption at the suitable "aggregate" level and the probabilistic assumption of the error term $\underset{\sim}{v}$ conditional on certain observable factors may not hold. This paper intends to provide a selective survey of the panel macroeconometric techniques that focus on controlling the impact of "unobserved heterogeneity" across individuals and over time to obtain valid inference on structures that are common across individuals and over time.

Panel data contain at least two dimensions, a cross-section dimension and a time series dimension. The multidimensional nature of panel data raises issues of statistical inference (e.g. Phillips & Moon (1999, 2000a, 2000b)). Moreover, because of the inertia in human behavior and institutional, and technological rigidities, a behavioral equation is more appropriately specified in *dynamic* form (Nerlove, 2000). Therefore, the focus of this paper is on the issues of statistical inference for a vector of dynamic interdependent variables. We shall consider both the reduced form and structural form approaches for modeling dynamic response. We shall consider issues of (i) estimating vector autoregressive model (VAR); (ii) testing of unit root or cointegration; (iii) statistical inference for dynamic structural equation; (iv) policy evaluation; and (v) aggregation and prediction. Because panel data is multidimensional, we pay special attention to the way that sample size increases on inference. In Sections 2 and 3 we discuss the reduced form approaches for modeling system of equations by considering panel stationary VAR, and nonstationary system, respectively. Unit root and cointegration tests are briefly discussed in Section 4. Section 5 discusses Cowles Commission structural modeling approach by decomposing $\underset{\sim}{w}_{it}$ into joint dependent variables $\underset{\sim}{y}_{it}$ and exogenous variables $\underset{\sim}{x}_{it}$. Section 6 demonstrates how one can use panel data to provide a "measurement without theory" approach to evaluate the policy impact. Section 7 discusses issues of aggregation and prediction. Concluding remarks are made in Section 8.

2. STATIONARY PANEL VECTOR AUTOREGRESSIVE MODELS

Economic magnitudes are often determined by the joint work of many factors. To take account of both the joint dependence of state variables as well as their dependence on past behavior, VAR have been proposed as a data-based approach to conveniently summarize the information contained in the data (e.g., Hsiao, 1979a, 1979b, 1982; Sims, 1980).

It is well known that time series properties of an $m \times 1$ vector, $\underset{\sim}{w}_{it}$, depend critically on whether the underlying processes are (trend) stationary or integrated or cointegrated. To ensure the time series property of $\underset{\sim}{w}_{it}$ containing intercepts and time trend term remains the same whether $\underset{\sim}{w}_{it}$ contains unit roots or not, we consider a model of the form,

$$\Phi_i(L)\,(\underset{\sim}{w}_{it} - \underset{\sim}{\eta}_i - \underset{\sim}{\delta} t) = \underset{\sim}{\epsilon}_{it} \tag{1}$$

where

$$\Phi_i(L) = I_m - \Phi_{i1}\, L - \ \ldots \ - \Phi_{ip_i}\, L^{p_i} \tag{2}$$

L denotes the lag operator, $L\underset{\sim}{w}_{it} = \underset{\sim}{w}_{i,t-1}$, and $\underset{\sim}{\epsilon}_{it}$ are independently distributed over i and t with mean 0 and covariance matrix Ω_i. For ease of exposition, we shall assume $p_i = 1$ and $\underset{\sim}{\delta} = \underset{\sim}{0}$. When the roots of $|\Phi_i(z)| = 0$ all lie outside the unit circle, the process is (trend) stationary. When some or all roots of $|\Phi_i(z)| = 0$ lie inside the unit circle, we say the process is nonstationary. We consider the case of stationary process in this section.

The individual-specific effects, $\underset{\sim}{\eta}_i$, and $\Phi_i(L)$ can either be treated as *fixed constants* or *random variables*. If they can be viewed as random draws from a common population and inference is on the population properties from which those in the data are considered to be a random sample, then it is more appropriate to consider the marginal inference on the observables by treating them as random variables (*random effects* inference). If $\underset{\sim}{\eta}_i$ and $\Phi_i(L)$ are from heterogeneous population, then it is more appropriate to make conditional inference, conditional on the *fixed effects*, $\underset{\sim}{\eta}_i$, and $\Phi_i(L)$. Unfortunately, without the specific knowledge of how the observables $\underset{\sim}{w}_{it}$ interact with the unobservables, it is hard to make a choice between the two.

The random effects inference needs to postulate the distribution of unobservables $\underset{\sim}{\eta}_i$ and Φ_i, $G(\eta_i, \Phi_i)$, and the computation of the marginal distribution can be complicated because

$$
\begin{aligned}
f(\underset{\sim}{w}_{io}, \ldots, \underset{\sim}{w}_{iT}) &= \int f(\underset{\sim}{w}_{io}, \ldots, \underset{\sim}{w}_{iT} \mid \underset{\sim}{\eta}_i, \Phi_i)\, \mathrm{d}G(\underset{\sim}{\eta}_i, \Phi_i) \\
&= \int \prod_{t=1}^{T} f(\underset{\sim}{w}_{it} \mid \underset{\sim}{w}_{i,t-1}, \eta_i, \Phi_i) f(w_{io} \mid \underset{\sim}{\eta}_i, \Phi_i)\, \mathrm{d}G(\underset{\sim}{\eta}_i, \Phi_i)
\end{aligned} \tag{3}
$$

involves multiple integration of $m(T+1)$ dimensions. However, conditional on $\underset{\sim}{\eta}_i$, Φ_i, under the independently, identically distributed (i.i.d.) assumption about $\underset{\sim}{\epsilon}_{it}$, the distribution of $f(\underset{\sim}{w}_{it} \mid \underset{\sim}{w}_{i,t-1}, \Phi_i, \underset{\sim}{\eta}_i)$ is independently distributed over time. Furthermore, the conditional inference, although is less efficient than the marginal inference, remains consistent even $\underset{\sim}{\eta}_i$ and Φ_i are indeed random so we shall concentrate on the *fixed effects* inference.

(a) "Homogeneous" panel VAR (PVAR) models

By "homogeneous" PVAR models we mean apart from the time-invariant but individual-varying intercept $\underset{\sim}{\alpha}_i = -(I_m - \Phi_i)\underset{\sim}{\eta}_i$, the slope coefficients, $\Phi_i = \Phi_j = \Phi$.

(i) Generalized Method of Moments (GMM)

Just as in the single equation case (e.g., Anderson & Hsiao, 1981, 1982), $\underset{\sim}{\alpha}_i = (I - \Phi)\underset{\sim}{\eta}_i$ can be eliminated by first differencing,

$$\Delta \underset{\sim}{w}_{it} = \Phi \Delta \underset{\sim}{w}_{i,t-1} + \Delta \underset{\sim}{\epsilon}_{it}, \quad t = 2, \ldots, T \tag{4}$$

where $\Delta = 1 - L$. Then we have the orthogonality conditions

$$E\left\{ (\Delta \underset{\sim}{w}_{it} - \Phi \Delta \underset{\sim}{w}_{i,t-1}) \underset{\sim}{q}'_{it} \right\} = \underset{\sim}{0}, \quad \text{for } t = 2, \ldots, T \tag{5}$$

where $\underset{\sim}{q}_{it} = (\underset{\sim}{w}'_{i0}, \ldots, \underset{\sim}{w}'_{i,t-2})'$. Therefore, an Arellano and Bond (1991) GMM method can be applied to obtain the consistent and asymptotically normally distributed estimator of Φ when T is fixed and N tends to infinity, provided none of the roots of $|I - \Phi_Z| = 0$ equals 1. However, if T also increases with N and $T/N \rightarrow c \neq 0$ as $N \rightarrow \infty$, then moment conditions (4) increase at order T^2. Following the derivation of Alvarez and Arellano (2003), one can show that the GMM estimator is asymptotically biased of order $\sqrt{T/N}$, when it is multiplied by the scale factor $\sqrt{NT}$. This asymptotic bias term leads to severe size distortion and needs to be corrected for valid inference (e.g., Hsiao & Zhang, 2013; Hsiao & Zhou, 2014).

(ii) (Transformed) Likelihood Approach[1]

We note that Eq. (4) is well defined given $\Delta \underset{\sim}{w}_{i1}$. However, $\Delta \underset{\sim}{w}_{i1}$ is random. Eq. (1) implies that

$$\Delta \underset{\sim}{w}_{i1} = -(I - \Phi) \underset{\sim}{w}_{i0} + \underset{\sim}{\epsilon}_{i1} * \tag{6}$$

Therefore, $E(\Delta \underset{\sim}{w}_{i1} \Delta \underset{\sim}{w}'_{i2}) = -\Omega$ and $E(\Delta \underset{\sim}{w}_{i1} \Delta \underset{\sim}{w}'_{it}) = \underset{\sim}{0}$ for $t > 2$. Assuming $\underset{\sim}{w}_{i0}$ has constant covariance matrix Ψ_0, then $E(\Delta \underset{\sim}{w}_{i1} \Delta \underset{\sim}{w}'_{i1}) = (I - \Phi)\Psi_0 (I - \Phi)' + \Omega = \Psi_1$. The joint likelihood is well defined and does not involve incidental parameters, $\underset{\sim}{\eta}_i$ or $\underset{\sim}{\alpha}_i$. The (quasi) likelihood function of $\Delta \underset{\sim}{w}'_i = (\Delta \underset{\sim}{w}'_{i1}, \ldots, \Delta \underset{\sim}{w}'_{iT})$ is given by

$$\prod_{i=1}^{N} (2\pi)^{-\frac{T}{2}} |\Omega^*|^{-\frac{1}{2}} \exp\left\{ -\frac{1}{2} \left(\Delta \underset{\sim}{w}_i - H_i \underset{\sim}{\phi} \right)' \Omega^{*-1} \left(\Delta \underset{\sim}{w}_i - H_i \underset{\sim}{\phi} \right) \right\} \tag{7}$$

where

$$H_i = G_i' \otimes I_m$$

$$G_i = (\underset{\sim}{0},\ \Delta \underset{\sim}{w}_{i1},\ \ldots, \Delta \underset{\sim}{w}_{i,T-1})$$

$$\underset{\sim}{\phi} = \text{vec}\,(\Phi')$$

$$\Omega^* = \begin{bmatrix} \Psi_1 & -\Omega & \underset{\sim}{0} & \cdot & \underset{\sim}{0} \\ -\Omega & 2\Omega & -\Omega & \cdot & \cdot \\ \underset{\sim}{0} & -\Omega & 2\Omega & \cdot & \cdot \\ \cdot & \cdot & \cdot & \cdot & \cdot \\ \cdot & \cdot & \cdot & \cdot & -\Omega \\ \underset{\sim}{0} & \underset{\sim}{0} & \cdot & \cdot & 2\Omega \end{bmatrix}.$$

Maximizing the logarithm of Eq. (7), $\ell(\underset{\sim}{\theta})$ with respect to $\underset{\sim}{\theta}' = (\underset{\sim}{\phi}', \underset{\sim}{\sigma}')$, where $\underset{\sim}{\sigma}$ denotes the unknown elements of Ω^* yields the (transformed) (quasi) maximum likelihood estimator (QMLE) (Binder, Hsiao, & Pesaran, 2005). The QMLE with properly formulated initial conditions is asymptotically unbiased independent of the way N or T or both tend to infinity (Hsiao & Zhou, 2014).

Conditional on Ω^*, the MLE of Φ is equivalent to the minimum distance estimator (MDE) that minimizing

$$\sum_{i=1}^{N} \left(\Delta \underset{\sim}{w}_i - H \underset{\sim}{\phi} \right)' \Omega^{*-1} \left(\Delta \underset{\sim}{w}_i - H_i \underset{\sim}{\phi} \right) \tag{8}$$

yields

$$\hat{\underset{\sim}{\phi}} = \left(\sum_{i=1}^{N} H_i' \Omega^{*-1} H_i \right)^{-1} \left(\sum_{i=1}^{N} H_i \Omega^{*-1} \Delta \underset{\sim}{w}_i \right). \tag{9}$$

The GMM estimator breaks down when some of the roots of $|I - \Phi_Z| = 0$ are equal to unity. To see this, suppose $\Phi = I_m$, then $\Delta \underset{\sim}{w}_{it} = \Delta \underset{\sim}{\epsilon}_{it}$, $\underset{\sim}{q}_{it}$ are no longer legitimate instruments. On the other hand, both the MLE and MDE always exist and are consistent whether $\underset{\sim}{w}_{it}$ contains unit roots or not. The MLE and MDE are asymptotically normally distributed independent of whether $\underset{\sim}{w}_{it}$ is (trend) stationary, integrated, or cointegrated as $N \to \infty$ and is asymptotically unbiased whether T is fixed or $\to \infty$.

Moreover, if the roots of $|I - \Phi_Z| = 0$ lie outside the unit circle, the MLE is asymptotically normally distributed with mean equal to Φ independent of the way N or T go to infinity (Hsiao & Zhang, 2013). Therefore, the conventional likelihood ratio test statistic or Wald type test statistic of unit root or the rank of cointegration can be approximated by chi-square statistics. Moreover, the limited Monte Carlo studies conducted by Binder et al. (2005) show that both the MLE and MDE perform very well in finite sample and dominate the conventional GMM, in particular, if the roots of $|I - \Phi_Z| = 0$ are near unity.

(b) "Heterogeneous" VAR Models

We shall say a VAR model "heterogeneous" if slope coefficients also vary across individuals, $\Phi_i \neq \Phi_j$ if $i \neq j$.

(i) Cross-Sectionally Independent Processes

When $\underset{\sim}{\epsilon}_{it}$ is independent over i with mean $\underset{\sim}{0}$ and unrestricted covariance matrix Ω_i and T is large, applying the least squares method to the system (1) equation by equation yields consistent and efficient estimates of $\Phi_i(L)$ and $\underset{\sim}{\alpha}_i$ if $T \to \infty$.

(ii) Cross-Sectionally Dependent Processes

When $\underset{\sim}{\epsilon}_{it}$ are cross-sectionally dependent, Eq. (1) can be put in Zellner's (1962) seemingly unrelated regression framework if N is fixed and T is large. We can first use the ith individual's time series observation to estimate $\Phi_i(L)$ and $\underset{\sim}{\alpha}_i$. Then use the estimated $\hat{\Phi}_i(L)$ and $\underset{\sim}{\alpha}_i$ to obtain estimated $\hat{\underset{\sim}{\epsilon}}_{it}$, $i = 1, \ldots, N$, $t = 1, \ldots, T$ and estimate $\Omega_{ij} = E(\underset{\sim}{\epsilon}_{it} \underset{\sim}{\epsilon}'_{jt})$ by

$$\hat{\Omega}_{ij} = \frac{1}{T} \sum_{t=1}^{T} \hat{\underset{\sim}{\epsilon}}_{it} \hat{\underset{\sim}{\epsilon}}'_{jt}. \tag{10}$$

Given $\hat{\Omega}_{ij}$, $i, j = 1, \ldots, N$, one can stack all N cross-sectionally Eq. (1) together and apply the feasible generalized least squares estimator to obtain the efficient estimate of $\Phi_i(L)$ and $\underset{\sim}{\alpha}_i$, $i = 1, \ldots, N$.

(iii) Global VAR (GVAR)

To obtain efficient estimates of $\Phi_i(L)$ using Zellner (1962) seemingly unrelated regression approach requires T to be considerably larger than N. In many macroeconomic applications, the number of time series observations, T, could be of the same magnitude as the number of cross-sectional dimensions, N. When N is large, it is not feasible to stack all Nm

equations together as a system. Pesaran, Schuermann, and Weiner (2004) propose a global VAR to accommodate dynamic cross-dependence by considering

$$\Phi_i(L)\left(\underset{\sim}{w}_{it} - \Gamma_i \underset{\sim}{w}^*_{it}\right) = \underset{\sim}{\varepsilon}_{it}, \quad i = 1, 2, \ldots, N \tag{11}$$

where

$$\underset{\sim}{w}^*_{it} = \sum_{j=1}^{N} r_{ij} \underset{\sim}{w}_{jt} \tag{12}$$

$$r_{ii} = 0, \sum_{j=1}^{N} r_{ij} = 1, \text{ and } \sum_{j=1}^{N} r_{ij}^2 \to 0 \text{ as } N \to \infty. \tag{13}$$

The weight r_{ij} could be $1/(N-1)$ for $i \neq j$, or constructed from trade value or other measures of some economic distance and could be time-varying. Just like the cross-sectionally mean augment regression approach proposed by Pesaran (2004), the global average $\underset{\sim}{w}^*_{it}$ is inserted into Eq. (1) to take account of the cross-sectional dependence. When $\underset{\sim}{w}^*_{i,t-s}$ can be treated as weakly exogenous (predetermined), the estimation of Eq. (11) for each i can proceed using standard time series estimation techniques (e.g., Pesaran, Shin, & Smith, 2000). Pesaran et al. (2004) show that the weak exogeneity assumption of $\underset{\sim}{w}^*_{it}$ hold for practically all countries except for the United States because of the United State's dominate position in the world. They also show that Eq. (11) yields better results than Eq. (1) when cross-sectional units are correlated.

3. COINTEGRATED PANEL MODELS AND VECTOR ERROR CORRECTION[2]

3.1. Properties of Cointegrated Processes

Many macro and financial data are nonstationary. The nonstationarity of a time series is usually represented by an integrated process of order d, $d \geq 1$, $I(d)$. A dth integrated process can be transformed into a stationary process by differencing the variable d-times, $(1-L)^d$ (e.g., Box & Jenkins,

1971). For instance, suppose all the elements of $\underset{\sim}{w}_{it}$ are $I(1)$, then $(1-L)\underset{\sim}{w}_{it}$ become stationary ($I(0)$ processes). However, differencing $\underset{\sim}{w}_{it}$ also removes the underlying long-run relations among the elements of $\underset{\sim}{w}_{it}$, which can have important economic implications. If $\underset{\sim}{w}_{it}$ are driven by some common nonstationary variables, one notable feature is that linear combinations of $\underset{\sim}{w}_{it}$ can remove these *common trends* and become stationary ($I(0)$). Such linear combinations capture the long-run relations among $\underset{\sim}{w}_{it}$ and are called "cointegrating" relations.

Let $\underset{\sim}{w}_{it}$ be an $m\times 1$ vector of random variables. We assume that each element of $\underset{\sim}{w}_{it}$, w_{jit}, is integrated of order 1, $I(1)$,

$$w_{jit} \sim I(1), \quad j=1,\ldots,m. \tag{14}$$

Following Engle and Granger (1987), we say that the elements of $\underset{\sim}{w}_{it}$ forming $r(\geq 1)$ cointegrating relations if there exist r linearly independent combinations of $\underset{\sim}{w}_{it}$ that are stationary $I(0)$,

$$C_i \underset{\sim}{w}_{it} = \underset{\sim}{u}_{it} \sim I(0) \tag{15}$$

where C_i denotes the $r\times m$ constant matrix with rank (C_i) = r, and $\underset{\sim}{u}_{it}$ denotes the $r\times 1$ random vectors with $E(\underset{\sim}{u}_{it})=0$, $E(\underset{\sim}{u}_{it}\underset{\sim}{u}'_{it})=\tilde{\Omega}_{ii}$, $E(\underset{\sim}{u}_{it}\underset{\sim}{u}'_{i,t-s})=\tilde{\Omega}_{is}$, and rank $(\tilde{\Omega}_{ii})=r$.

Rewriting $\underset{\sim}{\omega}_{it}$ as the sum of the impact of $(m-r)$ $I(1)$ common trends $\underset{\sim}{z}_{it}$ and stationary components, ξ_{it},

$$\underset{\sim}{w}_{it} = A_i \underset{\sim}{z}_{it} + \underset{\sim}{\xi}_{it}, \quad i=1,\ldots,N,\ t=1,\ldots,T \tag{16}$$

where

$$\underset{(m-r)\times 1}{\underset{\sim}{z}_{it}} \sim I(1) \tag{17}$$

and $A_i=(\underset{\sim}{a}'_i)$ is an $m\times(m-r)$ constant matrix. The cointegrating relations (15) imply that

$$C_i A_i = \underset{\sim}{0}, \quad i=1,\ldots,N. \tag{18}$$

If $A_i \neq \underset{\sim}{0}$ with rank $(A_i) = m - r$, $0 < r < m$ and $\underset{\sim}{z}_{it} \neq \underset{\sim}{z}_{jt}$, the $m \times 1$ $I(1)$ random variables $\underset{\sim}{w}_{it}$ are cointegrated. There exists an error correction representation (VEC) of $\underset{\sim}{w}_{it}$ (Engle & Granger, 1987),

$$\Delta \underset{\sim}{w}_{it} = \Pi_i^* \underset{\sim}{w}_{i,t-1} + \underset{\sim}{\epsilon}_{it}, \; i = 1, \ldots, N \tag{19}$$

where $\Delta = (1 - L)$ denotes the first difference operation, $\Delta \underset{\sim}{w}_{it} = \underset{\sim}{w}_{it} - \underset{\sim}{w}_{i,t-1}$, $\underset{\sim}{\epsilon}_{it}$ is independent, identically distributed with mean $\underset{\sim}{0}$ and covariance matrix Ω_{ii}, $\Pi_i^* = -(I_m - \Phi_i)$,

$$\text{rank}\left(\Pi_i^*\right) = r. \tag{20}$$

Decompose the $m \times m$ matrix Π_i into the product of two rank $r(m \times r)$ matrices, J_i and Λ_i,

$$\Pi_i^* = J_i \Lambda_i', \quad i = 1, \ldots, m. \tag{21}$$

The decomposition is not unique, $\Pi_i^* = J_i^* \Lambda_i^{*'}$, where $J_i^* = \Gamma_i F_i$, $\Lambda_i^* = \Lambda_i \, F_i'^{-1}$, for any $r \times r$ nonsingular matrix F_i. To uniquely define the cointegrating relations, Phillips (1991) chooses the normalization

$$\Lambda_i' = \left[I_r, \; \tilde{\Lambda}_i'\right] \tag{22}$$

where $\tilde{\Lambda}_i$ is an $(m - r) \times r$ constant matrix. The advantage of considering a vector error correction representation rather than PVAR (4) is that one can simultaneously consider the long-run (equilibrium) relations and short-run dynamics of $\underset{\sim}{w}_{it}$.

If the nonstationarity of $\underset{\sim}{w}_{it}$, $i = 1, \ldots, N$, is driven by the same common trends across i, i.e., if $\underset{\sim}{z}_{it} = \underset{\sim}{z}_{jt} = \underset{\sim}{z}_t$, it also implies that each element of $\underset{\sim}{w}_{it}$, w_{kt} is cointegrated across cross-sectional units. Let w_{kt} denote the $N \times 1$ vector of the kth element of $\underset{\sim}{w}_{it}$, w_{kit}, $(w_{k1t}, \ldots, w_{kNt})' = \underset{\sim}{w}_{kt}$ and $\underset{\sim}{\xi}_{kt} = (\xi_{k1t}, \ldots, \xi_{kNt})'$, $\underset{\sim}{\epsilon}_{kt} = (\epsilon_{k1t}, \ldots, \underset{\sim}{\epsilon}_{kNt})'$. Then

$$\underset{\sim}{w}_{kt} = A_k \underset{\sim}{z}_t + \underset{\sim}{\xi}_{kt}, \; k = 1, \ldots, m \tag{23}$$

where $A_k = (\underset{\sim}{a}_{ki}')$ denotes the $N \times (m - r)$ constant matrix of the cross-sectional stacked kth row of A_i. Suppose rank $(A_k) = d_k (\leq m - r)$, there also exists an $(m - d_k) \times m$ matrix C_k with rank $(m - d_k)$ such that

$$C_k A_k = \underset{\sim}{0}, \quad k = 1, \ldots, m. \tag{24}$$

Then

$$C_k \underset{\sim}{w}_{kt} = C_k \underset{\sim}{\xi}_{kt} \sim I(0). \tag{25}$$

In other words, with nonstationary panel data, there could be cointegration relations both over time and across individuals (Breitung & Pesaran, 2008).

3.2. Estimation

3.2.1. "Homogeneous" Cointegrating Relations

In the case when there is at most one cointegration relation among $I(1)\ \underset{\sim}{w}_{it}$, $i = 1, \ldots, N$, the "homogeneous" cointegration vector between $(w_{1it}, \underset{\sim}{\tilde{w}}'_{it})$, $(1, \beta')$ with individual-specific effects α_{1i} yields

$$w_{1it} = \underset{\sim}{\tilde{w}}'_{it} \underset{\sim}{\beta} + \alpha_{1i} + u_{1it} \tag{26}$$

where u_{1it} is stationary but independently distributed across i. The cointegrating vector $\underset{\sim}{\beta}$ can be estimated by the within estimator,

$$\begin{aligned} \hat{\underset{\sim}{\beta}} = & \left[\sum_{i=1}^{N} \sum_{t=1}^{T} \left(\underset{\sim}{\tilde{w}}_{it} - \underset{\sim}{\bar{\tilde{w}}}_i \right) \left(\underset{\sim}{\tilde{w}}_{it} - \underset{\sim}{\bar{\tilde{w}}}_i \right)' \right]^{-1} \\ & \times \left[\sum_{i=1}^{N} \sum_{t=1}^{T} \left(\underset{\sim}{\tilde{w}}_{it} - \underset{\sim}{\bar{\tilde{w}}}_i \right) (w_{1it} - \bar{w}_{1i}) \right] \end{aligned} \tag{27}$$

where $\underset{\sim}{\bar{w}}'_i = (\bar{w}_{1i}, \underset{\sim}{\bar{\tilde{w}}}'_i) = \frac{1}{T} \sum_{t=1}^{T} \underset{\sim}{w}'_{it}$. The least squares estimator converges to $\underset{\sim}{\beta}$ in the speed of $T\sqrt{N}$ and is asymptotically normally distributed if $N \to \infty$. However, the endogeneity and unit-root of $\underset{\sim}{\tilde{w}}_{it}$ leads to a nonzero asymptotic bias term of order $1/T$ when $\hat{\underset{\sim}{\beta}}$ is multiplied by the scale factor, $T\sqrt{N}$ (Kao & Chiang, 2000). The idea of Park (1992) and Phillips and Hansen (1990) fully modified estimator is suggested to correct the endogeneity effect,

$$w_{1it}^{+} = \tilde{\underset{\sim}{w}}_{it}'\underset{\sim}{\beta} + \alpha_{1i} + u_{1it}^{+} \tag{28}$$

where

$$w_{1it}^{+} = w_{1it} - \Omega_{u\Delta\tilde{w}}\Omega_{\Delta\tilde{w}}^{-1}\Delta\tilde{\underset{\sim}{w}}_{it} \tag{29}$$

$$u_{1it}^{+} = u_{1it} - \Omega_{u\Delta\tilde{w}}\Omega_{\Delta\tilde{w}}^{-1}\Delta\tilde{\underset{\sim}{w}}_{it} \tag{30}$$

and $\Omega_{u\Delta\tilde{w}} = \sum_{j=-\infty}^{\infty} E\left(u_{it}\Delta\tilde{\underset{\sim}{w}}'_{i,t-j}\right)$, $\Omega_{\Delta\tilde{w}} = \sum_{j=-\infty}^{\infty} E\left(\Delta\tilde{\underset{\sim}{w}}_{it}, \Delta\tilde{\underset{\sim}{w}}'_{i,t-j}\right)$ are the long run covariance matrix of u_{1it} and $\Delta\tilde{\underset{\sim}{w}}_{it}$, and $\Delta\tilde{\underset{\sim}{w}}_{it}$, respectively. The panel fully modified within estimator takes the form,

$$\begin{aligned}\hat{\underset{\sim}{\beta}}_{FM} = &\left[\sum_{i=1}^{N}\sum_{t=1}^{T}\left(\tilde{\underset{\sim}{w}}_{it} - \bar{\tilde{\underset{\sim}{w}}}_{i}\right)\left(\tilde{\underset{\sim}{w}}_{it} - \bar{\tilde{\underset{\sim}{w}}}_{i}\right)'\right]^{-1} \\ &\times\left[\sum_{i=1}^{N}\left(\sum_{t=1}^{T}\left(\tilde{\underset{\sim}{w}}_{it} - \bar{\tilde{\underset{\sim}{w}}}_{i}\right)w_{1it}^{+} - T\Delta_{\Delta\tilde{w}u}\right)\right]\end{aligned} \tag{31}$$

where $\Delta_{\Delta\tilde{w}u} = \sum_{j=0}^{\infty} E(\Delta\tilde{\underset{\sim}{w}}_{i,t-j}u_{1it})$. The correction terms $\Omega_{u\Delta\tilde{w}}$, $\Omega_{\Delta\tilde{w}}$, $\Delta_{\Delta\tilde{w}u}$ can be replaced by their consistent estimator. Kao and Chiang (2000) show that $T\sqrt{N}(\hat{\underset{\sim}{\beta}}_{FM} - \underset{\sim}{\beta})$ is asymptotically normally distributed with mean $\underset{\sim}{0}$ and covariance matrix $2\sigma_{u|\Delta\tilde{w}}^{2}\Omega_{\Delta\tilde{w}}^{-1}$, where $\sigma_{u|\Delta\tilde{w}}^{2} = \Omega_u - \Omega_{u\Delta\tilde{w}}\Omega_{\Delta\tilde{w}}^{-1}\Omega_{\Delta\tilde{w}u}$, $\Omega_u = \sum_{j=-\infty}^{\infty} E(u_{1it}u_{1i,t-j})$.

An alternative approach is to apply the dynamic within estimator to the lead-lag adjusted regression model (Phillips & Loretan, 1991; Saikkonen, 1991),

$$w_{1it} = \tilde{\underset{\sim}{w}}_{it}'\underset{\sim}{\beta} + \sum_{j=-q}^{q}\Delta\tilde{\underset{\sim}{w}}_{i,t-j}'\underset{\sim}{\gamma}_j + \alpha_{1i} + \tilde{u}_{1it} \tag{32}$$

where Westerlund (2005) suggests a data-based choice of truncation lag order q. Kao and Chiang (2000) show that the within estimator of Eq. (32) has the same asymptotic distribution as the panel fully modified within estimator. The Monte Carlo studies conduced by Kao and Chiang (2000) show that the (lead-lag adjusted) within estimator of Eq. (32) performs better than the panel fully modified estimator, probably because of the failure to obtain good estimates of $\Omega_{u\Delta\tilde{w}}$, $\Omega_{\Delta\tilde{w}}$, etc.

When there are more than one linearly independent cointegration relations among the elements of $\underset{\sim}{w}_{it}$, in principle, one can follow Phillips (1991) to normalize the r linearly independent cointegration relations in the form of Eq. (22), $\Lambda' = [I_r\ \tilde{\Lambda}']$, then apply the fully modified within estimator or the lead-lag adjusted within estimator equation by equation.

Alternatively, one can use the methods of estimating the fixed effects PVAR model discussed in Section 2 to obtain the consistent estimator of Φ_j's, then solving $\hat{\Lambda}$ from the estimated $\hat{\Phi}_j$'s. The error-correction representation of cointegrated system (6) gives $\Pi = -(I_m - \Phi)$. If rank $(\Pi) = r(>1)$, then we can write $\Pi = J\Lambda'$ where J and Λ are $m \times r$ with rank r. Then the cointegrating matrix Λ' is equal to

$$\Lambda' = (J'J)^{-1}J'\Pi. \tag{33}$$

If we choose the normalization $\Lambda' = [I_r\ \tilde{\Lambda}']$, then $J = \Pi_1$ and

$$\tilde{\Lambda}' = \left(\Pi_1'\Pi_1\right)^{-1}\Pi_1'\Pi \tag{34}$$

where Π_1 is the $m \times r$ matrix consisting of the first r columns of Π.

Although the above procedure is consistent, it is not efficient because the first stage estimator of Φ_j's has not taken into account the reduced rank restrictions on $\Pi = J\Lambda'$. One way to obtain efficient estimator of Φ_j is to apply constrained GMM or constrained MDE or constrained (transformed) MLE by minimizing the quadratic form of the moment conditions (5) or (8) or maximizing (7) subject to

$$\Lambda = H\underset{\sim}{\delta}_r + B_r \tag{35}$$

where H and B_r are, respectively, $m \times (m-r)$ and $m \times r$ matrices with known elements, and $\underset{\sim}{\delta}$ is a $(m-r) \times r$ matrix with unknown coefficients. In the case when $\Lambda' = \left[I_r\ \tilde{\Lambda}'\right]$, $H = [0, I_{m-r}]$, $\underset{\sim}{\delta}_r = \tilde{\Lambda}$, $B_r = [I_r, \underset{\sim}{0}]'$.

3.2.2. Heterogeneous Cointegrating System

If individual units are independent across i, the Johansen (1991) method can be applied to the time series data for each i to obtain the maximum likelihood estimator (MLE) of Eq. (19). There is no need for pooling.

When individual units are correlated, if N is fixed and T is large the covariance between $\underset{\sim}{\epsilon}_{it}$ and $\underset{\sim}{\epsilon}_{jt}$, Ω_{ij}, can simply be estimated by

$$\hat{\Omega}_{ij} = \frac{1}{T}\sum_{t=1}^{T} \underset{\sim}{\epsilon}_{it}\underset{\sim}{\epsilon}'_{jt} \tag{36}$$

where $\hat{\underset{\sim}{\epsilon}}_{it}$ can be constructed from Eq. (19) using the Johansen MLE estimates. Stacking the N cross-sectionally observed $\underset{\sim}{w}_{it}$ one after another yields

$$\Delta \underset{\sim}{w}_t = \tilde{\Pi}\underset{\sim}{w}_{t-1} + \underset{\sim}{u}_t \tag{37}$$

where $\underset{\sim}{w}'_t = \left(\underset{\sim}{w}'_{1t}, \ldots, \underset{\sim}{w}'_{Nt}\right)$,

$$\tilde{\Pi} = \begin{pmatrix} \Pi_1^* & \underset{\sim}{0} & \cdot & \cdot & \underset{\sim}{0} \\ \underset{\sim}{0} & \Pi_2^* & & & \underset{\sim}{0} \\ \cdot & & \cdot & & \\ \cdot & & & \cdot & \\ \underset{\sim}{0} & & & & \Pi_N^* \end{pmatrix} \tag{38}$$

and

$$\underset{\sim}{\epsilon}_t = \left(\underset{\sim}{\epsilon}'_{1t}, \ldots, \underset{\sim}{\epsilon}'_{Nt}\right)'.$$

Under the assumption that $\underset{\sim}{\epsilon}_{it}$ is independently normally distributed with mean $\underset{\sim}{0}$ and covariance matrix

$$\underset{Nm \times Nm}{\tilde{\Omega}} = \begin{pmatrix} \Omega_{11} & \Omega_{12} & \cdot & \cdot & \Omega_{1N} \\ \cdot & \Omega_{22} & \cdot & \cdot & \cdot \\ \cdot & \cdot & \cdot & \cdot & \cdot \\ \cdot & \cdot & \cdot & \cdot & \cdot \\ \Omega_{N1} & \cdot & & \cdot & \Omega_{NN} \end{pmatrix} \tag{39}$$

the log-likelihood function of $\Delta \underset{\sim}{w}_t$ is proportional to

$$-\frac{T}{2}\log|\tilde{\Omega}| - \frac{1}{2}tr\left[\Omega^{-1}\sum_{t=1}^{T}\left(\Delta \underset{\sim}{w}_t - \tilde{\Pi}\underset{\sim}{w}_{t-1}\right)\left(\Delta \underset{\sim}{w}_t - \tilde{\Pi}\underset{\sim}{w}_{t-1}\right)'\right]. \tag{40}$$

The MLE of Ω and Π are the solutions that simultaneously satisfy

$$\hat{\tilde{\Omega}} = \frac{1}{T}\sum_{t=1}^{T}\left(\Delta \underset{\sim}{w}_t - \hat{\tilde{\Pi}}\underset{\sim}{w}_{t-1}\right)\left(\Delta \underset{\sim}{w}_t - \hat{\tilde{\Pi}}\underset{\sim}{w}_{t-1}\right)' \tag{41}$$

and

$$\begin{pmatrix} \text{vec}\left(\hat{\Pi}_1^{*\prime}\right) \\ \text{vec}\left(\hat{\Pi}_2^{*\prime}\right) \\ \cdot \\ \cdot \\ \text{vec}\left(\hat{\Pi}_N^{*\prime}\right) \end{pmatrix} = \left(\sum_{t=1}^{T}\hat{\tilde{\Omega}}^{-1}\otimes \underset{\sim}{w}_{t-1}\underset{\sim}{w}_{t-1}'\right)^{-1} \times\left[\sum_{t=1}^{T}\left(\hat{\tilde{\Omega}}^{-1}\otimes \underset{\sim}{w}_{t-1}\right)\text{vec}\left(\Delta \underset{\sim}{w}_t\right)\right]. \tag{42}$$

Conditional on $\hat{\tilde{\Omega}}$, Eq. (42) is in the form of Zellner's (1962) seemingly unrelated regression estimator. Sequentially iterating between Eqs. (41) and (42) until convergence will result in the MLE of Π_i^* and $\tilde{\Omega}$.

However, if $\underset{\sim}{w}_{it}$ are cointegrated, then Π_i is subject to the restrictions of the form (21). Substituting Eq. (41) into Eq. (42) and making use of the relations (Magnus & Neudecker, 1999, p. 31)

$$\begin{aligned}\text{vec}\,(J_i\Lambda_i') &= (I_r\otimes J_i)\,\text{vec}\left(\Lambda_i'\right)\\ &= (\Lambda_i\otimes I_m)\,\text{vec}\,(J_i)\end{aligned} \tag{43}$$

we obtain the MLE of $(\text{vec}\,(\Lambda_1')', \ldots, \text{vec}\,(\Lambda_N')')'$ conditional on $\hat{\tilde{\Omega}}$ and $\hat{J}_i$, $i = 1, \ldots, N$,

$$\begin{pmatrix} \text{vec}\,(\hat{\Lambda}_1) \\ \cdot \\ \cdot \\ \text{vec}\,(\hat{\Lambda}_N) \end{pmatrix} = \left\{ \hat{Q}' \left[\hat{\tilde{\Omega}}^{-1} \otimes \left(\sum_{t=1}^{T} \underset{\sim}{w}_{t-1} \underset{\sim}{w}'_{t-1} \right) \right] \hat{Q} \right\}^{-1} \times \left\{ \hat{Q}' \left[\hat{\tilde{\Omega}}^{-1} \otimes I_{Nm} \right] \text{vec} \left(\sum_{t=1}^{T} \underset{\sim}{w}_{t-1} \Delta \underset{\sim}{w}'_t \right) \right\} \tag{44}$$

and the MLE of $(\text{vec}(\hat{J}'_1)', \ldots, \text{vec}\,(\hat{J}'_N)')'$ conditional on $\hat{\Omega}$ and $\hat{\Lambda}_i$, $i = 1, \ldots, N$,

$$\begin{pmatrix} \text{vec}\,(\hat{J}'_1) \\ \cdot \\ \cdot \\ \text{vec}\,(\hat{J}_N)' \end{pmatrix} = \left\{ \hat{P}' \left(\hat{\tilde{\Omega}}^{-1} \otimes \sum_{t=1}^{T} \underset{\sim}{w}_{t-1} \underset{\sim}{w}'_{t-1} \right) \hat{P} \right\}^{-1} \cdot \left\{ \hat{P}' \left(\hat{\tilde{\Omega}}^{-1} \otimes I_{Nm} \right) \text{vec} \left(\sum_{t=1}^{T} \underset{\sim}{w}_{t-1} \Delta \underset{\sim}{w}'_t \right) \right\} \tag{45}$$

where I_{Nm} denotes the $Nm \times Nm$ identity matrix,

$$\hat{Q} = \left[\left(\underset{\sim}{d}_1 \otimes \hat{J}_1 \right) \otimes \left(\underset{\sim}{d}_1 \otimes I_r \right), \ldots, \left(\underset{\sim}{d}_N \otimes \hat{J}_N \right) \otimes \left(\underset{\sim}{d}_N \otimes I_r \right) \right] \tag{46}$$

$$\hat{P} = \left[\left(\underset{\sim}{d}_1 \otimes I_m \right) \otimes \left(\underset{\sim}{d}_1 \otimes \hat{\Lambda}_1 \right), \ldots, \left(\underset{\sim}{d}_N \otimes I_m \right) \otimes \left(d_N \otimes \hat{\Lambda}_N \right) \right] \tag{47}$$

d_j denotes the jth column of I_N, and $\otimes$ denotes the Kronecker product. Therefore Groen and Kleiergen (2003) suggest the following iterative scheme to obtain the panel MLE:

1. Construct initial estimates $\hat{\Omega}^{(0)}$ and $\hat{J}_i^{(0)}$, $i = 1, \ldots, N$ from Eqs. (41) and (42), where the initial estimates of $\hat{J}_i^{(0)}$ are simply the first r columns of $\hat{\Pi}_i^{*(0)}$ under the normalization (22).
2. Construct estimates of Λ_i, $i = 1, \ldots, N$ from Eq. (44).

3. Revise the estimate of Π_i^* from Eq. (42) and revise the estimate of Ω from the revised estimate of $\hat{\Pi}_i^*$ using the formula in Eq. (41).
4. Revise the estimate of J_i given the revise estimator of Λ_i and Ω using Eq. (45).
5. Iterate steps 1–4 until the solution converges.

The MLE of Λ_i, $i=1, ..., N$ converges to their true values at rate T and their limiting distributions are mixed normal. Therefore, conventional Wald type test statistics on the null hypothesis of Λ_i is asymptotically chi-square distributed.

When the cointegrating matrix $\Lambda_i = \Lambda_j = \Lambda$, the common cointegrating matrix can be estimated by

$$\begin{aligned} \mathrm{vec}\,(\Lambda) &= \left(\tilde{Q}'\left(\hat{\tilde{\Omega}}^{-1} \otimes \sum_{t=1}^{T} \underset{\sim}{w}_{t-1}\underset{\sim}{w}'_{t-1}\right)\tilde{Q}\right)^{-1} \\ &\times \left(\tilde{Q}'\left(\hat{\tilde{\Omega}}^{-1} \otimes I_{Nm}\right) \mathrm{vec}\left(\sum_{t=1}^{T} \underset{\sim}{w}_{t-1}\Delta \underset{\sim}{w}'_t\right)\right) \end{aligned} \tag{48}$$

where $\tilde{Q}$ is of the form of $\hat{Q}$ with $\hat{J}_i$ replaced by ith row of I_N, $i=1, ..., N$. Because Λ_i or Λ is asymptotically mixed normally distributed, one can use the likelihood ratio test statistic to test the null hypothesis

$$\begin{aligned} & H_0 : \Lambda_1 = \Lambda_2 = \ldots = \Lambda_N = \Lambda \\ \text{versus} \quad & H_1 : \Lambda_i \neq \Lambda_j \end{aligned}$$

The likelihood ratio statistic is asymptotically chi-square distributed with $(N-1)r(m-r)$ degrees of freedom when $T \to \infty$.

When individual units contain individual-specific effects $\underset{\sim}{a}_i$ and p_i in Eq. (2) different from zero, one can follow Johansen (1991) to concentrate out constants and Φ_{is}^* by regressing $\Delta \underset{\sim}{w}_{it}$ and $\Delta \underset{\sim}{w}_{i,t-1}$ on the constants and $\Delta \underset{\sim}{w}_{i,t-s}$, $s=1, ..., p_i$, respectively, to obtain $\Delta \tilde{\underset{\sim}{w}}_{it}$ and $\Delta \underset{\sim}{w}_{i,t-1}$, then proceed to estimate J_i and Λ_i. Once the MLE of Γ_i, Λ_i, and Ω are obtained, the individual-specific constants and Φ_{ij}^* can then be obtained by regressing $(\Delta \tilde{\underset{\sim}{w}}_{it} - \hat{J}_i \hat{\Lambda}'_i \tilde{\underset{\sim}{w}}_{i,t-1})$ on constants, $\Delta \tilde{\underset{\sim}{w}}_{i,t-p_i-1}, ..., \Delta \tilde{\underset{\sim}{w}}_{i,t-1}$ using Zellner's (1962) seemingly unrelated regression method.

When N is large, it is not feasible to use either the likelihood approach or the Zellner (1962) unrelated regression framework to estimate either the homogeneous or the heterogeneous cointegration relations. Pesaran et al.

(2004) suggest using a global VAR (GVAR) ((11) – (13)) to filter out cross-sectional dependence. When w_{it}^* can be treated as weakly exogenous, the system (19) subject to the rank condition (22) for each i can be estimated using standard time series estimator techniques (e.g., Pesaran et al., 2000).

4. UNIT ROOT AND COINTEGRATION TESTS

4.1. Unit Root Tests

Panels have been used to analyze regional growth convergence (e.g., Bernard & Jones, 1996), exchange rate determination (e.g., testing of purchasing power parity hypothesis, Frankel & Rose, 1996), business cycle synchronization, etc. In such analysis the time series property of a variable is of significant interests to economists. If observed data are nonstationary, or contain unit roots, standard estimators will have nonstandard distributions as $T \to \infty$. The conventional Wald type test statistics can not be approximated well by t- or chi-square distributions (e.g., Dickey & Fuller, 1979, 1981; Phillips, 1986; Phillips & Durlauf, 1986). Computer simulations will have to be used to find the critical values under the null. In cases where N is fixed and T is large, standard time series techniques can be used and the panel aspect of the data does not pose new techniques. If N is large, panel data provides the possibility of invoking a version of central limit theorem along the cross-section dimension. Hence, contrary to the time series literature, the null hypothesis of panel unit root tests can be either under the null of unit root (no cointegration for the residual-based tests of cointegration) or under the null of stationarity (cointegration for the residual-based tests of cointegration) when $N \to \infty$ with either T fixed or $\to \infty$. When the null is formulated as containing a unit root, it is usually formulated in the form of

$$\Delta y_{it} = \gamma_i y_{i,t-1} + \sum_{\ell=1}^{p_i} \phi_{i\ell} \Delta y_{i,t-\ell} + \alpha_i + \epsilon_{it} \tag{49}$$

with the null,

$$H_0 : \gamma_1 = \gamma_2 = \cdots = \gamma_N = 0. \tag{50}$$

Under the assumption that ϵ_{it} are i.i.d. across i and over t, the test statistics are usually based on the average of augmented Dickey–Fuller test statics

(1979, 1981) (e.g., Levin, Lin, & Chu, 2002 (LL); Im, Pesaran, & Shin, 2003 (IPS); Westerlund & Larsson, 2012, etc.).

When ϵ_{it} are cross-sectionally dependent, the tests based on i.i.d. are subject to severe size distortion (e.g., Breitung & Das, 2008). Chang (2002) suggests using some nonlinear transformation of the lagged level variable, $y_{i,t-1}$, $F(y_{i,t-1})$, as an instrument (IV) for $y_{i,t-1}$ for the usual Dickey–Fuller type regression (49). As long as $F(\cdot)$ is regularly integreable, say $F(y_{i,t-1}) = y_{i,t-1}e^{-c_i|y_{i,\,t-1}|}$, where c_i is a positive constant, the IV t-ratio

$$Z_i = \frac{\hat{\gamma}_i - 1}{s(\hat{\gamma}_i)} \tag{51}$$

will converge to a standard normal when $T_i \to \infty$ where $s(\hat{\gamma}_i)$ is the standard error of the IV estimator $\hat{\gamma}_i$ and T_i denotes the time series observation of the ith unit because $F(y_{i,t-1})$ tends to zero as $y_{i,t-1}$ tends to $\pm\infty$, the non-stationarity of $y_{i,t-1}$ is eliminated. Moreover, the product of $F(y_{i,t-1})$ and $F(y_{j,t-1})$ from different cross-sectional units i and j are asymptotically uncorrelated even though $y_{i,t-1}$ and $y_{j,t-1}$ are correlated, therefore the average IV t-ratio statistic

$$S_N = \frac{1}{\sqrt{N}} \sum_{i=1}^{N} Z_i \tag{52}$$

possesses a standard normally limiting distribution as N also tends to infinity.

When y_{it} are correlated across cross-sectional units, Bai and Ng (2004, 2010) and Moon and Perron (2004) consider that the cross-correlations are driven by some common factors, $\underset{\sim}{f}_t = (f_{it}, \ldots, f_{kt})'$ that vary over time. Rewrite y_{it} as the sum of the impact of the common factors, $\underset{\sim}{b}_i'\underset{\sim}{f}_t$ and the idiosyncratic component, u_{ti},

$$y_{it} = \sum_{j=1}^{k} b_{ij} f_{jt} + u_{it} \tag{53}$$

where $\underset{\sim}{b}_i = (b_{i1}, \ldots, b_{ik})'$ is a $k \times 1$ vector of constants, u_{ti} is independent across i with mean zero. Bai and Ng (2004, 2010) and Moon and Perron (2004) propose to test unit roots in both $\underset{\sim}{f}_t$ and u_{it}. The factors are estimated from k principal components of Δy_{it}. Augmented Dickey–Fuller tests (ADF) are then applied to test if $\underset{\sim}{f}_t$ is integrated or not (I(1) v. I(0)). If it is found that the estimated factors contain unit roots and are not cointegrated, the N series are integrated of order 1. If the presence of a unit root in the factors is rejected, panel unit root tests such as Maddala and Wu (1999) P_λ or Choi (2001) P_m test is then applied to the defactored observations, u_{it}, $(y_{it} - \hat{\underset{\sim}{b}}'f_t)$.

If $\underset{\sim}{b}_i \neq \underset{\sim}{b}_j$ and $k=1$, Pesaran (2007) suggests augmenting Eq. (49) by the cross-sectional averaged values of $\bar{y}_{t-1} = \frac{1}{N}\sum_{i=1}^{N} y_{i,t-1}$ and $\Delta\bar{y}_{t-j} = \frac{1}{N}\sum_{i=1}^{N} \Delta y_{i,t-j}$,

$$\begin{aligned}\Delta y_{it} = \alpha_i + \delta_i t + \gamma_i y_{i,t-1} + \sum_{\ell=1}^{p_i} \phi_{i\ell}\Delta y_{i,t-\ell} \\ + c_i\bar{y}_{t-1} + \sum_{\ell=1}^{p_i} d_{i\ell}\Delta\bar{y}_{t-\ell} + e_{it}\end{aligned} \tag{54}$$

to filter out the cross-sectional dependency, then taking the average of separate unit root tests for N individual cross-section units of the augmented Dickey–Fuller t-ratios, τ_i, $\bar{\tau}$, as in Im et al. (2003).

When $k>1$, if there exist $K(\geq k-1)$ observed time series $\underset{\sim}{w}_{it}$, Kapetanios, Pesaran, and Yamagata (2011) and Pesaran et al. (2012) suggest further augmenting Eq. (49) by cross-sectional mean of $\underset{\sim}{w}_t$ and $\Delta\underset{\sim}{w}_{t-\ell}$

$$\begin{aligned}\Delta y_{it} = \alpha_i + \delta_{it} + \gamma_i y_{i,t-1} + \sum_{\ell=1}^{p_i} \Delta y_{i,t-\ell} \\ + \sum_{\ell=1}^{p_i} d_{i\ell}\Delta\bar{y}_{t-\ell} + W_t\underset{\sim}{\theta} + \epsilon_{it}, \quad i=1,\ldots,N\end{aligned} \tag{55}$$

where $W_t = (\Delta\underset{\sim}{w}_t', \Delta\underset{\sim}{w}_{t-1}', \ldots, \Delta\underset{\sim}{w}_{t-p_i-1}', \underset{\sim}{w}_{t-1}')$ and $\underset{\sim}{\theta}$ is an $mp_i \times 1$ vector of constants. Pesaran et al. (2012) suggest either constructing an IPS type test statistic by taking the average of t-statistics for $\gamma_i, i=1, \ldots, N$ or taking the average of the Sargan and Bhargava test statistic (SB) (1983),

$$\mathrm{SB}_i = T^{-2}\sum_{t=1}^{T}\frac{s_{it}^2}{\hat{\sigma}_i^2}, \quad i=1,\ldots,N \tag{56}$$

where

$$s_{it} = \sum_{s=1}^{t}\hat{\epsilon}_{is}, \hat{\sigma}^2 = \frac{\sum_{t=1}^{T}\hat{\epsilon}_{it}^2}{T-K^*}$$

$\hat{\epsilon}_{it}$ is the least squares residual of Eq. (55), and K^* is the number of the unknown constants in Eq. (55). Each of the SB_i converges to a functional of Brownian motion which is independent of the factors as well as their loadings. Pesaran et al. (2012) have provided the critical values of the augmented IPS and SB tests for $K = 0, 1, 2, 3$ and $p_i = 0,1, \ldots, 4$ for N, $T=20$, 30, 50, 70, 100, 200.

When the process of driving cross-section dependence is unknown, Choi and Chue (2007) suggest using a subsample testing procedure. They suggest to group the sample into a number of overlapping blocks of b time periods. Using all $(T-b+1)$ possible overlapping blocks, the critical value of a test statistic is estimated by the empirical distribution of the $(T-b+1)$ test statistics computed. Although the null distribution of the test statistic may depend on the unknown nuisance parameters when $T \to \infty$ and N fixed, the subsample critical values will converge in probability to the true critical values. The Monte Carlo simulation conducted by Choi and Chue (2007) show that the size of the subsample test is indeed robust against various forms of cross-section dependence.

When the null is formulated as of stationarity, the test statistics is usually constructed based on the average of Sargan–Bhargava (1983) statistics, which is formulated in the form of partial sum of y_{it} relative to the variance of Δy_{it},

$$Z = \frac{1}{\sqrt{N}} \sum_{i=1}^{N} (K_i - E(K_i)) \tag{57}$$

where

$$K_i = \frac{1}{T^2 \sigma_i^2} \sum_{t=1}^{T} S_{it}^2, \quad S_{it} = \frac{1}{\sqrt{T}} \sum_{s=1}^{t} y_{is}$$

and σ_i^2 is the variance of Δy_{it} (e.g., Hadri, 2000; Hadri & Larsson, 2005; Kwiastkowki et al., 1992).

Simulations conducted by Choi (2001, 2002) show that the empirical size of all the unit root tests is reasonably close to the nominal size and they all become more powerful as N increases. For further details, see Hsiao (2014, chapter 10.4).

4.2. Cointegration Tests

The existence of cointegration can be tested if the residuals of regressing one element of $\underset{\sim}{w}_{it}$ on the rest elements of $\underset{\sim}{w}_{it}$ contain a unit root or not. If the residuals are stationary, $\underset{\sim}{w}_{it}$ are cointegrated. In a time series framework, the null of time series unit root tests is unit root. In other words, the null is no cointegration.

Under the null of no cointegration, time series regression of the slope coefficients β fails to converge (Phillips, 1986). On the other hand, panels with large $\tilde{N}$ and large T can yield convergent estimate of $\underset{\sim}{\beta}$. If there is no cointegration, Kao (1999), using a sequential limit argument (first $T \to \infty$, followed by $N \to \infty$), has shown that the least squares estimator of Eq. (27) converges to $\Omega_{\Delta\tilde{w}}^{-1}\Omega_{\Delta\tilde{w}u}$. If there is cointegration, then the panel fully modified within estimator (31) or the within estimator for the lead-lag adjusted regression model (32) is consistent and asymptotically normally distributed. Moreover, since u_{it} is independently distributed across i, a version of the central limit theorem can be invoked on the cross-sectional average of a statistic. That is, even though a statistic could have different asymptotic properties depending on whether u_{it} contains a unit root or not along time series dimension, the properly scaled cross-sectional average of such a statistic is asymptotically normally distributed when $N \to \infty$. What this implies is that the panel null for the distribution of u_{it} could either be unit root (no cointegration) or stationary (cointegration).

McCoskey and Kao (1998) propose to test the null of cointegration using the statistic

$$\overline{LM} = \frac{\frac{1}{N}\sum_{i=1}^{N}\frac{1}{T^2}\sum_{t=1}^{T} S_{it}^{+2}}{s^{+2}} \tag{58}$$

where

$$S_{it}^{+} = \sum_{s=1}^{t} \hat{u}_{1is}, \quad s^{+2} = \frac{1}{NT}\sum_{i=1}^{N}\sum_{t=1}^{T} \hat{u}_{1it}^{+2}$$

$\hat{u}_{1it}$ are the estimated residuals of Eq. (26) with $\tilde{\beta}$ estimated by either Eq. (31) or applying the within estimator to Eq. (32) and $\hat{u}_{1it}^{+}$ is the estimated residual of Eq. (30). McCoskey and Kao (1998) show that $\sqrt{N}\,(\overline{LM})$ is asymptotically normally distributed with mean μ and variance σ_v^2, if individual units are independent of each other where μ and σ_v^2 can be found through Monte Carlo simulations.

Kao (1999) and Pedroni (1994) propose test cointegration under the null of no cointegration (residuals contain unit root). Kao (1999) proposes a modified Dicky–Fuller type test statistics to take account of correlations between regressors and error or serial correlations. Pedroni (1994) considers the unit root test statistic against "homogeneous" alternatives or "heterogeneous" alternative. For excellent surveys of panel unit root and cointegration tests, see Baltagi and Kao (2000), Banerjee (1999), Breitung and Pesaran (2008), Choi (2006), etc.

The residual-based tests can only tell if there exist cointegration relations among elements of $\underset{\sim}{w}_{it}$, they cannot tell the cointegration rank. For the "homogeneous" PVAR model, a test of the cointegration rank can be conducted by maximizing the (transformed) likelihood function (4) subject to either

$$\Lambda_r = H_r \underset{\sim}{\delta}_r + B_r \tag{59}$$

or

$$\Lambda_{r+q} = H_{t+1} \underset{\sim}{\delta}_{r+1} + B_{r+1} \tag{60}$$

where H_r and H_{r+1} are, respectively, $m \times (m-r)$ and $m \times (m-r-1)$ matrices with known elements, B_r and B_{r+1} are, respectively, $m \times r$ matrices with known elements, $\underset{\sim}{\delta}_r$ and $\underset{\sim}{\delta}_{r+1}$ are, respectively, $r \times m$ and $(r+1) \times m$ matrices with unknown elements. When T is fixed and $N \to \infty$, the likelihood ratio test statistic of cointegration rank r versus rank $(r+1)$ is asymptotically chi-square distributed with $(m-r)^2 - (m-r-1)^2 = 2(m-r) - 1$ degrees of freedom (Binder et.al., 2005). (Imposing Π to be of rank r leaves $m^2 - (m-r)^2$ unrestricted coefficient in Π).

5. DYNAMIC SIMULTANEOUS EQUATIONS MODELS

The discussions in previous sections, in particular, the panel VAR model (1), can be considered as a reduced form specification of the model

$$\Phi(L) \underset{\sim}{w}_{it} = \underset{\sim}{\alpha}_i + \underset{\sim}{\epsilon}_{it} \tag{61}$$

where

$$\Phi(L) = \Phi_0 + \Phi_1 L +, \ldots, + \Phi_p L^p \tag{62}$$

and

$$\Phi_0 \neq I_m. \tag{63}$$

For simplicity, we maintain the assumption that $\underset{\sim}{\epsilon}_{it}$ is i.i.d. across i and over t with covariance matrix Ω. When $\Phi_0 \neq I_m$, in addition to dynamic dependence, Eq. (61) also introduces contemporaneous dependence among elements of $\underset{\sim}{w}_{it}$. One will need prior information to identify an equation in the system, say the gth. If we assume that the prior information takes the form of exclusion restrictions, i.e., some variables are excluded from the gth equation. Let $\left[\Phi_{og}, \ldots, \Phi_{pg}\right]$ be the matrix formed from the columns of $[\Phi_0, \ldots, \Phi_p]$ that are zero on the gth row. The presence of $\underset{\sim}{\alpha}_i$ does not lead to any change in the necessary and sufficient condition for the identification of the gth equation of (61), i.e., (e.g., Hsiao, 1983; Hsiao & Zhou, 2014),

$$\text{rank}\left[\Phi_{og}, \ldots, \Phi_{pg}\right] = m - 1. \tag{64}$$

When an equation in (61) is identified, one can estimate that equation either through a method of moments approach or a likelihood approach. As an illustration. let $\underset{\sim}{w}'_{it} = (\underset{\sim}{y}'_{it}, \underset{\sim}{x}'_{it})$, where $\underset{\sim}{y}_{it}$ is $G \times 1$ and $\underset{\sim}{x}_{it}$ is $(m-G) \times 1$. Assume $p = 1$ and the first equation of the system (61) takes the form

$$y_{1it} = Y'_{it}\underset{\sim}{\phi}_{11,0} + Y'_{i,t-1}\underset{\sim}{\phi}_{11,1} + y_{1i,t-1}\gamma + \underset{\sim}{x}'_{it}\underset{\sim}{\beta} + \alpha_{1i} + \epsilon_{1it} \tag{65}$$

where (y_{1it}, Y'_{it}) denotes the sub-vector of $\underset{\sim}{y}_{it}$ that appears in the first equation. For notational ease we assume $\underset{\sim}{w}'_{i0} = (\underset{\sim}{y}'_{i0}, \underset{\sim}{x}'_{i0})$ are observable.

Taking the first difference of Eq. (65) to eliminate the individual-specific effects, α_{1i}, yields

$$\begin{aligned} \Delta y_{1it} &= \Delta Y'_{it}\phi_{11,0} + \Delta Y'_{i,t-1}\underset{\sim}{\phi}_{11,1} + \Delta y_{1i,t-1}\gamma + \Delta \underset{\sim}{x}'_{it}\underset{\sim}{\beta} + \Delta\epsilon_{1it} \\ &= \Delta \underset{\sim}{z}'_{it}\underset{\sim}{\theta} + \Delta\epsilon_{1it}, \quad i = 1, \ldots, N, \; t = 2, \ldots, T \end{aligned} \tag{66}$$

where $\Delta = (1 - L)$, L is the lag operator that shifts the variable back by one period, $Ly_{1it} = \underset{\sim}{y}_{1i,t-1}$, and $\underset{\sim}{z}'_{it} = (Y'_{it}, Y'_{i,t-1}, y_{1i,t-1}, \underset{\sim}{x}'_{it})$, $\underset{\sim}{\theta} = (\underset{\sim}{\phi}'_{11,0}, \underset{\sim}{\phi}'_{11,1}, \gamma, \underset{\sim}{\beta}')$. Under the assumption that $\underset{\sim}{\epsilon}_{it}$ is i.i.d. and $E(\underset{\sim}{x}_{it}\, \underset{\sim}{\epsilon}'_{it}) = \underset{\sim}{0}$, we have

$$E\underset{\sim}{q}_{it}\Delta\underset{\sim}{\epsilon}_{it}=\underset{\sim}{0} \tag{67}$$

where $\underset{\sim}{q}_{it}=(y_{1i0},\ Y'_{i0},\ \ldots,y_{1i,t-2},\ Y'_{1i,t-2},\ \underset{\sim}{x}'_{io},\ \ldots,\underset{\sim}{x}'_{iT})'$. Let

$$W_i=\begin{bmatrix} \underset{\sim}{q}_{i2} & \underset{\sim}{0} & \underset{\sim}{0} & \cdot & \underset{\sim}{0} \\ \underset{\sim}{0} & \underset{\sim}{q}_{i3} & \underset{\sim}{0} & \cdot & \underset{\sim}{0} \\ \cdot & \cdot & \cdot & \cdot & \underset{\sim}{0} \\ \underset{\sim}{0} & \cdot & \cdot & \cdot & \underset{\sim}{q}_{iT} \end{bmatrix} \tag{68}$$

be the $Q\times(T-1)$ block dimensional matrix, where Q denotes the dimension of $(\underset{\sim}{q}'_{i2},\ \ldots,\underset{\sim}{q}'_{iT})'$ Then

$$E\left(\underset{\sim}{W}_i\Delta\underset{\sim}{\epsilon}_{1i}\right)=0,\quad i=1,\ldots,N \tag{69}$$

where $\Delta\underset{\sim}{\epsilon}'_{1i}=(\Delta\epsilon_{1i2},\ \ldots,\Delta\epsilon_{1iT})$ with $E(\Delta\underset{\sim}{\epsilon}_{1i})=\underset{\sim}{0}$ and $E(\Delta\underset{\sim}{\epsilon}_{1i}\Delta\underset{\sim}{\epsilon}'_{1i})=\sigma_1^2\tilde{A}$, $\sigma_1^2=E(\underset{\sim}{\epsilon}_{1it}^2)$,

$$\tilde{A}=\begin{bmatrix} 2 & -1 & 0 & \cdot & 0 \\ -1 & 2 & -1 & \cdot & \cdot \\ 0 & -1 & 2 & \cdot & \cdot \\ \cdot & \cdot & \cdot & \cdot & \cdot \\ 0 & \cdot & \cdot & -1 & 2 \end{bmatrix}.$$

The Arellano and Bond (1991) GMM estimator of $\underset{\sim}{\theta}$ is to find $\hat{\underset{\sim}{\theta}}$ that minimizes

$$\left(\sum_{i=1}^{N}\Delta\underset{\sim}{\epsilon}'_{1i}\ W'_i\right)\left(\sum_{i=1}^{N}W_i\tilde{A}W'_i\right)^{-1}\left(\sum_{i=1}^{N}W_i\Delta\underset{\sim}{\epsilon}_{1i}\right). \tag{70}$$

When T is fixed and $N\to\infty$, $\sqrt{N}(\hat{\underset{\sim}{\theta}}_{\text{GMM}}-\underset{\sim}{\theta})$ is asymptotically normally distributed with mean $\underset{\sim}{0}$ and covariance matrix $\sigma_1^2\left(\frac{1}{N}\sum_{i=1}^{N}W_i\tilde{A}W'_i\right)^{-1}$. When T is also large and $\frac{T}{N}\to c\neq 0<\infty$ as $N,T\to\infty$, the process of removing individual-specific effects creates a second-order bias that becomes serious for large T because

$$E\left[\begin{pmatrix} \Delta Y_i' \\ \Delta Y_{i,-1}' \\ \Delta y_{1i,01} \end{pmatrix} W_i'\left(W_i\tilde{A}W_i'\right)^{-1}W_i\Delta \underset{\sim}{\epsilon}_{1i}\right] \neq 0 \tag{71}$$

and is of order log T. Akashi and Kunitomo (2012, 2014) show that the Arellano–Bond type GMM is inconsistent and asymptotically biased. Monte Carlo studies conducted by Akashi and Kunitomo (2012, 2014) show that the GMM estimator is badly biased when N and T are both large.

Alternatively, Hsiao and Zhou (2014) show that the likelihood approach with properly formulated initial value distribution for $\underset{\sim}{y}_{i0}$ yields an estimator that is asymptotically unbiased independent of the way N or T or both tend to infinity. However, maximizing the (transformed) likelihood function of $(\Delta\underset{\sim}{y}_{i2}, \ldots, \Delta\underset{\sim}{y}_{iT})$, $i=1,\ldots,N$, $t=2,\ldots,T$ under the false assumption that $\Delta\underset{\sim}{y}_{i1}$ are fixed constants is asymptotically unbiased only if N is fixed and T is large. If both N and T are large, the false (quasi) maximum likelihood estimator is asymptotically biased of order $\sqrt{N/T}$. Monte Carlo studies conducted by Hsiao and Zhou (2014) show that the reliability of statistical inference depends critically on the estimator that is asymptotically unbiased.

6. MACRO POLICY EVALUATION

Denote the outcome of the ith unit that received the treatment at time t by y_{it}^{1*} and the outcome not receiving the treatment by y_{it}^{0*}. If both y_{it}^{1*} and y_{it}^{0*} are observable, then treatment effect is simply

$$\Delta_{it} = y_{it}^{1*} - y_{it}^{0*} \tag{72}$$

One of the issues of evaluating the effectiveness of a macro policy is that we do not simultaneously observe y^{1*} and y^{0*}. Often, we only have time series data of the outcomes before the implementation of a policy and the outcomes after the implementation of a policy. However, many conditioning events have changed over time. For instance, one knows the outcomes of the U.S. economy before the 2008 financial crisis and the outcomes after the implementation of Fed's quantity easing policy, but one does not know what would have happened to the U.S. economy in the absence of Fed's quantity easing policy. The parametric approach to construct the counterfactuals, y_{it}^{0*}, after the year 2008 requires the conditional variables not affected by the changes in policy. The availability of panel data provides the possibility of measuring policy impact without relying on economic theory or macroeconometric model. Hsiao, Ching, and Wan (2012) propose a *measurement without theory* approach to evaluate the impact of macro policies by exploiting the dependence among cross-sectional units and noting that panel data not only contain observations of those before and after the implementation of a policy, but also contain time series information on those not subject to the policy intervention.

Let d_{it} be 1 if the ith unit received the treatment at time t and 0 if not. Then the observed y_{it} takes the form

$$y_{it} = d_{it} y_{it}^{1*} + (1 - d_{it}) y_{it}^{0*} \tag{73}$$

In other words, at time t one either observes y_{it}^{1*} or y_{it}^{0*}, not both. To measure the impact of a policy intervention at time t, one either has to construct the counterfactual of y_{it}^{1*} or y_{it}^{0*}. Suppose all N units at time t, $\underset{\sim}{y}_t = (y_{1t}, \ldots, y_{Nt})$ did not receive the treatment for $t = 1, \ldots, T_1$, i.e., $\underset{\sim}{y}_t = \underset{\sim}{y}^{0*}$, but from time period $T_1 + 1$ onwards, the first unit received treatment, $y_{1t} = y_{1t}^{1*}$, $t = T_1 + 1, \ldots, T$, while the rest of individuals did not, $y_{it} = y_{it}^{0*}$, $t = 1, \ldots, T$ for $i = 2, \ldots, N$. As long as

$$E(\varepsilon_{it} | d_{1t}) = 0, \; i = 2, \ldots, N \tag{74}$$

one can write

$$\begin{aligned} y_{1t}^{0*} &= E\left(y_{1t}^{0*} \mid \tilde{\underset{\sim}{y}}_t \right) + \eta_{1t}, \quad t = 1, \ldots, T \\ &= a + \underset{\sim}{c}' \tilde{\underset{\sim}{y}}_t + \eta_{1t} \end{aligned} \tag{75}$$

where $\tilde{\underset{\sim}{y}}_t = (y_{2t}, \ldots, y_{Nt})'$ and $E(\eta_{1t} \mid \tilde{\underset{\sim}{y}}_t) = 0$. It is shown by Hsiao et al. (2012) that minimizing

$$\frac{1}{T_1} \left(\underset{\sim}{y}_1^0 - \underset{\sim}{e} a - Y \underset{\sim}{c} \right)' A \left(\underset{\sim}{y}_1^0 - \underset{\sim}{e} a - Y \underset{\sim}{c} \right) \tag{76}$$

yields consistent estimates of a and $\underset{\sim}{c}$, where $\underset{\sim}{y}_1^0 = (y_{11}, \ldots, y_{1T_1})'$, $\underset{\sim}{e}$ is a $T_1 \times 1$ vector of 1's, Y is a $T_1 \times (N-1)$ matrix of T_1 time series observations of $\tilde{\underset{\sim}{y}}_t$, and A is a $T_1 \times T_1$ positive definite matrix. From the estimates $(\hat{a}, \hat{\underset{\sim}{c}}')$, one can construct the predicted value of the first unit in the absence of treatment, y_{1t}^{0*}, by

$$\hat{y}_{it}^{0*} = \hat{a} + \tilde{\underset{\sim}{c}}' \tilde{\underset{\sim}{y}}, \quad t = T_1 + 1, \ldots, T. \tag{77}$$

The treatment effect on the first unit can then be estimated by

$$\hat{\Delta}_{1t} = y_{1t} - \hat{y}_{1t}^{0*}, \quad t = T_1 + 1, \ldots, T. \tag{78}$$

Cross-sectional data provide measurement of policy intervention as a once-and-for-all impact. Panel data allow the policy impact to be evolutionary. If Δ_{1t} is serially correlated, but stationary, one can further model the time-varying treatment effects by an autoregressive moving average model using Box and Jenkins (1970) methodology

$$a(L)\, \hat{\Delta}_{1t} = \mu + \theta(L)\eta_t \tag{79}$$

where L is the lag operator, η_t is an i.i.d. process with zero mean and constant variance and the roots of $\theta(L) = 0$ lie outside the unit circle. If the roots of $a(L) = 0$ all lie outside the unit circle, the treatment effect is stationary, and the long-term treatment effect is

$$\Delta_1 = a(L)^{-1}\mu = \mu^*. \tag{80}$$

Condition (74) makes no claim about the relationship between d_{1t} and ε_{1t}. They can be correlated or uncorrelated. Here, all we need is that the jth unit's idiosyncratic components are independent of d_{1t} for $j \neq 1$.

7. AGGREGATION AND PREDICTIONS

Macroeconometrics modeling depends on the existence of stable relations among aggregate variables. Aggregation is a good simplification tool as long as micro relations are "homogeneous" (i.e., have identical parameter values) or the distribution of micro variables remains constant over time (e.g., Stoker, 1993; Theil, 1954). However, if the micro relation is dynamic and "heterogeneous," the dynamics of aggregate variables can be very different from the dynamics of disaggregate variables (e.g., Lewbel, 1994; Zaffaroni, 2001). For instance, consider a simple dynamic relation for micro units,

$$y_{it} = \gamma_i y_{i,t-1} + \underset{\sim}{x}'_{it} \underset{\sim}{\beta}_i + \alpha_i + u_{it}, \ |\gamma| < 1, \quad i = 1, \ldots, N \tag{81}$$

where u_{it} is i.i.d. with mean 0 and constant variance σ_u^2. Then the long-run relation between y and $\underset{\sim}{x}$ for each i is given by

$$y_{it} = \frac{1}{1-\gamma_i} \underset{\sim}{x}'_{it} \underset{\sim}{\beta}_i + \frac{\alpha_i}{1-\gamma_i} + \frac{1}{1-\gamma_i} u_{it}. \tag{82}$$

Let $\bar{y}_t = \sum_{i=1}^{N} y_{it}$, $\bar{\underset{\sim}{x}}_t = \sum_{i=1}^{N} \underset{\sim}{x}_{it}$, then

$$\bar{y}_t - \bar{\underset{\sim}{x}}'_t \underset{\sim}{b} - \alpha = v_t \tag{83}$$

has a stable relation (i.e., v_t is covariance stationary) if and only if either of the following conditions hold (Hsiao, Shen, & Fujiki, 2005):

$$\begin{aligned} &\text{(i)} \quad \frac{1}{1-\gamma_i} \underset{\sim}{\beta}_i = \frac{1}{1-\gamma_j} \underset{\sim}{\beta}_j \text{ for all } i \text{ and } j \\ &\text{or} \\ &\text{(ii)} \quad \text{if } \frac{1}{1-\alpha_i} \underset{\sim}{\beta}_i \neq \frac{1}{1-\gamma_j} \underset{\sim}{\beta}_j \end{aligned} \tag{84}$$

then $\underset{\sim}{x}'_t = (\underset{\sim}{x}'_{1t}, \ldots, \underset{\sim}{x}'_{Nt})$ must lie on the null space of D for all t, where

$$D' = \left(\frac{1}{1-\gamma_1} \underset{\sim}{\beta}'_1 - \underset{\sim}{b}', \frac{1}{1-\gamma_2} \underset{\sim}{\beta}'_2 - \underset{\sim}{b}', \ldots, \frac{1}{1-\gamma_N} \underset{\sim}{\beta}'_N - \underset{\sim}{b}' \right).$$

Panel data provide information on micro units over time that can be used to explore if conditions for stable aggregate relations hold. For instance, Hsiao et al. (2004) find that the estimated aggregate relations between Japan's money demand, GDP, and bond rate are unstable and sensitive to the time period covered. Depending on the sample period used, the estimated relationships are either of wrong sign or statistically insignificant or yield unbelievable magnitudes. They find the estimated long-run income elasticities are 75.23 for M1 and 11.04 for M2, respectively. They attribute these incredible results to the aggregation of "heterogeneous" micro units.

If micro units are "heterogeneous," two issues arise. First, shall one focus the analysis on micro units? Second, to predict the aggregate outcomes, shall one rely on the summation of micropredictions or rely on the prediction generated from the aggregate variables? The problem with micro analysis is that there are numerous micro relations to estimate while decision makers are only interested in the average outcomes. Moreover, there may not have enough time series observations to provide reliable estimates of micro relations. It appears that a random coefficients framework assuming $(\gamma_i, \underset{\sim}{\beta}_i')$ are independently distributed with constant mean $(\bar{\gamma}, \underset{\sim}{\beta}')$ and finite covariance matrix (e.g., Hsiao, 2014, chapter 6; Hsiao & Pesaran, 2008) provide a convenient framework to reconcile the issue of "heterogeneity" in aggregation while providing reasonable estimates of average relation. As a matter of fact, Hsiao, Shen, and Fujiki (2005) using a random coefficient framework for the analysis of Japanese disaggregate data (prefecture panel data) find that there is a stable average relation between money demand and income. The estimated short-run income elasticity for M1 and M2 is 0.88 and 0.47, respectively. The long-run income elasticity is 2.56 for M1 and 1.01 for M2. These results appear to be consistent with economic theory and the broadly observed facts about Japan. The average growth rate for M2 in the 1980s is about 9.34%. The inflation rate is 1.98%. The real M2 growth rate is 7.36%. The real growth rate of GDP during this period is 4.13%. Taking account the impact of 5-year bond rate fell from 9.332% at 1980.I to 5.767 at 1989.IV, the results are indeed very close to the estimated long-run income elasticities based on disaggregate data analysis.

If "heterogeneity" is indeed present in micro units, then shall we predict the aggregate outcome based on the summation of estimated micro relations or shall we predict the aggregate outcomes based on the estimated aggregate relations? Unfortunately, there is not much work on this specific issue. In choosing between whether to predict aggregate variables using aggregate (H_a) or disaggregate equations (H_d), Griliches and Grunfeld (1960) suggest using the criterion of:

$$\text{Choose } H_d \text{ if } \underset{\sim}{e}_d'\underset{\sim}{e}_d < \underset{\sim}{e}_a'\underset{\sim}{e}_a, \text{ otherwise choose } H_a \tag{85}$$

where $\underset{\sim}{e}_d$ and $\underset{\sim}{e}_a$ are the estimates of the errors in predicting aggregate outcomes under H_d and H_a, respectively. However, if cross-sectional units are cross-correlated, simple aggregation of individual unit forecasts may not be the optimal way of predicting aggregate (or average) outcomes.

For a discussion of optimal way of combining individual forecasts and related literature, see e.g. Hsiao and Wan (2014).

8. CONCLUDING REMARKS

This paper reviews the panel methodology to control the impact of unobserved heterogeneities among cross-sectional units to obtain valid inference for a dynamic system of stable relations, from both reduced form and structural form perspectives. However, many challenging methodological issues remain such as: (i) statistical properties of multi-dimensional statistics (Bai & Silverstein, 2004; Phillips & Moon, 1999, 2000a,b); (ii) nonlinear system; (iii) dynamic system with unobserved interactive effects (dynamic factor models) (e.g., Bai & Ng 2004; Phillips & Sul, 2003; Stock & Watson, 2002, 2005); (iv) fixed versus random effects inference with either N or T or both are large, etc. In addition, macroeconometric modeling depends on the existence of stable relations among aggregate variables. Summing the micro variables to yield aggregate variables does not lead to the distortion of fundamental economic relations only if certain "homogeneity" conditions among micro units hold. Panel data focus on individual outcomes. Information on disaggregate outcomes provide the possibility of investigating the source of discrepancies between the aggregate analysis and disaggregate analysis and find ways to reconcile the discrepancies (e.g., Hsiao et al., 2005).

NOTES

1. See Han and Phillips (2013) for the properties of transformed MLE when $|\Phi(z)| = 0$ contains unit roots or near unit roots.
2. This section is largely drawn from Hsiao (2014, chapter 10.3).

ACKNOWLEDGMENT

This work is partially supported by the China NSF grant #71131008. I would like to thank P. C. B. Phillips and a referee for their helpful comments.

REFERENCES

Akashi, K., & Kunitomo, N. (2012). Some properties of the LIML estimator in a dynamic panel structural equation. *Journal of Econometrics*, *166*, 167–183.

Akashi, K., & Kunitomo, N. (2014). The limited information maximum likelihood approach to dynamic structural equation models. *Annals of the Institute of Mathematical Statistics*. (forthcoming).

Alvarez, J., & Arellano, M. (2003). The time series and cross-section asymptotics of dynamic panel data estimators. *Econometrica*, *71*, 1121–1159.

Anderson, T. W., & Hsiao, C. (1981). Estimation of dynamic models with error components. *Journal of the American Statistical Association*, *76*, 598–606.

Arellano, M., & Bond, S. (1991). Some tests of specification for panel data: Monte Carlo evidence and an application to employment equations. *Review of Economic Studies*, *58*, 277–297.

Bai, J., & Ng, S. (2004). A panic on unit root tests and cointegration. *Econometrica*, *72*, 1127–1177.

Bai, J., & Ng, S. (2010). Panel unit root tests with cross-section dependence: A further investigation. *Econometric Theory*, *26*, 1088–1114.

Bai, Z. D., & Silverstein, J. W. (2004). CLT for linear statistics of large-dimensional sample covariance matrices. *Annals of Probability*, *32*, 553–605.

Baltagi, B. H., & Kao, C. (2000). Nonstationary panels, cointegration in panels and dynamic panels, A survey in nonstationary panels, panel cointegration and dynamic panels. In B. Baltagi (Ed.), *Advances in econometrics* (Vol. 15, pp. 7–52.). Amsterdam: JAI Press.

Banerjee, A. (1999). Panel data unit roots and cointegration: An overview. *Oxford Bulletin of Economics and Statistics*, *61*, 607–629.

Bernard, A., & Jones, C. (1996). Productivity across industries and countries: Time series theory and evidence. *Review of Economics and Statistics*, *78*, 135–146.

Binder, M., Hsiao, C., & Pesaran, M. H. (2005). Estimation and inference in short panel vector autoregression with unit roots and cointegration. *Econometric Theory*, *21*, 795–837.

Bodkin, R. G., Klein, L. R., & Marwah, K. (1991). *A history of macroeconometric model-building*. Hants. England: Edward Elgar.

Box, G. E. P., & Jenkins, G. M. (1970). *Time series analysis, forecasting and control*. San Francisco, CA: Holden Day.

Breitung, J., & Das, S. (2008). Panel unit roots under cross sectional dependence. *Statistica Nerrlandica*, *59*, 414–433.

Breitung, J., & Pesaran, M. H. (2008). Unit roots and cointegration in panels. In L. Matyas & P. Sevestre (Eds.), *The econometrics of panel data* (pp. 279–322). Berlin: Springer-Verlag.

Chang, Y. (2002). Nonlinear IV unit roots tests in panels with cross-sectional dependency. *Journal of Econometrics*, *110*, 261–292.

Choi, I. (2001). Unit root tests for panel data. *Journal of International Money and Finance*, *20*, 249–272.

Choi, I. (2002). Combination unit root tests for cross-sectionally correlated panels. In *Econometric theory and practice: Frontiers of analysis and applied research, essays in honor of P.C.B. Phillips*, Cambridge: Cambridge University Press.

Choi, I. (2006). Nonstationary panels. In K. Patterson, & T. C. Mills (Eds.), *Palgrave handbooks of econometrics* (Vol. 1, pp. 511–539). New York, NY: Palgrave Macmillan.

Choi, I., & Chue, T. K. (2007). Subsampling hypothesis tests for nonstationary panels with applications to exchange rates and stock prices. *Journal of Applied Econometrics*, *22*, 223–264.

Dickey, D. A., & Fuller, W. A. (1979). Distribution of the estimators for autoregressive time series with a unit root. *Journal of the American Statistical Association*, *74*, 427–431.

Dickey, D. A., & Fuller, W. A. (1981). Likelihood ratio statistics for autoregressive time series with a unit root. *Econometrica*, *49*, 1057–1072.

Engle, R. F., & Granger, C. W. J. (1987). Cointegration and error correction: Representation, estimation and testing. *Econometrica*, *55*, 251–276.

Frankel, J. A., & Rose, A. K. (1996). A panel project on purchasing power parity: Mean revision between and within countries. *Journal of International Economics*, *40*, 209–244.

Griliches, Z., & Grunfeld, Y. (1960). Is aggregation really bad? *Review of Economics and Statistics*, *42*, 1–13.

Groen, J. J. J., & Kleibergen, F. (2003). Likelihood-based cointegration analysis in panels of vector error-correction models. *Journal of Business and Economic Statistics*, *21*, 295–318.

Hadri, K. (2000). Testing for stationarity in heterogeneous panel data. *Econometrics Journal*, *3*, 148–161.

Hadri, K., & Larsson, R. (2005). Testing for stationarity in heterogeneous panel data where the time dimension is fixed. *Econometric Journal*, *8*, 55–69.

Han, C., & Phillips, P. C. B. (2013). First difference maximum likelihood and dynamic panel estimation. *Journal of Econometrics*, *175*, 35–45.

Hsiao, C. (1979a). Causality tests in econometrics. *Journal of Economic Dynamics and Control*, *1*, 321–346.

Hsiao, C. (1979b). Autoregressive modelling of Canadian money and income data. *Journal of the American Statistical Association*, *74*, 553–560.

Hsiao, C. (1982). Autoregressive modelling and causal ordering of economic variables. *Journal of Economic Dynamics and Control*, *4*, 243–259.

Hsiao, C. (1983). Identification. In Z. Griliches, & M. Intriligator (Eds.), *Handbook of econometrics* (Vol. 1, pp. 223–283). Amsterdam: North-Holland.

Hsiao, C. (2007). Panel data analysis – Advantages and challenges. *Test*, *16*, 1–22.

Hsiao, C. (2014). *Analysis of panel data* (3rd ed.). Cambridge: Cambridge University Press. (forthcoming).

Hsiao, C., Ching, H. S., & Wan, S. (2012). A panel data approach for program evaluation – measuring the benefits of political and economic integration of Hong Kong with mainland China. *Journal of Applied Econometrics*, *27*, 705–740.

Hsiao, C., & Pesaran, M. H. (2008). Random coefficients models. In L. Matayas, & P. Sevestre (Eds.), *The econometrics of panel data* (3rd ed., pp. 187–216). Berlin: Springer.

Hsiao, C., Shen, Y., & Fujiki, H. (2005). Aggregate vs. disaggregate data analysis – A Paradox in the estimation of money demand function of Japan under the low interest rate policy. *Journal of Applied Econometrics*, *20*, 579–601.

Hsiao, C., & Wan, S. K. (2014). Is there an otpimal forecast combination? *Journal of Econometrics*, *178*, 294–309.

Hsiao, C., & Zhang, J. (2013). MLE vs GMM for dynamic panel data models when both N and T are large. *Mimeo*.

Hsiao, C., & Zhou, Q. K. (2014). Statistical inference for panel dynamic simultaneous equations models. *Journal of Econometrics*. (forthcoming).

Johansen, S. (1991). Estimation and hypothesis testing of cointegration vectors in caussian vector autoregressive models. *Econometrica, 59*, 1551–1580.

Kao, C. (1999). Spurious regression and residual-based tests for cointegration in panel data. *Journal of Econometrics, 90*, 1–44.

Kao, C., & Chiang, M. H. (2000). On the estimation and inference of a cointegrated regression in panel data. In B. Baltagi (Ed.), *Advances in econometrics* (Vol. 15, pp. 161–168). Amsterdam: JAI Press.

Kwiatkowski, D., Phillips, P. C. B., Schmidt, P., & Shin, Y. (1992). Testing null hypothesis of stationarity against the alternative of a unit root. *Journal of Econometrics, 54*, 159–178.

Levin, A., Lin, C., & Chu, J. (2002). Unit root tests in panel data: Asymptotic and finite-sample properties. *Journal of Econometrics, 108*, 1–24.

Lewbel, A. (1994). Aggregation and simple dynamic. *American Economic Review, 84*, 905–918.

Maddala, G. S., & Wu, S. (1999). A comparative study of unit root tests with panel data and a new simple test. *Oxford Bulletin of Economics and Statistics, 61*, 631–652.

Magnus, J. R., & Neudecker, H. (1999). *Matrix differential calculus with applications in statistics and econometrics* (Rev. ed.). New York, NY: Wiley.

McCoskey, S., & Kao, C. (1998). A residual-based test of the null of cointegration in panel data. *Econometric Reviews, 17*, 57–84.

Moon, H. R., & Perron, B. (2004). Testing for a unit root in panels with dynamic factors. *Journal of Econometrics, 122*, 81–126.

Nerlove, M. (2000). An essay on the history of panel data econometrics. Paper presented at 2000 Panel Data Conference in Geneva.

Park, J. (1992). Canonical cointegrating regressions. *Econometrica, 60*, 119–143.

Pedroni, P. (1994). Panel cointegration: Asymptotic and finite sample properties of pooled time series tests with an application to the PPP hypothesis. *Econometric Theory, 20*, 597–625.

Pesaran, M. H. (2004). General diagnostic tests for cross-section dependence in panels, mimeo.

Pesaran, M. H. (2007). A simple panel unit root test in the presence of cross-section dependence. *Journal of Applied Econometrics, 22*, 265–312.

Pesaran, M. H., Schuermann, T., & Weiner, S. M. (2004). Modelling regional interdependencies using a global error-correlation macroeconometrics models. *Journal of Business and Economic Statistics, 22*, 129–162.

Pesaran, M. H., Shin, Y., & Smith, R. J. (2000). Structural analysis of vector error correction models with exogenous I(1) variables. *Journal of Econometrics, 97*, 293–343.

Pesaran, M. H., Smith, L. V., & Yamagata, T. (2012). Panel unit root tests in the presence of a multifactor error structure. *Mimeo*.

Phillips, P. C. B. (1986). Understanding spurious regressions in econometrics. *Journal of Econometrics, 33*, 311–340.

Phillips, P. C. B. (1991). Optimal inference in cointegrating systems. *Econometica, 59*, 283–306.

Phillips, P. C. B., & Durlauf, S. N. (1986). Multiple time series regression with integrated processes. *Review of Economic Studies, 53*, 473–496.

Phillips, P. C. B., & Hansen, B. E. (1990). Statistical inference in instrumental variables regression with *I*(1) processes. *Review of Economic Studies, 57*, 99–125.

Phillips, P. C. B., & Loretan, M. (1991). Estimating long-run economic equilibria. *Review of Economic Studies*, *58*, 407–436.

Phillips, P. C. B., & Moon, H. R. (1999). Linear regression limit theory for nonstationary panel data. *Econometrica*, *67*, 1057–1111.

Phillips, P. C. B., & Moon, H. R. (2000a). Nonstationary panel data analysis: An overview of some recent developments. *Econometric Reviews*, *19*, 263–286.

Phillips, P. C. B., & Moon, H. R. (2000b). Estimation of autoregressive roots near unity using panel data. *Econometric Theory*, *16*, 927–997.

Phillips, P. C. B., & Sul, D. (2003). Dynamic panel estimation and homogeneity testing under cross-section dependence. *Econometrics Journal*, *6*, 217–259.

Saikkonen, P. (1991). Asymptotically efficient estimation of cointegration regressions. *Econometric Theory*, *7*, 1–21.

Sargan, J. D., & Bhargava, A. (1983). Testing for residuals from least squares regression being generated by Gaussian random walk. *Econometrica*, *51*, 153–174.

Sims, C. (1980). Macroeconomic and reality. *Econometrica*, *48*, 1–48.

Stock, J. H., & Watson, M. W. (2002). Macroeconomic forecasting using diffusion indexes. *Journal of Business and Economic Statistics*, *20*, 147–162.

Stock, J. H., & Watson, M. W. (2005). Implications of dynamic factor models for var analysis. *mimeo*.

Stoker, T. M. (1993). Empirical approaches to the problem of aggregation over individuals. *Journal of Economic Literature*, *31*, 1827–1874.

Theil, H. (1954). *Linear aggregation of economic relations*. Amsterdam: North-Holland.

Westerlund, J. (2005). New simple tests for panel cointegration. *Econometric Reviews*, *24*, 297–331.

Westerlund, J., & Larsson, R. (2012). Testing for a unit root in random coefficient panel data model. *Journal of Econometrics*, *167*, 254–273.

Zaffaroni, P. (2001). Contemporaneous aggregation of linear dynamic models in large economies. Mimeo, Banca d'Italia.

Zellner, A. (1962). An efficient method of estimating seemingly unrelated regressions and tests for aggregation bias. *Journal of the American Statistical Association*, *57*, 348–368.

MEAN AVERAGE ESTIMATION OF DYNAMIC PANEL MODELS WITH NONSTATIONARY INITIAL CONDITION

John Chao[a], Myungsup Kim[b] and Donggyu Sul[c]

[a]*Department of Economics, University of Maryland, College Park, MD, USA*

[b]*Department of Economics, University of North Texas, Denton, TX, USA*

[c]*Department of Economics, University of Texas at Dallas, Richardson, TX, USA*

ABSTRACT

This paper proposes a new class of estimators for the autoregressive coefficient of a dynamic panel data model with random individual effects and nonstationary initial condition. The new estimators we introduce are weighted averages of the well-known first difference (FD) GMM/IV estimator and the pooled ordinary least squares (POLS) estimator. The proposed procedure seeks to exploit the differing strengths of the FD GMM/IV estimator relative to the pooled OLS estimator. In particular, the latter is inconsistent in the stationary case but is consistent and asymptotically normal with a faster rate of convergence than the former

Essays in Honor of Peter C. B. Phillips
Advances in Econometrics, Volume 33, 241–279

ISSN: 0731-9053/doi:10.1108/S0731-905320140000033008

when the underlying panel autoregressive process has a unit root. By averaging the two estimators in an appropriate way, we are able to construct a class of estimators which are consistent and asymptotically standard normal, when suitably standardized, in both the stationary and the unit root case. The results of our simulation study also show that our proposed estimator has favorable finite sample properties when compared to a number of existing estimators.

Keywords: Nonstationary initial condition; mean average estimator; smoothing threshold; POLS; FDIV

JEL classification: C33

1. INTRODUCTION

Pathbreaking research on the estimation of dynamic panel data models was done in the early 1980s by Nickell (1981) and by Anderson and Hsiao (1981, 1982). The former analyzed the bias properties of the least-squares dummy variable (LSDV) estimator and the pooled OLS estimator, whereas the latter two papers introduced the first-difference (FD) GMM/IV estimator. The three decades since these pioneering papers have witnessed the rapid development of the literature on dynamic panel regression. Among the important contributions to this literature are those of Arellano and Bond (1991), Ahn and Schmidt (1995), Arellano and Bover (1995), Kiviet (1995, 2007), Blundell and Bond (1998), Moon and Phillips (2000), Hahn and Kuersteiner (2002), Hsiao, Pesaran, and Tahmiscioglu (2002), Alvarez and Arellano (2003), Bun and Kiviet (2006), Phillips and Sul (2007), and Han, Phillips, and Sul (2011, 2014).

Within this vast literature, the work of Kiviet (2007) and Arellano (2003) have considered dynamic panel data settings with the most general form of nonstationary initial condition. In particular, they study a model of the form

$$y_{it} = a_i (1-\rho) + \rho y_{it-1} + \varepsilon_{it}, \quad y_{i0} = \alpha_0 + \alpha_1 a_i + \alpha_2 \varepsilon_{i0} \tag{1}$$

where $\varepsilon_{it} \sim$ i.i.d. $(0, \sigma^2)$ for $t \geq 0$ and $a_i \sim$ i.i.d. (μ_1, σ_a^2). Kiviet notes that modeling initial condition in this way results in three additional unknown parameters: α_0, α_1, α_2. Under this setting, Arellano (2003) shows that the following moment conditions hold regardless of the non-stationarity of the initial conditions and the restriction of time series heteroskedasticity.

$$\mathrm{E}\left[y_{it} - \rho y_{it-1} - \mu_1(1-\rho)\right] = 0 \tag{2}$$

$$\mathrm{E}\left[y_{it} - \rho y_{it-1} - \mu_1(1-\rho)\right]\left[\Delta y_{it-1} - \rho \Delta y_{it-2}\right] = 0 \tag{3}$$

$$\mathrm{E}\left[y_{it-s}\right]\left[\Delta y_{it} - \rho \Delta y_{it-1}\right] = 0 \text{ for } s > 2 \tag{4}$$

Using the moment conditions in Eqs. (2) through (4) yields consistency of GMM estimator. However, as is well-known, the moment condition becomes weaker as ρ approaches unity. Under stationary initial condition, several alternative estimators have been proposed to overcome the weak instrument problem. For example, Choi, Mark, and Sul (2010) use backward recursive mean adjustment to reduce the bias especially when ρ is near unity. Han et al. (2011, 2014) propose the "X-differencing" method for removing the unobserved effects, leading to consistent estimation of ρ in both the stable and the unit root case when stationarity of initial condition is assumed in the former case. However with nonstationary initial condition, this paper shows that the X-differencing estimator can be inconsistent.

The main objective of the current paper is to add to this impressive list of contributions by introducing a new class of estimators which can be shown to have good asymptotic properties when used to estimate a dynamic panel data regression with nonstationary initial condition. A main reason for considering nonstationary initial conditions is that they arise naturally in a number of situations where the panel data set is generated from laboratory experiments. Our estimation procedure is motivated by the observation that although it is well-known that the GMM/IV estimator is well-behaved in the case where $|\rho|$ is bounded away from one, this estimator suffers from a slower rate of convergence in the unit root case when $\rho = 1$, due to the weak instrument problem mentioned earlier. On the other hand, the pooled OLS estimator, while inconsistent in the case where $|\rho| < 1$, becomes consistent with a faster rate of convergence than the FD GMM/IV estimator in the unit root case when $N, T \to \infty$. The present paper seeks to exploit the differing strengths of GMM/IV vis-à-vis pooled OLS in different regions of the parameter space by introducing a class of mean average estimators which are weighted averages of these two estimators.

Several alternative weighting functions for mean average estimation are considered in our paper. In particular, we can generate different weighting functions based on taking alternative transformations of a class of information criteria used to evaluate the validity of the unit root hypothesis. The class of information criteria we consider are variants of the Bayesian Information Criterion (BIC). Alternative transformations which we consider include the logistic-type transformation, which has previously been used in Buckland, Burnham, and Augustin (1997), Burnham and Anderson (2002), Hjort and Claeskens (2003), Hansen (2007), and Chao (2014); although none of those papers consider the problem of estimating a dynamic panel data model, as we do here. In addition, we also consider a Gaussian type transformation which was originally introduced in Chao (2014).

The remainder of the paper proceeds as follows. In Section 2, we briefly discuss the dynamic panel regression studied in this paper and give the assumptions used in our subsequent large sample analysis. Section 3 of the paper provides some asymptotic results for the FD GMM/IV and the pooled OLS estimators. Section 4 introduces our mean average estimator and provides large sample results for this estimator. The results of a Monte Carlo study comparing different versions of the mean average estimator with several existing estimators are given in Section 5. We briefly conclude in Section 6 of the paper. Proofs and supporting lemmas are given in the appendix.

A few words on notations before we proceed. In this paper, we use $\Rightarrow$ to denote weak convergence and $\xrightarrow{p}$ to denote convergence in probability. In addition, we let χ^2_ν denote a chi-square random variable with ν degrees of freedom, and let $W_i(r)$, $r \in [0,1]$, denote the Wiener process, or standard Brownian motion.

2. MODEL AND ASSUMPTIONS

We consider the following dynamic panel data model written in unobserved components form

$$y_{it} = a_i + x_{it} \tag{5}$$

$$x_{it} = \rho x_{it-1} + \varepsilon_{it} \tag{6}$$

for $i=1, \dots N$ and $t=1, \dots, T$. Here, $\{y_{it}\}$ denotes the observed data, whereas a_i denotes an (unobserved) random effect and $\{x_{it}\}$ is generated by a latent AR(1) process. The initial condition for this model is given by

$$y_{i0}=a_i+x_{i0} \tag{7}$$

We make the following assumptions on the model given by Eqs. (5)–(7).

Assumption 1. (Idiosyncratic Errors)

(a) $\{\varepsilon_{it}\} \equiv \text{i.i.d. } (0, \sigma^2)$ across i and t, $\sigma^2>0$;
(b) $E\left[\varepsilon_{it}^4\right]<\infty$.

Assumption 2. (Random Effects)

(a) $\{a_i\} \equiv \text{i.i.d. } (\mu_1, \sigma_a^2)$ across i, $\sigma_a^2>0$;
(b) $E[a_i^4]<\infty$.

Assumption 3. (Initial Condition)

(a) $\{x_{i0}\} \equiv \text{i.i.d. } (m_1, \sigma_x^2)$ across i, $\sigma_x^2>0$;
(b) $E\left[x_{i0}^4\right]<\infty$.

Assumption 4.
ε_{it}, a_j, and x_{k0} are mutually independent for all i, j, k, and t.

Remarks.

(i) As Kiviet (2007) suggests, we can model the initial condition as (1). However, the initial conditions characterized there contain too many parameters. To simplify the parameterization, we consider the following latent AR(1) model.

$$y_{it}=a_i+x_{it}, \quad x_{it}=\rho x_{it-1}+\varepsilon_{it} \tag{8}$$

of which the regression specification at time $t=1$ can be rewritten as

$$y_{i1}=a_i\,(1-\rho)+\rho y_{i0}+\varepsilon_{i1} \tag{9}$$

Specifying the initial condition based on the latent model (8) is much easier than making such a specification based on the actual regression model given by Eq. (9). To see this, treat y_{i1} as the initial condition by setting $y_{i0}=0$ in Eq. (9), then we have $y_{i1}=a_i(1-\rho)+\varepsilon_{i1}$ and, thus, specifying the initial condition requires additional modeling of the first period error term ε_{i1}. Meanwhile let $x_{i0}=0$ and use the latent model (8), then we have $y_{i1}=a_i+x_{i1}$. Hence in this case, we only need to model x_{i1}. Define the steady state mean of y_{it} as $\lim_{t\to\infty} E(y_{it})=a_i$ Then the initial condition based on the latent model can be rewritten as $x_{i1}=y_{i1}-\lim_{t\to\infty} E(y_{it})$, which is more attractive in terms of economic interpretation. Now change the time from $t=1$ to $t=0$ and treat y_{i0} as the initial condition. Then we have

$$y_{i0}=\lim_{t\to\infty} E(y_{it})+x_{i0}=a_i+x_{i0}=c_i, \quad (say) \tag{10}$$

Note that $x_{i0}=\rho x_{i,-1}+\varepsilon_{i0}$. Hence, without loss of generality, we may let $\varepsilon_{i0}=0$. In this case, the latent model can be assumed to be

$$y_{it}=a_i+x_{i0}\rho^t+w_{it} \tag{11}$$

where

$$w_{it}=\sum_{j=0}^{t}\rho^j\varepsilon_{it-j} \text{ where } \varepsilon_{i0}=0 \tag{12}$$

Hence, in terms of the more general initial condition given in Kiviet (2007), our approach here leads to the particular specification $\alpha_0=x_{i0}$, $\alpha_1=1$, and $\alpha_2=0$. A basic but standard model can further be obtained by setting $x_{i0}=0$.

(ii) We can also allow for heterogeneous variance for ε_{it} across i, but for notational convenience we do not consider this extension here.

(iii) Note that Assumption 1 does not allow for cross-sectional dependence in the idiosyncratic errors $\{\varepsilon_{it}\}$. This assumption is reasonable in experimental games since subjects are randomly selected. It is also important to note that Assumption 1 does not imply cross-sectional independence among the experimental outcome y_{it}. Motivated by the possibility of common game setting and learning, the outcome variable is cross-sectionally correlated. In fact, the cross-sectional structure can be thought of as an approximate factor model. Observe that Eqs. (5)–(7) imply that

$$y_{it} = a_i + x_{i0}\rho^t + w_{it}$$

where

$$w_{it} = \sum_{j=0}^{t} \rho^j \varepsilon_{it-j}, \quad \text{with } \varepsilon_{i0} = 0$$

In this representation, the initial condition parameter x_{i0} can be interpreted as a factor loading coefficient and the learning parameter ρ^t can be taken to be a common factor. However, in the stationary case, the cross-sectional dependence goes away quickly since ρ^t decays to zero geometrically as t increases.

3. CONSISTENCY OF EXISTENT ESTIMATORS

There are many consistent estimators available when the initial condition is stationary. As we discussed in the section "Introduction", only FDIV estimator, which is using the last moment condition in Eq. (4), becomes consistent. Other GMM/IV estimator such as forward orthogonal demeaning by Arellano and Bover (1995) does not satisfy the moment conditions. Hence our interest is rather focusing on two existent estimators: Exact mean unbiased (EMU) estimator by Phillips and Sul (2007) and X-differencing estimator proposed by Han et al. (2011, 2014). Throughout this subsection, we consider only N asymptotics. That is, we consider a fixed T but let $N \rightarrow \infty$.

We assume researchers run the following panel AR(1) regression with fixed effects regardless of the true latent models.

$$y_{it} = \alpha_i + \rho y_{it-1} + \varepsilon_{it}, \quad t = 1, ..., T+1 \tag{13}$$

Even though y_{it} has a time varying mean, the panel AR(1) regression in Eq. (13) is not misspecified. To see this, we calculate the quasi-difference in y_{it} as

$$y_{it} - \rho y_{it-1} = [a_i + x_{i0}\rho^t + w_{it}] - [\rho a + x_{i0}\rho^t + \rho w_{it-1}] = a_i\,(1-\rho) + \varepsilon_{it}$$

3.1. Non-existence of MUE based on Within Group Estimator

First we consider the within group (WG) estimator. It is well-known that WG estimator suffers from the asymptotic bias with small T. Here we derive the exact bias form first and then see if the bias function is monotonic over ρ If so, we may consider the EMU estimator considered by Phillips and Sul (2007). First, define the WG estimator

$$\hat{\rho}_{\mathrm{WG}} = \frac{\sum^N \sum^T \tilde{y}_{it-1} \tilde{y}_{it}}{\sum^N \sum^T \tilde{y}_{it-1}^2}$$

and rewrite it as

$$\hat{\rho}_{\mathrm{WG}} - \rho = \frac{\sum^N \sum^T \tilde{y}_{it-1} \tilde{u}_{it}}{\sum^N \sum^T \tilde{y}_{it-1}^2} := \frac{A_{NT}}{B_{NT}} \tag{14}$$

Let $E_N = \mathrm{p}\lim_{N \to \infty}$. Then we have the following:

$$E_N A_{NT} = \left(-\frac{1}{1-\rho} + \frac{1-\rho^T}{(1-\rho)^2 T} \right) \sigma^2$$

but

$$E_N B_{NT} = \sigma_x^2 \left(\frac{\rho^2 (1-\rho^{2T})}{1-\rho^2} - \frac{\rho^2 (1-\rho^T)^2}{(1-\rho)^2 T} \right) + B_{1T}$$

$$B_{1T} = \sigma^2 \left(\frac{T}{1-\rho^2} - \frac{(1+\rho)^2 + \rho^2 - \rho^{2+2T}}{(1-\rho^2)^2} + \frac{\rho(1-\rho^T)(2+\rho-\rho^{1+T})}{(1-\rho^2)(1-\rho)^2 T} \right)$$

where B_{1T} is the expected value of the denominator term with stationary initial condition. Therefore the bias of the WG estimator under nonstationary initial condition is less than that under stationary initial condition since usually $E_N B_{NT}$ is less than B_{1T}. When T is large, the Nickell bias under nonstationary initial condition is given by

$$E_N (\hat{\rho}_{\mathrm{WG}} - \rho) = -\frac{1+\rho}{T} + O(T^{-2})$$

which is the same as the Nickell bias under stationary initial condition. It is due to the local nonstationarity of y_{it}.

Nonetheless, if the first derivative of a function does not change its sign, then the function is monotonic by definition. Alternatively, we can say if either maximum or minimum of the first derivatives of a function is negative or positive, respectively, then the function is monotonic. Let $\mathcal{B}_T = E_N(\hat{\rho}_{\mathrm{WG}} - \rho)$ and $\mathcal{C}_T = E_N\hat{\rho}_{\mathrm{WG}}$. Then $\mathcal{B}_T$ becomes the asymptotic inconsistency function of the WG estimators meanwhile $\mathcal{C}_T$ becomes the asymptotic mean function. We calculate numerically and find that $\mathcal{B}_T$ and $\mathcal{C}_T$ are not monotonic at all. Due to this non-monotonicity, the EMU estimator cannot exist.

3.2. Inconsistency of X-Differencing Estimator

The basic reason of why X-differencing method eliminates the bias completely with stationary initial conditions can be seen as follows. First consider the following cross differencing by using the $(s-1)$th and sth observations where $1 \le s < t-1$

$$y_{it} - y_{is-1} = \rho(y_{it-1} - y_{is}) + e_{it}, \quad \text{for} \quad e_{it} = x_{i0}(\rho^{s+1} - \rho^{s-1}) + (\rho - 1)w_{is-1} + \varepsilon_{is} + \varepsilon_{it}$$

Under stationary initial condition, $\mathrm{E}e_{it}(y_{it-1} - y_{is}) = 0$ for all $1 \le s < t-1$. However under nonstationary initial condition, this moment condition becomes invalid. That is,

$$\begin{aligned}\mathrm{E}e_{it}(y_{it-1} - y_{is}) &= m_2(\rho^{s+1} - \rho^{s-1})(\rho^{t-1} - \rho^{s}) \\ &\quad + \sigma^2\left[(\rho - 1)(\rho^{t+1} - \rho)\frac{\rho^2 - \rho^{2s-2}}{1 - \rho^2} + \rho^{t-s-1} - 1\right] \neq 0\end{aligned}$$

for all $1 \le s < t-1$.

To evaluate the inconsistency, we can consider only partial aggregation since full aggregation gives more inconsistency. The probability limit of the numerator term becomes by setting $s = 1$

$$\mathrm{E}_N \sum_{t=1}^{T-1} e_{it}(y_{it-1} - y_{i1}) = -\left[\sigma^2 - m_2(1 - \rho^2)\right]\rho T + O(1) \tag{15}$$

Meanwhile the probability limit of the denominator is given by

$$\mathrm{E}_N \sum\nolimits_{t=1}^{T-1} (y_{it-1} - y_{i1})^2 = \frac{m_2\rho^2 (1-\rho^2) + \sigma^2 (2-\rho^2)}{1-\rho^2} T + O(T^{-2}) \tag{16}$$

Finally the inconsistency of X-differencing estimator, $\hat{\rho}_{\mathrm{X}}$, becomes

$$E_N (\hat{\rho}_{\mathrm{X}} - \rho) = \frac{\rho (1-\rho^2)(\sigma^2 - m_2 (1-\rho^2))}{m_2\rho^2 (1-\rho^2) + \sigma^2 (2-\rho^2)} + O(T^{-1}) \tag{17}$$

Therefore the inconsistency of $\hat{\rho}_{\mathrm{X}}$ is dependent on many nuisance values of m_2 and σ^2.

4. ASYMPTOTIC PROPERTIES OF FD GMM/IV AND POOLED OLS ESTIMATORS

To motivate the construction of our proposed mean average estimator given in the next section, we first provide some preliminary asymptotic results on two well-known estimators, the FD GMM/IV estimator and the pooled OLS estimator. As proposed originally by Anderson and Hsiao (1981, 1982), the FD GMM/IV estimator uses y_{it-2} as an instrument to estimate the first differenced dynamic panel model

$$\Delta y_{it} = \rho \Delta y_{it-1} + \Delta \varepsilon_{it}$$

resulting in an estimator of the form

$$\hat{\rho}_{\mathrm{IV}} = \left(\sum_{i=1}^{N} \sum_{t=2}^{T} y_{it-2} \Delta y_{it-1} \right)^{-1} \left(\sum_{i=1}^{N} \sum_{t=2}^{T} y_{it-2} \Delta y_{it} \right) \tag{18}$$

On the other hand, running pooled OLS on the level specification

$$y_{it} = \alpha_i + \rho y_{it-1} + \varepsilon_{it}$$

results in the estimator

$$\hat{\rho}_{\text{pols}} = \left[\sum_{i=1}^{N}\sum_{t=2}^{T}\left(y_{it-1} - \overline{y}_{-1,N,T}\right)^2\right]^{-1}\left[\sum_{i=1}^{N}\sum_{t=2}^{T}\left(y_{it-1} - \overline{y}_{-1,N,T}\right)\left(y_{it} - \overline{y}_{N,T}\right)\right]$$

where

$$\overline{y}_{-1,N,T} = \frac{1}{N\,(T-1)}\sum_{i=1}^{N}\sum_{t=2}^{T} y_{it-1}, \quad \overline{y}_{N,T} = \frac{1}{N\,(T-1)}\sum_{i=1}^{N}\sum_{t=2}^{T} y_{it}$$

The asymptotic results we give below are for the case where N and T are both large, with the order of magnitude of T not exceeding that of N, as this covers many panel data settings of interest to economists. We consider both the case where the panel AR(1) process is stationary with $\rho \in (0, 1)$ and also the unit root case where $\rho = 1$.

Theorem 1. Suppose that Assumptions 1–4 hold. Then, the following statements are true.

(a) If $\rho \in (0, 1)$,

$$\sqrt{NT}\,(\hat{\rho}_{\text{IV}} - \rho) \Rightarrow N\,(0, 2\,[1 + \rho])$$

as $N, T \to \infty$ such that $T/N \to \kappa \in [0, \infty)$.

(b) If $\rho = 1$,

$$\sqrt{T}\,(\hat{\rho}_{IV} - 1) \Rightarrow 2\frac{\mathcal{Z}_1}{\mathcal{Z}_2}$$

as $N, T \to \infty$ such that $T/N \to \kappa \in [0,\infty)$. Here, $\mathcal{Z}_1 \equiv N(0, 1)$, $\mathcal{Z}_2 \equiv N(0, 1)$, and $\mathcal{Z}_1$ and $\mathcal{Z}_2$ are independent.

Theorem 2. Suppose that Assumptions 1–4 hold. Then, the following statements are true.

(a) If $\rho \in (0, 1)$,

$$\hat{\rho}_{\text{pols}} \xrightarrow{p} \rho + \frac{\sigma_a^2\,(1-\rho)(1-\rho^2)}{\sigma_a^2\,(1-\rho^2) + \sigma^2}$$

as $N, T \to \infty$ such that $T/N \to \kappa \in [0, \infty)$.

(b) If $\rho = 1$,

$$\sqrt{NT}\left(\hat{\rho}_{\text{pols}} - 1\right) \Rightarrow N(0, 2)$$

as $N, T \to \infty$ such that $T/N \to \kappa \in [0, \infty)$.

Remarks.

(i) Note that Theorems 1 and 2 show that the relative desirability of FD GMM/IV vis-à-vis the pooled OLS estimator depends on whether the panel AR(1) is stable or has a unit root. In the stable case, pooled OLS is inconsistent whereas FD GMM/IV is both consistent and asymptotically normal. On the other hand, in the unit root case, both FD GMM/IV and pooled OLS are consistent but the latter has a faster rate of convergence. In addition, in the unit root case, FD GMM/IV, due to the weak instrument problem, is no longer asymptotically normal and has a limiting distribution which is a scaled Cauchy distribution, being proportion to the ratio of two independent standard normal variates.

(ii) Note that some of the results reported in the above theorems are not completely new to this paper. In particular, part (b) of Theorem 1 has been shown recently by Phillips (2014). In related results, Kruiniger (2009) has also shown a Cauchy-like limiting distribution for the FD GMM/IV estimator in situations with persistent data where N is large and T is fixed.

5. MEAN AVERAGE ESTIMATOR

More precisely, the construction of our estimator begins with two existing estimators: the first difference IV estimator, $\hat{\rho}_{\text{IV}}$ and the pooled OLS estimator $\hat{\rho}_{\text{pols}}$. Our reason for choosing the pooled OLS estimator for this construction stems in part from its good finite sample properties in cases where ρ is close to unity. Some evidence of $\hat{\rho}_{\text{pols}}$'s good finite sample performance relative to other estimators for ρ close to unity is provided by our simulation study, whose results are reported below.

Given these estimators, our proposed mean average estimator can be written as

$$\hat{\rho}_{\text{avg}} = w_{IC}\hat{\rho}_{\text{IV}} + (1 - w_{IC})\,\hat{\rho}_{\text{pols}}$$

where w_{IC} is a weighting function based on a BIC-type information criterion, denoted by Δ_{IC} below. When the weighting function is based on the logistic-type transformation, we have the explicit expression

$$w_{IC,1} = \frac{1}{1 + \exp\{\frac{1}{2}\Delta_{\text{IC}}\}} \tag{19}$$

and when the Gaussian-type tranformation is used, we have

$$w_{\text{IC},2} = \Pr\,(\mathbb{Z} > \Delta_{\text{IC}}) \tag{20}$$

where $\mathbb{Z}$ denotes the standard normal random variable.

We also consider alternative specifications for Δ_{IC}. More specifically, we consider an information criterion of the general form

$$\Delta_{\text{IC}}\,(\alpha, \beta) \equiv \mathbb{T}_{N,T} + \alpha\,\ln(N) + \beta\,\ln(T)$$

where α and β are prespecified (positive) integers such that $\alpha \geq 1$, $\beta \geq 1$, and $\alpha + \beta > 2$ and where $\mathbb{T}_{N,T}$ denotes the usual t-statistic for testing the presence of a unit root in dynamic panel data model, i.e.,

$$\mathbb{T}_{N,T} = \frac{\hat{\rho}_{\text{pols}} - 1}{\sqrt{\hat{\sigma}^2 / \sum_{i=1}^{N}\sum_{t=1}^{T}\left(y_{it-1} - \frac{1}{NT}\sum_{i=1}^{N}\sum_{t=2}^{T} y_{it-1}\right)^2}}$$

Here, $\hat{\sigma}^2$ denotes some consistent estimator of σ^2, say

$$\hat{\sigma}^2 = \frac{1}{N\,(T-1)}\sum_{i=1}^{N}\sum_{t=2}^{T}\left(y_{it} - \bar{y}_i - \tilde{\rho}[y_{it-1} - \bar{y}_{i-1}]\right)^2$$

where

$$\bar{y}_i = \frac{1}{T-1}\sum_{t=2}^{T} y_{it}, \quad \bar{y}_{i-1} = \frac{1}{T-1}\sum_{t=2}^{T} y_{it-1}$$

Next, we analyze the asymptotic properties of this mean average estimator. To do so, we first introduce the following normalization function

$$\nu_{NT} = w_{IC}\left(\frac{2}{NT}\left[1+\hat{\rho}_{\mathrm{IV}}\right]\right)^{-1/2} + (1-w_{IC})\hat{\sigma}^{-1}\left[\sum_{i=1}^{N}\sum_{i=2}^{T}\left(y_{it-1}-\bar{y}_{NT}\right)^2\right]^{1/2}$$

Our main asymptotic result is given by the following theorem.

Theorem 3. Suppose that Assumptions 1–4 hold. Then, the following statements are true.

(a) If $\rho \in (0, 1)$,

$$\nu_{NT}\left(\hat{\rho}_{\mathrm{avg}} - \rho\right) \Rightarrow N(0, 1)$$

as $N, T \to \infty$ such that $T/N \to \kappa \in [0, \infty)$.

(b) *If* $\rho = 1$,

$$\nu_{NT}\left(\hat{\rho}_{\mathrm{avg}} - 1\right) \Rightarrow N(0, 1)$$

as $N, T \to \infty$ such that $T/N \to \kappa \in [0, \infty)$.

Note that Theorem 3 shows that the mean average estimator $\hat{\rho}_{\mathrm{avg}}$ improves upon both the FD GMM/IV and the pooled OLS estimator, in that when appropriately normalized, it has an asymptotic standard normal distribution in both the stable and the unit root case. It is also easily seen that it has a faster rate of convergence vis-à-vis the FD GMM/IV estimator when the underlying panel AR(1) process has a unit root.

6. MONTE CARLO SIMULATION

For our Monte Carlo study, we consider the following data generating process:

$$x_{i0} \sim \text{i.i.d. } N(5, 1), \quad a_i \sim \text{i.i.d. } N(1, 1), \quad \{\varepsilon_{it}\} \sim \text{i.i.d. } N(0, 1)$$

Parameters which have important impact on the finite sample performance of alternative estimators include ρ, N, T, and $m_1 = E[x_{i0}]$. In our study, we set $N = 100$ and vary $\rho = 0.7$, 0.8, 0.85, 0.9, 0.95 and $T = 10$, 20, 30, 50, 100.[1] To keep the dimension of the parameter space manageable, we also fix the mean of the initial condition, m_1, to be 5 in all our experiments. In unreported simulation results, we have found that our simulation results are not much affected by changes in m_1, except when m_1 is very small.

As mentioned earlier, we consider four versions of the mean average estimator. These alternative versions differ only in terms of the information criterion used in the weighting function. More specifically, given the general form of the information criterion used here, i.e.,

$$\Delta_{\text{IC}}(\alpha, \beta) = \mathbb{T}_{N,T} + \alpha \ln(N) + \beta \ln(T)$$

we consider four alternative specifications given by

$$\begin{array}{lll} \text{BIC1}: & \alpha = 1 & \beta = 1 \\ \text{BIC2}: & \alpha = 2 & \beta = 1 \\ \text{BIC3}: & \alpha = 2 & \beta = 2 \\ \text{BIC4}: & \alpha = 2 & \beta = 3 \end{array}$$

Note that of these four specifications, BIC4 carries the strongest penalty function against overparameterization and, everything else being equal, would tend to favor the more parsimonious unit root hypothesis. On the other hand, BIC1 has the weakest penalty function and, in consequence, most strongly favor the stable case. It follows that, of the four variants, the mean average estimator based on BIC4 would tend to put the heaviest weight on the POLS estimator in finite sample, whereas the estimator based on BIC1 would put a heavier weight on the FDIV estimator relative to the other three specifications.

Table 1 gives the sample mean of the simulated estimators over 2,000 replications. Looking at this table, we see that the WG estimator suffers from serious downward (asymptotic) bias, the POLS estimator shows a mild upward bias, whereas the X-differencing estimator exhibits a more significant upward bias. Also, in terms of bias, all four mean average estimators tend to perform better than WG, X-dif, and POLS; but the estimator with the smallest bias across all values of ρ examined under our experimental design is the FD GMM/IV estimator.

Table 1. Means of Various Estimators ($N = 100$).

ρ	T	WG	X-dif	POLS	FDIV	BIC1	BIC2	BIC3	BIC4
0.95	10	0.695	0.998	0.957	0.953	0.957	0.957	0.957	0.957
0.95	20	0.833	0.987	0.955	0.949	0.955	0.955	0.955	0.955
0.95	30	0.875	0.980	0.954	0.950	0.954	0.954	0.954	0.954
0.95	50	0.907	0.972	0.954	0.951	0.953	0.953	0.954	0.954
0.95	100	0.929	0.962	0.954	0.950	0.951	0.951	0.953	0.954
0.9	10	0.710	1.053	0.917	0.901	0.916	0.916	0.917	0.917
0.9	20	0.814	0.999	0.914	0.899	0.911	0.911	0.913	0.913
0.9	30	0.843	0.974	0.913	0.900	0.909	0.907	0.911	0.913
0.9	50	0.865	0.949	0.913	0.901	0.904	0.903	0.909	0.912
0.9	100	0.882	0.927	0.914	0.900	0.900	0.900	0.902	0.908
0.85	10	0.700	1.082	0.879	0.851	0.876	0.875	0.877	0.878
0.85	20	0.777	0.990	0.875	0.849	0.864	0.862	0.870	0.874
0.85	30	0.800	0.952	0.875	0.850	0.857	0.856	0.865	0.873
0.85	50	0.818	0.917	0.877	0.851	0.852	0.852	0.857	0.868
0.85	100	0.833	0.886	0.879	0.850	0.850	0.850	0.850	0.854
0.8	10	0.671	1.085	0.842	0.800	0.833	0.830	0.837	0.840
0.8	20	0.733	0.968	0.839	0.800	0.813	0.810	0.824	0.834
0.8	30	0.752	0.920	0.841	0.800	0.805	0.804	0.814	0.830
0.8	50	0.769	0.877	0.844	0.801	0.802	0.801	0.804	0.818
0.8	100	0.783	0.841	0.847	0.800	0.800	0.800	0.800	0.801
0.7	10	0.589	1.036	0.773	0.700	0.740	0.733	0.753	0.765
0.7	20	0.637	0.886	0.777	0.700	0.710	0.707	0.723	0.750
0.7	30	0.654	0.829	0.782	0.700	0.703	0.702	0.709	0.733
0.7	50	0.671	0.780	0.787	0.701	0.701	0.701	0.702	0.710
0.7	100	0.684	0.741	0.793	0.700	0.700	0.700	0.700	0.700

Table 2 gives the relative mean squared error (MSE) of the different estimators vis-à-vis that of the X-differencing estimator. Note first that variants of the mean average estimator based on BIC3 and BIC4 have uniformly better MSE than the X-differencing estimator across all data generating processes considered in our simulation study. The FD GMM/IV estimator also performs well in MSE and, in fact, does better than BIC3 and BIC4 in cases where $\rho = 0.7,\ 0.8$. However, the MSE of FD GMM/IV deteriorates dramatically as ρ moves closer to unity so that, when $\rho = 0.95$, FD GMM/IV not only performs much worse than BIC3 and BIC4 in terms of MSE but its MSE is also larger than that of the X-differencing estimator in this case. Note also that the mean average estimators also tend to perform better in terms of MSE than POLS, especially in cases where ρ is not so close to unity such as when $\rho = 0.7$ or 0.8.

Table 2. Relative Mean Squares Errors against X-Differencing ($N = 100$).

ρ	T	WG	X-dif	POLS	FDIV	BIC1	BIC2	BIC3	BIC4
0.95	10	18.22	1.000	0.069	2.071	0.069	0.069	0.069	0.069
0.95	20	8.574	1.000	0.055	1.383	0.056	0.057	0.055	0.055
0.95	30	5.734	1.000	0.056	1.329	0.059	0.063	0.056	0.056
0.95	50	3.737	1.000	0.071	1.499	0.107	0.141	0.072	0.070
0.95	100	2.755	1.000	0.149	2.467	1.022	1.288	0.225	0.147
0.9	10	1.508	1.000	0.022	0.120	0.021	0.021	0.021	0.021
0.9	20	0.768	1.000	0.027	0.131	0.026	0.027	0.026	0.027
0.9	30	0.610	1.000	0.041	0.170	0.045	0.054	0.037	0.040
0.9	50	0.513	1.000	0.083	0.250	0.148	0.170	0.079	0.076
0.9	100	0.484	1.000	0.291	0.485	0.464	0.471	0.375	0.204
0.85	10	0.425	1.000	0.020	0.038	0.018	0.017	0.019	0.019
0.85	20	0.276	1.000	0.037	0.057	0.027	0.028	0.029	0.034
0.85	30	0.252	1.000	0.068	0.082	0.052	0.057	0.043	0.057
0.85	50	0.242	1.000	0.168	0.129	0.116	0.120	0.092	0.102
0.85	100	0.250	1.000	0.659	0.260	0.258	0.259	0.252	0.212
0.8	10	0.209	1.000	0.025	0.022	0.019	0.017	0.021	0.023
0.8	20	0.166	1.000	0.059	0.039	0.027	0.028	0.032	0.047
0.8	30	0.165	1.000	0.123	0.059	0.049	0.052	0.045	0.075
0.8	50	0.170	1.000	0.332	0.095	0.092	0.093	0.086	0.100
0.8	100	0.187	1.000	1.360	0.196	0.196	0.196	0.195	0.187
0.7	10	0.114	1.000	0.050	0.015	0.021	0.018	0.030	0.041
0.7	20	0.121	1.000	0.174	0.032	0.029	0.029	0.036	0.083
0.7	30	0.134	1.000	0.410	0.051	0.049	0.050	0.049	0.095
0.7	50	0.149	1.000	1.192	0.085	0.085	0.085	0.084	0.090
0.7	100	0.175	1.000	5.053	0.184	0.184	0.184	0.184	0.183

7. CONCLUSION

In this paper, we introduce a new class of estimators, which are constructed by taking a weighted average of the FD GMM/IV and the pooled OLS estimators. We show that an advantage of this mean average estimator is that it is consistent and asymptotically normal when appropriately standardized, regardless of whether the underlying AR(1) process is stable or has a unit root. Our simulation study also shows that this estimator performs well in finite sample relative to a number of other estimators that have been proposed in the panel data literature.

NOTE

1. In an earlier version of our paper, we also reported Monte Carlo results for $N = 200$. Those results are qualitatively very similar to the results for $N = 100$; and, hence, at the request of a referee, we have now omitted those results. They are, however, available from us upon request.

REFERENCES

Ahn, S. C., & Schmidt, P. (1995). Efficient estimation of models for dynamic panel data. *Journal of Econometrics*, *68*, 29–51.

Alvarez, J., & Arellano, M. (2003). The time series and cross-section asymptotics of dynamic panel data estimators. *Econometrica*, *71*, 1121–1159.

Anderson, T. W., & Hsiao, C. (1981). Estimation of dynamic models with error components. *Journal of American Statistical Association*, *76*, 598–606.

Anderson, T. W., & Hsiao, C. (1982). Formulation and estimation of dynamic models using panel data. *Journal of Econometrics*, *18*, 47–82.

Arellano, M. (2003). *Panel data econometrics*. New York, NY: Oxford University Press.

Arellano, M., & Bond, S. (1991). Some tests of specification for panel data: Monte Carlo evidence and an application to employment equations. *Review of Economic Studies*, *58*, 277–297.

Arellano, M., & Bover, O. (1995). Another look at the instrumental variable estimation of error-components models. *Journal of Econometrics*, *68*, 29–51.

Billingsley, P. (1968). *Convergence of probability measures*. New York, NY: Wiley.

Blundell, R., & Bond, S. (1998). Initial conditions and moment restrictions in dynamic panel data models. *Journal of Econometrics*, *87*, 115–143.

Buckland, S. T., Burnham, K. P., & Augustin, N. H. (1997). Model selection: An integral part of inference. *Biometrics*, *53*, 603–618.

Bun, M. J. G., & Kiviet, J. F. (2006). The effects of dynamic feedbacks on LS and MM estimator accuracy in panel data models. *Journal of Econometrics*, *132*(2), 409–444.

Burnham, K. P., & Anderson, D. R. (2002). *Model selection and multimodel inference: A practical information-theoretic approach*. Berlin: Springer-Verlag.

Chao, J. C. (2014). Panel structural modeling with weak instrumentation and covariance restrictions. *Econometric Theory*, *30*, 839–881.

Choi, C. Y., Mark, N. C., & Sul, D. (2010). Bias reduction in dynamic panel data models by recursive mean adjustment under cross section dependence. *Oxford Bulletin of Economics and Statistics*, *72*(7), 567–599.

Hahn, J., & Kuersteiner, G. (2002). Asymptotically unbiased inference for a dynamic panel model with fixed effects when both N and T are large. *Econometrica*, *70*(4), 1639–1657.

Han, C., Phillips, P. C. B., & Sul, D. (2011). Uniform asymptotic normality in stationary and unit root autoregression. *Econometric Theory*, *27*(6), 1117–1151.

Han, C., Phillips, P. C. B., & Sul, D. (2014). X-differencing and dynamic panel model estimation. *Econometric Theory*, *30*(1), 201–251.

Hansen, B. E. (2007). Least squares model averaging. *Econometrica*, *75*, 1175–1189.

Hjort, N. L., & Claeskens, G. (2003). Frequentist model average estimators. *Journal of the American Statistical Association, 98*, 879–899.

Hsiao, C., Pesaran, M. H., & Tahmiscioglu, A. K. (2002). Maximum likelihood estimation of fixed effects dynamic panel data models covering short time periods. *Journal of Econometrics, 109*, 107–150.

Kiviet, J. F. (1995). On bias, inconsistency, and effciency of various etimators in dynamic panel data models. *Journal of Econometrics, 68*, 53–78.

Kiviet, J. F. (2007). Judging contending estimators by simulation: Tournaments in dynamic panel data models. In G. D. A. Phillips & E. Tzavalis (Eds.), *The refinement of econometric estimation and test procedures* (pp. 282–318). Cambridge: Cambridge University Press.

Kruiniger, H. (2009). GMM estimation of dynamic panel data models with persistent data. *Econometric Theory, 25*, 1348–1391.

Moon, H. R., & Phillips, P. C. B. (2000). Estimation of autoregressive roots near unity using panel data. *Econometric Theory, 16*, 927–997.

Nickell, S. (1981). Biases in dynamic models with fixed effects. *Econometrica, 49*, 1417–1426.

Phillips, P. C. B. (2014). Dynamic Panel GMM with Unit Root and Irrelevant Instruments: Exam Solution for Question A. Unpublished Manuscript, Yale University.

Phillips, P. C. B., & Moon, H. R. (1999). Linear regression limit theory for nonstationary panel data. *Econometrica, 67*(5), 1057–1111.

Phillips, P. C. B., & Sul, D. (2007). Bias in dynamic panel estimation with fixed effects, incidental trends, and cross section dependence. *Journal of Econometrics, 137*, 162–188.

APPENDIX

This appendix is divided into two parts. In the first part, we prove the main results of the paper. In the second part, we state and prove a number of supporting lemmas which are used in proving the main results. Throughout this appendix, we let C denote a generic positive constant that may be different in different uses.

Proofs of Theorems

Proof of Theorem 1. To show part (a), first write

$$\sqrt{NT}\,(\hat{\rho}_{\mathrm{IV}} - \rho) = \left(\frac{1}{NT}\sum_{i=1}^{N}\sum_{t=2}^{T} y_{it-2}\Delta y_{it-1}\right)^{-1} \frac{1}{\sqrt{NT}}\sum_{i=1}^{N}\sum_{t=2}^{T} y_{it-2}\Delta\varepsilon_{it}$$

Note that by tedious but straightforward calculations, we can show that

$$\frac{1}{NT}\sum_{i=1}^{N}\sum_{t=2}^{T} y_{it-2}\Delta y_{it-1} = -(1-\rho)\frac{1}{NT}\sum_{i=1}^{N}\sum_{t=2}^{T}\sum_{j=0}^{t-3}\sum_{k=0}^{t-3}\rho^{j+k}\varepsilon_{it-2-j}\varepsilon_{it-2-k} + O_p(T^{-1}) + O_p(N^{-1}) \xrightarrow{p} -\left[\frac{\sigma^2}{1+\rho}\right]$$

as $N, T \to \infty$ such that $T/N \to \kappa \in [0, \infty)$.

Next, note that

$$\frac{1}{\sqrt{NT}}\sum_{i=1}^{N}\sum_{t=2}^{T} y_{it-2}\Delta\varepsilon_{it} = \frac{1}{\sqrt{NT}}\sum_{i=1}^{N}\sum_{t=3}^{T} w_{it-2}\Delta\varepsilon_{it} + O_p(T^{-1/2})$$

where

$$w_{it-2} = \sum_{k=0}^{t-3}\rho^{k}\varepsilon_{it-2-k}$$

From the proof of Lemma A1 below, it is evident that

$$\frac{1}{\sqrt{NT}}\sum_{i=1}^{N}\sum_{t=3}^{T} w_{it-2}\Delta\varepsilon_{it} \Rightarrow N\left(0,\ \frac{2\sigma^4}{1+\rho}\right)$$

as $N, T \to \infty$ such that $T/N \to \kappa \in [0, \infty)$.

It follows by the Cramér Convergence Theorem that

$$\sqrt{NT}(\hat{\rho}_{\mathrm{IV}} - \rho) \Rightarrow -\left(\frac{1+\rho}{\sigma^2}\right) N\left(0, \frac{2\sigma^4}{1+\rho}\right) \equiv N\left(0, 2[1+\rho]\right)$$

as required.

Part (b) can be shown by modifying the argument given in Phillips (2014) for the case with Gaussian errors. For brevity, the proof is omitted here. ■

Proof of Theorem 2. To show part (a), write

$$\hat{\rho}_{\mathrm{pols}} - \rho = \left[\sum_{i=1}^{N}\sum_{t=2}^{T}\left(y_{it-1} - \bar{y}_{-1,N,T}\right)^2\right]^{-1} \sum_{i=1}^{N}\sum_{t=2}^{T}(y_{it-1} - \bar{y}_{-1,N,T})[a_i(1-\rho) + \varepsilon_{it}]$$

where

$$\bar{y}_{-1,N,T} = \frac{1}{N(T-1)}\sum_{i=1}^{N}\sum_{t=2}^{T} y_{it-1}, \quad \text{and} \quad \bar{y}_{N,T} = \frac{1}{N(T-1)}\sum_{i=1}^{N}\sum_{t=2}^{T} y_{it}$$

We can show by tedious but straightforward calculations that, as $N, T \to \infty$ such that $T/N \to \kappa \in [0, \infty)$,

$$\frac{1}{NT}\sum_{i=1}^{N}\sum_{t=2}^{T}\left(y_{it-1} - \bar{y}_{-1,N,T}\right)^2 = \sigma_a^2 + \frac{\sigma^2}{1-\rho^2} + O_p\left(T^{-1}\right) + O_p\left(\frac{1}{\sqrt{NT}}\right)$$

and

$$\frac{1}{NT}\sum_{i=1}^{N}\sum_{t=2}^{T}(y_{it-1}-\bar{y}_{-1,N,T})[a_i(1-\rho)+\varepsilon_{it}]=(1-\rho)\sigma_a^2+O_p\left(\frac{1}{T}\right)+O_p\left(\frac{1}{\sqrt{NT}}\right)$$

It follows by Slutsky's theorem that

$$\begin{aligned}\hat{\rho}_{\text{pols}}-\rho &=(1-\rho)\sigma_a^2\left[1+O_p\left(\frac{1}{T}\right)+O_p\left(\frac{1}{\sqrt{NT}}\right)\right]\left[\sigma_a^2+\frac{\sigma^2}{1-\rho^2}\right]^{-1}\\ &\xrightarrow{p}\frac{\sigma_a^2(1-\rho)(1-\rho^2)}{\sigma_a^2(1-\rho^2)+\sigma^2}\end{aligned}$$

as required.

To show part (b), write

$$\sqrt{N}T(\hat{\rho}_{\text{pols}}-1)=\left[\frac{1}{NT^2}\sum_{i=1}^{N}\sum_{t=2}^{T}(y_{it-1}-\bar{y}_{N,T})^2\right]^{-1}\frac{1}{\sqrt{N}T}\sum_{i=1}^{N}\sum_{t=2}^{T}(y_{it-1}-\bar{y}_{N,T})\varepsilon_{it}$$

By direct calculation and using Lemma A6 below, as $N,T\to\infty$ such that $T/N\to\kappa\in[0,\infty)$,

$$\begin{aligned}\sqrt{N}T(\hat{\rho}_{\text{pols}}-1) &=\left[\frac{\sigma^2}{2}+O_p\left(\frac{1}{T}\right)\right]^{-1}\left[\frac{1}{\sqrt{N}T}\sum_{i=1}^{N}\sum_{t=2}^{T}w_{it-1}\varepsilon_{it}+O_p\left(\frac{1}{\sqrt{T}}\right)\right]\\ &=\frac{2}{\sigma^2}\frac{1}{\sqrt{N}T}\sum_{i=1}^{N}\sum_{t=2}^{T}w_{it-1}\varepsilon_{it}\left[1+O_p\left(\frac{1}{\sqrt{T}}\right)\right]\\ &\Rightarrow\frac{2}{\sigma^2}N\left(0,\frac{\sigma^4}{2}\right)\equiv N(0,2)\end{aligned}$$

as required. ■

Proof of Theorem 3. We will prove this result only for the case where the weighting function is based on a logistic type transformation, i.e.,

$$w_{\mathrm{IC},1} = \frac{1}{1+\exp\left\{\frac{1}{2}\Delta_{\mathrm{IC}}\right\}}$$

Asymptotic results when the weight function is of the form given by Eq. (20) can be proved similarly; hence, for purposes of brevity, we omit its proof.

To proceed, consider first part (a), where we assume that $\rho \in (0, 1)$. In this case, note that by part (a) of Theorems 1 and 2 and Lemma A7, we have that

$$\sqrt{NT}(\hat{\rho}_{\mathrm{IV}} - \rho) \Rightarrow N\ \ (0, 2\,[1+\rho])$$

Moreover, in this case

$$\hat{\rho}_{\mathrm{pols}} = \rho + \frac{\sigma_a^2(1-\rho)(1-\rho^2)}{\sigma_a^2(1-\rho^2)+\sigma^2} + O_p(T^{-1})$$

and, by part (a) of Lemma A7 below, we have

$$\frac{\mathbb{T}_{NT}}{\sqrt{NT}} = \frac{\hat{\rho}_{\mathrm{pols}} - 1}{\sqrt{\hat{\sigma}^2 M_{yy}^{-1}}} \xrightarrow{p} -\sigma^{-1}\left[\sigma_a^2 + \frac{\sigma^2}{1-\rho^2}\right]^{1/2} \frac{\sigma^2(1-\rho)}{\sigma_a^2(1-\rho^2)+\sigma^2} < 0$$

as $N, T \to \infty$ such that $T/N \to \kappa \in [0, \infty)$. It follows that in this case,

$$\frac{\Delta_{IC}}{\sqrt{NT}} = \frac{\mathbb{T}_{NT}}{\sqrt{NT}} + \frac{\alpha \ln(N) + \beta \ln(T)}{\sqrt{NT}} = \frac{\mathbb{T}_{NT}}{\sqrt{NT}} + o(1) < 0 \quad \text{w.p.a.1.}$$

which implies that

$$w_{\mathrm{IC}} = \frac{1}{1+\exp\left\{\frac{1}{2}\sqrt{NT}\left(\Delta_{\mathrm{IC}}/\sqrt{NT}\right)\right\}} = 1 + O_p\left(\exp\left\{-C\sqrt{NT}\right\}\right)$$

for some constant $C > 0$. From this result, we further obtain

$$
\begin{aligned}
\nu_{NT}(\hat{\rho}_{\text{avg}} - \rho) = & \left\{ w_{\text{IC}} \left(\frac{2}{NT} [1 + \hat{\rho}_{\text{IV}}] \right)^{-1/2} \right. \\
& \left. + (1 - w_{\text{IC}}) \hat{\sigma}^{-1} \left[\sum_{i=1}^{N} \sum_{t=2}^{T} (y_{it-1} - \bar{y}_{NT})^2 \right]^{1/2} \right\} \\
& \times \left(w_{\text{IC}} \hat{\rho}_{\text{IV}} + (1 - w_{\text{IC}}) \hat{\rho}_{\text{pols}} - \rho \right) \\
= & \{ \sqrt{NT} [1 + O_p(\exp\{-C\sqrt{NT}\})] (2[1 + \hat{\rho}_{\text{IV}}])^{-1/2} \\
& + [1 - 1 + O_p(\exp\{-C\sqrt{NT}\})] O_p(\sqrt{NT}) \} \\
& \times \{ [1 + O_p(\exp\{-C\sqrt{NT}\})] \hat{\rho}_{\text{IV}} - \rho \\
& + [1 - 1 + O_p(\exp\{-C\sqrt{NT}\})] O_p(1) \} \\
= & \left[\sqrt{NT} (2[1 + \hat{\rho}_{\text{IV}}])^{-1/2} + O_p(\sqrt{NT} \exp\{-C\sqrt{NT}\}) \right] \\
& \times [\hat{\rho}_{\text{IV}} - \rho + O_p(\exp\{-C\sqrt{NT}\})] \\
= & (2[1 + \hat{\rho}_{\text{IV}}])^{-1/2} \sqrt{NT} (\hat{\rho}_{\text{IV}} - \rho_T) + O_p(\sqrt{NT} \exp\{-C\sqrt{NT}\}) \\
& \Rightarrow N(0, 1)
\end{aligned}
$$

which is the desired result for part (a).

Next, consider part (b), where we assume that $\rho = 1$. Now, by Theorem 1 part (b), as $N, T \to \infty$ such that $T/N \to \kappa \in [0, \infty)$,

$$
\sqrt{T}(\hat{\rho}_{\text{IV}} - \rho_{N,T}) \Rightarrow \frac{2\mathcal{Z}_1}{\mathcal{Z}_2}
$$

where $\mathcal{Z}_1 \equiv N(0, 1)$, $\mathcal{Z}_2 \equiv N(0, 1)$, and $\mathcal{Z}_1$ and $\mathcal{Z}_2$ are independent. Moreover, by Theorem 2 part (b) and Lemma A7,

$$
\sqrt{NT}(\hat{\rho}_{\text{pols}} - \rho_T) \Rightarrow N(0, 2)
$$

$$
\mathbb{T}_{NT} = O_p(1)
$$

as $N, T \to \infty$ such that $T/N \to \kappa \in [0, \infty)$.

It follows that in this case

$$
\frac{\Delta_{IC}}{\alpha \ln(N) + \beta \ln(T)} = \frac{\mathbb{T}_{NT}}{\alpha \ln(N) + \beta \ln(T)} + 1 \xrightarrow{p} 1
$$

which implies that

$$
\begin{aligned}
w_{\mathrm{IC}} &= \left[1+\exp\left\{\frac{1}{2}[\alpha\ln(N)+\beta\ln(T)]\frac{\Delta_{IC}}{\alpha\ln(N)+\beta\ln(T)}\right\}\right]^{-1}\\
&= \left[1+O_p\left(\exp\{(\alpha/2)\ln(N)+(\beta/2)\ln(T)\}\right)\right]^{-1}\\
&= \frac{1}{1+O_p\left(N^{\alpha/2}T^{\beta/2}\right)} = O_p\left(\frac{1}{N^{\alpha/2}T^{\beta/2}}\right)
\end{aligned}
$$

It follows that

$$
\begin{aligned}
&\nu_{NT}\left(\hat{\rho}_{\mathrm{avg}}-1\right)\\
&\quad=\left\{w_{\mathrm{IC}}\left(\frac{2}{NT}[1+\hat{\rho}_{\mathrm{IV}}]\right)^{-1/2}+(1-w_{\mathrm{IC}})\hat{\sigma}^{-1}\left[\sum_{i=1}^{N}\sum_{t=2}^{T}\left(y_{it-1}-\bar{y}_{NT}\right)^2\right]^{1/2}\right\}\\
&\quad\quad\times\left(w_{\mathrm{IC}}\hat{\rho}_{\mathrm{IV}}+(1-w_{\mathrm{IC}})\hat{\rho}_{\mathrm{pols}}-1\right)\\
&\quad=\left\{O_p\left(\frac{1}{N^{\alpha/2}T^{\beta/2}}\sqrt{NT}\right)+\left(1-O_p\left(\frac{1}{N^{\alpha/2}T^{\beta/2}}\right)\right)\hat{\sigma}^{-1}\right.\\
&\quad\quad\left.\times\left[\frac{1}{NT^2}\sum_{i=1}^{N}\sum_{t=2}^{T}\left(y_{it-1}-\bar{y}_{NT}\right)^2\right]^{1/2}\sqrt{N}T\right\}\\
&\quad\quad\times\left[\hat{\rho}_{\mathrm{pols}}-1+O_p\left(\frac{1}{N^{\alpha/2}T^{\beta/2}}\right)\right]\\
&\quad=\hat{\sigma}^{-1}\left[\frac{1}{NT^2}\sum_{i=1}^{N}\sum_{t=2}^{T}\left(y_{it-1}-\bar{y}_{NT}\right)^2\right]^{1/2}\sqrt{N}T\left(\hat{\rho}_{\mathrm{pols}}-\rho_T\right)\\
&\quad\quad+O_p\left(\frac{1}{N^{(\alpha-1)/2}T^{(\beta-1)/2}}\right)\\
&\quad=\hat{\sigma}^{-1}\left[\frac{\sigma^2}{2}+O_p\left(\frac{1}{T}\right)\right]^{1/2}\frac{2}{\sigma^2}\frac{1}{\sqrt{N}T}\sum_{i=1}^{N}\sum_{t=2}^{T}w_{it-1}\varepsilon_{it}\\
&\quad\quad+\hat{\sigma}^{-1}\left[\frac{\sigma^2}{2}+O_p\left(\frac{1}{T}\right)\right]^{1/2}O_p\left(\frac{1}{\sqrt{T}}\right)+O_p\left(\frac{1}{N^{(\alpha-1)/2}T^{(\beta-1)/2}}\right)
\end{aligned}
$$

so that

$$\nu_{NT}\left(\hat{\rho}_{\text{avg}} - 1\right) = \hat{\sigma}^{-1}\frac{\sigma}{\sqrt{2}}\frac{2}{\sigma^2}\frac{\sigma^2}{\sqrt{2}}\left(\frac{\sqrt{2}}{\sigma^2}\frac{1}{\sqrt{NT}}\sum_{i=1}^{N}\sum_{t=2}^{T} w_{it-1}\varepsilon_{it}\right) + o_p(1)$$

$$= \left(\frac{\sqrt{2}}{\sigma^2}\frac{1}{\sqrt{NT}}\sum_{i=1}^{N}\sum_{t=2}^{T} w_{it-1}\varepsilon_{it}\right) + o_p(1) \Rightarrow \mathcal{Z}$$

where $\mathcal{Z} \equiv N\,(0, 1)$, as required. ■

Supporting Lemmas

Lemma A1. Suppose that Assumptions 1–4 hold, and let $\rho \in (0, 1)$. Then, as $N, T \to \infty$ such that $T/N \to \kappa \in [0, \infty)$,

$$\frac{1}{\omega_{N,T}}\sum_{i=1}^{N}\sum_{t=3}^{T} w_{it-2}\Delta\varepsilon_{it} \Rightarrow N\,(0,\ 1)$$

where

$$w_{it-2} = \sum_{k=0}^{t-3}\rho^k\varepsilon_{it-2-k}, \quad \omega_{N,T}^2 = \sum_{i=1}^{N}\omega_{i,T}^2 = \sum_{i=1}^{N} E\left[\left(X_{i,T} + Y_{i,T}\right)^2\right]$$

and

$$X_{i,T} = \frac{1}{\sqrt{T}}\sum_{t=3}^{T}\varepsilon_{it-2}\varepsilon_{it-1}, \quad Y_{i,T} = (\rho - 1)\frac{1}{\sqrt{T}}\sum_{t=3}^{T} w_{it-3}\varepsilon_{it-1}$$

Proof:

To proceed, note first that, by Abel's partial summation formula,

$$\sum_{i=1}^{N}\sum_{t=3}^{T} w_{it-2}\Delta\varepsilon_{it} = \sum_{i=1}^{N}\left\{\sum_{t=3}^{T}(w_{it-3} - w_{it-2})\varepsilon_{it-1}\right\} + \sum_{i=1}^{N} w_{iT-2}\varepsilon_{iT} - \sum_{i=1}^{N} w_{i1}\varepsilon_{i2}$$

$$= \sum_{i=1}^{N}\sum_{t=4}^{T}\left(\sum_{k=0}^{t-4}\rho^k\varepsilon_{it-3-k} - \sum_{k=0}^{t-3}\rho^k\varepsilon_{it-2-k}\right)\varepsilon_{it-1}$$

$$+ \sum_{i=1}^{N}\sum_{k=0}^{T-3}\rho^k\varepsilon_{iT-2-k}\varepsilon_{iT} - \sum_{i=1}^{N}\varepsilon_{i1}\varepsilon_{i2}$$

Note that

$$E\left(\sum_{i=1}^{N}\sum_{k=0}^{T-3}\rho^k \varepsilon_{iT-2-k}\varepsilon_{iT}\right)^2 = \sum_{i=1}^{N}\sum_{j=1}^{N}\sum_{k=0}^{T-3}\sum_{\ell=0}^{T-3}\rho^k\rho^\ell E\left[\varepsilon_{iT-2-k}\varepsilon_{jT-2-\ell}\varepsilon_{iT}\varepsilon_{jT}\right]$$
$$= \sigma^4\sum_{i=1}^{N}\sum_{k=0}^{T-3}\rho^{2k} = \sigma^4 N\left[\frac{1-\rho^{2(T-2)}}{1-\rho^2}\right]$$

so that

$$\sum_{i=1}^{N}\sum_{k=0}^{T-3}\rho^k \varepsilon_{iT-2-k}\varepsilon_{iT} = O_p\left(\sqrt{N}\right)$$

Moreover,

$$E\left(\sum_{i=1}^{N}\varepsilon_{i1}\varepsilon_{i2}\right)^2 = \sum_{i=1}^{N}\sum_{j=1}^{N}E\left[\varepsilon_{i1}\varepsilon_{j1}\varepsilon_{i2}\varepsilon_{j2}\right] = \sigma^4 N$$

so that

$$\sum_{i=1}^{N}\varepsilon_{i1}\varepsilon_{i2} = O_p\left(\sqrt{N}\right)$$

It follows that

$$\frac{1}{\sqrt{NT}}\sum_{i=1}^{N}\sum_{t=3}^{T}w_{it-2}\Delta\varepsilon_{it} = \frac{1}{\sqrt{NT}}\sum_{i=1}^{N}\sum_{t=3}^{T}(w_{it-3}-w_{it-2})\varepsilon_{it-1} + O_p\left(\frac{1}{\sqrt{T}}\right)$$
$$= -\frac{1}{\sqrt{NT}}\sum_{i=1}^{N}\sum_{t=3}^{T}(\varepsilon_{it-2}-w_{it-3}+\rho w_{it-3})\varepsilon_{it-1} + O_p\left(\frac{1}{\sqrt{T}}\right)$$
$$= -\frac{1}{\sqrt{NT}}\sum_{i=1}^{N}\sum_{t=3}^{T}[\varepsilon_{it-2}+(\rho-1)w_{it-3}]\varepsilon_{it-1} + O_p\left(\frac{1}{\sqrt{T}}\right)$$

Now, let

$$\underline{U}_{N,T} = -\sum_{i=1}^{N} \left(X_{i,T} + Y_{i,T}\right)$$

where $X_{i,T}$ and $Y_{i,T}$ are as defined in the statement of the lemma. Next, note that

$$E\left[X_{i,T}\right] = \frac{1}{\sqrt{T}} \sum_{t=4}^{T} E[\varepsilon_{it-2}\varepsilon_{it-1}] = 0$$

$$E\left[Y_{i,T}\right] = (\rho - 1)\frac{1}{\sqrt{T}} \sum_{t=3}^{T} \sum_{k=0}^{t-3} \rho^k E[\varepsilon_{it-3-k}\varepsilon_{it-1}] = 0$$

thus,

$$E\left[\underline{U}_{N,T}\right] = -\sum_{i=1}^{N} \left(E\left[X_{i,T}\right] + E\left[Y_{i,T}\right]\right) = 0$$

In addition, note that

$$E\left[X_{i,T}^2\right] = \frac{1}{T} \sum_{t=4}^{T} \sum_{s=4}^{T} E[\varepsilon_{it-2}\varepsilon_{it-1}\varepsilon_{is-2}\varepsilon_{is-1}] = \frac{1}{T} \sum_{t=4}^{T} E\left[\varepsilon_{it-2}^2\right] E\left[\varepsilon_{it-1}^2\right]$$

$$= \sigma^4 \left(\frac{T-3}{T}\right) = \sigma^4 + O\left(\frac{1}{T}\right)$$

$$E\left[Y_{i,T}^2\right] = (\rho - 1)^2 \frac{1}{T} \sum_{t=3}^{T} \sum_{s=3}^{T} \sum_{k=0}^{t-3} \sum_{\ell=0}^{s-3} \rho^k \rho^\ell E[\varepsilon_{it-3-k}\varepsilon_{is-3-\ell}\varepsilon_{it-1}\varepsilon_{is-1}]$$

$$= \sigma^4 (1-\rho)^2 \frac{1}{T} \sum_{t=3}^{T} \sum_{k=0}^{t-3} \rho^{2k} = \sigma^4 \left(\frac{1-\rho}{1+\rho}\right) + O\left(\frac{1}{T}\right)$$

and

$$E\left[X_{i,T} Y_{i,T}\right] = (\rho - 1)\frac{1}{T} \sum_{t=3}^{T} \sum_{s=3}^{T} \sum_{k=0}^{t-3} \rho^k E[\varepsilon_{it-3-k}\varepsilon_{it-1}\varepsilon_{is-2}\varepsilon_{is-1}] = 0$$

It follows that

$$\omega_{i,T}^2 = E\left[(X_{i,T} + Y_{i,T})^2\right] = \frac{2\sigma^4}{1+\rho} + O\left(\frac{1}{T}\right)$$

$$\omega_{N,T}^2 = \sum_{i=1}^{N} \omega_{i,T}^2 = \frac{2\sigma^4}{1+\rho} N\left[1 + O\left(\frac{1}{T}\right)\right]$$

Hence, to prove the required result, it suffices to show that

$$\frac{U_{N,T}}{\omega_{N,T}} = \frac{1}{\omega_{N,T}/\sqrt{N}} \frac{-1}{\sqrt{N}} \sum_{i=1}^{N} (X_{i,T} + Y_{i,T}) \Rightarrow N(0,1)$$

as $N, T \to \infty$ such that $T/N \to \kappa \in [0, \infty)$. To show this, write

$$U_{N,T} = \frac{1}{\omega_{N,T}/\sqrt{N}} \frac{-1}{\sqrt{N}} \sum_{i=1}^{N} (X_{i,T} + Y_{i,T})$$

Next, by direct calculations, we have

$$\frac{\omega_{N,T}^2}{N} = \frac{1}{N} \sum_{i=1}^{N} \omega_{i,T}^2 = \frac{2\sigma^4}{1+\rho}\left[1 + O\left(\frac{1}{T}\right)\right] = \frac{2\sigma^4}{1+\rho} + O\left(\frac{1}{T}\right)$$

Since $0 < \sigma^4 < \infty$ by assumption, it follows that there exists a positive constant C,

$$0 < \frac{1}{C} \leq \frac{\omega_{N,T}}{\sqrt{N}} \leq C < \infty \text{ eventually as } N, T \to \infty$$

Hence, to show the asymptotic normality of $U_{N,T}$, it suffices to show that

$$\lim_{N,T\to\infty} \sum_{i=1}^{N} E\left[\frac{1}{\sqrt{N}} U_{N,T}\right]^4 = \lim_{N,T\to\infty} \frac{1}{N^2} \sum_{i=1}^{N} E\left[(X_{i,T} + Y_{i,T})^4\right] = 0$$

To show this, note first that by Loève's c_r inequality, we have that

$$\begin{aligned}\frac{1}{N^2}\sum_{i=1}^{N}E\left[\left(X_{i,T}+Y_{i,T}\right)^4\right] &\leq \frac{1}{N^2}\sum_{i=1}^{N}8\left\{E\left[\left(\frac{1}{\sqrt{T}}\sum_{t=4}^{T}\varepsilon_{it-2}\varepsilon_{it-1}\right)^4\right]\right. \\ &\quad \left.+E\left[\left((\rho-1)\frac{1}{\sqrt{T}}\sum_{t=3}^{T}\sum_{k=0}^{t-3}\rho^k\varepsilon_{it-2-k}\varepsilon_{it-1}\right)^4\right]\right\} \\ &= 8\frac{1}{N^2T^2}\sum_{i=1}^{N}E\left[\left(\sum_{t=4}^{T}\varepsilon_{it-2}\varepsilon_{it-1}\right)^4\right] \\ &\quad +8\frac{(\rho-1)^4}{N^2T^2}\sum_{i=1}^{N}E\left[\left(\sum_{t=3}^{T}\sum_{k=0}^{t-3}\rho^k\varepsilon_{it-2-k}\varepsilon_{it-1}\right)^4\right]\end{aligned}$$

Now,

$$\begin{aligned}E\left[\left(\sum_{t=4}^{T}\varepsilon_{it-2}\varepsilon_{it-1}\right)^4\right] &= \sum_{r=4}^{T}\sum_{s=4}^{T}\sum_{t=4}^{T}\sum_{u=4}^{T}E[\varepsilon_{ir-2}\varepsilon_{is-2}\varepsilon_{it-2}\varepsilon_{iu-2}\varepsilon_{ir-1}\varepsilon_{is-1}\varepsilon_{it-1}\varepsilon_{iu-1}] \\ &= \sum_{t=4}^{T}E\left[\varepsilon_{it-2}^4\right]E\left[\varepsilon_{it-1}^4\right] \\ &\quad +6\sum_{s=6}^{T}\sum_{t=4}^{s-2}E\left[\varepsilon_{is-2}^2\right]E\left[\varepsilon_{is-1}^2\right]E\left[\varepsilon_{it-2}^2\right]E\left[\varepsilon_{it-1}^2\right] \\ &\quad +6\sum_{t=4}^{T-1}E\left[\varepsilon_{it}^2\right]E\left[\varepsilon_{it-1}^4\right]E\left[\varepsilon_{it-2}^2\right] \\ &= \left(E\left[\varepsilon_{it-1}^4\right]\right)^2(T-3)+6\sigma^8\sum_{s=6}^{T}(s-5)+6E\left[\varepsilon_{it-1}^4\right]\sigma^4(T-4) \\ &= 6\sigma^8\frac{(T-5)(T-4)}{2}+\left(E\left[\varepsilon_{it-1}^4\right]\right)^2(T-3) \\ &\quad +6E\left[\varepsilon_{it-1}^4\right]\sigma^4(T-4) \\ &= 3\sigma^8T^2\left[1+O\left(\frac{1}{T}\right)\right]\end{aligned}$$

Moreover,

$$
\begin{aligned}
E&\left[\left(\sum_{t=3}^{T}\sum_{k=0}^{t-3}\rho^k\varepsilon_{it-2-k}\varepsilon_{it-1}\right)^4\right]\\
&=\sum_{r=3}^{T}\sum_{s=3}^{T}\sum_{t=3}^{T}\sum_{u=3}^{T}\sum_{h=0}^{r-3}\sum_{j=0}^{s-3}\sum_{k=0}^{t-3}\sum_{l=0}^{u-3}\rho^h\rho^j\rho^k\rho^\ell\\
&\quad\times E\left[\varepsilon_{ir-2-h}\varepsilon_{is-2-j}\varepsilon_{it-2-k}\varepsilon_{iu-2-\ell}\varepsilon_{ir-1}\varepsilon_{is-1}\varepsilon_{it-1}\varepsilon_{iu-1}\right]\\
&\le\overline{C}\left\{\sum_{t=3}^{T}\sum_{k=0}^{t-3}\rho^{4k}E\left[\varepsilon_{it-2-k}^4\right]E\left[\varepsilon_{it-1}^4\right]\right.\\
&\quad+\sum_{t=4}^{T}\sum_{s=3}^{t-1}\sum_{l=0}^{s-3}\rho^{2\ell}\rho^{2(t-s-1)}E\left[\varepsilon_{is-2-\ell}^2\right]E\left[\varepsilon_{is-1}^4\right]E\left[\varepsilon_{it-1}^2\right]\\
&\quad+\sum_{t=4}^{T}\sum_{s=3}^{t-1}\sum_{l=0}^{s-3}\rho^{2\ell}\rho^{2(t-s+\ell)}E\left[\varepsilon_{is-2-\ell}^4\right]E\left[\varepsilon_{is-1}^2\right]E\left[\varepsilon_{it-1}^2\right]\\
&\quad+\sigma^8\sum_{t=5}^{T}\sum_{s=4}^{t-1}\sum_{r=3}^{s-1}\sum_{h=0}^{r-3}\rho^h\rho^{t-s-1}\rho^{s-r-1}\rho^{t-r+h}\\
&\quad\left.+\sum_{t=5}^{T}\sum_{r=3}^{t-1}\sum_{h=0}^{r-3}\rho^h\rho^{2(t-r-1)}\rho^{t-r+h}\left|E\left[\varepsilon_{it-1}^3\right]\right|\left|E\left[\varepsilon_{ir-1}^3\right]\right|\sigma^2\right\}
\end{aligned}
$$

for some positive constant $\overline{C}$. Thus, given Assumption 1, there exists a positive constant C. From direct calculation, we have

$$
\begin{aligned}
E&\left[\left(\sum_{t=3}^{T}\sum_{K=0}^{t-3}\rho^k\varepsilon_{it-2-k}\varepsilon_{it-1}\right)^4\right]\\
&\le C\left[\sum_{t=3}^{T}\sum_{k=0}^{t-3}\rho^{4k}+\sum_{t=4}^{T}\sum_{s=3}^{t-1}\rho^{2(t-s-1)}\sum_{\ell=0}^{s-3}\rho^{2\ell}+\sum_{t=4}^{T}\sum_{s=3}^{t-1}\rho^{2(t-s)}\sum_{\ell=0}^{s-3}\rho^{4\ell}\right.\\
&\quad\left.+\sum_{t=5}^{T}\sum_{s=4}^{t-1}\sum_{r=3}^{s-1}\sum_{h=0}^{r-3}\rho^{2(t-r-1+h)}+\sum_{t=5}^{T}\sum_{r=3}^{t-1}\sum_{h=0}^{r-3}\rho^h\rho^{2(t-r-1)}\rho^{t-r+h}\right]\\
&=C\left[\sum_{t=3}^{T}\frac{1-\rho^{4(t-2)}}{1-\rho^4}+\sum_{t=4}^{T}\sum_{s=3}^{t-1}\rho^{2(t-1-s)}\frac{1-\rho^{2(s-2)}}{1-\rho^2}+\sum_{t=4}^{T}\sum_{s=3}^{t-1}\rho^{2(t-s)}\frac{1-\rho^{4(s-2)}}{1-\rho^4}\right.\\
&\quad\left.+\sum_{t=5}^{T}\sum_{s=4}^{t-1}\rho^{2(t-s)}\sum_{r=3}^{s-1}\rho^{2(s-1-r)}\frac{1-\rho^{2(r-2)}}{1-\rho^2}+\sum_{t=5}^{T}\rho^{3t}\sum_{r=3}^{t-1}\rho^{-(3r+2)}\frac{1-\rho^{2(r-2)}}{1-\rho^2}\right]\\
&=O(T)
\end{aligned}
$$

Hence,

$$\frac{1}{N^2}\sum_{i=1}^{N}E\left[\left(X_{i,T}+Y_{i,T}\right)^4\right] \leq 8\frac{1}{N^2T^2}\sum_{i=1}^{N}E\left[\left(\sum_{t=4}^{T}\varepsilon_{it-2}\varepsilon_{it-1}\right)^4\right] + 8\frac{(\rho-1)^4}{N^2T^2}\sum_{i=1}^{N}E\left[\left(\sum_{t=3}^{T}\sum_{k=0}^{t-3}\rho^k\varepsilon_{it-2-k}\varepsilon_{it-1}\right)^4\right]$$
$$= O\left(\frac{1}{N^2T^2}NT^2\right) + O\left(\frac{1}{N^2T^2}NT\right) = O\left(N^{-1}\right)$$

as required. ∎

Lemma A2.

(a)

$$\sum_{t=4}^{T}(t-1)\rho^{2(t-3)} = \frac{\rho}{2}\left\{\frac{2\rho-[2(T-3)+1]\rho^{2(T-3)}}{1-\rho} + \frac{\rho^2\left(1-\rho^{2(T-3)-1}\right)}{(1-\rho)^2}\right\} + \frac{2\rho^2\left(1-\rho^{2(T-3)}\right)}{1-\rho^2}$$

(b)

$$\sum_{t=5}^{T}\rho^{2(t-3)}(t-4)=\frac{\rho}{2}\left\{\frac{4\rho^3-[2(T-3)+1]\rho^{2(T-3)}}{1-\rho}+\frac{\rho^4\left(1-\rho^{2T-9}\right)}{(1-\rho)^2}-\frac{\rho^3\left(1-\rho^{2(T-4)}\right)}{1-\rho^2}\right\}$$

(c)

$$\sum_{t=5}^{T}(t-4)(t-3)\rho^{2(t-3)} = \frac{\rho^2}{4}\left\{\frac{12\rho^2-[2(T-3)+1]2(T-3)\rho^{2(T-3)-1}}{1-\rho} + \frac{8\rho^3-2[2(T-3)+1]\rho^{2(T-3)}}{(1-\rho)^2} + \frac{2\left[\rho^4-\rho^{2(T-3)+1}\right]}{(1-\rho)^3}\right\}$$
$$-\frac{\rho}{4}\left\{\frac{4\rho^3-[2(T-3)+1]\rho^{2(T-3)}}{1-\rho} + \frac{\rho^4-\rho^{2(T-3)+1}}{(1-\rho)^2}\right\}$$

Proof:
It is obvious, hence omitted.

Lemma A3. (Phillips & Moon, 1999, Theorem 3): Suppose that $Y_{i,T} = C_i Q_{i,T}$, where the $(m \times 1)$ random vectors $Q_{i,T}$ are i.i.d. $(0, \Sigma_T)$ across i for all T and the C_i are $(m \times m)$ nonzero and nonrandom matrices. Assume the following conditions hold.

(i) Let $\sigma_T^2 = \lambda_{\min}(\Sigma_T)$ and $\liminf_T \sigma_T^2 > 0$
(ii) $\max_{1 \le i \le n} \|C_i\|^2 / \lambda_{\min}\left(\sum_{i=1}^N C_i C_i'\right) = O(1/N)$ as $N \to \infty$
(iii) $\|Q_{i,T}\|^2$ are uniformly integrable in T
(iv) $\lim_{N,T} (1/N) \sum_{i=1}^N C_i \Sigma_T C_i' = \Omega > 0$

Then,

$$X_{N,T} = \frac{1}{\sqrt{N}} \sum_{i=1}^{N} Y_{i,T} \Rightarrow N(0, \Omega), \quad \text{as} \quad N, T \to \infty$$

Lemma A4. (Phillips & Moon, 1999, Corollary 1): Suppose that $Y_{i,T} = C_i Q_{i,T}$, where $Q_{i,T}$ are i.i.d. across i for all T, and the C_i are $(m \times m)$ nonrandom matrices for all i. Assume that $Q_{i,T}$ are integrable for all T and $Q_{i,T} \Rightarrow Q_i$ as $T \to \infty$. Assume that $C = \lim_N (1/N) \sum_{i=1}^N C_i$ exists. If $\|Q_{i,T}\|$ is uniformly integrable in T for all i, and if $\sup_i \|C_i\| < \infty$, then

$$\frac{1}{N} \sum_{i=1}^{N} Y_{i,T} \xrightarrow{p} CE[Q_i]$$

as $N, T \to \infty$.

Lemma A5. Suppose that Assumption 1 holds and define

$$w_{it-1} = \sum_{k=0}^{t-1} \varepsilon_{it-1-k}$$

with $\varepsilon_{i0} = 0$. Then,

(a) $\frac{1}{T} \sum_{t=2}^{T} w_{it-1} \varepsilon_{it} \Rightarrow \frac{\sigma^2}{2} \left[\chi_1^2 - 1\right] = \sigma^2 \int_0^1 W_i(r)\, \mathrm{d}W_i(r)$

as $T \to \infty$.

(b) $\frac{1}{T^2} \sum_{t=2}^{T} w_{it-1}^2 \Rightarrow \sigma^2 \int_0^1 [W_i(r)]^2 \mathrm{d}r$

as $T \to \infty$.

Joint weak convergence of (a) and (b) also apply.

Proof:
These results are well-known from the unit root literature, so we omit the proof. ■

Lemma A6. Suppose that Assumption 1 holds. Then,

(a) $\frac{1}{T}\sum_{t=2}^{T} w_{it-1}\varepsilon_{it} \Rightarrow N\left(0,\ \frac{\sigma^4}{2}\right)$

as $N, T \to \infty$ such that $T/N \to \kappa \in [0, \infty)$.

(b) $\frac{1}{NT^2}\sum_{i=1}^{N}\sum_{t=2}^{T} w_{it-1}^2 \xrightarrow{p} \frac{\sigma^2}{2}$

as $N, T \to \infty$ such that $T/N \to \kappa \in [0, \infty)$.

Proof:
To show part (a), we verify the conditions of Theorem 3 of Phillips and Moon (1999), given above as Lemma A3. To proceed, first define

$$Q_{i,T} = \frac{1}{T}\sum_{t=2}^{T} w_{it-1}\varepsilon_{it}$$

and note that by direct calculation

$$\begin{aligned}
\lim\inf_{T\to\infty} \sigma_T^2 &= \lim\inf_{T\to\infty} E\left[Q_{i,T}^2\right] = \lim_{T\to\infty} E\left[Q_{i,T}^2\right] \\
&= \lim_{T\to\infty}\frac{1}{T^2}\sum_{t=2}^{T}\sum_{s=2}^{T}\sum_{k=1}^{t-1}\sum_{\ell=1}^{s-1} E[\varepsilon_{ik}\varepsilon_{i\ell}\varepsilon_{it}\varepsilon_{is}] \\
&= \lim_{T\to\infty}\frac{1}{T^2}\sum_{t=2}^{T}\sum_{k=1}^{t-1} E\left[\varepsilon_{ik}^2\right]E\left[\varepsilon_{it}^2\right] \\
&= \sigma^4 \lim_{T\to\infty}\frac{T(T-1)}{2T^2} = \frac{\sigma^4}{2} > 0
\end{aligned}$$

so that condition (i) of Lemma A3 is satisfied. Moreover, in this case, we have

$$C_i = 1 \text{ for all } i$$

so that

$$\max_{1 \le i \le n} \|C_i\|^2/\lambda_{\min}\left(\sum_{i=1}^{N} C_i C_i'\right) = 1/N = O(1/N)$$

as required by condition (ii). Next, observe that by part (a) of Lemma A5, we have that as $T \to \infty$,

$$Q_{i,T} = \frac{1}{T}\sum_{t=2}^{T} w_{it-1}\varepsilon_{it} \Rightarrow \frac{\sigma^2}{2}\left[\chi_1^2 - 1\right] \equiv Q$$

so that by the continuous mapping theorem

$$Q_{i,T}^2 \Rightarrow Q^2 \equiv \frac{\sigma^4}{4}\left[\chi_1^2 - 1\right]^2, \text{ as } T \to \infty$$

In addition,

$$\begin{aligned} E\left[Q^2\right] &= \frac{\sigma^4}{4}\left\{E\left[\chi_1^2\right]^2 - 2E\left[\chi_1^2\right] + 1\right\} \\ &= \frac{\sigma^4}{4}\left\{Var\left[\chi_1^2\right] + \left(E\left[\chi_1^2\right]\right)^2 - 2E\left[\chi_1^2\right] + 1\right\} \\ &= \frac{\sigma^4}{4}\{2 + 1 - 2 + 1\} = \frac{\sigma^4}{2} \end{aligned}$$

and note that, as $T \to \infty$,

$$\lim_{T \to \infty} E\left[Q_{i,T}^2\right] = \sigma^4 \lim_{T \to \infty} \frac{T(T-1)}{2T^2} = \frac{\sigma^4}{2} = E\left[Q^2\right]$$

It follows from Theorem 5.4 of Billingsley (1968) that $\left\{Q_{i,T}^2\right\}$ is uniformly integrable, so that condition (iii) of Lemma A3 is satisfied. Finally, note that in this case

$$\lim_{N,T} (1/N)\sum_{i=1}^{N} C_i \Sigma_T C_i' = \lim_{N,T} (1/N)\sum_{i=1}^{N} E\left[Q_{i,T}^2\right] = \frac{\sigma^4}{2} > 0$$

so that condition (iv) is satisfied as well. It follows then from Lemma A3 that

$$Q_{i,T} = \frac{1}{T}\sum_{t=2}^{T} w_{it-1}\varepsilon_{it} \Rightarrow N\left(0, \frac{\sigma^4}{2}\right)$$

as $N, T \to \infty$.

To show part (b), we verify the conditions of Corollary 1 of Phillips and Moon (1999), given here as Lemma A4. To proceed, define now

$$Q_{i,T} = \frac{1}{T^2}\sum_{t=2}^{T} w_{it-1}^2$$

Note that $Q_{i,T}$ is integrable in light of Assumption 1 and by part (b) of Lemma A5, we have that, as $T \to \infty$

$$Q_{i,T} = \frac{1}{T^2}\sum_{t=2}^{T} w_{it-1}^2 \Rightarrow \sigma^2 \int_0^1 [W_i(r)]^2 \mathrm{d}r = Q_i$$

Again, we have in this case

$$C_i = 1 \quad \text{for all} \quad i$$

so that trivially,

$$C = \lim_N \; (1/N)\sum_{i=1}^{N} C_i = 1 < \infty$$

and

$$\sup_i \|C_i\| = 1 < \infty$$

Moreover, in this case,

$$\begin{aligned} E\left[\left|Q_{i,T}\right|\right] = E\left[Q_{i,T}\right] &= \frac{1}{T^2}\sum_{t=2}^{T} E\left[w_{it-1}^2\right] = \frac{1}{T^2}\sum_{t=2}^{T}\sum_{k=1}^{t-1}\sum_{\ell=1}^{t-1} E\left[\varepsilon_{ik}\varepsilon_{i\ell}\right] \\ &= \frac{1}{T^2}\sum_{t=2}^{T}\sum_{k=1}^{t-1} E\left[\varepsilon_{ik}^2\right] = \sigma^2 \frac{T\,(T-1)}{2T^2} \end{aligned}$$

so that, as $T \to \infty$,

$$\lim_{T\to\infty} E\left[\left|Q_{i,T}\right|\right] = \sigma^2 \lim_{T\to\infty} \frac{T(T-1)}{2T^2} = \frac{\sigma^2}{2} = \sigma^2 \int_0^1 E[W_i(r)]^2 \mathrm{d}r = E[Q_i] \text{ for all } i$$

It follows from Theorem 5.4 of Billingsley (1968) that $\{|Q_{i,T}|\}$ is uniformly integrable in T for all i. Hence, all the conditions of Lemma A4 are satisfied, and we deduce from this lemma that

$$\frac{1}{N}\sum_{i=1}^{N} Q_{i,T} = \frac{1}{NT^2}\sum_{i=1}^{N}\sum_{t=2}^{T} w_{it-1}^2 \xrightarrow{p} CE\,[Q_i] = \frac{\sigma^2}{2}$$

as $N, T \to \infty$. ■

Lemma A7. Under Assumptions 1–4, the following statements are true.

(a) If $\rho \in (0, 1)$,

$$\frac{\mathbb{T}_{NT}}{\sqrt{NT}} \xrightarrow{p} -\sigma^{-1}\left[\sigma_a^2 + \frac{\sigma^2}{1-\rho^2}\right]^{1/2} \frac{\sigma^2(1-\rho)}{\sigma_a^2(1-\rho^2)+\sigma^2} < 0$$

for any $\varepsilon > 0$, as $N, T \to \infty$ such that $T/N \to \kappa \in [0, \infty)$.

(b) If $\rho = 1$,

$$\mathbb{T}_{NT} \Rightarrow N\,(0, 1)$$

as $N, T \to \infty$ such that $T/N \to \kappa \in [0,\infty)$.

Proof:
To show (a), note that from part (a) of Theorem 2 that for $\rho \in (0, 1)$, we have that

$$\hat{\rho}_{\text{pols}} = \rho + \frac{\sigma_a^2(1-\rho)(1-\rho^2)}{\sigma_a^2(1-\rho^2)+\sigma^2} + O_p(T^{-1})$$

from which it follows that

$$\hat{\rho}_{\text{pols}} - 1 \xrightarrow{p} -\left[\frac{\sigma^2(1-\rho)}{\sigma_a^2(1-\rho^2)+\sigma^2}\right] < 0$$

as $N, T \to \infty$. Next, define

$$M_{yy} = \frac{1}{N(T-1)} \sum_{i=1}^{N} \sum_{t=2}^{T} \left(y_{it-1} - \overline{y}_{NT}\right)^2$$

and note that

$$M_{yy} \xrightarrow{p} \sigma_a^2 + \frac{\sigma^2}{1-\rho^2} > 0$$

in this case. Hence, it follows by the Slutsky Theorem that

$$\frac{\mathbb{T}_{NT}}{\sqrt{NT}} = \frac{\hat{\rho}_{\text{pols}} - 1}{\sqrt{\hat{\sigma}^2 M_{yy}^{-1}}} \xrightarrow{p} -\sigma^{-1}\left[\sigma_a^2 + \frac{\sigma^2}{1-\rho^2}\right]^{1/2} \frac{\sigma^2(1-\rho)}{\sigma_a^2(1-\rho^2)+\sigma^2} < 0$$

as required for part (a).

Next, consider part (b), where we assume that $\rho = 1$. In this case, by part (b) Theorem 2, we have

$$\sqrt{N}T\left(\hat{\rho}_{\text{pols}} - \rho_T\right) \Rightarrow N(0, 2)$$

as $N, T \to \infty$ such that $T/N \to \kappa \in [0, \infty)$. Moreover, in this case, we have

$$\frac{1}{NT^2} \sum_{i=1}^{N} \sum_{t=2}^{T} \left(y_{it-1} - \overline{y}_{NT}\right)^2 = \frac{1}{NT^2} \sum_{i=1}^{N} \sum_{t=2}^{T} w_{it-1}^2 + O_p\left(\frac{1}{T}\right) \xrightarrow{p} \frac{\sigma^2}{2}$$

It follows that

$$\mathbb{T}_{NT} = \frac{\hat{\rho}_{\text{pols}} - 1}{\sqrt{V(\hat{\rho}_{\text{pols}})}} \Rightarrow \frac{\sigma}{\sqrt{2}} \frac{N(0,2)}{\sigma} \equiv N\,(0,1)$$

where

$$V(\hat{\rho}_{\text{pols}}) = \hat{\sigma}^2 \left[\sum_{i=1}^{N} \sum_{t=2}^{T} \left(y_{it-1} - \overline{y}_{NT} \right)^2 \right]^{-1}$$

as $N, T \rightarrow \infty$ such that $T/N \rightarrow \kappa \in [0, \infty)$, thus, establishing the required result. ■

EFFICIENT ESTIMATION AND INFERENCE FOR DIFFERENCE-IN-DIFFERENCE REGRESSIONS WITH PERSISTENT ERRORS

Ryan Greenaway-McGrevy[a], Chirok Han[b] and Donggyu Sul[c]

[a]*Department of Economics, University of Auckland, Auckland, New Zealand*
[b]*Department of Economics, Korea University, Seoul, South Korea*
[c]*Department of Economics, University of Texas at Dallas, Richardson, TX, USA*

ABSTRACT

This paper is concerned with estimation and inference for difference-in-difference regressions with errors that exhibit high serial dependence, including near unit roots, unit roots, and linear trends. We propose a couple of solutions based on a parametric formulation of the error covariance. First stage estimates of autoregressive structures are obtained by using the Han, Phillips, and Sul (2011, 2013) X-differencing transformation. The X-differencing method is simple to implement and is unbiased in large N *settings. Compared to similar parametric methods,*

Essays in Honor of Peter C. B. Phillips
Advances in Econometrics, Volume 33, 281–302

ISSN: 0731-9053/doi:10.1108/S0731-905320140000033009

the approach is computationally simple and requires fewer restrictions on the permissible parameter space of the error process. Simulations suggest that our methods perform well in the finite sample across a wide range of panel dimensions and dependence structures.

Keywords: Treatment effects; difference-in-difference estimation; serial dependence; x-differencing; Cochrane-Orcutt transformation

JEL classification: C33

1. INTRODUCTION

This paper is concerned with estimating the following difference-in-difference (DD) regression with fixed effects and autoregressive errors of the form

$$y_{it} = \alpha_i + \lambda_t + \beta I_{it} + Z_{it}\gamma + \varepsilon_{it}, \; \varepsilon_{it} = \sum_{j=1}^{p} \rho_j \varepsilon_{it-j} + u_{it} \quad (1)$$

where $i=1, \ldots, N$; $t=1, \ldots, T$, α_i is a fixed effect, λ_t is a common time effect, I_{it} is the policy variable or treatment of interest (typically a binary or dummy variable), and Z_{it} is a vector of exogenous control variables. Within the DD literature focus typically centers on β – the coefficient on the dummy variable I_{it}. As emphasized in Bertrand, Duflo, and Mullainathan (2004, BDM), serial dependence in the error term ε_{it} generates problems for conducting valid statistical inference. Statistical tests may exhibit a size distortion if the serial dependence is not accounted for when constructing standard errors. By means of Monte Carlo simulations and pseudo-empirical applications, BDM show that inference based on the conventional OLS t-statistic over-rejects the null and suggest using robust covariance estimators to restore the size of the test for large N, small T panels.

BDM point out that much of the DD literature is potentially affected by this problem. Subsequent research has focused on HAC estimation with $T \to \infty$ in order to accommodate panel datasets with large T. Donald and Lang (2007), Hansen (2007a), Cameron, Miller, and Gelbach (2008), Bester, Conley, and Hansen (2011) and Miller, Cameron, and Gelbach (2011) all study estimators under large T asymptotics, and suggest various methods to obtain correctly sized tests for cases when T is larger than N.

Another strand of literature imposes a parametric serial dependence structure in order to simultaneously conduct valid inference and to gain more efficient point estimates. Bhargava, Franzini, and Narendranathan (1982) study a feasible generalized least squares (FGLS) method that relies on least squares (LS) estimation of an AR(1) process in the error. One potential drawback of the parameteric approach is that it relies on accurate first stage estimates of the autoregressive process, and it is well-known that LS estimators exhibit $O(T^{-1})$ bias and that the weak-instrument problem hampers instrumental variables (IV) methods in certain regions of the parameter space (Blundell & Bond, 1998). Although both Bhargava et al. (1982) and Hansen (2007b) correct the LS bias, their proposed method is computationally burdensome (requiring an iterative algorithm to correct for the bias exactly) and requires restrictions on the permissible parameter space in order for the inverted bias function to be unique (see Hansen, 2007b). For example, regions in the neighborhood of unity where the bias function is non-monotonic are excluded.

In this paper we provide some simple but effective methods to improve inference in DD regressions of the form of Eq. (1). Our suggested methods are based on the recently developed X-differencing estimator of autoregressive parameters proposed by Han, Phillips, and Sul (2011, 2014; HPS hereafter). We then transform the data using the fitted autoregressive parameters, using either an FGLS or Cochrane–Orcutt (CO) transformation, in order to remove serial dependence. Although the CO approach is less efficient than FGLS (due to the loss of initial observations in each time series), it is practically attractive and flexible, particularly if the data are highly persistent.

Three key features of our X-differencing-based approaches are appealing. First, the method is straightforward to apply and can be easily adopted by practitioners. Second, the method can be applied under fewer restrictions on the parameter space than bias-corrected LS or IV methods (e.g., it permits unit roots), and the efficiency gains relative to conventional LS can be substantial, particularly when the errors follow a unit root process and the CO transformation is used. This feature is particularly useful given that the typical dependent variable used in DD regressions – such as wages, consumption, employment, and healthcare expenditures (see BDM) – is highly persistent. Third, the estimator provides valid inference under a broad range of asymptotic sequences, requiring only that $N(T-p) \to \infty$.

Under large N frameworks (i.e., when $N \to \infty$), the X-differencing method delivers a consistent estimator of the autoregressive parameters, regardless of the size of T. Under small N frameworks (i.e., when N is fixed in the asymptotics) the method significantly attentuates the bias of the LS estimator (Han et al., 2011). (In large T, small N settings however, this bias is less of a concern, of course.) These features permit application of the methods in a variety of sample size settings, including both "long" and "short" panels.

The rest of the paper is constructed as follows. The next section defines the serial dependence issue, and suggests a solution how to correct this statistical problem. A small Monte Carlo simulation results are reported in Section 3. Section 4 summarizes the findings of this paper. Sample Stata codes are provided in the appendix.

2. ESTIMATION AND INFERENCE FOR AUTOREGRESSIVE ERROR STRUCTURES

In this section we consider models of the form of Eq. (1), where the innovation (u_{it}) to the AR(p) process (ε_{it}) is white noise, and the AR polynomial is permitted to have a unit root. There are two broad approaches considered in the literature for dealing with serial dependence: Correcting the standard errors of the LS estimator, or LS estimation based on transformed data (such as GLS).

The first approach is concerned with constructing covariance estimators that are robust to serial dependence. Nonparametric covariance estimators such as those based on clustering can often provide statistical tests with asymptotically correct sizes without relying on parametric assumptions on the error processes. The cost of this generality is that these require large N. When the number of groups (or clusters) is small, alternative methods are required. The nonparametric estimators proposed by Donald and Lang (2007), Hansen (2007a), Cameron et al. (2008), Bester et al. (2011) and Miller et al. (2011) permit both serial dependence and T to grow in the asymptotics. For example, Hansen (2007a) shows that under fixed N, large T asymptotics, using the clustered covariance matrix of Arellano (1987) to estimate the standard errors leads to a t-statistic that is asymptotically distributed as t_{N-1}. An additional problem under this approach is a potential efficiency loss if the errors are highly persistent. The convergence rate of the OLS estimator of β (in levels) becomes $\sqrt{N}$ rather than $\sqrt{NT}$ when either stochastic or non-stochastic trends are present in the error term, since identification essentially only comes from between group variation.

The second approach transforms the data in order to remove serial dependence before applying LS. This approach includes FGLS, weighted least squares, and the CO type correction. Wooldridge (2003) discusses random and fixed effects FGLS when the covariance matrix is estimated nonparametrically. It is worth noting that the (nonparametric) random and fixed effects FGLS estimators can be constructed as long as N is much larger than T. For each element of the $T \times T$ covariance matrix (or $(T-1) \times (T-1)$ matrix if the data have been differenced to eliminate the fixed effects) can be estimated by using cross-sectional average. To be specific, the sth, tth element of the covariance matrix, ω_{st}, of $\mathrm{E}\varepsilon_i\varepsilon_i' = \Omega_{T\times T}$ can be estimated consistently by taking the cross-sectional averages of the product of the regression residuals. As $N \to \infty$ with T fixed, it is easy to show that

$$\hat{\omega}_{st} = \frac{1}{N}\sum_{i=1}^{N} \hat{\varepsilon}_{is}\hat{\varepsilon}_{it} \to^{p} \omega_{st}$$

for each t and s. (For the fixed effects FGLS, the sample covariances of the differenced residuals are to be calculated.) However this nonparametric FGLS method would require the ratio condition of $T^2/N \to 0$ as $N,T \to \infty$ since the number of unknown parameters in the Ω matrix is $O(T^2)$ but the available information is just N.

Parametric assumptions are typically required if the restrictions on the asymptotic sequence are relaxed. The AR(p) structure embedded in the error of (1) is an example of such a parametric structure that has received attention in the extant literature (see, e.g., Bhargava et al., 1982; Hansen, 2007b; Kiefer, 1980). However it is well-known that the LS estimator of the ρ_js are inconsistent (or biased in the sense that the inconsistency goes away as $T \to \infty$). If this inconsistency is not corrected, then naturally the resulting covariance estimator is inconsistent. Bhargava et al. (1982) reduced the bias by utilizing the panel Durbin–Watson statistic. Meanwhile Hansen (2007b) proposes an exact mean unbiased (EMU) estimation by using an iterative estimation. The existence of EMU estimator requires that the binding function be monotonic, where the binding function, $B(\rho,T)$, is defined for AR(1) case as

$$B(\rho, T) = \rho + E(\hat{\rho} - \rho)$$

It is well-known that the binding function is not monotonic when ρ is near unity. Also in the AR(p) case, monotonicity does not generally hold when the sum of ρ_j is near unity.

The CO type correction also requires a bias correction. To be specific, the regression model in Eq. (1), ignoring the $Z_{it}\gamma$ and λ_t term, can be rewritten as

$$y_{it} - \sum_{j=1}^{p} \rho_j y_{it-j} = \alpha_i^* + \beta\left(I_{it} - \sum_{j=1}^{p} \rho_j I_{it-j}\right) + u_{it} \tag{2}$$

If u_{it} is free of serial dependence the limiting distribution of the standard OLS t-statistic becomes asymptotically standard normal. CO suggest using the regression residuals to estimate the unknown ρ_js. However, as discussed above, accurate estimation requires either a bias correction of the LS estimator or use of IV methods.

Another weakness of the above parametric approach is that the lag order is unknown and must be estimated. This can prove difficult in the presence of fixed effects when T is small (Lee, 2012). Moreover, as shown by Lee (2006), using a bias correction when the lag order is misspecified can exacerbate the bias of the LS estimator, rather than attenuate it. We discuss some consistent lag order selection methods in the following section.

2.1. FGLS with X-Differencing

We also adopt a parametric approach to dealing with the problem of serial dependence. However, we differ with the extant literature in that we make explicit use of the "X-differencing" method developed by Han et al. (2011, 2014) to estimate the AR(p) structure. The X-differencing method is a systematic differencing where the time lags on both sides of the equation are different, and proves to be effective in removing the nuisance fixed effects while also preserving the regressor-error uncorrelatedness. Specifically, the panel AR(p) equation $y_{it} = \alpha_i + \sum_{j=1}^{p} \rho_j y_{it-j} + u_{it}$ is transformed to $y_{it} - y_{is} = \sum_{j=1}^{p} \rho_j (y_{it-j} - y_{is+j}) + \text{error}_{it,s}$, and then for all t and s such that $t - s > p$, the transformed regressors and the transformed error are exactly uncorrelated under the assumption that Δy_{it} is covariance stationary and the AR(p) structure is correct. Now using this transformation, the autoregressive coefficients are consistently estimated regardless of the relative sizes of N and T. The estimators are consistent over a broad parameter space that includes unit roots in the autoregressive polynomial and there are no issues of non-monotonicity near the unit root.

Han, Phillips, and Sul (2013) show that the typical panel BIC estimation fails to identify the correct lag order. They suggest a couple of modified BICs and also the general to specific method with a data dependent p-value, and show that the suggested methods consistently estimate the correct lag order. The simplest of the modified BIC is as follows:

$$IC(k) = \hat{\sigma}^2(k) + k\frac{\ln\left(\sqrt{N}(T-k)\right)}{\sqrt{N}(T-k)}$$

where $\hat{\sigma}^2(k)$ denotes the mean squared residuals from the X-differencing regression with k lags of the dependent variable. Alternatively, the usual BIC may be applied to the sample truncated so that the same numbers of observations are used for all k.

Once the lag order and the AR coefficients are consistently estimated, the subsequent error covariance estimation and FGLS are straightforward. Following Hansen (2007b), we assume that the idiosyncratic error term ε_{it} of Eq. (1) is AR(p), i.e.,

$$\varepsilon_{it} = \sum_{j=1}^{p} \rho_j \varepsilon_{it-j} + u_{it}, \quad u_{i,t} \sim i.i.d.(0, \sigma^2) \tag{3}$$

The two procedures we consider are a fixed effects FGLS and a Cochrane–Orcutt (1949) type version, for which we need first to estimate ρ_j consistently. For this, we first get the residuals $y_{it} - \hat{\beta} I_{it} - Z_{it}\hat{\gamma}$ for some consistent $\hat{\beta}$ and $\hat{\gamma}$ such as least squares and first difference estimators,[1] and then cross sectionally de-mean them in order to remove the common time effects. Let these de-meaned residuals be denoted by $\hat{v}_{it}$. Run the pooled OLS regression on the X-differenced equation

$$\hat{v}_{it} - \hat{v}_{is} = \sum_{j=1}^{p} \rho_j (\hat{v}_{it-j} - \hat{v}_{is+j}) + \text{error}_{it,s}$$

stacked for all i, t, and s for $t - s > p$. Let $\hat{\rho}_j$ denote the resulting estimator. We have the following result.

Theorem 1. Suppose that y_{it} is generated according to Eq. (1) and ε_{it} is generated by Eq. (3). We assume that all regressors in Eq. (1) are strictly exogenous, and that ε_{it} is either (i) covariance stationary, or (ii) $\varepsilon_{it} = \varepsilon_{it-1} + w_{it}$, where w_{it} is covariance stationary. Then $\hat{\rho}_j$ is consistent for ρ_j for each j as $N(T - p - 1) \rightarrow \infty$.

See the appendix for a short proof of Theorem 1. Note that the homogeneity of β and γ in Eq. (1) is required for the consistency of the X-differencing estimator.

The theorem permits both covariance stationary and unit root processes in the regression errors. Thus the X-differencing estimation of the AR(p) error structure is applicable under a wider range of processes than the bias-corrected methods proposed by Bhargava et al. (1982) and Hansen (2007b) in at least two respects: First, it permits the case of a unit root. It is well-known that the LS bias function is discontinuous at unity, making the bias correction dependent on knowledge of whether the true process is stationary or integrated. Second, the restrictions necessary to map from the LS parameters to the true parameter values are not required (see Proposition 1 in Hansen, 2007b). In particular, it is well-known that the bias function becomes non-monotonic in the neighborhood of unity, meaning that there is no unique mapping for highly persistent but stationary processes.

Although the X-differencing estimator can be applied in the case of unit root errors, GLS transformation cannot. Define ρ as the sum of AR coefficients, i.e., $\rho = \sum_j^p \rho_j$. The GLS estimator does not exist when $\rho = 1$ since the covariance matrix is not invertible. Also White's correction may not work well unless the cross-sectional dimension is large. The CO approach provides a practical alternative in this situation.

2.2. Cochrane–Orcutt Transformation with X-Differencing

Drop the $Z_{it}\gamma$ and λ_t components from Eq. (1) for simplicity. The CO correction with X-differencing method becomes straightforward by replacing the ρ_j's by the X-differenced estimator $\hat{\rho}_{j,x}$ in Eq. (2). That is, the CO transformed regression with X-differencing is

$$y_{it} - \sum_{j=1}^{p} \hat{\rho}_{j,x} y_{it-j} = \tilde{\alpha}_i^* + \beta \left(I_{it} - \sum_{j=1}^{p} \hat{\rho}_{j,x} I_{it-j} \right) + u_{it}^+, \quad t = p+1, \ldots, T \tag{4}$$

where u_{it}^{+} is the implied regression error and, importantly, $\tilde{\alpha}_i^* = \left(1 - \sum_{j=1}^{p} \hat{\rho}_{j,x}\right)\alpha_i$ is common for all $t \geq p + 1$. By abandoning the first p observations, efficiency is lost on the one hand, but the fixed effects remain time-constant and the simple LSDV method can be used on the other hand. This second point is important because it allows us to use the same method for persistent data as well, in which case the first p observations are difficult to handle. Note that the conventional t-statistics have an $N(0,1)$ limiting distribution like in standard FGLS estimation due to the consistency of the X-differencing estimators (Han et al., 2014). The conventional t-statistic is defined as

$$t_{\hat{\beta}} = \frac{\hat{\beta}}{\sqrt{\hat{\sigma}_u^2(\tilde{X}'\tilde{X})^{-1}}}, \text{ for } \hat{\sigma}_u^2 = \frac{1}{(T-p-1)N}\sum_{i=1}^{N}\sum_{t=p+1}^{T}(\hat{u}_{it}^{+} - \overline{u}_i^{+})^2$$

where $\tilde{X}$ is the pooled matrix of the within-group transformed regressor, $\hat{u}_{it}^{+} = y_{it}^{+} - \hat{\beta}\tilde{I}_{it}^{+}$, and $\overline{u}_i^{+} = (T-p)^{-1}\sum_{t=p+1}^{T}\hat{u}_{it}^{+}$. Therefore panel robust covariance estimation needs not be used here.

When T is small, the CO type correction is less efficient compared to FGLS since the CO regressions do not use the first p observations. Due to this efficiency gain, the FGLS method has been popularly used and studied in the broader panel data literature (e.g., Baltagi & Li, 1991, 1992). Of course, if T is large enough, the efficiency loss by discarding the first p observations from each i under the CO method is negligible. In addition, a strength of the CO approach is that it can be used in cases when the GLS transformation matrix is not well-defined (i.e., when $\hat{\rho}_x = \sum_{j=1}^{p}\hat{\rho}_{j,x}$ is equal to or exceeds one).

2.3. Estimation and Inference for Alternative Dependence Structures

In the previous section, we discussed how to obtain a more accurate and powerful test statistic by utilizing the X-differencing method. However the asymptotic theory developed in the previous section is based on the crucial assumption that the error terms follow the data generating process given in Eq. (1). In this section, we consider regression errors that do not follow Eq. (1). We consider three cases.

The first case is that the error term does not follow a finite-order AR(p) but an AR(∞), for example, an ARMA(p,q) process. In this case, all parametric correction methods including Hansen (2007b) and X-differencing do not work "exactly." However, both parametric corrections can be used to approximate the serial dependence structure by permitting $p \to \infty$ as $T \to \infty$. Under this setting, Lee, Okui, and Shintani (2013) consider the inconsistency of various estimators. Particularly they show that the total bias of the LS estimator can be decomposed into truncation and fundamental biases, where the truncation bias arises due to the lag truncation and the fundamental bias is the Nickell (1981) bias (which disappears as $T \to \infty$ but not as $N \to \infty$). (GMM/IV estimators do not suffer from the fundamental bias. Hence as long as the truncation bias goes away as $T,p \to \infty$ jointly, the GMM/IV estimators are consistent.) For the X-differencing estimator, Han et al. (2014, Eq. (32)) provides a formula that relates the full aggregation of X-differences to the sum of cross-products (such as shown in the LS estimation) and the remainder for bias correction. It would thus be natural that Lee et al.'s (2013) results for bias-corrected LS should hold.

To examine the case in more detail, suppose that $y_{it} = a_i + z_{it}$, $z_{it} = \sum_{j=1}^{\infty} \rho_j z_{it-j} + \varepsilon_{it}$, but an AR(p) model is fitted by the X-differencing method. That is, $\tilde{y}_{it,s} \equiv y_{it} - y_{is}$ is regressed on $\tilde{y}_{it-1,s+1}, \ldots, \tilde{y}_{it-p,s+p}$ (with pooling over all t and s such that $t \geq s + p + 1$). Let $\tilde{\varepsilon}_{it,s}$ denote the associated error term, i.e., $\tilde{\varepsilon}_{it,s} = \tilde{y}_{it,s} - \sum_{j=1}^{p} \rho_j \tilde{y}_{it-j,s+j}$. Let $\gamma_j = E(z_{it} z_{it-j})$, which does not depend on t due to the maintained stationarity. (We discuss here the case with stationary z_{it} only.) Then the Yule–Walker equations imply that $\gamma_k = \sum_{j=1}^{\infty} \rho_j \gamma_{|k-j|}$. Because $\tilde{y}_{it,s} = z_{it} - z_{is}$, the expected cross-product of the kth regressor and the regression error is

$$
\begin{aligned}
E(\tilde{y}_{it-k,s+k} \tilde{\varepsilon}_{it,s}) &= 2\left[\left(\gamma_k - \sum_{j=1}^{p} \rho_j \gamma_{|k-j|}\right) - \left(\gamma_{t-s-k} - \sum_{j=1}^{p} \rho_j \gamma_{|t-s-k-j|}\right)\right] \\
&= 2 \sum_{j=p+1}^{\infty} \rho_j (\gamma_{|k-j|} - \gamma_{|t-s-k-j|})
\end{aligned} \tag{5}
$$

for $k = 1, \ldots p$. By the Markov inequality and the fact that $(a-b)^2 \leq 2(a^2 + b^2)$, we have

$$
|E(\tilde{y}_{it-k,s+k} \tilde{\varepsilon}_{it,s})| \leq 4 c_{2p} \left(\sum_{j=0}^{\infty} \gamma_j^2\right)^{1/2}
$$

for all k and p, where $c_{2p} = \left(\sum_{j=p+1}^{\infty} \rho_j^2\right)^{1/2}$. Let $\hat{\rho}_1, \ldots, \hat{\rho}_p$ be the X-differencing estimator, and let $\hat{\rho} = \sum_{j=1}^{p} \hat{\rho}_j$. Also let $\rho^{(p)} = \sum_{j=1}^{p} \rho_j$ and $\rho = \rho^{(\infty)}$. Then

$$\hat{\rho}-\rho^{(p)}=\mathbf{1}_p'\hat{\Gamma}_p^{-1}(NT_p^2)^{-1}\sum_{i=1}^{N}\sum_{t=p+2}^{T}\sum_{s=1}^{t-p-1}\tilde{w}_{it,s,p}\tilde{\varepsilon}_{it,s}$$

where $T_p=T-p$, $\hat{\Gamma}_p$ is the denominator matrix divided by NT_p^2, and $\tilde{w}_{it,s,p}=(\tilde{y}_{it-1,s+1},\ldots,\tilde{y}_{it-p,s+p})'$. Under the regularity that the smallest eigenvalue of Γ_p is bounded away from zero (technicality that is not dealt with here; see Lee et al., 2013), we have

$$\begin{aligned}|\hat{\rho}-\rho^{(p)}|^2 &\leq \frac{pC}{NT_p}\sum_{i=1}^{N}\sum_{t=p+2}^{T}\left(\frac{1}{T_p}\sum_{s=1}^{t-p-1}\tilde{w}_{it,s,p}\tilde{\varepsilon}_{it,s}\right)'\left(\frac{1}{T_p}\sum_{s=1}^{t-p-1}\tilde{w}_{it,s,p}\tilde{\varepsilon}_{it,s}\right)\\ &=pO(pc_{2p}^2)+pO_p(n_p^{-1}),\quad n_p\equiv N(T-p)\end{aligned}$$

as $p\to\infty$ and $n_p\to\infty$ for some universal constant $C<\infty$. Above the first bound on the second line is for the bias, and the second is for the variance. Thus, $\hat{\rho}=\rho^{(p)}+O_p(pc_{2p})+O_p\left(p^{1/2}n_p^{-1/2}\right)$. As $|\rho-\rho^{(p)}|\leq c_{1p}\equiv\sum_{j=p+1}^{\infty}|\rho_j|$, we have

$$|\hat{\rho}-\rho|=O\left(c_{1p}\right)+O\left(pc_{2p}\right)+O_p\left(p^{1/2}n_p^{-1/2}\right)$$

which implies that $\hat{\rho}$ is consistent for ρ as long as $p\to\infty$ and $p/n_p\to 0$ under the sufficient regularity conditions that $\sum_{j=1}^{\infty}|\rho_j|<\infty$ and $\sum_{j=1}^{\infty}j\rho_j^2<\infty$. These regularity conditions are satisfied for finite order ARMA processes because then ρ_j decays exponentially with j. Unbiased asymptotic distribution for $(n_p/p)^{1/2}(\hat{\rho}-\rho)$ requires a bit more: $(n_p/p)^{1/2}c_{1p}\to 0$ and $(pn_p)^{1/2}c_{2p}\to 0$. Usually c_{1p} and c_{2p} decay exponentially with p, thus these conditions are casually translated into that p is not too small compared to the total sample size $n_p=N(T-p)$. These conditions are much simpler than those for the estimators considered by Lee et al. (2013) because of the exact uncorrelatedness of the regressors and the regression error in the X-differenced equations for finite order panel AR models. More rigorous treatment would be called for in this regard but is not pursued here.

A second prominent case to consider is a factor error component structure such as that considered in Pesaran (2006), Bai (2009), and Greenaway-McGrevy, Han, and Sul (2012). Error component structures can generate forms of serial dependence that are not encompassed within the set of AR (p) models. For example, the sum of two AR(1) processes can be equivalently expressed as an ARMA(2,1) or an AR(∞). Using a factor augmented estimator may help simplify the problem, since the factor component of the error is controlled for in estimation. See, for example, Hagedorn, Karahan, Manovskii, and Mitman (2013).

However, for approaches that control for factors to the explained and explanatory variables (Greenaway-McGrevy et al., 2012; Pesaran, 2006, etc.), it is unclear how to estimate the common factors to binary variables as the common component would not be additive. This issue is left for future research.

The third case to consider is important for micro panel data but also is a difficult issue for theoretical econometricians. Suppose that the serial correlation of the error term arises from the inclusion of a small trend or integrated component. Typical outcome variables of interest in the DD literature are wages, employment, consumption, or medical expenditures, as Bertrand, Duflo, and Mullainathan (2004) point out. All these variables may exhibit (either stochastic or non-stochastic) trending behavior over time. In this case, the error term exhibits serious serial correlation. For instructive purposes, consider the following example.

Example (Trend Nonstationary)
Assume that the dependent variable, y_{it}, has the following simple latent structure:

$$y_{it} = a_i + b_i t + d_i \theta_t + e_{it} \tag{6}$$

where $\theta_t = \theta_{t-1} + \eta_t$, and all innovations are assumed to be $e_{it} \sim \text{i.i.d.}\left(0, \sigma_e^2\right)$, $b_i \sim \text{i.i.d.}\left(b, \sigma_b^2\right)$, and $d_i \sim \text{i.i.d.}\left(d, \sigma_d^2\right)$. If $d_i = 0$ for all i, then y_{it} is not serially correlated. Consider estimating the following simple dynamic regression:

$$y_{it} = c_i + \rho y_{it-1} + u_{it}$$

It is easy to show that the expectation of the within-group LS estimator is

$$E\hat{\rho}_T = 1 - \frac{12\sigma_e^2}{\left(b^2 + \sigma_b^2\right)T^2} + O(T^{-3})$$

so that as T increases, the estimated AR(1) coefficient approaches unity quite quickly. In applications however, the mean b and variance σ_b^2 of the trend coefficients are sufficiently small so that the point estimate of ρ is not in the neighborhood of unity, even with large T.

Of course, as T increases, the dominant term becomes the deterministic trend component so that the trending behavior can be seen obviously. Also even when there is no deterministic trend component, as T increases, the integrated series θ_t becomes the dominant term so that it becomes easy to detect such nonstationary behavior by using a typical panel unit root test. When T is not large, it is hard to rely on a formal statistical test to identify whether or not the dependent variable contains integrated components. However in this case, one can avoid this thorny issue by taking the first difference. That is,

$$\Delta y_{it} = b_i + \Delta\lambda_t + \beta\Delta I_{it} + \Delta u_{it}$$

where the fixed effects, b_i, capture the heterogeneous trend coefficients. Of course, the new regression error, Δu_{it}, may follow an ARMA(p,q) process rather than an AR(p). In this case, as we discussed before, one can increase the lag length for a large T.

FD removes the trend, so that GLS is feasible. For persistent but I(0) errors the induced (negative) serial correlation from over-differencing is corrected in the parametric FGLS or CO transformation. Although the FD errors do not in general follow a finite order AR(p) structure when the errors are AR(p), there should still be substantial efficiency gains from this approach. In this case lag estimation should be based on methods that find the best approximating model asymptotically (see Lee et al., 2013).

3. MONTE CARLO EXPERIMENTS

In this section we verify our asymptotic claims and investigate the finite sample performance of the suggested methods. The data generating process is given by

$$y_{it} = \beta I_{it} + \alpha_i + b_i t + d_i\theta_t + e_{it}$$

where

$$\theta_t = \theta_{t-1} + \eta_t, \quad e_{it} = \sum_{j=1}^{p} \rho_j e_{it-1} + u_{it}$$

We generate variables as follows:

$$\alpha_i \sim \text{i.i.d. } N(0,1),\ u_{it} \sim \text{i.i.d. } N(0,1),\ \eta_t \sim \text{i.i.d. } N\left(0,\sigma_\eta^2\right),\ b_i \sim \text{i.i.d. } N\left(0,\sigma_b^2\right),$$
$$\text{and } d_i \sim \text{i.i.d. } N\left(0,\sigma_d^2\right)$$

We set the initial observation of e_{i0} as i.i.d. $N(0,1/(1-\rho^2))$ and $\theta_0 = 0$. The binary variable, I_{it}, is generated from

$$I_{it} = 1\{x_{it} \geq 0\} \quad \text{where } x_{it} = \phi x_{it-1} + v_{it}$$

Under the alternative, we set $\beta = 0.1$. We consider two sets of values of σ_b^2 and σ_d^2. Under stationarity, both values are set to zero. Under I(1) errors, we set $\sigma_b = 0.01$ and $\sigma_d^2 = 1$ but vary σ_η from 0.05 to 0.2. These values are chosen based on PSID consumption expenditure data.

First we consider the case of stationary models. We consider $\rho = 0.5$, 0.8, 0.9 and $\phi = 0.8$, 0.9. Since the over-rejection of the null hypothesis with different N/T ratios is of interest, broadly two sets of T and N are considered. We set $T = 6$ or 100 and vary N. We report selected results here.

Table 1 shows the rejection rate under the null hypothesis. "GLS" refers to infeasible GLS where the true ρ value is known. Evidently, for small N

Table 1. Finite Sample Performance of Suggested Estimators for Stationary Errors under the Null Hypothesis: $\phi = 0.8$, $\rho = 0.8$, $\beta = 0$.

		Variance × 10^3					Rejection Rates (Nominal: 5%)				
			X-differencing		Hansen			X-differencing		Hansen	
N	T	WG	CO	FGLS	FGLS	GLS	WG	CO	FGLS	FGLS	GLS
10	6	264.66	169.77	145.35	152.32	140.57	0.164	0.079	0.082	0.095	0.071
25	6	95.35	55.99	48.83	50.25	48.15	0.087	0.064	0.060	0.067	0.059
50	6	45.97	24.72	22.36	22.85	22.25	0.066	0.049	0.051	0.053	0.050
100	6	23.23	13.44	11.84	11.98	11.79	0.069	0.062	0.063	0.063	0.062
200	6	10.96	6.33	5.62	5.68	5.61	0.056	0.047	0.055	0.056	0.056
400	6	5.47	3.19	2.84	2.87	2.84	0.049	0.051	0.053	0.058	0.053
5	100	89.91	14.41	14.37	14.37	14.32	0.209	0.081	0.076	0.075	0.075
6	100	74.91	12.43	12.32	12.33	12.26	0.181	0.086	0.083	0.082	0.083
7	100	59.66	9.80	9.74	9.76	9.72	0.159	0.072	0.071	0.071	0.069
8	100	52.39	7.86	7.80	7.81	7.79	0.131	0.061	0.058	0.059	0.059
9	100	43.92	7.32	7.22	7.22	7.22	0.116	0.063	0.059	0.060	0.058
10	100	39.94	6.21	6.17	6.17	6.18	0.115	0.057	0.055	0.055	0.055

all estimators except for the within-group estimator (labeled WG) based on the panel robust covariance estimator reject the null hypothesis at a rate similar to GLS. Both FGLS and CO methods reject the null hypothesis that $\beta=0$ slightly less than Hansen's FGLS estimator when T is small, but the difference is negligible. It is important to report that the over-rejection rate of the WG estimator is not dependent on the degree of serial dependence. Even when ρ is 0.5, the rejection frequencies of the WG estimator are similar to those for smaller values of ρ. Hence the finding of the over-rejection of the null hypothesis by BDM was not mainly due to high serial dependence of the regression errors but the small-N statistical properties of the panel robust covariance estimator which requires a large N for consistency. As long as N is large, the serial correlation has a negligible effect, as BDM report.

Table 2 reports the nominal power of the tests. Evidently, all estimators except the WG estimator with the panel robust covariance estimator perform very well. When T is small, the performance of CO with X-differencing is worse than GLS but better than WG in terms of variance for the considered data generating process. Of course, CO need not be more efficient than WG especially if the serial correlation in the error term is minor. In terms of power, the performance of CO with X-differencing is only slightly worse than FGLS estimators even when T is small.

Table 2. Comparison of Powers of Tests for Stationary Errors under the Alternative: $\phi=0.8$, $\rho=0.8$, $\beta=0.1$.

		Variance $\times10^3$					Rejection Rates (nominal 5%)				
			X-differencing		Hansen			X-differencing		Hansen	
N	T	WG	CO	FGLS	FGLS	GLS	WG	CO	FGLS	FGLS	GLS
10	6	264.66	169.77	145.35	152.32	140.57	0.166	0.091	0.098	0.118	0.094
25	6	95.35	55.99	48.83	50.25	48.15	0.112	0.088	0.096	0.106	0.094
50	6	45.97	24.72	22.36	22.85	22.25	0.103	0.095	0.106	0.116	0.107
100	6	23.23	13.44	11.84	11.98	11.79	0.114	0.142	0.173	0.180	0.172
200	6	10.96	6.33	5.62	5.68	5.61	0.162	0.222	0.277	0.284	0.274
400	6	5.47	3.19	2.84	2.87	2.84	0.275	0.421	0.488	0.492	0.486
5	100	89.91	14.41	14.37	14.37	14.32	0.231	0.176	0.173	0.176	0.173
6	100	74.91	12.43	12.32	12.33	12.26	0.209	0.201	0.199	0.200	0.198
7	100	59.66	9.80	9.74	9.76	9.72	0.182	0.225	0.224	0.221	0.222
8	100	52.39	7.86	7.80	7.81	7.79	0.172	0.226	0.226	0.226	0.226
9	100	43.92	7.32	7.22	7.22	7.22	0.150	0.246	0.245	0.245	0.244
10	100	39.94	6.21	6.17	6.17	6.18	0.141	0.265	0.270	0.269	0.272

Lastly, Table 3 provides the results for I(1) errors. We consider only three estimators: the WG estimator, first differenced LS estimator (FD), and first differenced CO estimator (FD-CO). The panel robust covariance estimator is used to construct t-statistics for the first two estimators. Meanwhile the standard t-test is used for the FD-CO. The fourth column in Table 3 reports the estimated means of the AR(1) coefficient from the Monte Carlo simulation. These are dependent on the value of σ_d and T: as either σ_d or T increases, the expected value of $\hat{\rho}$ increases. Note that the true ρ is set as 0.2. Evidently, the rejection rate of the null hypothesis of the WG estimator is reasonable when T is moderately large when the null is true ($\beta = 0$). It is a natural result since as long as N is large, the WG estimator provides accurate rejection rates. In terms of size distortion, FD-CO performs best. We do not report other FGLS estimators in Table 3 to save the space but their performances are very much similar to the FD-CO estimator. The power of the LS estimator does not improve with the size of T, because, as discussed above, the estimator converges at the $\sqrt{N}$ rate. Meanwhile both FD and FD-CO estimators reject the null more as T increases.

Table 3. Comparison of the First-Differenced CO with X-Differencing to other Estimators: $\rho = 0.2$, $\phi = 0.8$.

					Variance × 10^3			Rejection Rates		
$\beta = 0$	σ_d	T	N	$E(\hat{\rho})$	WG	FD	FD-CO	WG	FD	FD-CO
	0.05	10	50	0.926	271.20	37.18	31.54	0.101	0.127	0.084
	0.05	25	50	0.940	102.12	12.44	10.33	0.075	0.065	0.057
	0.05	50	50	0.945	49.23	5.96	5.07	0.059	0.055	0.055
	0.05	100	50	0.948	25.92	3.02	2.54	0.065	0.055	0.065
	0.2	10	50	0.937	358.89	37.60	33.46	0.104	0.124	0.080
	0.2	25	50	0.950	137.38	14.04	12.30	0.075	0.076	0.069
	0.2	50	50	0.954	73.23	6.58	5.76	0.062	0.055	0.055
	0.2	100	50	0.954	34.04	3.27	2.96	0.059	0.054	0.067
$\beta = 0.1$	0.05	10	50	0.926	266.38	34.10	29.98	0.117	0.173	0.138
	0.05	25	50	0.941	99.26	12.34	10.51	0.086	0.186	0.201
	0.05	50	50	0.946	48.67	6.23	5.30	0.085	0.261	0.325
	0.05	100	50	0.948	24.69	2.98	2.55	0.116	0.434	0.528
	0.2	10	50	0.937	374.72	37.07	32.34	0.117	0.164	0.118
	0.2	25	50	0.950	134.14	13.45	12.05	0.077	0.170	0.178
	0.2	50	50	0.953	67.71	6.75	5.91	0.085	0.252	0.286
	0.2	100	50	0.955	35.18	3.29	2.91	0.101	0.438	0.505

4. CONCLUDING REMARKS

In this paper we propose a simple parametric transformation for LS estimation of DD regressions that exhibit serially dependent errors. First stage estimates of autoregressive structures in the error are obtained by using the Han et al. (2011, 2014) X-differencing transformation of the panel, before applying an FGLS or CO type estimator of the regression equation. The X-differencing method is simple to implement and is unbiased in large N settings, and can be applied to both stationary and unit root error processes.

We also consider the case where the error processes exhibits either a non-stochastic or a stochastic trend. In this case we suggest first differencing the data before applying the X-differencing transformation to account for any residual serial dependence in the first-differenced series. This method can account for a wider variety of dependence structures in the error term than X-differencing in levels, including possible linear trends. The suggested method performs well in Monte Carlo studies.

NOTE

1. If ε_{it} is stationary, then both the least squares dummy variables (LSDV) and the first difference least squares (FD) estimators are consistent as the product NT approaches infinity. If $\varepsilon_{it} \sim I(1)$, the convergence rate of the FD estimator is $\sqrt{NT}$, and that of the LSDV estimator is $\sqrt{N}$. The latter can be shown by evaluating the maximal eigenvalue of the covariance matrix of $(\varepsilon_{i1}, \ldots, \varepsilon_{iT})'$, which is $O(T^2)$ because the sum of eigenvalues is bounded by the trace (Lütkepohl, 1996, section 5.3.1).

ACKNOWLEDGMENT

This paper was written for the presentation at the 14th Advances in Econometrics Conference in honor of Peter C.B. Phillips at Southern Methodist University on November 1–3, 2014. We thank Tom Fomby for organizing the conference and Yoosoon Chang and Joon Y. Park for preparing the conference program. We also thank Badi Baltagi for helpful comments. Research by Han was supported by Korea University (K1222321).

REFERENCES

Arellano, M. (1987). Computing robust standard errors for within-groups estimators. *Oxford Bulletin of Economics and Statistics*, *49*(4), 431–434.

Bai, J. (2009). Panel data models with interactive fixed effects. *Econometrica, 77*(4), 1229–1279.

Baltagi, B. H., & Li, Q. (1991). A transformation that will circumvent the problem of autocorrelation in an error component model. *Journal of Econometrics, 48*, 385–393.

Baltagi, B. H., & Li, Q. (1992). Prediction in the one-way error component model with serial correlation. *Journal of Forecasting, 11*, 561–567.

Bertrand, M., Duflo, E., & Mullainathan, S. (2004). How much should we trust differences-in-differences estimates? *Quarterly Journal of Economics, 119*(1), 249–275.

Bester, C. A., Conley, T. G., & Hansen, C. B. (2011). Inference with dependent data using cluster covariance estimators. *Journal of Econometrics, 165*(2), 137–151.

Bhargava, A., Franzini, L., & Narendranathan, W. (1982). Serial correlation and the fixed effects model. *Review of Economic Studies, 49*, 533–549.

Blundell, R., & Bond, S. (1998). Initial conditions and moment restrictions in dynamic panel data models. *Journal of Econometrics, 87*(1), 115–143.

Cameron, A. C., Miller, D. L., & Gelbach, J. B. (2008). Bootstrap-based improvements for inference with clustered errors. *Review of Economics and Statistics, 90*(3), 414–427.

Cochrane, D., & Orcutt, G. (1949). Application of least squares regression to relationships containing autocorrelated error terms. *Journal of the American Statistical Association, 44*(245), 32–61.

Donald, S. G., & Lang, K. (2007). Inference with differences-in-differences and other panel data. *Journal of Business and Economic Statistics, 89*(2), 221–233.

Greenaway-McGrevy, R., Han, C., & Sul, D. (2012). Asymptotic distribution of factor augmented estimators for panel regression. *Journal of Econometrics, 169*(1), 48–53.

Hagedorn, M., Karahan, F., Manovskii, I., & Mitman, K. (2013). *Unemployment benefits and unemployment in the great recession: The role of macro effects.* Working Paper No. 19499. Retrieved from http://www.nber.org/papers/w19499

Han, C., Phillips, P. C. B., & Sul, D. (2011). Uniform asymptotic normality in stationary and unit root autoregression. *Econometric Theory, 27*, 1117–1151.

Han, C., Phillips, P. C. B., & Sul, D. (2013). *Lag length selection in panel autoregression*, Mimeo, University of Texas at Dallas.

Han, C., Phillips, P. C. B., & Sul, D. (2014). X-differencing and dynamic panel model estimation. *Econometric Theory, 30*, 201–251.

Hansen, C. B. (2007a). Asymptotic properties of a robust variance matrix when T is large. *Journal of Econometrics, 141*, 597–620.

Hansen, C. B. (2007b). Generalized least squares inference in panel and multilevel models with serial correlation and fixed effects. *Journal of Econometrics, 140*, 670–694.

Kiefer, N. M. (1980). Estimation of fixed effect models for time series of cross-sections with arbitrary intertemporal covariance. *Journal of Econometrics, 14*, 195–202.

Lee, Y.-J., Okui, R., & Shintani, M. (2013). *Asymptotic inference for dynamic panel estimators of infinite order autoregressive processes.* Mimeo, Kyoto University.

Lee, Y.-S. (2006). *A general approach to bias correction in dynamic panel models under time series misspecification.* Mimeo, Yale University.

Lee, Y.-S. (2012). *Model selection in the presence of incidental parameters.* Manuscript, University of Michigan.

Lütkepohl, H. (1996). *Handbook of matrices.* John Wiley & Sons, Chichester.

Miller, D. L., Cameron, A. C., & Gelbach, J. B. (2011). Robust inference with multi-way clustering. *Journal of Business and Economic Statistics, 29*(2), 238–249.

Nickell, S. (1981). Biases in dynamic models with fixed effects. *Econometrica*, *49*, 1417–1426.

Pesaran, M. H. (2006). Estimation and inference in large heterogeneous panels with a multifactor error structure. *Econometrica*, *74*(4), 967–1012.

Wooldridge, J. M. (2003). Cluster-sample methods in applied econometrics. *American Economic Review*, *93*(2), 133–138.

APPENDIX

Proof of Theorem 1. Let $v_{it} = \alpha_i + \varepsilon_{it} + \lambda_t$; let $\ddot{v}_{it} = v_{it} - N^{-1}\sum_{j=1}^{N} v_{jt}$ and similarly define $\ddot{\alpha}_i$ and $\ddot{\varepsilon}_{it}$ so $\ddot{v}_{it} = \ddot{\alpha}_i + \ddot{\varepsilon}_{it}$. We have $\hat{v}_{it} = \ddot{v}_{it} - \ddot{X}_{it}'(\hat{\beta} - \beta)$, where $\ddot{X}_{it} = X_{it} - N^{-1}\sum_{k=1}^{N} X_{kt}$. When $\varepsilon_{it} = \sum_{j=1}^{p} \rho_j \varepsilon_{it-j} + u_{it}$, we have $\ddot{\varepsilon}_{it} = \sum_{j=1}^{p} \rho_j \ddot{\varepsilon}_{it-j} + \ddot{u}_{it}$, where $\ddot{u}_{it}$ is serially white noise. Thus, the moment conditions for X-differencing (Han et al., 2014, Eq. (7)) hold despite the presence of cross-sectional correlation in $\ddot{\varepsilon}_{it}$, and the consistency of the X-differencing estimator using $\ddot{v}_{it}$ instead of $\hat{v}_{it}$ follows from the convergences of $\sum_{i=1}^{N}\sum_{t=4}^{T}\sum_{s=1}^{t-3}(\ddot{\varepsilon}_{it-1} - \ddot{\varepsilon}_{is+1})^2$ and $\sum_{i=1}^{N}\sum_{t=4}^{T}\sum_{s=1}^{t-3}(\ddot{\varepsilon}_{it} - \ddot{\varepsilon}_{is})(\ddot{\varepsilon}_{it-1} - \ddot{\varepsilon}_{is+1})$ after appropriate normalization as $NT \to \infty$. (Note the convergence even with fixed N as long as $NT \to \infty$.) Now the result follows from the consistency of $\hat{\beta}$.

Construction of FGLS Estimator when $p \geq 2$. With consistent estimates of $\rho_1, \ldots, \rho_p$ available, we can then construct an FGLS estimator. When ε_{it} is stationary and Eq. (3) is satisfied, let $\gamma_j = E(\varepsilon_{it}\varepsilon_{it-j})/\sigma^2$. Then by standard text book algebra γ_j are determined by ρ_j as follows:

$$
\begin{aligned}
\gamma_0 &= \rho_1\gamma_1 + \rho_2\gamma_2 + \cdots + \rho_p\gamma_p + 1 \\
\gamma_1 &= \rho_1\gamma_0 + \rho_2\gamma_1 + \cdots + \rho_p\gamma_{p-1} \\
&\ \ \vdots \\
\gamma_p &= \rho_1\gamma_{p-1} + \rho_2\gamma_{p-2} + \cdots + \rho_p\gamma_0 \\
\gamma_j &= \rho_1\rho_{j-1} + \rho_2\gamma_{j-2} + \cdots + \rho_p\gamma_{j-p}, \quad j > p
\end{aligned}
$$

The first $p + 1$ identities are written as $\gamma_{0:p} = (A_1 + A_2)\gamma_{0:p} + (1,0,\ldots,0)'$, where $\gamma_{0:p} = (\gamma_0,\gamma_1,\ldots,\gamma_p)'$, A_1 is the $(p+1)\times(p+1)$ matrix whose ith row is $(0,\rho_i,\rho_{i+1},\ldots,\rho_p,0')$ with the first 0 being a scalar, and A_2 is the $(p+1)\times(p+1)$ matrix whose ith row is $(\rho_{i-1},\rho_{i-2},\ldots,\rho_1,0')$. Taking $p = 4$ as an illustrative example, we have

$$
A_1 = \begin{pmatrix} 0 & \rho_1 & \rho_2 & \rho_3 & \rho_4 \\ 0 & \rho_2 & \rho_3 & \rho_4 & 0 \\ 0 & \rho_3 & \rho_4 & 0 & 0 \\ 0 & \rho_4 & 0 & 0 & 0 \\ 0 & 0 & 0 & 0 & 0 \end{pmatrix}, \quad A_2 = \begin{pmatrix} 0 & 0 & 0 & 0 & 0 \\ \rho_1 & 0 & 0 & 0 & 0 \\ \rho_2 & \rho_1 & 0 & 0 & 0 \\ \rho_3 & \rho_2 & \rho_1 & 0 & 0 \\ \rho_4 & \rho_3 & \rho_2 & \rho_1 & 0 \end{pmatrix}
$$

So $(\gamma_0, \ldots \gamma_p)'$ is the first column of $(I - A_1 - A_2)^{-1}$, and the rest γ_j are obtained by recursion. One can then construct an estimate of $\Omega = \text{Toeplitz}(\gamma_0, \gamma_1, \ldots, \gamma_{T-1})$ using $\hat{\rho}_j$, and do the FGLS after first-differencing in order to eliminate the fixed effects. Specifically, letting $y_i = (y_{i1}, \ldots, y_{iT})'$, $X_i = (X_{i1}, \ldots, X_{iT})'$, and $\varepsilon_i = (\varepsilon_{i1}, \ldots, \varepsilon_{iT})'$, we have $y_i = X_i\beta + 1\alpha_i + \varepsilon_i$. Premultiplying the $(T-1) \times T$ first-differencing operator matrix Δ,

$$\Delta = \begin{pmatrix} -1 & 1 & 0 & \cdots & 0 & 0 \\ 0 & -1 & 1 & \cdots & 0 & 0 \\ \vdots & \vdots & \vdots & \ddots & 0 & 0 \\ 0 & 0 & 0 & \cdots & -1 & 1 \end{pmatrix}$$

so that the tth row of Δy_i is $y_{it} - y_{it-1}$, we have $\Delta y_i = \Delta X_i + \Delta\varepsilon_i$, where the fixed effects are eliminated. Then the error term $\Delta\varepsilon_i$ has covariance $\sigma^2 \Delta\Omega\Delta'$, and the FGLS estimator is

$$\hat{\beta}_{\text{fgls}} = \left[\sum_{i=1}^{N} X_i' \Delta' (\Delta\tilde{\Omega}\Delta')^{-1} \Delta X_i \right]^{-1} \sum_{i=1}^{n} X_i' \Delta' (\Delta\tilde{\Omega}\Delta')^{-1} \Delta y_i$$

where $\tilde{\Omega}$ is obtained by replacing ρ_j with $\hat{\rho}_j$ in the γ_j formulae. This estimator generalizes Bhargava et al.'s (1982) panel AR(1) FGLS to AR(p) and provides a simple alternative (requiring no numerical solutions and free from the non-monotonicity issue near unit root) to Hansen's (2007b) procedure. The $\hat{\beta}_{\text{fgls}}$ estimator has all the properties of FGLS estimators under regularity if Eq. (3) is true and ε_{it} is stationary.

The FGLS estimator can also be obtained by the following procedure. The equations are first transformed to

$$\tilde{y}_{it} = \tilde{X}_{it}'\beta + (1 - \rho^*)\alpha_i + \tilde{\varepsilon}_{it} \tag{A.1}$$

for $t = 1, \ldots, T$, so that $\tilde{\varepsilon}_{it}$ are serially uncorrelated, where $\rho^* = \sum_{j=1}^{p} \rho_j$. Precisely, for $t > p$, $\tilde{y}_{it} = y_{it} - \sum_{j=1}^{p} \rho_j y_{it-j}$, $\tilde{X}_{it} = X_{it} - \sum_{j=1}^{p} \rho_j X_{it-j}$, and $\tilde{\varepsilon}_{it} = u_{it}$ work, and for $t \leq p$, we can have $\tilde{y}_{it} = [y_{it} - (y_{i1}, \ldots, y_{it-1})\delta_t](1 - \rho^*)/(1 - 1'\delta_t)$ and $\tilde{X}_{it}$ and $\tilde{\varepsilon}_{it}$ are similarly obtained, where $\delta_t = \Gamma_t^{-1}(\gamma_t, \gamma_{t-1}, \ldots, \gamma_1)'$ and $\Gamma_t = \text{Toeplitz}(\gamma_0, \gamma_1, \ldots, \gamma_{t-1})$. Then $\tilde{\varepsilon}_{it}$ are serially uncorrelated but heteroskedastic. Especially, $E\tilde{\varepsilon}_{it}^2 = \sigma^2(1 - \rho^*)^2 h_t$, where $h_t = 1$ for

$t > p$, and $h_t = (-\delta_t', 1)\Gamma_t(-\delta_t', 1)'/(1 - 1'\delta_t)^2$ for $t \leq p$. This heteroskedasticity is unavoidable should the individual effects remain constant over time. Procedures as simple as LSDV would therefore not be available, and one should do GLS anyway after eliminating the fixed effects by first-differencing.

A CUSUM TEST FOR COMMON TRENDS IN LARGE HETEROGENEOUS PANELS

Javier Hidalgo[a] and Jungyoon Lee[b]

[a]Department of Economics, London School of Economics, London, UK
[b]Department of Economics, New College of the Humanities, London, UK

ABSTRACT

This paper examines a nonparametric CUSUM-type test for common trends in large panel data sets with individual fixed effects. We consider, as in Zhang, Su, and Phillips (2012), a partial linear regression model with unknown functional form for the trend component, although our test does not involve local smoothings. This conveniently forgoes the need to choose a bandwidth parameter, which due to a lack of a clear and sensible information criteria is difficult for testing purposes. We are able to do so after making use that the number of individuals increases with no limit. After removing the parametric component of the model, when the errors are homoscedastic, our test statistic converges to a Gaussian process whose critical values are easily tabulated. We also examine the consequences of having heteroscedasticity as well as discussing the problem of how to compute valid critical values due to the very complicated covariance structure of the limiting process. Finally, we present a small

Essays in Honor of Peter C. B. Phillips
Advances in Econometrics, Volume 33, 303–345

ISSN: 0731-9053/doi:10.1108/S0731-905320140000033010

Monte Carlo experiment to shed some light on the finite sample performance of the test.

Keywords: Common trends; large data set; partial linear models; bootstrap algorithms

JEL Classifications: C12; C13; C23

1. INTRODUCTION

One of the oldest issues and main concerns in time series is perhaps the study and modelling of their trend behaviour. The literature is large and vast, see for instance an overview by Phillips (2001), or more recently by White and Granger (2011) on some practicalities regarding trends for the purpose of, say, prediction. A huge amount of the literature has focused on the topic of stochastic versus deterministic trends. On the other hand, more recently there has been an interest on how analysis of macroeconomic data may benefit from using cross-sectional information. One of the earliest works is given by Phillips and Moon (1999) on testing for unit roots in panel data, see also the recent work on macroeconomic convergence by Phillips and Sul (2007), and Breitung and Pesaran (2008) for a survey on stochastic trends in panel data models. Recently there has also been a surge of interest on examining deterministic trending regression models. Among others and in a context with spatial dependence, see Robinson (2011a) who considers nonparametric trending models or Robinson (2011b) for a general parametric model where the trending regressors are of a non polynomial type t^{γ} with $\gamma > -1/2$. On the other hand, semiparametric models have been considered, see Gao and Hawthorne (2006) and in panel data models by Atak, Linton, and Xiao (2011) or Zhang, Su, and Phillips (2012) or Degas, Xu, Zhang, and Wu (2012). The work by Atak et al. (2011) assumes that the number of cross-section units is finite although the trending regression functions are common among the different units. On the contrary, the latter two references allow for the number of cross-section units to increase without limit and they consider a test for common trends, or, in the language of panel data analysis for homogeneity/poolability.

This paper belongs to the latter framework. More specifically, we are concerned with testing for common trends in the partial panel linear regression model

$$y_{it} = \beta' x_{it} + m_i(t/T) + \upsilon_{it}, \quad i = 1,\ldots,n, \quad t = 1,\ldots,T$$
$$\upsilon_{it} = \mu_i + \varepsilon_{it} \tag{1}$$

where $\{x_{it}\}_{t \geq 1}$, $i \in \mathbb{N}^+$, are k-vector of exogenous variables, $m_i(t/T)$ is left to be of unknown functional form, μ_i are the individual fixed effects and the error terms $\{\varepsilon_{it}\}_{t \geq 1}$, $i \in \mathbb{N}^+$, are sequences of zero mean random variables, possibly heteroscedastic. We shall remark that the reason not to introduce fixed time effects in Eq. (1) is because the tests are invariant to its presence, see Eq. (6) or (7) below. In addition, model (1) is a generalization of that discussed in Degras et al. (2012), where we have now some covariates x_{it} in the model. We are interested, to be more precise in the next section, on testing the hypothesis

$$H_0 : m_i(\tau) = m(\tau) \quad \text{for all } i \geq 1 \quad \text{and} \quad \tau \in [0, 1]$$

This hypothesis testing can be put into a much broader context of testing for equality among a set of curves, such as the conditional expectation and/or the dynamic structure in time series. More generally, our hypothesis can arise when we wish to decide how similar two or more groups of individuals are. When the number of curves is finite, there is a substantial literature. Relevant examples are the classical poolability test in panel data, see Hsiao (1986) and references therein, for parametric models, and Baltagi, Hidalgo, and Li (1996) in a nonparametric scenario. In a time series context, we can mention the work by Detter and Paparoditis (2009) and references there, where the interest is to decide whether the covariance structure is the same across the sequences.

Nowadays due to the amount of available data, it is not unrealistic to consider the number of series large or that they increase without limit. Among the latter framework, we can cite Jin and Su (2010) and Degras et al. (2012) and in a partially linear regression model the work by Zhang et al. (2012). Also it worth mentioning the recent work by Hidalgo and Souza (2013) who tested if the dynamic structure across sequences is the same.

It is worth noting that we can generalize our model (1) as

$$y_{it} = \beta' x_{it} + g_i(d_t) + \upsilon_{it}$$

where, as in Pesaran and Tosetti (2011) or more recently Bryan and Jenkins (2013), d_t has the interpretation of being a sequence of observed common effects/factors across individuals. See also Galvao and Kato

(2014), where d_t has the meaning of being fixed effects. With this interpretation, if $g_i(d_t) = g_i d_t$, say, we can regard the latest display model as a panel data with interactive fixed effects, so that our hypothesis becomes $g_i = g$, that is we are testing the existence of interactive effects versus a more standard additive fixed effects type of model. Bearing this in mind, we focus nevertheless on the case where $d_t = t/T$ merely for historical reasons, although our main results seem to hold true for the last displayed model.

We finish this section relating the results of the paper with the problem of classification with functional data sets, which is a topic of active research. The reason being that this paper tackles the problem of whether a set of curves, that is the trending functions, are the same or not among a set of individual units. Within the functional data analysis framework, this question translates into whether there is some common structure or if we can split the set (of curves) into several classes or groups. See classical examples in Ferraty and Vieu (2006), although their approach uses nonparametric techniques which we try to avoid so that the issues of how to choose a bandwidth parameter and/or the 'metric' to decide closeness are avoided. With this in mind, we believe that our approach can be used for a classification scheme. For instance, in economics are the trend components across different industries the same? In the language of functional data analysis, this is a problem of supervised classification which is nothing more than a modern name to one of the oldest statistical problems: namely to decide if an individual belongs to a particular population. The term supervised refers to the case where we have a 'training' sample which has been classified without error. Moreover, we can envisage that our methodology can be extended to problems dealing with functional data in a framework similar to those examined by Chan and Ogden (2009).

The remainder of the paper is organized as follows. In the next section, we introduce the test statistics and their limiting distributions in a model without the regressors x_{it}. Section 3 considers model (1), and we explicitly examine the consequences when we allow for heteroscedasticity, that is $E(\varepsilon_{it}) = \sigma_i^2$ for $i \in \mathbb{N}^+$. We show that the limiting process has quite a messy covariance structure to be of any use with real data sets. Because of this, we then examine a transformation to overcome the latter concern. Section 4 describes the local alternatives for which the tests have nontrivial power and their consistency. We also describe and show the validity of a bootstrap version of the test, as our simulation results illustrate that tests based on a subset of proposed statistics yield a very poor finite sample performance (see Table 2). Section 5 presents a Monte Carlo experiment to get some idea of the finite sample performance of our tests. Section 6 concludes and finally we confine the proofs to the appendix.

2. TESTING FOR HOMOGENEITY

As a starting point we shall first provide a test for common trends in the absence of exogenous regressors x_{it}. Our motivation comes from the fact that the results of Section 3 are then much easier to follow after those given in Theorems 1 and 2 below. So, we begin with the model

$$\begin{aligned} y_{it} &= m_i(t/T) + v_{it}, \quad i=1,\dots,n, \quad t=1,\dots,T \\ v_{it} &= \mu_i + \varepsilon_{it} \end{aligned} \tag{2}$$

with both n and T increasing to infinity.

The null hypothesis H_0 is

$$H_0 : m_i(\tau) = m(\tau) \quad \text{for all } i \geq 1; \quad \tau \in [0,1] \tag{3}$$

and the alternative hypothesis H_1 becomes

$$H_1 : 0 < \imath(n) = |\Lambda|/n < 1 \tag{4}$$

where $\Lambda = \{i : \mu(\Upsilon_i) > 0\}$ with $\Upsilon_i = \{\tau \in [0,1] : m_i(\tau) \neq m(\tau)\}$ and '$|A|$' denotes the cardinality of the set A and $\lambda(\Upsilon)$ denotes the Lebesgue measure of the set Υ. Λ denotes the set of individuals $i \geq 1$ for which $m_i(\tau)$ is different from the 'common' trend $m(\tau)$, and thus $\imath =: \imath(n)$ represents the proportion of sequences $i \geq 1$ for which $m_i(\tau) \neq m(\tau)$. One feature of Eq. (4) is that $\imath$ can be (asymptotically) negligible. More specifically, as we shall show in Section 4, the test has nontrivial power under local alternatives such that $\imath = O(n^{-1/2})$. This situation when $\imath \searrow 0$ can be of interest if we want to decide whether a new set of sequences share the same trending behaviour as the existing ones, or for 'supervised classification' purposes.

Before we state our results, let's introduce some regularity conditions.

Condition 1. (C1). $\{\varepsilon_{it}\}_{t \in \mathbb{Z}}$, $i \in \mathbb{N}^+$, are sequences of zero mean independent random variables with $E\varepsilon_{it}^2 = \sigma^2$ and finite fourth moments. In addition, the sequences $\{\varepsilon_{it}\}_{t \geq 1}$ and $\{\varepsilon_{jt}\}_{t \geq 1}$ are mutually independent for all $i \neq j$.

Condition 2. (C2). The functions $m_i(\tau)$ are bounded for all $i \in \mathbb{N}^+$.

$C1$ is standard, although stronger than we really need for our results to follow. An inspection of our proofs indicate that the results would follow provided some type of 'weak' dependence in both time and/or cross-sectional dimensions. The only main difference being that the asymptotic covariance structure of our statistics will be affected by its dependence. So, for simplicity and to ease arguments, we have decided to keep $C1$ as it stands. It is worth emphasizing that we do not assume that the sequences $\{\varepsilon_{it}\}_{t \in \mathbb{Z}}$, $i \in \mathbb{N}^+$ are identically distributed, although their first two moments are constant, although we shall discuss the consequences of allowing for heteroscedasticity in Section 3.

Regarding $C2$, we notice that we do not need any type of smoothness condition on the trend functions $m_i(\tau)$. We require only that they are bounded, although strictly speaking this is only needed when examining the consistency and local power of the tests.

Let's introduce now some notation used in the sequel of the paper. For arbitrary sequences $\{\varsigma_{it}\}_{t=1}^{T}$, $i \geq 1$, we define

$$\bar{\varsigma}_{\cdot t} = \frac{1}{n}\sum_{j=1}^{n} \varsigma_{jt}, \quad \bar{\varsigma}_{i\cdot} = \frac{1}{T}\sum_{s=1}^{T} \varsigma_{is}, \quad \bar{\varsigma}_{\cdot\cdot} = \frac{1}{Tn}\sum_{j=1}^{n}\sum_{s=1}^{T} \varsigma_{js} \tag{5}$$

For presentation reasons we shall consider separately the cases $\mu_i = 0$ and $\mu_i \neq 0$. The arguments needed in the latter case are lengthier, but they are based on those given when $\mu_i = 0$.

2.1. *The Case without Fixed Individual Effects* μ_i

Define

$$\tilde{m}_i(t/T) := y_{it} - \bar{y}_{\cdot t}, \quad i = 1, \cdots n, \quad t = 1, \ldots, T \tag{6}$$

$$\tilde{m}'_i(t/T) := y_{it} - \frac{1}{i-1}\sum_{j=1}^{i-1} y_{jt}, \quad i = 1, \cdots n, \quad t = 1, \ldots, T \tag{7}$$

The motivation to introduce the quantities (6) and (7) is that, under the null hypothesis H_0, it holds that $\bar{y}_{\cdot t} = m(t/T) + \bar{\varepsilon}_{\cdot t}$. So,

$$\tilde{m}_i\left(\frac{t}{T}\right) := \varepsilon_{it} - \overline{\varepsilon}_{\cdot t}; \quad \tilde{m}_i'\left(\frac{t}{T}\right) := \varepsilon_{it} - \frac{1}{i-1}\sum_{1=2}^{i-1} \varepsilon_{jt}$$

which do not depend on the trend function $m(\cdot)$ and they have zero mean. However, under the alternative hypothesis, $\tilde{m}_i(t/T)$ and $\tilde{m}_i'(t/T)$ will develop a mean different than zero, suggesting that tests based on Eqs. (6) and (7) will have the usual desirable statistical properties.

Hence, following ideas in Brown, Durbin, and Evans (1975), we base our test for homogeneity on

$$Q_{T,n,r,u} = \frac{1}{Tn}\sum_{t=1}^{[Tr]}\sum_{i=1}^{[nu]}(y_{it} - \overline{y}_{\cdot t})$$

$$Q'_{T,n,r,u} = \frac{1}{Tn}\sum_{t=1}^{[Tr]}\sum_{i=2}^{[nu]}\left(y_{it} - \frac{1}{i-1}\sum_{j=1}^{i-1} y_{jt}\right), \quad r, u \in [0, 1]$$

where $[c]$ denotes the integer part of a number c.

Let's introduce the following notation. We denote '$\Rightarrow_{D([0,1]^2)}$' weak convergence in the space $D([0, 1]^2)$, the space of continuous functions from the right and equipped with the Skorohod metric, given in Bickel and Wichura (1971, p. 1662). Recall that a two-parameter process $W(r, u)$ is said to be a Brownian sheet if it is a Gaussian process, satisfying $W(0, 0) = 0$ and

$$Cov(W(r_1, u_1), W(r_2, u_2)) = (r_1 \wedge r_2)(u_1 \wedge u_2)$$

where $(a_{1\wedge}a_2) = \min(a_1, a_2)$. We also introduce two-parameter process

$$B(r, u) = W(r, u) - uW(r, 1)$$

Theorem 1. Assuming $C1$, under H_0, we have that as T, $n \to \infty$,

$$\text{(a)} \quad \sqrt{Tn}\, Q_{T,n,r,u} \Rightarrow_{D([0,1]^2)} \sigma B(r, u), \quad r, u \in [0, 1] \tag{8}$$

$$\text{(b)} \quad \sqrt{Tn}\, Q'_{T,n,r,u} \Rightarrow_{D([0,1]^2)} \sigma W(r, u), \quad r, u \in [0, 1] \tag{9}$$

2.2. *The Case with Individual Fixed Effects* μ_i

When the individual fixed effects μ_i's are present in Eq. (2), we need to modify both $Q_{T,n,r,u}$ and $Q'_{T,n,r,u}$, as we need to remove them from the model. To that end, for all $t,u \in [0,1]$, consider

$$U_{T,n,r,u} = \frac{1}{Tn}\sum_{t=1}^{[Tr]}\sum_{i=1}^{[nu]}\{y_{it} - \bar{y}_{\cdot t} - \bar{y}_{i\cdot} + \bar{y}_{\cdot\cdot}\}$$

$$U'_{T,n,r,u} = \frac{1}{Tn}\sum_{t=2}^{[Tr]}\sum_{i=2}^{[nu]}\left\{y_{it} - \frac{1}{i-1}\sum_{j=1}^{i-1}y_{jt} - \frac{1}{t-1}\sum_{s=1}^{t-1}y_{is} + \frac{1}{(t-1)(i-1)}\sum_{j=1}^{i-1}\sum_{s=1}^{t-1}y_{js}\right\}$$

Let's introduce the two-parameter Gaussian process

$$B'(r,u) = W(r,u) - uW(r,1) - rW(1,u) + ruW(1,1)$$

which satisfies $B'(0,0)=0$, $B'(r,1)=0$, $B'(1,u)=0$ $\forall r,u \in [0,1]$ and

$$Cov(B'(r_1,u_1), B'(r_2,u_2)) = (r \wedge r_1)(1 - r_1 \vee r_2)(u_1 \wedge u_2)(1 - u_1 \vee u_2)$$

where $a_1 \vee a_2 = \max(a_1, a_2)$. The process $B'(r,u)$ is known as the *Brownian pillow*.

Theorem 2. Assuming $C1$, under H_0, we have that as T, $n \to \infty$

$$\textbf{(a)} \quad \sqrt{Tn}U_{T,n,r,u} \Rightarrow_{D([0,1]^2)} \sigma B'(r,u), \quad r,u \in [0,1] \tag{10}$$

$$\textbf{(b)} \quad \sqrt{Tn}U'_{T,n,r,u} \Rightarrow_{D([0,1]^2)} \sigma W(r,u), \quad r,u \in [0,1] \tag{11}$$

We now comment briefly on the results of Theorems 1 and 2. The first point to notice is that, as we mentioned in the abstract, we are able to avoid local smoothing in the estimation of the functions $m_i(\cdot)$, being the key that both n and T increase to infinity. We notice that both $\sqrt{Tn}U'_{T,n,r,u}$ and $\sqrt{Tn}Q'_{T,n,r,u}$ have the same asymptotic behaviour, which is not the case for $\sqrt{Tn}U_{T,n,r,u}$ and $\sqrt{Tn}Q_{Tn,r,u}$. This is somehow expected after we notice that both $y_{it} - \frac{1}{i-1}\sum_{j=1}^{i-1} y_{jt}$ and the term inside the braces in the definition of $U'_{T,n,r,u}$ have the same structure, more specifically they behave as martingale difference sequences. We just remark that $y_{it} - \frac{1}{i-1}\sum_{j=1}^{i-1} y_{jt}$ is nothing but the martingale transformation of $y_{it} - \overline{y}_{\cdot t}$.

2.3. *Tests for Homogeneity*

We put together results of Sections 2.1−2.2 to provide test statistics for homogeneity. To that end we denote by $g(\cdot)$ a continuous functional: $[0,1]^2 \to \mathbb{R}^+$. To implement the test(s) we need to estimate the variance σ^2. For that purpose, denote residuals by

$$e_{it}^{(1)} := y_{it} - \overline{y}_{\cdot t}; \quad e_{it}^{(2)} := y_{it} - \overline{y}_{\cdot t} - \overline{y}_{i\cdot} + \overline{y}_{\cdot\cdot}$$

depending on whether the model does not have or has individual fixed effects. As we mentioned earlier, under the H_0, we have that

$$e_{it}^{(1)} := \varepsilon_{it} - \overline{\varepsilon}_{\cdot t}; \quad e_{it}^{(2)} := \varepsilon_{it} - \overline{\varepsilon}_{\cdot t} - \overline{\varepsilon}_{i\cdot} + \overline{\varepsilon}_{\cdot\cdot}$$

In addition we estimate σ^2 by

$$\hat{\sigma}_{(\ell)}^2 := \frac{1}{Tn}\sum_{t=1}^{T}\sum_{i=1}^{n} e_{it}^{(\ell)2}, \quad \text{for} \quad \ell = 1, 2$$

Proposition 1. Assuming *C*1, under H_0, as $n, T \to \infty$, we have that

$$\hat{\sigma}_{(\ell)}^2 \to_p \sigma^2, \quad \text{for} \quad \ell = 1, 2$$

Proof. The proof is standard and so it is omitted. ■

Corollary 1. Assuming *C*1 − *C*2, under H_0, for any continuous functional $g(\cdot)$, as $T, n \to \infty$,

$$(a) \quad g\left(\sqrt{Tn}\frac{Q_{T,n,r,u}}{\hat{\sigma}_{(1)}}\right) \overset{d}{\Rightarrow} g(B(r,u)); \quad g\left(\sqrt{Tn}\frac{Q'_{T,n,r,u}}{\hat{\sigma}_{(1)}}\right) \overset{d}{\Rightarrow} g(W(r,u))$$

Table 1. Critical Values for α-Significance Level, n, $T = 10{,}000$.

α	0.1	0.075	0.05	0.025	0.01	0.005
$\sup_{r,u\in[0,1]}\lvert W(r,u)\rvert$	2.2187	2.3308	2.4781	2.7227	3.0282	3.2
$\sup_{r,u\in[0,1]}\lvert B(r,u)\rvert$	1.3419	1.3951	1.4677	1.5782	1.7106	1.8091
$\sup_{r,u\in[0,1]}\lvert B'(r,u)\rvert$	0.7777	0.8039	0.8372	0.8849	0.9515	0.9975

$$(b)\quad g\left(\sqrt{Tn}\frac{U_{T,n,r,u}}{\hat{\sigma}_{(2)}}\right) \overset{d}{\Rightarrow} g(B'(r,u)); \quad g\left(\sqrt{Tn}\frac{U'_{T,n,r,u}}{\hat{\sigma}_{(2)}}\right) \overset{d}{\Rightarrow} g(W(r,u))$$

Proof. The proof follows by standard arguments using the continuous mapping theorem, Theorems 1 and 2 and Proposition 1, so it is omitted. ■

One functional often employed to implement the test is the 'sup', that is

$$\sqrt{Tn} \sup_{r,u\in[0,1]} \left|\frac{U_{T,n,r,u}}{\hat{\sigma}_{(2)}}\right| \overset{d}{\Rightarrow} \sup_{r,u\in 0,1]} |B'(r,u)|$$

$$\sqrt{Tn} \sup_{r,u\in[0,1]} \left|\frac{U'_{T,n,r,u}}{\hat{\sigma}_{(2)}}\right| \overset{d}{\Rightarrow} \sup_{r,u\in 0,1]} |W(r,u)|$$

which corresponds to a Kolmogorov–Smirnov type of test.

Critical values for the supremum of absolute value of the three limiting processes are provided in Table 1 for various significance levels, which have been simulated with 20,000 iterations.

3. TEST OF COMMON TRENDS

We now revisit our model of interest (1). Recall that under the null hypothesis we can write Eq. (1) as

$$y_{it} = \beta' x_{it} + m(t/T) + v_{it}, \quad v_{it} = \mu_i + \varepsilon_{it} \tag{12}$$

It is obvious that if β were known, the problem of testing for homogeneity would be no different from that examined in Section 2. That is, we would test homogeneity in the model

$$y_{it} - x_{it}'\beta = : \upsilon_{it}$$
$$= m_i(t/T) + \mu_i + \varepsilon_{it}$$

replacing y_{it} there by υ_{it}. However β is unknown, so given an estimator $\hat{\beta}$, we might then consider instead

$$\hat{\upsilon}_{it} = : y_{it} - x_{it}'\hat{\beta} = x_{it}'(\hat{\beta} - \beta) + m(t/T) + \mu_i + \varepsilon_{it}$$

Thus, it is sensible to consider $U_{Tn,r,u}$ and $U'_{Tn,r,u}$ but with $\hat{\upsilon}_{it}$ replacing y_{it} there. More specifically, for $r,u \in [0,1]$, we define

$$\hat{U}_{T,n,r,u} = \frac{1}{Tn}\sum_{t=1}^{[Tr]}\sum_{i=1}^{[nu]}(\hat{\upsilon}_{it} - \bar{\hat{\upsilon}}_{\cdot t} - \bar{\hat{\upsilon}}_{i\cdot} + \bar{\hat{\upsilon}}_{\cdot\cdot}) \tag{13}$$

$$\hat{U}'_{T,n,r,u} = \frac{1}{Tn}\sum_{t=2}^{[Tr]}\sum_{i=2}^{[nu]}\left(\hat{\upsilon}_{it} - \frac{\sum_{j=1}^{i-1}\hat{\upsilon}_{js}}{i-1} - \frac{\sum_{s=1}^{t-1}\hat{\upsilon}_{is}}{t-1} + \frac{\sum_{j=1}^{i-1}\sum_{s=1}^{t-1}\hat{\upsilon}_{js}}{(i-1)(t-1)}\right)$$

So, we now look at how to estimate the slope parameters β in Eq. (12). For that purpose, given a generic sequence $\{\zeta_{it}\}_{i\geq 1, t\geq 1}$ and denoting by $\breve{\varsigma}_{it} : = \varsigma_{it} - \bar{\varsigma}_{\cdot t} - \bar{\varsigma}_{i\cdot} + \bar{\varsigma}_{\cdot\cdot}$, we have that under H_0, Eq. (12) becomes

$$\breve{y}_{it} = \beta'\breve{x}_{it} + \breve{\varepsilon}_{it}; \quad i = 1, \ldots, n; \quad t = 1, \ldots, T$$

so that we estimate β by least squares methods, that is

$$\hat{\beta} = \left(\sum_{t=1}^{T}\sum_{i=1}^{n}\breve{x}_{it}\breve{x}_{it}'\right)^{-1}\sum_{t=1}^{T}\sum_{i=1}^{n}\breve{x}_{it}\breve{y}_{it}$$

Observe that $\breve{\varsigma}_{it}$ removes the common trend and the fixed effects.

Condition 3. (C3). For all $i \in \mathbb{N}^+$, $\{x_{it}\}_{t\in\mathbb{Z}}$ are k-dimensional sequences of independent random variables mutually uncorrelated with the error sequences $\{\varepsilon_{it}\}_{t\in\mathbb{Z}}$, where $E(x_{it}) = \varkappa_i$, $\Sigma = E\{(x_{it} - \varkappa_i)(x_{it} - \varkappa_i)'\}$ and finite fourth moments.

Condition 4. (C4). T, $n \to \infty$ such that $T/n^2 \to 0$.

We have the following two results.

Theorem 3. Assuming $C1-C4$, under H_0, as $T,n\to\infty$,
$(Tn)^{1/2}(\hat{\beta}-\beta)\to^{d}\mathcal{N}(0,\sigma^2\Sigma^{-1})$

Theorem 4. Assuming $C1-C4$, under H_0, as $T,n\to\infty$ we have that for any continuous functional $g(\cdot)$,

$$\textbf{(a)}\quad g\left(\sqrt{Tn}\frac{\hat{U}_{T,n,r,u}}{\hat{\sigma}}\right)\overset{d}{\Rightarrow}g(B'(r,u));\quad \textbf{(b)}\quad g\left(\sqrt{Tn}\frac{\hat{U}'_{T,n,r,u}}{\hat{\sigma}}\right)\overset{d}{\Rightarrow}g(W(r,u))$$

where

$$\hat{\sigma}^2:=\frac{1}{Tn}\sum_{t=1}^{T}\sum_{i=1}^{n}(\hat{\upsilon}_{it}-\bar{\hat{\upsilon}}_{\cdot t}-\bar{\hat{\upsilon}}_{i\cdot}+\bar{\hat{\upsilon}}_{\cdot\cdot})^2$$

A typical continuous functional $g(\cdot)$ employed is the supremum, that is

$$(Tn)^{1/2}\sup_{r,u\in[0,1]}\left|\hat{\sigma}^{-1}\hat{U}'_{T,n,r,u}\right|\overset{d}{\to}\sup_{r,u\in[0,1]}\left|W(r,u)\right|$$

which corresponds to a Kolmogorov–Smirnov type of statistic.

Remark 1. The results of the previous theorem indicates that knowledge of β does not affect the asymptotic behaviour of our test.

3.1. Unequal Variance σ_i^2

We now look at the problem of testing for homogeneity with possible heterogeneous second moments in the error term. More specifically, we are concerned with testing for homogeneity when

Condition 5. (C5). For all $i\in\mathbb{N}^+$, $\{\varepsilon_{it}\}_{t\in\mathbb{Z}}$ are sequences of random variables as in $C1$ but such that $E\varepsilon_{it}^2=\sigma_i^2$ satisfying

$$\frac{1}{n}\sum_{i=1}^{n}\sigma_i^2\le C<\infty$$

We can be tempted to write $C5$ in a more traditional format as saying that $E(\varepsilon_{it}^2|x_{it})=\sigma^2(x_{it})$. However, $C3$ implies that the latter conditional variance would not play any relevant role on the asymptotic behaviour of any continuous functional of either $\hat{U}_{T,n,r,u}$ or $\hat{U}'_{T,n,r,u}$, in the sense that the asymptotic behaviour is that given in Theorem 4 but with a different scaling σ. On the other hand, this is not the case though, if the unconditional variance of $\{\varepsilon_{it}\}_{t\in\mathbb{Z}}$ is as stated in *C5* as Theorem 5 below shows. It is also worth mentioning that it is obvious how to handle the situation where we allow for trending variances, say $\sigma_i^2=\alpha_1+\alpha_2 i^\gamma$, as long as $\gamma<1$. This relaxation of *C5* is trivial and it only complicates the notation and arguments. Finally, similar caveats appear if *C5* we modified to say that $E\varepsilon_{it}^2=\sigma_t^2$. However, to save space we decided to keep *C5* as it stands.

Let's introduce the following notation

$$\sigma^2(u)=\lim_{n\to\infty}\frac{1}{n}\sum_{i=1}^{[nu]}\sigma_i^2$$

Theorem 5. Assuming *C3* and *C5*, under H_0 we have that as n, $T\to\infty$,

(a) $(Tn)^{1/2}\hat{U}_{T,n,r,u}\Rightarrow\mathcal{G}(r,u)$

(b) $(Tn)^{1/2}\hat{U}'_{T,n,r,u}\Rightarrow\mathcal{G}'(r,u)$

where $\mathcal{G}'(r,u)$ and $\mathcal{G}(r,u)$ are Gaussian processes with covariance structures $\Phi(r_1,u_1;r_2,u_2)$ given in (A.16) and

$$\begin{aligned}Cov(\mathcal{G}(r_1,u_1),\mathcal{G}(r_2,u_2)) &= (r_1\wedge r_2)(\sigma^2(u_1\wedge u_2)-u_2\sigma^2(u_1))\\ &\quad -r_1r_2u_2\sigma^2(u_1)-r_1r_2u_2\sigma^2(u_1\wedge u_2)\\ &\quad +u_1\sigma^2(u_2)(r_1r_2-(r_1\wedge r_2))\end{aligned}$$

respectively.

The results of Theorem 5 indicate that to obtain asymptotic critical values on functionals based on $(Tn)^{1/2}\hat{U}'_{T,n,r,u}$ and $(Tn)^{1/2}\hat{U}_{T,n,r,u}$ appear to be a daunting task. This is in view of the very complicated and complex covariance structure of the latter two processes. To overcome this type of problem, we envisage a procedure based on a transformation of $\hat{U}'_{T,n,r,u}$ or $\hat{U}_{T,n,r,u}$ in such a way that the transformed statistics will have a known (or at least simpler) covariance structure.

Denote the estimator of σ_i^2 by

$$\hat{\sigma}_i^2 = \frac{1}{T}\sum_{t=1}^{T}(\hat{\upsilon}_{it} - \overline{\hat{\upsilon}}_{\cdot t} - \overline{\hat{\upsilon}}_{i\cdot} - \overline{\hat{\upsilon}}_{\cdot\cdot})^2, \quad i=1,\ldots,n \tag{14}$$

It is quite standard in view of $C3$ and $C5$ to show that $\hat{\sigma}_i^2$ is a (pointwise) consistent estimator for σ_i^2 for all $i=1,\ldots, n$, and under $C3$ and $C5$ and under sufficient moment conditions, it is easily shown that

$$E(\hat{\sigma}_i^2 - \sigma_i^2)^{2p} = O(T^{-p}), \quad i=1,\ldots,n \tag{15}$$

So, for instance we modify $\hat{U}'_{T,n,r,u}$ to

$$\hat{U}^{\#}_{T,n,r,u} = \frac{1}{Tn}\sum_{t=1}^{[Tr]}\sum_{i=2}^{[nu]}\left(\frac{1}{\hat{\sigma}_i}\hat{\nu}_{it} - \frac{\sum_{j=1}^{i-1}\frac{1}{\hat{\sigma}_j}\hat{\upsilon}_{js}}{i-1} - \frac{\sum_{s=1}^{t-1}\frac{1}{\hat{\sigma}_i}\hat{\upsilon}_{is}}{t-1} + \frac{\sum_{j=1}^{i-1}\sum_{s=1}^{t-1}\frac{1}{\hat{\sigma}_j}\hat{\upsilon}_{js}}{(i-1)(t-1)}\right) \tag{16}$$

A similar transformation is obtained for $\hat{U}_{T,n,r,u}$. Now, Theorem 3 implies that the right side of Eq. (16) is

$$\frac{1}{Tn}\sum_{t=1}^{[Tr]}\sum_{i=2}^{[nu]}\left(\frac{1}{\hat{\sigma}_i}\varepsilon_{it} - \frac{\sum_{j=1}^{i-1}\frac{1}{\hat{\sigma}_j}\varepsilon_{js}}{i-1} - \frac{\sum_{s=1}^{t-1}\frac{1}{\hat{\sigma}_i}\varepsilon_{is}}{t-1} + \frac{\sum_{j=1}^{i-1}\sum_{s=1}^{t-1}\frac{1}{\hat{\sigma}_j}\varepsilon_{js}}{(i-1)(t-1)}\right) + o_p((Tn)^{-1/2})$$

uniformly in $r,u\in[0,1]$. Now, if we would have σ_i instead of $\hat{\sigma}_i$, the right hand side of the last displayed equation would be then what we had in Theorem 2 or 4, but with σ^2 replaced by 1 there, as we had that $\varepsilon_{it}/\sigma_i$ satisfies $C1$ but with unit variance. So, if

$$\frac{1}{Tn}\sum_{t=1}^{[Tr]}\sum_{i=2}^{[nu]}\left(\frac{1}{\hat{\sigma}_i} - \frac{1}{\sigma_i}\right)\varepsilon_{it} = o_p((Tn)^{-1/2}) \tag{17}$$

uniformly in $r,u \in [0,1]$, we then conclude that the modification given by $\hat{U}^{\#}_{Tn,r,u}$ leads to a statistic with a known covariance structure.

To that end, we first observe that by Eq. (15) and that $E\sup_{\ell=1,\ldots,q}|a_\ell| \le \left(\sum_{\ell=1}^{q} E|a_\ell|^k\right)^{1/k}$, we have that

$$\sup_{i=1,\ldots,n} |\hat{\sigma}_i^2 - \sigma_i^2| = O_p(n^{1/2p}T^{-1/2}) = o(1)$$

The latter uniform convergence, as opposed to pointwise consistency. But Eq. (17) is the case, because by Taylor's expansion,

$$\frac{1}{Tn}\sum_{t=1}^{[Tr]}\sum_{i=2}^{[nu]}\left\{\sum_{\ell=1}^{2p}(-1)^{\ell}\left(\frac{\hat{\sigma}_i - \sigma_i}{\sigma_i}\right)\right\}\varepsilon_{it}/\sigma_i + \frac{1}{Tn}\sum_{t=1}^{[Tr]}\sum_{i=2}^{[nu]}\left(\frac{\hat{\sigma}_i - \sigma_i}{\sigma_i}\right)^{2p+1}\frac{1}{\hat{\sigma}_i}\varepsilon_{it} \tag{18}$$

From here, suitable regularity conditions on how n and T increase to infinity and somewhat lengthy but routine algebra lead us to the claim in Eq. (17) and conclude that the transformation of $\hat{U}'_{Tn,\tau,\iota}$ given in $\hat{U}^{\#}_{Tn,r,u}$ will overcome the problematic issue of how to tabulate valid asymptotic critical values for our test.

4. ASYMPTOTIC PROPERTIES UNDER LOCAL ALTERNATIVE HYPOTHESIS – BOOTSTRAP

As usual, it is important to examine the behaviour of any test under alternative hypothesis and ultimately under local alternatives. We begin with the discussion under local alternatives, the consistency of the tests being a corollary. To that end, consider

$$H_l : \begin{cases} m_i(\tau) = m(\tau) + \dfrac{1}{T^{1/\xi}}\varrho_i(\tau) & \text{for all} \quad i \le \mathbf{I}(n) \\ m_i(\tau) = m(\tau) & \text{for all} \quad \mathbf{I}(n) < i \le n \end{cases} \tag{19}$$

Where $\varrho_i(\tau)$ is different than zero in $\Upsilon_i = \Upsilon$, a set of positive Lebesgue measure, $\xi \le 1/2$ and $\mathbf{I}(n) \le . \; Cn^{1/2}$, where C is a finite positive constant. It is worth remarking that we have assumed that Υ is the same for all $i \geq 1$ for notational simplicity. However in the Monte Carlo simulations we shall examine what happens with the power of the test when, given a particular alternative hypothesis, we permute the order of the cross-section units (see Table 8).

We begin with the test based on the statistic $U_{T,n,r,u}$ leaving the case with regressors x_{it} for later.

Proposition 2. Under H_i with $\xi = 1/2$ and $\mathbf{I}(n)=Cn^{1/2}$, assuming $C1$ and $C2$, we have that

$$(Tn)^{1/2} U_{T,n,r,u} \Rightarrow_{D([0,1]^2)} B'(r,u) + C^{1/2}\left(\int_{[0,r]\cap\Upsilon} \overline{\varrho}(\tau)d\tau - r\int_{\Upsilon} \overline{\varrho}(\tau)d\tau\right)$$

where $\overline{\varrho}(\tau) = \lim_{n\to\infty} n^{-1/2} \sum_{i=1}^{n^{1/2}} \varrho_i(\tau)$.

Proof. By definition we have that

$$U_{T,n,r,u} = \frac{1}{Tn}\sum_{t=1}^{[Tr]}\sum_{i=1}^{[nu]}(\varepsilon_{it} - \overline{\varepsilon}_{\cdot t} - \overline{\varepsilon}_{i\cdot} + \overline{\varepsilon}_{\cdot\cdot}) + \frac{1}{Tn}\sum_{t=1}^{[Tr]}\sum_{i=1}^{Cn^{1/2}}\left[\mathring{\varrho}_i(t/T) - \frac{1}{n}\sum_{j=1}^{Cn^{1/2}}\mathring{\varrho}_j(t/T)\right]$$

The second term on the right of the last displayed equality known as the drift function, is

$$\frac{1}{T^{3/2}n}\sum_{t=1}^{[Tr]}\sum_{i=1}^{Cn^{1/2}}\left(1 - \frac{1}{n}\right)\mathring{\varrho}_i(t/T)$$

So, we have that after we normalize $U_{T,n,r,u}$ by $(Tn)^{1/2}$ the latter displayed expression becomes

$$\frac{1}{T}\sum_{t=1}^{[Tr]}\frac{1}{n^{1/2}}\sum_{i=1}^{Cn^{1/2}}\mathring{\varrho}_i(t/T) \to C^{1/2}\left(\int_{[0,r]\cap\Upsilon} \bar{\mathring{\varrho}}(\tau)d\tau - r\int_{\Upsilon}\bar{\mathring{\varrho}}(\tau)d\tau\right)$$

Observe that we can interchange the limit in n and the integral using Lebesgue dominated convergence because $|\varrho_i(u)| \leq C$ for all $i \geq 1$. Recall that $C2$ implies that the functions $\varrho_i(\tau)$ are bounded. This concludes the proof of the proposition. ■

One immediate conclusion that we draw from Proposition 2 is that our tests detect local alternatives shrinking to the null hypothesis at a parametric rate $O(\mathrm{T}^{-1/2}n^{-1/2})$. A question of interest can be if test based on $U'_{Tn,r,u}$ can detect local alternatives when $\xi < 1/2$ and/or $\mathbf{I}$ is a finite integer. This type of alternatives can be useful for the purpose of, say, classification or whether we wish to decide if a new set of individuals, $i \leq \mathbf{I}$, shares the 'common' trend function $m(\tau)$.

To that end, we notice that the drift function in $(Tn)^{1/2}\mathrm{U}_{Tn,r,u}$ becomes

$$\frac{1}{T^{\xi+1/2}n^{1/2}}\sum_{t=1}^{[Tr]}\sum_{i=1}^{\mathbf{I}}\left(1-\frac{1}{n}\right)\mathring{\varrho}_i(t/T) \simeq \frac{1}{T^{\xi+1/2}n^{1/2}}\sum_{t=1}^{[T\tau]}\sum_{i=1}^{\mathbf{I}}\mathring{\varrho}_i(t/T)$$

$$\simeq \frac{T^{1/2-\xi}}{n^{1/2}}\int_{[0,r]\cap\Upsilon}\sum_{i=1}^{\mathbf{I}}\mathring{\varrho}_i(u)du$$

So, if $n \propto T^{1-2\xi}$, the drift function is nonzero and hence the test based on $\mathrm{U}_{Tn,r,u}$, and similarly for $U'_{T,n,r,u}$, have no trivial asymptotic power.

Another easy conclusion from Proposition 2 is that under fixed alternatives, since $\int_{[0,r]\cap\Upsilon}\bar{\mathring{\varrho}}(\tau)d\tau - r\int_{\Upsilon}\bar{\mathring{\varrho}}(\tau)d\tau$ is nonzero, $(Tn)^{-1/2}||\mathrm{U}_{T,n,r,u}||^{-1} \rightarrow_P 0$, so that tests based on $\mathrm{U}_{T,n,r,u}$ are consistent, so is $U'_{T,n,r,u}$.

We now discuss the local power for model (12). We begin by discussing the consequences on the asymptotic properties of the least squares estimator of β. To that end, recall that Eq. (12) under local alternatives with $\xi = 1/2$ and $\mathbf{I}(n)$ $Cn^{1/2}$ becomes

$$y_{it} = \beta' x_{it} + m_i(t/T) + v_{it}, \quad v_{it} = \mu_i + \varepsilon_{it}$$

so denoting

$$\mathring{m}_i(t/T) = m_i(t/T) - T^{-1}\sum_{s=1}^{T} m_i(s/T)$$

we have that standard manipulations yields

$$\hat{\beta}-\beta=\left(\sum_{t=1}^{T}\sum_{i=1}^{n}\breve{x}_{it}\breve{x}_{it}'\right)^{-1}\sum_{t=1}^{T}\sum_{i=1}^{n}\breve{x}_{it}\left\{\mathring{m}_i(t/T)-\frac{1}{n}\sum_{j=1}^{n}\mathring{m}_j(t/T)\right\}$$
$$+\left(\sum_{t=1}^{T}\sum_{i=1}^{n}\breve{x}_{it}\breve{x}_{it}'\right)^{-1}\sum_{t=1}^{T}\sum_{i=1}^{n}\breve{x}_{it}\varepsilon_{it} \tag{20}$$

But as we can take $Ex_{it}=0$, the only consequence on the asymptotic behaviour of $(Tn)^{1/2}(\hat{\beta}-\beta)$ is that the asymptotic variance will have an additional term coming from

$$\frac{1}{(Tn)^{1/2}}\sum_{i=1}^{n}\sum_{t=1}^{T}\breve{x}_{it}\left\{\mathring{m}_i(t/T)-\frac{1}{n}\sum_{j=1}^{n}\mathring{m}_j(t/T)\right\}$$

which is different than zero under fixed alternative hypothesis, whereas under the local alternatives it is clear to be $O_P(1)$ implying that the behaviour of $(Tn)^{1/2}(\hat{\beta}-\beta)$ is unchanged. The only condition for the latter is that $\varrho_i(\tau)$ is square integrable. See our comments after Corollary 2 below.

We now discuss the behaviour of $\hat{U}_{T,n,r,u}$ under the local alternatives in Eq. (19).

Corollary 2. Under H_l with $\xi=1/2$ and $\mathbf{l}(n)=Cn^{1/2}$ and assuming $C1-C4$, we have that

$$(Tn)^{1/2}\hat{U}_{T,n,r,u}\Rightarrow_{D([0,1]^2)}B'(r,u)+C^{1/2}\left(\int_{[0,r]\cap\Upsilon}\overline{\varrho}(\tau)\mathrm{d}\tau-r\int_{\Upsilon}\overline{\varrho}(\tau)\mathrm{d}\tau\right)$$

Proof. The proof follows easily in view of Eq. (20), comments that follow and Proposition 2, so it is omitted. ■

Corollary 2 then indicates that, as it was the case under the null hypothesis, the behaviour of the test is unaltered by the estimation of the slope parameters β under the local alternatives.

Finally, we need to discuss the consistency of the test(s). But this is a natural consequence of Proposition 2 and Corollary 2. The only difference, but this does not affect the consistency of the test, is that the distribution of $\hat{\beta}$ is different as it will have an additional term in its asymptotic variance coming from the asymptotic variance of first term on the right of Eq. (2), which by standard arguments yield to the expression

$$\Sigma^{-1} Var\left(\frac{1}{(Tn)^{1/2}}\sum_{t=1}^{T}\sum_{i=1}^{n} x_{it}\left\{\mathring{m}_i(t/T) - \frac{1}{n}\sum_{j=1}^{n}\mathring{m}_j(t/T)\right\}\right)\Sigma^{-1}$$

$$= \Sigma^{-1} \lim_{n,T\to\infty} \frac{1}{(Tn)^{1/2}}\sum_{t=1}^{T}\sum_{i=1}^{n}\left\{\mathring{m}_i(t/T) - \frac{1}{n}\sum_{j=1}^{n}\mathring{m}_j(t/T)\right\}^2$$

Again regarding the tests based on $(Tn)^{1/2}\hat{U}'_{T,n,r,u}$, we obtain the same type of conclusion proceeding as with $(Tn)^{1/2}\hat{U}_{T,n,r,u}$.

4.1. Bootstrap of the Test

In this subsection, we provide a valid bootstrap algorithm for our tests. In particular our main concern is to do so for the tests based on $\hat{U}_{T,n,r,u}$ (and $Q_{T,n,r,u}$) as our Monte Carlo experiment suggests a poor finite sample performance, especially when compared to those of $\hat{U}'_{T,n,r,u}$ (and $Q'_{T,n,r,u}$). To that end, because by $C1$ the errors ε_{it} are i.i.d., Efron's (1979) naive bootstrap would be appropriate. The bootstrap will have the following *three steps*:

STEP 1: For each $i = 1,\ldots, n$, denote by $\{\varepsilon^*_{it}\}_{t=1}^{T}$ a random sample of size T from the empirical distribution of $\{\hat{\varepsilon}_{it}\}_{t\geq 1, i\geq 1}$, where

$$\hat{\varepsilon}_{it} = \hat{\upsilon}_{it} - \bar{\hat{\upsilon}}_{i\cdot} - \bar{\hat{\upsilon}}_{\cdot t} + \bar{\hat{\upsilon}}_{\cdot\cdot}$$

Observe that by definition $\sum_{i=1}^{n}\sum_{t=1}^{T}\hat{\varepsilon}_{it} = 0$.

STEP 2: We compute our bootstrap panel model as

$$y^*_{it} = x'_{it}\hat{\beta} + \varepsilon^*_{it},\ i = 1,\ldots,n; \quad t = 1,\ldots,T$$

and the bootstrap least squares estimator as

$$\hat{\beta}^* = \left(\sum_{t=1}^{T}\sum_{i=1}^{n}\breve{x}_{it}\breve{x}'_{it}\right)^{-1}\sum_{t=1}^{T}\sum_{i=1}^{n}\breve{x}_{it}\breve{y}^*_{it}$$

STEP 3: Obtain the least squares residuals

$$\hat{\upsilon}^*_{it} = \breve{y}^*_{it} - \breve{x}'_{it}\hat{\beta}^*, \quad i = 1, ..., n; \quad t = 1, ..., T$$

and then compute the bootstrap analogues of $\hat{U}_{T,n,r,u}$ and $\hat{U}'_{T,n,r,u}$ with $\hat{\upsilon}^*_{it}$ replacing $\hat{\upsilon}_{it}$ there. That is, for r, $u \in [0,1]$, we define

$$\hat{U}^*_{T,n,r,u} = \frac{1}{Tn}\sum_{t=1}^{[Tr]}\sum_{i=1}^{[nu]}\left(\hat{\upsilon}^*_{it} - \overline{\hat{\upsilon}^*}_{\cdot t} - \overline{\hat{\upsilon}^*}_{i\cdot} - \overline{\hat{\upsilon}^*}_{\cdot\cdot}\right)$$

$$\hat{U}^{*'}_{T,n,r,u} = \frac{1}{Tn}\sum_{t=1}^{[Tr]}\sum_{i=1}^{[nu]}\left(\hat{\upsilon}^*_{it} - \frac{\sum_{j=1}^{i-1}\hat{\upsilon}^*_{js}}{i-1} - \frac{\sum_{s=1}^{t-1}\hat{\upsilon}^*_{is}}{t-1} + \frac{\sum_{j=1}^{i-1}\sum_{s=1}^{t-1}\hat{\upsilon}^*_{js}}{(i-1)(t-1)}\right)$$

Theorem 6. Assuming $C1-C4$, under the maintained hypothesis, as T, $n \to \infty$,

$$(Tn)^{1/2}(\hat{\beta}^* - \hat{\beta}) \xrightarrow{d} \mathcal{N}(0, \sigma^2\Sigma^{-1}), \quad (\textit{in probability})$$

We then have the following result.

Theorem 7. Assuming $C1-C4$, under the maintained hypothesis as T, $n \to \infty$.we have that for any continuous functional $g(\cdot)$,

$$\textbf{(a)} \quad g\left(\hat{\sigma}^{*-1}\sqrt{Tn}\hat{U}^*_{T,n,r,u}\right) \overset{d}{\Rightarrow} g(B'(r,u)), \quad (\textit{in probability})$$

$$\textbf{(b)} \quad g\left(\hat{\sigma}^{*-1}\sqrt{Tn}\hat{U}^{*'}_{T,n,r,u}\right) \overset{d}{\Rightarrow} g(W(r,u)) \quad (\textit{in probability})$$

where

$$\hat{\sigma}^{*2} := \frac{1}{Tn}\sum_{t=1}^{T}\sum_{i=1}^{n}\left(\hat{\upsilon}^*_{it} - \overline{\hat{\upsilon}^*}_{\cdot t} - \overline{\hat{\upsilon}^*}_{i\cdot} - \overline{\hat{\upsilon}^*}_{\cdot\cdot}\right)^2$$

5. MONTE CARLO STUDY

We now present results of a small Monte Carlo study to shed some light on the finite sample performance of our tests based on the statistics $Q_{T,n,r,u}$, $Q'_{T,n,r,u}$, $U_{T,n,r,u}$ and $U'_{T,n,r,u}$. All throughout the study, the results reported are based on 1,000 iterations. The sample sizes used were $T,n=20,30,50$.

We will only present the results for model (1), as those for (2) are qualitatively the same. So, we consider Eq. (1) given by

$$y_{it}=\beta' x_{it}+m_i(t/T)+v_{it}, \quad i=1,...,n, \quad t=1,...,T$$

$$v_{it}=\mu_i+\varepsilon_{it}$$

where μ_i,$\sim N(0,1)$,$i=1,\ldots,\ n-1$ with $\mu_n=-\sum_{j=1}^{n-1}\mu_j$ and $m(t/T)$=2log$(1+(t/T)^2)$. Recall that under H_0 $m_i(t/T)$=$m(t/T)$. For ε_{it}, we consider *i.i.d.* standard normal random variable as is the case for the regressors x_{it} and $\beta=2$. In all the tables $\hat{Q}$ and $\hat{Q}'$ stands the test in Section 3 with $\mu_{i=0}$ and the sup norm. Similarly, $\hat{U}$ and $\hat{U}'$ are those with μ_i as defined above.

Table 2 reports the Monte Carlo size at the 10, 5 and 1% nominal size, whereas Tables 3–8 reports the power of the different tests.

Table 2 suggests that the sizes of the test based on the asymptotic distribution are pretty good even for small samples for those tests based on the statistics $\hat{Q}'$ and $\hat{U}'$. However, the finite sample performance of the tests based on Q and U are very poor, in particular when we compare it with the performance obtained with $\hat{Q}'$ and $\hat{U}'$. Due to its poor small sample

Table 2. Monte Carlo Size of 10, 5 and 1% Tests.

nT	Test Stat	Asymptotic Test			Bootstrap Test		
400	$\hat{Q}$	0.026	0.01	0.001	0.118	0.051	0.003
	$\hat{Q}'$	0.1	0.049	0.009	0.129	0.062	0.01
	$\hat{U}$	0.028	0.016	0.006	0.155	0.092	0.025
	$\hat{U}'$	0.109	0.067	0.02	0.132	0.088	0.018
900	$\hat{Q}$	0.032	0.014	0.002	0.071	0.031	0.006
	$\hat{Q}'$	0.067	0.033	0.003	0.075	0.033	0.002
	$\hat{U}$	0.025	0.013	0.004	0.113	0.052	0.007
	$\hat{U}'$	0.092	0.044	0.012	0.116	0.048	0.012
2,500	$\hat{Q}$	0.069	0.03	0.005	0.116	0.062	0.006
	$\hat{Q}'$	0.087	0.043	0.005	0.099	0.043	0.006
	$\hat{U}$	0.049	0.025	0.009	0.111	0.07	0.024
	$\hat{U}'$	0.101	0.051	0.012	0.118	0.06	0.009

Table 3. Monte Carlo Power of 10, 5 and 1% Tests, Setting A, $b=0.5n$.

nT	Test Stat	Asymptotic Test			Bootstrap Test		
400	$\hat{Q}$	1	1	1	1	1	1
	$\hat{Q}'$	1	1	1	1	1	1
	$\hat{U}$	1	1	1	1	1	1
	$\hat{U}'$	0.996	0.988	0.963	0.998	0.988	0.96
900	$\hat{Q}$	1	1	1	1	1	1
	$\hat{Q}'$	1	1	1	1	1	1
	$\hat{U}$	1	1	1	1	1	1
	$\hat{U}'$	1	1	1	1	1	0.999
2,500	$\hat{Q}$	1	1	1	1	1	1
	$\hat{Q}'$	1	1	1	1	1	1
	$\hat{U}$	1	1	1	1	1	1
	$\hat{U}'$	1	1	1	1	1	1

Table 4. Monte Carlo Power of 10, 5 and 1% Tests, setting A, $b=0.75n$.

nT	Test Stat	Asymptotic Test			Bootstrap Test		
400	$\hat{Q}$	1	1	1	1	1	1
	$\hat{Q}'$	0.982	0.962	0.872	0.99	0.975	0.904
	$\hat{U}$	1	1	0.999	1	1	1
	$\hat{U}'$	0.806	0.72	0.52	0.817	0.723	0.547
900	$\hat{Q}$	1	1	1	1	1	1
	$\hat{Q}'$	1	1	1	1	1	1
	$\hat{U}$	1	1	1	1	1	1
	$\hat{U}'$	0.992	0.98	0.926	0.996	0.985	0.904
2,500	$\hat{Q}$	1	1	1	1	1	1
	$\hat{Q}'$	1	1	1	1	1	1
	$\hat{U}$	1	1	1	1	1	1
	$\hat{U}'$	1	1	1	1	1	1

performance, we decided to employ bootstrap methods to see if we can improve it. The table suggests that bootstrap test definitely improves the finite sample performance, being now tests based on, say, $\hat{Q}$ or $\hat{Q}'$ very similar on their behaviour.

Our next experiment deals with the power of the tests. We have considered four different settings of heterogeneity in the trend function m_i.

Setting A (single break point). Let b denote the break point, for which values $0.5n$ and $0.75n$ were tried. For $i=1,\ldots, b$, we set $m(t/T)=0$ for $t=1,\ldots, T/2$ and $m(t/T)=-1$ for $t=1+T/2,\ldots, T$. For $i=b+1,\ldots, n$, we set $m(t/T)=2\log(1+(t/T)^2)$, which ranges from 0 to around 1.4. Tables 3–4

Table 5. Monte Carlo Power of 10, 5 and 1% tests, setting B.

nT	Test Stat	Asymptotic Test			Bootstrap Test		
400	$\hat{Q}$	1	1	0.979	1	1	0.995
	$\hat{Q}'$	0.99	0.972	0.875	0.997	0.978	0.839
	$\hat{U}$	0.993	0.972	0.86	1	1	0.971
	$\hat{U}'$	0.86	0.772	0.543	0.873	0.789	0.503
900	$\hat{Q}$	1	1	1	1	1	1
	$\hat{Q}'$	1	1	1	1	1	1
	$\hat{U}$	1	1	1	1	1	1
	$\hat{U}'$	0.99	0.971	0.902	0.993	0.976	0.918
2,500	$\hat{Q}$	1	1	1	1	1	1
	$\hat{Q}'$	1	1	1	1	1	1
	$\hat{U}$	1	1	1	1	1	1
	$\hat{U}'$	1	1	1	1	1	1

Table 6. Monte Carlo Power of 10, 5 and 1% tests, setting C, $b=0.5n$.

nT	Test Stat	Asymptotic Test			Bootstrap Test		
400	$\hat{Q}$	1	1	1	1	1	1
	$\hat{Q}'$	1	1	1	1	1	1
	$\hat{U}$	0.997	0.99	0.972	1	0.999	0.997
	$\hat{U}'$	0.943	0.894	0.746	0.953	0.912	0.72
900	$\hat{Q}$	1	1	1	1	1	1
	$\hat{Q}'$	1	1	1	1	1	1
	$\hat{U}$	1	1	1	1	1	1
	$\hat{U}'$	0.999	0.999	0.99	0.999	0.998	0.985
2,500	$\hat{Q}$	1	1	1	1	1	1
	$\hat{Q}'$	1	1	1	1	1	1
	$\hat{U}$	1	1	1	1	1	1
	$\hat{U}'$	1	1	1	1	1	1

report the Monte Carlo power of the 10%, 5% and 1% tests under this setting.

Setting B (three break points). Let $b_1=0.25n, b_2=0.5n, b_3=0.75n$ be three break points. For $i=1,\dots, b_1$ and $i=b_2+1,\dots, b_3$, we set $m(t/T)=0$ for $t=1,\dots, T/2$ and $m(t/T)=-1$ for $t=1,\dots, T/2,\dots, T$. For $i=b_1+1,\dots, b_2$ and $i=b_3+1,\dots, n$, we let $m(t/T)=2\log(1+(t/T)^2)$. Table 5 reports the Monte Carlo power of the 10, 5 and 1% tests under this setting.

Setting C (single break point with linear trend functions). Let b denote the break point, for which values $0.5n$ and $0.75n$ were tried. For $i=1,\dots, b$, we

Table 7. Monte Carlo Power of 10, 5 and 1% Tests, Setting C, $b = 0.75n$.

nT	Test Stat	Asymptotic Test			Bootstrap Test		
400	$\hat{Q}$	1	1	1	1	1	1
	$\hat{Q}'$	1	1	1	1	1	1
	$\hat{U}$	0.945	0.897	0.718	0.991	0.982	0.916
	$\hat{U}'$	0.582	0.467	0.265	0.59	0.461	0.292
900	$\hat{Q}$	1	1	1	1	1	1
	$\hat{Q}'$	1	1	1	1	1	1
	$\hat{U}$	1	1	0.999	1	1	1
	$\hat{U}'$	0.891	0.822	0.637	0.902	0.834	0.57
2,500	$\hat{Q}$	1	1	1	1	1	1
	$\hat{Q}'$	1	1	1	1	1	1
	$\hat{U}$	1	1	1	1	1	1
	$\hat{U}'$	1	1	0.995	1	1	0.995

Table 8. Monte Carlo Power of 10, 5 and 1% Tests, Setting D.

nT	Test Stat	Asymptotic Test			Bootstrap Test		
400	$\hat{Q}$	0.152	0.071	0.012	0.39	0.182	0.045
	$\hat{Q}'$	0.493	0.323	0.096	0.52	0.362	0.135
	$\hat{U}$	0.084	0.033	0.008	0.354	0.182	0.024
	$\hat{U}'$	0.3	0.209	0.055	0.332	0.212	0.045
900	$\hat{Q}$	0.999	0.985	0.88	1	1	0.951
	$\hat{Q}'$	0.965	0.921	0.756	0.974	0.936	0.766
	$\hat{U}$	0.937	0.872	0.7	0.995	0.983	0.894
	$\hat{U}'$	0.738	0.608	0.371	0.751	0.638	0.412
2,500	$\hat{Q}$	1	1	0.999	1	1	1
	$\hat{Q}'$	1	1	0.996	1	1	0.999
	$\hat{U}$	1	0.998	0.947	1	1	0.996
	$\hat{U}'$	0.98	0.933	0.75	0.986	0.953	0.839

set $m(t/T) = 1 + t/T$, while for $i = b+1, \ldots, n$, we set $m(t/T) = 2 + 2t/T$. Tables 6–7 report the Monte Carlo power of the 10, 5 and 1% tests under this setting.

In Settings A and B above, the ordering of the i index was such that the break points neatly divide the sample into subgroups of the same trend functions. However, it is plausible in the real data that the ordering of i index is not so informative. This motivated us to consider the following setting.

Setting D (random permutation). For $i = 1, \ldots, n/2$, we set $m(t/T) = 0$ for $t = 1, \ldots, T/2$ and $m(t/T) = -1$ for $t = 1 + T/2, \ldots, T$, while for $i = 1 + n/2, \ldots, n$, we let $m(t/T)=2\log(1+(t/T)^2)$. After data has been generated, the i index was shuffled using random permutation. Table 8 reports the Monte Carlo power of the 10, 5 and 1% tests under this setting.

Across all settings, the Monte Carlo power results seem broadly similar between tests based on asymptotic and bootstrap critical values. Also, as with the size results, the presence of regressor and the resulting need for the first stage estimation of the parameter β has not much altered the Monte Carlo power results between the simple and partial linear models. The results improved with increasing sample sizes and the reported Monte Carlo powers were close to 1 at $T,n=50$ in all settings.

For both settings A and C which use a single break point, power performance was better when the break was at $0.5n$ compared to when it was $0.75n$. This is to be expected, since the former break point represents a further deviation away from the null of common trends/homogeneity than the latter.

For settings A, B and C in which the ordering of the i index is preserved, the worst power results were obtained by the $\hat{U}'$ statistic under the presence of individual fixed effects.

In Setting D, where the ordering of the i index was disturbed, the Monte Carlo results differ between particular realizations of the random permutation of i index and the ones reported in the tables appear to be quite standard. Monte Carlo power results are poorer for this setting when compared to others, highlighting the effect of the ordering of i index on our test statistics. It is encouraging that the power results improve considerably as the sample size increases even in this setting.

6. CONCLUSIONS

In this paper we have described and examined a simple test for common trends of unspecified functional form as the number of individuals increases. We were able to perform the test without resorting to nonparametric estimation techniques so that we avoid the uneasy issue of how to choose a bandwidth parameter in a testing procedure like ours. We have allowed the panel regression model to have covariates entering in a linear form. We discuss the consequences that the estimation of the slope parameters may have in the asymptotic behaviour of the test, finding that there were no consequences, so that the asymptotic behaviour of the test is not altered by the estimation of the parameters.

There are several interesting issues worth examining as those already mentioned in the introduction. One of them is how we can extend this methodology to the situation where the sample sizes T_i for the different sequences of individual units $i = 1, \ldots, n$, are not necessarily the same. We believe that the methodology in the paper can be implemented after some smoothing has been put in place, for instance, via splines. A second relevant extension is what happens when the errors exhibit cross-sectional and/or time dependence. We conjecture that, after inspection of our proofs, the main conclusions of our results will still hold true if they are 'weakly' dependent. However, the technical details to accomplish this and in particular those to obtain a consistent estimator of the asymptotic variance might be cumbersome and lengthy. We envisage, though, that it is possible to obtain a simple computational estimator of the long run variance of the test via bootstrap methods using results given in Section 3, together with those obtained by Chan and Ogden (2009). However the details are beyond the scope of this paper.

ACKNOWLEDGMENT

We thank for the comments of a referee which have led to a clearer version of the manuscript. Of course, any remaining errors are our sole responsibility.

REFERENCES

Atak, A., Linton, O., & Xiao, Z. (2011). A semiparametric panel model for unbalanced data with application to climate change in the United Kingdom. *Journal of Econometrics*, *164*, 92–115.

Baltagi, B., Hidalgo, J., & Li, Q. (1996). A nonparametric test for poolability using panel data. *Journal of Econometrics*, *75*, 345–367.

Bickel, P. J., & Wichura, M. J. (1971). Convergence criteria for multiparameter stochastic processes and some applications. *Annals of Mathematical Statistics*, *42*, 1656–1670.

Breitung, J., & Pesaran, M. H. (2008). Unit roots and cointegration in panels. In L. Matyas & P. Sevestre (Eds.), *The econometrics of panel data* (3rd ed., pp. 279–322). Berlin: Springer.

Brown, R. L., Durbin, J., & Evans, J. M. (1975). Techniques for testing the constancy of regression relationships over time. *Journal of Royal Statistical Society, Series B*, *37*, 149–192.

Bryan, M. L., & Jenkins, S. P. (2013). *Regression analysis of country effects using multilevel data: A cautionary tale*. Mimeo, Institute for Social and Economic Research.

Chang, C., & Ogden, R. D. (2009). Bootstrapping sums of independent but not identically distributed continuous processes with applications to functional data. *Journal of Multivariate Analysis*, *100*, 1291–1303.

Degras, D., Xu, Z., Zhang, T., & Wu, W. B. (2012). Testing for parallelism among trends in multiple time series. *IEEE Transactions on Signal Processing*, *60*, 1087–1097.

Detter, H., & Paparoditis, E. (2009). Bootstrapping frequency domain tests in multivariate time series with an application to testing equality of spectral densities. *Journal of Royal Statistical Society, Series B*, *71*, 831–857.

Efron, B. (1979). Bootstrap methods: Another look at the jackknife. *Annals of Statistics*, *7*, 1–26.

Ferraty, F., & Vieu, P. (2006). *Nonparametric functional data analysis: Theory and practice*. Berlin: Springer-Verlag.

Galvao, A. F., & Kato, K. (2014). Estimation and inference for linear panel data models under misspeci.cation when both n and T are large. *Journal of Business and Economic Statistics*, *32*, 285–309.

Gao, J., & Hawthorne, K. (2006). Semiparametric estimation and testing of the trend of temperature series. *The Econometrics Journal*, *9*, 332–355.

Hidalgo, J., & Souza, P. (2013). Testing for equality of an increasing number of spectral density functions. *Econometrics* (Forthcoming).

Hsiao, C. (1986). *Analysis of panel data*. New York, NY: Cambridge University Press.

Jin, S., & Su, L. (2010). *A nonparametric poolability test for panel data models with cross section dependence*. Mimeo, Singapore Management University.

Pesaran, M. H., & Yamagata, T. (2008). Testing slope heterogeneity in large panels. *Journal of Econometrics*, *142*, 50–93.

Phillips, P. C. B. (2001). Trending time series and macroeconomic activity: Some present and future challenges. *Journal of Econometrics*, *100*, 21–27.

Phillips, P. C. B., & Sul, D. (2007). Transition modeling and econometric convergence tests. *Econometrica*, *75*, 1771–1855.

Phillips, P. C. B., & Moon, R. (1999). Linear regression limit theory for nonstationary panel data. *Econometrica*, *67*, 1057–1111.

Robinson, P. M. (2011a). Asymptotic theory for nonparametric regression with spatial data. *Journal of Econometrics*, *165*, 5–19.

Robinson, P. M. (2011b). *Inference on power law spatial trends*. STICERD Working Paper (Preprint). London School of Economics.

Shao, J., & Tu, D. (1995). *The jackknife and bootstrap*. Berlin: Springer-Verlag.

White, H., & Granger, C. (2011). Consideration of trends in time series. *Journal of Time Series Econometrics*, *3*, 1–40.

Zhang, Y., Su, L., & Phillips, P. C. B. (2012). Testing for common trends in semiparametric panel data models with fixed effects. *Econometrics Journal*, *15*, 56–100.

APPENDIX

Proof of Theorem 1

Proof. We first notice that under H_0, we have that

$$\textbf{(a)} \quad Q_{T,n,r,u} = \frac{1}{Tn} \sum_{t=1}^{[Tr]} \sum_{i=1}^{[nu]} (\varepsilon_{it} - \overline{\varepsilon}_{\cdot t})$$

$$\textbf{(b)} \quad Q'_{T,n,r,u} = \frac{1}{Tn} \sum_{t=1}^{[Tr]} \sum_{i=2}^{[nu]} \left(\varepsilon_{it} - \frac{1}{i-1} \sum_{j=1}^{i-1} \varepsilon_{jt} \right), \quad r, u \in [0, 1]$$

We begin with part **(b)**. To show weak convergence in Eq. (9) we need to establish convergence of finite dimensional distributions and tightness. To that end, we first we establish that as $T,n \to \infty$,

$$E((Tn) Q'_{T,n,r_1,u_1} Q'_{T,n,r_2,u_2}) \to \sigma^2 (r_1 \wedge r_2)(u_1 \wedge u_2) \tag{A.1}$$

Denoting

$$z_{it} = : \varepsilon_{it} - \frac{1}{i-1} \sum_{j=1}^{i-1} \varepsilon_{jt} \tag{A.2}$$

we have

$$\sqrt{Tn} Q'_{T,n,r,u} = \sum_{t=1}^{[Tr]} \sum_{i=2}^{[nu]} z_{it}$$

Now, $C1$ and standard arguments imply that

$$E\{z_{i_1 t} z_{i_2 s}\} = 0 \tag{A.3}$$

if $i_1 \neq i_2$ and $t = s$. So, we have that

$$E\left(\sum_{t=1}^{[Tr_1]} \sum_{i=2}^{[nu_1]} z_{it} \sum_{t=1}^{[Tr_2]} \sum_{i=2}^{[nu_2]} z_{it} \right) = \sum_{t=1}^{[T(r_1 \wedge r_2)]} \sum_{i=2}^{[n(u_1 \wedge u_2)]} E(z_{it}^2)$$
$$\to \sigma^2 (r_1 \wedge r_2)(u_1 \wedge u_2)$$

which completes the proof of Eq. (A.1).

Next, we establish that the finite dimensional distributions (fidi) of $Q'_{T,n,r,u}$ converge to those of $\sigma W(r,u)$. As usual because the Cramer–Wold device, we only need to show the convergence in distribution of

$$\sqrt{Tn}Q'_{T,n,r,u} \xrightarrow{d} \sigma W(r,u), \quad r,u \in [0,1]$$

for any fixed r and u. We have already shown in Eq. (A.1) that $Var\left(\sqrt{Tn}Q'_{T,n,r,u}\right) \to \sigma^2 ru$. On the other hand, it is well-known that for any fixed t,

$$Z_{nt} = \frac{1}{\sqrt{n}} \sum_{i=2}^{[nu]} z_{it} \xrightarrow{d} \mathcal{N}(0,\sigma^2 u)$$

and as Z_{nt} and Z_{ns} are independent by $C1$, we conclude that

$$\frac{1}{\sqrt{T}} \sum_{t=1}^{[Tr]} Z_{nt} \xrightarrow{d} \mathcal{N}\left(0,\sigma^2 ur\right)$$

So, we have established the CLT when we take sequentially the limits in n and then in T. However, we need to show that this is the case when they are taken jointly. To that end, it suffices to verify that Z_{nt} satisfy the generalized Lindeberg–Feller condition: for any $\eta > 0$, as $T,n \to \infty$,

$$q_T(r) : = \sum_{t=1}^{[Tr]} E(Z_{nt}^2 I(|Z_{nt}| \geq \eta)) \to 0$$

see Theorem 2 in Phillips and Moon (1999), being a sufficient condition

$$E(Z_{nt}^4) = E\left(\frac{1}{\sqrt{n}} \sum_{i=2}^{[nu]} z_{it}\right)^4 \leq C \tag{A.4}$$

Proceeding as we did to show Eq. (A.1),

$$E(Z_{nt}^4) = \frac{3}{n^2}\left(\sum_{i=2}^{[nu]} Ez_{it}^2\right)^2 + \frac{1}{n^2}\sum_{i_1,\ldots,i_4=2}^{[nu]} cum(z_{i_1t}, z_{i_2t}, z_{i_3t}, z_{i_4t})$$

$$= 3\sigma^4(1+o(1)) + \frac{1}{n^2}\sum_{i_1,\ldots,i_4=2}^{[nu]} cum(\varepsilon_{i_1t}, \ldots, \varepsilon_{i_4t})$$

$$+ \frac{1}{n^2}\sum_{i_1,\ldots,i_4=2}^{[nu]} \frac{1}{\prod_{l=1}^{4} i_\ell - 1} cum\left(\sum_{j=1}^{i_1-1}\varepsilon_{jt}, \ldots, \sum_{j=1}^{i_4-1}\varepsilon_{jt}\right)$$

$$= 3\sigma^4 u^2 + O\left(\frac{\log^3 n}{n}\right)$$

So the sufficient condition (A.4) holds true and hence $\sqrt{Tn}Q'_{T,n,r,u} \xrightarrow{d} \sigma W(r,u)$.

To complete the proof of part **(b)**, we need to show tightness. For that purpose, define an *increment* of $Q'_{T,n,r,u}$ as follows. For $0 \le r_1 \le r_2 \le 1$ and $0 \le u_1 \le u_2 \le 1$,

$$\Delta'_{r_1,u_1,r_2,u_2} := \frac{1}{Tn}\sum_{t=[Tr_1]+1}^{[Tr_2]}\sum_{i=[nu_1]+1}^{[nu_2]} z_{it}$$

A sufficient condition for tightness, see Bickel and Wichura (1971), is

$$E((Tn)^2|\Delta'_{r_1,u_1,r_2,u_2}|^4) \le C\left(\frac{[Tr_2]-[Tr_1]}{T}\right)^2\left(\frac{[nu_2]-[nu_1]}{n}\right)^2 \tag{A.5}$$

where we can assume that $n^{-1} \le u_2 - u_2$ and $T^{-1} \le r_2 - r_1$ since otherwise the inequality in Eq. (A.5) would hold trivially. Now, proceeding as we did with Eq. (A.1), we have that the left side of Eq. (A.5) is

$$\frac{3}{T^2n^2}\left(\sum_{t=[Tr_1]+1}^{[Tr_2]}\sum_{i=[nu_1]+1}^{[nu_2]} Ez_{it}^2\right)^2 + \frac{1}{T^2n^2}\sum_{t_1,\ldots,t_4=[Tr_1]+1}^{[Tr_2]}\sum_{i_1,\ldots,i_4=[nu_1]+1}^{[nu_2]} cum(z_{i_1t_1}, z_{i_2t_2}, z_{i_3t_3}, z_{i_4t_4}) \tag{A.6}$$

By $C1$, we have that $cum(z_{i_1t}, z_{i_2t}, z_{i_3t}, z_{i_4t}) \neq 0$ only if $t_1 = \ldots = t_4$, so that the second term of Eq. (A.6) is

$$\frac{1}{T^2n^2}\sum_{t=[Tr_1]+1}^{[Tr_2]}\sum_{i_1,\ldots,i_4=[nu_1]+1}^{[nu_2]} cum(z_{i_1t}, z_{i_2t}, z_{i_3t}, z_{i_4t})$$

$$\leq C\left(\frac{[Tr_2]-[Tr_1]}{T}\right)^2\left\{\frac{1}{n^2}\sum_{i_1,\ldots,i_4=2}^{[nu]} cum(\varepsilon_{i_1t},\ldots,\varepsilon_{i_4t})\right.$$

$$\left.+\frac{1}{n^2}\sum_{i_1,\ldots,i_4=2}^{[nu]}\frac{1}{\prod_{l=1}^{4} i_\ell - 1} cum\left(\sum_{j=1}^{i_1-1}\varepsilon_{jt},\ldots,\sum_{j=1}^{i_4-1}\varepsilon_{jt}\right)\right\}$$

$$\leq C\left(\frac{[Tr_2]-[Tr_1]}{T}\right)^2\left(\frac{[nu_2]-[nu_1]}{n}\right)^2$$

On the other hand, the first term of Eq. (A.6) is also bounded by the far right side of the last displayed inequality. So this concludes the proof of the tightness condition and so part **(b)** of the theorem.

We now look at part **(a)**. The proof of part **(a)** proceeds similarly, if it is not easier, to that given in part **(b)** once we observe that

$$\begin{aligned}\sqrt{Tn}Q_{T,n,r,u} &= \frac{1}{\sqrt{Tn}}\sum_{t=1}^{[Tr]}\sum_{i=1}^{[un]}\left(\varepsilon_{it}-\frac{1}{n}\sum_{j=1}^{n}\varepsilon_{jt}\right)\\ &= \frac{1}{\sqrt{Tn}}\sum_{t=1}^{[Tr]}\sum_{i=1}^{[nu]}\varepsilon_{it} - u\frac{1}{\sqrt{Tn}}\sum_{t=1}^{[Tr]}\sum_{i=1}^{n}\varepsilon_{it}\end{aligned} \tag{A.7}$$

so that it is omitted. ■

Proof of Theorem 2

Proof. As in the proof of Theorem 1, we only handled explicitly part **(b)**, the proof of part **(a)** being similarly handled. Using Eq. (A.2) and then that

$$w_{it} = z_{it} - \frac{1}{t-1}\sum_{s=1}^{t-1} z_{is} \tag{A.8}$$

the notation given in the proof of Theorem 1, we have that

$$U'_{T,n,r,u} = \frac{1}{Tn}\sum_{t=2}^{[Tr]}\sum_{i=2}^{[nu]} w_{it}$$

Before we look at the structure of the second moments of $U'_{T,n,r,u}$, it is worth emphasizing that if $t \neq s$ for all i,j $E(w_{it}w_{js})=0$. Bearing this in mind together with Eq. (A.3), we then have

$$E\left(\sum_{t=1}^{[Tr_1]}\sum_{i=2}^{[nu_1]} w_{it} \sum_{t=1}^{[Tr_2]}\sum_{i=2}^{[nu_2]} w_{it}\right) = \sum_{t=1}^{[T(r_1\wedge r_2)]}\sum_{i=2}^{[n(u_1\wedge u_2)]} E(w_{it}^2)$$
$$\to \sigma^2(r_1\wedge r_2)(u_1\wedge u_2)$$

because by definition of w_{it} and $C1$, $E(w_{it}^2) = Ez_{it}^2(t/(t-1))$

Next, we examine the convergence in distribution of

$$\sqrt{Tn}U'_{T,n,r,u} = \frac{1}{\sqrt{Tn}}\sum_{t=2}^{[rT]}\sum_{i=2}^{[un]} w_{it}$$

As we argued in the proof of Theorem 1, for any fixed t, we have that

$$\frac{1}{\sqrt{n}}\sum_{i=2}^{[nu]} w_{it} \xrightarrow{d} \mathcal{N}\left(0,\sigma^2\left(1+\frac{1}{t-1}\right)u\right)$$

From here we obtain that

$$\frac{1}{\sqrt{T}}\sum_{t=2}^{[Tr]}\frac{1}{\sqrt{n}}\sum_{i=2}^{[nu]} w_{it} \xrightarrow{d} \mathcal{N}(0,\sigma^2 ru) \tag{A.9}$$

since the sequence $\frac{1}{\sqrt{n}}\sum_{i=2}^{[un]} w_{it}$ are independent in t by $C1$. However, we need to show that Eq. (A.9) also holds when the limit in n and T is taken jointly. To that end it suffices to show that

$$E\left(\frac{1}{\sqrt{n}}\sum_{i=2}^{[nu]} w_{it}\right)^4 \leq C$$

but the left side of the last displayed expression is

$$\begin{aligned}
&\frac{3}{n^2}\left(\sum_{i=2}^{[nu]} Ew_{it}^2\right)^2 + \frac{1}{n^2}\sum_{i_1,\ldots,i_4=2}^{[u_2n]} cum(w_{i_1t}, w_{i_2t}, w_{i_3t}, w_{i_4t}) \\
&= 3\sigma^4(1+o(1)) + \frac{1}{n^2}\sum_{i_1,\ldots,i_4=2}^{[nu]} cum(z_{i_1t},\ldots,z_{i_4t}) \\
&\quad + \frac{1}{n^2}\sum_{i_1,\ldots,i_4=2}^{[nu]} \frac{1}{\prod_{l=1}^{4} i_\ell - 1} cum\left(\sum_{j=1}^{i_1-1} z_{jt},\ldots,\sum_{j=1}^{i_4-1} z_{jt}\right) \\
&= 3\sigma^4u^2 + O\left(\frac{\log^3 n}{n}\right)
\end{aligned}$$

So, we conclude that Eq. (A.9) also holds when the limits are taking jointly.

To finish the proof it remains to verify the tightness condition of

$$\sqrt{Tn}U'_{T,n,r,u} = \frac{1}{\sqrt{Tn}}\sum_{t=2}^{[rT]}\sum_{i=2}^{[un]} w_{it}$$

To that end, and proceeding as in the proof of Theorem 1, it is enough to show that for $0 \leq r_1 \leq r_2 \leq 1$ and $0 \leq u_1 \leq u_2 \leq 1$,

$$\Delta'_{r_1,u_1,r_2,u_2} := \frac{1}{Tn}\sum_{t=[r_1T]+1}^{[r_2T]}\sum_{i=[u_1n]+1}^{[u_2n]} w_{it}$$

satisfies Eq. (A.5). The proof is essentially the same as that given for Eq. (A.5), that is Eq. (A.6), but with the obvious changes and so is omitted. This completes the proof of part **(b)**. The proof of part **(a)** is essentially the same as, if not easier than, that of part **(b)**, once we notice that

$$\begin{aligned}\sqrt{Tn}U_{T,n,r,u} &= \frac{1}{\sqrt{Tn}}\sum_{t=1}^{[Tr]}\sum_{i=1}^{[nu]}\left(z_{it} - \frac{1}{T}\sum_{s=1}^{T} z_{jt}\right)\\ &= \frac{1}{\sqrt{Tn}}\sum_{t=1}^{[Tr]}\sum_{i=1}^{[nu]}\varepsilon_{it} - u\frac{1}{\sqrt{Tn}}\sum_{t=1}^{[Tr]}\sum_{i=1}^{n}\varepsilon_{it}\\ &\quad - r\frac{1}{\sqrt{Tn}}\sum_{t=1}^{T}\sum_{i=1}^{[nu]}\varepsilon_{it} + ru\frac{1}{\sqrt{Tn}}\sum_{t=1}^{T}\sum_{i=1}^{n}\varepsilon_{it},\end{aligned}$$

and hence is omitted. ■

Proof of Theorem 3

Proof. The proof is quite standard after using Phillips and Moon (1999) results. First standard arguments indicate that

$$\frac{1}{nT}\sum_{i=1}^{n}\sum_{t=1}^{T}\breve{x}_{it}\breve{x}_{it}' \overset{P}{\to} \Sigma$$

Indeed this is the case because by $C3$, $(x_{it}-\varkappa_i)(x_{it}-\varkappa_i)'$ are i.i.d. sequences of random variables with finite second moments.

Next,

$$\begin{aligned}\frac{1}{(nT)^{1/2}}\sum_{i=1}^{n}\sum_{t=1}^{T}\breve{x}_{it}\varepsilon_{it} &= \frac{1}{(nT)^{1/2}}\sum_{i=1}^{n}\sum_{t=1}^{T}x_{it}\varepsilon_{it}\\ &\quad - \frac{1}{(nT)^{1/2}}\sum_{i=1}^{n}\sum_{t=1}^{T}\left(\frac{1}{T}\sum_{s=1}^{T}x_{is}\right)\varepsilon_{it}\{\overline{x}_{i\cdot} + \overline{x}_{\cdot t} - \overline{x}_{\cdot\cdot}\}\end{aligned}$$

where we have assumed that $\varkappa_i=0$ as the left side of the last displayed equality is invariant to the value of $\varkappa_i$. It is clear that the asymptotic behaviour of the left side of the last displayed equality is given by that of

$$\frac{1}{(nT)^{1/2}}\sum_{i=1}^{n}\sum_{t=1}^{T}x_{it}\varepsilon_{it} \tag{A.10}$$

To show that Eq. (A.10) converges in distribution to a normal random variable we employ Theorem 2 of Phillips and Moon (1999). But,

$$E\left(\frac{1}{T^{1/2}}\sum_{t=1}^{T}x_{it}\varepsilon_{is}\right)^4 \leq C$$

by $C1$, $C3$ and standard results. This concludes the proof of the theorem.■

Proof of Theorem 4

Proof. First by definition, we have that

$$\hat{U}'_{T,n,r,u}=\frac{1}{Tn}\sum_{t=1}^{[Tr]}\sum_{i=1}^{[nu]}\breve{\varepsilon}_{it}-(\hat{\beta}-\beta)'\frac{1}{Tn}\sum_{t=1}^{[Tr]}\sum_{i=1}^{[nu]}\breve{x}_{it}$$

So compared to what we had in the case of no regressors x_{it}, we have now the extra term $(\hat{\beta}-\beta)'\frac{1}{Tn}\sum_{t=1}^{[Tr]}\sum_{i=1}^{[nu]}\breve{x}_{it}$. But, as we can consider the situation where $E(x_{it})=\varkappa_i\equiv 0$ without loss of generality as $E\breve{x}_{it}=0$, we can easily conclude that

$$\sup_{r,u\in[0,1]}\left|\frac{1}{Tn}\sum_{t=1}^{[Tr]}\sum_{i=1}^{[nu]}\breve{x}_{it}\right|=o_p(1) \tag{A.11}$$

Indeed this is the case because for each $r,u\in[0,1]$ we have

$$\breve{\mathbb{X}}_{nT}(r,u)=:\frac{1}{Tn}\sum_{t=1}^{[Tr]}\sum_{i=1}^{[nu]}\breve{x}_{it}=o_p(1)$$

by ergodicity. On the other hand, the tightness condition of $\breve{\mathbb{X}}_{nT}(r,u)$ proceeds as that in Theorem 3. Thus, we conclude that

$$\hat{U}'_{T,n,r,u} = \frac{1}{Tn}\sum_{t=1}^{[Tr]}\sum_{i=1}^{[nu]}\breve{\varepsilon}_{it} + o_p((Tn)^{-1/2})$$

uniformly in $r,u \in [0,1]$, because by Theorem 4, $\hat{\beta}-\beta = O_p((Tn)^{-1/2})$. From here the proof of the theorem follows in a straightforward fashion. ■

Proof of Theorem 5

Proof. As we have done with the results in Theorems 1 and 3, we shall explicitly deal with the proof of part **(b)**, part **(a)** being similarly handled. To that end, we first notice that we still have that $(Tn)^{1/2}(\hat{\beta}-\beta) \to_d \mathcal{N}(0,\sigma^2\Sigma^{-1})$. Next, proceeding as in the proof of Theorem 4, and using the notation in Eqs. (A.2) and (A.8), we have that

$$\hat{U}'_{T,n,r,u} = \frac{1}{Tn}\sum_{t=1}^{[Tr]}\sum_{i=2}^{[nu]} w_{it} + o_p((Tn)^{-1/2})$$

uniformly in $r,u \in [0,1]$. However $C5$ will yield to the fact that, say $E(z_{it}z_{jt})$ can be different than zero even when $i \neq j$. Indeed for, standard algebra gives that

$$E(z_{it}z_{jt}) = \begin{cases} \sigma_i^2 + \dfrac{1}{(i-1)^2}\displaystyle\sum_{\ell=1}^{i-1}\sigma_\ell^2 & i=j \\ -\dfrac{1}{(ij)_+ - 1}\left(\sigma^2_{(ij)_-} - \dfrac{1}{(ij)_- - 1}\displaystyle\sum_{\ell=1}^{(ij)_- - 1}\sigma_\ell^2\right) & i \neq j \end{cases} \tag{A.12}$$

using the notation $(ij)_- = i \wedge j$ and $(ij)_+ = i \vee j$. On the other hand,

$$E(w_{it}w_{is}) = 0 \quad \text{if} \quad s \neq t \tag{A.13}$$

So, the latter two displayed expressions indicate that the covariance structure of $(Tn)^{1/2}\hat{U}'_{T,n,r,u}$ differs from when the second moments of ε_{it} are the same. Due to this, we now proceed to characterize the covariance structure of $(Tn)^{1/2}\hat{U}'_{T,n,r,u}$, that is

$$\frac{1}{Tn}E\left(\sum_{t=1}^{[Tr_1]}\sum_{i=2}^{[nu_1]} w_{it}\sum_{t=1}^{[Tr_2]}\sum_{i=2}^{[nu_2]} w_{it}\right) = \frac{1}{Tn}\sum_{t=1}^{[T(r_1\wedge r_2)]}\sum_{i=2}^{[nu_1]}\sum_{j=2}^{[nu_2]} E(w_{it}w_{jt}) \tag{A.14}$$

by Eq. (A.13). Now,

$$\begin{aligned} E(w_{it}w_{jt}) &= E\left\{\left(z_{it} - \frac{1}{t-1}\sum_{s=1}^{t-1} z_{is}\right)\left(z_{jt} - \frac{1}{t-1}\sum_{s=1}^{t-1} z_{js}\right)\right\} \\ &= E(z_{it}z_{jt}) + \frac{1}{(t-1)^2}\sum_{s=1}^{t-1} E(z_{is}z_{js}) \end{aligned}$$

because by $C1$, $E(z_{it}z_{js}) = 0$ if $t \neq s$. So, the right side of Eq. (A.14) is

$$\begin{aligned} &\frac{1}{Tn}\sum_{t=1}^{[T(r_1\wedge r_2)]}\sum_{i=2}^{[nu_1]}\sum_{j=1}^{[nu_2]}\left\{E(z_{it}z_{jt}) + \frac{1}{(t-1)^2}\sum_{s=1}^{t-1} E(z_{is}z_{js})\right\} \\ &= \frac{1}{Tn}\sum_{t=1}^{[T(r_1\wedge r_2)]}\sum_{i=2}^{[n(u_1\wedge u_2)]}\left\{Ez_{it}^2 + \frac{1}{(t-1)^2}\sum_{s=1}^{t-1} Ez_{is}^2\right\} \\ &\quad + \frac{1}{Tn}\sum_{t=1}^{[T(r_1\wedge r_2)]}\sum_{i=2}^{[nu_1]}\sum_{j\neq i}^{[nu_2]}\left\{E(z_{it}z_{jt}) + \frac{1}{(t-1)^2}\sum_{s=1}^{t-1} E(z_{is}z_{js})\right\} \end{aligned} \tag{A.15}$$

Now because Eq. (A.12), $\frac{1}{t-1}\sum_{s=1}^{t-1} Ez_{is}^2 \leq C$ and standard algebra gives that the first term on the right of Eq. (A.15) is

$$(r_1\wedge r_2)\frac{1}{n}\sum_{i=2}^{[n(u_1\wedge u_2)]} \sigma_i^2\left(1 + O\left(\frac{\log n}{n} + \frac{\log T}{T}\right)\right)$$

by Eq. (A.12). On the other hand, Eq. (A.12) implies that the contribution due to

$$\frac{1}{(t-1)^2}\sum_{s=1}^{t-1} E(z_{is}z_{js})$$

into the second term on the right of Eq. (A.15) is $O\left(\frac{\log n \log T}{T}\right)$, so that the behaviour of second term on the right of Eq. (A.15) is given by that of

$$\frac{1}{Tn}\sum_{t=1}^{[T(r_1\wedge r_2)]}\sum_{i=2}^{[nu_1]}\sum_{j\neq i}^{[nu_2]} E(z_{it}z_{jt})$$
$$= -(r_1\wedge r_2)\frac{1}{n}\sum_{i=2}^{[nu_1]}\sum_{j\neq i}^{[nu_2]}\left\{\frac{1}{(ij)_+ - 1}\left(\sigma^2_{(ij)_-} - \frac{1}{(ij)_- - 1}\sum_{\ell=1}^{(ij)_- - 1}\sigma^2_\ell\right)\right\}$$

Hence we conclude that the right side of Eq. (A.14) is governed by

$$(r_1\wedge r_2)\frac{1}{n}E\left(\sum_{i=1}^{[nu_1]}\sum_{j=1}^{[nu_2]} z_{it}z_{jt}\right)$$
$$=(r_1\wedge r_2)\frac{1}{n}\sum_{i=2}^{[nu_1]}\sum_{j=2}^{[nu_2]}E\left(\varepsilon_{i1} - \left(\sum_{\ell=i}^{[nu_1]}\frac{1}{\ell}\right)\varepsilon_{(i-1)1}\right)\left(\varepsilon_{j1} - \left(\sum_{\ell=j}^{[nu_2]}\frac{1}{\ell}\right)\varepsilon_{(j-1)1}\right)$$

which implies that as $n, T\nearrow\infty$, it is

$$(r_1\wedge r_2)\lim_{n\to\infty}\frac{1}{n}\sum_{i=2}^{[n(u_1\wedge u_2)]}\sigma_i^2\left(1+\log\left(\frac{i}{nu_1}\right)+\log\left(\frac{i}{nu_2}\right)+\log\left(\frac{i}{nu_1}\right)\log\left(\frac{i}{nu_2}\right)\right) \tag{A.16}$$

Next that the fidi of $(Tn)^{1/2}\hat{U}'_{T,n,r,u}$ converge in distribution to a Gaussian random variable with mean zero and variance

$$\Phi(r,u;r,u) = r\lim_{n\to\infty}\frac{1}{n}\sum_{i=2}^{[nu]}\sigma_i^2\left(1+2\log\left(\frac{i}{nu}\right)+\log^2\left(\frac{i}{nu}\right)\right)$$

proceeds as standard and it is nothing different to the proof under *C*1. Finally the tightness condition, for which a sufficient condition is

$$(Tn)^2 E\left(\sum_{t=[Tr_1]+1}^{[Tr_2]} \sum_{i=[nu_1]+1}^{[nu_2]} w_{it}\right)^4 \leq C(r_2 - r_1)^{1+\psi}(u_2 - u_1)^{1+\psi}$$

for some $\psi > 0$. Now the proof of Eq. (A.16) suggests that it suffices all we need to show that

$$(Tn)^2 E\left(\sum_{t=[Tr_1]+1}^{[Tr_2]} \sum_{i=[nu_1]+1}^{[nu_2]} \left(\varepsilon_{it} - \log\left(\frac{i}{n_2 u}\right)\varepsilon_{(i-1)t}\right)\right)^4 \leq C(r_2 - r_1)^{1+\psi}(u_2 - u_1)^{1+\psi}$$

However the proof of the last displayed inequality is almost routine by *C*3. This concludes the proof of part **(b)** of the theorem.

The proof of part **(a)** follows similarly after we notice that

$$\frac{1}{Tn} E\left(\sum_{t=1}^{[Tr_1]}\sum_{i=1}^{[nu_1]} \varepsilon_{it} \sum_{t=1}^{[Tr_2]}\sum_{i=1}^{[nu_2]} \varepsilon_{it}\right) = \frac{1}{Tn} \sum_{t=1}^{[T(r_1 \wedge r_2)]} \sum_{i=1}^{[n(u_1 \wedge u_2)]} E(\varepsilon_{it}\varepsilon_{jt})$$

$$= \frac{1}{Tn} \sum_{t=1}^{[T(r_1 \wedge r_2)]} \sum_{i=1}^{[n(u_1 \wedge u_2)]} \sigma_i^2$$

This concludes the proof of the theorem. ■

Proof of Theorem 6

Proof. By definition of $\hat{\beta}^*$ we have that

$$(Tn)^{1/2}(\hat{\beta}^* - \hat{\beta}) = \left(\frac{1}{Tn}\sum_{t=1}^{T}\sum_{i=1}^{n} \breve{x}_{it}\breve{x}'_{it}\right)^{-1} \frac{1}{(Tn)^{1/2}}\sum_{t=1}^{T}\sum_{i=1}^{n} \breve{x}_{it}\breve{\varepsilon}^*_{it}$$

So it suffices to show that

$$\frac{1}{(Tn)^{1/2}}\sum_{t=1}^{T}\sum_{i=1}^{n} \breve{x}_{it}\breve{\varepsilon}^*_{it} \xrightarrow{d} \mathcal{N}(0, \sigma^2\Sigma) \quad (in\ probability)$$

Arguing as we did in the proof of Theorem 4, say, it is clear that we only need to show that

$$\frac{1}{(Tn)^{1/2}}\sum_{t=1}^{T}\sum_{i=1}^{n}(x_{it}-\varkappa_i)\varepsilon_{it}^{*}\overset{d}{\to}\mathcal{N}(0,\sigma^2\Sigma)\quad (in\ probability)$$

But this is standard (see Shao & Tu 1995). ∎

Proof of Theorem 7

Proof. We would just show part **(a)**, with part **(b)** being similarly handled. From the continuous mapping theorem it suffices to show that

$$\sqrt{Tn}\hat{U}^{*'}_{T,n,r,u}=\frac{1}{\sqrt{Tn}}\sum_{t=1}^{[Tr]}\sum_{i=1}^{[nu]}\left(\hat{\upsilon}_{it}^{*}-\frac{\sum_{j=1}^{i-1}\hat{\upsilon}_{js}^{*}}{i-1}-\frac{\sum_{s=1}^{t-1}\hat{\upsilon}_{is}^{*}}{t-1}+\frac{\sum_{j=1}^{i-1}\sum_{s=1}^{t-1}\hat{\upsilon}_{js}^{*}}{(i-1)(t-1)}\right)$$

converges to (in probability) to $W(r,u)$. Denoting

$$z_{it}^{*}=:\varepsilon_{it}^{*}-\frac{1}{i-1}\sum_{j=1}^{i-1}\varepsilon_{jt}^{*},\quad w_{it}^{*}=:z_{it}^{*}-\frac{1}{t-1}\sum_{s=1}^{t-1}z_{is}^{*}$$

we write

$$\sqrt{Tn}\hat{U}^{*'}_{T,n,r,u}=\frac{1}{\sqrt{Tn}}\sum_{t=1}^{[Tr]}\sum_{i=2}^{[nu]}w_{it}^{*}$$

Now, because $\{\varepsilon_{it}^{*}\}_{t=1}^{T}$, $i\geq 1$, are i.i.d. sequences of random variables, $E^{*}\{z_{i_1t}^{*}z_{i_2s}^{*}\}=0$; $E^{*}\{w_{i_1t}^{*}w_{i_2s}^{*}\}=0$, which implies that

$$\begin{aligned}\frac{1}{Tn}E^{*}\left(\sum_{t=1}^{[Tr_1]}\sum_{i=2}^{[nu_1]}w_{it}^{*}\sum_{t=1}^{[Tr_2]}\sum_{i=2}^{[nu_2]}w_{it}^{*}\right)&=\frac{1}{Tn}\sum_{t=1}^{[T(r_1\wedge r_2)]}\sum_{i=2}^{[n(u_1\wedge u_2)]}E^{*}(w_{it}^{*2})\\&=(r_1\wedge r_2)(u_1\wedge u_2)\frac{1}{Tn}\sum_{t=1}^{T}\sum_{i=2}^{n}w_{it}^{2}\end{aligned}\qquad\text{(A.17)}$$

But the right side of Eq. (A.17) converges in probability to $(r_1 \wedge r_2)(u_1 \wedge u_2)\sigma^2$ by standard arguments.

Next, we establish that the finite dimensional distributions (fidi) of $\sqrt{Tn}\hat{U}^{*\prime}_{T,n,r,u}$ converge (in probability) to those of $\sigma W(r,u)$. As usual because the Cramer–Wold device, we only show the convergence in distribution of

$$\sqrt{Tn}\hat{U}^{*\prime}_{T,n,r,u} \xrightarrow{d} \sigma W(r,u), \quad r,u \in [0,1] \quad (\textit{in probability}) \tag{A.18}$$

for any fixed r and u. To that end, it is well-known that for any fixed t

$$W^*_{nt} = \frac{1}{\sqrt{n}}\sum_{i=2}^{[nu]} w^*_{it} \xrightarrow{d} \mathcal{N}(0,\sigma^2 u) \quad (\textit{in probability})$$

and as W^*_{nt} is independent of W^*_{ns} by construction, we conclude that

$$\frac{1}{\sqrt{T}}\sum_{t=1}^{[Tr]} W^*_{nt} \xrightarrow{d} \mathcal{N}(0,\sigma^2 ur), \quad (\textit{in probability})$$

So, we have established that when taking limits in n and then in T sequentially, it yields that $\sqrt{Tn}\hat{U}^{*\prime}_{T,n,r,u}$ converges in bootstrap distribution to $\sigma W(r,u)$. However, we need to show that this is the case when the limits in n and T are taken jointly. To that end, it suffices to verify that W^*_{nt} satisfy the generalized Lindeberg–Feller condition: for any $\eta > 0$, as $T,n \to \infty$,

$$\sum_{t=1}^{[Tr]} E^*(W^{*2}_{nt} I(|W^*_{nt}| \geq \eta)) \xrightarrow{P} 0$$

for which a sufficient condition is

$$E^*(W^{*4}_{nt}) = E^*\left(\frac{1}{\sqrt{n}}\sum_{i=2}^{[nu]} w^*_{it}\right)^4 = C_{nT} \tag{A.19}$$

with C_{nt} being an $O_p(1)$ sequence of random variables. By assumption,

$$
\begin{aligned}
E^*(W_{nt}^{*4}) = &\frac{3}{n^2}\left(\sum_{i=2}^{[nu]} E^*\omega_{it}^{*2}\right)^2 + \frac{1}{n^2}\sum_{i_1,\dots,i_4=2}^{[nu]} cum^*(\omega_{i_1t}^*, \omega_{i_2t}^*, \omega_{i_3t}^*, \omega_{i_4t}^*) \\
&3\left(\frac{1}{n}\sum_{i=2}^{n}\omega_{it}^2\right) + \frac{1}{n}\widehat{cum}(\varepsilon_{it}, \dots, \varepsilon_{it})(1+O_p(1)) \\
&+\frac{1}{n^2}\sum_{i_1,\dots,i_4=2}^{[nu]} \frac{1}{\prod_{l=2}^{4} i_l - 1}\sum_{j=1}^{i_1-1}\widehat{cum}(\varepsilon_{jt}, \dots, \varepsilon_{jt}) \\
\le\, & C_{nT}
\end{aligned}
$$

So, Eq. (A.19) holds true so does Eq. (A.18).

To complete the proof of part **(a)**, we need to show tightness. For that purpose, define an increment of $Q'_{T,n,r,u}$ as follows. For $0 \le r_1 \le r_2 \le 1$ and $0 \le u_1 \le u_2 \le 1$,

$$
\Delta_{r_1,u_1,r_2,u_2}^{*\prime} := \frac{1}{Tn}\sum_{t=[Tr_1]+1}^{[Tr_2]}\sum_{i=[nu_1]+1}^{[nu_2]} w_{it}^*
$$

A sufficient condition for tightness given by

$$
E^*((Tn)^2|\Delta_{r_1,u_1,r_2,u_2}^{*\prime}|^4) \le C_{nT}\left(\frac{[Tr_2]-[Tr_1]}{T}\right)^2\left(\frac{[nu_2]-[nu_1]}{n}\right)^2 \tag{A.20}
$$

and where $n^{-1} \le u_2 - u_1$ and $T^{-1} \le r_2 - r_1$ since otherwise Eq. (A.20) holds trivially. Now, proceeding as with Eq. (A.17), the left side of Eq. (A.20) is

$$
\begin{aligned}
&\frac{3}{T^2n^2}\left(\sum_{t=[Tr_1]+1}^{[Tr_2]}\sum_{i=[nu_1]+1}^{[nu_2]} Ew_{it}^{*2}\right)^2 \\
&+\frac{1}{T^2n^2}\sum_{t_1,\dots,t_4=[Tr_1]+1}^{[Tr_2]}\sum_{i_1,\dots,i_4=[nu_1]+1}^{[nu_2]} cum^*\left(w_{i_1t_1}^*, w_{i_2t_2}^*, w_{i_3t_3}^*, w_{i_4t_4}^*\right)
\end{aligned} \tag{A.21}
$$

By construction, $cum^*(w_{i_1t_1}^*, w_{i_2t_2}^*, w_{i_3t_3}^*, w_{i_4t_4}^*) \ne 0$ only if $t_1 = \dots = t_4$, so that the second term of Eq. (A.21) is bounded by

$$
\begin{aligned}
&C_{nT}\left(\frac{[Tr_2]-[Tr_1]}{T}\right)^2 \frac{1}{n^2} \sum_{i_1,\ldots,i_4=[nu_1]+1}^{[nu_2]} \Big\{\widehat{cum}(\varepsilon_{i_1t},\ldots,\varepsilon_{i_4t}) \\
&+\left(\prod_{l=1}^{4} i_\ell - 1\right)^{-1} \sum_{j=1}^{i_1-1} \widehat{cum}(\varepsilon_{jt},\ldots,\varepsilon_{jt})\Big\} \\
&\leq C_{nT}\left(\frac{[Tr_2]-[Tr_1]}{T}\right)^2 \left(\frac{[nu_2]-[nu_1]}{n}\right)^2
\end{aligned}
$$

On the other hand the first term of Eq. (A.21) is also bounded by the right side of Eq. (A.21). So this concludes the proof of the tightness condition and part **(a)** of the theorem. ■

TEST OF HYPOTHESES IN A TIME TREND PANEL DATA MODEL WITH SERIALLY CORRELATED ERROR COMPONENT DISTURBANCES

Badi H. Baltagi[a,c], Chihwa Kao[a] and Long Liu[b]

[a]*Department of Economics, Center for Policy Research, Syracuse University, Syracuse, New York, NY, USA*
[b]*Department of Economics, College of Business, University of Texas at San Antonio, San Antonio, TX, USA*
[c]*Department of Economics, Leicester University, Leicester, UK*

ABSTRACT

*This paper studies test of hypotheses for the slope parameter in a linear time trend panel data model with serially correlated error component disturbances. We propose a test statistic that uses a bias corrected estimator of the serial correlation parameter. The proposed test statistic which is based on the corresponding fixed effects feasible generalized least squares (*FE-FGLS*) estimator of the slope parameter has the standard normal limiting distribution which is valid whether the remainder error is*

Essays in Honor of Peter C. B. Phillips
Advances in Econometrics, Volume 33, 347–394

ISSN: 0731-9053/doi:10.1108/S0731-905320140000033011

$I(0)$ or $I(1)$. This performs well in Monte Carlo experiments and is recommended.

Keywords: Panel data; generalized least squares; time trend model; fixed effects; first difference; nonstationarity

JEL Classifications: C23; C33

1. INTRODUCTION

Panel data regression models with large cross-sectional and time-series dimensions have attracted much attention in recent years, e.g., see the surveys by Baltagi and Kao (2000), Phillips and Moon (2000), Choi (2006), and Breitung and Pesaran (2008) to mention a few.[1] Phillips and Moon (1999) provide *joint* asymptotic analysis of pooled estimators in panel regressions with nonstationary regressors when the underlying regression disturbances follow stationary processes. Under the additional condition, $n/T \to 0$, they show that sequential asymptotic results for their pooled estimators would be equivalent to the joint ones. Kao and Emerson (2004) and Baltagi, Kao, and Liu (2008) show that the asymptotics of the standard panel data estimators, like the fixed effects (FE), first-difference (FD), and generalized least squares (GLS) estimators of the slope coefficient depend crucially upon whether the error term is $I(0)$ or $I(1)$. For example, when the error term is $I(0)$, the FE and GLS estimators are asymptotically equivalent. However, when the error term is $I(1)$, this asymptotic equivalence breaks down and the GLS estimator is more efficient than the FE estimator. This paper considers fixed effects GLS (FE-GLS) based test statistics to test hypotheses regarding the slope parameter of a panel data time trend model where a priori knowledge as to whether the errors are $I(0)$ or $I(1)$ is not available.[2] We discuss the asymptotic properties of estimators of the autoregressive parameter and the corresponding fixed effects feasible GLS (FE-FGLS) estimators of the slope parameter. The main contribution of this paper is to introduce a FE-FGLS based test statistic which is robust when the error term is either $I(0)$ or $I(1)$.

The paper is organized as follows: Section 2 presents the panel data time trend model with an AR(1) error term. In Section 3, we discuss the FE-GLS estimator for this model and propose a test statistic that uses a bias corrected estimator of the serial correlation parameter and the corresponding FE-FGLS estimator of the regression parameter. Monte Carlo simulations are given in Section 4, while Section 5 provides the concluding remarks. All the proofs are given in the appendix. A few words on notation. All limits are taken sequentially as $T \to \infty$ and $n \to \infty$ unless otherwise specified. We use $(n, T) \to \infty$ to denote the *sequential limit*. Convergence in probability and distribution are denoted by $\xrightarrow{p}$ and $\xrightarrow{d}$, respectively. The limiting distribution of double indexed integrated processes has been extensively studied by Phillips and Moon (1999, 2000).

2. THE MODEL

Consider the following panel data time trend model:

$$y_{it} = \delta + \beta t + u_{it}, \quad i = 1, \ldots, n, \quad t = 1, \ldots, T \tag{1}$$

where $u_{it} = \mu_i + \nu_{it}$, and δ and β are scalars. We assume that the individual effects μ_i are random with $\mu_i \sim iid(0, \sigma_\mu^2)$ and ν_{it} following an AR(1) process which may or may not be stationary

$$\nu_{it} = \rho \nu_{it-1} + e_{it} \tag{2}$$

with $|\rho| \leq 1$, where e_{it} is a white noise process with variance σ_e^2. The μ_i's are independent of the ν_{it}'s for all i and t. This model has been studied by Baltagi and Krämer (1997), and Kao and Emerson (2004). In fact, Baltagi and Krämer (1997) showed the equivalence of OLS, GLS, and FE estimators for the panel data time trend model (1), but without serial correlation. Baltagi and Krämer (1997) also investigated the relative efficiency of the FD estimator with respect to the other estimators of β as $T \to \infty$. Kao and Emerson (2004) extended Baltagi and Krämer to model (1) with serially correlated remainder errors (2).[3] They showed that the FE estimator is asymptotically equivalent to GLS when the error term is $I(0)$ but that GLS is more efficient than FE when the error term is $I(1)$. Kao and Emerson show that the properties of the standard panel data estimators, like the FE, FD, and GLS estimators of β depend crucially upon the value of ρ.[4] When ν_{it} is $I(0)$, i.e., $\rho < 1$, the FE and GLS estimators are both $\sqrt{n}T^{3/2}$ consistent and asymptotically equivalent. However, when ν_{it} is $I(1)$, i.e., $\rho = 1$, this asymptotic equivalence breaks down and the GLS estimator is more efficient than the FE estimator. This has serious implications for applied research when ν_{it} is serially correlated and it is unknown whether the remainder disturbances are $I(0)$ or $I(1)$.[5]

In this paper, we are interested in testing

$$H_0 : \beta = \beta_0$$

without assuming knowledge of whether ν_{it} is $I(0)$ or $I(1)$.[6] Hypothesis testing on the slope of the trend has been studied in the econometric *time series* literature, e.g., Canjels and Watson (1997), Vogelsang and Fomby (2002), Bunzel and Vogelsang (2005), Roy, Falk, and Fuller (2004), and Perron and Yabu (2009). The focus of this paper is on the corresponding test in *panel data*. Consider the FE estimator of β, which is given by

$$\hat{\beta}_{\text{FE}} = \frac{\sum_{i=1}^{n} \sum_{t=1}^{T} (t - \bar{t})(y_{it} - \bar{y}_i)}{n \sum_{t=1}^{T} (t - \bar{t})^2} \tag{3}$$

where $\bar{t} = \frac{1}{T}\sum_{t=1}^{T} t$ and $\bar{y}_i = \frac{1}{T}\sum_{t=1}^{T} y_{it}$.[7] If ν_{it} is known to be $I(0)$, the t-statistic for the null hypothesis H_0 can be constructed using the FE estimator as follows:

$$t_{\text{FE}} = \frac{\hat{\beta}_{\text{FE}} - \beta_0}{\sqrt{\text{Var}\left(\hat{\beta}_{\text{FE}}\right)}} \tag{4}$$

where $\text{Var}\,(\hat{\beta}_{\text{FE}}) = \frac{\hat{\sigma}_v^2}{n \sum_{t=1}^{T} (t - \bar{t})^2}$ with $\hat{\sigma}_v^2 = \frac{1}{n(T-1)-1} \sum_{i=1}^{n} \sum_{t=2}^{T} \hat{\nu}_{it}^2$ and $\hat{\nu}_{it}$ are the within residuals from Eq. (1), i.e., $\hat{\nu}_{it} = (y_{it} - \bar{y}_{i.}) - \hat{\beta}_{\text{FE}}\,(t - \bar{t})$. The next theorem derives the limiting distribution of t_{FE} when the error term is $I(0)$ or $I(1)$.

Theorem 1. Assume $(n, T) \to \infty$,

1. *If* $|\rho| < 1$,

$$t_{\text{FE}} \xrightarrow{d} N(0, 1)$$

2. *If* $\rho = 1$,

$$\frac{1}{\sqrt{T}} t_{\text{FE}} \xrightarrow{d} N\left(0, \frac{3}{5}\right)$$

From Theorem 1, we note that t_{FE} in Eq. (4) will converge to a standard normal only when ν_{it} is $I(0)$, and t_{FE} will diverge when the error term is $I(1)$. This is not surprising since $\hat{\sigma}_\nu^2 = O_p(T)$, i.e., σ_ν^2 is *not identified* when ν_{it} is $I(1)$. If ν_{it} is known to be $I(1)$, then the optimal test for testing the null hypothesis H_0 is based on the t-statistic using the FD estimator, $\hat{\beta}_{\text{FD}}$, which is given by

$$\hat{\beta}_{\text{FD}} = \frac{1}{nT}\sum_{i=1}^{n}\sum_{t=1}^{T}\Delta y_{it} \tag{5}$$

where $\Delta y_{it} = y_{it} - y_{i,t-1}$. The corresponding t-statistic is given by

$$t_{\text{FD}} = \frac{\hat{\beta}_{\text{FD}} - \beta_0}{\sqrt{\text{Var}\left(\hat{\beta}_{\text{FD}}\right)}} \tag{6}$$

where $\text{Var}\,(\hat{\beta}_{\text{FD}}) = \hat{\sigma}_e^2/nT$ with $\hat{\sigma}_e^2 = \frac{1}{n(T-1)-1}\sum_{i=1}^{n}\sum_{t=2}^{T}(\Delta y_{it} - \hat{\beta}_{\text{FD}})^2$. The next theorem derives the limiting distribution of t_{FD} when the error term is $I(0)$ or $I(1)$

Theorem 2. Assume $(n, T) \to \infty$,

1. *If* $|\rho| < 1$,

$$\sqrt{T}t_{\text{FD}} \xrightarrow{d} N\left(0, \frac{1}{1-\rho}\right)$$

2. *If* $\rho = 1$,

$$t_{\text{FD}} \xrightarrow{d} N\,(0, 1)$$

The results of Theorem 2 show that $t_{\text{FD}} \xrightarrow{d} N\,(0, 1)$ when ν_{it} is in fact $I(1)$, under the null. On the other hand, $t_{\text{FD}} \xrightarrow{d} 0$ if ν_{it} is $I(0)$, under the null. In view of this and given that the order of integration of ν_{it} is *not known* in practice, it is natural to consider alternative robust test procedures.

3. THE FE-FGLS ESTIMATOR

Rewrite Eq. (1) in matrix form as

$$y = \delta \iota_{nT} + \beta x + u \tag{7}$$

with $u = Z_\mu \mu + v$, where $u' = (u_{11}, \ldots, u_{1T}, u_{21}, \ldots, u_{2T}, \ldots, u_{n1}, \ldots, u_{nT})$ with the observations stacked such that the slower index is over individuals and the faster index is over time. μ is an $n \times 1$ vector with typical element μ_i, $\mathbf{v}$ is an $nT \times 1$ vector with typical element ν_{it}, and $Z_\mu = I_n \otimes \boldsymbol{\iota}_T$, where I_n is an identity matrix of dimension n, $\boldsymbol{\iota}_T$ is a vector of ones of dimension T, and $\otimes$ denotes the Kronecker product. y is an $nT \times 1$ vector with typical element y_{it}, $x = \boldsymbol{\iota}_n \otimes x_i$, where $\boldsymbol{\iota}_n$ is a vector of ones of dimension n and $\mathbf{x}_i$ is a $T \times 1$ vector indicating a time trend with elements $(1, 2, \ldots, T)$. $\boldsymbol{\iota}_{nT}$ is a vector of ones of dimension nT. As shown in Baltagi and Li (1991), one can write the variance–covariance matrix as

$$\Phi = E(uu') = \sigma_\mu^2 \left(I_n \otimes \iota_T \iota_T' \right) + \sigma_e^2 (I_n \otimes \mathbf{A}) \tag{8}$$

where $\mathbf{A}$ is the variance–covariance matrix of ν_{it}, i.e.,

$$\mathbf{A} = \frac{1}{1-\rho^2} \begin{bmatrix} 1 & \rho & \rho^2 & \cdots & \rho^{T-1} \\ \rho & 1 & \rho & \cdots & \rho^{T-2} \\ \rho^2 & \rho & 1 & \cdots & \rho^{T-3} \\ \vdots & \vdots & \vdots & \ddots & \vdots \\ \rho^{T-1} & \rho^{T-2} & \rho^{T-3} & \cdots & 1 \end{bmatrix} \tag{9}$$

when $|\rho| < 1$ and

$$\mathbf{A} = \begin{bmatrix} 1 & 1 & 1 & \cdots & 1 \\ 1 & 2 & 2 & \cdots & 2 \\ 1 & 2 & 3 & \cdots & 3 \\ \vdots & \vdots & \vdots & \ddots & \vdots \\ 1 & 2 & 3 & \cdots & T \end{bmatrix}$$

when $\rho = 1$. When $|\rho| < 1$, one can easily verify that $\mathbf{A}^{-1} = \mathbf{C}'\mathbf{C}$, where

$$\mathbf{C}=\begin{bmatrix} \sqrt{1-\rho^2} & 0 & 0 & \cdots & 0 & 0 \\ -\rho & 1 & 0 & \cdots & 0 & 0 \\ 0 & -\rho & 1 & \cdots & 0 & 0 \\ \vdots & \vdots & \vdots & \ddots & \vdots & \vdots \\ 0 & 0 & 0 & -\rho & 1 & 0 \\ 0 & 0 & 0 & 0 & -\rho & 1 \end{bmatrix} \tag{10}$$

is the Prais–Winsten transformation matrix as in Baltagi and Li (1991). As suggested in Baltagi and Li (1991), one can apply the Prais–Winsten transformation matrix **C** to transform the remainder AR(1) disturbances into serially uncorrelated classical errors:

$$y^* = \delta\boldsymbol{\iota}_{nT}^* + \beta x^* + u^* \tag{11}$$

where $y^* = (I_n \otimes C)y$, $x^* = (I_n \otimes C)x = \boldsymbol{\iota}_n \otimes x_i^*$ with $x_i^* = Cx_i$ and $\boldsymbol{\iota}_{nT}^* = (I_n \otimes C)\boldsymbol{\iota}_{nT} = (1-\rho)(\boldsymbol{\iota}_n \otimes \boldsymbol{\iota}_T^{\alpha})$ using the fact that $C\boldsymbol{\iota}_T = (1-\rho)\boldsymbol{\iota}_T^{\alpha}$, where $\boldsymbol{\iota}_T^{\alpha'} = (\alpha, \boldsymbol{\iota}_{T-1}')$ and $\alpha = \sqrt{(1+\rho)/(1-\rho)}$. The transformed regression disturbances are in vector form

$$u^* = (I_n \otimes C)u = (I_n \otimes C\boldsymbol{\iota}_T)\mu + (I_n \otimes C)v = (1-\rho)\left(I_n \otimes \boldsymbol{\iota}_T^{\alpha}\right)\mu + v^* \tag{12}$$

where $v^* = (I_n \otimes C)v$. As shown in Baltagi and Li (1991), the variance–covariance matrix of the transformed disturbance is

$$\Phi^* = E\left(u^* u^{*'}\right) = \sigma_\mu^2 (1-\rho)^2 \left(I_n \otimes \boldsymbol{\iota}_T^{\alpha}\boldsymbol{\iota}_T^{\alpha'}\right) + \sigma_\varepsilon^2 (I_n \otimes I_T) \tag{13}$$

and

$$\sigma_\varepsilon \Phi^{*-1/2} = \frac{\sigma_\varepsilon}{\sigma_\alpha}\left(I_n \otimes \bar{J}_T^{\alpha}\right) + \left(I_n \otimes E_T^{\alpha}\right) \tag{14}$$

where $E_T^\alpha = I_T - \bar{J}_T^\alpha$, $\bar{J}_T^\alpha = \boldsymbol{\iota}_T^\alpha \boldsymbol{\iota}_T^{\alpha'}/d^2$, $d^2 = \boldsymbol{\iota}_T^{\alpha'}\boldsymbol{\iota}_T^\alpha = \alpha^2 + T - 1$, $\sigma_\alpha^2 = \sigma_e^2 + \theta\sigma_\mu^2$, and $\theta = d^2(1-\rho)^2$. Premultiplying the PW transformed observations in Eq. (11) by $\sigma_\varepsilon \Phi^{*-1/2}$, one gets

$$\sigma_\varepsilon \Phi^{*-1/2} y^* = \sigma_\varepsilon \Phi^{*-1/2} \delta \boldsymbol{\iota}_{nT}^* + \sigma_\varepsilon \Phi^{*-1/2} \beta x^* + \sigma_\varepsilon \Phi^{*-1/2} u^* \tag{15}$$

The least squares estimator of the transformed equation yields the GLS estimator $\hat{\beta}_{\mathrm{GLS}}$. As shown in Baltagi et al. (2008), $\hat{\beta}_{\mathrm{GLS}}$ has a faster converging speed than both the FE and FD estimators as $(n, T) \to \infty$. This is true whether ν_{it} and x_{it} are $I(1)$ or $I(0)$. Baltagi et al. (2011) further showed that the t-test statistic for $H_0 : \beta = \beta_0$ based on $\hat{\beta}_{\mathrm{GLS}}$ is always $N(0, 1)$ as $(n, T) \to \infty$.

A critical assumption for the GLS estimator is that $E(\mu_i | x_{it}) = 0$. It is well-known that when there is correlation between the regressors and the individual effects, GLS suffers from omitted variable bias, while FD and FE wipe out this source of endogeneity and remain consistent. In case of serial correlation, Baltagi et al. (2008) suggest a FE-GLS estimator that uses the within transformation to wipe out the $\mu_i^{'}$s and then runs GLS estimation to account for the serial correlation in the remainder error. Premultiplying Eq. (11) by $I_n \otimes E_T^\alpha$, one gets

$$\left(I_n \otimes E_T^\alpha\right) y^* = \left(I_n \otimes E_T^\alpha\right) x^* \beta + \left(I_n \otimes E_T^\alpha\right) \nu^* \tag{16}$$

using $E_T^\alpha \iota_T^\alpha = 0$. The least squares estimator of the transformed equation gives us the FE-GLS estimator, given by

$$\hat{\beta}_{\text{FE-GLS}} = \frac{x^{*\prime}\left(I_n \otimes E_T^\alpha\right) y^*}{x^{*\prime}\left(I_n \otimes E_T^\alpha\right) x^*} \tag{17}$$

It is worth pointing out that the FE-GLS encompasses both the within and FD estimators. To see this, note that

(i) If $\rho = 0$, and there is no serial correlation in the remainder error, we have $C = I_T$, $x^* = x$, $\alpha = 1$, $\iota_T^\alpha = \iota_T$ and hence $E_T^\alpha = E_T$, where $E_T = I_T - \bar{J}_T$ and $\bar{J}_T$ is a $T \times T$ matrix of $1/T$. The FE-GLS estimator in Eq. (17) reduces to the within estimator $\frac{x'(I_n \otimes E_T)y}{x'(I_n \otimes E_T)x}$.

(ii) Note also that $\bar{J}_T^\alpha$ can be rewritten as $\bar{J}_T^\alpha = l_T (l_T' l_T)^{-1} l_T'$, where $l_T = \sqrt{(1-\rho)}\iota_T^{\alpha\prime} = \sqrt{(1-\rho)}(\alpha, \iota_{T-1}') = (\sqrt{(1+\rho)}, \sqrt{(1-\rho)}\iota_{T-1}')$. If $\rho = 1$, we have $l_T' = (\sqrt{2}, 0_{T-1}')$ and hence $\bar{J}_T^\alpha = diag(1, 0, \cdots, 0)$ and $E_T^\alpha = I_T - \bar{J}_T^\alpha = \begin{bmatrix} 0 & 0_{T-1}' \\ 0_{T-1} & I_{T-1} \end{bmatrix}$.

Also, if $\rho = 0$, $\mathbf{C} = \begin{bmatrix} 0_T' \\ D \end{bmatrix}$ with $D = \begin{bmatrix} -1 & 1 & 0 & \cdots & 0 & 0 \\ \vdots & \vdots & \vdots & \ddots & \vdots & \vdots \\ 0 & 0 & 0 & -1 & 1 & 0 \\ 0 & 0 & 0 & 0 & -1 & 1 \end{bmatrix}$, which is the well-known first difference matrix. Hence $x^* = \left(I_n \otimes \begin{bmatrix} 0'_T \\ D \end{bmatrix}\right) x$ and $\begin{bmatrix} 0_T & D' \end{bmatrix}$ $\begin{bmatrix} 0 & 0'_{T-1} \\ 0_{T-1} & I_{T-1} \end{bmatrix} \begin{bmatrix} 0'_T \\ D \end{bmatrix} = D'D$. The FE-GLS estimator in Eq. (17) reduces to the FD estimator $\frac{x'(I_n \otimes D'D)y}{x'(I_n \otimes D'D)x}$.

From Eq. (17), we have

$$\hat{\beta}_{\text{FE-GLS}} - \beta = \frac{F_2}{F_1} \tag{18}$$

where $F_1 = x_i^{*\prime} x_i^* - \frac{(\iota_T^{\alpha\prime} x_i^*)^2}{d^2}$ and $F_2 = \frac{1}{n}\sum_{i=1}^n x_i^{*\prime} u_i^* - \frac{\iota_T^{\alpha\prime} x_i^*}{nd^2}\sum_{i=1}^n \iota_T^{\alpha\prime} u_i^*$. It is easy to show that $\text{Var}(\hat{\beta}_{\text{FE-GLS}}) = \frac{\sigma_e^2}{nF_1}$. Therefore,

$$t_{\text{FE-GLS}} = \frac{\hat{\beta}_{\text{FE-GLS}} - \beta}{\sqrt{\text{Var}\left(\hat{\beta}_{\text{FE-GLS}}\right)}} = \frac{F_2/F_1}{\sqrt{\sigma_e^2/(nF_1)}} = \frac{\sqrt{n}F_2}{\sqrt{\sigma_e^2 F_1}} \tag{19}$$

Note that both the FE-GLS estimator of β and its corresponding t-statistic do not depend on σ_μ^2 or σ_α^2. With a consistent estimator $\hat{\rho}$, the corresponding FE-FGLS estimator $\hat{\beta}_{\text{FE-FGLS}}$ is obtained by replacing C and E_T^α by their corresponding estimators $\hat{C}$ and $\hat{E}_T^\alpha$. As suggested by Baltagi and Li (1991), an estimator of σ_e^2 can be obtained as $\hat{\sigma}_e^2 = \frac{1}{n(T-1)}$ $\hat{u}^{*\prime}(I_n \otimes \hat{E}_T^\alpha)\hat{u}^*$, where $\hat{u}^*$ is an $nT \times 1$ vector of OLS residuals from the Prais–Winsten transformed regression using $\hat{\rho}$. The corresponding t-statistic based on the FE-FGLS estimator can be obtained from Eq. (19). The asymptotic properties are summarized in the following theorem

Theorem 3. Assume $(n, T) \to \infty$,

1. *When* $|\rho| < 1$, *if* $\hat{\rho} \xrightarrow{p} \rho$, *we have*
$$t_{\text{FE-FGLS}} \xrightarrow{d} N(0, 1)$$

2. *When* $\rho = 1$, *if* $T(\hat{\rho} - 1) \xrightarrow{p} \kappa$, *we have*

$$t_{\text{FE-FGLS}} \xrightarrow{d} N\left(0, \frac{\left(\kappa^2 - 3\kappa + 3\right)\left(\kappa^4 - 10\kappa^3 + 50\kappa^2 - 120\kappa + 120\right)}{10(\kappa^4 - 9\kappa^3 + 33\kappa^2 - 54\kappa + 36)}\right)$$

Theorem 3 implies that we need $k = 0$ when $\rho = 1$. Otherwise $t_{\text{FE-FGLS}}$ does not converge to a $N(0, 1)$. Baltagi and Li (1991) suggest estimating ρ using

$$\hat{\rho} = \frac{\sum_{i=1}^{n}\sum_{t=2}^{T}\hat{\nu}_{it}\hat{\nu}_{i,t-1}}{\sum_{i=1}^{n}\sum_{t=2}^{T}\hat{\nu}_{i,t-1}^{2}} \tag{20}$$

where $\hat{\nu}_{it}$ denotes the FE residual from Eq. (1) which is defined in Section 2. It can be obtained from a regression of $\hat{\nu}_{it}$ on $\hat{\nu}_{i,t-1}$. The asymptotics for $\hat{\rho}$ are given in the following theorem.

Theorem 4. Assume $(n, T) \to \infty$,

1. *If* $|\rho| < 1$,

$$\sqrt{nT}\left(\hat{\rho} - \rho + \frac{1+\rho}{T}\right) \xrightarrow{d} N(0, 1-\rho^2)$$

2. *If* $\rho = 1$,

$$\sqrt{nT}\left(\hat{\rho} - 1 + \frac{3}{T}\right) \xrightarrow{d} N\left(0, \frac{51}{5}\right)$$

The asymptotic distribution of $\hat{\rho}$ in Theorem 4 is actually the same as Theorems 2 and 4 in Hahn and Kuersteiner (2002) that discuss a dynamic panel data model. Also, the result for the case where $\rho = 1$ in Theorem 4 is the same as Theorem 2 in Kao (1999) which discusses the spurious panel data model. As we can see, the results from Theorem 4 : When $|\rho| < 1$, there is a bias of $(1+\rho)/T$ in $\hat{\rho}$, but it still implies $\hat{\rho} \xrightarrow{p} \rho$ as $(n, T) \to \infty$. When $\rho = 1$, $T(\hat{\rho} - 1)$ does not converge to zero in probability if there are individual effects in the model. Substituting $\kappa = -3$ into Theorem 3, one can verify that $\hat{\rho}$ suggested by Baltagi and Li (1991) leads to $t_{\text{FE-FGLS}} \xrightarrow{d} N\left(0, \frac{2989}{910}\right)$ when $\rho = 1$. This limits the usefulness of the FE-GLS estimator when the error term is $I(1)$ and there are individual effects in the panel model. This difference is due to the fact that μ_i can not be consistently estimated when the error term is $I(1)$ (see Kao & Emerson, 2004). To achieve $t_{\text{FE-FGLS}} \xrightarrow{d} N(0, 1)$, we need $\kappa = 0$.

Therefore, when $|\rho|<1$, a bias-corrected estimator of ρ is $\hat{\rho}+\frac{1+\hat{\rho}}{T}$. When $\rho = 1$, a bias-corrected estimator of ρ is $\hat{\rho}+\frac{3}{T}$. Combining the two cases, we suggest a bias-corrected estimator of ρ as follows:

$$\tilde{\rho}=\begin{cases}\hat{\rho}+\dfrac{1+\hat{\rho}}{T} & \text{if } 1-\hat{\rho}>\dfrac{3}{T}\\[2ex] 1 & \text{if } 1-\hat{\rho}\leq\dfrac{3}{T}\end{cases}$$

The asymptotics for $\tilde{\rho}$ are given in the following theorem.

Theorem 5. Assume $(n, T)\to\infty$,

1. *If* $|\rho|<1$,

$$\sqrt{nT}(\tilde{\rho}-\rho)\xrightarrow{d}N\left(0, 1-\rho^2\right)$$

2. *If* $\rho = 1$,

$$\sqrt{nT}(\tilde{\rho}-1)\xrightarrow{d}N\left(0, \frac{51}{5}\right)$$

Therefore, we have $t_{\text{FE-FGLS}}\xrightarrow{d}N(0, 1)$ using $\tilde{\rho}$ for both $|\rho|<1$ and $\rho = 1$.

In this section, we showed that the *t*-statistic based on FE-GLS is no longer robust if there are individual effects. Extra steps need to be taken to achieve the robustness when Eq. (1) includes individual effects.

3.1. The Model Without Individual Effects

Let us study the case where there are no individual effects, i.e., $\mu_i=0$ for all i. The variance–covariance matrix in Eq. (8) reduces to $\Phi=\sigma_e^2(I_n\otimes\mathbf{A})$ and hence $\Phi^{-1}=\frac{1}{\sigma_e^2}I_n\otimes\mathbf{A}^{-1}$. Eq. (11) reduces to

$$y^*=\delta\boldsymbol{\iota}_{nT}^*+\beta x^*+v^* \tag{21}$$

where the variance–covariance matrix of the transformed disturbance is $E(v^* v^{*\prime}) = \sigma_\varepsilon^2 (I_n \otimes I_T)$. The least squares estimator of the transformed equation yields the GLS estimator:

$$\hat{\beta}_{\text{GLS}} = \frac{x^{*\prime} M_{\iota^*_{nT}} y^*}{x^{*\prime} M_{\iota^*_{nT}} x^*} \tag{22}$$

where $M_{\iota^*_{nT}} = I_{nT} - \iota^*_{nT}(\iota^{*\prime}_{nT}\iota^*_{nT})\iota^{*\prime}_{nT} = I_{nT} - \bar{J}_n \otimes \bar{J}^\alpha_T$ using the fact that $\iota^*_{nT} = (1-\rho)(\iota_n \otimes \iota^\alpha_T)$. It is easy to see that $M_{\iota^*_{nT}} x^* = (I_{nT} - \bar{J}_n \otimes \bar{J}^\alpha_T)(\iota_n \otimes x^*_i) = \iota_n \otimes (x^*_i - \bar{J}^\alpha_T x^*_i) = (I_n \otimes E^\alpha_T)x^*$. This proves that $\hat{\beta}_{\text{GLS}}$ and $\hat{\beta}_{\text{FE-GLS}}$ are the same if there are no individual effects in the model. The t-statistic based on $\hat{\beta}_{\text{GLS}}$ is in turn the same as the one based on $\hat{\beta}_{\text{FE-GLS}}$ in Eq. (19), i.e.,

$$t_{\text{GLS}} = \frac{\sqrt{n}F_2}{\sqrt{\sigma_e^2 F_1}} \tag{23}$$

where F_1 and F_2 are defined in Eq. (18). Similar to Eq. (20) for the general model with individual effects, let

$$\hat{\rho} = \frac{\sum_{i=1}^n \sum_{t=2}^T \hat{u}_{it}\hat{u}_{i,t-1}}{\sum_{i=1}^n \sum_{t=2}^T \hat{u}^2_{i,t-1}} \tag{24}$$

where $\hat{u}_{it}$ is the OLS residual, i.e., $\hat{u}_{it} = (y_{it} - \bar{\bar{y}}) - \hat{\beta}_{OLS}(t - \bar{t})$ with $\bar{\bar{y}} = \frac{1}{nT}\sum_{i=1}^n \sum_{t=1}^T y_{it}$ and $\bar{t} = \frac{1}{T}\sum_{t=1}^T t$. Define $\hat{u}^*$ as an $nT \times 1$ vector of OLS residuals from the Prais–Winsten transformed regression using $\hat{\rho}$. An estimator of σ_e^2 is $\hat{\sigma}_e^2 = \frac{1}{nT}\hat{u}^{*\prime}\hat{u}^*$. Substituting $\hat{\rho}$ and $\hat{\sigma}_e^2$, the t-statistic corresponding to the FGLS estimator can be obtained from Eq. (23). The asymptotic properties are summarized in the following theorem.

Theorem 6. Assume $(n, T) \to \infty$,

1. *If* $|\rho| < 1$,

$$\sqrt{nT}\,(\hat{\rho} - \rho) \xrightarrow{d} N\left(0, 1 - \rho^2\right)$$

2. *If* $\rho = 1$,

$$T\,(\hat{\rho} - 1) \xrightarrow{p} N\,(0, 3)$$

Therefore, we have $t_{\text{FGLS}} \xrightarrow{d} N\,(0, 1)$ using $\hat{\rho}$ for both $|\rho| < 1$ and $\rho = 1$.

Table 1. Median, IQR, and RMSE of Estimators of ρ.

n	T	ρ	$\hat{\rho}$ Median	$\hat{\rho}$ IQR	$\hat{\rho}$ RMSE	$\tilde{\rho}$ Median	$\tilde{\rho}$ IQR	$\tilde{\rho}$ RMSE
500	20	0	0.000	0.013	0.010	0.050	0.014	0.051
		0.2	0.178	0.013	0.024	0.237	0.014	0.039
		0.4	0.354	0.013	0.047	0.422	0.013	0.024
		0.6	0.525	0.012	0.075	0.602	0.012	0.009
		0.8	0.686	0.010	0.115	0.770	0.011	0.031
		0.9	0.760	0.009	0.140	0.848	0.009	0.053
		1	0.857	0.007	0.143	1.000	0.000	0.000
500	50	0	0.000	0.008	0.006	0.020	0.008	0.021
		0.2	0.192	0.008	0.010	0.216	0.008	0.017
		0.4	0.382	0.008	0.018	0.410	0.008	0.012
		0.6	0.572	0.007	0.029	0.603	0.007	0.006
		0.8	0.758	0.006	0.042	0.793	0.006	0.008
		0.9	0.847	0.005	0.053	0.884	0.005	0.016
		1	0.941	0.003	0.059	1.000	0.022	0.016
50	500	0	0.000	0.009	0.006	0.002	0.009	0.007
		0.2	0.199	0.008	0.006	0.202	0.008	0.006
		0.4	0.398	0.008	0.006	0.401	0.008	0.006
		0.6	0.597	0.007	0.006	0.600	0.007	0.005
		0.8	0.796	0.005	0.006	0.800	0.005	0.004
		0.9	0.895	0.004	0.006	0.899	0.004	0.003
		1	0.994	0.001	0.006	0.998	0.003	0.003
10	100	0	−0.001	0.041	0.030	0.009	0.041	0.032
		0.2	0.195	0.041	0.031	0.207	0.041	0.031
		0.4	0.389	0.038	0.030	0.403	0.038	0.029
		0.6	0.585	0.034	0.029	0.601	0.034	0.025
		0.8	0.778	0.027	0.030	0.796	0.027	0.020
		0.9	0.873	0.021	0.031	0.892	0.022	0.018

Table 1. *(Continued)*

n	T	ρ	$\hat{\rho}$ Median	$\hat{\rho}$ IQR	$\hat{\rho}$ RMSE	$\tilde{\rho}$ Median	$\tilde{\rho}$ IQR	$\tilde{\rho}$ RMSE
		1	0.967	0.013	0.034	0.987	0.020	0.020
10	50	0	−0.004	0.057	0.042	0.016	0.058	0.046
		0.2	0.187	0.057	0.044	0.210	0.058	0.044
		0.4	0.378	0.054	0.046	0.405	0.055	0.041
		0.6	0.566	0.050	0.050	0.597	0.051	0.038
		0.8	0.753	0.041	0.056	0.788	0.042	0.033
		0.9	0.841	0.037	0.064	0.878	0.037	0.035
		1	0.934	0.026	0.069	0.973	0.041	0.041
50	10	0	−0.005	0.057	0.042	0.095	0.062	0.106
		0.2	0.152	0.060	0.065	0.268	0.066	0.083
		0.4	0.302	0.058	0.107	0.433	0.064	0.057
		0.6	0.440	0.055	0.165	0.584	0.061	0.048
		0.8	0.565	0.052	0.238	0.722	0.057	0.089
		0.9	0.632	0.050	0.271	0.795	0.055	0.113
		1	0.722	0.041	0.279	1.000	0.000	0.000
20	10	0	−0.003	0.088	0.065	0.097	0.097	0.120
		0.2	0.152	0.090	0.083	0.267	0.099	0.100
		0.4	0.299	0.089	0.120	0.429	0.098	0.078
		0.6	0.435	0.083	0.177	0.578	0.092	0.071
		0.8	0.559	0.079	0.248	0.714	0.087	0.107
		0.9	0.627	0.075	0.279	0.789	0.083	0.127
		1	0.716	0.068	0.288	1.000	0.151	0.112

Table 2. Size and Power of the t-Test for H_0: $\beta = 0$ ($n = 500$, $T = 20$).

ρ	β	FD	FE	FE-GLS	FE-FGLS_1	FE-FGLS_2
0	0.00	0.000	0.057	0.054	0.053	0.045
0	0.02	0.000	1.000	1.000	1.000	0.999
0	0.04	0.000	1.000	1.000	1.000	1.000
0	0.06	0.335	1.000	1.000	1.000	1.000
0	0.08	0.986	1.000	1.000	1.000	1.000
0	0.10	1.000	1.000	1.000	1.000	1.000
0.2	0.00	0.000	0.105	0.054	0.059	0.046
0.2	0.02	0.000	0.996	0.969	0.972	0.960
0.2	0.04	0.003	1.000	1.000	1.000	1.000
0.2	0.06	0.643	1.000	1.000	1.000	1.000
0.2	0.08	0.997	1.000	1.000	1.000	1.000
0.2	0.10	1.000	1.000	1.000	1.000	1.000
0.4	0.00	0.000	0.174	0.054	0.067	0.049
0.4	0.02	0.000	0.979	0.833	0.865	0.810
0.4	0.04	0.040	1.000	1.000	1.000	1.000
0.4	0.06	0.815	1.000	1.000	1.000	1.000
0.4	0.08	0.999	1.000	1.000	1.000	1.000
0.4	0.10	1.000	1.000	1.000	1.000	1.000
0.6	0.00	0.000	0.283	0.054	0.087	0.053
0.6	0.02	0.000	0.935	0.506	0.625	0.504
0.6	0.04	0.139	1.000	0.969	0.988	0.964
0.6	0.06	0.894	1.000	1.000	1.000	1.000
0.6	0.08	1.000	1.000	1.000	1.000	1.000
0.6	0.10	1.000	1.000	1.000	1.000	1.000
0.8	0.00	0.000	0.388	0.054	0.117	0.071
0.8	0.02	0.002	0.812	0.159	0.378	0.219
0.8	0.04	0.248	0.995	0.506	0.822	0.611
0.8	0.06	0.909	1.000	0.833	0.979	0.912
0.8	0.08	0.999	1.000	0.969	1.000	0.987
0.8	0.10	1.000	1.000	1.000	1.000	1.000
0.9	0.00	0.000	0.455	0.054	0.139	0.084
0.9	0.02	0.025	0.741	0.091	0.289	0.146
0.9	0.04	0.329	0.972	0.159	0.624	0.342
0.9	0.06	0.860	1.000	0.314	0.887	0.609
0.9	0.08	0.997	1.000	0.506	0.980	0.828
0.9	0.10	1.000	1.000	0.671	1.000	0.946
1	0.00	0.064	0.577	0.064	0.284	0.078
1	0.02	0.146	0.681	0.146	0.423	0.159
1	0.04	0.410	0.855	0.410	0.696	0.419
1	0.06	0.721	0.952	0.721	0.904	0.732
1	0.08	0.921	0.996	0.921	0.988	0.930
1	0.10	0.989	1.000	0.989	0.998	0.990

Theorem 6 shows that t_{FGLS} converges to $N(0,1)$, whether the error term is $I(0)$ or $I(1)$, when there are no individual effects in the model. This is an interesting result, i.e., the t-ratio based on FGLS effectively bridges the gap between the $I(0)$ and $I(1)$ error terms (if there are no individual effects in the model). This implies that inference on the slope parameter can be performed using the standard normal distribution if there are no individual effects. This is different from the pure time series model as in Perron and Yabu (2009) which requires a *super-efficient* estimate in order to achieve this goal. We know that this will change if there are individual effects in the

Table 3. Size and Power of the t-Test for $H_0 : \beta = 0$ ($n = 500$, $T = 50$).

ρ	β	FD	FE	FE-GLS	FE-FGLS$_1$	FE-FGLS$_2$
0	0.00	0.000	0.043	0.052	0.052	0.050
0	0.02	0.000	1.000	1.000	1.000	1.000
0	0.04	0.569	1.000	1.000	1.000	1.000
0	0.06	1.000	1.000	1.000	1.000	1.000
0.2	0.00	0.000	0.108	0.052	0.054	0.050
0.2	0.02	0.000	1.000	1.000	1.000	1.000
0.2	0.04	0.900	1.000	1.000	1.000	1.000
0.2	0.06	1.000	1.000	1.000	1.000	1.000
0.4	0.00	0.000	0.194	0.052	0.056	0.050
0.4	0.02	0.000	1.000	1.000	1.000	1.000
0.4	0.04	0.990	1.000	1.000	1.000	1.000
0.4	0.06	1.000	1.000	1.000	1.000	1.000
0.6	0.00	0.000	0.315	0.052	0.072	0.052
0.6	0.02	0.000	1.000	1.000	1.000	1.000
0.6	0.04	0.998	1.000	1.000	1.000	1.000
0.6	0.06	1.000	1.000	1.000	1.000	1.000
0.8	0.00	0.000	0.486	0.052	0.098	0.056
0.8	0.02	0.010	1.000	0.973	0.994	0.977
0.8	0.04	0.997	1.000	1.000	1.000	1.000
0.8	0.06	1.000	1.000	1.000	1.000	1.000
0.9	0.00	0.000	0.590	0.052	0.126	0.074
0.9	0.02	0.044	0.993	0.502	0.788	0.609
0.9	0.04	0.988	1.000	0.973	1.000	0.996
0.9	0.06	1.000	1.000	1.000	1.000	1.000
1	0.00	0.053	0.706	0.053	0.250	0.072
1	0.02	0.271	0.854	0.271	0.605	0.328
1	0.04	0.794	0.989	0.794	0.954	0.832
1	0.06	0.988	1.000	0.988	0.999	0.992
1	0.08	1.000	1.000	1.000	1.000	1.000

Note: Cases with power of 1.000 have been omitted after their first occurrence.

model. This is the more likely case in panel data with heterogeneity across individuals.

4. MONTE CARLO RESULTS

This section reports the results of Monte Carlo experiments designed to investigate the finite sample properties of the FE-FGLS based $t_{\text{FE-GLS}}$. The model is generated by

Table 4. Size-Adjusted Power of the t-Test for $H_0 : \beta = 0$ ($n = 500$, $T = 20$).

ρ	β	FD	FE	FE-GLS	FE-FGLS$_1$	FE-FGLS$_2$
0	0.02	0.780	1.000	0.999	0.999	0.999
0	0.04	0.999	1.000	1.000	1.000	1.000
0	0.06	1.000	1.000	1.000	1.000	1.000
0.2	0.02	0.801	0.986	0.961	0.962	0.961
0.2	0.04	0.999	1.000	1.000	1.000	1.000
0.2	0.06	1.000	1.000	1.000	1.000	1.000
0.4	0.02	0.780	0.930	0.815	0.826	0.811
0.4	0.04	0.998	1.000	1.000	1.000	1.000
0.4	0.06	1.000	1.000	1.000	1.000	1.000
0.6	0.02	0.700	0.716	0.472	0.525	0.480
0.6	0.04	0.996	0.998	0.961	0.975	0.962
0.6	0.06	1.000	1.000	1.000	1.000	1.000
0.8	0.02	0.500	0.409	0.136	0.231	0.171
0.8	0.04	0.968	0.936	0.472	0.679	0.551
0.8	0.06	1.000	1.000	0.815	0.960	0.873
0.8	0.08	1.000	1.000	0.961	1.000	0.980
0.8	0.1	1.000	1.000	0.999	1.000	1.000
0.9	0.02	0.308	0.234	0.073	0.131	0.099
0.9	0.04	0.852	0.734	0.136	0.402	0.268
0.9	0.06	0.997	0.975	0.289	0.740	0.512
0.9	0.08	1.000	1.000	0.472	0.946	0.752
0.9	0.1	1.000	1.000	0.647	0.992	0.920
1	0.02	0.117	0.095	0.117	0.115	0.111
1	0.04	0.373	0.293	0.373	0.363	0.356
1	0.06	0.687	0.598	0.687	0.674	0.658
1	0.08	0.900	0.844	0.900	0.892	0.891
1	0.1	0.983	0.957	0.983	0.982	0.983

Note: Cases with power of 1.000 have been omitted after their first occurrence.

$$y_{it} = \alpha + \beta t + \mu_i + v_{it}, \quad i = 1, \ldots, n, \quad t = 1, \ldots, T \tag{25}$$

with $\alpha = 5$, $\beta = 10$, $\mu_i \overset{iid}{\sim} N(0, 5)$, and $v_{it} = \rho v_{it-1} + e_{it}$, with ρ varying over the range (0, 0.2, 0.4, 0.6, 0.8, 0.9, 1), $v_{i0} = 0$, $e_{it} \overset{iid}{\sim} N(0, \sigma_e^2)$, and $\sigma_e^2 = 5$. The sample sizes (n, T) are (500,20), (500,50), (50,500), (10,100), (10,50), (50,10), and (20,10), respectively. For each experiment, we perform 1,000 replications. For each replication we estimate the model using: (i) FD: first-difference ignoring serial correlation; (ii) FE: fixed-effects ignoring serial correlation; (iii) FE-GLS: FE-GLS estimator using the true value of ρ; (iv) FE-FGLS$_1$: FE-FGLS estimator using $\hat{\rho}$ calculated by the method suggested in Baltagi and Li (1991); and (v) FE-FGLS$_2$: FE-FGLS estimator using a bias-corrected estimator $\tilde{\rho}$. Table 1 reports the median, interquantile range, and root mean squared error (RMSE) of estimators of $\hat{\rho}$ and $\tilde{\rho}$. Following Kelejian and Prucha (1999), RMSE is defined as $[\text{bias}^2 + (\text{IQR}/1.35)^2]^{1/2}$, where bias is the difference between the median and the true parameter value and IQR is the interquantile range. That is $\text{IQR} = c_1 - c_2$, where c_1 and c_2 are the 0.75 and 0.25 quantiles respectively. As explained in Kelejian and Prucha (1999), these characteristics are closely related to the standard measures of bias and RMSE but, unlike these measures, are assured to exist. When the true ρ is larger than 0.4, $\tilde{\rho}$ has smaller RMSE than $\hat{\rho}$. This is especially true when ρ is close to 1. For the first two

Table 5. Size-Adjusted Power of the t-Test for $H_0 : \beta = 0$ ($n = 500$, $T = 50$).

ρ	β	FD	FE	FE-GLS	FE-FGLS$_1$	FE-FGLS$_2$
0	0.02	1.000	1.000	1.000	1.000	1.000
0.2	0.02	1.000	1.000	1.000	1.000	1.000
0.4	0.02	1.000	1.000	1.000	1.000	1.000
0.6	0.02	1.000	1.000	1.000	1.000	1.000
0.8	0.02	1.000	0.998	0.970	0.984	0.975
0.8	0.04	1.000	1.000	1.000	1.000	1.000
0.9	0.02	0.979	0.884	0.492	0.652	0.554
0.9	0.04	1.000	1.000	0.970	0.998	0.989
0.9	0.06	1.000	1.000	1.000	1.000	1.000
1	0.02	0.265	0.248	0.265	0.254	0.260
1	0.04	0.792	0.734	0.792	0.782	0.776
1	0.06	0.987	0.973	0.987	0.987	0.986
1	0.08	1.000	1.000	1.000	0.999	0.999
1	0.1	1.000	1.000	1.000	1.000	1.000

Note: Cases with power of 1.000 have been omitted after their first occurrence.

Table 6. Size of the t-Test for $H_0 : \beta = 0$.

n	T	ρ	FD	FE	FE-GLS	FE-FGLS$_1$	FE-FGLS$_2$
50	500	0	0.000	0.059	0.060	0.056	0.057
		0.2	0.000	0.112	0.060	0.057	0.057
		0.4	0.000	0.192	0.060	0.057	0.057
		0.6	0.000	0.305	0.060	0.059	0.057
		0.8	0.000	0.507	0.060	0.060	0.059
		0.9	0.000	0.660	0.060	0.067	0.060
		1	0.054	0.910	0.054	0.168	0.064
10	100	0	0.000	0.047	0.050	0.044	0.046
		0.2	0.000	0.096	0.050	0.052	0.050
		0.4	0.000	0.175	0.050	0.053	0.052
		0.6	0.000	0.296	0.050	0.054	0.053
		0.8	0.000	0.465	0.050	0.070	0.056
		0.9	0.000	0.609	0.050	0.097	0.067
		1	0.064	0.802	0.064	0.198	0.083
10	50	0	0.000	0.049	0.047	0.041	0.037
		0.2	0.000	0.118	0.047	0.055	0.045
		0.4	0.000	0.209	0.047	0.063	0.049
		0.6	0.000	0.334	0.047	0.072	0.055
		0.8	0.000	0.476	0.047	0.111	0.067
		0.9	0.000	0.586	0.047	0.164	0.088
		1	0.047	0.753	0.047	0.215	0.087
50	10	0	0.000	0.051	0.042	0.036	0.025
		0.2	0.000	0.095	0.042	0.053	0.029
		0.4	0.000	0.153	0.042	0.067	0.037
		0.6	0.000	0.223	0.042	0.091	0.047
		0.8	0.000	0.297	0.042	0.126	0.057
		0.9	0.002	0.335	0.042	0.133	0.056
		1	0.037	0.424	0.037	0.131	0.044
20	10	0	0.000	0.050	0.041	0.035	0.030
		0.2	0.000	0.092	0.041	0.047	0.029
		0.4	0.000	0.139	0.041	0.063	0.035
		0.6	0.000	0.203	0.041	0.082	0.044
		0.8	0.002	0.278	0.041	0.116	0.058
		0.9	0.008	0.321	0.041	0.126	0.062
		1	0.053	0.399	0.053	0.119	0.073

(n, T) combinations, Tables 2 and 3 report the size and power of the t-test for $H_0 : \beta = 0$ corresponding to each estimator of β. Tables 4 and 5 report the size-adjusted power. Several conclusions emerge from these results. For the FD estimator, if $\rho = 1$, the size of the corresponding t-test is 0.064 when $n = 500$ and $T = 20$ and 0.053 when $n = 500$ and $T = 50$. However, the size is always zero for other values of ρ. For the FE estimator, if $\rho = 0$, the size of the corresponding t-test is 0.057 when $n=500$ and $T=20$ and 0.043 when $n=500$ and $T=50$. The size increases with ρ. This verifies the asymptotic results in Theorem 1. The standard deviation increases with ρ and decreases with T. This is consistent with the asymptotic results in Theorem 2. For the FE-FGLS estimators, the size of the corresponding t-test is too large for FE-FGLS$_1$, especially if $\rho > 0.4$ However, the t-test corresponding to FE-FGLS$_2$ has reasonable size and power, compared to FE-FGLS$_1$. Our simulation results confirm the robustness of $t_{\text{FE-FGLS}_2}$ using the bias-corrected estimator $\tilde{\rho}$. For the other (n, T) combinations, Tables 6 reports the size of the t-test for $H_0 : \beta = 0$ corresponding to each estimator. We can see that the results are robust to small samples and different ratios of n/T.

5. CONCLUSION

In this paper, we discuss test of hypotheses in a linear *time trend* panel data model with serially correlated error component disturbances. The error term could be either stationary or nonstationary. We consider estimation and testing using the FE, FD, and FE-GLS estimators. Different from the results in the pure time series case, the t-test based on FGLS always converges to $N(0, 1)$ no matter whether the error term is $I(0)$ or $I(1)$, when there are no individual effects in the model. When there are individual effects in the model, the t-statistic based on FE-GLS is no longer robust. We suggest a bias-corrected estimator of ρ to achieve robustness. We show that it performs well in Monte Carlo experiments and is recommended. While the focus of this paper is test of hypothesis in a simple linear trend panel data model with error components and serial correlation, it is important to extend this work to dynamic panel data models with cross-section dependence across the units. This should be the focus of future research.

NOTES

1. See also chapter 12 of Baltagi (2013) for a textbook treatment of this subject.
2. The results in this paper make use of the asymptotic results for a panel data time trend regression model studied by Kao and Emerson (2004).
3. One can extend the simple time trend model in this paper to a polynomial trend model by following similar steps as in section 6 of Emerson and Kao (2000).
4. Baltagi et al. (2008) study the asymptotic properties of OLS, FE, FD, and GLS in the random effects error components regression model with an

autocorrelated regressor and an autocorrelated remainder error (both of which can be stationary or nonstationary). They show that when the error term is $I(0)$ and the regressor is $I(0)$, the FE estimator is asymptotically equivalent to the GLS estimator and OLS is less efficient than GLS (due to a slower convergence speed). However, when the error term and the regressor are $I(1)$, GLS is more efficient than the FE estimator since GLS is $\sqrt{nT}$ consistent, while FE is $\sqrt{n}$ consistent. This implies that GLS is the preferred estimator under both cases (i.e., regression error is either $I(0)$ or $I(1)$).

5. One referee suggests testing the joint hypothesis: $H_0{:}\beta=0$ and $\rho=0$. Alternatively, testing the joint hypothesis: $H_0{:}\beta=0$ and $\rho=1$. Extending the results of this paper to these joint hypotheses is beyond the scope of this paper and should be subject for future research.

6. Baltagi, Kao, and Na (2011) also consider hypotheses testing in an I(0) or I(1) regressor case. However, the results in this paper for a *time trend* panel data model with serially correlated error component disturbances are different. For example, we show that the GLS based t-statistics with individual fixed effects have a different limiting distribution compared to that without the fixed effects.

7. Note that the FE and GLS estimators are asymptotically equivalent for this case, see Kao and Emerson (2004).

ACKNOWLEDGMENT

We would like to thank an anonymous referee and the editor Tom Fomby for their helpful suggestions.

REFERENCES

Baltagi, B. H. (2013). *Econometric analysis of panel data.* Chichester: Wiley.

Baltagi, B. H., & Kao, C. (2000). Nonstationary panels, cointegration in panels and dynamic panels: A survey. *Advances in Econometrics*, *15*, 7–51.

Baltagi, B. H., Kao, C., & Liu, L. (2008). Asymptotic properties of estimators for the linear panel regression model with random individual effects and serially correlated errors: The case of stationary and non-stationary regressors and residuals. *Econometrics Journal*, *11*, 554–572.

Baltagi, B. H., Kao, C., & Na, S. (2011). Test of hypotheses in panel data models when the regressor and disturbances are possibly nonstationary. *Advances in Statistical Analysis*, *95*, 329–350.

Baltagi, B. H., & Krämer, W. (1997). A simple linear trend model with error components, problem 97.2.1. *Econometric Theory*, *13*, 463.

Baltagi, B. H., & Li, Q. (1991). A transformation that will circumvent the problem of autocorrelation in an error component model. *Journal of Econometrics*, *52*, 371–380.

Breitung, J., & Pesaran, M. H. (2008). Unit roots and cointegration in panels. In L. Matyas & P. Sevestre (Eds.), *The econometrics of panel data: Fundamentals and recent developments in theory and practice* (Chap. 9, pp. 279–322). Berlin: Springer.

Bunzel, H., & Vogelsang, T. J. (2005). Powerful trend function tests that are robust to strong serial correlation with an application to the prebish singer hypothesis. *Journal of Business and Economic Statistics*, *23*, 381–394.

Canjels, E., & Watson, M. W. (1997). Estimating deterministic trends in the presence of serially correlated errors. *Review of Economics and Statistics*, *79*, 184–200.

Choi, I. (2006). Nonstationary panels. In T. C. Mills & K. Patterson (Eds.), *Palgrave handbooks of econometrics* (Vol. 1, pp. 511–539). London: Palgrave Macmillan.

Emerson, J., & Kao, C. (2000). *Testing for structural change of a time trend regression in panel data*. Center for Policy Research Working Papers 15. Center for Policy Research, Maxwell School, Syracuse University.

Hahn, J., & Kuersteiner, G. (2002). Asymptotically unbiased inference for a dynamic panel model with fixed effects when both n and t are large. *Econometrica*, *70*, 1639–1657.

Kao, C. (1999). Spurious regression and residual-based tests for cointegration in panel data. *Journal of Econometrics*, *90*, 1–44.

Kao, C., & Emerson, J. (2004). On the estimation of a linear time trend regression with a one-way error component model in the presence of serially correlated errors: Part I. *Journal of Probability and Statistical Science*, *2*, 213–243.

Kelejian, H. H., & Prucha, I. R. (1999). A generalized moments estimator for the autoregressive parameter in spatial model. *International Economic Review*, *40*, 509–533.

Perron, P., & Yabu, T. (2009). Estimating deterministic trends with an integrated or stationary noise component. *Journal of Econometrics*, *151*, 56–69.

Phillips, P. C. B., & Moon, M. (1999). Linear regression limit theory for nonstationary panel data. *Econometrica*, *67*, 1057–1111.

Phillips, P. C. B., & Moon, M. (2000). Nonstationary panel data analysis: An overview of some recent developments. *Econometric Reviews*, *19*, 263–286.

Roy, A., Falk, B., & Fuller, W. A. (2004). Testing for trend in the presence of autoregressive error. *Journal of the American Statistical Association*, *99*, 1082–1091.

Vogelsang, T. J., & Fomby, T. B. (2002). The application of size robust trend analysis to global warming temperature series. *Journal of Climate*, *15*, 117–123.

APPENDIX

A. Proof of Theorem 1

Proof. The proof of (1) is a textbook result and hence omitted here.

Consider (2). Recall $\hat{\sigma}_v^2 = \frac{1}{n(T-1)-1}\sum_{i=1}^n \sum_{t=2}^T \hat{\nu}_{it}^2$, where $\hat{\nu}_{it} = (y_{it} - \bar{y}_{i.}) - \hat{\beta}_{\text{FE}}(t-\bar{t}) = (v_{it} - \bar{v}_{i.}) - (\hat{\beta}_{\text{FE}} - \beta)(t-\bar{t})$. Hence

$$\frac{1}{T}\hat{\sigma}_v^2 \simeq \frac{1}{nT^2}\sum_{i=1}^n\sum_{t=2}^T \hat{\nu}_{it}^2 = \frac{1}{nT^2}\sum_{i=1}^n\sum_{t=2}^T (v_{it} - \bar{v}_{i.})^2$$
$$+ \frac{1}{nT^2}\left[\sqrt{nT}\left(\hat{\beta}_{\text{FE}} - \beta\right)\right]^2 \left\{\frac{1}{nT}\sum_{i=1}^n\sum_{t=2}^T (t-\bar{t})^2\right\}$$
$$- \frac{2}{n}\left[\sqrt{nT}\left(\hat{\beta}_{\text{FE}} - \beta\right)\right]\left\{\frac{1}{\sqrt{n}T^{5/2}}\sum_{i=1}^n\sum_{t=2}^T (v_{it} - \bar{v}_{i.})\,(t-\bar{t})\right\}$$

Notice that

$$\frac{1}{nT^2}\sum_{i=1}^n\sum_{t=2}^T (v_{it} - \bar{v}_{i.})^2 \xrightarrow{p} \frac{\sigma_e^2}{6}$$

by Eq. (C3) in Kao (1999),

$$\sqrt{nT}\left(\hat{\beta}_{\text{FE}} - \beta\right) \xrightarrow{d} N\left(0, \frac{6}{5}\sigma_e^2\right)$$

by Theorem 4 in Kao and Emerson (2004), and

$$\frac{1}{\sqrt{n}T^{5/2}}\sum_{i=1}^n\sum_{t=2}^T (v_{it} - \bar{v}_{i.})(t-\bar{t}) \xrightarrow{d} 3N\left(0, \frac{\sigma_e^2}{120}\right)$$

by an equation on p. 23 in Kao and Emerson (2004).

Hence we have

$$\frac{1}{T}\hat{\sigma}_v^2 \xrightarrow{p} \frac{\sigma_e^2}{6}$$

$$nT^2\text{Var}\left(\hat{\beta}_{\text{FE}}\right) = \frac{\frac{1}{T}\hat{\sigma}_v^2}{\frac{1}{nT^3}\sum_{i=1}^{n}\sum_{t=1}^{T}(t-\bar{t})^2} \xrightarrow{p} \frac{\sigma_e^2/6}{1/12} = 2\sigma_e^2$$

and therefore

$$\frac{1}{\sqrt{T}}t_{\text{FE}} = \frac{\sqrt{nT}\left(\hat{\beta}_{\text{FE}} - \beta\right)}{\sqrt{nT^2\text{Var}\left(\hat{\beta}_{\text{FE}}\right)}} \xrightarrow{d} \frac{N\left(0, \frac{6}{5}\sigma_e^2\right)}{\sqrt{2\sigma_e^2}} = N\left(0, \frac{3}{5}\right)$$

■

B. *Proof of Theorem 2*

Proof. Consider (1). Recall $\Delta y_{it} = \beta + \Delta v_{it}$ and hence $\Delta y_{it} - \hat{\beta}_{\text{FD}} = \Delta v_{it} - (\hat{\beta}_{\text{FD}} - \beta)$. We have

$$\begin{aligned}\hat{\sigma}_e^2 &\simeq \frac{1}{nT}\sum_{i=1}^{n}\sum_{t=2}^{T}\left(\Delta y_{it} - \hat{\beta}_{\text{FD}}\right)^2 = \frac{1}{nT}\sum_{i=1}^{n}\sum_{t=2}^{T}\left[\Delta v_{it} - \left(\hat{\beta}_{\text{FD}} - \beta\right)\right]^2 \\ &= \frac{1}{nT}\sum_{i=1}^{n}\sum_{t=2}^{T}(\Delta v_{it})^2 + \frac{1}{nT^2}\left[\sqrt{n}T\left(\hat{\beta}_{\text{FD}} - \beta\right)\right]^2 \\ &\quad - \frac{2}{\sqrt{n}T}\left[\sqrt{n}T\left(\hat{\beta}_{\text{FD}} - \beta\right)\right]\left(\frac{1}{nT}\sum_{i=1}^{n}\sum_{t=2}^{T}\Delta v_{it}\right)\end{aligned}$$

Notice that

$$\frac{1}{nT}\sum_{i=1}^{n}\sum_{t=2}^{T}(\Delta v_{it})^2 = (\rho-1)^2\frac{1}{nT}\sum_{i=1}^{n}\sum_{t=2}^{T}v_{i,t-1}^2 + \frac{1}{nT}\sum_{i=1}^{n}\sum_{t=2}^{T}e_{it}^2 + 2(\rho-1)\frac{1}{nT}\sum_{i=1}^{n}\sum_{t=2}^{T}v_{i,t-1}e_{it}$$

$$\xrightarrow{p} (\rho-1)^2\frac{\sigma_e^2}{1-\rho^2} + \sigma_e^2 + 0 = \frac{2\sigma_e^2}{1+\rho}$$

$$\frac{1}{nT}\sum_{i=1}^{n}\sum_{t=2}^{T}\Delta v_{it} \xrightarrow{p} 0$$

and

$$\sqrt{n}T\left(\hat{\beta}_{\text{FD}}-\beta\right) \xrightarrow{d} N\left(0, \frac{2\sigma_e^2}{1-\rho^2}\right)$$

by Theorem 3 in Kao and Emerson (2004).

Hence we have

$$nT\text{Var}\left(\hat{\beta}_{\text{FD}}\right) = \hat{\sigma}_e^2 \xrightarrow{p} \frac{2\sigma_e^2}{1+\rho}$$

and

$$\sqrt{T}t_{\text{FD}} = \frac{\sqrt{n}T\left(\hat{\beta}_{\text{FD}}-\beta_0\right)}{\sqrt{nT\text{Var}\left(\hat{\beta}_{\text{FD}}\right)}} \xrightarrow{d} \frac{N\left(0, \frac{2}{1-\rho^2}\sigma_e^2\right)}{\sqrt{\frac{2\sigma_e^2}{1+\rho}}} = N\left(0, \frac{1}{1-\rho}\right)$$

Part (2) can be shown easily following Kao and Emerson (2004) and hence omitted. ■

Lemma 1.

$$\mathbf{x}_i^{*'}\mathbf{x}_i^* = (1-\hat{\rho})^2\sum_{t=2}^{T}t^2 + 2\hat{\rho}(1-\hat{\rho})\sum_{t=2}^{T}t + \hat{\rho}^2(T-1) + (1-\hat{\rho}^2)$$

$$\hat{\boldsymbol{\iota}}_T^{\alpha'}\mathbf{x}_i^* = (1-\hat{\rho})\sum_{t=2}^{T}t + \hat{\rho}(T-1) + (1+\hat{\rho})$$

$$\begin{aligned}\mathbf{x}_i^{*'}\mathbf{v}_i^* &= (1-\hat{\rho}^2)\nu_{i1} + (1-\hat{\rho})(\rho-\hat{\rho})\sum_{t=2}^{T}t\nu_{i,t-1} \\ &\quad + \hat{\rho}(\rho-\hat{\rho})\sum_{t=2}^{T}\nu_{i,t-1} + (1-\hat{\rho})\sum_{t=2}^{T}te_{it} + \hat{\rho}\sum_{t=2}^{T}e_{it}\end{aligned}$$

$$\hat{\boldsymbol{\iota}}_T^{\alpha'}\mathbf{v}_i^* = (1+\hat{\rho})\nu_{i1} + (\rho-\hat{\rho})\sum_{t=2}^{T}\nu_{i,t-1} + \sum_{t=2}^{T}e_{it}$$

$$\mathbf{v}_i^{*'}\mathbf{v}_i^* = (1-\hat{\rho}^2)\nu_{i1}^2 + (\rho-\hat{\rho})^2\sum_{t=2}^{T}\nu_{i,t-1}^2 + 2(\rho-\hat{\rho})\sum_{t=2}^{T}\nu_{i,t-1}e_{it} + \sum_{t=2}^{T}e_{it}^2$$

Proof. Note that $\mathbf{x}_i^* = C\mathbf{x}_i = (\sqrt{1-\hat{\rho}^2},\ 2-\hat{\rho},\ 3-2\hat{\rho},\ \cdots, T-\hat{\rho}\,(T-1))'$ and $\hat{\boldsymbol{\iota}}_T^{\alpha} = (\hat{\alpha},\ 1, 1, \cdots, 1)'$ with $\hat{\alpha} = \sqrt{(1+\hat{\rho})/(1-\hat{\rho})}$. We have

$$\begin{aligned}
\mathbf{x}_i^{*'}\mathbf{x}_i^* &= (1-\hat{\rho}^2) + \sum_{t=2}^{T}[t-\hat{\rho}(t-1)]^2 = (1-\hat{\rho}^2) + \sum_{t=2}^{T}[(1-\hat{\rho})t+\hat{\rho}]^2 \\
&= (1-\hat{\rho})^2\sum_{t=2}^{T}t^2 + 2\hat{\rho}(1-\hat{\rho})\sum_{t=2}^{T}t + \hat{\rho}^2(T-1) + (1-\hat{\rho}^2) \\
\hat{\boldsymbol{\iota}}_T^{\alpha'}\mathbf{x}_i^* &= (1+\hat{\rho}) + \sum_{t=2}^{T}(t-\hat{\rho}(t-1)) = (1+\hat{\rho}) + \sum_{t=2}^{T}[(1-\hat{\rho})t+\hat{\rho}] \\
&= (1-\hat{\rho})\sum_{t=2}^{T}t + \hat{\rho}(T-1) + (1+\hat{\rho})
\end{aligned}$$

$$\begin{aligned}
\mathbf{x}_i^{*'}\mathbf{v}_i^* &= (1-\hat{\rho}^2)\nu_{i1} + \sum_{t=2}^{T}(t-\hat{\rho}(t-1))(\nu_{it}-\hat{\rho}\nu_{i,t-1}) \\
&= (1-\hat{\rho}^2)\nu_{i1} + \sum_{t=2}^{T}[(1-\hat{\rho})t+\hat{\rho}]\,[(\rho-\hat{\rho})\nu_{i,t-1}+e_{it}] \\
&= (1-\hat{\rho}^2)\nu_{i1} + (1-\hat{\rho})(\rho-\hat{\rho})\sum_{t=2}^{T}t\nu_{i,t-1} + \hat{\rho}(\rho-\hat{\rho}) \\
&\quad \sum_{t=2}^{T}\nu_{i,t-1} + (1-\hat{\rho})\sum_{t=2}^{T}te_{it} + \hat{\rho}\sum_{t=2}^{T}e_{it}
\end{aligned}$$

$$\begin{aligned}
\hat{\boldsymbol{\iota}}_T^{\alpha'}\mathbf{v}_i^* &= (1+\hat{\rho})\nu_{i1} + \sum_{t=2}^{T}(\nu_{it}-\hat{\rho}\nu_{i,t-1}) = (1+\hat{\rho})\nu_{i1} + \sum_{t=2}^{T}[(\rho-\hat{\rho})\nu_{i,t-1}+e_{it}] \\
&= (1+\hat{\rho})\nu_{i1} + (\rho-\hat{\rho})\sum_{t=2}^{T}\nu_{i,t-1} + \sum_{t=2}^{T}e_{it}
\end{aligned}$$

and

$$\begin{aligned}
\mathbf{v}_i^{*'}\mathbf{v}_i^* &= (1-\hat{\rho}^2)\nu_{i1}^2 + \sum_{t=2}^{T}(\nu_{it}-\hat{\rho}\nu_{i,t-1})^2 = (1-\hat{\rho}^2)\nu_{i1}^2 + \sum_{t=2}^{T}[(\rho-\hat{\rho})\nu_{i,t-1}+e_{it}]^2 \\
&= (1-\hat{\rho}^2)\nu_{i1}^2 + (\rho-\hat{\rho})^2\sum_{t=2}^{T}\nu_{i,t-1}^2 + 2(\rho-\hat{\rho})\sum_{t=2}^{T}\nu_{i,t-1}e_{it} + \sum_{t=2}^{T}e_{it}^2 \quad \blacksquare
\end{aligned}$$

C. Proof of Theorem 3

Proof. Consider part (1). For a fixed n, from Lemma 1, we have

$$\begin{aligned}\frac{1}{T^3}\mathbf{x}_i^{*'}\mathbf{x}_i^* &= (1-\hat{\rho})^2\left(\frac{1}{T^3}\sum_{t=1}^{T}t^2\right)+\frac{2}{T}\hat{\rho}(1-\hat{\rho})\left(\frac{1}{T^2}\sum_{t=1}^{T}t\right)\\ &\quad+\frac{1}{T^2}\left(\frac{T-1}{T}\right)\hat{\rho}^2+\frac{1}{T^3}(1-\hat{\rho}^2)\xrightarrow{p}\frac{(1-\rho)^2}{3}\end{aligned}$$

$$\frac{1}{T^2}\hat{\boldsymbol{\iota}}_T^{\alpha'}\mathbf{x}_i^* = (1-\hat{\rho})\left(\frac{1}{T^2}\sum_{t=1}^{T}t\right)+\frac{1}{T}\left(\frac{T-1}{T}\right)\hat{\rho}+\frac{1}{T^2}(1+\hat{\rho})\xrightarrow{p}\frac{1-\rho}{2}$$

$$\begin{aligned}\frac{1}{T^{3/2}}\mathbf{x}_i^{*'}\mathbf{v}_i^* &= \frac{1}{T^{3/2}}(1-\hat{\rho}^2)\nu_{i1}+(1-\hat{\rho})(\rho-\hat{\rho})\left(\frac{1}{T^{3/2}}\sum_{t=1}^{T}t\nu_{i,t-1}\right)\\ &\quad+\frac{1}{\sqrt{T}}\hat{\rho}(\rho-\hat{\rho})\left(\frac{1}{\sqrt{T}}\sum_{t=1}^{T}\nu_{i,t-1}\right)+(1-\hat{\rho})\left(\frac{1}{T^{3/2}}\sum_{t=1}^{T}te_{it}\right)\\ &\quad+\frac{1}{T}\hat{\rho}\left(\frac{1}{\sqrt{T}}\sum_{t=1}^{T}e_{it}\right)\xrightarrow{d}(1-\rho)\,\sigma_e\int rdW_i\end{aligned}$$

$$\frac{1}{\sqrt{T}}\hat{\boldsymbol{\iota}}_T^{\alpha'}\mathbf{v}_i^* = \frac{1}{\sqrt{T}}(1+\hat{\rho})\nu_{i1}+(\rho-\hat{\rho})\left(\frac{1}{\sqrt{T}}\sum_{t=1}^{T}\nu_{i,t-1}\right)+\frac{1}{\sqrt{T}}\sum_{t=1}^{T}e_{it}\xrightarrow{d}\sigma_e W_i(1)$$

$$\begin{aligned}\frac{1}{T}\mathbf{v}_i^{*'}\mathbf{v}_i^* &= (1-\hat{\rho}^2)\frac{1}{T}\nu_{i1}^2+(\rho-\hat{\rho})^2\frac{1}{T}\sum_{t=2}^{T}\nu_{i,t-1}^2+(\rho-\hat{\rho})\\ &\quad\frac{2}{T}\sum_{t=2}^{T}\nu_{i,t-1}e_{it}+\frac{1}{T}\sum_{t=2}^{T}e_{it}^2\xrightarrow{d}\sigma_e^2\end{aligned}$$

and

$$\frac{1}{T}\hat{d}^2 = \frac{T-1}{T}+\frac{1+\hat{\rho}}{T(1-\hat{\rho})}\xrightarrow{p}1$$

as $T \to \infty$, using $\frac{1}{T^3}\sum_{t=1}^{T} t^2 \xrightarrow{p} \frac{1}{3}$, $\frac{1}{T^2}\sum_{t=1}^{T} t \xrightarrow{p} \frac{1}{2}$, $\frac{1}{T^{3/2}}\sum_{t=1}^{T} t\nu_{i,t-1} \xrightarrow{d} \sigma_v \int rdW_i$, $\frac{1}{\sqrt{T}}\sum_{t=1}^{T} \nu_{i,t-1} \xrightarrow{d} \sigma_v W_i(1)$, $\frac{1}{T^{3/2}}\sum_{t=1}^{T} te_{it} \xrightarrow{d} \sigma_e \int rdW_i$, $\frac{1}{\sqrt{T}}\sum_{t=1}^{T} e_{it} \xrightarrow{d} \sigma_e W_i(1)$ and $\hat{\rho} \xrightarrow{p} \rho$. Therefore, for a fixed n, we have

$$\frac{1}{T^3}\hat{F}_1 = \frac{1}{T^3}\mathbf{x}_i^{*'}\mathbf{x}_i^* - \frac{T}{\hat{d}^2}\left(\frac{1}{T^2}\hat{\boldsymbol{\iota}}_T^{\alpha'}\mathbf{x}_i^*\right)^2 \xrightarrow{p} \frac{(1-\rho)^2}{3} - \left(\frac{1-\rho}{2}\right)^2 = \frac{(1-\rho)^2}{12}$$

and

$$\frac{\sqrt{n}}{T^{3/2}}\hat{F}_2 = \frac{1}{\sqrt{n}T^{3/2}}\sum_{i=1}^{n}\mathbf{x}_i^{*'}\mathbf{v}_i^* - \frac{\frac{1}{T^2}\hat{\boldsymbol{\iota}}_T^{\alpha'}x_i^*}{\frac{1}{T}\hat{d}^2}\left(\frac{1}{\sqrt{n}T}\sum_{i=1}^{n}\hat{\boldsymbol{\iota}}_T^{\alpha'}\mathbf{v}_i^*\right)$$

$$\times \xrightarrow{d} \frac{1}{\sqrt{n}}\sum_{i=1}^{n}\left[(1-\rho)\sigma_e\int rdW_i\right] - \left(\frac{1-\rho}{2}\right)\frac{1}{\sqrt{n}}\sum_{i=1}^{n}[\sigma_e W_i(1)]$$

$$= (1-\rho)\sigma_e\frac{1}{\sqrt{n}}\sum_{i=1}^{n}\left[\int rdW_i - \frac{1}{2}W_i(1)\right]$$

Since $\int rdW_i - \frac{1}{2}W_i(1) \sim N\left(0, \frac{1}{12}\right)$, we have $\frac{\sqrt{n}}{T^{3/2}}\hat{F}_2 \xrightarrow{d} N\left(0, \frac{(1-\rho)^2\sigma_e^2}{12}\right)$ as $(n, T) \to \infty$. It is easy to show that $\hat{\sigma}_e^2$ is consistent for σ_e^2. Finally, we have

$$t_{\text{FE-FGLS}} = \frac{\frac{\sqrt{n}}{T^{3/2}}\hat{F}_2}{\sqrt{\hat{\sigma}_e^2\frac{1}{T^3}\hat{F}_1}} \xrightarrow{d} \frac{N\left(0, \frac{(1-\rho)^2\sigma_e^2}{12}\right)}{\frac{(1-\rho)^2\sigma_e^2}{12}} = N(0, 1)$$

as $(n, T) \to \infty$

Consider part (2). For a fixed n, from Lemma 1, we have

$$\frac{1}{T}\mathbf{x}_i^{*'}\mathbf{x}_i^* = [T(1-\hat{\rho})]^2\left(\frac{1}{T^3}\sum_{t=2}^{T}t^2\right) + 2\hat{\rho}[T(1-\hat{\rho})]\left(\frac{1}{T^2}\sum_{t=2}^{T}t\right)$$

$$+ \hat{\rho}^2\left(\frac{T-1}{T}\right) + \frac{1}{T^2}\left[T(1-\hat{\rho}^2)\right] \xrightarrow{p} \frac{1}{3}\kappa^2 - \kappa + 1$$

$$\frac{1}{T}\hat{\boldsymbol{\iota}}_T^{\alpha'}\mathbf{x}_i^* = [T(1-\hat{\rho})]\left(\frac{1}{T^2}\sum_{t=1}^{T}t\right) + \hat{\rho}\left(\frac{T-1}{T}\right) + \frac{1}{T}(1+\hat{\rho}) \xrightarrow{p} -\frac{1}{2}\kappa + 1$$

$$\begin{aligned}\frac{1}{\sqrt{T}}\mathbf{x}_i^{*'}\mathbf{v}_i^* &= \left(\frac{1}{T^{3/2}}\right)[T(1-\hat{\rho})](1+\hat{\rho})\nu_{i1} + [T(1-\hat{\rho})]^2\left(\frac{1}{T^{5/2}}\sum_{t=1}^{T}t\nu_{i,t-1}\right)\\ &\quad + \hat{\rho}[T(1-\hat{\rho})]\left(\frac{1}{T^{3/2}}\sum_{t=1}^{T}\nu_{i,t-1}\right) + [T(1-\hat{\rho})]\left(\frac{1}{T^{3/2}}\sum_{t=1}^{T}te_{it}\right)\\ &\quad + \hat{\rho}\left(\frac{1}{\sqrt{T}}\sum_{t=1}^{T}e_{it}\right) \xrightarrow{d} \sigma_e\left[\kappa^2\int rW_i - \kappa\int W_i - \kappa\int rdW_i + W_i(1)\right]\end{aligned}$$

$$\begin{aligned}\frac{\mathbf{1}}{\sqrt{T}}\hat{\boldsymbol{\iota}}_T^{\alpha'}\mathbf{v}_i^* &= \frac{1}{\sqrt{T}}(1+\hat{\rho})\nu_{i1} + [T(1-\hat{\rho})]\left(\frac{1}{T^{3/2}}\sum_{t=1}^{T}\nu_{i,t-1}\right)\\ &\quad + \frac{1}{\sqrt{T}}\sum_{t=1}^{T}e_{it} \xrightarrow{d} \sigma_e\left[-\kappa\int W_i + W_i(1)\right]\end{aligned}$$

$$\begin{aligned}\frac{1}{T}\mathbf{v}_i^{*'}\mathbf{v}_i^* &= \frac{1+\hat{\rho}}{T}[T(1-\hat{\rho})]\frac{1}{T}\nu_{i1}^2 + \frac{1}{T^{3/2}}[T(1-\hat{\rho})]^2\frac{1}{T^{3/2}}\sum_{t=2}^{T}\nu_{i,t-1}^2\\ &\quad + \frac{1}{T}[T(1-\hat{\rho})]\frac{2}{T}\sum_{t=2}^{T}\nu_{i,t-1}e_{it} + \frac{1}{T}\sum_{t=2}^{T}e_{it}^2 \xrightarrow{d} \sigma_e^2\end{aligned}$$

and

$$\frac{T}{\hat{d}^2} = \frac{T}{\frac{1+\hat{\rho}}{1-\hat{\rho}} + T - 1} = \frac{T(1-\hat{\rho})}{2\hat{\rho} + T(1-\hat{\rho})} \xrightarrow{p} \frac{-\kappa}{2-\kappa}$$

as $T\to\infty$, using $\frac{1}{T^3}\sum_{t=1}^{T}t^2 \xrightarrow{p} \frac{1}{3}$, $\frac{1}{T^2}\sum_{t=1}^{T}t \xrightarrow{p} \frac{1}{2}$, $\frac{1}{T^{5/2}}\sum_{t=1}^{T}t\nu_{i,t-1} \xrightarrow{d} \int rW_i$, $\frac{1}{T^{3/2}}\sum_{t=1}^{T}\nu_{i,t-1} \xrightarrow{d} \int W_i$, $\frac{1}{T^{3/2}}\sum_{t=1}^{T}te_{it} \xrightarrow{d} \int rdW_i$, $\frac{1}{\sqrt{T}}\sum_{t=1}^{T}e_{it} \xrightarrow{d} W_i(1)$, and $T(1-\hat{\rho}) \xrightarrow{p} -\kappa$. Therefore, for a fixed n, we have

$$\begin{aligned}\frac{1}{T}\hat{F}_1 = \frac{1}{T}\mathbf{x}_i^{*'}\mathbf{x}_i^* - \frac{[T(1-\hat{\rho})]\left(\frac{1}{T}\hat{\boldsymbol{\iota}}_T^{\alpha'}\mathbf{x}_i^*\right)^2}{(1-\hat{\rho})\hat{d}^2} &\xrightarrow{p} \frac{1}{3}\kappa^2 - \kappa + 1 - \frac{-\kappa\left(-\frac{1}{2}\kappa+1\right)^2}{2-\kappa}\\ &= \frac{-\kappa^3 + 8\kappa^2 - 24\kappa + 24}{12(2-\kappa)}\end{aligned}$$

and

$$\sqrt{\frac{n}{T}}\hat{F}_2 = \frac{1}{\sqrt{nT}}\sum_{i=1}^{n}\mathbf{x}_i^{*'}\mathbf{v}_i^* - \frac{[T(1-\hat{\rho})]\left(\frac{1}{T}\hat{\boldsymbol{\iota}}_T^{\alpha'}\mathbf{x}_i^*\right)}{(1-\hat{\rho})\hat{d}^2}\left(\frac{1}{\sqrt{nT}}\sum_{i=1}^{n}\hat{\boldsymbol{\iota}}_T^{\alpha'}\mathbf{v}_i^*\right)$$

$$\xrightarrow{d} \frac{1}{\sqrt{n}}\sum_{i=1}^{n}\sigma_e\left[\kappa^2\int rW_i - \kappa\int W_i - \kappa\int rdW_i + W_i(1)\right]$$

$$-\frac{-\kappa\left(-\frac{1}{2}\kappa+1\right)}{2-\kappa}\frac{1}{\sqrt{n}}\sum_{i=1}^{n}\sigma_e\left[-\kappa\int W_i + W_i(1)\right]$$

$$= \frac{\sigma_e}{\sqrt{n}}\sum_{i=1}^{n}\left[\kappa^2\int rW_i - \kappa\int W_i - \kappa\int rdW_i + W_i(1) + \frac{\kappa}{2}\left(-\kappa\int W_i + W_i(1)\right)\right]$$

as T→∞. Since $\int rdW_i = W_i(1) - \int W_i$, $W_i(1) = \int dW_i$, $\int rW_i = \frac{1}{2}\int W_i dr^2 = \frac{1}{2}\left[W_i(1) - \int r^2 dW_i\right] = \frac{1}{2}\int(1-r^2)dW_i$, we know that

$$\kappa^2\int rW_i - \kappa\int W_i - \kappa\int rdW_i + W_i(1) + \frac{\kappa}{2}\left(-\kappa\int W_i + W_i(1)\right)$$

$$= \kappa^2\int rW_i + (1-\kappa)W_i(1) + \frac{\kappa}{2}\left(-\kappa\int W_i + W_i(1)\right)$$

$$= \int\left[-\frac{1}{2}\kappa^2 r^2 + \frac{1}{2}\kappa^2 r + \left(1 - \frac{1}{2}\kappa\right)\right]dW_i$$

which follows a normal distribution with zero mean and variance $\int\left[-\frac{1}{2}\kappa^2 r^2 + \frac{1}{2}\kappa^2 r + \left(1-\frac{1}{2}\kappa\right)\right]^2 dr = \frac{1}{120}\kappa^4 - \frac{1}{12}\kappa^3 + \frac{5}{12}\kappa^2 - \kappa + 1$. Hence

$$\sqrt{\frac{n}{T}}\hat{F}_2 \xrightarrow{d} \sigma_e N\left(0, \frac{1}{120}\kappa^4 - \frac{1}{12}\kappa^3 + \frac{5}{12}\kappa^2 - \kappa + 1\right)$$

as $(n, T) \to \infty$. It is easy to show that $\hat{\sigma}_e^2$ is consistent for σ_e^2. Finally, we have

$$t_{\text{FE-FGLS}}=\frac{\sqrt{\frac{n}{T}}\hat{F}_2}{\sqrt{\sigma_e^2\frac{1}{T}\hat{F}_1}}\xrightarrow{d}\frac{\sigma_e N\left(0,\ \frac{1}{120}\kappa^4-\frac{1}{12}\kappa^3+\frac{5}{12}\kappa^2-\kappa+1\right)}{\sigma_e\sqrt{\frac{\kappa^4-9\kappa^3+33\kappa^2-54\kappa+36}{12(\kappa^2-3\kappa+3)}}}$$
$$=N\left(0,\ \frac{(\kappa^2-3\kappa+3)(\kappa^4-10\kappa^3+50\kappa^2-120\kappa+120)}{10(\kappa^4-9\kappa^3+33\kappa^2-54\kappa+36)}\right)$$

as $(n,\ T)\to\infty$ ∎

Lemma 2.

$$\sum_{i=1}^{n}\sum_{t=2}^{T}\hat{\nu}_{i,t-1}^2=\sum_{i=1}^{n}\sum_{t=2}^{T}(v_{i,t-1}-\overline{v}_{i.})^2+\left(\hat{\beta}_{\text{FE}}-\beta\right)^2\sum_{i=1}^{n}\sum_{t=2}^{T}(t-1-\overline{t})^2$$
$$-2\left(\hat{\beta}_{\text{FE}}-\beta\right)\sum_{i=1}^{n}\sum_{t=2}^{T}(v_{i,t-1}-\overline{v}_{i.})\,(t-1-\overline{t})$$

and

$$\sum_{i=1}^{n}\sum_{t=2}^{T}(\hat{\nu}_{it}-\rho\hat{\nu}_{i,t-1})\hat{\nu}_{i,t-1}$$
$$=\left[\sum_{i=1}^{n}\sum_{t=2}^{T}e_{it}(v_{i,t-1}-\overline{v}_{i.})+(1-\rho)\sum_{i=1}^{n}\overline{v}_{i.}(v_{iT}-\overline{v}_{i.})\right]$$
$$-\rho\left(\hat{\beta}_{\text{FE}}-\beta\right)\left[(1-\rho)\sum_{i=1}^{n}\sum_{t=2}^{T}(v_{i,t-1}-\overline{v}_{i.})(t-\overline{t})-(2\rho-1)\sum_{i=1}^{n}(v_{iT}-\overline{v}_{i.})\right]$$
$$-\left(\hat{\beta}_{\text{FE}}-\beta\right)\left[\sum_{i=1}^{n}\sum_{t=2}^{T}e_{it}(t-1-\overline{t})+\frac{1}{2}(T-1)(1-\rho)\sum_{i=1}^{n}\overline{v}_{i.}\right]$$
$$+\left(\hat{\beta}_{\text{FE}}-\beta\right)^2\left[n(1-\rho)\sum_{t=2}^{T}(t-1-\overline{t})^2+\frac{1}{2}n(T-1)\right]$$

When $\rho=1$, it reduces to

$$\sum_{i=1}^{n}\sum_{t=2}^{T}\Delta\hat{\nu}_{it}\hat{\nu}_{i,t-1}=\sum_{i=1}^{n}\sum_{t=2}^{T}e_{it}(v_{i,t-1}-\overline{v}_{i.})-(\hat{\beta}_{\text{FE}}-\beta)\left[\sum_{i=1}^{n}(v_{iT}-\overline{v}_{i.})\right]$$
$$-(\hat{\beta}_{\text{FE}}-\beta)\left[\sum_{i=1}^{n}\sum_{t=2}^{T}e_{it}(t-1-\overline{t})\right]+\frac{n(T-1)}{2}\left(\hat{\beta}_{\text{FE}}-\beta\right)^2$$

Proof. Note that $\hat{\nu}_{it} = (y_{it} - \overline{y}_{i.}) - \hat{\beta}_{\text{FE}}(t - \overline{t}) = (v_{it} - \overline{v}_{i.}) - \left(\hat{\beta}_{\text{FE}} - \beta\right)(t - \overline{t})$ and hence

$$\sum_{i=1}^{n}\sum_{t=2}^{T}\hat{\nu}_{i,t-1}^{2} = \sum_{i=1}^{n}\sum_{t=2}^{T}(v_{i,t-1} - \overline{v}_{i.})^2 + \left(\hat{\beta}_{\text{FE}} - \beta\right)^2\sum_{i=1}^{n}\sum_{t=2}^{T}(t - 1 - \overline{t})^2 - 2\left(\hat{\beta}_{\text{FE}} - \beta\right)\sum_{i=1}^{n}\sum_{t=2}^{T}(v_{i,t-1} - \overline{v}_{i.})(t - 1 - \overline{t})$$

Also, we have

$$\begin{aligned}\hat{\nu}_{it} - \rho\hat{\nu}_{i,t-1} &= [(v_{it} - \overline{v}_{i.}) - \left(\hat{\beta}_{\text{FE}} - \beta\right)(t - \overline{t})] - \rho[(v_{i,t-1} - \overline{v}_{i.}) - \left(\hat{\beta}_{\text{FE}} - \beta\right)(t - 1 - \overline{t})] \\ &= e_{it} - (1-\rho)\overline{v}_{i.} - \left(\hat{\beta}_{\text{FE}} - \beta\right)[(1-\rho)(t - \overline{t}) + \rho]\end{aligned}$$

and hence

$$\begin{aligned}\sum_{i=1}^{n}\sum_{t=2}^{T}(\hat{\nu}_{it} - \rho\hat{\nu}_{i,t-1})\hat{\nu}_{i,t-1} &= \sum_{i=1}^{n}\sum_{t=2}^{T}[e_{it} - (1-\rho)\overline{v}_{i.} - \left(\hat{\beta}_{\text{FE}} - \beta\right)((1-\rho)(t - \overline{t}) + \rho)] \\ &\quad [(v_{i,t-1} - \overline{v}_{i.}) - \left(\hat{\beta}_{\text{FE}} - \beta\right)(t - 1 - \overline{t})] \\ &= \sum_{i=1}^{n}\sum_{t=2}^{T}(e_{it} - (1-\rho)\overline{v}_{i.})(v_{i,t-1} - \overline{v}_{i.}) \\ &\quad - \left(\hat{\beta}_{\text{FE}} - \beta\right) \\ &\quad \sum_{i=1}^{n}\sum_{t=2}^{T}(v_{i,t-1} - \overline{v}_{i.})((1-\rho)(t - \overline{t}) + \rho) \\ &\quad - \left(\hat{\beta}_{\text{FE}} - \beta\right)\sum_{i=1}^{n}\sum_{t=2}^{T}(e_{it} - (1-\rho)\overline{v}_{i.})(t - 1 - \overline{t}) + \left(\hat{\beta}_{\text{FE}} - \beta\right)^2 \\ &\quad \sum_{i=1}^{n}\sum_{t=2}^{T}((1-\rho)(t - \overline{t}) + \rho)(t - 1 - \overline{t}) \\ &= I + II + III + IV\end{aligned}$$

It is easy to see that

$$\begin{aligned}I &= \sum_{i=1}^{n}\sum_{t=2}^{T}(e_{it} - (1-\rho)\overline{v}_{i.})\,(v_{i,t-1} - \overline{v}_{i.}) \\ &= \sum_{i=1}^{n}\sum_{t=2}^{T}e_{it}(v_{i,t-1} - \overline{v}_{i.}) - (1-\rho)\sum_{i=1}^{n}\sum_{t=2}^{T}\overline{v}_{i.}(v_{i,t-1} - \overline{v}_{i.}) \\ &= \sum_{i=1}^{n}\sum_{t=2}^{T}e_{it}(v_{i,t-1} - \overline{v}_{i.}) + (1-\rho)\sum_{i=1}^{n}\overline{v}_{i.}(v_{iT} - \overline{v}_{i.})\end{aligned}$$

using $\sum_{t=2}^{T}(v_{i,t-1}-\overline{v}_{i.})=\left[\sum_{t=1}^{T}(v_{it}-\overline{v}_{i.})\right]-(v_{iT}-\overline{v}_{i.})=-(v_{iT}-\overline{v}_{i.})$. For term *II*, we have

$$\begin{aligned}\sum_{i=1}^{n}\sum_{t=2}^{T}(v_{i,t-1}-\overline{v}_{i.})((1-\rho)(t-\overline{t})+\rho) &= (1-\rho)\sum_{i=1}^{n}\sum_{t=2}^{T}(v_{i,t-1}-\overline{v}_{i.})(t-\overline{t})\\ &\quad+(2\rho-1)\sum_{i=1}^{n}\sum_{t=2}^{T}(v_{i,t-1}-\overline{v}_{i.})\\ &= (1-\rho)\sum_{i=1}^{n}\sum_{t=2}^{T}(v_{i,t-1}-\overline{v}_{i.})(t-\overline{t})\\ &\quad-(2\rho-1)\sum_{i=1}^{n}(v_{iT}-\overline{v}_{i.})\end{aligned}$$

For term *III*, we have

$$\begin{aligned}\sum_{i=1}^{n}\sum_{t=2}^{T}(e_{it}-(1-\rho)\overline{v}_{i.})(t-1-\overline{t}) &= \sum_{i=1}^{n}\sum_{t=2}^{T}e_{it}(t-1-\overline{t})-(1-\rho)\sum_{i=1}^{n}\overline{v}_{i.}\sum_{t=2}^{T}(t-1-\overline{t})\\ &= \sum_{i=1}^{n}\sum_{t=2}^{T}e_{it}(t-1-\overline{t})+\frac{1}{2}(T-1)(1-\rho)\sum_{i=1}^{n}\overline{v}_{i.}\end{aligned}$$

since $\sum_{t=2}^{T}(t-1-\overline{t})=\left[\sum_{t=1}^{T}(t-\overline{t})\right]-(T-\overline{t})=-(T-\overline{t})=-\frac{T-1}{2}$. For term *IV*, we have

$$\begin{aligned}\sum_{i=1}^{n}\sum_{t=2}^{T}((1-\rho)(t-\overline{t})+\rho)(t-1-\overline{t}) &= n\sum_{t=2}^{T}((1-\rho)(t-1-\overline{t})+1)(t-1-\overline{t})\\ &= n(1-\rho)\sum_{t=2}^{T}(t-1-\overline{t})^2+n\sum_{t=2}^{T}(t-1-\overline{t})\\ &= n(1-\rho)\sum_{t=2}^{T}(t-1-\overline{t})^2+\frac{1}{2}n(T-1)\end{aligned}$$

Therefore,

$$\begin{aligned}\sum_{i=1}^{n}\sum_{t=2}^{T}(\hat{v}_{it}-\rho\hat{v}_{i,t-1})\hat{v}_{i,t-1} &= \left[\sum_{i=1}^{n}\sum_{t=2}^{T}e_{it}(v_{i,t-1}-\overline{v}_{i.})+(1-\rho)\sum_{i=1}^{n}\overline{v}_{i.}(v_{iT}-\overline{v}_{i.})\right]\\ &\quad-\rho\left(\hat{\beta}_{\mathrm{FE}}-\beta\right)\left[(1-\rho)\sum_{i=1}^{n}\sum_{t=2}^{T}(v_{i,t-1}-\overline{v}_{i.})(t-\overline{t})-(2\rho-1)\sum_{i=1}^{n}(v_{iT}-\overline{v}_{i.})\right]\\ &\quad-\left(\hat{\beta}_{\mathrm{FE}}-\beta\right)\left[\sum_{i=1}^{n}\sum_{t=2}^{T}e_{it}(t-1-\overline{t})+\frac{1}{2}(T-1)(1-\rho)\sum_{i=1}^{n}\overline{v}_{i.}\right]\\ &\quad+\left(\hat{\beta}_{\mathrm{FE}}-\beta\right)^2\left[n(1-\rho)\sum_{t=2}^{T}(t-1-\overline{t})^2+\frac{1}{2}n(T-1)\right]\end{aligned}$$

D. Proof of Theorem 4

Proof. Note that

$$\hat{\rho}-\rho=\frac{\sum_{i=1}^{n}\sum_{t=2}^{T}(\hat{\nu}_{it}-\rho\hat{\nu}_{i,t-1})\hat{\nu}_{i,t-1}}{\sum_{i=1}^{n}\sum_{t=2}^{T}\hat{\nu}_{i,t-1}^{2}}$$

Consider (1). First, from Lemma 2, we have

$$\frac{1}{nT}\sum_{i=1}^{n}\sum_{t=2}^{T}\hat{\nu}_{i,t-1}^{2}=\frac{1}{nT}\sum_{i=1}^{n}\sum_{t=2}^{T}(v_{i,t-1}-\overline{v}_{i.})^{2}+\frac{1}{nT}\left[\sqrt{n}T^{3/2}\left(\hat{\beta}_{\text{FE}}-\beta\right)\right]^{2}$$
$$\left[\frac{1}{T^{3}}\sum_{t=2}^{T}(t-1-\bar{t})^{2}\right]-\frac{2}{nT}[\sqrt{n}T^{3/2}\left(\hat{\beta}_{\text{FE}}-\beta\right)]$$
$$\left[\frac{1}{\sqrt{n}T^{3/2}}\sum_{i=1}^{n}\sum_{t=2}^{T}(v_{i,t-1}-\overline{v}_{i.})(t-1-\bar{t})\right]$$

Notice that

$$\frac{1}{nT}\sum_{i=1}^{n}\sum_{t=2}^{T}(v_{i,t-1}-\overline{v}_{i.})^{2}\xrightarrow{p}\frac{\sigma_{e}^{2}}{1-\rho^{2}}$$

by Lemma 3.1 in Baltagi et al. (2008),

$$\sqrt{n}T^{3/2}\left(\hat{\beta}_{\text{FE}}-\beta\right)\xrightarrow{d}N\left(0,\ \frac{12\sigma_{e}^{2}}{(1-\rho)^{2}}\right)$$

by Theorem 3 in Kao and Emerson (2004) and

$$\frac{1}{\sqrt{n}T^{3/2}}\sum_{i=1}^{n}\sum_{t=2}^{T}(v_{i,t-1}-\overline{v}_{i.})(t-1-\bar{t})\xrightarrow{d}N\left(0,\ \frac{\sigma_{e}^{2}}{12(1-\rho)^{2}}\right)$$

by an equation on p. 17 in Kao and Emerson (2004).

Hence we have

$$\frac{1}{nT}\sum_{i=1}^{n}\sum_{t=2}^{T}\hat{\nu}_{i,t-1}^{2}\xrightarrow{p}\frac{\sigma_{e}^{2}}{1-\rho^{2}}$$

Also, we have

$$
\begin{aligned}
\frac{1}{\sqrt{nT}}\sum_{i=1}^{n}\sum_{t=2}^{T}(\hat{v}_{it}-\rho\hat{v}_{i,t-1})\hat{v}_{i,t-1} =& \frac{1}{\sqrt{nT}}\sum_{i=1}^{n}\sum_{t=2}^{T}e_{it}(v_{i,t-1}-\overline{v}_{i.}) \\
&+\frac{1-\rho}{\sqrt{nT}}\sum_{i=1}^{n}\overline{v}_{i.}(v_{iT}-\overline{v}_{i.})-\frac{\rho}{\sqrt{nT}}\left[\sqrt{n}T^{3/2}\left(\hat{\beta}_{\mathrm{FE}}-\beta\right)\right] \\
&\left[\frac{1-\rho}{\sqrt{n}T^{3/2}}\sum_{i=1}^{n}\sum_{t=2}^{T}(v_{i,t-1}-\overline{v}_{i.})(t-\overline{t})-\frac{2\rho-1}{T^{3/2}}\left(\frac{1}{\sqrt{n}}\sum_{i=1}^{n}(v_{iT}-\overline{v}_{i.})\right)\right] \\
&-\frac{1}{\sqrt{nT}}\left[\sqrt{n}T^{3/2}\left(\hat{\beta}_{\mathrm{FE}}-\beta\right)\right] \\
&\left[\frac{1}{\sqrt{n}T^{3/2}}\sum_{i=1}^{n}\sum_{t=2}^{T}e_{it}(t-1-\overline{t})+\frac{1}{\sqrt{T}}\frac{(1-\rho)(T-1)}{2T}\left(\frac{1}{\sqrt{n}}\sum_{i=1}^{n}\overline{v}_{i.}\right)\right] \\
&+\frac{1}{\sqrt{nT}}\left[\sqrt{n}T^{3/2}\left(\hat{\beta}_{\mathrm{FE}}-\beta\right)\right]^2 \\
&\left[(1-\rho)\left[\frac{1}{T^3}\sum_{t=2}^{T}(t-1-\overline{t})^2\right]+\frac{1}{T^2}\left(\frac{T-1}{2T}\right)\right] \\
&= I+II+III+IV
\end{aligned}
$$

Consider I: Notice that

$$
\begin{aligned}
\frac{1}{\sqrt{nT}}\sum_{i=1}^{n}\sum_{t=2}^{T}e_{it}\left(v_{i,t-1}-\overline{v}_{i.}\right)+\sqrt{\frac{n}{T}\frac{\sigma_e^2}{1-\rho}} &= \frac{1}{\sqrt{nT}}\sum_{i=1}^{n}\sum_{t=2}^{T}e_{it}v_{i,t-1}-\sqrt{\frac{n}{T}}\left(\frac{1}{n}\sum_{i=1}^{n}\sum_{t=2}^{T}e_{it}\overline{v}_{i.}-\frac{\sigma_e^2}{1-\rho}\right) \\
&\xrightarrow{d}\sigma_e^2 N\left(0,\frac{1}{1-\rho^2}\right)
\end{aligned}
$$

using

$$
\frac{1}{\sqrt{nT}}\sum_{i=1}^{n}\sum_{t=2}^{T}e_{it}v_{i,t-1}\xrightarrow{d}\sigma_e^2 N\left(0,\frac{1}{1-\rho^2}\right)
$$

and

$$
\sqrt{n}\left(\frac{1}{n}\sum_{i=1}^{n}\sum_{t=2}^{T}e_{it}\overline{v}_{i.}-\frac{\sigma_e^2}{1-\rho}\right)\xrightarrow{d}N\left(0,\lim_{(n,T)\to\infty}\mathrm{Var}\left(\sum_{t=2}^{T}e_{it}\overline{v}_{i.}\right)\right)
$$

by the Lindeberg–Feller central limit theorem and

$$E\left(\sum_{t=2}^{T} e_{it}\overline{v}_{i.}\right) = E\left(\frac{1}{T}\sum_{t=1}^{T}\sum_{s=2}^{T} v_{it}e_{is}\right) = \frac{1}{T}\sum_{t=1}^{T}\sum_{s=2}^{t} E(v_{it}e_{is})$$
$$= \frac{1}{T}\sum_{t=1}^{T}\sum_{j=0}^{t-1} \rho^{j}\sigma_e^2 = \frac{\sigma_e^2}{1-\rho}$$

Together with the fact that

$$\frac{1}{\sqrt{nT}}\sum_{i=1}^{n} \overline{v}_{i.}(v_{iT} - \overline{v}_{i.}) = \frac{1}{\sqrt{nT}}\sum_{i=1}^{n} \overline{v}_{i.}v_{iT} - \frac{1}{\sqrt{nT}}\sum_{i=1}^{n} \overline{v}_{i.}^2 \xrightarrow{p} 0$$

we have

$$I + \sqrt{\frac{n}{T}}\frac{\sigma_e^2}{1-\rho} \xrightarrow{d} \sigma_e^2 N\left(0, \frac{1}{1-\rho^2}\right)$$

Consider *II*: By Theorem 3 in Kao and Emerson (2000), we have

$$\sqrt{n}T^{3/2}\left(\hat{\beta}_{\mathrm{FE}} - \beta\right) \xrightarrow{d} N\left(0, \frac{12\sigma_e^2}{(1-\rho)^2}\right)$$

Also it is easy to show that

$$\frac{1}{\sqrt{n}T^{3/2}}\sum_{i=1}^{n}\sum_{t=2}^{T}(v_{i,t-1} - \overline{v}_{i.})(t - \overline{t}) \xrightarrow{d} N\left(0, \frac{\sigma_e^2}{12(1-\rho)^2}\right)$$

and

$$\frac{1}{\sqrt{n}}\sum_{i=1}^{n}(v_{iT} - \overline{v}_{i.}) = O_p(1)$$

Hence the term $II = o_p(1)$.

Consider *III*: By an equation on p. 17 in Kao and Emerson (2004), we have

$$\frac{1}{\sqrt{n}T^{3/2}}\sum_{i=1}^{n}\sum_{t=2}^{T}e_{it}(t-1-\bar{t})\xrightarrow{d}N\left(0,\frac{\sigma_e^2}{12}\right)$$

Also it is easy to show that

$$\frac{1}{\sqrt{n}}\sum_{i=1}^{n}\bar{v}_{i.}=O_p(1)$$

Hence the term $III=o_p(1)$.

Consider IV: It is easy to show that

$$\frac{1}{nT^3}\sum_{i=1}^{n}\sum_{t=2}^{T}(t-\bar{t})^2\xrightarrow{p}\frac{1}{12}$$

and hence the term $IV=o_p(1)$.

Hence we have

$$\frac{1}{\sqrt{nT}}\sum_{i=1}^{n}\sum_{t=2}^{T}(\hat{v}_{it}-\rho\hat{v}_{i,t-1})\hat{v}_{i,t-1}+\sqrt{\frac{n}{T}}\frac{\sigma_e^2}{1-\rho}\xrightarrow{d}\sigma_e^2N\left(0,\frac{1}{1-\rho^2}\right)$$

Therefore,

$$\sqrt{nT}\left(\hat{\rho}-\rho+\frac{1+\rho}{T}\right)=\frac{\frac{1}{\sqrt{nT}}\sum_{i=1}^{n}\sum_{t=2}^{T}(\hat{v}_{it}-\rho\hat{v}_{i,t-1})\hat{v}_{i,t-1}+\sqrt{\frac{n}{T}}\frac{\sigma_e^2}{1-\rho}}{\frac{1}{nT}\sum_{i=1}^{n}\sum_{t=2}^{T}\hat{v}_{i,t-1}^2}+o_p(1)$$

$$\xrightarrow{d}\frac{\sigma_e^2N\left(0,\frac{1}{1-\rho^2}\right)}{\frac{\sigma_e^2}{1-\rho^2}}+o_p(1)=N\left(0,1-\rho^2\right)$$

as $(n,T)\to\infty$.

Next we show part (2). First, from Lemma 2, we have

$$\begin{aligned}\frac{1}{nT^2}\sum_{i=1}^{n}\sum_{t=2}^{T}\hat{\nu}_{i,t-1}^2 &= \frac{1}{nT^2}\sum_{i=1}^{n}\sum_{t=2}^{T}(v_{i,t-1}-\overline{v}_{i.})^2 - \frac{2}{n}\left[\sqrt{nT}\left(\hat{\beta}_{\mathrm{FE}}-\beta\right)\right]\\ &\frac{1}{\sqrt{n}T^{5/2}}\sum_{i=1}^{n}\sum_{t=2}^{T}[(t-1-\overline{t})(v_{it}-\overline{v}_{i.})]\\ &+\frac{1}{n}\left[nT\left(\hat{\beta}_{\mathrm{FE}}-\beta\right)^2\right]\frac{1}{T^3}\sum_{t=2}^{T}(t-1-\overline{t})^2\end{aligned}$$

Notice that

$$\sqrt{nT}\left(\hat{\beta}_{\mathrm{FE}}-\beta\right)\xrightarrow{d}N\left(0,\frac{6}{5}\sigma_e^2\right)$$

by Theorem 4 in Kao and Emerson (2004),

$$\begin{aligned}\frac{1}{\sqrt{n}T^{5/2}}\sum_{i=1}^{n}\sum_{t=2}^{T}[(t-1-\overline{t})(v_{i,t-1}-\overline{v}_{i.})] &= \frac{1}{\sqrt{n}T^{5/2}}\sum_{i=1}^{n}\sum_{t=2}^{T}[(t-1-\overline{t})v_{i,t-1}]\\ &\xrightarrow{d}N\left(0,\frac{\sigma_e^2}{120}\right)=O_p(1)\end{aligned}$$

by an equation on p. 23 in Kao and Emerson (2004), and

$$\frac{1}{nT^3}\sum_{i=1}^{n}\sum_{t=2}^{T}(t-1-\overline{t})^2\to\frac{1}{12}$$

Hence we have

$$\frac{1}{nT^2}\sum_{i=1}^{n}\sum_{t=2}^{T}\hat{\nu}_{i,t-1}^2=\frac{1}{nT^2}\sum_{i=1}^{n}\sum_{t=2}^{T}(v_{i,t-1}-\overline{v}_{i.})^2+o_p(1)$$

Next, from Lemma 2, we have

$$\begin{aligned}\frac{1}{\sqrt{n}T}\sum_{i=1}^{n}\sum_{t=2}^{T}\Delta\hat{\nu}_{it}\hat{\nu}_{i,t-1} &= \frac{1}{\sqrt{n}T}\sum_{i=1}^{n}\sum_{t=2}^{T}e_{it}(v_{i,t-1}-\overline{v}_{i.}) \\ &\quad - \frac{1}{\sqrt{n}T}\left[\sqrt{n}T\left(\hat{\beta}_{\mathrm{FE}}-\beta\right)\right]\left[\frac{1}{\sqrt{n}}\sum_{i=1}^{n}\frac{1}{\sqrt{T}}(v_{iT}-\overline{v}_{i.})\right] \\ &\quad - \frac{1}{\sqrt{n}}\left[\sqrt{n}T\left(\hat{\beta}_{\mathrm{FE}}-\beta\right)\right]\left[\frac{1}{\sqrt{n}T^{3/2}}\sum_{i=1}^{n}\sum_{t=2}^{T}e_{it}(t-1-\overline{t})\right] \\ &\quad + \frac{1}{\sqrt{n}T}\frac{T-1}{2T}\left[\sqrt{n}T\left(\hat{\beta}_{\mathrm{FE}}-\beta\right)\right]^{2}\end{aligned}$$

Notice that

$$\frac{1}{nT}\sum_{i=1}^{n}\sum_{t=2}^{T}e_{it}(v_{i,t-1}-\overline{v}_{i.})\xrightarrow{p}-\frac{\sigma_e^2}{2}$$

by Eq. (C5) in Kao (1999),

$$\frac{1}{\sqrt{n}}\sum_{i=1}^{n}\frac{1}{\sqrt{T}}(v_{iT}-\overline{v}_{i.})=\frac{1}{\sqrt{n}}\sum_{i=1}^{n}\left(\frac{v_{iT}}{\sqrt{T}}\right)-\frac{1}{\sqrt{n}}\sum_{i=1}^{n}\left(\frac{1}{T^{3/2}}\sum_{t=2}^{T}v_{it}\right)\xrightarrow{p}0$$

$$\frac{1}{\sqrt{n}T^{3/2}}\sum_{i=1}^{n}\sum_{t=2}^{T}e_{it}(t-1-\overline{t})\xrightarrow{d}N\left(0,\frac{\sigma_e^2}{12}\right)$$

by an equation on p. 17 in Kao and Emerson (2004), and

$$\sqrt{n}T\left(\hat{\beta}_{\mathrm{FE}}-\beta\right)\xrightarrow{d}N\left(0,\frac{6}{5}\sigma_e^2\right)$$

by Theorem 4 in Kao and Emerson (2004).

Hence we have

$$\frac{1}{\sqrt{n}T}\sum_{i=1}^{n}\sum_{t=2}^{T}\Delta\hat{\nu}_{it}\hat{\nu}_{i,t-1}=\frac{1}{\sqrt{n}T}\sum_{i=1}^{n}\sum_{t=2}^{T}e_{it}(v_{i,t-1}-\overline{v}_{i.})+o_p(1)$$

Therefore,

$$\sqrt{n}T(\hat{\rho}-1)=\frac{\frac{1}{\sqrt{n}T}\sum_{i=1}^{n}\sum_{t=2}^{T}\Delta\hat{v}_{it}\hat{v}_{i,t-1}}{\frac{1}{nT^2}\sum_{i=1}^{n}\sum_{t=2}^{T}\hat{v}_{i,t-1}^2}=\frac{\frac{1}{\sqrt{n}T}\sum_{i=1}^{n}\sum_{t=2}^{T}e_{it}(v_{i,t-1}-\overline{v}_{i.})}{\frac{1}{nT^2}\sum_{i=1}^{n}\sum_{t=2}^{T}(v_{i,t-1}-\overline{v}_{i.})^2}+o_p(1)$$

as $(n,T)\to\infty$. As shown in Eq. (C5) in Kao (1999),

$$\frac{1}{T}\sum_{t=2}^{T}e_{it}(v_{i,t-1}-\overline{v}_{i.})\xrightarrow{d}\zeta_{3i}$$

with $E(\zeta_{3i})=-\sigma_e^2/2$ and $\mathrm{Var}(\zeta_{3i})=\sigma_e^4/12$. Also, as shown in Eq. (C2) in Kao (1999),

$$\frac{1}{T^2}\sum_{t=2}^{T}(v_{i,t-1}-\overline{v}_{i.})^2\xrightarrow{d}\zeta_{4i}$$

with $E(\zeta_{4i})=\sigma_e^2/6$ and $\mathrm{Var}(\zeta_{4i})=\sigma_e^4/45$. By Eq. (C10) in Kao (1999), we know

$$\sqrt{n}T(\hat{\rho}-1)-\sqrt{n}\frac{-\frac{\sigma_e^2}{2}}{\frac{\sigma_e^2}{6}}\xrightarrow{d}N\left(0,\ \frac{\frac{\sigma_e^4}{12}}{\left(\frac{\sigma_e^2}{6}\right)^2}+\frac{\left(\frac{\sigma_e^2}{2}\right)^2}{\left(\frac{\sigma_e^2}{6}\right)^4}\left(\frac{\sigma_e^4}{45}\right)\right)$$

It simplifies to

$$\sqrt{n}T\left(\hat{\rho}-1-\frac{3}{T}\right)\xrightarrow{d}N\left(0,\ \frac{51}{5}\right)$$

as $(n,T)\to\infty$.

E. Proof of Theorem 5

Proof. Let $S=\{T(1-\hat{\rho})>3\}$ and $\overline{S}=\{T(1-\hat{\rho})\leq 3\}$. Consider (1). When $|\rho|<1$, it suffices to show that $\sqrt{n}T(\tilde{\rho}-\rho)-\sqrt{n}T\left(\hat{\rho}-\rho+\frac{1+\hat{\rho}}{T}\right)=\sqrt{n}T\left(\tilde{\rho}-\hat{\rho}-\frac{1+\hat{\rho}}{T}\right)\xrightarrow{p}0$. We have

$$\lim_{(n,T)\to\infty}\Pr\left(\left|\sqrt{nT}\left(\tilde{\rho}-\hat{\rho}-\frac{1+\hat{\rho}}{T}\right)\right|>\varepsilon\right) = \lim_{(n,T)\to\infty}\Pr\left(\left|\sqrt{nT}\left(\tilde{\rho}-\hat{\rho}-\frac{1+\hat{\rho}}{T}\right)\right|>\varepsilon|S\right)\Pr(S)$$
$$+\lim_{(n,T)\to\infty}\Pr\left(\left|\sqrt{nT}\left(\tilde{\rho}-\hat{\rho}-\frac{1+\hat{\rho}}{T}\right)\right|>\varepsilon|\overline{S}\right)\Pr(\overline{S})$$

The first term is zero given that, if S is true, we have $\tilde{\rho}=\hat{\rho}+1+\hat{\rho}/T$ so that $\Pr\left(\left|\sqrt{nT}\left(\tilde{\rho}-\hat{\rho}-\frac{1+\hat{\rho}}{T}\right)\right|>\varepsilon|S\right)=0$. The second term is zero since $\sqrt{nT}(\hat{\rho}-\rho+\frac{1+\rho}{T})=O_p(1)$ implies

$$T(1-\hat{\rho})-3 = T(1-\rho)+\sqrt{\frac{T}{n}}\left[\sqrt{nT}\left(\hat{\rho}-\rho+\frac{1+\rho}{T}\right)\right]-3-(1+\rho)$$
$$= T(1-\rho)+O_p\left(\sqrt{\frac{T}{n}}\right)+o_p(1)\to\infty$$

and hence $\Pr(\overline{S})\to 0$ as $T\to\infty$. Therefore, $\Pr\left(\left|\sqrt{nT}\left(\tilde{\rho}-\hat{\rho}-\frac{1+\hat{\rho}}{T}\right)\right|>\varepsilon\right)\to 0$ as $(n,T)\to\infty$. Consider (2). When $|\rho|<1$, we have

$$\lim_{(n,T)\to\infty}\Pr\left(\left|\sqrt{n}T(\tilde{\rho}-1)\right|>\varepsilon\right) = \lim_{(n,T)\to\infty}\Pr\left(\left|\sqrt{n}T(\tilde{\rho}-1)\right|>\varepsilon|S\right)\Pr(S)$$
$$+\lim_{(n,T)\to\infty}\Pr\left(\left|\sqrt{n}T(\tilde{\rho}-1)\right|>\varepsilon|\overline{S}\right)\Pr(\overline{S})$$

Now the fact that $\sqrt{n}T\left(\hat{\rho}-1+\frac{3}{T}\right)=O_p(1)$ implies $\Pr(S)\to 0$ as $(n,T)\to\infty$, so that the first term is zero. For the second term, if $\overline{S}$ is true, $\tilde{\rho}=1$ so that $\Pr\left(\left|\sqrt{n}T(\tilde{\rho}-1)\right|>\varepsilon|\overline{S}\right)=0$. Thus, $\Pr(\left|\sqrt{n}T(\tilde{\rho}-1)\right|>\varepsilon)\to 0$ as $(n,T)\to\infty$. ■

Lemma 3.

$$\sum_{i=1}^{n}\sum_{t=2}^{T}\hat{u}_{i,t-1}^2=\sum_{i=1}^{n}\sum_{t=2}^{T}(v_{i,t-1}-\overline{\overline{v}})^2+\left(\hat{\beta}_{OLS}-\beta\right)^2\sum_{i=1}^{n}\sum_{t=2}^{T}(t-1-\bar{t})^2$$
$$-2\left(\hat{\beta}_{OLS}-\beta\right)\sum_{i=1}^{n}\sum_{t=2}^{T}(t-1-\bar{t})(v_{i,t-1}-\overline{\overline{v}})$$

and

$$\begin{aligned}\sum_{i=1}^{n}\sum_{t=2}^{T}(\hat{u}_{it}-\rho\hat{u}_{i,t-1})\hat{u}_{i,t-1} &= \sum_{i=1}^{n}\sum_{t=2}^{T}[(e_{it}-(1-\rho)\bar{\bar{v}})\,(v_{i,t-1}-\bar{\bar{v}})] \\ &+ \left(\hat{\beta}_{OLS}-\beta\right)\sum_{i=1}^{n}\sum_{t=2}^{T}[(t-1-\bar{t})(e_{it}-(1-\rho)\bar{\bar{v}})] \\ &+ \left(\hat{\beta}_{OLS}-\beta\right)\sum_{i=1}^{n}\sum_{t=2}^{T}[((1-\rho)(t-\bar{t})+\rho)(v_{i,t-1}-\bar{\bar{v}})] \\ &+ \left(\hat{\beta}_{OLS}-\beta\right)^2\sum_{i=1}^{n}\sum_{t=2}^{T}[(t-1-\bar{t})((1-\rho)(t-\bar{t})+\rho)]\end{aligned}$$

When $\rho = 1$, *it reduces to*

$$\begin{aligned}\sum_{i=1}^{n}\sum_{t=2}^{T}\Delta\hat{u}_{it}\hat{u}_{i,t-1} &= \sum_{i=1}^{n}\sum_{t=2}^{T}[e_{it}(v_{i,t-1}-\bar{\bar{v}})] + \left(\hat{\beta}_{OLS}-\beta\right)\sum_{i=1}^{n}\sum_{t=2}^{T}(t-1-\bar{t})e_{it} \\ &+ \left(\hat{\beta}_{OLS}-\beta\right)\sum_{i=1}^{n}\sum_{t=2}^{T}(v_{i,t-1}-\bar{\bar{v}}) \\ &+ \left(\hat{\beta}_{OLS}-\beta\right)^2\sum_{i=1}^{n}\sum_{t=2}^{T}(t-1-\bar{t})\end{aligned}$$

where $\Delta\hat{u}_{it} = \hat{u}_{it} - \hat{u}_{i,t-1}$.

Proof. Since $\hat{u}_{it} = (y_{it} - \bar{\bar{y}}) - \hat{\beta}_{OLS}(t-\bar{t}) = (v_{it} - \bar{\bar{v}}) - \left(\hat{\beta}_{OLS}-\beta\right)(t-\bar{t})$, where $\bar{\bar{y}} = \frac{1}{nT}\sum_{i=1}^{n}\sum_{t=1}^{T} y_{it}$ and $\bar{\bar{v}} = \frac{1}{nT}\sum_{i=1}^{n}\sum_{t=1}^{T} v_{it}$ and hence

$$\begin{aligned}\hat{u}_{it}-\rho\hat{u}_{i,t-1} &= \left[(v_{it}-\bar{\bar{v}}) - \left(\hat{\beta}_{OLS}-\beta\right)(t-\bar{t})\right] \\ &\quad -\rho\left[(v_{i,t-1}-\bar{\bar{v}}) - \left(\hat{\beta}_{OLS}-\beta\right)(t-1-\bar{t})\right] \\ &= e_{it} - (1-\rho)\bar{\bar{v}} - \left(\hat{\beta}_{OLS}-\beta\right)[(t-\rho(t-1)) - (1-\rho)\bar{t}] \\ &= e_{it} - (1-\rho)\bar{\bar{v}} - \left(\hat{\beta}_{OLS}-\beta\right)[(1-\rho)(t-\bar{t})+\rho]\end{aligned}$$

Results in Lemma 3 can be easily obtained. ■

Lemma 4. *We have*

$$\sqrt{n}T^{3/2}\left(\hat{\beta}_{OLS}-\beta\right) \xrightarrow{d} N\left(0, \frac{12\sigma_e^2}{(1-\rho)^2}\right)$$

when $|\rho| < 1$ *and*

$$\sqrt{nT}\left(\hat{\beta}_{OLS} - \beta\right) \xrightarrow{d} N\left(0, \frac{6}{5}\sigma_e^2\right)$$

when $\rho = 1$

Proof. Using $u_{it} = \mu_i + v_{it}$, we have

$$\hat{\beta}_{OLS} - \beta = \frac{\sum_{i=1}^{n}\sum_{t=1}^{T}(t-\bar{t})u_{it}}{\sum_{i=1}^{n}\sum_{t=1}^{T}(t-\bar{t})^2} = \frac{\sum_{i=1}^{n}\sum_{t=1}^{T}(t-\bar{t})v_{it}}{\sum_{i=1}^{n}\sum_{t=1}^{T}(t-\bar{t})^2}$$

since $\sum_{i=1}^{n}\sum_{t=1}^{T}(t-\bar{t})\mu_i = \sum_{i=1}^{n}\mu_i\sum_{t=1}^{T}(t-\bar{t}) = 0$. By Theorems 3 and 4 in Kao and Emerson (2004), we have the asymptotic property of $\hat{\beta}_{OLS}$ in Lemma 4.

F. Proof of Theorem 6

Proof. Consider (1). Note that

$$\hat{\rho} - \rho = \frac{\sum_{i=1}^{n}\sum_{t=2}^{T}(\hat{u}_{it} - \rho\hat{u}_{i,t-1})\hat{u}_{i,t-1}}{\sum_{i=1}^{n}\sum_{t=2}^{T}\hat{u}_{i,t-1}^2}$$

From Lemma 3, we have

$$\begin{aligned}\frac{1}{nT}\sum_{i=1}^{n}\sum_{t=2}^{T}\hat{u}_{i,t-1}^2 &= \frac{1}{nT}\sum_{i=1}^{n}\sum_{t=2}^{T}(v_{i,t-1} - \bar{\bar{v}})^2 + \frac{1}{nT}\left[\sqrt{n}T^{3/2}\left(\hat{\beta}_{OLS} - \beta\right)\right]^2 \\ &\left[\frac{1}{nT^3}\sum_{i=1}^{n}\sum_{t=2}^{T}(t-1-\bar{t})^2\right] - \frac{2}{nT}\left[\sqrt{n}T^{3/2}\left(\hat{\beta}_{OLS} - \beta\right)\right] \\ &\left[\frac{1}{\sqrt{n}T^{3/2}}\sum_{i=1}^{n}\sum_{t=2}^{T}(t-1-\bar{t})(v_{it} - \bar{\bar{v}})\right]\end{aligned}$$

Notice that

$$\frac{1}{nT}\sum_{i=1}^{n}\sum_{t=2}^{T}(v_{i,t-1} - \bar{\bar{v}})^2 \xrightarrow{p} \frac{\sigma_e^2}{1-\rho^2}$$

from Lemma 3.1 of Baltagi et al. (2008),

$$\frac{1}{nT^3}\sum_{i=1}^{n}\sum_{t=2}^{T}(t-1-\bar{t})^2 \xrightarrow{p} \frac{1}{12}$$

$$\begin{aligned}\frac{1}{\sqrt{n}T^{3/2}}\sum_{i=1}^{n}\sum_{t=2}^{T}(t-1-\bar{t})(v_{it}-\bar{\bar{v}}) &= \frac{1}{\sqrt{n}T^{3/2}}\sum_{i=1}^{n}\sum_{t=2}^{T}(t-1-\bar{t})v_{it} \\ &\quad + o_p(1) \xrightarrow{d} \frac{\sigma_e^2}{1-\rho^2}N\left(0, \frac{1}{12}\right)\end{aligned}$$

and

$$\sqrt{n}T^{3/2}\left(\hat{\beta}_{OLS}-\beta\right) \xrightarrow{d} N\left(0, \frac{12\sigma_e^2}{(1-\rho)^2}\right)$$

by Lemma 4.

Hence we have

$$\frac{1}{nT}\sum_{i=1}^{n}\sum_{t=2}^{T}\hat{u}_{i,t-1}^2 \xrightarrow{p} \frac{\sigma_e^2}{1-\rho^2}$$

as $(n, T) \to \infty$. Also, from Lemma 3, we have

$$\begin{aligned}\frac{1}{\sqrt{nT}}\sum_{i=1}^{n}\sum_{t=2}^{T}(\hat{u}_{it}-\rho\hat{u}_{i,t-1})\hat{u}_{i,t-1} &= \frac{1}{\sqrt{nT}}\sum_{i=1}^{n}\sum_{t=2}^{T}[(e_{it}-(1-\rho)\bar{\bar{v}})(v_{i,t-1}-\bar{\bar{v}})] \\ &\quad + \frac{1}{\sqrt{nT}}\left[\sqrt{n}T^{3/2}\left(\hat{\beta}_{OLS}-\beta\right)\right] \\ &\quad \frac{1}{\sqrt{n}T^{3/2}}\sum_{i=1}^{n}\sum_{t=2}^{T}[(t-1-\bar{t})(e_{it}-(1-\rho)\bar{\bar{v}})] \\ &\quad + \frac{1}{\sqrt{nT}}\left[\sqrt{n}T^{3/2}\left(\hat{\beta}_{OLS}-\beta\right)\right] \\ &\quad \frac{1}{\sqrt{n}T^{3/2}}\sum_{i=1}^{n}\sum_{t=2}^{T}[((1-\rho)(t-\bar{t})+\rho)(v_{i,t-1}-\bar{\bar{v}})] \\ &\quad + \frac{1}{\sqrt{nT}}\left[\sqrt{n}T^{3/2}\left(\hat{\beta}_{OLS}-\beta\right)\right]^2 \\ &\quad \frac{1}{nT^3}\sum_{i=1}^{n}\sum_{t=2}^{T}[(t-1-\bar{t})((1-\rho)(t-\bar{t})+\rho)]\end{aligned}$$

Notice that

$$\frac{1}{\sqrt{nT}}\sum_{i=1}^{n}\sum_{t=2}^{T}\left[(e_{it}-(1-\rho)\bar{\bar{v}})(v_{i,t-1}-\bar{\bar{v}})\right] = \frac{1}{\sqrt{nT}}\sum_{i=1}^{n}\sum_{t=2}^{T}e_{it}v_{i,t-1}-\frac{1}{\sqrt{nT}}\left(\sqrt{nT}\bar{\bar{v}}\right)$$
$$\left[\frac{1}{\sqrt{nT}}\sum_{i=1}^{n}\sum_{t=2}^{T}e_{it}+(1-\rho)\frac{1}{\sqrt{nT}}\sum_{i=1}^{n}\sum_{t=2}^{T}v_{i,t-1}\right]$$
$$+\frac{1}{\sqrt{nT}}(1-\rho)\left(\sqrt{nT}\bar{\bar{v}}\right)^{2}\xrightarrow{d}\sigma_e^2 N\left(0,\frac{1}{1-\rho^2}\right)+o(1)$$

$$\frac{1}{\sqrt{n}T^{3/2}}\sum_{i=1}^{n}\sum_{t=2}^{T}\left[(t-1-\bar{t})(e_{it}-(1-\rho)\bar{\bar{v}})\right] = \frac{1}{\sqrt{n}T^{3/2}}\sum_{i=1}^{n}\sum_{t=2}^{T}[(t-1-\bar{t})e_{it}]$$
$$+o_p(1)\xrightarrow{d}\sigma_e^2 N\left(0,\frac{1}{12}\right)$$

$$\frac{1}{nT^3}\sum_{i=1}^{n}\sum_{t=2}^{T}[(t-1-\bar{t})((1-\rho)(t-\bar{t})+\rho)] = (1-\rho)\frac{1}{nT^3}\sum_{i=1}^{n}\sum_{t=2}^{T}(t-\bar{t})^2$$
$$+o_p(1)\xrightarrow{p}\frac{1-\rho}{12}$$

and

$$\sqrt{n}T^{3/2}\left(\hat{\beta}_{OLS}-\beta\right)\xrightarrow{d}N\left(0,\frac{12\sigma_e^2}{(1-\rho)^2}\right)$$

by Lemma 4.

Hence we have

$$\frac{1}{\sqrt{nT}}\sum_{i=1}^{n}\sum_{t=2}^{T}(\hat{u}_{it}-\rho\hat{u}_{i,t-1})\hat{u}_{i,t-1}\xrightarrow{d}\sigma_e^2 N\left(0,\frac{1}{1-\rho^2}\right)$$

as $(n,T)\to\infty$. Therefore,

$$\sqrt{nT}(\hat{\rho}-\rho) = \frac{\frac{1}{\sqrt{nT}}\sum_{i=1}^{n}\sum_{t=2}^{T}(\hat{u}_{it}-\rho\hat{u}_{i,t-1})\hat{u}_{i,t-1}}{\frac{1}{nT}\sum_{i=1}^{n}\sum_{t=2}^{T}\hat{u}_{i,t-1}^2}\xrightarrow{d}\frac{\sigma_e^2 N\left(0,\frac{1}{1-\rho^2}\right)}{\frac{\sigma_e^2}{1-\rho^2}}$$
$$=N(0,1-\rho^2)$$

as $(n, T) \to \infty$.

Consider (2). Note that

$$\hat{\rho} - 1 = \frac{\sum_{i=1}^{n} \sum_{t=2}^{T} \Delta \hat{u}_{it} \hat{u}_{i,t-1}}{\sum_{i=1}^{n} \sum_{t=2}^{T} \hat{u}_{i,t-1}^2}$$

From Lemma 3, we have

$$\begin{aligned}\frac{1}{nT^2} \sum_{i=1}^{n} \sum_{t=2}^{T} \hat{u}_{i,t-1}^2 &= \frac{1}{nT^2} \sum_{i=1}^{n} \sum_{t=2}^{T} (v_{i,t-1} - \bar{\bar{v}})^2 + \frac{1}{n} \left[nT \left(\hat{\beta}_{OLS} - \beta \right) \right]^2 \\ &\left[\frac{1}{nT^3} \sum_{i=1}^{n} \sum_{t=2}^{T} (t - 1 - \bar{t})^2 \right] - \frac{2}{n} \left[\sqrt{n}T \left(\hat{\beta}_{OLS} - \beta \right) \right] \\ &\left[\frac{1}{\sqrt{n}T^{5/2}} \sum_{i=1}^{n} \sum_{t=2}^{T} (t - 1 - \bar{t})(v_{i,t-1} - \bar{\bar{v}}) \right]\end{aligned}$$

Notice that

$$\frac{1}{nT^2} \sum_{i=1}^{n} \sum_{t=2}^{T} (v_{i,t-1} - \bar{\bar{v}})^2 \xrightarrow{p} \frac{\sigma_e^2}{2}$$

by Eq. (C3) in Kao (1999),

$$\sqrt{n}T \left(\hat{\beta}_{OLS} - \beta \right) \xrightarrow{d} N\left(0, \frac{6}{5}\sigma_e^2\right)$$

by Lemma 4,

$$\begin{aligned}\frac{1}{\sqrt{n}T^{5/2}} \sum_{i=1}^{n} \sum_{t=2}^{T} (t - 1 - \bar{t})(v_{i,t-1} - \bar{\bar{v}}) &= \frac{1}{\sqrt{n}T^{5/2}} \sum_{i=1}^{n} \sum_{t=2}^{T} [(t - 1 - \bar{t}) v_{i,t-1}] \\ &+ o_p(1) \xrightarrow{d} N\left(0, \frac{\sigma_e^2}{120}\right)\end{aligned}$$

by an equation on p. 23 in Kao and Emerson (2004) and

$$\frac{1}{nT^3}\sum_{i=1}^{n}\sum_{t=2}^{T}(t-1-\bar{t})^2 \to \frac{1}{12}$$

Hence we have

$$\begin{aligned}\frac{1}{nT^2}\sum_{i=1}^{n}\sum_{t=2}^{T}\hat{u}_{i,t-1}^2 &= \frac{1}{nT^2}\sum_{i=1}^{n}\sum_{t=2}^{T}(v_{i,t-1}-\bar{\bar{v}})^2 + \frac{1}{n}\left[nT\left(\hat{\beta}_{OLS}-\beta\right)\right]^2 \\ &\left[\frac{1}{nT^3}\sum_{i=1}^{n}\sum_{t=2}^{T}(t-1-\bar{t})^2\right] - \frac{2}{n}\left[\sqrt{n}T\left(\hat{\beta}_{OLS}-\beta\right)\right] \\ &\left[\frac{1}{\sqrt{n}T^{5/2}}\sum_{i=1}^{n}\sum_{t=2}^{T}(t-1-\bar{t})(v_{i,t-1}-\bar{\bar{v}})\right] \xrightarrow{p} \frac{\sigma_e^2}{6}\end{aligned}$$

as $(n, T) \to \infty$. Also, from Lemma 3,

$$\begin{aligned}\frac{1}{\sqrt{n}T}\sum_{i=1}^{n}\sum_{t=2}^{T}\Delta\hat{u}_{it}\hat{u}_{i,t-1} &= \frac{1}{\sqrt{n}T}\sum_{i=1}^{n}\sum_{t=2}^{T}\left[e_{it}(v_{i,t-1}-\bar{\bar{v}})\right] + \frac{1}{\sqrt{n}}\left[\sqrt{n}T\left(\hat{\beta}_{OLS}-\beta\right)\right] \\ &\left[\frac{1}{\sqrt{n}T^{3/2}}\sum_{i=1}^{n}\sum_{t=2}^{T}(t-1-\bar{t})e_{it}\right] + \frac{1}{T^{3/2}}\left[\sqrt{n}T\left(\hat{\beta}_{OLS}-\beta\right)\right] \\ &\left[\frac{1}{\sqrt{n}T^{3/2}}\sum_{i=1}^{n}\sum_{t=2}^{T}(v_{i,t-1}-\bar{\bar{v}})\right] + \frac{1}{\sqrt{n}T}\left[\sqrt{n}T\left(\hat{\beta}_{OLS}-\beta\right)\right]^2 \\ &\left[\frac{1}{nT}\sum_{i=1}^{n}\sum_{t=2}^{T}(t-1-\bar{t})\right]\end{aligned}$$

Notice that

$$\begin{aligned}\frac{1}{\sqrt{n}T}\sum_{i=1}^{n}\sum_{t=2}^{T}\left[e_{it}(v_{i,t-1}-\bar{\bar{v}})\right] &= \frac{1}{\sqrt{n}T}\sum_{i=1}^{n}\sum_{t=2}^{T}e_{it}v_{it} - \frac{1}{\sqrt{n}}\left(\frac{1}{\sqrt{nT}}\sum_{i=1}^{n}\sum_{t=2}^{T}e_{i,t-1}\right) \\ &\left(\frac{1}{\sqrt{n}T^{3/2}}\sum_{i=1}^{n}\sum_{t=2}^{T}v_{it}\right) \xrightarrow{d} N\left(0, \frac{\sigma_e^2}{12}\right)\end{aligned}$$

$$\frac{1}{\sqrt{n}T^{3/2}}\sum_{i=1}^{n}\sum_{t=2}^{T}(t-1-\bar{t})e_{it}\xrightarrow{d}N\left(0,\frac{\sigma_e^2}{12}\right)$$

$$\frac{1}{\sqrt{n}T^{3/2}}\sum_{i=1}^{n}\sum_{t=2}^{T}(v_{i,t-1}-\bar{\bar{v}})\xrightarrow{d}N\left(0,\frac{\sigma_e^2}{3}\right)$$

and

$$\sqrt{nT}\left(\hat{\beta}_{OLS}-\beta\right)\xrightarrow{d}N\left(0,\frac{6}{5}\sigma_e^2\right)$$

by Lemma 4 and

$$\frac{1}{nT}\sum_{i=1}^{n}\sum_{t=2}^{T}(t-1-\bar{t})\xrightarrow{p}\frac{1}{2}$$

Hence we have

$$\frac{1}{\sqrt{nT}}\sum_{i=1}^{n}\sum_{t=2}^{T}\Delta\hat{u}_{it}\hat{u}_{i,t-1}\xrightarrow{d}N\left(0,\frac{\sigma_e^2}{12}\right)$$

as $(n,T)\to\infty$. Therefore,

$$\sqrt{n}T(\hat{\rho}-1)=\frac{\frac{1}{\sqrt{nT}}\sum_{i=1}^{n}\sum_{t=2}^{T}\Delta\hat{u}_{it}\hat{u}_{i,t-1}}{\frac{1}{nT^2}\sum_{i=1}^{n}\sum_{t=2}^{T}\hat{u}_{i,t-1}^2}\xrightarrow{d}\frac{1}{\sigma_e^2/6}N\left(0,\frac{\sigma_e^2}{12}\right)=N(0,3)$$

as $(n,T)\to\infty$. ■

PART III
ISSUES IN ECONOMETRIC THEORY

LIMIT THEORY AND INFERENCE ABOUT CONDITIONAL DISTRIBUTIONS

Purevdorj Tuvaandorj and Victoria Zinde-Walsh

Department of Economics, McGill University, CIREQ, CIRANO, Montreal, Canada

ABSTRACT

We consider conditional distribution and conditional density functionals in the space of generalized functions. The approach follows Phillips (1985, 1991, 1995) who employed generalized functions to overcome non-differentiability in order to develop expansions. We obtain the limit of the kernel estimators for weakly dependent data, even under non-differentiability of the distribution function; the limit Gaussian process is characterized as a stochastic random functional (random generalized function) on the suitable function space. An alternative simple to compute estimator based on the empirical distribution function is proposed for the generalized random functional. For test statistics based on this estimator, limit properties are established. A Monte Carlo experiment demonstrates good finite sample

Essays in Honor of Peter C. B. Phillips
Advances in Econometrics, Volume 33, 397–423

ISSN: 0731-9053/doi:10.1108/S0731-905320140000033012

performance of the statistics for testing logit and probit specification in binary choice models.

Keywords: Conditional distribution; generalized functions; empirical distribution function; specification testing; bootstrap

JEL classification: C14

1. INTRODUCTION

This paper treats the conditional distribution (and conditional density) as elements in the spaces of generalized functions; this endows functions with well-defined generalized derivatives and permits expansions even when the functions are not differentiable in the ordinary sense. The generalized function approach was utilized in a number of papers by P. C. B. Phillips (1985, 1991, 1995), where the results were based on expansions in situations involving lack of differentiability. In the space of generalized functions the differentiation operator is always defined and is continuous; this is exploited in developing expansions. Here the methodology of generalized functions provides a means to derive limit processes for estimators of conditional distributions and densities.

The asymptotic properties of the kernel estimators of conditional distribution and conditional density are established in the literature only under restrictive smoothness and support assumptions. Existence and smoothness of the marginal density, $f_x(x)$, as well as differentiability (possibly twice – see, e.g., Li & Racine, 2007; Pagan & Ullah, 1999) of the joint distribution, $F_{x,y}(x, y)$, or of the conditional distribution, $F_{y|x}(x, y)$, is typically assumed. There are several problems with making such assumptions: first, both from a theoretical economic modeling perspective and from empirical evidence smoothness may be violated (kinks, spikes in hazard functions), second, smoothness assumptions are practically impossible to test, third, if smoothness is indeed violated there is no clear indication as to the pointwise behavior of the estimator under such a misspecification. The question then arises: what is the limit process of the kernel estimator of the conditional distribution and conditional density functions when the usual smoothness assumptions are violated?

The precise answer is provided when we consider these estimators in spaces of generalized functions; the limit process is a Gaussian random functional (generalized random function) on a given space of smooth functions; convergence is at a parametric rate. Although the limit process can no longer be interpreted pointwise (as in the case, e.g., the density does not exist), it provides the possibility for inference which utilizes convergence at a parametric rate to a Gaussian process. In the i.i.d. case the limit process was obtained in Zinde-Walsh (2013); here the result is extended to stationary mixing processes.

Our derivation suggests a simpler estimator that can be used in place of the kernel estimator; the estimator is based on the empirical distribution function that is easy to compute and has the same limit process as the kernel estimator in the space of generalized functions. It has the additional advantage of being unbiased.

We use the results about the limit process in generalized functions to propose test statistics for testing distributional hypotheses. We focus here on testing a parametric conditional distribution. The test differs from the conditional Kolmogorov (CK) test of Andrews (1997) and related tests that use the difference between the empirical joint distribution and the joint distribution constructed from the parametric conditional. We approach the conditional distribution via differentiation rather than integration (implicit in the CK test); this is made possible by generalized functions. Our statistic cannot exploit the sup norm since generalized functions are not defined pointwise, instead we construct a joint Gaussian process of values of the functional (indexed by several functions) and construct a χ^2 type statistic based on that (it would also be possible to use a supremum of the values of the functional). Our statistic similarly to CK suffers from the dependence arising from estimation of the parameters in the null distribution and requires performing bootstrap.

We perform a small numerical investigation of the approximation quality of the limit Gaussian process in finite samples and find that it provides a fairly good approximation to the distribution of the values of the functional (generalized function) for different choices of possible distributions even for very moderate sample sizes.

We also investigate the finite sample properties of our test for probit and logit specifications in a binary choice model. The Monte Carlo experiment provides good size properties (similar in behavior to those of CK in Andrews (1997)) in moderate samples. The test has good power in moderate sized samples; the alternatives we considered are similar to Stute and Zhu (2005).

The following notation is used throughout the paper: $\overset{d}{\rightarrow}$ and $\overset{p}{\rightarrow}$ stand for convergence in distribution (weak convergence) and in probability, respectively, $\|\cdot\|$ denotes the Euclidean norm. For the space of d_v times differentiable functions on $\mathbb{R}^{\mathrm{d}_v}$ or its open subspace W, define the differentiation operator $\partial^{\mathrm{d}_v} \equiv \frac{\partial^{\mathrm{d}_v}}{\partial v_1 \ldots \partial v_{\mathrm{d}_v}}$ that provides for any function g the derivative $\frac{\partial^{\mathrm{d}_v} g(v)}{\partial v_1 \ldots \partial v_{\mathrm{d}_v}}$.

1.1. The Space of Generalized Functions

The definitions of spaces of generalized functions that are used here are based on Gel'fand and Shilov (1964).

Consider a space of well-behaved "test" functions such as the space $D_\infty(\mathbb{R}^{d_x})$ of infinitely differentiable functions with bounded support, or any of the spaces $D_m(\mathbb{R}^{d_x})$ of m times continuously differentiable functions (with bounded support); sometimes the domain of definition can be an open subset W of $\mathbb{R}^{d_x}$, typically here W denotes $(0, 1)^{d_x} \subset \mathbb{R}^{d_x}$. Denote the generic space by $D(W)$; convergence in $D(W)$ is defined as follows: a sequence $\psi_n \in D(W)$ converges to zero if all ψ_n are defined on a common bounded support in W and ψ_n as well as all the l-th order derivatives (with $l \leq m$ for D_m or all $l < \infty$ for D_∞) converge uniformly to zero. Another space of test functions is $S(\mathbb{R}^{d_x})$ where the support of the infinitely differentiable functions is not necessarily bounded but the functions go to zero at infinity faster than any power (and all their derivatives have the same property); this was the space used in Phillips (1991, 1995).

The space of generalized functions is the dual space, $D^*(W)$, the space of linear continuous functionals on $D(W)$ with the value of the functional $f \in D^*(W)$ for a function $\psi \in D(W)$ denoted by (f, ψ). This is a linear space with the weak topology defined as follows: a sequence of elements of $D^*(W)$ converges if the sequence of values of the functionals converges for any function from $D(W)$: a sequence f_n converges to f if for any $\psi \in D(W)$ convergence $(f_n, \psi) \to (f, \psi)$ holds. Whenever some space $D_1 \subset D_2$, the inclusion $D_2^* \subset D_1^*$ holds for the dual spaces. The space of generalized functions in Phillips (1991, 1995), $S^*(\mathbb{R}^{d_x})$, is included in $D^*(\mathbb{R}^{d_x}) : S^*(\mathbb{R}^{d_x}) \subset D^*(\mathbb{R}^{d_x})$; the results here apply in that space as well.

Assume that functions in $D(W)$, $W \subseteq \mathbb{R}^{d_x}$, are suitably differentiable, e.g., at least d_x times continuously differentiable. Then for any $\psi \in D(W)$, $F \in D^*$, and the differentiation operator ∂^{d_x}, define a generalized derivative $f \in D^*; f = \partial^{d_x} F$ as the functional with values given by

$$(f, \psi) = (-1)^{d_x} (F, \partial^{d_x} \psi). \tag{1}$$

The differentiation operator in the space of generalized functions is continuous.

Suppose that F is a probability distribution function on $\mathbb{R}^{d_x}$, then it is a regular locally summable function with

$$(F, \psi) = \int \dots \int F(x_1, \dots, x_{d_x})\psi(x_1, \dots, x_{d_x})dx_1 \dots dx_{d_x},$$

where the integral exists by the properties of F. Then the value on the right-hand side of Eq. (1) is provided by integration

$$(F, \partial^{d_x}\psi) = \int \dots \int F(x_1, \dots, x_{d_x})\partial^{d_x}\psi(x_1, \dots, x_{d_x})\, dx_1 \dots dx_{d_x}.$$

Thus the functional that gives the generalized derivative: $f = \partial^{d_x}F$, the generalized density function, is fully defined. If f exists as a regular function, then it is defined as a generalized function by

$$(f, \psi) = \int \dots \int f(x_1, \dots, x_{d_x})\psi(x_1, \dots, x_{d_x})dx_1 \dots dx_{d_x};$$

it is then easy to check integrating by parts that Eq. (1) holds.

2. MAIN RESULT

2.1. Conditional Distribution and Density as Generalized Functions

Here conditioning is limited to conditioning on a variable or vector in a joint distribution, that is given a joint distribution function $F_{x,y}(\cdot,\cdot)$ on $\mathbb{R}^{d_x} \times \mathbb{R}^{d_y}$ where d_x and d_y are the dimensions of x and y, define a (generalized) function $F_{y|x}(\cdot,\cdot)$ that represents the conditional distribution of y given x. The conditional distribution function may not exist for every point x. Denote by F_x and F_y the marginal distribution functions of x and y, respectively. Note that although support of the random y belongs to $\mathbb{R}^{d_y}$ it could be a discrete set of points, thus we do not restrict y to be continuously distributed.

The generalized function representation is derived by considering copula functions (see Zinde-Walsh, 2013). Represent $F_{x,y}(x, y) = C_{F_x,F_y}(F_x(x), F_y(y))$, where $C_{F_x,F_y}(\cdot,\cdot)$ is the copula function (Sklar, 1973). If the marginal $F_x(x)$ is a continuous function, the copula function is uniquely defined in its first argument. If the marginal is not continuous, the copula function is no longer unique; following Darsow, Nguyen, and Olsen (1992) in the case when the distribution is discrete or discrete/continuous, select the copula function obtained by linear interpolation. Then our interest is in

$$\lim_{\tilde{\Delta}\to 0} \frac{C_{F_x,F_y}(a+\tilde{\Delta}, b) - C_{F_x,F_y}(a,b)}{\tilde{\Delta}}.$$

Since the copula function is differentiable with respect to each argument (and provides the appropriate value for the conditional distribution even at a mass point as shown in Darsow et al., 1992) the derivative $\frac{\partial C_{F_x,F_y}}{\partial F_x}$ is a regular function. However, the copula function is not easily obtainable and estimable and also often cannot be further differentiated to provide a conditional density. This is why we consider generalized derivatives that significantly simplify both derivation and estimation. Consider the copula function as a generalized function on $D((0,1)^{d_x})\times D(\mathbb{R}^{d_y})$; as a functional applied to $\psi_{x,y}=\psi_x(x_1,\ldots,x_{d_x})\psi_y(y_1,\ldots,y_{d_y})\in D((0,1)^{d_x})\times D(\mathbb{R}^{d_y})$ it defines the value

$$\begin{aligned}(C_{F_x,F_y},\psi) &= \int\ldots\int C_{F_x,F_y}(F_x, F_y(y))\psi_x(F_{x_1},\ldots,F_{x_{d_x}})\\ &\quad\times\psi_y(y_1,\ldots,y_{d_y})\mathrm{d}F_{x_1}\ldots\mathrm{d}F_{x_{d_x}}\mathrm{d}y_1\ldots\mathrm{d}y_{d_y}\\ &= \int\ldots\int F_{x,y}(x, y)\psi_x(F_{x_1},\ldots,F_{x_{d_x}})\\ &\quad\times\psi_y(y_1,\ldots,y_{d_y})\mathrm{d}F_{x_1}\ldots\mathrm{d}F_{x_{d_x}}\mathrm{d}y_1\ldots\mathrm{d}y_{d_y}.\end{aligned}$$

Define the conditional distribution $F_{y|x}$ as a functional on $D((0,1)^{d_x})\times D(\mathbb{R}^{d_y})$ through the generalized derivative $\frac{\partial C_{F_x,F_y}}{\partial F_x}$. For any $\psi_{x,y}\in D((0,1)^{d_x})\times D(\mathbb{R}^{d_y})$ the value of the functional is

$$\begin{aligned}(F_{y|x},\psi_{x,y}) &= (-1)^{d_x}\int\ldots\int C_{F_x,F_y}(F_x,F_y(y))\partial^{d_x}\psi_x(F_{x_1},\ldots,F_{x_{d_x}})\\ &\quad\times\psi_y(y_1,\ldots,y_{d_y})\mathrm{d}F_{x_1}\ldots\mathrm{d}F_{x_{d_x}}\mathrm{d}y_1\ldots\mathrm{d}y_{d_y}\\ &= (-1)^{d_x}\int\ldots\int F_{x,y}(x, y)\partial^{d_x}\psi_x(F_{x_1},\ldots,F_{x_{d_x}})\\ &\quad\times\psi_y(y_1,\ldots,y_{d_y})\mathrm{d}F_{x_1}\ldots\mathrm{d}F_{x_{d_x}}\mathrm{d}y_1\ldots\mathrm{d}y_{d_y}.\end{aligned} \tag{2}$$

To define conditional density $f_{y|x}$ as a generalized function, one would have

$$\begin{aligned}(f_{y|x},\psi_{x,y}) &= (-1)^{d_x+d_y}\int\ldots\int F_{x,y}(x, y)\partial^{d_x}\psi_x(F_{x_1},\ldots,F_{x_{d_x}})\\ &\quad\times\partial^{d_y}\psi_y(y_1,\ldots,y_{d_y})\mathrm{d}F_{x_1}\ldots\mathrm{d}F_{x_{d_x}}\mathrm{d}y_1\ldots\mathrm{d}y_{d_y}.\end{aligned} \tag{3}$$

When $(F_{y|x}, \psi_x)$ exists as a pointwise function of y, one can consider the conditional distribution $F_{y|x}$ as a functional on $D((0,1)^{d_x})$ only. The representation is convenient in that it involves only distribution functions (and not the copula function). Using more concise notation for the multivariate functions and integrals, we express Eq. (2) as

$$\left(F_{y|x}, \psi_{x,y}\right) = (-1)^{d_x} \int\int F_{x,y}(x, y)\, \partial^{d_x}\psi_x(F_x)\psi_y(y)dF_x dy;$$

a similar formula holds for Eq. (3).

Note that, as in Zinde-Walsh (2013) it is possible to consider F_x to be either a vector function $F_x = \left(F_{x_1}, \dots, F_{x_{d_x}}\right)'$ or a scalar function F_x of the vector $x = \left(x_1, \dots, x_{d_x}\right)'$; in the latter case, without loss of generality we can express $F_{y|x}$ as a generalized function on $D\,(0,1) \times D\left(\mathbb{R}^{d_y}\right)$ as

$$\left(F_{y|x}, \psi_{x,y}\right) = -\int\int F_{x,y}(x, y)\, \partial\psi_x(F_x)\psi_y(y)dF_x dy. \tag{4}$$

2.2. *The Limit Process of the Kernel Estimator of Conditional Distribution*

Recall the usual kernel estimator of conditional distribution:

$$\begin{aligned}\tilde{F}_{y|x}(x, y) &= \frac{\sum_{t=1}^{n} G\left(\frac{y - y_t}{h_y}\right) k\left(\frac{x_t - x}{h}\right)}{\sum_{t=1}^{n} k\left(\frac{x_t - x}{h}\right)} \\ &= \frac{\frac{1}{n}\sum_{t=1}^{n} G\left(\frac{y - y_t}{h_y}\right) \frac{1}{h^{d_x}} k\left(\frac{x_t - x}{h}\right)}{\tilde{f}_x(x)},\end{aligned} \tag{5}$$

where G is the integral of a kernel function g that satisfies assumptions similar to those on k otherwise it is assumed to be the indicator function $1(\cdot)$. The kernel functions satisfy the usual assumptions.

Assumption 1. The kernel functions k and g are bounded, smooth, symmetric density functions on bounded support on $\mathbb{R}^{d_x}$ and $\mathbb{R}^{d_y}$, respectively.

To simplify exposition we assume that each component of vector x is associated with the same (scalar) bandwidth parameter h; it is not difficult to generalize to the case of distinct bandwidths.

In Zinde-Walsh (2013) the case of independent observations was examined. Here we consider assumptions that relax the independence condition allowing for some weak form of dependence to which Donsker's theorem (see, e.g., van der Vaart & Wellner, 1996) applies. The following assumption summarizes the regularity condition.

Assumption 2. The process $\{(x_t', y_t')'\}_{t=1}^{\infty} \in \mathbb{R}^{d_x+d_y}$ is strictly stationary and α-mixing with distribution function $F_{x,y}(x, y)$ and mixing coefficient $\alpha(\tau)$ that satisfies $\alpha(\tau) = O(\tau^{-1-\varepsilon})$ for some $\varepsilon > 0$.

Denote the empirical distribution function by $\hat{F}_{\cdot}(\cdot)$; our proof employs limit results for empirical distributions. A remarkable result of Rio (2000) says that the mixing rate stated in Assumption 2, while being independent of the dimension of the vector $(x_t', y_t')'$, d_x+d_y, is sufficient for weak convergence of the empirical process $\sqrt{n}(\hat{F}_{x,y}(\cdot,\cdot) - F_{x,y}(\cdot,\cdot))$ to a tight Gaussian process. It is clear that the same property holds for $\sqrt{n}(\hat{F}_x(\cdot) - F_x(\cdot))$. Let U_x and $U_{x,y}$ be zero mean Gaussian processes with covariance functions

$$\Gamma_x(\xi_1, \xi_2) = \sum_{t=1}^{\infty} \mathrm{Cov}\,[1(x_1 \leq \xi_1)1(x_t \leq \xi_2)], \quad \xi_1, \xi_2 \in \mathbb{R}^{d_x} \tag{6}$$

and

$$\Gamma_{x,y}(\xi_1, \xi_2) = \sum_{t=1}^{\infty} \mathrm{Cov}[1((x_1', y_1')' \leq \xi_1)1((x_t', y_t')' \leq \xi_2)], \quad \xi_1, \xi_2 \in \mathbb{R}^{d_x+d_y} \tag{7}$$

respectively. Define for any v by d^v the d_x dimensional vector operator of differentiation

$$d^v = \left(\frac{\partial}{\partial v_1}, \ldots, \frac{\partial}{\partial v_{d_x}}\right).$$

Denote for a vector A and a vector B of dimension d_x by $J(A, B)$ the scalar product $\Sigma_{i=1}^{d_x} A_i B_i$. The multivariate integrals are over the appropriate spaces $D((0, 1)^{d_x}) \times \mathbb{R}^{d_y}$. The following theorem provides the limit process for the kernel estimator of the conditional distribution.

Theorem 1. Suppose that Assumptions 1 and 2 hold, and the bandwidth parameter h satisfies $h=cn^{-\delta}$ for some $\delta>1/4$. Then the estimator $\tilde{F}_{y|x}(x, y)$ as a generalized random function on $D((0,1)^{d_x})\times D(\mathbb{R}^{d_y})$ converges at $n^{1/2}$ rate to the conditional distribution generalized function $F_{y|x}(x, y)$ defined by Eq. (2) as $n\to\infty$; the limit process for $\sqrt{n}(\tilde{F}_{y|x}-F_{y|x})$ is given by a $\psi_{x,y}\in D((0,1)^{d_x})\times D(\mathbb{R}^{d_y})$ indexed random functional, $Q_{y|x}$ with

$$\begin{aligned}(Q_{y|x}, \psi_{x,y}) = (-1)^{d_x}\Big[&\int\int F_{x,y}J\left(d^{F_x}\partial^{d_x}\psi_x(F_x), U_x\right)\psi_y(y)dF_x dy \\ &+\int\int F_{x,y}\partial^{d_x}\psi_x(F_x)\psi_y(y)dU_x dy \\ &+\int\int \partial^{d_x}\psi_x(F_x)\psi_y(y)U_{x,y}dF_x dy\Big],\end{aligned} \tag{8}$$

where U_x and $U_{x,y}$ are Gaussian processes of dimensions d_x and d_x+d_y, and covariance functions given in Eqs. (6) and (7) correspondingly to F_x and $F_{x,y}$; as a generalized random process the limit process $Q_{y|x}$ of $\sqrt{n}(\tilde{F}_{y|x}-F_{y|x})$ is Gaussian with mean functional zero and covariance bilinear functional C, given, for any (suppressing the subscripts x, y) $\psi_1, \psi_2\in D((0,1)^{d_x})\times D(\mathbb{R}^{d_y})$, by

$$(C, (\psi_1, \psi_2)) = \mathrm{Cov}\left[(Q_{y|x}, \psi_1), (Q_{y|x}, \psi_2)\right].$$

The proof of Theorem 1 generalizes the proof of Theorem 3 in Zinde-Walsh (2013) to weakly dependent data, and relies on expansions in the space of generalized functions to control the bias functional.

We obtain the asymptotic distribution of the kernel estimators for weakly dependent data, even under non-differentiability of the distribution function; the limit Gaussian process is characterized as a stochastic random functional (random generalized function) on the suitable function space; the usual kernel estimator (with suitable undersmoothing) converges at a parametric rate in the space of generalized functions.

Thus the question of what happens when the kernel estimator is used in the case when the assumptions that justify the asymptotic distribution pointwise are violated is answered here: the estimator consistently estimates the generalized conditional distribution function. In consequence, the choice of bandwidth and kernel functions does not play a particular role for the asymptotic result to hold; the same limit process would be obtained if the kernel estimators were replaced by the empirical distribution functions. The latter is unbiased and more attractive from a computational viewpoint because the estimator of the generalized conditional distribution function becomes simply an average of functions evaluated at different observations, thus numerical integration is not required.

2.3. Estimators of the Conditional Distribution and Conditional Density that Exploit the Space of Generalized Functions

The proof of Theorem 1 demonstrates that the limit process of the usual kernel estimator in the space of generalized functions provides values for the functional that are identical to those obtained from an estimator based on empirical distribution function. Specifically, for $\hat{F}_{y|x}$ that is defined as a functional in the space of generalized functions by its values

$$(\hat{F}_{y|x}, \psi_{x,y}) = (-1)^{d_x} \int \dots \int \hat{F}_{x,y}(x, y) \partial^{d_x} \psi_x(\hat{F}_{x_1}, \dots, \hat{F}_{x_{d_x}}) \times \psi_y(y_1, \dots, y_{d_y}) d\hat{F}_{x_1} \dots d\hat{F}_{x_{d_x}} dy_1 \dots dy_{d_y},$$

the limit process is the same as for $\tilde{F}_{y|x}$ defined in Eq. (8). This provides an estimator for the values of the functional which does not rely on a denominator, and is more stable and asymptotically unbiased.

As pointed out in Zinde-Walsh (2013), if the interest is only in the conditional distribution, we may restrict consideration to the value for ψ_x function only and consider the values $(-1)^{d_x} E_{\hat{F}_x}(\hat{F}_{x,y}(x, y) \partial^{d_x} \psi_x(\hat{F}_{x_1}, \dots, \hat{F}_{x_{d_x}}))$ as estimators for the functional $(F_{y|x}, \psi_x)$ for every y. This is appropriate since the generalized functions approach is applied to compensate for possible non-differentiability and in the conditional distribution differentiation is applied with respect to x only. Of course, if the interest is in conditional density, then differentiation with respect to y is also required and then the values of the functional need to be constructed for $\psi_{x,y}$, a function that is smooth in y as well as in F_x. This gives us the value for the estimator of the density functional

$$(\tilde{f}_{y|x}, \psi_{x,y}) = (-1)^{d_x + d_y} \int \dots \int \tilde{F}_{x,y}(x, y) \partial^{d_x} \psi_x(\tilde{F}_{x_1}, \dots, \tilde{F}_{x_{d_x}}) \times \partial^{d_y} \psi_y(y_1, \dots, y_{d_y}) d\tilde{F}_{x_1} \dots d\tilde{F}_{x_{d_x}} dy_1 \dots dy_{d_y}. \quad (9)$$

2.4. The Limit Process for the Kernel Estimator of Generalized Conditional Density Function

Similarly to Theorem 1 the following theorem provides the limit process for the estimator of the conditional density function defined in Eq. (9).

Theorem 2. Let Assumptions 1 and 2 hold, and the bandwidth parameter h satisfy $h = cn^{-\delta}$ for some $\delta > 1/4$. The estimator $\tilde{f}_{y|x}(x, y)$ as a generalized random function on $D((0,1)^{d_x}) \times D(\mathbb{R}^{d_y})$ converges at $n^{1/2}$ rate to the conditional density generalized function $f_{y|x}(x, y)$ defined by Eq. (3) as $n \to \infty$; the limit process for $\sqrt{n}(\tilde{f}_{y|x} - f_{y|x})$ on $D((0,1)^{d_x}) \times D(\mathbb{R}^{d_y})$ is given by a $\psi_{x,y}$ indexed random functional, $M_{y|x}$ with

$$
\begin{aligned}
(M_{y|x}, \psi_{x,y}) = (-1)^{d_x + d_y}\Big[& \int\int F_{x,y} J\left(d^{F_x} \partial^{d_x} \psi_x(F_x), U_x\right) \partial^{d_y} \psi_y(y) dF_x dy \\
& + \int\int F_{x,y} \partial^{d_x} \psi_x(F_x) \partial^{d_y} \psi_y(y) dU_x dy \\
& + \int\int \partial^{d_x} \psi_x(F_x) U_{x,y} \partial^{d_y} \psi_y(y) dF_x dy \Big],
\end{aligned}
$$

where U_x and $U_{x,y}$ are zero mean Gaussian processes of dimensions d_x and $d_x + d_y$, and covariance functions given in Eqs. (6) and (7) correspondingly to F_x and $F_{x,y}$; as a generalized random process the limit process $M_{y|x}$ of $\sqrt{n}(\tilde{f}_{y|x} - f_{y|x})$ is Gaussian with mean functional zero and covariance bilinear functional C, given, for any ψ_1, ψ_2, by

$$
(C, (\psi_1, \psi_2)) = \mathrm{Cov}\left[(M_{y|x}, \psi_1), (M_{y|x}, \psi_2)\right].
$$

3. TESTING A PARAMETRIC FORM OF CONDITIONAL DISTRIBUTION

This section examines the problem of testing parametric functional form. The null hypothesis maintains that

$$
H_0 : F_{y|x}(x, y) = F_{y|x}(x, y; \theta_0) \quad \text{for some} \quad \theta_0 \in \Theta \subseteq \mathbb{R}^p,
$$

where $F_{y|x}(x, y; \theta_0)$ is a parametric conditional distribution function, and Θ denotes the parameter space. Let $\hat{\theta}$ denote the asymptotically normal maximum likelihood estimator (MLE) of θ_0. We consider a test statistic based on the difference between nonparametric and parametric linear functional estimators:

$$S_n(\hat{\theta}) = \sqrt{n} \begin{pmatrix} \left(\hat{F}_{y|x} - F_{y|x}\,(x,\ y;\ \hat{\theta}),\ \psi_{1x}\right) \\ \vdots \\ \left(\hat{F}_{y|x} - F_{y|x}\,(x,\ y;\ \hat{\theta}),\ \psi_{Lx}\right) \end{pmatrix}. \tag{10}$$

We estimate $\left(F_{y|x},\ \psi_x\right)$ employing Eq. (4) with empirical distribution functions, $\hat{F}_{x,y}$ and $\hat{F}_x$ to estimate the joint and the marginal distributions, thus

$$\int \hat{F}_{x,y}(x, y)\partial^{d_x}\psi_x\left(\hat{F}_x\right)d\hat{F}_x = \frac{1}{n}\sum_{t=1}^{n} \hat{F}_{x,y}(x_t,\ y)\partial^{d_x}\psi_x\left(\hat{F}_x(x_t)\right) \tag{11}$$

and

$$\int F_{y|x}\left(x,\ y;\ \hat{\theta}\right)\psi_x\left(\hat{F}_x\right)d\hat{F}_x = \frac{1}{n}\sum_{t=1}^{n} F_{y|x}(x_t,\ y;\ \hat{\theta})\psi_x\left(\hat{F}_x(x_t)\right), \tag{12}$$

hence no numerical integration is required for the estimation of the linear functionals. Without loss of generality, we show the asymptotic normality for $L = 1$. From Eqs. (11) and (12) we have for $y = \bar{y}$ fixed

$$\begin{aligned} S_n(\hat{\theta}) &= \sqrt{n}\left(\hat{F}_{y|x}(x,\ \bar{y}) - F_{y|x}(x,\ \bar{y};\ \hat{\theta}),\ \psi_x\right) \\ &= \sqrt{n}\left(\int \hat{F}_{x,y}(x,\ \bar{y})\partial^{d_x}\psi_x(\hat{F}_x)d\hat{F}_x - \int F_{y|x}(x,\ \bar{y};\ \hat{\theta})\psi_x(\hat{F}_x)d\hat{F}_x\right) \\ &= \frac{1}{\sqrt{n}}\sum_{t=1}^{n}\left(\hat{F}_{x,y}(x_t,\ \bar{y})\partial^{d_x}\psi_x(\hat{F}_x(x_t)) - F_{y|x}\,(x_t,\ \bar{y};\ \hat{\theta})\psi_x(\hat{F}_x(x_t))\right). \end{aligned}$$

To determine the asymptotic distribution of $S_n(\hat{\theta})$, write

$$\begin{aligned} \sqrt{n}\left(\hat{F}_{y|x}(x,\ \bar{y}) - F_{y|x}(x,\ \bar{y};\ \hat{\theta}),\ \psi_x\right) &= \sqrt{n}\left(\hat{F}_{y|x}(x,\ \bar{y}) - F_{y|x}(x,\ \bar{y};\ \theta_0),\ \psi_x\right) \\ &\quad - \sqrt{n}\left(F_{y|x}(x,\ \bar{y};\ \hat{\theta}) - F_{y|x}(x,\ \bar{y};\ \theta_0),\ \psi_x\right). \end{aligned} \tag{13}$$

The limiting distribution of the first term on the right-hand side of Eq. (13) is given by $(Q_{y|x}, \psi_x)$ in Eq. (8). Upon linearization, the second term is shown to follow normal distribution asymptotically under some regularity conditions. It will then follow that $S_n(\hat{\theta})$ has a limit Gaussian distribution with a variance that can be consistently estimated by some estimator $\hat{\Sigma}$, and the statistic defined by

$$T_n(\hat{\theta}) = S_n(\hat{\theta})'\hat{\Sigma}^{-1}S_n(\hat{\theta}) \tag{14}$$

is asymptotically χ_1^2 distributed under the null hypothesis. Since the statistic is asymptotically pivotal, bootstrap is a natural alternative to tests based on the limit χ^2 distribution and could provide refinement. Define

$$H_n(\theta) = \frac{1}{n}\sum_{t=1}^{n}\frac{\partial F_{y|x}}{\partial\theta'}(x_t, \bar{y}; \theta)\psi_x(F_x(x_t)).$$

The formal regularity conditions under which we establish the limiting distribution of the parametric component of $S_n(\hat{\theta})$ are stated in the following assumption.

Assumption 3. (a) $\hat{\theta} \xrightarrow{p} \theta_0$ with $\theta_0 \in$ interior(Θ), $\Theta \subseteq \mathbb{R}^p$. (b) $F_{y|x}(x, y; \theta)$ is continuously differentiable with respect to θ in some neighborhood $\mathcal{N}$ of θ_0 and admits a density function $f_{y|x}(x, y; \theta)$. (c) The log-likelihood function $\ell_n(\theta) = \sum_{t=1}^{n} \log f_{y|x}(x_t, y_t; \theta)$ is twice continuously differentiable in $\mathcal{N}$ with first and second order derivatives $\partial\ell_n(\theta)/\partial\theta$ and $\partial^2\ell_n(\theta)/\partial\theta\partial\theta'$ respectively. (d) $(1/\sqrt{n})\partial\ell_n(\theta_0)/\partial\theta \xrightarrow{d} N[0, I(\theta_0)]$ where $I(\theta_0)$ is nonsingular and finite, and $I(\theta)$ is continuous at θ_0. (e) $\sup_{\|h\|\leq\delta}|-(1/n)\partial^2\ell_n(\theta_0 + h/\sqrt{n})/\partial\theta\partial\theta' - I(\theta_0)| = o_p(1)$ where $\delta > 0$ is finite and $h \in \mathbb{R}^p$. (f) $\sup_{\theta\in\mathcal{N}}\|H_n(\theta) - H(\theta)\| \xrightarrow{p} 0$ with $H(\theta)$ continuous at θ_0.

The regularity conditions concerning the likelihood function and the MLE are standard (see, e.g., Theorem 3.1 of Newey & McFadden, 1994). Assumption 3 (f) is a local uniform convergence condition similar to (e) and is implied by the conditions under which the uniform law of large numbers for $H_n(\theta)$ holds. For i.i.d. data, this condition could be replaced by local uniform integrability of $(\partial F_{y|x}/\partial\theta')(x_t, \bar{y}; \theta)$ on $\mathcal{N}$ as in Lemma 4.3 of Newey and McFadden (1994). The next result characterizes the asymptotic distribution of the linear functional estimator when the parameter θ_0 is estimated by the MLE $\hat{\theta}$.

Proposition 1. Let Assumptions 2 and 3 hold. Under the null hypothesis that $H_0 : F_{y|x}(x, y) = F_{y|x}(x, y; \theta_0)$ for some $\theta_0 \in \Theta$, we have, as $n \to \infty$

$$S_n(\hat{\theta}) \xrightarrow{d} (Q_{y|x}, \psi_x) - [Z + \int F_{y|x}(x, \bar{y}; \theta_0) J \left(\mathrm{d}^{F_x}\psi_x(F_x), U_x\right) \mathrm{d}F_x + \int F_{y|x}(x, \bar{y}; \theta_0) \psi_x(F_x) \mathrm{d}U_x] \tag{15}$$

where $Z \sim N\left[0, H(\theta_0) I(\theta_0)^{-1} H(\theta_0)'\right]$.

4. SIMULATIONS

This section presents simulation evidence on the performance of estimators and test statistics. We use eq. (11) for the estimation of $\left(F_{y|x}, \psi_x\right)$:

$$(\hat{Q}_{y|x}, \psi_x) = -\int \hat{F}_{x,y} \partial\psi_x(\hat{F}_x) \mathrm{d}\hat{F}_x = -\frac{1}{n}\sum_{t=1}^{n} \hat{F}_{x,y}(x_t, y) \partial\psi_x\left(\hat{F}_x(x_t)\right)$$

following Eq. (4). All calculations were carried out in R Version 3.0.2 (R Development Core Team, 2013).

4.1. Numerical Evaluation of Test Function Selection

We conduct a simple experiment to explore which test function provides better results for the distribution of estimated values of the functional. We generate several joint distributions similar to those considered by Donoho and Johnstone (1995): y_t is generated according to

$$y_t = \frac{g(x_t)}{s_g} + u_t, \quad x_t \sim \text{Uniform}[0, 1], \quad u_t \sim N[0, \sigma^2], \quad t = 1, \ldots, n,$$

where s_g is the standard deviation of $g(x_t)$. The functions used are

$$\text{HeaviSine}: \quad g(x) = 4\sin 4\pi x - \text{sign}(x - 0.3) - \text{sign}(0.72 - x);$$

$$\text{Blocks}: \quad g(x) = \sum_{j=1}^{11} h_j \varphi(x - \tau_j), \quad \varphi(x) = \frac{1}{2}(1 + \text{sign}(x)),$$

$$\tau = (0.1, 0.13, 0.15, 0.23, 0.25, 0.40, 0.44, 0.65, 0.76, 0.78, 0.81),$$

$$h = (4, -5, 3, -4, 5, -4.2, 2.1, 4.3, -3.1, 2.1, -4.2);$$

$$\text{Bumps}: \quad g(x) = \sum_{j=1}^{11} h_j \varphi\left(\frac{x - \tau_j}{w_j}\right), \quad \varphi(x) = \frac{1}{(1 + |x|)^4},$$

$$\tau = (0.1, 0.13, 0.15, 0.23, 0.25, 0.40, 0.44, 0.65, 0.76, 0.78, 0.81),$$

$$h = (4, 5, 3, 4, 5, 4.2, 2.1, 4.3, 3.1, 5.1, 4.2),$$

$$w = (0.005, 0.005, 0.006, 0.01, 0.01, 0.03, 0.01, 0.01, 0.005, 0.008, 0.005);$$

$$\text{Doppler}: \quad g(x) = \sqrt{x(1 - x)} \sin\left(\frac{2\pi(1 + \varepsilon)}{x + \varepsilon}\right), \quad \varepsilon = 0.05.$$

In the simulation experiment, the following functions are used as test functions: quadratic $\psi_x(x) = x(1 - x)1(0 \le x \le 1)$, quartic $\psi_x(x) = x^2(1 - x)^2 1(0 \le x \le 1)$, and bump $\psi_x(x) = \exp(-1/x(1 - x))1(0 \le x \le 1)$. The number of simulated samples is $N = 1{,}000$, and $n = 50$. The values of y at which the linear functional $(F_{y|x}, \psi_x)$ is estimated are 21 equidistant grid points on $[-5, 5]$. We average the values of $\sqrt{n}$ times the absolute bias and $\sqrt{n}$ times the root mean squared error (RMSE) over the grid points.

The results are reported in Table 1. On comparing $\sigma = 2$ to $\sigma = 1$, we see that the absolute bias and the RMSE of the test functions are stable for Blocks and Bumps, greater for Doppler, and somewhat lower for HeaviSine when $\sigma = 2$. The bump function (see Fig. 1) outperforms the quadratic and quartic functions in terms of bias and RMSE in all cases, so we shall proceed with this function for the example studied in Section 4.2.

Choosing a test function ψ_x with good properties is obviously an important problem that calls for a further investigation. In general, an optimal choice of test function is likely to be specific to the problem at hand, and a considerable effort would be required for determining such functions.

Table 1. Mean Absolute Bias and RMSE of Estimators of $(F_{y|x}, \psi_x)$ over 1,000 Simulated Samples of Size $n = 50$.

$\sigma=1$	HeaviSine		Blocks		Bumps		Doppler	
Test Functions	Bias	RMSE	Bias	RMSE	Bias	RMSE	Bias	RMSE
Quadratic	0.151	0.162	0.452	0.457	0.454	0.458	0.072	0.087
Quartic	0.032	0.035	0.096	0.097	0.097	0.098	0.009	0.014
Bump	0.007	0.008	0.020	0.021	0.020	0.021	0.002	0.003
$\sigma=2$	HeaviSine		Blocks		Bumps		Doppler	
Test functions	Bias	RMSE	Bias	RMSE	Bias	RMSE	Bias	RMSE
Quadratic	0.122	0.146	0.473	0.481	0.465	0.472	0.248	0.262
Quartic	0.021	0.027	0.100	0.102	0.099	0.101	0.046	0.050
Bump	0.005	0.007	0.021	0.022	0.021	0.021	0.010	0.011

4.2. A Test of Parametric Specification in a Binary Choice Model

The specification we use in the simulation is

$$P(y_t = 1|x_t) = \Psi\left(x_t'\theta + c\left(\sum_{j=1}^{p}|x_{tj}|\right)\right) \qquad t = 1, \dots, n, \tag{16}$$

where $x_t = (x_{t1}, \dots, x_{tp})' \sim N[0, I_p]$ and Ψ is either the logistic ($\Psi(u) = \exp(u)/(1+\exp(u))$ or the standard normal (probit) CDF. The logit or probit model under the null hypothesis has $c = 0$. The alternative is generated with $c = 0.5, 1, 2, 3$. The parameter values are $\theta = (-1/\sqrt{2}, 1/\sqrt{2})'$ for $p=2$, and $\theta = (-1/\sqrt{3}, 1/\sqrt{3}, -1/\sqrt{3})$ for $p=3$. The logit design and the parameter configurations $c=1, 2, 3$ follow Stute and Zhu (2005); we consider additionally the probit model and a closer alternative with $c=0.5$.

Since, for $0 \le \bar{y} < 1$, $F_{y|x}(x_t, \bar{y}; \theta) = P(y_t \le \bar{y}|x_t, \theta) = P(y_t = 0|x_t, \theta)$, it suffices to determine the asymptotic distribution of the test statistic at a single value, say $\bar{y} = 0.5$, in which case the corresponding test statistics S_n and T_n are asymptotically normal and chi-square distributed, respectively. The test based on the statistic S_n is a percentile bootstrap type

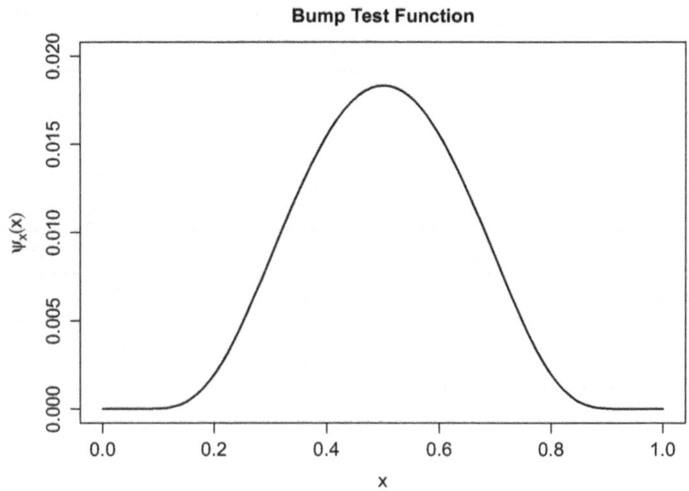

Fig. 1. Bump Test Function.

procedure; we generate $B = 199$ bootstrap samples $\{(x_t', y_t^*)'\}_{t=1}^n$ according to $P(y_t^* = 1) = \Psi(x_t'\hat{\theta})$ where $\hat{\theta}$ is the MLE of θ, and compute the bootstrap statistics $S_{n,j}^*$, $j = 1, \ldots, B$. We then reject the null hypothesis at level 5% if S_n is outside the (0.025,0.975) range of the bootstrap distribution. To construct the statistic T_n, the sample mean $\overline{S}^*$ of $S_{n,j}^*, j = 1,\ldots, B$ is subtracted off from S_n to correct the finite sample bias, and Σ is estimated by the sample covariance of the bootstrap samples, $\text{Var}(S_n^*)$. The test rejects at 5% level if the statistic $T_n = (S_n - \overline{S}^*)^2 / \text{Var}(S_n^*)$ is greater than the 0.95 quantile of χ_1^2 distribution. The number of replications is $N =$ 1,000 as before.

We report the estimated size and powers of the tests in Tables 2 and 3. We generally note that though both tests are undersized, the S_n test provides an improvement bringing the size closer to nominal. Also, the sizes of the tests improve as the sample size increases. Despite the low probability of rejection under the null, the power is substantial in both models. The percentile bootstrap test based on S_n dominates the asymptotic test T_n in terms of the power. Furthermore, in every case, the powers of the tests S_n and T_n are greater than those reported by Stute and Zhu (2005) for the logit model with $c = 1, 2, 3$.

Table 2. The Null Rejection Frequency under Eq. (16) with $c = 0$ at 5% Level.

Logit	$p = 2$		$p = 3$	
Test Statistics	S_n	T_n	S_n	T_n
$n = 50$	0.032	0.025	0.032	0.030
$n = 100$	0.030	0.039	0.041	0.030
Probit	$p = 2$		$p = 3$	
Test statistics	S_n	T_n	S_n	T_n
$n = 50$	0.039	0.033	0.025	0.022
$n = 100$	0.051	0.041	0.034	0.031

Table 3. Powers of Tests for H_0: (16) with c = 0 against H_1: (16) with $c =$ 0.5, 1, 2, 3. at 5% Level.

Logit Model								
Test Statistics	S_n	T_n	S_n	T_n	S_n	T_n	S_n	T_n
$p = 2$	$c = 0.5$		$c = 1$		$c = 2$		$c = 3$	
$n = 50$	0.315	0.207	0.623	0.486	0.737	0.645	0.752	0.658
$n = 100$	0.521	0.423	0.790	0.735	0.827	0.805	0.830	0.803
$p = 3$	$c = 0.5$		$c = 1$		$c = 2$		$c = 3$	
$n = 50$	0.659	0.533	0.915	0.873	0.945	0.919	0.950	0.927
$n = 100$	0.924	0.883	0.992	0.989	0.996	0.992	0.996	0.990
Probit Model								
$p = 2$	$c = 0.5$		$c = 1$		$c = 2$		$c = 3$	
$n = 50$	0.526	0.369	0.741	0.656	0.749	0.661	0.756	0.675
$n = 100$	0.746	0.677	0.844	0.815	0.837	0.806	0.849	0.811
$p = 3$	$c = 0.5$		$c = 1$		$c = 2$		$c = 3$	
$n = 50$	0.881	0.789	0.944	0.905	0.947	0.935	0.957	0.946
$n = 100$	0.979	0.972	0.997	0.989	0.991	0.988	0.995	0.992

5. CONCLUSION

This paper establishes the asymptotic properties of estimators of conditional distribution and density functions for stationary mixing data by treating them as elements of the space of generalized functions.

Accordingly, no smoothness restriction is needed for the validity of asymptotic distribution of the proposed estimators; the possible irregularities associated with the distribution and density functions are smoothed out through the use of an appropriate test function. The computationally inexpensive linear functional estimator that is based on the empirical distribution performs satisfactorily for a moderate size sample. The percentile bootstrap procedure based on the proposed estimator is applied to testing functional form in the binary choice model and has good size and power properties in the simulations conducted.

ACKNOWELDGEMENT

The authors thank the participants of the 14th Advances in Econometrics Conference and especially Brendan Beare, and an anonymous referee, the editors Yoosoon Chang and Joon Park for helpful comments and suggestions. The authors gratefully acknowledge support of this research from the Fonds de recherche sur la société et la culture (Québec).

REFERENCES

Andrews, D. W. K. (1997). A conditional Kolmogorov test. *Econometrica, 65*, 1097–1128.

Andrews, D. W. K. (1999). Estimation when a parameter is on a boundary. *Econometrica, 67*, 1341–1383.

Darsow, W. F., Nguyen, B., & Olsen, E. T. (1992). Copulas and Markov processes. *Illinois Journal of Mathematics, 36*(4), 600–642.

Donoho, D. L., & Johnstone, I. M. (1995). Adapting to unknown smoothness via wavelet shrinkage. *Journal of the American Statisitcal Association, 90*(432), 1200–1224.

Gel'fand, I. M., & Shilov, G. E. (1964). *Generalized functions: Properties and operations* (Vol. 1–2). San Diego: Academic Press.

Li, Q., & Racine, J. S. (2007). *Nonparametric econometrics: Theory and practice*. Princeton, NJ: Princeton University Press.

Newey, W. K., & McFadden, D. (1994). Large sample estimation and hypothesis testing. In R. F. Engle & D. L. McFadden (Eds.), *Handbook of econometrics* (Vol. 4, Chap. 36, pp. 2111–2245). Amsterdam: Elsevier Science.

Pagan, A., & Ullah, A. (1999). *Nonparametric econometrics,* Themes in modern econometrics. Cambridge, U.K.: Cambridge University Press.

Phillips, P. C. B. (1985). A theorem on the tail behaviour of probability distributions with an application to the stable family. *Canadian Journal of Economics, 18*(1), 58–65.

Phillips, P. C. B. (1991). A shortcut to LAD estimator asymptotics. *Econometric Theory, 7*, 450–463.

Phillips, P. C. B. (1995). Robust nonstationary regression. *Econometric Theory, 11*, 450–463.

R Development Core Team. (2013). *R: A language and environment for statistical computing* R *foundation for statistical computing*. Vienna, Austria. ISBN 3-900051-07-0.

Rio, E. (2000). *Théorie asymptotique des processus aléatoires faiblement dépendants*. In *Mathématiques and applications* (Vol. 31). Berlin: Springer.

Sklar, A. (1973). Random variables, joint distribution functions, and copulas. *Kybernetika*, *9*(6), 449–460.

Stute, W., & Zhu, L.-X. (2005). Nonparametric checks for single-index models. *The Annals of Statistics*, *33*(3), 1048–1083.

van der Vaart, A. W., & Wellner, J. A. (1996). *Weak convergence and empirical processes*. Springer-Verlag, New York: Springer.

Zinde-Walsh, V. (2013). Nonparametric functionals as generalized functions," arXiv:1303. 1435.

APPENDIX: PROOFS

Theorem 1. For any $\psi_x \in D((0,1)^{d_x})$, by the lemma in Zinde-Walsh (2013) the value of the functional $(\tilde{F}_{y|x}, \psi_x)$ is well defined by

$$(\tilde{F}_{y|x}, \psi_x) = (-1)^{d_x} \int \frac{1}{n}\sum_{t=1}^{n} G\left(\frac{y-y_t}{h_y}\right) K\left(\frac{x_t-x}{h}\right) \partial d_x \psi_x \left(\frac{1}{n}\sum_{t=1}^{n} K\left(\frac{x_t-x}{h}\right)\right) \mathrm{d}\left(\frac{1}{n}\sum_{t=1}^{n} K\left(\frac{x_t-x}{h}\right)\right),$$

where G and K are integrals of the kernel functions g and k. Write

$$\int \tilde{F}_{x,y} \partial^{d_x} \psi_x(\tilde{F}_x)\, \mathrm{d}\tilde{F}_x = \int \hat{F}_{x,y} \partial^{d_x} \psi_x(\hat{F}_x)\, \mathrm{d}\hat{F}_x + \left[\int \tilde{F}_{x,y} \partial^{d_x} \psi_x(\tilde{F}_x)\, \mathrm{d}\tilde{F}_x - \int \hat{F}_{x,y} \partial^{d_x} \psi_x(\hat{F}_x)\, \mathrm{d}\hat{F}_x\right].$$

Calculating the bias by expansions, we find

$$\int \tilde{F}_{x,y} \partial^{d_x} \psi_x\, (\tilde{F}_x)\, \mathrm{d}\tilde{F}_x - \int \hat{F}_{x,y} \partial^{d_x} \psi_x(\hat{F}_x)\, \mathrm{d}\hat{F}_x = O_p(h^2).$$

Clearly,

$$\int \hat{F}_{x,y} \partial^{d_x} \psi_x(\hat{F}_x) \mathrm{d}\hat{F}_x = \left[\int F_{x,y} \partial^{d_x} \psi_x(\hat{F}_x) \mathrm{d}F_x + \int F_{x,y} \partial^{d_x} \psi_x(\hat{F}_x) \mathrm{d}(\hat{F}_x - F_x)\right] + \left[\int (\hat{F}_{x,y} - F_{x,y}) \partial^{d_x} \psi_x(\hat{F}_x) \mathrm{d}F_x + \int (\hat{F}_{x,y} - F_{x,y}) \partial^{d_x} \psi(\hat{F}_x) \mathrm{d}(\hat{F}_x - F_x)\right]. \tag{A.1}$$

By Taylor expansion,

$$\partial^{d_x} \psi_x(\hat{F}_x(x)) = \partial^{d_x} \psi_x(F_x(x)) + \sum_{i=1}^{d_x} \frac{\partial}{\partial F_{x_i}} \partial^{d_x} \psi_x(F_x) \left(\hat{F}_{x_i}(x) - F_{x_i}(x)\right) + r(\hat{F}_x(x) - F_x(x)), \tag{A.2}$$

where $x^2 r(x) \to 0$ as $x \to 0$, and by the Mean Value theorem

$$\partial^{d_x}\psi_x(\hat{F}_x(x)) = \partial^{d_x}\psi_x(F_x(x)) + \sum_{i=1}^{d_x}\frac{\partial}{\partial F_{x_i}}\partial^{d_x}\psi_x\left(\overline{F}_x\right)\left(\hat{F}_{x_i}(x) - F_{x_i}(x)\right) \tag{A.3}$$

where $\overline{F}_x \in (0, 1)^{d_x}$ is a mixture of $\hat{F}_x$ and F_x. Then the first term in eq. (A.1) can be written as

$$\begin{aligned}\int F_{x,y}\partial^{d_x}\psi_x(\hat{F}_x)\mathrm{d}F_x &= \int F_{x,y}\partial^{d_x}\psi_x(F_x)\mathrm{d}F_x + \int F_{x,y}J\left(\mathrm{d}^{F_x}\partial^{d_x}\psi_x(F_x), \hat{F}_x - F_x\right)\mathrm{d}F_x \\ &+ \int F_{x,y}\partial^{d_x}\psi_x(F_x)r(\hat{F}_x - F_x)\mathrm{d}F_x.\end{aligned}$$

Using Eq. (A.3), the remaining terms in Eq. (A.1) become

$$\begin{aligned}\int F_{x,y}\partial^{d_x}\psi_x(\hat{F}_x)\, d(\hat{F}_x - F_x) &= \int F_{x,y}\partial^{d_x}\psi_x(F_x)\, d(\hat{F}_x - F_x) \\ &+ \int F_{x,y}J\left(\mathrm{d}^{F_x}\partial^{d_x}\psi_x\left(\overline{F}_x\right),\ \hat{F}_x - F_x\right) d(\hat{F}_x - F_x),\end{aligned} \tag{A.4}$$

$$\begin{aligned}\int (\hat{F}_{x,y} - F_{x,y})\partial^{d_x}\psi_x(\hat{F}_x)\,\mathrm{d}F_x &= \int (\hat{F}_{x,y} - F_{x,y})\partial^{d_x}\psi_x(F_x)\,\mathrm{d}F_x \\ &+ \int (\hat{F}_{x,y} - F_{x,y})J\left(\mathrm{d}^{F_x}\partial^{d_x}\psi_x(\overline{F}_x),\ \hat{F}_x - F_x\right)\mathrm{d}F_x\end{aligned} \tag{A.5}$$

and

$$\begin{aligned}\int (\hat{F}_{x,y} - F_{x,y})\partial^{d_x}\psi_x(\hat{F}_x)d(\hat{F}_x - F_x) &= \int (\hat{F}_{x,y} - F_{x,y})\partial^{d_x}\psi_x(F_x)\mathrm{d}(\hat{F}_x - F_x) \\ &+ \int (\hat{F}_{x,y} - F_{x,y})J\left(\mathrm{d}^{F_x}\partial^{d_x}\psi_x(\overline{F}_x), \hat{F}_x - F_x\right)\mathrm{d}(\hat{F}_x - F_x).\end{aligned} \tag{A.6}$$

By properties of $\psi_x \in D(W)$, the function $\mathrm{d}^{F_x}\partial^{d_x}\psi_x(\overline{F}_x)$ is bounded. By weak convergence of the empirical distribution function for multivariate α-mixing processes (see Theorem 7.3 of Rio, 2000),

$$\sqrt{n}(\hat{F}_{x,y} - F_{x,y}) \xrightarrow{d} U_{x,y}, \quad \sqrt{n}(\hat{F}_x - F_x) \xrightarrow{d} U_x,$$

where $U_{x,y}$ and U_x are Gaussian processes with dimension $\mathrm{d}_x+\mathrm{d}_y$ and d_x respectively. Then we can express $\sqrt{n}(\hat{F}_{y|x}-F_{y|x},\ \psi_x)$ as

$$Q_\psi\left(\sqrt{n}(\hat{F}_x-F_x),\ \sqrt{n}(\hat{F}_{x,y}-F_{x,y})\right)+\sqrt{n}R\left(\sqrt{n}(\hat{F}_x-F_x),\ \sqrt{n}(\hat{F}_{x,y}-F_{x,y})\right),$$

where

$$\begin{aligned}Q_\psi\left(\sqrt{n}(\hat{F}_x-F_x),\ \sqrt{n}(\hat{F}_{x,y}-F_{x,y})\right)=&\int F_{x,y}\partial^{\mathrm{d}_x}\psi_x(F_x)\,\mathrm{d}\sqrt{n}(\hat{F}_x-F_x)\\&+\int\sqrt{n}(\hat{F}_{x,y}-F_{x,y})\partial^{\mathrm{d}_x}\psi_x(F_x)\,\mathrm{d}F_x\\&+\int F_{x,y}J\left(\mathrm{d}^{F_x}\partial^{\mathrm{d}_x}\psi_x(F_x),\ \sqrt{n}(\hat{F}_x-F_x)\right)\mathrm{d}F_x\end{aligned}$$

and $R(\cdot,\cdot)$ is a bounded function. Since the function Q_ψ is continuous in its arguments, by substituting the limiting Gaussian processes for the arguments of $Q_\psi(\cdot,\cdot)$ we obtain $\sqrt{n}(\hat{F}_{y|x}-F_{y|x},\ \psi_x)\xrightarrow{\mathrm{d}}(Q_{y|x},\ \psi_x)=Q_\psi(U_x,\ U_{x,y})$. For any (omitting the subscript x) $\psi_1,\ldots,\psi_l\in D(W)$, the joint limiting Gaussian process for

$$\sqrt{n}\left(\hat{F}_{y|x}-F_{y|x},\ \psi_l\right),\ \ldots,\sqrt{n}\left(\hat{F}_{y|x}-F_{y|x},\ \psi_l\right)$$

is similarly derived from the joint process of $Q_{\psi_1}(U_x,\ U_{x,y}),\ldots,$ $Q_{\psi_1}(U_x,\ U_{x,y})$. The mean of the process is zero since Q_ψ is linear in its arguments and the covariance is given by $\mathrm{Cov}\left(Q_{\psi_1}(U_x,\ U_{x,y}),\ Q_{\psi_2}(U_x,\ U_{x,y})\right)=\mathrm{Cov}\left((Q_{y|x},\ \psi_1),\ (Q_{y|x},\ \psi_2)\right)$. Since by assumption $h^2=o(n^{-1/2})$, the limiting process on $D(W)$ is fully described by $Q_{y|x}$. Since $\psi_{x,y}$ is a product function, this implies (8). ■

Theorem 2. By proceeding similarly to Theorem 1, we have, for any $\psi\in D((0,1)^{\mathrm{d}_x})\times D(\mathbb{R}^{\mathrm{d}_y})$,

$$(\tilde{f}_{y|x},\ \psi_{x,y})=(-1)^{\mathrm{d}_x+\mathrm{d}_y}\int\int\tilde{F}_{x,y}(x,\ y)\partial^{\mathrm{d}_x}\psi_x(\tilde{F}_x)\partial^{\mathrm{d}_y}\psi_y(y)\,\mathrm{d}\tilde{F}_x\,\mathrm{d}y.$$

Decompose

$$\begin{aligned}&\int\int\tilde{F}_{x,y}(x,y)\partial^{\mathrm{d}_x}\psi_x(\tilde{F}_x)\partial^{\mathrm{d}_y}\psi_y(y)\mathrm{d}\tilde{F}_x\mathrm{d}y\\&=\int\int\hat{F}_{x,y}(x,y)\partial^{\mathrm{d}_x}\psi_x(\hat{F}_x)\partial^{\mathrm{d}_y}\psi_y(y)\mathrm{d}\hat{F}_x\mathrm{d}y\\&\quad+\left[\int\int\tilde{F}_{x,y}(x,y)\partial^{\mathrm{d}_x}\psi_x(\tilde{F}_x)\partial^{\mathrm{d}_y}\psi_y(y)\mathrm{d}\tilde{F}_x\mathrm{d}y-\int\int\hat{F}_{x,y}(x,y)\partial^{\mathrm{d}_x}\psi_x(\hat{F}_x)\partial^{\mathrm{d}_y}\psi_y(y)\mathrm{d}\hat{F}_x\mathrm{d}y\right].\end{aligned}$$

The second term in the bracket is $O_p(h^2)$. Write the first term as

$$\int\int \hat{F}_{x,y}\partial^{d_x}\psi_x(\hat{F}_x)\partial^{d_y}\psi_y\, d\hat{F}_x\, dy$$

$$= \int\int F_{x,y}\partial^{d_x}\psi_x(\hat{F}_x)\partial^{d_y}\psi_y\, dF_x\, dy \tag{A.7}$$

$$+ \int\int F_{x,y}\partial^{d_x}\psi_x(\hat{F}_x)\partial^{d_y}\psi_y\, d(\hat{F}_x - F_x)\, dy \tag{A.8}$$

$$+ \int\int (\hat{F}_{x,y} - F_{x,y})\partial^{d_x}\psi_x(\hat{F}_x)\partial^{d_y}\psi_y\, dF_x\, dy \tag{A.9}$$

$$+ \int\int (\hat{F}_{x,y} - F_{x,y})\partial^{d_x}\psi_x(\hat{F}_x)\partial^{d_y}\psi_y\, d(\hat{F}_x - F_x)\, dy. \tag{A.10}$$

For Eq. (A.7), using Eq. (A.2) we have

$$\begin{aligned}\int\int F_{x,y}\partial^{d_x}\psi_x(\hat{F}_x)\partial^{d_y}\psi_y dF_x dy &= \int\int F_{x,y}\partial^{d_x}\psi_x(F_x)\partial^{d_y}\psi_y dF_x dy \\ &+ \int\int F_{x,y}J\left(d^{F_x}\partial^{d_x}\psi_x(F_x), \hat{F}_x - F_x\right)\partial^{d_y}\psi_y dF_x dy \\ &+ \int\int F_{x,y}r(\hat{F}_x - F_x)\partial^{d_y}\psi_y dF_x dy.\end{aligned}$$

The first term in the right hand side of the above expression is the true value of the functional. When scaled by factor $\sqrt{n}$, the second term converges in distribution to $\int\int F_{x,y}J(d^{F_x}\partial^{d_x}\psi_x(F_x), U_x)\, \partial^{d_y}\psi_y\, dU_x\, dy$ and the third term is negligible. From Eqs. (A.3), (A.8) and (A.9) become

$$\begin{aligned}\int\int F_{x,y}\partial^{d_x}\psi_x(\hat{F}_x)\partial^{d_y}\psi_y d(\hat{F}_x - F_x)dy &= \int\int F_{x,y}\partial^{d_x}\psi_x(F_x)\partial^{d_y}\psi_y d(\hat{F}_x - F_x)dy \\ &+ \int\int F_{x,y}J\left(d^{F_x}\partial^{d_x}\psi_x(\overline{F}_x), \hat{F}_x - F_x\right)\partial^{d_y}\psi_y d(\hat{F}_x - F_x)dy\end{aligned}$$

and

$$\begin{aligned}\int\int (\hat{F}_{x,y} - F_{x,y})\partial^{d_x}\psi_x(\hat{F}_x)\partial^{d_y}\psi_y dF_x dy &= \int\int (\hat{F}_{x,y} - F_{x,y})\partial^{d_x}\psi_x(F_x)\partial^{d_y}\psi_y dF_x dy \\ &+ \int\int (\hat{F}_{x,y} - F_{x,y})J\left(d^{F_x}\partial^{d_x}\psi_x(\overline{F}_x), \hat{F}_x - F_x\right)\partial^{d_y}\psi_y dF_x dy.\end{aligned}$$

Only the first terms on right hand side of the above expressions converge in distribution to nondegenerate random variables given by

$$\int\int F_{x,y}\partial^{d_x}\psi_x(F_x)\partial^{d_y}\psi_y(y)\,dU_x\,dy \quad\text{and}\quad \int\int U_{x,y}\partial^{d_x}\psi_x(F_x)\partial^{d_y}\psi_y(y)\,dF_x\,dy$$

respectively. Finally, we see that (A.10) is negligible by writing

$$\begin{aligned}\int\int(\hat{F}_{x,y}-F_{x,y})\partial^{d_x}\psi_x(\hat{F}_x)\partial^{d_y}\psi_y\,d(\hat{F}_x-F_x)dy &= \int\int(\hat{F}_{x,y}-F_{x,y})\partial^{d_x}\psi_x(F_x)\partial^{d_y}\psi_y\,d(\hat{F}_x-F_x)dy\\ &\quad+\int\int(\hat{F}_{x,y}-F_{x,y})J(d^{F_x}\partial^{d_x}\psi_x(\overline{F}_x),\hat{F}_x-F_x)\\ &\quad\times\partial^{d_y}\psi_y\,d(\hat{F}_x-F_x)dy.\end{aligned}$$

Taken together,

$$\begin{aligned}\sqrt{n}(\tilde{f}_{y|x}-f_{y|x},\psi_{x,y}) \xrightarrow{d} (-1)^{d_x+d_y}\Bigg[&\int\int F_{x,y}J(d^{F_x}\partial^{d_x}\psi_x\,(F_x),\,U_x)\,\partial^{d_y}\psi_y\,dU_x\,dy\\ &+\int\int F_{x,y}\partial^{d_x}\psi_x(F_x)\partial^{d_y}\psi_y(y)\,dU_x\,dy\\ &+\int\int \partial^{d_x}\psi_x(F_x)U_{x,y}\partial^{d_y}\psi_y(y)\,dF_x\,dy\Bigg].\end{aligned}$$

■

Proposition 1. Recall the decomposition (13):

$$\begin{aligned}&\sqrt{n}\left[\int\hat{F}_{x,y}(x,\,\overline{y})\partial^{d_x}\psi_x(\hat{F}_x)\,d\hat{F}_x - F_{y|x}(x,\,\overline{y};\,\hat{\theta})\psi_x(\hat{F}_x)\,d\hat{F}_x\right]\\ &=\sqrt{n}\left[\int\hat{F}_{x,y}(x,\,\overline{y})\partial^{d_x}\psi_x(\hat{F}_x)\,d\hat{F}_x - \int F_{x,y}(x,\,\overline{y})\partial^{d_x}\psi_x(F_x)\,dF_x\right]\\ &\quad-\sqrt{n}\left[\int F_{y|x}(x,\,\overline{y};\,\hat{\theta})\psi_x(\hat{F}_x)\,d\hat{F}_x - \int F_{y|x}(x,\,\overline{y};\,\theta_0)\psi_x(F_x)\,dF_x\right].\end{aligned}$$

By Theorem 1, the first component converges in distribution to $(Q_{y|x},\,\psi_x)$. Write the second term as

$$\sqrt{n}\left[\int F_{y|x}(x,\,\overline{y};\,\hat{\theta})\psi_x(\hat{F}_x)\,d\hat{F}_x - \int F_{y|x}(x,\,\overline{y};\,\theta_0)\psi_x(F_x)\,dF_x\right].$$

$$= \sqrt{n} \int F_{y|x}(x,\ \bar{y};\ \theta_0)\psi_x(F_x)\ \mathrm{d}(\hat{F}_x - F_x) \tag{A.11}$$

$$+ \sqrt{n} \int F_{y|x}(x,\ \bar{y};\ \theta_0)\ (\psi_x(\hat{F}_x) - \psi_x(F_x))\ \mathrm{d}\hat{F}_x \tag{A.12}$$

$$+ \sqrt{n} \int (F_{y|x}(x,\ \bar{y};\ \hat{\theta}) - F_{y|x}(x,\ \bar{y};\ \theta_0))\ \psi_x(\hat{F}_x)\ \mathrm{d}\hat{F}_x. \tag{A.13}$$

We find the limiting distribution of each term in the above expression separately. For Eq. (A.11), we have

$$\sqrt{n} \int F_{y|x}(x,\ \bar{y};\ \theta_0)\psi_x(F_x)\ \mathrm{d}(\hat{F}_x - F_x) \xrightarrow{d} \int F_{y|x}(x,\ \bar{y};\ \theta_0)\psi_x(F_x)\ \mathrm{d}U_x \tag{A.14}$$

as $n \to \infty$. On writing Eq. (A.12) as

$$\begin{aligned}\sqrt{n} \int F_{y|x}(x,\bar{y};\theta_0)(\psi_x(\hat{F}_x) - \psi_x(F_x))\mathrm{d}\hat{F}_x &= \sqrt{n} \int F_{y|x}(x,\bar{y};\theta_0)(\psi_x(\hat{F}_x) - \psi_x(F_x))\mathrm{d}F_x \\ &+ \sqrt{n} \int F_{y|x}(x,\bar{y};\theta_0)\,(\psi_x(\hat{F}_x) - \psi_x(F_x))\mathrm{d}(\hat{F}_x - F_x)\end{aligned}$$

and applying the Mean Value theorem $\psi_x(\hat{F}_x) - \psi_x(F_x) = J\left(\mathrm{d}^{F_x}\psi_x(\overline{F}_x),\ \hat{F}_x - F_x\right)$ and $\sqrt{n}(\hat{F}_x - F_x) \xrightarrow{d} U_x$ to each term in the last equation,

$$\begin{aligned}&\sqrt{n} \int F_{y|x}(x,\ \bar{y};\ \theta_0)(\psi_x(\hat{F}_x) - \psi_x(F_x))\ \mathrm{d}\hat{F}_x \\ &= \int F_{y|x}(x,\ \bar{y};\ \theta_0)J\ \left(\mathrm{d}^{F_x}\psi_x(F_x),\ \sqrt{n}(\hat{F}_x - F_x)\right)\ \mathrm{d}F_x + o_P(1) \\ &\xrightarrow{d} \int F_{y|x}(x,\ \bar{y};\ \theta_0)J\ (\mathrm{d}^{F_x}\psi_x(F_x),\ U_x)\ \mathrm{d}F_x.\end{aligned} \tag{A.15}$$

Assumptions 3(a)–(e) imply $\sqrt{n}(\hat{\theta} - \theta_0) = O_p(1)$ (see Andrews, 1999, Theorem 1, van der Vaart & Wellner, 1996 Chapter 3.4). Expanding the score function around the true parameter value and using Assumption 3 (d) and (e), we have $\sqrt{n}(\hat{\theta} - \theta_0) = I(\theta_0)^{-1}(1/\sqrt{n})\partial\ell_n(\theta_0)/\partial\theta + o_p(1) \xrightarrow{d} N[0, I(\theta_0)^{-1}]$. Then Eq. (A.13) becomes

$$
\begin{aligned}
&\sqrt{n}\int (F_{y|x}(x,\ \bar{y};\ \hat{\theta}) - F_{y|x}(x,\ \bar{y};\ \theta_0))\ \psi_x\ (\hat{F}_x)\ \mathrm{d}\hat{F}_x \\
&= \frac{1}{n}\sum_{t=1}^{n}\sqrt{n}(F_{y|x}(x_t,\ \bar{y};\ \hat{\theta}) - F_{y|x}(x_t,\ \bar{y};\ \theta_0))\ \psi_x\ (\hat{F}_x(x_t)) \\
&= \frac{1}{n}\sum_{t=1}^{n}\frac{\partial F_{y|x}}{\partial\theta'}(x_t,\ \bar{y};\ \overline{\theta})\ \psi_x\ (\hat{F}_x(x_t))\sqrt{n}(\hat{\theta} - \theta_0) \\
&= \frac{1}{n}\sum_{t=1}^{n}\frac{\partial F_{y|x}}{\partial\theta'}(x_t,\ \bar{y};\ \overline{\theta})\psi_x\ (F_x(x_t))\sqrt{n}(\hat{\theta} - \theta_0) + o_p(1) \\
&= H_n(\overline{\theta})I(\theta_0)^{-1}\frac{1}{\sqrt{n}}\frac{\partial \ell_n(\theta_0)}{\partial\theta} + o_p(1),
\end{aligned}
$$

where the second equality is due to the Mean Value expansion around θ_0 with $\overline{\theta}$ being a convex combination of $\hat{\theta}$ and θ_0, and the third equality follows by expanding $\psi_x(\hat{F}_x(x_t))$ around $\psi_x(F_x(x_t))$ and using $\sqrt{n}(\hat{F}_x - F_x) = O_p(1)$, $\sqrt{n}(\hat{\theta} - \theta_0) = O_p(1)$ in conjunction with Assumptions 3 (a) and (b). Since from Assumption 3 (a) and (g)

$$
H_n(\overline{\theta}) = \frac{1}{n}\sum_{t=1}^{n}\frac{\partial F_{y|x}}{\partial\theta'}(x_t,\ \bar{y};\ \overline{\theta})\psi_x(F(x_t)) \xrightarrow{p} H(\theta_0);
$$

using Slutsky's lemma we obtain

$$
\sqrt{n}\int (F_{y|x}(x, \bar{y}; \hat{\theta}) - F_{y|x}(x, \bar{y}; \theta_0))\psi_x(\hat{F}_x)\mathrm{d}\hat{F}_x \xrightarrow{d} Z \sim N\left[0, H(\theta_0)I(\theta_0)^{-1}H(\theta_0)'\right] \tag{A.16}
$$

as $n \to \infty$. Finally, it follows from Eqs. (A.14), (A.15), and (A.16) that under the null hypothesis

$$
S_n(\hat{\theta}) \xrightarrow{d} (Q_{y|x}, \psi_x) - (Z + \int F_{y|x}(x, \bar{y}; \theta_0)J\left(\mathrm{d}^{F_x}\psi_x(F_x), U_x\right)\mathrm{d}F_x + \int F_{y|x}(x, \bar{y}; \theta_0)\psi_x(F_x)\mathrm{d}U_x)
$$

as required. ■

ON THE LIMITING AND EMPIRICAL DISTRIBUTIONS OF IV ESTIMATORS WHEN SOME OF THE INSTRUMENTS ARE ACTUALLY ENDOGENOUS

Jan F. Kiviet[a] and Jerzy Niemczyk[b]

[a]*Division of Economics, Nanyang Technological University, Singapore, Republic of Singapore; University of Amsterdam, Amsterdam, the Netherlands*

[b]*European Central Bank, Frankfurt, Germany*

ABSTRACT

IV estimation is examined when some instruments may be invalid. This is relevant because the initial just-identifying orthogonality conditions are untestable, whereas their validity is required when testing the orthogonality of additional instruments by so-called overidentification restriction tests. Moreover, these tests have limited power when samples are small, especially when instruments are weak. Distinguishing between conditional and unconditional settings, we analyze the limiting distribution of inconsistent IV and examine normal first-order asymptotic approximations to

Essays in Honor of Peter C. B. Phillips
Advances in Econometrics, Volume 33, 425–490

ISSN: 0731-9053/doi:10.1108/S0731-905320140000033013

its density in finite samples. For simple classes of models we compare these approximations with their simulated empirical counterparts over almost the full parameter space. The latter is expressed in measures for: model fit, simultaneity, instrument invalidity, and instrument weakness. Our major findings are that for the accuracy of large sample asymptotic approximations instrument weakness is much more detrimental than instrument invalidity. Also, IV estimators obtained from strong but possibly invalid instruments are usually much closer to the true parameter values than those obtained from valid but weak instruments.

Keywords: Empirical density; inconsistent estimators; invalid instruments; (un)conditional asymptotic distribution; weak instruments

JEL Classifications: C13; C15; C30

1. INTRODUCTION

When in a regression model some of the explanatory variables are contemporaneously correlated with the disturbance term, and this correlation is unknown, then one needs further variables in order to find consistent estimators by the method of moments. These instrumental variables should have a known (usually zero) correlation with the disturbances. If this is the case they provide moment conditions (called orthogonality conditions when the correlation is zero) that make it possible to obtain consistent instrumental variable (IV) estimators. In practice, however, it is difficult to assess whether an explanatory or an external variable excluded from the explanatory variables is uncorrelated with the disturbance term indeed, since such an orthogonality test for the validity of candidate instruments is viable only when just identification or overidentification by valid instruments has been assumed already. Thus, econometric methodology is handicapped due to the unfortunate prerequisite that some non-econometric methodology should provide first some truly valid instrumental variables, in number at least as large as the number of unknown coefficients (k) to be estimated. The validity of the initial k instruments is statistically untestable. Moreover, orthogonality tests of additional candidate instrumental variables will have reasonable power only when the instruments employed and those under test are not too weak (are sufficiently correlated with the regressors) and the sample size is substantial. Therefore, it seems very likely that IV estimation will often be employed when some of the instruments are in fact invalid. Then the IV estimator for the structural parameters will be inconsistent, even when the structural equation itself is correctly specified regarding the parameters of interest; moreover, standard and weak-instrument robust coefficient restriction tests will be unreliable.[1] Here we examine the magnitude of some consequences of using invalid instruments and analyze the determining factors of these consequences both in large and in finite samples.

In this paper we consider general (and in much more detail some simple specific) forms of static linear structural equations and corresponding partial reduced form systems in covariance stationary variables and examine the IV estimator when actually some of its exploited orthogonality conditions do not hold. We cover the general case where the number of moment conditions exploited (l), thus the valid and invalid conditions together, is at least as large as the number of unknown coefficients, i.e., we consider the (alleged) over or just identified case ($l \geq k$). We focus on the distribution of such a possibly invalid IV estimator for a single structural equation that itself has been specified correctly in the sense that its implied vector of error terms is IID (independent and identically distributed) with unconditional expectation equal to zero.[2] In addition to the expression for the inconsistency of the IV estimator in terms of parameters and data moments, we also examine its limiting distribution under standard large sample asymptotics. Unlike for consistent estimators this limiting distribution depends on whether or not one conditions on exogenous variables. The resulting analytic first-order asymptotic approximations to the actual distribution of inconsistent IV estimators in finite samples are compared by simulation experiments with the actual estimator distribution for widely varying model parameter values.

Despite its obvious relevance, the analysis of IV estimators employing invalid instruments has not received very much attention in the literature. Yet, the special case of inconsistent OLS has been addressed in various studies. Goldberger (1964, p. 359) examines for IIN (independent and identically normally distributed) regressors the unconditional limiting distribution and obtains the inconsistency and asymptotic variance. In an unpublished paper, Rothenberg (1972), conditioning on the unobserved means of the regressors, derives the limiting distribution of OLS when some regressors are affected by measurement errors. From this result Hausman (1978, formula 2.11) obtains the limiting distribution of OLS in a simultaneous equation with $k=1$, while conditioning on the explanatory part of the reduced form equation. The same case can be found as a problem exercise in Phillips and Wickens (1978, Question 6.10). In their solution they indicate (but do not solve) the complexities of obtaining the variance of the limiting distribution. The analysis of the much more general problem of obtaining the limiting distribution of an inconsistent instrumental variables estimator has received attention too. For one equation from a normal linear dynamic simultaneous system with serial correlation this was taken up by Hendry (1979), and further examined in Maasumi and Phillips (1982) and Hendry (1982). These three studies seek a so-called control variate, which has the same limiting distribution, and examine its potential to enhance the effectiveness of Monte Carlo simulation findings by response surface analysis. The focus in these three studies is on the unconditional distribution of inconsistent IV estimation assuming normality of all variables involved, whereas ours will primarily be on the conditional distribution rendering distributional assumptions on predetermined variables redundant. Much more recently Bound, Jaeger and Baker (1995, p. 444) and Hahn and Hausman (2005) have examined effects of (locally) invalid instruments in simple linear one regressor models, i.e., $k=1$, and Hall and Inoue (2003) the consequences of misspecification in a general nonlinear GMM context. Ashley (2009) derives the counterpart of Golberger's unconditional result for inconsistent 2SLS applied to an alleged just identified model ($l=k$) and demonstrates how it can be used in practice to produce inference on structural parameters by exposing its sensitivity to varying assumptions on the correlation of instruments and disturbances.

Our major analytic result will be an explicit formula for the asymptotic variance of inconsistent 2SLS in case $l \geq k \geq 1$, which does not require an assumption on nor estimates of higher-order population moments of genuinely exogenous components of the model, because we condition on their sample realizations. In principle, this conditional variance is smaller (in a matrix sense) than the corresponding unconditional variance, and hence more attractive, provided one is interested in inference that refers more directly to the actually observed data and less to a putative multivariate data generating system on all the variables involved. This conditional variance is obtained here by extending the approach introduced by Rothenberg (1972) for inconsistent OLS estimators, also followed for OLS estimation of a simultaneous equation in Kiviet and Niemczyk (2007, 2012) and Kiviet (2013), which complete some initial results obtained in Joseph and Kiviet (2005). For some simple cases we examine any discrepancies between conditional and unconditional asymptotic distributions and their simulated finite sample counterparts. We do not resort to the response surface technique, but to (dynamic) graphical techniques. These allow to cover almost the entire parameter space, in which we do not put the DGP parameters on the axes but transformations of these which much more directly convey the basic model characteristics, being: degree of simultaneity, instrument strength, instrument invalidity, model fit, and sample size. Whereas much of the recent literature on weak instruments focusses on developing appropriate tests and confidence sets when instruments are weak but valid, see for instance Hahn and Inoue (2002) and Andrews and Stock (2007), the present study analyzes and illustrates properties of the distribution of standard coefficient estimators when instruments may be both weak and invalid.

The analysis of the exact finite sample properties of consistent IV estimators has a long history. Early contributions are Sawa (1969), Mariano (1973), and Phillips (1980, 1983). More recent contributions (and further references) can be found in, for instance, Phillips (2006) and Hillier (2006). Some of our numerical findings illustrate the effects of instrument weakness on the finite sample density of consistent IV estimators, which have been studied before by Woglom (2001), who focusses on just identified IV estimators, and by Forchini (2006), who gives further theoretical underpinnings in case of overidentification. Here, we supplement these findings with illustrations for the case of invalid instruments, also addressing the yet underexposed effects of conditioning. Apart from providing general insights into the consequences of employing invalid instruments, the results might also provide a stepping stone toward the development of alternative operational empirical conditional inference techniques in the same vein as is provided in Ashley (2009) on the basis of inconsistent unconditional just-identified IV and in Kiviet (2013) on the basis of inconsistent unconditional OLS.

From our simulations we establish that invalid but not very weak instruments yield IV estimators which have a distribution in small samples that is rather close to the analytic large-sample asymptotic approximations derived here. Hence, the distribution of these estimators is often close to normal, but when inconsistent it has its probability mass centered around the pseudo-true-value instead of the true value. Even when instruments are weak but the sample size is not too small we establish that the accuracy of the normal conditional asymptotic distribution is not all that bad, whereas standard large-sample asymptotics of the unconditional distribution can be very poor, as had already been established for the valid instrument case. More importantly, though, for both valid and invalid instruments we also find that when the instrument is weak the probability mass of the actual distribution of instrumental variable estimators is generally much closer to the true value of the coefficient than indicated by these much too flat asymptotic approximations. For valid but rather weak instruments it had already been established that the finite sample distribution of IV can be skewed, and that it becomes bimodal for very strong simultaneity, whereas for extreme weakness (i.e., close to underidentification) the dispersion explodes and the median moves away from the true parameter value toward the probability limit of OLS. We find that skewness, bimodality, and a median away from the pseudo-true-value may occur for much more moderate weakness and simultaneity when instruments are invalid. Note, however, that in practice one can easily avoid using weak instruments, since weakness (unlike validity) can straightforwardly be assessed. Because the invalid IV estimator is reasonably well behaved for reasonably strong instruments, a tentative conclusion is that it seems more promising to attempt to produce accurate inference from IV estimators based on strong (as in OLS) but possibly invalid instruments, than on valid but weak instruments; (see also Kiviet, 2013). In the latter case, not only is the standard asymptotic approximation poor, but also the actual behavior of the distribution of the estimator is rather erratic and has much larger estimation errors than invalid but strong instruments produce. Thus, even when its actual behavior could be adequately approximated by alternative weak-instrument asymptotic methods, this consistent weak instruments based IV estimator may well have a less attractive actual distribution than an inconsistent one based on strong but invalid instruments.

The structure of this paper is as follows. In Section 2 we introduce the model and the statistical assumptions on all instrumental and explanatory variables involved. Focussing on the alleged overidentified case we consider the generalized IV or 2SLS estimator and derive its inconsistency and conditional limiting distribution (proofs in appendices) for the case where all variables are covariance stationary. Next, these results are specialized for the just identified case, for which we make comparisons with the unconditional limiting distribution. These explicit limiting distributions are then compared with the more implicit results of Maasoumi and Phillips (1982), Hendry (1982), and Hall and Inoue (2003). Section 3 contains graphic illustrations of both the asymptotic and finite sample distributions in specific simple ($k = 1$) models, and we illustrate the consequences and some advantages of conditioning. Moreover, we compare the performance of valid and invalid IV with OLS. The latter uses always extremely strong but possibly invalid instruments. In separate subsections we examine models with $l = 1$ and with $l = 2$. Substantial attention is paid to obtaining a transparent design for simulating the data for these models and instruments and to establishing any invariance and symmetry properties of the estimators over the parameter space. Instead of presenting extensive tables, we present a few series of 2D and 3D graphs in print, and we provide dynamic multidimensional visualization techniques to present our findings more effectively via links to the web through animations on a monitor. Section 4 concludes and conjectures on how to use the obtained results in practice.

2. MODEL, ASSUMPTIONS AND THEOREMS

Before we define our framework in full detail, we will first sketch a broad outline. We consider data generating processes for variables for which n observations have been collected in the rows of $y=(y_1,\ldots,y_n)'$, $X = (x_1,\ldots, x_n)'$ and $Z=(z_1,\ldots,z_n)'$. The full column rank matrices X and Z have k and l columns respectively, with $l \geq k$; also $Z'X$ has full column rank. For $i=1,\ldots,$ n column vector x_i contains the explanatory variables for y_i in a linear structural model, which is well-specified in a sense that implies $\varepsilon_i = y_i - x_i'\beta \sim \text{IID}(0,\sigma_\varepsilon^2)$ with $\sigma_\varepsilon > 0$ for a true and unique β. The l variables collected in Z will be used as instrumental variables for estimating the k structural parameters of interest β of model

$$y = X\beta + \varepsilon \tag{1}$$

However, not all these instruments are necessarily valid. Some elements of z_i may be correlated with ε_i. Moreover, some of the z_i may only be weakly correlated with some or all elements of x_i, whereas some correspond to (or are spanned by) columns of Z and hence are extremely strongly correlated with elements of x_i. All variables are stationary and we denote their non-centered second moment matrices as $\sum_{x'x}$, $\sum_{z'x}$, and $\sum_{z'z}$, respectively, which all three are assumed to have full column rank.

In this framework the generalized instrumental variable (GIV) or two-stage least-squares estimator of β exists and is given by

$$\hat{\beta}_{\text{GIV}} = \left[X'Z(Z'Z)^{-1}Z'X\right]^{-1}X'Z(Z'Z)^{-1}Z'y = (\hat{X}'\hat{X})^{-1}\hat{X}'y \tag{2}$$

where we introduced the notation

$$\hat{X} \equiv Z\hat{\Pi} = Z(Z'Z)^{-1}Z'X \tag{3}$$

Here $\hat{\Pi} = (Z'Z)^{-1}Z'X$ contains the OLS coefficient estimates of the first-stage regressions. The probability limit for $n \to \infty$ of $\hat{\beta}_{\text{GIV}}$ exists and can be expressed as

$$\begin{aligned}\beta^*_{\text{GIV}} &\equiv \text{plim}\hat{\beta}_{\text{GIV}}\\ &= \beta + \text{plim}\left[X'Z(Z'Z)^{-1}Z'X\right]^{-1}X'Z(Z'Z)^{-1}Z'\varepsilon \\ &= \beta + \sigma^2_\varepsilon[\Sigma_{X'Z}\Sigma^{-1}_{Z'Z}\Sigma_{Z'X}]^{-1}\Sigma_{X'Z}\Sigma^{-1}_{Z'Z}\zeta\end{aligned} \tag{4}$$

where $\zeta \equiv \sigma_\varepsilon^{-2}\text{plim}n^{-1}Z'\varepsilon = \sigma_\varepsilon^{-2}E(z_i'\varepsilon_i)$, $\forall i$. Vector β^*_{GIV} is also known as the pseudo-true-value of $\hat{\beta}_{\text{GIV}}$. We shall denote the inconsistency of $\hat{\beta}_{\text{GIV}}$ as

$$\ddot{\beta}_{\text{GIV}} \equiv \beta^*_{\text{GIV}} - \beta = \sigma^2_\varepsilon \Sigma^{-1}_{\hat{X}'\hat{X}}\Pi'\zeta \tag{5}$$

where we used $\Sigma_{\hat{X}'\hat{X}} \equiv \Sigma_{X'Z}\Sigma^{-1}_{Z'Z}\Sigma_{Z'X}$ and $\Pi \equiv \text{plim}(Z'Z)^{-1}Z'X = \Sigma^{-1}_{Z'Z}\Sigma_{Z'X}$. Note that the GIV estimator is consistent $(\beta^*_{\text{GIV}} = \beta)$ if and only if $\Pi'\zeta = 0$, so in particular when $\zeta = 0$ or in the pathological case that $\zeta \neq 0$ but is in the $l-k$ dimensional subspace orthogonal to the space spanned by the columns of Π.

Since $\Pi=[E(Z'Z)]-^1E(Z'X)$, we may write

$$X = Z\Pi + V \tag{6}$$

where $E(Z'V)=O$. This establishes (without imposing any restrictions) an orthogonal (in a stochastic sense) decomposition of X. Only when $\zeta = 0$ (i.e., when all instruments are valid) and when Z includes all the predetermined variables from the (here not specified) complete simultaneous system then Eq. (6) would contain all the reduced form equations for all the endogenous regressors in X. In our set-up, though, where Z may contain invalid instruments, these will often just be pseudo reduced form equations.

In a similar way as we decomposed X "orthogonally" with respect to the matrix Z, we may decompose both Z and V with respect to the vector ε. Since $E(Z'\varepsilon) = n\sigma^2_\varepsilon\zeta$ this yields

$$Z = \overline{Z} + \varepsilon\zeta', \textit{with } E\left(\overline{Z}'\varepsilon\right) = 0 \tag{7}$$

and

$$V = \overline{V} + \varepsilon\nu', \textit{with } E\left(\overline{V}'\nu\right) = 0 \tag{8}$$

where $\nu \equiv n^{-1}\sigma_\varepsilon^{-2}E(V'\varepsilon)$. Substituting these in Eq. (6) yields for the regressor matrix X another "orthogonal" decomposition (now not with respect to Z but with respect to ε)

$$X = (\overline{Z} + \varepsilon\zeta')\Pi + \overline{V} + \varepsilon\nu' = \overline{Z}\Pi + \nu' + \varepsilon(\zeta'\Pi + \nu') = \overline{X} + \varepsilon\xi' \quad (9)$$

where $\overline{X} \equiv \overline{Z}\Pi + \overline{V}$ and $\xi \equiv \Pi\zeta + \nu$, with $E(\overline{X}'\varepsilon) = 0$.

Note that for the observations on subject (or at time period) i, i.e., (y_i, x_i', z_i'), all information not conflated with ε_i is embodied in $\overline{z}_i'$ (the components of z_i' which are uncorrelated with ε_i) and $\overline{x}_i' = \overline{z}_i\Pi + \overline{\nu}_i'$ (where $\overline{\nu}_i$ contains those components of the pseudo reduced form disturbances which are uncorrelated with ε_i). The variables in the columns of $\overline{Z}$ and $\overline{X}$ are exogenous (with respect to ε). Apart from their columns corresponding with known zero elements in ζ and ξ they are unobservable, and thus $\overline{Z}$ and $\overline{X}$ do not establish a feasible information set. Nevertheless, we will demonstrate that it is viable to derive statistical – albeit unfeasible – results when conditioning on $\overline{Z}$ and $\overline{X}$. This is useful too, because it represents the benchmark for the situation where inference is not meant to refer to the population from which $\overline{Z}$ and $\overline{X}$ are drawn, but just to their actual realizations in the sample.

The parametrization and regularity conditions introduced above, supplemented with a series of conditional expectation assumptions, form the formal framework under which we will derive a conditional asymptotic variance of inconsistent IV estimators. This framework is defined as follows.

Framework A. *We have for observations $i = 1,...,n$: (i) the structural equation $y_i = x_i'\beta + \varepsilon_i$ and the alleged instruments z_i', with (ii) $E(x_i\varepsilon_i) = \sigma_\varepsilon^2\xi$ and $E(z_i\varepsilon_i) = \sigma_\varepsilon^2\zeta$, where the $k \times 1$ vector ξ parametrizes simultaneity and the $l \times 1$ vector ζ parametrizes instrument invalidity, whereas (iii) the disturbances are mutually uncorrelated and have the finite conditional moments $E(\varepsilon_i|\overline{X},\overline{Z}) = 0$, $E(\varepsilon_i^2|\overline{X},\overline{Z}) = \sigma_\varepsilon^2$ $E(\varepsilon_i^3|\overline{X},\overline{Z}) = \mu_3\sigma_\varepsilon^3$ and $E(\varepsilon_i^4|\overline{X},\overline{Z}) = \mu_4\sigma_\varepsilon^4$ where $\overline{X} \equiv X - \varepsilon\xi'$ and $\overline{Z} \equiv Z - \varepsilon\zeta'$. Moreover, (iv) $\forall i$ $E(x_ix_i') = \Sigma_{X'X} \equiv \text{plim}_{n\to\infty} n^{-1}X'X$, $E(z_iz_i') = \Sigma_{Z'Z} \equiv \text{plim}_{n\to\infty} n^{-1}Z'Z$ and $E(z_ix_i') = \Sigma_{Z'X} \equiv \text{plim}_{n\to\infty} n^{-1}Z'X$ all have full column rank, and also (v) $X'X$, $Z'Z$, and $Z'X$ all have full column rank with probability one.*

Note that if $\xi_j = 0$ for some $j \in \{1,...k\}$ then the jth regressor in X is exogenous or predetermined and will establish a valid instrument; otherwise, when $\xi_j \neq 0$, the jth regressor is endogenous. Likewise, if $\zeta_g = 0$ for some $g \in \{1,...,l\}$ then the g-th column of Z establishes a valid instrument, and an invalid instrument otherwise. Note that this framework does not allow that either X or Z or both include lagged dependent variables. Our major result concerns the asymptotic variance of inconsistent instrumental variables estimation of β, conditional on the exogenous variables $\overline{X}$ and $\overline{Z}$ (hence, not requiring a distributional assumption on $\overline{X}$ and $\overline{Z}$). The unconditional asymptotic variance will only be examined for the case $l = k$ under normality.

In the special case $l = k$ of (alleged) just identification the above GIV results specialize to simple IV, i.e.,

$$\hat{\beta}_{\mathrm{IV}} = \left(Z'X\right)^{-1} Z'y, \beta^{*}_{\mathrm{IV}} = \beta + \sigma_{\varepsilon}^{2} \Sigma_{Z'X}^{-1} \zeta, \ddot{\beta}_{\mathrm{IV}} = \sigma_{\varepsilon}^{2} \Sigma_{Z'X}^{-1} \zeta \tag{10}$$

When in fact $Z = X$ (all regressors are used as instruments), i.e., $\zeta = \xi$, then IV specializes to OLS, giving

$$\hat{\beta}_{\mathrm{OLS}} = \left(X'X\right)^{-1} X'y, \beta^{*}_{\mathrm{OLS}} = \beta + \sigma_{\varepsilon}^{2} \Sigma_{X'X}^{-1} \xi, \ddot{\beta}_{\mathrm{OLS}} = \sigma_{\varepsilon}^{2} \Sigma_{X'X}^{-1} \xi \tag{11}$$

For the sake of simplicity, we start with deriving special results for models with disturbances that have 3rd and 4th moments corresponding to those of the normal distribution. Therefore, we also specify

Framework B. *This specializes Framework A to the case:* $\mu_3 = 0$ *and* $\mu_4 = 3$.

With increasing sample size the estimator $\hat{\beta}_{\mathrm{GIV}}$ tends to β^{*}_{GIV}, instead of β. Therefore, in order to establish its limiting distribution we should not focus on $\sqrt{n}\left(\hat{\beta}_{\mathrm{GIV}} - \beta\right)$, but choose a center of the distribution that tends to β^{*}_{GIV} too, see Rothenberg (1972). The derivations are relatively smooth if we center at

$$\beta^{*}_{n,\mathrm{GIV}} \equiv \sigma_{\varepsilon}^{2} S_{\hat{X}'\hat{X}}^{-1} P' \tag{12}$$

where $S_{\hat{X}'\hat{X}} \equiv S'_{Z'X} S_{Z'Z}^{-1} S_{Z'X}$, $P \equiv S_{Z'Z}^{-1} S_{Z'X}$ with

$$S_{Z'Z} \equiv n^{-1} E\left(Z'Z\right) = n^{-1} \overline{Z}'\overline{Z} + \sigma_{\varepsilon}^{2} \zeta\zeta' \text{ and } S_{Z'X} \equiv n^{-1} E\left(Z'X\right) = n^{-1} \overline{Z}'\overline{X} + \sigma_{\varepsilon}^{2} \zeta\xi' \tag{13}$$

Note that $\mathrm{plim}\beta^{*}_{n,\mathrm{GIV}} = \beta^{*}_{\mathrm{GIV}}$. For GIV estimators we obtain the following result on its convergence in distribution (proof in Appendix A).

Theorem 1. *In Framework B and conditional on the exogenous variables* $\overline{X}$ *and* $\overline{Z}$ *we have* $n^{1/2}\left(\hat{\beta}_{\mathrm{GIV}} - \beta^{*}_{n,\mathrm{GIV}}\right) \xrightarrow{d} \mathcal{N}\left(0, V^{\mathrm{CN}}_{\mathrm{GIV}}\right)$, *with*

$$
\begin{aligned}
V_{\text{GIV}}^{\text{CN}} = {} & \sigma_\varepsilon^2 c_5(1-c_3+c_4)\Sigma_{\hat{X}'\hat{X}}^{-1} + \sigma_\varepsilon^2 c_4^2 \Sigma_{\hat{X}'\hat{X}}^{-1}\Sigma_{X'X}\Sigma_{\hat{X}'\hat{X}}^{-1} \\
& - c_4[\Sigma_{\hat{X}'\hat{X}}^{-1}\Sigma_{X'X}\ddot{\beta}_{\text{GIV}}\ddot{\beta}_{\text{GIV}}' + \ddot{\beta}_{\text{GIV}}\ddot{\beta}_{\text{GIV}}'\Sigma_{X'X}\Sigma_{\hat{X}'\hat{X}}^{-1}] \\
& + \sigma_\varepsilon^4 c_4(1-2c_4)\Sigma_{\hat{X}'\hat{X}}^{-1}\xi\xi'\Sigma_{\hat{X}'\hat{X}}^{-1} \\
& + \sigma_\varepsilon^2 c_4(1-2c_5)[\Sigma_{\hat{X}'\hat{X}}^{-1}\xi\ddot{\beta}_{\text{GIV}}' + \ddot{\beta}_{\text{GIV}}\xi'\Sigma_{\hat{X}'\hat{X}}^{-1}] \\
& + \left[c_5(1-2c_5) - c_3 + \sigma_\varepsilon^{-2}\left(\ddot{\beta}_{\text{GIV}}'\Sigma_{X'X}\ddot{\beta}_{\text{GIV}}\right)\right]\ddot{\beta}_{\text{GIV}}\ddot{\beta}_{\text{GIV}}'
\end{aligned}
$$

where $c_1 \equiv \sigma_\varepsilon^2\zeta'\Sigma_{Z'Z}^{-1}\zeta$, $c_2 \equiv \zeta'\Pi\ddot{\beta}_{\text{GIV}}$, $c_3 \equiv \xi'\ddot{\beta}_{\text{GIV}}$, $c_4 \equiv c_1 - c_2$ and $c_5 \equiv 1 - c_3 - c_4$.

The superindex CN of $V_{\text{GIV}}^{\text{CN}}$ indicates that it refers to the conditional limiting distribution and to the case where the disturbances are "almost normal", because $\mu_3 = 0$ and $\mu_4 = 3$. The limiting distribution of $\hat{\beta}_{\text{GIV}}$ is still genuinely normal when instruments are invalid, although no longer centered at β but at the pseudo-true-value β_{GIV}^*. When all instruments are valid ($\zeta = 0$) then $\beta_{\text{GIV}}^* = \beta$, $\ddot{\beta}_{\text{GIV}} = 0$ and $c_1 = c_2 = c_3 = 0$, giving $c_4 = 0$ and $c_5 = 1$, so that Theorem 1 specializes to the standard result $n^{1/2}(\hat{\beta}_{\text{GIV}} - \beta) \xrightarrow{d} \mathcal{N}(0, \sigma_\varepsilon^2\Sigma_{\hat{X}'\hat{X}}^{-1})$. Note that when $\zeta = 0$ the asymptotic variance of $\hat{\beta}_{\text{GIV}}$ is not determined by the simultaneity ξ, because $\Sigma_{\hat{X}'\hat{X}} = \Sigma_{X'Z}\Sigma_{Z'Z}^{-1}\Sigma_{Z'X} = \Sigma_{\overline{X}'\overline{Z}}\Sigma_{\overline{Z}'\overline{Z}}^{-1}\Sigma_{\overline{Z}'\overline{X}}$. However, when instruments are invalid ($\zeta \neq 0$) then $\Sigma_{Z'X} = \Sigma_{\overline{Z}'\overline{X}} + \sigma_\varepsilon^2\zeta\xi'$ and $\Sigma_{Z'Z} = \Sigma_{\overline{Z}'\overline{Z}} + \sigma_\varepsilon^2\zeta\zeta'$, thus $\Sigma_{\hat{X}'\hat{X}}$ is now determined by both ξ and ζ. When fitting X to Z, while the $\varepsilon\xi'$ part of X is not (asymptotically) orthogonal to Z due to its component $\varepsilon\zeta'$, this does not only lead to the inconsistency, but also to the many extra terms in the asymptotic conditional variance.

When $l = k$ and GIV specializes to IV we have $\zeta'\Pi\ddot{\beta}_{\text{IV}} = \sigma_\varepsilon^2\zeta'\Sigma_{Z'Z}^{-1}\Sigma_{Z'X}\Sigma_{Z'X}^{-1}\zeta = \sigma_\varepsilon^2\zeta'\Sigma_{Z'Z}^{-1}\zeta$, so $c_1 = c_2$, $c_4 = 0$, and $c_5 = 1 - c_3$. This leads to substantial simplification, giving:

Corollary 1. *In Framework B for the special case $l = k$ we have that conditional on $\overline{X}$ and $\overline{Z}$ we have* $n^{1/2}\left(\hat{\beta}_{\text{IV}} - \beta_{n,\text{IV}}^*\right) \xrightarrow{d} \mathcal{N}\left(0, V_{\text{IV}}^{\text{CN}}\right)$, *with*

$$
V_{\text{IV}}^{\text{CN}} = \sigma_\varepsilon^2(1-c_3)^2\Sigma_{Z'X}^{-1}\Sigma_{Z'Z}\Sigma_{X'Z}^{-1} - \left[(1-c_3)^2 - \sigma_\varepsilon^2\zeta'\Sigma_{Z'X}^{-1}\Sigma_{\overline{X}'\overline{X}}\Sigma_{X'Z}^{-1}\zeta\right]\ddot{\beta}_{\text{IV}}\ddot{\beta}_{\text{IV}}'
$$

where $\beta_{n,\text{IV}}^* \equiv \beta + \sigma_\varepsilon^2 S_{Z'X}^{-1}\zeta$ and $c_3 \equiv \xi'\ddot{\beta}_{\text{IV}} = \sigma_\varepsilon^2\xi'\Sigma_{Z'X}^{-1}\zeta$.

When all instruments are valid ($\zeta = 0$) this result specializes to the standard result $n^{1/2}(\hat{\beta}_{\text{IV}} - \beta) \xrightarrow{d} N(0, \sigma_\varepsilon^2 \Sigma_{Z'X}^{-1} \Sigma_{Z'Z} \Sigma_{X'Z}^{-1})$, which is also true unconditionally and for nonnormal disturbances. Since for arbitrary ζ and ξ the scalar $\sigma_\varepsilon^2 \xi' \Sigma_{Z'X}^{-1} \zeta$ can either be positive or negative, no general conclusions can be drawn on the behavior of $V_{\text{IV}}^{\text{CN}}$ in comparison to the reference case $\sigma_\varepsilon^2 \Sigma_{Z'X}^{-1} \Sigma_{Z'Z} \Sigma_{X'Z}^{-1}$. Depending on the particular parametrization and data moment matrices the conditional asymptotic variance of individual coefficient estimates may either increase or decrease, due to $\xi \neq 0$ and $\zeta \neq 0$. When $Z = X$, which gives $\zeta = \xi$ and $\hat{\beta}_{\text{IV}} = \hat{\beta}_{\text{OLS}}$, the resulting $V_{\text{IV}}^{\text{CN}} = V_{\text{OLS}}^{\text{CN}}$ is the same as the formula for the conditional asymptotic variance found for an inconsistent OLS estimator when the disturbances are (almost) normal, as earlier derived in Kiviet and Niemczyk (2007, 2012).

Next, we look at the case where the disturbances may have general 3*rd* and 4*th* moment (proof in Appendix B). Let ι be an $n \times 1$ vector of unit elements. Upon defining

$$\Sigma_{Z'\iota} \equiv \text{plim}\, n^{-1} Z' \iota = \text{plim}\, n^{-1} \bar{Z}' \iota \equiv \Sigma_{\bar{Z}'\iota}$$

$$\Sigma_{X'\iota} \equiv \text{plim}\, n^{-1} X' \iota = \text{plim}\, n^{-1} \bar{X}' \iota \equiv \Sigma_{\bar{X}'\iota}$$

we find (superindex CP indicates conditional on $\bar{X}$ and $\bar{Z}$ with IID disturbances following a Pearson distribution):

Theorem 2. *In Framework A and conditional on* $\bar{X}$ *and* $\bar{Z}$ *we have* $n^{1/2}(\hat{\beta}_{\text{GIV}} - \beta^*_{n,\text{GIV}}) \xrightarrow{d} \mathcal{N}(0, V_{\text{GIV}}^{\text{CP}})$, *where* $V_{\text{GIV}}^{\text{CP}}$ *is equal to* $V_{\text{GIV}}^{\text{CN}}$, *given in Theorem 1, plus two additional terms. When* $\mu_4 \neq 3$ *an additional term is*

$$(\mu_4 - 3)\left\{\sigma_\varepsilon^4 c_4^2 \Sigma_{\hat{X}'\hat{X}}^{-1} \xi \xi' \Sigma_{\hat{X}'\hat{X}}^{-1} + \sigma_\varepsilon^2 c_4 c_5 [\ddot{\beta}_{\text{GIV}} \xi' \Sigma_{\hat{X}'\hat{X}}^{-1} + \Sigma_{\hat{X}'\hat{X}}^{-1} \xi \ddot{\beta}_{\text{GIV}}'] + c_5^2 \ddot{\beta}_{\text{GIV}} \ddot{\beta}_{\text{GIV}}'\right\}$$

where $c_4 \equiv \sigma_\varepsilon^2 \zeta' \Sigma_{Z'Z}^{-1} \zeta - \zeta' \Pi \ddot{\beta}_{\text{GIV}}$ and $c_5 \equiv 1 - \xi' \ddot{\beta}_{\text{GIV}} - c_4$. *When* $\mu_3 \neq 0$ *another additional term is*

$$\begin{aligned}
&\mu_3 \Big\{ c_4 \Big[\sigma_\varepsilon^3 c_4 \Sigma_{\hat{X}'\hat{X}}^{-1} \Sigma_{X'\iota} \xi' \Sigma_{\hat{X}'\hat{X}}^{-1} - \sigma_\varepsilon \ddot{\beta}_{\text{GIV}} \ddot{\beta}_{\text{GIV}}' \Sigma_{X'\iota} \xi' \Sigma_{\hat{X}'\hat{X}}^{-1} + \sigma_\varepsilon^3 c_5 \Sigma_{\hat{X}'\hat{X}}^{-1} \Pi' \Sigma_{Z'\iota} \xi' \Sigma_{\hat{X}'\hat{X}}^{-1} \\
&\quad + \left(\sigma_\varepsilon^3 \Sigma_{\hat{X}'\hat{X}}^{-1} \xi - \sigma_\varepsilon \ddot{\beta}_{\text{GIV}}\right) \left(\sigma_\varepsilon^2 \zeta' - \ddot{\beta}_{\text{GIV}}' \Sigma_{X'Z}\right) \Sigma_{Z'Z}^{-1} \Sigma_{Z'\iota} \xi' \Sigma_{\hat{X}'\hat{X}}^{-1} \Big] \\
&\quad + c_5 \Big[\sigma_\varepsilon c_4 \Sigma_{\hat{X}'\hat{X}}^{-1} \Sigma_{X'\iota} \ddot{\beta}_{\text{GIV}}' - \sigma_\varepsilon^{-1} \ddot{\beta}_{\text{GIV}}' \Sigma_{X'\iota} \ddot{\beta}_{\text{GIV}} \ddot{\beta}_{\text{GIV}}' + \sigma_\varepsilon c_5 \Sigma_{\hat{X}'\hat{X}}^{-1} \Pi' \Sigma_{Z'\iota} \ddot{\beta}_{\text{GIV}}' \\
&\quad + \left(\sigma_\varepsilon \Sigma_{\hat{X}'\hat{X}}^{-1} \xi - \sigma_\varepsilon^{-1} \ddot{\beta}_{\text{GIV}}\right) \left(\sigma_\varepsilon^2 \zeta' - \ddot{\beta}_{\text{GIV}}' \Sigma_{X'Z}\right) \Sigma_{Z'Z}^{-1} \Sigma_{Z'\iota} \ddot{\beta}_{\text{GIV}}' \Big]
\end{aligned}$$

$$
\begin{aligned}
&+c_4\Big[\sigma_\varepsilon^3 c_4 \Sigma_{\hat{X}'\hat{X}}^{-1}\xi\Sigma_{X'\iota}'\Sigma_{\hat{X}'\hat{X}}^{-1} - \sigma_\varepsilon\Sigma_{\hat{X}'\hat{X}}^{-1}\xi\Sigma_{X'\iota}'\ddot{\beta}_{\text{GIV}}\ddot{\beta}_{\text{GIV}}' + \sigma_\varepsilon^3 c_5 \Sigma_{\hat{X}'\hat{X}}^{-1}\xi\Sigma_{Z'\iota}'\Pi\Sigma_{\hat{X}'\hat{X}}^{-1} \\
&+\Sigma_{\hat{X}'\hat{X}}^{-1}\xi\Sigma_{Z'\iota}'\Sigma_{Z'Z}^{-1}(\sigma_\varepsilon^2\zeta - \Sigma_{Z'X}\ddot{\beta}_{\text{GIV}})\left(\sigma_\varepsilon^3\xi'\Sigma_{\hat{X}'\hat{X}}^{-1} - \sigma_\varepsilon\ddot{\beta}_{\text{GIV}}'\right)\Big] \\
&+c_5\Big[\sigma_\varepsilon c_4\ddot{\beta}_{\text{GIV}}\Sigma_{X'\iota}'\Sigma_{\hat{X}'\hat{X}}^{-1} - \sigma_\varepsilon^{-1}\ddot{\beta}_{\text{GIV}}'\Sigma_{X'\iota}\ddot{\beta}_{\text{GIV}}\ddot{\beta}_{\text{GIV}}' + \sigma_\varepsilon c_5\ddot{\beta}_{\text{GIV}}\Sigma_{Z'\iota}'\Pi\Sigma_{\hat{X}'\hat{X}}^{-1} \\
&\qquad +\ddot{\beta}_{\text{GIV}}\Sigma_{Z'\iota}'\Sigma_{Z'Z}^{-1}(\sigma_\varepsilon^2\zeta - \Sigma_{Z'X}\ddot{\beta}_{\text{GIV}})\left(\sigma_\varepsilon\xi'\Sigma_{\hat{X}'\hat{X}}^{-1} - \sigma_\varepsilon^{-1}\ddot{\beta}_{\text{GIV}}'\right)\Big]\Big\}
\end{aligned}
$$

When all the instruments are valid ($\zeta = 0$) this result again collapses to the standard one, i.e., $V_{\text{GIV}}^{\text{CP}} = \sigma_\varepsilon^2\Sigma_{\hat{X}'\hat{X}}^{-1}$, which highlights that normality of the disturbances is not a requirement for the standard normal limiting distribution of $\hat{\beta}_{\text{GIV}}$.

For the special case $l = k$ Theorem 2 yields:

Corollary 2. *In Framework A for the special case $l = k$ we have that conditional on $\overline{X}$ and $\overline{Z}$ we have $n^{1/2}(\hat{\beta}_{\text{IV}} - \beta_{n,\text{IV}}^*) \xrightarrow{d} \mathcal{N}(0, V_{\text{IV}}^{\text{CP}})$, with*

$$
\begin{aligned}
V_{\text{IV}}^{\text{CP}} &= \sigma_\varepsilon^2 c_5^2 \Sigma_{Z'X}^{-1}\Sigma_{Z'Z}\Sigma_{X'Z}^{-1} + \mu_3\sigma_\varepsilon c_5^2\left[\Sigma_{Z'X}^{-1}\Sigma_{Z'\iota}\ddot{\beta}_{\text{IV}}' + \ddot{\beta}_{\text{IV}}\Sigma_{Z'\iota}'\Sigma_{X'Z}^{-1}\right] \\
&\quad - \left[(5-\mu_4)c_5^2 + 2c_5\left(\mu_3\sigma_\varepsilon^{-1}\ddot{\beta}_{\text{IV}}'\Sigma_{X'\iota} - 1\right) + 1 - \sigma_\varepsilon^{-2}\ddot{\beta}_{\text{IV}}'\Sigma_{X'X}\ddot{\beta}_{\text{IV}}\right]\ddot{\beta}_{\text{IV}}\ddot{\beta}_{\text{IV}}'
\end{aligned}
$$

where $c_5 \equiv 1 - \xi'\ddot{\beta}_{\text{IV}} = 1 - \sigma_\varepsilon^2\xi'\Sigma_{Z'X}^{-1}\zeta$.

It shows that an increase (decrease) in the kurtosis leads to a larger (smaller) asymptotic variance. Of course, for $\mu_3 = 0$ and $\mu_4 = 3$ this result simplifies to that of Corollary 1.

In the proofs of the above theorems we employ a lemma which is a straightforward extension of the simple CLT (central limit theorem): Let v_i be a $k \times 1$ random vector such that $E(v_i) = 0$, $E(v_i v_i') = V_i$, and $E(v_i v_h') = O$ for $i \neq h = 1,\ldots,n$, then $n^{1/2}\overline{v} \xrightarrow{d} \mathcal{N}(0, \lim_{n\to\infty}\overline{V})$, where $\overline{v} = n^{-1}\sum_{i=1}^n v_i$ and $\overline{V} = n^{-1}\sum_{i=1}^n V_i$. We employ the following generalized version.

Lemma. *Let ω be a $k \times 1$ nonrandom vector and $W = (w_1,\ldots,w_n)'$ a $n \times m$ random matrix with w_i being stationary $\forall i$, whereas the $n \times 1$ vector $\varepsilon = (\varepsilon_1,\ldots,\varepsilon_n)'$ has mutually uncorrelated elements for which $E(\varepsilon_i|W) = 0$, $E(\varepsilon_i^2|W) = \sigma_\varepsilon^2$, $E(\varepsilon_i^3|W) = \mu_3\sigma_\varepsilon^3$ and, $E(\varepsilon_i^4|W) = \mu_4\sigma_\varepsilon^4$. Then for the $k \times 1$ vector $v_i = w_i\varepsilon_i + \omega(\varepsilon_i^2 - \sigma_\varepsilon^2)$ we have $E(v_i|W) = 0$, $E(v_i v_i'|W) = V_i = \sigma_\varepsilon^2 w_i w_i' + \mu_3\sigma_\varepsilon^3(w_i\omega' + \omega w_i') + (\mu_4 - 1)\sigma_\varepsilon^4\omega\omega'$, whereas $E(v_i v_h'|W) = O$ for $i \neq h$, so that for $n^{-1/2}\sum_{i=1}^n v_i = n^{-1/2}[W'\varepsilon + \omega(\varepsilon'\varepsilon - n\sigma_\varepsilon^2)]$ a CLT implies that conditional on W*

$$n^{1/2}\bar{v} \xrightarrow{d} \mathcal{N}\left(0,\sigma_\varepsilon^2\Sigma_{W'W} + \mu_3\sigma_\varepsilon^3\left(\Sigma_{W'\iota}\omega' + \omega\Sigma_{\iota'W}\right) + \left(\mu_4 - 1\right)\sigma_\varepsilon^4\omega\omega'\right)$$

where $\Sigma_{W'W} \equiv \text{plim}\, n^{-1}W'W = E\left(w_i w_i'\right)$ *and* $\Sigma_{W'\iota} \equiv \Sigma_{\iota'W}' \equiv \text{plim}\, n - 1W'\iota = E(w_i)$ $\forall i$, *with* ι *a* $n \times 1$ *vector of unit elements.*

The principle difference between the conditional approach followed above and the results obtained in Maasoumi and Phillips (1982) is the following. Instead of simplifying (by conditioning) formula (A.7) of Appendix A into an expression to which the above Lemma applies and from which the asymptotic variance directly follows, they substitute Eq. (A.7) in Eq. (A.4) and then rewrite it as $n^{1/2}Hvec[n^{-1}F'F - E(n^{-1}F'F)]$, in which H is a $k \times nm$ transformation matrix determined by selection and data moment matrices and parameters, whereas the random zero mean vectorized object is obtained from the $n \times m$ matrix F, which contains all the n observations on all the m variables (both endogenous and predetermined) from a multi-equation dynamic simultaneous system with serial correlation. This expression constitutes the control variate that has the same unconditional limiting distribution as a single equation GIV estimator in which invalid instruments are being used. Next they sketch how under normality of all the m variables (including any exogenous and predetermined variables) and exploiting a spectral density matrix its variance could be established. Hence, they do not provide an explicit formula and only consider the unconditional asymptotic variance under normality. This also applies to the result in Hendry (1982), who provides algebraic instructions on how the unconditional asymptotic variance can be computed when all variables are normal. Note, though, that evaluation of the unconditional asymptotic variance, like the conditional one, is unfeasible in the sense that it requires substitution of the values of unobserved parameters.

The results in Theorems 1 and 2 in fact address special cases of Theorem 2 in Hall and Inoue (2003, p. 369). The latter theorem is more general, but more implicit at the same time. It concerns GMM estimation (both 1-step and 2-step) of a possibly nonlinear misspecified model and expresses its asymptotic variance matrix in a few model characteristics and a matrix Ω. This matrix, which is left unspecified, is the variance of the limiting distribution of a $k + 2l$ vector, say v^*, which in our particular setting specializes to

$$v^* \equiv \begin{pmatrix} n^{-1/2}\left[Z'\left(y - X\beta^*_{\text{GIV}}\right) - n\text{plim}\, n^{-1}Z'\left(y - X\beta^*_{\text{GIV}}\right)\right] \\ n^{1/2}\left(n^{-1}X'Z - \Sigma_{X'Z}\right)\Sigma_{Z'Z}^{-1}\text{plim}\, n^{-1}Z'(y - X\beta^*_{\text{GIV}}) \\ n^{1/2}\left[(n^{-1}Z'Z)^{-1} - \Sigma_{Z'Z}^{-1}\right]\text{plim}\, n^{-1}Z'(y - X\beta^*_{\text{GIV}}) \end{pmatrix} \xrightarrow{d} \mathcal{N}(0, \Omega)$$

How Ω should be obtained and whether or not it is supposed to represent the unconditional or the conditional variance they do not mention. It can be shown, though, that in our model

$$n^{1/2}\left(\hat{\beta}_{\mathrm{GIV}} - \beta^{*}_{n,\mathrm{GIV}}\right) = \Sigma^{-1}_{\hat{X}'\hat{X}}\left(\Pi' \quad I_k \quad \Sigma_{X'Z}\right)v^{*} + o_p(1) \tag{14}$$

and thus the conditional asymptotic variance of GIV that we obtained can indeed be expressed in $\sum_{Z'X}$, $\sum_{Z'Z}$, and Ω (which we did express for our linear model explicitly in $\sum_{Z'Z}$, $\sum_{Z'Z}$, ξ, ζ, μ_3, μ_4, and σ^2_ε). The added value of our results is that some general conclusions could be drawn on the joint effects of simultaneity, instrument invalidity, and disturbance kurtosis on the limiting distribution of GIV and, because they are explicit in parameters and data moments, they allow to depict the numerical effects of those various characteristics, as we will show in the next section.

When $l = k$ and the data are IID, it is relatively straightforward to generalize the result by Goldberger (1964, p. 359) on inconsistent OLS and obtain the unconditional limiting distribution of the IV estimator when some instruments are invalid. Subtracting from all components in the model their unconditional expectation, and thus removing the intercept (if present) from both the model and the set of instruments, the remaining regressors all have expectation zero. Still using the same notation for the model (although it may now have one regressor less), we consider also the alternative model specification

$$y = X\beta + \varepsilon = X\beta^{*}_{\mathrm{IV}} + u \tag{15}$$

where $u \equiv \varepsilon - X\ddot{\beta}_{\mathrm{IV}}$. Because now $E(x_i) = 0$, we have $E(u_i) = E(\varepsilon_i) - E(x_i')\ddot{\beta}_{\mathrm{IV}} = 0$, and also $\sigma^2_u \equiv E(u_i^2) = \sigma^2_\varepsilon(1 - 2\ddot{\beta}'_{\mathrm{IV}}\xi) + \ddot{\beta}'_{\mathrm{IV}}\Sigma_{X'X}\ddot{\beta}_{\mathrm{IV}}$, $E(u_iu_j) = 0$ for $i \neq j$, whereas $E(z_iu_i) = \sigma^2_\varepsilon\zeta - E(z_ix_i')\ddot{\beta}_{\mathrm{IV}} = \sigma^2_\varepsilon\zeta - \Sigma_{Z'X}\ddot{\beta}_{\mathrm{IV}} = 0$. Thus, the instruments Z are valid in this alternative model specification, whereas for $l > k$ this would not generally be true. Ashley (2009) derives the variance of the unconditional limiting distribution of the IV estimator of β^{*}_{IV}, which in the general IID case involves a great many fourth order moments. He also shows how it simplifies when all regressors, instruments, and the disturbances are normal, in particular when $l = k = 1$. This latter case we will examine more closely in the next section.

3. ILLUSTRATIONS

To illustrate the analytical asymptotic findings obtained in the foregoing section, we will calculate the various formulas for particular models and show the corresponding normal densities over relevant parts of the parameter space. In addition, we will simulate these models and depict the empirical density of the estimators to check the relevance and accuracy of the first-order asymptotic approximations in finite samples. We will also compare IV and GIV estimators (using possibly invalid and possibly weak instruments) with OLS. The latter estimator always uses extremely strong instruments that at the same time are invalid in case of simultaneity.

The limiting distributions obtained in the foregoing section are all of the generic form $n^{1/2}(\hat{\beta}-\beta_n^*) \xrightarrow{d} \mathcal{N}(0,V)$ and they imply a first-order approximation to the distribution of $\hat{\beta}$ in finite samples which can be expressed as

$$\hat{\beta} \overset{a}{\sim} \mathcal{N}(\beta+\ddot{\beta}, n^{-1}V) \tag{16}$$

This entails a first-order asymptotic approximation to the bias or mean error of $\hat{\beta}$ equal to $\ddot{\beta}=\beta^*-\beta$ and to the mean squared error (AMSE) given by

$$\text{AMSE}(\hat{\beta}) \equiv n^{-1}V + \ddot{\beta}\ddot{\beta}' \tag{17}$$

The actual values of $\ddot{\beta}$ and of (the square root of) AMSE($\hat{\beta}$) can be computed for any n and any given values of the model parameters and relevant data moments. To find out how accurate the first-order asymptotic approximation (17) is, it should be compared with corresponding Monte Carlo estimates obtained from a series of realizations of $\hat{\beta}$ in simulated finite samples. However, these cannot be achieved in the standard way when $\hat{\beta}$ does not have finite first or second moments in finite samples, as is the case for GIV when $l - k \leq 1$. Then, irrespective of the number of Monte Carlo replications employed, the sample moments from Monte Carlo experiments are not informative as they do not converge. Appropriate alternatives for the mean error and for the root mean squared error are then the median error and the median of the absolute error.

For a scalar estimator $\hat{\beta}$ of β the median error ME($\hat{\beta}$) and the median absolute error MAE($\hat{\beta}$) are defined as

$$\begin{aligned} &\Pr\left\{(\hat{\beta}-\beta) \leq \text{ME}(\hat{\beta})\right\} = 0.5 \\ &\Pr\left\{|\hat{\beta}-\beta| \leq \text{MAE}(\hat{\beta})\right\} = 0.5 \end{aligned} \tag{18}$$

From a series of R independent Monte Carlo realizations $\hat{\beta}^{(r)}$ (r = 1,..., R) we estimate ME($\hat{\beta}$) by sorting the values ($\hat{\beta}^{(r)} - \beta$) and taking the median value, and similarly for MAE($\hat{\beta}$), taking the median of the sorted $|\hat{\beta}^{(r)} - \beta|$ values. Of course, AMSE($\hat{\beta}$) is not the natural asymptotic counterpart of the Monte Carlo estimate of MAE($\hat{\beta}$) We assess the (scalar) asymptotic version AMSE($\hat{\beta}$) of MAE($\hat{\beta}$) in the following way. Let the CDF of the normal approximation to the distribution of $\hat{\beta} - \beta$ be indicated by $\Phi_{\ddot{\beta},\sigma_{\hat{\beta}}}(x)$. Then, for $m \equiv$ AMAE($\hat{\beta}$), we have

$$\begin{aligned} 0.5 &= \Pr\left\{|\hat{\beta} - \beta| \leq m\right\} = 1 - \Pr\left\{|\hat{\beta} - \beta| > m\right\} \\ &= 1 - \Pr\left\{\hat{\beta} - \beta > m\right\} - \Pr\left\{\hat{\beta} - \beta < -m\right\} \\ &= \Pr\left\{\hat{\beta} - \beta < m\right\} - \Pr\left\{\hat{\beta} - \beta < -m\right\} \\ &\stackrel{a}{=} \Phi_{\ddot{\beta},\sigma_{\hat{\beta}}}(m) - \Phi_{\ddot{\beta},\sigma_{\hat{\beta}}}(-m) \end{aligned}$$

so that we can solve[3] m from

$$\Phi_{\ddot{\beta},\sigma_{\hat{\beta}}}(m) = 0.5 + \Phi_{\ddot{\beta},\sigma_{\hat{\beta}}}(-m) \tag{19}$$

Below we will examine the empirical finite sample distribution of scalar $\hat{\beta}_{\text{GIV}}$ and compare it with $\hat{\beta}_{\text{GIV}} \overset{a}{\sim} \mathcal{N}(\beta + \ddot{\beta}_{\text{GIV}}, n^{-1} V_{\text{GIV}}^{\text{CN}})$. In addition, for various estimators $\hat{\beta}_{\text{GIV}}$ (including $\hat{\beta}_{\text{IV}}$ and $\hat{\beta}_{\text{OLS}}$), we examine $\text{MAE}(\hat{\beta}_{\text{GIV}})$ and compare it with $\text{AMAE}(\hat{\beta}_{\text{GIV}})$ over almost the entire parameter space of two simple classes of models. Employing normally distributed disturbances[4], we examined these models under Framework B only.

3.1. A Simple Just Identified Model

We commence by considering the most basic example one can think of, viz. a model with one regressor (k = 1) and one instrument (l = 1), which is either weak or strong and possibly invalid. The two variables x and z, together with the dependent variable y, are supposed to be jointly IID with zero mean and finite second moments. Hence, the variables are stationary and our Theorems 1 and 2 apply. This model has often been examined in the past. Recently in Woglom (2001) and Hillier (2006), and for $l \geq 1$ in Bound et al. (1995) and Hahn and Hausman (2005). Though, only the latter two papers consider (locally) invalid instruments.

We first evaluate the relevant expressions for the conditional limiting distribution given in Corollary 1. In the model with $k = l = 1$ we can simplify the notation considerably, by writing σ_x^2 for $\sum x'x$, σ_{xz} or $\rho_{xz}\sigma_x\sigma_z$ for $\sum z'x$, etc. Using $\zeta = \sigma_{z\varepsilon}/\sigma_\varepsilon^2$ and $\xi = \sigma_{x\varepsilon}/\sigma_\varepsilon^2$ we obtain

$$\begin{aligned} \ddot{\beta}_{\text{IV}} &= \beta_{\text{IV}}^* - \beta = \sigma_\varepsilon^2 \Sigma_{Z'X}^{-1} \zeta = \frac{\sigma_{z\varepsilon}}{\sigma_{xz}} = \frac{\rho_{z\varepsilon}}{\rho_{xz}} \frac{\sigma_\varepsilon}{\sigma_x} \\ c_3 &= \sigma_\varepsilon^2 \xi' \Sigma_{Z'X}^{-1} \zeta = \frac{1}{\sigma_\varepsilon^2} \frac{\sigma_{z\varepsilon}\sigma_{x\varepsilon}}{\sigma_{xz}} = \frac{\rho_{z\varepsilon}\rho_{x\varepsilon}}{\rho_{xz}} \\ \ddot{\beta}_{\text{IV}}' \Sigma_{X'X} \ddot{\beta}_{\text{IV}} &= \sigma_\varepsilon^4 \zeta' \Sigma_{Z'X}^{-1} \Sigma_{X'X} \Sigma_{X'Z}^{-1} \zeta = \sigma_{z\varepsilon}^2 \frac{\sigma_x^2}{\sigma_{xz}^2} = \sigma_\varepsilon^2 \frac{\rho_{z\varepsilon}^2}{\rho_{xz}^2} \end{aligned} \tag{20}$$

giving in the case where the disturbances are (almost) normally distributed

$$V_{\text{IV}}^{\text{CN}} = \frac{\sigma_\varepsilon^2}{\sigma_x^2} \frac{(1-\rho_{z\varepsilon}^2)(\rho_{xz} - \rho_{z\varepsilon}\rho_{x\varepsilon})^2 + \rho_{z\varepsilon}^4 (1-\rho_{x\varepsilon}^2)}{\rho_{xz}^4} \tag{21}$$

The expression for the inconsistency $\ddot{\beta}_{\text{IV}}$ shows that its sign is determined by the sign of $\rho_{z\varepsilon}/\rho_{xz}$, whereas its magnitude is inversely related to the strength of the instrument (cf. Bound et al., 1995). $V_{\text{IV}}^{\text{CN}}$ is unaffected by the signs of $\rho_{z\varepsilon}$, $\rho_{x\varepsilon}$, and ρ_{xz} as long as the sign of the product $\rho_{z\varepsilon}\rho_{x\varepsilon}\rho_{xz}$ remains the same, or when either $\rho_{x\varepsilon}$ or $\rho_{z\varepsilon}$ is zero. Self-evidently, $V_{\text{IV}}^{\text{CN}}$ diverges for ρ_{xz} approaching zero.

For this simple model we find from Ashley (2009, formula 15) for the unconditional asymptotic variance under normality

$$V_{\text{IV}}^{\text{UN}} = \frac{\sigma_\varepsilon^2}{\sigma_x^2} \frac{(\rho_{xz} - \rho_{z\varepsilon}\rho_{x\varepsilon})^2 + \rho_{z\varepsilon}^2 (1-\rho_{x\varepsilon}^2)}{\rho_{xz}^4} \tag{22}$$

which makes immediately clear that the conditional asymptotic variance (21) is smaller if $\rho_{z\varepsilon} \neq 0$, as expected.

We now set out to design the Monte Carlo. Without loss of generality we may focus in this model on the case $\beta = 1$. This is just a normalization and not a restriction, because we can imagine that we started off from a model $y_i = \beta^{\#} x_i^{\#} + \varepsilon_i$, with $\beta^{\#} \neq 0$, and rescaled the explanatory variable such that $x_i = x_i^{\#}/\beta^{\#}$.

An important characteristic of the model is the signal-to-noise ratio (SN), which is taken as

$$\mathrm{SN} = \frac{\beta^2 \sigma_x^2}{\sigma_\varepsilon^2} = \frac{\sigma_x^2}{\sigma_\varepsilon^2} \tag{23}$$

From Eqs. (20) and (21) we find that $V_{\mathrm{IV}}^{\mathrm{CN}}$ and $\ddot{\beta}$ are proportional to (the square root of) the inverse of SN. In fact, after the normalization $\beta = 1$, in this simple model the approximation to the distribution of the IV estimator $\hat{\beta}_{\mathrm{IV}} \sim^{a} \mathcal{N}\left(\beta + \ddot{\beta}, n^{-1} V_{\mathrm{IV}}^{\mathrm{CN}}\right)$ is completely determined by n and the four model characteristics ρ_{xz}, $\rho_{x\varepsilon}$, $\rho_{z\varepsilon}$, and SN.

Next, we focus on obtaining an appropriate data generating scheme for this model to be used in the simulations. In the notation of Section 2 it is given by

$$\left.\begin{aligned} y_i &= \beta x_i + \varepsilon_i \\ x_i &= \bar{x}_i + \xi \varepsilon_i \\ z_i &= \bar{z}_i + \zeta \varepsilon_i \end{aligned}\right\} \tag{24}$$

where ξ and ζ are scalars. In order to obtain $(\varepsilon_i, x_i, z_i)' \sim \mathrm{IID}(0, \Omega)$, with appropriate 3×3 covariance matrix Ω, we can first generate $v_i = (v_{i,1}, v_{i,2}, v_{i,3}' \sim \mathrm{IID}(0, I_3)$ and then parameterize as follows:

$$\begin{aligned} \varepsilon_i &= \sigma_\varepsilon v_{i,1} \\ \bar{x}_i &= \alpha_1 v_{i,2} \\ \bar{z}_i &= \alpha_2 v_{i,2} + \alpha_3 v_{i,3} \end{aligned}$$

This provides full generality. The coefficient α_1 determines $\sigma_{\bar{x}}^2$, whereas $E(\bar{x}_i \varepsilon_i) = 0$, as it should. Also $E(\bar{z}_i \varepsilon_i) = 0$ and α_2 and α_3 enable any correlation between $\bar{x}_i$ and $\bar{z}_i$ and any value of $\sigma_{\bar{z}}^2$. The above implies

$$\begin{pmatrix} \varepsilon_i \\ x_i \\ z_i \end{pmatrix} = \Omega^{1/2} v_i = \begin{pmatrix} \sigma_\varepsilon & 0 & 0 \\ \sigma_\varepsilon \xi & \alpha_1 & 0 \\ \sigma_\varepsilon \zeta & \alpha_2 & \alpha_3 \end{pmatrix} \begin{pmatrix} v_{i,1} \\ v_{i,2} \\ v_{i,3} \end{pmatrix} \tag{25}$$

Note that the zero elements do not entail restrictions on Ω, because $\Omega^{1/2}$ is nonunique and a lower-triangular form with positive diagonal elements can be found for any positive definite Ω.

In this simple model with $k = l = 1$ we have

$$\hat{\beta}_{IV} = \frac{\sum z_i y_i}{\sum z_i x_i} = \beta + \frac{\sum z_i \varepsilon_i}{\sum z_i x_i} \tag{26}$$

which clarifies that, irrespective of the sample size, the distribution of $\hat{\beta}_{IV}$ is invariant to the scale of z_i. We may also change the sign of all the z_i without affecting $\hat{\beta}_{IV}$. Therefore, we may restrict ourselves in the illustrations to cases with $\rho_{xz} > 0$ (the case $\rho_{xz} = 0$ leads to underidentification and was already excluded in the assumptions). Since the distribution of $\hat{\beta}_{IV} - \beta$ becomes just its mirror-image when all x_i are changed in sign, we shall also restrict ourselves to cases where $\rho_{z\varepsilon} \geq 0$, because of the following reasoning. The value of ρ_{xz} is invariant to changing the signs of all x_i and z_i values. Hence, for any value of $\rho_{xz} > 0$ the distribution of $\hat{\beta}_{IV} - \beta$ for $\rho_{z\varepsilon} \leq 0$ and arbitrary positive or negative value of $\rho_{x\varepsilon}$ is equivalent with the distribution of $-(\hat{\beta}_{IV} - \beta)$ for $-\rho_{z\varepsilon} \geq 0$ and $-\rho_{x\varepsilon}$. It is also obvious that σ_x and σ_ε do not affect the distribution of $\hat{\beta}_{IV}$ separately, but only through their ratio. Hence, without loss of generality, we can impose some genuine equality restrictions on the six parameters of Ω. For these we choose

$$\sigma_\varepsilon = 1 \tag{27}$$

$$\sigma_z^2 = \zeta^2 + \alpha_2^2 + \alpha_3^2 = 1 \tag{28}$$

By Eq. (27) we normalize all results with respect to σ_ε, and Eq. (23) simplifies to

$$\text{SN} = \sigma_x^2 \tag{29}$$

Because any GIV estimator is invariant to the scale of the instruments (only the space spanned by the instruments is relevant) we may impose Eq. (28), which will be used to obtain the value

$$\alpha_3 = \left| \left(1 - \zeta^2 - \alpha_2^2\right)^{1/2} \right| \tag{30}$$

where, without loss of generality, we may stick to positive values for α_3 as long as $v_{i,3}$ is symmetrically distributed. For similar reasons we would get observationally equivalent data realizations if both α_1 and α_2 would be changed in sign. Therefore, below we will restrict ourselves to just positive values for both α_1 and α_3.

The above yields the following data (co)variances and correlations:

$$\begin{aligned} &\sigma_x^2 = \xi^2 + \alpha_1^2 && \sigma_y^2 = \xi^2 + 2\xi + 1 + \alpha_1^2 \\ &\sigma_{x\varepsilon} = \xi && \rho_{x\varepsilon} = \xi / \sqrt{\xi^2 + \alpha_1^2} \\ &\sigma_{z\varepsilon} = \zeta && \rho_{z\varepsilon} = \zeta \\ &\sigma_{xz} = \xi\zeta + \alpha_1\alpha_2 && \rho_{xz} = (\xi\zeta + \alpha_1\alpha_2) / \sqrt{\xi^2 + \alpha_1^2} \end{aligned} \tag{31}$$

Note that these, after the normalizations $\beta = 1$, $\sigma_\varepsilon = 1$, and $\sigma_z = 1$, depend on only four free parameters of the data generating process (DGP), viz. ξ, ζ, α_1, and α_2. As we already established, the expressions for inconsistency in Eq. (20) and asymptotic variance (21) evaluated under $\mu_3 = 0$ and $\mu_4 = 3$ (the *3rd* and *4th* moment of $v_{i,1}$) depend on just four characteristics too, viz. on $\rho_{x\varepsilon}$, $\rho_{z\varepsilon}$, ρ_{xz}, and $\mathrm{SN} = \sigma_x^2$. The latter four can be used in this simple model as a base for the Monte Carlo design parameter space, since they determine the parameters of the DGP through the relationships

$$\begin{aligned} &\zeta = \rho_{z\varepsilon} \\ &\xi = \rho_{x\varepsilon}\sigma_x \\ &\alpha_1 = \sigma_x \left| \left(1 - \rho_{x\varepsilon}^2\right)^{1/2} \right| \\ &\alpha_2 = \left(\rho_{xz} - \rho_{x\varepsilon}\rho_{z\varepsilon}\right) / \left| \left(1 - \rho_{x\varepsilon}^2\right)^{1/2} \right| \end{aligned} \tag{32}$$

from which α_3 follows directly via Eq. (30). This reparametrization[5] is useful, because the parameters $\rho_{x\varepsilon}$, $\rho_{z\varepsilon}$, ρ_{xz}, and SN have a direct econometric interpretation, viz. the degree of simultaneity, instrument (in)validity, and instrument strength, whereas SN is directly related to the model fit, which can be expressed as SN/(SN + 1). We prefer to avoid to use the "concentration parameter" as one of the relevant characteristics of this model in the present context, because this concept refers exclusively to the case where all instruments are valid.

From the above it follows that by varying the four parameters $|\rho_{x\varepsilon}| < 1, 0 \leq \rho_{z\varepsilon} < 1, 0 < \rho_{xz} < 1$, and $0 < \sigma_x^2 / \left(\sigma_x^2 + 1\right) < 1$, we can examine the limiting and finite sample (un)conditional distributions of $\hat{\beta}_{\mathrm{IV}}$ over the entire parameter space of this model. Note, however, that not all values of these parameters will be admissible. For example, when $\rho_{x\varepsilon}$ is large and $\rho_{z\varepsilon}$ is small, this cannot be compatible with ρ_{xz} being very large. Moreover, σ_x has just an effect on the scale of $\ddot{\beta}_{\mathrm{IV}}$, $V_{\mathrm{IV}}^{\mathrm{CN}}$, V_{IV}^{U}, and $\hat{\beta}_{\mathrm{IV}} - \beta$ so we may choose just one fixed value for σ_x and from these findings the results for any value of σ_x can be obtained simply by rescaling. In our calculations and simulations we will fix SN = 10, yielding a population fit of the model of 10/11 = 0.909.

In the simulations we took $v_i \sim \text{IIN}(0,I_3)$ and used 2,000,000 replications. From the results we may expect to get quick insights into issues as the following. For which combinations of the five design parameter values is: (a) the actual density of $\hat{\beta}_{\text{IV}}$ close to normal (symmetric, unimodal, etc.), (b) the actual median of $\hat{\beta}_{\text{IV}}$ close to β^*_{IV}, (c) the actual tail behavior of $\hat{\beta}_{\text{IV}}$ reasonably well represented by that of the asymptotic normal approximation, and (d) how does the magnitude of the actual estimation errors depend on the design parameters. Hence, we will assess the correspondences and differences in shape, location, and spread of the asymptotic and the empirical distributions, both for the conditional and the unconditional distributions. Since in this just identified model the IV estimator does not have finite moments, we know that even if the instruments are valid, the asymptotic approximation will not capture the fat tails of the finite sample distribution.

For our results on the simulated conditional distribution only one arbitrary draw of the series $v_{i,2}$ and $v_{i,3}$ has been used. However, because such a single random realization will not yield two series which have an actual sample correlation of zero and a sample variance of one, this implies that we would loose full control over the actual values of SN and of the strength of the instrument. We overcame this problem by transforming these single draws of two n-element vectors v_j by replacing one by its residuals after regressing on the other and by normalizing them, such that they obtained zero sample mean, zero sample correlation, and inner-product n. Naturally, when establishing the conditional asymptotic distribution by evaluating $\ddot{\beta}_{\text{IV}}$ and $V_{\text{IV}}^{\text{CN}}$, one has to replace σ_{xz} by $\bar{x}'\bar{z}/n + \sigma_\varepsilon^2\zeta\xi$ and σ_x^2 by $\bar{x}'\bar{x}/n + \sigma_\varepsilon^2\xi^2$ Due to our transformation of the v_j series $\bar{x}'\bar{x} = \alpha_1^2 v_2' v_2 = n\alpha_1^2$ and likewise $\bar{x}'\bar{z} = n\alpha_1\alpha_2$ yielding exactly the same numerical values for σ_{xz} and σ_x^2 as for the unconditional case. Therefore, the assessment of the standard asymptotic distribution when $\rho_{z\varepsilon} = 0$ will be the same for the conditional and unconditional case, which would not occur for untransformed single realizations of $\bar{x}$ and $\bar{z}$; and, for $\rho_{z\varepsilon} \neq 0$, our "standardized" results will underexpose the effects of conditioning.

In order to find out how accurate the first-order asymptotic approximations are, actual values of $\ddot{\beta}_{\text{IV}}$ and of AMAE($\hat{\beta}_{\text{IV}}$) can now be calculated for any set of compatible values of n, $\rho_{x\varepsilon}$, $\rho_{z\varepsilon}$, ρ_{xz}, and σ_x, and they can be compared with corresponding Monte Carlo estimates obtained from $\hat{\beta}_{\text{IV}}$ realizations in simulated finite samples. Before we present these summarizing characteristics, we will first examine the actual density functions themselves.

The Figs. 1 through 4 consider $\rho_{xz} = 0.8, 0.4, 0.1, 0.02$ respectively. Each figure contains for $n = 50, 200, 2{,}000$ a set of 8 panels, so 24 in total. The 8 panels depict in two rows densities for the four cases $\rho_{x\varepsilon} = -0.3, 0, 0.3, 0.6$, with next to each other results for $\rho_{z\varepsilon} = 0$ and $\rho_{z\varepsilon} = 0.2$ respectively. All these panels present three or four densities, viz. for the actual empirical conditional distribution (*solid line*), for the unconditional finite sample distribution (*dashed line*), and for the available asymptotic approximations. For these, either both the conditional and unconditional distributions are available and equivalent (then we use *circles*), or if different and available the conditional asymptotic distribution (*squares*) and the unconditional (*diamonds*) are presented separately. These asymptotic distributions have been taken as $\hat{\beta}_{\text{IV}} \overset{a}{\sim} \mathcal{N}(\beta + \ddot{\beta}_{\text{IV}}, n^{-1}V)$, where V is given by Eqs. (21) or (22) respectively.

In Fig. 1 $\rho_{xz} = 0.8$, so the instrument is far from weak. The panels in columns 1 and 3 have $\rho_{z\varepsilon} = 0$, i.e., the instrument is valid and the standard asymptotic result applies for both conditional and unconditional distributions. In columns 2 and 4 $\rho_{z\varepsilon} = 0.2$, i.e., the instrument is (mildly) invalid, hence the IV estimator is inconsistent and the asymptotic approximations differ for the conditional and unconditional cases. From Fig. 1 we find that for a relatively strong instrument the resemblance between corresponding actual and approximated distributions is quite remarkable even for sample sizes as small as $n = 50$, but for the sample sizes considered we already note some differences between conditional and unconditional distributions when $\rho_{z\varepsilon} \neq 0$. In Fig. 2, where $\rho_{xz} = 0.4$, we note that due to the weaker instrument the actual distributions display some skewness, especially when sample size is small, except for $\rho_{x\varepsilon} = \rho_{z\varepsilon} = 0$. By its very nature, such skewness is completely overlooked by the first-order normal approximations. Hence, although any inconsistency and the dispersion of the actual distributions (which both increased due to the weaker instrument) are quite well approximated, the actual behavior in the tails of the distribution may be over or under stated by standard asymptotic approximations. In Fig. 3 where the instrument is weak we note more pronounced skewness when both $\rho_{x\varepsilon} \neq 0$ and $\rho_{z\varepsilon} \neq 0$. The actual unconditional distribution is approximated well only for a really large sample. On the other hand, especially when $\rho_{x\varepsilon} \geq 0$ and $\rho_{z\varepsilon}$ 0, the conditional asymptotic approximation is remarkably accurate. For a much weaker instrument, Fig. 4 shows that even for large sample size the actual distributions may become bimodal, unlike their normal first-order approximations. Only for $\rho_{x\varepsilon} = 0$ and $\rho_{z\varepsilon} = 0$ the standard asymptotic approximation captures the actual conditional distribution very well, even when the sample size is small. When the instrument is invalid and the sample size gets larger the approximation of the conditional distribution is found to be better than that of the unconditional one. When the instrument is very weak,

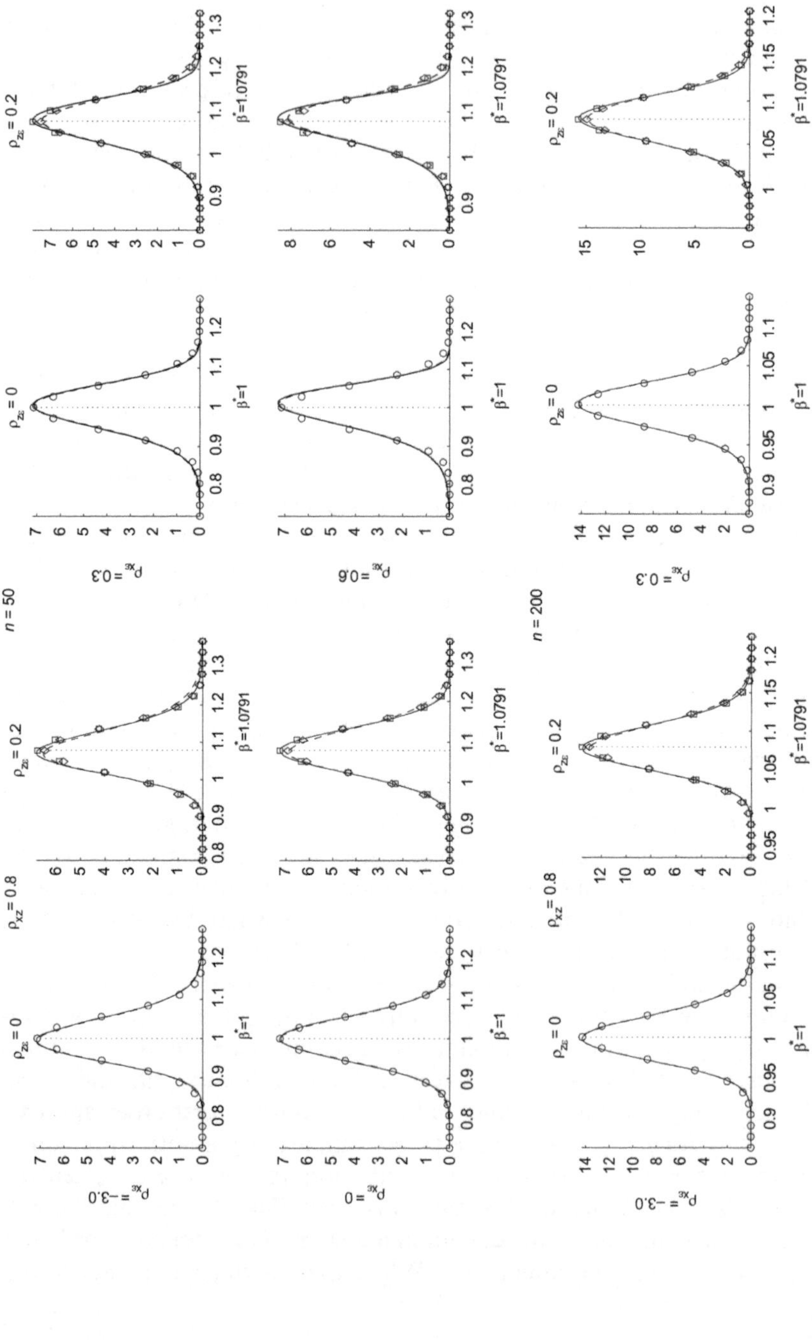

Fig. 1. Densities for $k = l = 1$; $\beta = 1$; $\sigma_x^{2}/\sigma_\varepsilon^{2} = 10$; $\rho_{XZ} = 0.8$ (actual:– = cond., –– = uncond.; asymptotic: = □ = cond., ◇ = uncond., ○ = both).

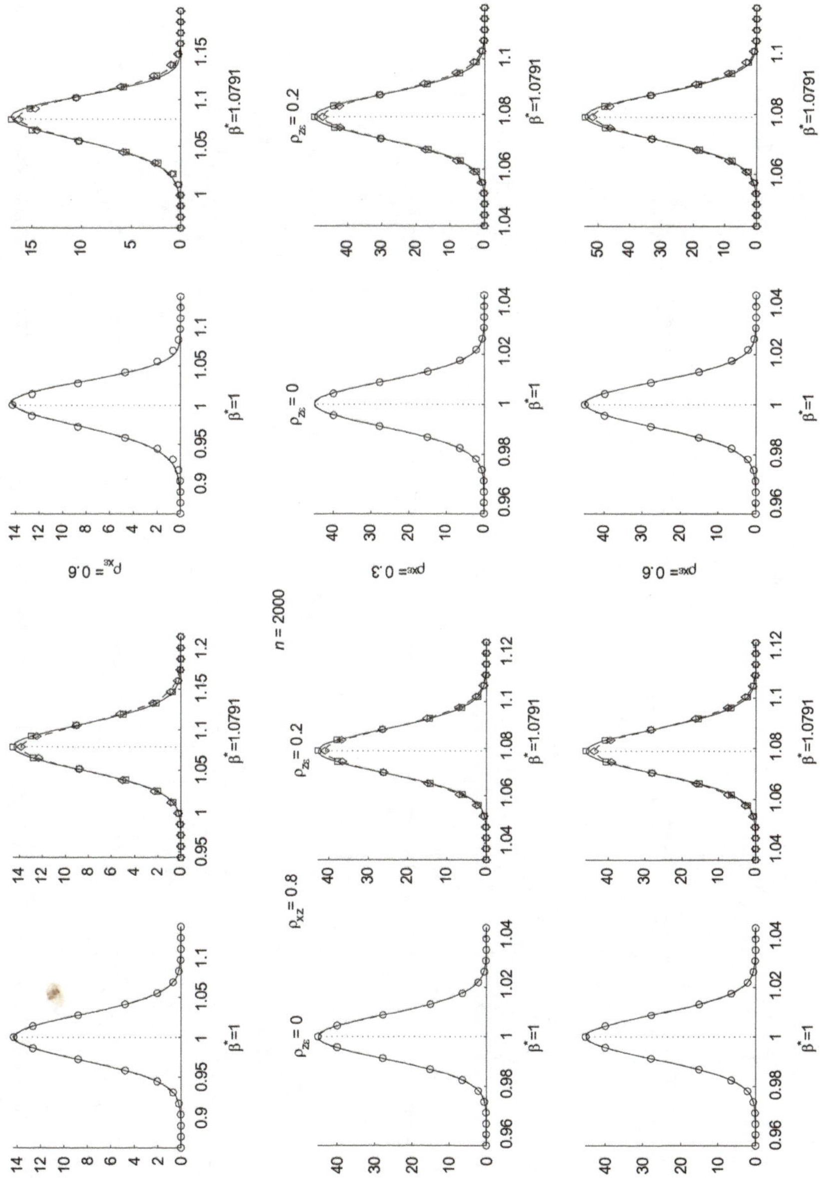

Fig. 1. (*Continued*)

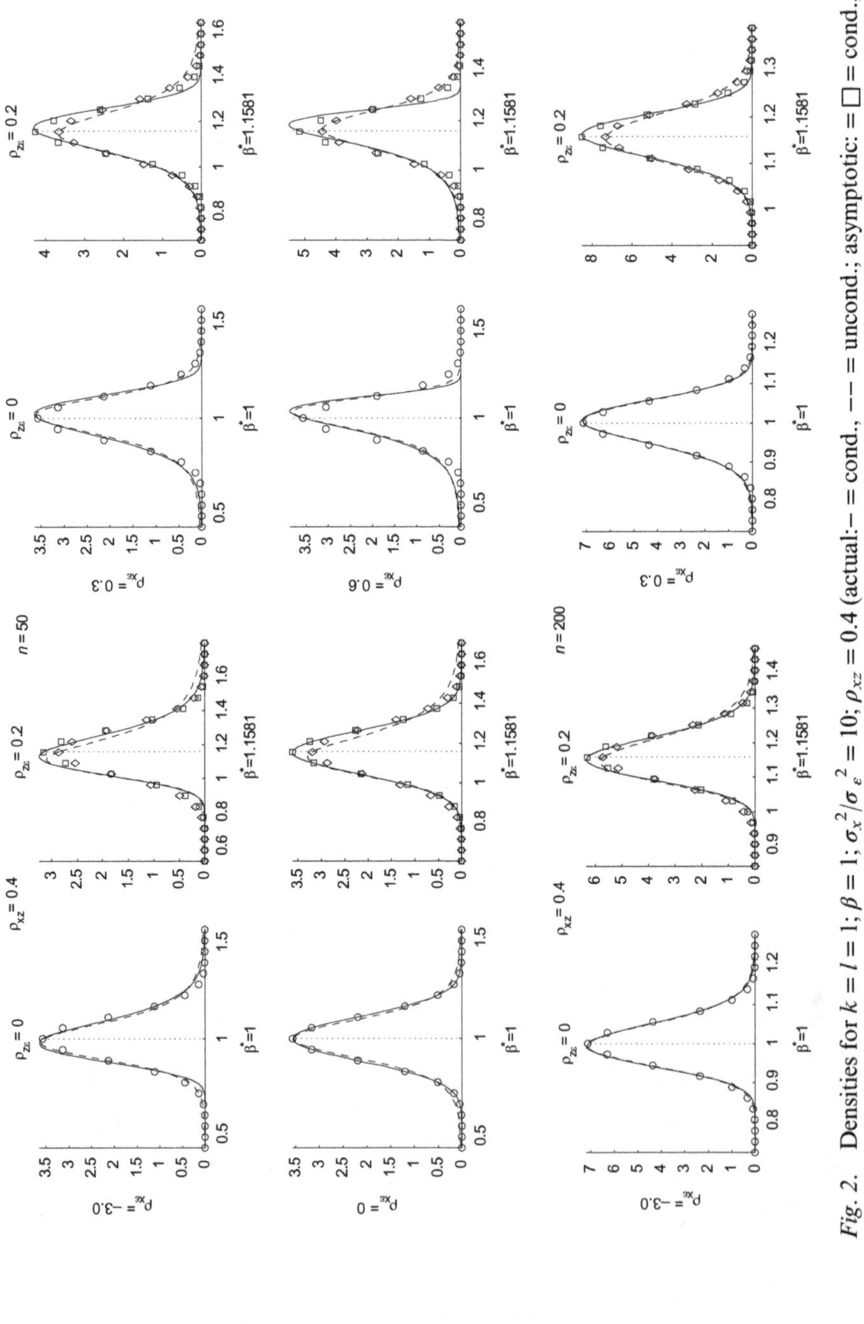

Fig. 2. Densities for $k = l = 1$; $\beta = 1$; $\sigma_x^2/\sigma_\varepsilon^2 = 10$; $\rho_{xz} = 0.4$ (actual:– = cond., –– = uncond.; asymptotic: = □ = cond., ◇ = uncond., ○ = both).

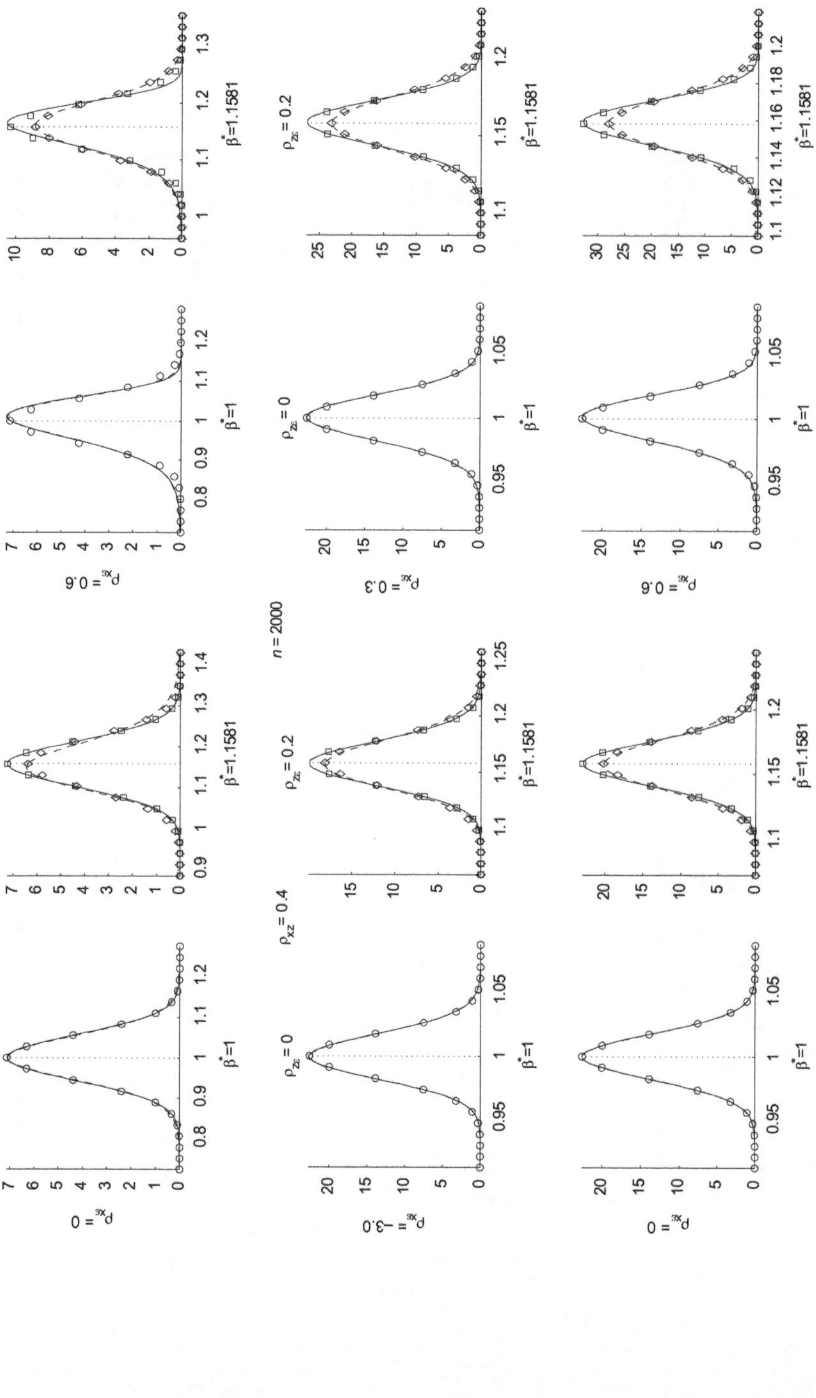

Fig. 2. (Continued)

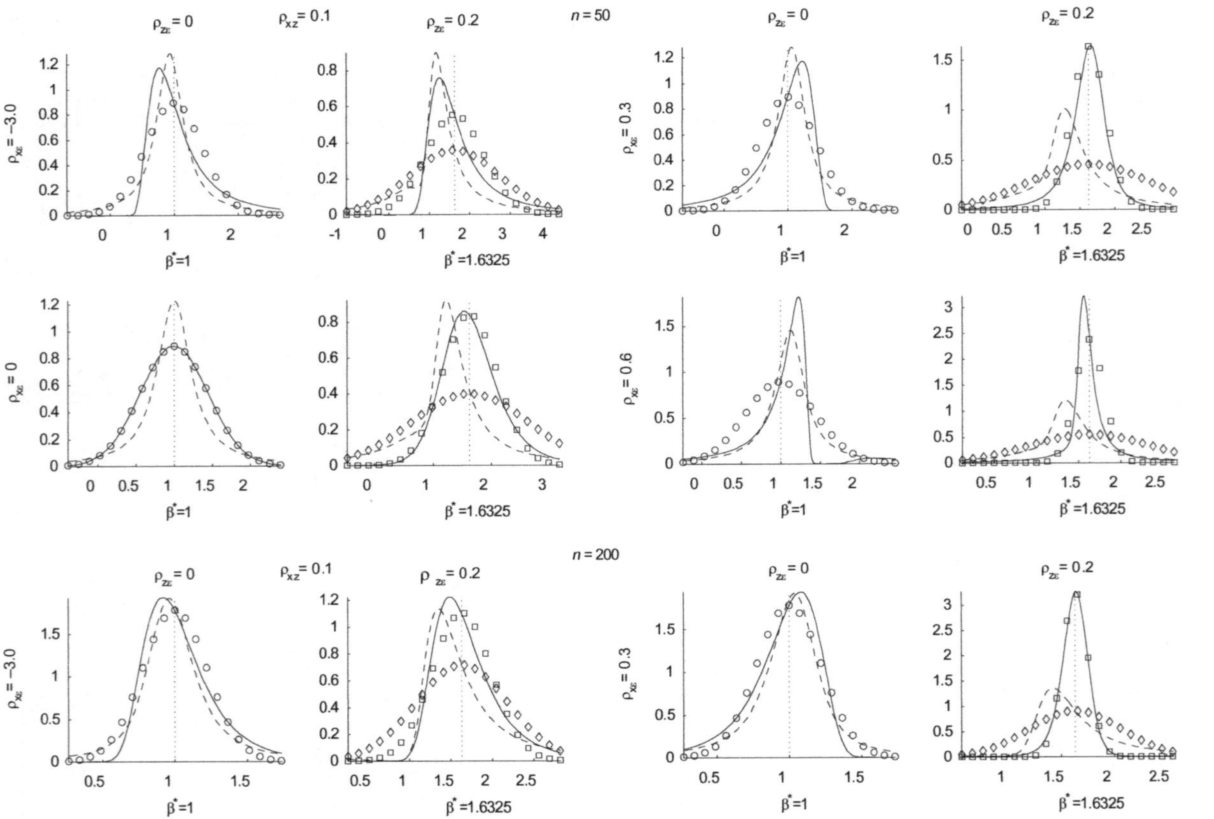

Fig. 3. Densities for $k = l = 1$; $\beta = 1$; $\sigma_x^2/\sigma_\varepsilon^2 = 10$; $\rho_{xz} = 0.1$ (actual:– = cond., –– = uncond.; asymptotic: □ = cond., ◇ = uncond., ○ = both).

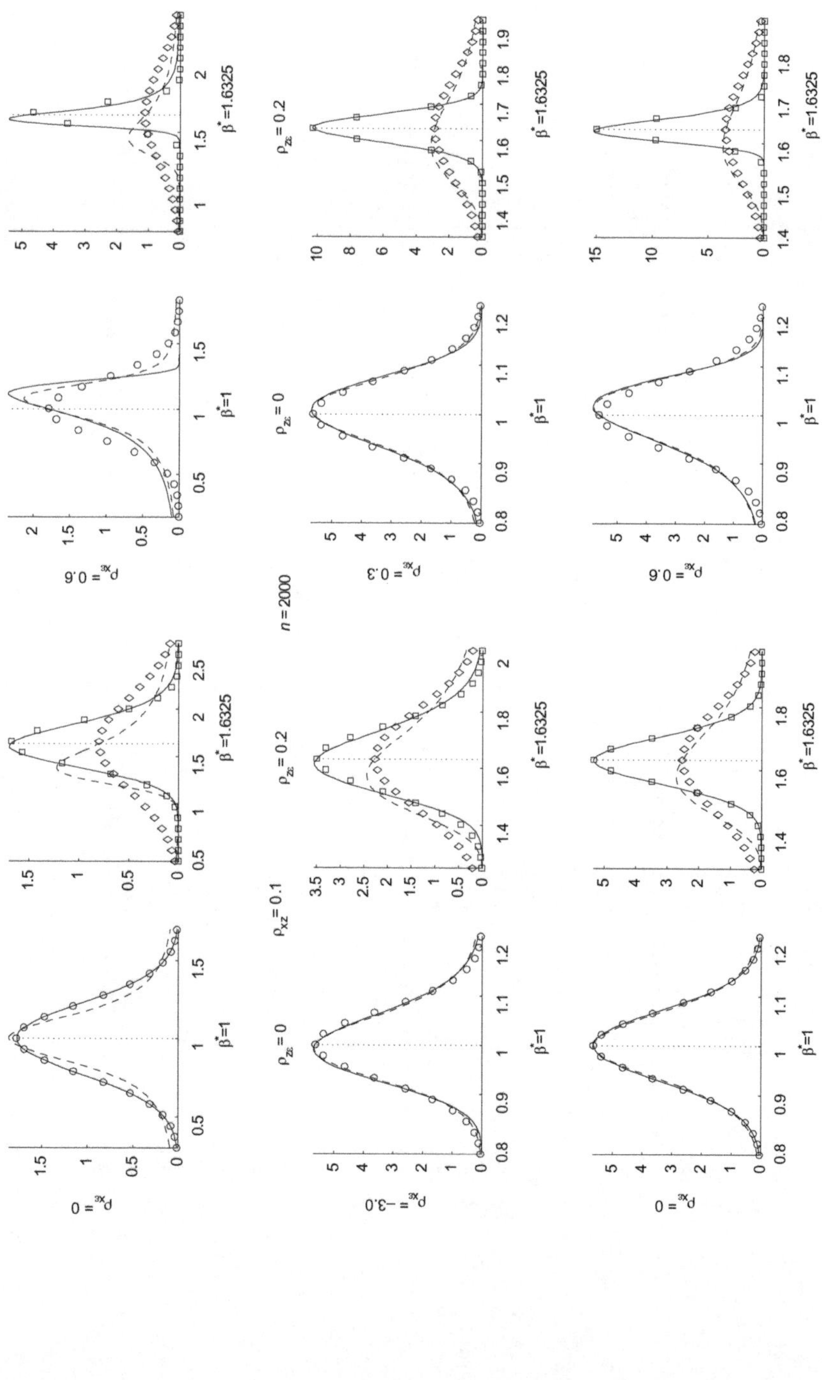

Fig. 3. (*Continued*)

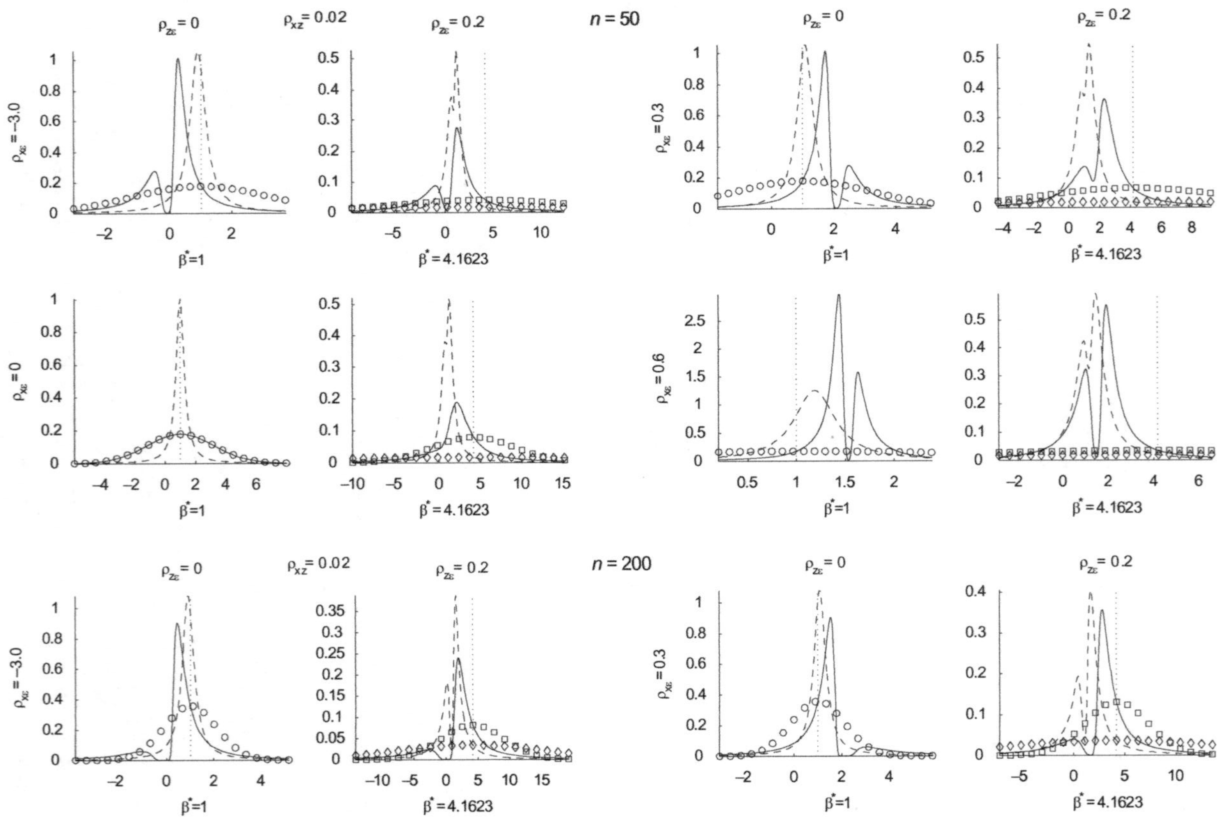

Fig. 4. Densities for $k = l = 1$; $\beta = 1$; $\sigma_x^2/\sigma_\varepsilon^2 = 10$; $\rho_{xz} = 0.02$ (actual:– = cond., –– = uncond.; asymptotic: □ = cond., ◇ = uncond., ○ = both).

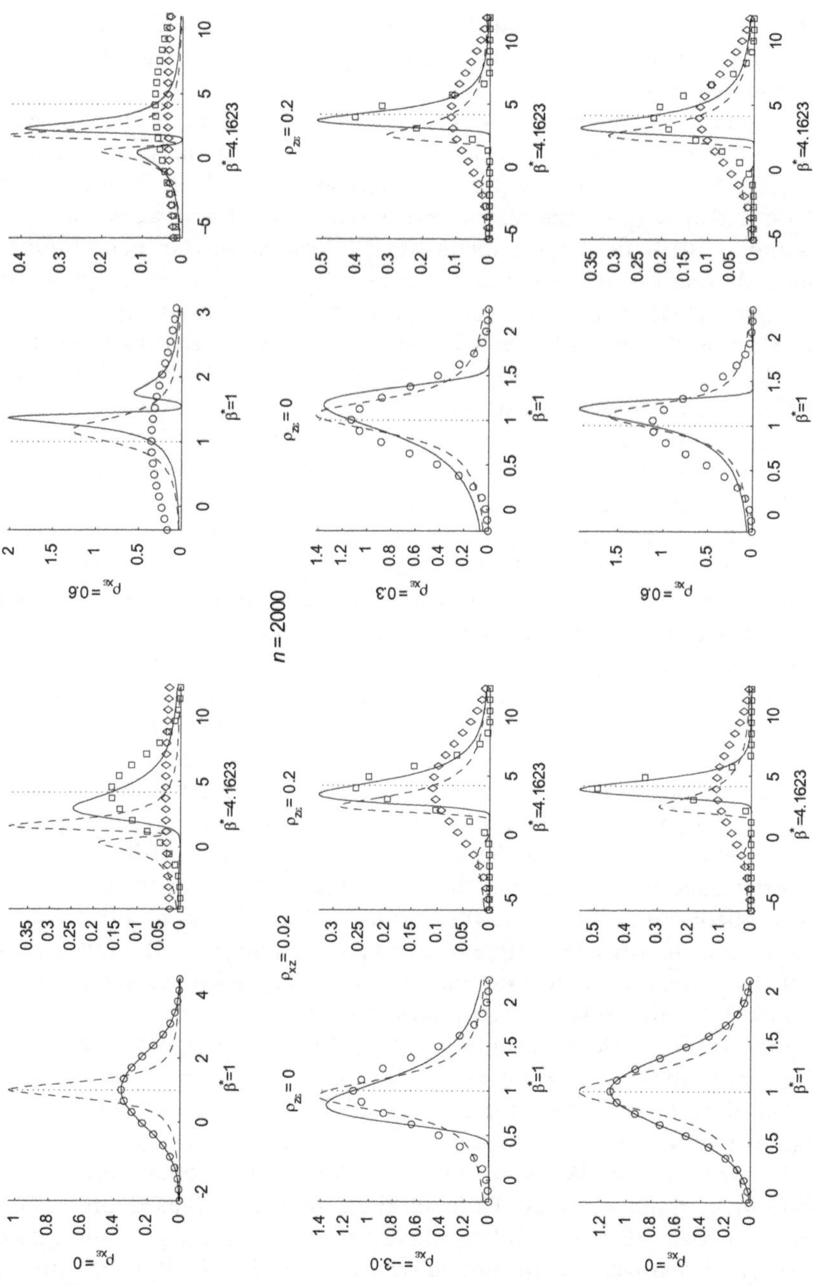

Fig. 4. (*Continued*)

whether valid or not, the actual distributions become so widely dispersed and wrongly located that they compare very unfavorably with that of a much stronger instrument, even if this were not valid.

The magnitude of the (median) bias of consistent IV and of OLS in relation to the effects of weakness of the instrument has been analyzed by many authors, see Sawa (1969) and (further references in) Hillier (2006). From Fig. 4 we find that when the instrument is both invalid and weak then the finite sample distribution of the inconsistent IV estimator (both conditional and unconditional) is not centered at the pseudo-true-value. Surprisingly, it is often quite close to the true value (also when the instrument is not so weak), whereas the distribution becomes bimodal when the instrument is very weak. Maddala and Jeong (1992), Woglom (2001), Hillier (2006), and Forchini (2006) show that bimodality of the unconditional consistent IV estimator occurs for much more severe simultaneity than examined here, viz. for $\rho_{x\varepsilon} = 0.99$, whereas Phillips (2006) shows that it is omnipresent in the simple Keynesian model where simultaneity is always severe. We find that the conditional distribution may be bimodal for much smaller values of $\rho_{x\varepsilon}$. For moderate degree of simultaneity our findings also suggest that using instruments that are both weak and invalid may lead to bimodality in small samples, irrespective of whether one conditions or not.

From Figs. 1 through 4 we conclude that, irrespective of whether the instruments are valid or not, one should avoid to use standard first-order large sample asymptotics when instruments are really weak. If one replaces the weak instrument with a strong one that is invalid (which is always possible by reverting to OLS), one obtains an inconsistent estimator, such as depicted in the $\rho_{z\varepsilon} = 0.2$ columns of Fig. 1. Not only are asymptotic approximations very accurate here, but also the actual distributions are much better concentrated around the true value than that of the consistent estimators depicted in the $\rho_{z\varepsilon} = 0$ columns of Figs. 3 and 4. For $n = 50$ most of the inconsistent IV estimates for $\rho_{z\varepsilon} = 0.2$ and $\rho_{xz} = 0.8$ fall within the (0.9, 1.2) interval for all examined values of $\rho_{x\varepsilon}$, whereas this range is close to (0, 2) for the consistent estimates when $\rho_{xz} = 0.1$.

A wider picture of the major findings from Figs. 1 through 4 on the conditional distribution will be given now by scanning the median absolute error over almost the full parameter space of this simple model. Fig. 5 provides an overview in 16 diagrams of the (in)accuracy of the asymptotic conditional distribution of IV as an approximation to the actual conditional distribution in finite samples. Each of these diagrams (based on 50,000 replications) cover all compatible positive values of $\rho_{x\varepsilon}$ and ρ_{xz}, and relate to a particular relatively small sample size, viz. $n = 20$, 50, 100, 200, and a

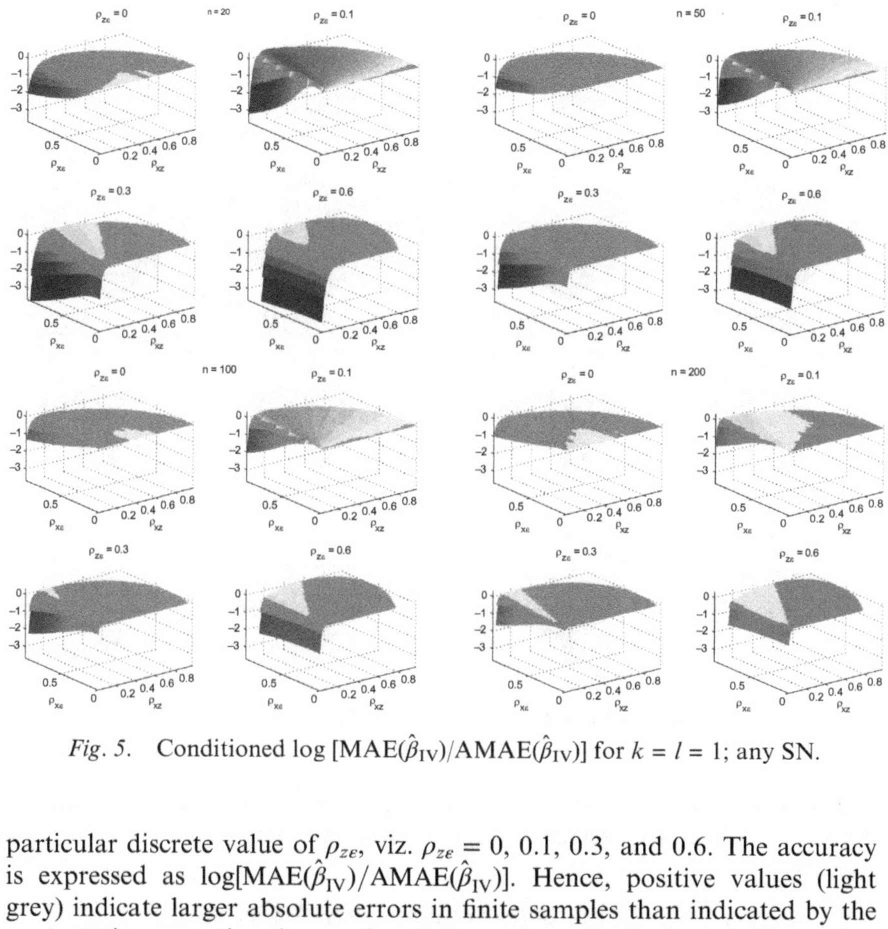

Fig. 5. Conditioned log [MAE($\hat{\beta}_{\text{IV}}$)/AMAE($\hat{\beta}_{\text{IV}}$)] for $k = l = 1$; any SN.

particular discrete value of $\rho_{z\varepsilon}$, viz. $\rho_{z\varepsilon} = 0$, 0.1, 0.3, and 0.6. The accuracy is expressed as $\log[\text{MAE}(\hat{\beta}_{\text{IV}})/\text{AMAE}(\hat{\beta}_{\text{IV}})]$. Hence, positive values (light grey) indicate larger absolute errors in finite samples than indicated by the asymptotic approximation and negative values (dark grey) indicate that standard asymptotics is too pessimistic about the absolute errors of $\hat{\beta}_{\text{IV}}$ in finite samples. This log-ratio is invariant regarding the value of $\text{SN} = \sigma_x^2/\sigma_\varepsilon^2$. We find that the approximation is quite good, even for $n = 20$, as long as the instrument is not very weak.

Fig. 6 examines $\log[\text{MAE}(\hat{\beta}_{\text{OLS}})/\text{MAE}(\hat{\beta}_{\text{IV}})]$, which is also invariant with respect to SN. It shows that in finite samples the absolute estimation errors committed by OLS are larger than those of IV only when $\rho_{x\varepsilon}$ and ρ_{xz} are both large. Of course, the area where IV beats OLS gets smaller for larger $\rho_{z\varepsilon}$. We also note that OLS may beat IV by a much larger margin (when the instrument is weak and the simultaneity not so serious) than IV will

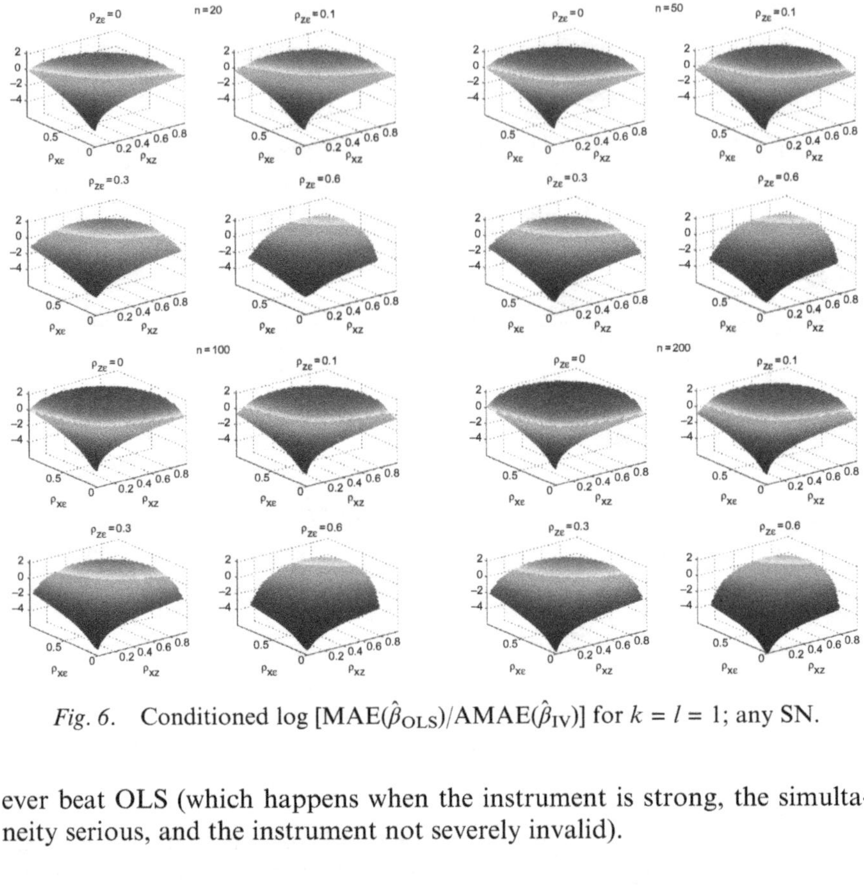

Fig. 6. Conditioned log [MAE($\hat{\beta}_{\mathrm{OLS}}$)/AMAE($\hat{\beta}_{\mathrm{IV}}$)] for $k = l = 1$; any SN.

ever beat OLS (which happens when the instrument is strong, the simultaneity serious, and the instrument not severely invalid).

3.2. A Simple Overidentified Model

The model of the above subsection can be extended such that we have two instruments $z_{i,1}$ and $z_{i,2}$, i.e., $l = 2$ and $\zeta = (\zeta_1,\zeta_2)'$. First, we examine by which minimal set of data moments the limiting distribution is determined in this model. Again we assume that all variables in the regression have been scaled such that $\beta = 1$ and $\sigma_\varepsilon^2 = 1$, whereas the instruments Z have been transformed such that $\Sigma_{Z'Z} = I$ (while still spanning the original subspace). Such an orthonormal base for this subspace is nonunique, and without loss of generality we may choose one in which only $z_{i,1}$ is possibly correlated with ε_i, so that $\zeta_2 = 0$. This implies that

$$\Sigma_{X'Z}\Sigma_{Z'Z}^{-1}\Sigma_{Z'\varepsilon} = \sigma_{\hat{x}\varepsilon} = \sigma_{xz_1}\sigma_{z_1\varepsilon} = \rho_{xz_1}\rho_{z_1\varepsilon}\sigma_x \tag{33}$$

where, of course, $\rho_{z_1\varepsilon} = \zeta_1$. Now the various entries in the formula of Theorem 1 specialize to

$$\Sigma_{X'X} = \sigma_x^2 > 0$$
$$\Sigma_{\hat{X}'\hat{X}} = \sigma_{\hat{x}}^2 = \rho_{x\hat{x}}^2 \sigma_x^2 > 0$$
$$\ddot{\beta}_{\text{GIV}} = \sigma_\varepsilon^2 \Sigma_{\hat{X}'\hat{X}}^{-1} \Sigma_{X'Z} \Sigma_{Z'Z}^{-1} \Sigma_{Z'\varepsilon} = \frac{\sigma_{\hat{x}\varepsilon}}{\sigma_{\hat{x}}^2} = \frac{\rho_{xz_1}\rho_{z_1\varepsilon}\sigma_x}{\rho_{x\hat{x}}^2 \sigma_x^2} = \frac{\rho_{xz_1}\rho_{z_1\varepsilon}}{\rho_{x\hat{x}}^2 \sigma_x}$$
$$c_1 = \sigma_\varepsilon^2 \Sigma_{\varepsilon'Z} \Sigma_{Z'Z}^{-1} \Sigma_{Z'\varepsilon} = \rho_{z_1\varepsilon}^2 \tag{34}$$
$$c_2 = \sigma_\varepsilon^2 \Sigma_{\varepsilon'Z} \Sigma_{Z'Z}^{-1} \Sigma_{Z'X} \Sigma_{\hat{X}'\hat{X}}^{-1} \Sigma_{X'Z} \Sigma_{Z'Z}^{-1} \Sigma_{Z'\varepsilon} = \rho_{\hat{x}\varepsilon}^2 = \frac{\rho_{xz_1}^2 \rho_{z_1\varepsilon}^2}{\rho_{x\hat{x}}^2}$$
$$c_3 = \Sigma_{\varepsilon'X} \ddot{\beta}_{\text{GIV}} = \frac{\rho_{x\varepsilon}\rho_{\hat{x}\varepsilon}\sigma_x}{\sigma_{\hat{x}}} = \frac{\rho_{x\varepsilon}\rho_{\hat{x}\varepsilon}}{\rho_{x\hat{x}}} = \frac{\rho_{x\varepsilon}\rho_{xz_1}\rho_{z_1\varepsilon}}{\rho_{x\hat{x}}^2}$$

from which c_4 and c_5 readily follow. From the above we conclude that the limiting distribution of Theorem 1 is fully determined by (and varies with) the five data moments: σ_x, $\rho_{x\hat{x}}$, $\rho_{x\varepsilon}$, $\rho_{z_1\varepsilon}$, and ρ_{xz_1}. However, in the special case $\rho_{z_1\varepsilon} = 0$ the minimal set of parameters is just one dimensional, because $\rho_{x\hat{x}}\sigma_x$ suffices. For the general case we find

$$\begin{aligned} V_{\text{GIV}}^{\text{CN}} = {} & \frac{\sigma_\varepsilon^2}{\sigma_x^2 \rho_{x\hat{x}}^2} \left[\left(1 - \rho_{z_1\varepsilon}^4\right) + \rho_{z_1\varepsilon} \frac{\gamma_1}{\rho_{x\hat{x}}^2} + \rho_{z_1\varepsilon}^2 \rho_{xz_1}^2 \frac{\gamma_2}{\rho_{x\hat{x}}^4} + 2\rho_{z_1\varepsilon}^4 \rho_{xz_1}^4 \frac{\gamma_3}{\rho_{x\hat{x}}^6} \right] \\ & + \frac{\sigma_\varepsilon^2}{\sigma_x^4 \rho_{x\hat{x}}^4} \rho_{z_1\varepsilon}^4 \left(1 - \frac{\rho_{xz_1}^2}{\rho_{x\hat{x}}^2}\right) \left[1 - 2\rho_{z_1\varepsilon}^2 \left(1 - \frac{\rho_{xz_1}^2}{\rho_{x\hat{x}}^2}\right)\right] \end{aligned} \tag{35}$$

where

$$\gamma_1 = \rho_{z_1\varepsilon}^3 - 2\rho_{x\varepsilon}\rho_{xz_1}(1 + \rho_{z_1\varepsilon}^2 - 2\rho_{z_1\varepsilon}^4) - \rho_{xz_1}^2(\rho_{z_1\varepsilon} - 5\rho_{z_1\varepsilon}^3 + 2\rho_{z_1\varepsilon}^5)$$
$$\gamma_2 = \rho_{x\varepsilon}^2 + 4\rho_{z_1\varepsilon}\rho_{x\varepsilon}\rho_{xz_1} - 4\rho_{z_1\varepsilon}^2[1 + 3\rho_{z_1\varepsilon}\rho_{x\varepsilon}\rho_{xz_1} - \rho_{x\varepsilon}^2 + \rho_{xz_1}^2(1 - \rho_{z_1\varepsilon}^2)]$$
$$\gamma_3 = 2 - (\rho_{x\varepsilon} - \rho_{z_1\varepsilon}\rho_{xz_1})(3\rho_{x\varepsilon} - \rho_{z_1\varepsilon}\rho_{xz_1})$$

Note that this variance is invariant to sign changes of the correlations as long as the sign of $\rho_{z_1\varepsilon}\rho_{x\varepsilon}\rho_{xz_1}$ is not affected, or when either $\rho_{x\varepsilon}$ or $\rho_{z_1\varepsilon}$ is zero. The sign of the inconsistency $\ddot{\beta}_{\text{GIV}}$ is determined by the sign of $\rho_{z_1\varepsilon}\rho_{xz_1}$. For given values of $\rho_{x\hat{x}}$ and $\rho_{z_1\varepsilon}$ the magnitude of $\ddot{\beta}_{\text{GIV}}$ is a multiple of ρ_{xz_1}, so it will be large when the invalid instrument is relatively strong. For the special case $\rho_{xz_1} = \rho_{x\hat{x}}$ i.e., the second instrument is orthogonal to x, the variance formula specializes to

$$\frac{\sigma_\varepsilon^2}{\sigma_x^2} \frac{\left(1 - \rho_{z_1\varepsilon}^2\right)\left(\rho_{xz_1} - \rho_{z_1\varepsilon}\rho_{x\varepsilon}\right)^2 + \rho_{z_1\varepsilon}^4\left(1 - \rho_{x\varepsilon}^2\right)}{\rho_{xz_1}^4} \tag{36}$$

which, not surprisingly, corresponds to Eq. (21).

Next we examine whether, apart from n, the same number of parameters is required to obtain in all generality the finite sample distribution of GIV by generating the appropriate data processes. For that purpose the schemes (24) and (25) can be extended as follows. Let now $v_i \sim \text{IID}(0, I_4)$. Again we take $\varepsilon_i = v_{i,1}$ and, again restricting ourselves to positive α_1 for symmetrically distributed v_i, we have

$$x_i = \xi v_{i,1} + \alpha_1 v_{i,2} = \sigma_x \left[\rho_{x\varepsilon} v_{i,1} + \left| \left(1 - \rho_{x\varepsilon}^2\right)^{1/2} \right| v_{i,2} \right] \tag{37}$$

with $\sigma_x^2 = \text{SN}$ (this is all similar to the earlier example with $l = 1$). Now, however, we have to compose the $l = 2$ instruments as

$$z_{i,1} = \zeta_1 v_{i,1} + \alpha_2 v_{i,2} + \alpha_3 v_{i,3} + \alpha_4 v_{i,4}$$

$$z_{i,2} = \zeta_2 v_{i,1} + \alpha_5 v_{i,2} + \alpha_6 v_{i,3} + \alpha_7 v_{i,4}$$

These entail full generality, because they allow both instruments to have any correlation with the disturbance ε_i, any correlation with the regressor x_i, and any mutual correlation. Since it is only the space spanned by these two instruments that matters for $\hat{\beta}_{\text{GIV}}$, we may replace $z_{i,2}$ by a linear combination of $z_{i,1}$ and $z_{i,2}$ such that it no longer depends on $v_{i,1}$. This corresponds to taking $\zeta_2 = 0$ and reinterpreting α_5, α_6, and α_7. Hence, the general case of two possibly invalid instruments can be represented fully by that of one valid and one possibly invalid instrument, as we already argued above from the asymptotic perspective. Now we can perform a similar operation with respect to $z_{i,1}$, such that we may impose $\alpha_4 = 0$. Next, rescaling the instruments such that they have unit variance leads to the generating schemes

$$\left.\begin{aligned} z_{i,1} &= \zeta_1 v_{i,1} + \alpha_2 v_{i,2} + \left| \left(1 - \zeta_1^2 - \alpha_2^2\right)^{1/2} \right| v_{i,3} \\ z_{i,2} &= \alpha_5 v_{i,2} + \alpha_6 v_{i,3} + \left| \left(1 - \alpha_5^2 - \alpha_6^2\right)^{1/2} \right| v_{i,4} \end{aligned}\right\} \tag{38}$$

Due to the symmetry of v_i generality is maintained when we restrict ourselves to cases where particular coefficients are nonnegative. This extends to α_2 and α_5, because the space spanned by the instruments does not change by multiplying all elements by -1, yielding

$$0 \le \alpha_2 \le 1, 0 \le \alpha_5 \le 1 \tag{39}$$

We also maintain full generality by imposing zero covariance on the two instruments, which implies $\alpha_2 \alpha_5 + \alpha_6 \left(1 - \zeta_1^2 - \alpha_2^2\right)^{1/2} = 0$, from which we find

$$\alpha_6 = -\alpha_2\alpha_5\left(1-\zeta_1^2-\alpha_2^2\right)^{-1/2} \tag{40}$$

So, for given values of σ_x, $\rho_{x\varepsilon}$, and $\rho_{z_1\varepsilon}=\zeta_1$ we would be able to generate data according to Eqs. (37) and (38) if we also knew α_2 and α_5.

The asymptotic overall strength of the two instruments can be controlled by the population R^2 of the regression of x on $Z=(z_1,z_2)$, which is

$$R_{xZ}^2 = \frac{\Sigma_{x'Z}\Sigma_{Z'Z}^{-1}\Sigma_{Z'x}}{\sigma_x^2} \tag{41}$$

Note that

$$\rho_{x\hat{x}}^2 = \frac{\left(\Sigma_{x'Z}\Sigma_{Z'Z}^{-1}\Sigma_{Z'x}\right)^2}{\sigma_x^2\sigma_{\hat{x}}^2} = \frac{\sigma_{\hat{x}}^2}{\sigma_x^2} = R_{xZ}^2 \tag{42}$$

and, since we imposed $\Sigma_{Z'Z}=I$, we have

$$\rho_{x\hat{x}}^2 = \frac{\Sigma_{x'Z}\Sigma_{Z'x}}{\sigma_x^2} = \rho_{xz_1}^2 + \left(1-\rho_{x\varepsilon}^2\right)\alpha_5^2$$

$$\rho_{xz_1} = \rho_{x\varepsilon}\rho_{z_1\varepsilon} + \left|(1-\rho_{x\varepsilon}^2)^{1/2}\right|\alpha_2$$

From these we can express the (nonnegative) values of α_5 and α_2 as

$$\alpha_5 = \left|\left(\frac{\rho_{x\hat{x}}^2-\rho_{xz_1}^2}{1-\rho_{x\varepsilon}^2}\right)^{1/2}\right| \tag{43}$$

and

$$\alpha_2 = \left|\frac{\rho_{xz_1}-\rho_{x\varepsilon}\rho_{z_1\varepsilon}}{\left(1-\rho_{x\varepsilon}^2\right)^{1/2}}\right| \tag{44}$$

from which α_6 follows directly by evaluating Eq. (40).

Hence, we can scan the finite sample distribution of GIV for this class of model for any n over its entire parameter space by simulating data for all compatible values of σ_x, $\rho_{x\hat{x}}$ $\rho_{x\varepsilon}$, ρ_{xz_1}, and $\rho_{z_1\varepsilon}$. Here again, these are found to be the data moments that characterize the asymptotic distribution. They determine ξ and α_1 as in Eq. (32) and α_2, α_5, and α_6 via Eqs. (44), (43), and (40), respectively. We may restrict ourselves to cases where $\rho_{x\hat{x}}>0$ (since the coefficients of the simulation design are just determined by $\rho_{x\hat{x}}^2$). Note that the coefficients of the data generation process, notably α_2, are unaffected (thus yielding the same distribution of $\hat{\beta}_{\text{GIV}}$) if both $\rho_{z_1\varepsilon}$ and ρ_{xz_1} are changed in sign. Therefore, we will only examine cases with $\rho_{xz_1} \geq 0$ However, we shall also just examine nonnegative values of $\rho_{z_1\varepsilon}$, because when the distribution of ε is symmetric changing the signs of both $\rho_{z_1\varepsilon}$ and $\rho_{x\varepsilon}$ yields the mirror image of the distribution of $\hat{\beta}_{\text{GIV}}$. In line with the just identified model the distribution of $\hat{\beta}_{\text{GIV}} - \beta$ for $\rho_{z_1\varepsilon} \leq 0$ is equivalent with the distribution of $-(\hat{\beta}_{\text{GIV}} - \beta)$ for $-\rho_{z_1\varepsilon} \geq 0$ and $-\ \rho_{x\varepsilon}$, because: If we change the signs of $\rho_{z_1\varepsilon}$, $\rho_{x\varepsilon}$, and all ε_i then the variables x_i, $z_{i,1}$, $z_{i,2}$ and thus $\hat{x}_i$ remain the same, whereas $\hat{\beta}_{\text{GIV}} - \beta = \hat{x}_i\varepsilon_i/\hat{x}_i^2$ changes sign.

In the special case that no instrument is invalid we have $\zeta_1 = \rho_{z_1\varepsilon} = 0$ in Eq. (38). Thus full generality is maintained by making $z_{i,2}$ independent of $v_{i,3}$, giving $\alpha_6 = 0$, and zero covariance of the two instruments implies now $\alpha_2\alpha_5 = 0$. Hence, we may choose $\alpha_5 = 0$, resulting in the simplified generating schemes

$$\begin{aligned} z_{i,1} &= \alpha_2 v_{i,2} + \left(1 - \alpha_2^2\right)^{1/2} v_{i,3} \\ z_{i,2} &= v_{i,4} \end{aligned} \tag{45}$$

These imply $\rho_{xz_1} = \rho_{x\hat{x}}$ and $\alpha_2 = \left|\rho_{x\hat{x}}(1 - \rho_{x\varepsilon}^2)^{-1/2}\right|$ instead of Eq. (44). Hence, when $\zeta = 0$ the finite sample distribution is determined by just three parameters (viz. σ_x, $\rho_{x\varepsilon}$, and $\rho_{x\hat{x}}$) instead of five (apart from n), whereas the limiting distribution just depends on $\sigma_{\hat{x}}^2 = \rho_{x\hat{x}}^2\sigma_x^2$.

In all calculations we again fixed SN = 10 (which here too has only a multiplicative effect, i.e., just affects the scale of the densities). For the conditional distribution we used the same draws for $v_{i,2}$ and $v_{i,3}$ as in the previous example, and added a $v_{i,4}$ and used the same strategy regarding normalizing and orthogonalizing them. Since $l - k = 1$, GIV does have a finite first moment now, and for $l > k$ we do not have an explicit formula for the unconditional asymptotic variance when $\rho_{z_1\varepsilon} \neq 0$. Figs. 7 through 10 present illustrative densities for $\rho_{x\hat{x}} = 0.8$, 0.4, 0.1, 0.02 respectively. Again we examine n = 50, 200, 2,000 and as before we chose values $\rho_{x\varepsilon} = -\ 0.3$, 0.0, 0.3, 0.6 and $\rho_{z_1\varepsilon} = \zeta_1 = 0.0, 0.2$, whereas we fixed $\rho_{xz_1} = \rho_{x\hat{x}}/2$. Hence, z_1 provides half of the joint strength of the instruments, and we omitted cases where $\rho_{xz_1} = \rho_{x\hat{x}}$ (and $\rho_{xz_2} = 0$) Although we already established that the latter cases yield similar asymptotic results as obtained for $k = l = 1$, from the simulations we found that the finite sample densities do differ slightly from the "no finite moments" case, and more so for a weaker instrument z_1.

Fig. 7 shows that for strong instruments the available asymptotic approximations are reasonably accurate, but slightly less so for small sample size in Fig. 8 where the instruments are weaker. For really weak instruments we note from Figs. 9 and 10 that the asymptotic approximations for the

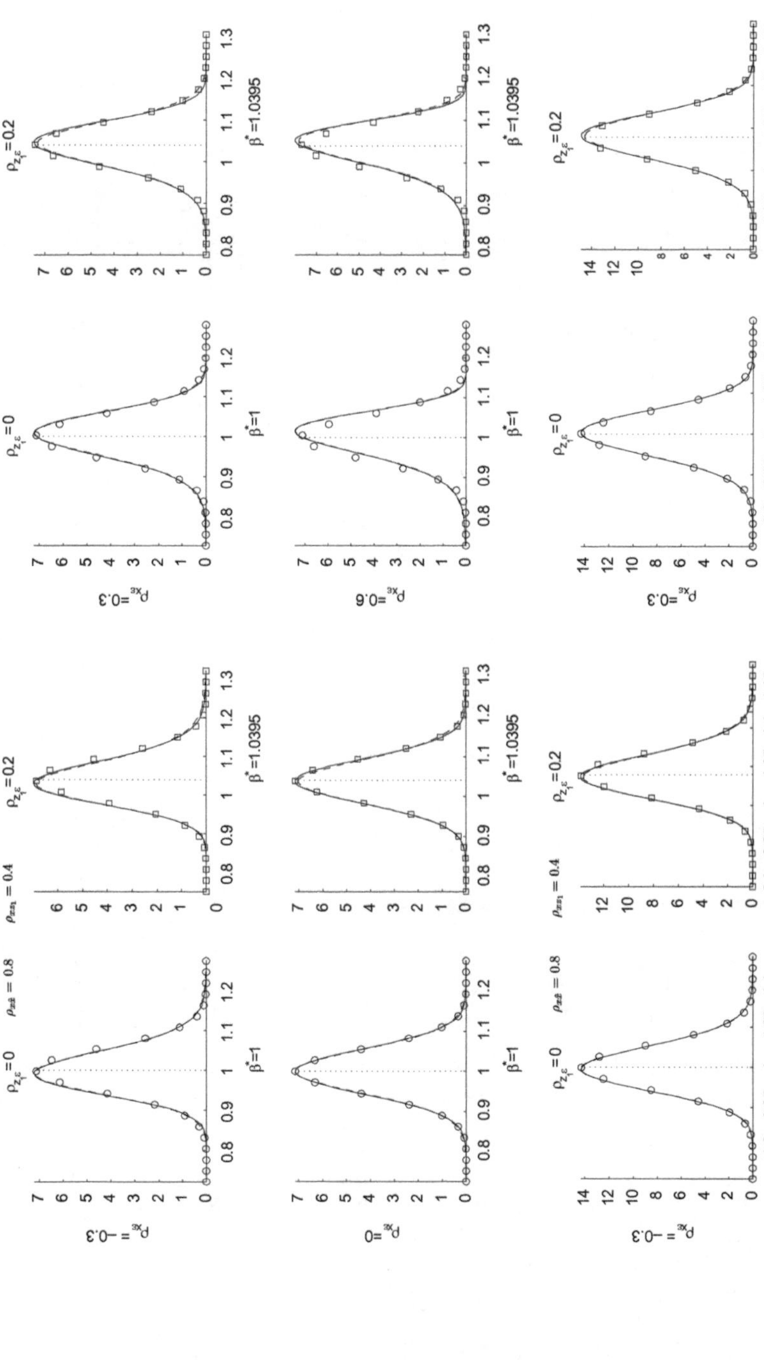

Fig. 7. Densities for $l-1=k=1$; $\beta=1$; $\sigma_x^{\,2}/\sigma_\varepsilon^{\,2}=10$; $\rho_{x\hat{x}}=0.8$; $\rho_{xz_1}=0.4$ (actual:– = cond., –– = uncond.; asymptotic: □ = Cond., ○ = both cond. and uncond.).

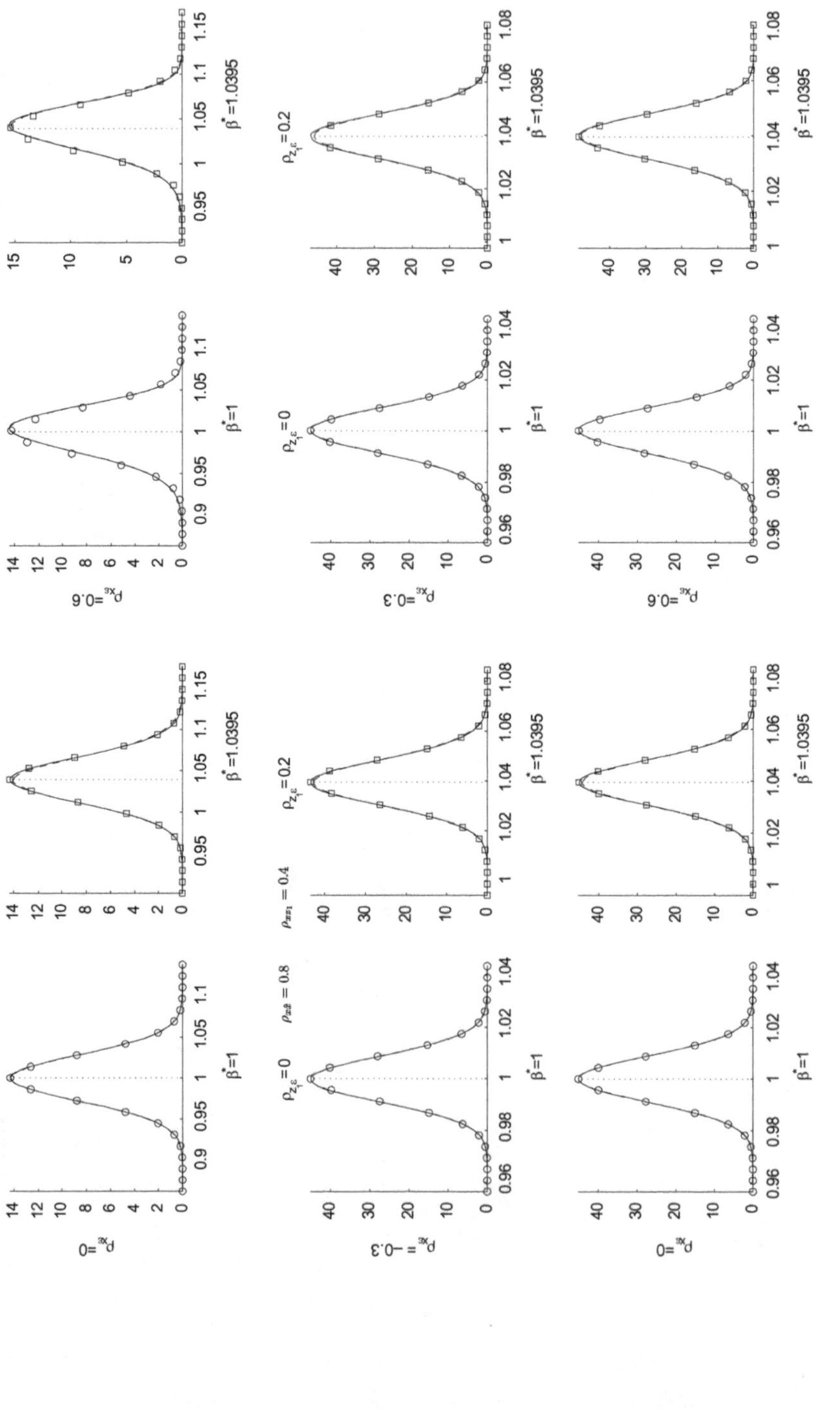

Fig. 7. *(Continued)*

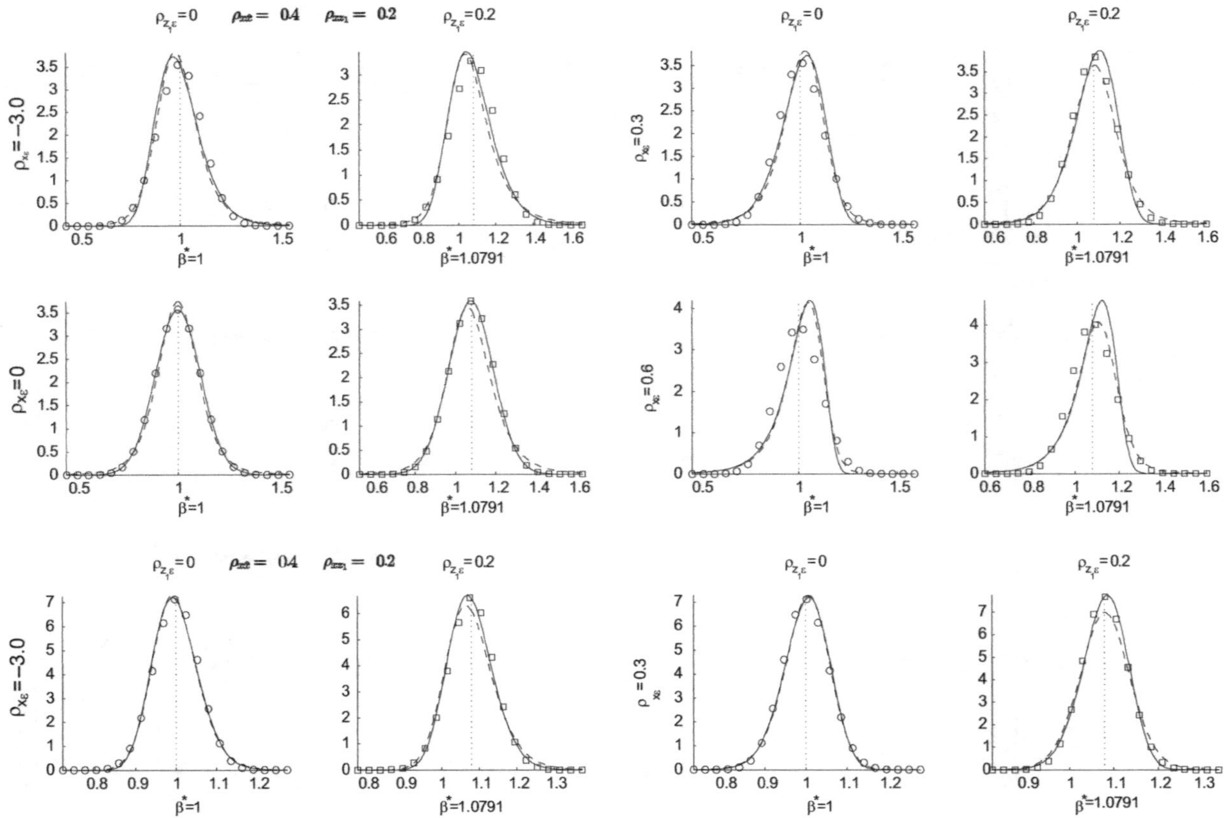

Fig. 8. Densities for $l - 1 = k = 1$; $\beta = 1$; $\sigma_x^2/\sigma_\varepsilon^2 = 10$; $\rho_{x\hat{x}} = 0.4$; $\rho_{xz_1} = 0.2$ (actual:– = cond., –– = uncond.; asymptotic: □ = cond., ○ = both cond. and uncond.).

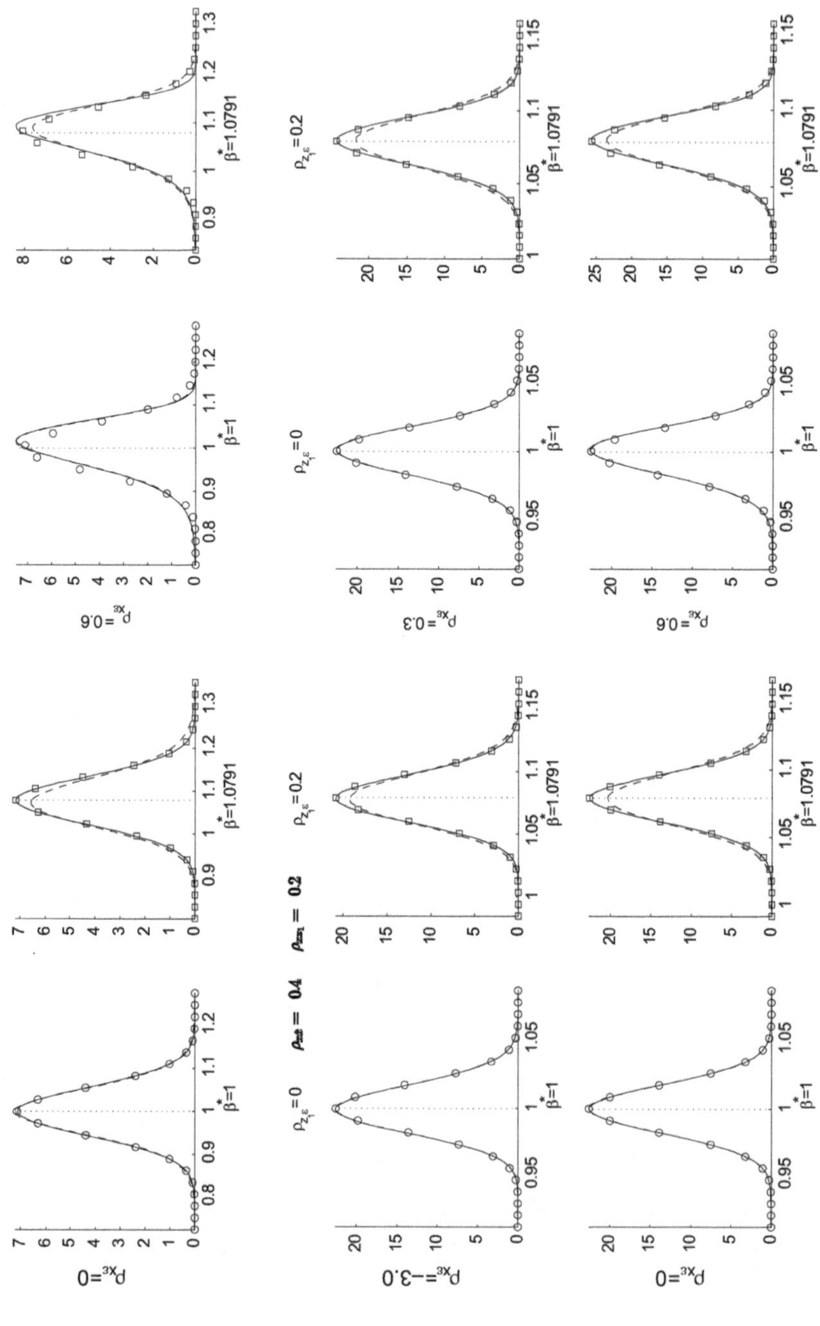

Fig. 8. *(Continued)*

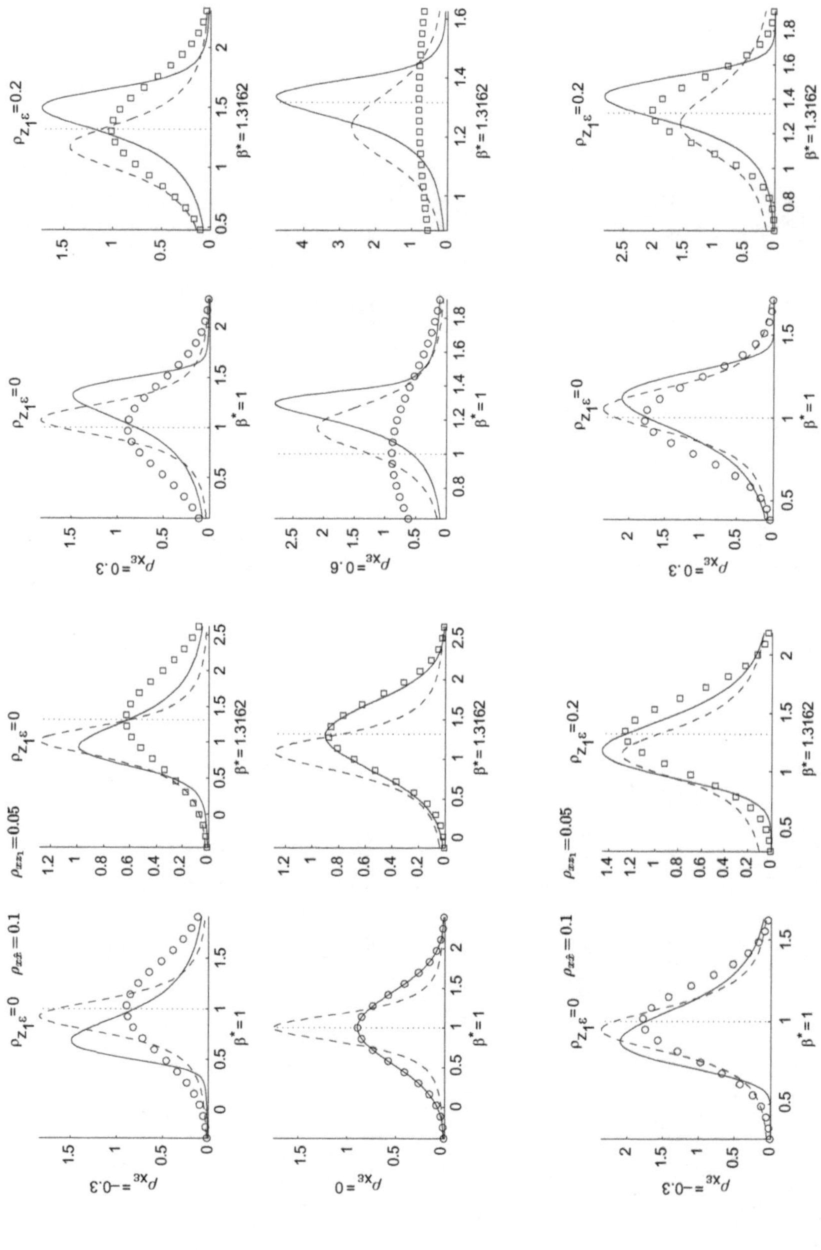

Fig. 9. Densities for $l-1=k=1$; $\beta=1$; $\sigma_x^{\ 2}/\sigma_\varepsilon^{\ 2}=10$; $\rho_{x\hat{x}}=0.1$; $\rho_{xz_1}=0.05$ (actual:– = cond., -- = uncond.; Asymptotic: □ = cond., ○ = both cond. and uncond.).

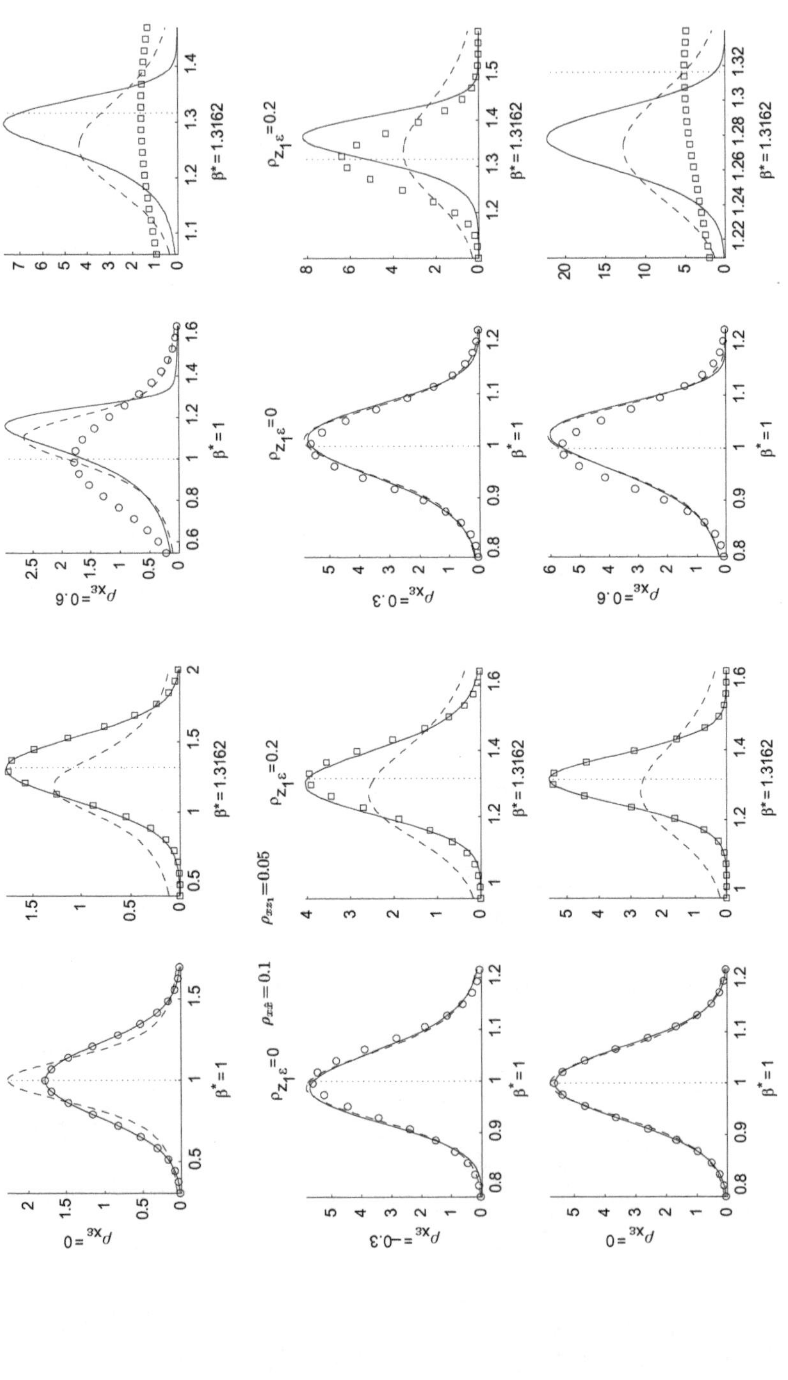

Fig. 9. (*Continued*)

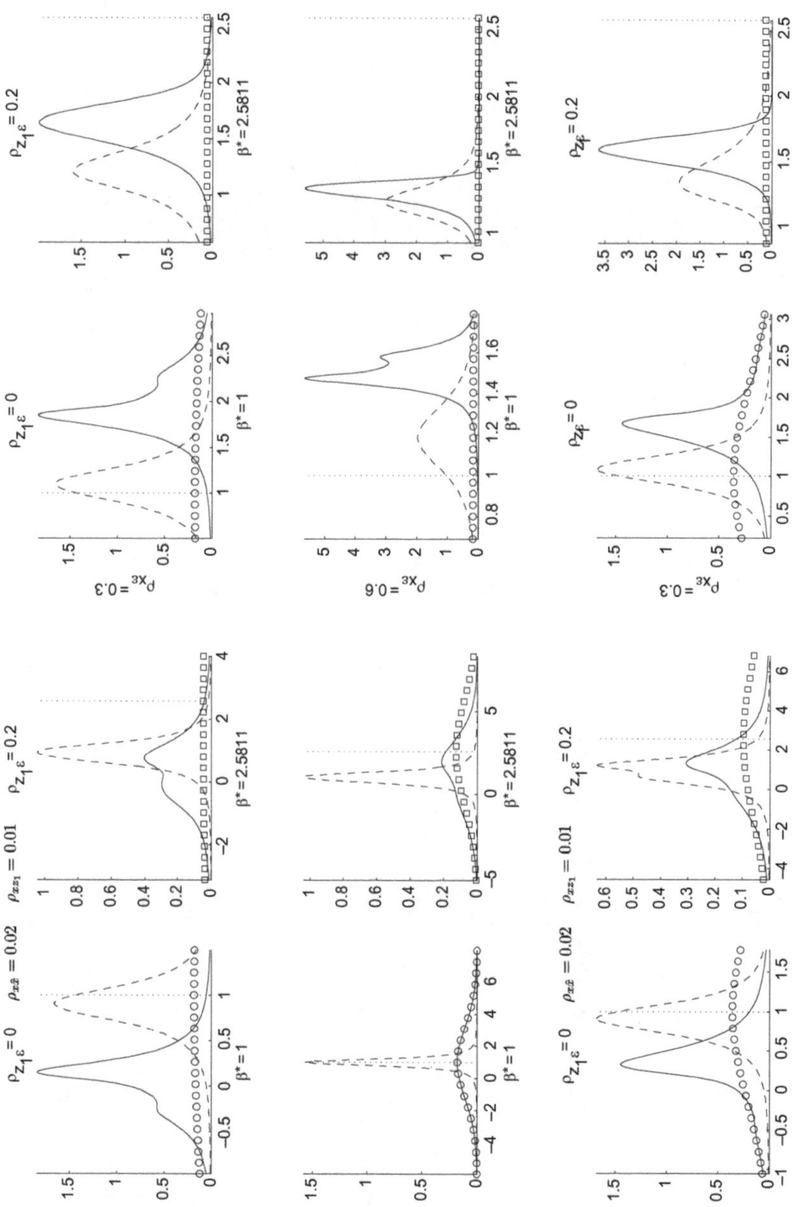

Fig. 10. Densities for $l - 1 = k = 1$; $\beta = 1$; $\sigma_x^{\ 2}/\sigma_\varepsilon^{\ 2} = 10$; $\rho_{x\hat{x}} = 0.02$; $\rho_{xz_1} = 0.01$ (actual:– = cond., –– = uncond.; asymptotic: □ = cond., ○ = both cond. and uncond.).

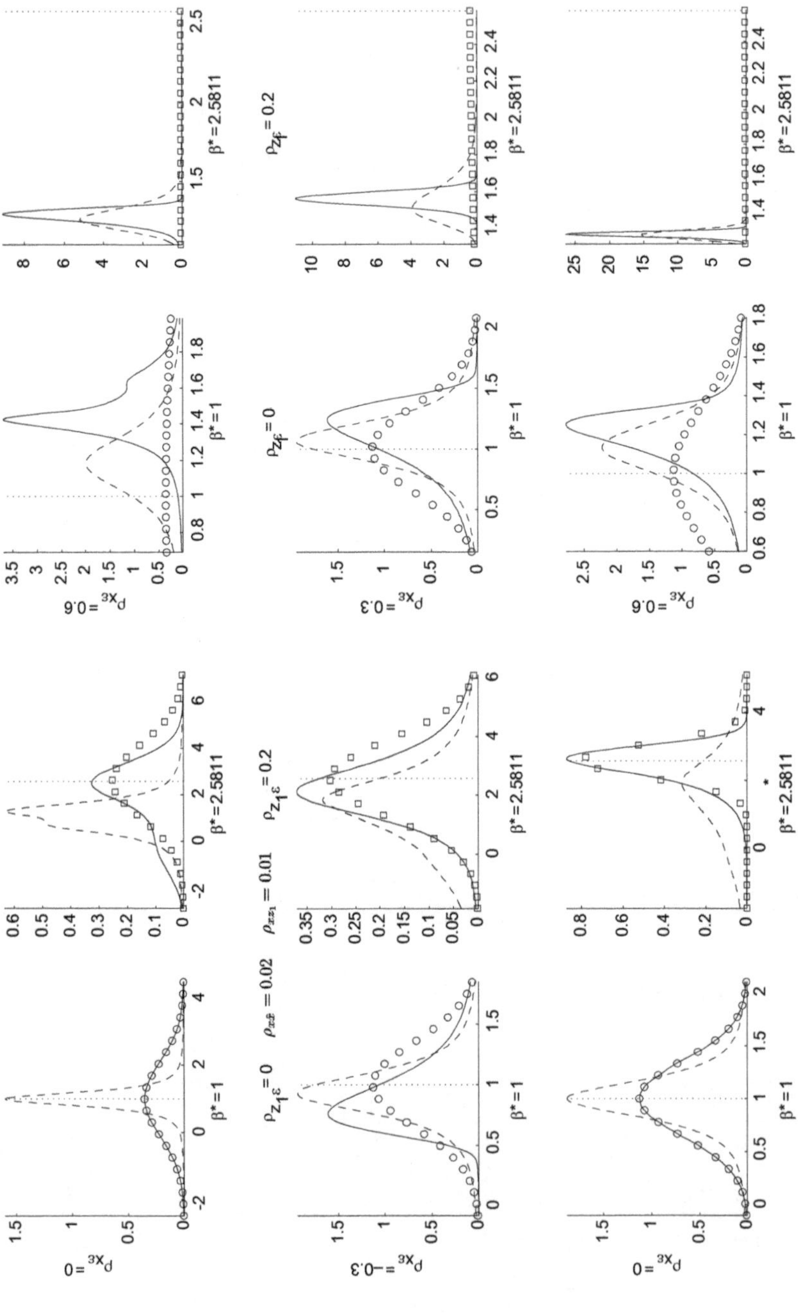

Fig. 10. (*Continued*)

conditional distribution are very accurate when $\rho_{x\varepsilon} = 0$, but are much too pessimistic regarding the inter quartile range otherwise. Forchini (2006) suspects bimodality in the overidentified model when the instruments are valid but weak; for $\rho_{x\hat{x}} = 0.02$ we establish that to be the case, especially for the conditional distribution, and also for the unconditional distribution when there is an invalid instrument. When both instruments are valid and $\rho_{x\hat{x}} = 0.02$ the $l = 2$ case produces estimators which are substantially more efficient than the corresponding $l = 1$ estimators in Fig. 4. This seems at odds with the findings in Donald and Newey (2001) which suggest that efficiency benefits when weak instruments are discarded. Note, however, that their analysis assumes that the number of instruments grows at a smaller rate than the sample size, whereas in our experiments the number of instruments is fixed.

Finally, we look again at median absolute error results. Fig. 11 gives for this model a more global impression of the remarkable accuracy of the conditional asymptotic approximation even in very small samples. However,

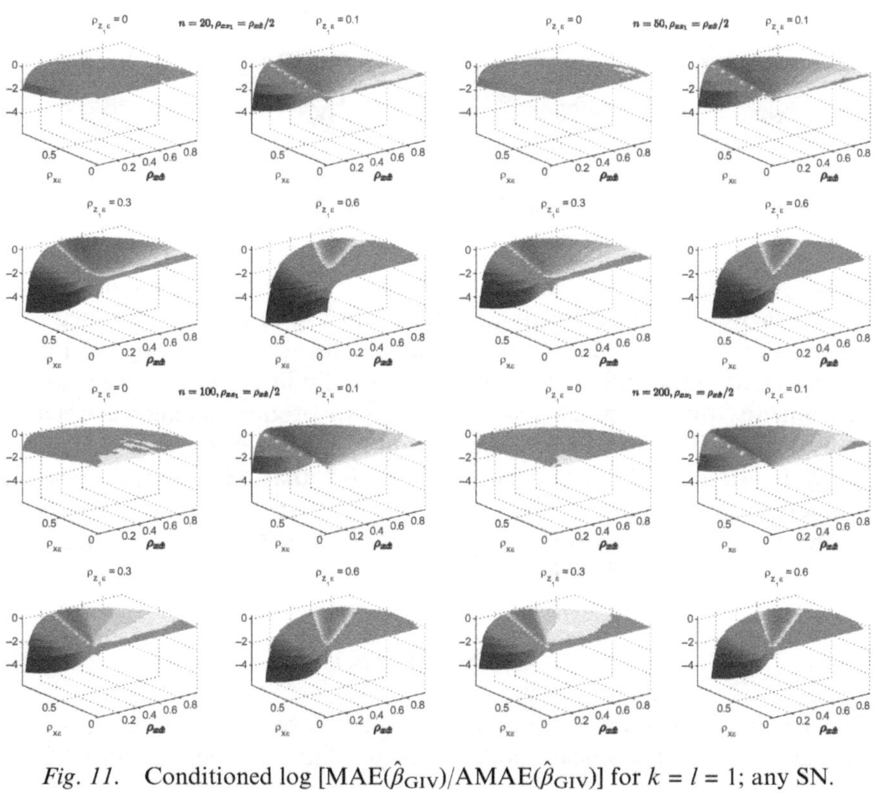

Fig. 11. Conditioned log [MAE($\hat{\beta}_{\text{GIV}}$)/AMAE($\hat{\beta}_{\text{GIV}}$)] for $k = l = 1$; any SN.

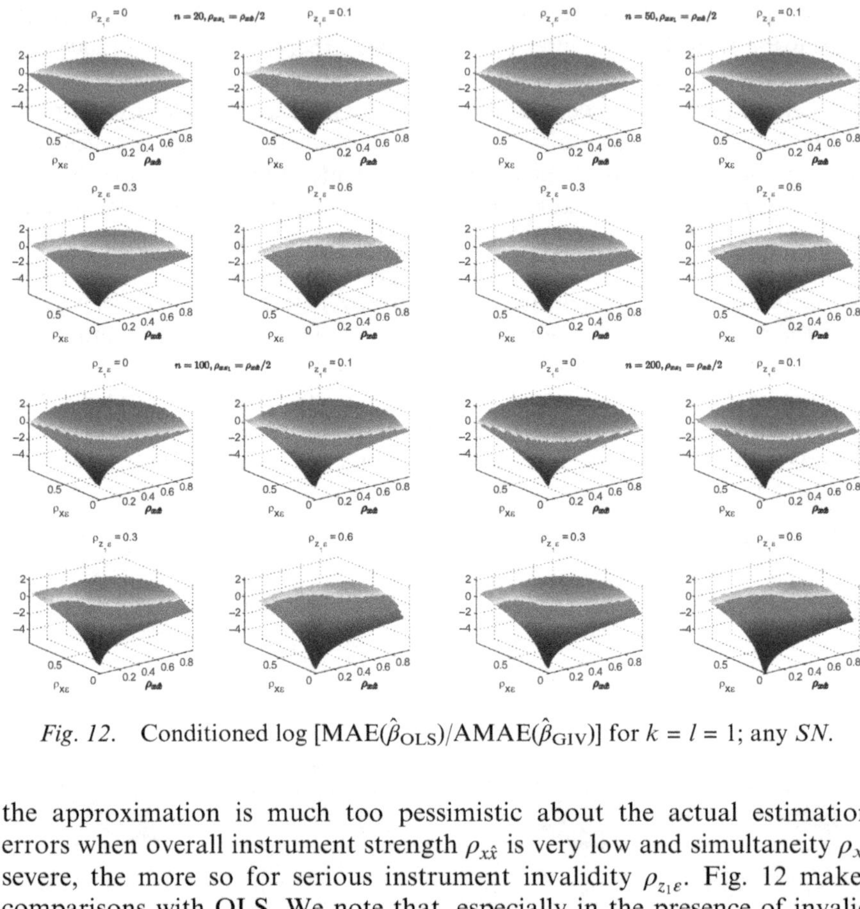

Fig. 12. Conditioned log [MAE($\hat{\beta}_{\text{OLS}}$)/AMAE($\hat{\beta}_{\text{GIV}}$)] for $k = l = 1$; any *SN*.

the approximation is much too pessimistic about the actual estimation errors when overall instrument strength $\rho_{x\hat{x}}$ is very low and simultaneity $\rho_{x\varepsilon}$ severe, the more so for serious instrument invalidity $\rho_{z_1\varepsilon}$. Fig. 12 makes comparisons with OLS. We note that, especially in the presence of invalid instruments, there is much scope for OLS to produce smaller estimation errors than GIV. Anyhow, our simulation results do not generally support the conclusion by Hahn and Hausman (2005) that 2SLS is the preferred estimator when $n \geq 100$ and $\rho^2_{x\hat{x}} \geq 0.1$ They arrive at this conclusion by comparing second-order asymptotic approximations to MSE, whereas ours are obtained from simulating the actual distributions.

4. CONCLUSIONS

The asymptotic variance of a consistent method of moments estimator for the coefficients of a linear model does just involve the variance of the disturbances and an expression involving population data moments. For these moments consistent estimates obtained from the sample data are being substituted when estimating this variance. Usually, it is inconsequential whether or not one considers exogenous regressors as fixed or as random realizations. For models where all observations are IID we demonstrated that when the estimator is inconsistent due to exploiting invalid moment conditions, a relevant random vector series (to which the central limit theorem can be applied in order to obtain the limiting distribution) has elements which are no longer linear but quadratic in the disturbance. Therefore the asymptotic variance also involves third and fourth order moments of the disturbances. Moreover, conditioning on exogenous variables generally has consequences for the variance expression of the limiting distribution of inconsistent estimators, which, although still normal, are now centered at the pseudo-true-value (true coefficient plus inconsistency). It remains a challenge to generalize the explicit results obtained here for IID data and IV estimators, to time-series models and GMM estimators, such as for dynamic panel data models.

We examined the accuracy of our analytic large sample results by comparing them with the simulated actual behavior of instrumental variable estimators in finite samples. Through a reparametrization of the structural and reduced form coefficients into parameters that directly express the degree of simultaneity, the degree of (in)validity of the instrument(s), the strength of the instrument(s), and the signal-to-noise ratio of the model, and by condensing the numerical results into graphic displays, it proved possible to produce a rather complete taxonomy of the behavior of the examined instrumental variables estimators over their full (but low dimensional) parameter space.

There is a quickly expanding literature on the shortcomings of standard large sample asymptotic approximations to the distribution of IV and GMM estimators and tests when the sample size is small or moderate and some of the instruments are weak but valid, and how alternative and better approximations could be obtained. The present study shows that it is possible to obtain an explicit large sample asymptotic approximation to the distribution of method of moments estimators, also when some of the exploited moment conditions are invalid. Not surprisingly, however, that approximation is found to be vulnerable too, when instruments are weak. One option now would be to replace it by an approximation that aims to cope with weakness of instruments. However, our illustrations also suggest an alternative approach in which the employment of weak instruments, which in general yield unattractive biased estimators with widely dispersed and often bimodal distributions, is abandoned altogether. We have shown that exclusively exploiting strong instruments, even if these constitute invalid instruments, often yields much smaller absolute estimation errors in comparison with those obtained on the basis of weak instruments. For that situation we have produced here a very accurate approximation to the finite sample distribution. But, to render this approximation feasible one requires information on the simultaneity parameter ξ and the instrument invalidity parameter ζ. That seems hard to obtain, and if such information was available other estimators than those obtained by minimizing an (in)appropriate method of moments criterion function might be better for producing accurate inference on the coefficient β. However, the now available explicit though unfeasible conditional and unconditional asymptotic distributions of possibly inconsistent estimators can always be used to produce a sensitivity analysis of OLS or IV inference under alternative assumptions regarding the degree of simultaneity and of instrument invalidity.

NOTES

1. See Murray (2006), Small (2007), Berkowitz, Caner, and Ying Fang (2008, 2012), and Guggenberger (2012).

2. Also the conditional distribution is assumed IID with zero expectation provided no endogenous regressors nor any invalid instruments are included in the conditioning set. An alternative point of departure is chosen in Hale, Mariano, and Ramage (1980), Rhodes and Westbrook (1981), Knight (1982), and Skeels (1995) where instruments are invalid due to omitted regressors.

3. Since $m=\Phi^{-1}_{\ddot{\beta},\sigma_{\hat{\beta}}}\left[0.5+\Phi_{\ddot{\beta},\sigma_{\hat{\beta}}}(-m)\right]$, we employed the iterative scheme, $m_0 = 0$, $m_{i+1}=\Phi^{-1}_{\ddot{\beta},\sigma_{\hat{\beta}}}\left[0.5+\Phi_{\ddot{\beta},\sigma_{\hat{\beta}}}(-m_i)\right]$ for $i = 0,1,\ldots$ until convergence. When $\ddot{\beta}=0$ no iteration is required since $m=\Phi^{-1}_{0,\sigma_{\hat{\beta}}}(0.75)$ conforms to the quartile.

4. This document contains a few series of graphs only; more complete and animated pictures are available via the web, see https://sites.google.com/site/homepagejfk/

5. For more background regarding the role of the simulation design parameter space and its relationship with the data generating process parameter space see Kiviet (2011).

REFERENCES

Andrews, D. W. K., & Stock, J. H. (2007). Inference with weak instruments. In R. Blundell, W. K. Newey, & T. Persson (Eds.), *Advances in economics and econometrics, theory and applications: Ninth World congress of the econometric society* (Vol. 3, 122–173). Cambridge, UK: Cambridge University Press.

Ashley, R. (2009). Assessing the credibility of instrumental variables inference with imperfect instruments via sensitivity analysis. *Journal of Applied Econometrics*, *24*, 325–337.

Berkowitz, D., Caner, M., & Fang, Y. (2008). Are "nearly exogenous instruments" reliable? *Economics Letters*, *101*, 20–23.

Berkowitz, D., Caner, M., & Fang, Y. (2012). The validity of instruments revisited. *Journal of Econometrics*, *166*, 255–266.

Bound, J., Jaeger, D. A., & Baker, R. M. (1995). Problems with instrumental variable estimation when the correlation between the instruments and the endogenous explanatory variable is weak. *Journal of the American Statistical Association*, *90*, 443–450.

Donald, S. G., & Newey, W. K. (2001). Choosing the number of instruments. *Econometrica*, *69*, 1161–1191.

Forchini, G. (2006). On the bimodality of the exact distribution of the TSLS estimator. *Econometric Theory*, *22*, 932–946.

Goldberger, A. S. (1964). *Econometric theory*. New York, NY: Wiley.

Guggenberger, P. (2012). On the asymptotic size distortion of tests when instruments locally violate the exogeneity assumption. *Econometric Theory*, *28*, 387–421.

Hahn, J., & Hausman, J. A. (2005). IV estimation with valid and invalid instruments. *Annales d'Économie et de Statistique*, *79/80*, 25–57.

Hahn, J., & Inoue, A. (2002). A Monte Carlo comparison of various asymptotic approximations to the distribution of instrumental variables estimators. *Econometric Reviews*, *21*, 309–336.

Hale, C., Mariano, R. S., & Ramage, J. G. (1980). Finite sample analysis of misspecification in simultaneous equation models. *Journal of the American Statistical Association*, *75*, 418–427.

Hall, A. R., & Inoue, A. (2003). The large sample behaviour of the generalized method of moments estimator in misspecified models. *Journal of Econometrics*, *114*, 361–394.

Hausman, J. A. (1978). Specification tests in econometrics. *Econometrica*, *46*, 1251–1271.

Hendry, D. F. (1979). The behaviour of inconsistent instrumental variables estimators in dynamic systems with autocorrelated errors. *Journal of Econometrics*, *9*, 295–314.

Hendry, D. F. (1982). A reply to professors Maasoumi and Phillips. *Journal of Econometrics*, *19*, 203–213.

Hillier, G. (2006). Yet more on the exact properties of IV estimators. *Econometric Theory*, *22*, 913–931.

Joseph, A. S., & Kiviet, J. F. (2005). Viewing the relative efficiency of IV estimators in models with lagged and instantaneous feedbacks. *Journal of Computational Statistics and Data Analysis*, *49*, 417–444.

Kiviet, J. F. (2011). Monte Carlo simulation for econometricians. *Foundations and Trends in Econometrics*, *5*, 1–181.

Kiviet, J. F. (2013). Identification and inference in a simultaneous equation under alternative information sets and sampling schemes. *The Econometrics Journal*, *16*, S24–S59.

Kiviet, J. F., & Niemczyk, J. (2007). The asymptotic and finite sample distributions of OLS and simple IV in simultaneous equations. *Journal of Computational Statistics and Data Analysis*, *51*, 3296–3318.

Kiviet, J. F., & Niemczyk, J. (2012). Comparing the asymptotic and empirical (un)conditional distributions of OLS and IV in a linear static simultaneous equation. *Journal of Computational Statistics & Data Analysis*, *56*, 3567–3586.

Knight, J. L. (1982). A note on finite sample analysis of misspecifcation in simultaneous equation models. *Economics Letters*, *9*, 275–279.

Maasumi, E., & Phillips, P. C. B. (1982). On the behavior of inconsistent instrumental variable estimators. *Journal of Econometrics*, *19*, 183–201.

Maddala, G. S., & Jeong, J. (1992). On the exact small sample distribution of the instrumental variable estimator. *Econometrica*, *60*, 181–183.

Mariano, R. S. (1973). Approximations to the distribution functions of the ordinary least-squares and two-stage least-squares estimators in the case of two included endogenous variables. *Econometrica*, *41*, 67–77.

Murray, M. P. (2006). Avoiding invalid instruments and coping with weak instruments. *Journal of Economic Perspectives*, *20*, 111–132.

Phillips, P. C. B. (1980). The exact distribution of instrumental variable estimators in an equation containing $n+1$ endogenous variables *Econometrica*, *48*, 861–878.

Phillips, P. C. B. (1983). Exact small sample theory in the simultaneous equations model. In Z. Griliches & M. D. Intriligator (Eds.), *Handbook of econometrics* (Vol. 1, pp. 449–516). Amsterdam: North-Holland.

Phillips, P. C. B. (2006). A remark on bimodality and weak instrumentation in structural equation estimation. *Econometric Theory*, *22*, 947–960.

Phillips, P. C. B., & Wickens, M. R. (1978). *Exercises in econometrics*. Cambridge, MA: Philip Allen and Ballinger.

Rhodes, G. F., & Westbrook, M. D. (1981). A study of estimator densities and performance under misspecifcation. *Journal of Econometrics*, *16*, 311–337.

Rothenberg, T. J. (1972). *The asymptotic distribution of the least squares estimator in the errors in variables model*. Unpublished mimeo.

Sawa, T. (1969). The exact sampling distribution of ordinary least squares and two-stage least squares estimators. *Journal of the American Statistical Association*, *64*, 923–937.

Skeels, C. L. (1995). Instrumental variables estimation in misspecified single equations. *Econometric Theory*, *11*, 498–529.

Small, D. S. (2007). Sensitivity analysis for instrumental variables regression with overidentifying restrictions. *Journal of the American Statistical Society*, *102*, 1049–1058.

Woglom, G. (2001). More results on the exact small sample properties of the instrumental variable estimator. *Econometrica*, *69*, 1381–1389.

APPENDIX A: PROOF OF THEOREM 1

Centering around $\beta^*_{n,\mathrm{GIV}}$ defined in Eq. (12) we obtain

$$\sqrt{n}\left(\hat{\beta}_{\mathrm{GIV}} - \beta^*_{n,\mathrm{GIV}}\right) = \sqrt{n}\left[\left(\hat{X}'\hat{X}\right)^{-1}\hat{X}'\varepsilon - \sigma^2_\varepsilon S^{-1}_{\hat{X}'\hat{X}} P'\zeta\right] \tag{A.1}$$

To find the limiting distribution we shall rewrite the right-hand side of Eq. (A.1) such that we can invoke the Lemma given at the end of Section 2. Below we first show that Eq. (A.1) can be rewritten as

$$\sqrt{n}\left(\hat{\beta}_{\mathrm{GIV}} - \beta^*_{n,\mathrm{GIV}}\right) = \left(\frac{1}{n}\hat{X}'\hat{X}\right)^{-1}\frac{1}{\sqrt{n}}\left[W'\varepsilon + \omega(\varepsilon'\varepsilon - n\sigma^2_\varepsilon)\right] + o_p(1) \tag{A.2}$$

for appropriate $n \times k$ matrix W, with $E(W'\varepsilon) = 0$, and nonrandom $k \times 1$ vector ω. Invoking also a theorem often attributed to Cramér, the Lemma then yields

$$\sqrt{n}\left(\hat{\beta}_{\mathrm{GIV}} - \beta^*_{n,\mathrm{GIV}}\right) \xrightarrow{d} N\left[0, \sigma^2_\varepsilon \Sigma^{-1}_{\hat{X}'\hat{X}}\left(\mathrm{plim}_{n\to\infty}\frac{1}{n}W'W + 2\sigma^2_\varepsilon\omega\omega'\right)\Sigma^{-1}_{\hat{X}'\hat{X}}\right] \tag{A.3}$$

upon assuming $\mu_3 = 0$ and $\mu_4 = 3$.

We first set out to rewrite Eq. (A.1) in the form Eq. (A.2). We easily obtain

$$\begin{aligned}\sqrt{n}\left(\hat{\beta}_{\mathrm{GIV}} - \beta^*_{n,\mathrm{GIV}}\right) &= \sqrt{n}\left(\hat{X}'\hat{X}\right)^{-1}\left[\hat{\Pi}'(Z'\varepsilon - n\sigma^2_\varepsilon\zeta) + n\sigma^2_\varepsilon\hat{\Pi}'\zeta - \sigma^2_\varepsilon\hat{X}'\hat{X}S^{-1}_{\hat{X}'\hat{X}}P'\zeta\right] \\ &= \left(\frac{1}{n}\hat{X}'\hat{X}\right)^{-1}\frac{1}{\sqrt{n}}\left\{\hat{\Pi}'\left[\overline{Z}'\varepsilon + (\varepsilon'\varepsilon - n\sigma^2_\varepsilon)\zeta\right] + n\sigma^2_\varepsilon\left[\hat{\Pi}' - \frac{1}{n}\hat{X}'\hat{X}S^{-1}_{\hat{X}'\hat{X}}P'\right]\zeta\right\}\end{aligned} \tag{A.4}$$

For the second expression between square brackets in the final line of Eq. (A.4) we find

$$\begin{aligned}\hat{\Pi}' - \frac{1}{n}\hat{X}'\hat{X}S^{-1}_{\hat{X}'\hat{X}}S_{X'Z}S^{-1}_{Z'Z} &= \hat{\Pi}'\left(S_{Z'Z} - \frac{1}{n}Z'Z\right)S^{-1}_{Z'Z} + \left(\frac{1}{n}X'Z - \frac{1}{n}\hat{X}'\hat{X}S^{-1}_{\hat{X}'\hat{X}}S_{X'Z}\right)S^{-1}_{Z'Z} \\ &= \hat{\Pi}'\left(S_{Z'Z} - \frac{1}{n}Z'Z\right)S^{-1}_{Z'Z} + \left(\frac{1}{n}X'Z - S_{X'Z}\right)S^{-1}_{Z'Z} + \left(S_{\hat{X}'\hat{X}} - \frac{1}{n}\hat{X}'\hat{X}\right)S^{-1}_{\hat{X}'\hat{X}}S_{X'Z}S^{-1}_{Z'Z}\end{aligned} \tag{A.5}$$

Its third term contains a factor which can be decomposed as

$$
\begin{aligned}
& S_{\hat{X}'\hat{X}} - \frac{1}{n}\hat{X}'\hat{X} \\
&= S_{X'Z}S_{Z'Z}^{-1}S_{Z'X} - \hat{\Pi}'\frac{1}{n}Z'X \\
&= \left(S_{X'Z}S_{Z'Z}^{-1} - \hat{\Pi}'\right)S_{Z'X} - \hat{\Pi}'\left(\frac{1}{n}Z'X - S_{Z'X}\right) \\
&= \left\{\left(S_{X'Z} - \frac{1}{n}X'Z\right)S_{Z'Z}^{-1} - \frac{1}{n}X'Z\left[\left(\tfrac{1}{n}Z'Z\right)^{-1} - S_{Z'Z}^{-1}\right]\right\}S_{Z'X} - \hat{\Pi}'\left(\frac{1}{n}Z'X - S_{Z'X}\right) \\
&= \left\{\left(S_{X'Z} - \frac{1}{n}X'Z\right)S_{Z'Z}^{-1} - \hat{\Pi}'\left[\left(S_{Z'Z} - \frac{1}{n}Z'Z\right)S_{Z'Z}^{-1}\right]\right\}S_{Z'X} - \hat{\Pi}'\left(\frac{1}{n}Z'X - S_{Z'X}\right)
\end{aligned}
\tag{A.6}
$$

Now substituting the decompositions obtained in Eqs. (A.5) and (A.6) into the expression within curly brackets in the final line of Eq. (A.4), and next using $\hat{\Pi} = \Pi + O_p(n^{-1/2})$, $P = \Pi + O_p(n^{-1/2})$, and $\ddot{\beta}_{n,\text{GIV}} = \ddot{\beta}_{\text{GIV}} + O_p(n^{-1/2})$, we obtain

$$
\begin{aligned}
& \hat{\Pi}'\left[\overline{Z}'\varepsilon + (\varepsilon'\varepsilon - n\sigma_\varepsilon^2)\zeta\right] + n\sigma_\varepsilon^2\left[\hat{\Pi}' - \frac{1}{n}\hat{X}'\hat{X}S_{\hat{X}'\hat{X}}^{-1}S_{X'Z}S_{Z'Z}^{-1}\right]\zeta \\
&= \hat{\Pi}'\left[\overline{Z}'\varepsilon + (\varepsilon'\varepsilon - n\sigma_\varepsilon^2)\zeta\right] \\
&+ n\sigma_\varepsilon^2\hat{\Pi}'\left(S_{Z'Z} - \frac{1}{n}Z'Z\right)S_{Z'Z}^{-1}\zeta + n\sigma_\varepsilon^2\left(\frac{1}{n}X'Z - S_{X'Z}\right)S_{Z'Z}^{-1}\zeta + n\left(S_{\hat{X}'\hat{X}} - \frac{1}{n}\hat{X}'\hat{X}\right)\ddot{\beta}_{n,\text{GIV}} \\
&= \Pi'\left[\overline{Z}'\varepsilon + (\varepsilon'\varepsilon - n\sigma_\varepsilon^2)\zeta\right] - n\sigma_\varepsilon^2\Pi'\left(\frac{1}{n}Z'Z - S_{Z'Z}\right)S_{Z'Z}^{-1}\zeta + n\sigma_\varepsilon^2\left(\frac{1}{n}X'Z - S_{X'Z}\right)S_{Z'Z}^{-1}\zeta \\
&- n\left(\frac{1}{n}X'Z - S_{X'Z}\right)\Pi\ddot{\beta}_{\text{GIV}} + n\Pi'\left(\frac{1}{n}Z'Z - S_{Z'Z}\right)\Pi\ddot{\beta}_{\text{GIV}} - n\Pi'\left(\frac{1}{n}Z'X - S_{Z'X}\right)\ddot{\beta}_{\text{GIV}} + O_p(1)
\end{aligned}
\tag{A.7}
$$

All the six terms of Eq. (A.7) are $O_p(n^{1/2})$ and will, after premultiplication by $n^{-1/2}\left(\frac{1}{n}\hat{X}'\hat{X}\right)^{-1}$, affect the limiting distribution of $\hat{\beta}_{\text{GIV}}$.

In deriving in a more general context such a limiting distribution Hendry (1979, formula 16) takes into account only terms similar to the first and sixth of Eq. (A.7). Hence, he incorrectly neglects four of the six $O_p(n^{1/2})$ terms of Eq. (A.7), as demonstrated by Maasoumi and Phillips (1982, formula 17), who also show that this only affects the $l > k$ case. From Eq. (A.7) it can easily be seen that in the special case $l = k$ terms 2 and 5, and 3 and 4 cancel. Maasoumi and Phillips (1982) and Hendry (1982) provide algebra by which, exploiting formulas related to Eqs. (A.4) and (A.7), the unconditional limiting distribution of the GIV estimator can be obtained for one equation of a particular simultaneous dynamic system with first order serial correlation involving an arbitrary number of endogenous and autoregressive predetermined variables, which are all assumed to be normally distributed.

We will here obtain an explicit result for the particular situation described by our Frameworks A and B, while conditioning on the (latent) predetermined variables. Hence, we do not make an assumption on the distribution of $\overline{X}$ and $\overline{Z}$, but make the substitutions

$$\begin{aligned}\frac{1}{n}Z'Z - S_{Z'Z} &= \frac{1}{n}\overline{Z}'\overline{Z} + \frac{1}{n}\overline{Z}'\varepsilon\zeta' + \frac{1}{n}\zeta\varepsilon'\overline{Z} + \frac{1}{n}\zeta\varepsilon'\varepsilon\zeta' - \frac{1}{n}\overline{Z}'\overline{Z} - \sigma_\varepsilon^2\zeta\zeta' \\ &= \frac{1}{n}\overline{Z}'\varepsilon\zeta' + \frac{1}{n}\zeta\varepsilon'\overline{Z} + \frac{1}{n}(\varepsilon'\varepsilon - n\sigma_\varepsilon^2)\zeta\zeta'\end{aligned}$$

$$\frac{1}{n}X'Z - S_{X'Z} = \frac{1}{n}\overline{X}'\varepsilon\zeta' + \frac{1}{n}\xi\varepsilon'\overline{Z} + \frac{1}{n}(\varepsilon'\varepsilon - n\sigma_\varepsilon^2)\xi\zeta'$$

in the final expression given for Eq. (A.7), which yields

$$\begin{aligned}&\Pi'\overline{Z}'\varepsilon + (\varepsilon'\varepsilon - n\sigma_\varepsilon^2)\Pi'\zeta - \sigma_\varepsilon^2\Pi'\overline{Z}'\varepsilon\zeta' S_{Z'Z}^{-1}\zeta - \sigma_\varepsilon^2\Pi'\zeta\varepsilon'\overline{Z}S_{Z'Z}^{-1}\zeta - \sigma_\varepsilon^2\Pi'(\varepsilon'\varepsilon - n\sigma_\varepsilon^2)\zeta\zeta' S_{Z'Z}^{-1}\zeta \\ &+ \sigma_\varepsilon^2\overline{X}'\varepsilon\zeta' S_{Z'Z}^{-1}\zeta + \sigma_\varepsilon^2\xi\varepsilon'\overline{Z}S_{Z'Z}^{-1}\zeta + \sigma_\varepsilon^2(\varepsilon'\varepsilon - n\sigma_\varepsilon^2)\zeta' S_{Z'Z}^{-1}\zeta + \Pi'\overline{Z}'\varepsilon\zeta'\Pi\ddot{\beta}_{\text{GIV}} + \Pi'\zeta\varepsilon'\overline{Z}\Pi\ddot{\beta}_{\text{GIV}} \\ &+ \Pi'(\varepsilon'\varepsilon - n\sigma_\varepsilon^2)\zeta\zeta'\Pi\ddot{\beta}_{\text{GIV}} - \overline{X}'\varepsilon\zeta'\Pi\ddot{\beta}_{\text{GIV}} - \xi\varepsilon'\overline{Z}\Pi\ddot{\beta}_{\text{GIV}} - (\varepsilon'\varepsilon - n\sigma_\varepsilon^2)\xi\zeta'\Pi\ddot{\beta}_{\text{GIV}} - \Pi'\zeta\varepsilon'\overline{X}\ddot{\beta}_{\text{GIV}} \\ &- \Pi'\overline{Z}'\varepsilon\xi'\ddot{\beta}_{\text{GIV}} - \Pi'(\varepsilon'\varepsilon - n\sigma_\varepsilon^2)\zeta\xi'\ddot{\beta}_{\text{GIV}} + O_p(1)\end{aligned}$$

This can be further simplified by using

$$c_1 \equiv \sigma_\varepsilon^2 \zeta' \Sigma_{Z'Z}^{-1} \zeta$$

$$c_2 \equiv \zeta' \Pi \ddot{\beta}_{\text{GIV}} = \sigma_\varepsilon^2 \zeta' \Sigma_{Z'Z}^{-1} \Sigma_{Z'X} \Sigma_{\hat{X}'\hat{X}}^{-1} \Sigma_{X'Z} \Sigma_{Z'Z}^{-1} \zeta$$

$$c_3 \equiv \xi' \ddot{\beta}_{\text{GIV}}$$

giving

$$\begin{aligned}
&\Pi'\overline{Z}'\varepsilon + (\varepsilon'\varepsilon - n\sigma_\varepsilon^2)\Pi'\zeta - c_1\Pi'\overline{Z}'\varepsilon - \sigma_\varepsilon^2\Pi'\zeta\zeta'\Sigma_{Z'Z}^{-1}\overline{Z}'\varepsilon - c_1(\varepsilon'\varepsilon - n\sigma_\varepsilon^2)\Pi'\zeta \\
&+ c_1\overline{X}'\varepsilon + \sigma_\varepsilon^2\xi\zeta'\Sigma_{Z'Z}^{-1}\overline{Z}'\varepsilon + c_1(\varepsilon'\varepsilon - n\sigma_\varepsilon^2)\xi + c_2\Pi'\overline{Z}'\varepsilon + \Pi'\zeta\ddot{\beta}_{\text{GIV}}'\Pi'\overline{Z}'\varepsilon + c_2(\varepsilon'\varepsilon - n\sigma_\varepsilon^2)\Pi'\zeta \\
&- c_2\overline{X}'\varepsilon - \xi\ddot{\beta}_{\text{GIV}}'\Pi'\overline{Z}'\varepsilon - c_2(\varepsilon'\varepsilon - n\sigma_\varepsilon^2)\xi - \Pi'\zeta\ddot{\beta}_{\text{GIV}}'\overline{X}'\varepsilon - c_3\Pi'\overline{Z}'\varepsilon - c_3(\varepsilon'\varepsilon - n\sigma_\varepsilon^2)\Pi'\zeta + o_p(n^{1/2}) \\
&\qquad = \left[c_4 I_k - \Pi'\zeta\ddot{\beta}_{\text{GIV}}'\right]\overline{X}'\varepsilon + \left[c_5\Pi' + (\xi - \Pi'\zeta)\left(\sigma_\varepsilon^2\zeta' - \ddot{\beta}_{\text{GIV}}'\Sigma_{X'Z}\right)\Sigma_{Z'Z}^{-1}\right]\overline{Z}'\varepsilon \\
&\qquad + (c_4\xi + c_5\Pi'\zeta)(\varepsilon'\varepsilon - n\sigma_\varepsilon^2) + O_p(1)
\end{aligned} \tag{A.8}$$

where $c_4 \equiv c_1 - c_2$ and $c_5 \equiv 1 - c_3 - c_4$.

Note that Eq. (A.8) re-expresses the factor in curly brackets in the final line of Eq. (A.4). We want to derive its limiting distribution after scaling by the factor $1/\sqrt{n}$, so we may neglect the remainder term. Defining the $k \times k$ matrix Θ_1, the $k \times l$ matrix Θ_2, and the $k \times 1$ vector ω, such that

$$\Theta_1 \equiv c_4 I_k - \Pi'\zeta\ddot{\beta}_{\text{GIV}}' \tag{A.9}$$

$$\Theta_2 \equiv c_5\Pi' + (\xi - \Pi'\zeta)\left(\sigma_\varepsilon^2\zeta' - \ddot{\beta}_{\text{GIV}}'\Sigma_{X'Z}\right)\Sigma_{Z'Z}^{-1}$$

$$\omega \equiv c_4\xi + c_5\Pi'\zeta$$

we can now invoke the Lemma with

$$W' = \Theta_1\overline{X}' + \Theta_2\overline{Z}' \tag{A.10}$$

For the case $\mu_3 = 0$ and $\mu_4 = 3$ we then obtain, conditioning on $\overline{X}$ and $\overline{Z}$, the limiting distribution

$$\frac{1}{\sqrt{n}}\left[\Theta_1\overline{X}'\varepsilon + \Theta_2\overline{Z}'\varepsilon + \omega(\varepsilon'\varepsilon - n\sigma_\varepsilon^2)\right] \xrightarrow{d} \mathcal{N}(0, \sigma_\varepsilon^2 V_0)$$

where

$$V_0 = \Theta_1\Sigma_{\overline{X}'\overline{X}}\Theta_1' + \Theta_2\Sigma_{\overline{Z}'\overline{Z}}\Theta_2' + 2\sigma_\varepsilon^2\omega\omega' + \Theta_1\Sigma_{\overline{X}'\overline{Z}}\Theta_2' + \Theta_2\Sigma_{\overline{Z}'\overline{X}}\Theta_1' \tag{A.11}$$

In evaluating V_0 we make use of

$$\begin{aligned}
\Sigma_{\overline{Z}'\overline{Z}} &\equiv \text{plim}\, n^{-1}\overline{Z}'\overline{Z} = \Sigma_{Z'Z} - \sigma_\varepsilon^2\zeta\zeta' \\
\Sigma_{\overline{X}'\overline{X}} &\equiv \text{plim}\, n^{-1}\overline{X}'\overline{X} = \Sigma_{X'X} - \sigma_\varepsilon^2\xi\xi' \\
\Sigma_{\overline{Z}'\overline{X}} &\equiv \text{plim}\, n^{-1}\overline{Z}'\overline{X} = \Sigma_{Z'X} - \sigma_\varepsilon^2\zeta\xi' \\
\Sigma_{\overline{X}'\overline{Z}} &\equiv \text{plim}\, n^{-1}\overline{X}'\overline{Z} = \Sigma_{\overline{Z}'\overline{X}}'
\end{aligned}$$

and find that V_0 can be expressed as

$$\begin{aligned}
&\left[c_4 I_k - \Pi'\zeta\ddot{\beta}_{\text{GIV}}'\right](\Sigma_{X'X} - \sigma_\varepsilon^2\xi\xi')\left[c_4 I_k - \ddot{\beta}_{\text{GIV}}\zeta'\Pi\right] \\
&+ \left[c_5\Pi' + (\xi - \Pi'\zeta)\left(\sigma_\varepsilon^2\zeta' - \ddot{\beta}_{\text{GIV}}'\Sigma_{X'Z}\right)\Sigma_{Z'Z}^{-1}\right](\Sigma_{Z'Z} - \sigma_\varepsilon^2\zeta\zeta') \\
&\times\left[c_5\Pi + \Sigma_{Z'Z}^{-1}(\sigma_\varepsilon^2\zeta - \Sigma_{Z'X}\ddot{\beta}_{\text{GIV}})(\xi' - \zeta'\Pi)\right] \\
&+ 2\sigma_\varepsilon^2\left[c_4\xi + c_5\Pi'\zeta\right]\left[c_4\xi' + c_5\zeta'\Pi\right] \\
&+ \left[c_4 I_k - \Pi'\zeta\ddot{\beta}_{\text{GIV}}'\right](\Sigma_{X'Z} - \sigma_\varepsilon^2\xi\zeta')\left[c_5\Pi + \Sigma_{Z'Z}^{-1}(\sigma_\varepsilon^2\zeta - \Sigma_{Z'X}\ddot{\beta}_{\text{GIV}})(\xi' - \zeta'\Pi)\right] \\
&+ \left[c_5\Pi' + (\xi - \Pi'\zeta)\left(\sigma_\varepsilon^2\zeta' - \ddot{\beta}_{\text{GIV}}'\Sigma_{X'Z}\right)\Sigma_{Z'Z}^{-1}\right](\Sigma_{Z'X} - \sigma_\varepsilon^2\zeta\xi')\left[c_4 I_k - \ddot{\beta}_{\text{GIV}}\zeta'\Pi\right]
\end{aligned}$$

Next, we examine these five terms of V_0 one by one. The first one is

$$
\begin{aligned}
& c_4^2(\Sigma_{X'X} - \sigma_\varepsilon^2\xi\xi') - c_4(\Sigma_{X'X} - \sigma_\varepsilon^2\xi\xi')\ddot{\beta}_{\mathrm{GIV}}\zeta'\Pi \\
& - c_4\Pi'\zeta\ddot{\beta}_{\mathrm{GIV}}'(\Sigma_{X'X} - \sigma_\varepsilon^2\xi\xi') + \Pi'\zeta\ddot{\beta}_{\mathrm{GIV}}'(\Sigma_{X'X} - \sigma_\varepsilon^2\xi\xi')\ddot{\beta}_{\mathrm{GIV}}\zeta'\Pi \\
= & c_4^2\Sigma_{X'X} - \sigma_\varepsilon^2 c_4^2\xi\xi' - c_4\Sigma_{X'X}\ddot{\beta}_{\mathrm{GIV}}\zeta'\Pi + \sigma_\varepsilon^2 c_3c_4\xi\zeta'\Pi \\
& - c_4\Pi'\zeta\ddot{\beta}_{\mathrm{GIV}}'\Sigma_{X'X} + \sigma_\varepsilon^2 c_3c_4\Pi'\zeta\xi' + \left(\ddot{\beta}_{\mathrm{GIV}}'\Sigma_{X'X}\ddot{\beta}_{\mathrm{GIV}} - \sigma_\varepsilon^2 c_3^2\right)\Pi'\zeta\zeta'\Pi
\end{aligned}
$$

the second is

$$
\begin{aligned}
& \left[c_5\Pi'\Sigma_{Z'Z} + (\xi - \Pi'\zeta)\left(\sigma_\varepsilon^2\zeta' - \ddot{\beta}_{\mathrm{GIV}}'\Sigma_{X'Z}\right)\right]\left[c_5\Pi + \Sigma_{Z'Z}^{-1}(\sigma_\varepsilon^2\zeta - \Sigma_{Z'X}\ddot{\beta}_{\mathrm{GIV}})(\xi' - \zeta'\Pi)\right] \\
& -\sigma_\varepsilon^2\left[c_5\Pi'\zeta\zeta' + (\xi - \Pi'\zeta)\left(\sigma_\varepsilon^2\zeta' - \ddot{\beta}_{\mathrm{GIV}}'\Sigma_{X'Z}\right)\Sigma_{Z'Z}^{-1}\zeta\zeta'\right]\left[c_5\Pi + \Sigma_{Z'Z}^{-1}(\sigma_\varepsilon^2\zeta - \Sigma_{Z'X}\ddot{\beta}_{\mathrm{GIV}})(\xi' - \zeta'\Pi)\right]
\end{aligned}
$$

$$
\begin{aligned}
= & c_5^2\Pi'\Sigma_{Z'Z}\Pi + c_5(\xi - \Pi'\zeta)\left(\sigma_\varepsilon^2\zeta'\Pi - \ddot{\beta}_{\mathrm{GIV}}'\Sigma_{X'Z}\Pi\right) + (\sigma_\varepsilon^2 c_5\Pi'\zeta - c_5\Pi'\Sigma_{Z'X}\ddot{\beta}_{\mathrm{GIV}})(\xi' - \zeta'\Pi) \\
& + (\xi - \Pi'\zeta)\left(\sigma_\varepsilon^2\zeta'\Sigma_{Z'Z}^{-1} - \ddot{\beta}_{\mathrm{GIV}}'\Pi'\right)(\sigma_\varepsilon^2\zeta - \Sigma_{Z'X}\ddot{\beta}_{\mathrm{GIV}})(\xi' - \zeta'\Pi) \\
& -\sigma_\varepsilon^2 c_5\left[c_5\Pi'\zeta\zeta'\Pi + (\xi - \Pi'\zeta)\left(\sigma_\varepsilon^2\zeta' - \ddot{\beta}_{\mathrm{GIV}}'\Sigma_{X'Z}\right)\Sigma_{Z'Z}^{-1}\zeta\zeta'\Pi\right] \\
& -\sigma_\varepsilon^2\left[c_5\Pi'\zeta\zeta' + (\xi - \Pi'\zeta)(c_1\zeta' - c_2\zeta')\right]\left[(\sigma_\varepsilon^2\Sigma_{Z'Z}^{-1}\zeta - \Pi\ddot{\beta}_{\mathrm{GIV}})(\xi' - \zeta'\Pi)\right]
\end{aligned}
$$

$$
\begin{aligned}
= & c_5^2\Pi'\Sigma_{Z'Z}\Pi + \sigma_\varepsilon^2 c_5\xi\zeta'\Pi - \sigma_\varepsilon^2 c_5\Pi'\zeta\zeta'\Pi - c_5\xi\ddot{\beta}_{\mathrm{GIV}}'\Sigma_{X'Z}\Pi + c_5\Pi'\zeta\ddot{\beta}_{\mathrm{GIV}}'\Sigma_{X'Z}\Pi \\
& + \sigma_\varepsilon^2 c_5\Pi'\zeta\xi' - c_5\Pi'\Sigma_{Z'X}\ddot{\beta}_{\mathrm{GIV}}\xi' - \sigma_\varepsilon^2 c_5\Pi'\zeta\zeta'\Pi + c_5\Pi'\Sigma_{Z'X}\ddot{\beta}_{\mathrm{GIV}}\zeta'\Pi \\
& + (\xi - \Pi'\zeta)\left(\sigma_\varepsilon^2\zeta'\Sigma_{Z'Z}^{-1} - \ddot{\beta}_{\mathrm{GIV}}'\Pi'\right)(\sigma_\varepsilon^2\zeta\xi' - \Sigma_{Z'X}\ddot{\beta}_{\mathrm{GIV}}\xi') \\
& - (\xi - \Pi'\zeta)\left(\sigma_\varepsilon^2\zeta'\Sigma_{Z'Z}^{-1} - \ddot{\beta}_{\mathrm{GIV}}'\Pi'\right)(\sigma_\varepsilon^2\zeta\zeta'\Pi - \Sigma_{Z'X}\ddot{\beta}_{\mathrm{GIV}}\zeta'\Pi) \\
& - \sigma_\varepsilon^2 c_5\left[c_5\Pi'\zeta\zeta'\Pi + (\xi - \Pi'\zeta)(c_1\zeta'\Pi - c_2\zeta'\Pi)\right] \\
& - \sigma_\varepsilon^2\left[c_5\Pi'\zeta\zeta' + (\xi - \Pi'\zeta)(c_1\zeta' - c_2\zeta')\right](\sigma_\varepsilon^2\Sigma_{Z'Z}^{-1}\zeta\xi' - \Pi\ddot{\beta}_{\mathrm{GIV}}\xi') \\
& + \sigma_\varepsilon^2\left[c_5\Pi'\zeta\zeta' + (\xi - \Pi'\zeta)(c_1\zeta' - c_2\zeta')\right](\sigma_\varepsilon^2\Sigma_{Z'Z}^{-1}\zeta\zeta'\Pi - \Pi\ddot{\beta}_{\mathrm{GIV}}\zeta'\Pi)
\end{aligned}
$$

$$
\begin{aligned}
&= c_5\Pi'\Sigma_{Z'Z}\Pi + \sigma_\varepsilon^2 c_5 \xi\zeta'\Pi - \sigma_\varepsilon^2 c_5 \Pi'\zeta\zeta'\Pi - \sigma_\varepsilon^2 c_5 \xi\zeta'\Pi + \sigma_\varepsilon^2 c_5 \Pi'\zeta\zeta'\Pi \\
&+ \sigma_\varepsilon^2 c_5 \Pi'\zeta\xi' - \sigma_\varepsilon^2 c_5 \Pi'\zeta\xi' - \sigma_\varepsilon^2 c_5 \Pi'\zeta\zeta'\Pi + \sigma_\varepsilon^2 c_5 \Pi'\zeta\zeta'\Pi \\
&+ (\xi - \Pi'\zeta)\left(\sigma_\varepsilon^2 c_1 \xi' - \sigma_\varepsilon^2 c_2 \xi'\right) - (\xi - \Pi'\zeta)\left(\sigma_\varepsilon^2 c_2 \xi' - \sigma_\varepsilon^2 \ddot{\beta}_{\mathrm{GIV}}' \Pi'\zeta\xi'\right) \\
&- (\xi - \Pi'\zeta)\left(\sigma_\varepsilon^2 c_1 \zeta'\Pi - \sigma_\varepsilon^2 c_2 \zeta'\Pi\right) + (\xi - \Pi'\zeta)\left(\sigma_\varepsilon^2 c_2 \zeta'\Pi - \sigma_\varepsilon^2 \ddot{\beta}_{\mathrm{GIV}}' \Pi'\zeta\zeta'\Pi\right) \\
&- \sigma_\varepsilon^2 c_5 (c_5 \Pi'\zeta\zeta'\Pi + c_1 \xi\zeta'\Pi - c_1 \Pi'\zeta\zeta'\Pi - c_2 \xi\zeta'\Pi + c_2 \Pi'\zeta\zeta'\Pi) \\
&- \sigma_\varepsilon^2 \left[c_1 c_5 \Pi'\zeta\xi' + (\xi - \Pi'\zeta) c_1 c_4 \xi'\right] + \sigma_\varepsilon^2 \left[c_2 c_5 \Pi'\zeta\xi' + (\xi - \Pi'\zeta) c_2 c_4 \xi'\right] \\
&+ \sigma_\varepsilon^2 \left[c_1 c_5 \Pi'\zeta\zeta'\Pi + c_1 c_4 (\xi\zeta'\Pi - \Pi'\zeta\zeta'\Pi)\right] - \sigma_\varepsilon^2 \left[c_2 c_5 \Pi'\zeta\zeta'\Pi + c_2 c_4 (\xi\zeta'\Pi - \Pi'\zeta\zeta'\Pi)\right]
\end{aligned}
$$

$$
\begin{aligned}
&= c_5^2 \Sigma_{\hat{X}'\hat{X}} + \sigma_\varepsilon^2 c_4 \xi\xi' - \sigma_\varepsilon^2 c_4 \Pi'\zeta\xi' - \sigma_\varepsilon^2 c_2 \xi\xi' + \sigma_\varepsilon^2 c_2 \xi\xi' \\
&- \sigma_\varepsilon^2 c_4 \xi\zeta'\Pi + \sigma_\varepsilon^2 c_4 \Pi'\zeta\zeta'\Pi + \sigma_\varepsilon^2 (c_4 - c_5) c_5 \Pi'\zeta\zeta'\Pi - \sigma_\varepsilon^2 c_4 c_5 \xi\zeta'\Pi \\
&- \sigma_\varepsilon^2 c_4 c_5 \Pi'\zeta\xi' - \sigma_\varepsilon^2 c_4^2 \xi\xi' + \sigma_\varepsilon^2 c_4^2 \Pi'\zeta\xi' + \sigma_\varepsilon^2 c_4 c_5 \Pi'\zeta\zeta'\Pi + \sigma_\varepsilon^2 c_4^2 \xi\zeta'\Pi - \sigma_\varepsilon^2 c_4^2 \Pi'\zeta\zeta'\Pi
\end{aligned}
$$

$$
\begin{aligned}
= c_5^2 \Sigma_{\hat{X}'\hat{X}} &+ \sigma_\varepsilon^2 c_4 (1 - c_4) \xi\xi' + \sigma_\varepsilon^2 c_4 (c_4 - 1 - c_5) \Pi'\zeta\xi' + \sigma_\varepsilon^2 c_4 (c_4 - 1 - c_5) \xi\zeta'\Pi \\
&- \sigma_\varepsilon^2 \left[c_4 (c_4 - 1 - 2c_5) + c_5^2\right] \Pi'\zeta\zeta'\Pi
\end{aligned}
$$

the third is

$$
2\sigma_\varepsilon^2 c_4^2 \xi\xi' + 2\sigma_\varepsilon^2 c_4 c_5 \Pi'\zeta\xi' + 2\sigma_\varepsilon^2 c_4 c_5 \xi\zeta'\Pi + 2\sigma_\varepsilon^2 c_5^2 \Pi'\zeta\zeta'\Pi
$$

the fourth is

$$
\begin{aligned}
&\left[c_4 \Sigma_{X'Z} - \Pi'\zeta\ddot{\beta}_{\mathrm{GIV}}' \Sigma_{X'Z}\right]\left[c_5 \Pi + \Sigma_{Z'Z}^{-1} (\sigma_\varepsilon^2 \zeta - \Sigma_{Z'X} \ddot{\beta}_{\mathrm{GIV}}) (\xi' - \zeta'\Pi)\right] \\
&- \left[\sigma_\varepsilon^2 c_4 \xi\zeta' - \sigma_\varepsilon^2 \Pi'\zeta\ddot{\beta}_{\mathrm{GIV}}' \xi\zeta'\right]\left[c_5 \Pi + \Sigma_{Z'Z}^{-1} (\sigma_\varepsilon^2 \zeta - \Sigma_{Z'X} \ddot{\beta}_{\mathrm{GIV}}) (\xi' - \zeta'\Pi)\right]
\end{aligned}
$$

$$= c_4c_5\Sigma_{X'Z}\Pi - c_5\Pi'\zeta\ddot{\beta}'_{\mathrm{GIV}}\Sigma_{X'Z}\Pi + \sigma_\varepsilon^2 c_4\Sigma_{X'Z}\Sigma_{Z'Z}^{-1}\zeta\xi' - c_4\Sigma_{X'Z}\Sigma_{Z'Z}^{-1}\Sigma_{Z'X}\ddot{\beta}_{\mathrm{GIV}}\xi'$$
$$- \sigma_\varepsilon^2 c_4\Sigma_{X'Z}\Sigma_{Z'Z}^{-1}\zeta\zeta'\Pi + c_4\Sigma_{X'Z}\Sigma_{Z'Z}^{-1}\Sigma_{Z'X}\ddot{\beta}_{\mathrm{GIV}}\zeta'\Pi - \sigma_\varepsilon^2 c_2\Pi'\zeta\xi'$$
$$+ \Pi'\zeta\ddot{\beta}'_{\mathrm{GIV}}\Sigma_{X'Z}\Sigma_{Z'Z}^{-1}\Sigma_{Z'X}\ddot{\beta}_{\mathrm{GIV}}\xi' + \sigma_\varepsilon^2 c_2\Pi'\zeta\zeta'\Pi - \Pi'\zeta\ddot{\beta}'_{\mathrm{GIV}}\Sigma_{X'Z}\Sigma_{Z'Z}^{-1}\Sigma_{Z'X}\ddot{\beta}_{\mathrm{GIV}}\zeta'\Pi$$
$$- \sigma_\varepsilon^2 c_4c_5\xi\zeta'\Pi + \sigma_\varepsilon^2 c_3c_5\Pi'\zeta\zeta'\Pi - \sigma_\varepsilon^2 c_1c_4\xi\xi' + \sigma_\varepsilon^2 c_1c_3\Pi'\zeta\xi' + \sigma_\varepsilon^2 c_2c_4\xi\xi'$$
$$- \sigma_\varepsilon^2 c_2c_3\Pi'\zeta\xi' + \sigma_\varepsilon^2 c_1c_4\xi\zeta'\Pi - \sigma_\varepsilon^2 c_1c_3\Pi'\zeta\zeta'\Pi - \sigma_\varepsilon^2 c_2c_4\xi\zeta'\Pi + \sigma_\varepsilon^2 c_2c_3\Pi'\zeta\zeta'\Pi$$

$$= c_4c_5\Sigma_{X'Z}\Pi - \sigma_\varepsilon^2 c_5\Pi'\zeta\zeta'\Pi + \sigma_\varepsilon^2 c_4\Pi'\zeta\xi' - \sigma_\varepsilon^2 c_4\Pi'\zeta\xi' - \sigma_\varepsilon^2 c_4\Pi'\zeta\zeta'\Pi + \sigma_\varepsilon^2 c_4\Pi'\zeta\zeta'\Pi$$
$$- \sigma_\varepsilon^2 c_2\Pi'\zeta\xi' + \sigma_\varepsilon^2 c_2\Pi'\zeta\xi' + \sigma_\varepsilon^2 c_2\Pi'\zeta\zeta'\Pi - \sigma_\varepsilon^2 c_2\Pi'\zeta\zeta'\Pi$$
$$+ \sigma_\varepsilon^2 c_4(c_4 - c_5)\xi\zeta'\Pi + \sigma_\varepsilon^2 c_3(c_5 - c_4)\Pi'\zeta\zeta'\Pi - \sigma_\varepsilon^2 c_4^2\xi\xi' + \sigma_\varepsilon^2 c_3c_4\Pi'\zeta\xi'$$

$$= c_4c_5\Sigma_{\hat{X}'\hat{X}} - \sigma_\varepsilon^2 c_4^2\xi\xi' + \sigma_\varepsilon^2 c_4(c_4 - c_5)\xi\zeta'\Pi + \sigma_\varepsilon^2 c_3c_4\Pi'\zeta\xi' + \sigma_\varepsilon^2 c_3(c_5 - c_4)\Pi'\zeta\zeta'\Pi$$
$$- \sigma_\varepsilon^2 c_5\Pi'\zeta\zeta'\Pi$$

and the final fifth one is the transpose of the fourth. Collecting all terms we find

$$V_0 = c_4^2\Sigma_{X'X} - \sigma_\varepsilon^2 c_4^2\xi\xi' - c_4\Sigma_{X'X}\ddot{\beta}_{\mathrm{GIV}}\zeta'\Pi + \sigma_\varepsilon^2 c_3c_4\xi\zeta'\Pi - c_4\Pi'\zeta\ddot{\beta}'_{\mathrm{GIV}}\Sigma_{X'X}$$
$$+ \sigma_\varepsilon^2 c_3c_4\Pi'\zeta\xi' + \left(\ddot{\beta}'_{\mathrm{GIV}}\Sigma_{X'X}\ddot{\beta}_{\mathrm{GIV}} - \sigma_\varepsilon^2 c_3^2\right)\Pi'\zeta\zeta'\Pi + (1 - c_4 - c_3)^2\Sigma_{\hat{X}'\hat{X}}$$
$$+ \sigma_\varepsilon^2 c_4(1 - c_4)\xi\xi' + \sigma_\varepsilon^2 c_4(2c_4 + c_3 - 2)\Pi'\zeta\xi' + \sigma_\varepsilon^2 c_4(2c_4 + c_3 - 2)\xi\zeta'\Pi$$
$$- \sigma_\varepsilon^2\left[c_4(c_4 - 1 - 2c_5) + c_5^2\right]\Pi'\zeta\zeta'\Pi + 2\sigma_\varepsilon^2 c_4^2\xi\xi' + 2\sigma_\varepsilon^2 c_4c_5\Pi'\zeta\xi' + 2\sigma_\varepsilon^2 c_4c_5\xi\zeta'\Pi$$
$$+ 2\sigma_\varepsilon^2 c_5^4\Pi'\zeta\zeta'\Pi + 2c_4c_5\Sigma_{\hat{X}'\hat{X}} - 2\sigma_\varepsilon^2 c_4^2\xi\xi' + \sigma_\varepsilon^2 c_4(c_4 + c_3 - c_5)\xi\zeta'\Pi$$
$$+ \sigma_\varepsilon^2 c_4(c_4 + c_3 - c_5)\Pi'\zeta\xi' + 2\sigma_\varepsilon^2 c_3(c_2 - c_1 + c_5)\Pi'\zeta\zeta'\Pi - 2\sigma_\varepsilon^2 c_5\Pi'\zeta\zeta'\Pi$$

$$
\begin{aligned}
&= c_4^2\Sigma_{X'X} + 2c_4c_5\Sigma_{\hat{X}'\hat{X}} + c_5^2\Sigma_{\hat{X}'\hat{X}} - c_4\Sigma_{X'X}\ddot{\beta}_{\mathrm{GIV}}\zeta'\Pi - c_4\Pi'\zeta\ddot{\beta}'_{\mathrm{GIV}}\Sigma_{X'X}\\
&-\sigma_\varepsilon^2c_4^2\xi\xi' + \sigma_\varepsilon^2c_4(1-c_4)\xi\xi' + 2\sigma_\varepsilon^2c_4^2\xi\xi' - 2\sigma_\varepsilon^2c_4^2\xi\xi'\\
&+\sigma_\varepsilon^2c_3c_4\xi\zeta'\Pi + \sigma_\varepsilon^2c_4(2c_4+c_3-2)\xi\zeta'\Pi + 2\sigma_\varepsilon^2c_4c_5\xi\zeta'\Pi + \sigma_\varepsilon^2c_4(c_4+c_3-c_5)\xi\zeta'\Pi\\
&+\sigma_\varepsilon^2c_3c_4\Pi'\zeta\xi' + \sigma_\varepsilon^2c_4(2c_4+c_3-2)\Pi'\zeta\xi' + 2\sigma_\varepsilon^2c_4c_5\Pi'\zeta\xi' + \sigma_\varepsilon^2c_4(c_4+c_3-c_5)\Pi'\zeta\xi'\\
&+\left(\ddot{\beta}'_{\mathrm{GIV}}\Sigma_{X'X}\ddot{\beta}_{\mathrm{GIV}} - \sigma_\varepsilon^2c_3^2\right)\Pi'\zeta\zeta'\Pi - \sigma_\varepsilon^2\left[c_4(c_4-1-2c_5)+c_5^2\right]\Pi'\zeta\zeta'\Pi\\
&+2\sigma_\varepsilon^2c_5^2\Pi'\zeta\zeta'\Pi + 2\sigma_\varepsilon^2c_3(c_2-c_1+c_5)\Pi'\zeta\zeta'\Pi - 2\sigma_\varepsilon^2c_5\Pi'\zeta\zeta'\Pi
\end{aligned}
$$

$$
\begin{aligned}
&= c_4^2\Sigma_{X'X} + (2c_4+c_5)c_5\Sigma_{\hat{X}'\hat{X}} - c_4\Sigma_{X'X}\ddot{\beta}_{\mathrm{GIV}}\zeta'\Pi - c_4\Pi'\zeta\ddot{\beta}'_{\mathrm{GIV}}\Sigma_{X'X}\\
&\quad + \sigma_\varepsilon^2c_4(1-2c_4)\xi\xi' + \sigma_\varepsilon^2c_4(c_4+c_3-c_5)\xi\zeta'\Pi + \sigma_\varepsilon^2c_4(c_4+c_3-c_5)\Pi'\zeta\xi'\\
&\quad + \ddot{\beta}'_{\mathrm{GIV}}\Sigma_{X'X}\ddot{\beta}_{\mathrm{GIV}}\Pi'\zeta\zeta'\Pi\\
&\quad + \sigma_\varepsilon^2\left\{-c_3^2 - \left[c_4(c_4-1-2c_5)+c_5^2\right] + 2c_5^2 + 2c_3(c_5-c_4) - 2c_5\right\}\Pi'\zeta\zeta'\Pi
\end{aligned}
$$

$$
\begin{aligned}
&= c_4^2\Sigma_{X'X} + \left[(1-c_3)^2 - c_4^2\right]\Sigma_{\hat{X}'\hat{X}} - c_4\Sigma_{X'X}\ddot{\beta}_{\mathrm{GIV}}\zeta'\Pi - c_4\Pi'\zeta\ddot{\beta}'_{\mathrm{GIV}}\Sigma_{X'X}\\
&\quad + \sigma_\varepsilon^2c_4(1-2c_4)\xi\xi'\\
&\quad + \sigma_\varepsilon^2c_4(1-2c_5)\xi\zeta'\Pi + \sigma_\varepsilon^2c_4(1-2c_5)\Pi'\zeta\xi' + \left(\ddot{\beta}'_{\mathrm{GIV}}\Sigma_{X'X}\ddot{\beta}_{\mathrm{GIV}}\right)\Pi'\zeta\zeta'\Pi\\
&\quad + \sigma_\varepsilon^2[c_5(1-2c_5)-c_3]\Pi'\zeta\zeta'\Pi
\end{aligned}
$$

Thus, the asymptotic variance of the (generalized) GIV estimator (A.3) is

$$
\begin{aligned}
V_{\mathrm{GIV}}^{\mathrm{CN}} &= \sigma_\varepsilon^2\left[(1-c_3)^2 - c_4^2\right]\Sigma_{\hat{X}'\hat{X}}^{-1} + \sigma_\varepsilon^2c_4^2\Sigma_{\hat{X}'\hat{X}}^{-1}\Sigma_{X'X}\Sigma_{\hat{X}'\hat{X}}^{-1}\\
&- c_4\left[\Sigma_{\hat{X}'\hat{X}}^{-1}\Sigma_{X'X}\ddot{\beta}_{\mathrm{GIV}}\ddot{\beta}'_{\mathrm{GIV}} + \ddot{\beta}_{\mathrm{GIV}}\ddot{\beta}'_{\mathrm{GIV}}\Sigma_{X'X}\Sigma_{\hat{X}'\hat{X}}^{-1}\right] + \sigma_\varepsilon^4c_4[1-2c_4]\Sigma_{\hat{X}'\hat{X}}^{-1}\xi\xi'\Sigma_{\hat{X}'\hat{X}}^{-1}\\
&+ \sigma_\varepsilon^2c_4(1-2c_5)\left[\Sigma_{\hat{X}'\hat{X}}^{-1}\xi\ddot{\beta}'_{\mathrm{GIV}} + \ddot{\beta}_{\mathrm{GIV}}\xi'\Sigma_{\hat{X}'\hat{X}}^{-1}\right]\\
&+ \left[c_5(1-2c_5) - c_3 + \sigma_\varepsilon^{-2}\left(\ddot{\beta}'_{\mathrm{GIV}}\Sigma_{X'X}\ddot{\beta}_{\mathrm{GIV}}\right)\right]\ddot{\beta}_{\mathrm{GIV}}\ddot{\beta}'_{\mathrm{GIV}}
\end{aligned}
$$

which gives the result of Theorem 1.

Note that when $k = l$ we have $c_1 = c_2$, so $c_4 = 0$ and $c_5 = 1 - c_3$, and so the variance simplifies to

$$\begin{aligned} V_{\mathrm{IV}}^{\mathrm{CN}} &= \sigma_\varepsilon^2 c_5^2 \Sigma_{\hat{X}'\hat{X}}^{-1} + \left[(1-c_3)(2c_3-1) - c_3 + \sigma_\varepsilon^{-2}\left(\ddot{\beta}_{\mathrm{IV}}' \Sigma_{X'X} \ddot{\beta}_{\mathrm{IV}}\right)\right] \ddot{\beta}_{\mathrm{IV}} \ddot{\beta}_{\mathrm{IV}}' \\ &= \sigma_\varepsilon^2 c_5^2 \Sigma_{\hat{X}'\hat{X}}^{-1} - \left[2c_3^2 - 2c_3 + 1 - \sigma_\varepsilon^{-2}\left(\ddot{\beta}_{\mathrm{IV}}' \Sigma_{X'X} \ddot{\beta}_{\mathrm{IV}}\right)\right] \ddot{\beta}_{\mathrm{IV}} \ddot{\beta}_{\mathrm{IV}}' \end{aligned}$$

which is the result of Corollary 1.

APPENDIX B: PROOF OF THEOREM 2

When $\mu_4 \neq 3$ then there is an additional contribution to the asymptotic variance for which we have to evaluate $\sigma_\varepsilon^4 \omega\omega'$ In obtaining the third term of Eq. (A.11) we already found

$$\omega\omega' = c_4^2 \xi\xi' + c_4 c_5 \Pi' \zeta\xi' + c_4 c_5 \xi\zeta' \Pi + c_5^2 \Pi' \zeta\zeta' \Pi$$

so

$$\begin{aligned}
&\sigma_\varepsilon^4 \Sigma_{\hat{X}'\hat{X}}^{-1} \omega\omega' \Sigma_{\hat{X}'\hat{X}}^{-1} \\
&\quad = \sigma_\varepsilon^4 c_4^2 \Sigma_{\hat{X}'\hat{X}}^{-1} \xi\xi' \Sigma_{\hat{X}'\hat{X}}^{-1} + \sigma_\varepsilon^4 c_4 c_5 \Sigma_{\hat{X}'\hat{X}}^{-1} \Pi' \zeta\xi' \Sigma_{\hat{X}'\hat{X}}^{-1} \\
&\qquad + \sigma_\varepsilon^4 c_4 c_5 \Sigma_{\hat{X}'\hat{X}}^{-1} \xi\zeta' \Pi \Sigma_{\hat{X}'\hat{X}}^{-1} + \sigma_\varepsilon^4 c_5^2 \Sigma_{\hat{X}'\hat{X}}^{-1} \Pi' \zeta\zeta' \Pi \Sigma_{\hat{X}'\hat{X}}^{-1} \\
&\quad = \sigma_\varepsilon^4 c_4^2 \Sigma_{\hat{X}'\hat{X}}^{-1} \xi\xi' \Sigma_{\hat{X}'\hat{X}}^{-1} + \sigma_\varepsilon^2 c_4 c_5 \ddot{\beta}_{\mathrm{GIV}} \xi' \Sigma_{\hat{X}'\hat{X}}^{-1} + \sigma_\varepsilon^2 c_4 c_5 \Sigma_{\hat{X}'\hat{X}}^{-1} \xi \ddot{\beta}_{\mathrm{GIV}}' \\
&\qquad + c_5^2 \ddot{\beta}_{\mathrm{GIV}} \ddot{\beta}_{\mathrm{GIV}}'
\end{aligned}$$

In the overall asymptotic variance this term has factor $\mu_4 - 1$. The expression for $V_{\mathrm{GIV}}^{\mathrm{CP}}$ already contains it with factor 2, so the additional term given in Theorem 4 has factor $\mu_4 - 3$.

When $\mu_3 \neq 0$ there is another additional contribution to the asymptotic variance, for which we have to evaluate

$$\mu_3 \sigma_\varepsilon^3 \left(\Sigma_{W'\iota} \omega' + \omega \Sigma_{\iota' W} \right)$$

Since

$$\begin{aligned}
W'\iota &= \Theta_1 \overline{X}' \iota + \Theta_2 \overline{Z}' \iota = c_4 \overline{X}' \iota - \Pi' \zeta \ddot{\beta}_{\mathrm{GIV}}' \overline{X}' \iota + c_5 \Pi' \overline{Z}' \iota \\
&\quad + (\xi - \Pi' \zeta) \left(\sigma_\varepsilon^2 \zeta' - \ddot{\beta}_{\mathrm{GIV}}' \Sigma_{X'Z} \right) \Sigma_{Z'Z}^{-1} \overline{Z}' \iota
\end{aligned}$$

we find

$$\Sigma_{W'\iota} = c_4 \Sigma_{X'\iota} - \Pi' \zeta \ddot{\beta}_{\mathrm{GIV}}' \Sigma_{X'\iota} + c_5 \Pi' \Sigma_{Z'\iota} + (\xi - \Pi' \zeta) \left(\sigma_\varepsilon^2 \zeta' - \ddot{\beta}_{\mathrm{GIV}}' \Sigma_{X'Z} \right) \Sigma_{Z'Z}^{-1} \Sigma_{Z'\iota}$$

and with $\omega' = c_4\xi' + c_5\zeta'\Pi$, we obtain

$$\Sigma_{W'\iota}\omega' = c_4\left[c_4\Sigma_{X'\iota}\xi' - \Pi'\zeta\ddot{\beta}'_{\mathrm{GIV}}\Sigma_{X'\iota}\xi' + c_5\Pi'\Sigma_{Z'\iota}\xi' + (\xi - \Pi'\zeta)\left(\sigma_\varepsilon^2\zeta' - \ddot{\beta}'_{\mathrm{GIV}}\Sigma_{X'Z}\right)\Sigma_{Z'Z}^{-1}\Sigma_{Z'\iota}\xi'\right]$$

$$+ c_5\left[c_4\Sigma_{X'\iota}\zeta'\Pi - \Pi'\zeta\ddot{\beta}'_{\mathrm{GIV}}\Sigma_{X'\iota}\zeta'\Pi + c_5\Pi'\Sigma_{Z'\iota}\zeta'\Pi + (\xi - \Pi'\zeta)\right.$$

$$\left.\left(\sigma_\varepsilon^2\zeta' - \ddot{\beta}'_{\mathrm{GIV}}\Sigma_{X'Z}\right)\Sigma_{Z'Z}^{-1}\Sigma_{Z'\iota}\zeta'\Pi\right]$$

Thus,

$$\sigma_\varepsilon^3\Sigma_{\hat{X}'\hat{X}}^{-1}\Sigma_{W'\iota}\omega'\Sigma_{\hat{X}'\hat{X}}^{-1}$$

$$= \sigma_\varepsilon^3 c_4\left[c_4\Sigma_{\hat{X}'\hat{X}}^{-1}\Sigma_{X'\iota}\xi'\Sigma_{\hat{X}'\hat{X}}^{-1} - \Sigma_{\hat{X}'\hat{X}}^{-1}\Pi'\zeta\ddot{\beta}'_{\mathrm{GIV}}\Sigma_{X'\iota}\xi'\Sigma_{\hat{X}'\hat{X}}^{-1} + c_5\Sigma_{\hat{X}'\hat{X}}^{-1}\Pi'\Sigma_{Z'\iota}\xi'\Sigma_{\hat{X}'\hat{X}}^{-1}\right.$$

$$\left.+ \left(\Sigma_{\hat{X}'\hat{X}}^{-1}\xi - \Sigma_{\hat{X}'\hat{X}}^{-1}\Pi'\zeta\right)\left(\sigma_\varepsilon^2\zeta' - \ddot{\beta}'_{\mathrm{GIV}}\Sigma_{X'Z}\right)\Sigma_{Z'Z}^{-1}\Sigma_{Z'\iota}\xi'\Sigma_{\hat{X}'\hat{X}}^{-1}\right]$$

$$+ \sigma_\varepsilon^3 c_5\left[c_4\Sigma_{\hat{X}'\hat{X}}^{-1}\Sigma_{X'\iota}\zeta'\Pi\Sigma_{\hat{X}'\hat{X}}^{-1} - \Sigma_{\hat{X}'\hat{X}}^{-1}\Pi'\zeta\ddot{\beta}'_{\mathrm{GIV}}\Sigma_{X'\iota}\zeta'\Pi\Sigma_{\hat{X}'\hat{X}}^{-1} + c_5\Sigma_{\hat{X}'\hat{X}}^{-1}\Pi'\Sigma_{Z'\iota}\zeta'\Pi\Sigma_{\hat{X}'\hat{X}}^{-1}\right.$$

$$\left.+ \left(\Sigma_{\hat{X}'\hat{X}}^{-1}\xi - \Sigma_{\hat{X}'\hat{X}}^{-1}\Pi'\zeta\right)\left(\sigma_\varepsilon^2\zeta' - \ddot{\beta}'_{\mathrm{GIV}}\Sigma_{X'Z}\right)\Sigma_{Z'Z}^{-1}\Sigma_{Z'\iota}\zeta'\Pi\Sigma_{\hat{X}'\hat{X}}^{-1}\right]$$

$$= c_4\left[\sigma_\varepsilon^3 c_4\Sigma_{\hat{X}'\hat{X}}^{-1}\Sigma_{X'\iota}\xi'\Sigma_{\hat{X}'\hat{X}}^{-1} - \sigma_\varepsilon\ddot{\beta}_{\mathrm{GIV}}\ddot{\beta}'_{\mathrm{GIV}}\Sigma_{X'\iota}\xi'\Sigma_{\hat{X}'\hat{X}}^{-1} + \sigma_\varepsilon^3 c_5\Sigma_{\hat{X}'\hat{X}}^{-1}\Pi'\Sigma_{Z'\iota}\xi'\Sigma_{\hat{X}'\hat{X}}^{-1}\right.$$

$$\left.+ \left(\sigma_\varepsilon^3\Sigma_{\hat{X}'\hat{X}}^{-1}\xi - \sigma_\varepsilon\ddot{\beta}_{\mathrm{GIV}}\right)\left(\sigma_\varepsilon^2\zeta' - \ddot{\beta}'_{\mathrm{GIV}}\Sigma_{X'Z}\right)\Sigma_{Z'Z}^{-1}\Sigma_{Z'\iota}\xi'\Sigma_{\hat{X}'\hat{X}}^{-1}\right]$$

$$+ c_5\left[\sigma_\varepsilon c_4\Sigma_{\hat{X}'\hat{X}}^{-1}\Sigma_{X'\iota}\ddot{\beta}'_{\mathrm{GIV}} - \sigma_\varepsilon^{-1}\ddot{\beta}'_{\mathrm{GIV}}\Sigma_{X'\iota}\ddot{\beta}_{\mathrm{GIV}}\ddot{\beta}'_{\mathrm{GIV}} + \sigma_\varepsilon c_5\Sigma_{\hat{X}'\hat{X}}^{-1}\Pi'\Sigma_{Z'\iota}\ddot{\beta}'_{\mathrm{GIV}}\right.$$

$$\left.+ \left(\sigma_\varepsilon\Sigma_{\hat{X}'\hat{X}}^{-1}\xi - \sigma_\varepsilon^{-1}\ddot{\beta}_{\mathrm{GIV}}\right)\left(\sigma_\varepsilon^2\zeta' - \ddot{\beta}'_{\mathrm{GIV}}\Sigma_{X'Z}\right)\Sigma_{Z'Z}^{-1}\Sigma_{Z'\iota}\ddot{\beta}'_{\mathrm{GIV}}\right]$$

and the additional term is then equal to μ_3 multiplied by

$$
\begin{aligned}
&\sigma_\varepsilon^3 \Sigma_{\hat{X}'\hat{X}}^{-1} [\Sigma_{W'\iota}\omega' + \omega \Sigma_{\iota' W}] \Sigma_{\hat{X}'\hat{X}}^{-1} \\
&= c_4 \Big\{ \sigma_\varepsilon^3 c_4 \Sigma_{\hat{X}'\hat{X}}^{-1} \Sigma_{X'\iota} \xi' \Sigma_{\hat{X}'\hat{X}}^{-1} - \sigma_\varepsilon \ddot{\beta}_{\text{GIV}} \ddot{\beta}_{\text{GIV}}' \Sigma_{X'\iota} \xi' \Sigma_{\hat{X}'\hat{X}}^{-1} + \sigma_\varepsilon^3 c_5 \Sigma_{\hat{X}'\hat{X}}^{-1} \Pi' \Sigma_{Z'\iota} \xi' \Sigma_{\hat{X}'\hat{X}}^{-1} \\
&+ \left(\sigma_\varepsilon^3 \Sigma_{\hat{X}'\hat{X}}^{-1} \xi - \sigma_\varepsilon \ddot{\beta}_{\text{GIV}} \right) \left(\sigma_\varepsilon^2 \zeta' - \ddot{\beta}_{\text{GIV}}' \Sigma_{X'Z} \right) \Sigma_{Z'Z}^{-1} \Sigma_{Z'\iota} \xi' \Sigma_{\hat{X}'\hat{X}}^{-1} \Big\} \\
&+ c_5 \Big[\sigma_\varepsilon c_4 \Sigma_{\hat{X}'\hat{X}}^{-1} \Sigma_{X'\iota} \ddot{\beta}_{\text{GIV}}' - \sigma_\varepsilon^{-1} \ddot{\beta}_{\text{GIV}} \Sigma_{X'\iota} \ddot{\beta}_{\text{GIV}} \ddot{\beta}_{\text{GIV}}' + \sigma_\varepsilon c_5 \Sigma_{\hat{X}'\hat{X}}^{-1} \Pi' \Sigma_{Z'\iota} \ddot{\beta}_{\text{GIV}}' \\
&+ \left(\sigma_\varepsilon \Sigma_{\hat{X}'\hat{X}}^{-1} \xi - \sigma_\varepsilon^{-1} \ddot{\beta}_{\text{GIV}} \right) \left(\sigma_\varepsilon^2 \zeta' - \ddot{\beta}_{\text{GIV}}' \Sigma_{X'Z} \right) \Sigma_{Z'Z}^{-1} \Sigma_{Z'\iota} \ddot{\beta}_{\text{GIV}}' \Big] \\
&+ c_4 \Big[\sigma_\varepsilon^3 c_4 \Sigma_{\hat{X}'\hat{X}}^{-1} \xi \Sigma_{X'\iota}' \Sigma_{\hat{X}'\hat{X}}^{-1} - \sigma_\varepsilon \Sigma_{\hat{X}'\hat{X}}^{-1} \xi \Sigma_{X'\iota}' \ddot{\beta}_{\text{GIV}} \ddot{\beta}_{\text{GIV}}' + \sigma_\varepsilon^3 c_5 \Sigma_{\hat{X}'\hat{X}}^{-1} \xi \Sigma_{Z'\iota}' \Pi \Sigma_{\hat{X}'\hat{X}}^{-1} \\
&+ \Sigma_{\hat{X}'\hat{X}}^{-1} \xi \Sigma_{Z'\iota}' \Sigma_{Z'Z}^{-1} (\sigma_\varepsilon^2 \zeta - \Sigma_{Z'X} \ddot{\beta}_{\text{GIV}}) \left(\sigma_\varepsilon^3 \xi' \Sigma_{\hat{X}'\hat{X}}^{-1} - \sigma_\varepsilon \ddot{\beta}_{\text{GIV}}' \right) \Big] \\
&+ c_5 \Big[\sigma_\varepsilon c_4 \ddot{\beta}_{\text{GIV}} \Sigma_{X'\iota}' \Sigma_{\hat{X}'\hat{X}}^{-1} - \sigma_\varepsilon^{-1} \ddot{\beta}_{\text{GIV}} \Sigma_{X'\iota} \ddot{\beta}_{\text{GIV}} \ddot{\beta}_{\text{GIV}}' + \sigma_\varepsilon c_5 \ddot{\beta}_{\text{GIV}} \Sigma_{Z'\iota}' \Pi \Sigma_{\hat{X}'\hat{X}}^{-1} \\
&+ \ddot{\beta}_{\text{GIV}} \Sigma_{Z'\iota}' \Sigma_{Z'Z}^{-1} (\sigma_\varepsilon^2 \zeta - \Sigma_{Z'X} \ddot{\beta}_{\text{GIV}}) \left(\sigma_\varepsilon \xi' \Sigma_{\hat{X}'\hat{X}}^{-1} - \sigma_\varepsilon^{-1} \ddot{\beta}_{\text{GIV}}' \right) \Big]
\end{aligned}
$$

This expression can be simplified slightly when we assume that both matrices X and Z have a first column of ones. Then

$$\Sigma_{\hat{X}'\hat{X}}^{-1} \Sigma_{X'\iota} = e_{k,1}$$

$$\Pi' \Sigma_{Z'\iota} = \Sigma_{X'Z} \Sigma_{Z'Z}^{-1} \Sigma_{Z'\iota} = \Sigma_{X'Z} e_{l,1}$$

where $e_{f,g}$ denotes an $f \times 1$ unit vector which has all elements equal to zero apart from a unit element in position g. This yields

$$\sigma_\varepsilon^3\Sigma_{\hat{X}'\hat{X}}^{-1}[\Sigma_{W'\iota}\omega' + \omega\Sigma_{\iota'W}]\Sigma_{\hat{X}'\hat{X}}^{-1}$$

$$= c_4\Big\{\sigma_\varepsilon^3 c_4 e_{k,1}\xi'\Sigma_{\hat{X}'\hat{X}}^{-1} - \sigma_\varepsilon\ddot{\beta}_{\text{GIV}}\ddot{\beta}_{\text{GIV}}'\Sigma_{X'\iota}\xi'\Sigma_{\hat{X}'\hat{X}}^{-1} + \sigma_\varepsilon^3 c_5\Sigma_{\hat{X}'\hat{X}}^{-1}\Sigma_{X'Z}e_{l,1}\xi'\Sigma_{\hat{X}'\hat{X}}^{-1}$$

$$+ \left(\sigma_\varepsilon^3\Sigma_{\hat{X}'\hat{X}}^{-1}\xi - \sigma_\varepsilon\ddot{\beta}_{\text{GIV}}\right)\left(\sigma_\varepsilon^2\zeta' - \ddot{\beta}_{\text{GIV}}'\Sigma_{X'Z}\right)e_{l,1}\xi'\Sigma_{\hat{X}'\hat{X}}^{-1}\Big\}$$

$$+ c_5\Big[\sigma_\varepsilon c_4 e_{k,1}\ddot{\beta}_{\text{GIV}}' - \sigma_\varepsilon^{-1}\ddot{\beta}_{\text{GIV}}'\Sigma_{X'\iota}\ddot{\beta}_{\text{GIV}}\ddot{\beta}_{\text{GIV}}' + \sigma_\varepsilon c_5\Sigma_{\hat{X}'\hat{X}}^{-1}\Sigma_{X'Z}e_{l,1}\ddot{\beta}_{\text{GIV}}'$$

$$+ \left(\sigma_\varepsilon\Sigma_{\hat{X}'\hat{X}}^{-1}\xi - \sigma_\varepsilon^{-1}\ddot{\beta}_{\text{GIV}}\right)\left(\sigma_\varepsilon^2\zeta' - \ddot{\beta}_{\text{GIV}}'\Sigma_{X'Z}\right)e_{l,1}\ddot{\beta}_{\text{GIV}}'\Big]$$

$$+ c_4\Big[\sigma_\varepsilon^3 c_4\Sigma_{\hat{X}'\hat{X}}^{-1}\xi e_{k,1}' - \sigma_\varepsilon\Sigma_{\hat{X}'\hat{X}}^{-1}\xi\Sigma_{X'\iota}'\ddot{\beta}_{\text{GIV}}\ddot{\beta}_{\text{GIV}}' + \sigma_\varepsilon^3 c_5\Sigma_{\hat{X}'\hat{X}}^{-1}\xi\Sigma_{X'Z}e_{l,1}'\Sigma_{\hat{X}'\hat{X}}^{-1}$$

$$+ \Sigma_{\hat{X}'\hat{X}}^{-1}\xi e_{l,1}'(\sigma_\varepsilon^2\zeta - \Sigma_{Z'X}\ddot{\beta}_{\text{GIV}})\left(\sigma_\varepsilon^3\xi'\Sigma_{\hat{X}'\hat{X}}^{-1} - \sigma_\varepsilon\ddot{\beta}_{\text{GIV}}'\right)\Big]$$

$$+ c_5\Big[\sigma_\varepsilon c_4\ddot{\beta}_{\text{GIV}}e_{k,1}' - \sigma_\varepsilon^{-1}\ddot{\beta}_{\text{GIV}}'\Sigma_{X'\iota}\ddot{\beta}_{\text{GIV}}\ddot{\beta}_{\text{GIV}}' + \sigma_\varepsilon c_5\ddot{\beta}_{\text{GIV}}e_{l,1}'\Sigma_{Z'X}\Sigma_{\hat{X}'\hat{X}}^{-1}$$

$$+ \ddot{\beta}_{\text{GIV}}e_{l,1}'(\sigma_\varepsilon^2\zeta - \Sigma_{Z'X}\ddot{\beta}_{\text{GIV}})\left(\sigma_\varepsilon\xi'\Sigma_{\hat{X}'\hat{X}}^{-1} - \sigma_\varepsilon^{-1}\ddot{\beta}_{\text{GIV}}'\right)\Big]$$

When $k = l$, i.e., $c_1 = c_2$, $c_5 = 1 - c_3$, $\Pi\Sigma_{\hat{X}'\hat{X}}^{-1} = \Sigma_{X'Z}^{-1}$, and $\sigma_\varepsilon^2\zeta - \Sigma_{Z'X}\ddot{\beta}_{\text{IV}} = 0$, $V_{\text{GIV}}^{\text{CP}}$ specializes to the expression

$$V_{\text{IV}}^{\text{CP}} = \sigma_\varepsilon^2 c_5^2\Sigma_{Z'X}^{-1}\Sigma_{Z'Z}\Sigma_{X'Z}^{-1} - \left[2c_5^2 - 2c_5 + 1 - \sigma_\varepsilon^{-2}\left(\ddot{\beta}_{\text{IV}}'\Sigma_{X'X}\ddot{\beta}_{\text{IV}}\right)\right]\ddot{\beta}_{\text{IV}}\ddot{\beta}_{\text{IV}}'$$

$$+ (\mu_4 - 1)c_5^2\ddot{\beta}_{\text{IV}}\ddot{\beta}_{\text{IV}}' - 2\mu_3 c_5\sigma_\varepsilon^{-1}\ddot{\beta}_{\text{IV}}'\Sigma_{X'\iota}\ddot{\beta}_{\text{IV}}\ddot{\beta}_{\text{IV}}'$$

$$+ \mu_3\sigma_\varepsilon c_5^2\left[\Sigma_{Z'X}^{-1}\Sigma_{Z'\iota}\ddot{\beta}_{\text{IV}}' + \ddot{\beta}_{\text{IV}}\Sigma_{Z'\iota}'\Sigma_{X'Z}^{-1}\right] = \sigma_\varepsilon^2 c_5^2\Sigma_{Z'X}^{-1}\Sigma_{Z'Z}\Sigma_{X'Z}^{-1}$$

$$+ \mu_3\sigma_\varepsilon c_5^2\left[\Sigma_{Z'X}^{-1}\Sigma_{Z'\iota}\ddot{\beta}_{\text{IV}}' + \ddot{\beta}_{\text{IV}}\Sigma_{Z'\iota}'\Sigma_{X'Z}^{-1}\right] - \Big[(3 - \mu_4)c_5^2 + 2c_5\left(\mu_3\sigma_\varepsilon^{-1}\ddot{\beta}_{\text{IV}}'\Sigma_{X'\iota} - 1\right)$$

$$+ 1 - \sigma_\varepsilon^{-2}\left(\ddot{\beta}_{\text{IV}}'\Sigma_{X'X}\ddot{\beta}_{\text{IV}}\right)\Big]\ddot{\beta}_{\text{IV}}\ddot{\beta}_{\text{IV}}'$$

TESTING THE EQUALITY OF TWO POSITIVE-DEFINITE MATRICES WITH APPLICATION TO INFORMATION MATRIX TESTING☆

Jin Seo Cho[a] and Halbert White[b]

[a]*School of Economics, Yonsei University, Seoul, South Korea*
[b]*Department of Economics, University of California – San Diego, La Jolla, CA, USA*

ABSTRACT

We provide a new characterization of the equality of two positive-definite matrices **A** *and* **B**, *and we use this to propose several new computationally convenient statistical tests for the equality of two unknown positive-definite matrices. Our primary focus is on testing the information matrix equality (e.g. White, 1982, 1994). We characterize the asymptotic behavior of our new trace-determinant information matrix test statistics under the null and the alternative and investigate their finite-sample performance for a variety of models: linear regression, exponential duration,*

☆A glossary of notation and the program codes written in GAUSS for our simulations are available at: http://web.yonsei.ac.kr/jinseocho/research.htm

Essays in Honor of Peter C. B. Phillips
Advances in Econometrics, Volume 33, 491–556

ISSN: 0731-9053/doi:10.1108/S0731-905320140000033014

probit, and Tobit. The parametric bootstrap suggested by Horowitz (1994) delivers critical values that provide admirable level behavior, even in samples as small as n = 50. Our new tests often have better power than the parametric-bootstrap version of the traditional IMT; when they do not, they nevertheless perform respectably.

Keywords: Matrix equality; information matrix test; eigenvalues; trace; determinant

JEL classifications: C01; C12; C52

1. INTRODUCTION

Testing the equality of two positive-definite matrices, say **A** and **B**, has a distinguished history in multivariate statistics. Wilks (1935) showed that for data drawn from two independent multivariate normal samples, the likelihood ratio (LR) test for independence is a ratio of the determinants of the two maximum-likelihood covariance matrix estimators. This finding stimulated investigation of other determinant-based tests. For example, Pillai and Nagarsenker (1972) and Das Gupta, and Giri (1973) examined the properties of a class of determinant ratio tests for equal covariance matrices. Other researchers have studied tests based on the trace of two covariance matrix estimators. Roy (1953), Pillai and Jayachandran (1968), and Nagao (1973, 1974) developed trace-based tests and compared their performance to that of determinant-based tests.

Mauchly (1940) considered a related but weaker hypothesis, sphericity, i.e., that $\mathbf{A} = d\mathbf{B}$ for some unknown $d > 0$. For normal data, the LR statistic is a function of both the estimated traces and determinants.

Testing the equality of two positive-definite matrices also plays a central role in model specification analysis. Specifically, when a probability model used for maximum-likelihood estimation is correctly specified, the information matrix equality $\mathbf{A} = \mathbf{B}$ holds, where **A** is the opposite of the average log-likelihood Hessian and **B** is the average of the outer product of the log-likelihood scores, both evaluated at the true parameter (see, e.g., Fisher, 1922, 1925). White (1982) proposed an information matrix test (IMT) for model misspecification based on a comparison of estimates of the elements of **A** and **B**. The omnibus or nondirectional IMT compares all the nonredundant elements of **A** and **B**, yielding an asymptotic chi-squared test statistic. Directional specification tests (e.g., for conditional heteroskedasticity, skewness, or kurtosis) are obtained by comparing selected elements of **A** and **B**, also yielding asymptotic chi-squared tests.

The intuitive appeal and generality of this proposal led to an extensive body of work studying the properties of the IMT, including papers of Chesher (1983), Lancaster (1984), Orme (1988, 1990), Taylor (1987), Hall (1987), Chesher and Spady (1991), Horowitz (1994), and Dhaene and Hoorelbeke (2004), among others. One early finding was negative: Taylor (1987) and Orme (1990), among others, showed that previously proposed IMTs typically suffered from extreme level distortions, so much so as to render them impractical for empirical application. Chesher and Spady (1991) showed that these level distortions can be resolved by employing higher-order expansions for the IMT. As Horowitz (1994) pointed out, however, this approach is extremely cumbersome because it involves higher-order cumulants, making it impractical for all but the simplest models. Instead, Horowitz proposed use of the parametric bootstrap. This method is computationally straightforward, and, as Horowitz's Monte Carlo experiments show, parametric bootstrap-based IMTs exhibit outstanding level performance, even for modest sample sizes and in cases where the test statistic is not pivotal. Furthermore, it has power properties similar to those exhibited by level distortion-adjusted IMTs. The parametric bootstrap has been the preferred method for IMT implementation since its introduction. Nevertheless, it is unclear whether the parametric bootstrap still works well for other non-pivotal tests not used by Horowitz in his Monte Carlo experiments.

Until recently, little or no attention has been paid to the possibility of constructing IMTs based on the trace or determinant of **A** and **B**. To the best of our knowledge, Golden, Henley, White, and Kashner (2013) were the first to systematically investigate this possibility by proposing IMTs based on functions of the log eigenspectra of **A** and **B**, including tests based on the trace and determinant. A major contribution of the present paper is to extend this line of inquiry by proposing tests of $\mathbf{A}=\mathbf{B}$ based on trace and determinant properties that *characterize* the equality of two positive-definite matrices. This characterization, namely that $\mathbf{A}=\mathbf{B}$ if and only if or $\det(\mathbf{BA}^{-1})^{1/k}=k^{-1}\mathrm{tr}(\mathbf{BA}^{-1})=1$, or $\det(\mathbf{AB}^{-1})^{1/k}=k^{-1}\mathrm{tr}(\mathbf{AB}^{-1})=1$, is apparently new; we have not been able to find its applications elsewhere. It is remarkably simple, and it is striking in that it enables an omnibus[1] IMT based on a comparison of only two quantities, regardless of the matrix dimension. This result also applies to the classical problem of testing the equality of two covariance matrices, but without requiring data to be generated by the multivariate normal distribution.

The resulting computational simplicity of these new trace-determinant tests is by itself appealing. As we further show, implementation using the parametric bootstrap yields tests with outstanding level performance, which implies that the parametric bootstraps show excellent performance even for our non-pivotal test statistics.

To date, the IMT literature has focused mostly on the level properties of the IMT. Here, we further contribute to the extant literature by studying the power properties of standard IMTs, other related tests, and our new trace-determinant IMTs by using the parametric bootstrap. Specifically, we examine the power of the various tests to detect misspecification in four models: linear regression, exponential duration, probit, and Tobit. We find that our new trace-determinant tests often outperform previous tests. When they do not, they nevertheless perform respectably. In addition, we examine the local power properties of our new tests and associate them with the standard LR statistics testing for covariance equality and sphericity under the multivariate normal distribution condition.

The plan of the paper is as follows. In Section 2, we state the lemma characterizing the equality of two positive-definite matrices, discuss its implications for information matrix testing, and propose three related IMTs. In Section 3, we study the asymptotic behavior of our test statistics under the null, alternative, and local alternative hypotheses. We also examine how our test statistics are interrelated with the LR test under the classical multivariate normal distribution condition and discuss implementation considerations; following Horowitz (1994), we recommend use of the parametric bootstrap. In Section 4, we investigate by Monte Carlo experiments the finite-sample level, power, and local power of our new trace-determinant IMTs, the Chesher (1983) and Lancaster (1984) IMTs, and some related tests. Section 5 contains a summary and concluding remarks. Mathematical proofs and additional assumptions are gathered in the Mathematical Appendix.

Before proceeding, we present the following notational details. A function will always be denoted using an empty argument: a function mapping f from $\mathscr{X}$ to $\mathscr{Y}$ will be denoted by $f(\cdot)$ or $f : \mathscr{X} \mapsto \mathscr{Y}$. When f alone is used, this denotes a variable in a Euclidean space. Also, for notational simplicity, we denote $f'(x)|_{x=x_*}$ by $f'(x_*)$ and let $\partial_x f(x)$ and $\partial^2_{x,y} f(x,y)$ denote $(\partial/\partial x)f(x)$ and $(\partial^2/\partial x \partial y)f(x,y)$, respectively. We use the following simple facts without reference: $\text{tr}[\mathbf{AB}] = \text{tr}[\mathbf{BA}]$, $\det[\mathbf{AB}] = \det[\mathbf{A}]\det[\mathbf{B}]$, and $\det[\mathbf{A}^{-1}] = 1/\det[\mathbf{A}]$.

2. A BASIC LEMMA AND ITS TESTING IMPLICATIONS

Our tests for the equality of two positive-definite matrices are based on the following simple but striking lemma.

Lemma 1. Let $\mathbf{A}$ and $\mathbf{B}$ be real positive-definite $k \times k$ matrices with $k \in \mathbb{N}$. Then $\mathbf{A} = \mathbf{B}$ if and only if

$$\det\left[\mathbf{A}^{-1/2}\mathbf{B}\mathbf{A}^{-1/2}\right]^{1/k} = 1 \text{ and } \mathrm{tr}\left[\mathbf{A}^{-1/2}\mathbf{B}\mathbf{A}^{-1/2}\right]/k = 1$$

where $\mathbf{A}^{-1/2}$ is the real positive-definite $k \times k$ matrix square root of $\mathbf{A}^{-1}$. □

Thus, $\mathbf{A} = \mathbf{B}$ whenever the geometric and arithmetic means of the eigenvalues of $\mathbf{A}^{-1/2}\mathbf{B}\mathbf{A}^{-1/2}$ both equal 1. We state the result in terms of $\mathbf{A}^{-1/2}\mathbf{B}\mathbf{A}^{-1/2}$ to make it obvious that this matrix has real positive eigenvalues. Equivalently, with $\mathbf{D} := \mathbf{B}\mathbf{A}^{-1}$, $\mathbf{A} = \mathbf{B}$ if and only if $\det(\mathbf{D})^{1/k} = k^{-1}$ $\mathrm{tr}(\mathbf{D}) = 1$. To the best of our knowledge, one of the exercise questions in Magnus and Neudecker (1999) is closest to ours; this states that for any positive semi-definite matrix $\mathbf{M}$, $\det[\mathbf{M}]^{1/k} = \mathrm{tr}[\mathbf{M}]/k$ if and only if $\mathbf{M}$ is proportional to $\mathbf{I}$. As another characterization, Strawderman (1994) also show that $\mathbf{A} = \mathbf{B}$ if and only if $k^{-1}\mathrm{tr}(\mathbf{D}) = 1$ and $k^{-1}\mathrm{tr}(\mathbf{D}^2) = 1$.

No IMT exists using Lemma 1, although similar motivations using eigenvalues exist. Bera (1986) and Bera and Hall (1991) regarded eigenvalues as key elements for testing two equal positive-definite matrices. They focused on the eigenvalues of $\mathbf{A} - \mathbf{B}$ and used their distances to test the equality of $\mathbf{A}$ and $\mathbf{B}$. Similarly, many tests using the eigenvalues can be developed, although developing a general theory on their applications is not straightforward, mainly due to their non-differentiability.

To apply Lemma 1, we construct statistics testing any two of the following hypotheses:

$$\mathrm{tr}[\mathbf{D}]/k = 1 \tag{1}$$

$$\det[\mathbf{D}]^{1/k} = 1 \tag{2}$$

$$\mathrm{tr}[\mathbf{D}]/k = \det[\mathbf{D}]^{1/k} \tag{3}$$

Any two of these imply the other. Thus, to test

$$\mathbb{H}_0 : \mathbf{A} = \mathbf{B} \text{ versus } \mathbb{H}_1 : \mathbf{A} \neq \mathbf{B}$$

we consider three equivalent hypotheses, each of which yields a corresponding test statistic:

$$\mathbb{H}_0^{(1)} : \text{tr}[\mathbf{D}]/k = 1 \text{ and } \det[\mathbf{D}]^{1/k} = 1 \quad \text{vs.} \quad \mathbb{H}_1^{(1)} : \text{tr}[\mathbf{D}]/k \neq 1 \text{ or } \det[\mathbf{D}]^{1/k} \neq 1$$

$$\mathbb{H}_0^{(2)} : \text{tr}[\mathbf{D}]/k = 1 \text{ and } \text{tr}[\mathbf{D}]/k = \det[\mathbf{D}]^{1/k} \text{ vs. } \mathbb{H}_1^{(2)} : \text{tr}[\mathbf{D}]/k \neq 1 \text{ or } \text{tr}[\mathbf{D}]/k \neq \det[\mathbf{D}]^{1/k}$$

$$\mathbb{H}_0^{(3)} : \det[\mathbf{D}]^{1/k} = 1 \text{ and } \text{tr}[\mathbf{D}]/k = \det[\mathbf{D}]^{1/k} \text{ vs. } \mathbb{H}_1^{(3)} : \text{tr}[\mathbf{D}]/k \neq 1 \text{ or } \text{tr}[\mathbf{D}]/k \neq \det[\mathbf{D}]^{1/k}$$

Clearly, $\mathbb{H}_0^{(1)}$ tests (1) and (2), $\mathbb{H}_0^{(2)}$ tests (1) and (3), and $\mathbb{H}_0^{(3)}$ tests (2) and (3).

To define test statistics corresponding to $\mathbb{H}_0^{(1)} - \mathbb{H}_0^{(3)}$, let $\mathbf{A}_n$ and $\mathbf{B}_n$ be consistent estimators for $\mathbf{A}$ and $\mathbf{B}$, and write $\mathbf{D}_n := \mathbf{B}_n \mathbf{A}_n^{-1}$. Each test statistic combines two of the following:

$$T_n := \text{tr}[\mathbf{D}_n]/k - 1; \quad D_n := \det[\mathbf{D}_n]^{1/k} - 1; \text{ and } S_n := \text{tr}[\mathbf{D}_n]/k - \det[\mathbf{D}_n]^{1/k}$$

When $\mathbf{A} = \mathbf{B}$, the consistency of $(\mathbf{A}_n, \mathbf{B}_n)$ implies that each of these should be negligible in probability. For the estimators $(\mathbf{A}_n, \mathbf{B}_n)$ studied here, it turns out that $\mathbf{A} = \mathbf{B}$ implies $T_n = O_{\mathbb{P}}(n^{-1/2})$, $D_n = O_{\mathbb{P}}(n^{-1/2})$, and $S_n = O_{\mathbb{P}}(n^{-1})$, as we show in Lemma 3 below.

The given hypotheses and statistics are essential in testing $\mathbb{H}_0$ against $\mathbb{H}_1$ when the eigenvalues of $\mathbf{BA}^{-1}$ are exploited. We do not need to consider any other transformation of the eigenvalues. As pointed out by Bera (1986) and Bera and Hall (1991), the eigenvalues of $\mathbf{A} - \mathbf{B}$ can be transformed into many statistics in various ways. Instead, our statistics simply focus on the trace and determinant of $\mathbf{BA}^{-1}$ without introducing any exceptional case for $\mathbf{A} = \mathbf{B}$. In addition, our statistics do not estimate eigenvectors. The level and power properties of their tests critically depend upon the way to estimate the eigenvectors, as in Bera and Hall (1991). Strawderman (1994) also considers another testing principle using his characterization. Comparing these test statistics with ours is left as a future research topic.

Consider the following statistics, corresponding to $\mathbb{H}_0^{(1)} - \mathbb{H}_0^{(3)}$:

$$\mathscr{B}_n^{(1)} := nk^2 \left(\frac{1}{2} T_n^2 + \frac{1}{2} D_n^2 \right); \quad \mathscr{B}_n^{(2)} := 2nk \left(\frac{1}{2} T_n^2 + S_n \right);$$

$$\text{and } \mathscr{B}_n^{(3)} := 2nk \left(\frac{1}{2} D_n^2 + S_n \right)$$

Under $\mathbb{H}_0$, each of these is bounded but not negligible in probability. Note that T_n and D_n are squared, while S_n is not. This is due to their different orders of convergence. The coefficient 1/2 multiplying T_n^2 and D_n^2 ensures a straightforward asymptotic null distribution, and $S_n \geq 0$ because the arithmetic mean is always greater than or equal to the geometric mean.

To apply these methods to information matrix testing, we can let $\hat{\boldsymbol{\theta}}_n$ be the (quasi-) maximum-likelihood ((Q)ML) estimator (White, 1982) consistent for $\boldsymbol{\theta}_*$, an interior element of $\Theta \subset \mathbb{R}^k$, such that

$$\sqrt{n}(\hat{\boldsymbol{\theta}}_n - \boldsymbol{\theta}_*) \overset{\text{A}}{\sim} N[\mathbf{0},\ \mathbf{A}_*{}^{-1}\mathbf{B}_*\mathbf{A}_*{}^{-1}]$$

Here, $\mathbf{A}_*$ is the negative Hessian matrix of the (quasi-) likelihood function at $\boldsymbol{\theta}_*$, and $\mathbf{B}_*$ is the asymptotic covariance matrix of the (quasi-) log-likelihood scores. Correct specification implies the information matrix equality, $\mathbf{A}_* = \mathbf{B}_*$, under mild regularity conditions, justifying the classical maximum-likelihood covariance matrix estimators. Thus, if we let $\mathbf{A}(\cdot)$ and $\mathbf{B}(\cdot)$ be continuous functions of $\boldsymbol{\theta}$ (i.e., $\mathbf{A} : \Theta \mapsto \mathbb{R}^{k \times k}$ and $\mathbf{B} : \Theta \mapsto \mathbb{R}^{k \times k}$), we can test $\mathbf{A}_* := \mathbf{A}(\boldsymbol{\theta}_*) = \mathbf{B}_* := \mathbf{B}(\boldsymbol{\theta}_*)$ using estimators $\hat{\mathbf{A}}_n := \mathbf{A}_n(\hat{\boldsymbol{\theta}}_n)$ and $\hat{\mathbf{B}}_n := \mathbf{B}_n(\hat{\boldsymbol{\theta}}_n)$, where $\mathbf{A}_n(\cdot)$ and $\mathbf{B}_n(\cdot)$ are sample analogs of $\mathbf{A}(\cdot)$ and $\mathbf{B}(\cdot)$. We also let $\hat{\mathbf{D}}_n := \hat{\mathbf{B}}_n \hat{\mathbf{A}}_n^{-1}$ and define

$$\hat{T}_n := \text{tr}[\hat{\mathbf{D}}_n]/k - 1; \quad \hat{D}_n := \det[\hat{\mathbf{D}}_n]^{1/k} - 1; \text{ and } \hat{S}_n := \text{tr}[\hat{\mathbf{D}}_n]/k - \det[\hat{\mathbf{D}}_n]^{1/k}$$

from which we construct

$$\hat{\mathscr{B}}_n^{(1)} := nk^2\left(\frac{1}{2}\hat{T}_n^2 + \frac{1}{2}\hat{D}_n^2\right); \quad \hat{\mathscr{B}}_n^{(2)} := 2nk\left(\frac{1}{2}\hat{T}_n^2 + \hat{S}_n\right); \text{ and}$$

$$\hat{\mathscr{B}}_n^{(3)} := 2nk\left(\frac{1}{2}\hat{D}_n^2 + \hat{S}_n\right)$$

As it turns out, estimating $\boldsymbol{\theta}_*$ using $\hat{\boldsymbol{\theta}}_n$ impacts the asymptotic null behavior of our test statistics, introducing certain additive terms.

Furthermore, we notice that the dimension condition can be relaxed to handle general cases. That is, as we detail below, our constructions are valid even when $\Theta \subset \mathbb{R}^{\ell}$ with $\ell \in \mathbb{N}$. We, therefore, suppose this from now on and impose $l = k$ when testing the information matrix equality.

We also consider the simpler but important special case of testing the equality of the population covariance matrices of $\mathbf{a}(Y_t,\mathbf{X}_t)$ and $\mathbf{b}(Y_t,\mathbf{X}_t)$, where $\mathbf{a}(Y_t,\mathbf{X}_t)$ and $\mathbf{b}(Y_t,\mathbf{X}_t)$ are possibly nonlinear transformations of $(Y_t,\mathbf{X}_t)$. For this, we compare two sample covariance matrices $\tilde{\mathbf{A}}_n$ and $\tilde{\mathbf{B}}_n$, defined as

$$\tilde{\mathbf{A}}_n := \hat{\Sigma}_{\mathbf{a},n} - \hat{\boldsymbol{\mu}}_{\mathbf{a},n}\hat{\boldsymbol{\mu}}'_{\mathbf{a},n}, \quad \text{and} \quad \tilde{\mathbf{B}}_n := \hat{\Sigma}_{\mathbf{b},n} - \hat{\boldsymbol{\mu}}_{\mathbf{b},n}\hat{\boldsymbol{\mu}}'_{\mathbf{b},n}$$

where, for the given vector-valued functions $\mathbf{a}(\cdot,\cdot)$ and $\mathbf{b}(\cdot,\cdot)$,

$$\hat{\boldsymbol{\mu}}_{\mathbf{a},n} := n^{-1}\sum_{t=1}^{n}\mathbf{a}(Y_t,\mathbf{X}_t) \qquad \hat{\Sigma}_{\mathbf{a},n} := n^{-1}\sum_{t=1}^{n}\mathbf{a}(Y_t,\mathbf{X}_t)\mathbf{a}(Y_t,\mathbf{X}_t)'$$

$$\hat{\boldsymbol{\mu}}_{\mathbf{b},n} := n^{-1}\sum_{t=1}^{n}\mathbf{b}(Y_t,\mathbf{X}_t) \quad \text{and} \quad \hat{\Sigma}_{\mathbf{b},n} := n^{-1}\sum_{t=1}^{n}\mathbf{b}(Y_t,\mathbf{X}_t)\mathbf{b}(Y_t,\mathbf{X}_t)'$$

Here, $(\hat{\boldsymbol{\mu}}_{\mathbf{a},n},\hat{\Sigma}_{\mathbf{a},n},\hat{\boldsymbol{\mu}}_{\mathbf{b},n},\hat{\Sigma}_{\mathbf{b},n})$ is consistent for $(\boldsymbol{\mu}_{\mathbf{a},*},\Sigma_{\mathbf{a},*},\boldsymbol{\mu}_{\mathbf{b},*},\Sigma_{\mathbf{b},*}) := (E[\mathbf{a}(Y_t,\mathbf{X}_t)], E[\mathbf{a}(Y_t,\mathbf{X}_t)\mathbf{a}(Y_t,\mathbf{X}_t)'], E[\mathbf{b}(Y_t,\mathbf{X}_t)], E[\mathbf{b}(Y_t,\mathbf{X}_t)\mathbf{b}(Y_t,\mathbf{X}_t)'])$, and the other regularity conditions are provided in the appendix for our test statistics defined in Theorem 2 below.

3. TEST STATISTIC ASYMPTOTIC BEHAVIOR

3.1. Asymptotic Null Behavior

To examine the asymptotic null behavior of $\hat{T}_n$, $\hat{D}_n$, and $\hat{S}_n \equiv \hat{T}_n - \hat{D}_n$, we impose the following regularity conditions.

Assumption 1. (i) $(\Omega, \mathcal{F}, \mathbb{P})$ is a complete probability space;

(ii) for $\ell \in \mathbb{N}$, $\Theta \subset \mathbb{R}^{\ell}$ is a compact convex set with nonempty interior; and

(iii) there is a sequence of measurable mappings $\{\hat{\boldsymbol{\theta}}_n : \Omega \mapsto \Theta\}$ consistent for a unique $\boldsymbol{\theta}_* \in int(\Theta)$. □

Assumption 2. (i) For $k \in \mathbb{N}$, the symmetric matrix mapping $\mathbf{A} : \Theta \mapsto \mathbb{R}^{k\times k}$ is in $\mathscr{C}^{(2)}(\Theta)$ and is such that $\mathbf{A}_* := \mathbf{A}(\boldsymbol{\theta}_*)$ is positive definite; and

(ii) the symmetric matrix mapping $\mathbf{B} : \Theta \mapsto \mathbb{R}^{k\times k}$ is in $\mathscr{C}^{(2)}(\Theta)$ and is such that $\mathbf{B}_* := \mathbf{B}(\boldsymbol{\theta}_*)$ is positive definite. □

Assumption 3. (i) There are symmetric matrix estimators $\mathbf{A}_n(\cdot)$ and $\mathbf{B}_n(\cdot)$ consistent for $\mathbf{A}(\cdot)$ and $\mathbf{B}(\cdot)$, respectively, uniformly on Θ; and

(ii) $\sqrt{n}[(\hat{\boldsymbol{\theta}}_n - \boldsymbol{\theta}_*)', \text{vech}[\mathbf{A}_n - \mathbf{A}_*]' \text{ vech}[\mathbf{B}_n - \mathbf{B}_*]']' \overset{\text{A}}{\sim} N(0, \Omega_*)$, where $\mathbf{A}_n := \mathbf{A}_n(\boldsymbol{\theta}_*)$, $\mathbf{B}_n := \mathbf{B}_n(\boldsymbol{\theta}_*)$, and Ω_* is a $(k^2 + k + l) \times (k^2 + k + l)$ positive semi-definite matrix. □

Here, vech$(\cdot)$ is used in Assumption 3(ii) to accommodate the symmetry of $\mathbf{A}_n$, $\mathbf{A}_*$, $\mathbf{B}_n$, and $\mathbf{B}_*$. An appropriate central limit theorem (CLT) typically ensures Assumption 3(ii). Also, $\mathbf{A}_n$ and $\mathbf{B}_n$ used for defining T_n, D_n, and S_n correspond to $\mathbf{A}_n(\boldsymbol{\theta}_*)$ and $\mathbf{B}_n(\boldsymbol{\theta}_*)$, respectively. That is, these are estimators with known parameters. Similarly, we have $\mathbf{D}_n := \mathbf{B}_n(\boldsymbol{\theta}_*)\mathbf{A}_n(\boldsymbol{\theta}_*)^{-1}$. Finally, $l = k$ when testing the information matrix equality, and the first $k \times k$ block of Ω_* is equal to $\mathbf{A}_*^{-1}\mathbf{B}_*\mathbf{A}_*^{-1}$.

To simplify notation, we let $\mathbf{M}_n := \mathbf{A}_*^{-1}(\mathbf{B}_n - \mathbf{A}_n)$ and $\mathbf{S}_{j,*} := \mathbf{A}_*^{-1}(\partial_j \mathbf{B}_* - \partial_j \mathbf{A}_*)$ for $j = 1, \ldots, \ell$, where $\partial_j \mathbf{B}_* := (\partial/\partial\theta_j)\mathbf{B}_*$ and $\partial_j \mathbf{A}_* := (\partial/\partial\partial_j)\mathbf{A}_*$. We also write

$$\mathbf{K}_n := \mathbf{M}_n + \sum_{j=1}^{\ell} (\hat{\theta}_{j,n} - \theta_{j,*})\mathbf{S}_{j,*}$$

The $k \times k$ statistic $\mathbf{K}_n$ plays the central role in determining the asymptotic distributions of all our test statistics. Given Assumption 3(ii), $\mathbf{M}_n = O_{\mathbb{P}}(n^{-1/2})$, $(\hat{\boldsymbol{\theta}}_n - \boldsymbol{\theta}_*) = O_{\mathbb{P}}(n^{-1/2})$, and $\mathbf{K}_n = O_{\mathbb{P}}(n^{-1/2})$. Furthermore, Assumption 3(ii) implies that $\mathbf{K}_n$ is asymptotically a $k \times k$ matrix of normal random variables. We omit deriving the asymptotic covariance matrix of $\mathbf{K}_n$. This is mainly because we will implement our testing by using the parametric bootstrap, which renders estimation of the covariance matrix unnecessary.

We obtain asymptotic approximations by applying Taylor expansions to $\hat{T}_n$ and $\hat{D}_n$. The following lemma relies on first-order expansions.

Lemma 2. Given Assumptions 1, 2, 3, and $\mathbb{H}_0$,

(i) $\hat{T}_n = \text{tr}[\mathbf{K}_n]/k + o_{\mathbb{P}}(n^{-1/2})$;
(ii) $\hat{D}_n = \text{tr}[\mathbf{K}_n]/k + o_{\mathbb{P}}(n^{-1/2})$; and
(iii) $\hat{S}_n \equiv \hat{T}_n - \hat{D}_n = o_{\mathbb{P}}(n^{-1/2})$ □

Given Assumption 3, both $\hat{T}_n$ and $\hat{D}_n$ are $O_{\mathbb{P}}(n^{-1/2})$ under $\mathbb{H}_0$, and their asymptotic null distributions are normal. Asymptotic null distributions for $\hat{T}_n^2$ and $\hat{D}_n^2$ follow straightforwardly. In contrast, a first-order approximation is not sufficient to obtain an asymptotic distribution for $\hat{S}_n$, regardless of whether there are estimated parameters, as $\hat{S}_n = o_{\mathbb{P}}(n^{-1/2})$.

To fully specify the null behavior of our statistics, it turns out that next-order expansions for $\text{tr}[\hat{\mathbf{D}}_n]$ and $\det[\hat{\mathbf{D}}_n]$ are required as in Cho and White (2007). For these, we write $\mathbf{W}_n := \mathbf{B}_*^{-1}(\mathbf{B}_n - \mathbf{B}_*)$, $\mathbf{U}_n := \mathbf{A}_*^{-1}(\mathbf{A}_n - \mathbf{A}_*)$, and, for $i, j = 1, \ldots, l$, $\mathbf{G}_{j,n} := \mathbf{B}_*^{-1}\partial_j(\mathbf{B}_n - \mathbf{B}_*)$ and $\mathbf{H}_{j,n} := \mathbf{A}_*^{-1}\partial_j(\mathbf{A}_n - \mathbf{A}_*)$. We also write $\partial_{ji}^2 := \partial^2/\partial\theta_j\partial\theta_i$, and we impose the following conditions.

Assumption 4. (i) For $j = 1, \ldots, l$, $\partial_j\mathbf{A}_n(\cdot)$ and $\partial_j\mathbf{B}_n(\cdot)$ are consistent for $\partial_j\mathbf{A}(\cdot)$ and $\partial_j\mathbf{B}(\cdot)$, uniformly on Θ; and

(ii) for $i, j = 1, \ldots, l$, $\partial_{ji}^2\mathbf{A}_n(\cdot)$ and $\partial_{ji}^2\mathbf{B}_n(\cdot)$ are consistent for $\partial_{ji}^2\mathbf{A}(\cdot)$ and $\partial_{ji}^2\mathbf{B}(\cdot)$, uniformly on Θ. □

Assumption 5. For $j = 1, \ldots, l$, $\mathbf{H}_{j,n} O_{\mathbb{P}}(n^{-1/2})$ and $\mathbf{G}_{j,n} = O_{\mathbb{P}}(n^{-1/2})$. □

Assumptions 4 and 5 easily hold for many interesting models such as those considered in Section 4.

The following lemma provides the required second-order asymptotic approximations. For this, we let $\mathbf{J}_{j,n} := \mathbf{G}_{j,n} - \mathbf{H}_{j,n}$, we let ∇_θ^2 denote the Hessian operator with respect to $\boldsymbol{\theta}$, and we define $\mathbf{D}_* := \mathbf{B}_*\mathbf{A}_*^{-1}$.

Lemma 3. Given Assumptions 1, 2, 3, 4, 5, and $\mathbb{H}_0$,

(i) $\hat{T}_n = \hat{T}_n^\star + o_{\mathbb{P}}(n^{-1})$, where $\hat{T}_n^\star := \hat{T}_{n,1}^\star + \hat{T}_{n,2}^\star$, $\hat{T}_{n,1}^\star := \frac{1}{k}\text{tr}[\mathbf{K}_n]$, and

$$\hat{T}_{n,2}^\star := -\frac{1}{k}\text{tr}[\mathbf{K}_n\mathbf{U}_n] + \frac{1}{k}\left[\text{tr}\left[\mathbf{J}_{j,n} - \mathbf{M}_n\mathbf{A}_*^{-1}\partial_j\mathbf{A}_*\right]\right]'(\hat{\boldsymbol{\theta}}_n - \boldsymbol{\theta}_*)$$

$$+ \frac{1}{2k}(\hat{\boldsymbol{\theta}}_n - \boldsymbol{\theta}_*)'\nabla_\theta^2\text{tr}[\mathbf{D}_*](\hat{\boldsymbol{\theta}}_n - \boldsymbol{\theta}_*)$$

with $\hat{T}_{n,1}^\star = O_{\mathbb{P}}(n^{-1/2})$ and $\hat{T}_{n,2}^\star = O_{\mathbb{P}}(n^{-1})$;

(ii) $\hat{D}_n = \hat{D}_n^\star + o_{\mathbb{P}}(n^{-1})$, where $\hat{D}_n^\star := \hat{D}_{n,1}^\star + \hat{D}_{n,2}^\star$, $\hat{D}_{n,1}^\star := \frac{1}{k}\text{tr}[\mathbf{K}_n]$, and

$$\hat{D}_{n,2}^\star := \frac{1}{2k}\left(\frac{1}{k} - 1\right)\text{tr}[\mathbf{K}_n]^2 + \frac{1}{2k}\left(\text{tr}[\mathbf{M}_n]^2 + \text{tr}\left[\mathbf{U}_n^2\right] - \text{tr}\left[\mathbf{W}_n^2\right]\right)$$

$$+ \frac{1}{k}\left[\text{tr}\left[\mathbf{J}_{j,n} + \mathbf{U}_n\mathbf{A}_*^{-1}\partial_j\mathbf{A}_* - \mathbf{W}_n\mathbf{A}_*^{-1}\partial_j\mathbf{B}_*\right]\right]'(\hat{\boldsymbol{\theta}}_n - \boldsymbol{\theta}_*)$$

$$+ \frac{1}{k}\left[\text{tr}[\mathbf{M}_n]\text{tr}\left[\mathbf{S}_{j,*}\right]\right]'(\hat{\boldsymbol{\theta}}_n - \boldsymbol{\theta}_*)$$

$$+ \frac{1}{2k}(\hat{\boldsymbol{\theta}}_n - \boldsymbol{\theta}_*)'\nabla_\theta^2\det[\mathbf{D}_*](\hat{\boldsymbol{\theta}}_n - \boldsymbol{\theta}_*)$$

with $\hat{D}_{n,1}^\star = O_{\mathbb{P}}(n^{-1/2})$ and $\hat{D}_{n,2}^\star = O_{\mathbb{P}}(n^{-1})$;

(iii) $\hat{S}_n = \hat{S}_n^{\star} + o_{\mathbb{P}}(n^{-1})$, where

$$\hat{S}_n^{\star} := -\frac{1}{2k}\left(\frac{1}{k}-1\right)\mathrm{tr}[\mathbf{K}_n]^2 - \frac{1}{2k}(\mathrm{tr}[\mathbf{M}_n]^2 - \mathrm{tr}[\mathbf{M}_n^2])$$
$$+\frac{1}{k}\mathrm{tr}\left[\mathbf{M}_n\sum_{j=1}^{l}(\hat{\theta}_{j,n}-\theta_{j,*})\mathbf{S}_{j,*}\right] - \frac{1}{k}\mathrm{tr}[\mathbf{M}_n]\mathrm{tr}\left[\sum_{j=1}^{l}(\hat{\theta}_{j,n}-\theta_{j,*})\mathbf{S}_{j,*}\right]$$
$$+\frac{1}{2k}\mathrm{tr}\left[\left(\sum_{j=1}^{l}(\hat{\theta}_{j,n}-\theta_{j,*})\mathbf{S}_{j,*}\right)^2\right] - \frac{1}{2k}\mathrm{tr}\left[\sum_{j=1}^{l}(\hat{\theta}_{j,n}-\theta_{j,*})\mathbf{S}_{j,*}\right]^2$$

with $\hat{S}_n^{\star} = O_{\mathbb{P}}(n^{-1})$. □

Here, we let $[V_j]$ say, denote a vector $\mathbf{V}$ with jth row element V_j.

These results suffice to obtain asymptotic distributions for our test statistics. First, the asymptotic null distribution of $\hat{\mathscr{B}}_n^{(1)}$ is easily obtained from Lemma 2(i, ii), because

$$\hat{\mathscr{B}}_n^{(1)} := nk^2\left(\frac{1}{2}\hat{T}_n^2 + \frac{1}{2}\hat{D}_n^2\right) = n(\mathrm{tr}[\mathbf{K}_n])^2 + o_{\mathbb{P}}(1)$$

Given that $\sqrt{n}(n)^{1/2}\mathrm{tr}[\boldsymbol{K}_n]$ is asymptotically normal by Assumption 3, the asymptotic null distribution of $\hat{\mathscr{B}}_n^{(1)}$ is the square of a normal random variable. Second, we can combine Lemma 2(i) and Lemma 3(iii) to obtain the asymptotic null distribution of $\hat{\mathscr{B}}_n^{(2)}$. This follows from

$$\hat{\mathscr{B}}_n^{(2)} = n\left\{\mathrm{tr}[\mathbf{K}_n]^2 - (\mathrm{tr}[\mathbf{M}_n]^2 - \mathrm{tr}[\mathbf{M}_n^2]) + 2\mathrm{tr}\left[\mathbf{M}_n\sum_{j=1}^{l}(\hat{\theta}_{j,n}-\theta_{j,*})\mathbf{S}_{j,*}\right]\right.$$
$$+\mathrm{tr}\left[\left(\sum_{j=1}^{l}(\hat{\theta}_{j,n}-\theta_{j,*})\mathbf{S}_{j,*}\right)^2\right]$$
$$\left.-2\mathrm{tr}[\mathbf{M}_n]\mathrm{tr}\left[\sum_{j=1}^{l}(\hat{\theta}_{j,n}-\theta_{j,*})\mathbf{S}_{j,*}\right] - \mathrm{tr}\left[\sum_{j=1}^{l}(\hat{\theta}_{j,n}-\theta_{j,*})\mathbf{S}_{j,*}\right]^2\right\} + o_{\mathbb{P}}(1)$$
$$= n\left\{\mathrm{tr}\left[\left(\sum_{j=1}^{l}(\hat{\theta}_{j,n}-\theta_{j,*})\mathbf{S}_{j,*}\right)^2\right] + 2\mathrm{tr}\left[\left(\sum_{j=1}^{l}(\hat{\theta}_{j,n}-\theta_{j,*})\mathbf{S}_{j,*}\right)\mathbf{M}_n\right] + \mathrm{tr}[\mathbf{M}_n^2]\right\}$$
$$+ o_{\mathbb{P}}(1) = n\,\mathrm{tr}[\mathbf{K}_n^2] + o_{\mathbb{P}}(1)$$

The asymptotic null approximation of $\hat{\mathscr{B}}_n^{(3)}$ is obtained in the same way. The definition of $\hat{\mathscr{B}}_n^{(3)}$ and the approximation for $\hat{D}_n$ give $\hat{\mathscr{B}}_n^{(3)} = n\text{tr}[\mathbf{K}_n^2] + o_{\mathbb{P}}(1)$, so that $\hat{\mathscr{B}}_n^{(2)} - \hat{\mathscr{B}}_n^{(3)} = o_{\mathbb{P}}(1)$ under $\mathbb{H}_0$.

We summarize these results as follows.

Theorem 1. Given Assumptions 1, 2, 3, 4, 5, and $\mathbb{H}_0$:

(i) $\hat{\mathscr{B}}_n^{(1)} = n\text{tr}[\mathbf{K}_n]^2 + o_{\mathbb{P}}(1)$;
(ii) $\hat{\mathscr{B}}_n^{(2)} = n\text{tr}[\mathbf{K}_n^2] + o_{\mathbb{P}}(1)$; and
(iii) $\hat{\mathscr{B}}_n^{(3)} = n\text{tr}[\mathbf{K}_n^2] + o_{\mathbb{P}}(1)$. □

For the case in which $\tilde{\mathbf{A}}_n$ and $\tilde{\mathbf{B}}_n$ are sample covariance matrices, replacing $\mathbf{A}_*$ and $\mathbf{B}_*$ to provide $\tilde{\mathbf{M}}_n$, we have a simplified result that does not involve $\hat{\boldsymbol{\theta}}_n$: we have

Theorem 2. Given Assumptions A1, A2, A3, and $\mathbb{H}_0$,

(i) $\tilde{\mathscr{B}}_n^{(1)} = n\text{tr}\left[\tilde{\mathbf{M}}_n\right]^2 + o_{\mathbb{P}}(1)$;
(ii) $\tilde{\mathscr{B}}_n^{(2)} = n\text{tr}\left[\tilde{\mathbf{M}}_n^2\right] + o_{\mathbb{P}}(1)$; and
(iii) $\tilde{\mathscr{B}}_n^{(3)} = n\text{tr}\left[\tilde{\mathbf{M}}_n^2\right] + o_{\mathbb{P}}(1)$, where

$$\tilde{\mathscr{B}}_n^{(1)} := nk^2\left(\frac{1}{2}\tilde{T}_n^2 + \frac{1}{2}\tilde{D}_n^2\right);\ \tilde{\mathscr{B}}_n^{(2)} := 2nk\left(\frac{1}{2}\tilde{T}_n^2 + \tilde{S}_n\right);\ \tilde{\mathscr{B}}_n^{(3)} := 2nk\left(\frac{1}{2}\tilde{D}_n^2 + \tilde{S}_n\right);$$

and $\tilde{\mathbf{M}}_n := \mathbf{A}_*^{-1}(\tilde{\mathbf{B}}_n - \tilde{\mathbf{A}}_n)$ with $\tilde{T}_n := \text{tr}[\tilde{\mathbf{D}}_n]/k - 1$; $\tilde{D}_n := \det[\tilde{\mathbf{D}}_n]^{1/k} - 1$; $\tilde{S}_n := \text{tr}[\tilde{\mathbf{D}}_n]/k - \det[\tilde{\mathbf{D}}_n]^{1/k}$; and $\tilde{\mathbf{D}}_n := \tilde{\mathbf{B}}_n\tilde{\mathbf{A}}_n^{-1}$. □

To obtain this result, we write

$$\sqrt{n}(\tilde{\mathbf{A}}_n - \mathbf{A}_*) = \sqrt{n}(\hat{\Sigma}_{\mathbf{a},n} - \Sigma_{\mathbf{a},*}) - \sqrt{n}(\hat{\boldsymbol{\mu}}_{\mathbf{a},n} - \boldsymbol{\mu}_{\mathbf{a},*})\hat{\boldsymbol{\mu}}_{\mathbf{a},n}' - \sqrt{n}\boldsymbol{\mu}_{\mathbf{a},*}(\hat{\boldsymbol{\mu}}_{\mathbf{a},n} - \boldsymbol{\mu}_{\mathbf{a},*})'$$

and

$$\sqrt{n}(\tilde{\mathbf{B}}_n - \mathbf{B}_*) = \sqrt{n}(\hat{\Sigma}_{\mathbf{b},n} - \Sigma_{\mathbf{b},*}) - \sqrt{n}(\hat{\boldsymbol{\mu}}_{\mathbf{b},n} - \boldsymbol{\mu}_{\mathbf{b},*})\hat{\boldsymbol{\mu}}_{\mathbf{b},n}' - \sqrt{n}\boldsymbol{\mu}_{\mathbf{b},*}(\hat{\boldsymbol{\mu}}_{\mathbf{b},n} - \boldsymbol{\mu}_{\mathbf{b},*})'$$

and require that the multivariate CLT applies to $\sqrt{n}[\text{vech}[(\hat{\Sigma}_{\mathbf{a},n} - \Sigma_{\mathbf{a},*})]', \text{vech}[(\hat{\Sigma}_{\mathbf{b},n} - \Sigma_{\mathbf{b},*})]', (\hat{\boldsymbol{\mu}}_{\mathbf{a},n} - \boldsymbol{\mu}_{\mathbf{a},*})', (\hat{\boldsymbol{\mu}}_{\mathbf{b},n} - \boldsymbol{\mu}_{\mathbf{b},*})']'$. The difference between Theorems 1 and 2 is that, due to the structure of $\tilde{\mathbf{A}}_n$ and $\tilde{\mathbf{B}}_n$, $\hat{\boldsymbol{\theta}}_n$ no longer plays an explicit role. Consequently, $\tilde{\mathbf{M}}_n$ replaces $\boldsymbol{K}_n$. We state the referenced regularity conditions in the appendix. Because the proof of Theorem 2 closely parallels that of Theorem 1, we omit this from the appendix.

3.2. Asymptotic Behavior under the Alternative

We next examine the asymptotic behavior of $\hat{T}_n$, $\hat{D}_n$, and $\hat{S}_n$ under the alternative. To simplify notation, for $j=1, \ldots, l$, we let $\mathbf{P}_n := \mathbf{W}_n - \mathbf{U}_n$ and $\mathbf{R}_{j,*} := \mathbf{B}_*^{-1}\partial_j\mathbf{B}_* - \mathbf{A}_*^{-1}\partial_j\mathbf{A}_*$; these definitions correspond to $\boldsymbol{M}_n$ and $\boldsymbol{S}_{j,*}$. Under $\mathbb{H}_0$, $\mathbf{P}_n = \mathbf{M}_n$ and $\mathbf{R}_{j,*} = \mathbf{S}_{j,*}$. We also let

$$\mathbf{L}_n := \mathbf{P}_n + \sum_{j=1}^{l}(\hat{\theta}_{j,n} - \theta_{j,*})\mathbf{R}_{j,*}$$

so that $\mathbf{L}_n = \mathbf{K}_n$ under $\mathbb{H}_0$. In particular, $\mathbf{P}_n = O_{\mathbb{P}}(n^{-1/2})$ and $\mathbf{L}_n = O_{\mathbb{P}}(n^{-1/2})$ by Assumptions 3 and 5, even under the alternative. For the next result, we let $T_* := k^{-1}\mathrm{tr}[\mathbf{D}_*] - 1$ and $D_* := \det[\mathbf{D}_*]^{1/k} - 1$. Recall that $\mathbf{D}_* := \mathbf{B}_*\mathbf{A}_*^{-1}$. We also note that $T_* \geq D_*$ from the property that the arithmetic mean is always greater than or equal to the geometric mean.

Lemma 4. Given Assumptions 1, 2, 3, 4, and 5, the following hold:

(i)
$$\begin{aligned}\hat{T}_n = {} & T_* + \frac{1}{k}\mathrm{tr}\left[\mathbf{L}_n\mathbf{A}_*^{-1}\mathbf{B}_*\right] - \frac{1}{k}\mathrm{tr}\left[\mathbf{L}_n\mathbf{U}_n\mathbf{A}_*^{-1}\mathbf{B}_*\right] \\ & + \frac{1}{k}[\mathrm{tr}\left[\left(\mathbf{J}_{j,n} - \mathbf{P}_n\mathbf{A}_*^{-1}\partial_j\mathbf{A}_*\right)\mathbf{A}_*^{-1}\mathbf{B}_*\right]]'(\hat{\boldsymbol{\theta}}_n - \boldsymbol{\theta}_*) \qquad (4) \\ & + \frac{1}{2k}(\hat{\boldsymbol{\theta}}_n - \boldsymbol{\theta}_*)'\nabla^2_{\boldsymbol{\theta}}\mathrm{tr}[\mathbf{D}_*](\hat{\boldsymbol{\theta}}_n - \boldsymbol{\theta}_*) + o_{\mathbb{P}}(n^{-1});\end{aligned}$$

(ii)
$$\begin{aligned}\det[\mathbf{D}_*]^{-\frac{1}{k}}\hat{D}_n = {} & \det[\mathbf{D}_*]^{-\frac{1}{k}}D_* + \frac{1}{k}\mathrm{tr}[\mathbf{L}_n] + \frac{1}{2k}\left(\frac{1}{k} - 1\right)\mathrm{tr}[\mathbf{L}_n]^2 \\ & + \frac{1}{k}\mathrm{tr}[\mathbf{P}_n][\mathrm{tr}\left[\mathbf{R}_{j,*}\right]]'(\hat{\boldsymbol{\theta}}_n - \boldsymbol{\theta}_*) + \frac{1}{2k}(\mathrm{tr}[\mathbf{P}_n]^2 + \mathrm{tr}\left[\mathbf{U}_n^2\right] - \mathrm{tr}\left[\mathbf{W}_n^2\right]) \\ & + \frac{1}{k}[\mathrm{tr}\left[\mathbf{J}_{j,n} + \mathbf{U}_n\mathbf{A}_*^{-1}\partial_j\mathbf{A}_* - \mathbf{W}_n\mathbf{B}_*^{-1}\partial_j\mathbf{B}_*\right]]'(\hat{\boldsymbol{\theta}}_n - \boldsymbol{\theta}_*) \\ & + \frac{1}{2k}\det[\mathbf{D}_*]^{-1}(\hat{\boldsymbol{\theta}}_n - \boldsymbol{\theta}_*)'\nabla^2_{\boldsymbol{\theta}}\det[\mathbf{D}_*](\hat{\boldsymbol{\theta}}_n - \boldsymbol{\theta}_*) + o_{\mathbb{P}}(n^{-1}) \qquad (5)\end{aligned}$$

■

Lemma 3 follows easily from Lemma 4 given $\mathbb{H}_0$. Under $\mathbb{H}_0$, $T_* = D_* = 0$, $\mathbf{L}_n = \mathbf{K}_n$, $\mathbf{P}_n = \mathbf{M}_n$, $\mathbf{A}_*^{-1}\mathbf{B}_* = \mathbf{I}$, $\det[\mathbf{D}_*] = 1$, and $\mathbf{R}_{j,*} = \mathbf{S}_{j,*}$ for each j = 1,2, ..., l. Using these, we obtain Lemma 3 from Lemma 4. We also note that only the second terms on the right of Eqs. (4) and (5) are $O_{\mathbb{P}}(n^{-1/2})$; the rest are $O_{\mathbb{P}}(n^{-1})$. Thus, asymptotic behavior under the alternative is mainly determined by the first two terms in each case. It follows that the behavior of $\hat{S}_n := \hat{T}_n - \hat{D}_n$ is similarly determined. We have

Corollary 1. Given Assumptions 1, 2, 3, 4, and 5,

(i) if for all $d > 0$, $\mathbf{B}_* \neq d\mathbf{A}_*$, $\hat{S}_n = (T_* - D_*) + \frac{1}{k}\mathrm{tr}\left[(\mathbf{A}_*^{-1}\mathbf{B}_* - \det[\mathbf{D}_*]^{\frac{1}{k}}\mathbf{I})\mathbf{L}_n\right] + o_{\mathbb{P}}(n^{-1/2})$; and
(ii) if for some $d_* > 0$, $\mathbf{B}_* = d_*\mathbf{A}_*$, $\hat{S}_n = -\frac{d_*}{2k^2}\mathrm{tr}\left[\mathbf{L}_n\right]^2 + \frac{d_*}{2k}\mathrm{tr}\left[\mathbf{L}_n^2\right] + o_{\mathbb{P}}(n^{-1})$.

□

Although Corollary 1 follows easily from Lemma 4, we provide its proof in the appendix to make the role of the second-order derivatives clear. Indeed, $\mathrm{tr}\left[(\mathbf{A}_*^{-1}\mathbf{B}_* - \det[\mathbf{D}_*]^{\frac{1}{k}}\mathbf{I})\mathbf{L}_n\right] = 0$ if and only if $\mathbf{B}_*$ is proportional to $\mathbf{A}_*$. Also, if $\mathbf{B}_* = d_*\mathbf{A}_*$, then $T_* = D_* = d_* - 1$. We use this fact in obtaining Corollary 1(*ii*), which implies that $\hat{S}_n = O_{\mathbb{P}}(n^{-1})$. This suggests that the analysis of the statistics under the alternative must separately treat the cases where $\mathbf{B}_*$ *is* proportional to $\mathbf{A}_*$ and where $\mathbf{B}_*$ is *not* proportional to $\mathbf{A}_*$. In terms of correct model specification, the literature typically assumes that for some d_*, $\mathbf{B}_* = d_*\mathbf{A}_*$ by assuming that conditional disturbances obey conditional homoskedasticity.

The power properties of our test statistics now follow easily. We have

$$\hat{\mathscr{B}}_n^{(1)} = \frac{nk^2}{2}(T_*^2 + D_*^2) + nk\left(\mathrm{tr}\left[\left(T_*\mathbf{A}_*^{-1}\mathbf{B}_* + D_*\det[\mathbf{D}_*]^{\frac{1}{k}}\mathbf{I}\right)\mathbf{L}_n\right]\right) + O_{\mathbb{P}}(1) \quad (6)$$

from the definition of $\hat{\mathscr{B}}_n^{(1)}$ and Lemma 4. The first term is $O(n)$, and the second is $O_{\mathbb{P}}(\sqrt{n})$. Thus, for any $c_n = o(n)$, $\lim_{n\to\infty}\mathbb{P}\left(\hat{\mathscr{B}}_n^{(1)} \geq c_n\right) = 1$.

As seen above, the behaviors of $\hat{\mathscr{B}}_n^{(2)}$ and $\hat{\mathscr{B}}_n^{(3)}$ depend on whether $\mathbf{B}_*$ is proportional to $\mathbf{A}_*$. Specifically, we cannot expect power from $\hat{S}_n$ if $\mathbf{B}_*$ is proportional to $\mathbf{A}_*$. When $\mathbf{B}_*$ is not proportional to $\mathbf{A}_*$, we have

$$\hat{\mathscr{B}}_n^{(2)} = nk(T_*^2 + 2T_* - 2D_*) + 2n\mathrm{tr}\left[\left[(T_*+1)\mathbf{A}_*^{-1}\mathbf{B}_* - \det[\mathbf{D}_*]^{\frac{1}{k}}\mathbf{I}\right]\mathbf{L}_n\right] + O_{\mathbb{P}}(1) \text{ and} \quad (7)$$

$$\hat{\mathscr{B}}_n^{(3)} = nk(D_*^2 - 2D_* + 2T_*) + 2n\{(D_*+1)(D_*-1)\mathrm{tr}[\mathbf{L}_n] + \mathrm{tr}[\mathbf{A}_*^{-1}\mathbf{B}_*\mathbf{L}_n]\} + O_{\mathbb{P}}(1) \quad (8)$$

by the definitions of $\hat{\mathscr{B}}_n^{(2)}$ and $\hat{\mathscr{B}}_n^{(3)}$, Lemma 4, and Corollary 1(*i*). The first term of $\hat{\mathscr{B}}_n^{(2)}$ is $O(n)$ if $T_*^2 + 2T_* - 2D_* \neq 0$, and that of $\hat{\mathscr{B}}_n^{(3)}$ is $O(n)$ if $D_*^2 - 2D_* + 2T_* \neq 0$. The second terms are $O_{\mathbb{P}}(\sqrt{n})$. Also, if $T_* \neq D_*$, $T_* > D_*$ from the inequality of the arithmetic and geometric means. Using this, we can obtain the power properties of $\hat{\mathscr{B}}_n^{(2)}$ and $\hat{\mathscr{B}}_n^{(3)}$ as follows: if $T_*^2 + 2T_* - 2D_* > 0$, for the same $c_n = o(n)$ as above, $\lim_{n\to\infty} \mathbb{P}(\hat{\mathscr{B}}_n^{(2)} \geq c_n) = 1$; and if $D_*^2 + 2T_* - 2D_* > 0$, $\lim_{n\to\infty}\mathbb{P}(\hat{\mathscr{B}}_n^{(3)} \geq c_n) = 1$. Here, we do not have to consider the absolute values of $\hat{\mathscr{B}}_n^{(2)}$ and $\hat{\mathscr{B}}_n^{(3)}$, as the sign of $T_*^2 + 2T_* - 2D_*$ or of $D_*^2 + 2T_* - 2D_*$ cannot be negative. A two-sided test is therefore inappropriate in general.

Furthermore, we can compare the global powers of the tests using the power properties. First, we compare $\hat{\mathscr{B}}_n^{(2)}$ with $\hat{\mathscr{B}}_n^{(3)}$. The leading term of $\hat{\mathscr{B}}_n^{(2)}$ diverges more rapidly than $\hat{\mathscr{B}}_n^{(3)}$ if and only if $|T_*| > |D_*|$. Second, the leading term of $\hat{\mathscr{B}}_n^{(1)}$ diverges more rapidly than $\hat{\mathscr{B}}_n^{(3)}$ if and only if $\frac{k}{2}(T_*^2 + D_*^2) > D_*^2 + 2(T_* - D_*)$. Likewise, the leading term of $\hat{\mathscr{B}}_n^{(1)}$ diverges more rapidly than $\hat{\mathscr{B}}_n^{(2)}$ if and only if $\frac{k}{2}(T_*^2 + D_*^2) > T_*^2 + 2(T_* - D_*)$. From these aspects, it follows that the global powers of the tests are interrelated in $3!(=6)$ different ways.

- Condition A: $|T_*| \geq |D_*|$, $\frac{k}{2}(T_*^2 + D_*^2) \geq D_*^2 + 2(T_* - D_*)$, and $\frac{k}{2}(T_*^2 + D_*^2) \geq T_*^2 + 2(T_* - D_*)$;
- Condition B: $|T_*| \geq |D_*|$, $\frac{k}{2}(T_*^2 + D_*^2) \geq D_*^2 + 2(T_* - D_*)$, and $\frac{k}{2}(T_*^2 + D_*^2) \leq T_*^2 + 2(T_* - D_*)$;
- Condition C: $|T_*| \geq |D_*|$, $\frac{k}{2}(T_*^2 + D_*^2) \leq D_*^2 + 2(T_* - D_*)$, and $\frac{k}{2}(T_*^2 + D_*^2) \leq T_*^2 + 2(T_* - D_*)$;
- Condition D: $|T_*| \leq |D_*|$, $\frac{k}{2}(T_*^2 + D_*^2) \leq D_*^2 + 2(T_* - D_*)$, and $\frac{k}{2}(T_*^2 + D_*^2) \leq T^{*2} + 2(T_* - D_*)$;
- Condition E: $|T_*| \leq |D_*|$, $\frac{k}{2}(T_*^2 + D_*^2) \leq D_*^2 + 2(T_* - D_*)$, and $\frac{k}{2}(T_*^2 + D_*^2) \geq T_*^2 + 2(T_* - D_*)$;
- Condition F: $|T_*| \leq |D_*|$, $\frac{k}{2}(T_*^2 + D_*^2) \geq D_*^2 + 2(T_* - D_*)$, and $\frac{k}{2}(T_*^2 + D_*^2) \geq T_*^2 + 2(T_* - D_*)$.

Under different conditions, the tests behave differently. For example, if (T_*, D_*) satisfies Condition F, the leading term of $\hat{\mathscr{B}}_n^{(1)}$ is greater than those of $\hat{\mathscr{B}}_n^{(2)}$ and $\hat{\mathscr{B}}_n^{(3)}$, and the leading term of $\hat{\mathscr{B}}_n^{(3)}$ is greater than that of $\hat{\mathscr{B}}_n^{(2)}$. Thus, for $c_n = o(n)$, $\lim_{n\to\infty}\mathbb{P}\left(\hat{\mathscr{B}}_n^{(1)} \geq \hat{\mathscr{B}}_n^{(3)} + c_n \geq \hat{\mathscr{B}}_n^{(2)} + c_n\right) = 1$, or, for notational simplicity, we may denote this as $\hat{\mathscr{B}}_n^{(1)} \gtrsim \hat{\mathscr{B}}_n^{(3)} \gtrsim \hat{\mathscr{B}}_n^{(2)}$. Table 1 summarizes the global power relationships arranged by Conditions A–F.

Table 1. Global Power Relationships.

Conditions for (T_*, D_*)	Relationships
A	$\hat{\mathscr{B}}_n^{(2)} \gtrsim \hat{\mathscr{B}}_n^{(1)} \gtrsim \hat{\mathscr{B}}_n^{(3)}$
B	$\hat{\mathscr{B}}_n^{(1)} \gtrsim \hat{\mathscr{B}}_n^{(3)} \gtrsim \hat{\mathscr{B}}_n^{(2)}$
C	$\hat{\mathscr{B}}_n^{(2)} \gtrsim \hat{\mathscr{B}}_n^{(3)} \gtrsim \hat{\mathscr{B}}_n^{(1)}$
D	$\hat{\mathscr{B}}_n^{(3)} \gtrsim \hat{\mathscr{B}}_n^{(2)} \gtrsim \hat{\mathscr{B}}_n^{(1)}$
E	$\hat{\mathscr{B}}_n^{(3)} \gtrsim \hat{\mathscr{B}}_n^{(1)} \gtrsim \hat{\mathscr{B}}_n^{(2)}$
F	$\hat{\mathscr{B}}_n^{(1)} \gtrsim \hat{\mathscr{B}}_n^{(2)} \gtrsim \hat{\mathscr{B}}_n^{(3)}$

The table shows the power orders of $\hat{\mathscr{B}}_n^{(1)}$, $\hat{\mathscr{B}}_n^{(2)}$, and $\hat{\mathscr{B}}_n^{(3)}$ under Conditions A to F. These orders are obtained by the divergence rates of the test statistics given by Eqs. (6), (7), and (8). This implies that if the sample size is fairly large and (T_*,D_*) belongs to the region indexed by F, say, then $\hat{\mathscr{B}}_n^{(1)}$ is more powerful than $\hat{\mathscr{B}}_n^{(2)}$, and $\hat{\mathscr{B}}_n^{(3)}$ is more powerful than $\hat{\mathscr{B}}_n^{(3)}$.

These global power behaviors provide guidance for selecting better tests. From the given condition, $(\hat{T}_n - 1, \hat{D}_n - 1) \to (T_*, D_*)$ in probability, so that if $(\hat{T}_n - 1, \hat{D}_n - 1)$ satisfies Condition A, say, we should expect better power properties from $\hat{\mathscr{B}}_n^{(1)}$ than from the other tests. As another example, if $T_* = D_*$ under $\mathbb{H}_1$, Conditions A or F holds, and the others do not hold. This implies that $\hat{\mathscr{B}}_n^{(1)}$ or $\hat{\mathscr{B}}_n^{(2)}$ are globally most powerful.

The dimension of $\hat{\mathbf{A}}_n$ or $\hat{\mathbf{B}}_n$ also delivers various power properties. Fig. 1 shows how the space of (T_*,D_*) is partitioned into the regions satisfying Conditions A–F for $k=2$, 3, 4, 10, 20, and 50. For example, if (T_*,D_*) belongs to the region indexed by D, this implies that Condition D governs the data. Here, only the region below the 45-degree line is considered because T_* has to be greater than or equal to D_*. As we can see from Fig. 1, the regions governed by Conditions B, C, D, and E get smaller and eventually vanish to the origin as k tends to infinity. Most space is indexed by A or F. This fact implies that if $(\hat{T}_n, \hat{D}_n)$ is moderately different from the origin and the number of the dimension is fairly large, $\hat{\mathscr{B}}_n^{(1)}$ or $\hat{\mathscr{B}}_n^{(2)}$ delivers more powerful results. We can also see that the regions indexed by E and F are relatively smaller than other regions when k is small.

Now suppose that for some $d_*(\neq 1)$, $\mathbf{B}_* = d_*\mathbf{A}_*$. The definitions of $\hat{\mathscr{B}}_n^{(1)}$, $\hat{\mathscr{B}}_n^{(2)}$, and $\hat{\mathscr{B}}_n^{(3)}$, Lemma 4, and Corollary 1(ii) imply that

$$\hat{\mathscr{B}}_n^{(1)} = nk^2(d_* - 1)^2 + 2nk(d_* - 1)d_*\text{tr}[\mathbf{L}_n] + O_{\mathbb{P}}(1); \quad (9)$$

$$\hat{\mathscr{B}}_n^{(2)} = nk(d_* - 1)^2 + 2n(d_* - 1)d_*\text{tr}[\mathbf{L}_n] + O_{\mathbb{P}}(1); \quad \text{and} \quad (10)$$

$$\hat{\mathscr{B}}_n^{(3)} = nk(d_* - 1)^2 + 2n(d_* - 1)d_*\text{tr}[\mathbf{L}_n] + O_{\mathbb{P}}(1) \quad (11)$$

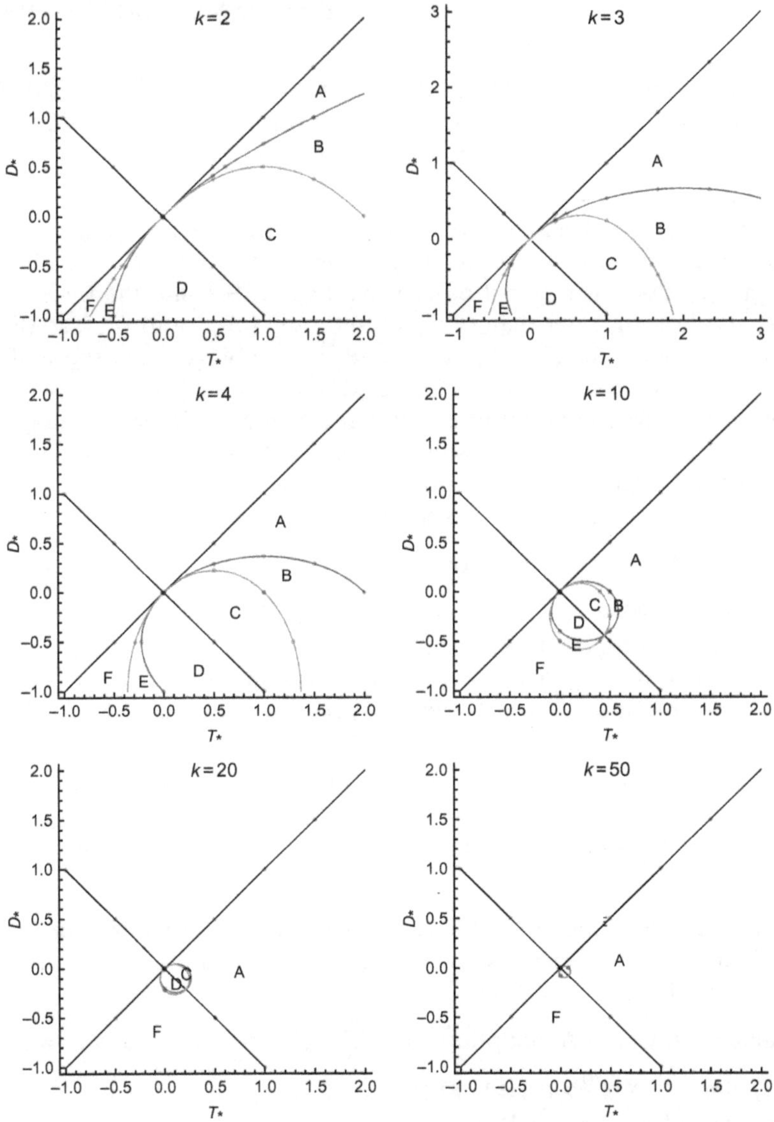

Fig. 1. Partitioned Space of (T_*, D_*). For $k = 2, 3, 4, 10, 20$, and 50, This Figure Shows the Space of (T_*, D_*) Partitioned by the Conditions A–F. For Example, if (T_*, D_*) Belongs to the Region Indexed by A, We Have that $\hat{\mathscr{B}}_n^{(2)} \gtrsim \hat{\mathscr{B}}_n^{(1)} \gtrsim \hat{\mathscr{B}}_n^{(3)}$ in Probability by Table 1. As Another Case, if (T_*, D_*) Belongs to the Region Indexed by B, We Have that $\hat{\mathscr{B}}_n^{(1)} \gtrsim \hat{\mathscr{B}}_n^{(3)} \gtrsim \hat{\mathscr{B}}_n^{(2)}$ in Probability by Table 1. We Also Observe that the Number of Parameters (k) Matters in Partitioning the Space of (T_*, D_*). As k Tends to Infinity, Most Space of (T_*, D_*) is Indexed by A and F.

Alternatively, we can also obtain these results from Eqs. (6), (7), and (8) by letting $\mathbf{B}_* = d_*\mathbf{A}_*$ for $d_* \neq 1$. The first terms on the right are $O(n)$, and the second are $O_{\mathbb{P}}(\sqrt{n})$. Thus, for any $c_n = o(n)$, $\lim_{n\to\infty}\mathbb{P}(\hat{\mathscr{B}}_n^{(2)} \geq c_n) = 1$ and $\lim_{n\to\infty}\mathbb{P}(\hat{\mathscr{B}}_n^{(3)} \geq c_n) = 1$.

We can also compare the global powers of the tests in a similar manner to the general case. First, the leading terms of $\hat{\mathscr{B}}_n^{(2)}$ and $\hat{\mathscr{B}}_n^{(3)}$ are identical. This implies that their global powers are similar. Second, the leading term of $\hat{\mathscr{B}}_n^{(1)}$ is always greater than or equal to those of $\hat{\mathscr{B}}_n^{(2)}$ and $\hat{\mathscr{B}}_n^{(3)}$, so that we can always expect the global power of $\hat{\mathscr{B}}_n^{(1)}$ to be bigger than those of $\hat{\mathscr{B}}_n^{(2)}$ and $\hat{\mathscr{B}}_n^{(3)}$. Thus, we obtain that $\lim_{n\to\infty}\mathbb{P}(\hat{\mathscr{B}}_n^{(1)} \geq \max\,[\hat{\mathscr{B}}_n^{(2)}, \hat{\mathscr{B}}_n^{(3)}] + c_n) = 1$. When there is additional information that for some d_*, $\mathbf{B}_* = d_*\mathbf{A}_*$ (e.g., conditional homoskedasticity in testing correct model specification), the testing results of $\hat{\mathscr{B}}_n^{(1)}$ should be more valuable than the other tests.

We summarize these results as follows.

Theorem 3. Given Assumptions 1, 2, 3, 4, 5, and $\mathbb{H}_1$, for any $c_n = o(n)$,

(i) $\lim_{n\to\infty}\mathbb{P}(\hat{\mathscr{B}}_n^{(i)} \geq c_n) = 1$, where $i = 1,2$, and 3; and

(ii) when for all $d > 0$, $\mathbf{B}_* \neq d\mathbf{A}_*$,

(ii.a) $\lim_{n\to\infty}\mathbb{P}(\hat{\mathscr{B}}_n^{(2)} \geq \hat{\mathscr{B}}_n^{(3)} + c_n) = 1$ if and only if $|T_*| > |D_*|$;

(ii.b) $\lim_{n\to\infty}\mathbb{P}(\hat{\mathscr{B}}_n^{(1)} \geq \hat{\mathscr{B}}_n^{(2)} + c_n) = 1$ if and only if $(\frac{k}{2} - 1)T_*^2 + \frac{k}{2}D_*^2 - 2(T_* - D_*) > 0$;

(ii.c) $\lim_{n\to\infty}\mathbb{P}(\hat{\mathscr{B}}_n^{(1)} \geq \hat{\mathscr{B}}_n^{(3)} + c_n) = 1$ if and only if $(\frac{k}{2} - 1)D_*^2 + \frac{k}{2}T_*^2 - 2(T_* - D_*) > 0$;

(iii) when for some $d_* > 0$, $\mathbf{B}_* = d_*\mathbf{A}_*$, $\lim_{n\to\infty}\mathbb{P}(\hat{\mathscr{B}}_n^{(1)} \geq \max[\hat{\mathscr{B}}_n^{(2)}, \hat{\mathscr{B}}_n^{(3)}] + c_n) = 1$. □

The results are similar for the case when the estimators are sample covariance matrices: for the case in which $\tilde{\mathbf{A}}_n$ and $\tilde{\mathbf{B}}_n$ are sample covariance matrices, we have

Theorem 4. Given Assumptions A1, A2, A3, and $\mathbb{H}_1$, for any $c_n = o(n)$,

(i) $\lim_{n\to\infty}\mathbb{P}(\tilde{\mathscr{B}}_n^{(i)} \geq c_n) = 1$, where $i = 1,2,3$;

(ii) when for all $d > 0$, $\mathbf{B}_* \neq d\mathbf{A}_*$,

(ii.a) $\lim_{n\to\infty}\mathbb{P}(\tilde{\mathscr{B}}_n^{(2)} \geq \tilde{\mathscr{B}}_n^{(3)} + c_n) = 1$ if and only if $|T_*| > |D_*|$;

(ii.b) $\lim_{n\to\infty}\mathbb{P}(\tilde{\mathscr{B}}_n^{(1)} \geq \tilde{\mathscr{B}}_n^{(2)} + c_n) = 1$ if and only if $(\frac{k}{2} - 1)T_*^2 + \frac{k}{2}D_*^2 - 2(T_* - D_*) > 0$;

(ii.c) $\lim_{n\to\infty}\mathbb{P}(\tilde{\mathscr{B}}_n^{(1)} \geq \tilde{\mathscr{B}}_n^{(3)} + c_n) = 1$ if and only if $(\frac{k}{2} - 1)D_*^2 + \frac{k}{2}T_*^2 - 2(T_* - D_*) > 0$;

(iii) when for some $d_* > 0$, $\mathbf{B}_* = d_*\mathbf{A}_*$, $\lim_{n\to\infty}\mathbb{P}(\tilde{\mathscr{B}}_n^{(1)} \geq \max\left[\tilde{\mathscr{B}}_n^{(2)}, \tilde{\mathscr{B}}_n^{(3)}\right] + c_n) = 1$. □

Because we explained earlier the key idea of Theorem 3 and because the proof of Theorem 4 closely parallels that of Theorem 3, we omit their proofs from the appendix.

3.3. Asymptotic Behavior under the Local Alternative

The tests we consider here are consistent under the alternative as we analyzed in the previous subsection. Their local powers, which we consider in this subsection, can be similarly analyzed.

There can be many local alternatives to the null hypothesis. An analytically convenient local alternative is constructed by letting $\mathbf{B}_{*,n}$ approach $\mathbf{A}_*$. To keep our presentation concise, we consider the following Pitman type local alternative:

$$\mathbb{H}_a^{(1)} : \mathbf{B}_{*,n} = \mathbf{B}_* + n^{-1/2}\overline{\mathbf{B}}_* \quad \text{and} \quad \mathbf{B}_* = \mathbf{A}_*$$

where $\overline{\mathbf{B}}_* := \overline{\mathbf{B}}(\boldsymbol{\theta}_*)$, and $\overline{\mathbf{B}}(\cdot)$ is a continuously differentiable function of $\boldsymbol{\theta}$. That is, $\overline{\mathbf{B}} : \Theta \mapsto \mathbb{R}^{k\times k}$. If $\overline{\mathbf{B}}_* = \mathbf{0}$, the local alternative $\mathbb{H}_a^{(1)}$ reduces to the null hypothesis. Therefore, as n tends to infinity, $\mathbf{B}_{*,n}$ approaches $\mathbf{B}_*$, and the two matrices become identical.

The motivation for considering $\mathbb{H}_a^{(1)}$ is that it has a simple form. Our statistics defined by $\hat{T}_n$, $\hat{D}_n$, and $\hat{S}_n$ have the core element $\mathbf{B}_{*,n}\mathbf{A}_*^{-1}$ under $\mathbb{H}_a^{(1)}$, and this feature simplifies the analysis of $\mathbf{B}_{*,n}\mathbf{A}_*^{-1}$ without losing the insights of the tests. If we had considered the following local alternative:

$$\mathbb{H}_a^{(2)} : \mathbf{A}_{*,n} = \mathbf{A}_* + n^{-1/2}\overline{\mathbf{A}}_* \quad \text{and} \quad \mathbf{B}_* = \mathbf{A}_*$$

where $\overline{\mathbf{A}}_* := \overline{\mathbf{A}}(\boldsymbol{\theta}_*)$ and $\overline{\mathbf{A}} : \Theta \mapsto \mathbb{R}^{k\times k}$, the analysis becomes more complicated. This also implies that there are many local alternatives other than $\mathbb{H}_a^{(1)}$, and they can be used to examine the local powers of the tests in other directions.

Before examining the asymptotic behaviors of $\hat{T}_n$, $\hat{D}_n$, and $\hat{S}_n$ under $\mathbb{H}_a^{(1)}$, we first fix our ideas by defining notations relevant to our discussions. We let $\mathbf{W}_{o,n} := \mathbf{B}_*^{-1}(\mathbf{B}_n - \mathbf{B}_{*,n})$, which is identical to $\mathbf{A}_*^{-1}(\mathbf{B}_n - \mathbf{B}_{*,n})$ under $\mathbb{H}_a^{(1)}$:

$$\mathbf{M}_{o,n} := \mathbf{W}_{o,n} - \mathbf{U}_n$$

$$\mathbf{K}_{o,n} := \mathbf{M}_{o,n} + \sum_{j=1}^{l} \left(\hat{\theta}_{j,n} - \theta_{j,*}\right) \mathbf{S}_{j,*}$$

$$\mathbf{J}_{j,o,n} := \mathbf{G}_{j,o,n} - \mathbf{H}_{j,n} := \mathbf{B}_*^{-1} \partial_j (\mathbf{B}_n - \mathbf{B}_{*,n}) - \mathbf{H}_{j,n}$$

$$\begin{aligned} \hat{T}_{o,n} :=& \frac{1}{k} \mathrm{tr}\left[\boldsymbol{K}_{o,n}(\mathbf{I} - \mathbf{U}_n)\right] + \frac{1}{k}\left[\mathrm{tr}\left[\mathbf{J}_{j,o,n} - \mathbf{M}_{o,n}\mathbf{A}_*^{-1}\partial_j \mathbf{A}_*\right]\right]'(\hat{\boldsymbol{\theta}}_n - \boldsymbol{\theta}_*) \\ &+ \frac{1}{2k}(\hat{\boldsymbol{\theta}}_n - \boldsymbol{\theta}_*)' \nabla_{\boldsymbol{\theta}}^2 \mathrm{tr}[\mathbf{D}_*](\hat{\boldsymbol{\theta}}_n - \boldsymbol{\theta}_*) \end{aligned}$$

$$\begin{aligned} \hat{D}_{o,n} :=& \frac{1}{k}\mathrm{tr}\left[\mathbf{K}_{o,n}\right] + \frac{1}{2k}\left(\frac{1}{k} - 1\right)\mathrm{tr}[\mathbf{K}_{o,n}]^2 + \frac{1}{2k}\left(\mathrm{tr}[\mathbf{M}_{o,n}]^2 + \mathrm{tr}\left[\mathbf{U}_n^2\right] - \mathrm{tr}\left[\mathbf{W}_{o,n}^2\right]\right) \\ &+ \frac{1}{k}\left[\mathrm{tr}\left[\mathbf{J}_{j,o,n} + \mathbf{U}_n \mathbf{A}_*^{-1}\partial_j \mathbf{A}_* - \mathbf{W}_{o,n}\mathbf{A}_*^{-1}\partial_j \mathbf{B}_*\right]\right]'(\hat{\boldsymbol{\theta}}_n - \boldsymbol{\theta}_*) \\ &+ \frac{1}{k}\left[\mathrm{tr}\left[\mathbf{M}_{o,n}\right]\mathrm{tr}\left[\mathbf{S}_{j,*}\right]\right]'(\hat{\boldsymbol{\theta}}_n - \boldsymbol{\theta}_*) + \frac{1}{2k}(\hat{\boldsymbol{\theta}}_n - \boldsymbol{\theta}_*)'\nabla_{\boldsymbol{\theta}}^2 \det[\mathbf{D}_*](\hat{\boldsymbol{\theta}}_n - \boldsymbol{\theta}_*) \end{aligned}$$

$$\begin{aligned} \hat{S}_{o,n} :=& -\frac{1}{2k}\left(\frac{1}{k} - 1\right)\mathrm{tr}[\mathbf{K}_{o,n}]^2 - \frac{1}{2k}\left(\mathrm{tr}[\mathbf{M}_{o,n}]^2 - \mathrm{tr}\left[\mathbf{M}_{o,n}^2\right]\right) \\ &+ \frac{1}{k}\mathrm{tr}[\mathbf{M}_{o,n}\sum_{j=1}^{l}(\hat{\theta}_{j,n} - \theta_{j,*})\mathbf{S}_{j,*}] - \frac{1}{k}\mathrm{tr}\left[\mathbf{M}_{o,n}\right]\mathrm{tr}\left[\sum_{j=1}^{l}(\hat{\theta}_{j,n} - \theta_{j,*})\mathbf{S}_{j,*}\right] \\ &+ \frac{1}{2k}\mathrm{tr}\left[\left(\sum_{j=1}^{l}(\hat{\theta}_{j,n} - \theta_{j,*})\mathbf{S}_{j,*}\right)^2\right] - \frac{1}{2k}\mathrm{tr}\left[\sum_{j=1}^{l}(\hat{\theta}_{j,n} - \theta_{j,*})\mathbf{S}_{j,*}\right]^2 \end{aligned}$$

Note that they are identical to the previous statistics if $\overline{\mathbf{B}}_* = \mathbf{0}$. All these statistics are defined to capture the local asymptotic behaviors of the previous statistics. Mainly, their difference stems from that the key parameter of interest is not $\mathbf{B}_*$ but $\mathbf{B}_{*,n}$, so that it is now $\sqrt{n}(\mathbf{B}_n - \mathbf{B}_{*,n})$ that obeys the CLT asymptotically.

We formally impose the following assumptions.

Assumption 6. (i) There are symmetric matrix estimators $\mathbf{A}_n(\cdot)$ and $\mathbf{B}_n(\cdot)$ consistent for $\mathbf{A}(\cdot)$ and $\mathbf{B}(\cdot)$, respectively, uniformly on Θ; and

(ii) $\sqrt{n}[(\hat{\boldsymbol{\theta}}_n - \boldsymbol{\theta}_*)', \text{vech}[\mathbf{A}_n - \mathbf{A}_*]', \text{vech}[\mathbf{B}_n - \mathbf{B}_{*,n}]']' \overset{A}{\sim} N(\mathbf{0}, \boldsymbol{\Omega}_*)$, where $\mathbf{A}_n := \mathbf{A}_n(\boldsymbol{\theta}_*)$, $\mathbf{B}_n := \mathbf{B}_n(\boldsymbol{\theta}_*)$, and $\boldsymbol{\Omega}_*$ is a $(k^2 + k + l) \times (k^2 + k + l)$ positive semi-definite matrix. □

Assumption 7. For $j = 1, \ldots, l$, $\mathbf{H}_{j,n} = O_{\mathbb{P}}(n^{-1/2})$ and $\mathbf{G}_{j,o,n} = O_{\mathbb{P}}(n^{-1/2})$. □

Assumption 8. The symmetric mapping $\overline{\mathbf{B}} : \Theta \mapsto \mathbb{R}^{k \times k}$ is in $\mathscr{C}^{(1)}(\Theta)$ and is such that $\overline{\mathbf{B}}_* := \overline{\mathbf{B}}(\boldsymbol{\theta}_*)$ is positive definite. □

Assumptions 6 and 7 are provided to replace Assumptions 3 and 5, respectively. We replaced the key parameter $\mathbf{B}_*$ with $\mathbf{B}_{*,n}$, so that we can expect $\mathbf{W}_{o,n}$, $\mathbf{M}_{o,n}$, $\mathbf{K}_{o,n}$, $\mathbf{J}_{j,o,n}$, $\hat{T}_{o,n}$, $\hat{D}_{o,n}$, and $\hat{S}_{o,n}$ under $\mathbb{H}_a^{(1)}$ to have asymptotic behaviors identical to those of $\mathbf{W}_n$, $\mathbf{M}_n$, $\mathbf{K}_n$, $\mathbf{J}_{j,n}$, $\hat{T}_n$, $\hat{D}_n$, and $\hat{S}_n$ under $\mathbb{H}_0$, respectively. Therefore, all of them are $O_{\mathbb{P}}(n^{-1/2})$ under $\mathbb{H}_a^{(1)}$. Furthermore, Assumption 8 is added to endow the local parameter $\overline{\mathbf{B}}_*$ with an appropriate structure of positive definiteness.

The following lemma shows the asymptotic expansions of the statistics under the local alternative.

Lemma 5. Given Assumptions 1, 2, 4, 6, 7, 8, and $\mathbb{H}_a^{(1)}$

(i)

$$\hat{T}_n = \hat{T}_{o,n} + \frac{1}{\sqrt{n}k}\{\text{tr}[\mathbf{N}_*] - \text{tr}[\mathbf{N}_*\mathbf{U}_n] + [\text{tr}[\mathbf{A}_*^{-1}(\partial_j\overline{\mathbf{B}}_*) - \mathbf{N}_*\mathbf{A}_*^{-1}(\partial_j\mathbf{A}_*)]]'(\hat{\boldsymbol{\theta}}_n - \boldsymbol{\theta}_*)\}$$
$$+ o_{\mathbb{P}}(n^{-1})$$

where $\mathbf{N}_* := \mathbf{B}_*^{-1}\overline{\mathbf{B}}_*$;

(ii)

$$\hat{D}_n = \hat{D}_{o,n} + \frac{1}{\sqrt{n}k}\{\text{tr}[\mathbf{N}_*] - \text{tr}[\mathbf{N}_*\mathbf{W}_{o,n}] + [\text{tr}[\mathbf{C}_{j,*}]]'(\hat{\boldsymbol{\theta}}_n - \boldsymbol{\theta}_*)\}$$
$$+ \frac{1}{\sqrt{n}k^2}\text{tr}[\mathbf{N}_*]\text{tr}[\mathbf{K}_{o,n}] - \frac{1}{2nk}\text{tr}[\mathbf{N}_*^2] + \frac{1}{2nk^2}\text{tr}[\mathbf{N}_*]^2 + o_{\mathbb{P}}(n^{-1})$$

where $\mathbf{C}_{j,*} := \mathbf{B}_*^{-1}\partial_j\overline{\mathbf{B}}_* - \mathbf{N}_*\mathbf{B}_*^{-1}(\partial_j\mathbf{B}_*)$; and

(iii)

$$\hat{S}_n = \hat{S}_{o,n} + \frac{1}{\sqrt{n}k}\{\text{tr}[\mathbf{N}_*\mathbf{M}_{o,n}] + [\text{tr}[\mathbf{N}_*\mathbf{S}_{j,*}]]'(\hat{\boldsymbol{\theta}}_n - \boldsymbol{\theta}_*)\}$$
$$- \frac{1}{\sqrt{n}k^2}\text{tr}[\mathbf{N}_*]\text{tr}[\mathbf{K}_{o,n}] + \frac{1}{2nk}\text{tr}[\mathbf{N}_*^2] - \frac{1}{2nk^2}\text{tr}[\mathbf{N}_*]^2 + o_{\mathbb{P}}(n^{-1})$$

□

Proving Lemma 5 is not difficult. Using Lemma 4 and the expansion that $(\mathbf{I}-n^{-1/2}\mathbf{B}_*^{-1}(-\overline{\mathbf{B}}_*))^{-1}=\mathbf{I}-n^{-1/2}\mathbf{B}_*^{-1}\overline{\mathbf{B}}_*+n^{-1}\mathbf{B}_*^{-1}\overline{\mathbf{B}}_*\mathbf{B}_*^{-1}\overline{\mathbf{B}}_*+\ldots$ provides the proof of Lemma 5. Here, this expansion is applicable because for sufficiently large n, $\|n^{-1/2}\mathbf{B}_*^{-1}(-\overline{\mathbf{B}}_*)\|<1$.

The local asymptotic behaviors of the statistics in Lemma 5 are not identical. Lemmas 5(i and ii) imply that $\sqrt{n}k\hat{T}_n=\mathrm{tr}[\mathbf{N}_*]+O_{\mathbb{P}}(1)$ and $\sqrt{n}k\hat{D}_n=\mathrm{tr}[\mathbf{N}_*]+O_{\mathbb{P}}(1)$, whereas $2nk^2\hat{S}_n=k\mathrm{tr}[\mathbf{N}_*^2]-\mathrm{tr}[\mathbf{N}_*]^2+O_{\mathbb{P}}(1)$ by Lemma 5(iii). Using these features, we derive the following theorem.

Theorem 5. Given Assumptions 1, 2, 4, 6, 7, 8, and $\mathbb{H}_a^{(1)}$,

(i) $\hat{\mathscr{B}}_n^{(1)}=\mathrm{tr}[\mathbf{N}_*+\sqrt{n}\mathbf{K}_{o,n}]^2+o_{\mathbb{P}}(1)$;
(ii) $\hat{\mathscr{B}}_n^{(2)}=\mathrm{tr}[(\mathbf{N}_*+\sqrt{n}\mathbf{K}_{o,n})^2]+o_{\mathbb{P}}(1)$; and
(iii) $\hat{\mathscr{B}}_n^{(3)}=\mathrm{tr}[(\mathbf{N}_*+\sqrt{n}\mathbf{K}_{o,n})^2]+o_{\mathbb{P}}(1)$ □

We note that Theorem 1 can also be derived from Theorem 5 if we let $\overline{\mathbf{B}}_*=\mathbf{0}$. In addition, the local parameter $\mathbf{N}_*$ is added to $\sqrt{n}\mathbf{K}_{o,n}$ as a location parameter. Theorem 5 further implies that the local power of $\hat{\mathscr{B}}_n^{(1)}$ is not automatically acquired. The product of two positive-definite matrices is not necessarily positive definite, so that $\mathbf{N}_*:=\mathbf{B}_*^{-1}\overline{\mathbf{B}}_*$ can have $\mathrm{tr}[\mathbf{N}_*]=0$, implying that $\hat{\mathscr{B}}_n^{(1)}$ may not have local power for such a case. Similarly, if $\mathrm{tr}[\mathbf{N}_*^2]=0$, $\hat{\mathscr{B}}_n^{(2)}$ and $\hat{\mathscr{B}}_n^{(3)}$ do not have local powers, either. For them to have their local powers, it is necessary to have $\mathrm{tr}[\mathbf{N}_*]\neq 0$ and $\mathrm{tr}[\mathbf{N}_*^2]\neq 0$.

When $\tilde{\mathbf{A}}_n$ and $\tilde{\mathbf{B}}_n$ are sample covariance matrices, we have

Corollary 2. Given Assumptions A1, A2, A4, A5, and $\mathbb{H}_a^{(1)}$,

(i) $\tilde{\mathscr{B}}_n^{(1)}=\mathrm{tr}[(\mathbf{N}_*+\sqrt{n}\tilde{\mathbf{M}}_{o,n})]^2+o_{\mathbb{P}}(1)$;
(ii) $\tilde{\mathscr{B}}_n^{(2)}=\mathrm{tr}[(\mathbf{N}_*+\sqrt{n}\tilde{\mathbf{M}}_{o,n})^2]+o_{\mathbb{P}}(1)$; and
(iii) $\tilde{\mathscr{B}}_n^{(3)}=\mathrm{tr}[(\mathbf{N}_*+\sqrt{n}\tilde{\mathbf{M}}_{o,n})^2]+o_{\mathbb{P}}(1)$ and $\tilde{\mathscr{B}}_n^{(2)}-\tilde{\mathscr{B}}_n^{(3)}=o_{\mathbb{P}}(1)$, where $\tilde{\mathbf{M}}_{o,n}:=\mathbf{A}_*^{-1}(\tilde{\mathbf{B}}_n-\mathbf{B}_{*,n})-\mathbf{A}_*^{-1}(\tilde{\mathbf{A}}_n-\mathbf{A}_*)$. □

As before, $\tilde{\mathbf{M}}_{o,n}$ replaces $\mathbf{K}_{o,n}$ because $\hat{\boldsymbol{\theta}}_n$ no longer plays an explicit role. The referenced regularity conditions are in the appendix. As the proof of Corollary 2 is parallel to that of Theorem 5, we omit it from the appendix.

3.4. The Trace-Determinant Tests and the Likelihood Ratio Tests

In this section, we consider how the trace-determinant tests are associated with the LR test statistic under the local alternative. The LR test statistic gives reasonable power in all directions under the local alternative, and it is uniformly most powerful under some restrictive assumptions (e.g., proposition 15.2 of van der Vaart, 2000). This motivates us to compare the trace-determinant test statistics with the LR test statistic.

For the purpose of comparison, we first assume a particular distribution. Specifically, an independently and identically distributed (IID) multivariate normal random variable is assumed. We assume this because the LR test can be easily computed for the equality of two matrices. In particular, the normal distribution condition enables the LR test to be associated with the trace and determinant tests. As it turns out, our tests can be reformulated into a test which is asymptotically equivalent to the LR test.

We consider two different null hypotheses to examine the LR test. First, Nagao (1967) and Nagarsenker and Pillai (1973) tested whether the covariance matrix is equal to a specified matrix under the same data condition. We exploit their results to examine the LR test. Second, Mauchly (1940) assumed a similar condition to ours and examined the LR statistic to test whether the covariance matrix of the random variable is a diagonal matrix with the same diagonal elements. We consider the LR test under the same condition and examine how the LR test is associated with our test statistics.

Before investigating the LR test, we first define statistics relevant to our investigations and provide their asymptotic behaviors under the local alternative. We first let $\hat{Q}_n := \ln[\mathrm{tr}[\hat{\mathbf{D}}_n]/k]$ and $\hat{L}_n := \ln[\det(\hat{\mathbf{D}}_n)]/k$. They are the logarithms of the trace and the determinant, respectively, so that $\hat{T}_n$ and $\hat{D}_n$ now correspond to $\hat{Q}_n$ and $\hat{L}_n$, respectively. We next let $\hat{W}_n := \hat{Q}_n - \hat{L}_n$ and $\hat{M}_n := \hat{T}_n - \hat{L}_n$. The motivations of these statistics are identical to $\hat{S}_n$. As the same roles are played by $\hat{Q}_n$ and $\hat{T}_n$, we are able to define two different test statistics with identical roles. The following lemma provides their asymptotic behaviors under the local alternative.

Lemma 6. Given Assumptions 1, 2, 4, 6, 7, 8, and $\mathbb{H}_a^{(1)}$,

(i)
$$\hat{L}_n = \frac{1}{\sqrt{nk}}\mathrm{tr}[\mathbf{N}_*] - \frac{1}{\sqrt{nk}}\mathrm{tr}\left[\mathbf{N}_*\mathbf{W}_{o,n}\right] + \frac{1}{\sqrt{nk}}\left[\mathrm{tr}\left[\mathbf{C}_{j,*}\right]\right]'(\hat{\boldsymbol{\theta}}_n - \boldsymbol{\theta}_*)$$
$$- \frac{1}{2nk}\mathrm{tr}\left[\mathbf{N}_*^2\right] - \frac{1}{2k^2}\mathrm{tr}\left[\mathbf{K}_{o,n}\right]^2 + \hat{D}_{o,n} + o_{\mathbb{P}}(n^{-1});$$

(ii)
$$\hat{Q}_n = \frac{1}{\sqrt{nk}}\mathrm{tr}[\mathbf{N}_*] - \frac{1}{\sqrt{nk}}\mathrm{tr}[\mathbf{N}_*\mathbf{U}_n] + \frac{1}{\sqrt{nk}}\left[\mathrm{tr}\left[\mathbf{A}_*^{-1}\partial_j\overline{\mathbf{B}}_* - \mathbf{N}_*\mathbf{A}_*^{-1}\partial_j\mathbf{A}_*\right]\right]'(\hat{\boldsymbol{\theta}}_n - \boldsymbol{\theta}_*)$$
$$- \frac{1}{2nk}\mathrm{tr}\left[\mathbf{N}_*^2\right] - \frac{1}{2k^2}\mathrm{tr}[\mathbf{K}_{o,n}]^2 - \frac{1}{\sqrt{nk^2}}\mathrm{tr}[\mathbf{N}_*]\mathrm{tr}\left[\mathbf{K}_{o,n}\right] + \hat{T}_{o,n} + o_{\mathbb{P}}(n^{-1});$$

(iii) $\hat{M}_n = \frac{1}{2nk}\mathrm{tr}\left[\left(\mathbf{N}_* + \sqrt{n}\mathbf{K}_{o,n}\right)^2\right] + + o_{\mathbb{P}}(n^{-1})$; and

(iv) $\hat{W}_n = \frac{1}{2nk}\mathrm{tr}\left[\left(\mathbf{N}_* + \sqrt{n}\mathbf{K}_{o,n}\right)^2\right] - \frac{1}{2nk^2}\mathrm{tr}\left[\mathbf{N}_* + \sqrt{n}\mathbf{K}_{o,n}\right]^2 + o_{\mathbb{P}}(n^{-1})$. □

Proving Lemma 6 is straightforward. We note that $\hat{L}_n = \ln[\hat{D}_n + 1]$ and $\hat{Q}_n = \ln[\hat{T}_n + 1]$, and Lemma 5 already provided the asymptotic behaviors of $\hat{D}_n$ and $\hat{T}_n$. We exploit them to prove Lemma 6(i and ii). The asymptotic behaviors of $\hat{M}_n$ and $\hat{W}_n$ are obtained by combining these results with Lemma 5(i and ii). The statistics $\hat{M}_n$ and $\hat{W}_n$ form the expansion of the LR statistic as we detail below.

In this section, we also provide assumptions distinct from those in the previous section.

Assumption 9. $\{\mathbf{X}_t \in \mathbb{R}^k\}$ is a set of IID multivariate normal random variables such that $\mathbf{X}_t \sim N(\boldsymbol{\theta}_*, \mathbf{B}_*)$ such that $\boldsymbol{\theta}_* \in \mathbb{R}^k$. □

Here, it follows that $k = l$ by the normal distribution condition. Although this assumption is too strong for general data and we can easily generalize the assumption, we stick to this condition so that a direct comparison of the tests can be made in a straightforward manner. Given Assumption 9, if we let $L_n(\boldsymbol{\theta}, \mathbf{B})$ be the likelihood, the ML estimator is

$$\hat{\boldsymbol{\theta}}_n := \frac{1}{n}\sum_{t=1}^{n}\mathbf{X}_t \quad \text{and} \quad \hat{\mathbf{B}}_n := \frac{1}{n}\sum_{t=1}^{n}(\mathbf{X}_t - \hat{\boldsymbol{\theta}}_n)(\mathbf{X}_t - \hat{\boldsymbol{\theta}}_n)'$$

and the maximum-likelihood is obtained as $L_n(\hat{\boldsymbol{\theta}}_n, \hat{\mathbf{B}}_n) = (2\pi)^{-nk/2}(\det[\hat{\mathbf{B}}_n])^{-n/2}\exp(-nk/2)$. In addition to this, we further impose the following assumption on an estimator $\hat{\mathbf{A}}_n$.

Assumption 10. (i) There is a symmetric matrix estimator $\mathbf{A}_n(\cdot)$ consistent for $\mathbf{A}(\cdot)$ uniformly on Θ;

(ii) the symmetric matrix mapping $\mathbf{A} : \Theta \mapsto \mathbb{R}^{k \times k}$ is in $\mathscr{C}^{(2)}(\Theta)$ and is such that $\mathbf{A}_* := \mathbf{A}(\boldsymbol{\theta}_*)$ is positive definite;

(iii) for $j = 1, \ldots, l$, $\partial_j \mathbf{A}_n(\cdot)$ is consistent for $\partial_j \mathbf{A}(\cdot)$ uniformly on Θ;

(iv) for $i, j = 1, \ldots, l$, $\partial^2_{ji}\mathbf{A}_n(\cdot)$ is consistent for $\partial^2_{ji}\mathbf{A}(\cdot)$;

(v) for $j = 1, \ldots, l$, $\mathbf{H}_{j,n} = O_{\mathbb{P}}(n^{-1/2})$;

(vi) $\sqrt{n}[(\hat{\boldsymbol{\theta}}_n - \boldsymbol{\theta}_*)', \mathrm{vech}[\mathbf{A}_n - \mathbf{A}_*]', \mathrm{vech}[\mathbf{B}_n - \mathbf{B}_{*,n}]']' \overset{A}{\sim} N(\mathbf{0}, \boldsymbol{\Omega}_*)$, where $\mathbf{A}_n := \mathbf{A}_n(\boldsymbol{\theta}_*)$, $\mathbf{B}_n := \mathbf{B}_n(\boldsymbol{\theta}_*)$, and $\boldsymbol{\Omega}_*$ is a $(k^2 + k + l) \times (k^2 + k + l)$ positive semi-definite matrix; and

(vii) The symmetric mapping $\overline{\mathbf{B}} : \Theta \mapsto \mathbb{R}^{k \times k}$ is in $\mathscr{C}^{(1)}(\Theta)$ and is such that $\overline{\mathbf{B}}_* := \overline{\mathbf{B}}(\boldsymbol{\theta}_*)$ is positive definite. □

The conditions in Assumption 10 are virtually identical assumptions on $\hat{\mathbf{A}}_n$ in the previous sections. We slightly modified the structure to fit Assumption 9.

When testing the unknown covariance matrix $\boldsymbol{B}_*$, we consider it to be identical to $\mathbf{A}_*$, which can be consistently estimated by $\hat{\mathbf{A}}_n$. That is, we are interested in testing $\mathbf{B}_* = \mathbf{A}_*$ as before, so that we are supposing the same environment as in Theorem 5.

Given this, the LR test can be easily obtained. If we let $L_n(\boldsymbol{\theta},\mathbf{B})$ be the likelihood, the maximum-likelihood constrained by $\mathbf{B} = \hat{\mathbf{A}}_n$ is obtained as $L_n(\hat{\boldsymbol{\theta}}_n, \hat{\mathbf{A}}_n) = (2\pi)^{-nk/2}(\det[\hat{\mathbf{A}}_n])^{-n/2}\exp\left(-\frac{nk}{2}\text{tr}\left[\hat{\mathbf{A}}_n^{-1}\hat{\mathbf{B}}_n\right]\right)$, and the LR test defined as $\mathscr{LR}_n^{(1)} := 2\{\ln[L_n(\hat{\boldsymbol{\theta}}_n, \hat{\mathbf{B}}_n)] - \ln[L_n(\hat{\boldsymbol{\theta}}_n, \hat{\mathbf{A}}_n)]\}$ has the following asymptotic behavior under the local alternative.

Theorem 6. Given Assumptions 9, 10, and $\mathbb{H}_a^{(1)}$,

(i) $\mathscr{LR}_n^{(1)} = \frac{1}{2}\text{tr}\left[(\mathbf{N}_* + \sqrt{n}\mathbf{K}_{o,n})^2\right] + o_{\mathbb{P}}(n^{-1})$;
(ii) $\mathscr{LR}_n^{(1)} = \frac{1}{2}\hat{\mathscr{B}}_n^{(2)} + o_{\mathbb{P}}(n^{-1})$; and
(iii) $\mathscr{LR}_n^{(1)} = \frac{1}{2}\hat{\mathscr{B}}_n^{(3)} + o_{\mathbb{P}}(n^{-1})$. □

Therefore, Theorem 6(*i*) implies that the LR test is asymptotically equivalent to $nk\hat{M}_n$ under the local alternative.

Mauchly (1940) tested the sphericity assumption under the same condition as above. That is, he tested whether for some d_*, $\mathbf{B}_* = d_*\mathbf{A}_*$. Here, $\mathbf{B}_*$, $\mathbf{A}_*$, and d_* are unknown, and $\mathbf{A}_*$ can be consistently estimated by $\hat{\mathbf{A}}_n$ as before, so that the relevant local alternative hypothesis is given as follows: for some d_*, $\mathbb{H}_a^{(s)} : \mathbf{B}_{*,n} = \mathbf{B}_* + n^{-1/2}\overline{\mathbf{B}}_*$ and $\mathbf{B}_* = d_*\mathbf{A}_*$.

The sphericity assumption can be associated with our test statistics, too. The constrained maximum-likelihood is obtained by maximizing $L_n(\boldsymbol{\theta}, d\hat{\mathbf{A}}_n)$ with respect to $\boldsymbol{\theta}$ and d, and it turns out equal to $L_n(\tilde{\boldsymbol{\theta}}_n, \tilde{d}_n\hat{\mathbf{A}}_n) = (2\pi)^{-nk/2}(\text{tr}[\hat{\mathbf{A}}_n^{-1}\hat{\mathbf{B}}_n]/k)^{-nk/2}(\det[\hat{\mathbf{A}}_n])^{-n/2}\exp(-nk/2)$, where $(\tilde{\boldsymbol{\theta}}_n, \tilde{d}_n)$ is the constrained ML estimator. Specifically, $(\tilde{\boldsymbol{\theta}}_n, \tilde{d}_n) = (\hat{\boldsymbol{\theta}}_n, \text{tr}\left[\hat{\mathbf{A}}_n^{-1}\hat{\mathbf{B}}_n\right]/k)$, and the LR test is obtained as $\mathscr{LR}_n^{(2)} := 2\{\ln[L_n(\hat{\boldsymbol{\theta}}_n, \hat{\mathbf{B}}_n)] - \ln[L_n(\tilde{\boldsymbol{\theta}}_n, \tilde{d}_n\hat{\mathbf{A}}_n)]\}$. The LR test has the following asymptotic behavior under the local alternative.

Theorem 7. Given Assumptions 9, 10, and $\mathbb{H}_a^{(s)}$,

(i) $\mathscr{LR}_n^{(2)} = \frac{1}{2}\left(\text{tr}\left[(\mathbf{N}_* + \sqrt{n}\mathbf{K}_{o,n})^2\right] - \frac{1}{k}\text{tr}\left[\mathbf{N}_* + \sqrt{n}\mathbf{K}_{o,n}\right]^2\right) + o_{\mathbb{P}}(n^{-1})$;
(ii) $\mathscr{LR}_n^{(2)} = \frac{1}{2}\left(\hat{\mathscr{B}}_n^{(2)} - \frac{1}{k}\hat{\mathscr{B}}_n^{(1)}\right) + o_{\mathbb{P}}(n^{-1})$; and
(iii) $\mathscr{LR}_n^{(2)} = \frac{1}{2}\left(\hat{\mathscr{B}}_n^{(3)} - \frac{1}{k}\hat{\mathscr{B}}_n^{(1)}\right) + o_{\mathbb{P}}(n^{-1})$. ■

Theorem 7(*i*) implies that the LR test is asymptotically equivalent to $nk\hat{W}_n$ under the local alternative.

We can see that the trace-determinant tests form the major components of the LR tests obtained under different circumstances from Theorems 6 and 7. They provide several further implications. First, the meanings of the trace-determinant tests become clear by using the LR test statistics. If we let $\mathscr{LR}_n^{(3)} := 2\{\ln[L_n(\tilde{\boldsymbol{\theta}}_n, \tilde{d}_n\hat{\mathbf{A}}_n)] - \ln[L_n(\tilde{\boldsymbol{\theta}}_n, \hat{\mathbf{A}}_n)]\}$, $\mathscr{LR}_n^{(1)} \equiv \mathscr{LR}_n^{(2)} + \mathscr{LR}_n^{(3)}$, and this implies that $\mathscr{LR}_n^{(1)}$ is the sum of $\mathscr{LR}_n^{(2)}$ and $\mathscr{LR}_n^{(3)}$ such that $\mathscr{LR}_n^{(3)}$ tests whether the sphericity parameter (d_*) is one. Second, the asymptotic behavior of $\mathscr{LR}_n^{(3)}$ is determined from this. That is, $\mathscr{LR}_n^{(3)} = \frac{1}{2k}\text{tr}\,[\mathbf{N}_* + \sqrt{n}\mathbf{K}_{o,n}]^2 + o_{\mathbb{P}}(n^{-1})$ under the local alternative, so that $\mathscr{LR}_n^{(3)} = \frac{1}{2k}\hat{\mathscr{B}}_n^{(1)} + o_{\mathbb{P}}(n^{-1})$. Finally, therefore, $\frac{1}{2}(\hat{\mathscr{B}}_n^{(2)} - \frac{1}{k}\hat{\mathscr{B}}_n^{(1)})$ or $\frac{1}{2}(\hat{\mathscr{B}}_n^{(3)} - \frac{1}{k}\hat{\mathscr{B}}_n^{(1)})$ tests the sphericity condition, and $\frac{1}{2k}\hat{\mathscr{B}}_n^{(1)}$ tests the sphericity parameter condition under the given conditions, so that testing the equal covariance matrix condition can be accomplished by summing the two test statistics: $\frac{1}{2}(\hat{\mathscr{B}}_n^{(2)} - \frac{1}{k}\hat{\mathscr{B}}_n^{(1)})$ and $\frac{1}{2k}\hat{\mathscr{B}}_n^{(1)}$; or $\frac{1}{2}(\hat{\mathscr{B}}_n^{(3)} - \frac{1}{k}\hat{\mathscr{B}}_n^{(1)})$ and $\frac{1}{2k}\hat{\mathscr{B}}_n^{(1)}$.

3.5. Implementation Considerations

The previous literature provides useful guidance for implementing our tests. As Taylor (1987) and Orme (1990), among others, have pointed out, the level distortions of the classical IMTs can be huge. A major reason for this is the ill-conditioning of the estimated asymptotic covariance matrix used to form the IMT (see, e.g., Golden et al., 2013). We may therefore expect that our test statistics will suffer from similar finite-sample level distortions. Chesher and Spady (1991) examined higher-order expansions of the IMT as a way to reduce the finite-sample level distortion. Their Monte Carlo experiments showed that these methods can work well. As Horowitz (1994) pointed out, however, this approach is extremely cumbersome because it requires use of higher-order cumulants, which differ from model to model. This suggests that higher-order approximations and methods that estimate an asymptotic covariance matrix should be avoided.

The parametric bootstrap proposed by Horowitz (1994) avoids both of these pitfalls, and, as Horowitz showed, gives tests with negligible finite-sample level distortions, even for small sample sizes and when the tests are non-pivotal. The parametric bootstrap is also appealing because it can deliver well-behaved asymptotic critical values for our statistics, despite their nonstandard asymptotic distributions and non-pivotal properties. Furthermore, the Monte Carlo experiments by Horowitz showed that powers obtained by the parametric bootstrap are very close to those obtained by correcting level distortions; on this fact, he suggested using the parametric bootstrap to compare powers of IMT statistics. In particular, the parametric bootstrap is appealing when comparing various IMTs, given that the maximum-likelihood-based approach is hard to apply to construct IMTs. Thus, we implement the parametric bootstrap to apply our tests.

The use of the parametric bootstrap is theoretically justified by the fact that the asymptotic approximations of $\hat{T}_n$, $\hat{D}_n$, and $\hat{S}_n$ are already derived. More specifically, Lemma 4 and Corollary 1 show that the distributions of $\hat{T}_n$, $\hat{D}_n$, and $\hat{S}_n$ are mainly determined by their own location parameters and $\mathbf{L}_n := \mathbf{B}_*^{-1}(\mathbf{B}_n - \mathbf{B}_*) - \mathbf{A}_*^{-1}(\mathbf{A}_n - \mathbf{A}_*) + \sum_{j=1}^{l}(\hat{\theta}_{j,n} - \theta_{j,*})\mathbf{R}_{j,*}$, which are zeros and $\mathbf{K}_n$, respectively, under $\mathbb{H}_0$. Furthermore, Assumption 3(ii) implies that $\mathbf{L}_n$ asymptotically follows a normal distribution, implying that the asymptotic distributions of $\hat{T}_n$, $\hat{D}_n$, and $\hat{S}_n$ are well defined under the null and are first-order correct. These observations, along with the arguments given by Horowitz (1994), justify use of the parametric bootstrap.

Although the parametric bootstrap is well known, we explain its procedure in order for our paper to be self-contained and to fix our test statistics. We proceed as follows:

1. Given the model $\mathcal{M} := \{f(\cdot|\cdot, \boldsymbol{\theta}) : \boldsymbol{\theta} \in \Theta\}$ for $\mathbf{Y}_t|\mathbf{X}_t$, obtain the (Q)MLE $\hat{\boldsymbol{\theta}}_n$ by maximizing $\mathrm{L}_n(\cdot)$ on $\boldsymbol{\Theta}$, where $L_n(\boldsymbol{\theta}) := n^{-1}\sum_{t=1}^{n} \ell_t(\boldsymbol{\theta})$ and $\ell_t(\boldsymbol{\theta}) := \log[f(\mathrm{Y}_t|\mathbf{X}_t, \boldsymbol{\theta})]$, with IID $\{(\mathrm{Y}_t, \mathbf{X}'_t)' \in \mathbb{R}^{1+d}\}$;
2. Estimate $\mathbf{A}_*$ and $\mathbf{B}_*$ as $\hat{\mathbf{A}}_n := -\nabla_{\boldsymbol{\theta}}^2 L_n(\hat{\boldsymbol{\theta}}_n)$ and $\hat{\mathbf{B}}_n := n^{-1}\sum_{t=1}^{n} \nabla_{\boldsymbol{\theta}}\ell_t(\hat{\boldsymbol{\theta}}_n)\nabla'_{\boldsymbol{\theta}}\ell_t(\hat{\boldsymbol{\theta}}_n)$. Using these, compute $\hat{\mathscr{B}}_n^{(1)}$, $\hat{\mathscr{B}}_n^{(2)}$, and $\hat{\mathscr{B}}_n^{(3)}$;
3. For each $\mathbf{X}_t$, generate B independent samples of Y_t^b from $f(\cdot|\mathbf{X}_t, \hat{\boldsymbol{\theta}}_n)$, yielding data sets $(Y_t^b, \mathbf{X}_t)$, $t = 1, 2, \ldots, n$, $b = 1, 2, \ldots, B$;
4. Form the bootstrap (Q)MLE $\hat{\boldsymbol{\theta}}_n^b$ by maximizing $L_n^b(\cdot) := n^{-1}\sum_{t=1}^{n} \ell_t^b(\cdot)$, where $\ell_t^b(\boldsymbol{\theta}) := \log[f(Y_t^b|\mathbf{X}_t, \boldsymbol{\theta})]$. Compute $\mathbf{A}_n^b := -\nabla_{\boldsymbol{\theta}}^2 L_n^b(\hat{\boldsymbol{\theta}}_n^b)$ and $\mathbf{B}_n^b := n^{-1}\sum_{t=1}^{n} \nabla_{\boldsymbol{\theta}}\ell_t^b(\hat{\boldsymbol{\theta}}_n^b)\nabla'_{\boldsymbol{\theta}}\ell_t^b(\hat{\boldsymbol{\theta}}_n^b)$, and use these to form test statistics $\mathscr{B}_n^{(1),b}$, $\mathscr{B}_n^{(2),b}$, and $\mathscr{B}_n^{(3),b}$;
5. Estimate p-values by $\hat{p}_n^{(1)} := B^{-1}\sum_{b=1}^{B} I(\mathscr{B}_n^{(1),b} \geq \hat{\mathscr{B}}_n^{(1)})$, $\hat{p}_n^{(2)} := B^{-1}\sum_{b=1}^{B} I(\mathscr{B}_n^{(2),b} \geq \hat{\mathscr{B}}_n^{(2)})$, and $\hat{p}_n^{(3)} := B^{-1}\sum_{b=1}^{B} I(\mathscr{B}_n^{(3),b} \geq \hat{\mathscr{B}}_n^{(3)})$, respectively.
6. If the estimated p-values are less than the prespecified level of significance, we reject the null; otherwise, we do not.

4. MONTE CARLO EXPERIMENTS

In this section, we examine the performance of our statistics when applied to a variety of parametric models, estimated by quasi-maximum-likelihood applied to IID data. We consider four different models: linear regression, exponential duration, probit, and Tobit.[2]

Our Monte Carlo experiments replicate the steps of the parametric bootstrap multiple times. When a test statistic, $\hat{\mathscr{B}}_n^{(1)}$, say, is evaluated using the parametric bootstrap, we also write this as $\hat{\mathscr{B}}_n^{(1,p)}$.

4.1. Linear Regression

Suppose that data are generated as

$$Y_t = \mathbf{X}'_t\boldsymbol{\beta}_* + U_t$$

where $U_t|\mathbf{X}_t \sim N(0,\sigma_*^2)$. We estimate the unknown $\boldsymbol{\beta}_*$ using the normal MLE with the typical model element $Y_t|\mathbf{X}_t \sim N(\mathbf{X}'_t\boldsymbol{\beta}, \sigma^2)$. We consider the case when $\mathbf{X}_t = (1,X_t)'$ and $X_t \sim N(0,1)$.

We compare our tests to other familiar test statistics. Specifically, we consider Chesher's (1983) and Lancaster's (1984) IMT,[3] denoted IM_n. We also consider Jarque and Bera's (1987) test for the normality of U_t, denoted JB_n. Both IM_n and JB_n obey standard chi-square distributions asymptotically under the null. We also apply the parametric bootstrap to these tests, denoted IM_n^p and JB_n^p.

We present our simulation results in Table 2. Here, we take $\boldsymbol{\beta}_* = (0.5,1)'$ with $\sigma_*^2 = 1$. We let $B = 1{,}000$ and perform 20,000 Monte Carlo replications. The simulation results under the null can be summarized as follows. First, our tests based on the parametric bootstrap perform quite well, with nominal levels closely comparable to actual levels even for $n = 50$. As expected, IM_n performs quite poorly, exhibiting the familiar level distortions. In contrast, JB_n performs much better, although it does suffer modest level distortion for smaller samples. The parametric bootstrap nicely fixes these problems. Only IM_n is adversely affected by increasing the number of parameters.

To examine power, we conduct further Monte Carlo experiments using six different alternative DGPs:

- ALT 1: $U_t|\mathbf{X}_t \sim N(0,\exp(\mathbf{X}'_t\boldsymbol{\beta}_*))$;
- ALT 2: $U_t|\mathbf{X}_t \sim N(0,\exp(2\mathbf{X}'_t\boldsymbol{\beta}_*))$;
- ALT 3: $U_t|\mathbf{X}_t \sim MxN(-1,1;1,1;0.5)$;
- ALT 4: $U_t|\mathbf{X}_t \sim MxN(-1.5,1;1.5,1;0.5)$;

Table 2. Levels of the Test Statistics (Number of Repetitions: 20,000; Number of Bootstrap Repetitions: 1,000; Model: $Y_t = \mathbf{X}_t'\boldsymbol{\beta} + U_t$ and $U_t \sim N(0, \sigma^2)$; DGP: $Y_t = \mathbf{X}_t'\boldsymbol{\beta}_* + U_t$ and $U_t \sim N(0, \sigma_*^2)$, $\mathbf{X}_t = (1, X_t)'$, and $X_t \sim N(0, 1)$).

Statistics	Levels \ n	50	100	200	400	600	800	1,000	2,000
$\hat{\mathscr{B}}_n^{(1,p)}$	1%	1.07	1.02	1.03	1.05	1.21	1.18	1.06	1.01
	5%	5.32	5.42	4.99	5.12	5.25	5.33	4.98	5.01
	10%	10.48	10.23	9.82	10.06	10.06	10.44	9.86	10.14
$\hat{\mathscr{B}}_n^{(2,p)}$	1%	1.02	1.12	1.13	1.12	1.08	1.13	1.07	1.06
	5%	5.00	5.10	4.95	5.29	5.28	5.22	4.86	5.20
	10%	9.81	10.23	10.16	10.19	10.46	10.30	9.83	10.23
$\hat{\mathscr{B}}_n^{(3,p)}$	1%	1.06	1.08	1.14	1.15	1.01	1.14	1.04	1.02
	5%	5.02	5.15	4.84	5.25	5.33	5.21	4.89	5.09
	10%	9.90	10.10	9.97	10.30	10.51	10.24	9.85	10.17
IM_n	1%	36.93	25.91	16.68	10.40	7.98	6.51	5.73	3.43
	5%	53.28	40.14	28.45	20.22	16.45	14.15	13.22	9.60
	10%	62.79	49.01	36.45	27.38	23.51	20.86	19.61	15.56
JB_n	1%	1.62	1.90	1.76	1.78	1.37	1.54	1.33	1.13
	5%	3.51	4.21	4.48	4.87	5.04	4.96	4.92	4.88
	10%	5.22	6.70	7.61	8.58	9.15	9.40	9.28	9.68
IM_n^p	1%	1.11	1.05	0.97	1.08	1.11	1.03	1.08	1.01
	5%	5.14	5.15	4.97	4.85	5.06	5.15	5.27	5.03
	10%	10.37	10.00	9.86	9.80	10.16	9.98	10.35	9.89
JB_n^p	1%	1.09	1.15	1.06	1.21	1.05	1.25	1.03	0.98
	5%	4.73	5.09	4.98	5.30	5.35	5.24	5.05	4.96
	10%	9.91	10.16	9.94	9.98	10.23	10.45	10.12	10.06

- ALT 5: $U_t|\mathbf{X}_t \sim t_{30}$; and
- ALT 6: $U_t|\mathbf{X}_t \sim t_{20}$.

Here, $Z \sim MxN(a,b;c,d;p)$ denotes a mixed normal distribution where $Z \sim N(a,b)$ with probability p and $Z \sim N(c,d)$ with probability $1 - p$.

Although the normal model is correctly specified for the conditional mean, the conditional variance or conditional distribution is misspecified for these alternatives. The first two alternatives exhibit conditional heteroskedasticity, with the first closer to the null than the second. The next two alternatives have PDFs with two peaks and dispersed distributions. The third is closer to the null than the fourth. The final two alternatives have fat tails, with the first closer to the null than the second.

We present our simulation results in Table 3. The results are for the nominal 5% level, obtained using the parametric bootstrap, and are

Table 3. Powers of the Test Statistics (Level of Significance: 5%; Number of Repetitions: 5,000; Number of Bootstrap Repetitions: 1,000; Model: $Y_t = \mathbf{X}_t'\boldsymbol{\beta} + U_t$ and $U_t \sim N(0, \sigma^2)$; DGP: $Y_t = \mathbf{X}_t'\boldsymbol{\beta}_* + U_t$, $\mathbf{X}_t = (1, X_t)'$, and $X_t \sim N(0, 1)$).

Statistics \ n	50	100	200	400	600	800	1,000	2,000
			$U_t \vert \mathbf{X}_t \sim N(0, \exp(\mathbf{X}_t'\boldsymbol{\beta}_*))$					
$\hat{\mathscr{B}}_n^{(1,p)}$	53.68	80.76	97.48	100.0	100.0	100.0	100.0	100.0
$\hat{\mathscr{B}}_n^{(2,p)}$	87.62	99.64	100.0	100.0	100.0	100.0	100.0	100.0
$\hat{\mathscr{B}}_n^{(3,p)}$	89.29	99.74	100.0	100.0	100.0	100.0	100.0	100.0
IM_n^p	22.22	88.64	100.0	100.0	100.0	100.0	100.0	100.0
JB_n^p	50.82	78.94	96.98	99.98	100.0	100.0	100.0	100.0
			$U_t \vert \mathbf{X}_t \sim N(0, \exp(2\mathbf{X}_t'\boldsymbol{\beta}_*))$					
$\hat{\mathscr{B}}_n^{(1,p)}$	96.18	99.96	100.0	100.0	100.0	100.0	100.0	100.0
$\hat{\mathscr{B}}_n^{(2,p)}$	99.94	100.0	100.0	100.0	100.0	100.0	100.0	100.0
$\hat{\mathscr{B}}_n^{(3,p)}$	99.98	100.0	100.0	100.0	100.0	100.0	100.0	100.0
IM_n^p	80.72	100.0	100.0	100.0	100.0	100.0	100.0	100.0
JB_n^p	94.44	99.92	100.0	100.0	100.0	100.0	100.0	100.0
			$U_t \vert \mathbf{X}_t \sim 0.5{\cdot}N(-1, 1) + 0.5{\cdot}N(1, 1)$					
$\hat{\mathscr{B}}_n^{(1,p)}$	9.42	14.90	25.32	44.92	63.18	76.76	85.14	99.32
$\hat{\mathscr{B}}_n^{(2,p)}$	1.04	1.32	3.98	23.78	48.18	70.44	84.76	99.70
$\hat{\mathscr{B}}_n^{(3,p)}$	1.60	2.64	8.94	32.16	55.24	75.56	87.38	99.76
IM_n^p	16.10	25.90	43.72	67.08	81.20	90.20	95.20	99.86
JB_n^p	0.88	1.04	7.80	36.84	65.28	83.28	92.80	99.94
			$U_t \vert \mathbf{X}_t \sim 0.5{\cdot}N(-1.5, 1) + 0.5{\cdot}N(1.5, 1)$					
$\hat{\mathscr{B}}_n^{(1,p)}$	33.46	59.90	88.34	99.62	99.98	100.0	100.0	100.0
$\hat{\mathscr{B}}_n^{(2,p)}$	1.84	15.16	74.88	99.76	100.0	100.0	100.0	100.0
$\hat{\mathscr{B}}_n^{(3,p)}$	7.40	34.86	85.60	99.88	100.0	100.0	100.0	100.0
IM_n^p	51.86	82.42	97.42	99.98	100.0	100.0	100.0	100.0
JB_n^p	0.58	20.40	86.90	99.96	100.0	100.0	100.0	100.0
				$U_t\mathbf{X}_t \sim t_{30}$				
$\hat{\mathscr{B}}_n^{(1,p)}$	5.40	7.40	8.94	11.96	16.44	18.00	20.86	34.70
$\hat{\mathscr{B}}_n^{(2,p)}$	8.14	10.08	12.24	15.54	20.58	22.26	24.90	39.98
$\hat{\mathscr{B}}_n^{(3,p)}$	8.18	9.50	11.66	14.80	19.44	21.34	23.92	38.86
IM_n^p	4.14	3.32	2.72	2.28	1.86	2.24	2.84	5.78
JB_n^p	8.68	10.76	14.02	18.04	23.14	25.34	28.46	45.82
				$U_t\mathbf{X}_t \sim t_{20}$				
$\hat{\mathscr{B}}_n^{(1,p)}$	2.32	6.40	9.14	13.80	17.70	22.92	26.66	48.82
$\hat{\mathscr{B}}_n^{(2,p)}$	0.08	0.20	1.04	4.20	8.80	14.70	20.44	45.00
$\hat{\mathscr{B}}_n^{(3,p)}$	0.06	0.16	0.56	2.66	6.30	11.86	17.24	42.10
IM_n^p	4.00	2.76	2.12	1.62	1.70	2.58	3.46	14.86
JB_n^p	10.68	15.34	19.90	29.78	37.64	44.18	51.84	74.14

somewhat nuanced. First, with conditional heteroskedasticity, our tests perform better than the others. $\hat{\mathscr{B}}_n^{(2,p)}$ and $\hat{\mathscr{B}}_n^{(3,p)}$ outperform $\hat{\mathscr{B}}_n^{(1,p)}$. Second, with normal mixture disturbances, the best test is IM_n^p, followed by $\hat{\mathscr{B}}_n^{(1,p)}$, which noticeably outperforms $\hat{\mathscr{B}}_n^{(2,p)}$ and $\hat{\mathscr{B}}_n^{(3,p)}$ in smaller samples. JB_n^p underperforms in smaller samples, although it catches up in larger samples. The t-distribution alternatives are harder for all tests to detect, as these alternatives are not as far from the null. The JB_n^p test is best, followed fairly closely by our trace-determinant tests. Overall, it appears that our tests are consistent against these alternatives, sometimes performing best and otherwise performing respectably.

We also conduct other experiments to examine the global powers of the trace-determinant tests. More specifically, Table 1 shows how the most powerful test is globally determined by the conditions for (T_*, D_*). As the sample size increases, the leading terms in Eqs. (6), (7), and (8) become the main factors to determine the powers. We investigate this by Monte Carlo experiments. For this purpose, we use the following procedure: First, for each DGP and sample size, we estimate (T_*, D_*) by Monte Carlo simulations. The number of replications is 10,000. This experiment is conducted to avoid the difficulties in computing (T_*, D_*) analytically. Second, we predict the most powerful test by using this estimate and Table 1. Third, we compare the empirical powers in Table 3 with our predictions and indicate the results as follows: if the prediction is correct (resp. wrong), we denote this by "○" (resp. "●"); and if all three tests reject the null hypothesis, so that we cannot say which one is the most powerful test, we denote this by "Δ." If the global powers are effectively determined by Table 1, "○" should eventually appear as the sample size increases.

The results of this experiment are contained in Table 4. For ALTs 1, 3, 4, and 5, "○" is observed more frequently, or it appears eventually as the sample size increases before all three tests reject the null. On the other hand, for ALTs 2 and 6, the most powerful test is not correctly predicted by the global power patterns.

These wrong predictions occur mainly because (T_*, D_*) is too close to the other regions. For example, the estimated (T_*, D_*) of ALT 6 is approximately (0.0608,0.0544) when $n = 2{,}000$, and it belongs to the region indexed by C, which predicts $\hat{\mathscr{B}}_n^{(2,p)}$ to be the most powerful test statistic. Nevertheless, this value is very close to the origin, whose neighbors are the regions indexed by A, B, and D. We can see this from the second panel of Fig. 1. Under Conditions A, B, and D, $\hat{\mathscr{B}}_n^{(2,p)}$, $\hat{\mathscr{B}}_n^{(1,p)}$, and $\hat{\mathscr{B}}_n^{(3,p)}$ are the most powerful test statistics, respectively, so that the null hypothesis can also be frequently rejected by $\hat{\mathscr{B}}_n^{(1,p)}$ and $\hat{\mathscr{B}}_n^{(3,p)}$. This leads to the wrong

Table 4. Prediction of the Most Powerful Test. (Model: $Y_t = \mathbf{X}_t'\boldsymbol{\beta} + U_t$ and $U_t \sim N(0, \sigma^2)$).

$\mathbf{X}_t$	Alternatives \ n	50	100	200	400	600	800	1,000	2,000
$(1, X_t)'$	ALT 1	●	●	○	Δ	Δ	Δ	Δ	Δ
	ALT 2	●	●	Δ	Δ	Δ	Δ	Δ	Δ
	ALT 3	●	●	●	●	●	●	○	○
	ALT 4	●	●	●	○	○	Δ	Δ	Δ
	ALT 5	○	●	○	○	○	○	○	○
	ALT 6	●	●	●	●	●	●	●	●

The table shows the results of the most powerful tests predicted by Table 1. "○" and "●" indicate that the prediction is correct and wrong, respectively. "Δ" indicates that the prediction of the most powerful test cannot be properly made because $\hat{\mathscr{B}}_n^{(1,p)}$, $\hat{\mathscr{B}}_n^{(2,p)}$, and $\hat{\mathscr{B}}_n^{(3,p)}$ all reject the null.

prediction, and it also explains why one test does not have a dominant power over the other tests, as we can see from Table 3.

We also conducted parallel simulations with $\mathbf{X}_t$ drawn from a uniform distribution and/or $\mathbf{X}_t = (1, X_t, Z_t)'$ with $(X_t, Z_t)' \sim N(\mathbf{0}, \mathbf{I}_2)$. The results were almost identical, so we do not report them here.

4.2. Exponential Duration

Next, we consider duration structures following a conditionally exponential distribution. The DGP is

$$Y_t|(\delta_t, \mathbf{X}_t) \sim \mathrm{Exp}(\delta_t \exp(\mathbf{X}'_t \boldsymbol{\beta}_*))$$

where "Exp" stands for the exponential distribution, and $\mathbf{X}_t = X_t$ with $X_t \sim N(0,1)$, as before. We assume that δ_t is not observable and that the researcher observes only Y_t and $\mathbf{X}_t$. The conditional distribution of $Y_t|\mathbf{X}_t$ is the exponential if δ_t is a constant with probability one. Otherwise, the simple exponential model is misspecified. We consider the following null and alternative DGPs for δ_t:

- NULL (Constant case): $\delta = 1$ with probability 1;
- ALT 1 (Discrete): $\delta_t \sim$ DM(0.7370,1.9296;0.5);
- ALT 2 (Gamma): $\delta_t \sim$ Gamma(5,5);
- ALT. 3 (Log-normal): $\delta_t \sim$ Log-normal $(-\ln(1.2)/2, \ln(1.2))$;

- ALT 4 (Uniform I): $\delta_t \sim$ Uniform[0.30053,2.3661]; and
- ALT 5 (Uniform II): $\delta_t \sim$ Uniform[1,5/3],

where DM(a,b;p) denotes a discrete mixture with $P(\delta_t = a) = p$ and $P(\delta_t = b) = 1 - p$. These DGPs are identical to those considered by Cho and White (2010) and Cho, Cheong, and White (2011). In each case, we let $\boldsymbol{\beta}_*$ be the unit vector.

The alternative DGPs represent various forms of unobservable heterogeneity, a subject of considerable interest in the literature. As Heckman and Singer (1984) pointed out, unobservable heterogeneity can have serious adverse consequences for estimation and inference. Among others, Lancaster (1979) developed a test for unobserved heterogeneity; Lancaster's test is designed to detect misspecifications in the direction of a gamma distribution. The other three DGPs also represent alternative lines of inquiry in the literature. See Cho and White (2010) for further discussion.

We suppose that the researcher specifies a model for $Y_t|\mathbf{X}_t$ that treats δ_t as a constant:

$$\{f(\cdot|\cdot : \alpha, \boldsymbol{\beta}) : f(y|\mathbf{x} : \alpha, \boldsymbol{\beta}) = \alpha \exp(\mathbf{x}'\boldsymbol{\beta}) \exp(-\alpha \exp(\mathbf{x}'\boldsymbol{\beta})y), (\alpha, \boldsymbol{\beta}) \in \Theta\}$$

where Θ is a parameter space for $(\alpha,\boldsymbol{\beta})$ such that each parameter has a lower bound and upper bound equal to 0 and 10, respectively. Thus, the above model is correctly specified only for the first DGP and misspecified for the others. The parameter space is relatively large, ensuring that the probability limits of the (Q)MLEs are interior to Θ. We test model misspecification using our tests, the Chesher (1983) and Lancaster (1984), and Lancaster's (1979) Lagrange multiplier test for unobserved heterogeneity, which we denote LM_n. As before, we also consider parametric bootstrap versions of the IMTs and Lancaster's (1979) LM test, denoted LM_n^p.

Our simulation results appear in Tables 5 and 6. Table 5 focuses on the null behavior of the tests, whereas Table 6 shows the behaviors under the alternative. Here, $B = 1{,}000$, and we perform 20,000 Monte Carlo replications. We summarize the results as follows. The levels for all parametric bootstrap procedures are good, with actual levels close to nominal levels. Except for IM_n, we observe similar null behavior in Table 5.

Second, we see from Table 6 that our tests outperform IM_n^p and LM_n^p for every alternative DGP. Among our tests, the most powerful test for smaller samples is $\hat{\mathscr{B}}_n^{(2,p)}$, followed by $\hat{\mathscr{B}}_n^{(3,p)}$ and $\hat{\mathscr{B}}_n^{(1,p)}$, in that sequence. In particular, the finite sample power of LM_n^p is very weak. Even when we apply the

Table 5. Levels of the Test Statistics. (Number of Repetitions: 20,000; Number of Bootstrap Repetitions: 1,000; Model: $Y_t|\mathbf{X}_t \sim \text{Exp}(\alpha \exp(\mathbf{X}_t'\boldsymbol{\beta}))$; DGP: $Y_t|\mathbf{X}_t \sim \text{Exp}(\alpha_* \exp(\mathbf{X}_t'\boldsymbol{\beta}_*))$, $\mathbf{X}_t = X_t$, and $X_t \sim N(0, 1)$).

Statistics	Levels \ n	50	100	200	400	600	800	1,000	2,000
$\hat{\mathscr{B}}_n^{(1,p)}$	1%	1.15	1.02	1.01	0.90	1.10	1.15	1.05	1.21
	5%	5.12	5.00	4.89	5.45	5.16	5.38	4.99	5.35
	10%	10.53	10.25	9.77	10.30	10.50	10.67	9.97	10.25
$\hat{\mathscr{B}}_n^{(2,p)}$	1%	1.13	1.05	1.04	0.90	1.13	1.11	1.05	1.17
	5%	5.15	4.92	4.88	5.40	5.11	5.44	4.96	5.17
	10%	10.20	9.93	9.96	10.00	10.35	10.74	10.25	10.24
$\hat{\mathscr{B}}_n^{(3,p)}$	1%	1.11	1.05	1.06	0.95	1.17	1.09	1.05	1.15
	5%	5.20	5.03	4.82	5.45	5.19	5.53	4.93	5.20
	10%	10.20	10.12	9.89	9.75	10.30	10.84	10.12	10.27
IM_n	1%	16.47	16.08	12.76	10.90	10.16	8.94	8.30	5.89
	5%	33.79	31.29	26.67	22.55	20.09	18.05	17.01	13.26
	10%	45.36	41.41	35.53	30.30	27.28	25.45	23.77	19.49
LM_n	1%	30.65	19.77	12.14	7.98	5.70	4.96	3.92	2.79
	5%	35.54	24.99	17.24	12.64	9.84	9.24	8.08	7.01
	10%	39.01	28.26	20.90	16.22	13.61	13.12	12.02	11.11
IM_n^p	1%	1.09	1.11	1.09	1.05	1.16	1.18	1.16	1.12
	5%	5.04	4.96	4.95	4.95	5.11	5.37	5.33	5.33
	10%	9.96	10.12	9.83	9.05	10.26	10.26	10.52	10.31
LM_n^p	1%	1.03	1.06	1.11	1.11	1.03	1.20	1.02	1.04
	5%	5.38	4.91	5.09	5.53	5.17	5.21	4.98	5.33
	10%	10.34	9.92	9.81	10.41	9.74	10.38	9.95	10.48

parametric bootstrap to LM_n, it can yield poor performance under the alternative. This indicates that choosing the appropriate IMT is important to have better finite sample properties. Our IMTs appear to avoid the poor properties. This ordering changes in larger samples.

We finally examine the predictions of the most powerful test by using the global powers. The process is the same as in the linear regression case. The prediction results are contained in Table 7, which shows that many alternative DGPs exhibit correct predictions as the sample size increases. On the other hand, a wrong prediction is obtained for ALT 5.

The reason for this wrong prediction is the same as before. That is, (T_*,D_*) is too close to other regions. The estimated (T_*,D_*) using 2,000 observations is approximately (0.0401,0.0382), and this value belongs to the region indexed by C but is also very close to the regions indexed by A, B, and D. We can see this from the first panel of Fig. 1. Thus, the null hypothesis is frequently rejected by the other test statistics.

Table 6. Powers of the Test Statistics (Level of Significance: 5%; Number of Repetitions: 5,000; Number of Bootstrap Repetitions: 1,000; Model: $Y_t|\mathbf{X}_t \sim \text{Exp}(\alpha \exp(\mathbf{X}_t'\boldsymbol{\beta}))$; DGP: $Y_t|(\delta_t, \mathbf{X}_t) \sim \text{Exp}(\delta_t \exp(\mathbf{X}_t'\boldsymbol{\beta}_*))$, $\mathbf{X}_t = X_t$, and $X_t \sim N(0, 1)$).

Statistics \ n	50	100	200	400	600	800	1,000	2,000
			$\delta_t \sim$ DM(0.7370, 1.9296; 0.5)					
$\hat{\mathscr{B}}_n^{(1,p)}$	15.52	28.12	48.46	74.44	88.94	95.72	98.16	99.98
$\hat{\mathscr{B}}_n^{(2,p)}$	20.84	30.38	47.60	71.60	86.86	94.40	97.56	100.0
$\hat{\mathscr{B}}_n^{(3,p)}$	17.72	28.00	45.88	76.48	86.34	94.20	97.52	100.0
IM_n^p	0.92	0.54	0.72	6.44	24.98	53.44	75.84	99.96
LM_n^p	0.80	0.20	0.02	0.02	1.24	17.42	60.20	100.0
			$\delta_t \sim$ Gamma(5,5)					
$\hat{\mathscr{B}}_n^{(1,p)}$	21.14	37.32	62.04	87.14	96.42	98.64	99.48	100.0
$\hat{\mathscr{B}}_n^{(2,p)}$	27.10	42.38	63.82	86.72	95.94	98.72	99.58	100.0
$\hat{\mathscr{B}}_n^{(3,p)}$	24.44	39.80	62.20	86.20	95.76	98.62	99.54	100.0
IM_n^p	1.74	1.32	1.80	8.88	26.56	51.54	73.38	99.20
LM_n^p	0.68	0.26	0.02	0.00	0.08	2.44	16.22	87.58
			$\delta_t \sim$ LN(−ln(1.2)/2,ln(1.2))					
$\hat{\mathscr{B}}_n^{(1,p)}$	14.06	14.06	41.68	67.20	84.46	90.58	95.72	99.98
$\hat{\mathscr{B}}_n^{(2,p)}$	19.46	19.46	43.82	66.54	83.12	89.62	94.90	99.90
$\hat{\mathscr{B}}_n^{(3,p)}$	17.08	17.08	42.36	65.10	82.44	89.26	94.72	99.90
IM_n^p	1.68	1.68	0.94	2.66	10.80	24.68	44.64	96.73
LM_n^p	0.96	0.42	0.18	0.00	0.08	1.98	16.24	98.68
			$\delta_t \sim U$(0.30053,2.3661)					
$\hat{\mathscr{B}}_n^{(1,p)}$	32.96	53.62	82.44	97.34	99.50	99.96	99.98	100.0
$\hat{\mathscr{B}}_n^{(2,p)}$	40.72	57.30	82.76	97.38	99.60	99.98	100.0	100.0
$\hat{\mathscr{B}}_n^{(3,p)}$	36.08	54.70	81.54	97.14	99.58	99.98	100.0	100.0
IM_n^p	1.12	1.94	5.72	32.98	71.00	91.02	97.90	100.0
LM_n^p	0.02	0.06	0.00	0.00	0.38	6.68	31.44	97.76
			$\delta_t \sim U$(1,5/3)					
$\hat{\mathscr{B}}_n^{(1,p)}$	4.78	5.54	6.36	7.56	8.44	10.00	9.62	13.90
$\hat{\mathscr{B}}_n^{(2,p)}$	5.62	7.06	7.52	8.20	8.74	10.20	10.02	12.84
$\hat{\mathscr{B}}_n^{(3,p)}$	5.32	6.68	7.20	7.92	8.52	9.88	9.68	12.50
IM_n^p	4.32	3.76	3.34	3.44	2.84	2.78	3.00	2.58
LM_n^p	4.10	4.00	2.84	2.20	1.82	1.48	1.08	2.54

We also conducted experiments using $\mathbf{X}_t \sim N(\mathbf{0},\mathbf{I}_2)$ and/or the Weibull specifications studied by Cho and White (2010) and Cho et al. (2011) for the same DGPs, and we obtained similar level and power patterns. We omit reporting these results for the sake of brevity. Thus, our parametric bootstrap tests appear promising for detecting unobserved heterogeneity in duration models.

Table 7. Prediction of the Most Powerful Test. Model: $Y_t|\mathbf{X}_t \sim \text{Exp}\left(\alpha \exp\left(\mathbf{X}_t'\boldsymbol{\beta}\right)\right)$.

$\mathbf{X}_t$	Alternatives \ n	50	100	200	400	600	800	1,000	2,000
$(1,X_t)'$	ALT 1	○	○	●	●	●	●	●	○
	ALT 2	○	●	○	●	●	○	○	Δ
	ALT 3	○	○	○	●	●	●	●	○
	ALT 4	○	○	○	○	○	○	○	Δ
	ALT 5	●	●	○	○	○	○	○	●

The table shows the results of the most powerful tests predicted by Table 1. "○" and "●" indicate that the prediction is correct and wrong, respectively. "Δ" indicates that the prediction of the most powerful test cannot be properly made because $\hat{\mathscr{B}}_n^{(1,p)}$, $\hat{\mathscr{B}}_n^{(2,p)}$, and $\hat{\mathscr{B}}_n^{(3,p)}$ all reject the null.

4.3. Probit

For our third experiment, we consider a probit specification, as did Horowitz (1994).

Again, we consider $\mathbf{X}_t=(1,X_t)'$, where $X_t \sim N(0,1)$. The probit model has the typical element

$$f(Y_t|\mathbf{X}_t;\boldsymbol{\beta})=\Phi(\mathbf{X}_t'\boldsymbol{\beta})$$

where Φ is the standard normal CDF. We take $\boldsymbol{B}=[-5,\ 5]$.

We examine the following four DGPs in our experiments:

- NULL: $Y_t|\mathbf{X}_t \sim \text{Probit}(\mathbf{X}_t'\boldsymbol{\beta}_*)$;
- ALT 1: $Y_t|\mathbf{X}_t \sim \text{Probit}(\mathbf{X}_t'\boldsymbol{\beta}_*/\exp(0.5\mathbf{X}_t'\boldsymbol{\beta}_*))$;
- ALT 2: $Y_t|\mathbf{X}_t \sim \text{Probit}((\mathbf{X}_t'\boldsymbol{\beta}_*)^2)$; and
- ALT 3: $Y_t|\mathbf{X}_t \sim \text{Logit}(\mathbf{X}_t'\boldsymbol{\beta}_*)$

where "Probit($\mathbf{X}_t'\boldsymbol{\beta}_*$)" denotes that the conditional distribution of $Y_t|\mathbf{X}_t$ satisfies $P(Y_t=1|\mathbf{X}_t)=\Phi(\mathbf{X}_t'\boldsymbol{\beta}_*)$. The model is correctly specified for the first DGP but misspecified for the rest. "Logit($\mathbf{X}_t'\boldsymbol{\beta}_*$)" denotes that the conditional distribution of $Y_t|\mathbf{X}_t$ satisfies $P(Y_t=1|\mathbf{X}_t)=\{1+\exp(\mathbf{X}_t'\boldsymbol{\beta}_*)\}^{-1}$. We take $\boldsymbol{\beta}_*=(0.5,1)'$.

We conduct the same simulations as before, and we again compare our tests to parametric bootstrap versions of the Chesher (1983) and Lancaster (1984) IMT. As the asymptotic covariance matrix for the full IMT is singular, we drop redundant terms.

Table 8. Levels of the Test Statistics. (Number of Repetitions: 10,000; Number of Bootstrap Repetitions: 500; Model: $Y_t|\mathbf{X}_t \sim \text{Probit}(\mathbf{X}_t'\boldsymbol{\beta})$; DGP: $Y_t|\mathbf{X}_t \sim \text{Probit}(\mathbf{X}_t'\boldsymbol{\beta}_*)$, $\mathbf{X}_t = (1, X_t)'$, and $X_t \sim N(0, 1)$).

Statistics	Levels \ n	50	100	200	300	400	500	600	700
$\hat{\mathscr{B}}_n^{(1,p)}$	1%	0.99	1.00	1.26	1.29	1.20	1.09	1.16	1.38
	5%	2.95	4.20	5.07	4.98	5.20	5.13	4.87	5.11
	10%	6.85	8.61	9.98	9.80	10.40	9.64	9.79	10.20
$\hat{\mathscr{B}}_n^{(2,p)}$	1%	0.96	1.07	1.20	1.14	1.28	1.18	1.08	1.27
	5%	3.89	4.36	4.96	4.87	5.10	5.01	4.82	5.11
	10%	7.21	8.67	9.62	9.66	10.41	9.52	9.42	10.10
$\hat{\mathscr{B}}_n^{(3,p)}$	1%	0.79	0.92	1.19	1.16	1.31	1.14	1.10	1.25
	5%	3.04	4.20	5.02	4.74	5.11	4.84	4.76	5.06
	10%	6.51	8.47	9.49	9.53	10.38	9.68	9.36	10.06
IM_n	1%	35.98	28.89	21.72	1.68	1.52	12.13	11.34	10.51
	5%	53.38	42.48	31.94	27.03	25.30	20.87	19.50	18.51
	10%	61.85	49.87	39.17	33.91	31.63	26.94	25.66	25.12
IM_n^p	1%	0.58	0.80	1.10	1.10	1.06	1.01	1.26	1.14
	5%	3.54	4.52	5.00	5.19	5.37	4.89	5.35	5.27
	10%	8.01	9.40	9.96	9.88	10.60	9.50	9.94	10.41

We present our simulation results in Tables 8 and 9. Table 8 presents the null behaviors of the test statistics, and Table 9 examines the alternatives. Here, the number of bootstrap replications is $B = 500$. We conduct 10,000 Monte Carlo replications under the null and 3,000 under the alternative.

We summarize the results as follows. As before, the levels of all the parametric bootstrap tests accord well with nominal values, and again the raw IM_n statistic performs poorly. With regard to power, IM_n^p performs best for the third DGP in smaller samples, although it is dominated in the other two cases. Overall, the trace-determinant tests perform respectably.

We also examine the global powers of the test statistics as before. For all alternative DGPs, Table 10 shows that as the sample size increases, "O" is observed more frequently or eventually before all three tests reject the null, implying that Table 1 correctly predicts the most powerful test statistic.

We also conducted experiments using $\mathbf{X}_t := (1, X_t, Z_t)'$ and $(X_t, Z_t)' \sim N(\mathbf{0}, \mathbf{I}_2)$ and obtained similar level and power patterns. We omit reporting these results for the sake of brevity.

Table 9. Powers of the Test Statistics (Level of Significance: 5%; Number of Repetitions: 3,000; Number of Bootstrap Repetitions: 500. Model: $Y_t|\mathbf{X}_t \sim \text{Probit}(\mathbf{X}_t'\boldsymbol{\beta})$; DGP: $\mathbf{X}_t = (1, X_t)'$ and $X_t \sim N(0,\ 1)$).

Statistics\n	50	100	200	300	400	500	600	700
			$Y_t|\mathbf{X}_t \sim \text{Probit}(\mathbf{X}_t'\boldsymbol{\beta}_*/\exp(0.5\mathbf{X}_t'\boldsymbol{\beta}_*))$					
$\hat{\mathscr{B}}_n^{(1,p)}$	9.03	15.40	22.13	27.10	34.93	38.83	43.93	47.73
$\hat{\mathscr{B}}_n^{(2,p)}$	15.86	38.90	71.23	89.86	97.06	99.16	99.90	99.96
$\hat{\mathscr{B}}_n^{(3,p)}$	14.03	37.93	71.16	90.06	97.10	99.30	99.90	99.96
IM_n^p	6.93	27.80	67.93	90.00	97.40	99.63	99.93	100.0
			$Y_t|\mathbf{X}_t \sim \text{Probit}\left((\mathbf{X}_t'\boldsymbol{\beta}_*)^2\right)$					
$\hat{\mathscr{B}}_n^{(1,p)}$	25.56	70.00	92.83	97.96	99.40	99.70	99.93	99.96
$\hat{\mathscr{B}}_n^{(2,p)}$	36.46	93.50	100.0	100.0	100.0	100.0	100.0	100.0
$\hat{\mathscr{B}}_n^{(3,p)}$	45.53	95.43	100.0	100.0	100.0	100.0	100.0	100.0
IM_n^p	63.96	97.96	100.0	100.0	100.0	100.0	100.0	100.0
			$Y_t|\mathbf{X}_t \sim \text{Logit}(\mathbf{X}_t'\boldsymbol{\beta}_*)$					
$\hat{\mathscr{B}}_n^{(1,p)}$	3.36	4.40	5.20	6.03	7.13	7.70	7.80	7.60
$\hat{\mathscr{B}}_n^{(2,p)}$	3.70	4.30	5.20	6.50	6.93	7.20	7.73	8.26
$\hat{\mathscr{B}}_n^{(3,p)}$	2.96	3.93	4.90	6.56	6.90	7.06	7.63	7.90
IM_n^p	1.53	3.43	3.60	4.33	3.73	3.33	4.13	3.80

4.4. Tobit

As a final experiment, we consider the Tobit model. Horowitz (1994) also examined the performance of the IMT for the Tobit model, describing it as a successful application of the parametric bootstrap.

The experimental design is similar to that for the probit model. As before, $\mathbf{X}_t = (1, X_t)'$, where $X_t \sim N(0,1)$. The Tobit model has the typical element

$$Y_t = \max[0, \mathbf{X}_t'\boldsymbol{\beta} + U_t]$$

where $U_t \sim N(0,\sigma^2)$. Again, we take $\boldsymbol{B} = [-5,\ 5]$, and we let σ lie between 0.1 and 10. The unknown parameters $\boldsymbol{\beta}$ and σ are estimated by (Q)ML estimation. We consider the following four DGPs:

- NULL: $Y_t = \max[0, \mathbf{X}'_t\boldsymbol{\beta}_* + U_t]$ and $U_t|\boldsymbol{X}_t \sim N(0,1)$;
- ALT 1: $Y_t = \max[0, \mathbf{X}'_t\boldsymbol{\beta}_* + U_t]$ and $U_t|\mathbf{X}_t \sim N(0, \exp(0.5\mathbf{X}'_t\boldsymbol{\beta}_*))$;
- ALT 2: $Y_t = \max[0, (\mathbf{X}_t'\boldsymbol{\beta}_*)^2 + U_t]$ and $U_t|\boldsymbol{X}_t \sim N(0,1)$; and
- ALT 3: $Y_t = \max[0, \mathbf{X}_t'\boldsymbol{\beta}_* + U_t]$ and $U_t|\boldsymbol{X}_t \sim t_{30}$.

Table 10. Prediction of the Most Powerful Test. (Model: $Y_t|\mathbf{X}_t \sim \text{Probit}(\mathbf{X}_t'\boldsymbol{\beta})$).

$\mathbf{X}_t$	Alternatives \ n	50	100	200	300	400	500	600	700
$(1, X_t)'$	ALT 1	O	O	O	●	●	●	O	O
	ALT 2	O	O	O	O	O	O	O	O
	ALT 3	O	O	O	●	●	●	●	O

The table shows the results of the most powerful tests predicted by Table 1. "O" and "●" indicate that the prediction is correct and wrong, respectively.

Table 11. Levels of the Test Statistics. (Number of Repetitions: 10,000; Number of Bootstrap Repetitions: 500; Model: $Y_t = \max[0, \mathbf{X}_t'\boldsymbol{\beta} + U_t]$ and $U_t \sim N(0, \sigma^2)$; DGP: $Y_t = \max[0, \mathbf{X}_t'\boldsymbol{\beta}_* + U_t]$, $\mathbf{X}_t = (1, X_t)'$, and $(X_t, U_t)' \sim N(\mathbf{0}, \mathbf{I}_2)$).

Statistics	Levels \ n	50	100	200	300	400
$\hat{\mathscr{B}}_n^{(1,p)}$	1%	0.92	1.32	1.15	1.20	1.04
	5%	4.90	5.25	4.99	5.45	4.97
	10%	10.07	10.49	10.18	10.32	10.05
$\hat{\mathscr{B}}_n^{(2,p)}$	1%	0.99	1.17	1.03	1.22	0.98
	5%	4.79	4.93	4.87	4.68	5.06
	10%	9.31	9.57	9.75	9.62	10.37
$\hat{\mathscr{B}}_n^{(3,p)}$	1%	0.95	1.27	1.07	1.18	1.03
	5%	4.79	4.84	4.92	4.83	5.10
	10%	9.31	9.73	9.65	9.80	10.30
IM_n	1%	52.43	41.72	30.54	24.60	20.66
	5%	69.66	56.86	44.81	37.67	32.94
	10%	77.01	65.59	52.92	45.76	41.25
IM_n^p	1%	1.09	1.16	1.21	1.39	1.20
	5%	4.65	5.84	6.00	5.88	5.21
	10%	10.15	11.86	11.35	11.29	9.53

We let $\boldsymbol{\beta}_* = (0,1)'$. Thus, the Tobit model is correctly specified for the first DGP and misspecified for the others.

We again compare our tests with parametric bootstrap versions of the Chesher (1983) and Lancaster (1984) IMT. As before, we drop redundant terms.

The results appear in Tables 11 and 12. Table 11 contains results for levels, and Table 12 reports results for the alternatives. As for the probit case, the number of bootstrap replications is $B = 500$, with 10,000 Monte Carlo replications under the null and 3,000 under the alternatives.

Table 12. Powers of the Test Statistics (Level of Significance: 5%. Number of Repetitions: 3,000. Number of Bootstrap Repetitions: 500. Model: $Y_t = \max\left[0, \mathbf{X}_t'\boldsymbol{\beta}_* + U_t\right]$ and $U_t \sim N(0, \sigma^2)$; DGP: $\mathbf{X}_t = (1, X_t)'$ and $X_t \sim N(0, 1)$).

Statistics \ n	50	100	200	300	400
	$Y_t = \max\left[0, \mathbf{X}_t'\boldsymbol{\beta}_* + U_t\right]$ and $U_t \vert \mathbf{X}_t \sim N(0, \exp(0.5\mathbf{X}_t'\boldsymbol{\beta}_*))$				
$\hat{\mathscr{B}}_n^{(1,p)}$	32.30	50.63	75.26	88.73	94.46
$\hat{\mathscr{B}}_n^{(2,p)}$	62.96	89.66	99.73	99.93	100.0
$\hat{\mathscr{B}}_n^{(3,p)}$	64.80	91.43	99.73	100.0	100.0
IM_n^p	8.33	24.00	92.76	99.90	100.0
	$Y_t = \max\left[0, (\mathbf{X}_t'\boldsymbol{\beta}_*)^2 + U_t\right]$ and $U_t \vert \mathbf{X}_t \sim N(0, 1)$				
$\hat{\mathscr{B}}_n^{(1,p)}$	81.76	98.36	99.96	100.0	100.0
$\hat{\mathscr{B}}_n^{(2,p)}$	80.03	98.56	99.96	100.0	100.0
$\hat{\mathscr{B}}_n^{(3,p)}$	76.13	97.90	99.96	100.0	100.0
IM_n^p	37.43	62.23	87.63	96.10	98.53
	$Y_t = \max\left[0, \mathbf{X}_t'\boldsymbol{\beta}_* + U_t\right]$ and $U_t \vert \mathbf{X}_t \sim t_{30}$				
$\hat{\mathscr{B}}_n^{(1,p)}$	5.00	6.33	7.76	8.63	9.63
$\hat{\mathscr{B}}_n^{(2,p)}$	7.26	8.16	9.86	10.70	13.20
$\hat{\mathscr{B}}_n^{(3,p)}$	6.96	7.73	9.26	10.56	12.63
IM_n^p	4.36	4.80	4.30	4.20	2.66

Table 13. Prediction of the Most Powerful Test. (Model $Y_t = \max\left[0, \mathbf{X}_t'\boldsymbol{\beta} + U_t\right]$ and $U_t \sim N(0, \sigma^2)$).

$\mathbf{X}_t$	Alternatives \ n	50	100	200	300	400
$(1, X_t)'$	ALT 1	●	●	●	●	○
	ALT 2	●	○	○	Δ	Δ
	ALT 3	●	●	○	○	○

The table shows the results of the most powerful tests predicted by Table 1. "○" and "●" indicate that the prediction is correct and wrong, respectively. "Δ" indicates that the prediction of the most powerful test cannot be properly made because $\hat{\mathscr{B}}_n^{(1,p)}$, $\hat{\mathscr{B}}_n^{(2,p)}$, and $\hat{\mathscr{B}}_n^{(3,p)}$ all reject the null.

Again, we see that all the parametric bootstrap tests have levels close to nominal, while IM_n does not perform well. In each alternative, our new tests outperform IM_n^p.

We also predict the most powerful test statistic using the global powers as before. For all the alternative DGPs we consider here, Table 13 shows that as the sample size increases, Table 1 correctly predicts the most powerful test statistic. This is affirmed from the fact that as the sample size increases, "○" is more frequently observed, or it appears eventually before "Δ" is observed.

We also conducted experiments using $\mathbf{X}_t := (1, X_t, Z_t)'$ and $(X_t, Z_t)' \sim N(\mathbf{0}, \mathbf{I}_2)$ and obtained similar level and power patterns. We omit reporting these results for the sake of brevity.

5. CONCLUSION

We provide a new characterization of the equality of two positive-definite matrices **A** and **B**, namely that $\det(\mathbf{BA}^{-1})^{1/k} = k^{-1}\mathrm{tr}(\mathbf{BA}^{-1}) = 1$, and we use this to propose several new, computationally convenient statistical tests for the equality of two unknown positive-definite matrices. Our primary focus is on testing the information matrix equality (e.g., White, 1982, 1994), where the matrices **A** and **B** depend on underlying parameters that require estimation. We characterize the asymptotic behavior of our test statistics under the null, alternative, and local alternative, and we investigate their finite-sample performance for a variety of models: linear regression, exponential duration, probit, and Tobit. Although our statistics have nonstandard asymptotic distributions, the parametric bootstrap easily accommodates these and delivers critical values that provide admirable level behavior, even in samples as small as $n = 50$. Reinforcing Horowitz's (1994) findings, we find that the parametric bootstrap also eradicates the well-documented poor level performance of the traditional IMT in all of our experiments. Our new tests often have better power than the traditional IMT; when they do not, they nevertheless perform respectably. In particular, the trace-determinant tests are always better than the conventional IMTs for duration data.

The simplicity, reliable level performance, and respectable power properties of our new parametric bootstrap trace-determinant IMTs remove the obstacles that might have previously dissuaded researchers from applying an IMT. Our findings here, and the versatility of information matrix testing methods generally, lead us to strongly recommend routine application of parametric bootstrap-based IMTs.

NOTES

1. Directional versions can be constructed by selecting suitable submatrices of **A** and **B**.

2. GAUSS codes for the linear regression, exponential duration, Weibull duration, probit, and Tobit models are downloadable at the following http://web.yonsei.ac.kr/jinseocho/research.htm

3. To construct this IMT, we need to include the first-order and second-order derivatives as testing components. Nevertheless, including the second-order derivative with respect to the intercept coefficient yields a singular covariance matrix. We thus omit this redundant term.

ACKNOWLEDGMENTS

The second author (Halbert White) had passed away before the final version was completed. The first author would like to acknowledge his contributions to this paper. He formed the outlines of the current paper. In addition, the authors are most grateful to the co-editors, Yoosoon Chang, Tom Fomby, and Joon Y. Park, and one anonymous referee. We also acknowledge helpful discussions with Anil Bera, Stephane Bonhomme, Richard Golden, Steven Henley, Atsushi Inoue, Jinook Jeong, Kiho Jeong, Michael Kashner, Hak Bae Lee, Jin Lee, Ki Young Park, Sang Soo Park, Peter C.B. Phillips, Robert Strawderman, Yoon Jae Whang, Byoungsam Yoo, Victoria Zinde-Walsh, and other participants at the 14th Advances in Econometrics Conference in Honor of Peter C.B. Phillips (Southern Methodist University, 2013), the Economics Joint Conference 2012, and the 17th Joint Workshop of Yonsei University, Hokkaido University (Hokkaido University, 2012), and KEA International Conference (Korea University, 2012). Also, Taeyoun Kim and Myungkoo Song provided excellent research assistance for our Monte Carlo experiments.

REFERENCES

Anderson, T. (2003). *An introduction to multivariate statistical analysis*. Hoboken, NJ: Wiley.

Bera, A. (1986). *Model specification test through eigenvalues*. Mimeo, Department of Economics, University of Illinois.

Bera, A., & Hall, A. (1991). *An eigenvalue based test for heteroskedasticity*. Mimeo, Department of Economics, University of Illinois.

Chesher, A. (1983). Information matrix test. *Economics Letters*, *13*, 45–48.

Chesher, A., & Spady, R. (1991). Asymptotic expansions of the information matrix test statistic. *Econometrica*, *59*, 787–815.

Cho, J. S., Cheong, T. U., & White, H. (2011). Experience with the weighted bootstrap in testing for unobserved heterogeneity in exponential and Weibull duration models. *Journal of Economic Theory and Econometrics*, *22*(2), 60–91

Cho, J. S., & White, H. (2007). Testing for regime switching. *Econometrica, 75*, 1671–1720.

Cho, J. S., & White, H. (2010). Testing for unobserved heterogeneity in exponential and Weibull duration models. *Journal of Econometrics, 157*, 458–480.

Das Gupta, S., & Giri, N. (1973). Properties of tests concerning covariance matrices of normal distributions. *Annals of Statistics, 1*, 1222–1224.

Dhaene, G., & Hoorelbeke, D. (2004). The information matrix test with bootstrap-based covariance matrix estimation. *Economics Letters, 82*, 341–347.

Fisher, R. (1922). On the mathematical foundations of theoretical statistics. *Philosophical Transactions of the Royal Society, A, 222*, 309–368.

Fisher, R. (1925). Theory of statistical estimation. *Proceedings of the Cambridge Philosophical Society, 22*, 700–725.

Golden, R., Henley, S., White, H., & Kashner, T. (2013). New directions in information matrix testing: Eigenspectrum tests. In N. R. Swanson, & X. Chen (Eds.), *Causality, prediction, and specification analysis: Recent advances and future directions: essays in honour of H. L. White, Jr.* (pp. 145–177). New York, NY: Springer.

Hall, A. (1987). The information matrix test for the linear model. *Review of Economic Studies, 54*, 257–263.

Heckman, J., & Singer, B. (1984). A method of minimizing the impact of distributional assumptions in econometric models of duration data. *Econometrica, 52*, 271–320.

Horowitz, J. (1994). Bootstrap-based critical values for the information matrix test. *Journal of Econometrics, 61*, 395–411.

Jarque, C., & Bera, A. (1987). A test for normality of observations and regression residuals. *International Statistical Review, 55*, 163–218.

Lancaster, T. (1979). Econometric methods for the duration of unemployment. *Econometrica, 47*, 939–956.

Lancaster, T. (1984). The covariance matrix of the information matrix test. *Econometrica, 52*, 1052–1053.

Magnus, J., & Neudecker, H. (1999). *Matrix differential calculus with applications in statistics and econometrics*. Chichester: Wiley.

Mauchly, J. (1940). Significance test for sphericity of a normal *n*-variable distribution. *Annals of Mathematical Statistics, 11*, 204–209.

Nagao, H. (1967). Monotonicity of the modified likelihood ratio test for a covariance matrix. *Journal of Science of the Hiroshima University. Series A-I, 31*, 147–150.

Nagao, H. (1973). On some test criteria for covariance matrix. *Annals of Statistics, 1*, 700–709.

Nagao, H. (1974). Asymptotic non-null distributions of two test criteria for equality of covariance matrices under local alternatives. *Annals of the Institute of Statistical Mathematics, 26*, 395–402.

Nagarsenker, B. N., & Pillai, K. C. S. (1973). The distribution of the sphericity test criterion. *Journal of Multivariate Analysis, 3*, 226–235.

Orme, C. (1988). The calculation of the information matrix test for binary data models. *The Manchester School, 56*, 370–376.

Orme, C. (1990). The small-sample performance of the information-matrix test. *Journal of Econometrics, 46*, 309–331.

Pillai, K., & Jayachandran, K. (1968). Power comparison of tests of equality of two covariance matrices based on four criteria. *Biometrika, 55*, 335–342.

Pillai, K., & Nagarsenker, B. (1972). On the distribution of a class of statistics in multivariate analysis. *Journal of Multivariate Analysis, 2*, 96–114.

Roy, S. (1953). On a heuristic method of test construction and its use in multivariate analysis. *Annals of Mathematical Statistics*, *24*, 220–238.

Strawderman, R. (1994). A note on necessary and sufficient conditions for proving that a random symmetric matrix converges to a given limit. *Statistics & Probability Letters*, *21*, 367–370.

Taylor, L. (1987). The size bias of White's information matrix test. *Economics Letters*, *24*, 63–67.

van der Vaart, A. (2000). *Asymptotic statistics*. New York, NY:Cambridge University Press.

White, H. (1982). Maximum likelihood estimation of misspecified models. *Econometrica*, *50*, 1–26.

White, H. (1994). *Estimation, inference and specification analysis*. New York, NY: Cambridge University Press.

Wilks, S. (1935). On the independence of *k* sets of normally distributed statistical variables. *Econometrica*, *3*, 309–326.

APPENDIX

A.1. Proofs

Proof of Lemma 1. If $\mathbf{A}=\mathbf{B}$, then clearly $[\det(\mathbf{A}^{-1/2}\mathbf{B}\mathbf{A}^{-1/2})]^{1/k}= \mathrm{tr}(\mathbf{A}^{-1/2}\mathbf{B}\mathbf{A}^{-1/2})/k=1$.

For the converse, we have that $[\det(\mathbf{A}^{-1/2}\mathbf{B}\mathbf{A}^{-1/2})]^{1/k}= \mathrm{tr}(\mathbf{A}^{-1/2}\mathbf{B}\mathbf{A}^{-1/2})/k$. Equivalently, $\left(\prod_{j=1}^{k}\lambda_j\right)^{1/k}=k^{-1}\sum_{j=1}^{k}\lambda_j$, where λ_j, $j=1,\ldots,k$, are the real nonnegative eigenvalues of $A^{-1/2}\mathbf{B}\mathbf{A}^{-1/2}$. It is wellknown that equality of the geometric and arithmetic means follows if and only if the elements of the means are identical, i.e., $\lambda_1=\ldots=\lambda_k=\lambda$, say. As $[\det(\mathbf{A}^{-1/2}\mathbf{B}\mathbf{A}^{-1/2})]^{1/k}=1$, we have $[\det(\mathbf{A}^{-1/2}\mathbf{B}\mathbf{A}^{-1/2})]^{1/k}=\lambda=1$. That is, $\mathbf{A}^{-1/2}\mathbf{B}\mathbf{A}^{-1/2}$ has eigenvalues identically equal to 1, so that $\mathbf{A}^{-1/2}\mathbf{B}\mathbf{A}^{-1/2}=\mathbf{C}\mathbf{I}\mathbf{C}'=\mathbf{I}$, where $\mathbf{C}$ is the orthonormal matrix of the eigenvectors of $\mathbf{A}^{-1/2}\mathbf{B}\mathbf{A}^{-1/2}$. Now $\mathbf{A}^{-1/2}\mathbf{B}\mathbf{A}^{-1/2}=\mathbf{I}$ implies $\mathbf{A}^{1/2}\mathbf{A}^{-1/2}\mathbf{B}\mathbf{A}^{-1/2}\mathbf{A}^{1/2}=\mathbf{A}^{1/2}\mathbf{A}^{1/2}$, which simplifies to $\mathbf{B}=\mathbf{A}$. ■

Before proving our results, we first state some useful lemmas, allowing us to avoid repeating certain arguments. We provide proofs only for those lemmas that are not elementary.

Lemma A1. Given Assumptions 1, 2, and 3,

(i) $\mathbf{A}_n^{-1}-\mathbf{A}_*^{-1}=-\mathbf{U}_n\mathbf{A}_*^{-1}+\mathbf{U}_n^2\mathbf{A}_*^{-1}+o_{\mathbb{P}}(n^{-1})$;
(ii) $\mathbf{B}_n^{-1}-\mathbf{B}_*^{-1}=-\mathbf{W}_n\mathbf{B}_*^{-1}+\mathbf{W}_n^2\mathbf{B}_*^{-1}+o_{\mathbb{P}}(n^{-1})$;
(iii) $\mathbf{D}_n-\mathbf{D}_*=\mathbf{B}_*\mathbf{P}_n(\mathbf{I}-\mathbf{U}_n)\mathbf{A}_*^{-1}+o_{\mathbb{P}}(n^{-1})$, where $\boldsymbol{P}_n:=\mathbf{W}_n-\mathbf{U}_n$; and
(iv) if $\mathbb{H}_0$ further holds, $\mathbf{D}_n-\mathbf{D}_*=\mathbf{B}_*\mathbf{M}_n(\mathbf{I}-\mathbf{U}_n)\mathbf{A}_*^{-1}+o_{\mathbb{P}}(n^{-1})$. □

Proof of Lemma A1. (i) We apply exercise 13.21 of Abadir and Magnus (2005): $d\mathbf{X}^{-1}=-\mathbf{X}^{-1}(d\mathbf{X})\,\mathbf{X}^{-1}$, so that $d^2\mathbf{X}^{-1}=-d\mathbf{X}^{-1}(d\mathbf{X})\,\mathbf{X}^{-1}-\mathbf{X}^{-1}(d^2\mathbf{X})\mathbf{X}^{-1}-\mathbf{X}^{-1}(d\mathbf{X})d\mathbf{X}^{-1}$. This implies that the second-order approximation of $\mathbf{X}^{-1}-\mathbf{X}_o^{-1}$ is obtained as $d\mathbf{X}^{-1}+\frac{1}{2}d^2\mathbf{X}^{-1}=-\mathbf{X}_o^{-1}(d\mathbf{X})\mathbf{X}_o^{-1}+\{\mathbf{X}_o^{-1}(d\mathbf{X})\mathbf{X}_o^{-1}(d\mathbf{X})\mathbf{X}_o^{-1}\}-\frac{1}{2}\mathbf{X}_o^{-1}\,(d^2\mathbf{X})\mathbf{X}_o^{-1}$ where $d\mathbf{X}$ captures $(\mathbf{X}-\mathbf{X}_o)$.

We now obtain the second-order approximation of $\mathbf{A}_n^{-1}-\mathbf{A}_*^{-1}$ by letting $\mathbf{X}_o=\mathbf{A}_*$ and $d\mathbf{X}=\mathbf{A}_n-\mathbf{A}_*$, where the remainder term is $o_{\mathbb{P}}(n^{-1})$ from the fact that $\mathbf{A}_n-\mathbf{A}_*=O_{\mathbb{P}}(n^{-1/2})$. We also use the definition of $\mathbf{U}_n:=\mathbf{A}_*^{-1}(\mathbf{A}_n-\mathbf{A}_*)$ and obtain the desired result.

(ii) The proof is identical to (*i*). We can replace $\mathbf{A}_n$, $\mathbf{A}_*$, and $\mathbf{U}_n$ with $\mathbf{B}_n$, $\mathbf{B}_*$, and $\mathbf{W}_n$, respectively.

(iii) We note the following identity: $\mathbf{D}_n - \mathbf{D}_* \equiv (\mathbf{B}_n - \mathbf{B}_*)\mathbf{A}_*^{-1} + (\mathbf{B}_n - \mathbf{B}_*)(\mathbf{A}_n^{-1} - \mathbf{A}_*^{-1}) + \mathbf{B}_*(\mathbf{A}_n^{-1} - \mathbf{A}_*^{-1})$. By reasoning analogous to Lemma A1(i) for $(\mathbf{A}_n^{-1} - \mathbf{A}_*^{-1})$ we obtain $(\mathbf{B}_n - \mathbf{B}_*)\mathbf{U}_n^2\mathbf{A}_*^{-1} = O_{\mathbb{P}}(n^{-3/2})$. This yields the desired approximation.

(iv) We have $\mathbf{P}_n = \mathbf{M}_n$ in (iii) under $\mathbb{H}_0$. This completes the proof. ∎

Lemma A2. Given Assumptions 1, 2, and 3,

(i) $\det[\mathbf{A}_n] - \det[\mathbf{A}_*] = \det[\mathbf{A}_*]\left(\mathrm{tr}[\mathbf{U}_n] + \frac{1}{2}\mathrm{tr}\left[\mathbf{U}_n\right]^2 - \frac{1}{2}\mathrm{tr}\left[\mathbf{U}_n^2\right]\right) + o_{\mathbb{P}}(n^{-1})$;

(ii) $\det[\mathbf{B}_n] - \det[\mathbf{B}_*] = \det[\mathbf{B}_*]\left(\mathrm{tr}[\mathbf{W}_n] + \frac{1}{2}\mathrm{tr}\left[\mathbf{W}_n\right]^2 - \frac{1}{2}\mathrm{tr}\left[\mathbf{W}_n^2\right]\right) + o_{\mathbb{P}}(n^{-1})$;

(iii) $\det[\mathbf{A}_n]^{-1} - \det[\mathbf{A}_*]^{-1} = -\det[\mathbf{A}_*]^{-1}$
$\left(\mathrm{tr}[\mathbf{U}_n] + \frac{1}{2}\mathrm{tr}[\mathbf{U}_n]^2 - \frac{1}{2}\mathrm{tr}\left[\mathbf{U}_n^2\right]\right) + o_{\mathbb{P}}(n^{-1})$;

(iv) $\det[\mathbf{D}_n] - \det[\mathbf{D}_*] = \det[\mathbf{D}_*]$
$\left\{\mathrm{tr}[\mathbf{P}_n] + \frac{1}{2}\mathrm{tr}\left[\mathbf{P}_n\right]^2 - \frac{1}{2}(\mathrm{tr}\left[\mathbf{W}_n^2\right] - \mathrm{tr}\left[\mathbf{U}_n^2\right])\right\} + o_{\mathbb{P}}(n^{-1})$; and

(v) if $\mathbb{H}_0$ further holds, $\det[\mathbf{D}_n] - 1 = \mathrm{tr}[\mathbf{M}_n] + \frac{1}{2}(\mathrm{tr}[\mathbf{M}_n])^2 - \frac{1}{2}(\mathrm{tr}\left[\mathbf{W}_n^2\right] - \mathrm{tr}\left[\mathbf{U}_n^2\right]) + o_{\mathbb{P}}(n^{-1})$. □

Proof of Lemma A2. (i) By exercise 13.32 of Abadir and Magnus (2005): $d|\mathbf{X}| = |\mathbf{X}|\mathrm{tr}(\mathbf{X}^{-1}d\mathbf{X})$. This also implies that $d^2|\mathbf{X}| = d|\mathbf{X}|\mathrm{tr}(\mathbf{X}^{-1}d\mathbf{X}) + |\mathbf{X}|d\mathrm{tr}(\mathbf{X}^{-1}d\mathbf{X}) = |\mathbf{X}|\mathrm{tr}(\mathbf{X}^{-1}d\mathbf{X})^2 + |\mathbf{X}|\mathrm{tr}(d\mathbf{X}^{-1}\ d\mathbf{X} + \mathbf{X}^{-1}d^2\mathbf{X})$. We also note that $d\mathbf{X}^{-1} = -\ \mathbf{X}^{-1}(d\mathbf{X})\mathbf{X}^{-1}$ by exercise 13.21 of Abadir and Magnus (2005). Thus, $d^2|\mathbf{X}| = |\mathbf{X}|\{\mathrm{tr}(\mathbf{X}^{-1}d\mathbf{X})^2 - \mathrm{tr}[\mathbf{X}^{-1}(d\mathbf{X})\mathbf{X}^{-1}d\mathbf{X}] + \mathrm{tr}[X^{-1}d^2\mathbf{X}]\}$, which implies that the second-order approximation of $|\mathbf{X}| - |\mathbf{X}_o|$ is obtained as $d|\mathbf{X}| + \frac{1}{2}d^2|\mathbf{X}| = |\mathbf{X}_o|\mathrm{tr}(\mathbf{X}_o^{-1}d\mathbf{X}) + \frac{1}{2}|\mathbf{X}_o|\left\{\mathrm{tr}(\mathbf{X}_o^{-1}d\mathbf{X})^2 - \mathrm{tr}\left[\mathbf{X}_o^{-1}(d\mathbf{X})\mathbf{X}_o^{-1}d\mathbf{X}\right] + \mathrm{tr}\left[\mathbf{X}_o^{-1}d^2\mathbf{X}\right]\right\}$, where $d\mathbf{X}$ captures $(\mathbf{X} - \mathbf{X}_o)$.

We now apply this result by letting $\mathbf{X}_o$, $|\mathbf{X}_o|$, and $d\mathbf{X}$ be $\mathbf{A}_*$, det $[\mathbf{A}_*]$, and $\mathbf{A}_n - \mathbf{A}_*$, respectively. Thus,

$$\begin{aligned}\det[\mathbf{A}_n] - \det[\mathbf{A}_*] = &\det[\mathbf{A}_*]\mathrm{tr}[\mathbf{A}_*^{-1}(\mathbf{A}_n - \mathbf{A}_*)] \\ &+ \frac{1}{2}\det[\mathbf{A}_*]\{\mathrm{tr}[\mathbf{A}_*^{-1}(\mathbf{A}_n - \mathbf{A}_*)]^2 \\ &- \mathrm{tr}[\mathbf{A}_*^{-1}(\mathbf{A}_n - \mathbf{A}_*)\mathbf{A}_*^{-1}(\mathbf{A}_n - \mathbf{A}_*)]\} + o_{\mathbb{P}}(n^{-1})\end{aligned}$$

where the final terms are obtained from Assumption 3, that $(\mathbf{A}_n - \mathbf{A}_*) = O_{\mathbb{P}}(n^{-1/2})$. Finally, we note that $\mathbf{U}_n := \mathbf{A}_*^{-1}(\mathbf{A}_n - \mathbf{A}_*)$, so that $\det[\mathbf{A}_n] - \det[\mathbf{A}_*] = \det[\mathbf{A}_*]\left(\mathrm{tr}[\mathbf{U}_n] + \frac{1}{2}\mathrm{tr}\left[\mathbf{U}_n\right]^2 - \frac{1}{2}\mathrm{tr}\left[\mathbf{U}_n^2\right]\right) + o_{\mathbb{P}}(n^{-1})$.

(ii) We apply the same argument, replacing $\mathbf{A}_n$, $\mathbf{A}_*$, and $\mathbf{U}_n$ with $\mathbf{B}_n$, $\mathbf{B}_*$, and $\mathbf{W}_n$, respectively.

(iii) Applying Taylor's expansion gives $\det[\mathbf{A}_n]^{-1} - \det[\mathbf{A}_*]^{-1} = -\det[\mathbf{A}_*]^{-2}(\det[\mathbf{A}_n] - \det[\mathbf{A}_*]) + \det[\mathbf{A}_*]^{-3}(\det[\mathbf{A}_n] - \det[\mathbf{A}_*])^2 + o_{\mathbb{P}}(n^{-1})$ using Assumption 3, that $(\mathbf{A}_n - \mathbf{A}_*) = O_{\mathbb{P}}(n^{-1/2})$. Replacing $(\det[\mathbf{A}_n] - \det[\mathbf{A}_*])$ with the expression in Lemma 2(*i*) and rearranging gives the desired result.

(iv) We note that $\det[\mathbf{D}_n] - \det[\mathbf{D}_*] = \det[\mathbf{B}_n]/\det[\mathbf{A}_n] - \det[\mathbf{B}_*]/\det[\mathbf{A}_*]$ by the definitions of $\mathbf{D}_n$ and $\mathbf{D}_*$, so that the following identity holds:

$$\det[\mathbf{D}_n] - \det[\mathbf{D}_*] \equiv \frac{1}{\det[\mathbf{A}_*]}(\det[\mathbf{B}_n] - \det[\mathbf{B}_*]) + \left(\frac{1}{\det[\mathbf{A}_n]} - \frac{1}{\det[\mathbf{A}_*]}\right)(\det[\mathbf{B}_n] - \det[\mathbf{B}_*]) + \left(\frac{1}{\det[\mathbf{A}_n]} - \frac{1}{\det[\mathbf{A}_*]}\right)\det[\mathbf{B}_*]$$

Using Lemma A2(ii and iii) and rearranging the terms according to the rate of convergence gives the result.

(v) We note that $\mathbf{P}_n = \mathbf{M}_n$ under $\mathbb{H}_0$. The desired result follows from Lemma A2(iv). ■

Lemma A3. Given Assumptions 1, 2, and 3,

(i) $\nabla_{\boldsymbol{\theta}}\mathrm{tr}[\mathbf{D}_n] = [\mathrm{tr}[\mathbf{R}_{j,n}\mathbf{A}_n^{-1}\mathbf{B}_n]]$, where $\mathbf{R}_{j,n} := \mathbf{B}_n^{-1}\partial_j\mathbf{B}_n - \mathbf{A}_n^{-1}\partial_j\mathbf{A}_n$;

(ii) $\nabla_{\boldsymbol{\theta}}\mathrm{tr}[\mathbf{D}_*] = [\mathrm{tr}[\mathbf{R}_{j,*}\mathbf{A}_*^{-1}\mathbf{B}_*]]$, where $\mathbf{R}_{j,*} := \mathbf{B}_*^{-1}\partial_j\mathbf{B}_* - \mathbf{A}_*^{-1}\partial_j\mathbf{A}_*$; and

(iii) if $\mathbb{H}_0$ further holds, $\nabla_{\boldsymbol{\theta}}\mathrm{tr}[\mathbf{D}_*] = [\mathrm{tr}[\mathbf{S}_{j,*}]]$. □

Proof of Lemma A3. (i) By the fact that $\partial_j\mathbf{A}_n^{-1} = -\mathbf{A}_n^{-1}(\partial_j\mathbf{A}_n)\mathbf{A}_n^{-1}$ and the definition of $\mathbf{D}_n := \mathbf{B}_n\mathbf{A}_n^{-1}$, the desired result holds.

(ii) The proof is the same as that of (i). That is, $\mathbf{D}_* := \mathbf{B}_*\mathbf{A}_*^{-1}$ and $\partial_j\mathbf{A}_*^{-1} = -\mathbf{A}_*^{-1}(\partial_j\mathbf{A}_*)\mathbf{A}_*^{-1}$

(iii) If $\mathbb{H}_0$ holds, $\mathbf{B}_*\mathbf{A}_*^{-1} = \mathbf{I}$, so that $\nabla_{\boldsymbol{\theta}}\mathrm{tr}[\mathbf{D}_*] = [\mathrm{tr}[(\partial_j\mathbf{B}_* - \partial_j\mathbf{A}_*)\mathbf{A}_*^{-1}]] = [\mathrm{tr}[\mathbf{S}_{j,*}]]$. ■

Lemma A4. Given Assumptions 1, 2, 3, and 4,

(i) $\nabla_{\boldsymbol{\theta}}\det[\mathbf{D}_n] = \det[\mathbf{D}_n][\mathrm{tr}[\mathbf{R}_{j,n}]]$;

(ii) $\nabla_{\boldsymbol{\theta}}\det[\mathbf{D}_*] = \det[\mathbf{D}_*][\mathrm{tr}[\mathbf{R}_{j,*}]]$;

(iii) if $\mathbb{H}_0$ further holds, $\nabla_{\boldsymbol{\theta}}\det[\mathbf{D}_*] = [\mathrm{tr}[\mathbf{S}_{j,*}]]$;

(iv) $\nabla_{\boldsymbol{\theta}}(\det[\mathbf{D}_n] - \det[\mathbf{D}_*]) = \det[\mathbf{D}_*]\{\mathrm{tr}[\mathbf{P}_n][\mathrm{tr}\ [\mathbf{R}_{j,*}]] + [\mathrm{tr}[\mathbf{A}_*^{-1}(\partial_j\mathbf{A}_*)\mathbf{U}_n - \mathbf{B}_*^{-1}(\partial_j\mathbf{B}_*)\mathbf{W}_n]] + [\mathrm{tr}[\mathbf{J}_{j,n}]]\} + o_{\mathbb{P}}(n^{-1/2})$; and

(v) if $\mathbb{H}_0$ further holds, $\nabla_{\boldsymbol{\theta}}(\det[\mathbf{D}_n] - \det[\mathbf{D}_*]) = \mathrm{tr}[\mathbf{M}_n][\mathrm{tr}[\mathbf{S}_{j,*}]] + [\mathrm{tr}[\mathbf{A}_*^{-1}\{(\partial_j\mathbf{A}_*)\mathbf{U}_n - (\partial_j\mathbf{B}_*)\mathbf{W}_n\}]] + [\mathrm{tr}[\mathbf{J}_{j,n}]] + o_{\mathbb{P}}(n^{-1/2})$. □

Proof of Lemma A4. (i) By exercise 13.32 of Abadir and Magnus (2005): $d|\mathbf{X}| = |\mathbf{X}|\mathrm{tr}(\mathbf{X}^{-1}d\mathbf{X})$, with $d|\mathbf{X}|$ be $\partial_j\det[\mathbf{D}_n]$, and $\partial_j\det[\mathbf{D}_n] = \det[\mathbf{D}_n]\,\mathrm{tr}[\mathbf{D}_n^{-1}\partial_j\mathbf{D}_n]$. Also, $\partial_j\mathbf{D}_n = (\partial_j\mathbf{B}_n)\mathbf{A}_n^{-1} - \mathbf{B}_n\mathbf{A}_n^{-1}(\partial_j\mathbf{A}_n)\mathbf{A}_n^{-1}$. If we combine these, $\partial_j\det[\mathbf{D}_n] = \det[\mathbf{D}_n]\mathrm{tr}[\mathbf{R}_{j,n}]$, and the definition of the gradient yields the result.

(ii) We repeat the proof of (*i*), replacing the subscript "*n*" with the subscript "*".

(iii) Under $\mathbb{H}_0$, $\det[\mathbf{D}_*] = 1$ and $\mathbf{A}_* = \mathbf{B}_*$, so that $\partial_j\det[\mathbf{D}_*] = \mathrm{tr}[\mathbf{A}_*^{-1}\partial_j\mathbf{B}_* - \mathbf{A}_*^{-1}\partial_j\mathbf{A}_*] = \mathrm{tr}[\mathbf{S}_{j,*}]$.

(iv) We note the following identity:

$$\begin{aligned}\nabla_{\boldsymbol{\theta}}(\det[\mathbf{D}_n] - \det[\mathbf{D}_*]) \equiv\ & (\det[\mathbf{D}_n] - \det[\mathbf{D}_*])[\mathrm{tr}[\mathbf{R}_{j,n}]] \\ & + \det[\mathbf{D}_*][\mathrm{tr}[\mathbf{B}_n^{-1}\partial_j\mathbf{B}_n - \mathbf{B}_*^{-1}\partial_j\mathbf{B}_*]] - \det[\mathbf{D}_*] \\ & \times[\mathrm{tr}[\mathbf{A}_n^{-1}\partial_j\mathbf{A}_n - \mathbf{A}_*^{-1}\partial_j\mathbf{A}_*]]\end{aligned} \tag{A.1}$$

We examine the asymptotic approximation of each component in the RHS. First, Lemma A2(*iv*) implies that $\det[\mathbf{D}_n] - \det[\mathbf{D}_*] = \det[\mathbf{D}_*](\mathrm{tr}[\mathbf{P}_n]) + o_{\mathbb{P}}(n^{-1/2})$. Thus,

$$(\det[\mathbf{D}_n] - \det[\mathbf{D}_*])[\mathrm{tr}[\mathbf{R}_{j,n}]] = \det[\mathbf{D}_*](\mathrm{tr}[\mathbf{P}_n])[\mathrm{tr}[\mathbf{R}_{j,*}]] + o_{\mathbb{P}}(n^{-1/2}) \tag{A.2}$$

by Assumptions 3 and 4. Second, we note that

$$\begin{aligned}\mathbf{B}_n^{-1}\partial_j\mathbf{B}_n - \mathbf{B}_*^{-1}\partial_j\mathbf{B}_* &\equiv (\mathbf{B}_n^{-1} - \mathbf{B}_*^{-1})\partial_j\mathbf{B}_n + \mathbf{B}_*^{-1}\partial_j(\mathbf{B}_n - \mathbf{B}_*) \\ &= -\mathbf{W}_n\mathbf{B}_*^{-1}\partial_j\mathbf{B}_* + \mathbf{B}_*^{-1}\partial_j(\mathbf{B}_n - \mathbf{B}_*) + o_{\mathbb{P}}(n^{-1/2})\end{aligned} \tag{A.3}$$

where the last equality holds by Lemma A1(ii). Third, it follows similarly that

$$\mathbf{A}_n^{-1}\partial_j\mathbf{A}_n - \mathbf{A}_*^{-1}\partial_j\mathbf{A}_* = -\mathbf{U}_n\mathbf{A}_*^{-1}\partial_j\mathbf{A}_* + \mathbf{A}_*^{-1}\partial_j(\mathbf{A}_n - \mathbf{A}_*) + o_{\mathbb{P}}(n^{-1/2}). \quad \text{(A.4)}$$

Finally, we plug Eqs. (A.2), (A.3), and (A.4) into Eq. (A.1) and obtain

$$\begin{aligned}\nabla_\theta(\det[\mathbf{D}_n] - \det[\mathbf{D}_*]) &= \det[\mathbf{D}_*]\{\mathrm{tr}[\mathbf{P}_n][\mathrm{tr}[\mathbf{R}_{j,*}]] + [\mathrm{tr}[\mathbf{A}_*^{-1}(\partial_j\mathbf{A}_*)\mathbf{U}_n - \mathbf{B}_*^{-1}(\partial_j\mathbf{B}_*)\mathbf{W}_n]]\}\\ &\quad + \det[\mathbf{D}_*][\mathrm{tr}[\mathbf{B}_*^{-1}\partial_j(\mathbf{B}_n - \mathbf{B}_*) - \mathbf{A}_*^{-1}\partial_j(\mathbf{A}_n - \mathbf{A}_*)]] + o_{\mathbb{P}}(n^{-1/2})\end{aligned} \quad \text{(A.5)}$$

Here, we note that $\mathbf{B}_*^{-1}\partial_j(\mathbf{B}_n - \mathbf{B}_*) - \mathbf{A}_*^{-1}\partial_j(\mathbf{A}_n - \mathbf{A}_*) = \mathbf{G}_{j,n} - \mathbf{H}_{j,n} = \mathbf{J}_{j,n}$ by the definitions of $\mathbf{G}_{j,n}$, $\mathbf{H}_{j,n}$ and $\mathbf{J}_{j,n}$. This yields the desired result.

(v) Under $\mathbb{H}_0$, $\det[\mathbf{D}_*] = 1$ and $\mathbf{P}_n = \mathbf{M}_n$. Also, $\mathrm{tr}[\mathbf{W}_n\mathbf{B}_*^{-1}\partial_j\mathbf{B}_* - \mathbf{U}_n\mathbf{A}_*^{-1}\partial_j\mathbf{A}_*] = \mathrm{tr}[\mathbf{A}_*^{-1}(\partial_j\mathbf{B}_*)\mathbf{W}_n - \mathbf{A}_*^{-1}(\partial_j\mathbf{A}_*)\mathbf{U}_n]$ and $\mathrm{tr}[\mathbf{B}_*^{-1}\partial_j\mathbf{B}_* - \mathbf{A}_*^{-1}\partial_j\mathbf{A}_*] = \mathrm{tr}[\mathbf{A}_*^{-1}(\partial_j\mathbf{B}_* - \partial_j\mathbf{A}_*)] = \mathrm{tr}[\mathbf{S}_{j,*}]$. ■

Lemma A5. Given Assumptions 1 and 2,

(i) $\partial^2_{ji}\mathrm{tr}[\mathbf{D}_*] = \mathrm{tr}[\mathbf{A}_*^{-1}\mathbf{B}_*\{(\mathbf{B}_*^{-1}\partial^2_{ji}\mathbf{B}_* - \mathbf{A}_*^{-1}\partial^2_{ji}\mathbf{A}_*) - (\mathbf{R}_{j,*}\mathbf{A}_*^{-1}\partial_i\mathbf{A}_* + \mathbf{R}_{i,*}\mathbf{A}_*^{-1}\partial_j\mathbf{A}_*)\}]$; and

(ii) if $\mathbb{H}_0$ further holds, $\partial^2_{ji}\mathrm{tr}[\mathbf{D}_*] = \mathrm{tr}[[\mathbf{A}_*^{-1}(\partial^2_{ji}\mathbf{B}_* - \partial^2_{ji}\mathbf{A}_*) - (\mathbf{S}_{j,*}\mathbf{A}_*^{-1}\partial_i\mathbf{A}_* + \mathbf{S}_{i,*}\mathbf{A}_*^{-1}\partial_j\mathbf{A}_*)]]$. □

Proof of Lemma A5. (i) Some tedious algebra shows that

$$\begin{aligned}\partial^2_{ji}\mathbf{D}_* = {} & (\partial^2_{ji}\mathbf{B}_*)\mathbf{A}_*^{-1} - (\partial_i\mathbf{B}_*)\mathbf{A}_*^{-1}(\partial_j\mathbf{A}_*)\mathbf{A}_*^{-1} - (\partial_j\mathbf{B}_*)\mathbf{A}_*^{-1}(\partial_i\mathbf{A}_*)\mathbf{A}_*^{-1}\\ & + \mathbf{B}_*\mathbf{A}_*^{-1}(\partial_j\mathbf{A}_*)\mathbf{A}_*^{-1}(\partial_i\mathbf{A}_*)\mathbf{A}_*^{-1} - \mathbf{B}_*\mathbf{A}_*^{-1}(\partial^2_{ij}\mathbf{A}_*)\mathbf{A}_*^{-1}\\ & + \mathbf{B}_*\mathbf{A}_*^{-1}(\partial_i\mathbf{A}_*)\mathbf{A}_*^{-1}(\partial_j\mathbf{A}_*)\mathbf{A}_*^{-1}\end{aligned}$$

so that

$$\begin{aligned}\partial^2_{ji}\mathrm{tr}[\mathbf{D}_*] = {} & \mathrm{tr}[\mathbf{B}_*\mathbf{A}_*^{-1}[(\partial_j\mathbf{A}_*)\mathbf{A}_*^{-1}(\partial_i\mathbf{A}_*)\mathbf{A}_*^{-1} + (\partial_i\mathbf{A}_*)\mathbf{A}_*^{-1}(\partial_j\mathbf{A}_*)\mathbf{A}_*^{-1}]]\\ & - \mathrm{tr}[(\partial_j\mathbf{A}_*)\mathbf{A}_*^{-1}(\partial_i\mathbf{B}_*)\mathbf{A}_*^{-1} + (\partial_j\mathbf{B}_*)\mathbf{A}_*^{-1}(\partial_i\mathbf{A}_*)\mathbf{A}_*^{-1}] + \mathrm{tr}[[(\partial^2_{ji}\mathbf{B}_*)\\ & - (\partial^2_{ij}\mathbf{A}_*)\mathbf{A}_*^{-1}\mathbf{B}_*]\mathbf{A}_*^{-1}]\end{aligned}$$

We now rearrange this using the definitions of $\mathbf{R}_{j,*}$ and $\mathbf{R}_{i,*}$, yielding the desired result.

(ii) We note that $\mathbf{R}_{j,*} = \mathbf{S}_{j,*}$ and $\mathbf{R}_{i,*} = \mathbf{S}_{i,*}$ under $\mathbb{H}_0$. This completes the proof. ■

Lemma A6. Given Assumptions 1 and 2,

(i) $\partial^2_{ji}\det[\mathbf{D}_*] = \det[\mathbf{D}_*]\quad\{\mathrm{tr}[\mathbf{R}_{i,*}]\mathrm{tr}[\mathbf{R}_{j,*}] + \mathrm{tr}[\mathbf{B}_*^{-1}\partial^2_{ji}\mathbf{B}_* - \mathbf{A}_*^{-1}\partial^2_{ji}\mathbf{A}_* - \mathbf{R}_{i,*}\mathbf{B}_*^{-1}(\partial_j\mathbf{B}_*) - \mathbf{R}_{j,*}\mathbf{A}_*^{-1}\partial_i\mathbf{A}_*]\}$; and

(ii) if $\mathbb{H}_0$ also holds,

$\partial^2_{ji}\det[\mathbf{D}_*] = \mathrm{tr}[\mathbf{S}_{i,*}]\mathrm{tr}[\mathbf{S}_{j,*}] + \mathrm{tr}[\mathbf{A}_*^{-1}(\partial^2_{ji}\mathbf{B}_* - \partial^2_{ji}\mathbf{A}_*) - \mathbf{S}_{i,*}\mathbf{B}_*^{-1}(\partial_j\mathbf{B}_*) - \mathbf{S}_{j,*}\mathbf{A}_*^{-1}\partial_i\mathbf{A}_*]$. □

Proof of Lemma A6. (i) From the proof of Lemma A4 (ii), $\partial_i\det[\mathbf{D}_*] = \det[\mathbf{D}_*]\mathrm{tr}[\mathbf{R}_{i,*}]$. Therefore,

$$\partial^2_{ji}\det[\mathbf{D}_*] = \mathrm{tr}[\mathbf{R}_{i,*}]\partial_j\det[\mathbf{D}_*] + \det[\mathbf{D}_*]\mathrm{tr}[\partial_j\mathbf{B}_*^{-1}\partial_i\mathbf{B}_* + \mathbf{B}_*^{-1}\partial^2_{ji}\mathbf{B}_* - \partial_j\mathbf{A}_*^{-1}\partial_i\mathbf{A}_* - \mathbf{A}_*^{-1}\partial^2_{ji}\mathbf{A}_*].$$

Now replace ∂j $\det[\mathbf{D}_*]$ $\partial_j(\mathbf{B}_*^{-1})$, and $\partial_j(\mathbf{A}_*^{-1})$ with $\det[\mathbf{D}_*]\mathrm{tr}[\mathbf{R}_{j,*}]$, $-\mathbf{B}_*^{-1}(\partial_j\mathbf{B}_*)\mathbf{B}_*^{-1}$, and $-\mathbf{A}_*^{-1}(\partial_j\mathbf{A}_*)\mathbf{A}_*^{-1}$, respectively. Using the definitions of $\mathbf{R}_{j,*}$ and $\mathbf{R}_{i,*}$ and rearranging yields the desired result.

(ii) Under $\mathbb{H}_0$, $\mathbf{A}_* = \mathbf{B}_*$ and $\mathbf{B}_*\mathbf{A}_*^{-1} = \mathbf{I}$. Further, $\mathbf{R}_{j,*} = \mathbf{S}_{j,*}$ and $\mathbf{R}_{i,*} = \mathbf{S}_{i,*}$ ■

Proof of Lemma 2. Lemma 3 implies Lemma 2. ■

Lemma A7. Given Assumptions 1, 2, and $\mathbb{H}_0$, $\nabla^2_{\theta}\mathrm{tr}[\mathbf{D}_*] - \nabla^2_{\theta}\det[\mathbf{D}_*] = [\mathrm{tr}[\mathbf{S}_{j,*}\mathbf{S}_{i,*}] - \mathrm{tr}[\mathbf{S}_{j,*}]\mathrm{tr}[\mathbf{S}_{i,*}]]$. □

Proof of Lemma A7. We apply Lemmas A5(ii) and A6(ii) and obtain

$$\begin{aligned}\partial^2_{ji}\mathrm{tr}([\mathbf{D}_*] - \det[\mathbf{D}_*]) &= \mathrm{tr}[\mathbf{A}_*^{-1}\partial_j\mathbf{A}_*\mathbf{A}_*^{-1}\partial_i\mathbf{A}_*] - \mathrm{tr}[\mathbf{A}_*^{-1}\partial_j\mathbf{B}_*\mathbf{A}_*^{-1}\partial_i\mathbf{A}_*]\\ &\quad - \mathrm{tr}[\mathbf{A}_*^{-1}\partial_j\mathbf{A}_*\mathbf{A}_*^{-1}\partial_i\mathbf{B}_*] + \mathrm{tr}[\mathbf{A}_*^{-1}\partial_j\mathbf{B}_*\mathbf{A}_*^{-1}\partial_i\mathbf{B}_*]\\ &\quad - \mathrm{tr}[\mathbf{S}_{j,*}]\mathrm{tr}[\mathbf{S}_{i*}] = \mathrm{tr}[\mathbf{S}_{j,*}\mathbf{S}_{i,*}] - \mathrm{tr}[\mathbf{S}_{j,*}]\mathrm{tr}[\mathbf{S}_{i,*}]\end{aligned}$$

Therefore, $\nabla^2_{\theta}\mathrm{tr}[\mathbf{D}_*] - \nabla^2_{\theta}\det[\mathbf{D}_*] = [\mathrm{tr}[\mathbf{S}_{j,*}\mathbf{S}_{i,*}] - \mathrm{tr}[\mathbf{S}_{j,*}]\mathrm{tr}[\mathbf{S}_{i,*}]]$. This completes the proof. ■

Proof of Lemma 3. (i) Note that $\mathrm{tr}[\hat{\mathbf{D}}_n - \mathbf{D}_*] = \mathrm{tr}[\hat{\mathbf{D}}_n - \mathbf{D}_n] + \mathrm{tr}[\mathbf{D}_n - \mathbf{D}_*]$ and Lemma 1(iii) gives

$$\mathrm{tr}[\mathbf{D}_n] - \mathrm{tr}[\mathbf{D}_*] = \mathrm{tr}[\mathbf{P}_n\mathbf{A}_*^{-1}\mathbf{B}_*] - \mathrm{tr}[\mathbf{P}_n\mathbf{U}_n\mathbf{A}_*^{-1}\mathbf{B}_*] + o_{\mathbb{P}}(n^{-1}) \qquad \text{(A.6)}$$

We next consider the approximation of $(\hat{\mathbf{D}}_n - \mathbf{D}_n)$. Applying a Taylor expansion gives

$$\mathrm{tr}\left[\hat{\mathbf{D}}_n - \mathbf{D}_n\right] = \nabla'_{\boldsymbol{\theta}}\mathrm{tr}[\mathbf{D}_n]\tilde{\boldsymbol{\theta}}_n + \frac{1}{2}\tilde{\boldsymbol{\theta}}'_n\nabla^2_{\boldsymbol{\theta}}\mathrm{tr}[\mathbf{D}_*]\tilde{\boldsymbol{\theta}}_n + o_{\mathbb{P}}(n^{-1}) \tag{A.7}$$

where $\tilde{\boldsymbol{\theta}}_n :=\hat{\boldsymbol{\theta}}_n - \boldsymbol{\theta}_*$. We also note that

$$\nabla'_{\boldsymbol{\theta}}\mathrm{tr}[\mathbf{D}_n]\tilde{\boldsymbol{\theta}}_n = \nabla'_{\boldsymbol{\theta}}\mathrm{tr}[\mathbf{D}_*]\tilde{\boldsymbol{\theta}}_n + \nabla'_{\boldsymbol{\theta}}(\mathrm{tr}[\mathbf{D}_n] - \mathrm{tr}[\mathbf{D}_*])\tilde{\boldsymbol{\theta}}_n + o_{\mathbb{P}}(n^{-1}) \tag{A.8}$$

and

$$\nabla_{\boldsymbol{\theta}}\mathrm{tr}[\mathbf{D}_*] = [\mathrm{tr}[\mathbf{R}_{j,*}\mathbf{A}_*^{-1}\mathbf{B}_*]] \tag{A.9}$$

by Lemma A3(ii). Further, applying Lemma A3(i and ii) implies that

$$\begin{aligned}\nabla_{\boldsymbol{\theta}}(\mathrm{tr}[\mathbf{D}_n] - \mathrm{tr}[\mathbf{D}_*]) = {} & [\mathrm{tr}[(\partial_j\mathbf{B}_n)\mathbf{A}_n^{-1} - (\partial_j\mathbf{B}_*)\mathbf{A}_*^{-1}]] \\ & - [\mathrm{tr}[\mathbf{B}_n\mathbf{A}_n^{-1}(\partial_j\mathbf{A}_n)\mathbf{A}_n^{-1} - \mathbf{B}_*\mathbf{A}_*^{-1}(\partial_j\mathbf{A}_*)\mathbf{A}_*^{-1}]]\end{aligned} \tag{A.10}$$

We examine each element in Eq. (A.10) separately. The first term in Eq. (A.10) is

$$\begin{aligned}&(\partial_j\mathbf{B}_n)\mathbf{A}_n^{-1} - (\partial_j\mathbf{B}_*)\mathbf{A}_*^{-1} \\ &\qquad \equiv \partial_j(\mathbf{B}_n - \mathbf{B}_*)\mathbf{A}_*^{-1} + \partial_j(\mathbf{B}_n - \mathbf{B}_*)(\mathbf{A}_n^{-1} - \mathbf{A}_*^{-1}) + (\partial_j\mathbf{B}_*)(\mathbf{A}_n^{-1} - \mathbf{A}_*^{-1})\end{aligned}$$

We now apply Lemma A1(i) and obtain

$$(\partial_j\mathbf{B}_n)\mathbf{A}_n^{-1} - (\partial_j\mathbf{B}_*)\mathbf{A}_*^{-1} = \partial_j(\mathbf{B}_n - \mathbf{B}_*)\mathbf{A}_*^{-1} - (\partial_j\mathbf{B}_*)\mathbf{U}_n\mathbf{A}_*^{-1} + o_{\mathbb{P}}(n^{-1/2}) \tag{A.11}$$

For the second term in Eq. (A.10), note that

$$\begin{aligned}&\mathbf{B}_n\mathbf{A}_n^{-1}(\partial_j\mathbf{A}_n)\mathbf{A}_n^{-1} - \mathbf{B}_*\mathbf{A}_*^{-1}(\partial_j\mathbf{A}_*)\mathbf{A}_*^{-1} \\ &\qquad \equiv (\mathbf{B}_n - \mathbf{B}_*)\mathbf{A}_n^{-1}(\partial_j\mathbf{A}_n)\mathbf{A}_n^{-1} + \mathbf{B}_*(\mathbf{A}_n^{-1} - \mathbf{A}_*^{-1})(\partial_j\mathbf{A}_n)\mathbf{A}_n^{-1} \\ &\qquad\quad + \mathbf{B}_*\mathbf{A}_*^{-1}\partial_j(\mathbf{A}_n - \mathbf{A}_*)\mathbf{A}_n^{-1} + \mathbf{B}_*\mathbf{A}_*^{-1}(\partial_j\mathbf{A}_*)(\mathbf{A}_n^{-1} - \mathbf{A}_*^{-1})\end{aligned}$$

and apply Lemma 3(i) and the definitions of $\mathbf{W}_n$ and $\mathbf{H}_{j,n}$ to obtain

$$\begin{aligned}&\mathbf{B}_n\mathbf{A}_n^{-1}(\partial_j\mathbf{A}_n)\mathbf{A}_n^{-1} - \mathbf{B}_*\mathbf{A}_*^{-1}(\partial_j\mathbf{A}_*)\mathbf{A}_*^{-1} \\ &\quad = \mathbf{B}_*\mathbf{W}_n\mathbf{A}_*^{-1}(\partial_j\mathbf{A}_*)\mathbf{A}_*^{-1} - \mathbf{B}_*\mathbf{U}_n\mathbf{A}_*^{-1}(\partial_j\mathbf{A}_*)\mathbf{A}_*^{-1} \\ &\quad\quad + \mathbf{B}_*\mathbf{H}_{j,n}\mathbf{A}_*^{-1} - \mathbf{B}_*\mathbf{A}_*^{-1}(\partial_j\mathbf{A}_*)\mathbf{U}_n\mathbf{A}_*^{-1} + o_{\mathbb{P}}(n^{-1/2})\end{aligned} \tag{A.12}$$

We now subtract Eq. (A.12) from Eq. (A.11) to obtain the approximation of the RHS in Eq. (A.10) as follows:

$$\nabla_\theta(\mathrm{tr}[\mathbf{D}_n]-\mathrm{tr}[\mathbf{D}_*]) = [\mathrm{tr}[\{\mathbf{J}_{j,n}-\mathbf{P}_n\mathbf{A}_*^{-1}\partial_j\mathbf{A}_*-\mathbf{R}_{j,*}\mathbf{U}_n\}\mathbf{A}_*^{-1}\mathbf{B}_*]]+o_{\mathbb{P}}(n^{-1/2}) \tag{A.13}$$

where letting $\mathbf{J}_{j,n}: = \mathbf{G}_{j,n}-\mathbf{H}_{j,n}$, $\mathbf{G}_{j,n} := \mathbf{B}_*^{-1}\partial_j(\mathbf{B}_n-\mathbf{B}_*)$, $\mathbf{P}_n := \mathbf{W}_n-\mathbf{U}_n$, and $\mathbf{R}_{j,*} := \mathbf{B}_*^{-1}\partial_j\mathbf{B}_*-\mathbf{A}_*^{-1}\partial_j\mathbf{A}_*$. We now plug Eqs. (A.9) and (A.13) into Eq. (A.8) and obtain

$$\nabla_\theta'\mathrm{tr}[\mathbf{D}_n]\tilde{\boldsymbol{\theta}}_n = [\mathrm{tr}[\mathbf{R}_{j,*}\mathbf{A}_*^{-1}\mathbf{B}_*+\{\mathbf{J}_{j,n}-\mathbf{P}_n\mathbf{A}_*^{-1}\partial_j\mathbf{A}_*-\mathbf{R}_{j,*}\mathbf{U}_n\}\mathbf{A}_*^{-1}\mathbf{B}_*]]'\tilde{\boldsymbol{\theta}}_n+o_{\mathbb{P}}(n^{-1})$$

Plugging this into Eq. (A.7) yields

$$\begin{aligned}\mathrm{tr}[\hat{\mathbf{D}}_n-\mathbf{D}_n] &= [\mathrm{tr}[\mathbf{R}_{j,*}\mathbf{A}_*^{-1}\mathbf{B}_*+\{\mathbf{J}_{j,n}-\mathbf{P}_n\mathbf{A}_*^{-1}\partial_j\mathbf{A}_*-\mathbf{R}_{j,*}\mathbf{U}_n\}\mathbf{A}_*^{-1}\mathbf{B}_*]]'\tilde{\boldsymbol{\theta}}_n\\ &\quad+\frac{1}{2}\tilde{\boldsymbol{\theta}}_n'\nabla_\theta^2\mathrm{tr}[\mathbf{D}_*]\tilde{\boldsymbol{\theta}}_n+o_{\mathbb{P}}(n^{-1})\end{aligned} \tag{A.14}$$

We now combine Eqs. (A.6) and (A.14) and obtain

$$\begin{aligned}\mathrm{tr}[\hat{\mathbf{D}}_n]-\mathrm{tr}[\mathbf{D}_*] &= \mathrm{tr}[\mathbf{L}_n\mathbf{A}_*^{-1}\mathbf{B}_*]-\mathrm{tr}[\mathbf{L}_n\mathbf{U}_n\mathbf{A}_*^{-1}\mathbf{B}_*]+[\mathrm{tr}[(\mathbf{J}_{j,n}-\mathbf{P}_n\mathbf{A}_*^{-1}\partial_j\mathbf{A}_*)\mathbf{A}_*^{-1}\mathbf{B}_*]]'\tilde{\boldsymbol{\theta}}_n\\ &\quad+\frac{1}{2}\tilde{\boldsymbol{\theta}}_n'\nabla_\theta^2\mathrm{tr}[\mathbf{D}_*]\tilde{\boldsymbol{\theta}}_n+o_{\mathbb{P}}(n^{-1})\end{aligned} \tag{A.15}$$

where we let $\mathbf{L}_n : = \mathbf{P}_n+\sum_{j=1}^{l}\tilde{\theta}_{j,n}\mathbf{R}_{j,*}$. Finally, imposing $\mathbb{H}_0$ implies that $\mathbf{L}_n = \mathbf{M}_n+\sum_{j=1}^{l}\tilde{\theta}_{j,n}\mathbf{S}_{j,*}$, $\mathbf{A}_*^{-1}\mathbf{B}_* = \mathbf{I}$, and $\mathbf{P}_n = \mathbf{M}_n$, so that the desired result follows.

(ii) We note that

$$\det[\hat{\mathbf{D}}_n]^{\frac{1}{k}}-\det[\mathbf{D}_*]^{\frac{1}{k}} \equiv \left(\det[\hat{\mathbf{D}}_n]^{\frac{1}{k}}-\det[\mathbf{D}_n]^{\frac{1}{k}}\right)+\left(\det[\mathbf{D}_n]^{\frac{1}{k}}-\det[\mathbf{D}_*]^{\frac{1}{k}}\right) \tag{A.16}$$

We separately examine the approximation for each term of the RHS and then combine them under the null.

First, we consider $\det[\mathbf{D}_n]^{\frac{1}{k}}-\det[\mathbf{D}_*]^{\frac{1}{k}}$. We note that

$$\begin{aligned}\det[\mathbf{D}_n]^{\frac{1}{k}}-\det[\mathbf{D}_*]^{\frac{1}{k}} &= \frac{1}{k}\det[\mathbf{D}_*]^{\frac{1}{k}-1}(\det[\mathbf{D}_n]-\det[\mathbf{D}_*])\\ &\quad+\frac{1}{2k}\left(\frac{1}{k}-1\right)\det[\mathbf{D}_*]^{\frac{1}{k}-2}(\det[\mathbf{D}_n]-\det[\mathbf{D}_*])^2+o_{\mathbb{P}}(n^{-1})\end{aligned}$$

by a second-order Taylor expansion. We apply Lemma A2(iv) to obtain

$$\det[\mathbf{D}_n]^{\frac{1}{k}} - \det[\mathbf{D}_*]^{\frac{1}{k}} = \det[\mathbf{D}_*]^{\frac{1}{k}}\left\{\frac{1}{k}\mathrm{tr}[\mathbf{P}_n] + \frac{1}{2k^2}\mathrm{tr}[\mathbf{P}_n]^2 - \frac{1}{2k}(\mathrm{tr}\left[\mathbf{W}_n^2\right] - \mathrm{tr}\left[\mathbf{U}_n^2\right])\right\} + o_{\mathbb{P}}(n^{-1}) \tag{A.17}$$

Next, we approximate $\det[\hat{\mathbf{D}}_n]^{1/k} - \det[\mathbf{D}_n]^{1/k}$. A second-order Taylor expansion gives

$$\begin{aligned}\det[\hat{\mathbf{D}}_n]^{\frac{1}{k}} - \det[\mathbf{D}_n]^{\frac{1}{k}} &= \frac{1}{k}\det[\mathbf{D}_n]^{\frac{1}{k}-1}\nabla'_\theta \det[\mathbf{D}_n]\tilde{\boldsymbol{\theta}}_n + \frac{1}{2k}\det[\mathbf{D}_n]^{\frac{1}{k}-1}\tilde{\boldsymbol{\theta}}'_n\nabla^2_\theta\det[\mathbf{D}_n]\tilde{\boldsymbol{\theta}}_n \\ &+ \frac{1}{2k}\left(\frac{1}{k}-1\right)\det[\mathbf{D}_n]^{\frac{1}{k}-2}\{\nabla'_\theta\det[\mathbf{D}_n]\tilde{\boldsymbol{\theta}}_n\}^2 + o_{\mathbb{P}}(n^{-1})\end{aligned} \tag{A.18}$$

Here, each term on the RHS can be approximated as follows: we have

$$\det[\mathbf{D}_n]^{\frac{1}{k}-2}\{\tilde{\boldsymbol{\theta}}'_n\nabla_\theta\det[\mathbf{D}_n]\}^2 = \det[\mathbf{D}_*]^{\frac{1}{k}}\left\{\tilde{\boldsymbol{\theta}}'_n[\mathrm{tr}[\mathbf{R}_{j,*}]]\right\}^2 + o_{\mathbb{P}}(n^{-1}) \tag{A.19}$$

by Assumption 4 and Lemma A4(i, ii), and

$$\det[\mathbf{D}_n]^{\frac{1}{k}-1}\tilde{\boldsymbol{\theta}}'_n\nabla^2_\theta\det[\mathbf{D}_n]\tilde{\boldsymbol{\theta}}_n = \det[\mathbf{D}_*]^{\frac{1}{k}-1}\tilde{\boldsymbol{\theta}}'_n\nabla^2_\theta\det[\mathbf{D}_*]\tilde{\boldsymbol{\theta}}_n + o_{\mathbb{P}}(n^{-1}) \tag{A.20}$$

Here, we have used Assumption 3. Also, we can decompose the main part of the first term on the RHS as

$$\begin{aligned}\det[\mathbf{D}_n]^{\frac{1}{k}-1}\nabla'_\theta\det[\mathbf{D}_n]\tilde{\boldsymbol{\theta}}_n &\equiv \det[\mathbf{D}_*]^{\frac{1}{k}-1}\nabla'_\theta\det[\mathbf{D}_*]\tilde{\boldsymbol{\theta}}_n \\ &+ \left(\det[\mathbf{D}_n]^{\frac{1}{k}-1} - \det[\mathbf{D}_*]^{\frac{1}{k}-1}\right)\nabla'_\theta\det[\mathbf{D}_*]\tilde{\boldsymbol{\theta}}_n \\ &+ \det[\mathbf{D}_n]^{\frac{1}{k}-1}(\nabla'_\theta\det[\mathbf{D}_n] - \nabla'_\theta\det[\mathbf{D}_*])\tilde{\boldsymbol{\theta}}_n\end{aligned} \tag{A.21}$$

We examine the approximation of each term on the RHS of Eq. (A.21): (*a*) the first term is

$$\det[\mathbf{D}_*]^{\frac{1}{k}-1}\nabla'_\theta\det[\mathbf{D}_*]\tilde{\boldsymbol{\theta}}_n = \det[\mathbf{D}_*]^{\frac{1}{k}}\left[\mathrm{tr}\left[\mathbf{R}_{j,*}\right]\right]'\tilde{\boldsymbol{\theta}}_n \tag{A.22}$$

by Lemma A4(ii); (*b*) the second term on the RHS of Eq. (A.21) can be written as

$$\left(\det[\mathbf{D}_n]^{\frac{1}{k}-1} - \det[\mathbf{D}_*]^{\frac{1}{k}-1}\right)\nabla'_\theta \det[\mathbf{D}_*]\tilde{\boldsymbol{\theta}}_n$$

$$= \left(\frac{1}{k}-1\right)\det[\mathbf{D}_*]^{\frac{1}{k}-2}(\det[\mathbf{D}_n]-\det[\mathbf{D}_*])\nabla'_\theta\det[\mathbf{D}_*]\tilde{\boldsymbol{\theta}}_n + o_{\mathbb{P}}(n^{-1}) \quad \text{(A.23)}$$

$$= \left(\frac{1}{k}-1\right)\det[\mathbf{D}_*]^{\frac{1}{k}}\mathrm{tr}[\mathbf{P}_n]\left[\mathrm{tr}\left[\mathbf{R}_{j,*}\right]\right]'\tilde{\boldsymbol{\theta}}_n + o_{\mathbb{P}}(n^{-1})$$

by Lemmas A2(iv) and A4(ii); (*c*) the final term on the RHS of Eq. (A.21) can be written as

$$\det[\mathbf{D}_n]^{\frac{1}{k}-1}(\nabla'_\theta\det[\mathbf{D}_n]-\nabla'_\theta\det[\mathbf{D}_*])\tilde{\boldsymbol{\theta}}_n = \det[\mathbf{D}_*]^{\frac{1}{k}}\mathrm{tr}[\mathbf{P}_n]\left[\mathrm{tr}\left[\mathbf{R}_{j,*}\right]\right]'\tilde{\boldsymbol{\theta}}_n + \det[\mathbf{D}_*]^{\frac{1}{k}}$$
$$\times[\mathrm{tr}[\mathbf{J}_{j,n}+\mathbf{U}_n\mathbf{A}_*^{-1}\partial_j\mathbf{A}_*-\mathbf{W}_n\mathbf{B}_*^{-1}\partial_j\mathbf{B}_*]]'\tilde{\boldsymbol{\theta}}_n + o_{\mathbb{P}}(n^{-1}) \quad \text{(A.24)}$$

by Lemma A4(iv); (*d*) we now plug Eq. (A.22), (A.23), and (A.24) into Eq. (A.21) and obtain

$$\det[\mathbf{D}_n]^{\frac{1}{k}-1}\nabla'_\theta\det[\mathbf{D}_n]\tilde{\boldsymbol{\theta}}_n = \det[\mathbf{D}_*]^{\frac{1}{k}}\left\{1+k^{-1}\mathrm{tr}[\mathbf{P}_n]\right\}[\mathrm{tr}\left[\mathbf{R}_{j,*}\right]]'\tilde{\boldsymbol{\theta}}_n$$
$$+\det[\mathbf{D}_*]^{\frac{1}{k}}\left[\mathrm{tr}\left[\mathbf{J}_{j,n}+\mathbf{U}_n\mathbf{A}_*^{-1}\partial_j\mathbf{A}_*-\mathbf{W}_n\mathbf{B}_*^{-1}\partial_j\mathbf{B}_*\right]\right]'\tilde{\boldsymbol{\theta}}_n + o_{\mathbb{P}}(n^{-1}) \quad \text{(A.25)}$$

Plugging Eqs. (A.19), (A.20), and (A.25) into Eq. (A.18) gives

$$\det[\hat{\mathbf{D}}_n]^{\frac{1}{k}} - \det[\mathbf{D}_n]^{\frac{1}{k}} = \frac{1}{k}\det[\mathbf{D}_*]^{\frac{1}{k}}\left\{1+\frac{1}{k}\mathrm{tr}[\mathbf{P}_n]\right\}[\mathrm{tr}\left[\mathbf{R}_{j,*}\right]]'\tilde{\boldsymbol{\theta}}_n$$
$$+\frac{1}{k}\det[\mathbf{D}_*]^{\frac{1}{k}}[\mathrm{tr}\left[\mathbf{J}_{jn}+\mathbf{U}_n\mathbf{A}_*^{-1}\partial_j\mathbf{A}_*-\mathbf{W}_n\mathbf{B}_*^{-1}\partial_j\mathbf{B}_*\right]]'\tilde{\boldsymbol{\theta}}_n$$
$$+\frac{1}{2k}\left(\frac{1}{k}-1\right)\det[\mathbf{D}_*]^{\frac{1}{k}}\{[\mathrm{tr}[\mathbf{R}_{j,*}]]'\tilde{\boldsymbol{\theta}}_n\}^2+\frac{1}{2k}\det[\mathbf{D}_*]^{\frac{1}{k}-1}\tilde{\boldsymbol{\theta}}'_n\nabla^2_\theta\det[\mathbf{D}_*]\tilde{\boldsymbol{\theta}}_n+o_{\mathbb{P}}(n^{-1}) \quad \text{(A.26)}$$

Summing Eqs. (A.17) and (A.26) then gives

$$\det[\mathbf{D}_*]^{-\frac{1}{k}}\{\det[\hat{\mathbf{D}}_n]^{1/k}-\det[\mathbf{D}_*]^{1/k}\}=\frac{1}{k}\mathrm{tr}[\mathbf{L}_n]+\frac{1}{2k}\left(\frac{1}{k}-1\right)\mathrm{tr}[\mathbf{L}_n]^2$$
$$+\frac{1}{k}\mathrm{tr}[\mathbf{P}_n]\mathrm{tr}[\sum_{j=1}^{l}\tilde{\theta}_{j,n}\mathbf{R}_{j,*}]+\frac{1}{2k}(\mathrm{tr}[\mathbf{P}_n]^2+\mathrm{tr}\left[\mathbf{U}_n^2\right]-\mathrm{tr}\left[\mathbf{W}_n^2\right])$$
$$+\frac{1}{k}[\mathrm{tr}\left[\mathbf{J}_{j,n}+\mathbf{U}_n\mathbf{A}_*^{-1}\partial_j\mathbf{A}_*-\mathbf{W}_n\mathbf{B}_*^{-1}\partial_j\mathbf{B}_*\right]]'\tilde{\boldsymbol{\theta}}_n+\frac{1}{2k}\det[\mathbf{D}_*]^{-1}\tilde{\boldsymbol{\theta}}_n'\nabla_{\boldsymbol{\theta}}^2\det[\mathbf{D}_*]\tilde{\boldsymbol{\theta}}_n+o(n^{-1}) \tag{A.27}$$

Here, we let $\mathbf{L}_n := \mathbf{P}_n + \sum_{j=1}^{l}(\hat{\theta}_{j,n}-\theta_{j,*})\mathbf{R}_{j,*}$. This reduces to the desired result by noting that $\det[\mathbf{D}_*]=1$, $\mathbf{L}_n=\mathbf{K}_n$, $\mathbf{P}_n=\mathbf{M}_n$, and $\mathbf{R}_{j,*}=\mathbf{S}_{j,*}$ under $\mathbb{H}_0$.

(iii) By the definitions of $\hat{T}_n^*$ and $\hat{D}_n^*$, it also follows that $\hat{S}_n^*=\hat{T}_n^*-\hat{D}_n^*$, so that

$$\hat{S}_n^*=-\frac{1}{2k}\left(\frac{1}{k}-1\right)\mathrm{tr}[\mathbf{K}_n]^2-\frac{1}{k}\mathrm{tr}[\mathbf{K}_n\mathbf{U}_n]-\frac{1}{2k}(\mathrm{tr}[\mathbf{M}_n]^2+\mathrm{tr}\left[\mathbf{U}_n^2\right]-\mathrm{tr}\left[\mathbf{W}_n^2\right])$$
$$-\frac{1}{k}[\mathrm{tr}\left[\mathbf{M}_n\mathbf{A}_*^{-1}\partial_j\mathbf{A}_*+\mathbf{U}_n\mathbf{A}_*^{-1}\partial_j\mathbf{A}_*-\mathbf{W}_n\mathbf{A}_*^{-1}\partial_j\mathbf{B}_*\right]]'\tilde{\boldsymbol{\theta}}_n-\frac{1}{k}[\mathrm{tr}[\mathbf{M}_n]\mathrm{tr}\left[\mathbf{S}_{j,*}\right]]'\tilde{\boldsymbol{\theta}}_n$$
$$+\frac{1}{2k}\tilde{\boldsymbol{\theta}}_n'(\nabla_{\boldsymbol{\theta}}^2\mathrm{tr}[\mathbf{D}_*]-\nabla_{\boldsymbol{\theta}}^2\det[\mathbf{D}_*])\tilde{\boldsymbol{\theta}}_n$$

Here, Lemma 7 implies that $(\nabla_{\boldsymbol{\theta}}^2\mathrm{tr}[\mathbf{D}_*]-\nabla_{\boldsymbol{\theta}}^2\det[\mathbf{D}_*])=[\mathrm{tr}[\mathbf{S}_{j,*}\mathbf{S}_{i,*}]-\mathrm{tr}[\mathbf{S}_{j,*}]\mathrm{tr}[\mathbf{S}_{i,*}]]$. Therefore,

$$\frac{1}{2k}\tilde{\boldsymbol{\theta}}_n'(\nabla_{\boldsymbol{\theta}}^2\mathrm{tr}[\mathbf{D}_*]-\nabla_{\boldsymbol{\theta}}^2\det[\mathbf{D}_*])\tilde{\boldsymbol{\theta}}_n=\frac{1}{2k}\mathrm{tr}\left[\left(\sum_{j=1}^{l}(\hat{\theta}_{j,n}-\theta_{j,*})\mathbf{S}_{j,*}\right)^2\right]-\frac{1}{2k}\mathrm{tr}\left[\sum_{j=1}^{l}(\hat{\theta}_{j,n}-\theta_{j,*})\mathbf{S}_{j,*}\right]^2 \tag{A.28}$$

Next, we note that $\mathbf{M}_n=\mathbf{W}_n-\mathbf{U}_n$ and $\mathbf{K}_n=\mathbf{M}_n+\sum^{j=1l}(\hat{\theta}_{j,n}-\theta_{j,*})\mathbf{S}_{j,*}$ under $\mathbb{H}_0$, so that

$$-\frac{1}{2k}(\mathrm{tr}[\mathbf{U}_n^2]-\mathrm{tr}[\mathbf{W}_n^2])=\frac{1}{2k}\mathrm{tr}[\mathbf{M}_n^2]+\frac{1}{k}\mathrm{tr}[\mathbf{M}_n\mathbf{U}_n] \tag{A.29}$$

and

$$-\frac{1}{k}\mathrm{tr}[\mathbf{K}_n\mathbf{U}_n]=-\frac{1}{k}\mathrm{tr}[\mathbf{M}_n\mathbf{U}_n]-\frac{1}{k}\mathrm{tr}\left[\mathbf{U}_n\sum_{j=1}^{l}(\hat{\theta}_{j,n}-\theta_{j,*})\mathbf{S}_{j,*}\right] \tag{A.30}$$

Finally, we note that under $\mathbb{H}_0$,

$$\frac{1}{k}\mathrm{tr}\left[\mathbf{M}_n\mathbf{A}_*^{-1}\partial_j\mathbf{A}_*+\mathbf{U}_n\mathbf{A}_*^{-1}\partial_j\mathbf{A}_*-\mathbf{W}_n\mathbf{A}_*^{-1}\partial_j\mathbf{B}_*\right]=-\frac{1}{k}\mathrm{tr}\left[\mathbf{M}_n\mathbf{S}_{j,*}+\mathbf{U}_n\mathbf{S}_{j,*}\right] \tag{A.31}$$

We now replace these new representations in Eqs. (A.28), (A.29), (A.30), and (A.31) and rearrange the terms to obtain the desired result. ■

Proof of Lemma 4. The given claims are already proven by Eqs. (A.15) and (A.27). ■

Proof of Corollary 1. We let $\mathbf{Q}_n := \left(\mathbf{A}_*^{-1}\mathbf{B}_* - \det[\mathbf{D}_*]^{\frac{1}{k}}\mathbf{I}\right)$ for notational simplicity. We also have $\hat{S}_n=(T_*-D_*)+\alpha_n+\beta_n+o_{\mathbb{P}}(n^{-1})$, where $\alpha_n:=\alpha_n^{(1)}+\alpha_n^{(2)}$, $\alpha_n^{(1)}:=\frac{1}{k}\mathrm{tr}[\mathbf{Q}_n\mathbf{L}_n]$

$$\alpha_n^{(2)}:=\frac{1}{k}\left[\mathrm{tr}\left[\mathbf{Q}_n\mathbf{J}_{j,n}\right]]'\tilde{\boldsymbol{\theta}}_n-\frac{1}{k}\tilde{\boldsymbol{\theta}}_n'\left[\mathrm{tr}\left[\mathbf{Q}_n\mathbf{R}_{j,*}\mathbf{A}_*^{-1}\partial_i\mathbf{A}_*+\mathbf{Q}_n(\mathbf{B}_*^{-1}\partial_{ji}^2\mathbf{B}_*-\mathbf{A}_*^{-1}\partial_{ji}^2\mathbf{A}_*)\right]\right]'\tilde{\boldsymbol{\theta}}_n$$

and

$$\begin{aligned}\beta_n :=& -\frac{1}{k}\mathrm{tr}\left[\mathbf{A}_*^{-1}\mathbf{B}_*\mathbf{L}_n\mathbf{U}_n\right]-\det[\mathbf{D}_*]^{\frac{1}{k}}\left\{\frac{1}{2k^2}\mathrm{tr}[\mathbf{L}_n]^2-\frac{1}{2k}\mathrm{tr}\left[\mathbf{W}_n^2-\mathbf{U}_n^2\right]\right\}\\ &-\frac{1}{k}[\mathrm{tr}\left[\mathbf{A}_*^{-1}\mathbf{B}_*\mathbf{P}_n\mathbf{A}_*^{-1}\partial_j\mathbf{A}_*\right]]'\tilde{\boldsymbol{\theta}}_n+\frac{1}{k}\det[\mathbf{D}_*]^{\frac{1}{k}}[\mathrm{tr}\left[\mathbf{U}_n\mathbf{R}_{j,*}+\mathbf{P}_n\mathbf{B}_*^{-1}\partial_j\mathbf{B}_*\right]]'\tilde{\boldsymbol{\theta}}_n\\ &+\frac{1}{2k}\det[\mathbf{D}_*]^{\frac{1}{k}}\tilde{\boldsymbol{\theta}}_n'\left[\mathrm{tr}\left[\mathbf{R}_{j,*}\mathbf{R}_{i,*}\right]\right]\tilde{\boldsymbol{\theta}}_n\end{aligned}$$

by Lemmas 4, A5, and A6.

(i) It is not hard to see that $\alpha_n^{(1)} = O_{\mathbb{P}}(n^{-1/2})$, $\alpha_n^{(2)} = O_{\mathbb{P}}(n^{-1})$, and $\beta_n = O_{\mathbb{P}}(n^{-1})$. Thus, $\hat{S}_n = (T_* - D_*) + \alpha_n^{(1)} + o_{\mathbb{P}}(n^{-1/2}) = (T_* - D_*) + \frac{1}{k}\mathrm{tr}[(\mathbf{A}_*^{-1}\mathbf{B}_* - \det[\mathbf{D}_*]^{\frac{1}{k}}\mathbf{I})\mathbf{L}_n] + o_{\mathbb{P}}(n^{-1/2})$ by the definition of $\mathbf{Q}_n$.

(ii) If for some $d_* > 0$, $\mathbf{B}_* = d_*\mathbf{A}_*$, $\det[\mathbf{D}_*]^{\frac{1}{k}} = d_*$, and $\mathbf{Q}_n = \mathbf{0}$. Also, $T_* = D_*$, $\alpha_n = 0$, and

$$\beta_n = -\frac{d_*}{2k^2}\mathrm{tr}[\mathbf{L}_n]^2 - \frac{d_*}{k}\mathrm{tr}[\mathbf{L}_n\mathbf{U}_n] + \frac{d_*}{2k}\mathrm{tr}\left[\mathbf{W}_n^2 - \mathbf{U}_n^2\right] + \frac{d_*}{2k}\tilde{\boldsymbol{\theta}}_n'\left[\mathrm{tr}\left[\mathbf{R}_{j,*}\mathbf{R}_{i,*}\right]\right]\tilde{\boldsymbol{\theta}}_n$$

$$+ \frac{d_*}{k}\left[\mathrm{tr}\left[\mathbf{U}_n\mathbf{R}_{j,*} + \mathbf{P}_n(\mathbf{B}_*^{-1}\partial_j\mathbf{B}_* - \mathbf{A}_*^{-1}\partial_j\mathbf{A}_*)\right]\right]'\tilde{\boldsymbol{\theta}}_n$$

Here, we let $\mathbf{L}_n := \mathbf{W}_n - \mathbf{U}_n + \sum_{j=1}^{l}\tilde{\theta}_{j,n}\mathbf{R}_{j,*}$ and $\mathbf{R}_{j,*} := \mathbf{B}_*^{-1}\partial_j\mathbf{B}_* - \mathbf{A}_*^{-1}\partial_j\mathbf{A}_*$, so that

$$\beta_n = -\frac{d_*}{2k^2}\mathrm{tr}[\mathbf{L}_n]^2 + \frac{d_*}{2k}\mathrm{tr}\left[(\mathbf{W}_n - \mathbf{U}_n)^2 + 2(\mathbf{W}_n - \mathbf{U}_n)\sum_{j=1}^{l}\tilde{\theta}_{j,n}\mathbf{R}_{j,*} + \left(\sum_{j=1}^{l}\tilde{\theta}_{j,n}\mathbf{R}_{j,*}\right)^2\right]$$

Finally, we note that $\mathrm{tr}[\mathbf{L}_n^2] = \mathrm{tr}\left[\mathbf{W}_n^2 + \mathbf{U}_n^2 - 2\mathbf{W}_n\mathbf{U}_n + 2(\mathbf{W}_n - \mathbf{U}_n)\sum_{j=1}^{l}\tilde{\theta}_{j,n}\mathbf{R}_{j,*} + \left(\sum_{j=1}^{\ell}\tilde{\theta}_{j,n}\mathbf{R}_{j,*}\right)^2\right]$, yielding

$$\beta_n = -\frac{d_*}{2k^2}\mathrm{tr}[\mathbf{L}_n]^2 + \frac{d_*}{2k}\mathrm{tr}\left[\mathbf{L}_n^2\right]$$

This completes the proof. ■

The following lemmas are useful in examining the test statistics under the local alternative: $\mathbb{H}_a^{(1)}$.

Lemma A8. Given the same conditions as in Lemma 5 and $\mathbb{H}_a^{(1)}$,

(i) $\mathbf{B}_{*,n}^{-1} = \mathbf{B}_*^{-1} - n^{-1/2}\mathbf{N}_*\mathbf{B}_*^{-1} + O(n^{-1})$;

(ii) $\mathrm{tr}\left[\mathbf{B}_{*,n}\mathbf{A}_*^{-1}\right] = k + n^{-1/2}\mathrm{tr}[\mathbf{N}_*]$;

(iii) $\tilde{\mathbf{R}}_{j,*,n} = \mathbf{S}_{j,*} + n^{-1/2}\mathbf{C}_{j,*} + O(n^{-1})$, where $\tilde{\mathbf{R}}_{j,*,n} := \mathbf{B}_{*,n}^{-1}\partial_j\mathbf{B}_{*,n} - \mathbf{A}_*^{-1}\partial_j\mathbf{A}_*$;

(iv) $\tilde{\mathbf{P}}_n = \mathbf{M}_{o,n} - n^{-1/2}\mathbf{N}_*\mathbf{W}_{o,n} + O_{\mathbb{P}}(n^{-3/2})$, where $\tilde{\mathbf{P}}_n := \mathbf{B}_{*,n}^{-1}(\mathbf{B}_n - \mathbf{B}_{*,n}) - \mathbf{A}_*^{-1}(\mathbf{A}_n - \mathbf{A}_*)$;

(v) $\tilde{\mathbf{L}}_n = \mathbf{K}_{o,n} + n^{-1/2}\sum_{j=1}^{l}\left(\hat{\theta}_{j,n} - \theta_{j,*}\right)\mathbf{C}_{j,*} - n^{-1/2}\mathbf{N}_*\mathbf{W}_{o,n} + O_{\mathbb{P}}\left(n^{-3/2}\right)$, where $\tilde{\mathbf{L}}_n := \tilde{\mathbf{P}}_n + \sum_{j=1}^{l}\left(\hat{\theta}_{j,n} - \theta_{j,*}\right)\tilde{\mathbf{R}}_{j,*,n}$;

(vi) $\mathrm{tr}\left[\tilde{\mathbf{L}}_n\mathbf{A}_*^{-1}\mathbf{B}_{*,n}\right] = \mathrm{tr}\left[\mathbf{K}_{o,n}\right] + n^{-1/2}\mathrm{tr}\left[\sum_{j=1}^{l}\left(\hat{\theta}_{j,n}-\theta_{j,*}\right)\{\mathbf{S}_{j,*}\mathbf{N}_*+\mathbf{C}_{j,*}\} - \mathbf{U}_n\mathbf{N}_*\right] + O_{\mathbb{P}}\left(n^{-3/2}\right)$;

(vii) $\mathrm{tr}\left[\tilde{\mathbf{L}}_n\mathbf{U}_n\mathbf{A}_*^{-1}\mathbf{B}_{*,n}\right] = \mathrm{tr}\left[\mathbf{K}_{o,n}\mathbf{U}_n\right] + O_{\mathbb{P}}\left(n^{-3/2}\right)$; and

(viii) $\tilde{\mathbf{J}}_{j,n} = \mathbf{J}_{j,o,n} + O_{\mathbb{P}}\left(n^{-1}\right)$, where $\tilde{\boldsymbol{J}}_{j,n} := \boldsymbol{B}_{*,n}^{-1}\partial_j\left(\boldsymbol{B}_n - \boldsymbol{B}_{*,n}\right) - \boldsymbol{A}_*^{-1}\partial_j\left(\boldsymbol{A}_n - \boldsymbol{A}_*\right)$. □

Proof of Lemma A8. (i) From the definition of $\mathbf{B}_{*,n}$, $\mathbf{B}_{*,n} = \mathbf{B}_*\left(\mathbf{I} - n^{-1/2}\mathbf{B}_*^{-1}\left(-\overline{\mathbf{B}}_*\right)\right)$, so that $\mathbf{B}_{*,n}^{-1} = \left(\mathbf{I} - n^{-1/2}\mathbf{B}_*^{-1}\left(-\overline{\mathbf{B}}_*\right)\right)^{-1}\mathbf{B}_*^{-1}$. We also note that when the sample size n is moderately large, all eigenvalues of $n^{-1/2}\mathbf{B}_*^{-1}\left(-\overline{\mathbf{B}}_*\right)$ are less than one in modulus, so that

$$\left(\mathbf{I} - n^{-1/2}\mathbf{B}_*^{-1}\left(-\overline{\mathbf{B}}_*\right)\right)^{-1} = \mathbf{I} - n^{-1/2}\mathbf{B}_*^{-1}\overline{\mathbf{B}}_* + n^{-1}\mathbf{B}_*^{-1}\overline{\mathbf{B}}_*\mathbf{B}_*^{-1}\overline{\mathbf{B}}_* + \ldots.$$

This implies that $\mathbf{B}_{*,n}^{-1} = \mathbf{B}_*^{-1} - n^{-1/2}\mathbf{N}_*\mathbf{B}_*^{-1} + n^{-1}\mathbf{N}_*^2\mathbf{B}_*^{-1} + \ldots$. The desired result follows from this.

(ii) Under $\mathbb{H}_a^{(1)}$, $\mathbf{B}_{*,n}\mathbf{A}_*^{-1} = \mathbf{I} + n^{-1/2}\overline{\mathbf{B}}_*\mathbf{B}_*^{-1}$. Thus, $\mathrm{tr}\left[\mathbf{B}_{*,n}\mathbf{A}_*^{-1}\right] = k + n^{-1/2}\mathrm{tr}[\mathbf{N}_*]$.

(iii) Using Lemma A8(i) and $\mathbf{B}_{*,n}$, $\mathbf{B}_{*,n}^{-1}\partial_j\mathbf{B}_{*,n} = \left(\mathbf{B}_*^{-1} - n^{-1/2}\mathbf{N}_*\mathbf{B}_*^{-1}\right) \times \left(\partial_j\mathbf{B}_* + n^{-1/2}\partial_j\overline{\mathbf{B}}_*\right) + O\left(n^{-1}\right) = \mathbf{B}_*^{-1}\partial_j\mathbf{B}_* + n^{-1/2}\mathbf{C}_{j,*} + O\left(n^{-1}\right)$. Also, under $\mathbb{H}_a^{(1)}$, $\mathbf{A}_* = \mathbf{B}_*$. Thus, the desired result follows by the definition of $\mathbf{S}_{j,*}$.

(iv) Using Lemma A8(i) and the definition of $\mathbf{W}_{o,n} := \mathbf{B}_*^{-1}\left(\mathbf{B}_n - \mathbf{B}_{*,n}\right)$, $\tilde{\mathbf{P}}_n = \left(\mathbf{B}_*^{-1} - n^{-1/2}\mathbf{N}_*\mathbf{B}_*^{-1} + O\left(n^{-1}\right)\right)\left(\mathbf{B}_n - \mathbf{B}_{*,n}\right) - \mathbf{A}_*^{-1}(\mathbf{A}_n - \mathbf{A}_*) = \mathbf{M}_{o,n} - n^{-1/2}\mathbf{N}_*\mathbf{W}_{o,n} + O_{\mathbb{P}}\left(n^{-3/2}\right)$.

(v) From the definition of $\tilde{\mathbf{L}}_n$, $\tilde{\mathbf{L}}_n = \tilde{\mathbf{P}}_n + \sum_{j=1}^{l}\left(\hat{\theta}_{j,n} - \theta_{j,*}\right)\tilde{\mathbf{R}}_{j,*,n}$. Lemmas A8(iii and iv) now imply that $\tilde{\mathbf{L}}_n = \mathbf{M}_{o,n} - n^{-1/2}\mathbf{N}_*\mathbf{W}_{o,n} + \sum_{j=1}^{l}\left(\hat{\theta}_{j,n} - \theta_{j,*}\right)\mathbf{S}_{j,*} + n^{-1/2}\sum_{j=1}^{l}\left(\hat{\theta}_{j,n} - \theta_{j,*}\right)\mathbf{C}_{j,*} + O_{\mathbb{P}}\left(n^{-3/2}\right)$.

(vi) From the definition of $\tilde{\mathbf{L}}_n$, $\tilde{\mathbf{L}}_n\mathbf{A}_*^{-1}\mathbf{B}_{*,n} = \tilde{\mathbf{P}}_n\mathbf{A}_*^{-1}\mathbf{B}_{*,n} + \sum_{j=1}^{l} \times \left(\hat{\theta}_{j,n} - \theta_{j,*}\right)\tilde{\mathbf{R}}_{j,*,n}\mathbf{A}_*^{-1}\mathbf{B}_{*,n}$. We examine the traces of the terms in the RHS. First, $\mathrm{tr}\left[\tilde{\mathbf{P}}_n\mathbf{A}_*^{-1}\mathbf{B}_{*,n}\right] = \mathrm{tr}\left[\mathbf{W}_{o,n} - \mathbf{U}_n\right] - n^{-1/2}\mathrm{tr}[\mathbf{U}_n\mathbf{N}_*] = \mathrm{tr}\left[\mathbf{M}_{o,n}\right] - n^{-1/2}\mathrm{tr}[\mathbf{U}_n\mathbf{N}_*]$ by noting that $\mathrm{tr}\left[\mathbf{B}_{*,n}^{-1}\left(\mathbf{B}_n - \mathbf{B}_{*,n}\right)\mathbf{A}_*^{-1}\mathbf{B}_{*,n}\right] = \mathrm{tr}\left[\mathbf{A}_*^{-1}\left(\mathbf{B}_n - \mathbf{B}_{*,n}\right)\right] = \mathrm{tr}\left[\mathbf{W}_{o,n}\right]$. Second, using Lemma A8(iii), $\sum_{j=1}^{l}\left(\hat{\theta}_{j,n} - \theta_{j,*}\right)\tilde{\mathbf{R}}_{j,*,n}\mathbf{A}_*^{-1}\mathbf{B}_{*,n} = \sum_{j=1}^{l}\left(\hat{\theta}_{j,n} - \theta_{j,*}\right)\mathbf{S}_{j,*} + n^{-1/2} \times$

$\sum_{j=1}^{l}\left(\hat{\theta}_{j,n}-\theta_{j,*}\right)\mathbf{S}_{j,*}\,\mathbf{N}_{*}+n^{-1/2}\sum_{j=1}^{l}\left(\hat{\theta}_{j,n}-\theta_{j,*}\right)\mathbf{C}_{j,*}+O_{\mathbb{P}}\left(n^{-3/2}\right)$. Therefore, if we add these two terms and note that $\mathbf{K}_{o,n}=\mathbf{M}_{o,n}+\sum_{j=1}^{l}\left(\hat{\theta}_{j,n}-\theta_{j,*}\right)\mathbf{S}_{j,*}$, the desired result follows.

(vii) From the proof of Lemma A8(*v*), $\tilde{\mathbf{L}}_n=\mathbf{K}_{o,n}+O_{\mathbb{P}}\left(n^{-1}\right)$. This implies that $\tilde{\mathbf{L}}_n\mathbf{U}_n=\mathbf{K}_{o,n}\mathbf{U}_n+O_{\mathbb{P}}\left(n^{-3/2}\right)$, so that we can conclude that $\text{tr}\left[\tilde{\mathbf{L}}_n\mathbf{U}_n\mathbf{A}_*^{-1}\mathbf{B}_{*,n}\right]=\text{tr}\left[\mathbf{K}_{o,n}\mathbf{U}_n\mathbf{A}_*^{-1}\mathbf{B}_{*,n}\right]+O_{\mathbb{P}}\left(n^{-3/2}\right)$.

(viii) By Lemma 8(i), it trivially holds. This completes the proof. ■

Lemma A9. Given the same conditions as in Lemma 5 and $\mathbb{H}_a^{(1)}$,

(i) $\det\left[\mathbf{B}_{*,n}\right]=\det[\mathbf{B}_*]+n^{-1/2}\det[\mathbf{B}_*]\text{tr}[\mathbf{N}_*]+\frac{1}{2n}\det[\mathbf{B}_*]\left\{\text{tr}[\mathbf{N}_*]^2-\text{tr}\left[\mathbf{N}_*^2\right]\right\}+O\left(n^{-3/2}\right)$;

(ii) $\det\left[\mathbf{B}_{*,n}\mathbf{A}_*^{-1}\right]=1+n^{-1/2}\text{tr}[\mathbf{N}_*]+\frac{1}{2n}\left\{\text{tr}[\mathbf{N}_*]^2-\text{tr}\left[\mathbf{N}_*^2\right]\right\}+O\left(n^{-3/2}\right)$; and

(iii) $\det\left[\mathbf{B}_{*,n}\mathbf{A}_*^{-1}\right]^{1/k}=1+\frac{1}{\sqrt{n}k}\text{tr}[\mathbf{N}_*]+\frac{1}{2nk}\left\{\text{tr}[\mathbf{N}_*]^2-\text{tr}\left[\mathbf{N}_*^2\right]\right\}+\frac{1}{2nk}\left(\frac{1}{k}-1\right)\text{tr}[\mathbf{N}_*]^2+O\left(n^{-3/2}\right)$. □

Proof of Lemma A9. (i) We can apply Taylor's expansion to the determinant. That is,

$$\det\left[\mathbf{B}_{*,n}\right]=\det[\mathbf{B}_*]+\det[\mathbf{B}_*]\text{tr}\left[\mathbf{B}_*^{-1}(\mathbf{B}_{*,n}-\mathbf{B}_*)\right]+\frac{\det[\mathbf{B}_*]}{2}\left\{\text{tr}\left[\mathbf{B}_*^{-1}(\mathbf{B}_{*,n}-\mathbf{B}_*)\right]^2-\text{tr}\left[\mathbf{B}_*^{-1}(\mathbf{B}_{*,n}-\mathbf{B}_*)\mathbf{B}_*^{-1}(\mathbf{B}_{*,n}-\mathbf{B}_*)\right]\right\}+o_{\mathbb{P}}\left(n^{-1}\right)$$

We also note that $\mathbf{B}_{*,n}-\mathbf{B}_*=n^{-1/2}\overline{\mathbf{B}}_*$, and plugging this into the above equation now yields the desired result.

(ii) By Lemma A9(i) and the facts that $\det\left[\mathbf{B}_{*,n}\mathbf{A}_*^{-1}\right]=\det\left[\mathbf{B}_{*,n}\right]/\det[\mathbf{A}_*]$ and $\det[\mathbf{B}_*]=\det[\mathbf{A}_*]$, the desired result follows by dividing the equation in Lemma A9(i) with $\det[\mathbf{A}_*]$.

(iii) If we expand the power function $x^{1/k}$ around 1,

$$x^{1/k}=1+\frac{1}{k}(x-1)+\frac{1}{2k}\left(\frac{1}{k}-1\right)(x-1)^2+\ldots.$$

We now let x be $\det\left[\mathbf{B}_{*,n}\mathbf{A}_*^{-1}\right]$ and instead plug its expansion in Lemma A9(ii) into this equation. Next, we arrange the terms in the

RHS according to their convergence rates. The desired result follows from this. ■

Proof of Lemma 5. (i) As the key parameter is now $\mathbf{B}_{*,n}$, we approximate $\hat{T}_n$ around $\mathbf{A}_*$ and $\mathbf{B}_{*,n}$ using Lemma 4(i). Then,

$$\hat{T}_n = \frac{1}{k}\mathrm{tr}\left[\mathbf{B}_{*,n}\mathbf{A}_*^{-1}\right] - 1 + \frac{1}{k}\mathrm{tr}\left[\tilde{\mathbf{L}}_n\mathbf{A}_*^{-1}\mathbf{B}_{*,n}\right] - \frac{1}{k}\mathrm{tr}\left[\tilde{\mathbf{L}}_n\mathbf{U}_n\mathbf{A}_*^{-1}\mathbf{B}_{*,n}\right]$$

$$+ \frac{1}{k}\left[\mathrm{tr}\left[\left(\tilde{\mathbf{J}}_{j,n} - \tilde{\mathbf{P}}_n\mathbf{A}_*^{-1}\partial_j\mathbf{A}_*\right)\mathbf{A}_*^{-1}\mathbf{B}_{*,n}\right]\right]'\left(\hat{\boldsymbol{\theta}}_n - \boldsymbol{\theta}_*\right)$$

$$+ \frac{1}{2k}\left(\hat{\boldsymbol{\theta}}_n - \boldsymbol{\theta}_*\right)'\nabla_{\boldsymbol{\theta}}^2\mathrm{tr}\left[\boldsymbol{B}_{*,n}\boldsymbol{A}_*^{-1}\right]\left(\hat{\boldsymbol{\theta}}_n - \boldsymbol{\theta}_*\right) + o_{\mathbb{P}}(n^{-1})$$

We note that the asymptotic approximation of the first line in this equation is provided in Lemma A8(iii, vi, and vii). In addition, Lemma A8 provides the asymptotic expansions of $\tilde{\mathbf{P}}_n$ and $\tilde{\mathbf{K}}_{j,n}$, so that

$$\frac{1}{k}\left[\mathrm{tr}\left[\left(\tilde{\mathbf{J}}_{j,n} - \tilde{\mathbf{P}}_n\mathbf{A}_*^{-1}\partial_j\mathbf{A}_*\right)\mathbf{A}_*^{-1}\mathbf{B}_{*,n}\right]\right]'\left(\hat{\boldsymbol{\theta}}_n - \boldsymbol{\theta}_*\right)$$

$$+ \frac{1}{2k}\left(\hat{\boldsymbol{\theta}}_n - \boldsymbol{\theta}_*\right)'\nabla_{\boldsymbol{\theta}}^2\mathrm{tr}\left[\mathbf{B}_{*,n}\mathbf{A}_*^{-1}\right]\left(\hat{\boldsymbol{\theta}}_n - \boldsymbol{\theta}_*\right)$$

$$= \frac{1}{k}\left[\mathrm{tr}\left[\left(\tilde{\mathbf{J}}_{j,o,n} - \mathbf{M}_{o,n}\mathbf{A}_*^{-1}\partial_j\mathbf{A}_*\right)\mathbf{A}_*^{-1}\mathbf{B}_{*,n}\right]\right]'\left(\hat{\boldsymbol{\theta}}_n - \boldsymbol{\theta}_*\right)$$

$$+ \frac{1}{2k}\left(\hat{\boldsymbol{\theta}}_n - \boldsymbol{\theta}_*\right)'\nabla_{\boldsymbol{\theta}}^2\mathrm{tr}\left[\mathbf{D}_*^{-1}\right]\left(\hat{\boldsymbol{\theta}}_n - \boldsymbol{\theta}_*\right) + o_{\mathbb{P}}(n^{-1})$$

Therefore, if we collect all these results, it is not hard to obtain that

$$\hat{T}_n = \hat{T}_{o,n} + \frac{1}{\sqrt{n}k}\{\mathrm{tr}[\mathbf{N}_*] - \mathrm{tr}[\mathbf{N}_*\mathbf{U}_n]$$

$$+ [\mathrm{tr}[\mathbf{A}_*^{-1}(\partial_j\overline{\mathbf{B}}_*) - \mathbf{N}_*\mathbf{A}_*^{-1}(\partial_j\overline{\mathbf{A}}_*)]]'(\hat{\boldsymbol{\theta}}_n - \boldsymbol{\theta}_*)\} + o_{\mathbb{P}}(n^{-1})$$

using the definition of $\hat{T}_{o,n}$. This is the desired result.

(ii) The proof is almost identical. If we approximate $\hat{D}_n$ around $\mathbf{A}_*$ and $\mathbf{B}_{*,n}$ using Lemma 4(ii),

$$\hat{D}_n = \det\left[\mathbf{B}_{*,n}\mathbf{A}_*^{-1}\right]^{\frac{1}{k}} - 1 + \frac{1}{k}\det\left[\mathbf{B}_{*,n}\mathbf{A}_*^{-1}\right]^{\frac{1}{k}}\mathrm{tr}\left[\tilde{\mathbf{L}}_n\right] + \frac{1}{2k}\left(\frac{1}{k}-1\right)\det\left[\mathbf{B}_{*,n}\mathbf{A}_*^{-1}\right]^{\frac{1}{k}}\mathrm{tr}\left[\tilde{\mathbf{L}}_n\right]^2$$

$$+\frac{1}{k}\det\left[\mathbf{B}_{*,n}\mathbf{A}_*^{-1}\right]^{\frac{1}{k}}\mathrm{tr}\left[\tilde{\mathbf{P}}_n\right]\left[\mathrm{tr}\left[\tilde{\mathbf{R}}_{j,*,n}\right]\right]'\left(\hat{\boldsymbol{\theta}}_n - \boldsymbol{\theta}_*\right) + \frac{1}{2k}\det\left[\mathbf{B}_{*,n}\mathbf{A}_*^{-1}\right]^{\frac{1}{k}}$$

$$\times\left(\mathrm{tr}\left[\tilde{\mathbf{P}}_n\right]^2 + \mathrm{tr}\left[\mathbf{U}_n^2\right] - \mathrm{tr}\left[\tilde{\mathbf{W}}_n^2\right]\right)$$

$$+\frac{1}{k}\det\left[\mathbf{B}_{*,n}\mathbf{A}_*^{-1}\right]^{\frac{1}{k}}\left[\mathrm{tr}\left[\tilde{\mathbf{J}}_{j,n} + \mathbf{U}_n\mathbf{A}_*^{-1}\partial_j\mathbf{A} - \tilde{\mathbf{W}}_n\mathbf{B}_*^{-1}\partial_j\mathbf{B}_*\right]\right]'\left(\hat{\boldsymbol{\theta}}_n - \boldsymbol{\theta}_*\right)$$

$$+\frac{1}{2k}\det\left[\mathbf{B}_{*,n}\mathbf{A}_*^{-1}\right]^{\frac{1}{k}-1}\left(\hat{\boldsymbol{\theta}}_n - \boldsymbol{\theta}_*\right)'\nabla_{\boldsymbol{\theta}}^2\det\left[\mathbf{B}_{*,n}\mathbf{A}_*^{-1}\right]\left(\hat{\boldsymbol{\theta}}_n - \boldsymbol{\theta}_*\right) + o_{\mathbb{P}}(n^{-1})$$

where $\tilde{\mathbf{W}}_n := \mathbf{B}_{*,n}^{-1}(\mathbf{B}_n - \mathbf{B}_{*,n})$. We note that the last three lines of this equation is $O_{\mathbb{P}}(n^{-1})$, so that they can be reformulated into

$$\frac{1}{k}\mathrm{tr}\left[\mathbf{M}_{o,n}\right]\left[\mathrm{tr}\left[\mathbf{S}_{j,*}\right]\right]'\left(\hat{\boldsymbol{\theta}}_n - \boldsymbol{\theta}_*\right) + \frac{1}{2k}\left(\mathrm{tr}\left[\mathbf{M}_{o,n}\right]^2 + \mathrm{tr}\left[\mathbf{U}_n^2\right] - \mathrm{tr}\left[\mathbf{W}_{o,n}^2\right]\right)$$

$$+\frac{1}{k}\left[\mathrm{tr}\left[\mathbf{J}_{j,o,n} + \mathbf{U}_n\mathbf{A}_*^{-1}\partial_j\mathbf{A}_* - \mathbf{W}_{o,n}\mathbf{A}_*^{-1}\partial_j\mathbf{B}_*\right]\right]'\left(\hat{\boldsymbol{\theta}}_n - \boldsymbol{\theta}_*\right)$$

$$+\frac{1}{2k}\left(\hat{\boldsymbol{\theta}}_n - \boldsymbol{\theta}_*\right)'\nabla_{\boldsymbol{\theta}}^2\det[\mathbf{D}_*]\left(\hat{\boldsymbol{\theta}}_n - \boldsymbol{\theta}_*\right) + O_{\mathbb{P}}\left(n^{-3/2}\right)$$

under $\mathbb{H}_a^{(1)}$. On the other hand, the first line of the equation is formed by $\det\left[\mathbf{B}_{*,n}\mathbf{A}_*^{-1}\right]$ and $\mathrm{tr}\left[\tilde{\mathbf{L}}_n\right]$, and their asymptotic expansions are given in Lemmas A8(v) and A9(iii), respectively. Using these, we obtain that

$$\det\left[\mathbf{B}_*,n\mathbf{A}_*^{-1}\right]^{\frac{1}{k}} - 1 + \frac{1}{k}\det\left[\mathbf{B}_{*,n}\mathbf{A}_*^{-1}\right]^{\frac{1}{k}}\mathrm{tr}\left[\tilde{\mathbf{L}}_n\right] + \frac{1}{2k}\left(\frac{1}{k}-1\right)\det\left[\mathbf{B}_{*,n}\mathbf{A}_*^{-1}\right]^{\frac{1}{k}}\mathrm{tr}\left[\tilde{\mathbf{L}}_n\right]^2$$

$$=\frac{1}{k}\mathrm{tr}\left[\tilde{\mathbf{K}}_{o,n}\right] + \frac{1}{\sqrt{n}k}\mathrm{tr}[\mathbf{N}_*] + \frac{1}{2k}\left(\frac{1}{k}-1\right)\mathrm{tr}\left[\tilde{\mathbf{K}}_{o,n}\right]^2 - \frac{1}{\sqrt{n}k}\mathrm{tr}\left[\mathbf{N}_*\mathbf{W}_{o,n}\right]$$

$$+\frac{1}{\sqrt{n}k}\left[\mathrm{tr}\left[\mathrm{C}_{j,*}\right]\right]'\left(\hat{\boldsymbol{\theta}}_n - \boldsymbol{\theta}_*\right) + \frac{1}{\sqrt{n}k^2}\mathrm{tr}[\mathbf{N}_*]\mathrm{tr}\left[\mathbf{K}_{o,n}\right]$$

$$+\frac{1}{2nk^2}\mathrm{tr}[\mathbf{N}_*]^2 - \frac{1}{2nk}\mathrm{tr}\left[\mathbf{N}_*^2\right] + O_{\mathbb{P}}\left(n^{-3/2}\right)$$

We now combine them and note the definition of $\hat{D}_{o,n}$ to obtain the desired result.

(iii) Using the definition of $\hat{S}_n := \hat{T}_n - \hat{D}_n$, we rearrange the terms according to their convergence rates. Using the fact that $\mathbf{S}_{j,*} := \mathbf{B}_*^{-1}\partial_j\mathbf{B}_* - \mathbf{A}_*^{-1}\partial\mathbf{A}_*$ under $\mathbb{H}_a^{(1)}$, we can derive the desired result. This completes the proof. ■

Proof of Theorem 5. (i) From Lemma 5, we note that

$$k\sqrt{n}\hat{T}_n = \text{tr}[\mathbf{N}_*] + k\sqrt{n}\hat{T}_{o,n} + O_{\mathbb{P}}\left(n^{-1/2}\right)$$

and $k\sqrt{n}\hat{D}_n = \text{tr}[\mathbf{N}_*] + k\sqrt{n}\hat{D}_{o,n} + O_{\mathbb{P}}(n^{-1/2})$, so that

$$\frac{nk^2}{2}\left(\hat{T}_n^2 + \hat{D}_n^2\right) = \text{tr}[\mathbf{N}_*]^2 + k\sqrt{n}(\hat{T}_{o,n} + \hat{D}_{o,n})\text{tr}[\mathbf{N}_*] + \frac{k^2 n}{2}\left(\hat{T}_{o,n}^2 + \hat{D}_{o,n}^2\right) + O_{\mathbb{P}}\left(n^{-1/2}\right)$$

Also, $\hat{T}_{o,n} = \frac{1}{k}\text{tr}\left[\mathbf{K}_{o,n}\right] + O_{\mathbb{P}}(n^{-1})$ and $\hat{D}_{o,n} = \frac{1}{k}\text{tr}\left[\mathbf{K}_{o,n}\right] + O_{\mathbb{P}}(n^{-1})$ by the definitions of $\hat{T}_{o,n}$ and $\hat{D}_{o,n}$ and the given conditions. Thus, it follows that

$$\frac{nk^2}{2}\left(\hat{T}_n^2 + \hat{D}_n^2\right) = \text{tr}[\mathbf{N}_*]^2 + 2\sqrt{n}\text{tr}\left[\mathbf{K}_{o,n}\right]\text{tr}[\mathbf{N}_*] + n\text{tr}\left[\mathbf{K}_{o,n}\right]^2 + O_{\mathbb{P}}\left(n^{-1/2}\right)$$

and we note that $\hat{\mathscr{B}}_n^{(1)} := \frac{nk^2}{2}\left(\hat{T}_n^2 + \hat{D}_n^2\right)$, implying that $\hat{\mathscr{B}}_n^{(1)} = \left(\text{tr}[\mathbf{N}_*] + \sqrt{n}\text{tr}\left[\mathbf{K}_{o,n}\right]\right)^2 + O_{\mathbb{P}}\left(n^{-1/2}\right) = \left(\text{tr}\left[\mathbf{N}_* + \sqrt{n}\mathbf{K}_{o,n}\right]\right)^2 + O_{\mathbb{P}}(n^{-1/2})$. This is the desired result.

(ii) By Lemma 5(i), $\sqrt{n}\hat{T}_n = \frac{1}{k}\text{tr}[\mathbf{N}_*] + \frac{\sqrt{n}}{k}\text{tr}\left[\mathbf{K}_{o,n}\right] + O_{\mathbb{P}}(n^{-1/2})$, so that

$$nk\hat{T}_n^2 = \frac{1}{k}\text{tr}[\mathbf{N}_*]^2 + \frac{n}{k}\text{tr}\left[\mathbf{K}_{o,n}\right]^2 + \frac{2\sqrt{n}}{k}\text{tr}[\mathbf{N}_*]\text{tr}\left[\mathbf{K}_{o,n}\right] + O_{\mathbb{P}}\left(n^{-1/2}\right)$$

Next, Lemma 5(iii) implies that

$$2nk\hat{S}_n = \mathrm{tr}\left[\mathbf{N}_*^2\right] + n\mathrm{tr}\left[\mathbf{K}_{o,n}^2\right] - \frac{1}{k}\mathrm{tr}[\mathbf{N}_*]^2 - \frac{n}{k}\mathrm{tr}\left[\mathbf{K}_{o,n}\right]^2$$
$$- \frac{2\sqrt{n}}{k}\mathrm{tr}[\mathbf{N}_*]\mathrm{tr}\left[\mathbf{K}_{o,n}\right] + 2\sqrt{n}\mathrm{tr}\left[\mathbf{N}_*\mathbf{M}_{o,n}\right]$$
$$+ 2\sqrt{n}\left[\mathrm{tr}\left[\mathbf{N}_*\mathbf{A}_*^{-1}(\partial_j\mathbf{B}_* - \partial_j\mathbf{A}_*)\right]\right]'\left(\hat{\boldsymbol{\theta}}_n - \boldsymbol{\theta}_*\right) + O_{\mathbb{P}}\left(n^{-1/2}\right)$$

Thus, if we add $nk\hat{T}_n^2$ to $2nk\hat{S}_n$,

$$nk\hat{T}_n^2 + 2nk\hat{S}_n = \mathrm{tr}[\mathbf{N}_*^2] + n\mathrm{tr}[\mathbf{K}_{o,n}^2] + 2\sqrt{n}\Big\{\mathrm{tr}[\mathbf{N}_*\mathbf{M}_{o,n}]$$
$$+ \left[\mathrm{tr}\left[\mathbf{N}_*\mathbf{A}_*^{-1}\left(\partial_j\mathbf{B}_* - \partial_j\mathbf{A}_*\right)\right]\right]'\left(\hat{\theta}_{j,n} - \theta_{j,*}\right)\Big\} + O_{\mathbb{P}}\left(n^{-1/2}\right)$$

We now note that

$$\mathrm{tr}\left[\mathbf{N}_*\mathbf{M}_{o,n}\right] + \left[\mathrm{tr}\left[\mathbf{N}_*\mathbf{A}_*^{-1}\left(\partial_j\mathbf{B}_* - \partial_j\mathbf{A}_*\right)\right]\right]'\left(\hat{\boldsymbol{\theta}}_n - \boldsymbol{\theta}_*\right) = \mathrm{tr}\left[\mathbf{N}_*\mathbf{K}_{o,n}\right]$$

so that $\hat{\mathscr{B}}_n^{(2)} = nk\hat{T}_n^2 + 2nk\hat{S}_n = \mathrm{tr}\left[\mathbf{N}_*^2\right] + 2\sqrt{n}\mathrm{tr}\left[\mathbf{N}_*\mathbf{K}_{o,n}\right] + n\mathrm{tr}\left[\mathbf{K}_{o,n}^2\right] + O_{\mathbb{P}}\left(n^{-1/2}\right)$, implying that $\hat{\mathscr{B}}_n^{(2)} = \mathrm{tr}\left[\left(\mathbf{N}_* + \sqrt{n}\mathbf{K}_{o,n}\right)^2\right] + o_{\mathbb{P}}(1)$, as desired.

(iii) By Lemma 5(ii), $\sqrt{n}\hat{D}_n = \frac{1}{k}\mathrm{tr}[\mathbf{N}_*] + \frac{\sqrt{n}}{k}\mathrm{tr}\left[\mathbf{K}_{o,n}\right] + O_{\mathbb{P}}\left(n^{-1/2}\right)$, and this expansion is the same as that of $\sqrt{n}\hat{T}_n$. We can thus conclude that $\hat{\mathscr{B}}_n^{(3)}$ has the same asymptotic expansion as $\hat{\mathscr{B}}_n^{(2)}$. This completes the proof. ∎

Proof of Lemma 6. (i) We note that $\hat{L}_n = \ln\left[\hat{D}_n + 1\right]$ and $\hat{D}_n = O_{\mathbb{P}}\left(n^{-1/2}\right)$. We now approximate $\hat{L}_n$ around 1 by using Taylor's expansion, which yields that

$$\hat{L}_n = \hat{D}_n - \frac{1}{2}\hat{D}_n^2 + o_{\mathbb{P}}\left(n^{-1}\right) \tag{A.32}$$

Given this, Lemma 5(ii) provides the asymptotic expansion of $\hat{D}_n$, so that it follows that

$$\frac{1}{2}\hat{D}_n^2 = \frac{1}{2nk^2}\mathrm{tr}[\mathbf{N}_*]^2 + \frac{1}{2k^2}\mathrm{tr}\left[\mathbf{K}_{o,n}\right]^2 + \frac{1}{\sqrt{n}k^2}\mathrm{tr}[\mathbf{N}_*]\mathrm{tr}\left[\mathbf{K}_{o,n}\right] + o_{\mathbb{P}}\left(n^{-1}\right) \tag{A.33}$$

We now combine the results in Lemma 5(ii) and Eq. (A.33) with Eq. (A.32), and this yields the desired result.

(ii) We note that $\hat{Q}_n = \ln\left[\hat{T}_n + 1\right]$ and $\hat{T}_n = O_{\mathbb{P}}\left(n^{-1/2}\right)$. We now approximate $\hat{Q}_n$ around 1 by Taylor's expansion, and we obtain that

$$\hat{Q}_n = \hat{T}_n - \frac{1}{2}\hat{T}_n^2 + o_{\mathbb{P}}\left(n^{-1}\right) \quad \text{(A.34)}$$

We further note that

$$\hat{T}_n^2 = \frac{1}{nk^2}\mathrm{tr}[\mathbf{N}_*]^2 + \frac{1}{k^2}\mathrm{tr}\left[\mathbf{K}_{o,n}\right]^2 + \frac{2}{\sqrt{n}k^2}\mathrm{tr}[\mathbf{N}_*]\mathrm{tr}\left[\mathbf{K}_{o,n}\right] + o_{\mathbb{P}}\left(n^{-1}\right) \quad \text{(A.35)}$$

and combine this with Lemma 5(i) according to Eq. (A.34). This gives the desired result.

(iii) We simply combine the results in Lemmas 5(i) and 6(ii) by using the definition of $\hat{M}_n$. This shows that

$$\hat{M}_n = \frac{1}{2kn}\mathrm{tr}\left[\left(\mathbf{N}_* + \sqrt{n}\mathbf{K}_{o,n}{}^2\right)\right] + \frac{1}{2k^2}\mathrm{tr}\left[\mathbf{K}_{o,n}\right]^2 - \frac{1}{2k}\mathrm{tr}\left[\mathbf{K}_{o,n}^2\right] + \hat{S}_{o,n} + o_{\mathbb{P}}\left(n^{-1}\right)$$

We next substitute $\hat{S}_{o,n}$ in this equation with its definition. Most terms are canceled by others, and the only surviving term is $\mathrm{tr}[(\mathbf{N}_* + \sqrt{n}\mathbf{K}_{o,n}{}^2)]/(2kn) + o_{\mathbb{P}}\left(n^{-1}\right)$.

(iv) We combine the results in Lemma 6(i and ii) by using the definition of $\hat{W}_n$. Then, it follows that

$$\begin{aligned}\hat{W}_n &= \hat{Q}_n - \hat{L}_n \\ &= \frac{1}{2nk}\mathrm{tr}\left[\left(\mathbf{N}_* + \sqrt{n}\mathbf{K}_{o,n}{}^2\right)\right] - \frac{1}{2nk^2}\mathrm{tr}\left[\mathbf{N}_* + \sqrt{n}\mathbf{K}_{o,n}\right]^2 \\ &\quad + \frac{1}{2k^2}\mathrm{tr}\left[\mathbf{K}_{o,n}\right]^2 - \frac{1}{2k}\mathrm{tr}\left[\mathbf{K}_{o,n}^2\right] + \hat{S}_{o,n} + o_{\mathbb{P}}\left(n^{-1}\right)\end{aligned}$$

We now use the definition of $\hat{S}_{o,n}$ to obtain the desired result. This completes the proof. ∎

Proof of Theorem 6. (i) We note that

$$\mathscr{LR}_n^{(1)} = 2\left\{\ln\left[L_n\left(\hat{\boldsymbol{\theta}}_n, \hat{\mathbf{B}}_n\right)\right] - \ln\left[L_n\left(\hat{\boldsymbol{\theta}}_n, \hat{\mathbf{A}}_n\right)\right]\right\} = nk(\hat{T}_n - \hat{L}_n)$$
$$= nk\hat{M}_n = \frac{1}{2}\mathrm{tr}\left[\left(\mathbf{N}_* + \sqrt{n}\mathbf{K}_{o,n}{}^2\right)\right] + o_{\mathbb{P}}(n^{-1})$$

by Lemma 6(ii).

(ii and iii) The desired results follow from Theorem 6(*i*) and Theorem 5(ii and iii). ■

Proof of Theorem 7. (i) We note that

$$\mathscr{LR}_n^{(2)} = -n\ln\left[\det(\hat{\mathbf{B}}_n)\right] + nk\ln\left[\mathrm{tr}\left[\hat{\mathbf{A}}_n^{-1}\hat{\mathbf{B}}_n\right]/k\right] + n\ln\left[\det\left(\hat{\mathbf{A}}_n\right)\right]$$
$$= n\left(k\ln\left[\mathrm{tr}\left[\hat{\mathbf{A}}_n^{-1}\hat{\mathbf{B}}_n\right]/k\right] - \ln\left[\det\left(\hat{\mathbf{A}}_n^{-1}\hat{\mathbf{B}}_n\right)\right]\right)$$
$$= n\left(k\hat{Q}_n - k\hat{L}_n\right) = nk\hat{W}_n$$

Given this, the desired result holds by Lemma 6(iv).

(ii and iii) We can combine Theorem 7(i) with Theorem 5 to complete the proof. ■

A.2. Additional Assumptions for Theorem 2

Assumption A1. $(\Omega, \mathcal{F}, \mathbb{P})$ is a complete probability space. □

Assumption A2. (i) For $k \in \mathbb{N}$, the symmetric matrix $\mathbf{A}_* := E\left[\mathbf{a}(Y_t, \mathbf{X}_t)\mathbf{a}(Y_t, \mathbf{X}_t)'\right] - E[\mathbf{a}(Y_t, \mathbf{X}_t)]E\left[\mathbf{a}(Y_t, \mathbf{X}_t)'\right]$ is positive definite; and

(ii) the symmetric matrix $\mathbf{B}_* := E\left[\mathbf{b}(Y_t, \mathbf{X}_t)\mathbf{b}(Y_t, \mathbf{X}_t)'\right] - E[\mathbf{b}(Y_t, \mathbf{X}_t)] E\left[\mathbf{b}(Y_t, \mathbf{X}_t)'\right]$ is positive definite. □

Assumption A3. (i) The estimators $\tilde{\mathbf{A}}_n$ and $\tilde{\mathbf{B}}_n$ are consistent for $\mathbf{A}_*$ and $\mathbf{B}_*$, respectively; and

(ii) $\sqrt{n}\left[\mathrm{vech}\left[(\hat{\Sigma}_{\mathbf{a},n} - \Sigma_{\mathbf{a},*})\right]', \mathrm{vech}\left[(\hat{\Sigma}_{\mathbf{b},n} - \Sigma_{\mathbf{b},*})\right]', (\hat{\boldsymbol{\mu}}_{\mathbf{a},n} - \boldsymbol{\mu}_{\mathbf{a},*})', (\hat{\boldsymbol{\mu}}_{\mathbf{b},n} - \boldsymbol{\mu}_{\mathbf{b},*})'\right]' \overset{A}{\sim} N(\mathbf{0}, \Upsilon_*)$, where Υ_* is a $(k^2 + 3k) \times (k^2 + 3k)$ positive semi-definite matrix. □

Assumption A4. (i) The estimators $\tilde{\mathbf{A}}_n$ and $\tilde{\mathbf{B}}_n$ are consistent for $\mathbf{A}_*$ and $\mathbf{B}_*$, respectively; and

(ii) $\sqrt{n}\left[\text{vech}\left[(\hat{\Sigma}_{\mathbf{a},n}-\Sigma_{\mathbf{a},*})\right]',\text{vech}\left[(\hat{\Sigma}_{\mathbf{b},n}-\Sigma_{\mathbf{b},*,n})\right]',(\hat{\boldsymbol{\mu}}_{\mathbf{a},n}-\boldsymbol{\mu}_{\mathbf{a},*})',(\hat{\boldsymbol{\mu}}_{\mathbf{b},n}-\boldsymbol{\mu}_{\mathbf{b},*,n})'\right]' \overset{A}{\sim} N(\mathbf{0},\Upsilon_*)$, where Υ_* is a $(k^2+3k)\times(k^2+3k)$ positive semi-definite matrix. □

Assumption A5. The symmetric mapping $\overline{\mathbf{B}}_*$ is positive definite. □

MINIMAX ESTIMATION OF NONREGULAR PARAMETERS AND DISCONTINUITY IN MINIMAX RISK

Kyungchul Song

Vancouver School of Economics, University of British Columbia, Vancouver, Canada

ABSTRACT

When a parameter of interest is nondifferentiable in the probability, the existing theory of semiparametric efficient estimation is not applicable, as it does not have an influence function. Song (2014) recently developed a local asymptotic minimax estimation theory for a parameter that is a nondifferentiable transform of a regular parameter, where the transform is a composite map of a continuous piecewise linear map with a single kink point and a translation-scale equivariant map. The contribution of this paper is twofold. First, this paper extends the local asymptotic minimax theory to nondifferentiable transforms that are a composite map of a Lipschitz continuous map having a finite set of nondifferentiability points and a translation-scale equivariant map. Second, this paper investigates the discontinuity of the local asymptotic minimax risk in the true

Essays in Honor of Peter C. B. Phillips
Advances in Econometrics, Volume 33, 557–585

ISSN: 0731-9053/doi:10.1108/S0731-905320140000033015

probability and shows that the proposed estimator remains to be optimal even when the risk is locally robustified not only over the scores at the true probability, but also over the true probability itself. However, the local robustification does not resolve the issue of discontinuity in the local asymptotic minimax risk.

Keywords: Nonregular parameters; semiparametric efficiency; local asymptotic minimax estimation; translation-scale equivariant maps

JEL Classifications: C01; C13; C14; C44

1. INTRODUCTION

Statistical inference on a parameter begins by choosing an appropriate estimator. For a finite dimensional parameter defined under local asymptotic normal experiments, it has become nearly a standard practice in statistics and econometrics to establish the optimality of an estimator through semiparametric efficiency, where optimality is expressed through a variance bound. An estimator is taken to be optimal if it is asymptotically normal with its asymptotic variance achieving the bound. The literature along this approach is vast in statistics and econometrics.

A mathematical analysis of asymptotic optimal inference began with the celebrated paper by Wald (1943). While the approach of local asymptotic minimax estimation has appeared in the previous literature (e.g., Chernoff, 1956; Le Cam, 1953), major breakthroughs were made by Hájek (1972) and Le Cam (1972). Koshevnik and Levit (1976), Levit (1978), Pfanzagl and Wefelmeyer (1982), Begun, Hall, Huang, and Wellner (1983), and Chamberlain (1987) extended asymptotic efficient estimation to nonparametric and semiparametric models. See also van der Vaart (1988, 1991) for further developments in this direction, and Newey (1990) for results that are relevant to econometrics. A general account of this approach is found in monographs such as Bickel, Klaassen, Rikov, and Wellner (1993), and in later chapters of van der Vaart and Wellner (1996) and van der Vaart (1998). While the references so far mostly focus on local asymptotic normal experiments (as this paper does), optimal estimation theory in local asymptotic mixed normal experiments has also received attention in the literature (see Basawa & Scott, 1983; Jeganathan, 1982). In econometrics, Phillips (1991) developed optimal inference theory for cointegrating regression models using the framework of local asymptotic mixed normal experiments.

The existing notion of semiparametric efficiency is not directly applicable, when the parameter is not differentiable in the probability that identifies the parameter. Nondifferentiable parameters do not merely constitute a pathological case, for one can easily encounter such a parameter when the parameter (denoted by $\theta \in \mathbf{R}$) is defined through a nondifferentiable transform of another parameter vector, say, $\beta \in \mathbf{R}^d$. For example, the parameter of interest might take the form of $\theta = \max\{\beta_1, \ldots, \beta_d\}$ or $\theta = \min\{\beta_1, \ldots, \beta_d\}$, where $\beta_1, \ldots, \beta_d$ are average treatment effects from different treatment regimes or mean squared prediction errors from different predictive models, or boundaries of multiple intervals. (As for the last example, Chernozhukov, Lee, & Rosen, 2013 called the parameter an intersection bound. Examples of such bounds are found in Haile & Tamer, 2003; Manski & Tamer, 2002 among many others.) The difficulty with estimation theory for such nondifferentiable parameters is emphasized by Doss and Sethuraman (1989). See Hirano and Porter (2012) for a general impossibility result for such parameters.

This paper focuses on the problem of optimal estimation when the parameter is nondifferentiable in a particular way. More specifically, this paper focuses on a parameter of interest in $\mathbf{R}$ which takes the following form:

$$\theta = (f \circ g)(\beta) \tag{1}$$

where $\beta \in \mathbf{R}^d$ is a regular parameter for which a semiparametric efficiency bound is well defined, g is a translation-scale equivariant map, and f is a continuous map that is potentially nondifferentiable. While the paper focuses on this particular way that nondifferentiability arises, it accommodates various nondifferentiable parameters that are relevant in empirical researches.

A recent work by the author (Song, 2014) focuses on the case of f being a continuous piecewise linear map *with a single kink point*, and has demonstrated that the existing semiparametric efficient estimation can be extended to this case of nonregular parameter θ through a local asymptotic minimax approach. While the result applies to various examples of nonregular parameters used in econometrics, the restriction on f excludes some interesting examples as discussed below.

Example 1 (Maximal Treatment Effects under Constraints). Suppose that there are J treatments and β_j's are treatment effect parameters such as average treatment effects or average treatment effects on the treated. We define the maximal treatment effect to be

$$\theta_1 = \max_{1 \le j \le J} \beta_j$$

Suppose that we have prior information that the treatment effect is nonnegative but bounded by certain known constant $C > 0$, e.g., from previous studies. Taking it into consideration, one may take the parameter of interest to be

$$\theta = \min\{\max\{\theta_1, 0, C\}$$ ■

Example 2 (Bounded Absolute Average Derivatives). Let Y be the observed outcome variable and X a covariate vector. The average derivative with respect to the first entry of X is defined to be

$$\beta = \int \frac{\partial \mathbf{E}[Y|X=x]}{\partial x_1} dF(x)$$

where F denotes the distribution function of X. Suppose that we are interested in the magnitude of the effect with prior information (obtained from previous studies) that this magnitude cannot be larger than $C > 0$. Then one may consider estimating the following parameter

$$\theta = \min\{|\beta|, C\}$$

which incorporates the prior information. ■

This paper extends the theory to the case where f is Lipschitz continuous yet potentially nondifferentiable at a finite number of points. Thus the above examples and many others are also incorporated in the theory. As in Song (2014), it turns out that the local asymptotic minimax estimator takes the following form:

$$\hat{\theta}_{mx} \equiv f\left(g(\tilde{\beta}) + \frac{\hat{c}^*}{\sqrt{n}} \right) \tag{2}$$

where $\hat{c}^*$ is an *optimal bias adjustment term*, and $\tilde{\beta}$ is a semiparametrically efficient estimator of β. The optimal bias adjustment term can be determined by simulating the local asymptotic minimax risk.

Some researches in the literature have suggested various methods of bias adjustment and reported improved performances see, e.g., Chernozhukov, Lee, & Rosen, 2013; Haile & Tamer, 2003). The approach of Song (2014) and this paper is distinct in the sense that it determines the optimal bias adjustment explicitly through theory of local asymptotic minimax estimation.

The resulting local asymptotic minimax risk for the kind of nonregular parameters considered in this paper is discontinuous in the underlying true probability in general. Such a discontinuity arises as a consequence of applying the asymptotic theory in the local asymptotic minimax approach to the nondifferentiable parameters. If this discontinuity is purely an artifact of the asymptotic device employed here, the notion of optimality based on it may not be appropriate for the finite sample decision problem.

When the asymptotic distribution of a test statistic or an estimator exhibits discontinuity in the underlying true probability, it is a common practice to consider an alternative asymptotic theory along a sequence of probabilities local around the true probability. Mostly, this alternative asymptotics involves a localization parameter which continuously "bridges" two distributions across the discontinuity point. The most common example of this approach is local asymptotic power analysis in hypothesis tests, where one adopts a sequence of probabilities that converge to a probability that belongs to the null hypothesis. A similar approach is found in local to unity models (Stock, 1991), weakly identified models (Staiger & Stock, 1997), and more recently, models of various moment inequality restrictions (Andrews & Guggenberger, 2009) among many others.

Following the same spirit in the context of local asymptotic minimax estimation, this paper explores a local robustification of the risk, where the risk is further robustified against a local perturbation of the true probability. Somewhat unexpectedly, the local asymptotic minimax risk remains unchanged after this local robustification of the risk. On the one hand, this means that the local asymptotic minimax estimator in Eq. (2) retains its optimality under this robustification, as long as the efficient estimator $\tilde{\beta}$, after location-scale normalization, converges in distribution uniformly over the true probabilities. On the other hand, the discontinuity of the risk in the true probability is not resolved by the local robustification approach. Hence there may be a gap between the finite sample risk and its asymptotic version and the gap does not close uniformly over all the probabilities even in the limit. It remains an open question whether this renders the whole apparatus of the local asymptotic minimax theory dubious in practice when the parameter is nondifferentiable.

The rest of the paper is structured as follows. In Section 2, the paper defines the scope of this paper by introducing assumptions about f, g, β, and the set of underlying probabilities that identify β. In Section 3, the paper gives a characterization of local asymptotic minimax risk, and proposes a general method to construct a local asymptotic minimax estimator. In Section 4, the paper considers a local robustification of the local asymptotic minimax risk, and shows that the results of Section 3 mostly remain unchanged. Section 5 concludes the paper. The mathematical proofs of the paper's results appear in the appendix.

A word of notation. Let $\mathbf{1}_d$ be a $d \times 1$ vector of ones with $d \geq 2$. For a vector $\mathbf{x} \in \mathbf{R}^d$ and a scalar c, we simply write $\mathbf{x} + c = \mathbf{x} + c\mathbf{1}_d$, or write $\mathbf{x} = c$ instead of $\mathbf{x} = c\mathbf{1}_d$. For $\mathbf{x} \in \mathbf{R}^d$, the notation max($\mathbf{x}$) (or min($\mathbf{x}$)) means the maximum (or the minimum) over the entries of the vector $\mathbf{x}$. We let $\overline{\mathbf{R}} = [-\infty, \infty]$ and view it as a two-point compactification of $\mathbf{R}$, and let $\overline{\mathbf{R}}^d$ be the product of its d copies, so that $\overline{\mathbf{R}}^d$ itself is a compactification of $\mathbf{R}^d$. (e.g., Dudley, 2002, p. 74) We follow the convention to set $\infty \cdot 0 = 0$ and $(-\infty) \cdot 0 = 0$. A supremum and an infimum of a nonnegative map over an empty set are set to be 0 and ∞ respectively.

2. NONDIFFERENTIABLE TRANSFORMS OF A REGULAR PARAMETER

2.1. Nondifferentiable Transforms

First, we begin with conditions for f and g in Eq. (1).

Assumption 1. (i) The map $g : \mathbf{R}^d \to \mathbf{R}$ is Lipschitz continuous, and satisfies the following.

(a) (Translation Equivariance) For each $c \in \mathbf{R}$ and $\mathbf{x} \in \mathbf{R}^d$, $g(\mathbf{x} + c) = g(\mathbf{x}) + c$.
(b) (Scale Equivariance) For each $u \geq 0$ and $\mathbf{x} \in \mathbf{R}^d$, $g(u\mathbf{x}) = ug(\mathbf{x})$.
(c) (Directional Derivatives) For each $\mathbf{z} \in \mathbf{R}^d$ and $\mathbf{x} \in \mathbf{R}^d$,

$$\tilde{g}(\mathbf{x}; \mathbf{z}) \equiv \lim_{t \downarrow 0} t^{-1}(g(\mathbf{x} + t\mathbf{z}) - g(\mathbf{x}))$$

exists.

(ii) The map $f : \overline{\mathbf{R}} \to \overline{\mathbf{R}}$ is Lipschitz continuous and nonconstant on $\mathbf{R}$, and is continuously differentiable except at a finite number of points in $\mathbf{R}$, with a Lipschitz continuous derivative.

Assumption 1(i) is the same as Assumption 1(i) of Song (2014) but the requirement for f is now substantially generalized by Assumption 1(ii). To give a sense of the map g, consider the following examples.

Example 1. (a) $g(\mathbf{x}) = \mathbf{s}'\mathbf{x}$, where $\mathbf{s} \in S_1 \equiv \{\mathbf{s} \in \mathbf{R}^d\text{: } \mathbf{s}'\mathbf{1}_d = 1\}$ and $\mathbf{1}_d$ is the d-dimensional vector of ones.

(b) $g(\mathbf{x}) = \max(\mathrm{x})$ or $g(\mathrm{x}) = \min(\mathrm{x})$.
(c) $g(\mathbf{x}) = \max\{\min(\mathbf{x}_1), \mathbf{x}_2\}$, where $\mathbf{x}_1$ and $\mathbf{x}_2$ are (possibly overlapping) subvectors of $\mathbf{x}$.
(d) $g(\mathbf{x}) = \max(\mathbf{x}_1) + \max(\mathbf{x}_2)$, $g(\mathrm{x}) = \min(\mathbf{x}_1) + \min(\mathbf{x}_2)$, $g(\mathbf{x}_1) = \max(\mathbf{x}_1) + \min(\mathbf{x}_2)$, or $g(\mathbf{x}) = \max(\mathbf{x}_1) + \mathrm{s}'\mathbf{x}_2$ with $s \in S_1$.

Thus the examples of the parameters θ in the form (1) are as follows.

Example 2. (a) $\theta = |\max\{\beta_1, \beta_2\}|$

(b) $\theta = |\beta_1 - 1|$.
(c) $\theta = \min\{\max\{\beta, 0\}, 1\}$.
(d) $\theta = \min\{|\beta|, 1\}$.
(e) $\theta = \max\{\min\{\max\{\beta_1, \beta_2\}, 1\}, 0\}$.

The framework of Song (2014) requires that f be a piecewise linear map with a single kink point, and hence excludes the examples of (c)–(e). In example (c), the parameter θ is β censored at 0 and 1. In example (d), the parameter of interest is the absolute value of $|\beta|$ censored at 1.

One might ask whether the representation of parameter θ as a composition map $f \circ g$ of β in Eq. (1) with f and g satisfying Assumption 1 is unique. Lemma 1 of Song (2014) gives an affirmative answer. As we shall see later, the asymptotic risk bound involves g and the optimal estimators involve the maps f and g. This uniqueness result removes ambiguity that can potentially arise when θ has multiple equivalent representations with different maps f and g. When $d \geq 2$, the roles of f and g cannot be interchanged. When $d = 1$, Assumption 1(i) requires that $g(x) = x$. Hence in general the roles of f and g cannot be interchanged.

2.2. Local Asymptotic Normality and Regularity of β

We introduce briefly conditions for probabilities that identify β, in a manner adapted from van der Vaart (1991) and van der Vaart and Wellner (1996) (see Section 3.11, pp. 412–422.) The exposition here mostly follows Song (2014). Let $\mathscr{P} \equiv \{P_\alpha : \alpha \in \mathscr{A}\}$ be a family of distributions on a measurable space $(\mathscr{X}, \mathscr{G})$ indexed by $\alpha \in \mathscr{A}$, where the set $\mathscr{A}$ is a subset of a Euclidean space or an infinite dimensional space. We assume that we have i.i.d. draws $Y_1,...,Y_n$ from $P_{\alpha_0} \in \mathscr{P}$ so that $\boldsymbol{X}_n \equiv (Y_1,...,Y_n)$ is distributed as $P^n_{\alpha_0}$. Let $\mathscr{P}(P_{\alpha_0})$ be the collection of maps $t \to P_{\alpha_t}$ such that for some $h \in L_2(P_{\alpha_0})$,

$$\int \left\{ \frac{1}{t}(\mathrm{d}P^{1/2}_{\alpha_t} - \mathrm{d}P^{1/2}_{\alpha_0}) - \frac{1}{2} h \mathrm{d}P^{1/2}_{\alpha_0} \right\}^2 \to 0, \quad \text{as} \quad n \to \infty \tag{3}$$

When this convergence holds, we say that P_{α_t} is *differentiable in quadratic mean* to P_{α_0}, call $h \in L_2(P_{\alpha_0})$ a *score function* associated with this convergence, and call the set of all such h's a *tangent set*, denoting it by $T(P_{\alpha_0})$. We assume that the tangent set is a linear subspace of $L_2(P_{\alpha_0})$. Taking $\langle \cdot,\cdot \rangle$ to be the usual inner product in $L_2(P_{\alpha_0})$, we view $(H, \langle \cdot,\cdot \rangle)$, with $H \equiv T(P_{\alpha_0})$, as a subspace of a separable Hilbert space. For each $h \in H$, $n \in \mathbb{N}$, and $\alpha_h \in \mathscr{A}$ such that $\alpha_h = 0$ when $h = 0$, let $P_{\alpha_0 + \alpha_h/\sqrt{n}}$ be probabilities converging to P_{α_0} (as in Eq. (3)) as $n \to \infty$ having h as its score. We simply write $P_{n,h} = P^n_{\alpha_0 + \alpha_h/\sqrt{n}}$ and consider sequences of such probabilities $\{P_{n,h}\}_{n \geq 1}$ indexed by $h \in H$. (See van der Vaart (1991); van der Vaart & Wellner (1996), Section 3.11 for details.) Differentiability in quadratic mean and i.i. d. assumption imply local asymptotic normality (LAN): for any $h \in H$,

$$\log \frac{\mathrm{d}P_{n,h}}{\mathrm{d}P_{n,0}} = \zeta_n(h) - \frac{1}{2} \langle h, h \rangle$$

where for each $h, h' \in H$,

$$[\zeta_n(h), \zeta_n(h')] \xrightarrow{d} [\zeta(h), \zeta(h')], \quad \text{under}\{P_{n,0}\}$$

and $\zeta(\cdot)$ is a centered Gaussian process on H with covariance function $\mathbf{E}[\zeta(h_1)\zeta(h_2)] = \langle h_1, h_2 \rangle$. (See the proof of Lemma 3.10.11 of van der Vaart & Wellner (1996).) Local asymptotic normality reduces the decision problem to one in which an optimal decision is sought under a single Gaussian shift experiment $\mathscr{E} = (\mathscr{X}, \mathscr{G}, P_h; h \in H)$, where P_h is such that $\log \mathrm{d}P_h/\mathrm{d}P_0 = \zeta(h) - \frac{1}{2}\langle h, h \rangle$.

We assume that β is identified by P_α, $\alpha \in \mathscr{A}$, and write $\beta_n(h) = \beta(P_{\alpha_0 + \alpha_h/\sqrt{n}})$, regarding the parameter as an $\mathbf{R}^d$-valued map on H. As a sequence of maps on H, we assume that there exists a continuous linear $\mathbf{R}^d$-valued map, $\dot{\beta}$, on H such that for any $h \in H$,

$$\sqrt{n}(\beta_n(h) - \beta_n(0)) \to \dot{\beta}(h) \tag{4}$$

as $n \to \infty$. In other words, $\beta_n(h)$ is *regular* in the sense of van der Vaart and Wellner (1996, Section 3.11).

As is well known the functional $\dot{\beta}$ determines the efficiency bound for β. Let e_m be a $d \times 1$ vector whose mth entry is one and the other entries are zero. Certainly $\mathbf{e}'_m\dot{\beta}(\cdot)$ defines a continuous linear functional on H, and hence there exists $\dot{\beta}^*_m \in \overline{H}$ such that $\mathbf{e}'_m\dot{\beta}(h) = \langle \dot{\beta}^*_m, h\rangle$, $h \in H$. Then $||\dot{\beta}^*_m||^2 = \langle \dot{\beta}^*_m, \dot{\beta}^*_m\rangle$ represents the asymptotic variance bound of the parameter $\beta_m = \mathbf{e}'_m\beta$. Let Σ be a $d \times d$ matrix whose (m,k)th entry is given by $\langle \dot{\beta}^*_m, \dot{\beta}^*_k\rangle$. Throughout this paper, we assume that Σ is invertible. The inverse of matrix Σ is called the semiparametric efficiency bound for β. (See Bickel, et al. (1993) for ways to compute Σ.)

3. LOCAL ASYMPTOTIC MINIMAX ESTIMATION

3.1. Loss Functions

For a decision $d \in \mathbf{R}$ and the object of interest $\theta \in \mathbf{R}$, we consider the following form of a loss function:

$$L(d, \theta) \equiv \tau(|d - \theta|) \tag{5}$$

where $\tau : \mathbf{R} \to \mathbf{R}$ is a map that satisfies the following assumption.

Assumption 2. (i) $\tau(\cdot)$ is increasing on $[0,\infty)$, $\tau(0) = 0$, and there exists $\bar{\tau} \in (0,\infty]$ such that $\tau^{-1}([0,y])$ is bounded in $[0,\infty)$ for all $0 < y < \bar{\tau}$.

(ii) For each $M > 0$, there exists $C_M > 0$ such that for all $x,y \in \boldsymbol{R}$,

$$|\tau_M(x) - \tau_M(y)| \le C_M|x - y| \tag{6}$$

where $\tau_M(\cdot) \equiv \min\{\tau(\cdot), M\}$.

The condition in Eq. (6) allows unbounded loss functions. The class of loss functions in this paper is mostly appropriate for the problem of optimal estimation, but excludes some other types of decision problems. For example, it excludes the hypothesis testing type loss function $\tau(|d - \theta|) = 1\{|d - \theta| > c\}$, $c \in \mathbf{R}$.

3.2. Pointwise Local Asymptotic Minimax Theory

First, we develop local asymptotic minimax theory for each *fixed* α_0, and call it *pointwise local asymptotic minimax theory*, because the asymptotic approximation is pointwise at each α_0. Let

$$\theta_n(h) \equiv (f \circ g)(\beta_n(h))$$

and, given any estimator $\hat{\theta}$ which is a measurable function of $\mathbf{X}_n$, we define its *local maximal risk*: for each $b \in [0,\infty)$,

$$\mathcal{R}_{n,b}(\hat{\theta}) \equiv \sup_{h \in H_{n,b}} \mathbf{E}_h \left[\tau(|\sqrt{n}\{\hat{\theta} - \theta_n(h)\}|) \right] \tag{7}$$

where $H_{n,b} \equiv \{h \in H : \|\beta_n(h) - \beta_n(0)\| \leq b/\sqrt{n}\}$, and $\mathbf{E}_h$ denotes expectation under $P_{n,h}$.

Suppose that a Lipschitz continuous map $f : \overline{\mathbf{R}} \to \overline{\mathbf{R}}$ that satisfies Assumption 1(ii) is given. Let $\mathcal{Y} \subset \mathbf{R}$ be the set of differentiability points of f in $\mathbf{R}$. By Assumption 1(ii), the set $\mathcal{Y}$ is dense in $\mathbf{R}$. We define for each $x \in \mathbf{R}$

$$\bar{f}'(x) \equiv \lim_{\varepsilon \downarrow 0} \sup_{y \in [x-\varepsilon, x+\varepsilon] \cap \mathcal{Y}} |f'(y)|$$

where $f'(y)$ denotes the first order derivative of f at y. Certainly, the limit always exists by Assumption 1(ii), and hence $\bar{f}'(x)$ is well defined for both differentiable and nondifferentiable points. At a nondifferentiable point x, it is equivalent to define $\bar{f}'(x)$ to be the maximum of the absolute left derivative and absolute right derivative. One may consider various alternative concepts of generalized derivatives (e.g., see Clarke, Ledyaev, Stern, & Wolenski, 1998), but the definition $\bar{f}'(x)$ is simple enough for our purpose. The following result is a generalization of Theorem 1 in Song (2014).

Theorem 1. Suppose that Assumptions 1–2 hold. Then for any sequence of estimators $\hat{\theta}$,

$$\sup_{b \in [0,\infty)} \liminf_{n \to \infty} \mathcal{R}_{n,b}(\hat{\theta}) \geq \inf_{c \in \mathbf{R}} B(c)$$

where

$$B(c) \equiv \sup_{\mathbf{r} \in \mathbf{R}^d} \mathbf{E}\left[\tau(\bar{f}'(g(\beta_0))|\tilde{g}_0(Z+\mathbf{r}) - \tilde{g}_0(\mathbf{r}) + c|)\right]$$

The main feature of the local asymptotic risk bound in Theorem 1 is that it involves infimum over a line, instead of infimum over an infinite dimensional space. This convenient form is due to the same argument in Song (2014) based on the purification result of Dvoretsky, Wald, and Wolfowitz (1951) in zero sum games. This form is crucial for simulating the risk lower bound when we construct a local asymptotic minimax estimator, as explained below.

We consider an optimal estimator of θ that achieves the bound in Theorem 1. The procedure here is adapted from the proposal by Song (2014). Suppose that we are given a consistent estimator $\hat{\Sigma}$ of Σ and a semiparametrically efficient estimator $\tilde{\beta}$ of β which satisfy the following assumptions.

Assumption 3. (i) For each $\varepsilon > 0$, there exists $a > 0$ such that

$$\text{limsup}_{n \to \infty} \text{sup}_{h \in H} P_{n,h}\{\sqrt{n}||\hat{\Sigma} - \Sigma|| > a\} < \varepsilon$$

(ii) For each $t \in \mathbf{R}^d$, $\text{sup}_{h \in H} \left| P_{n,h}\{\sqrt{n}(\tilde{\beta} - \beta_n(h)) \leq t\} - P\{Z \leq t\} \right| \to 0$ as $n \to \infty$.

Assumption 3 imposes $\sqrt{n}$-consistency of $\hat{\Sigma}$ and convergence in distribution of $\sqrt{n}(\tilde{\beta} - \beta_n(h))$, both uniform over $h \in H$. The uniform convergence can often be verified through the central limit theorem uniform in $h \in H$.

For a fixed large $M_1 > 0$, we define

$$\hat{\theta}_{mx} \equiv f\left(g(\tilde{\beta}) + \frac{\hat{c}_{M_1}}{\sqrt{n}} \right)$$

where $\hat{c}_{M_1}$ is a bias adjustment term constructed from the simulations of the risk lower bound in Theorem 1, as we explain now.

To simulate the risk lower bound in Theorem 1, we first draw $\{\xi_i\}_{i=1}^L$ i.i.d. from $N(0, I_d)$. Since $\tilde{g}_0(\cdot)$ depends on β_0 that is unknown to the researcher, we first construct a consistent estimator of $\tilde{g}_0(\cdot)$. Take a sequence $\varepsilon_n \to 0$ such that $\sqrt{(n)}\varepsilon_n \to \infty$ as $n \to \infty$. Examples of ε_n are $\varepsilon_n = n^{-1/3}$ or $\varepsilon_n = n^{-1/2} \log n$. Let

$$\hat{g}_n(\mathbf{z}) \equiv g\left(\mathbf{z} + \varepsilon_n^{-1}(\tilde{\beta} - g(\tilde{\beta}))\right)$$

Then it is not hard to see that $\hat{g}_n(\mathbf{z})$ is consistent for $\tilde{g}_0(\mathbf{z})$. Define

$$\hat{a}_n \equiv \sup_{x \in [g(\tilde{\beta}) - \varepsilon_n, g(\tilde{\beta}) + \varepsilon_n] \cap \mathcal{Y}} |f'(x)|$$

Let

$$\hat{B}_{M_1}(c) \equiv \sup_{\mathbf{r} \in [-M_1, M_1]^d} \frac{1}{L} \sum_{i=1}^{L} \tau_{M_1}\left(\hat{a}_n \left| \hat{g}_n(\hat{\Sigma}^{1/2}\xi_i + \mathbf{r}) - \hat{g}_n(\mathbf{r}) + c \right|\right) \tag{8}$$

Then we define

$$\hat{c}_{M_1} \equiv \frac{1}{2}\{\sup \hat{E}_{M_1} + \inf \hat{E}_{M_1}\} \tag{9}$$

where, with $\eta_{n,L} \to 0$, $\eta_{n,L}(\sqrt{L} + \varepsilon_n\sqrt{n} + \varepsilon_n^{-1}) \to \infty$ as n, $L \to \infty$, and

$$\hat{E}_{M_1} \equiv \left\{ c \in [-M_1, M_1] : \hat{B}_{M_1}(c) \leq \inf_{c_1 \in [-M_1, M_1]} \hat{B}_{M_1}(c_1) + \eta_{n,L} \right\}$$

The following theorem affirms that $\hat{\theta}_{mx}$ is local asymptotic minimax for $\theta = g(\beta)$. (For technical facility, we follow a suggestion by Strasser (1985, p. 440) and consider a truncated loss: $\tau_M(\cdot) = \min\{\tau(\cdot), M\}$ for large M.)

Theorem 2. Suppose that Assumptions 1–3 hold. Then, for any $M > 0$ and any $M_1 \geq$ M that constitutes constant $\hat{c}_{M_1}$,

$$\sup_{b \in [0,\infty)} \limsup_{n \to \infty} \mathcal{R}_{n,b,M}(\hat{\theta}_{mx}) \leq \inf_{c \in \mathbf{R}} B(c)$$

where $\mathcal{R}_{n,b,M}(\hat{\theta}_{mx})$ *coincides with* $\mathcal{R}_{n,b}(\hat{\theta}_{mx})$ *with* $\tau(\cdot)$ *replaced by* $\min\{\tau(\cdot), M\}$.

Therefore, the risk lower bound

$$\inf_{c \in \mathbf{R}} B(c)$$

in Theorem 1 is sharp. We call it the *local asymptotic minimax risk* in this paper.

When $\tau(x) = |x|^p$, for some $p \geq 1$, the minimizer of $B(c)$ does not depend on the shape of f. Hence, in constructing $\hat{B}_{M_1}(c)$ in Eq. (8), it suffices to take $\hat{a}_n = 1$.

Similarly in Song (2014), when $\theta = g(\beta)$ is a regular parameter, taking the form of $g(\beta) = \mathbf{s}'\beta$ with $\mathbf{s} \in S_1$, the local asymptotic minimax risk bound becomes

$$\inf_{c \in \mathbf{R}} \mathbf{E}\left[\tau(\bar{f}'(\mathbf{s}'\beta_0))|\mathbf{s}'Z + c|)\right] = \mathbf{E}\left[\tau(\bar{f}'(\mathbf{s}'\beta_0)|\mathbf{s}'Z|)\right]$$

where the equality above follows by Anderson's Lemma. In this case, it suffices to set $\hat{c}^*_{M_1} = 0$, for the infimum over $c \in \mathbf{R}$ is achieved at $c = 0$. This is true regardless of whether f is symmetric around zero or not.

4. DISCONTINUITY IN THE LOCAL ASYMPTOTIC MINIMAX RISK

4.1. Local Robustification

The local asymptotic minimax risk $\inf_{c \in \mathbf{R}} B(c)$ depends on β_0 discontinuously in general. This is easily seen from the form of $B(c)$, for we may have $\bar{f}'(x)$ and $\bar{f}'(y)$ stay apart, even as x and y get closer to each other.[1] This discontinuity may imply that the local asymptotic minimax approach may serve as a poor approximation of a finite sample risk bound.

We consider an alternative approach of optimality that is robustified against a local perturbation of $\beta_0 = \beta(P_{\alpha_0})$ (i.e., of $\alpha_0 \in \mathscr{A}$). Note that Ibragimov and Khas'minski (1986) pointed out the desirability of local robustification with respect to such an initial parameter β_0.

For each $\mathbf{y} \in \mathbf{R}^d$ and a positive sequence $\varepsilon_n \downarrow 0$, define

$$\mathscr{A}(\alpha_0; \varepsilon_n) \equiv \{\alpha \in \mathscr{A} : ||\beta(P_\alpha) - \beta(P_{\alpha_0})|| \leq \varepsilon_n\}$$

The set $\mathscr{A}(\alpha_0; \varepsilon_n)$ is the collection of α's such that the regular parameter vectors $\beta(P_\alpha)$ and $\beta(P_{\alpha_0})$ are close to each other. Then define the local maximal risk under local robustification: for each $b \in [0,\infty)$, and a positive sequence $\varepsilon_n \downarrow 0$,

$$\mathcal{R}_{n,b}(\hat{\theta}; \varepsilon_n) \equiv \sup_{\alpha_1 \in \mathscr{A}(\alpha_0;\varepsilon_n)} \sup_{h \in H_{n,b}(\alpha_1)} \mathbf{E}_{h,\alpha_1}\left[\tau(|\sqrt{n}\{\hat{\theta} - \theta_n(h)\}|)\right]$$

where $\mathbf{E}_{h,\alpha_1}$ denotes the expectation under $P_{n,h,\alpha_1} \equiv P_{\alpha_1+\alpha_h/\sqrt{n}}$ and

$$H_{n,b}(\alpha_1) \equiv \{h \in H : ||\beta_n(h) - \beta(P_{\alpha_1})|| \leq b/\sqrt{n}\}$$

Then certainly by Theorem 1, we have for any sequence of estimators $\hat{\theta}$,

$$\sup_{b \in [0,\infty)} \liminf_{n \to \infty} \mathcal{R}_{n,b}(\hat{\theta}; \varepsilon_n) \geq \inf_{c \in \mathbf{R}} B(c)$$

The main question is whether this lower bound is sharp. For this, we show that the optimal estimator $\hat{\theta}_{mx}$ continues to achieve this lower bound, when Assumption 3 is strengthened as follows.

Assumption 3′. (i) There exists $M > 0$ such that

$$\text{limsup}_{n\to\infty}\text{sup}_{\alpha\in\mathcal{A}}\text{sup}_{h\in H}P_{n,h,\alpha}\{\sqrt{n}||\hat{\Sigma} - \Sigma|| > M\} < \varepsilon$$

(ii) For each $t \in \mathbf{R}^d$,

$$\sup_{\alpha\in\mathcal{A}} \sup_{h\in H} \left|P_{n,h,\alpha}\{\sqrt{n}(\tilde{\beta} - \beta_n(h)) \leq t\} - P\{Z \leq t\}\right| \to 0$$

as $n \to \infty$.

Assumption 3′ strengthens the uniformity in convergence in Assumption 3 to that over $\alpha \in \mathcal{A}$. In many cases, it is not hard to verify this condition.

Theorem 3. Suppose that Assumptions 1–2 and 3′ hold. Then for each $\varepsilon_n \downarrow 0$ such that $\varepsilon_n\sqrt{n} \to \infty$, as $n \to \infty$, for any sequence of estimators $\hat{\theta}$, and for any $M_1 > M$ such that M_1 constitutes $\hat{c}_{M_1}$,

$$\lim_{M\uparrow\infty} \sup_{b\in[0,\infty)} \limsup_{n\to\infty} \mathcal{R}_{n,b,M}(\hat{\theta}_{mx}; \varepsilon_n) \leq \inf_{c\in\mathbf{R}} B(c)$$

The result of Theorem 3 shows that the local asymptotic minimax risk

$$\inf_{c\in\mathbf{R}} B(c) \tag{10}$$

remains unchanged, even when we locally robustify the maximal risk, and that the estimator $\hat{\theta}_{mx}$ continues to satisfy the local asymptotic minimaxity after local robustification. At the same time, local robustification does not resolve the issue of discontinuity in the local asymptotic minimax risk.

5. DISCUSSION

To understand the result of Theorem 3, let us consider localization with a fixed Pitman direction. First, let $\alpha_0 \in \mathscr{A}$ be as before such that $\beta(P_{\alpha_0}) = \beta_0$, and consider

$$\alpha_n(\delta) = \alpha_0 + \frac{\delta}{\sqrt{n}} \tag{11}$$

where $\delta \in \mathscr{A}$ is a Pitman direction. We assume that $\{P_{\alpha_n(\delta)}\}_{n=1}^{\infty}$ is quadratic mean differentiable at P_{α_0} with a score $h_\delta \in H$. Then, we have

$$\begin{aligned}\beta(P_{\alpha n(\delta)}) &= \beta(P_{\alpha 0}) + \beta(P_{\alpha 0 + \delta/\sqrt{n}}) - \beta(P_{\alpha 0}) \\ &= \beta(P_{\alpha 0}) + \frac{\dot{\beta}(h_\delta)}{\sqrt{n}} + o(n^{-1/2})\end{aligned}$$

by the regularity of β. In other words, the Pitman direction δ for $\alpha_n(\delta)$ is now translated into the Pitman direction $\dot{\beta}(h_\delta)$ for $\beta(P_{\alpha_n(\delta)})$.

Recall that the local asymptotic minimax risk arises as a consequence of robustification against all the scores $h \in H$ at P_{α_0}. Since Σ is invertible, the range of $\dot{\beta}$ (when $\dot{\beta}$ is extended to a completion $\overline{H}$ of H) is equal to $\mathbf{R}^d$, i.e., for any $\mathbf{r} \in \mathbf{R}^d$, there exists $h \in \overline{H}$ such that $\dot{\beta}(h) = \mathbf{r}$. Therefore, robustification against all the Pitman directions such that $\{P_{\alpha_n(\delta)}\}_{n=1}^{\infty}$ is quadratic mean differentiable at P_{α_0} is equivalent to robustification against all the $\sqrt{n}$-converging Pitman deviations from β_0. Thus the local robustification against Pitman deviations from β is already incorporated in the results of local asymptotic minimax risk in Theorems 1 and 2.[2] This is why local robustification around β_0 does not alter the results.

One might suggest considering a single Pitman direction δ and focusing on a sequence of probabilities $\{P_{\alpha_n(\delta)}\}_{n=1}^{\infty}$, derive the local asymptotic minimax risk in a way that depends on δ, and see if the risk continuously depends on δ. This approach is analogous to many other approaches used to deal with discontinuity of asymptotic distributions such as Pitman local asymptotic power analysis, local-to-unity models, and weak identification. However, such an approach in this context counters to the basic motivation of the local asymptotic minimax approach, because restricting attention to a single sequence of probabilities fails to robustify the decision problem properly against local perturbations of the underlying probability and hence fails to exclude superefficient estimators.[3]

6. CONCLUSION

This paper focuses on the problem of optimal estimation for a parameter that is a nondifferentiable transform of a regular parameter. First, this paper extends the results of Song (2014) allowing for a more general class of nondifferentiable transforms. Second, this paper investigates the issue of discontinuity in local asymptotic minimax risk, and considers the approach of local robustification of the true probability. As it turns out, the local robustification does not alter the local asymptotic minimax risk. This means that the optimal estimator remains optimal under this additional dimension of local robustification. On the other hand, it also means that the discontinuity in the minimax risk is not resolved by the local robustification. Hence, there still remains the question of whether local asymptotic minimax theory gives a good approximation of a finite sample decision problem when the parameter is nondifferentiable. A full investigation of this issue is relegated to a future research.

NOTES

1. While nondifferentiability of f yields discontinuity in the minimax risk in most cases, there are counterexamples. For example, when $f(a) = |a|$, we have $\bar{f}'(a) = 1$ for all $a \in \mathbf{R}$, and if further $g(\beta) = \mathbf{s}'\beta$, the minimax risk is continuous in α_0, although f is nondifferentiable at 0.

2. In fact, Theorem 3 is stronger than this, because for each $\bar{\delta} \in (0,\infty)$, $\mathscr{A}(\alpha_0; \bar{\delta}/\sqrt{n}) \mathscr{A}(\alpha_0; \varepsilon_n)$, from some large n on.

3. A still alternative way is an approach of global robustification, where one robustifies against all a_0's in A. The problem with this approach is that the minimax decision problem often becomes trivial, with the minimax risk being infinity. Such a trivial case arises, e.g., when $\sup_{x \in \mathbf{R}} \bar{f}'(x) = \infty$. This is the case when $f(x) = x^2$ for example.

ACKNOWLEDGMENT

This research was supported by the Social Sciences and Humanities Research Council of Canada.

REFERENCES

Andrews, D. W. K., & Guggenberger, P. (2009). Validity of subsampling and "Plug-in Asymptotic" inference for parameters defined by moment inequalities. *Econometric Theory*, *25*, 669–709.

Basawa, I. V., & Scott, D. J. (1983). *Asymptotic optimal inference for non-ergodic models*. New York, NY: Springer-Verlag.

Begun, J. M., Hall, W. J., Huang, W.-M., & Wellner, J. A. (1983). Information and asymptotic efficiency in parametric-nonparametric models. *Annals of Statistics*, *11*, 432–452.

Bickel, P. J., Klaassen, A. J., Ritov, Y., & Wellner, J. A. (1993). *Efficient and adaptive estimation for semiparametric models*. New York, NY: Springer-Verlag.

Chamberlain, G. (1987). Asymptotic efficiency in estimation with conditional moment restrictions. *Journal of Econometrics*, *34*, 305–334.

Chernoff, H. (1956). Large sample theory: Parametric case. *Annals of Mathematical Statistics*, *27*, 1–22.

Chernozhukov, V., Lee, S., & Rosen, A. (2013). Intersection bounds: Estimation and inference. *Econometrica*, *81*, 667–737.

Clarke, F. H., Ledyaev, Y. S., Stern, R. J., & Wolenski, P. R. (1998). *Nonsmooth analysis and control theory*. New York, NY: Springer-Verlag.

Doss, H., & Sethuraman, J. (1989). The price of bias reduction when there is no unbiased estimate. *Annals of Statistics*, *17*, 440–442.

Dudley, R. M. (2002). *Real analysis and probability*. New York, NY: Cambridge University Press.

Dvoretsky, A., Wald, A., & Wolfowitz, J. (1951). Elimination of randomization in certain statistical decision procedures and zero-sum two-person games. *Annals of Mathematical Statistics*, *22*, 1–21.

Haile, P. A., & Tamer, E. (2003). Inference with an incomplete model of English auctions. *Journal of Political Economy*, *111*, 1–51.

Hájek, J. (1972). Local asymptotic minimax and admissibility in estimation. *Proceedings of the 6th Berkeley Symposium in Mathematical Statistics and Probability*, *1*, 175–194.

Hirano, K., & Porter, J. (2012). Impossibility results for nondifferentiable functionals. *Econometrica*, *80*, 1769–1790.

Ibragimov, I. A., & Khas'minski, R. Z. (1986). A uniform condition of local asymptotic normality. *Journal of Soviet Mathematics*, *34*, 1427–1432.

Jeganathan, P. (1982). On the asymptotic theory of estimation when the limit of likelihood ratios is mixed normal. *Sankya, Series A*, *44*, 173–212.

Koshevnik, Y. A., & Levit, B. Y. (1976). On a non-parametric analogue of the information matrix. *Theory of Probability and Its Applications*, *21*, 738–753.

Le Cam, L. (1953). On some asymptotic properties of maximum likelihood estimates and related Bayes' estimates. *University of California Publications in Statistics*, *1*, 277–330.

Le Cam, L. (1972). Limits of experiments. *Proceedings of the 6th Berkeley Symposium in Mathematical Statistics and Probability*, *1*, 245–265.

Levit, B. Y. (1978). Infinite-dimensional informational lower bounds. *Theory of Probability and Its Applications*, *23*, 388–394.

Manski, C. F., & Tamer, E. (2002). Inference on regressions with interval data on a regressor or outcome. *Econometrica*, *70*, 519–546.

Newey, W. K. (1990). Semiparametric efficiency bounds. *Journal of Applied Econometrics*, *5*, 99–135.

Pfanzagl, J. (with the assistance of Wefelmeyer, W.) (1982). *Contributions to a general asymptotic statistical theory, lecture notes in statistics* (Vol. 13). New York, NY: Springer-Verlag.

Phillips, P. C. B. (1991). Optimal inference in cointegrated systems. *Econometrica*, *59*, 283–306.

Song, K. (2014). Local asymptotic minimax estimation of nonregular parameters with translation-scale equivariant maps. *Journal of Multivariate Analysis*, *125*, 136–158.

Staiger, D., & Stock, J. H. (1997). Instrumental variables regression with weak instruments. *Econometrica*, *65*, 557–586.

Stock, J. H. (1991). Confidence intervals for the largest autoregressive root in US macroeconomic time series. *Journal of Monetary Economics*, *28*, 435–459.

Strasser, H. (1985). *Mathematical theory of statistics*. New York, NY: Walter de Gruyter.

van der Vaart, A. W. (1988). *Statistical estimation in large sample spaces*. Amsterdam: CWI Tracts 44.

van der Vaart, A. W. (1991). On differentiable functionals. *Annals of Statistics*, *19*, 178–204.

van der Vaart, A. W. (1998). *Asymptotic statistics*. New York, NY: Cambridge University Press.

van der Vaart, A. W., & Wellner, J. A. (1996). *Weak convergence and empirical processes*. New York, NY: Springer-Verlag.

Wald, A. (1943). Tests of statistical hypothesis concerning several parameters when the number of observations is large. *Transactions of the American Mathematical Society*, *54*, 426–482.

APPENDIX: MATHEMATICAL PROOFS

Proof of Theorem 1. As in the proof of Lemma 3 of Song (2014), we begin by fixing $r \in \boldsymbol{R}^d$ so that for some $h' \in \overline{H}$, $\mathbf{r} = \dot{\beta}(h')$. (Existence of such $h' \in \overline{H}$ for each $r \in \boldsymbol{R}^d$ follows from the condition that Σ is invertible.) Also fix $h \in H$ such that $\langle h,h' \rangle = 0$. We write

$$\begin{aligned} &\sqrt{n}\{\hat{\theta} - f(g(\beta_n(h+h')))\} \\ &= \sqrt{n}\{\hat{\theta} - f(g(\beta_n(h')))\} - \sqrt{n}\{f(g(\beta_n(h+h'))) - f(g(\beta_n(h')))\} \end{aligned}$$

Suppose first that f is continuously differentiable at $g(\beta_0)$. Then by Assumption 1(ii), we have $x_1 < x_2$ such that $x_1 < g(\beta_0) < x_2$, where f is continuously differentiable on $[x_1, x_2]$. Furthermore, by regularity of β and Lipschitz continuity of g, we have

$$g(\beta_n(h+h')) = g(\beta_n(h+h') - \beta_0 + \beta_0) \to g(\beta_0) \tag{A.1}$$

as $n \to \infty$. Therefore, we note that from some large n on, by the mean value theorem,

$$\begin{aligned} &\sqrt{n}\{f(g(\beta_n(h+h'))) - f(g(\beta_0))\} \\ &= \sqrt{n} f'(a_n(h,h'))\, \{g(\beta_n(h+h')) - g(\beta_0)\} \end{aligned}$$

where $a_n(h,h') \equiv t_n\{g(\beta_n(h + h') - g(\beta_0)\} + g(\beta_0)$ for some $t_n \in [0,1]$. From Eq. (A.1), we have

$$a_n(h,h') \to g(\beta_0), \quad \text{as} \quad n \to \infty$$

From Eq. (A.10) of Song (2014) on page 149, we also find that

$$\sqrt{n}\{g(\beta_n(h+h')) - g(\beta_n(h'))\} = \tilde{g}_0(\dot{\beta}(h) + \mathbf{r}) - \tilde{g}_0(\mathbf{r}) + o(1) \tag{A.2}$$

Since f' is continuous at $g(\beta_0)$ and $\dot{\beta}$ is bounded, we combine these results to deduce that

$$\begin{aligned} &\sqrt{n}\{f(g(\beta_n(h+h'))) - f(g(\beta_n(h')))\} \\ &\to f'(g(\beta_0))(\tilde{g}_0(\dot{\beta}(h) + \mathbf{r}) - \tilde{g}_0(\mathbf{r})) \end{aligned} \tag{A.3}$$

as $n \to \infty$.

For any sequence of estimators $\hat{\theta}$, the sequence $\{\hat{\theta}\}_{n\geq 1}$ is uniformly tight in $\overline{\mathbf{R}}$, and hence by using the LAN property and Eq. (A.3), applying Prohorov's Theorem and Lemma A4 of Song (2014), we find that for each subsequence of $\{n\}$, there exists a further subsequence $\{n'\}$ such that under $\{P_{n',h'}\}$,

$$\begin{bmatrix} \sqrt{n'}\left\{\hat{\theta}-g(\beta_{n'}(h+h'))\right\} \\ \log dP_{n',h+h'}/dP_{n',h'} \end{bmatrix} \overset{d}{\to} \begin{bmatrix} V-f'(g(\beta_0))\left(\tilde{g}_0(\dot{\beta}(h)+\mathbf{r})-\tilde{g}_0(\mathbf{r})\right) \\ \zeta(h)-\frac{1}{2}\langle h,h\rangle \end{bmatrix}$$

where $V\in\overline{\mathbf{R}}$ is a random variable having a potentially deficient distribution. The rest of the proof can be proceeded precisely as in the proofs of Lemma 3 and Theorem 1 of Song (2014).

Second, suppose that f is not continuously differentiable at $g(\beta_0)$. Since there is a finite number of nondifferentiability points for f, we have x_1, $x_2\in\mathbf{R}$ such that $x_1 < g(\beta_0) < x_2$, and f is continuously differentiable on $[x_1,g(\beta_0))$ and $(g(\beta_0),x_2]$ by Assumption 1(ii).

As previously, we choose arbitrary $\mathbf{r}\in\mathbf{R}^d$ so that for some $h'\in H$, $\mathbf{r}=\dot{\beta}(h')$, and fix $b/2\geq ||h'||\cdot||\dot{\beta}^*||$. Now, define

$$H^*_{n,b,1}\equiv\{h\in H^*_{n,b}: R_n(h)\geq 0, \quad \text{and} \qquad H^*_{n,b,2}\equiv\{h\in H^*_{n,b}: R_n(h)\leq 0$$

where $H^*_{n,b}\equiv\{h\in H_{n,b}:\langle h,h'\rangle=0$ and $R_n(h)\equiv g(\beta_n(h+h'))-g(\beta_0)$, and observe that for all $h\in H$,

$$|R_n(h)|\to 0 \tag{A.4}$$

as $n\to\infty$. (This is Eq. (A.31) of Song (2014). See the arguments for details.) Thus we have for each $h\in H$, as $n\to\infty$,

$$\begin{aligned} &1\left\{h\in H^*_{n,b,1}\right\}\to 1\{h\in H_b\} \quad \text{and} \\ &1\left\{h\in H^*_{n,b,2}\right\}\to 1\{h\in H_b\}, \end{aligned} \tag{A.5}$$

where $H_b\equiv\{h\in H: ||\dot{\beta}(h)||\leq b\}$.

Note that

$$\begin{aligned}&\lim_{b\to\infty}\ \liminf_{n\to\infty}\ \sup_{h\in H_{n,b}} \mathbf{E}_h\left[\tau_M(|\sqrt{n}\{\hat{\theta}-f(g(\beta_n(h)))|)\right]\\ \geq\ &\max_{l=1,2}\ \lim_{b\to\infty}\ \liminf_{n\to\infty}\ \sup_{h\in H^*_{n,b/2,l}} \mathbf{E}_h\left[\tau_M(|\sqrt{n}\{\hat{\theta}-f(g(\beta_n(h)))|)\right]\end{aligned} \tag{A.6}$$

Due to the liminf and supremum over $h\in H^*_{n,b/2,l}$ (where the supremum over an empty set of a nonnegative function is taken to be zero), it suffices to focus on $h\in H$ such that $h\in H^*_{n,b/2,1}$ or $h\in H^*_{n,b/2,2}$, eventually from some large n on.

For each $h\in H^*_{n,b,1}$, we have

$$g(\beta_0)\leq g(\beta_n(h+h'))$$

and by the mean-value theorem,

$$\begin{aligned}&\sqrt{n}\{f(g(\beta_n(h+h')))-f(g(\beta_0))\}\\ &=f'_+(g(\beta_0)+t_n)\sqrt{n}(g(\beta_n(h+h'))-g(\beta_0))\end{aligned}$$

where $t_n \geq 0$ and $t_n \leq g(\beta_n(h + h')) - g(\beta_0)$ and $f'_+(x)$ denotes the right derivative of f at x. By using Eq. (A.2) and the Lipschitz continuity of f' on $(g(\beta_0),x_2]$, for any $h\in H$, such that $h\in H^*_{n,b/2,1}$ eventually, we have

$$\sqrt{n}\{f(g(\beta_n(h+h')))-f(g(\beta_n(h')))\}\to f'_+(g(\beta_0))(\tilde{g}_0(\dot{\beta}(h)+\mathbf{r})-\tilde{g}_0(\mathbf{r}))$$

as $n\to\infty$.

Therefore, for any $h\in H$, such that $h\in H^*_{n,b/2,1}$ eventually, and for each subsequence of $\{n\}$, there exists a further subsequence $\{n'\}$ such that under $\{P_{n',h'}\}$,

$$\begin{bmatrix}\sqrt{n'}\{\hat{\theta}-f(g(\beta_{n'}(h+h')))\}\\ \log dP_{n',h+h'}/dP_{n',h'}\end{bmatrix}\overset{d}{\to}\begin{bmatrix}V_+ - f'_+(g(\beta_0))(\tilde{g}_0(\dot{\beta}(h)+\mathbf{r})-\tilde{g}_0(\mathbf{r}))\\ \zeta(h)-\frac{1}{2}\langle h,h\rangle\end{bmatrix}$$

where $V_+ \in \overline{\mathbf{R}}$ is a random variable having a potentially deficient distribution. Using Eq. (A.5) and following the same arguments as in the proofs of Lemma 3 and Theorem 1 of Song (2014), we deduce that

$$\begin{aligned} &\lim_{b\to\infty} \liminf_{n\to\infty} \sup_{h\in H^*_{n,b/2,1}} \mathbf{E}_h\left[\tau_M\left(\left|\sqrt{n}\{\hat{\theta} - f(g(\beta_n(h)))\right|\right)\right] \\ &\geq \inf_{c\in\mathbf{R}} \sup_{\mathbf{r}\in\mathbf{R}^d} \mathbf{E}[\tau(|f'_+(g(\beta_0))||\tilde{g}_0(Z+\mathbf{r}) - \tilde{g}_0(\mathbf{r}) + c|)] \end{aligned} \tag{A.7}$$

Similarly, for any $h\in H$, such that $h\in H^*_{n,b/2,2}$ eventually, we have

$$\sqrt{n}\{f(g(\beta_n(h_n+h'))) - f(g(\beta_n(h')))\} \to f'_-(g(\beta_0))(\tilde{g}_0(\dot{\beta}(h)+\mathbf{r}) - \tilde{g}_0(\mathbf{r}))$$

as $n \to \infty$, where $f'_-(x)$ denotes the left derivative of f at x. Hence similarly as before, for any $h\in H$, such that $h\in H^*_{n,b/2,2}$ eventually, and for each subsequence of $\{n\}$, there exists a further subsequence $\{n'\}$ such that under $\{P_{n',h'}\}$,

$$\begin{bmatrix} \sqrt{n'}\{\hat{\theta} - f(g(\beta_{n'}(h+h')))\} \\ \log dP_{n',h+h'}/dP_{n',h'} \end{bmatrix} \overset{d}{\to} \begin{bmatrix} V_- - f'_-(g(\beta_0))(\tilde{g}_0(\dot{\beta}(h)+\mathbf{r}) - \tilde{g}_0(\mathbf{r})) \\ \zeta(h) - \frac{1}{2}\langle h, h\rangle \end{bmatrix}$$

where $V_- \in \overline{\mathbf{R}}$ is a random variable having a potentially deficient distribution. Using Eq. (A.5) and following the same arguments as in the proofs of Lemma 3 and Theorem 1 of Song (2014), we deduce that

$$\begin{aligned} &\lim_{b\to\infty} \liminf_{n\to\infty} \sup_{h\in H^*_{n,b/2,2}} \mathbf{E}_h\left[\tau_M\left(\left|\sqrt{n}\{\hat{\theta} - f(g(\beta_n(h)))\right|\right)\right] \\ &\geq \inf_{c\in\mathbf{R}} \sup_{\mathbf{r}\in\mathbf{R}^d} \mathbf{E}[\tau(|f'_-(g(\beta_0))||\tilde{g}_0(Z+\mathbf{r}) - \tilde{g}_0(\mathbf{r}) + c|)] \end{aligned} \tag{A.8}$$

Combining the bounds in Eqs. (A.7) and (A.8) into Eq. (A.6), we conclude that

$$\begin{aligned} &\lim_{b\to\infty} \liminf_{n\to\infty} \sup_{h\in H_{n,b}} \mathbf{E}_h\left[\tau_M\left(|\sqrt{n}\{\hat{\theta} - f(g(\beta_n(h)))|\right)\right] \\ &\geq \max\{\Psi(a_+), \Psi(a_-)\} \end{aligned} \tag{A.9}$$

where, for $a \geq 0$,

$$\Psi(a) \equiv \inf_{c \in \mathbf{R}} \sup_{\mathbf{r} \in \mathbf{R}^d} \mathbf{E}[\tau(a|\tilde{g}_0(Z+\mathbf{r}) - \tilde{g}_0(\mathbf{r}) + c|)]$$

and

$$a_+ \equiv |f'_+(g(\beta_0))| \quad \text{and} \quad a_- \equiv |f'_-(g(\beta_0))|$$

Since $\Psi(a)$ is an increasing function of a on $[0,\infty)$, the last bound is equal to

$$\Psi(\max\{a_+, a_-\})$$

Since f' is Lipschitz continuus on $[x_1, g(\beta_0))$ and $(g(\beta_0), x_2]$ by Assumption 1(ii), we have

$$a_+ = \lim_{y \downarrow 0} |f'(g(\beta_0)+y)| = \lim_{\varepsilon \downarrow 0} \sup_{0<y\leq\varepsilon} |f'(g(\beta_0)+y)| \quad \text{and}$$
$$a_- = \lim_{y \downarrow 0} |f'(g(\beta_0)-y)| = \lim_{\varepsilon \downarrow 0} \sup_{0<y\leq\varepsilon} |f'(g(\beta_0)-y)|$$

Since max function is continuous,

$$\begin{aligned}\max\{a_+, a_-\} &= \lim_{\varepsilon \downarrow 0} \max\left\{ \sup_{0<y\leq\varepsilon} |f'(g(\beta_0)+y)|, \sup_{0<y\leq\varepsilon} |f'(g(\beta_0)-y)| \right\} \\ &= \lim_{\varepsilon \downarrow 0} \sup_{y \in -\varepsilon,\varepsilon] \setminus \{0\}} |f'(g(\beta_0)+y)| = \bar{f}'(g(\beta_0))\end{aligned}$$

Thus we have a desired lower bound. ■

For a given $M_1 > 0$, define

$$B_{M_1}(c) \equiv \sup_{\mathbf{r} \in \mathbf{R}^d} \mathbf{E}\left[\tau_{M_1}(a_0|\tilde{g}_0(Z+\mathbf{r}) - \tilde{g}_0(\mathbf{r}) + c|)\right]$$

where $a_0 \equiv \bar{f}'(g(\beta_0))$, and let

$$E_{M_1} \equiv \left\{ c \in [-[M_1, M_1] : B_{M_1}(c) \leq \inf_{c_1 \in [-[M_1, M_1]} B_{M_1}(c_1) \right\}$$

Define $c_{M_1} \equiv 0.5\{\max E_{M_1} + \min E_{M_1}\}$. We also define

$$\overline{g}_n(\mathbf{z}) \equiv g(\mathbf{z} + \varepsilon_n^{-1}(\beta_0 - g(\beta_0)))$$

for $\mathbf{z} \in \mathbf{R}^d$, and

$$\overline{B}_{M_1}(c) \equiv \sup_{\mathbf{r} \in [-M_1, M_1]^d} \frac{1}{L} \sum_{i=1}^{L} \tau_{M_1}(\hat{a}_n | \overline{g}_n(\hat{\Sigma}^{1/2} \xi_i + \mathbf{r}) - \overline{g}_n(\mathbf{r}) + c|)$$

$$\tilde{B}_{M_1}(c) \equiv \sup_{\mathbf{r} \in [-M_1, M_1]^d} \frac{1}{L} \sum_{i=1}^{L} \tau_{M_1}(a_0 | \overline{g}_n(\Sigma^{1/2} \xi_i + \mathbf{r}) - \overline{g}_n(\mathbf{r}) + c|)$$

and

$$B_{M_1}^*(c) \equiv \sup_{\mathbf{r} \in [-M_1, M_1]^d} \mathbf{E}\left[\tau_{M_1}(a_0 | \overline{g}_n(\Sigma^{1/2} \xi_i + \mathbf{r}) - \overline{g}_n(\mathbf{r}) + c|)\right]$$

We also define

$$E_{M_1}^* \equiv \left\{ c \in [-M_1, M_1] : B_{M_1}^*(c) \leq \inf_{c_1 \in [-M_1, M_1]} B_{M_1}^*(c_1) \right\}$$

Lemma A1. Suppose that Assumptions 1(i), 2, and 3 hold.

(i) *As* $K \to \infty$,

$$\lim_{n \to \infty} \sup_{h \in H} P_{n,h} \left\{ \sup_{c \in [-M_1, M_1]} |B_{M_1}^*(c) - \hat{B}_{M_1}(c)| > K(L^{-1/2} + n^{-1/2} \varepsilon_n^{-1} + \varepsilon_n) \right\} \to 0$$

(ii) *As* $n \to \infty$

$$\sup_{c \in [-M_1, M_1]} |B_{M_1}^*(c) - B_{M_1}(c)| \to 0$$

Proof. (i) As shown in the proof of Lemma A5 of Song (2014), we find that as $K \to \infty$,

$$\lim_{n \to \infty} \sup_{h \in H} P_{n,h} \left\{ \sup_{\mathbf{z} \in \mathbf{R}^d} |\overline{g}_n(\mathbf{z}) - \hat{g}_n(\mathbf{z})| > K n^{-1/2} \varepsilon_n^{-1} \right\} \to 0$$

Therefore, as $K \to \infty$,

$$\lim_{n\to\infty} \sup_{h\in H} P_{n,h}\left\{ \sup_{c\in[-M_1,M_1]} |\overline{B}_{M_1}(c) - \hat{B}_{M_1}(c)| > Kn^{-1/2}\varepsilon_n^{-1} \right\} \to 0$$

We show that

$$\lim_{n\to\infty} \sup_{h\in H} P_{n,h}\{|\hat{a} - a_0| > K\varepsilon_n\} \to 0 \tag{A.10}$$

as $K \to \infty$. Let us define for $\varepsilon > 0$,

$$a_0(\varepsilon) = \sup_{x\in[g(\beta_0)-\varepsilon, g(\beta_0)+\varepsilon]\cap\mathcal{Y}} |f'(x)|$$

Also, for any $\tilde{\varepsilon}_n \downarrow 0$ such that $\tilde{\varepsilon}_n/\varepsilon_n \to 0$ and $\tilde{\varepsilon}_n\sqrt{n} \to \infty$ as $n \to \infty$, we have that

$$\inf_{h\in H} P_{n,h}\{|g(\tilde{\beta}) - g(\beta_0)| \le C\tilde{\varepsilon}_n\} \to 1$$

for some $C > 0$. Therefore, with probability approaching one (uniformly over $h \in H$),

$$\left|\hat{a}_n - a_0(\tilde{\varepsilon}_n)\right| \le \sup_{x\in[g(\tilde{\beta})-\varepsilon_n, g(\tilde{\beta})+\varepsilon_n]\cap\mathcal{Y}} |f'(x)|$$

$$- \sup_{x\in[g(\beta_0)-\tilde{\varepsilon}_n/2, g(\beta_0)+\tilde{\varepsilon}_n/2]\cap\mathcal{Y}} |f'(x)|$$

The last difference is bounded by $C\varepsilon_n$ for some $C > 0$, by the assumption that the derivative f' is Lipschitz continuous on $\mathcal{Y}$. Furthermore, we have

$$|a_0(\varepsilon) - a_0| \le C\varepsilon$$

for $C > 0$ that does not depend on β_0, because f is independent of β_0 and f' is Lipschitz continuous on $\mathcal{Y}$. Thus we obtain Eq. (A.10), and following the proof of Lemma A5 of Song (2014), we conclude that

$$\lim_{n\to\infty} \sup_{h\in H} P_{n,h}\left\{ \sup_{c\in[-M_1,M_1]} |\tilde{B}_{M_1}(c) - \overline{B}_{M_1}(c)| > K\{n^{-1/2} + \varepsilon_n\} \right\} \to 0 \quad \text{and}$$

$$\lim_{n\to\infty} P\left\{ \sup_{c\in[-M_1,M_1]} |B^*_{M_1}(c) - \tilde{B}_{M_1}(c)| > K(L^{-1/2} + n^{-1/2}) \right\} \to 0$$

as $K \to \infty$. Combining these results, we obtain the desired result.

(ii) The proof is precisely the same as the proof of Lemma A6 of Song (2014). ∎

The following lemma deals with the discrepancy between $\hat{c}_{M_1}$ and c_{M_1}.

Lemma A2. *Suppose that Assumptions 1(i), 2, and 3 hold. Then there exists M_0 such that for any $M_1 > M_0$, and any $\varepsilon > 0$,*

$$\sup_{h\in H} P_{n,h}\{|\hat{c}_{M_1} - c_{M_1}| > \varepsilon\} \to 0$$

as n, $L \to \infty$ jointly.

Proof of Lemma A2. The proof essentially modifies that of Lemma A7 of Song (2014). From the latter proof, it suffice to show (a) and (b) in the proof of Lemma A7 of Song (2014) for our context. We can derive these using Lemma A1 precisely in the same way. ∎

Proof of Theorem 2. Take $\tilde{\varepsilon}_n \downarrow 0$ such that $\tilde{\varepsilon}_n/\varepsilon_n \to 0$ but $\tilde{\varepsilon}_n\sqrt{n} \to \infty$. Then, observe that

$$\inf_{h\in H} P_{n,h}\left\{ \left| g(\tilde{\beta}) - g(\beta_0) + \frac{\hat{c}_{M_1}}{\sqrt{n}} \right| \leq C\tilde{\varepsilon}_n \right\} \to 1$$

for some constant $C > 0$ that does not depend on $h\in H$ by Assumption 3 (i) and Lipschitz continuity of g and the fact that

$$\frac{|\hat{c}_{M_1}|}{\sqrt{n}} \leq \frac{M_1}{\sqrt{n}} = O(n^{-1/2})$$

as $n \to \infty$ for each fixed $M_1 > 0$. Then, with probability approaching one,

$$\begin{aligned} \left|\sqrt{n}\{\hat{\theta}_{mx} - f(g(\beta_n(h)))\}\right| &\leq a_n \left| g(\tilde{\beta}) - g(\beta_n(h)) + \frac{\hat{c}_{M_1}}{\sqrt{n}} \right| \\ &= a_n \left| g(\tilde{\beta}) - g(\beta_n(h)) + \frac{c_{M_1}}{\sqrt{n}} \right| + o_P(n^{-1/2}) \end{aligned} \tag{A.11}$$

where

$$a_n \equiv \sup_{x \in [g(\beta_0) - \tilde{\varepsilon}_n/2, g(\beta_0) + \tilde{\varepsilon}_n/2] \cap \mathcal{Y}} |f'(x)| \tag{A.12}$$

and o_P (1) is uniform over $h \in H$. The last equality follows by Assumption 3(i), Lipschitz continuity of f, and Lemma A1. Note that the supremum in Eq. (A.12) is monotone decreasing in n, so that

$$a_n \to \bar{f}'(g(\beta_0)) \tag{A.13}$$

as $n \to \infty$.

Therefore, using (Eq. A.11) and following precisely the same proof as that of Theorem 2 in Song (2014), we have

$$\limsup_{n \to \infty} \sup_{h \in H_{n,b}} \mathbf{E}_h \left[\tau_M \left(|\sqrt{n}\{\hat{\theta}_{mx} - f(g(\beta_n(h)))\}| \right) \right]$$

$$\leq \limsup_{n \to \infty} \sup_{\mathbf{r} \in \mathbf{R}^d} \mathbf{E}\left[\tau_M(a_n |\tilde{g}_0(Z + \mathbf{r}) - \tilde{g}_0(\mathbf{r}) + c_{M_1}|) \right]$$

By (Eq. A.13), the last term is bounded by

$$\begin{aligned} &\sup_{\mathbf{r} \in \mathbf{R}^d} \mathbf{E}[\tau_{M_1}(\bar{f}'(g(\beta_0)) |\tilde{g}_0(Z + \mathbf{r}) - \tilde{g}_0(\mathbf{r}) + c_{M_1}|)] \\ = &\inf_{c \in [-M_1, M_1]} \sup_{\mathbf{r} \in \mathbf{R}^d} \mathbf{E}[\tau_{M_1}(\bar{f}'(g(\beta_0)) |\tilde{g}_0(Z + \mathbf{r}) - \tilde{g}_0(\mathbf{r}) + c|)] \end{aligned}$$

The last equality follows by the definition of c_{M_1}. Finally, we increase $M_1 \uparrow \infty$ to obtain the desired result. ■

Proof of Theorem 3. First, due to Assumption 3′, the convergences in Lemmas A1 and A2 are uniform over $\alpha_0 \in \mathcal{A}$. Take $\tilde{\varepsilon}_n \downarrow 0$ such that $\tilde{\varepsilon}_n/\varepsilon_n \to 0$ but $\tilde{\varepsilon}_n\sqrt{n} \to \infty$. For each $\alpha \in \mathcal{A}$, let

$$\beta_\alpha = \beta_\alpha(P_\alpha)$$

Then, observe that by Assumption 3′(i), Lipschitz continuity of g,

$$\inf_{\alpha \in \mathcal{A}_n(\alpha_0;\varepsilon_n)} \inf_{h \in H} P_{n,h,\alpha}\left\{\left|g(\beta_\alpha) - g(\beta_\alpha) + \frac{\hat{c}_{M_1}}{\sqrt{n}}\right| \leq C\tilde{\varepsilon}_n\right\} \to 1$$

for some constant $C > 0$ that does not depend on $h \in H$ or $\alpha \in \mathcal{A}$. Then, we have

$$\left|\sqrt{n}\{\hat{\theta}_{mx} - f(g(\beta_n(h)))\}\right| \leq \overline{a}_n\left|g(\tilde{\beta}) - g(\beta_n(h)) + \frac{c_{M_1}}{\sqrt{n}}\right| + o_P(n^{-1/2})$$

where $o_P(1)$ is uniform over $h \in H$ and over $\alpha \in \mathcal{A}$, and

$$\overline{a}_n \equiv \sup_{\alpha \in \mathcal{A}_n(\alpha_0;\varepsilon_n)} \sup_{x \in g(\beta_\alpha) - \tilde{\varepsilon}_n, g(\beta_\alpha) + \tilde{\varepsilon}_n] \cap \mathcal{Y}} |f'(x)|$$

(Recall that $\beta_n(h) = \beta(P_{\alpha + \alpha_h/\sqrt{n}})$ and hence it depends on $\alpha \in \mathcal{A}$.)

Similarly as in the proof of Theorem 2,

$$\begin{aligned}
&\limsup_{n \to \infty} \sup_{\alpha \in \mathcal{A}_n(\alpha_0;\varepsilon_n)} \sup_{h \in H_{n,b}} \mathbf{E}_h\left[\tau_M\left(|\sqrt{n}\{\hat{\theta}_{mx} - f(g(\beta_n(h)))\}|\right)\right] \\
\leq\ &\limsup_{n \to \infty} \sup_{\mathbf{r} \in \mathbf{R}^d} \mathbf{E}[\tau_M(\overline{a}_n|\tilde{g}_0(Z + \mathbf{r}) - \tilde{g}_0(\mathbf{r}) + c_{M_1}|)] \\
\leq\ &\sup_{\mathbf{r} \in \mathbf{R}^d} \mathbf{E}[\tau_M(\overline{a}_{n_0}|\tilde{g}_0(Z + \mathbf{r}) - \tilde{g}_0(\mathbf{r}) + c_{M_1}|)]
\end{aligned}$$

for any fixed $n_0 \geq 1$. The last inequality follows because $\varepsilon_n \downarrow 0$ and $\tilde{\varepsilon}_n \downarrow 0$ as $n \to \infty$, and $\overline{a}_n$ and $\mathcal{A}_n(\alpha_0; \varepsilon_n)$ are decreasing in n. We send $n_0 \to \infty$ and apply the monotone convergence theorem to obtain the last bound as

$$\sup_{\mathbf{r} \in \mathbf{R}^d} \mathbf{E}[\tau_{M_1}(\bar{f}'(\beta_0)|\tilde{g}_0(Z+\mathbf{r}) - \tilde{g}_0(\mathbf{r}) + c_{M1}|)]$$
$$= \inf_{c \in [-M_1, M_1]} \sup_{\mathbf{r} \in \mathbf{R}^d} \mathbf{E}[\tau_{M_1}(\bar{f}'(\beta_0)|\tilde{g}_0(Z+\mathbf{r}) - \tilde{g}_0(\mathbf{r}) + c|)]$$

Finally, we increase $M_1 \uparrow \infty$ to obtain the desired result.

THE GAP BETWEEN THE CONDITIONAL WAGE DISTRIBUTIONS OF INCUMBENTS AND THE NEWLY HIRED EMPLOYEES: DECOMPOSITION AND UNIFORM ORDERING

Esfandiar Maasoumi[a], Melinda Pitts*[b] and Ke Wu[c]

[a]*Department of Economics, Emory University, Atlanta, GA, USA*
[b]*Federal Reserve Bank of Atlanta, Atlanta, GA, USA*
[c]*Department of Economics, Emory University, Atlanta, GA, USA*

ABSTRACT

We examine the cardinal gap between wage distributions of the incumbents and newly hired workers based on entropic distances which are well-defined welfare theoretic measures. Decomposition of several effects is achieved by identifying several counterfactual distributions of different

*The views expressed here are the authors and not necessarily those of the Federal Reserve Bank of Atlanta or the Federal Reserve System.

Essays in Honor of Peter C. B. Phillips
Advances in Econometrics, Volume 33, 587–612

ISSN: 0731-9053/doi:10.1108/S0731-905320140000033016

groups. These go beyond the usual Oaxaca–Blinder decompositions at the (linear) conditional means. Much like quantiles, these entropic distances are well-defined inferential objects and functions whose statistical properties have recently been developed. Going beyond these strong rankings and distances, we consider weak uniform ranking of these wage outcomes based on statistical tests for stochastic dominance. The empirical analysis is focused on employees with at least 35 hours of work in the 1996–2012 monthly Current Population Survey (CPS). Among others, we find incumbent workers enjoy a better distribution of wages, but the attribution of the gap to wage inequality and human capital characteristics varies between quantiles. For instance, highly paid new workers are mainly due to human capital components, and in some years, even better wage structure.

Keywords: Wage gap; metric entropy distance; stochastic dominance; counterfactual analysis; human capital; inequality

JEL Classifications: I31; C43

1. INTRODUCTION

Wage differentials among different types of workers, e.g., the gender earnings gap, wage differences between immigrants and natives, etc., have drawn much attention from labor economists and policy makers. There is an extensive literature on labor market outcomes, much of it focused on the analysis of the wage gap at the mean, median, and other quantiles of the wage distribution. More recently, techniques have been provided for identifying entire distributions and general functions of the distributions. These techniques provide the backdrop for the current paper's approach. One central object of inference in this paper is a summary measure of the "distance" between the entire distributions of interest. Our proposed summary measure makes clear that all other measures of the gap between two distributions are special, and all imply and are implied by well-defined welfare functions. Seen in this light, comparison at the mean, median, or any particular quantile would appear to place too much weight on a part of the population, or too equal a weight everywhere. For example, Blau and Kahn (2006) documented the slowing convergence of the gender gap at the mean, median, and 90th percentile levels. Albrecht, Björklund, and Vroman (2003) looked at wages differentials at different parts of the distribution to see whether the gender gap is larger in the upper tail than in the lower tail of the wage distribution due to a "glass ceiling" effect in Sweden. Kampkötter and Sliwka (2011) investigated average wage differences between newly hired and incumbent employees. While these focused examinations are informative and useful, recent papers have examined the wage differentials at the entire distribution level. For example, Massoumi and Wang (2012) employed a metric entropy measure proposed by Granger, Maasoumi, and Racine (2004) to examine the gender wage gap based on the metric distance between two distributions. The measure is the metric member of the Generalized Entropy class of measures with very credible welfare theoretic foundations.

All measures of the gap provide strong ranking of outcome distributions since they are based on implicit "cardinal" welfare or weighting functions. They are inevitably subjective even though some are less extreme than others. In view of this, we explore weak uniform rankings based on the concept of stochastic dominance which allow assessments over entire classes of welfare functions. We do so by rigorous statistical tests for various orders of dominance.

A key issue of interest is about the decomposition of observed gaps and rankings in order to identify the factors that underlie the overall wage differentials. Specifically, are those differentials associated with inequality or discrimination in the wage structure, or are they due to human capital composition effect. The classic decomposition method is due to Oaxaca (1973) and Blinder (1973). It is a regression-based method focusing on linear conditional mean decomposition. One major limitation of the Oaxaca–Blinder procedure, discussed by Barsky, Bound, Charles, and Lupton (2002), is that the decomposition provides consistent estimates of the structure and composition effect only under the assumption that the conditional expectation is linear. As suggested by Barsky et al. (2002), an alternative nonparametric decomposition may be based on propensity score reweighting methods, as advocated in DiNardo, Fortin, and Lemieux (1996). The key advantage of this reweighting approach is that it identifies the counterfactual distribution under less restrictive assumptions and hence can easily be applied to more general distributional statistics, rather than the simple mean and quantiles.

Several recent papers, e.g., Firpo, Fortin, and Lemieux (2007), Massoumi and Wang (2012), have applied this reweighting method for wage gap decompositions. Following the recent approach, this paper decomposes the wage gap between newly hired and incumbent employees across the entire distribution. The wage differences between newly hired and incumbent employees is a less studied topic in labor economics. The seminal work of Doeringer and Piore (1985) provided a theoretical foundation in this area, claiming that the incumbent wage could partially be determined by internal labor markets. Following the work of Baker, Gibbs, and Holmstrom (1994), many empirical studies investigated the wage structure of the internal labor markets. But very few studies have been done to examine the difference between the wage structure of the internal labor markets and that of the external labor markets. Studying the differential is very important because it sheds light on how much external market forces could determine the wage formation within firms. It could also potentially serve as an indicator of competitiveness of labor markets, since wage differentials between new hires and incumbents with identical characteristics should not exist in perfectly competitive labor markets.

This paper's analysis focuses on a sample of employed workers. As we do not address the issue of selection into the labor market, this work is only generalizable to the work force and not the population as a whole. The plan of the rest of the paper is as follows. In Section 2 the decomposition and counterfactual approach is explained. Section 2.1 introduces the idea of decomposition with a general distributional function. Section 2.2 discusses the Oaxaca–Blinder decomposition that employs linear conditional expectations as the functional form. Section 2.3 talks about a metric entropy measure and its welfare implications. Section 3 discusses the empirical and analytical methodologies in detail, i.e., the stochastic dominance tests and the propensity score reweighting method used to identify counterfactual distributions. Section 4 explains how to construct the linked CPS monthly data set used in the paper. Section 5 gives the results to the stochastic dominance tests and counterfactual analysis. The conclusion is in Section 6.

2. THE DECOMPOSITION PROBLEM

A key question of interest in this paper is how to decompose the distributional wage gap between incumbent and newly hired employees into a composition effect, corresponding to differences in the covariates between the two groups, and a wage structure effect corresponding to differences in the return to the covariates. In this section, we present a general theoretical framework illustrating the decomposition at the distributional level. We also link this decomposition to the more popular Oaxaca–Blinder decomposition method. We then propose to apply an entropy metric, a distributional statistic that could summarize differences between two distributions, to measure the structure and composition effects, and present its welfare function underpinnings.

2.1. Decomposition with General Distributional Function

The outcome variable of interest is the log hourly wage. We have two groups of workers, the incumbent group denoted as group 0 and the new hire group denoted as group 1. Let $ln(w^0)$ and $ln(w^1)$ denote the log wages of incumbent and newly hired employees, respectively. We observe a random sample of $N = N_0 + N_1$ workers. N_0 denotes the sample size of incumbents and N_1 is the sample size of the newly hired employees. Let $F_0(y) \equiv Pr[ln(w^0) \leq y]$ represents the cumulative distribution function (CDF) of $ln(w^0)$ and $f_0(y)$ is the corresponding probability density function (PDF). The same notations apply to the log wages of newly hired employees.

The wage structure of the incumbent group is denoted by g_0 and that of the newly hired group is denoted by g_1. Individual wages are determined nonparametrically by both observed characteristics X_i and unobserved characteristics ε_i via the unknown wage structure functions g_D,

$$ln\left(w_i^D\right) = g_D(X_i, \varepsilon_i) \quad \text{for } D = 0, 1 \tag{1}$$

This nonparametric approach avoids imposing distributional assumptions or specific functional forms, which allow for very flexible interactions among X_i and ε_i. We only assume that $(ln(w),X,D)$ have some unknown joint distribution. Under such specification, the wage differential is assumed to be associated to two primary sources: (1) differences in observed human capital characteristics X_i (e.g., education, age, etc.), and unobserved human capital characteristics ε_i (e.g., innate ability). However, under the unconfoundedness assumption elaborated in the next section, the composition effect only comes from differences in X_i and differences in the wage structures, $g_D(\cdot)$.

With observed data, we can identify the conditional distribution of a new hire's log hourly wage, $ln\left(w^1\right)|X, D = 1 \overset{d}{\sim} F_{1|X}$, and the conditional distribution of the incumbent's log hourly wage, $ln\left(w^0\right)|X, D = 0 \overset{d}{\sim} F_{0|X}$. With certain further assumptions discussed later, we are able to identify the conditional counterfactual distribution of $ln\left(w^0\right)|X, D = 1 \overset{d}{\sim} F_{C|X}$ using the aforementioned propensity score reweighting method. The conditional counterfactual distribution $F_{C|X}$ is the wage distribution that would have been observed under the wage structure of group 0, but with the distribution of observed and unobserved characteristics of group 1. Accordingly, the unconditional (on X) distributions are denoted as F_1, F_0, *and* F_c. We analyze the distributional wage gap between groups 0 and 1 using some distributional function. Following Firpo et al. (2007), we denote ν as a function of the conditional joint distribution of $(ln(w^1), ln(w^0))|D$, i.e., $\nu : F_\nu \rightarrow \mathbb{R}$, where F_ν belongs to a class of distribution functions that satisfy $\forall F \in F_\nu$ and $||\nu(F)|| < +\infty$. Under this specification, the distributional wage gap between two groups can be written in terms of ν:

$$\Delta_O^\nu = \nu(F_1) - \nu(F_0) = \nu_1 - \nu_0 \tag{2}$$

We can then further decompose Eq. (2) into two parts, given that X is not evenly distributed across the two groups:

$$\Delta_O^\nu = (\nu_1 - \nu_C) + (\nu_C - \nu_0) = \Delta_S^\nu + \Delta_X^\nu \tag{3}$$

where the first term Δ_S^ν reflects the wage structure effect, meaning the effect caused by changing $g_1(\cdot,\cdot)$ to $g_0(\cdot,\cdot)$ while holding characteristics $(X,\varepsilon)|D = 1$ constant. The other term Δ_X^ν indicates the composition effect, which is the effect from changing the distribution of characteristics from $(X,\varepsilon)|D = 1$ to $(X,\varepsilon)|D = 0$, while keeping the "wage structure" $g_0(\cdot,\cdot)$ constant.

2.2. Oaxaca–Blinder Decomposition as a Linear Conditional Expectation Case

With such settings, we can include Oaxaca–Blinder decomposition as a special case, where the ν function is the mathematical expectation $\mathbb{E}$. Under the assumption that the conditional expectation takes linear form, we have

$$\mathbb{E}\left[ln\left(w_i^D\right)|X\right] \equiv X_i\beta_D, \quad \text{for } D = 0, 1 \tag{4}$$

Then the expected wage gap between the "treated" and untreated group, Δ_O^μ, can be written as

$$\begin{aligned}
\Delta_O^{\mu} &= \mathbb{E}_x[\mathbb{E}[(ln(w)|X,\ D=1)] - \mathbb{E}_x[\mathbb{E}[(ln(w)|X,\ D=0)] \\
&= \mathbb{E}[ln(w)|D=1] - \mathbb{E}[ln(w)|D=0] \\
&= \mathbb{E}[X|D=1]\beta_1 - \mathbb{E}[X|D=0]\beta_0 \\
&= \mathbb{E}[X|D=1](\beta_1 - \beta_0) + (\mathbb{E}[X|D=1] - \mathbb{E}[X|D=0])\beta_0 \\
&\equiv \Delta_S^{\mu} + \Delta_X^{\mu}
\end{aligned}$$

The second line follows from the Law of Iterated Expectations. Note that the decomposition in the fourth line uses group 1 as the base group. The counterfactual outcome indicates the mean wage that would have been observed under the wage structure of group 0, but with X from group 1, can directly be computed by $\mathbb{E}[X|D=1]\beta_0$, which is the counterpart of ν_C in Eq. (3). Δ_S^{μ} is the mean wage structure effect and accordingly Δ_X^{μ} stands for the mean composition effect. The Oaxaca–Blinder decomposition is very appealing empirically due to its ease of estimation and interpretation. However, as Barsky et al. (2002) pointed out, consistent estimates of both effects rely on the assumption of the linear structure, which is restrictive. Moreover, Kline (2011) showed that the counterfactual mean identified by the Oaxaca–Blinder method constitutes a propensity score reweighting estimator based upon a linear model for the conditional odds of being treated. Therefore, the Oaxaca–Blinder decomposition is indeed a special linear case of propensity score reweighting method. By applying the reweighting method generally, we impose less structure and hence lead to more robust inference.

3. EMPIRICAL METHODOLOGY

3.1. A Metric Entropy Measure of the Wage Gap

A comparison of means is implicitly based on a welfare/weighting function that is additive and attaches equal weight to each wage earner. Among others, this implicit welfare function imposes infinite substitutability. Assessment at the median, or any other quantile is justified by even more radical welfare weighting schemes. To overcome these limitations we choose more general distributional functions that could summarize information along the whole distribution. Several commonly used information-based entropy measures such as Shannon's entropy and Kullback–Leibler relative entropy are good candidates for such distributional functions. They are well analyzed in the field of income inequality where the corresponding welfare functions are identified. For instance, an axiomatic approach to "ideal" inequality measures, equivalently welfare functions, or risk averse utility functions, renders the class of Generalized Entropy as ideal. Further additive decomposition requirements render Shannon's entropy, and Theil's measures of inequality as "best." (For example, see Bourguignon, 1979; Maasoumi, 1986; Shorrocks, 1978). Inequality measures are divergence measures between any distribution and a uniform (rectangular) size distribution representing perfect equality. The latter is eliminated when the difference between the "inequalities" of two wage distributions is computed. However, entropy divergence measures are generally not metric since they violate the triangular inequality. Hence they are not proper measures of distance. This paper uses a metric entropy measure S_ρ proposed by Granger et al. (2004) as the specific distributional ν function, which is a normalization of the "Bhattacharya–Matusita–Hellinger" measure of distance. It is the one member of the Generalized Entropy family that is a metric. It is given by

$$S_\rho = \frac{1}{2}\int_{-\infty}^{\infty}\left(f_1^{\frac{1}{2}} - f_0^{\frac{1}{2}}\right)^2 \mathrm{d}y \tag{5}$$

This measure has several desirable properties: (1) it is well defined for both continuous and discrete variables[1]; (2) it is normalized to 0 if two distributions are equal and lies between 0 and 1; (3) it satisfies the properties of a metric and hence is a true measure of distance; and (4) it is invariant under continuous and strictly increasing transformation on the underlying variables. Note that the natural log of earnings is used throughout this paper. Since the logarithm is a strictly increasing function, the findings of this paper are invariant whether using the raw wages or the log form. Following Granger et al. (2004) and Maasoumi and Racine (2002), we consider a kernel-based nonparametric implementation of the entropy measure shown in Eq. (5).

3.2. *Stochastic Dominance*

Using S_ρ as the distributional distance measure, we can estimate the distance between original wage distribution and counterfactual wage distribution, and thus the distributional wage structure and composition effects. However, this analysis is still subjective as it would reflect the social welfare based on the Generalized Entropy function.

In order to compare the different wage distributions robustly, and relative to large classes of welfare functions, we need to examine Stochastic Dominance rankings. First-order Stochastic Dominance corresponds to a class (denoted as U_1) of all (increasing) von Neumann–Morgenstern type of social welfare functions u such that welfare is increasing in wages (i.e. $u' > 0$), and the second-order Stochastic Dominance test corresponds to the class of social welfare functions in U_1 such that $u'' \leq 0$ (i.e., concavity), denoted as U_2. Concavity implies an aversion to higher dispersion (or inequality) of wages across workers. In this paper, we focus on the one-dimensional social welfare function of only earnings.

Case 1. First-Order Dominance: Incumbent employee wage distribution First-Order Stochastically Dominates newly hired employee wage distribution (denoted as $ln(w^0)$ FSD $ln(w^1)$) if and only if

1. $E[u(ln(w^0))] \geq E[u(ln(w^1))]$ for all $u \in U_1$ with strict inequality for some u;
2. Or, $F_0(y) \leq F_1(y)$ for all y with strict inequality for some y.

Case 2. Second-Order Dominance: Incumbent wage distribution Second-Order Stochastically Dominates newly hired employee wage distribution (denoted as $ln(w^0)$ SSD $ln(w^1)$) if and only if

1. $E[u(ln(w^0))] \geq E[u(ln(w^1))]$ for all $u \in U_2$ with strict inequality for some u;
2. Or, $\int_{-\infty}^{y} F_0(t)dt \leq \int_{-\infty}^{y} F_1(t)dt$ for all y with strict inequality for some y.

The stochastic dominance tests used in this paper are based on a generalized Kolmogorov–Smirnov test as discussed in Linton, Maasoumi, and Whang (2005). The test statistics for FSD and SSD are given by

$$d = \sqrt{\frac{N_0 N_1}{N_0 + N_1}} \min\{\sup[F_0(y) - F_1(y)], \quad \sup[F_1(y) - F_0(y)]\} \tag{6}$$

$$s = \sqrt{\frac{N_0 N_1}{N_0 + N_1}} \min\left\{\sup \int_{-\infty}^{y} [F_0(t) - F_1(t)]dt, \quad \sup \int_{-\infty}^{y} [F_1(t) - F_0(t)]dt\right\} \tag{7}$$

When we report the empirical test results in Section 5, we denote sup $[F_0(y) - F_1(y)]$ as $d_{1,\max}$ and $\sup[F_1(y) - F_0(y)]$ as $d_{2,\max}$. We report both

$d_{1,\max}$ and $d_{2,\max}$ along with the test statistic d for clarity of interpretation. $s_{1,\max}$ and $s_{2,\max}$ are similarly defined. In empirical applications, the CDFs are replaced with their empirical counterparts. The empirical CDFs are given by $\widehat{F_d(y)} = \frac{1}{N_d}\sum_{i=1}^{N_d} I\left(ln(w_i^d) \leq y\right), \quad d=0,1$, where $I(\cdot)$ is an indicator function. The underlying distribution of the test statistics are generally unknown and depend on the data. Following Maasoumi and Heshmati (2000), simple bootstrap technique based on 199 replications are employed to obtain the empirical distribution of the test statistics.

3.3. Identification of the Counterfactual Distributions

The fundamental question this paper addresses is to identify the wage structure and composition effects through the identification of counterfactual wage distributions, and determine which effect dominates the wage differential. We consider the following counterfactual situation: holding the human capital characteristics of the newly hired workers constant, if we change their wage structure to the wage structure of the incumbents, would the counterfactual wage distribution be different from the original one? If so, would the counterfactual wage distribution stochastically dominate the original one in terms of welfare? If we find such dominance in the first or second order, we would conclude that the wage structures are different and the internal wage structure is better. Similarly, we could also check whether the wage gap is due to differences in human capital characteristics by changing the distribution of the newly hired employees' characteristics to that of the incumbents, holding their wage structure unchanged. To conduct such counterfactual analysis, we follow the propensity score reweighting methods as discussed in Firpo (2007) to identify the counterfactual distributions mentioned above. Simple bootstrap with replacement is applied to obtain the statistical significance of the dominance tests. Specifically, we want to identify the distributions of the following two counterfactual outcomes:

$$ln\left(w_i^{c1}\right) = g_0(X_i, \varepsilon_i)|D=1 \quad \text{(counterfactual outcome \#1)} \tag{8}$$

$$ln\left(w_i^{c2}\right) = g_1(X_i, \varepsilon_i)|D=0 \quad \text{(counterfactual outcome \#2)} \tag{9}$$

The benchmark outcome we considered is the conditional wage distribution of the new hires $ln(w_i^1) = g_1(X_{i1}, \varepsilon_{i1})$. The counterfactual outcome #1, $ln(w_i^{c1})$, indicates the hypothetical unobserved wage of the newly hired employees if they were paid under the incumbent wage structure. Comparing the benchmark wage $ln(w_i^1)$ to $ln(w_i^{c1})$ using the S_ρ measure would yield the wage structure effect Δ_S^ν as in Eq. (3). Comparing distributional distance between $ln(w_i^{c1})$ and the incumbent wage $ln(w_i^0)$ would give us the composition effect, denoted by Δ_X^ν in Eq. (3). However, that would require using $ln(w_i^0)$ as the benchmark. For ease of interpretation, we choose to use $ln(w_i^1)$ as the benchmark when identifying both effects and construct counterfactual outcome #2 $ln(w_i^{c2})$, which indicates the hypothetical wage of the newly hired employees if they had the characteristics of the incumbents. With the new hire wage as the benchmark, S_ρ measure of $ln(w_i^1) - ln(w_i^{c2})$ gives the composition effect that are reported in empirical applications in Section 5.

Firpo (2007) proved that under certain assumptions, such counterfactual distributions are identified. Following Firpo (2007) and Firpo et al. (2007), we make similar assumptions:

1. Unconfoundedness: Suppose (Y,D,X) have a joint distribution, where Y is the outcome and D is a dummy indicating treatment: (Y_1, Y_0) and D are jointly independent conditional on $X = x$.
2. Common support: For all $x \in X$, $0 < P_r\{D = 1|X = x\} := p(x) < 1$.

Assumption 1 means that fixing the values of observable human capital characteristics X, the distribution of the wage outcome or the error term ε is independent of whether one is incumbent or newly hired. Assumption 2 rules out the possibilities that some specific x belongs only to either one of the two worker groups and hence such x can predict the probability of being treated perfectly.

The counterfactual distribution of $ln(w_i^{c1})$ could be identified by the following propensity score reweighting methods discussed in Firpo (2007).

$$F_{c1} = \mathbb{E}[\omega_{c1}(D_1, X) \cdot I[(ln(w_i) \leq y)] \tag{10}$$

where $\omega_{c1}(D_1,X) = ((p_1(x))/(1 - p_1(x)))((1 - D_1)/(p_1))$, D_1 is a treatment dummy variable taking the value of 1 for incumbent employees, $p_1(x) = Pr\{D_1 = 1|X = x\}$ is the propensity score, $p_1 = Pr\{D_1 = 1\} = \mathbb{E}[p_1(X)]$ is the marginal probability of being treated. In practice, we will estimate the propensity score parametrically using a logit model.[2] Applying the weights $\omega_{c1}(D_1,X)$ gives us the counterfactual distribution of $ln\left(w_i^{c1}\right)$. Identifying the distribution of counterfactual outcome $ln\left(w_i^{c2}\right)$, F_{c2}, is similar, but we need to take newly hired employees as the treated group. Let D_2 be the treatment dummy taking the value of 1 for new hires.

$$F_{c2} = \mathbb{E}[\omega_{c2}(D_2, X) \cdot I[(ln(w_i) \leq y)] \tag{11}$$

where $\omega_{c2}(D_2,X) = ((p_2(x))/(1 - p_2(x)))((1 - D_2)/(p_2))$, $p_2(x)$ and p_2 are similarly defined as in the previous case.[3] Applying the weights $\omega_{c2}(D_2,X)$ gives us the counterfactual distribution of $ln\left(w_i^{c2}\right)$. Once we identify the counterfactual distributions of interest, we can then perform stochastic dominance tests to compare those counterfactual distributions with the original distribution.

4. DATA

The data used in this paper come from 1996–2012 monthly Current Population Survey (CPS). The monthly CPS is a survey of a probability sample of housing units. Although the CPS is designed to be a cross-sectional survey, it does not survey a completely new set of housing units every month. The sample is divided into eight representative rotation groups. Therefore, a typical housing unit in the sample is interviewed in eight different months, given no attrition during survey period. If a housing unit is randomly selected into monthly CPS for the first time, it will be interviewed for four consecutive months, followed by an eight-month break, and then be surveyed for another four consecutive months. The rotation group could be identified by the CPS variable "month in sample" (MIS).

The CPS sample design actually allows us to longitudinally link a household in sample over eight different months. Following methods as discussed in Madrian and Lefgren (1999), we conducted one-month matching for all the eligible rotation groups (MIS = 2–4 or 6–8) in each monthly sample, i.e., linking those eligible subsamples with their previous month observations.[4] In our sample, the matching rate for those eligible groups is over 90 % on average.[5] Using this longitudinally linked data set, we could identify the incumbent and newly hired employees. Since we are interested in the wage differentials, we first restrict our sample to individuals of working age, i.e., those who aged from 18 to 64. Then we keep those who remained full-time employed (35 hours per week or above) in both month $t-1$ and month t. Among those full-time workers, we define incumbent workers to be those who stayed with the same employer from month $t-1$ to t. The newly hired employees are defined to be those who changed their employer from month $t-1$ and t, i.e., workers that switched to a new job with a new employer at time t.[6]

Following the literature (e.g., Massoumi & Wang, 2012), we use the log of hourly wages, measured by an individual's weekly wage income divided by the number of hours worked per week. Note that, as we mentioned above, the metric entropy measure of the wage differential and stochastic dominance tests are invariant to the logarithm transformation, while many conventional measures are not. The observed human capital variables used in the counterfactual analysis include age, age squared, gender, education (five education groups: less than high school, high school, some college, college, graduate), marital status, ethnicity, and region (Northeast, Midwest, South, and West). The Occupation variable is grouped into three categories: high-skill (managerial and professional occupations); medium-skill (technician, technical production, sales, and administrative support occupations); and low-skill (other occupations such as maintenance, construction, and farming occupations).

5. RESULTS

5.1. Baseline Analysis

5.1.1. Trend of the Wage Differential between Internal and External Labor Markets

Table 1 shows various measures of the log wage differences between the incumbent and newly hired employees, i.e., $ln(w^0) - ln(w^1)$. The second column in the table reports the distributional measure of the wage gap S_ρ. Since S_ρ is a normalized metric taking on values between 0 and 1, for easy interpretation we report the original results multiplied by 100 throughout the paper. Under the null hypothesis of no difference between incumbent and new hire wage distributions, we calculate the statistical significance of the S_ρ measure using 199 simple bootstrap replications. The p-values are reported in the third column. The other columns in Table 1 report conventional measures (e.g., mean, median, and quantiles at various levels) of

Table 1. Entropy Measures of Wage Differentials.

Year	$S_p \times 100$	p of S_p	Mean	10th	25th	50th	75th	90th
1996	0.97	(0.00)	0.14	0.09	0.13	0.14	0.13	0.11
1997	1.47	(0.00)	0.15	0.13	0.16	0.18	0.17	0.08
1998	1.11	(0.00)	0.13	0.08	0.15	0.20	0.11	0.04
1999	1.14	(0.00)	0.13	0.15	0.12	0.17	0.13	0.07
2000	0.93	(0.00)	0.11	0.07	0.17	0.12	0.07	0.07
2001	0.69	(0.00)	0.10	0.07	0.12	0.11	0.08	0.04
2002	1.03	(0.00)	0.10	0.11	0.11	0.13	0.08	0.04
2003	0.95	(0.00)	0.11	0.13	0.12	0.14	0.10	0.04
2004	0.62	(0.00)	0.10	0.06	0.08	0.12	0.13	0.07
2005	0.97	(0.00)	0.12	0.06	0.14	0.12	0.12	0.12
2006	0.98	(0.00)	0.14	0.09	0.10	0.15	0.14	0.14
2007	0.50	(0.00)	0.10	0.09	0.15	0.11	0.08	0.06
2008	0.65	(0.01)	0.09	0.06	0.13	0.12	0.07	0.03
2009	1.24	(0.00)	0.11	0.11	0.18	0.16	0.06	0.09
2010	0.64	(0.00)	0.07	0.10	0.11	0.13	0.04	−0.08
2011	0.59	(0.03)	0.08	0.05	0.07	0.07	0.08	0.09
2012	0.65	(0.00)	0.09	0.06	0.13	0.11	0.08	0.05

Note: Columns (2)–(3) report metric entropy measure of distributional distance and its p-values respectively. The p-values are obtained from 199 simple bootstrap under the null hypothesis of no difference between incumbent and new hire wage distributions.

earning differentials commonly used in the literature. We can see that both the traditional measures and the metric entropy measure S_ρ imply that there exists wage differentials between those two groups of workers for all the years in sample. The distributional distances are statistically significant at 5% in 2011 and at 1% in remaining years. The mean differences and all the quantile differences except for the 90th quantile in 2010, are all positive, clearly showing wage gaps in favor of the incumbent employees However, it is hard to tell a clear trend over time for any of these measures and even harder to tell whether our new measure shows a different pattern of the time trend from other traditional measures.

The S_ρ measure and other conventional measures are not directly comparable. Thus, to enable easy comparisons, we normalize all these measures by setting the value in the year of 1996 to 100 and computing the normalized values. The plot of these normalized values of S_ρ, mean, median, 25th, and 75th percentiles is shown in Fig. 1. As shown in the graph, other than the 75th percentile, the traditional measures display similar time trends as the S_ρ entropy measure. In order to check how the wage differentials fit with macro business cycles, we plot the recession periods with

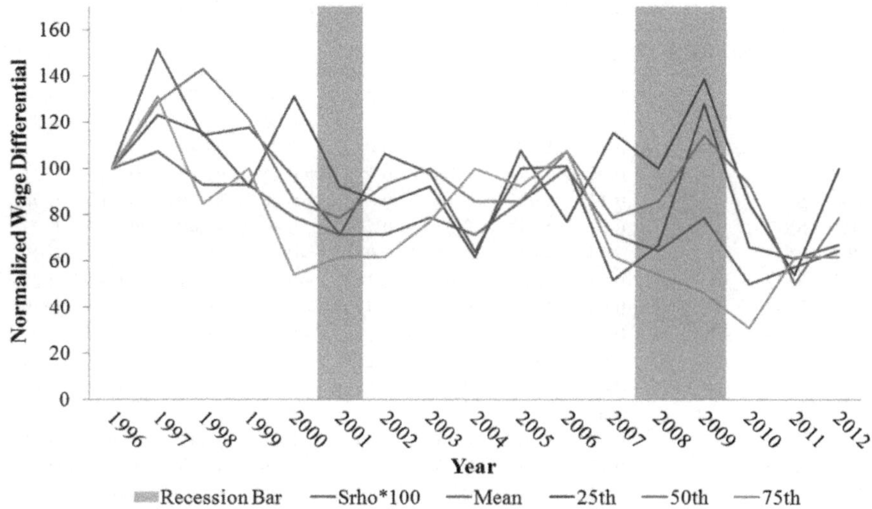

Fig. 1. Time Trend of Wage Differential with Business Cycle Indicator.

shaded vertical bars in the figure. During the sample period, March 2001–November 2001 and December 2007–June 2009 are considered as recession periods by the NBER. Since our measures are computed at yearly frequency, we roughly pick 2001, 2008, and 2009 as the recession years and the three years are indicated by the shaded bars in Fig. 1. The line plots do not show very clear cyclical patterns, but all measures, except the 75th percentile of wage differentials do seem to increase during the recent great recession period from 2008 to 2009. During the great recession the level of payroll employment fell by 5.4%, more than four times the employment decline faced in the 2001 recession.[7] Many firms reduced or halted hiring, which reduced the bargaining power of those job seekers. So the newly hired employees may have had to accept lower wages, which increases the wage gaps between the incumbent and the newly hired workers.

5.1.2. Stochastic Dominance Test Results

As discussed above, these measures of the gender gap could not give a clear ranking of the earnings distributions in terms of social welfare. Therefore, in Table 2 we present the stochastic dominance test results. The second column labeled Observed Ranking details if the distributions can be ranked in either the first or second order, where FSD is short for First-order

Table 2. Stochastic Dominance Test Results.

Year	Observed Rank	$d_{1,\max}$	$d_{2,\max}$	d	$P(d<0)$	$s_{1,\max}$	$s_{2,\max}$	s	$P(d<0)$
1996	FSD	−0.03	5.15	−0.03	0.30	−0.04	104.05	−0.04	0.94
1997	SSD	0.06	6.30	0.06	0.25	−0.05	110.07	−0.05	0.99
1998	SSD	0.11	5.47	0.11	0.04	−0.05	98.14	−0.05	0.87
1999	SSD	0.06	5.78	0.06	0.19	−0.05	93.93	−0.05	0.81
2000	SSD	0.11	4.96	0.11	0.05	−0.06	86.00	−0.06	0.96
2001	SSD	0.01	4.39	0.01	0.43	−0.06	80.49	−0.06	0.97
2002	SSD	0.24	4.48	0.24	0.01	−0.06	76.70	−0.06	0.99
2003	SSD	0.07	4.20	0.07	0.14	−0.05	71.31	−0.05	0.87
2004	FSD	−0.06	4.27	−0.06	0.41	−0.06	68.43	−0.06	0.79
2005	SSD	0.09	4.54	0.09	0.18	−0.09	73.32	−0.09	0.92
2006	SSD	0.08	4.62	0.08	0.21	−0.09	95.11	−0.09	0.94
2007	FSD	−0.06	3.88	−0.06	0.55	−0.07	67.61	−0.07	0.87
2008	FSD	−0.03	4.16	−0.03	0.48	−0.08	55.20	−0.08	0.98
2009	SSD	0.38	3.56	0.38	0.00	−0.04	61.14	−0.04	0.76
2010	SSD	0.45	2.76	0.45	0.01	−0.06	47.83	−0.06	0.93
2011	SSD	0.07	2.13	0.07	0.09	−0.07	35.03	−0.07	0.54
2012	SSD	0.01	3.34	0.01	0.21	−0.06	47.96	−0.06	0.64

Stochastic Dominance and SSD stands for Second-order Stochastic Dominance. The columns labeled $Pr[d \leq 0]$ and $Pr[s \leq 0]$ report the probabilities of the test statistics (of the first-and second-order dominance tests respectively) to be non-positive based on the simple bootstrap with replacement for 199 replications. The probability serves a similar role as p-values in any hypothesis test, but the interpretation is reversed. For example, if we observe FSD (SSD) and $Pr[d \leq 0]$ ($Pr[s \leq 0]$) is 0.95, then it means that the test statistic is statistically significant at 5% level (p-value = 0.05).

From Table 2, we can see that the wage distribution of incumbents lies predominantly to the right of the wage distribution of new hires, meaning that incumbent workers enjoy higher level of wages. For all the years in the sample, we find stochastic dominance relations either in the first or second order. In 4 out of 17 years (1996, 2004, 2007, and 2008), we find the wage distribution of incumbent workers to empirically dominates, in a first-order sense, the wage distribution among newly hired workers, but such dominance relation is not statistically significant in any of the four years. For the remaining years, highly significant second-order dominance is found in the years of 1997, 2000–2002, and 2008, with confidence level greater than 0.95. This suggests that any worker with a social welfare function in the class U_2 (increasing and concave in wage) would prefer the incumbent distribution to the new hire distribution in those five years. Such dominance ranking is only possible when we account for an aversion to higher dispersion in the welfare criteria. This finding is quite interesting because those significant second-order dominance cases mainly occurred around recession periods (2001 and 2008 are recession years). Second-order dominance indicates that starting from the very left tail of the wage distribution, incumbent workers are better paid than newly hired workers at most quantiles. This is in line with the findings of Oreopoulos, von Wachter, and Heisz (2006), who found that young graduates entering the labor market in a recession suffer significant initial earnings losses. SSD also suggests that at the far right tail of the wage distribution, some newly hired workers could be paid better than their incumbent counterparts. One possible explanation could be the differences in human capital characteristics. Those who managed to find highly paid jobs during a recession may have very strong human capital characteristics. We will further test this hypothesis using counterfactual analysis in a latter section.

5.2. Counterfactual Analysis

Table 3 reports the estimated wage structure effect, i.e., the wage gap caused by the inequality in the pay structure. Metric entropy and traditional measures of the log wage differences between the newly hired employees and their counterfactual outcome #1, i.e., $ln(w^1) - ln(w^{c1})$, are presented. The p-values of S_ρ measure are calculated using the same bootstrap method as applied in Table 1. From Table 3, we can see that most means and quantiles in almost all years except for 2011 are negative, which means that the counterfactual wages under the incumbent's wage structure while keeping new employee characteristics unchanged are generally better than actual wages those new hires earn. The distributional distance measured by S_ρ is smaller and less significant than the distance between $ln(w^0)$ and $ln(w^{c1})$, as it only reflects the wage structure effect.

Table 4 reports dominance test results of the actual wage distribution of the new hires versus the counterfactual wage distribution #1. Recall that this comparison identifies the difference of the wage structures between the external and internal labor markets. Any finding of stochastic dominance indicates the inequality in the pay structure instead of the differences in human capital characteristics. We find the counterfactual wage distribution #1 SSD the original wage distribution of the new hires for all the years in sample, except for the year of 2011, which means that if the newly hired workers were paid under incumbent wage structure, such outcomes are

Table 3. Measures of Differences between New Hire and New Hire Counterfactual #1 Distributions.

Year	$S_\rho \times 100$	p of S_ρ	Mean	10th	25th	50th	75th	90th
1996	0.34	(.03)	−0.06	−0.05	−0.07	−0.06	−0.05	−0.02
1997	0.77	(.00)	−0.07	−0.09	−0.11	−0.10	−0.08	0.00
1998	0.47	(.01)	−0.05	−0.04	−0.06	−0.09	−0.03	0.04
1999	0.47	(.01)	−0.06	−0.07	−0.06	−0.09	−0.04	0.00
2000	0.46	(.01)	−0.03	−0.07	−0.11	−0.04	0.00	0.04
2001	0.32	(.05)	−0.03	−0.00	−0.04	−0.04	−0.01	0.05
2002	0.47	(.00)	−0.03	−0.07	−0.08	−0.05	0.00	0.00
2003	0.38	(.06)	−0.02	−0.08	−0.05	−0.05	0.00	0.05
2004	0.23	(.25)	−0.03	−0.05	−0.03	−0.05	−0.04	0.03
2005	0.36	(.04)	−0.04	−0.06	0.00	−0.04	−0.03	−0.03
2006	0.28	(.17)	−0.03	0.00	−0.04	−0.07	−0.02	−0.00
2007	0.19	(.58)	−0.03	−0.05	−0.10	−0.03	−0.02	0.03
2008	0.37	(.17)	−0.03	−0.06	−0.07	−0.05	0.00	0.07
2009	0.63	(.00)	−0.04	−0.07	−0.09	−0.08	0.00	−0.00
2010	0.40	(.11)	−0.00	−0.05	−0.04	−0.03	0.04	0.12
2011	0.47	(.00)	0.01	0.00	0.00	0.04	0.04	0.01
2012	0.33	(.06)	−0.03	−0.02	−0.04	−0.03	0.01	0.00

Note: Columns (2)–(3) report metric entropy measure of distributional distance and its p-values respectively. The p-values are obtained from 199 simple bootstrap under the null hypothesis of no difference between the new hire and their counterfactual #1 wage distributions.

Table 4. Stochastic Dominance Test Results, Counterfactual #1.

Year	Observed Rank	$d_{1,\max}$	$d_{2,\max}$	d	$P(d<0)$	$s_{1,\max}$	$s_{2,\max}$	s	$P(d<0)$
1996	SSD	14.22	0.58	0.58	0.05	240.39	−0.28	−0.28	0.85
1997	SSD	17.43	0.73	0.73	0.03	261.86	−0.25	−0.25	0.96
1998	SSD	16.37	2.39	2.39	0.01	206.92	−0.25	−0.25	0.71
1999	SSD	15.41	1.31	1.31	0.01	201.00	−0.46	−0.46	0.60
2000	SSD	11.39	1.92	1.92	0.00	156.57	−0.34	−0.34	0.88
2001	SSD	8.80	2.64	2.64	0.02	132.64	−0.30	−0.30	0.89
2002	SSD	9.60	2.66	2.66	0.00	136.40	−0.26	−0.26	0.81
2003	SSD	9.20	2.70	2.70	0.00	123.87	−0.26	−0.26	0.72
2004	SSD	8.55	1.16	1.16	0.01	109.38	−0.32	−0.32	0.61
2005	SSD	10.93	1.43	1.43	0.01	143.21	−0.34	−0.34	0.77
2006	SSD	12.29	1.38	1.38	0.01	159.84	−0.45	−0.45	0.91
2007	SSD	9.16	1.75	1.75	0.03	104.39	−0.33	−0.33	0.73
2008	SSD	11.21	3.73	3.73	0.00	113.81	−0.43	−0.43	0.94
2009	SSD	11.15	3.16	3.16	0.00	155.81	−0.28	−0.28	0.63
2010	SSD	5.33	7.22	5.33	0.00	98.05	−0.29	−0.29	0.46
2011	None	3.39	4.66	3.39	0.00	29.92	25.71	25.71	0.16
2012	SSD	8.42	0.85	0.85	0.00	80.50	−0.22	−0.22	0.43

preferred at least for those with social welfare functions in the class of U_2. As indicated by the bootstrapped probabilities, those dominance relations are statistically significant in 1997, 2006, and 2008, with confidence level greater than 0.9 and are close to significant in 2000 and 2001. Second-order dominance indicates that such findings holds mainly at the lower tail of the wage distribution, while at the upper tail, the wage structure of those new hires may actually be better than those of the incumbents, so such counterfactual wages may be lower than their actual wages for those highly paid new employees. To further test this finding, in the following section we divide our sample into two subgroups, higher and lower wage groups, and conducted counterfactual analysis respectively.

Table 5 reports the estimated composition effect, i.e., the wage gap caused by the differences human capital characteristics. S_ρ and conventional measures of the log wage differences between the newly hired employees and their counterfactual outcome #2, i.e., $ln(w^1)-ln(w^{c2})$, are reported. From the table we can see that all the means and quantiles in all

Table 5. Measures of Difference between New Hire and New Hire Counterfactual #2 Distributions.

Year	$S_\rho \times 100$	p of S_ρ	Mean	10th	25th	50th	75th	90th
1996	0.27	(0.53)	−0.08	−0.04	−0.07	−0.07	−0.08	−0.08
1997	0.28	(0.59)	−0.08	−0.09	−0.07	−0.10	−0.14	−0.08
1998	0.29	(0.64)	−0.08	−0.04	−0.06	−0.13	−0.10	−0.06
1999	0.28	(0.44)	−0.08	−0.07	−0.03	−0.09	−0.12	−0.11
2000	0.23	(0.48)	−0.08	−0.06	−0.11	−0.05	−0.09	−0.08
2001	0.24	(0.08)	−0.08	0.00	−0.05	−0.10	−0.09	−0.08
2002	0.28	(0.42)	−0.09	−0.05	−0.11	−0.10	−0.10	−0.10
2003	0.23	(0.50)	−0.07	−0.07	−0.05	−0.09	−0.10	−0.07
2004	0.27	(0.66)	−0.08	−0.06	−0.03	−0.11	−0.12	−0.08
2005	0.26	(0.14)	−0.08	−0.06	−0.01	−0.07	−0.10	−0.11
2006	0.29	(0.05)	−0.09	−0.03	−0.04	−0.10	−0.11	−0.12
2007	0.26	(0.26)	−0.08	−0.05	−0.10	−0.09	−0.10	−0.07
2008	0.20	(0.97)	−0.07	−0.03	−0.08	−0.10	−0.11	−0.06
2009	0.25	(0.68)	−0.09	−0.07	−0.09	−0.11	−0.11	−0.12
2010	0.19	(0.80)	−0.08	−0.05	−0.07	−0.09	−0.10	−0.09
2011	0.19	(0.98)	−0.07	−0.04	−0.05	−0.08	−0.09	−0.10
2012	0.20	(0.51)	−0.07	−0.00	−0.06	−0.10	−0.09	−0.10

Note: Columns (2)−(3) report metric entropy measure of distributional distance and its p-values respectively. The p-values are obtained from 199 simple bootstrap under the null hypothesis of no difference between the new hire and their counterfactual #2 wage distributions.

the years in the sample are negative, which indicates that the counterfactual wages under the incumbent characteristics while keeping new hire's wage structure unchanged are generally better than actual wages of the new hires. We conclude that the differences in human capital characteristics between the incumbents and new hires also contributed to their wage gap. The distributional distance measured by S_ρ is a little smaller and less significant than those reported in Table 3, which means that the estimated composition effect is smaller compared to the estimated wage structure effect.

Table 6 reports the stochastic dominance test results from the comparison between the actual wage distribution of the new hires versus the counterfactual wage distribution #2. Note that this comparison identifies the wage gap caused by differences in human capital characteristics. As shown in the table, we find the counterfactual wage distribution #2 FSD the actual new hire wage distribution in all years. However, such first-order dominance relations are not statistically significant. FSD always indicates SSD, but those second-order dominance relations are largely insignificant as well. Hence we have found some evidence for differences in human capital characteristics, but the evidence is not quite strong. The data seem to tell us that even though there is some difference in human capital between incumbent and newly hired workers, such a difference is not large enough to be statistically meaningful.

Table 6. Stochastic Dominance Test Results, Counterfactual #2.

Year	Observed Rank	$d_{1,\max}$	$d_{2,\max}$	d	$P(d < 0)$	$s_{1,\max}$	$s_{2,\max}$	s	$P(d < 0)$
1996	FSD	14.50	−0.30	−0.30	0.21	303.47	−0.30	−0.30	0.47
1997	FSD	14.80	−0.29	−0.29	0.18	303.02	−0.29	−0.29	0.38
1998	FSD	15.24	−0.26	−0.26	0.16	340.35	−0.30	−0.30	0.48
1999	FSD	14.62	−0.45	−0.45	0.21	293.55	−0.45	−0.45	0.51
2000	FSD	13.78	−0.25	−0.25	0.14	285.84	−0.37	−0.37	0.51
2001	FSD	14.62	−0.29	−0.29	0.17	295.95	−0.29	−0.29	0.52
2002	FSD	15.84	−0.33	−0.33	0.36	344.21	−0.41	−0.41	0.77
2003	FSD	13.85	−0.26	−0.26	0.15	301.62	−0.26	−0.26	0.43
2004	FSD	15.42	−0.25	−0.25	0.25	274.34	−0.32	−0.32	0.87
2005	FSD	15.22	−0.22	−0.22	0.31	255.04	−0.27	−0.27	0.58
2006	FSD	15.64	−0.26	−0.26	0.34	375.20	−0.26	−0.26	0.81
2007	FSD	15.40	−0.25	−0.25	0.10	281.80	−0.56	−0.56	0.53
2008	FSD	13.37	−0.34	−0.34	0.11	220.90	−0.46	−0.46	0.47
2009	FSD	13.66	−0.28	−0.28	0.20	297.15	−0.28	−0.28	0.54
2010	FSD	12.28	−0.22	−0.22	0.21	284.13	−0.22	−0.22	0.51
2011	FSD	11.90	−0.39	−0.39	0.22	244.62	−0.42	−0.42	0.59
2012	FSD	12.49	−0.25	−0.25	0.33	216.75	−0.25	−0.25	0.71

5.3. Counterfactual Analysis of Different Wage Groups

In this section, we report the findings of counterfactual analysis for different wage groups. We used the weighted median wage of our sample, $18.5 per hour, as the cut-off point. Higher wage group consists of workers with wages above the median, and the rest are in the lower wage group.

5.3.1. Counterfactual Analysis of Higher Wage Group

We conducted the two kinds of counterfactual analysis again for the higher wage workers. The findings are reported in Tables 7 and 8. In line with Table 6, Table 8 also indicates a first-order distributional wage premium of human capital characteristics in favor of the incumbents. But still, among higher paid workers, such an edge is also not statistically significant, neither is the second-order dominance relation significant for any year in sample. We have our most interesting finding in Table 7, which summarizes the wage gap caused by inequality in wage structure for higher paid workers. In many years, we find that the newly hired worker's wage distribution and the counterfactual wage distribution # 1 are generally unrankable. However, we do find second-order dominance relations in the years of 1997, 2000, 2001, 2003, 2008, 2010, and 2011. More notably, the

Table 7. Stochastic Dominance Test Results Counterfactual #1 (Higher Wage Workers).

Year	Observed Rank	$d_{1,\max}$	$d_{2,\max}$	d	$P(d<0)$	$s_{1,\max}$	$s_{2,\max}$	s	$P(d<0)$
1996	None	2.09	3.17	2.09	0.00	0.26	40.10	0.26	0.26
1997	SSD	1.85	3.10	1.85	0.10	−0.30	49.34	−0.30	0.65
1998	None	0.80	6.16	0.80	0.06	0.80	118.62	0.80	0.18
1999	None	0.34	6.09	0.34	0.03	0.14	79.75	0.14	0.38
2000	SSD	1.05	3.50	1.05	0.15	−0.65	80.04	−0.65	0.47
2001	SSD	1.38	5.59	1.38	0.00	−0.39	100.11	−0.39	0.51
2002	None	0.23	4.42	0.23	0.07	0.23	118.22	0.23	0.23
2003	SSD	0.46	4.28	0.46	0.00	−0.61	102.91	−0.61	0.46
2004	None	1.72	5.78	1.72	0.00	3.52	30.94	3.52	0.16
2005	None	0.76	4.63	0.76	0.02	0.66	56.92	0.66	0.14
2006	None	2.59	2.61	2.59	0.00	11.49	38.30	11.49	0.23
2007	None	5.66	2.16	2.16	0.02	21.11	0.63	0.63	0.18
2008	SSD	0.44	7.88	0.44	0.03	−0.18	104.73	−0.18	0.59
2009	None	4.27	6.15	4.27	0.02	10.85	121.45	10.85	0.14
2010	SSD	0.33	11.37	0.33	0.00	−0.83	315.47	−0.83	0.82
2011	SSD	2.01	2.83	2.01	0.00	−0.35	18.44	−0.35	0.30
2012	None	4.34	1.83	1.83	0.00	15.58	0.55	0.55	0.13

Table 8. Stochastic Dominance Test Results Counterfactual #2 (Higher Wage Workers).

Year	Observed Rank	$d_{1,\max}$	$d_{2,\max}$	d	$P(d < 0)$	$s_{1,\max}$	$s_{2,\max}$	s	$P(d < 0)$
1996	FSD	14.50	−0.30	−0.30	0.18	303.47	−0.30	−0.30	0.39
1997	FSD	14.80	−0.29	−0.29	0.12	303.02	−0.29	−0.29	0.37
1998	FSD	15.24	−0.26	−0.26	0.12	340.35	−0.30	−0.30	0.41
1999	FSD	14.62	−0.45	−0.45	0.21	293.55	−0.45	−0.45	0.42
2000	FSD	13.78	−0.25	−0.25	0.16	285.84	−0.37	−0.37	0.54
2001	FSD	14.62	−0.29	−0.29	0.19	295.95	−0.29	−0.29	0.42
2002	FSD	15.84	−0.33	−0.33	0.32	344.21	−0.41	−0.41	0.76
2003	FSD	13.85	−0.26	−0.26	0.19	301.62	−0.26	−0.26	0.49
2004	FSD	15.42	−0.25	−0.25	0.32	274.34	−0.32	−0.32	0.81
2005	FSD	15.22	−0.22	−0.22	0.36	255.04	−0.27	−0.27	0.66
2006	FSD	15.64	−0.26	−0.26	0.34	375.20	−0.26	−0.26	0.75
2007	FSD	15.40	−0.25	−0.25	0.12	281.80	−0.56	−0.56	0.41
2008	FSD	13.37	−0.34	−0.34	0.11	220.90	−0.46	−0.46	0.60
2009	FSD	13.66	−0.28	−0.28	0.15	297.15	−0.28	−0.28	0.49
2010	FSD	12.28	−0.22	−0.22	0.15	284.13	−0.22	−0.22	0.45
2011	FSD	11.90	−0.39	−0.39	0.22	244.62	−0.42	−0.42	0.59
2012	FSD	12.49	−0.25	−0.25	0.20	216.75	−0.25	−0.25	0.60

dominance relations reversed direction. The wage distribution of newly hired workers empirically dominates, in a second-order sense, the counterfactual wage distribution # 1. Although they are largely statistically insignificant, the reverse of the dominance relations, to some degree, confirmed our hypothesis that certain highly paid new workers actually enjoyed a better wage structure than their incumbent counterparts, the so-called "new hire premium" in the literature. For workers with a social welfare function in the class U_2, the counterfactual case that replaces new hire's wage structure with that of incumbernt workers, while keeping their characteristics constant, would actually make those new hires worse off.

5.3.2. *Counterfactual Analysis of Lower Wage Group*

The results of counterfactual analysis for the lower paid group are reported in Tables 9 and 10. Table 10 shows similar results as Table 6, indicating better human capital characteristics among incumbent workers with hourly wage lower than \$18.5.

Table 9 reports the stochastic dominance test results between the original wage distribution of the new hires and the counterfactual wage distribution #1 among lower paid group. We have some interesting findings here. In the years of 1996, 1997, 2000–2003, and 2005–2009, the counterfactual

Table 9. Stochastic Dominance Test Results for Lower Wage Workers, Counterfactual #1.

Year	Observed Rank	$d_{1,\max}$	$d_{2,\max}$	d	$P(d<0)$	$s_{1,\max}$	$s_{2,\max}$	s	$P(d<0)$
1996	FSD	13.34	−0.13	−0.13	0.15	365.28	−0.22	−0.22	0.84
1997	FSD	18.51	−0.22	−0.22	0.83	544.61	−0.26	−0.26	0.92
1998	SSD	18.00	0.47	0.47	0.04	402.38	−0.20	−0.20	0.70
1999	None	15.13	0.19	0.19	0.13	388.87	0.64	0.64	0.21
2000	FSD	13.52	−0.17	−0.17	0.58	394.86	−0.23	−0.23	0.71
2001	FSD	10.85	−0.23	−0.23	0.55	287.80	−0.25	−0.25	0.84
2002	FSD	11.11	−0.26	−0.26	0.46	327.00	−0.29	−0.29	0.81
2003	FSD	10.37	−0.01	−0.01	0.29	293.57	−0.20	−0.20	0.68
2004	SSD	8.33	0.90	0.90	0.04	198.47	−0.23	−0.23	0.31
2005	FSD	8.71	−0.26	−0.26	0.11	202.16	−0.26	−0.26	0.40
2006	FSD	12.60	−0.31	−0.31	0.38	243.86	−0.52	−0.52	0.84
2007	FSD	10.71	−0.15	−0.15	0.17	222.28	−0.24	−0.24	0.36
2008	FSD	10.11	−0.03	−0.03	0.35	246.93	−0.17	−0.17	0.90
2009	FSD	10.45	−0.01	−0.01	0.34	268.62	−0.19	−0.19	0.71
2010	SSD	6.42	0.03	0.03	0.15	200.86	−0.21	−0.21	0.72
2011	SSD	6.46	1.14	1.14	0.01	148.40	−0.19	−0.19	0.39
2012	None	8.91	0.64	0.64	0.01	177.41	0.77	0.77	0.28

Table 10. Stochastic Dominance Test Results for Lower Wage Workers, Counterfactual#2.

Year	Observed Rank	$d1_{,\max}$	$d_{2,\max}$	d	$P(d<0)$	$s_{1,\max}$	$s_{2,\max}$	s	$P(d<0)$
1996	FSD	14.50	−0.30	−0.30	0.11	303.47	−0.30	−0.30	0.46
1997	FSD	14.80	−0.29	−0.29	0.10	303.02	−0.29	−0.29	0.36
1998	FSD	15.24	−0.26	−0.26	0.22	340.35	−0.30	−0.30	0.53
1999	FSD	14.62	−0.45	−0.45	0.20	293.55	−0.45	−0.45	0.46
2000	FSD	13.78	−0.25	−0.25	0.13	285.84	−0.37	−0.37	0.46
2001	FSD	14.62	−0.29	−0.29	0.22	295.95	−0.29	−0.29	0.62
2002	FSD	15.84	−0.33	−0.33	0.31	344.21	−0.41	−0.41	0.76
2003	FSD	13.85	−0.26	−0.26	0.12	301.62	−0.26	−0.26	0.48
2004	FSD	15.42	−0.25	−0.25	0.31	274.34	−0.32	−0.32	0.85
2005	FSD	15.22	−0.22	−0.22	0.30	255.04	−0.27	−0.27	0.65
2006	FSD	15.64	−0.26	−0.26	0.46	375.20	−0.26	−0.26	0.77
2007	FSD	15.40	−0.25	−0.25	0.11	281.80	−0.56	−0.56	0.41
2008	FSD	13.37	−0.34	−0.34	0.09	220.90	−0.46	−0.46	0.46
2009	FSD	13.66	−0.28	−0.28	0.19	297.15	−0.28	−0.28	0.55
2010	FSD	12.28	−0.22	−0.22	0.19	284.13	−0.22	−0.22	0.54
2011	FSD	11.90	−0.39	−0.39	0.17	244.62	−0.42	−0.42	0.65
2012	FSD	12.49	−0.25	−0.25	0.15	216.75	−0.25	−0.25	0.62

wage distribution #1 empirically dominates, in a first-order sense, the wage distribution of newly hired workers. In the years of 1998, 2004, 2010, and 2011, the counterfactual wage distribution #1 empirically dominates, in a second-order sense, the wage distribution of newly hired workers. First-order dominance relation is largely insignificant, but in 1997 and 2008, the second-order dominance relations are statistically significant, with p-values less than 0.1. The findings indicate that for lower wage workers, the counterfactual wage distribution #1 are preferred compared to the actual new hire wage distribution for workers with a social welfare function in the class of U_2 in both years. The significant dominance relation in 2008, provides a strong evidence that during the recent great recession year, lower wage new hired workers suffer from a much worse pay structure than that of the incumbents. It is an indicator showing that the external labor market deteriorates much more than the internal labor market during the recent recession.

CONCLUSION

This paper employs a distribution-based, entropy metric to measure the wage differentials between incumbent and newly hired employees. The entropy measure incorporates the differences at the entire distribution level and thus gives a better picture on wage comparison. We also use stochastic dominance tests to rank those wage distributions based on social welfare. We find that the incumbent workers are generally paid better than the newly hired worker in any year from 1996 to 2012. Further counterfactual analysis shows that the wage gap could be attributed to both the inequality in wage structures and the differences in human capital characteristics, depending on a worker's wage level. For highly paid new workers, the wage gap mainly comes from the differences in human capital characteristics and those new hires tend to enjoy a better wage structure than the incumbents in certain years. For lower paid new workers, the wage differential comes from both gap in human capital characteristics and the inequality in wage structure. Especially in the recent recession year 2008, those lower wage new hires suffer more from the significantly worse wage structure than that of the incumbents.

NOTES

1. For discrete variables, $S_\rho = \frac{1}{2}\sum\left(p_1^{1/2} - p_0^{1/2}\right)$.
2. Nonparametric kernel regression can also be used to estimate the propensity score, which allows more flexible dependence relations among independent and dependent variables.
3. Note that under such setting, $p_1(x) + p_2(x) = 1$ and $p_1 + p_2 = 1$.
4. In 1995, the Census made some changes to CPS sample ID variable, which led to very poor matching rates for that year, so we chose 1996 as the starting year to circumvent the problem.
5. One shortcoming of this linked data is that we can only follow workers who remain in the same household. Thus any new hire that moved in order to take a new job could not be matched in this data set.
6. We also exclude those with hourly wage less than or equal to $1, because those extremely low wages are likely be due to misreporting.
7. Authors' calculation. *Source:* BLS, Haver Analytics.

REFERENCES

Albrecht, J., Björklund, A., & Vroman, S. (2003). Is there a glass ceiling in Sweden? *Journal of Labor Economics, 21*(1), 145–177.

Baker, G., Gibbs, M., & Holmstrom, B. (1994). The internal economics of the firm: Evidence from personnel data. *The Quarterly Journal of Economics, 109*(4), 881–919.

Barsky, R., Bound, J., Ko'Charles, K., & Lupton, J. P. (2002). Accounting for the black–white wealth gap: A nonparametric approach. *Journal of the American Statistical Association, 97*(459), 663–673.

Blau, F. D., & Kahn, L. M. (2006). The US gender pay gap in the 1990s: Slowing convergence. *Industrial and Labor Relations Review, 60*(1), 45–66.

Blinder, A. S. (1973). Wage discrimination: Reduced form and structural estimates. *Journal of Human Resources, 18*(4)(Autumn), 436–455.

Bourguignon, F. (1979). Decomposable income inequality measures. *Econometrica: Journal of the Econometric Society, 47*(4), 901–920.

DiNardo, J., Fortin, N. M., & Lemieux, T. (1996). Labor market institutions and the distribution of wages, 1973–1992: A semiparametric approach. *Econometrica, 64*(5), 1001–1044.

Doeringer, P. B., & Piore, M. J. (1985). *Internal labor markets and manpower analysis.* Armonk, NY: ME Sharpe.

Firpo, S. (2007). Efficient semiparametric estimation of quantile treatment effects. *Econometrica 75*(1), 259–276.

Firpo, S., Fortin, N., & Lemieux, T. (2007). *Decomposing wage distributions using recentered influence function regressions.* Working Paper.

Granger, C. W., Maasoumi, E., & Racine, J. (2004). A dependence metric for possibly nonlinear processes. *Journal of Time Series Analysis, 25*(5), 649–669.

Kampkötter, P., & Sliwka, D. (2011). Wage premia for newly hired employees: Theory and evidence.

Kline, P. (2011). Oaxaca-Blinder as a reweighting estimator. *American Economic Review*, *101*(3), 532–537.

Linton, O., Maasoumi, E., & Whang, Y. J. (2005). Consistent testing for stochastic dominance under general sampling schemes. *The Review of Economic Studies*, *72*(3), 735–765.

Maasoumi, E. (1986). The measurement and decomposition of multi-dimensional inequality. *Econometrica: Journal of the Econometric Society*, *54*(4)(July), 991–997.

Maasoumi, E., & Heshmati, A. (2000). Stochastic dominance amongst Swedish income distributions. *Econometric Reviews*, *19*(3), 287–320.

Maasoumi, E., & Racine, J. (2002). Entropy and predictability of stock market returns. *Journal of Econometrics*, *107*(1), 291–312.

Madrian, B. C., & Lefgren, L. J. (1999). *A note on longitudinally matching Current Population Survey (CPS) respondents*. NBER Technical Working Papers 0247, National Bureau of Economic Research, Inc. URL. Retrieved from http://ideas.repec.org/p/nbr/nberte/0247.html

Massoumi, E. & Wang, L. (2012). *The gender earnings gap: Measurement and analysis*. Working Paper.

Oaxaca, R. (1973). Male-female wage differentials in urban labor markets. *International economic review*, *14*(3), 693–709.

Oreopoulos, P., von Wachter, T., & Heisz, A. (2006). *The short- and long-term career effects of graduating in a recession: Hysteresis and heterogeneity in the market for college graduates*. Working Paper No. 12159, National Bureau of Economic Research. URL. Retrieved from http://www.nber.org/papers/w12159

Shorrocks, A. F. (1978). The measurement of mobility. *Econometrica: Journal of the Econometric Society*, 1013–1024.

PART IV
THEORY AND APPLICATION OF TIME SERIES

DEVIANCE INFORMATION CRITERION FOR COMPARING VAR MODELS

Tao Zeng[a], Yong Li[b] and Jun Yu[c]

[a]*Economics and Management School, Wuhan University, Wuhan, China*
[b]*Hanqing Advanced Institute of Economics and Finance, Renmin University of China, Beijing, China*
[c]*School of Economics and Lee Kong Chian School of Business, Singapore Management University, Singapore, Republic of Singapore*

ABSTRACT

Vector Autoregression (VAR) has been a standard empirical tool used in macroeconomics and finance. In this paper we discuss how to compare alternative VAR models after they are estimated by Bayesian MCMC methods. In particular we apply a robust version of deviance information criterion (RDIC) recently developed in Li, Zeng, and Yu (2014b) to determine the best candidate model. RDIC is a better information criterion than the widely used deviance information criterion (DIC) when latent variables are involved in candidate models. Empirical analysis using US data shows that the optimal model selected by RDIC can be different from that by DIC.

Essays in Honor of Peter C. B. Phillips
Advances in Econometrics, Volume 33, 615–637

ISSN: 0731-9053/doi:10.1108/S0731-905320140000033017

Keywords: Bayes factor; DIC; VAR models; Markov Chain Monte Carlo

JEL Classifications: C11; C12; G12

1. INTRODUCTION

In the past 30 years, Vector Autoregression (VAR) has been widely used to capture the linear interdependencies among multiple time series of macroeconomic variables and financial variables. Consequently, VAR models have evolved as a standard tool for evaluating the monetary policy, for predicting macroeconomic variables and financial variables, and for the impulse response analysis. In VAR, each variable has an equation explaining its evolution based on its own lags and the lags of the other variables. Unfortunately, typically economic theory is silent about the choice of the lag length and hence such a choice must be determined by data at hand. When the lag length is not small and when the system is of moderate size, there is a large number of parameters in VAR and, hence, the identification and the estimation of VAR may be a formidable task (see, e.g., Ni & Sun, 2003).

In large cross-sections of time series, factor models, with a small number of common latent factors, have been employed to alleviate the problem of a large number of parameters (see, e.g., Bernanke & Boivin, 2003; Boivin & Ng, 2005; Forni, Hallin, Lippi, & Reichlin, 2003; Stock & Watson, 2002a, 2002b). Obviously, an important choice is the number of common factors. More often than not, the common factors are assumed to follow a VAR model. In this case, another important choice is the lag length. As in the case of the basic VAR models, usually economic theory does not offer guidance to choose the lag length in the factor VAR models. Once again, how many lags to be used is an important empirical question.

Frequentist's inferential approaches have proven difficult for estimating some VAR models. Consequently, Bayesian approaches have been increasingly popular for estimating VAR models (see e.g., Bai & Wang, 2012; Bernanke, Boivin, & Eliasz, 2005; Koop & Korobilis, 2009; Kose, Otrok, & Whiteman, 2003, 2008; Otrok & Whiteman, 1998). In particular, with the advance of MCMC algorithms and expanded computing facility, Bayesian MCMC methods have been routinely used for estimating VAR.

The question we ask in this paper is the following. After a set of candidate VAR models have been estimated by MCMC, with some candidate models involving latent common factors, how should one select the optimal model? Model comparison is one of the most important statistical inferences that one has to face (see, e.g., Phillips, 1995, 1996). In the Bayesian literature, Bayes factor (BF) (Kass & Raftery, 1995) is arguably the most popular tool for Bayesian model comparison. However, BF is subject to some theoretical drawbacks as well as some computational limitations. For instance, it suffers from the well-known Jeffreys–Lindley paradox (see Robert, 2001; Li & Yu, 2012). For another example, calculation of BF requires the evaluation of marginal likelihood. For some VAR models, marginal likelihood involves high-dimensional integrations numerically. This is the case for the factor VAR models when factors are latent. Consequently, the implementation of BF entails high computational cost.

As an alternative approach to BF, a recent contribution to Bayesian model comparison is the deviance information criterion (DIC) of Spiegelhalter, Best, Carlin, and van der Linde (2002). DIC can be understood as the Bayesian version of the Akaike information criterion (AIC, Akaike, 1973). As shown in Spiegelhalter et al. (2002), DIC is relatively simple to compute from the MCMC output, compared with BF. Moreover, it is immune to the Jeffreys–Lindley paradox.

However, as pointed out by Li, Zeng, and Yu (2014b), the original DIC, developed by Spiegelhalter et al. (2002) and implemented in a Bayesian software WinBUGS, is not asymptotically justified for models that involve latent variables. Consequently, Li et al. (2014b) advocated the use of a robust version of DIC (RDIC) for comparing models involving latent variables. In this paper, we examine the performance of DIC and RDIC for comparing VAR models, with and without latent variables.

The paper is organized as follows. In Section 2, we introduce the VAR models and review the Bayesian MCMC methods. Section 3 reviews DIC and RDIC and shows how to calculate RDIC for the VAR models. Section 4 compares DIC and RDIC using real data. Section 5 concludes the paper. Appendix collects the derivations needed for computing RDIC.

2. BAYESIAN ANALYSIS OF VAR MODELS

In this section, we first give a simple description of the VAR models. The basic VAR(p) model is of the form

$$y_t = a_0 + \sum_{j=1}^{p} A_j y_{t-j} + \varepsilon_t \tag{1}$$

where y_t is an $N \times 1$ vector containing T observations, ε_t an $N \times 1$ vector of errors which is i.i.d. $N(0,\Sigma)$, a_0 an $N \times 1$ vector of intercepts, A_j an $N \times N$ matrix of coefficients, and p the lag length.

The above VAR model can also be written in the matrix form

$$y = XA + E$$

or

$$Y = (I_M \otimes X)\alpha + \varepsilon$$

where y is a $T \times N$ matrix which stacks the T observations on each dependent variable in columns next to one another, $E = (\varepsilon_1, \varepsilon_2, \ldots, \varepsilon_T)'$, $x_t = (1, y'_{t-1}, \ldots, y'_{t-p})'$ and $X = (x'_1, \ldots, x'_T)'$, a $T \times K$ matrix, $K = 1 + Np$, $A = (a_0, A_1, \ldots, A_p)'$, $Y = vec(y)$, $\alpha = vec(A)$, $\varepsilon = vec(E) \sim N(0, \Sigma \otimes I_T)$.

VAR may not be parsimonious since there may be a great many coefficients in it. With the typical sample size for macroeconomic variables, it is not easy to obtain reliable estimates when the dimension of the parameter space is very large. Bayesian estimation is attractive because the prior information provides a logical and formally consistent way of introducing shrinkage to reduce the over-parametrizations problem (Koop & Korobilis, 2009).

Following Koop and Korobilis (2009), for a given lag length p, we implement Bayesian analysis with the natural conjugate priors:

$$\alpha | \Sigma \sim N(0, \Sigma \otimes \underline{V})$$

and

$$\Sigma^{-1} \sim Wishart\left(\underline{S}^{-1}, \underline{v}\right)$$

where

$$\alpha = vec(A), \ \ \underline{V} = 10 \times I_K, \ \ \underline{S}^{-1} = I_N, \ \ \underline{v} = N + 1$$

As a result, the posterior distribution is

$$\alpha | \Sigma, y \sim N(\widehat{\alpha}, \Sigma \otimes (X'X)^{-1})$$

and

$$\Sigma^{-1}|\mathbf{y} \sim Wishart(S^{-1}, T-K-N-1)$$

where $\hat{A} = (X'X)^{-1}X'\mathbf{y}$, $\hat{\alpha} = vec(\hat{A})$, and $S = (\mathbf{y} - X\hat{A})'(\mathbf{y} - X\hat{A})$.

To reduce the dimensionality of the parameter space in Eq. (1), one may consider introducing a smaller number of dynamic factors, f_t, so that

$$y_t = L\boldsymbol{f}_t + e_t \tag{2}$$

$$\boldsymbol{f}_t = \Phi_1\boldsymbol{f}_{t-1} + \cdots + \Phi_h\boldsymbol{f}_{t-h} + \varepsilon_t \tag{3}$$

where $\boldsymbol{f}_t$ is the $q \times 1$ ($q < N$) latent dynamic factor which follows a VAR specification, L the $N \times q$ dynamic factor loading, Φ_j the $q \times q$ matrix, e_t i.i.d. $N(0,\Sigma)$, and ε_t i.i.d. $N(0,Q)$. We assume $\{e_t\}_{t=1}^{T}$ is independent of $\{\varepsilon_t\}_{t=1}^{T}$. Following Bai and Wang (2012), we assume the number of dynamic factors q does not depend on h. To achieve the identification of the factor VAR model, we set the upper $q \times q$ block of L to an identity matrix, that is,

$$L = \begin{bmatrix} I_q \\ * \end{bmatrix}$$

This identification restriction was also used in Bernanke et al. (2005).

For the basic VAR models, the likelihood function, $p(\mathbf{y}|\boldsymbol{\theta})$, has an analytical form, where the observed data is denoted as $\mathbf{y} = (y_1, \ldots, y_T)'$ and $\boldsymbol{\theta}$ contains the model parameters. Hence, the posterior distribution $p(\boldsymbol{\theta}|\mathbf{y})$ is easy to obtain, that is,

$$p(\boldsymbol{\theta}|\mathbf{y}) \propto p(\mathbf{y}|\boldsymbol{\theta})p(\boldsymbol{\theta})$$

For the factor VAR model, denote the latent factors $\boldsymbol{f} = (f_1, f_2, \ldots, f_T)'$. In this case, the likelihood function involves unobserved dynamic factors, that is,

$$p(\mathbf{y}|\boldsymbol{\theta}) = \int p(\mathbf{y}, \boldsymbol{f}|\boldsymbol{\theta})\mathrm{d}\boldsymbol{f}$$

where $p(\mathbf{y}, \boldsymbol{f}|\boldsymbol{\theta})$ is the so-called complete data likelihood function. Not surprisingly, the estimation of the factor VAR model is more difficult by the classical estimation procedures.

However, with the help of the data-augmentation strategy of Tanner and Wong (1987) and the MCMC techniques, Bayesian approach can easily provide the full likelihood inference of the factor VAR model. The idea is to augment the parameter space from $\boldsymbol{\theta}$ to $(\boldsymbol{\theta}, \boldsymbol{f})$. As a result, given p, h, and q, the new posterior distribution is

$$p(\boldsymbol{\theta},\boldsymbol{f}|\boldsymbol{y}) \propto p(\boldsymbol{\theta},\boldsymbol{f},\boldsymbol{y}) = p(\boldsymbol{y}|\boldsymbol{\theta},\boldsymbol{f})p(\boldsymbol{f}|\boldsymbol{\theta})p(\boldsymbol{\theta}) \tag{4}$$

where

$$p(\boldsymbol{y}|\boldsymbol{\theta},\boldsymbol{f}) = \prod_{t=1}^{T} p(\boldsymbol{y}_t|\boldsymbol{\theta},\boldsymbol{f})$$

$$p(\boldsymbol{f}|\boldsymbol{\theta}) = p(\boldsymbol{f}_0|\boldsymbol{\theta}) \prod_{t=1}^{T} p(\boldsymbol{f}_t|\boldsymbol{f}_{t-1},\boldsymbol{\theta})$$

MCMC techniques may be used to obtain random samples from the posterior distribution (4). Bayesian estimates of $\boldsymbol{\theta}$ and the latent volatilities $\boldsymbol{f}$ can be obtained easily via the corresponding means of random samples. Specifically, let $\{\boldsymbol{\theta}^{(j)},\boldsymbol{f}^{(j)}, j=1,2, \ldots, J\}$ be the efficient random samples generated from the joint posterior distribution $p(\boldsymbol{\theta},\boldsymbol{f}|\boldsymbol{y})$ after discarding the burn-in samples. Then the posterior mean of $\boldsymbol{\theta},\boldsymbol{f}$ can be obtained by

$$\hat{\boldsymbol{\theta}} = \frac{1}{J}\sum_{j=1}^{J}\boldsymbol{\theta}^{(j)}, \quad \hat{\boldsymbol{f}} = \frac{1}{J}\sum_{j=1}^{J}\boldsymbol{f}^{(j)} \tag{5}$$

Similarly, the posterior variance of $\boldsymbol{\theta}$ can be obtained by

$$\widehat{Var}(\boldsymbol{\theta}|\boldsymbol{y}) = \frac{1}{J-1}\sum_{j=1}^{J}(\boldsymbol{\theta}^{(j)} - \hat{\boldsymbol{\theta}})(\boldsymbol{\theta}^{(j)} - \hat{\boldsymbol{\theta}})'$$

3. DEVIANCE INFORMATION CRITERION FOR VAR MODELS

In the Bayesian literature, there are two popular tools for model comparison. The first one is BF (Kass & Raftery, 1995), while the other is DIC (Spiegelhalter et al., 2002). Given two candidate models M_1 and M_2, BF is given by

$$B_{12} = \frac{p(y|M_1)}{p(y|M_2)} \tag{6}$$

where $p(y|M_k), k = 1,2$ is the marginal likelihood of M_k, and can be obtained by integrating over the support of the parameters and latent states, that is,

$$p(y|M_k) = \int_{\Omega_k \cup \Omega_\omega} p(y, f|\theta_k, M_k) p(\theta_k|M_k) \mathrm{d}f \mathrm{d}\theta_k, \quad \theta_k \in \Omega_k, \quad k = 1,2$$

However, if a vague prior is adopted, BF suffers from the Jeffreys–Lindley paradox. As pointed out by Kass and Raftery (1995), when a proper prior with a very large spread is used to represent the prior ignorance, this behavior will force the BF to favor its competitive model; see Example 1 in Li, Zeng, and Yu (2014a) for an illustration of this problem.

Moreover, calculation of BF in general necessitates the evaluation of marginal likelihood which is a marginalization over the parameter vectors in each candidate model. When the dimension of the parameter space is large, the high-dimensional integration entails high computational cost.

DIC was recently proposed and heuristically justified by Spiegelhalter et al. (2002) based on the classical asymptotic theory.[1] It is calculated in a Bayesian software WinBUGS and widely used in the Bayesian community to compare alternative models. The basic form of DIC can be expressed as follows:

$$\mathrm{DIC} = D(\bar{\theta}) + 2P_D = \overline{D(\theta)} + P_D \tag{7}$$

$$D(\bar{\theta}) = -2 \log p(y|\bar{\theta}), \overline{D(\theta)} = -2 \int \log p(y|\theta) p(\theta|y) \mathrm{d}\theta \tag{8}$$

$$P_D = -2 \int [\log p(y|\theta) - \log p(y|\bar{\theta})] p(\theta|y) \mathrm{d}\theta = \overline{D(\theta)} - D(\bar{\theta}) \tag{9}$$

where $\bar{\theta}$ is the Bayesian estimator, $\overline{D(\theta)}$ a Bayesian measure of fit which may be better considered as a measure of "adequacy," and P_D a Bayesian measure of model complexity. One advantage of DIC is that it is immune to Jeffreys–Lindley paradox. However, it is important to point out that DIC addresses how well the posterior might predict future data generated by the same mechanism that gave rise to the observed data. This is different from BF which addresses how observed data are predicted by the priors. Perhaps this difference makes DIC more suitable for comparing alternative VAR models when the primary objective of VAR is forecasting.

When the likelihood function $p(\boldsymbol{y}|\boldsymbol{\theta})$ is available in closed-form, MCMC is easy to implement and DIC is easy to calculate. For a VAR model with latent variables, to facilitate MCMC simulations, the *data augmentation* strategy is often used, as shown in Section 2. With *data augmentation*, Spiegelhalter et al. (2002) suggested the following way to compute DIC:

$$\text{DIC}^* = D^*(\bar{\boldsymbol{\theta}},\bar{\boldsymbol{f}}) + 2P_D^* = \overline{D^*(\boldsymbol{\theta},\boldsymbol{f})} + P_D^* \tag{10}$$

$$D^*(\bar{\boldsymbol{\theta}},\bar{\boldsymbol{f}}) = -2\log p(\boldsymbol{y}|\bar{\boldsymbol{\theta}},\bar{\boldsymbol{f}}) \tag{11}$$

$$\overline{D^*(\boldsymbol{\theta},\boldsymbol{f})} = -2\int \log p(\boldsymbol{y}|\boldsymbol{\theta},\boldsymbol{f})p(\boldsymbol{\theta},\boldsymbol{f}|\boldsymbol{y})\mathrm{d}\boldsymbol{\theta}\mathrm{d}\boldsymbol{f} \tag{12}$$

$$P_D^* = -2\int [\log p(\boldsymbol{y}|\boldsymbol{\theta},\boldsymbol{f}) - \log p(\boldsymbol{y}|\bar{\boldsymbol{\theta}},\bar{\boldsymbol{f}})]p(\boldsymbol{\theta},\boldsymbol{f}|\boldsymbol{y})\mathrm{d}\boldsymbol{\theta}\mathrm{d}\boldsymbol{f} \tag{13}$$

where $\bar{\boldsymbol{f}}$ the Bayesian estimator of $\boldsymbol{f}$. Obviously, the latent variables $\boldsymbol{f}$ are treated in the same way as $\boldsymbol{\theta}$. This treatment greatly facilitates the calculation of DIC* from an MCMC output when the new likelihood function, $p(\boldsymbol{y}|\boldsymbol{\theta},\boldsymbol{f})$, is available in closed-form, a case for the factor VAR model.

While computationally tractable, unfortunately, *data augmentation* invalidates the theoretical underpinnings of DIC* since it makes the likelihood function, $p(\boldsymbol{y}|\boldsymbol{\theta},\boldsymbol{f})$, nonregular. This is because the dimension of the parameter space $(\boldsymbol{\theta}, \boldsymbol{f})$ increases as the sample size increases. In particular, the nonregular likelihood problem does not lead to the asymptotic normality in the posterior distribution of $(\boldsymbol{\theta}, \boldsymbol{f})$. Moreover, DIC* can be highly sensitive to nonlinear transformations of latent variables and distributional representations of model specification. In a recent study, Chan and Grant (2014) showed that DIC* has a larger variability than DIC in the context of latent variable models.

To overcome this problem, Li et al. (2014b) proposed a robust version of DIC (RDIC) for comparing latent variable models. RDIC is easy to compute and robust to nonlinear transformations of latent variables and distributional representations of model specification. The RDIC is given by

$$\text{RDIC} = D(\overline{\boldsymbol{\theta}}) + 2\mathbf{tr}\{\mathbf{I}(\overline{\boldsymbol{\theta}})V(\overline{\boldsymbol{\theta}})\} = D(\overline{\boldsymbol{\theta}}) + 2P_{RD} \tag{14}$$

where

$$P_{RD} = \mathbf{tr}\{\mathbf{I}(\overline{\boldsymbol{\theta}})V(\overline{\boldsymbol{\theta}})\} \tag{15}$$

with **tr** denoting the trace of a matrix,

$$\mathbf{I}(\boldsymbol{\theta}) = -\frac{\partial^2 \log p(\mathbf{y}|\boldsymbol{\theta})}{\partial\boldsymbol{\theta}\partial\boldsymbol{\theta}'},\ V(\overline{\boldsymbol{\theta}}) = E\left[(\boldsymbol{\theta}-\overline{\boldsymbol{\theta}})(\boldsymbol{\theta}-\overline{\boldsymbol{\theta}})'|\mathbf{y}\right]$$

Under regular conditions, Li et al. (2014b) showed that $P_{RD} = P_D + o_p(1)$, $\text{RDIC} = \text{DIC} + o_p(1)$, where DIC, RDIC, P_D, and P_{RD} are defined in Eqs. (7), (14), (9), and (15), respectively. The conditions include the regular conditions to the Bayesian large sample theory (see, e. g., Chen, 1985). In addition, it is required that the data generating process is stationary and that the model is regular so that the standard maximum likelihood theory can be applied.

We should point out that RDIC is different from Takeuchi information criterion (TIC, Takeuchi, 1976) which is defined as

$$\text{TIC} = -2\log p(\mathbf{y}|\hat{\boldsymbol{\theta}}_{ML}) + 2\mathbf{tr}\{\mathbf{J}(\hat{\boldsymbol{\theta}}_{ML})\mathbf{I}^{-1}(\hat{\boldsymbol{\theta}}_{ML})\}$$

where $y^{t-1} = (y_1, y_2, \ldots, y_{t-1})$, $\hat{\boldsymbol{\theta}}_{ML}$ is the ML estimator of $\boldsymbol{\theta}$, $\mathbf{J}(\hat{\boldsymbol{\theta}}_{ML})$ is a consistent estimate of the long run variance. TIC can be equivalently written as

$$\text{TIC} = -2\log p(\mathbf{y}|\hat{\boldsymbol{\theta}}_{ML}) + 2\mathbf{tr}\{\mathbf{I}(\hat{\boldsymbol{\theta}}_{ML})\widehat{\Sigma}(\hat{\boldsymbol{\theta}}_{ML})\}$$

where

$$\widehat{\Sigma}(\hat{\boldsymbol{\theta}}_{ML}) = \mathbf{I}^{-1}(\hat{\boldsymbol{\theta}}_{ML})\mathbf{J}(\hat{\boldsymbol{\theta}}_{ML})\mathbf{I}^{-1}(\hat{\boldsymbol{\theta}}_{ML})$$

is the so-called sandwich covariance matrix for $\hat{\boldsymbol{\theta}}_{ML}$. Although $\mathbf{tr}\{\mathbf{I}(\overline{\theta})V(\overline{\theta})\}$ and $\mathbf{tr}\{\mathbf{I}(\hat{\boldsymbol{\theta}}_{ML})\widehat{\Sigma}(\hat{\boldsymbol{\theta}}_{ML})\}$ are similar, a closer comparison of them shows important differences. First, $\mathbf{tr}\{\mathbf{I}(\hat{\boldsymbol{\theta}}_{ML})\hat{\Sigma}(\hat{\boldsymbol{\theta}}_{ML})\}$ in TIC is based on the ML estimation, whereas $\mathbf{tr}\{\mathbf{I}(\bar{\boldsymbol{\theta}})V(\bar{\boldsymbol{\theta}})\}$ in RDIC is based on the Bayesian estimation. Second, $\hat{\Sigma}(\hat{\boldsymbol{\theta}}_{ML})$ in TIC requires the inversion of the matrix $I(\boldsymbol{\theta})$. When the dimension of $\boldsymbol{\theta}$ is high, $I(\boldsymbol{\theta})$ may be difficult to invert. However, in RDIC, there is no need to invert any matrix. Third, like AIC, RDIC requires the model be correctly specified, but TIC relaxes this assumption.

It should be pointed out that, like AIC, RDIC does not have the consistent property for the true model. This is different from the Bayesian information criterion such as BIC (Schwarz, 1978) that approximates BF in large sample (Kass & Raftery, 1995). Compared to BF, hence, we expect RDIC tends to choose less parsimonious models. This comparison is similar to between of AIC and BIC.

The RDIC clearly requires the evaluation of the observed information matrix and the second derivative of the observed-data likelihood function. For most latent variable models, the observed-data likelihood function does not have a closed-from expression so that the second derivatives are difficult to evaluate. However, with the help of the EM algorithm, the second derivatives can be easily approximated. In particular, under the mild regularity conditions, Louis (1982) derived the observed information matrix as

$$\begin{aligned}\mathbf{I}(\boldsymbol{\theta}) &= E_{f|y,\theta}\left\{-\frac{\partial^2 \log p(\mathbf{y},\boldsymbol{f}|\boldsymbol{\theta})}{\partial\boldsymbol{\theta}\partial\boldsymbol{\theta}'}\right\} - Var_{\mathbf{f}|\mathbf{y},\theta}\left\{\frac{\partial \log p(\mathbf{y},\boldsymbol{f}|\boldsymbol{\theta})}{\partial\boldsymbol{\theta}}\right\}\\ &= E_{f|y,\theta}\left\{-\frac{\partial^2 \log p(\mathbf{y},\boldsymbol{f}|\boldsymbol{\theta})}{\partial\boldsymbol{\theta}\partial\boldsymbol{\theta}'} - \frac{\partial \log p(\mathbf{y},\boldsymbol{f}|\boldsymbol{\theta})}{\partial\boldsymbol{\theta}}\frac{\partial \log p(\mathbf{y},\boldsymbol{f}|\boldsymbol{\theta})}{\partial\boldsymbol{\theta}'}\right\}\\ &\quad + E_{f|y,\theta}\left(\frac{\partial \log p(\mathbf{y},\boldsymbol{f}|\boldsymbol{\theta})}{\partial\boldsymbol{\theta}}\right)E_{f|y,\theta}\left(\frac{\partial \log p(\mathbf{y},\boldsymbol{f}|\boldsymbol{\theta})}{\partial\boldsymbol{\theta}'}\right)\end{aligned}$$

where the expectations are taken with respect to the conditional distribution of $\boldsymbol{f}$ given $\boldsymbol{y}$ and $\boldsymbol{\theta}$. Hence, the information matrix can be approximated by

$$\begin{aligned}&E_{f|y,\theta}\left\{-\frac{\partial^2 \log p(\mathbf{y},\boldsymbol{f}|\boldsymbol{\theta})}{\partial\boldsymbol{\theta}\partial\boldsymbol{\theta}'} - \frac{\partial \log p(\mathbf{y},\boldsymbol{f}|\boldsymbol{\theta})}{\partial\boldsymbol{\theta}}\frac{\partial \log p(\mathbf{y},\boldsymbol{f}|\boldsymbol{\theta})}{\partial\boldsymbol{\theta}'}\right\}\\ &\approx -\frac{1}{M}\sum_{m=1}^{M}\left\{\frac{\partial^2 \log p(\mathbf{y},\boldsymbol{f}^{(m)}|\boldsymbol{\theta})}{\partial\boldsymbol{\theta}\partial\boldsymbol{\theta}'} + \frac{\partial \log p(\mathbf{y},\boldsymbol{f}^{(m)}|\boldsymbol{\theta})}{\partial\boldsymbol{\theta}}\frac{\partial \log p(\mathbf{y},\boldsymbol{f}^{(m)}|\boldsymbol{\theta})}{\partial\boldsymbol{\theta}'}\right\}\end{aligned}$$

$$E_{f|y,\theta}\left(\frac{\partial \log p(y,f|\theta)}{\partial \theta}\right) \approx \frac{1}{M}\sum_{m=1}^{M}\frac{\partial \log p(y,f^{(m)}|\theta)}{\partial \theta}$$

For more details, one can refer to Li et al. (2014b).

In this paper, we calculate DIC, DIC*, and RDIC for the basic VAR models and the VAR models with latent variables. For the basic VAR model, all three statistics are easy to compute and $P_D = P_D^*$, DIC = DIC*. For the factor VAR models, DIC is computationally much more demanding than DIC* and RDIC. DIC* is routinely reported in the literature.

4. EMPIRICAL STUDY

In this section, we will determine the optimal lag length in the basic VAR model (q) and optimal lag length in the factor VAR model (h) using real data. In particular, we fit both the basic VAR models and the factor VAR models to the quarterly U.S. data on the inflation rate π_t (the annual percentage change in a chain-weighted price index), the unemployment rate u_t (the seasonally adjusted unemployment rate), and the interest rate r_t (the yield on the three month Treasury bill rate). The data have been previously used by Koop and Korobilis (2009) and Koop and Potter (2011). The sample period is from 1953Q1 to 2006Q3.

We first use DIC, DIC*, and RDIC to select the optimal lag in the basic VAR model. In the empirical analysis, $y_t = (\pi_t, u_t, r_t)$ and $N = 3$. The prior is set at

$$\underline{V} = 10 \times I_K, \quad \underline{S}^{-1} = I_M, \quad \underline{\nu} = N + 1$$

For the basic VAR models, we allow nine different lag lengths, i.e., $p = 1, \ldots, 9$. Without latent variables in the models, DIC = DIC*.

To compute DIC, we draw 12,000 samples from the posterior distribution and discard the first 2,000 draws. Since both the posterior distribution and the second-order derivatives have the analytical form, we can easily compute RDIC using the posterior mean of the parameters. Table 1 reports DIC, P_D, RDIC, and P_{RD} for the candidate models. Several conclusions can be drawn from Table 1. First, both RDIC and DIC suggest that $p = 6$ is the best model. Second, RDIC and DIC take nearly identical values in all the candidate models. This is not surprising since there is no latent variable in the basic VAR models.

Table 1. Model Selection Results for the Basic VAR Models.

P	1	2	3	4	5	6	7	8	9
P_D	17.53	26.53	35.75	45.24	54.93	**64.78**	75.23	85.92	96.77
DIC	857.72	730.86	725.17	725.87	680.3	**672.15**	676.15	687.11	681.88
P_{RD}	17.31	26.13	35.17	44.47	53.99	**63.58**	73.91	84.64	95.01
$RDIC$	857.28	730.06	724.06	724.34	678.41	**669.76**	673.5	684.53	679.01

We then fit the data to the one-factor VAR model for $h=1,2,3,4$. With the latent variables involved, DIC is no longer the same as DIC*. To select the optimal lag length, we use DIC, DIC*, and RDIC. For simplicity, we assume R to be a diagonal matrix. The priors are similar to those used in Bernanke et al. (2005), namely,

$$\Sigma_{ii} \sim IG(3, 0.001), \quad L_i \sim N(0, \Sigma_{ii} \times I_q)$$

$$vec(\Phi)|Q \sim N(0, Q \otimes \Omega_0), \quad Q \sim Inverse-Wishart(Q_0, q+2)$$

where $\sum_{ii}$ is the ith diagonal element of R and L_i is the ith row of $L(i>q)$, $\Phi = (\Phi_1, \ldots, \Phi_h)$. See Bernanke et al. (2005) for the construction of Ω_0 and Q_0.

Although DIC is in general difficult to calculate for latent variable models, in this particular case, it can be obtained by using the Kalman filter. Of course, DIC is computationally much more expensive to compute than DIC* and RDIC. Using the Gibbs sampler, we sample 22,000 random observations from the corresponding posterior distributions. We discard the first 2,000 observations and keep the following 20,000 as the effective samples from the posterior distribution of the parameters.

Table 2 reports DIC, P_D, DIC^*, P^*_D, RDIC, and P_{RD}. Some findings arise from Table 2. First, both RDIC and DIC suggest that $h=2$ is the best model, whereas DIC* selects $h=3$. Second, RDIC and DIC take nearly identical values in all the candidate models. However, they take quite different values from DIC*. This difference arises because the latent variables are included into the parameter space in DIC*. As previously explained, such an expansion of the parameter space undermines the theoretical justification of DIC* and should not be used to compare alternative models. In this particular case, the use of DIC* will select too big a model although it is not clear if this is the common feature of DIC* in general. Li et al. (2014b) also report evidence that DIC* ranks the same models with different representations differently.

Table 2. Model Selection Results for the Factor VAR Models.

h	1	2	3	4
P_D^*	216	243	233	238
DIC^*	2294	1966	**1941**	1942
P_{RD}	5.34	4.65	6.06	6.2
$RDIC$	2120.68	**1879.1**	1882.12	1880.1
P_D	5.8131	5.9328	6.8114	7.3254
DIC	2121.9	**1881.7**	1884	1882.3

5. CONCLUSION

This paper uses a robust deviance information criteria (RDIC) to determine the optimal lag length in the basic VAR models and in the factor VAR models. When the latent variable is treated as parameters to facilitate Bayesian parameter estimation, the widely used DIC lacks theoretical justification. This is because the justification of DIC relies on the validity of the standard Bayesian asymptotic theory. In particular, when the latent variable is treated as parameters, the number of parameters increases with the number of observations, making the likelihood nonregular. In the empirical analysis, we show that in the basic VAR model where there is no latent variable, DIC and RDIC select the same optimal model. However, in the factor VAR model where the factors are latent, DIC and RDIC select the different optimal model.

NOTE

1. The rigorous asymptotical justification of DIC is given in Li et al. (2014b). Let $\mathbf{y}_{rep} = (\mathbf{y}_{1,rep}, \mathbf{y}_{2,rep}, \ldots, \mathbf{y}_{n,rep})$ be the independent replicate data generated by the same mechanism that gives rise to the observed data $\mathbf{y}$. Spiegelhalter et al. (2002, p. 604) proposed to choose the loss function $\mathrm{L}(\mathbf{y}_{rep}, \mathbf{y}) = -2\log p(\mathbf{y}_{rep} | \bar{\theta}(\mathbf{y}))$. Li et al. (2014b) showed that such a loss function cannot be used to justify DIC. By choosing the loss function as $\mathbf{L}(\mathbf{y}_{rep}, \mathbf{y}) = -2\log\, p(\mathbf{y}_{rep} | \mathbf{y})$, under regular conditions, Li et al. (2014b) asymptotically justified DIC.

ACKNOWLEDGEMENTS

Li gratefully acknowledges the financial support by the Fundamental Research Funds for the Central Universities, and the Research Funds of

Renmin University of China. Yu thanks the Singapore Ministry of Education for Academic Research Fund under grant number MOE2011-T2-2-096. We acknowledge the helpful comments from a referee and the participants at a conference in honor of Peter C. B. Phillips held at Southern Methodist University on November 1–3, 2013.

REFERENCES

Akaike, H. (1973). Information theory and an extension of the maximum likelihood principle. In B. N. Petrov & F. Caski (Eds.), *Second international symposium on information theory* (Vol. 1, pp. 267–281). Akademiai Kiado, Budapest.

Bai, J., & Wang, P. (2012). Identification and Bayesian estimation of dynamic factor models. *Journal of Business and Economic Statistics*, forthcoming.

Bernanke, B. S., & Boivin, J. (2003). Monetary policy in a data-rich environment. *Journal of Monetary Economics*, *50*, 525–546.

Bernanke, B. S., Boivin, J., & Eliasz, P. (2005). Measuring the effects of monetary policy: A factor-augmented vector autoregressive (FAVAR) approach. *The Quarterly Journal of Economics*, *120*, 387–422.

Boivin, J., & Ng, S. (2005). Understanding and comparing factor-based forecasts. *International Journal of Central Banking*, *1*, 117–151.

Chan, J. C. C., & Grant, A. L. (2014). Issues in Comparing Stochastic Volatility Models Using the Deviance Information Criterion. Research School of Economics, Australian National University, Working Paper.

Chen, C. F. (1985). On asymptotic normality of limiting density functions with Bayesian implications. *Journal of the Royal Statistical Society, Series B*, *47*, 540–546.

Forni, M., Hallin, M., Lippi, M., & Reichlin, L. (2003). Do financial variables help forecasting inflation and real activity in the euro area? *Journal of Monetary Economics*, *50*, 1243–1255.

Kass, R. E., & Raftery, A. E. (1995). Bayes factors. *Journal of the American Statistical Association*, *90*, 773–795.

Koop, G., & Korobilis, D. (2009). Bayesian multivariate time series methods for empirical macroeconomics. *Foundations and Trends® in Econometrics*, *3*, 267–358.

Koop, G., & Potter, S. M. (2011). Time varying VARs with inequality restrictions. *Journal of Economic Dynamics and Control*, *35*, 1126–1138.

Kose, M. A., Otrok, C., & Whiteman, C. H. (2003). International business cycles: World, region, and country-specific factors. *American Economic Review*, *93*, 1216–1239.

Kose, M. A., Otrok, C., & Whiteman, C. H. (2008). Understanding the evolution of world business cycles. *Journal of International Economics*, *75*, 110–130.

Li, Y., & Yu, J. (2012). Bayesian hypothesis testing in latent variable models. *Journal of Econometrics*, *166*, 237–246.

Li, Y., Zeng, T., & Yu, J. (2014a). A new approach to Bayesian hypothesis testing. *Journal of Econometrics*, *178*, 602–612.

Li, Y., Zeng, T., & Yu, J. (2014b). Robust deviation information criterion for latent variable models. School of Economics, Singapore Management University, Working Paper.

Louis, T. A. (1982). Finding the observed information matrix when using the EM algorithm. *Journal of the Royal Statistical Society, Series B, 44*, 226–233.

Magnus, J., & Neudecker, H. (1999). *Matrix differential calculus with applications in statistics and econometrics*. Chichester: Wiley.

Ni, S., & Sun, D. (2003). Noninformative priors and frequentist risks of Bayesian estimators of vector-autoregressive models. *Journal of Econometrics, 115*, 159–197.

Otrok, C., & Whiteman, C. H. (1998). Bayesian leading indicators: Measuring and predicting economic conditions in Iowa. *International Economic Review, 39*, 997–1014.

Phillips, P. C. B. (1995). Bayesian model selection and prediction with empirical applications. *Journal of Econometrics, 69*, 289–331.

Phillips, P. C. B. (1996). Econometric model determination. *Econometrica, 64*, 763–812.

Robert, C. (2001). *The bayesian choice: From decision-theoretic foundations to computational implementation*. Springer.

Schwarz, G. (1978). Estimating the dimension of a model. *Annals of Statistics, 6*(2), 461–464.

Spiegelhalter, D. J., Best, N. G., Carlin, B. P., & van der Linde, A. (2002). Bayesian measures of model complexity and fit. *Journal of the Royal Statistical Society, Series B, 64*, 583–639.

Stock, J. H., & Watson, M. W. (2002a). Forecasting using principal components from a large number of predictors. *Journal of the American Statistical Association, 97*, 1167–1179.

Stock, J. H., & Watson, M. W. (2002b). Macroeconomic forecasting using diffusion indexes. *Journal of Business & Economic Statistics, 20*, 147–162.

Takeuchi, K. (1976). Distribution of Informational Statistics and a Criterion of Model Fitting. *Suri-Kagaku (Mathematical Sciences), 153*, 13–18. (in Japanese).

Tanner, M., & Wong, W. (1987). The calculation of posterior distributions by data augmentation. *Journal of the American Statistical Association, 82*, 528–540.

APPENDIX

A.1. The Derivation of RDIC for the Basic VAR(p) Models

The log-likelihood function for VAR(p) model is

$$\log p(\mathbf{y}|\Sigma, A) = -\frac{TN}{2}\ln 2\pi - \frac{T}{2}\ln|\Sigma| - \frac{1}{2}tr\left[\Sigma^{-1}(\mathbf{y}-XA)'(\mathbf{y}-XA)\right]$$

Using the matrix differentiation rules of Magnus and Neudecker (1999), the first-order derivative is

$$D_A \log p(\mathbf{y}|\Sigma, A) = \left[vec\left(\left(\frac{1}{2}(\Sigma^{-1'} + \Sigma^{-1})(\mathbf{y}-XA)'X\right)'\right)\right]'$$

$$D_\Sigma \log p(\mathbf{y}|\Sigma, A) = \left[vec\left(\left(-\frac{T}{2}\Sigma^{-1} + \frac{1}{2}\Sigma^{-1}(\mathbf{y}-XA)'(\mathbf{y}-XA)\Sigma^{-1}\right)'\right)\right]$$

and the second-order derivatives are

$$D_{AA} \log p(\mathbf{y}|\Sigma, A) = -\frac{1}{2}((\Sigma^{-1'} + \Sigma^{-1}) \otimes X'X)$$

$$D_{A\Sigma} \log p(\mathbf{y}|\Sigma, A) = -\frac{1}{2}K_{NK}\left(\left[(\mathbf{y}-XA)'X\right]' \otimes I_N\right)(K_{NN} + I_{NN})(\Sigma^{-1} \otimes \Sigma^{-1})$$

$$D_{\Sigma A} \log p(\mathbf{y}|\Sigma, A) = D_{A\Sigma} \log p(\mathbf{y}|\Sigma, A)$$

$$D_{\Sigma\Sigma} \log p(\mathbf{y}|\Sigma, A) = K_{NN}\left\{\begin{array}{c} \frac{T}{2}\frac{1}{2}((\Sigma^{-1})' \otimes \Sigma^{-1} + (\Sigma^{-1})' \otimes \Sigma^{-1}) \\ -\frac{1}{2}\left(\begin{array}{c} \left(\Sigma^{-1}(\mathbf{y}-XA)'(\mathbf{y}-XA)\Sigma^{-1}\right)' \otimes \Sigma^{-1} \\ +(\Sigma^{-1})' \otimes \left(\Sigma^{-1}(\mathbf{y}-XA)'(\mathbf{y}-XA)\Sigma^{-1}\right) \end{array}\right) \end{array}\right\}$$

where K_{NN} is the commutation matrix for a matrix with N rows and N columns. Since Σ is symmetric, define $V\Sigma = vech(\Sigma)$ and we have an index matrix $D_{V\Sigma}(\Sigma)$ which is defined as

$$D_{V\Sigma}(\Sigma) = diag(R_1, R_2, \ldots R_m, \ldots, R_N)$$

where

$$R_k = \begin{bmatrix} 0_{(m-1)\times(N-m+1)} \\ I_{N-m+1} \end{bmatrix}_{N\times(N-m+1)}$$

Hence, the derivatives are

$$D_A \log p(\mathbf{y}|\Sigma, A) = \left[vec\left(\left(\frac{1}{2}(\Sigma^{-1'} + \Sigma^{-1})(\mathbf{y} - XA)'X \right)' \right) \right]$$

$$D_{V\Sigma} \log p(\mathbf{y}|\Sigma, A) = D_\Sigma \log p(\mathbf{y}|\Sigma, A) \times D_{V\Sigma}(\Sigma)$$

$$D_{AA} \log p(\mathbf{y}|\Sigma, A) = -\frac{1}{2}((\Sigma^{-1'} + \Sigma^{-1}) \otimes X'X)$$

$$D_{AV\Sigma} \log p(\mathbf{y}|\Sigma, A) = D_{A\Sigma} \log p(\mathbf{y}|\Sigma, A) \times D_{V\Sigma}(\Sigma)$$

$$D_{V\Sigma A} \log p(\mathbf{y}|\Sigma, A) = D'_{AV\Sigma} \log p(\mathbf{y}|\Sigma, A)$$

$$\begin{aligned} D_{V\Sigma V\Sigma} \log p(\mathbf{y}|\Sigma, A) &= (D_{V\Sigma}(\Sigma)' \otimes I_1) \times D_{\Sigma\Sigma} \log p(\mathbf{y}|\Sigma, A) \times D_{V\Sigma}(\Sigma) \\ &= D_{V\Sigma}(\Sigma)' \times D_{\Sigma\Sigma} \log p(\mathbf{y}|\Sigma, A) \times D_{V\Sigma}(\Sigma) \end{aligned}$$

A.2. The Derivation of RDIC for the Factor VAR Model

The model can be written in matrix form

$$y_t = Lf_t + e_t$$

$$f_t = \Phi F_{t-1} + \varepsilon_t$$

where $\Phi = (\Phi_1, \Phi_2, \ldots, \Phi_h)$, $\mathbf{F}_t = (f_t', \ldots, f_{t-h+1}')'$.

The complete data log-likelihood function is

$$\begin{aligned} \log f(\mathbf{y}, \mathbf{f}|L, \Sigma, \Phi, Q) = &-\frac{NT + q(T-h)}{2} \log 2\pi - \frac{T}{2} \log|\Sigma| \\ &- \frac{1}{2} \mathbf{tr}\left[\Sigma^{-1}(\mathbf{y} - \mathbf{f}L')'(\mathbf{y} - \mathbf{f}L')\right] \\ &- \frac{T-h}{2} \log|Q| - \frac{1}{2} \mathbf{tr}\left[Q^{-1}(\mathbf{f}_{+1} - \mathbf{f}_{-1}\Phi')'(\mathbf{f}_{+1} - \mathbf{f}_{-1}\Phi')\right] \end{aligned}$$

where $f_{+1}=[f_{h+1},\ f_{h+2},\ \ldots,\ f_T]'$, $f_{-1}=[F_h,\ F_{h+1},\ \ldots\ F_{T-1}]'$. Denote this function by $\varphi(L, \Sigma, \Phi, Q)$. We now derive the first and second derivative of it.

The first-order derivatives of $\varphi(L, \Sigma, \Phi, Q)$

Whenever there is no confusion, we denote $\varphi(L, \Sigma, \Phi, Q)$ simply by φ. The derivative of $\varphi(L, \Sigma, \Phi, Q)$ with respect to L is

$$\begin{aligned}
d_L(\varphi) &= d\left(-\frac{1}{2}\mathbf{tr}\left[\Sigma^{-1}(y-fL')'(y-fL')\right]\right)\\
&= -\frac{1}{2}\mathbf{tr}\{-\Sigma^{-1}(dL)f'(y-fL')+\Sigma^{-1}(y-fL')'(-f(dL)')\}\\
&= \frac{1}{2}\mathbf{tr}\{\Sigma^{-1}dLf'(y-fL')+\Sigma^{-1}(y-fL')'f(dL)'\}\\
&= \frac{1}{2}\mathbf{tr}\{f'(y-fL')\Sigma^{-1}dL+dLf'(y-fL')(\Sigma^{-1})'\}\\
&= \frac{1}{2}\mathbf{tr}\{f'(y-fL')((\Sigma^{-1})'+\Sigma^{-1})dL\}\\
&= \mathbf{tr}(\tilde{c}dL)
\end{aligned}$$

where

$$\tilde{c}=\frac{1}{2}f'(\mathbf{y}-fL')((\Sigma^{-1})'+\Sigma^{-1})$$

Taking the *vec* operation, we get

$$d\left(vec\left(-\frac{1}{2}\mathbf{tr}\left[\Sigma^{-1}(y-fL')'(y-fL')\right]\right)\right)=d(vec(\varphi))=(vec(\tilde{c})')'d(vec(L))$$

The first derivative of $\varphi(L, \Sigma, \Phi, Q)$ is

$$D_L(\varphi)=\left(vec\left(\left[\frac{1}{2}f'(y-fL')((\Sigma^{-1})'+\Sigma^{-1})\right]'\right)\right)'$$

Similarly, we have

$$D_\Sigma(\varphi) = \left(vec\left(-\frac{T-s}{2}\Sigma^{-1} + \frac{1}{2}\Sigma^{-1}(y - fL')'(y - fL)\Sigma^{-1}\right)'\right)'$$

$$D_\Phi(\varphi) = \left(vec\left(\left[\frac{1}{2}f'_{-1}(f_{+1} - f_{-1}\Phi')((Q^{-1})' + Q^{-1})\right]'\right)\right)'$$

$$D_Q(\varphi) = \left(vec\left(-\frac{T-h}{2}Q^{-1} + \frac{1}{2}Q^{-1}(f_{+1} - f_{-1}\Phi')'(f_{+1} - f_{-1}\Phi')Q^{-1}\right)'\right)'$$

The second-order derivatives of $\varphi(L, \Sigma, \Phi, Q)$
The first-order derivative of $\tilde{c}$ is

$$d\tilde{c} = d\left(\frac{1}{2}f'(y - fL')((\Sigma^{-1})' + \Sigma^{-1})\right) = -\frac{1}{2}f'f(dL)'((\Sigma^{-1})' + \Sigma^{-1})$$

And the second-order derivative is

$$\begin{aligned} d_L^2\varphi &= \mathbf{tr}(d\tilde{c} * dL) \\ &= \mathbf{tr}\left(-\frac{1}{2}f'f(dL)'((\Sigma^{-1})' + \Sigma^{-1})dL\right) \end{aligned}$$

Then, we have

$$D_{L,L}(\varphi) = -\frac{1}{2}(f'f \otimes ((\Sigma^{-1})' + \Sigma^{-1}))$$

$$H = G(T) = T', \quad T = S(\Sigma) = \frac{1}{2}f'(y - fL')((\Sigma^{-1})' + \Sigma^{-1})$$

$$D(G(T)) = K_{qN}$$

$$D(S(\Sigma)) = I_N \otimes (f'(y - fL')) \cdot \left(-\frac{1}{2}(K_{NN} + I_{NN})\right) \cdot ((\Sigma^{-1})' \otimes \Sigma^{-1})$$

$$DH(\Sigma) = (DG(T))(DS(\Sigma))$$

where K_{qm} is the commutation matrix for a matrix with q rows and N columns. Thus, we have

$$D_{L,\Sigma}(\varphi)=\frac{\partial D_L(\varphi)}{(\partial vec\Sigma)'}=(DG(T))(DS(\Sigma))$$

$$=K_{qN}\cdot I_N\otimes(f'(y-fL'))\cdot\left(-\frac{1}{2}(K_{NN}+I_{NN})\right)\cdot((\Sigma^{-1})'\otimes\Sigma^{-1})$$

$$D_{L,\Phi}(\varphi)=0$$

$$D_{L,Q}(\varphi)=0$$

$$D_{\Sigma,\Sigma}(\varphi)=K_{NN}\cdot\begin{pmatrix}\frac{T-s}{2}\cdot\frac{1}{2}((\Sigma^{-1})'\otimes\Sigma^{-1}+(\Sigma^{-1})'\otimes\Sigma^{-1})\\ -\frac{1}{2}\begin{pmatrix}(\Sigma^{-1}(y-fL')'(y-fL')\Sigma^{-1})'\otimes\Sigma^{-1}\\ +(\Sigma^{-1})'\otimes(\Sigma^{-1}(y-fL')'(y-fL')\Sigma^{-1})\end{pmatrix}\end{pmatrix}$$

$$D_{\Sigma,\Phi}(\varphi)=0$$

$$D_{\Sigma,Q}(\varphi)=0$$

$$D_{\Phi,Q}(\varphi)=K_{qq}\cdot(I_K\otimes f'_{-1}(f_{+1}-f_{-1}\Phi'))\cdot\left(-\frac{1}{2}(K_{qq}+I_{qq})\right)\cdot((Q^{-1})'\otimes Q^{-1})$$

$$D_{\Phi,\Phi}(\varphi)=-\frac{1}{2}(f'_{-1}f_{-1}\otimes((Q^{-1})'+Q^{-1}))$$

$$D_{Q,Q}(\varphi)=K_{KK}\left(\frac{T-s}{4}((Q^{-1})'\otimes Q^{-1}+(Q^{-1})'\otimes Q^{-1})-\frac{1}{2}M\right)$$

where

$$\begin{aligned}M=&Q^{-1}(f_{+1}-f_{-1}\Phi')'(f_{+1}-f_{-1}\Phi')Q^{-1'}\otimes Q^{-1}\\&+(Q^{-1})'\otimes(\Sigma^{-1}(f_{+1}-f_{-1}\Phi')'(f_{+1}-f_{-1}\Phi')Q^{-1})\end{aligned}$$

The special structure of the parameter matrices

Let

$$L^* = vec(\overline{L}), \quad \Sigma^* = diag(\Sigma), \quad \Phi^* = vec(\Phi), \quad Q^* = vech(Q)$$

where $\overline{L}$ is the last $(N\text{-}q) \times q$ block of L. We now obtain the derivative of these parameter matrices.

The first-order derivatives are as follows:

$$D_{L^*}(\varphi) = D_L(\varphi) \cdot D_{L^*}(L(L^*)) = D_L(\varphi) \cdot \dot{I}_{L^*}$$

$$D_{\Sigma^*}(\varphi) = D_\Sigma(\varphi) \cdot D_{\Sigma^*}(\Sigma(\Sigma^*)) = D_\Sigma(\varphi) \cdot \dot{I}_{\Sigma^*}$$

$$D_{\Phi^*}(\varphi) = D_\Phi(\varphi) \cdot \dot{I}_{\Phi^*}$$

$$D_{Q^*}(\varphi) = D_Q(\varphi) \cdot \dot{I}_{Q^*}$$

The second-order derivatives are as follows:

$$\begin{aligned}
D_{L^*,L^*}(\varphi) &= D_{L^*}(D_{L^*}(\varphi)) = D_{L^*}(D_L(\varphi) \cdot \dot{I}_{L^*}) \\
&= (\dot{I}'_{L^*} \otimes I_1) \cdot D_{L^*}(D_L(\varphi)) \\
&= (\dot{I}'_{L^*} \otimes I_1) \cdot D_{L,L}(\varphi) \cdot \dot{I}_{L^*}
\end{aligned}$$

$$\begin{aligned}
D_{L^*,\Sigma^*}(\varphi) &= D_{\Sigma^*}(D_{L^*}(\varphi)) = D_{\Sigma^*}(D_L(\varphi) \cdot \dot{I}_{L^*}) \\
&= (\dot{I}'_{L^*} \otimes I_1) \cdot D_{\Sigma^*}(D_L(\varphi)) \\
&= (\dot{I}'_{L^*} \otimes I_1) \cdot D_\Sigma(D_L(\varphi)) \cdot D_{\Sigma^*}(\Sigma(\Sigma^*)) \\
&= \dot{I}'_{L^*} \cdot D_{L,\Sigma}(\varphi) \cdot \dot{I}_{\Sigma^*}
\end{aligned}$$

$$D_{L^*,\Phi^*}(\varphi) = 0$$

$$D_{L^*,Q^*}(\varphi) = 0$$

$$\begin{aligned}
D_{\Sigma^*,\Sigma^*}(\varphi) &= D_{\Sigma^*}(D_{\Sigma^*}(\varphi)) = D_{\Sigma^*}(D_\Sigma(\varphi) \cdot \dot{I}_{\Sigma^*}) \\
&= \dot{I}'_{\Sigma^*} \otimes I_1 \cdot D_{\Sigma^*}(D_\Sigma(\varphi)) \\
&= \dot{I}'_{\Sigma^*} \cdot D_\Sigma(D_\Sigma(\varphi)) \cdot \dot{I}_{\Sigma^*}
\end{aligned}$$

$$D_{\Sigma^*,\Phi^*}(\varphi)=0$$

$$D_{\Sigma^*,Q^*}(\varphi)=0$$

$$D_{\Phi^*,\Phi^*}(\varphi)=\dot{I}'_{\Phi^*}\cdot(D_{\Phi,\Phi}(\varphi))\cdot\dot{I}_{\Phi^*}$$

$$D_{\Phi^*,Q^*}(\varphi)=\dot{I}'_{\Phi^*}\cdot(D_{\Phi,Q}(\varphi))\cdot\dot{I}_{Q^*}$$

$$D_{Q^*,Q^*}(\varphi)=\dot{I}'_{Q^*}\cdot D_{Q,Q}(\varphi)\cdot\dot{I}_{Q^*}$$

where $D_{L^*}(L(L^*))=\dot{I}_{L^*}$, $D_{\Sigma^*}(\Sigma(\Sigma^*))=\dot{I}_{\Sigma}$.
For $\dot{I}_{L^*}$ which is a block diagonal matrix, we have

$$\dot{I}_{L^*}=diag(P_1,P_2,\ldots,P_q)$$

where

$$P_i=\begin{bmatrix}0_{q\times(N-q)}\\ I_{N-q}\end{bmatrix}$$

And for $\dot{I}_{\Sigma^*}$, which is an $N^2\times N$ matrix whose nth column has 1 in the $((n-1)\times N+n)$th row and other elements are all zeros. For $\dot{I}_{\Phi^*}$, we have

$$\dot{I}_{\Phi^*}=I_{q^*q}$$

For $\dot{I}_{Q^*}$, we have

$$\dot{I}_{Q^*}=diag(R_1,R_2,\ldots R_k,\ldots,R_q)$$

where

$$R_k=\begin{bmatrix}0_{(k-1)\times(q-k+1)}\\ I_{q-k+1}\end{bmatrix}_{q\times(q-k+1)}$$

since Q is symmetric.

The first-order derivative matrix of the complete-data likelihood with respect to L^*,Σ^*,Φ^*,Q^* is

$$vec(\begin{bmatrix}D_{L^*}(\varphi) & D_{\Sigma^*}(\varphi) & D_{\Phi^*}(\varphi) & D_{Q^*}(\varphi)\end{bmatrix})$$

The second-order derivative matrix of the complete data likelihood with respect to $L^*, \Sigma^*, \Phi^*, Q^*$ is

$$\begin{bmatrix} D_{L^*,L^*}(\varphi) & D_{L^*,\Sigma^*}(\varphi) & 0 & 0 \\ D_{\Sigma^*,L^*}(\varphi) & D_{\Sigma^*,\Sigma^*}(\varphi) & 0 & 0 \\ 0 & 0 & D_{\Phi^*,\Phi^*}(\varphi) & D_{\Phi^*,Q^*}(\varphi) \\ 0 & 0 & D_{Q^*,\Phi^*}(\varphi) & D_{Q^*,Q^*}(\varphi) \end{bmatrix}$$

STABLE LIMIT THEORY FOR THE VARIANCE TARGETING ESTIMATOR

Igor Vaynman and Brendan K. Beare

Department of Economics, University of California – San Diego, La Jolla, CA, USA

ABSTRACT

The variance targeting estimator (VTE) for generalized autoregressive conditionally heteroskedastic (GARCH) processes has been proposed as a computationally simpler and misspecification-robust alternative to the quasi-maximum likelihood estimator (QMLE). In this paper we investigate the asymptotic behavior of the VTE when the stationary distribution of the GARCH process has infinite fourth moment. Existing studies of historical asset returns indicate that this may be a case of empirical relevance. Under suitable technical conditions, we establish a stable limit theory for the VTE, with the rate of convergence determined by the tails of the stationary distribution. This rate is slower than that achieved by the QMLE. The limit distribution of the VTE is nondegenerate but singular. We investigate the use of subsampling techniques for

Essays in Honor of Peter C. B. Phillips
Advances in Econometrics, Volume 33, 639–672

ISSN: 0731-9053/doi:10.1108/S0731-905320140000033018

inference, but find that finite sample performance is poor in empirically relevant scenarios.

Keywords: GARCH; variance targeting; heavy tails

JEL Classifications: C220; C580

1. INTRODUCTION

It is now widely recognized that the distributions of many economic and financial variables are heavy tailed. The relevance of heavy tailed laws for the study of price series was emphasized in early contributions by Mandelbrot (1963) and Fama (1963). Major theoretical advances in the study of heavy tailed phenomena were made over the following decades in various areas of applied mathematics, but it was perhaps not until a series of papers by P. C. B. Phillips and M. Loretan in the 1990s that these advances were brought into the mainstream of the econometric literature. Phillips (1990) studied the impact of infinite variance innovations on his now well-known nonparametric correction for serial dependence (Phillips, 1987) when testing for a unit root. Phillips and Loretan (1991) considered the behavior of the Durbin–Watson statistic in regression models with infinite variance residuals, while Phillips and Loretan (1995) considered the behavior of various diagnostic tests for covariance stationarity in the presence of heavy tails. Loretan and Phillips (1994) estimated the tail decay rates for various stock market and exchange rate return series. Their findings were broadly consistent with the return series having finite second moment but infinite fourth moment. In subsequent years there has been an enormous effort by economists and econometricians to better understand the impact of heavy tails on economic decision making and econometric procedures. Ibragimov (2009) provides a helpful discussion of much of this literature, and examines the profound implications of heavy tails for portfolio diversification strategies.

In this paper we are concerned with the impact of heavy tails on a popular estimator for the generalized autoregressive conditionally heteroskedastic (GARCH) model of Bollerslev (1986). GARCH models have been widely used to capture the time variation in volatility found in financial return series. Estimation of GARCH models is typically achieved by quasi-maximum likelihood estimation (QMLE) under a synthetic assumption of Gaussian innovations. There is a large literature examining the asymptotic properties of the QMLE when innovations have finite fourth moment; key papers include Weiss (1986), Lee and Hansen (1994), Lumsdaine (1996), Berkes, Horváth, and Kokoszka (2003), Francq and Zakoïan (2004), and Robinson and Zaffaroni (2006). In the more delicate case where the innovations have infinite fourth moment, Hall and Yao (2003) and Mikosch and Straumann (2006) established a stable limit theory for the QMLE. The monograph of Straumann (2005) provides a high level discussion of the asymptotic behavior of the QMLE in both the light and heavy tailed cases.

The variance targeting estimator (VTE) is a two-step estimation procedure for GARCH models that is sometimes used as an alternative to the QMLE. The method originates with Engle and Mezrich (1996) and was studied briefly by Kristensen and Linton (2004) and in more depth by Francq, Horváth, and Zakoïan (2011). It is based on a reparametrization of GARCH in which the unconditional variance takes the place of the volatility equation intercept. In the first step the unconditional variance is estimated by the sample variance. In the second step the remaining parameters are estimated by maximizing the restricted quasi-likelihood function given the unconditional variance estimated in the first step. The resulting estimator is therefore a hybrid of QMLE and the method of moments. While inefficient relative to the QMLE, the VTE has two useful properties: it is computationally faster than the QMLE, and it provides a consistent estimate of the unconditional variance even in the presence of model misspecification. This latter property is especially important, since accurate estimation of the unconditional variance is critical for policy relevant measures such as value-at-risk at medium to long horizons.

A useful analysis of the VTE in the case where the stationary distribution of the GARCH process has finite fourth moment is presented in Francq et al. (2011). However, there is to our knowledge no published paper that characterizes the asymptotic distribution of the VTE when the stationary distribution has infinite fourth moment. We provide such a characterization in this paper. Empirical results of Loretan and Phillips (1994) and others suggest that this case may be the relevant one for many financial applications. Moreover, the dynamic structure of GARCH processes is such that, even when innovations are Gaussian and therefore have finite moments of all orders, the fourth moment of the stationary distribution may be infinite. The link between the tail behavior of innovations and the tail behavior of the stationary distribution is provided by Kesten's theorem, as we will see later.

The primary difficulty in characterizing the behavior of the VTE when the fourth moment of the stationary distribution is infinite is that the central limit theorem is no longer applicable to the sample variance. Instead, a stable limit theory for the sample variance may be derived using point process techniques developed by Resnick (1987) for iid data, extended by Davis and Hsing (1995) and Davis and Mikosch (1998) to weakly dependent univariate and multivariate processes respectively, and applied by Mikosch and Stărică (2000) and Basrak, Davis, and Mikosch (2002) to GARCH processes. We find that the stable limit of the sample variance computed in the first step of the VTE dominates the asymptotic behavior of the parameter estimates computed in the second step of the VTE. The asymptotic distribution of the full VTE is nondegenerate but singular, and consists of a stable law distributed over a line in multidimensional space. The rate of convergence of the VTE to this distribution is determined by the tail behavior of the stationary distribution, and is necessarily slower than the rate of convergence of the QMLE, which is governed by the tail behavior of the innovations. This contrasts with the light tailed case, where Francq et al. (2011) have shown that the VTE and QMLE converge at the same rate. We investigate the use of subsampling to approximate the limiting stable law of the VTE, as in Politis, Romano, and Wolf (1999), but find that finite sample performance is poor in empirically relevant scenarios.

A recent working paper of Hill and Renault (2012) demonstrates that a tail trimmed version of the VTE may be asymptotically normal even in the presence of heavy tails. Since our results reflect somewhat negatively on the performance of the VTE under heavy tails, they point to the potential importance of techniques such as tail trimming that may reduce the sensitivity of the VTE to extreme realizations.

The remainder of the paper is organized as follows. In Section 2 we review known properties of GARCH processes, devoting particular attention to multivariate regular variation and to the weak convergence of GARCH-based point processes. This material has been developed largely outside the pages of econometrics journals, and we hope that some readers may find our brief review a useful entry point to the literature. Limit theory for VTE is presented in Section 3: we review known results for the light tailed case, and present new results for the heavy tailed case. We investigate the use of subsampling for inference in Section 4, and conclude in Section 5. Some proofs and technical lemmas are collected together in the Mathematical Appendix.

2. GARCH: DEFINITION AND PROPERTIES

Let $(\eta_t)_{t\in\mathbb{Z}}$ be an iid sequence of centered random variables, and let $p, q \in \mathbf{N}$. For notational convenience, we write η for η_t where appropriate.

A stationary sequence of pairs of random variables $(y_t, h_t)_{t\in\mathbb{Z}}$, with each h_t nonnegative, is said to be a GARCH(p, q) process with innovations (η_t) if it satisfies the equations

$$y_t = h_t\eta_t \tag{1}$$

$$h_t^2 = c + \sum_{i=1}^{p} a_i y_{t-i}^2 + \sum_{j=1}^{q} b_j h_{t-j}^2 \tag{2}$$

for all $t\in\mathbb{Z}$, and if it is nonanticipatory, meaning that each y_t can be represented as a measurable function of the current and past innovations $(\eta_s)_{s\leq t}$. We refer to (y_t) as the return process and (h_t) as the volatility process. The GARCH process is parameterized by $\boldsymbol{\theta}=(c,\ \boldsymbol{\lambda},\ P_\eta)$, where $\boldsymbol{\lambda}=(a_1,\ \ldots,\ a_p,\ b_1,\ \ldots,\ b_q)$, and P_η is the law of η. The parameter space is $\Gamma=\Gamma_1\times\Gamma_2\times\Gamma_3$, where $c\in\Gamma_1$, $\boldsymbol{\lambda}\in\Gamma_2$, and $P_\eta\in\Gamma_3$. We define Γ_1, Γ_2, and Γ_3 as follows.

(i) $\Gamma_1=(0,\ \infty)$.
(ii) $\Gamma_2=\left\{\boldsymbol{\lambda}\in[0,\infty)^{p+q} : \sum_{i=1}^{p} a_i + \sum_{j=1}^{q} b_j < 1 \quad \text{and} \quad \sum_{i=1}^{p} a_i > 0\right\}$.
(iii) $\Gamma_3=\{P_\eta : \mathbb{E}\eta=0,\ \mathbb{E}\,\eta^2=1,\ P_\eta$ has positive density on $\mathbb{R}$, and there exists $\kappa\in(1,\infty]$ such that $\mathbb{E}(\eta^2)^\kappa=\infty$ and $\mathbb{E}(\eta^2)^{\kappa'}<\infty$ for all $\kappa'\in[0,\ \kappa)\}$.

We next review known properties of GARCH(p,q) processes with $\boldsymbol{\theta}\in\Gamma$. More extensive reviews may be found in Lindner (2009) and Davis and Mikosch (2009).

2.1. Stochastic Recurrence Equation Representation

The GARCH(p,q) model can be nested in the more general framework of stochastic recurrence equations (SREs) in the following way. If q or p is less than 2, then embed the GARCH(p, q) process in a GARCH ($2\vee p, 2\vee q$) process with $a_i=0$ for $i > p$ and $b_j=0$ for $j>q$. Let $d=p+q-1$, and define the sequence of $d\times 1$ random vectors $(\mathbf{X}_t)_{t\in\mathbb{Z}}$ by

$$\mathbf{X}_t = (h_{t+1}^2,\ h_t^2, \ldots,\ h_{t-q+2}^2,\ y_t^2,\ y_{t-1}^2, \ldots,\ y_{t-p+2}^2)', \tag{3}$$

and the iid sequence of random $d\times d$ matrices $(\mathbf{A}_t)_{t\in\mathbb{Z}}$ and constant $d\times 1$ vector $\mathbf{B}$ by

$$\mathbf{A}_t = \begin{bmatrix} a_1\eta_t^2+b_1 & b_2 & \cdots & b_{q-1} & b_q & a_2 & \cdots & a_{p-1} & a_p \\ 1 & 0 & \cdots & 0 & 0 & 0 & \cdots & 0 & 0 \\ 0 & 1 & \cdots & 0 & 0 & 0 & \cdots & 0 & 0 \\ \vdots & \vdots & \ddots & \vdots & \vdots & \vdots & \ddots & \vdots & \vdots \\ 0 & 0 & \cdots & 1 & 0 & 0 & \cdots & 0 & 0 \\ \eta_t^2 & 0 & \cdots & 0 & 0 & 0 & \cdots & 0 & 0 \\ 0 & 0 & \cdots & 0 & 0 & 1 & \cdots & 0 & 0 \\ \vdots & \vdots & \ddots & \vdots & \vdots & \vdots & \ddots & \vdots & \vdots \\ 0 & 0 & \cdots & 0 & 0 & 0 & \cdots & 1 & 0 \end{bmatrix}, \quad \mathbf{B} = \begin{bmatrix} c \\ 0 \\ 0 \\ \vdots \\ 0 \\ 0 \\ 0 \\ \vdots \\ 0 \end{bmatrix}. \tag{4}$$

Then $\mathbf{X}_t$ satisfies the SRE

$$\mathbf{X}_t = \mathbf{A}_t \mathbf{X}_{t-1} + \mathbf{B}. \tag{5}$$

The SRE representation of the GARCH(p, q) model has been instrumental in providing general conditions for the existence of a stationary nonanticipatory solution to Eqs. (1) and (2), as well as establishing mixing conditions and describing the behavior of the tails of the marginal distributions of the squared returns y_t^2 and squared volatilities h_t^2. Building on results of Nelson (1990), Bougerol and Picard (1992) showed that if $c > 0$, there exists a unique stationary nonanticipatory solution to the SRE (5) if and only if

$$\gamma := \inf\left\{\frac{1}{n}\mathbb{E}\log\|\mathbf{A}_1\cdots\mathbf{A}_n\| : n \in \mathbb{N}\right\} < 0, \tag{6}$$

where $\|\cdot\|$ is the operator norm induced by some norm on $\mathbb{R}^d$. γ is referred to as the top Lyapunov exponent of $(\mathbf{A}_t)$, and its sign is invariant to the choice of norm on $\mathbb{R}^d$. When $\boldsymbol{\theta} \in \Gamma$ we have $\gamma < 0$, and the solution to Eq. (5) is given by

$$\mathbf{X}_t = \mathbf{B} + \sum_{k=1}^{\infty} \mathbf{A}_t \cdots \mathbf{A}_{t-k+1}\mathbf{B}. \tag{7}$$

As $(\mathbf{X}_t)$ is stationary, for convenience we will write $\mathbf{X}$ for $\mathbf{X}_t$ when appropriate. Boussama (1998, Theorem 3.4.2) showed that when P_η has positive density in a neighborhood of the origin, as it must when $\boldsymbol{\theta} \in \Gamma$, $(\mathbf{X}_t)$ is

β-mixing (absolutely regular), with an exponential decay rate of mixing coefficients. See Carrasco and Chen (2002) for further results on the mixing properties of GARCH(p,q) processes.

2.2. Parametrization by Unconditional Variance

When $\boldsymbol{\theta} \in \Gamma$ the unconditional variance of y_t is finite and given by

$$\sigma^2 : = \mathrm{Var}(y_t) = \mathbb{E}y_t^2 = c\left(1 - \sum_{i=1}^{p} a_i - \sum_{j=1}^{q} b_j\right)^{-1}. \tag{8}$$

It is therefore equivalent to parameterize the GARCH(p,q) model by $\boldsymbol{\theta} = (\sigma^2, \boldsymbol{\lambda}, P_\eta)$, and let $c(\sigma^2, \boldsymbol{\lambda}) = \sigma^2\left(1 - \sum_{i=1}^{p} a_i - \sum_{j=1}^{q} b_j\right)$. The existence of a finite unconditional variance is the primary reason to restrict the parameter space by requiring $\sum_{i=1}^{p} a_i + \sum_{j=1}^{q} b_j < 1$; this condition is not in fact necessary for the top Lyapunov exponent γ to be negative. A necessary but insufficient condition for $\gamma < 0$ is $\sum_{j=1}^{q} b_j < 1$ (Bougerol & Picard, 1992, Corollary 2.3). However, VTE is clearly not appropriate when $\mathbb{E}y_t^2 = \infty$, and hence we restrict the parameter space for $\boldsymbol{\lambda}$ to Γ_2.

2.3. Multivariate Regular Variation

Loosely, a random vector $\mathbf{X}$ exhibits multivariate regular variation if the tail probability decays like a power law in any direction. In the univariate case, regular variation is often defined in terms of the tail behavior of distribution functions, but in the multivariate case it is more natural to use convergence of measures.

We now briefly define vague convergence of Radon measures. A more detailed account of this subject may be found in Kallenberg (1983, pp. 168–171) or Resnick (1987, pp. 139–149). Let E be a locally compact second countable Hausdorff space equipped with a σ-algebra $\mathcal{E}$, and let $C_K^+(E)$ denote the class of all continuous functions $f: E \rightarrow \mathbb{R}_+$ with compact support. A measure μ on E is *Radon* if $\mu(A) < \infty$ for all relatively compact $A \in \mathcal{E}$. Let $M_+(E)$ denote the collection of Radon measures on E. A topology on $M_+(E)$ can be generated by using as a base the collection of finite intersections of sets $\{\mu \in M_+(E) : \int_E f \mathrm{d}\mu \in (s,t)\}$, $f \in C_K^+(E)$, $0<s<t<\infty$. This construction maps the usual topology of open intervals on $\mathbb{R}$ into a topology on $M_+(E)$ via the Lebesgue integral. The topology generated is known as the *vague topology*, and under this topology $M_+(E)$ is separable and completely metrizable (Kallenberg, 1983, Theorem 15.7.7). We write $\xrightarrow{v}$ to signify convergence in the vague topology, or *vague convergence*.

Note that vague convergence is a more general notion than weak convergence, which we denote by $\xrightarrow{w}$. The latter deals with classes of bounded measures on E, while measures in $M_+(E)$ need only be finite on relatively compact sets. Indeed, for bounded measures $\mu, \mu_1, \mu_2 ... \in M_+(E)$, $\mu_n \xrightarrow{w} \mu$ if and only if $\mu_n \xrightarrow{v} \mu$ and $\mu_n(E) \to \mu(E)$ (Kallenberg, 1983, Theorem 15.7.6).

We can now define multivariate regular variation in terms of the vague convergence of a sequence of Radon measures on the state space $E = \overline{\mathbb{R}}^d \backslash \{\mathbf{0}\}$ equipped with the Borel σ-algebra $\mathcal{E} = \mathcal{B}(\overline{\mathbb{R}}^d \backslash \{\mathbf{0}\})$, where $\overline{\mathbb{R}} = \mathbb{R} \cup \{-\infty, \infty\}$. In this space, Borel sets bounded away from $\mathbf{0}$ are relatively compact; this is the purpose of puncturing the usual space $\overline{\mathbb{R}}^d$ at the origin. An $\mathbb{R}^d$ valued random vector $\mathbf{X}$ is said to be *multivariate regularly varying* with index $\alpha \in (0,\infty)$ if the following condition is satisfied.

(i) There exists a sequence $(a_n) \uparrow \infty$ and a nonnull $\mu \in M_+(\overline{\mathbb{R}}^d \backslash \{\mathbf{0}\})$ such that

$$n\mathbb{P}(a_n^{-1}\mathbf{X} \in \cdot) \xrightarrow{v} \mu(\cdot) \quad \text{as } n \to \infty, \tag{9}$$

and $\mu(sB) = s^{-\alpha}\mu(B)$ for all $s > 0$ and all relatively compact $B \in \mathcal{B}(\overline{\mathbb{R}}_+^d \backslash \{\mathbf{0}\})$.

Alternatively, given a norm $|\cdot|$ on $\mathbb{R}^d$, we may define multivariate regular variation of $\mathbf{X}$ in terms of the weak convergence of a sequence of bounded measures on the unit sphere $\mathbb{S}^{d-1} = \{x \in \mathbb{R}^d : |x| = 1\}$.

(ii) There exists a probability measure Θ on $\mathbb{S}^{d-1}$ such that, for all $s > 0$,

$$\frac{\mathbb{P}(|\mathbf{X}| > sx, \mathbf{X}/|\mathbf{X}| \in \cdot)}{\mathbb{P}(|\mathbf{X}| > x)} \xrightarrow{w} s^{-\alpha}\Theta(\cdot) \quad \text{as } x \to \infty. \tag{10}$$

Conditions (i) and (ii), taken from Resnick (1986, p. 69), are equivalent. Further equivalent characterizations are given by Resnick (2004). Condition (i) illustrates nicely the utility of vague convergence when characterizing the tail behavior of $\mathbf{X}$: if $A \in \mathcal{B}(\overline{\mathbb{R}}^d \backslash \{\mathbf{0}\})$ is relatively compact, it is bounded away from $\mathbf{0}$, and so for large n the probability of the event $a_n^{-1}\mathbf{X} \in A$ depends only on the tail behavior of $\mathbf{X}$. The Radon measure μ in condition (i) satisfies $\mu\{x : |x| > s, x/|x| \in \cdot\} = cs^{-\alpha}\Theta(\cdot)$ for all $s > 0$, where

$c > 0$ and Θ is the probability measure in condition (ii). Θ is called the *spectral measure* of $\mathbf{X}$, and captures the tail dependency between the components of $\mathbf{X}$, as well as the relative likelihood of positive and negative extremes. We see from condition (ii) that when $\mathbf{X}$ is multivariate regularly varying with index α we have $\mathbb{P}(|\mathbf{X}|>x)=x^{-\alpha}L(x)$, where L is a slowly varying function.

The representation of the GARCH(p,q) model as a SRE provides insights into the tail behavior of $\mathbf{X}_t$ via the theory developed by Kesten (1973), as demonstrated in Basrak et al. (2002, Theorem 3.1). Although Kesten's theorems are stated in terms of univariate regular variation of linear combinations of $\mathbf{X}_t$, results of Basrak et al. (2002) and Boman and Lindskog (2009, Corollary 2) show the connection with multivariate regular variation. These results are summarized in the following theorem, adapted from Davis and Mikosch (2009, Theorem 1). The binary relation $\sim$ indicates that the ratio of two quantities tends to one as x (or n, depending on context) tends to infinity.

Theorem 1. Suppose $\boldsymbol{\theta} \in \Gamma$, and let $(\mathbf{X}_t)$ be the unique stationary solution to the SRE (5). Then, writing $\mathbf{X}$ for $\mathbf{X}_t$, the following statements are true.

(i) $\mathbf{X}$ is multivariate regularly varying with index $\alpha \in (1, \kappa)$.
(ii) For all $\mathbf{a} \in \mathbb{R}^d \setminus \{\mathbf{0}\}$, we have $\mathbb{P}(\mathbf{a}'\mathbf{X} > x) \sim w(\mathbf{a})x^{-\alpha}$ for some $w(\mathbf{a}) \in [0,\infty)$. Moreover, if $\mathbf{a} \in [0,\infty)^d \setminus \{\mathbf{0}\}$, then $w(\mathbf{a}) > 0$.
(iii) $\mathbb{P}(|\mathbf{X}|>x) \sim cx^{-\alpha}$ for some $c \in (0,\infty)$.

Note that the regular variation of $|\mathbf{X}|$ in Theorem 1(iii) is of the special kind where the slowly varying function $L(x)=x^{\alpha}\mathbb{P}(|\mathbf{X}|>x)$ converges to a constant. Let the sequence (a_n) satisfy

$$n\mathbb{P}(|\mathbf{X}|>a_n) \to 1 \quad \text{as } n \to \infty. \tag{11}$$

Then $\mathbb{P}(|\mathbf{X}|>x) \sim cx^{-\alpha}$ implies that $a_n \sim (cn)^{1/\alpha}$. Letting $\mathbf{a}$ in Theorem 1(iii) be the unit vector for the $(q + 1)$th or 2nd coordinate, we see that $n\mathbb{P}(y_t^2 > a_n) \to c_y$ and $n\mathbb{P}(h_t^2 > a_n) \to c_h$ for constants $c_y, c_h \in (0,\infty)$. The sequence (a_n) therefore controls the tails of y_t^2 and h_t^2, and in fact by Karamata's theorem (Bingham, Goldie, & Teugels, 1989, Theorem 1.5.11) we have

$$\frac{n}{a_n^{\gamma}}\mathbb{E}((y_t^2)^{\gamma}1(y_t^2 \le a_n\varepsilon)) \to \frac{c_y\alpha\varepsilon^{\gamma-\alpha}}{\gamma-\alpha}, \quad \frac{n}{a_n^{\gamma}}\mathbb{E}((h_t^2)^{\gamma}1(h_t^2 \le a_n\varepsilon)) \to \frac{c_h\alpha\varepsilon^{\gamma-\alpha}}{\gamma-\alpha} \tag{12}$$

as $n \to \infty$, for all $\gamma > \alpha$ and $\varepsilon > 0$.

In general, the index of regular variation α is given by Kesten's theorem as the unique solution to the equation

$$\lim_{n\to\infty} n^{-1}\log\mathbb{E}\|\mathbf{A}_n\cdots\mathbf{A}_1\|^{\alpha}=0. \tag{13}$$

For the GARCH(1,1) model (13) simplifies to $\mathbb{E}(a_1\eta^2+b_1)^{\alpha}=1$, which can be solved by simulation or direct computation of the expectation if (a_1,b_1,P_η) are known. However, it is difficult to determine α in the more general GARCH(p,q) model. That $\alpha > 1$ is clear since $\mathbb{E}y_t^2<\infty$, while $\alpha < \kappa$ follows from the fact that $\mathbb{E}\|\mathbf{A}_n\cdots\mathbf{A}_1\|^{\kappa'}=\infty$ for $\kappa' \geq \kappa$.

2.4. Point Process Convergence

Point process theory deals with the weak convergence of distributions over spaces of Radon counting measures, and is a powerful tool for establishing limit theory for weakly dependent sequences of random variables whose finite dimensional distributions are multivariate regularly varying. Here we review a few basic elements of this theory that are key to establishing certain results on VTE presented in the following section. For general information on point process theory, see Kallenberg (1983) and Resnick (1987).

Return for a moment to the general setting where our state space E is some locally compact second countable Hausdorff space equipped with a σ-algebra $\mathcal{E}$. A Radon measure $\mu\in M_+(E)$ is said to be a Radon *counting* measure on E if $\mu(A)\in\mathbb{N}\cup\{0,\infty\}$ for all $A\in\mathcal{E}$. Let $M_p(E)$ be the set of Radon counting measures on E, and equip $M_p(E)$ with the σ-algebra $\mathcal{M}_p(E)$ generated by the vague topology. Every $\mu\in M_p(E)$ can be represented as $\mu=\sum_{i\in I}\delta_{x_i}$, a countable sum of Dirac measures concentrated at the points $(x_i)_{i\in I}$ in E. These points need not be distinct: x_i has multiplicity $\mu(\{x_i\})$. If I is empty then μ is the null measure. Since μ is Radon, $(x_i)_{i\in I}$ can have no accumulation point in E.

A *point process* on E is a random element of $M_p(E)$; that is, a measurable map N from a probability space $(\Omega,\mathcal{F},\mathbb{P})$ to the measurable space $(M_p(E),\mathcal{M}_p(E))$. One very important class of point processes is the family of Poisson processes. A point process N is said to be a *Poisson process* if both of the following statements are true.

(i) For any $k\in\mathbb{N}$, if $A_1,\ldots, A_k\in\mathcal{E}$ are mutually disjoint sets, then $N(A_1),\ldots, N(A_k)$ are mutually independent random variables.

(ii) There is a Radon measure $\mu \in M_+(E)$, called the *intensity measure* of N, such that, for any $A \in \mathcal{E}$ and any $k \in \mathbb{N} \cup \{0\}$,

$$\mathbb{P}(N(A)=k)=\begin{cases} e^{-\mu(A)}\mu(A)^k/k! & \text{if } \mu(A)<\infty \\ 0 & \text{if } \mu(A)=\infty. \end{cases} \tag{14}$$

Given any $\mu \in M_+(E)$, we may construct a Poisson process on E with intensity measure μ, and its distribution is uniquely determined by μ (Resnick, 1987, Proposition 3.6).

Let us now consider the more concrete setting where we have state space $E=\overline{\mathbb{R}}_+^d\backslash\{\mathbf{0}\}$ equipped with the Borel σ-algebra $\mathcal{E}=\mathcal{B}(\overline{\mathbb{R}}_+^d\backslash\{\mathbf{0}\})$, where $\overline{\mathbb{R}}_+:=[0,\infty]$. The unique stationary solution $(\mathbf{X}_t)$ to the SRE (5) generates a sequence of point processes on $\overline{\mathbb{R}}_+^d\backslash\{\mathbf{0}\}$ given by

$$N_n=\sum_{t=1}^{n}\delta_{\mathbf{X}_t/a_n}, \quad n\in\mathbb{N}, \tag{15}$$

where (a_n) is a sequence satisfying Eq. (11). Basrak et al. (2002) have shown by appealing to Davis and Mikosch (1998, Theorem 2.8), itself a multivariate extension of Davis and Hsing (1995, Theorem 2.7), that the sequence of point processes N_n converges weakly to a limiting point process N on $\overline{\mathbb{R}}_+^d\backslash\{\mathbf{0}\}$. We summarize their results in the following theorem.

Theorem 2. Suppose $\boldsymbol{\theta}\in\Gamma$, and let $(\mathbf{X}_t)$ be the unique stationary solution to the SRE (5). Then the sequence of point processes N_n defined in Eq. (15) satisfies $N_n \xrightarrow{w} N$ in the vague topology, where N is a point process on $\overline{\mathbb{R}}_+^d\backslash\{\mathbf{0}\}$ admitting the representation

$$N=\sum_{i=1}^{\infty}\sum_{j=1}^{\infty}\delta_{P_i\mathbf{Q}_{ij}}. \tag{16}$$

Here,

(i) $\sum_{i=1}^{\infty}\delta_{P_i}$ is a Poisson process on $(0,\infty)$ with absolutely continuous intensity measure $\nu(dy)=\zeta\alpha y^{-\alpha-1}dy$, where $\alpha\in(1,\kappa)$ is the index of multivariate regular variation of $\mathbf{X}$, and $\zeta\in(0,1]$.

(ii) $\sum_{j=1}^{\infty}\delta_{\mathbf{Q}_{ij}}$, $i\in\mathbb{N}$, is an iid sequence of point processes on $\overline{\mathbb{R}}_+^d\backslash\{\mathbf{0}\}$ taking values in the set $\{\mu\in M_p(\overline{\mathbb{R}}_+^d\backslash\{\mathbf{0}\}):\mu(\{\mathbf{x}:|\mathbf{x}|>1\})=0$ and $\mu(\mathbb{S}^{d-1})>0\}$.

(iii) The point processes $\sum_{i=1}^{\infty}\delta_{P_i}$ and $\sum_{j=1}^{\infty}\delta_{\mathbf{Q}_{ij}}$, $i\in\mathbb{N}$, are mutually independent.

Eq. (16) is known as the *cluster representation* of N (Davis & Hsing, 1995, Corollary 2.4), while ζ is the *extremal index* of $(|\mathbf{X}_t|)$ (Leadbetter & Rootzén, 1988, pp. 438–440). The point process convergence $N_n \xrightarrow{w} N$ plays a key role in a number of studies of the asymptotic behavior of statistics based on heavy tailed GARCH processes. Davis and Mikosch (1998), Mikosch and Stărică (2000), and Basrak et al. (2002) used point process methods to establish a stable limit theory for the sample autocovariances and autocorrelations of ARCH(1), GARCH(1,1), and GARCH (p,q) processes respectively, while Mikosch and Straumann (2006) used point process methods to study the asymptotic behavior of the QMLE for GARCH(p,q) models when innovations are heavy tailed. In the following section we will use Theorem 2 to develop limit theory for a self-normalized version of the VTE for GARCH(p,q) models with heavy tailed marginal distributions.

3. LIMIT THEORY FOR THE VTE

In this section we investigate the asymptotic behavior of the VTE for the GARCH(p,q) model. We review known results on the VTE applicable when $\mathbb{E}y_t^4 < \infty$, and present new results covering the more problematic case $\mathbb{E}y_t^4 = \infty$.

3.1. Estimator and Assumptions

The VTE is a two-step estimator of the parameters $\boldsymbol{\nu} = (\sigma^2, \boldsymbol{\lambda})$ in the GARCH(p,q) model. In the first step, the mean square of the sample $y_1, \ldots, y_n$ is computed and used as an estimator for the unconditional variance, σ^2. Define the first step estimator as

$$\hat{\sigma}_n^2 = n^{-1} \sum_{t=1}^{n} y_t^2. \tag{17}$$

We will refer to $\hat{\sigma}_n^2$ as the *sample variance*. In the second step, the remaining parameters $\boldsymbol{\lambda}$ are estimated by maximizing the Gaussian quasi-likelihood of the sample, with σ^2 restricted to the estimate $\hat{\sigma}_n^2$ computed in the first step.

For $\boldsymbol{\nu}\in\Gamma_1\times\Gamma_2$ and $t=1,\dots, n$, define the *feasible* conditional volatility $\tilde{\mathfrak{h}}_t^2(\boldsymbol{\nu})$ as

$$\tilde{\mathfrak{h}}_t^2(\boldsymbol{\nu})=\begin{cases} c(\boldsymbol{\nu})+\sum_{i=1}^{p} a_i y_{t-i}^2+\sum_{j=1}^{q} b_j\tilde{\mathfrak{h}}_{t-j}^2(\boldsymbol{\nu}) & \text{if } p\vee q<t\leq n \\ \sigma^2 & \text{if } 1\leq t\leq p\vee q. \end{cases} \tag{18}$$

The second step Gaussian quasi-likelihood is

$$\mathcal{L}_n(\boldsymbol{\lambda})=\prod_{t=1}^{n}\frac{1}{\sqrt{2\pi\tilde{\mathfrak{h}}_t^2(\hat{\sigma}_n^2,\boldsymbol{\lambda})}}\exp\left(-\frac{y_t^2}{2\tilde{\mathfrak{h}}_t^2(\hat{\sigma}_n^2,\boldsymbol{\lambda})}\right), \tag{19}$$

and the quasi-log-likelihood is

$$\begin{aligned}\log\mathcal{L}_n(\boldsymbol{\lambda})&=-\frac{1}{2}\sum_{t=1}^{n}\left(\log 2\pi\tilde{\mathfrak{h}}_t^2(\hat{\sigma}_n^2,\boldsymbol{\lambda})+\frac{y_t^2}{\tilde{\mathfrak{h}}_t^2(\hat{\sigma}_n^2,\boldsymbol{\lambda})}\right)\\ &=\frac{n}{2}\log 2\pi-\frac{1}{2}\sum_{t=1}^{n}\tilde{\ell}_t(\hat{\sigma}_n^2,\boldsymbol{\lambda}),\end{aligned} \tag{20}$$

where

$$\tilde{\ell}_t(\boldsymbol{\nu})=\log\tilde{\mathfrak{h}}_t^2(\boldsymbol{\nu})+\frac{y_t^2}{\tilde{\mathfrak{h}}_t^2(\boldsymbol{\nu})}. \tag{21}$$

The second step estimator $\hat{\boldsymbol{\lambda}}_n$ is given by any measurable solution of

$$\log\mathcal{L}_n(\hat{\boldsymbol{\lambda}}_n)=\max_{\lambda\in\Lambda}\log\mathcal{L}_n(\boldsymbol{\lambda}), \tag{22}$$

where the solution space $\Lambda\subset\Gamma_2$ satisfies Assumption 1 below. The *variance targeting estimator* is then $\hat{\boldsymbol{\nu}}_n=(\hat{\sigma}_n^2,\hat{\boldsymbol{\lambda}}_n)$.

Let c_0, σ_0^2, (a_{0i}), (b_{0j}), and $P_{\eta,0}$ denote the true values of the unknown parameters c, σ^2, (a_i), (b_j), and P_η respectively, and let $\boldsymbol{\lambda}_0=(a_{01},\dots, a_{0p}, b_{01},\dots, b_{0q})$, $\boldsymbol{\nu}_0=(\sigma_0^2,\boldsymbol{\lambda}_0)$, and $\boldsymbol{\theta}_0=(\boldsymbol{\nu}_0,P_{\eta,0})$. We impose the following conditions on $\boldsymbol{\theta}_0$ and Λ.

Assumption 1. (i) $\boldsymbol{\theta}_0 \in \Gamma$. (ii) Λ is a compact subset of Γ_2 whose interior contains $\boldsymbol{\lambda}_0$. (iii) $\mathscr{A}(x) = \sum_{i=1}^{p} a_{0i} x^i$ and $\mathcal{B}(x) = 1 - \sum_{j=1}^{q} b_{0j} x^j$ are coprime in the set of polynomials with real coefficients.

Part (i) of Assumption 1 suffices for the various nice properties of GARCH processes discussed in Section 2, while conditions resembling (ii) are a standard ingredient for the study of extremum estimators. Condition (iii) is an identification condition used by Berkes et al. (2003, Theorem 2.5) to rule out observationally equivalent submodels of the GARCH(p,q) specification.

3.2. Weak Convergence of the VTE

Strong consistency of the VTE has been shown by Francq et al. (2011, Theorem 2.1) under conditions more general than Assumption 1. We will study weak convergence of suitable normalizations of the VTE, paying particular attention to the self-normalized quantity

$$\boldsymbol{S}_n = \frac{\sqrt{n}(\hat{\boldsymbol{\nu}}_n - \boldsymbol{\nu}_0)}{\tau_n}, \quad \text{where} \quad \tau_n^2 = \frac{1}{n}\sum_{t=1}^{n} y_t^4. \tag{23}$$

Since $\boldsymbol{\theta}_0 \in \Gamma$, Theorem 1 implies that y_t^2 is regularly varying with index $\alpha \in (1,\infty)$. Normalization of $n^{1/2}(\hat{\boldsymbol{\nu}}_n - \boldsymbol{\nu}_0)$ by τ_n is useful because the rate at which $\hat{\boldsymbol{\nu}}_n$ converges to $\boldsymbol{\nu}_0$ depends on α. If $\alpha \in (2,\infty)$ we have $\mathbb{E}y_t^4 < \infty$. In this case, $\hat{\boldsymbol{\nu}}_n$ converges to $\boldsymbol{\nu}_0$ at the rate $n^{1/2}$ and τ_n converges to a nonzero finite limit, so that $\boldsymbol{S}_n$ has a nondegenerate weak limit. On the other hand, if $\alpha \in (1,2)$ we have $\mathbb{E}y_t^4 = \infty$. We will see that in this case $\hat{\boldsymbol{\nu}}_n$ converges to $\boldsymbol{\nu}_0$ at a rate slower than $n^{1/2}$, but τ_n diverges to infinity at just the right rate to ensure that $\boldsymbol{S}_n$ continues to have a nondegenerate weak limit. This facilitates the use of subsampling techniques for inference (Politis et al., 1999) that do not require α to be estimated, as we will see in Section 4. Following related papers on heavy tailed GARCH processes by Davis and Mikosch (1998), Mikosch and Stărică (2000), and Basrak et al. (2002), we exclude from consideration the borderline case $\alpha = 2$, where y_t^2 has infinite variance and yet remains in the domain of attraction of the normal distribution. Significant additional technical challenges arise when $\alpha = 2$.

The case $\mathbb{E}y_t^4 = \infty$ is not merely an intellectual curiosity, and occurs for empirically plausible parameter values even if the innovations (η_t) are assumed to be Gaussian. In Fig. 1 we partition the parameter space of the stationary GARCH(1,1) model according to whether $\mathbb{E}y_t^4 < \infty$ or $\mathbb{E}y_t^4 = \infty$; the former is true if and only if $\mathbb{E}(a_1\eta^2 + b_1)^2 < 1$. The partition displayed in

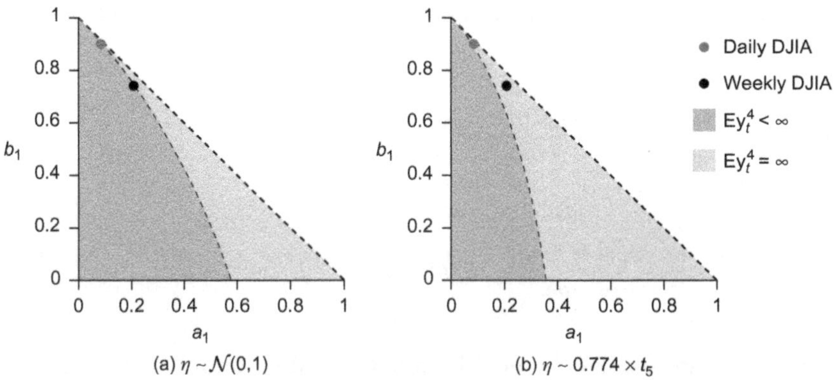

Fig. 1. Regions of the GARCH(1,1) parameter space in which $\mathbb{E}y_t^4$ is finite or infinite. *Note*: The partition of the parameter space is valid for $\mathbb{E}\eta^4 = 3$ in panel (a), and for $\mathbb{E}\eta^4 \approx 7.83$ in panel (b). Parameters for daily or weekly returns on the Dow Jones Industrial Average index are the QMLEs reported by Francq et al. (2011, Tables 6–7).

panel (a) obtains when $\eta \sim \mathcal{N}(0,1)$ (or $\mathbb{E}\eta^4 = 3$), while the partition in panel (b) is valid for $\eta \sim 0.774 \times t_5$ (or $\mathbb{E}\eta^4 \approx 7.83$). We identify points in the parameter space corresponding to estimates reported by Francq et al. (2011) for daily and weekly returns on the Dow Jones Industrial Average (DJIA) index. Even in panel (a), where the innovation density is standard normal, we see that $\mathbb{E}y_t^4 = \infty$ over a large region of the parameter space. Moreover, the parameter estimates for daily and weekly DJIA returns lie extremely close to the threshold of the regions of finite and infinite fourth moment. In panel (b), where the innovation distribution is heavier tailed, the region in which $\mathbb{E}y_t^4 = \infty$ takes up a larger share of the parameter space. The parameter estimates for weekly DJIA returns now lie squarely within the region where $\mathbb{E}y_t^4 = \infty$, while the estimates for daily returns remain close to the threshold.

3.2.1. Preliminary Results

We shall review some useful preliminary results that hold regardless of whether $\mathbb{E}y_t^4 < \infty$ or $\mathbb{E}y_t^4 = \infty$. Since $\hat{\boldsymbol{\lambda}}_n$ is strongly consistent for $\boldsymbol{\lambda}_0$, and $\boldsymbol{\lambda}_0$ lies in the interior of Λ, we know that, for sufficiently large n, $\hat{\boldsymbol{\lambda}}_n$ solves the first order condition

$$\mathbf{0} = \frac{\partial}{\partial \boldsymbol{\lambda}} \log \mathcal{L}_n(\hat{\boldsymbol{\lambda}}_n) = -\frac{1}{2} \sum_{t=1}^{n} \frac{\partial \tilde{\ell}_t(\hat{\boldsymbol{\nu}}_n)}{\partial \boldsymbol{\lambda}}. \tag{24}$$

For each $i=1,\ldots,p+q$, a Taylor expansion of $\partial\tilde{\ell}_t(\hat{\boldsymbol{\nu}}_n)/\partial\lambda_i$ around $\boldsymbol{\nu}=\boldsymbol{\nu}_0$ yields

$$0=\sum_{t=1}^{n}\left(\frac{\partial\tilde{\ell}_t(\boldsymbol{\nu}_0)}{\partial\lambda_i}+\frac{\partial^2\tilde{\ell}_t(\boldsymbol{\nu}_i^*)}{\partial\lambda_i\partial\boldsymbol{\nu}'}(\hat{\boldsymbol{\nu}}_n-\boldsymbol{\nu}_0)\right) \tag{25}$$

$$=\sum_{t=1}^{n}\frac{\partial\tilde{\ell}_t(\boldsymbol{\nu}_0)}{\partial\lambda_i}+\boldsymbol{J}_n^{(i)}n(\hat{\boldsymbol{\lambda}}_n-\boldsymbol{\lambda}_0)+K_n^{(i)}n(\hat{\sigma}_n^2-\sigma_0^2), \tag{26}$$

where $\boldsymbol{\nu}_i^*$ lies on the line segment between $\hat{\boldsymbol{\nu}}_n$ and $\boldsymbol{\nu}_0$, and

$$\boldsymbol{J}_n^{(i)}=\frac{1}{n}\sum_{t=1}^{n}\frac{\partial^2\tilde{\ell}_t(\boldsymbol{\nu}_i^*)}{\partial\lambda_i\partial\boldsymbol{\lambda}'},\quad K_n^{(i)}=\frac{1}{n}\sum_{t=1}^{n}\frac{\partial^2\tilde{\ell}_t(\boldsymbol{\nu}_i^*)}{\partial\lambda_i\partial\sigma^2}. \tag{27}$$

Let $\boldsymbol{J}_n$ denote the $(p+q)\times(p+q)$ matrix with ith row $\boldsymbol{J}_n^{(i)}$, and let $\boldsymbol{K}_n$ denote the $(p+q)\times 1$ vector with ith element $K_n^{(i)}$.

To examine the asymptotic behavior of $\hat{\boldsymbol{\lambda}}_n$, it is useful to approximate the sequences $(\tilde{\mathfrak{h}}_t(\boldsymbol{\nu}))$ and $(\tilde{\ell}_t(\boldsymbol{\nu}))$ by stationary ergodic sequences. To that end, define the *infeasible* conditional volatility as the unique stationary solution to

$$\mathfrak{h}_t^2(\boldsymbol{\nu})=c(\boldsymbol{\nu})+\sum_{i=1}^{p}a_iy_{t-i}^2+\sum_{j=1}^{q}b_j\mathfrak{h}_{t-j}^2(\boldsymbol{\nu}), \tag{28}$$

and note that $\mathfrak{h}_t(\boldsymbol{\nu}_0)=h_t^2$. Also define $\ell_t(\boldsymbol{\nu})$, the infeasible analog to $\tilde{\ell}_t(\boldsymbol{\nu})$, as

$$\ell_t(\boldsymbol{\nu})=\log\mathfrak{h}_t^2(\boldsymbol{\nu})+\frac{y_t^2}{\mathfrak{h}_t^2(\boldsymbol{\nu})}. \tag{29}$$

Lemma 1. Under Assumption 1, $\boldsymbol{J}_n\overset{a.s.}{\to}\boldsymbol{J}$ and $\boldsymbol{K}_n\overset{a.s.}{\to}\boldsymbol{K}$ as $n\to\infty$, where

$$\boldsymbol{J}=\mathbb{E}\left(\frac{\partial^2\ell_t(\boldsymbol{\nu}_0)}{\partial\boldsymbol{\lambda}\partial\boldsymbol{\lambda}'}\right),\quad \boldsymbol{K}=\mathbb{E}\left(\frac{\partial^2\ell_t(\boldsymbol{\nu}_0)}{\partial\boldsymbol{\lambda}\partial\sigma^2}\right). \tag{30}$$

Further, the matrix $\boldsymbol{J}$ is nonsingular.

Lemma 1 follows from the proof of Francq and Zakoïan (2004, Theorem 2.2), specifically items (ii), (iv), and (vi). Although Francq and Zakoïan assume that $\mathbb{E}\eta^4 < \infty$, this assumption is not used to show the claims of Lemma 1. The parametrization used by Francq and Zakoïan is $(c,\boldsymbol{\lambda})$, but their arguments apply directly to our equivalent parametrization $(\sigma^2,\boldsymbol{\lambda})$. Nonsingularity of $\boldsymbol{J}$ depends critically on the identification condition given in Assumption 1(iii).

3.2.2. Weak Convergence with Finite Fourth Moment

When $\mathbb{E}y_t^4 < \infty$, a central limit theorem for martingale difference sequences may be used to demonstrate that the VTE converges at the rate $n^{1/2}$ to a Gaussian limit. The following theorem is a slightly modified version of Francq et al. (2011, Theorem 2.1), and uses the fact that $\tau_n^2 \overset{a.s.}{\to} \mathbb{E}y_t^4 = (\mathbb{E}h_t^4)(\mathbb{E}\eta_t^4)$ by the ergodic theorem.

Theorem 3. Under Assumption 1, if $\mathbb{E}y_t^4 < \infty$ then

$$\sqrt{n}(\hat{\boldsymbol{\nu}}_n - \boldsymbol{\nu}_0) \overset{w}{\to} \mathcal{N}\left(\mathbf{0}, (\mathbb{E}\eta_t^4 - 1)\boldsymbol{\Sigma}\right) \quad \text{and} \quad \boldsymbol{S}_n \overset{w}{\to} \mathcal{N}\left(\mathbf{0}, \left(\frac{1}{\mathbb{E}h_t^4} - \frac{1}{\mathbb{E}y_t^4}\right)\boldsymbol{\Sigma}\right),$$

where the nonsingular matrix $\boldsymbol{\Sigma}$ is given by

$$\boldsymbol{\Sigma} = \begin{bmatrix} D & -D\boldsymbol{K}'\boldsymbol{J}^{-1} \\ -D\boldsymbol{J}^{-1}\boldsymbol{K} & \boldsymbol{J}^{-1} + D\boldsymbol{J}^{-1}\boldsymbol{K}\boldsymbol{K}'\boldsymbol{J}^{-1} \end{bmatrix}, \quad D = C^2\mathbb{E}h_t^4,$$

$$C = \frac{\sigma_0^2}{c_0}\left(1 - \sum_{j=1}^{q} b_{0j}\right).$$

For details of the proof, see Francq et al. (2011). There it is shown further that the VTE is asymptotically less efficient than the QMLE, which also converges at the rate $n^{1/2}$ to a Gaussian limit.

3.2.3. Weak Convergence with Infinite Fourth Moment

When $\mathbb{E}y_t^4 = \infty$, the results of Francq et al. (2011) establishing asymptotic normality of the VTE are no longer applicable. We will show that a suitable normalization of the VTE nevertheless converges weakly to a stable limit. As discussed earlier, we focus on the case where the index of regular variation α appearing in Theorem 1 satisfies $\alpha \in (1,2)$, and rule out the troublesome borderline case $\alpha = 2$.

Let (a_n) be a sequence satisfying Eq. (11), and define

$$U_n = a_n^{-1} \sum_{t=1}^{n} (y_t^2 - \mathbb{E}y_t^2), \quad V_n = a_n^{-2} \sum_{t=1}^{n} y_t^4. \tag{31}$$

Recall that $a_n \sim cn^{1/\alpha}$ for some $c > 0$. A random variable X is said to be *α-stable* if it has characteristic function

$$\mathbb{E}\ \exp(itX) = \begin{cases} \exp\left(i\mu t - |\varsigma t|^{\alpha}\ (1 - i\beta \mathrm{sgn}(t) \tan(\pi\alpha/2))\right) & \text{if } \alpha \neq 1 \\ \exp\left(i\mu t - |\varsigma t|\ (1 + i\beta(2/\pi)\mathrm{sgn}(t)\ln|t|)\right) & \text{if } \alpha = 1. \end{cases} \tag{32}$$

The parameters μ, ς, and β signify location, scale, and skew respectively. See Samorodnitsky and Taqqu (1994) for further discussion of stable distributions.

Theorem 4. Under Assumption 1, if $\alpha \in (1,2)$ then

$$(U_n, V_n) \overset{w}{\to} (U, V), \tag{33}$$

where U is a nondegenerate α-stable random variable and V is a strictly positive $\alpha/2$-stable random variable.

Results similar to Theorem 4 have appeared in prior literature. Basrak et al. (2002, Theorem 3.6) proved that $U_n \overset{w}{\to} U$ under the additional requirement that $\mathbb{E}\eta^4 < \infty$, which is assumed in Eq. (3.5) in their paper. Similar results were proved by Davis and Mikosch (1998) and Mikosch and Stărică (2000) for the ARCH(1) and GARCH(1,1) models respectively. Here we relax the requirement that $\mathbb{E}\eta^4 < \infty$ by appealing to a moment inequality for martingales due to von Bahr and Esseen (1965). Another result similar to Theorem 4 appeared in Kokoszka and Wolf (2004, Theorem 2), but imposes a symmetry condition that makes it inapplicable here due to the nonnegativity of y_t^2.

We now give a brief proof of Theorem 4, relegating details to technical lemmas in the Mathematical Appendix. The main ideas are due to Davis and Hsing (1995), and provide a nice illustration of the utility of the point process methods discussed in Section 2.4.

Proof of Theorem 4. Following Basrak et al. (2002, pp. 110–111), we begin by noting that $U_n = U_n^* + o_p(1)$, where

$$U_n^* = Ca_n^{-1} \sum_{t=1}^{n} h_t^2(\eta_t^2 - 1), \tag{34}$$

and C was defined in Theorem 3. To isolate the effect of the extreme realizations of y_t^2 and h_t^2 on (U_n^*, V_n), we consider the censored partial sums

$$U_{n\varepsilon}^* = Ca_n^{-1} \sum_{t=1}^{n} h_t^2(\eta_t^2 - 1)1(h_t^2 > \varepsilon a_n), \quad V_{n\varepsilon} = a_n^{-2} \sum_{t=1}^{n} y_t^4 1(y_t^2 > \varepsilon a_n), \tag{35}$$

where $\varepsilon > 0$. Observe that $(U_{n\varepsilon}^*, V_{n\varepsilon}) = T_\varepsilon(N_n)$, where N_n is the point process defined in Eq. (15) and $T_\varepsilon : M_p(\overline{\mathbb{R}}_+^d \backslash \{\mathbf{0}\}) \to \mathbb{R}^2$ is the map

$$T_\varepsilon\left(\sum_{i=1}^{\infty} \delta_{\mathbf{x}_i}\right) = \left(C \sum_{i=1}^{\infty} (x_{i,q+1} - x_{i,2})1(x_{i,2} > \varepsilon), \sum_{i=1}^{\infty} x_{i,q+1}^2 1(x_{i,q+1} > \varepsilon)\right). \tag{36}$$

Theorem 2 states that $N_n \xrightarrow{w} N$, where N satisfies the cluster representation (16). Thanks to the ε-trimming in Eq. (36), it can be shown (see Lemma A.2) that T_ε is continuous on a subset of $M_p(\overline{\mathbb{R}}_+^d \backslash \{\mathbf{0}\})$ inhabited by N with probability one, and so an application of the continuous mapping theorem yields

$$(U_{n\varepsilon}^*, V_{n\varepsilon}) \xrightarrow{w} T_\varepsilon(N) \quad \text{as } n \to \infty. \tag{37}$$

Careful inspection of the characteristic function of $T_\varepsilon(N)$ (see Lemma A.3) reveals that

$$T_\varepsilon(N) \xrightarrow{w} (U, V) \quad \text{as } \varepsilon \to 0. \tag{38}$$

A result of Billingsley (1968, Theorem 3.2) allows us to combine Eqs. (37) and (38) to obtain $(U_n, V_n) \xrightarrow{w} (U, V)$ as $n \to \infty$, provided that the censoring of partial sums is asymptotically negligible in the sense that, for any $\delta > 0$,

$$\lim_{\varepsilon \to 0} \limsup_{n \to \infty} \mathbb{P}(|U_n^* - U_{n\varepsilon}^*| \geq \delta) = 0 \tag{39}$$

and

$$\lim_{\epsilon\to 0}\limsup_{n\to\infty}\mathbb{P}(|V_n - V_{n\varepsilon}|\geq\delta)=0. \tag{40}$$

Eqs. (39) and (40) can be proved (see Lemma A.1) using Karamata's theorem and a moment inequality of von Bahr and Esseen (1965). ■

The following corollary to Theorem 4 may be obtained by writing $n^{1/2}(\hat{\sigma}_n^2 - \sigma_0^2)/\tau_n = U_n/V_n^{1/2}$ and applying the continuous mapping theorem.

Corollary 1. Under Assumption 1, if $\alpha\in(1,2)$ then

$$\frac{\sqrt{n}(\hat{\sigma}_n^2-\sigma_0^2)}{\tau_n}\xrightarrow{w} W := U/V^{1/2}. \tag{41}$$

Comparing Theorem 4 and Corollary 1, we see that normalizing by τ_n has the effect of eliminating the unknown scaling sequence (a_n). The limiting distribution W is unknown, but may in principle be approximated using subsampling, as we will see in the next section.

Having established the limiting behavior of the sample variance computed in the first step of the variance targeting method, we proceed to the second step in which the Gaussian quasi-likelihood is maximized subject to $\sigma^2 = \hat{\sigma}_n^2$. Rearranging the Taylor expansion (26), we obtain

$$na_n^{-1}(\hat{\boldsymbol{\lambda}}_n - \boldsymbol{\lambda}_0) = -\boldsymbol{J}_n^{-1}\boldsymbol{K}_n na_n^{-1}(\hat{\sigma}_n^2-\sigma_0^2) - \boldsymbol{J}_n^{-1}na_n^{-1}\boldsymbol{Y}_n, \tag{42}$$

where $\boldsymbol{J}_n$ is a.s. invertible for large enough n, and

$$\boldsymbol{Y}_n = \frac{1}{n}\sum_{t=1}^{n}\frac{\partial\tilde{\ell}_t(\boldsymbol{\nu}_0)}{\partial\boldsymbol{\lambda}}. \tag{43}$$

Lemma 1 ensures that $\boldsymbol{J}_n^{-1}\boldsymbol{K}_n \xrightarrow{a.s.} \boldsymbol{J}^{-1}\boldsymbol{K}$ and $\boldsymbol{J}_n^{-1}\xrightarrow{a.s.}\boldsymbol{J}^{-1}$, while Theorem 4 ensures that, when $\alpha\in(1,2)$, $na_n^{-1}(\hat{\sigma}_n^2-\sigma_0^2)\xrightarrow{w} U$. It may also be shown that $\boldsymbol{Y}_n$ converges to zero at a rate determined by the index κ characterizing the tail behavior of the squared innovations η^2. This rate turns out to be faster than na_n^{-1}, so $na_n^{-1}\boldsymbol{Y}_n$ vanishes, and the limit distribution of the normalized VTE concentrates on a line in $\mathbb{R}^{p+q+1}$.

Theorem 5. Under Assumption 1, if $\alpha \in (1,2)$ then

$$na_n^{-1}(\hat{\boldsymbol{\nu}}_n - \boldsymbol{\nu}_0) \xrightarrow{w} \begin{bmatrix} 1 \\ -\boldsymbol{J}^{-1}\boldsymbol{K} \end{bmatrix} U \quad \text{and} \quad \boldsymbol{S}_n \xrightarrow{w} \begin{bmatrix} 1 \\ -\boldsymbol{J}^{-1}\boldsymbol{K} \end{bmatrix} W, \tag{44}$$

where U and W are the weak limits in Theorem 4 and Corollary 1.

Theorem 5 is proved in the Mathematical Appendix. A consequence of Theorem 5 is that, if $\alpha \in (1,2)$ and $\boldsymbol{J}^{-1}\boldsymbol{K}$ has nonzero elements, then the VTE is consistent at the rate $n^{1-1/\alpha}$. This compares unfavorably to the rate of consistency achieved by the QMLE, shown by Mikosch and Straumann (2006) under similar technical conditions to be $n^{1/2}$ if $\kappa > 2$ or $n^{1-1/\kappa}L(n)$ if $\kappa \in (1,2)$, for some slowly varying L. No such discrepancy arises when $\alpha > 2$: as discussed earlier, Francq et al. (2011) showed that the VTE and QMLE are both consistent at the rate $n^{1/2}$. Since $\kappa > \alpha$, our results indicate that the efficiency loss associated with the VTE may be more severe in the heavy tailed case.

4. INFERENCE VIA SUBSAMPLING

We have seen that the Gaussian limit theory established for the VTE by Francq et al. (2011) breaks down in the heavy tailed case $\alpha \in (1,2)$. In this section we investigate the use of subsampling methods to assign robust confidence intervals to the VTE. We describe the construction of subsampling confidence intervals in Section 4.1, and numerically assess their finite sample performance in Section 4.2.

4.1. Construction of Subsampling Confidence Intervals

Theorems 3 and 5 indicate that the elements of the self-normalized quantity $\boldsymbol{S}_n$ converge weakly to what are typically nondegenerate limit distributions. As discussed by Politis et al. (1999, chap.11), subsampling can be used to estimate these limit distributions without having to first estimate the rate of convergence of the sample variance. For $i = 1,\ldots, p+q+1$, let $\nu_0^{(i)}$ denote the ith element of $\boldsymbol{\nu}_0$, let $S_n^{(i)}$ denote the ith element of $\boldsymbol{S}_n$, and let $F_n^{(i)}$ denote the cdf of $S_n^{(i)}$. Let $m = m_n$ be a sequence of block sizes satisfying $m \to \infty$ and $m/n \to 0$ as $n \to \infty$, and let $\hat{\boldsymbol{\nu}}_{nt}$ be the VTE of $\boldsymbol{\nu}_0$ computed using the block of observations $(y_t, \ldots, y_{t+m-1})$. The subsampled version of $S_n^{(i)}$ for this block of observations is given by $S_{nt}^{(i)} = m^{1/2}(\hat{\nu}_{nt}^{(i)} - \hat{\nu}_n^{(i)})/\tau_{nt}$, where $\tau_{nt}^2 = m^{-1}\sum_{j=t}^{t+m-1} y_j^4$, and $\hat{\nu}_{nt}^{(i)}$ is the ith element of $\hat{\boldsymbol{\nu}}_{nt}$. Our subsampling approximation to $F_n^{(i)}$ is

$$\hat{F}_n^{(i)}(x) = \frac{1}{n-m+1}\sum_{t=1}^{n-m+1} 1(S_{nt}^{(i)} \leq x), \quad x \in \mathbb{R}. \tag{45}$$

For $s \in (0,1)$, let $c_n^{(i)}(s) = \inf\{x : \hat{F}_n^{(i)}(x) \geq s\}$, the s-quantile of $\hat{F}_n^{(i)}$. The next result provides an asymptotic justification for using $c_n^{(i)}(s)$ to form confidence intervals for $\nu_0^{(i)}$.

Theorem 6. Under Assumption 1, if $\alpha \in (1,2) \cup (2,\infty)$ then for $i = 1, \ldots, p + q + 1$ and $s \in (0,1)$ we have

$$\lim_{n\to\infty} \mathbb{P}(S_n^{(i)} \leq c_n(1-s)) = 1 - s, \tag{46}$$

provided that the $(i-1)$th element of $\boldsymbol{J}^{-1}\boldsymbol{K}$ is nonzero in the case that $i \geq 2$ and $\alpha \in (1,2)$.

Theorem 6 is proved in the Mathematical Appendix. The condition on $\boldsymbol{J}^{-1}\boldsymbol{K}$ is made to rule out the possibility that the line on which the asymptotic distribution of the VTE concentrates is perfectly orthogonal to one of the coordinate axes. In this case we would have a degenerate limit for the corresponding element of $\boldsymbol{S}_n$, making the usual justification for subsampling inapplicable. Excluding this possibility, Theorem 6 implies that the equal tailed confidence interval for $\nu_0^{(i)}$,

$$[\hat{\nu}_n^{(i)} - n^{-1/2}\tau_n c_n^{(i)}(1-s/2), \hat{\nu}_n^{(i)} + n^{-1/2}\tau_n c_n^{(i)}(s/2)], \tag{47}$$

has limiting coverage probability equal to the nominal level $1-s$. A simple modification of Theorem 6 may be used to show that the symmetric confidence interval for $\nu_0^{(i)}$,

$$[\hat{\nu}_n^{(i)} - n^{-1/2}\tau_n \tilde{c}_n^{(i)}(1-s), \hat{\nu}_n^{(i)} + n^{-1/2}\tau_n \tilde{c}_n^{(i)}(1-s)], \tag{48}$$

where $\tilde{c}_n^{(i)}(1-s) = \inf\{x : \tilde{F}_n^{(i)}(x) \geq 1-s\}$ and $\tilde{F}_n^{(i)}(x) = \frac{1}{n-m+1}\sum_{t=1}^{n-m+1} 1(|S_{nt}^{(i)}| \leq x)$, also has limiting coverage probability $1-s$ when $S_n^{(i)}$ has nondegenerate limit.

4.2. Finite Sample Performance

Here we present the results of a simulation study used to assess the finite sample performance of the subsampling confidence intervals discussed in the previous subsection. We focus on tests of the null hypothesis $\sigma^2 = \sigma_0^2$ based on equal tailed and symmetric confidence intervals for σ_0^2. This parameter is easier to deal with because we need to only compute the estimator $\hat{\sigma}_n^2$, which is a simple average. Confidence intervals for the other GARCH parameters require numerical optimization in the second step quasi-maximum likelihood estimation, which can be burdensome in the context of a Monte Carlo study of subsampling approximation.

We consider a variety of configurations of sample sizes, block sizes, nominal sizes, parameter values, and error distributions in our simulations. Specifically, we consider sample sizes $n \in \{500, 2500\}$, block sizes $m \in \{10, 25, 50, 100\}$, and nominal sizes $s \in \{0.05, 0.1\}$. We confine ourselves to the GARCH(1,1) model with $\sigma_0^2 = 1$, $b_{01} = 0.85$, and $a_{01} \in \{0.06, 0.1, 0.14\}$; note that this implies $a_{01} + b_{01} \in \{0.91, 0.95, 0.99\}$. We consider three innovation distributions: the $\mathcal{N}(0,1)$ distribution and the Student t_p distribution with $p \in \{3, 5\}$ degrees of freedom, scaled to have unit variance. The t_3 distribution has infinite fourth moment, the t_5 distribution has finite fourth moment but infinite absolute fifth moment, and the $\mathcal{N}(0,1)$ distribution has finite moments of all orders. The sample sizes and parameter values we use are chosen to be relevant for typical financial applications: in Fig. 1, the permitted values of a_{01} and b_{01} lie in roughly the same part of the parameter space as the estimates using daily DJIA returns. Automated selection rules for the block size m have been proposed by Politis et al. (1999) and Kokoszka and Wolf (2004), but these are difficult to implement within a large Monte Carlo study, so we instead consider subsampling performance over a range of fixed block sizes.

The results of our simulations are reported in Tables 1, 2, and 3. Each table includes results for a single innovation distribution. Alongside the parameter value a_{01}, we report the corresponding value of α implied by Kesten's theorem. The numbers reported in the last four columns of each table are the null rejection rates for testing $\sigma^2 = \sigma_0^2$; that is, the rate at which our $(1-s)$-level subsampling confidence intervals for σ_0^2 do not include σ_0^2. These rates are computed over 2,000 experimental replications.

We draw four main conclusions from the results reported in Tables 1, 2, and 3.

1. For many parameter configurations, null rejection rates are far above nominal size.

Table 1. Finite sample size of subsampling tests of $H_0 : \sigma^2 = \sigma_0^2$ for the GARCH(1,1) model with $\sigma_0^2 = 1$, $a_{01} \in \{0.06, 0.1, 0.14\}$, $b_{01} = 0.85$, and $\eta \sim \mathcal{N}(0,\ 1)$.

			Subsampling Block Size			
Sample Size	Nominal Size	Test Type	$m = 10$	$m = 25$	$m = 50$	$m = 100$
$a_0 = 0.06$, $\alpha \approx 10.70$						
500	0.05	Equal tailed	0.15	0.12	0.12	0.20
500	0.05	Symmetric	0.02	0.05	0.08	0.15
500	0.10	Equal tailed	0.20	0.17	0.17	0.23
500	0.10	Symmetric	0.05	0.11	0.14	0.20
2,500	0.05	Equal tailed	0.15	0.11	0.08	0.08
2,500	0.05	Symmetric	0.00	0.02	0.04	0.06
2,500	0.10	Equal tailed	0.19	0.16	0.13	0.12
2,500	0.10	Symmetric	0.04	0.08	0.09	0.11
$a_0 = 0.10$, $\alpha \approx 4.54$						
500	0.05	Equal tailed	0.23	0.20	0.20	0.26
500	0.05	Symmetric	0.06	0.10	0.12	0.18
500	0.10	Equal tailed	0.29	0.26	0.25	0.30
500	0.10	Symmetric	0.14	0.16	0.19	0.23
2,500	0.05	Equal tailed	0.23	0.17	0.13	0.11
2,500	0.05	Symmetric	0.02	0.04	0.05	0.06
2,500	0.10	Equal tailed	0.27	0.22	0.19	0.17
2,500	0.10	Symmetric	0.09	0.11	0.11	0.12
$a_0 = 0.14$, $\alpha \approx 1.54$						
500	0.05	Equal tailed	0.46	0.45	0.44	0.47
500	0.05	Symmetric	0.37	0.37	0.37	0.41
500	0.10	Equal tailed	0.54	0.51	0.49	0.50
500	0.10	Symmetric	0.44	0.43	0.42	0.44
2,500	0.05	Equal tailed	0.37	0.35	0.32	0.29
2,500	0.05	Symmetric	0.27	0.26	0.25	0.25
2,500	0.10	Equal tailed	0.47	0.44	0.39	0.36
2,500	0.10	Symmetric	0.37	0.34	0.32	0.32

2. Null rejection rates are much greater at larger values of a_{01}. When $a_{01} = 0.14$, so that $a_{01} + b_{01} = 0.99$, the null rejection rate is always above 0.25 even when innovations are Gaussian, and often rises above 0.5 when innovations have the (rescaled) t_3 distribution.
3. Null rejection rates are generally greater at larger values of α, but the value of a_{01} seems to be the more important factor determining rejection rates. This can be seen by comparing the null rejection rates in Table 1 with $a_{01} = 0.14$ and in Table 3 with $a_{01} = 0.06$. The former group of rejection rates are in all cases substantially greater than the

Table 2. Finite sample size of subsampling tests of $H_0 : \sigma^2 = \sigma_0^2$ for the GARCH(1,1) model with $\sigma_0^2 = 1$, $a_{01} \in \{0.06, 0.1, 0.14\}$, $b_{01} = 0.85$, and $\eta \sim t_5$.

			Subsampling Block Size			
Sample Size	Nominal Size	Test Type	$m=10$	$m=25$	$m=50$	$m=100$
$a_0=0.06$, $\alpha \approx 2.45$						
500	0.05	Equal tailed	0.15	0.13	0.15	0.22
500	0.05	Symmetric	0.01	0.05	0.08	0.15
500	0.10	Equal tailed	0.19	0.18	0.19	0.26
500	0.10	Symmetric	0.05	0.10	0.14	0.19
2,500	0.05	Equal tailed	0.16	0.12	0.10	0.09
2,500	0.05	Symmetric	0.00	0.01	0.03	0.05
2,500	0.10	Equal tailed	0.20	0.16	0.15	0.15
2,500	0.10	Symmetric	0.02	0.05	0.07	0.09
$a_0=0.10$, $\alpha \approx 2.08$						
500	0.05	Equal tailed	0.20	0.20	0.21	0.29
500	0.05	Symmetric	0.07	0.11	0.16	0.22
500	0.10	Equal tailed	0.25	0.25	0.26	0.33
500	0.10	Symmetric	0.14	0.18	0.21	0.27
2,500	0.05	Equal tailed	0.22	0.19	0.16	0.14
2,500	0.05	Symmetric	0.03	0.05	0.07	0.09
2,500	0.10	Equal tailed	0.27	0.25	0.23	0.22
2,500	0.10	Symmetric	0.08	0.10	0.12	0.14
$a_0=0.14$, $\alpha \approx 1.24$						
500	0.05	Equal tailed	0.43	0.45	0.47	0.52
500	0.05	Symmetric	0.41	0.43	0.45	0.49
500	0.10	Equal tailed	0.51	0.51	0.51	0.55
500	0.10	Symmetric	0.49	0.50	0.50	0.53
2,500	0.05	Equal tailed	0.32	0.34	0.34	0.33
2,500	0.05	Symmetric	0.30	0.32	0.33	0.35
2,500	0.10	Equal tailed	0.42	0.42	0.42	0.42
2,500	0.10	Symmetric	0.40	0.41	0.40	0.41

latter group, but α is equal to 1.54 in the former group and 1.44 in the latter group.

4. The tests based on symmetric confidence intervals tend to control size better than those based on equal tailed confidence intervals.

In view of the above findings, it is difficult for us to recommend the use of subsampling confidence intervals in practical implementations of the VTE for which the sample sizes and parameter values used in our simulations appear to be relevant. We did find more encouraging results for the symmetric confidence intervals at sample sizes of $n = 50{,}000$ observations, but this seems of limited interest from a practical perspective.

Table 3. Finite sample size of subsampling tests of $H_0 : \sigma^2 = \sigma_0^2$ for the GARCH(1,1) model with $\sigma_0^2 = 1$, $a_{01} \in \{0.06, 0.1, 0.14\}$, $b_{01} = 0.85$, and $\eta \sim t_3$.

Sample Size	Nominal Size	Test Type	Subsampling Block Size $m = 10$	$m = 25$	$m = 50$	$m = 100$
$a_0 = 0.06$, $\alpha \approx 1.44$						
500	0.05	Equal tailed	0.10	0.13	0.19	0.30
500	0.05	Symmetric	0.05	0.12	0.18	0.25
500	0.10	Equal tailed	0.16	0.20	0.24	0.33
500	0.10	Symmetric	0.12	0.19	0.24	0.29
2,500	0.05	Equal tailed	0.10	0.10	0.10	0.12
2,500	0.05	Symmetric	0.01	0.05	0.09	0.13
2,500	0.10	Equal tailed	0.14	0.16	0.19	0.22
2,500	0.10	Symmetric	0.05	0.13	0.17	0.20
$a_0 = 0.10$, $\alpha \approx 1.13$						
500	0.05	Equal tailed	0.16	0.23	0.29	0.38
500	0.05	Symmetric	0.15	0.23	0.29	0.37
500	0.10	Equal tailed	0.25	0.29	0.34	0.43
500	0.10	Symmetric	0.25	0.31	0.36	0.42
2,500	0.05	Equal tailed	0.12	0.13	0.15	0.17
2,500	0.05	Symmetric	0.06	0.11	0.14	0.18
2,500	0.10	Equal tailed	0.18	0.21	0.23	0.25
2,500	0.10	Symmetric	0.13	0.18	0.21	0.24
$a_0 = 0.14$, $\alpha \approx 1.08$						
500	0.05	Equal tailed	0.50	0.55	0.59	0.65
500	0.05	Symmetric	0.53	0.58	0.60	0.65
500	0.10	Equal tailed	0.57	0.60	0.63	0.67
500	0.10	Symmetric	0.61	0.63	0.65	0.68
2,500	0.05	Equal tailed	0.36	0.41	0.44	0.46
2,500	0.05	Symmetric	0.40	0.46	0.47	0.50
2,500	0.10	Equal tailed	0.45	0.50	0.51	0.52
2,500	0.10	Symmetric	0.50	0.52	0.54	0.55

5. CONCLUSION

In this paper we have studied the VTE for the GARCH(p,q) model, devoting particular attention to the heavy tailed case where $\mathbb{E}y_t^4 = \infty$. Prior research by Francq et al. (2011) has demonstrated that in the light tailed case the VTE typically has a larger asymptotic variance than the QMLE, but enjoys a degree of robustness toward model misspecification. Our results indicate that in the heavy tailed case, the loss of efficiency associated with the VTE can be more severe, with the rate of consistency slower than the rate achieved by the QMLE. Moreover, the limit distribution of the VTE is non-Gaussian, invalidating the use of confidence intervals based on Gaussian approximation. Though subsampling techniques can in principle be used to generate asymptotically valid confidence intervals for the VTE, our numerical simulations indicate that the finite sample performance of these confidence intervals can be extremely poor at realistic sample sizes and parameter values. Taken together, our results indicate that the VTE should be used with caution in applications where heavy tails are suspected, particularly if valid statistical inference (as opposed to mere consistency) is a primary concern.

ACKNOWLEDGMENTS

We thank the anonymous referee and seminar participants at Southern Methodist University for helpful comments.

REFERENCES

Basrak, B., Davis, R. A., & Mikosch, T. (2002). Regular variation of GARCH processes. *Stochastic Processes and their Applications*, *99*, 95–115.

Berkes, I., Horváth, L., & Kokoszka, P. (2003). GARCH processes: Structure and estimation. *Bernoulli*, *9*, 201–227.

Billingsley, P. (1968). *Convergence of probability measures*. New York, NY: Wiley.

Bingham, N. H., Goldie, C. M., & Teugels, J. L. (1989). *Regular variation*. Cambridge: Cambridge University Press.

Bollerslev, T. (1986). Generalized autoregressive conditional heteroskedasticity. *Journal of Econometrics*, *31*, 307–327.

Boman, J., & Lindskog, F. (2009). Support theorems for the radon transform and Cramér-Wold theorems. *Journal of Theoretical Probability*, *22*, 683–710.

Bougerol, P., & Picard, N. (1992). Stationarity of GARCH processes and of some nonnegative time series. *Journal of Econometrics*, *52*, 115–127.

Boussama, F. (1998). *Ergodicité, mélange et estimation dans le modéles GARCH*. Doctoral thesis, Université Paris 7.

Carrasco, M., & Chen, X. (2002). Mixing and moment properties of various GARCH and stochastic volatility models. *Econometric Theory*, *18*, 17–39.

Davis, R. A., & Hsing, T. (1995). Point process and partial sum convergence for weakly dependent random variables with infinite variance. *Annals of Probability*, *23*, 879–917.

Davis, R. A., & Mikosch, T. (1998). The sample autocorrelations of heavy-tailed processes with applications to ARCH. *Annals of Statistics*, *26*, 2049–2080.

Davis, R. A., & Mikosch, T. (2009). Extreme value theory for GARCH processes. In T. G. Anderson, R. A. Davis, J. -P. Kreiß, & T. Mikosch (Eds.), *Handbook of financial time series*. New York, NY: Springer.

Engle, R. F., & Mezrich, J. (1996). GARCH for groups. *Risk*, *9*, 36–40.

Fama, E. F. (1963). Mandelbrot and the stable Paretian hypothesis. *Journal of Business*, *36*, 420–429.

Francq, C., Horváth, L., & Zakoïan, J.-M. (2011). Merits and drawbacks of variance targeting in GARCH models. *Journal of Financial Econometrics*, *9*, 619–656.

Francq, C., & Zakoïan, J.-M. (2004). Maximum likelihood estimation of pure GARCH and ARMA-GARCH processes. *Bernoulli*, *10*, 605–637.

Hall, P., & Yao, Q. (2003). Inference in ARCH and GARCH models with heavy tailed errors. *Econometrica*, *71*, 285–317.

Hill, J. B., & Renault, E. (2012). *Variance targeting for heavy tailed time series*. Working Paper, Chapel Hill, NC: University of North Carolina.

Ibragimov, R. (2009). Portfolio diversification and value at risk under thick-tailedness. *Quantitative Finance*, *9*, 565–580.

Kallenberg, O. (1983). *Random measures* (3rd ed.). London: Academic Press.

Kesten, H. (1973). Random difference equations and renewal theory for products of random matrices. *Acta Mathematica*, *131*, 207–248.

Kokoszka, P., & Wolf, M. (2004). Subsampling the mean of heavy-tailed dependent observations. *Journal of Time Series Analysis*, *25*, 217–234.

Kristensen, D., & Linton, O. (2004). Consistent standard errors for target variance approach to GARCH estimation. *Econometric Theory*, *20*, 990–993.

Leadbetter, M. R., & Rootzén, H. (1988). Extremal theory for stochastic processes. *Annals of Probability*, *16*, 431–478.

Lee, S. -W., & Hansen, B. E. (1994). Asymptotic theory for the GARCH(1,1) quasi-maximum likelihood estimator. *Econometric Theory*, *10*, 29–52.

Lindner, A. M. (2009). Stationarity, mixing, distributional properties and moments of GARCH(p,q) processes. In T. G. Anderson, R. A. Davis, J. -P. Kreiß, & T. Mikosch (Eds.), *Handbook of financial time series*. New York, NY: Springer.

Loretan, M., & Phillips, P. C. B. (1994). Testing the covariance stationarity of heavy-tailed time series: An overview of the theory with applications to several financial datasets. *Journal of Empirical Finance*, *1*, 211–248.

Lumsdaine, R. L. (1996). Consistency and asymptotic normality of the quasi-maximum likelihood estimator in IGARCH(1,1) and covariance stationary GARCH(1,1) models. *Econometrica*, *64*, 575–596.

Mandelbrot, B. (1963). The variation of certain speculative prices. *Journal of Business*, *36*, 394–419.

Mikosch, T., & Stărică, C. (2000). Limit theory for the sample correlations and extremes of a GARCH(1,1) process. *Annals of Statistics*, *28*, 1427–1451.

Mikosch, T., & Straumann, D. (2006). Stable limits of martingale transforms with application to the estimation of GARCH parameters. *Annals of Statistics*, *34*, 493–522.

Nelson, D. B. (1990). Stationarity and persistence in the GARCH(1,1) model. *Econometric Theory*, *6*, 318–334.

Phillips, P. C. B. (1987). Time series regression with a unit root. *Econometrica*, *55*, 277–301.

Phillips, P. C. B. (1990). Time series regression with a unit root and infinite-variance errors. *Econometric Theory*, *6*, 44–62.

Phillips, P. C. B., & Loretan, M. (1991). The Durbin-Watson ratio under infinite-variance errors. *Journal of Econometrics*, *47*, 85–114.

Phillips, P. C. B., & Loretan, M. (1995). On the theory of testing covariance stationarity under moment condition failure. In G. S. Maddala, P. C. B. Phillips, & T. N. Srinivasan (Eds.), *Advances in econometrics and quantitative economics. Essays in honor of Professor C. R. Rao*. Oxford: Blackwell.

Politis, D. N., Romano, J. P., & Wolf, M. (1999). *Subsampling*. New York, NY: Springer.

Resnick, S. I. (1986). Point processes, regular variation and weak convergence. *Advances in Applied Probability*, *18*, 66–138.

Resnick, S. I. (1987). *Extreme values, regular variation, and point processes*. New York, NY: Springer-Verlag.

Resnick, S. I. (2004). On the foundations of multivariate heavy-tail analysis. *Journal of Applied Probability*, *41*, 191–212.

Robinson, P. M., & Zaffaroni, P. (2006). Pseudo-maximum likelihood estimation of ARCH (∞) models. *Annals of Statistics*, *34*, 1049–1074.

Samorodnitsky, G., & Taqqu, M. S. (1994). *Stable non-Gaussian random processes: Stochastic models with infinite variance*. New York, NY: Chapman and Hall.

Straumann, D. (2005). *Estimation in conditionally heteroskedastic time series*. Lecture Notes in Statistics. Berlin: Springer.

von Bahr, B., & Esseen, C.-G. (1965). Inequalities for the rth absolute moment of a sum of random variables, $1 \leq r \leq 2$. *Annals of Mathematical Statistics*, *36*, 299–303.

Weiss, A. A. (1986). Asymptotic theory for ARCH models: Estimation and testing. *Econometric Theory*, *2*, 107–131.

APPENDIX A. MATHEMATICAL APPENDIX

Lemma A.1. Under Assumption 1, if $\alpha \in (1,2)$ then Eqs. (39) and (40) hold for $\delta > 0$.

Proof of Lemma A.1. To prove Eq. (39), we fix $\gamma \in (\alpha, \kappa \wedge 2)$ and use Markov's inequality to write

$$\mathbb{P}\left(\left|a_n^{-1}\sum_{t=1}^{n} h_t^2(\eta_t^2 - 1)1(h_t^2 \le \varepsilon a_n)\right| > \delta\right) \le (\delta a_n)^{-\gamma}\mathbb{E}|M_n|^{\gamma}, \tag{A.1}$$

where $M_n = \sum_{t=1}^{n} h_t^2(\eta_t^2 - 1)1(h_t^2 \le \varepsilon a_n)$. Since $\mathbb{E}(M_{n+1}|M_n) = M_n$ a.s. for each $n \in \mathbb{N}$, and $\gamma \in (1,2)$, we may apply the moment inequality of von Bahr and Esseen (1965, Theorem 2) to obtain

$$\mathbb{E}|M_n|^{\gamma} \le 2\sum_{t=1}^{n}\mathbb{E}|h_t^2(\eta_t^2 - 1)1(h_t^2 \le \varepsilon a_n)|^{\gamma} = 2n\mathbb{E}(h_t^{2\gamma}1(h_t^2 \le \varepsilon a_n))\mathbb{E}|\eta_t^2 - 1|^{\gamma}. \tag{A.2}$$

Combining Eqs. (A.1), (A.2), and (12), a consequence of Karamata's theorem, we find that

$$\begin{aligned}\limsup_{n\to\infty} \mathbb{P}(|U_n^* - U_{n\varepsilon}^*| > \delta) &= \limsup_{n\to\infty} \mathbb{P}\left(C\left|a_n^{-1}\sum_{t=1}^{n} h_t^2(\eta_t^2 - 1)1(h_t^2 \le \varepsilon a_n)\right| > \delta\right) \\ &\le \frac{2(\delta/C)^{-\gamma}c_h\alpha\varepsilon^{\gamma-\alpha}}{\gamma - \alpha}\mathbb{E}|\eta^2 - 1|^{\gamma}. \end{aligned}\tag{A.3}$$

Since $\gamma < \kappa$ we have $\mathbb{E}\left|\eta_1^2 - 1\right|^{\gamma} < \infty$, and so we obtain Eq. (39) by letting $\varepsilon \to 0$.

The proof of Eq. (40) is similar, but uses a more elementary inequality in place of von Bahr and Esseen (1965, Theorem 2). We fix $\gamma \in (\alpha/2, 1)$ and use Markov's inequality to write

$$\mathbb{P}\left(a_n^{-2}\sum_{t=1}^{n} y_t^4 1(y_t^2 \le \varepsilon a_n) > \delta\right) \le (\delta a_n^2)^{-\gamma}\mathbb{E}\left|\sum_{t=1}^{n} y_t^4 1(y_t^2 \le \varepsilon a_n)\right|^{\gamma}. \tag{A.4}$$

The inequality $\left(\sum_{i=1}^{n} c_i\right)^s \leq \sum_{i=1}^{n} c_i^s$, valid for $c_i \geq 0$ and $s \in [0,1]$, yields

$$\mathbb{E}\left|\sum_{t=1}^{n} y_t^4 1(y_t^2 \leq \varepsilon a_n)\right|^{\gamma} \leq n\mathbb{E}((y_t^4)^{\gamma} 1(y_t^2 \leq \varepsilon a_n)). \tag{A.5}$$

Combining Eqs. (A.4), (A.5), and (12), we obtain

$$\limsup_{n\to\infty} \mathbb{P}(|V_n - V_{n\varepsilon}| > \delta) = \limsup_{n\to\infty} \mathbb{P}\left(a_n^{-2}\sum_{t=1}^{n} y_t^4 1(y_t^2 \leq \varepsilon a_n) > \delta\right) \tag{A.6}$$

$$\leq \frac{\delta^{-\gamma} c_y \alpha \varepsilon^{2\gamma-\alpha}}{2\gamma - \alpha}, \tag{A.7}$$

and Eq. (40) follows by letting $\varepsilon \to 0$. ■

Lemma A.2. Under Assumption 1, if $\alpha \in (1,2)$ then, for any $\varepsilon > 0$, T_ε is continuous on a subset of $M_p(\overline{\mathbb{R}}_+^d \backslash \{\mathbf{0}\})$ inhabited by N with probability one.

Proof of Lemma A.2. Let $B_\varepsilon = \{\mathbf{x} \in \overline{\mathbb{R}}_+^d : \max(x_2, x_{p+1}) > \varepsilon\}$ and $A_\varepsilon = \{m \in M_p(\overline{\mathbb{R}}_+^d \backslash \{\mathbf{0}\}) : m(\partial B_\varepsilon) = 0\}$, and consider a sequence $m_1, m_2, \ldots \in \overline{\mathbb{R}}_+^d \backslash \{\mathbf{0}\}$ with $m_n \xrightarrow{v} m \in A_\varepsilon$. B_ε is bounded away from the origin and hence relatively compact, so a result of Resnick (1987, Proposition 3.13) ensures that, for all n sufficiently large, we may label the points of m_n and m in B_ε by $(\mathbf{x}_1^{(n)}, \ldots, \mathbf{x}_k^{(n)}), (\mathbf{x}_1, \ldots, \mathbf{x}_k) \in B_\varepsilon^k$, with $k = m(B_\varepsilon)$, and for each $i = 1, \ldots, k$ we have $\mathbf{x}_i^{(n)} \to \mathbf{x}_i$. Since $T_\varepsilon(m_n)$ and $T_\varepsilon(m)$ depend only on the points $(\mathbf{x}_1^{(n)}, \ldots, \mathbf{x}_k^{(n)})$ and $(\mathbf{x}_1, \ldots, \mathbf{x}_k)$ respectively, it is clear from Eq. (36) that $T_\varepsilon(m_n) \to T_\varepsilon(m)$. Thus T_ε is continuous on A_ε. The limiting point process N satisfies the cluster representation (16) given in Theorem 2, so we may write $\mathbb{P}(N \notin A_\varepsilon) = \mathbb{P}(P_i \mathbf{Q}_{ij} \in \partial B_\varepsilon$ for some $i,j) \leq \sum_{i,j} \mathbb{P}(P_i \mathbf{Q}_{ij} \in \partial B_\varepsilon)$. Since $\sum_i \delta_{P_i}$ is Poisson with absolutely continuous intensity, each P_i must be a continuous random variable. Further, each P_i is independent of each $\mathbf{Q}_{ij}$. We thus have $\mathbb{P}(P_i \mathbf{Q}_{ij} \in \partial B_\varepsilon) = 0$, and hence $\mathbb{P}(N \notin A_\varepsilon) = 0$. ■

Lemma A.3. Under Assumption 1, if $\alpha \in (1,2)$ then $T_\varepsilon(N) \xrightarrow{w} (U, V)$ as $\varepsilon \to 0$.

Proof of Lemma A.3. Let $\phi_\varepsilon : \mathbb{R}^2 \to \mathbb{C}$ denote the characteristic function of $(U_\varepsilon, V_\varepsilon) := T_\varepsilon(N)$. We will show that ϕ_ε converges to some $\phi : \mathbb{R}^2 \to \mathbb{C}$ that is continuous at the origin by showing that, as $\varepsilon \to 0$, $\phi_\varepsilon(t)$ is Cauchy at all fixed $t \in \mathbb{R}^2$, and uniformly Cauchy in a neighborhood of the origin. It then follows from the Lévy continuity theorem that $T_\varepsilon(N)$ converges weakly to a pair of random variables with characteristic function ϕ. Let $A = \{t \in \mathbb{R}^2 : |t_1| \vee |t_2| \leq 1\}$. We will show that ϕ_ε is uniformly Cauchy on A: for any $\eta > 0$, there exists an $\varepsilon > 0$ such that

$$\sup_{0<u<v<\varepsilon} \sup_{t \in A} |\phi_v(t) - \phi_u(t)| < \eta. \tag{A.8}$$

Observe that, for any $\delta > 0$,

$$\begin{aligned} |\phi_v(t) - \phi_u(t)| &\leq \mathbb{E}(g(t,u,v) 1(|U_v - U_u| \vee |V_v - V_u| \leq \delta)) \\ &\quad + \mathbb{E}(g(t,u,v) 1(|U_v - U_u| \vee |V_v - V_u| > \delta)), \end{aligned} \tag{A.9}$$

where we have defined

$$g(t,u,v) = |\exp(i(t_1 U_v + t_2 V_v)) - \exp(i(t_1 U_u + t_2 V_u))| \tag{A.10}$$

$$= \sqrt{2 - 2\cos(t_1(U_v - U_u) + t_2(V_v - V_u))}. \tag{A.11}$$

For $t \in A$ and small enough $\delta > 0$ we have $g(t,u,v) \leq \sqrt{2 - 2\cos(2\delta)} < \eta/2$ when $|U_v - U_u| \vee |V_v - V_u| \leq \delta$. Thus the first term on the right-hand side of Eq. (A.9) is less than $\eta/2$ for small enough δ. Fix such a δ; it remains to show that the second term is less than $\eta/2$ for small enough $\varepsilon > 0$. Since $0 \leq g \leq 2$, it suffices to find $\varepsilon > 0$ such that

$$\sup_{0<u<v<\varepsilon} \mathbb{P}(|U_v - U_u| \vee |V_v - V_u| > \delta) < \eta/4. \tag{A.12}$$

Let $\tilde{T}_{uv} = |T_v^{(1)} - T_u^{(1)}| \vee |T_v^{(2)} - T_u^{(2)}|$, where $T_\varepsilon^{(1)}$ and $T_\varepsilon^{(2)}$ denote the first and second components of T_ε. Lemma A.2 ensures that $\tilde{T}_{uv}$ is continuous on a subset of $M_p(\overline{\mathbb{R}}_+^d \setminus \{\mathbf{0}\})$ inhabited by N with probability one. Thus, from the continuous mapping theorem and the weak convergence $N_n \xrightarrow{w} N$ given by Theorem 2, we have $\tilde{T}_{uv}(N_n) \xrightarrow{w} \tilde{T}_{uv}(N)$. Consequently,

$$\mathbb{P}(|U_v - U_u| \vee |V_v - V_u| > \delta) = \mathbb{P}(\tilde{T}_{uv}(N) > \delta) = \lim_{n \to \infty} \mathbb{P}(\tilde{T}_{uv}(N_n) > \delta). \tag{A.13}$$

Observe that

$$\begin{aligned}\tilde{T}_{uv}(N_n) = |U^*_{nv} - U^*_{nu}| \vee |V_{nv} - V_{nu}| \leq |U^*_n - U^*_{nv}| + |U^*_n - U^*_{nu}| \\ + |V_n - V_{nv}| + |V_n - V_{nu}|.\end{aligned} \tag{A.14}$$

It follows from Eq. (A.14) and Lemma A.1 that $\sup_{0<u<v<\varepsilon}\lim_{n\to\infty}$ $\mathbb{P}(\tilde{T}_{uv}(N_n) > \delta) = 0$. In view of Eq. (A.13), this establishes the validity of Eq. (A.12), and we conclude that ϕ_ε is uniformly Cauchy on A. A slight modification of the foregoing argument establishes that $\phi_\varepsilon(t)$ is Cauchy at each fixed $t = (t_1, t_2)$: first choose $\delta = \delta(t)$ small enough that $g(t, u, v) \leq \sqrt{2 - 2\cos(2\delta(|t_1| \vee |t_2|))} < \eta/2$ when $|U_v - U_u| \vee |V_v - V_u| \leq \delta$, and then choose ε small enough that Eq. (A.12) is valid. We conclude that $T_\varepsilon(N)$ converges weakly to a pair of random variables. One can show that the first of these random variables is α-stable by arguing as in Davis and Hsing (1995, p. 898), and that the second is $\alpha/2$-stable and positive by arguing as in Kokoszka and Wolf (2004, pp. 231–232). ■

Proof of Theorem 5. In view of Theorem 4, Corollary 1, and the remarks preceding the statement of Theorem 5, it suffices for us to show that $na_n^{-1}\mathbf{Y}_n = o_p(1)$. Begin by writing

$$na_n^{-1}\mathbf{Y}_n = a_n^{-1}\sum_{t=1}^{n}\frac{\partial\ell_t(\boldsymbol{\nu}_0)}{\partial\boldsymbol{\lambda}} + a_n^{-1}\sum_{t=1}^{n}\left(\frac{\partial\ell_t(\boldsymbol{\nu}_0)}{\partial\boldsymbol{\lambda}} - \frac{\partial\tilde{\ell}_t(\boldsymbol{\nu}_0)}{\partial\boldsymbol{\lambda}}\right). \tag{A.15}$$

The second term on the right-hand side of Eq. (A.15) is $o_p(1)$ by item (iv) in the proof of Theorem 2.2 of Francq and Zakoïan (2004). It remains to show that the first term is $o_p(1)$. Fix $i \in \{1, \ldots, p+q\}$. Differentiating Eq. (29) with respect to λ_i we see that

$$\frac{\partial\ell_t(\boldsymbol{\nu}_0)}{\partial\lambda_i} = (1 - \eta_t^2)\left(\frac{1}{h_t^2}\frac{\partial\mathfrak{h}_t^2(\boldsymbol{\nu}_0)}{\partial\lambda_i}\right), \tag{A.16}$$

and differentiating Eq. (28) we see further that $0 \leq h_t^{-2}\partial\mathfrak{h}_t^2(\boldsymbol{\nu}_0)/\partial\lambda_i < \lambda_{0i}^{-1} < \infty$. Fix $\gamma \in (\alpha, \kappa \wedge 2)$, so that $\mathbb{E}|1 - \eta^2|^\gamma < \infty$ and $na_n^{-\gamma} \to 0$ as $n \to \infty$. Proceeding as in the proof of Lemma A.1 and applying the inequalities of Markov and of von Bahr and Esseen to the martingale difference sequence $(\partial \ell_t(\boldsymbol{\nu}_0)/\partial \lambda_i)$, we obtain

$$\mathbb{P}\left(\left|a_n^{-1}\sum_{t=1}^{n}\frac{\partial \ell_t(\boldsymbol{\nu}_0)}{\partial \lambda_i}\right|>\delta\right)\leq 2(\delta\lambda_{0i})^{-\gamma}na_n^{-\gamma}\mathbb{E}|1-\eta^2|^\gamma \xrightarrow{p} 0 \qquad \text{(A.17)}$$

as $n \to \infty$, for any $\delta > 0$. Thus the first term on the right-hand side of Eq. (A.15) is also $o_p(1)$, and $na_n^{-1}\boldsymbol{Y}_n = o_p(1)$ as claimed. ■

Proof of Theorem 6. This follows immediately from a result of Kokoszka and Wolf (2004, Theorem 1) if we can find sequences u_n and v_n with $u_n/v_n = n^{1/2}$ such that $S_n^{(i)}$, $u_n(\hat{\nu}_n^{(i)} - \nu_0^{(i)})$, and $v_n\tau_n$ have atomless weak limits. In the light tailed case $\alpha \in (2,\infty)$ we set $u_n = n^{1/2}$ and $v_n = 1$, and the desired weak convergence then follows from Theorem 3 and the ergodic theorem. In the heavy tailed case $\alpha \in (1,2)$ we set $u_n = na_n^{-1}$ and $v_n = n^{1/2}a_n^{-1}$, and the desired weak convergence then follows from Theorems 4 and 5. The requirement that the $(i-1)$th element of $\boldsymbol{J}^{-1}\boldsymbol{K}$ is nonzero when $i \geq 2$ ensures that the weak limits of $S_n^{(i)}$ and $u_n(\hat{\nu}_n^{(i)} - \nu_0^{(i)})$ given by Theorem 5 are not degenerate at zero. ■

ASSESSING THE POWER OF LONG-HORIZON PREDICTIVE TESTS IN MODELS OF BULL AND BEAR MARKETS

Alex Maynard and Dongmeng Ren

Department of Economics, University of Guelph, Guelph, Canada

ABSTRACT

We compare the finite sample power of short- and long-horizon tests in nonlinear predictive regression models of regime switching between bull and bear markets, allowing for time varying transition probabilities. As a point of reference, we also provide a similar comparison in a linear predictive regression model without regime switching. Overall, our results do not support the contention of higher power in longer horizon tests in either the linear or nonlinear regime switching models. Nonetheless, it is possible that other plausible nonlinear models provide stronger justification for long-horizon tests.

Keywords: Predictive regression; long-horizon regression; regime-switching; nonlinear; stock return predictability

JEL classifications: G12; G14; C51; C53; C58

Essays in Honor of Peter C. B. Phillips
Advances in Econometrics, Volume 33, 673–711

ISSN: 0731-9053/doi:10.1108/S0731-905320140000033019

1. INTRODUCTION

Long-horizon predictive regression tests have been the subject of substantial interest in both empirical finance and financial econometrics, following influential applications to stock return predictability, (Campbell & Shiller, 1988; Fama & French, 1988b), exchange rate prediction (Chinn & Meese, 1995; Mark, 1995), and the term structure of interest rates (Cutler, Poterba, & Summers, 1991; Fama & Bliss, 1987). The strong empirical results, including large R-squares and t-statistics, observed in long-horizon stock return regressions have been particularly influential in the finance literature, as one of several important findings leading to the conclusion by the Royal Swedish Academy of Sciences (2013) Nobel Press release that

> There is no way to predict the price of stocks and bonds over the next few days or weeks. But it is quite possible to foresee the broad course of these prices over longer periods, such as the next three to five years.

Similarly, in his survey article, Cochrane (1999) cites the predictability of stock returns at long horizons as one of the three most important new facts in finance.

This paper asks whether there is any long-horizon power advantage in empirically plausible nonlinear models using valid econometric tests. In particular, we compare the power of short- and long-horizon predictive regressions under the assumption that the data is generated by nonlinear Hamilton (1989) style regime switching models. These models have been successfully used for some time to model long-term swings in foreign currency exchange rates (Bollen, Gray, & Whaley, 2000; Cheung & Erlandsson, 2005; Dewachter, 2001; Engel & Hamilton, 1990). A more recent literature develops similar models to capture bull and bear runs (or multiple states) in stock markets (Chauvet & Potter, 2000; Guidolin & Hyde, 2010; Guidolin & Timmermann, 2005; Maheu & McCurdy, 2000; Maheu, McCurdy, & Song, 2012). Schaller and Norden (1997) and Guidolin and Timmermann (2005) estimate predictive regressions with regime switches. To our knowledge, no one has considered the power of long-horizon regressions in these models, although Kilian (1999) mentions this avenue.

Overall, our results are not supportive of long-horizon regression. Long-horizon tests can show modest size-adjusted power gains using a standard t-test in the linear model. Using more powerful tests, we find no power advantages at long horizons. Short-horizon tests have as good or better power. Long-horizons tests fare no better (and often worse) in bull/bear regime shift models, even when the regressor is predictive of the regime shift itself. In the context of long-horizon IVX tests, we find that the power comparison depends on both the horizon and the tuning parameter determining the degree of filtering used to create the instrument. Nonetheless, we find that with a good choice of this tuning parameter, the short run IVX can provide as good or better power as its long run counterpart in both linear and regime switching predictive regression settings.

The remainder of the paper is organized as follows: Section 2 reviews the literature and provides the background and motivation for our study. In Section 3 we introduce the regime shifting predictive regression model that is used as a data generating process for our power comparison. Section 4 describes the data. Section 5 presents the empirical estimates of the regime shift model used to anchor our simulations. Section 6 describes the short- and long-horizon specifications and tests employed in the power comparisons. Section 7 provides an extensive simulated power comparison of short- and long-horizon regressions using two different long-horizon specifications and several long-horizon tests.

2. LITERATURE, BACKGROUND, AND MOTIVATION

The dependent variables in long-horizon regressions are typically multiyear asset returns observed at a monthly or quarterly frequency, defined by

$$r_{t+k}^{k} = \sum_{j=1}^{k} r_{t+j} \tag{1}$$

where k is the horizon period and r_t is the one period return. The long-horizon return is regressed on a predetermined predictor x_t, such as a dividend or earnings price ratio, resulting in the long-horizon regression specification

$$r_{t+k}^{k} = \beta_0(k) + \beta_1(k)x_t + \varepsilon_{1,t+k}^{k} \tag{2}$$

with tests for long-horizon predictability based on the restriction

$$H_0 : \beta_1(k) = 0 \tag{3}$$

The special case in which $k = 1$ corresponds to the short-horizon predictive regression

$$r_{t+1} = \beta_0 + \beta_1 x_t + \varepsilon_{1,t+1} \tag{4}$$

which has also generated substantial interest. Although predetermined, valuation predictors, such as the dividend and earnings price ratios, tend to be both persistent and highly endogenous. Following Cavanagh, Elliott, and Stock (1995), they have been traditionally modeled using the local-to-unity process (Chan & Wei, 1987; Phillips, 1987) and this has more recently been generalized to include mildly integrated processes (Phillips & Lee, 2012; Phillips & Magdalinos, 2007). The long horizon, persistence, and endogeneity combine to create a nonstandard inference problem. They have thus generated an increasing interest in financial econometrics, including the development of new long-horizon tests (Hjalmarsson, 2012; Liu & Maynard, 2007; Phillips & Lee, 2013; Valkanov, 2003).

Although his interest in this particular problem appears fairly recent, it seems fair to say that Professor Peter C. B. Phillips has made at least three very important contributions to this literature. The first contribution is an indirect contribution. In fact, the long-horizon regression provides one of many nice examples of the useful insights that can be gained from the nonstationary asymptotics developed in very large part by Professor Phillips. The empirical results from these regressions appear remarkably strong and are of clear importance to economics and finance. At the same time, early simulation studies detect substantial size distortion (Goetzmann & Jorion, 1993; Kim & Nelson, 1993). Allowing the horizon to increase with k and modeling the predictor as a near unit root, Valkanov (2003) uses the tools of (near) nonstationary asymptotics to provide a clear explanation for the size distortion observed in earlier studies. In his framework, the regressor x_t on the right hand side of Eq. (2) is near integrated, while the dependent variable (1) is partially summed since k grows with the sample size, T. Consequently, under the null hypothesis in Eq. (3), the asymptotics resemble in certain respects the spurious regression asymptotics of Phillips (1986), helping to explain both the size distortion and large t and R-squared statistics in empirical applications.

Further insights are provided by Hjalmarsson (2012), who shows that when the regression coefficient from the long-horizon regression is scaled by k it shares the same second order endogeneity bias as the short-horizon regression estimator of β_1 in Eq. (4). Often referred to as the Stambaugh (1999) bias, following Cavanagh et al. (1995) this bias is perhaps best understood by viewing the large sample behavior of the predictive regression in Eq. (4) as a special case of cointegrating regression asymptotics (Park & Phillips, 1988, 1989; Phillips, 1991; Phillips & Hansen, 1990, inter alia), generalized to near unit roots (Chan & Wei, 1987; Phillips, 1987, 1988). Thus, the underlying theoretical frameworks developed earlier by

Professor Phillips have been employed to provide a great deal of insight into this important empirical application.

More recently, Professor Phillips has made two important direct contributions to this literature. One of the challenges in predictive regression is that, if the predictor is modelled as a near unit root process, the asymptotic distribution of the test statistic typically depends on the local-to-unity parameter which cannot be estimated. Until recently, many of the econometric methods that have been designed to provide inference in predictive regression, including long-horizon regressions, rely on a Bonferroni bound employing a first stage confidence interval for the local-to-unity parameter based on the inversion of a unit root test as in Stock (1991). Phillips (2014) has recently uncovered serious concerns with this approach, showing that the Stock (1991) confidence interval for the local-to-unity parameter has zero asymptotic coverage when the data generating process is stationary. This can lead to the invalidity of the resulting Bonferroni based tests when the true process is mildly integrated or stationary.

In a new major breakthrough, Phillips and Magdalinos (2007) generalize the local-to-unity model to allow for mildly integrated processes and Magdalinos and Phillips (2009) use this new theory to propose an alternative solution to the predictive regression known as the IVX method, which uses a mildly filtered version of the predictor as an instrument. Their solution altogether eliminates the endogeneity bias and dependence on an unknown local-to-unity parameter without reliance on Bonferroni methods. It continues to work for stationary and mildly integrated regressors and is easily extended to multivariate settings.[1] Phillips and Lee (2013) have recently proposed a long-horizon version of the IVX method, using a rearranged version of the long-horizon specification suggested in Jegadeesh (1991).

While the econometric literature discussed above is primarily concerned with understanding or eliminating the size distortion in long-horizon predictive regression, in this paper we are interested in the power of long-horizon specifications relative to their short-run counterparts in Eq. (4). This has been a controversial question, with the presumed power advantages of long-horizon regressions both strongly criticized in Boudoukh, Richardson, and Whitelaw (2008), and valiantly defended by Cochrane (2008).

There seems to be an unstated assumption in much of the early empirical literature that predictive regressions are more powerful at longer horizons, perhaps due to economic intuition or simply as a result of the stronger empirical results reported at longer horizons (see, e.g., Campbell, Lo, &

MacKinlay, 1997, chap. 7). This proposition is stated more directly in Campbell (2001). Several works provide support for this conjecture (Campbell, 2001; Cochrane, 2008; Kilian & Taylor, 2003; Mark & Sul, 2006; Wohar & Rapach, 2005), while others question the power advantage of longer horizons (Ang & Bekaert, 2007; Boudoukh et al., 2008; Hjalmarsson, 2008, 2012).

With a few exceptions, the power properties of long-horizon regressions have mainly been examined assuming that the true model for returns is given by a short-horizon linear model similar to Eq. (4) (Campbell, 2001; Cochrane, 2008; Hjalmarsson, 2008, 2012; Mark & Sul, 2006; Valkanov, 2003). In this case, as both Campbell (2001) and Hjalmarsson (2012) remark, the short-horizon regression in Eq. (4) is a correctly specified model. This may lead one to question the advantage of Eq. (2), relative to the correctly specified regression in Eq. (4). Nonetheless, as Campbell (2001), Mark and Sul (2006), and Cochrane (2008) all astutely note, the short-horizon regression loses power in the realistic case in which the valuation predictors are both highly persistent and contemporaneously correlated with the residual. They argue that the long-horizon regression offers power improvements in this case.

In fact, this combination of near unit root regressor with contemporaneous endogeneity, gives rise to second order biases in Eq. (4), resulting in both size distortion and power loss (Campbell & Yogo, 2006; Phillips, 1991; Phillips & Hansen, 1990). However, this arguably reflects only an inefficient use of the information in Eq. (4) by OLS-based tests that are suboptimal in the combined presence of endogeneity and (near) nonstationarity. Since more efficient short-run estimators and more powerful short-run tests are now available (Campbell & Yogo, 2006; Jansson & Moreira, 2006; Magdalinos & Phillips, 2009, inter alia) one can still argue that there is no inherent power advantage to the long-horizon specification when the true model is the linear short-horizon predictive regression. In our simulated power comparisons we do find some small size-adjusted power improvements using OLS-based tests when the true model is linear, but these improvements disappear when more powerful tests are used. Hjalmarsson (2012) also provides some results to support this contention.

In our view, any inherent advantage to the long-horizon specification could only arise under nonlinear alternatives to Eq. (4). In this case, neither Eq. (4) nor Eq. (2) is correctly specified, so that the long run specification in Eq. (2) may plausibly provide a better approximation to the true, but unknown, nonlinear alternative. Kilian (1999) similarly argues that "the observed pattern of p-values is inconsistent with a linear model." Yet, we are aware of relatively little literature which investigates the power of long-horizon specifications when the data generating process is nonlinear. Kilian and Taylor (2003) and Wohar and Rapach (2005) simulate power using a nonlinear ESTAR model for the predictor finding power advantages at longer horizons. On the other hand, Ang and Bekaert (2007) simulate power in a nonlinear present value model, but find long-horizon regressions to be less powerful. Marmer (2008) shows that predictability is present only in the short run in the case when the predictive component of returns is a general integral transformation of a nonstationary predictor.[2]

We compare the power of long- and short-horizon predictive tests in the case when the true model is characterized by regime switching between bull and bear markets. We assume that the econometrician does not know the true model and tests predictability using standard linear predictive models without regime shifting in both the short- and long-horizon specifications. Since neither linear regression is correctly specified, it is no longer obvious that a powerful short-horizon test should outperform a long-horizon test. In fact, since the states are themselves persistent, with a probability of switching between states that depends on the predictor, it seems a priori plausible that the long-horizon regressions might outperform the short-horizon regressions without the Markov-switching component.

3. REGIME SWITCHING PREDICTIVE REGRESSIVE MODELS

We consider the following regime switching model

$$r_{t+1} = \beta_0(s_t) + \beta_1(s_t)x_t + \sigma_1(s_t)\varepsilon_{t+1} \tag{5}$$

where the state $s_t \in 1 \ldots N$ is a first order Markov process with transition probabilities

$$p_{ij} = \text{Prob}\,(s_t = j | s_{t-1} = i) \tag{6}$$

When $N = 1$ and there is just one single state, then the regime switching model specializes to the standard linear predictive model

$$r_{t+1} = \beta_0 + \beta_1 x_t + \sigma_1 \varepsilon_{t+1} \tag{7}$$

In order to allow the predictor to predict transitions between states, as well as returns within states, we focus our attention on a model with time varying transition probabilities. Following Ding (2012), we model them as (where Φ is the CDF of $N(0,1)$)

$$p_{ij,t} = \Pi_{l=1}^{j-1}\left(1 - q_{il,t}\right)q_{ij,t} \tag{8}$$

$$q_{ij,t} = \begin{cases} \Phi\left(\theta_{0,ij} + \theta_{1,ij}x_{t-1}\right) & \text{for} \quad 1<j<N-1 \\ 1 & \text{for} \quad j=N \end{cases}$$

This formulation allows us to model the transition probabilities as a function of the predictor, while still ensuring that these probabilities appropriately sum to one. For example, in the two-state model $N=2$, this simplifies to

$$p_{i1,t} = q_{i1,t} = \Phi(\theta_{0,i1} + \theta_{1,i1}x_{t-1}) \tag{9}$$

$$p_{i2,t} = 1 - p_{i1,t} \tag{10}$$

in which x_t may help predict transitions between bull and bear states.

To provide an economic interpretation, we follow the literature in referring to the states as bull and bear states in the two state model and as bull, normal, and bear states in the three state model. To avoid any ambiguity, we define the bull and bear states, respectively, as the states with highest and lowest values of the estimated intercept $\hat{\beta}_0(s_t)$ in Eq. (5).

3.1. Persistent, Endogenous Regressors

Although predetermined, common valuation predictors, such as the dividend or earnings price ratios, are both persistent and endogenous. It is typically difficult to reject unit roots in these variables. Yet, taken literally, a unit root in these predictors may not seem natural from a financial modeling perspective. Moreover, time series unit root tests are, by design, not consistent against near unit root alternatives. Accordingly, the local-to-unity or near unit root models (Chan & Wei, 1987; Phillips, 1987, 1988) have been increasingly used to model the predictor. This class of models has been recently generalized by Phillips and Magdalinos (2007) to include mildly integrated series. Consider, for simplicity, a first order autoregressive process for the predictor

$$x_t = \rho_0 + \rho_1 x_{t-1} + v_t \tag{11}$$

A very general formulation for ρ_1 is provided by Phillips and Lee (2013), who model ρ_1 as

$$\rho_1 = 1 + c/T^{\eta} \tag{12}$$

Eq. (12) specializes to a unit root process, in the case when $c=0$, a near integrated process when $\eta=1$ and $c<0$ and a mildly integrated series when $0<\eta<1$.[3]

In order to realistically capture the endogeneity in the data, we follow the linear predictive regression literature in modeling the innovations as contemporaneously correlated with correlation $\delta = \text{corr}\ (\varepsilon_t, v_t)$:

$$(\varepsilon_t, v_t/\sigma_2)' \sim \text{i.i.d.} \left(0, \begin{bmatrix} 1 & \delta \\ \delta & 1 \end{bmatrix} \right) \tag{13}$$

This error structure is common in both the predictive regression and regime shift literatures. In the absence of regime shift, it nonetheless has the disadvantage of imposing homoskedasticity. In our context, we allow for the conditional return variance $\sigma_1^2(s_t)$ to vary across states. Incorporating time varying conditional heteroskedasticity within states could further enhance the realism of the model, although possibly at the cost of complicating its estimation.

4. DATA AND VARIABLES

Our study is based on 1,048 monthly observations of the excess return, including dividends, and the dividend price ratio on the S&P 500 price index starting in July 1926 and ending in October 2013. The stock return and dividend data are maintained by Robert Shiller and are combined with the monthly risk free rate maintained by Kenneth French. The monthly dividends are linearly interpolated from yearly totals. Defining the level of the S&P 500 price index by P_t, dividends by D_t, and the risk free rate by i_t, we define the excess return as

$$r_t = ln\left(\frac{P_t + D_t}{P_{t-1}}\right) - i_t \tag{14}$$

Following common practice (see, e.g., Campbell et al., 1997, chap. 7; Fama & French, 1988a), we sum the monthly dividends over the past 12 months to obtain

$$dp_t = ln\left(\frac{D_t + D_{t-1} + \ldots D_{t-11}}{P_t}\right) \tag{15}$$

Dividends are often summed as in Eq. (15) on account of their strong seasonality. Although not standard practice, this could also be achieved by a yearly average of dividends. It is possible that smoothing the dividends may also mitigate any bias from the linear interpolation of yearly dividends. [4]

Following Schaller & Norden, (1997, footnote 14, p. 14), who estimate a regime switching predictive model with fixed coefficients, we then standardize dp_t to have zero-mean and unit variance in order to define our predictor as

$$x_t = \left(dp_t - \overline{d}p_t\right)/\hat{\sigma}_{dpt} \tag{16}$$

where $\overline{d}p_t$ and $\hat{\sigma}_{dp_t}$ are the sample mean and standard deviation of dp_t respectively. Although this normalization is not typical in the linear predictive regression literature, we also find that it leads to a somewhat better fit and more easily interpretable parameters when estimating a regime switching predictive regression model.

If dp_t is (near) nonstationary, it will have an infinite range, tending to take values far from zero. Without the normalization in Eq. (16), this would lead the transition probabilities, defined as an asymptotically homogeneous function of the predictor in Eq. (8),[5] to cluster at zero or one depending on the signs of θ_1 and x_t. By normalizing the standard error, we avoid this problem. On the other hand, this normalization would present additional challenges for asymptotic inference in the regime shift model, since x_t is a function of the dividend price ratio process in Eq. (15), which may itself be characterized by a near unit root, in which case the standard deviation in Eq. (16) is increasing in sample size. We leave these developments for future work. In this paper, we simply employ the parameter estimates of the regime switching model to parameterize the data generating process used in our simulated power analysis.

5. EMPIRICAL ESTIMATES

Before turning to the regime switching regression model, we first estimate a regime switching model for the mean and variance of the excess return in Eq. (14). In this way, we explore the distinct properties of the returns in the bear, bull, and normal states of the market. This also allows us to assess the significance of the coefficients and the fit of the regime switching model, without the additional complications induced by time varying transition probabilities and the inclusion of a persistent predictive regressor.

Tables 1 and 2 respectively show the estimated coefficients and transition coefficients in the pure regime switching model without predictors. Table 1 provides the estimates of $\beta_0(s_t)$ and $\sigma_1(s_t)$ for each state s_t, when restricting $\beta_1(s_t)=0$ in Eq. (5). Likewise, Table 2 provides estimates of the coefficients of the transition probabilities in Eq. (8), which are non-time varying in the absence of a predictor.[6] Standard errors are given in parenthesis.

For the purposes of comparison, we include the results for the single state model in column 2 of Table 1.[7] This shows a mean monthly (log) excess return for the S&P500 of 0.0051, or approximately 6 percent on an annual basis, over the entire sample period and a return variance of 0.0021. Columns 3 and 4 show the estimated bear and bull state values for the two state model. The mean return in the bull state is substantially higher than in the bear state, whereas the variance of the bear state is nearly nine times as high as that of the bull state, reflecting the greater turbulence that occurs during market downturns. In both cases, the difference between the estimates in the two states is several times bigger than the larger of the two standard errors, lending statistical support to the observation that the market behaves differently during bear and bull states. In the three state model (columns 5–7), the bull and bear states capture the more substantial rallies and downturns, with calmer periods absorbed by the normal state. Consequently, the three state models shows a much larger differential between average returns in the bull and bear markets. The bear market again shows the greatest volatility, while the bull state has the lowest return variance.

Table 1. Estimated Model Coefficients in Regime Switching Models without Predictors.

	Single State Model	Two State Model		Three State Model		
s_t	N/A	Bull	Bear	Bull	Normal	Bear
$\hat{\beta}_0(s_t)$	0.0051	0.0103	−0.0223	0.0105	0.0027	−0.0284
	(0.0014)	(0.0010)	(0.0078)	(0.0011)	(0.0042)	(0.0123)
$\hat{\sigma}_1^2(s_t)$	0.0021	0.0008	0.0074	0.0008	0.0021	0.0095
	(0.2184)	(0.0001)	(0.0000)	(0.0000)	(0.0003)	(0.0009)
H-Q IC	−3.3378	−3.6928			−3.6797	

The table shows the estimated expected return $\hat{\beta}_0(s_t)$ and variance $\hat{\sigma}_1^2(s_t)$ for each possible value of the state s_t. In other words, it shows the estimated coefficients in a restricted version (5), in which $\beta_1(s_t)=0$. Standard errors are given in parenthesis. The bottom line provides the value of the Hannan and Quinn (1979) information criteria (H-Q IC), with a lower value indicating a better penalized fit.

Table 2. Transition Probability Model Coefficients in Regime Switching Model without Predictors.

	Intercepts				
	Two state model		Three state model		
s_t/s_{t-1}	Bull (i=1) $\hat{\theta}_{0,11}$	Bear (i=2) $\hat{\theta}_{0,21}$	Bull (i=1) $\hat{\theta}_{0,1j}$	Normal (i=2) $\hat{\theta}_{0,2j}$	Bear (i=3) $\hat{\theta}_{0,3j}$
Bull (j=1)	1.8780	−1.0058	2.2325	−1.9328	−1.5921
	(0.1264)	(0.1459)	(0.1326)	(0.3365)	(0.3114)
Normal (j=2)			−1.9567	2.2392	−1.4603
			(3.4577)	(0.6587)	(0.3455)

The table entries show the estimated intercepts in (8), the model for the transition probabilities in (5), which are non-time varying in the absence of a predictor. Standard errors are given in parenthesis.

Columns 2–3 of Table 2 show the estimated intercepts in the model for the transition probabilities between bear and bull states in the two state model. Both states are quite persistent, but the probability of switching from bear to bull state in any period is substantially higher than the probability of switching from bull to bear. This reflects the greater duration of bull states. Columns 4–6 of the same table provide the coefficients of the transition probabilities for the three state model. All three states are again persistent, but the normal and bull states are more persistent than the bear state. In all cases, the standard errors suggest that the estimates are reasonably precise.

The last row of Table 1 shows the Hannan and Quinn (1979) information criteria (H-Q IC) for each model, with lower, more negative values denoting a better penalized fit.[8] Both regime switching models are strongly favored relative to the single state model and the two state model shows a slight improvement over the three state model.[9]

We now include the dividend price ratio as a state-dependent predictor for the returns themselves in Eq. (5).[10] This arguably allows for a more realistic specification of the predictive regression model, which incorporates the difference in expected return and variance across the bear and bull states. It also allows for the predictive power of the dividend price ratio to vary across states. In addition, we allow the dividend price ratio to help predict the transition probability between bear and bull states via its inclusion in the model for the time varying transition probabilities in Eq. (8). To the extent that valuation variables may predict transitions between bull and bear markets, this may have stronger practical implications than return predictions within a given state.

Drawing inference in the regime shift predictive regression model is presumably complicated by a similar second order bias as in the linear predictive regression model. Deriving techniques that avoid second order bias and size distortion in this highly nonlinear model is a worthy goal for future research, but lies beyond both the scope and needs of our current paper, in which we require only consistent model estimates in order to anchor our simulated power comparisons in Section 7. In a related context, Gonzalo and Pitarakis (2012) develop an IVX-based predictive regression test with structural breaks. Although their model differs in a number of important respects from that in Eqs. (5) and (8), their finding offers general support for the existence of breaks or regime changes in predictive regression.

Table 3 shows the parameters estimates and standard errors in parenthesis in the regime switching predictive regression model (5) with time varying transition probabilities given by Eq. (8). The results for the two state model are shown in columns 3–4. As in Table 1, the bull state has a higher mean return, whereas the bear state has a higher standard deviation. The predictive power of the dividend yield (if significant) is also about seven times as large in the bear state as in the bull state. Gonzalo and Pitarakis (2012) recently come to a similar conclusion in a model of predictive regression with structural breaks. In the three state model shown in columns 5–7, it is the bear state in which the dividend yield is most strongly predictive, with the coefficient on the dividend price ratio positive but estimated with a large standard error.

Table 3. Coefficient Estimates in Regime Switching Predictive Regression Model with Time Varying Transition Probabilities.

	Single State Model	Two State Model		Three State Model		
s_t=:	N/A	Bull	Bear	Bull	Normal	Bear
$\hat{\beta}_0(s_t)$	0.0057	0.0110	−0.0274	0.0153	0.0028	−0.0028
	(0.0015)	(0.0012)	(0.0089)	(0.0013)	(0.0034)	(0.0095)
$\hat{\beta}_1(s_t)$	0.0018	0.0020	0.0144	0.0036	0.0032	0.0065
	(0.0013)	(0.0010)	(0.0070)	(0.0012)	(0.0029)	(0.0062)
$\hat{\sigma}_1^2(s_t)$	0.0021	0.0009	0.0074	0.0007	0.0014	0.0075
	(0.0010)	(0.0001)	(0.0010)	(0.0001)	(0.0002)	(0.0007)
H-Q IC	−3.3396	−3.6911		−3.6478		

The table entries show the estimates of the coefficients in the regime switching predictive regression model (5) for each possible value of the state s_t. Standard errors are given in parenthesis. The bottom line provides the value of the Hannan and Quinn (1979) information criteria (H-Q IC), with a lower value indicating a better penalized fit. Note that the inclusion of the dividend price ratio as a predictor may induce a predictive regression problem, a solution for which has yet to be provided in this regime switching model. Therefore, standard errors can only be relied on as a rough indicator of the estimation variance, but should not be employed to draw formal inferences.

Table 4 shows the estimates and standard errors for the parameters in Eq. (8) governing the transition probabilities. Here, we focus our comments on the two state model in columns 2–3, whose parameters are the most readily interpretable, as seen from Eq. (9). The first panel provides the estimates of the intercepts (the $\theta_{0,ij}$ in Eq. (8)). The diagonal element of the intercepts ($\hat{\theta}_{0,11}$) is large and positive, while the off-diagonal element ($\hat{\theta}_{0,21}$) is negative. This indicates that the states are again persistent, with a relatively small probability of switching in any single period. The second panel in Table 4 shows the slope coefficients (the $\theta_{1,ij}$ in Eq. (8)). The positive estimate of $\hat{\theta}_{1,11}$ in the second column suggests that the conditional probability of remaining in a bull market is highest when the dividend price ratio is large. Put another way, a switch from bull to bear market, possibly via a market crash, appears more likely when the stocks are highly valued relative to dividends (low dividend price ratio). The negative estimate of $\hat{\theta}_{1,21}$ suggests that the transition from bear to bull market is also more likely when stocks are relatively higher valued. This may reflect the observation that bull markets sometimes end in sudden crashes, whereas the transition from bear to bull often follows a more gradual market rally, which allows the stock prices to partially recover prior to the onset of the next bull market.

The last row of Table 3 shows the Hannan and Quinn (1979) information criteria (H-Q IC) for each model. The inclusion of the dividend price

Table 4. Time Varying Transition Probability Model Coefficients in Regime Switching Predictive Regression Model.

Intercepts					
	Two state model		Three state model		
s_t/s_{t-1}	Bull (i=1) $\hat{\theta}_{0,11}$	Bear (i=2) $\hat{\theta}_{0,21}$	Bull (i=1) $\hat{\theta}_{0,1j}$	Normal (i=2) $\hat{\theta}_{0,2j}$	Bear (i=3) $\hat{\theta}_{0,3j}$
Bull (j=1)	2.2589	−1.0872	2.0002	−2.0033	−1.9870
	(0.2272)	(0.2035)	(0.2090)	(0.3422)	(0.2724)
Normal (j=2)			−1.9965	2.0148	−1.9790
			(2.6658)	(0.3991)	(0.3856)
Slope Coefficients					
	Two state model		Three state model		
s_t/s_{t-1}	Bull (i=1) $\hat{\theta}_{1,11}$	Bear(i=2) $\hat{\theta}_{1,21}$	Bull (i=1) $\hat{\theta}_{1,1j}$	Normal (i=2) $\hat{\theta}_{1,2j}$	Bear (i=3) $\hat{\theta}_{1,3j}$
Bull (j=1)	0.3356	−0.3296	0.0139	0.0063	−0.0145
	(0.1478)	(0.1732)	(0.1675)	(0.4277)	(0.3006)
Normal (j=2)			−0.0033	−0.0023	−0.0095
			(1.9531)	(0.3386)	(0.4061)

The table entries show the estimates of the coefficients in (8), the model for the time transition probabilities in the regime switching predictive regression model (5). Standard errors are given in parenthesis. Note that the inclusion of the dividend price ratio as a predictor may induce a predictive regression problem, a solution for which has yet to be provided in this regime switching model. Therefore, standard errors can only be relied on as a rough indicator of the estimation variance, but should not be employed to draw formal inferences.

ratio leads to a lower H-Q IC in all models, although it is unclear if the difference is significant. Among the models with the dividend price ratio included in Table 3, the two state model has the lowest H-Q IC. Its value is substantially lower than the single state model or linear predictive regression. The two state model also has a somewhat better fit than the three state model. We therefore employ the two state model with the dividend price ratio as our baseline model in which to anchor our simulations in Section 7. Fig. 1 shows the fitted probabilities of a bear state in this model, with the calendar date shown on the horizontal axis and the major market downturns listed in the figure caption. Although during a majority of the time the probability of the bear state is low, the model appears to identify nearly all of the major historical downturns and/or market crashes as bear states. Indeed, it would appear to do quite a good job in capturing the major periods that most market observers would classify as bear states.

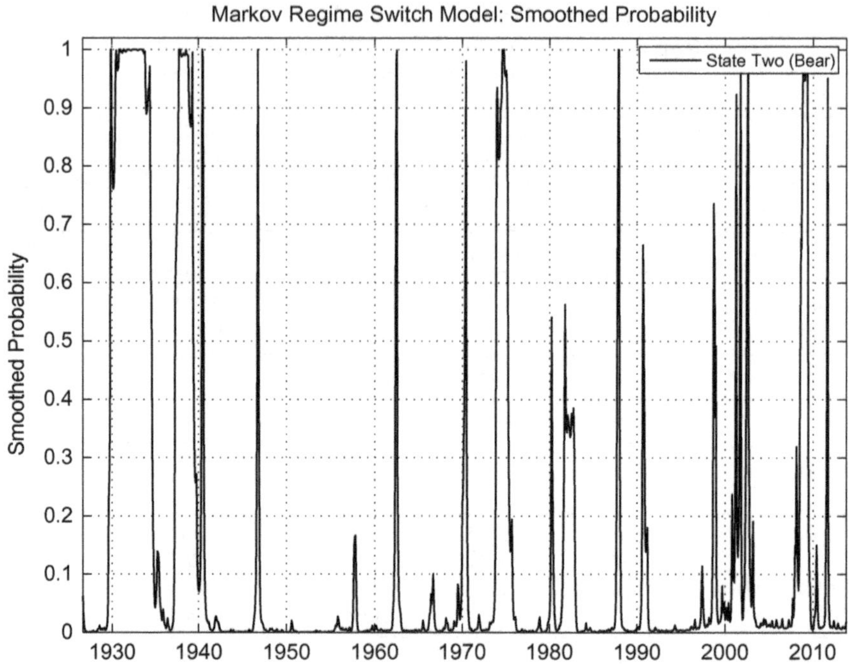

Fig. 1. Fitted Bear State Probabilities in Two State Regime Switching Predictive Regression Model with Time Varying Transition Probabilities. Major Market Downturns: 1929–1933 The Great Depression; 1937–1938 Recession; 1945 End of the War Recession; 1960–1961 Recession; 1969–1970 Recession; 1973–1975 Oil Crisis; Early 1980s Recession; Early 1990s Recession; Early 2000s Recession; December 2007–June 2009 Great Recession.

6. LONG-HORIZON REGRESSION SPECIFICATIONS AND TESTS

In the simulated power exercise that follows, the empirical researcher is not assumed to know the true model. Instead it is assumed that either a short or long-horizon linear predictive regression is employed as an empirical specification. In particular, we consider two long-horizon specifications from the literature, both of which share the same null hypothesis, but which differ in the formulation of their alternative. Both involve the choice of a horizon length (k), which in some asymptotic analysis is modeled as a function of the sample size T (Phillips & Lee, 2013; Valkanov, 2003) and in others taken to be arbitrarily large, but fixed, as in Hjalmarsson (2011). A fairly general formulation covering both of these possibilities is given by

$$k = \lambda T^{\nu} \quad \text{for} \quad 0 \leq \nu \leq 1, \quad \lambda > 0, \quad \text{and } \lambda \mathbf{I}(\nu \neq 0) \leq 1 \tag{17}$$

where $\mathbf{I}()$ denotes the indicator function. In Eq. (17), $\nu = 0$ corresponds to a fixed horizon as in Hjalmarsson (2011), ($\nu = 1$, $0 < \lambda < 1$) corresponds to a horizon that grows at a fixed fraction of sample size as in Valkanov (2003), and ($\lambda = 1$, $0 < \nu < 1$) allows a horizon that grows more slowly than T, as in Phillips and Lee (2013).

6.1. Standard Long-Horizon Specification

One of the most common versions of the long-horizon specification is given by Eq. (2), in which r_{t+k}^{k} is the long-horizon (k period) return in Eq. (1). The null hypothesis of non-predictability is tested via a test of the parameter restriction in Eq. (3) under the maintained hypothesis[11] that

$$E_t \varepsilon_{1,t+k}^{k} = 0 \tag{18}$$

6.2. Rearranged Long-Horizon Regression

We also consider a rearrangement of this regression originally proposed by Cochrane (1991) and Jegadeesh (1991) and given by

$$r_{t+k} = \beta_0^*(k) + \beta_1^*(k) x_t^k + \varepsilon_{t+k}^{*,k} \tag{19}$$

in which a one period return is regressed on the long-horizon (or partially summed) regressor

$$x_t^k = \sum_{j=1}^{k} x_{t+k-j} \tag{20}$$

The null hypothesis of non-predictability is then tested using the coefficient restriction

$$H_0 : \beta_1^*(k) = 0 \tag{21}$$

under the maintained assumption that

$$E_t \varepsilon^{*,k}_{t+1} = 0 \tag{22}$$

Liu and Maynard (2007) use this same rearranged regression to propose an exact nonparametric test of long-horizon predictability based on a sign test. Phillips and Lee (2013) employ this specification to provide a long-horizon version of the IVX solution to the predictive regression problem.

Since x_t^k is realized at time $t+k-1$, the rearranged regression in Eq. (19) can also be viewed as a short-horizon regression that uses a long history of the predictor x_t as its regressor. Note, however, that the temporal distance between the one period component returns and one period component predictors in the two regressions, (2) and (19), are the same. That is, $(r_{t+k}, x_t^k) = (r_{t+k}, x_{t+k-1} + x_{t+k-2} + \ldots + x_t)$ and $(r_{t+k}^k, x_t) = (r_{t+1} + r_{t+2} + \ldots r_{t+k}, x_t)$ both involve spacings of 1,2,... *and k* periods between r_t and x_t. Therefore, when (r_t, x_t) are jointly covariance stationary the rearrangement in Eq. (19) can be motivated by expressing $\beta_1(k) = \text{cov}(r_{t+k}^k, x_t)/\text{var}(x_t)$ and $\beta_1^*(k) = \text{cov}(r_{t+k}, x_t^k)/\text{var}(x_t^k)$ and noting that the covariances in the numerator are equivalent. In other words, the null hypotheses that $\beta_1(k) = 0$ and that $\beta_1^*(k) = 0$ impose the same orthogonality restriction, viz. $\text{cov}(r_{t+k}^k, x_t) = \text{cov}(r_{t+k}, x_t^k) = 0$. More generally, even when x_t is not stationary, under the maintained hypothesis in Eq. (22), Liu and Maynard (2007) and Phillips and Lee (2013) show that the null hypothesis Eq. (21) of the rearranged specification implies the original null hypothesis in Eq. (3), together with the maintained assumption Eq. (18).[12] Therefore, the two formulations test the same null hypothesis, but may have different power implications under the alternative hypothesis.

6.3. Long-Horizon Tests for the Standard Specification

We are not currently aware of a valid existing method of testing Eq. (3) using the traditional long-horizon formulation in Eq. (2) under the general specifications Eq. (12) and Eq. (17) for the persistence of predictor, x_t and the choice of the horizon k. Nevertheless, this specification is of particular interest since it is perhaps the mostly widely used in the empirical literature. Within the confines of the local-to-unity model, which imposes $\eta = 1$ in Eq. (12), Valkanov (2003) and Hjalmarsson (2011) provide long-horizon predictive tests based on Eq. (2) employing local-to-unity asymptotics and Bonferroni bounds procedures.

Valkanov (2003) provides the asymptotic distribution of the standard t-test for testing the restriction (3) in Eq. (2) under a local-to-unity asymptotic specification for x_t (12, with $\eta = 1$) and a horizon that grows at a fixed fraction of the sample size ($v = 1$ in Eq. (17)). For a given value of the local-to-unity parameter c, this provides for a correct critical value for the standard test statistic, scaled by the square-root of the sample size. However, since the critical value depends on c, which cannot be consistently estimated in a time series context, a Bonferroni procedure based on a first stage confidence interval is employed. This approach is therefore similar in spirit to the short-horizon predictive test of Cavanagh et al. (1995). Both employ a standard test statistic (possibly after rescaling) with corrected critical values.

Hjalmarsson (2011) instead corrects the test statistic by providing a second order endogeneity correction to the estimator of $\beta_1(k)$ on which the test is based. This is accomplished via an augmented regression of the type first introduced by Phillips (1991)[13]

$$r_{t+k}^k = \beta_0(k) + \beta_1(k)x_t + \phi(k)\Delta_c x_t^k + \varepsilon_{1,t+k}^{+,k} \quad \text{where} \tag{23}$$

$$\Delta_c x_t^k = \sum_{j=1}^{k} \left(x_{t-k+j} - \left(1 + \frac{c}{T}\right) x_{t-k+j-1} \right) = \sum_{j=1}^{k} v_{t-k+j}$$

The inclusion of the term $\Delta_c x_t^k$ in Eq. (23)[14] removes the endogeneity bias in the estimate of $\beta_1(k)$ in Eq. (23), denoted by $\hat{\beta}_1^+(k)$. Although the distribution of $\hat{\beta}_1^+(k)$ still depends on the horizon length k, it does so in a simple way. As is well explained in Boudoukh et al. (2008), under the null hypothesis in Eq. (3), estimates of $\beta_1(k)$ are approximately proportional to k. Consequently, Hjalmarsson (2011) shows that when rescaled by the horizon length, $\hat{\beta}_1^+(k)/k$ has a mixed normal null limiting distribution whose variance no longer depends on k. Likewise, letting $t_k^+(c)$ denote the standard t-statistic associated with the test of $H_0 : \beta_1(k) = 0$ in Eq. (23), he shows that

$$t_k^+(c)/\sqrt{k} \to_d N(0, 1) \tag{24}$$

under the null hypothesis, justifying the use of standard critical values.

In the simulations below, we will refer to $t_k^+(c)/\sqrt{k}$ as the "oracle" version of Hjalmarsson's (2011) test. It is infeasible in practice, because the augmentation $\Delta_c x_t^k$ depends on the unknown value of c. In practice, a

Bonferroni bound based on a first-stage confidence interval for c is therefore required in order to draw inference. Denoting this confidence interval, with confidence level $1-\alpha_1$ by $\left(\underline{c}_{\alpha_1}, \overline{c}_{\alpha_1}\right)$ a feasible, yet conservative version of the test rejects if

$$t_{k,\min}^{+}/\sqrt{k} = \inf_{c \in \left(\underline{c}_{\alpha_1}, \overline{c}_{\alpha_1}\right)} t_k^{+}(c)/\sqrt{k} > z_{\alpha_2} \tag{25}$$

where $z_{\alpha 2}$ is the standard normal critical value associated with the significance level α_2, such that $\alpha_1+\alpha_2=\alpha$, where α is the desired significance level of the test. In other words, a rejection occurs for the Bonferroni bounds test only if it occurs for every possible value of c in the first stage confidence interval. The requirement that $\alpha_1+\alpha_2=\alpha$ can lead to overly conservative tests and in practice adjustments to α_1 are typically recommended in order to keep the test from becoming too conservative (Campbell & Yogo, 2006; Cavanagh et al., 1995). In implementing this test, we select α_1 according to the recommendations in Hjalmarsson (2011), to which we refer the reader for further details. In the linear predictive regression context, Hjalmarsson (2012) finds that his test has better power properties than the earlier test by Valkanov (2003). Thus, we employ this version of the test of the restriction (3) in Eq. (2).

In an important recent paper, Phillips (2014) has shown that the Stock (1991) confidence interval for the local-to-unity parameter c has zero asymptotic coverage when the data generating process is stationary. This can lead to either invalidity or excessive conservatism of Bonferroni procedures based on a first stage confidence interval for c, when the true process is mildly integrated ($\eta<1$ in Eq. (12)) or stationary. Although Hjalmarsson (2011) employs an alternative first stage bound, based on Chen and Deo (2009), his simulations do indicate that his test becomes increasingly conservative for large negative values of c, particularly at long horizons.

We address this in several respects. First, for all of our simulations, we compare the power of the test across the oracle version in Eq. (24), in addition to the Bonferroni version in Eq. (25). Although the oracle version of the test is not feasible, this allows us to assess whether any of the power comparisons across horizons is driven primarily by the implementation of the Bonferroni bound. More importantly, we include power comparisons for the new IVX-based long-horizon test of Phillips and Lee (2013). This is the first regression-based long-horizon test that we are aware of which does not require Bonferroni bounds. Since it is based not on Eq. (2), but rather on the rearranged regression (19), we discuss its implementation in the next section. Currently, we are not aware of any IVX test based on the original long-horizon specification in Eq. (2). Given the emphasis in the empirical literature on the specification in Eq. (2), we feel that it is important to include feasible tests based on this specification in our power comparisons.

6.4. Long-Horizon IVX Test for the Rearranged Specification

Phillips and Lee (2013) develop an IVX estimator and predictive test for use in the long-horizon context, employing the rearranged regression in Eq. (19). They refer to their test as the long-horizon IVX (LHIVX) test. As mentioned above, unlike other long-horizon regression based tests, the LHIVX test does not rely on Bonferroni bounds or first stage confidence intervals for c. Instead it provides a single test statistic with a standard normal limit distribution yielding simple inference. Consequently, its validity is not restricted to the local-to-unity model, and it is easily applied in multivariate contexts. Indeed, Phillips and Lee (2013) allow for a very general model of the persistence in x_t as in Eq. (12).

IVX-based tests employ an instrument that is a mildly filtered version of the original regressor x_t. The instrument is filtered enough so that the endogeneity term is not present in the limit distribution of the instrumental variable estimator, but not so much that it unduly reduces the instrument strength. An important theoretical foundation for its development is Phillips and Magdalinos (2007)'s generalization of the local-to-unity framework to allow for mildly integrated variables. The instrument is designed to be a mildly integrated regressor ($\eta < 1$ in Eq. (12)). This intermediate persistence of the instrument is crucial to the success of the IVX approach, since an I(1) or local-to-unity based instrument would still be subject to an endogeneity bias that depends on c, whereas an I(0) instrument would only be weakly correlated with an I(1) regressor.

We will focus on the case of a single regressor, since this is the case we consider in Section 7. In the short-horizon case, when $k = 1$ in Eq. (19), their IVX instrument is defined as the mildly filtered series

$$\tilde{z}_t = \sum_{j=1}^{T} (1 + c_z/T^{\delta_z})^{(t-j)} \Delta x_j \tag{26}$$

where $c_z < 0$ and $0 < \delta_z < 1$ are specified by the researcher. In the context of the long-horizon regression when $k > 1$ in Eq. (19), Phillips and Lee (2013) propose the long-horizon instrument

$$\tilde{z}_t^k = \sum_{j=1}^{k} \tilde{z}_{t+j-1} \tag{27}$$

which is partially summed in the same way as the regressor in Eq. (20). Under an additional rate condition that guides the choice of c_z and δ_z, Phillips and Lee (2013) show that their estimator is asymptotically mixed normal, resulting in standard normal or chi-squared inference over the wide range of persistence levels for x_t in Eq. (12), including mildly integrated, nearly integrated, integrated, mildly explosive, and locally explosive models.

7. POWER OF LONG-HORIZON REGRESSION IN LINEAR AND REGIME SWITCHING PREDICTIVE REGRESSION MODELS

We provide a simulation-based comparison of the power of short- and long-horizon linear regression predictive tests when the true model is given by the regime switching model in Eq. (5) with persistent endogenous regressors as in Eqs. (11−13). As a point of comparison, we also provide results when the data is generated from the short-horizon linear predictive regression Eq. (7).

The regime switching model has a good number of parameters associated with it. In order to ensure that we simulate from a realistic parameterization of the model, we use the estimates in Table 3 to set the default values of the parameters in Eq. (5). Similarly, we use the estimates in Table 4 to simulate the model for the time varying transition probabilities in Eq. (8). We focus on the two regime ($N=2$) model, which appears to have the best fit, but also compare it to the linear predictive regression ($N=1$).[15] In the model for x_t, the parameters in Eq. (12) are not estimable and there is a genuine uncertainty regarding the persistence of valuation predictors such as the dividend price ratio. We consider two specifications of Eq. (12): ($c=-2.5$, $\eta=1$) and ($c=-20$, $\eta=1$). The first represents a case in which the series is almost as persistent as a unit root, whereas the second represents the case of a much less persistent series. The innovations for return and predictor series are drawn from Eq. (13) using a multivariate normal distribution with correlation $\delta=-0.95$, which is typical of valuation predictors, such as the dividend price ratio.[16] We consider $T=200$ as a fairly small sample and $T=1{,}048$, the sample size in our data set described in Section 4. All simulation results are based on 2,000 replications.

We restrict certain parameters under the null hypothesis. In the linear predictive regression it is typical to test the null hypothesis that $\beta_1=0$ in Eq. (7) under the maintained assumption that $E_t\varepsilon_{t+1}=0$, which is equivalent to the non-predictability condition $E_t r_{t+1}=\beta_0$.[17] We enforce the same non-predictability condition when imposing the null hypothesis in the regime switching model. This implies both zero slope coefficients in all states and intercepts that do not vary across states, i.e.,

$$H_0 : \begin{pmatrix} \beta_0(s_t) \\ \beta_1(s_t) \end{pmatrix} = \begin{pmatrix} \beta_{0,0} \\ 0 \end{pmatrix} \quad \text{for all states } s_t \tag{28}$$

For $\beta_{0,0}$, the null value of β_0, we take a weighted average of our empirical estimates of $\beta_0(s_t)$ across the N states, where the weights are given by the unconditional state probabilities implied by the transition probabilities in Eq. (8) evaluated at the mean value of the predictor $\bar{x}$.

In order to provide a power curve, rather than simply power at a single point in the alternative, we allow the parameters that are restricted under the null hypothesis to drift back toward their default (estimated) values under the alternative hypothesis, i.e.,

$$H_A : \begin{pmatrix} \beta_0(s_t) \\ \beta_1(s_t) \end{pmatrix} = \begin{pmatrix} \beta_{0,0} \\ 0 \end{pmatrix} + \frac{\gamma}{T^{(1+v_2)/2}} \begin{pmatrix} \beta_0^*(s_t) - \beta_{0,0} \\ \beta_1^*(s_t) \end{pmatrix} \tag{29}$$

where $\beta_0^*(s_t)$ and $\beta_1^*(s_t)$ are the default values of the parameters taken from the empirical estimates in each state shown in Table 4. The value of γ determines the distance from the null hypothesis and is allowed to vary across the horizontal axis. The value of v_2 is specified below for each test.

Although the data is generated from the regime switching predictive regression model, we do not assume that the empirical researcher knows that this is the true model. Rather, our interest lies in comparing the power of the most common short- and long-horizon linear predictive regressions when the data is generated by a plausible nonlinear model, such as the regime switching predictive regression model. We compare the power of the long- and short-horizon regressions using the two well-known long-horizon specifications, the standard long-horizon regression Eq. (2), and the rearranged long-horizon regression Eq. (19), discussed in Section 6. We consider only the empirically relevant positive, one-sided alternatives $H_A : \beta_1(k) > 0$ or $H_A : \beta_1^*(k) > 0$ respectively to the null restrictions Eq. (3) and Eq. (21). To keep our comparisons easily viewable, in each figure we compare the power curve for the short-horizon specification $k = 1$ to two long-horizon specifications, where k is chosen according to Eq. (17). The choice of λ and ν are discussed separately below for each test.

In the case of the standard long-horizon regression Eq. (2), we simulate power comparisons across three different tests:

- Although the OLS-based test is invalid in our framework and highly sized distorted, it has nonetheless been influential in the literature. It is therefore of some interest to know whether longer horizon versions of the test lead to any power improvements or whether they merely aggravate size distortion. Thus we compare size-adjusted power of the OLS-based test between long- and short-horizon tests.
- As an alternative test that has conservative size within the confines of the local-to-unity model, we consider the feasible, Bonferroni version of the rescaled, endogeneity corrected tests of Hjalmarsson (2011) using the test statistic $t^+_{k,\min}/\sqrt{k}$ in Eq. (25). Since this test is not oversized, we compare power rather than size-adjusted power in this case.[18]
- Since Phillips (2014) has pointed out some important shortcomings with many of the existing Bonferroni-based approaches to predictive testing and Hjalmarsson (2011) reports that when c is large negative, the Bonferroni version of his test becomes more conservative at larger horizons, we also provide results for the oracle version of the same test in Eq. (24). Although the oracle version is of course infeasible, it helps us to ensure that none of the comparison are solely driven by the influence of the Bonferroni bounds in the feasible version of the test.

In the case of the rearranged regression, we compare two additional tests.

- We compare size-adjusted power in an OLS-based test of the rearranged regression.
- More interestingly, we also compare the power (without size-adjustment) of the IVX and LHIVX tests of Phillips and Lee (2013) discussed in Section 6.

Since this results in a great many power curves, we include only a few of the curves to illustrate our main findings below. Additional results, that generally confirm the main conclusions arrived at below, are available from the authors upon request. These include results using both the smaller sample size of $T = 200$ and the lower persistence parameter of $c = -20$.

7.1. Power Comparisons Based on the Standard Long-Horizon Specification

We first compare the size-adjusted power of short- and long-horizon tests based on Eq. (2) for the OLS-based test. We also compare power for both the Bonferroni and oracle versions of Hjalmarsson's (2011) test discussed in Section 6.3. Since these tests have nontrivial power against $O_p(T^{-1})$ alternatives, we set $v_2 = 1$ in Eq. (29). Similarly, we set $v = 1$ in Eq. (17) when selecting k and take $\lambda = 0.05$ and 0.010, resulting in values of $k = 10$ and $k = 20$ when $T = 200$ and $k = 52$ and $k = 104$ when $T = 1{,}048$. In all cases we compare to $k = 1$.

7.1.1. True Model Is a Linear Predictive Regression

Fig. 2 (using $T = 1{,}048$) provides the size-adjusted power curves of standard t-test when $k = 1$ and $k = 52$ and $k = 105$ when the true model is the linear predictive model in Eq. (7). The three curves are generally quite similar.

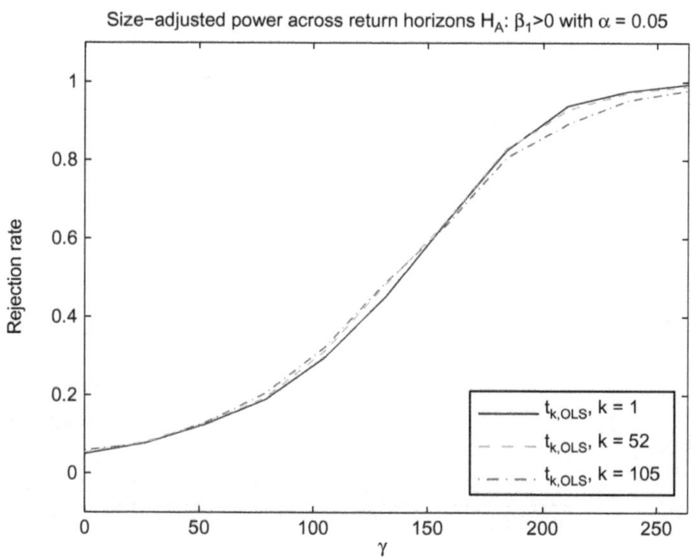

Fig. 2. The Size-Adjusted Power of the OLS Based Predictive Test when the Return is Generated from the Linear Predictive Regression Model in Eq. (7), the Predictor is Generated by the Local-to-Unity process in Eqs. (11) and (12) with $c = -2.5$, and the Residuals Are Generated from Eq. (13) Using a Multivariate Normal Distribution with $\delta = -0.95$. We Set $T = 1{,}048$.

A small power advantage to the longer horizon tests is detectable toward the middle of the power curve ($50 < \gamma < 150$). The OLS-based test does not make efficient use of the endogeneity between the regression error and regressor innovation, which may explain why there is room for some slight power advantages to the long-horizon specification. We next turn to the oracle version of Hjalmarsson's (2011) test in Fig. 3, which makes optimal use of this endogeneity within the confines of the linear predictive model with local-to-unity predictor. With the use of this more powerful test, the slight advantage of the long-horizon test disappears. The short-horizon is more powerful throughout the power curve. The dominance of the short-horizon test remains even after the test is made feasible using its Bonferroni implementation in Fig. 4. This confirms that when the true model is linear and the short-run regression is therefore correctly specified, the long-horizon tests should not be able to provide power improvements to efficient versions of the short-horizon test.

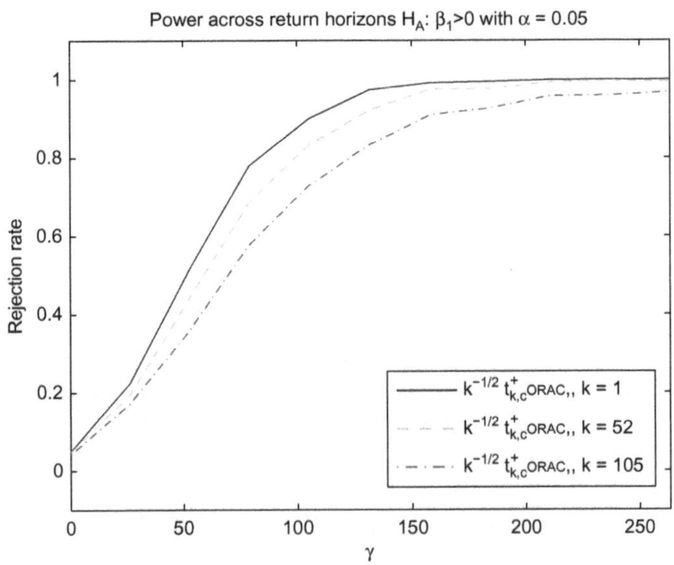

Fig. 3. The Power of the Oracle-Based Predictive Test when the Return is Generated from the Linear Predictive Regression Model in Eq. (7), the Predictor Is Generated by the Local-to-Unity Process in Eqs. (11) and (12) with $c = -2.5$, and the Residuals Are Generated from Eq. (13) Using a Multivariate Normal Distribution with $\delta = -0.95$. We Set $T = 1{,}048$.

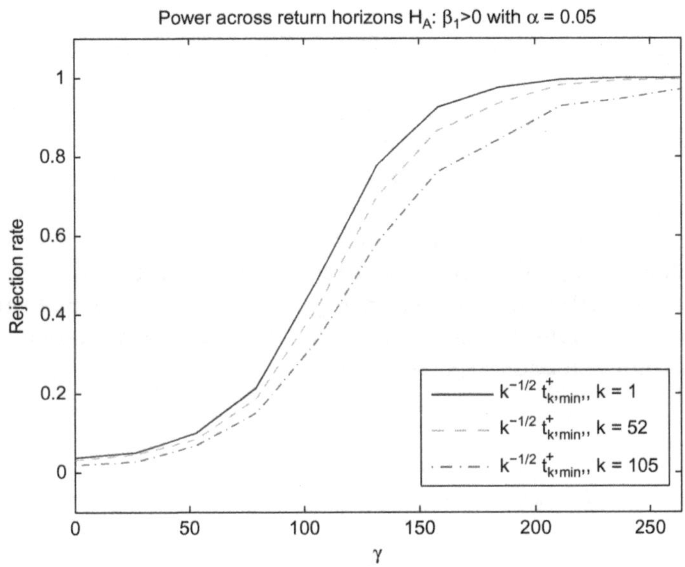

Fig. 4. The Power of the Bonferroni-Based Predictive Test when the Return Is Generated from the Linear Predictive Regression Model in Eq. (7), the Predictor Is Generated by the Local-to-Unity Process in Eqs. (11) and (12) with $c=-2.5$, and the Residuals Are Generated from Eq. (13) Using a Multivariate Normal Distribution with $\delta=-0.95$. We Set $T=1{,}048$.

7.1.2. True Model Is a Regime Switching Predictive Regression

We now consider the same comparisons in the regime switching predictive regression model, in which the regressor can be predictive for both the transition probabilities of switching between regimes and the return outcomes within regimes. In this case, both the short- and long-horizon models are inherently misspecified and act only as linear approximations to the true nonlinear model. In principle, there is no reason to argue that the long-horizon model couldn't provide an improved approximation and better power than the short-horizon model. Indeed, it would seem surprising if there were not some nonlinear models for which this is the case. The practical question that we now address is whether, using simulations based on empirical estimates of the regime switching model, we obtain power improvements at longer horizons. Put another way, if the regime switching model were the true model, would we be more likely to detect the resulting return predictability at longer horizons?

Our results suggest that this is not the case. Long-horizons tests fare no better (and sometimes worse) when the data is generated from nonlinear regime shift models, capturing bear/bull markets. We find this result even when allowing the regressor to be predictive of the regime shift itself. The OLS test, shown in Fig. 5 (using $T = 1{,}048$), again shows modest size-adjusted power advantages at long-horizons close to the null hypothesis, whereas the short-horizon test has the best power for distant alternatives. However, the short-horizon test continues to show the best power over the entire alternative in both the oracle and Bonferroni versions of Hjalmarsson's (2011) test, shown in Figs. 6 and 7. Thus, even in this non-linear model, the long-horizon tests do not provide a power advantage over their short-horizon counterparts.

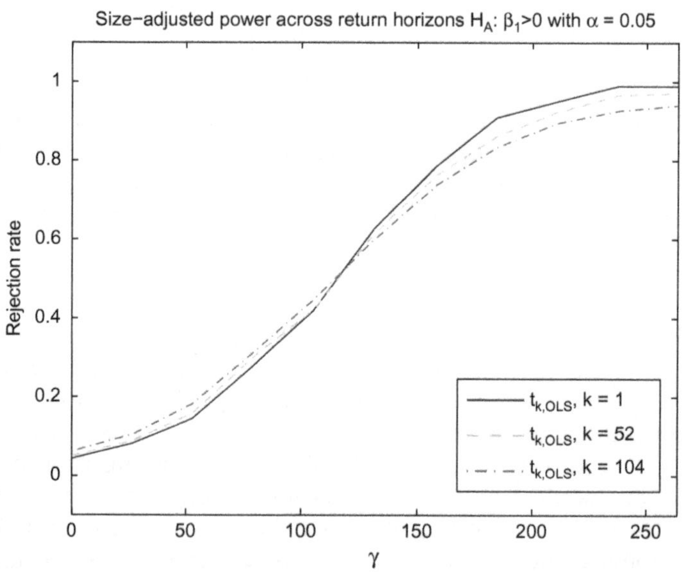

Fig. 5. The Size-Adjusted Power of the OLS-Based Predictive Test when the True Return Model Is the Two-State Regime Switching Model in Eq. (5) with Time Varying Transition Probabilities Given by Eq. (8), the Predictor Is Generated by the Local-to-Unity Process in Eqs. (11) and (12) with $c = -2.5$, and the Residuals Are Generated from Eq. (13) Using a Multivariate Normal Distribution with $\delta = -0.95$. We Set $T = 1{,}048$.

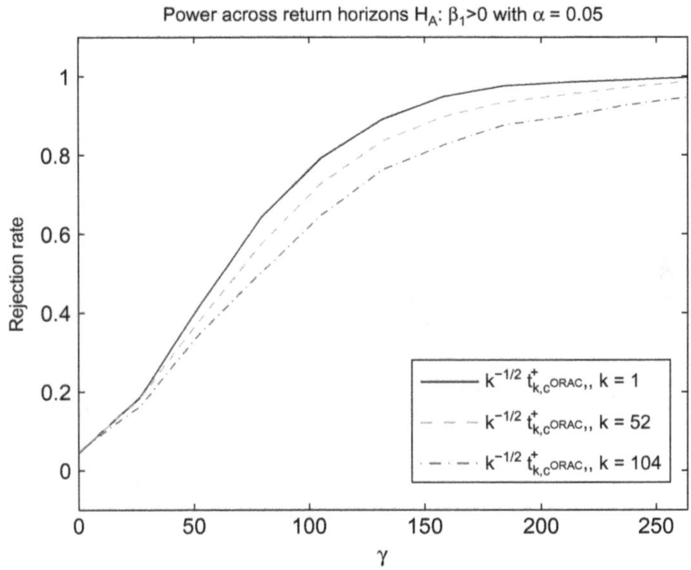

Fig. 6. The Power of the Oracle-Based Predictive Test when the True Return Model Is the Two-State Regime Switching Model in Eq. (5) with Time Varying Transition Probabilities Given by Eq. (8), the Predictor Is Generated by the Local-to-Unity Process in Eqs. (11) and (12) with $c=-2.5$, and the Residuals Are Generated from Eq. (13) Using a Multivariate Normal Distribution with $\delta=-0.95$. We Set $T=1{,}048$.

7.2. Power Comparisons Based on Rearranged Long-Horizon Specification

We now compare power across horizons in the rearranged long-horizon empirical specification in Eq. (19), with our primary focus on the IVX and LHIVX estimators discussed in Section 6. For the short-horizon IVX, $k=1$. For the LHIVX, Phillips and Lee (2013) consider return horizons that grow more slowly than sample size ($\nu<1$ in Eq. (17)). We fix $\lambda=1$ and consider both $\nu=0.80$ and $\nu=0.90$, resulting in values of $k=69$ and $k=117$ when $T=200$ and $k=260$ and $k=522$ when $T=1{,}048$. Phillips and Lee (2013) show that their test is divergent against alternatives of the rate $T^{-1/2}k^{-1/2}=T^{-(1+\nu)/2}$. Therefore, we set $\nu=0.80$ in the specification of the local alternative in Eq. (29), where γ again varies across the horizontal axis. Following both the recommendations of Phillips and Lee (2012, 2013) we

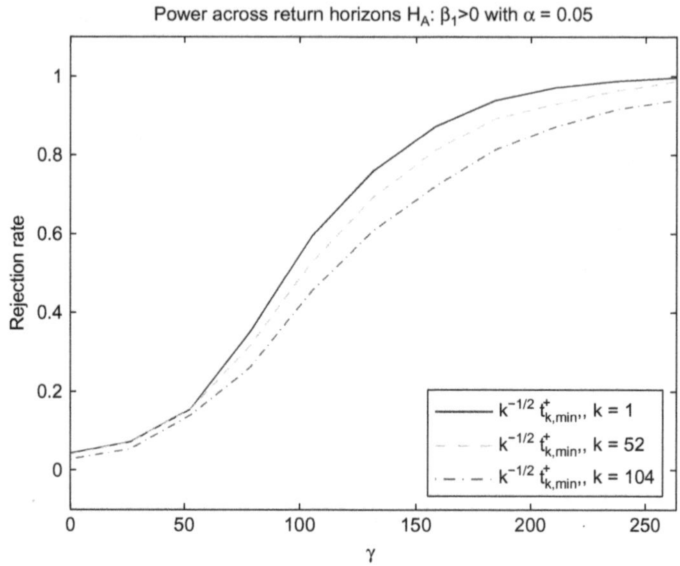

Fig. 7. The Power of the Bonferroni-Based Predictive Test when the True Return Model Is the Two-State Regime Switching Model in Eq. (5) with Time Varying Transition Probabilities Given by Eq. (8), the Predictor Is Generated by the Local-to-Unity Process in Eqs. (11) and (12) with $c=-2.5$, and the Residuals Are Generated from Eq. (13) Using a Multivariate Normal Distribution with $\delta=-0.95$. We Set $T=1,048$.

set $c_z=-5.0$. The selection of δ_Z in Eq. (26) requires slightly more attention. For the short-horizon IVX, Phillips and Lee (2012) recommend a value of δ_Z between 0.75 and 0.95. For the long-horizon regression, rate restrictions require $\delta_Z<\nu$ in Eq. (17) and Phillips and Lee (2013) suggest $\delta_Z=\nu-0.05$. Therefore, we employ $\delta_Z=0.75$ when $\nu=0.80$ and $\delta_Z=0.85$ when $\nu=0.90$. We compare these to two versions of the short-horizon IVX: $k=1$ with $\delta_Z=0.75$ and $k=1$ with $\delta_Z=0.85$. With these choices, we use recommended values of δ_Z in all cases and we can compare the short- and long-horizon regressions holding δ_Z fixed.

The LHIVX is a newly introduced test and we are not aware of any finite sample power results for the test even in the linear model, so it is interesting to compare its performance across horizons and choices of δ_Z. Fig. 8 provides this comparison in the linear predictive model for $T=1,048$ and $c=-2.5$. Of the two long-horizon tests, it is interesting to note that using $\nu=0.80$ (k = 261) with $\delta_Z=0.75$ has both better size and power than

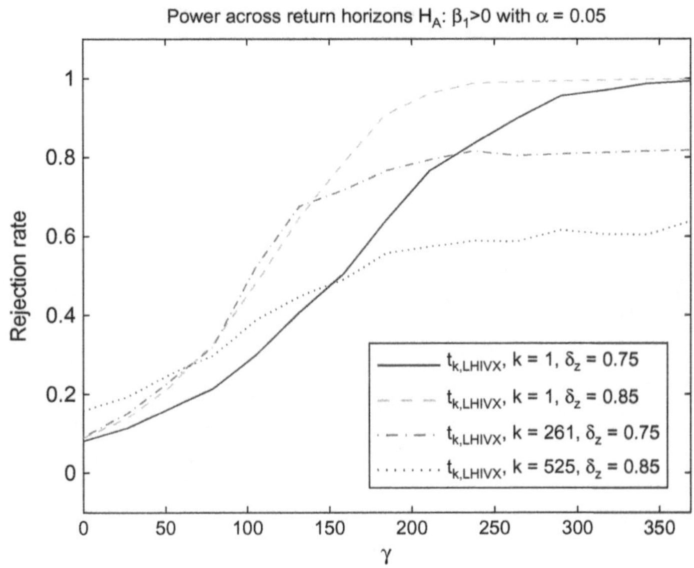

Fig. 8. The Power of the LHIVX Test in a Linear Predictive Regression Model. We Plot Power for Both $k=1$ and for k Given by Eq. (17) with $\lambda=1$ and $\nu=0.75$ and $\nu=0.90$. The Horizontal Axis Shows the Value of γ in Eq. (29) with $\nu_2=0.80$. Here We Set $c=-2.5$, $c_z=-5.0$, and $T=1{,}048$.

the test employing $\nu=0.90$ ($k=525$). This result was not expected, but it may be that $\nu=0.90$ comes too close to the restriction that $\nu<1$. In fact, the LHIVX test with $\nu=0.80$ and $\delta_Z=0.75$ has very good local power, dominating the short-horizon IVX test with the same value of δ_Z for $\gamma<200$. However, when using a larger value of $\delta_Z=0.85$, the short-horizon test does as well as the long-horizon test near the null hypothesis and provides better power further into the alternative. These results are interesting in that they highlight the important interplay between the choice of δ_Z and the horizon. Yet, overall they still suggest that with a good choice of δ_Z the short-horizon IVX can provide as much or more power than its long-horizon counterpart.

In Fig. 9, we next investigate the power of the LHIVX test when the data is generated by the regime switching model. The general conclusions do not change. The LHIVX test with $\nu=0.80$ ($k=250$) and the short-horizon IVX test with $\delta_Z=0.85$ are equally good and improve on the other two tests near the null hypothesis, while the short-horizon test with $\delta_Z=0.85$ appears to be the best further along the power curve.

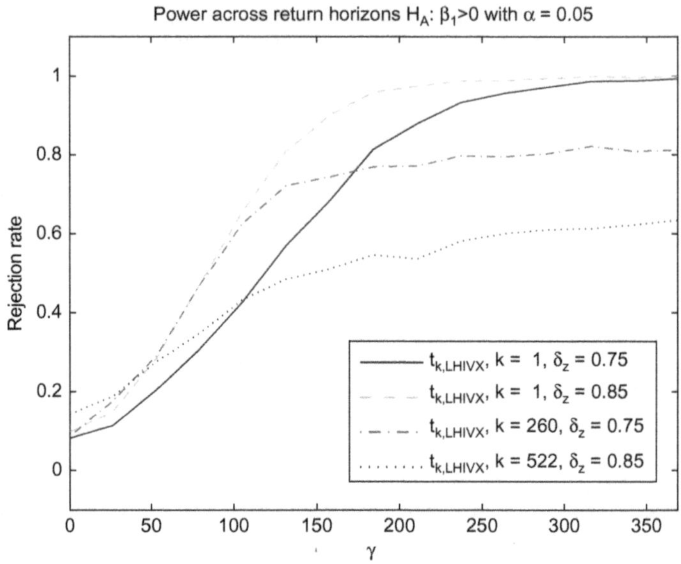

Fig. 9. The Power of the LHIVX Test in the Two-State Regime Switching Model with Time Varying Transition Probabilities. We Plot Power for Both $k=1$ and for k Given by Eq. (17) with $\lambda=1$ and $v=0.75$ and $v=0.90$. The Horizontal Axis Shows the Value of γ in Eq. (29) with $v_2=0.80$. Here We Set $c=-2.5$, $c_z=-5.0$, and $T=1{,}048$.

Overall, when the short-horizon test is efficient or based on a good selection of δ_Z, our simulations show little evidence of power improvements from longer horizon tests in either the linear predictive regression or the regime switching predictive regression model.

8. CONCLUSION

There has been much debate in the literature regarding the presumed power advantages of long-horizon regressions. With a few notable exceptions, most of this debate has taken place within the context of a linear predictive model as the true data generating process. In this case, long-horizon regression tests may have power advantages over short-horizon tests that do not fully exploit the information in the model, especially the contemporaneous endogeneity between the regressor innovation and the regression residual.

On the other hand, it seems unlikely that they would have advantages over more efficient short-horizon tests when a linear short-horizon model is the true model.

The class of nonlinear models is so large that it would not be surprising if one could find nonlinear models which are better approximated by long-horizon than short-horizon regression models. However, this would only seem to provide practical support for the long-horizon approach if both the nonlinear model that supports it and its parameter values are realistic. This argues in favor of a comparison based on simulations from an estimated nonlinear model that has already received support in the empirical literature.

In this paper we compare the power of short- and long-horizon tests in both the linear model and an empirically plausible nonlinear model, involving regime switching predictive regression with time varying transition probabilities that are also a function of the predictor. Previous empirical literature has shown this model to be successful in capturing the bull and bear states long observed by market participants. We use our empirical estimates to anchor our simulations in a realistic manner.

We then compare the power of short- and long-horizon tests when the true model is given by the estimated regime switching predictive regression model. As a point of reference, we provide similar comparisons when the data is generated by a linear regression model. We make these comparisons using two different versions of the long-horizon regressions: the standard long-horizon regression in Eq. (2), which has a long-horizon dependent variable and the rearranged long-horizon regression in Eq. (19), which uses a long-horizon predictor. Accordingly, we also consider two different recent long-horizon tests, the Hjalmarsson (2011) test and the Phillips and Lee (2013) long-horizon IVX (LHIVX) test. In addition, we compare size-adjusted power for the influential, though size-distorted, OLS-based tests used in much of the earlier empirical work. We also make comparisons using an infeasible, oracle version of the Hjalmarsson (2011) test.

Taken as a whole, our results are not overly supportive of the long-horizon regressions. In the case of the standard long-horizon specification, we find that that long-horizon regressions can provide at best a modest improvement in size-adjusted power using OLS-based tests. However, in more powerful versions of the tests, such as the oracle version of the Hjalmarsson (2011) test, or even its Bonferroni counterpart, the short-horizon test shows better power in both the linear and regime switching predictive tests.

In the context of the rearranged regression, the power of the LHIVX test depends on both the horizon and the parameter δ_Z, which determines the extent of the mild filtering used in the creation of the instrument. The theoretical results provide more flexibility in selecting this parameter at short horizons than in long horizons. For some choices of δ_Z the long-horizon IVX test can provide more power close to the null hypothesis than its short-horizon counterpart. However, with a better choice of δ_Z, we find that the short-horizon IVX is generally more powerful than the LHIVX, even close to the null hypothesis. The advantage to the short-horizon test increases as we move further from the null hypothesis.

Overall, our results support the contention that the higher power of long-horizon regressions may simply be a "myth" as argued by Boudoukh et al. (2008). On the other hand, regime switching models are not the only plausibly nonlinear models that could be considered in making these comparisons. Contrary to our results, improved power has been found in long-horizon regressions when using a nonlinear ESTAR model as the data generating process (Kilian & Taylor, 2003; Wohar & Rapach, 2005). Models incorporating financial bubbles (Evans, 1991; Phillips, Shi, & Yu, 2014) might also support the conjecture of improved power at longer horizons and this could be an interesting avenue for future research. More general theoretical results on the relative power of long horizon tests in nonlinear models might be possible in the general framework of Park and Phillips (1999).

NOTES

1. It also solves the much more general problem of cointegration with near integrated regressors, see Elliott (1998).
2. Kasparis, Andreou, and Phillips (2012) and Cai and Gao (2013) find evidence of nonlinear predictive power in the dividend yield for stock returns, while the results in Juhl (2014) are suggestive, but insignificant. Gonzalo and Pitarakis (2012) find evidence of structural breaks in the predictive regression relationship. However, none of these papers considers the implications for long-horizon predictive tests.
3. Locally ($c > 0$, $\eta = 1$) and mildly ($c > 0$, $0 < \eta < 1$) explosive processes are also allowed for in Eq. (12).
4. Recent research by Ghysels and Miller (2014) uncovers potentially serious bias in the use of interpolated data in the context of cointegration testing.
5. See Park and Phillips (1999).
6. Omitting the predictor restricts $\theta_{1,ij} = 0$ in Eq. (8) for all i,j.
7. We are grateful to Marcelo Perlin for use of his MATLAB code for the estimation of the fixed transition probability Markov Switching Models. His code is available online and documented in Perlin (2012).
8. Guidolin and Hyde (2010) similarly employ the H-Q IC to aid the selection of the number of states in a regime switching model.

9. In additional results, omitted for brevity, a marginally better H-Q IC value was obtained in the four state, but at the cost of large standard errors, resulting in the poor identification of a number of the model coefficients.

10. We are grateful to Zhuangxin Ding for use of his MATLAB code. As documented in Ding (2012), this code extends Perlin's (2012) original code in order to allow for time varying transition probabilities. In order to verify that global maximums were obtained, we compared estimation results and likelihood values across several perturbations to our initial starting values for the optimizations.

11. The maintained hypothesis in Eq. (18) ensures the r_{t+k} is unpredictable under the null in Eq. (3). We refer to it as a maintained hypothesis, since it is not usually explicitly tested in this literature.

12. As explained in Liu and Maynard (2007), Eqs. (21) and (22) imply $E_{t+j-1}r_{t+j} = \beta_0^*(k)$ and therefore $E_t r_{t+k} = k\beta_0(k)$, which is equivalent to Eqs. (3) and (18). See also Phillips and Lee (2013) for an insightful explanation of the relationship between the two long-horizon specifications.

13. In Eq. (23) the estimator $\beta_1^+(k)$ is equivalent to a local-to-unity version of the fully modified Phillips and Hansen (1990) estimator specialized to the context of the long-horizon predictive regression.

14. Due to the inclusion of this term, we include a plus in the superscript of $\varepsilon_{1,t+k}^{+,k}$ to distinguish it from $\varepsilon_{1,t+k}^{k}$.

15. We have also rerun many of our results using a three regime version of our model, based on earlier estimates, obtaining qualitatively similar results. A minor update to Tables 3–4 was made when reviewing the page proofs. Given the minor nature of the changes we do not anticipate that this would influence our power comparisons implemented prior to this update.

16. We estimate $\delta = -0.9424$ in the linear predictive regression using our data.

17. Since, following much of the literature, we do not impose $\beta_0 = 0$, this could be more precisely referred to as the null hypothesis of non-time varying predictability. The nonzero intercept allows for a non-time varying risk premium and accommodates the positive average returns that have been recorded over long historical periods.

18. In principle, it is not clear whether any of the tests we consider here are correctly sized when the residual variance $\sigma_1^2(s_t)$ varies across states under the null hypothesis. However, this does not appear to be an important practical concern in any of our simulations.

ACKNOWLEDGMENT

This paper was prepared for the 2013 Advances in Econometrics Conference: Essays in Honor of Peter C. B. Phillips held at the Southern Methodist University. We thank the conference participants, participants at the 2014 Meeting of the Canadian Economic Association, Erik Hjalmarsson, and Leo Michelis for useful discussion. We are grateful to the editors, Joon Park and Yoosoon Chang, and to an anonymous referee for very helpful comments and suggestions that have substantially improved the paper. We gratefully acknowledge the use of code provided by Erik Hjalmarsson and code made available online by Zhuanxin Ding and Marcelo Perlin. Maynard thanks the SSHRC for research funding.

REFERENCES

Ang, A., & Bekaert, G. (2007). Stock return predictability: Is it there? *Review of Financial Studies*, *20*(3), 651–707.

Bollen, N. P. B., Gray, S. F., & Whaley, R. E. (2000). Regime switching in foreign exchange rates: Evidence from currency option prices. *Journal of Econometrics*, *94*(1–2), 239–276.

Boudoukh, J., Richardson, M., & Whitelaw, R. (2008). The myth of long-horizon predictability. *The Review of Financial Studies*, *21*(4), 1577–1605.

Cai, B., & Gao, J. (2013). *Hermite series estimation in nonlinear cointegrating models*. Working Paper No. 17/13. Department of Econometrics and Business Statistics, Monash University.

Campbell, J., Lo, A., & MacKinlay, C. (1997). *The econometrics of financial markets*. Princeton, N.J: Princeton University Press.

Campbell, J. Y. (2001). Why long horizons? A study of power against persistent alternatives. *Journal of Empirical Finance*, *8*, 459–491.

Campbell, J. Y., & Shiller, R. (1988). The dividend-price ratio and expectations of future dividends and discount factors. *Review of Financial Studies*, *1*(3), 195–228.

Campbell, J. Y., & Yogo, M. (2006). Efficient tests of stock return predictability. *Journal of Financial Economics*, *81*(1), 27–60.

Cavanagh, C. L., Elliott, G., & Stock, J. H. (1995). Inference in models with nearly integrated regressors. *Econometric Theory*, *11*, 1131–1147.

Chan, N. H., & Wei, C. Z. (1987). Asymptotic inference for nearly nonstationary AR(1) processes. *Annals of Statistics*, *15*(3), 1050–1063.

Chauvet, M., & Potter, S. (2000). Coincident and leading indicators of the stock market. *Journal of Empirical Finance*, *7*(1), 87–111.

Chen, W. W., & Deo, R. S. (2009). The restricted likelihood ratio test at the boundary in autoregressive series. *Journal of Time Series Analysis*, *30*(6), 618–630.

Cheung, Y.-W., & Erlandsson, U. G. (2005). Exchange rates and Markov switching dynamics. *Journal of Business & Economic Statistics*, *23*, 314–320.

Chinn, M. D., & Meese, R. A. (1995). Banking on currency forecasts: How predictable is change in money? *Journal of International Economics*, *38*(1–2), 161–178.

Cochrane, J. (1991). Volatility tests and efficient markets: A review essay. *Journal of Monetary Economics*, *27*, 463–487.

Cochrane, J. H. (1999). New facts in finance. *Economic Perspectives, Federal Reserve Bank of Chicago*, *23*(3), 36–58.

Cochrane, J. H. (2008). The dog that did not bark: A defense of return predictability. *The Review of Financial Studies*, *21*(4), 1533–1575.

Cutler, D. M., Poterba, J. M., & Summers, L. H. (1991). Speculative dynamics. *Review of Economic Studies*, *58*(3), 529–546.

Dewachter, H. (2001). Can Markov switching models replicate chartist profits in the foreign exchange market? *Journal of International Money and Finance*, *20*(1), 25–41.

Ding, Z. (2012). *An implementation of markov regime switching model with time varying transition probabilities in MATLAB*. Retrieved from http://ssrn.com/abstract=2083332 or http://dx.doi.org/10.2139/ssrn.2083332

Elliott, G. (1998). On the robustness of cointegration methods when regressors have almost unit roots. *Econometrica*, *66*, 149–158.

Engel, C., & Hamilton, J. D. (1990). Long swings in the dollar: Are they in the data and do markets know it? *American Economic Review*, *80*(4), 689–713.

Evans, G. W. (1991). Pitfalls in testing for explosive bubbles in asset prices. *American Economic Review*, *81*(4), 922–930.

Fama, E., & French, K. (1988a). Dividend yields and expected stock returns. *Journal of Financial Economics*, *22*, 3–25.

Fama, E., & French, K. (1988b). Permanent and temporary components of stock prices. *Journal of Political Economy*, *96*, 246–273.

Fama, E. F., & Bliss, R. R. (1987). The information in long-maturity forward rates. *American Economic Review*, *77*(4), 680–692.

Ghysels, E., & Miller, J. I. (2014). *On the size distortion from linearly interpolating low-frequency series for cointegration tests*. Unpublished manuscript.

Goetzmann, W. N., & Jorion, P. (1993). Testing the predictive power of dividend yields. *Journal of Finance*, *48*(2), 663–679.

Gonzalo, J., & Pitarakis, J.-Y. (2012). Regime-specific predictability in predictive regressions. *Journal of Business & Economic Statistics*, *30*(2), 229–241.

Guidolin, M., & Hyde, S. (2010). Can VAR models capture regime shifts in asset returns? A long-horizon strategic asset allocation perspective. *Journal of Banking and Finance*, *36*(3), 695–716.

Guidolin, M., & Timmermann, A. (2005). Economic implications of bull and bear regimes in U.K. stock and bond returns. *Economic Journal*, *115*(500), 111–143.

Hamilton, J. D. (1989). A new approach to the economic analysis of nonstationary time series and the business cycle. *Econometrica*, *57*, 357–384.

Hannan, E. J., & Quinn, B. (1979). The determination of the order of an autoregression. *Journal of the Royal Statistical Society Series B 41*, 190–195.

Hjalmarsson, E. (2008). Interpreting long-horizon estimates in predictive regressions. *Finance Research Letters*, *5*(2), 104–117.

Hjalmarsson, E. (2011). New methods for inference in long-horizon regressions. *Journal of Financial and Quantitative Analysis*, *46*(3), 815–839.

Hjalmarsson, E. (2012). Some curious power properties of long-horizon tests. *Finance Research Letters*, *9*, 81–91.

Jansson, M., & Moreira, M. J. (2006). Optimal inference in regression models with nearly integrated regressors. *Econometrica*, *74*, 681–714.

Jegadeesh, N. (1991). Seasonality in stock price mean reversion: Evidence from the U.S. and the U.K. *Journal of Finance*, *46*, 1427–1444.

Juhl, T. (2014). A nonparametric test of the predictive regression model. *Journal of Business & Economic Statistics*, *32*(3), 387–394.

Kasparis, I., Andreou, E., & Phillips, P. C. B. (2012). *Nonparametric predictive regression*. Cowles Foundation Discussion Papers 1878. Cowles Foundation for Research in Economics, Yale University.

Kilian, L. (1999). Exchange rates and monetary fundamentals: What do we learn from long-horizon regressions? *Journal of Applied Econometrics*, *14*(5), 491–510.

Kilian, L., & Taylor, M. P. (2003). Why is it so difficult to beat the random walk forecast of exchange rates? *Journal of International Economics*, *60*(1), 85–107.

Kim, M. J., & Nelson, C. R. (1993). Predictable stock returns: The role of small sample bias. *Journal of Finance*, *48*, 641–662.

Liu, W., & Maynard, A. (2007). A new application of exact non-parametric methods to long-horizon predictability tests. *Studies in Nonlinear Dynamics & Econometrics*, *11*(1), Article 7.

Magdalinos, T., & Phillips, P. C. B. (2009). *Econometric inference in the vicinity of unity*. CoFie Working Paper No. 7, Singapore Management University.

Maheu, J. M., & McCurdy, T. H. (2000). Identifying bull and bear markets in stock returns. *Journal of Business & Economic Statistics*, *18*(1), 100–112.

Maheu, J. M., McCurdy, T. H., & Song, Y. (2012). Components of bull and bear markets: Bull corrections and bear rallies. *Journal of Business & Economic Statistics*, *30*(3), 391–403.

Mark, N. C. (1995). Exchange rates and fundamentals: Evidence on long-horizon predictability. *American Economic Review*, *85*(1), 201–218.

Mark, N. C., & Sul, D. (2006). *The power of long-horizon predictive tests*. Technical report. Department of Economics, Ohio State University.

Marmer, V. (2008). Nonlinearity, nonstationarity, and spurious forecasts. *Journal of Econometrics*, *142*(1), 1–27.

Park, J., & Phillips, P. C. B. (1999). Asymptotics for nonlinear transformations of integrated time series. *Econometric Theory*, *15*, 269–298.

Park, J. Y., & Phillips, P. C. B. (1988). Statistical inference in regressions with integrated processes: Part 1. *Econometric Theory*, *4*(3), 468–497.

Park, J. Y., & Phillips, P. C. B. (1989). Statistical inference in regressions with integrated processes: Part 2. *Econometric Theory*, *5*, 95–131.

Perlin, M. (2012). *MS Regress–The MATLAB package for Markov regime switching models*. Available at SSRN: http://ssrn.com/abstract=1714016 or http://dx.doi.org/10.2139/ssrn.1714016

Phillips, P. C. B. (1986). Understanding spurious regression in econometrics. *Journal of Econometrics*, *33*, 311–340.

Phillips, P. C. B. (1987). Towards a unified asymptotic theory for autoregression. *Biometrika*, *74*, 535–547.

Phillips, P. C. B. (1988). Regression theory for near-integrated time series. *Econometrica*, *56*, 1021–1043.

Phillips, P. C. B. (1991). Optimal inference in cointegrated systems. *Econometrica*, *59*, 283–306.

Phillips, P. C. B. (2014). On confidence intervals for autoregressive roots and predictive regression. *Econometrica*, *82*(3), 1177–1195.

Phillips, P. C. B., & Hansen, B. E. (1990). Statistical inference in instrumental variables regression with I(1) processes. *Review of Economic Studies*, *57*, 99–125.

Phillips, P. C. B., & Lee, J. H. (2012). *Robust econometric inference with mixed integrated and mildly explosive regressors*. Technical report. Department of Economics, Yale University.

Phillips, P. C. B., & Lee, J. H. (2013). Predictive regression under various degrees of persistence and robust long-horizon regression. *Journal of Econometrics*, *177*(2), 250–264.

Phillips, P. C. B., & Magdalinos, T. (2007). Limit theory for moderate deviations from a unit root. *Journal of Econometrics*, *136*(1), 115–130.

Phillips, P. C. B., Shi, S., & Yu, J. (2014). Specification sensitivity in right-tailed unit root testing for explosive behavior. *Oxford Bulletin of Economics and Statistics*, *76*(3), 315–333.

Royal Swedish Academy of Sciences. (2013). The Sveriges Riksbank Prize in Economic Sciences in memory of Alfred Nobel 2013: Eugene F Fama, Lars Peter Hansen, Robert J Shiller. Press Release.

Schaller, H., & Norden, S. V. (1997). Regime switching in stock market returns. *Applied Financial Economics*, *7*(2), 177–191.

Stambaugh, R. F. (1999). Predictive regressions. *Journal of Financial Economics*, *54*, 375–421.

Stock, J. H. (1991). Confidence intervals for the largest autoregressive root in U.S. macroeconomic time series. *Journal of Monetary Economics*, *28*, 435–439.

Valkanov, R. (2003). Long-horizon regressions: Theoretical results and applications. *Journal of Financial Economics*, *68*, 201–232.

Wohar, M. E., & Rapach, D. E. (2005). Valuation ratios and long-horizon stock price predictability. *Journal of Applied Econometrics*, *20*(3), 327–344.

IDIOSYNCRATIC VOLATILITY, EXPECTED WINDFALL, AND THE CROSS-SECTION OF STOCK RETURNS

Chi Wan[a] and Zhijie Xiao[b]

[a]*Department of Accounting and Finance, University of Massachusetts, Boston, MA, USA*

[b]*Department of Economics, Boston College, Chestnut Hill, MA, USA*

ABSTRACT

This paper analyzes the roles of idiosyncratic risk and firm-level conditional skewness in determining cross-sectional returns. It is shown that the traditional EGARCH estimates of conditional idiosyncratic volatility may bring significant finite sample estimation bias in the presence of non-Gaussianity. We propose a new estimator that has more robust sampling performance than the EGARCH MLE in the presence of heavy-tail or skewed innovations. Our cross-sectional portfolio analysis demonstrates that the idiosyncratic volatility puzzle documented by Ang, Hodrick, Xiang, and Zhang (2006) exists intertemporally. We conduct further analysis to solve the puzzle. We show that two factors idiosyncratic variance and individual conditional skewness play important roles

Essays in Honor of Peter C. B. Phillips
Advances in Econometrics, Volume 33, 713–749

ISSN: 0731-9053/doi:10.1108/S0731-905320140000033020

in determining cross-sectional returns. A new concept, the "expected windfall," is introduced as an alternate measure of conditional return skewness. After controlling for these two additional factors, we solve the major piece of this puzzle: Our cross-sectional regression tests identify a positive relationship between conditional idiosyncratic volatility and expected returns for over 99% of the total market capitalization of the NYSE, NASDAQ, and AMEX stock exchanges.

Keywords: Idiosyncratic volatility; conditional skewness; robust estimation; quantile regression

JEL Classifications: G10; C01; C02; G32

1. INTRODUCTION

The asset pricing theory of incomplete markets predicts a positive idiosyncratic volatility effect: investors should command higher expected return for bearing higher idiosyncratic risks. In the presence of costly information, Merton (1987) provides a theoretical framework where firms with high idiosyncratic volatility require high expected returns to compensate investors for holding imperfectly diversified portfolios. Some behavioral models like Barberis and Huang (2001) also predict that stocks with higher idiosyncratic volatility should earn higher expected returns. In addition, the role of idiosyncratic risk in determining stock returns has gained further importance given the evidence of Campebell, Lettau, Malkiel, and Xu (2001) who find that there have been noticeable increases in both firm level volatility and the number of stocks needed to achieve a specific level of diversification over time.

However, empirical studies have yielded mixed results on idiosyncratic volatility and there has been a lively debate on the role of idiosyncratic risk in determining cross-sectional stock returns. Ang, Hodrick, Xing, and Zhang (AHXZ, 2006) find that stocks with high idiosyncratic volatility in the current month subsequently earn abnormally low returns the following month. More specifically, AHXZ find a −1.06% difference in raw average monthly returns between the two extreme quintile stock portfolios with the highest/lowest idiosyncratic volatilities. Moreover, AHXZ (2006) show that this negative idiosyncratic volatility effect is robust after controlling for other risk factors and occurs internationally across 23 developed markets. Since this negative idiosyncratic volatility effect is inconsistent with most asset pricing theories, AHXZ (2006) findings are referred to as an "idiosyncratic volatility puzzle," and have attracted much attention.

Fu (2009), Spiegel and Wang (2005), and others criticize the use of an OLS model in the estimation of idiosyncratic volatility as it may not be able to capture the leverage effect and the time variation in the idiosyncratic volatility process. They further argue that the relationship between risk and returns should be studied intertemporally. As AHXZ (2006) primarily focus on the relationship between realized idiosyncratic volatilities and future returns, Fu (2009), on the other hand, stresses that the negative idiosyncratic volatility effect documented by AHXZ (2006) may not imply the same intertemporal effect involving conditional idiosyncratic volatility. Fu (2009) models the firm level idiosyncratic volatility with an EGARCH specification and presents a positive relationship between conditional idiosyncratic volatility and cross-sectional expected returns. Similarly, Spiegel and Wang (2006) sort stocks into 10 portfolios, based on the forecasted idiosyncratic volatility from an EGARCH model and find the exact opposite effect from AHXZ: namely, stocks with high idiosyncratic volatility earn high average returns. More specifically, they show that the difference in raw average monthly returns between the decile portfolio that contains stocks with the highest idiosyncratic volatilities and the decile portfolio that contains the lowest idiosyncratic volatility stocks is 1.33%.

Given the contradictory evidence of the idiosyncratic risk effect on cross-sectional returns, the purpose of the present study is to investigate the relationship between conditional idiosyncratic volatility and cross-sectional expected stock returns in an effort to shed light on the lively debate about the idiosyncratic volatility effect.

First, we argue that the traditional MLE estimation of EGARCH based on Gaussian assumption is highly unrealistic at the level of the individual stock. Our empirical analysis rejects Gaussianity at the 5% significance level for over 90% of the stocks traded on the NYSE, NASDAQ, and AMEX and distribution of individual stocks are quite heterogeneous. Our Monte Carlo evidence also indicates that the traditional EGARCH estimation based on the unified (over all stocks) normality assumption may cause a severe estimation error in EGARCH estimates of conditional idiosyncratic volatility and may prove misleading in the empirical analysis. The positive idiosyncratic volatility effect reported by Fu (2009), Spiegel and Wang (2006), and Eiling (2006) disappears after relaxing the Gaussian innovation assumption on stock return processes.

Second, we propose an alternative estimator for conditional volatility that is robust to error distributions. The proposed method does not require a specific distributional assumption on the stock return process. Most importantly, we allow individual stocks to have a firm specific return distribution. Therefore, the present model is capable of capturing distinctive features among different stock return processes, including nonzero skewness and excess kurtosis. Monte Carlo evidence indicates that the proposed estimator of conditional idiosyncratic volatility substantially outperforms the conventional estimator in the presence of non-Gaussianity.

Third, based on the more robust estimator, our cross-sectional portfolio analysis confirms that the negative idiosyncratic volatility effect documented by AHXZ (2006) also exists intertemporally. In other words, stocks with high conditional idiosyncratic volatilities yield low average returns. These findings are opposite of the findings reported by Fu (2009) and Spiegel and Wang (2006). We find that a long–short trading strategy that longs stocks with the lowest conditional idiosyncratic volatility and shorts those with the highest generates an average monthly return of 1.53% from July 1964 to December 2006.

Fourth, we take a further step to solve the puzzle. Our study reveals that previous studies of the idiosyncratic volatility effect fail to take into account two important factors. The first factor is the existence of a nonlinear relationship between idiosyncratic risk and returns. Portfolio analysis demonstrates that the average returns for portfolios sorted on conditional idiosyncratic volatility quite steady and slightly increase among the first few low volatility portfolios before dropping precipitously for portfolios with small stocks with excessively high levels of idiosyncratic volatility, leading to the large return difference between the two extreme portfolios.[1] The second factor is that conditional skewness may play an important role in determining stock returns, especially for low-price small stocks. We find that stocks with high idiosyncratic volatility are small stocks with low prices. Chen, Hong, and Stein (2001) and Duffee (2002a, 2002b) show that small stocks have more positively skewed returns than do large ones. Moreover, a low-price stock is more likely to have a positively skewed return distribution than a high-price stock. Therefore, a low-price small stock is more likely to exhibit lottery-like behavior by realizing an uncommon windfall profit.

According to the equilibrium model of Barberis and Huang (2008), the securities capable of delivering windfall profits may be over-priced and consequently expected to earn low returns. This might help to explain why high idiosyncratic volatility stocks have low returns if those stocks are expected to realize windfall profits. In this paper, we introduce the "expected windfall" as an alternative measure for individual stock skewness. The expected windfall is an analogue to the expected shortfall while focusing exclusively on the most profitable and most unlikely returns. More specifically, for a given percentage such as 95% the expected windfall is the conditional mean of returns given the realized return among the best 5% of all possible outcomes.

After taking into account these two additional factors, we solve the major piece of the idiosyncratic volatility puzzle by presenting strong empirical evidence of a positive relationship between conditional idiosyncratic volatility and expected returns using cross-section Fama–MacBeth regression tests. In particular, after controlling for the non-monotonicity in idiosyncratic volatility and individual stock conditional skewness, we discover a positive idiosyncratic volatility effect for stocks comprising 99% of the total market capitalization. This positive idiosyncratic volatility effect is consistent with the prediction of most asset pricing theories and behavioral models. While the negative idiosyncratic volatility effect concentrates among "penny-like" stocks, the most volatile, low-price, micro-cap stocks with an average monthly idiosyncratic volatility of 19%, an average stock price of $7.63, an average market capitalization of $93 million, and comprise less than 1% of the total market capitalization. In addition, we find that stocks expected to realize extraordinary returns by having a large expected windfall are overpriced and expected to earn low returns. This finding provides strong empirical support for the theoretical model of Barberis and Huang (2008).

The reminder of this paper proceeds as follows. We study estimation of conditional idiosyncratic volatility in Section 2. It is demonstrated that, for 90% of stocks, the Gaussian assumption used in EGARCH estimation is rejected at the 5% significance level. A robust method to estimate conditional idiosyncratic volatility is proposed in Section 2. A Monte Carlo investigation reveals the advantage of the proposed method when the errors are non-Gaussian. Section 3 presents the results of portfolio analysis based on the robust estimation of idiosyncratic volatility. Section 4 performs cross-sectional regression tests to investigate the role of idiosyncratic risk in determining expected stock returns at the average level. Section 5 summarizes the results and concludes.

2. ESTIMATION OF CONDITIONAL IDIOSYNCRATIC VOLATILITY

Conditional volatility plays an essential role in finance. The literature on estimating conditional volatility is large. Many existing methods of volatility estimation in econometrics and finance are Maximum Likelihood Estimation (MLE) based on the assumption that financial returns have normal or conditionally normal distributions. However, there is accumulating evidence that financial time series such as returns are not well approximated by Gaussian models. In particular, it is frequently found that market returns display negative skewness and excess kurtosis. Extreme realizations of returns can adversely affect the performance of estimation and inference designed for Gaussian conditions; this is particularly true of ARCH and GARCH models whose estimation of conditional variances are very sensitive to large innovations.

In this section, we study estimation of conditional volatility and its impact on empirical analysis. We first revisit the traditional MLE method based on Gaussian return innovations in EGARCH specifications. We tested the Gaussian assumption at the stock level and find that this assumption is rejected at the 5% significance level for over 90% of the stocks traded on major markets. Monte Carlo evidence indicates that MLE based on this unrealistic assumption may provide poor finite sample performance and undermine the empirical results of the previous literature. To accommodate the non-Gaussian feature in return distributions, we propose a more robust method based on quantile regression.

The data in our analysis are from the CRSP database. Monthly returns for stocks traded on the NYSE, AMEX, and NASDAQ from July 1964 to December 2006 are collected. The monthly risk free interest rate and three Fama–French factors are downloaded from the Kenneth R. French online data library. Firms are required to have at least 60 consecutive return observations to be included in estimation. The sample consists of 1,926,356 return observations for 12,051 firms over the 510 months.

2.1. Revisiting the EGARCH Estimations for Conditional Idiosyncratic Volatility

Fu (2009) and Spiegel and Wang (2006) describe the time series of firm level idiosyncratic volatility using an EGARCH specification. More specifically, for stock i, the monthly return innovation $u_{i,t}$ is measured against the monthly Fama–French three factor model. The logarithm of conditional variance is specified as Eq. (3) and stock return innovations are assumed to be normally distributed. The EGARCH model is fitted using the maximum likelihood method with return observations for every stock. The model is

$$r_{i,t} - r_{f,t} = \alpha_i + \beta_{i,\mathrm{MKT}}\mathrm{MKT}_t + \beta_{i,\mathrm{SMB}}\mathrm{SMB}_t + \beta_{i,\mathrm{HML}}\mathrm{HML}_t + u_{i,t} \tag{1}$$

$$u_{i,t} = \sigma_{i,t}\varepsilon_{i,t}, \text{ where } \varepsilon_{i,t} \sim \mathrm{iid}N(0,1) \tag{2}$$

$$\ln\sigma_{i,t}^2 = a_i + \sum_{l=1}^{p} b_{i,l}\ln\sigma_{i,t-l}^2 + \sum_{k=1}^{q} c_{i,k}[\theta\varepsilon_{i,t-k} + \gamma(|\varepsilon_{i,t-k}| - \sqrt{2/\pi})] \tag{3}$$

With EGARCH estimates of conditional idiosyncratic volatility, Fu (2009) and Spiegel and Wang (2006) report a positive relationship between conditional idiosyncratic volatility and cross-sectional returns. Since this positive idiosyncratic volatility effect is consistent with the prediction of asset pricing theories, the existence of the idiosyncratic volatility puzzle uncovered by AHXZ (2006) is dismissed.

The unified assumption of Gaussian innovations, however, casts doubt on the finite sample accuracy of the EGARCH estimates of conditional idiosyncratic volatility of Fu (2009) and Spiegel and Wang (2006). Such a unified normality assumption across stocks is oversimplified in omitting the long-observed and well-documented high skewness and excess kurtosis in stock return processes. See, e.g., Harvey and Siddique (2000) for analysis of US monthly stock returns. In addition, Bollerslev (1987) shows that the excess kurtosis of the stock return process is not just a result of changing volatility as it still exists after returns are normalized by their estimated conditional volatility. Gaussian-based MLE can create serious finite sample estimation errors for parameter estimation and volatility prediction when the innovation distribution differs from normality.

We first check the normality on the return distributions. There is a large literature on testing for normality. Two important features of non-normality are nonzero skewness and excess kurtosis. Statistical tests for normality have been proposed based on these two important index (see, e.g., D'Agostino, Balanger, & D'Agostino, 1990; Jarque & Bera, 1980. We check the assumption of Gaussian innovations at the individual stock level based on skewness and kurtosis. In particular, we consider tests for the following null hypotheses: $H_{01}: skew = 0$; $H_{02}: ExKur = 0$; and $H_{03}: Normality$. Summarized results for individual stock returns are reported in Table 1.

As shown in Table 1, at the 1% (5%) significance level, the null hypothesis of zero skewness is rejected by 73.8% (80.7%) of stocks; and the null hypothesis of no excess kurtosis is also rejected for 79.7% (87.5%) of stocks.

Table 1. Tests for the Gaussian Innovation Assumption of the EGARCH Specification.

	$\alpha = 1\%$	$\alpha = 5\%$
H_0 : *skew* = 0	73.8%	80.7%
H_0 : *ExKur* = 0	79.7%	87.5%
H_0 : *Normality*	83.3%	90.3%

The Gaussian innovation assumption of the EGARCH specification is tested for stocks traded on the NYSE, NASDAQ, and AMEX over the time span of July 1964 to December 2006. The stocks are required to have at least 60 monthly consecutive return observations to be eligible for the estimation and tests. The second row, labeled H_0 : *Skew* = 0, refers to the percentages of stocks for which the null hypothesis of zero skewness of return innovations is rejected at the 1% and 5% significance levels, respectively. The third row, labeled H_0 : *ExKur* = 0, refers to the percentage of stocks for which the null hypothesis of no excess kurtosis of return innovations is rejected at the 1% and 5% significance levels. The last row, labeled H_0:*Normality*, refers to the overall percentage of stocks for which the null hypothesis of normality of return innovations is rejected at the 1% and 5% significance levels.

Overall, the normality assumption on stock return innovations is rejected at the 1% (5%) significance level for over 83.3% (90.3%) of stocks traded on the NYSE, NASDAQ, and AMEX. Therefore, the Gaussian innovation assumption at the individual firm level is highly unrealistic and may introduce severe finite sample estimation error in the EGARCH estimates of conditional idiosyncratic volatility, and may bias the empirical results of Fu (2009) and Spiegel and Wang (2006) since they assume that for every stock i the time series of return innovations $\{\varepsilon_{i,t}\}_t$ is normally distributed.[2]

2.2. Linear TGARCH Specification

In this paper, we propose a robust volatility estimation method based on a combination of quantile regression and minimum distance estimation. The proposed method does not impose distributional assumptions on the stock return process. In addition, we allow individual stocks to have firm-specific return distributions that may be skewed, with or without fat tails, and may vary across stocks. The proposed method is also relatively easy to implement and Monte Carlo evidence indicates that it has good sampling performance.

Although our proposed robust method applies to general models, we consider the GARCH model in this paper. GARCH models, originally proposed by Engle (1982) and Bollerslev (1986), have proven to be highly successful in modeling financial data, and are arguably the most widely used models in financial applications. Since then, a variety of GARCH models have been proposed by various researchers, including the EGARCH model of Nelson (1991) and the linear GARCH model of Taylor (1986). In the original quadratic form of the GARCH model we say that u_t follows a GARCH(p,q) process if $u_t = \sigma_t \cdot \varepsilon_t$, where $\sigma_t^2 = \beta_0 + \beta_1 \sigma_{t-1}^2 + \cdots + \beta_p \sigma_{t-p}^2 + \gamma_1 u_{t-1}^2 + \cdots + \gamma_q u_{t-q}^2$, and ε_t is an iid sequence of mean zero Gaussian random variables. As noted by Duffie and Pan (1997), maximum likelihood estimation of this form of the GARCH model has the potential disadvantage that it is overly sensitive to extreme returns. For example, if we consider a market crash, extreme daily absolute returns may be 10–20 times the "normal" daily fluctuation, so the quadratic form of GARCH model yields a return effect which is 100–400 times the normal variance. This not only causes "overshooting" in volatility forecasting, but also carries this influence far into the future. As an alternative, Taylor (1986) suggested a linear GARCH model, in which u_t follows a GARCH(p,q) process with $u_t = \sigma_t \cdot \varepsilon_t$, where

$$\sigma_t = \beta_0 + \beta_1 \sigma_{t-1} + \cdots + \beta_p \sigma_{t-p} + \gamma_1 |u_{t-1}| + \cdots + \gamma_q |u_{t-q}| \tag{4}$$

The quadratic GARCH model seems computationally more convenient than the linear GARCH model, but linear GARCH may be more appropriate in modeling financial returns.

Another important feature in financial time series is the asymmetry in return distributions. To take into account this feature, asymmetric or threshold GARCH models have been proposed (see, e.g., Glosten, Jagannathan, & Runkle, 1993, Zakovian). Such models have been found to be adequate for capturing both conditional heteroscedasticity and the asymmetric volatility effect in asset returns by Engle and Ng (1993) and Bekaert and Wu (2000).

To better capture both the time persistence and the asymmetric effect of the conditional volatility process, we use the linear Threshold GARCH (TGARCH) model to describe firm-level monthly idiosyncratic volatility. Thus, the volatility process is described by

$$u_{i,t} = \sigma_{i,t} \varepsilon_{i,t}, \text{where } \varepsilon i, t \sim \text{iid} \big| F_i(0,1) \tag{5}$$

$$\sigma_{i,t} = \beta_{i,0} + \beta_{i,1} \sigma_{i,t-1} + \gamma_{i,1} |u_{i,t-1}| + \gamma_{i,2} |u_{i,t-1}| \times I(u_{i,t-1} < 0) \tag{6}$$

where $\beta_{i,0}$, $\beta_{i,1}$, and $\gamma_{i,1}$ are GARCH(1,1) parameters and parameter $\gamma_{2,i}$ captures the leverage effect documented by Nelson (1991) and Engle and Ng (1993). For the ith stock, $F_i\,(\cdot)$ denotes the *firm-specific* cumulative density function of return innovations $\{\varepsilon_{i,t}\}_{t=1}^{T_i}$ that may be skewed with or without excess kurtosis (fat-tails). For standardization purpose, we assume that ε_t is iid with mean zero and unit variance. An important feature in this model is that we do not make any assumption on the specific form of $F_i\,(\cdot)$ and allow return innovations to have firm-specific underlying distributions that can vary across stocks and thus are better capable of capturing potential distinctive features.

2.3. A Robust Estimator of Conditional Idiosyncratic Volatility

The linear TGARCH structure is less sensitive to extreme returns, but it is more difficult to handle mathematically and computationally than the quadratic GARCH model. In this paper, we propose an approach based on quantile regressions, which has some relative advantage in handling the linear structure and has the important property that it is relatively robust to distributional assumptions. See Koenker and Zhao (1996) and Xiao and Koenker (2009) for studies on quantile regressions on different types of models.

Quantile regression method has the important property that it is robust to distributional assumptions. This property is inherited from the robustness property of the ordinary sample quantiles. Quantile estimation is only influenced by the local behavior of the conditional distribution of the response near the specified quantile. As a result, the result estimated from quantile regression is not sensitive to outlier observations. Such a property is especially attractive in financial applications since many financial data such as portfolio returns or log returns are usually heavy-tailed and asymmetrically distributed.

Given the linear TGARCH[3] model (5), let $\alpha_i=(\beta_{i,0},\beta_{i,1},\gamma_{i,1},\gamma_{i,2})$, and

$$x_{i,t}=(1,\sigma_{i,t-1},|u_{i,t-1}|,|u_{i,t-1}|1(u_{i,t-1}<0))'$$

then $\sigma_{i,t}=\alpha_i' x_{i,t}$. Let $\mathcal{F}_{t-1}$ represents information up to time $t-1$, the τth conditional quantile of y_t is given by $Q_{u_{i,t}}(\tau|\mathcal{F}_{t-1})=H(x_{it},\theta_i(\tau))$, where $\theta_i(\tau)=\left(\alpha_i',F^{-1}(\tau)\right)'$, and

$$\begin{aligned}H(x_{it},\theta_i(\tau))=&\beta_{i,0}F^{-1}(\tau)+\beta_{i,1}\sigma_{i,t-1}F^{-1}(\tau)+\gamma_{i,1}|u_{i,t-1}|F^{-1}(\tau)+\gamma_{i,2}|u_{i,t-1}|\\&\times I(u_{i,t-1}<0)F^{-1}(\tau)\end{aligned}$$

We propose the following robust estimator for conditional idiosyncratic volatility.

Step 1: For each stock i, we first estimate the linear TGARCH model of $u_{i,t}$ at the τth quantile based on the following nonlinear quantile regression estimation:

$$\min_{\theta_i} \sum_t \rho_\tau(u_{it} - H(x_{it}, \theta_i)) \tag{7}$$

and denote the estimate at the τth quantile as $\hat{\theta}_i(\tau)$. In principle, an estimate for the conditional volatility $\sigma_{i,t}$ can be obtained from the above quantile regression at a particular τ (say, $\tau = 0.5$). To improve efficiency, we conduct the above estimation based on a range of quantiles, and obtain the final estimator by appropriately aggregating information over all quantiles in the following step. Such an aggregation is important in practice. In applications, this also helps to reduce numerical instability.

Step 2: Once we obtain the linear TGARCH estimates $\hat{\theta}_i(\tau)$ at different quantiles, we combine information over multiple quantiles in estimation to obtain a globally coherent estimate of the TGARCH parameters. This is accomplished most easily using minimum distance methods[4] as in Xiao and Koenker (2009). Denote the vector of the linear TGARCH estimators $\hat{\theta}_i(\tau)$ as $\hat{\pi}_i$, i.e., $\hat{\pi}_i = [\hat{\theta}_i(\tau_1)^\top, \cdots, \hat{\theta}_i(\tau_K)^\top]^\top$, and let

$$\mathbf{a}_i = [\beta_{i,0}, \beta_{i,1}, \gamma_{i,1}, \gamma_{i,2}, F_i^{-1}(\tau_1), \cdots, F_i^{-1}(\tau_K)]^\top$$

The relationship between π_i and $\mathbf{a}_i$ can be easily written out as a function

$$\pi_i = B\mathbf{a}_i$$

where

$$B = \begin{bmatrix} B_1 \\ B_2 \\ \vdots \\ B_K \end{bmatrix}, B_i = \begin{bmatrix} I_4 & 0_{4\times K} \\ 0_{1\times 4} & \iota_{i,K} \end{bmatrix}$$

and $\iota_{i,K}$ is a $K \times 1$ vector whose ith element is 1, and other elements are 0:

$$\iota_{i,K} = (0, \cdots, 0, \underset{\substack{\uparrow \\ i\text{th element}}}{1}, 0, \cdots, 0)$$

We consider the following estimator for the vector $\mathbf{a}_i$ that combines information over the K quantile estimates $\hat{\theta}_i(\tau)$:

$$\tilde{\mathbf{a}}_i = \arg\min_{\mathbf{a}_i} (\hat{\pi}_i - B\mathbf{a}_i)^{\top}(\hat{\pi}_i - B\mathbf{a}_i) \tag{8}$$

Solving the problem (8), we obtain $\tilde{\mathbf{a}}_i = [B^{\top}B]^{-1}B^{\top}\hat{\pi}_i$.

Step 3: Using the TGARCH estimates from the second step, the conditional idiosyncratic volatility can then be estimated as $\sigma_{i,t}(\hat{\beta}_i, \hat{\gamma}_i)$.

We give the statistical properties such as consistency and limiting distributions of this estimator in the appendix. A sketch of proofs is also provided in the appendix.

In practice, we may consider iteration of the above quantile-based method. In particular, let the estimated idiosyncratic volatility from the above quantile regression be $\sigma_{i,t}(\hat{\beta}_i, \hat{\gamma}_i)$. The estimates of return innovations $\hat{\varepsilon}_{i,t}$ can be immediately computed as the ratio between idiosyncratic shocks $\hat{u}_{i,t}$ and idiosyncratic volatility $\hat{\sigma}_{i,t}$. Then, the τth quantile of underlying distribution of ε, i.e., $Q_{\varepsilon_i}(\tau)$, can be updated from the empirical quantile of the ratios $\hat{\varepsilon}_{i,t}$, this is equivalent to solving the following linear quantile regression,

$$\min_{\xi} \sum_{t=1}^{T_i} \rho_{\tau}(\hat{\varepsilon}_{i,t} - \xi) \tag{9}$$

With the estimated value $Q_{\varepsilon_i}(\tau)$ of the τth quantile of $F_i(\tau)$, the GARCH coefficients are updated by solving the first nonlinear quantile regression. That is, the two quantile regressions Eqs. (7) and (9) can be iterated to achieve finite sample improvement.

2.4. A Robustness Comparison of GARCH Volatility Estimates

We perform a Monte Carlo study to compare the sampling performance of the proposed quantile-regression based estimator with that of the traditional maximum likelihood estimator. We are particularly interested in the robustness property of these estimators in the presence of skewed and/or heavy-tailed return distributions.

Since our sample contains monthly stock returns from July 1964 to December 2006 (510 months in total) and we require firms to have at least 60 return observations to be included in the sample, the number of firms' monthly returns varies from 60 to 510. Hence, we employ 1,000 simulations with sample size T, which takes value of 60, 300, or 500. More specifically, we generate time series using (i) a EGARCH(1,1) model, (ii) a GARCH(1,1) model, and (iii) a Quadratic TGARCH(1,1) model with different innovation distributions, including (1) normal distribution, (2) t distribution with degree of freedom 5, (3) t distribution with degree of freedom 3, (4) skewed t distribution with degree of freedom 3 and a skewness parameter 3, and (5) skewed t distribution with degree of freedom 3 and a skewness parameter 5. Given different data generating processes, we estimate return volatility using both the maximum likelihood method with a normality assupmtion as employed in Fu (2009) and Spiegel and Wang (2006) and the proposed quantile-regression based method. Note that the volatility process of the former method is correctly specified in EGARCH model, while that of the latter is all misspecified in three GARCH-type models.

Table 2 reports the mean squared errors (MSE) and the percent deviations (PD) for maximum likelihood estimates and our proposed estimates, respectively. As shown in Table 2, Panel A, when both the volatility process (EGARCH) and innovation distribution (normal distribution) are correctly specified, maximum likelihood estimates of return volatility have smaller mean-squared errors than estimates based on the proposed quantile-regression based method. However, the sampling performance of maximum likelihood estimates deteriorates dramatically in the presence of misspecified innovation distributions. For instance, if return innovations are skewed with heavy-tail as in skewed-t distribution, the maximum likelihood estimates display substantially large mean-squared errors. While the quantile-regression based method is able to produce accurate volatility estimates for different data generating processes, and the accuracy of volatility estimates is largely unaffected by different return distributions and misspecification in volatility equation. The PD of two estimation techniques, as reported in Table 2, Panel B, confirms the accuracy and robustness of our quantile-regression based volatility estimates when returns are nonnormal. In conclusion, our quantile-regression based method provides much more robust conditional volatility estimates across different return processes that are potentially skewed with fat tails. This result is not surprising, since our newly proposed method does not rely on innovation distribution assumptions in volatility estimation. Moreover, the comparisons show that the misspecification in volatility process have little impact on the estimation performance of the proposed estimator.

Table 2. Robustness Comparison of Conditional Volatility Estimation.

Innovation Dist.	Sample Size	EGARCH(1,1) MLE	EGARCH(1,1) Robust Est.	GARCH(1,1) MLE	GARCH(1,1) Robust Est.	QTGARCH(1,1) MLE	QTGARCH(1,1) Robust Est.
Panel A: MSE							
Normal	60	9.30×10^{-4}	8.05×10^{-3}	1.00×10^{-2}	1.33×10^{-2}	1.21×10^{-1}	8.05×10^{-3}
	300	7.91×10^{-4}	3.22×10^{-3}	4.30×10^{-3}	4.74×10^{-3}	3.13×10^{-3}	3.22×10^{-3}
	500	7.88×10^{-4}	2.29×10^{-3}	3.11×10^{-3}	4.52×10^{-3}	2.83×10^{-3}	2.85×10^{-3}
$t(df=5)$	60	1.08×10^{-2}	1.29×10^{-2}	1.70×10^{-1}	2.30×10^{-2}	8.18×10^{-2}	1.29×10^{-2}
	300	8.04×10^{-3}	6.75×10^{-3}	1.98×10^{-2}	9.89×10^{-3}	2.39×10^{-2}	6.75×10^{-3}
	500	1.09×10^{-1}	5.32×10^{-3}	8.95×10^{-2}	7.97×10^{-3}	9.30×10^{-1}	5.32×10^{-3}
$t(df=3)$	60	2.83×10^{-3}	2.01×10^{-2}	4.27×10^{-1}	2.72×10^{-2}	8.20×10^{-2}	2.01×10^{-2}
	300	2.45×10^{-1}	9.65×10^{-3}	7.98×10^{-1}	1.45×10^{-2}	2.98×10^{-2}	9.65×10^{-3}
	500	5.18×10^{-1}	8.79×10^{-3}	1.65×10^{-2}	1.33×10^{-2}	5.05×10^{-2}	8.79×10^{-3}
$sk.t(df=3,$	60	3.19×10^{-3}	7.87×10^{-3}	7.22×10^{-2}	1.21×10^{-2}	4.48×10^{-1}	7.87×10^{-3}
$s=3)$	300	1.24×10^{-1}	7.30×10^{-3}	4.73×10^{-2}	1.39×10^{-2}	5.85×10^{-1}	7.30×10^{-3}
	500	6.91×10^{-1}	8.80×10^{-3}	3.24×10^{-1}	1.5×10^{-2}	4.72×10^{-1}	8.80×10^{-3}
$sk.t(df=3,$	60	4.00×10^{-1}	1.60×10^{-2}	1.35×10^{-1}	2.75×10^{-2}	9.69×10^{-1}	1.60×10^{-2}
$s=5)$	300	3.41×10^{-3}	6.05×10^{-3}	7.23×10^{-1}	1.01×10^{-2}	8.51×10^{-1}	6.05×10^{-3}
	500	5.20×10^{-1}	5.56×10^{-3}	3.63×10^{-1}	9.33×10^{-3}	4.95×10^{-1}	5.56×10^{-3}
Panel B: PD							
Normal	60	0.171	0.203	0.152	0.182	0.433	0.171
	300	0.097	0.194	0.084	0.101	0.087	0.097
	500	0.090	0.177	0.071	0.092	0.080	0.090
$t(df=5)$	60	0.257	0.201	0.274	0.216	0.260	0.202
	300	0.210	0.133	0.118	0.135	0.114	0.133
	500	0.242	0.110	0.093	0.113	0.101	0.111
$t(df=3)$	60	0.288	0.254	0.802	0.264	0.310	0.254
	300	0.244	0.148	0.149	0.153	0.135	0.148
	500	0.260	0.147	0.131	0.151	0.132	0.147
$sk.t(df=3,$	60	0.330	0.201	0.321	0.206	0.588	0.201
$s=3)$	300	0.279	0.153	0.197	0.155	0.215	0.150
	500	0.285	0.138	0.608	0.144	0.212	0.139
$sk.t(df=3,$	60	0.395	0.226	0.312	0.237	0.962	0.226
$s=5)$	300	0.247	0.145	0.495	0.147	0.339	0.145
	500	0.516	0.142	0.274	0.147	0.181	0.140

Panel A shows the mean square errors (MSE) and Panel B shows the percent deviation (PD) of the maximum likelihood estimates with a Gaussian innovation assumption (reported in the column labeled "MLE") and that of the proposed quantile regression based estimates (reported in the column labeled "Robust Est."). We employ 1,000 simulations with sample size taking values of 60, 300, or 500. More specifically, we generate time series using (i) a EGARCH(1,1) model, (ii) a GARCH(1,1) model, and (iii) a Quadratic TGARCH(1,1) model with different innovation distributions, including (1) normal distribution, (2) t distribution with degree of freedom 5, (3) t distribution with degree of freedom 3, (4) skewed t distribution with degree of freedom 3 and a skewness parameter 3, and (5) skewed t distribution with degree of freedom 3 and a skewness parameter 5.

3. AN EMPIRICAL ANALYSIS BASED ON MORE ROBUST VOLATILITY ESTIMATORS

In this section, we reestimate conditional idiosyncratic volatility using the proposed robust volatility estimator and conduct a cross-sectional portfolio analysis based on our new idiosyncratic volatility estimates. Our firm-level cross-sectional analysis shows that the negative idiosyncratic volatility effect documented by AHXZ (2006) still exists intertemporally. In other words, the portfolios containing stocks with the highest level of conditional idiosyncratic volatility earn low average returns. A further analysis finds two additional factors that help to explain the pricing anomaly: (1) the relationship between conditional idiosyncratic volatility and returns is non-linear; and (2) firm-level conditional skewness is also priced in stock returns. However, previous studies did not take these two factors into consideration in analyzing the return volatility relationship.

We follow recent studies and measure idiosyncratic shocks as residuals after fitting the Fama and French (1993) three-factor model. More specifically, for the ith stock, monthly excess returns are regressed on the monthly Fama–French three-factor model:

$$r_{i,t}-r_{f,t}=\alpha_i+\beta_{i,\mathrm{MKT}}\mathrm{MKT}_t+\beta_{i,\mathrm{SMB}}\mathrm{SMB}_t+\beta_{i,\mathrm{HML}}\mathrm{HML}_t+u_{i,t},t=1,\ldots,T_i \quad (10)$$

where T_i is the number of available monthly return observations and $u_{i,t}$ are the idiosyncratic shocks estimated as residuals from fitting the market model. The linear TGARCH model is used to capture both the time persistence and the asymmetric effect of the conditional volatility process, as described by Eqs. (5) and (6).

Given the previously described data, for the ith stock, monthly idiosyncratic shocks $u_{i,t}$ are estimated as residuals after fitting the market model with all available monthly returns. The ith stock conditional idiosyncratic volatility $\sigma_{i,t}$ is then estimated using the proposed robust estimation method.

In our analysis, quantile regression for individual stocks are estimated at different values of τ and the averaged conditional idiosyncratic volatility across quantiles are used to combine information over different quantiles. In particular, the linear TGARCH model is estimated at its 5, 25, 75, and 95% quantiles, and the average idiosyncratic volatility across these four quantiles is used as a robust estimate for the firm-level conditional idiosyncratic volatility.[5]

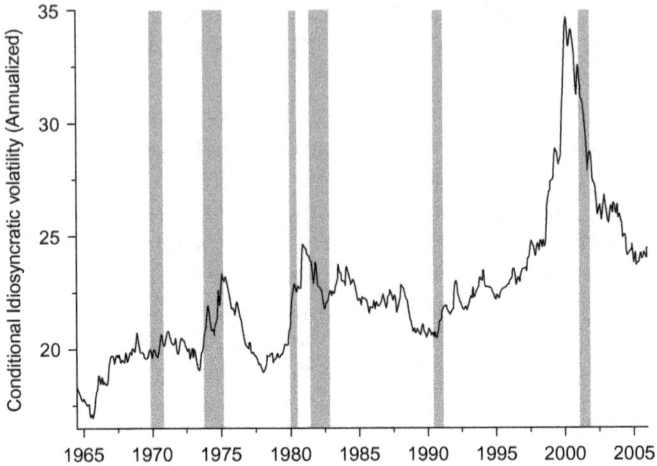

Fig. 1. The Time Trend of Aggregated Idiosyncratic Volatility.

Fig. 1 plots the annualized value weighted conditional idiosyncratic volatility across stocks from July 1964 to December 2006. It can be seen that the level of idiosyncratic volatility increased to a historically high level between 1998 and 2002 and returned to a rather normal level with a continuously decreasing trend starting in 2003.[6]

3.1. Firm-Level Cross-Sectional Analysis: The Volatility Puzzle

We next conduct a cross-sectional portfolio analysis to examine whether idiosyncratic risk has predictive power over stock returns. To determine the contemporaneous relationship between idiosyncratic risk and returns, stocks are sorted into 10 value-weighted portfolios based on our robust estimates of conditional idiosyncratic volatility. The procedure is as follows. At the end of each month, stocks are sorted based on their conditional volatility estimates for next month. We then divide the stocks evenly into 10 portfolios, such that portfolio 1 contains the 10% of stocks expected to have the lowest level of idiosyncratic volatilities over the next month, while portfolio 10 contains the 10% of stocks that have the highest level of conditional idiosyncratic volatility over the next month. For convenience, we call them decile portfolios. The portfolio weights are determined as proportional to firm market value, the product of monthly closing stock price, and the number of outstanding shares. Each month, these 10 decile portfolios are rebalanced. Portfolio returns as well as other useful information are then recorded.

Panel A in Table 3 presents the average conditional idiosyncratic volatility, average returns, return standard deviations, and the average market shares, average stock prices, average (log of) firm sizes, and average book-to-market ratios for 10 decile portfolios over the sample period between July 1964 and December 2006. As reported in column 1 (Table 3), the average monthly conditional idiosyncratic volatilities monotonically increase from 3.9% for decile portfolio 1 to 22.41% for decile portfolio 10. Surprisingly, there are low average returns to decile portfolios containing stocks with high conditional idiosyncratic volatilities. A long–short trading strategy that longs stocks with the lowest conditional idiosyncratic volatility and shorts stocks with the highest generates an average monthly return of 1.53% from July 1964 to December 2006. This return difference is statistically significant with a *t*-statistic of 4.19 reported in the last row of Panel A. The cross-sectional portfolio analysis presents a strong negative intertemporal relationship between conditional idiosyncratic risk and average stock returns based on the analysis of two extreme decile portfolios. This result is exactly opposite to the positive idiosyncratic volatility effect reported by Fu (2009) and Spiegel and Wang (2006) where stocks are sorted by EGARCH estimates of conditional idiosyncratic volatility.

Table 3 also displays distinct patterns for the average size, book-to-market ratio, and stock price of decile portfolios sorted by conditional idiosyncratic volatility. More specifically, as stocks become more volatile, the average conditional idiosyncratic volatility increases from 3.92% to 22.41%, while the average market share drops from 31.03% to less than 1%. In addition to small market capitalization, stocks with high conditional idiosyncratic volatility tend to have low average stock prices and low book-to-market ratios. In general, stocks with low (high) conditional idiosyncratic volatility are large (small) firms with high (low) stock prices and high (low) book-to-market ratios.

As a robustness check, the above cross-sectional portfolio analysis is repeated using only the stocks traded on the NYSE to mitigate the concern that the observed patterns are simply driven by small stocks traded on the NASDAQ and AMEX. As reported in Table 3, Panel B, the cross-section pricing anomaly remains. In particular, the return difference between decile portfolio 1 and decile portfolio 10 is −0.83% per month. This value is statistically significant with a *t*-statistic of −2.83. Therefore, excluding stocks traded on NASDAQ and AMEX changes neither the observed negative

Table 3. Portfolios Sorted by Conditional Idiosyncratic Volatility.

Panel A: Portfolios Sorted by Conditional Idiosyncratic Volatility

Rank	Average IVol (%)	Average return (%)	SD (%)	Mkt. share	Stock price	In(Size)	*B*/*M*
1 (*low*)	3.92	1.02	3.69	31.04	42.71	5.80	1.05
2	5.59	0.93	4.16	25.27	67.51	5.96	1.08
3	6.76	1.06	4.59	15.44	33.44	5.67	0.81
4	7.88	1.02	5.22	9.87	27.10	5.31	0.84
5	9.03	0.99	5.82	6.89	23.36	4.96	0.88
6	10.34	0.91	6.57	4.69	19.83	4.58	0.89
7	11.82	1.01	7.24	3.03	16.59	4.19	0.92
8	13.67	0.78	8.31	1.92	13.36	3.80	0.92
9	16.24	0.25	8.54	1.22	10.40	3.40	0.85
10 (*high*)	22.41	−0.51	9.49	0.63	6.86	2.83	0.77
10 − 1		−1.53					
		[−4.19]					

Panel B: Portfolios Sorted by Conditional Idiosyncratic Volatility (NYSE Only)

Rank	Average IVol (%)	Average return (%)	SD (%)	Mkt. share (%)	Average price	In(Size)	*B*/*M*
1 (*low*)	3.66	1.04	3.74	25.36	51.52	6.69	1.10
2	5.14	0.93	4.03	22.73	113.76	6.82	1.59
3	6.03	0.98	4.41	15.94	82.57	6.69	1.07
4	6.82	1.00	4.62	11.21	42.19	6.38	0.75
5	7.60	1.05	4.97	7.62	32.15	6.05	0.78
6	8.43	1.01	5.45	5.67	28.95	5.77	0.80
7	9.35	0.87	5.73	4.38	25.89	5.50	0.83
8	10.49	0.90	6.41	3.44	22.38	5.24	0.83
9	12.21	0.99	7.32	2.29	18.83	4.88	0.83
10 (*high*)	16.90	0.21	8.10	1.36	13.91	4.33	0.78
10 − 1		−0.83					
		[−2.83]					

This table presents the average conditional idiosyncratic volatility (column 1), average monthly return (column 2) and the return standard deviation (column 3) for the 10 portfolios sorted by conditional idiosyncratic volatility. The fourth column shows the average market share for each portfolio. The fifth column shows the average stock price within portfolios. The sixth and seventh columns report the average log market capitalization and the book-to-market ratio of firms within portfolios. The last row in each panel, labeled 10−1, refers to the return difference between Portfolio 10 and Portfolio 1 with the *t*-statistic reported in square brackets. The sample period is from June 1964 through December 2006.

idiosyncratic volatility effect nor the fact that volatile stocks tend to have small market capitalizations, low stock prices, and low book-to-market ratios.

In summary, using the proposed robust conditional idiosyncratic volatility estimates, the cross-sectional portfolio analysis shows that the negative idiosyncratic volatility effect, documented by AHXZ (2006), exists intertemporally. That is, stocks with the highest conditional idiosyncratic volatilities yield the lowest average returns.[7] This negative intertemporal idiosyncratic volatility effect is opposite to the results of Fu (2009) and Spiegel and Wang (2006), where conditional volatility is estimated from an EGARCH model based on Gaussian MLE. The idiosyncratic volatility puzzle becomes even more puzzling.

3.2. *Idiosyncratic Volatility Effect: More than a Linear Effect*

To solve the volatility puzzle, we take a closer look at the cross-sectional behavior of returns. One of the observations is that the effect of idiosyncratic volatility on stock returns is not linear. As shown in Table 3, Panel A, the average returns for decile portfolios sorted on conditional idiosyncratic volatility are steady and even slightly increasing within the first seven decile portfolios of stocks with a relatively lower level of idiosyncratic risk. The average portfolio returns drop precipitously as the level of idiosyncratic risk increases even higher among decile portfolios 8, 9, and 10, which comprise only 3.77% of total market capitalization of stocks traded on major markets. And the drops in average returns among the last three decile portfolios eventually lead to a large negative return difference of −1.53% per month between the two extreme decile portfolios.[8] In addition, this nonmonotonicity of idiosyncratic volatility becomes even clearer after excluding the relatively small stocks traded on the NASDAQ and AMEX. As shown in Table 3, Panel B, the observed large negative return difference is simply driven by the drop in the last decile portfolio that comprises less than 1.5% of total market capitalization.

Fig. 2 plots average returns versus average idiosyncratic volatility for decile portfolios sorted on conditional idiosyncratic volatility. The solid line plots the relationship for portfolios formed with stocks traded on NYSE, NASDAQ, and AMEX, while the dashed line plots the relationship for stocks traded only on the NYSE. It presents a nonlinear effect of idiosyncratic volatility on stock returns, and the nonlinearity is robust after excluding stocks traded on AMEX and NASDAQ. Given the fact that the

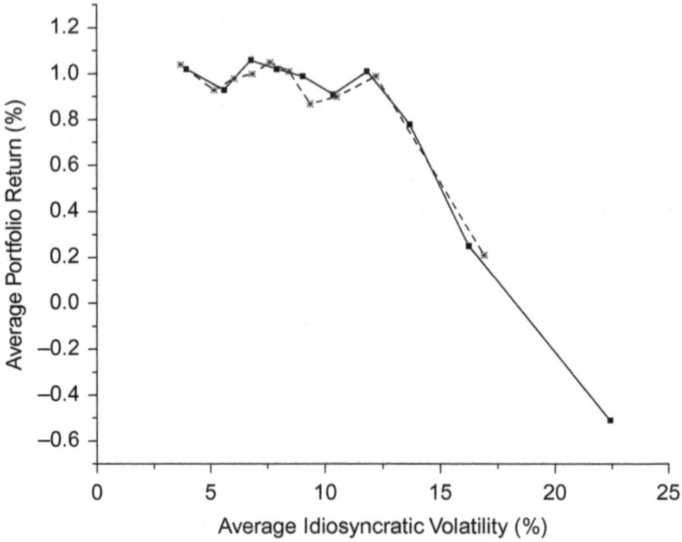

Fig. 2. The Nonlinear Relation Between Idiosyncratic Volatility and the Average Portfolio Return.

portfolios with an excessively high level of conditional idiosyncratic volatility only contribute a small proportion of the total market share, the cross-sectional portfolio analysis focusing exclusively on the two extreme portfolios may not be able to fully reveal the true effect of idiosyncratic volatility. In fact, as reported in Panels A and B of Table 3, the idiosyncratic volatility effect is ambiguous within the first seven decile portfolios, which comprise over 95% of the total market share of stocks traded on the three major markets. However, previous studies have not considered this nonlinear effect of idiosyncratic volatility on stock returns.

3.3. Firm-Level Conditional Skewness

Table 3 also presents another intriguing result: stocks with high idiosyncratic risk are relatively small-cap stocks with low prices. As shown in Panel A of Table 3, stocks in decile portfolio 10 have an average conditional idiosyncratic volatility of 22.41% per month and an average stock price of \$6.86 per share.[9] In addition, the 10% most risky stocks comprise only 0.63% of total market capitalization on average.

Given the fact that shareholders have limited liability, the stock return distribution is positively skewed. Moreover, Chen et al. (2001) and Duffee (2002a, 2002b) show that small stocks have more positively skewed returns than large stocks. Low-price stock return distributions should also skew to the right, given the already low stock prices. Intuitively, given the very limited downside risk of a stock price that is already low, investors may decide to hold low-price stocks as out-of-the-money options or simply as lotteries, if they are expected to realize extraordinary returns. As a result, individual skewness especially for low-price small-cap stocks could play a very important role in determining future returns. Barberis and Huang (2008) study the implications of the cumulative prospect theory (CPT) of Tversky and Kahneman (1992) on security prices. They present a theoretical model where investors overweight the tail probabilities and take a substantial undiversified position in securities that exhibit lottery-like characteristics and are expected to generate windfall gains. They show that such lottery-like securities may be overpriced and subsequently yield low returns. Therefore, low returns for volatile stocks might be partially explained by large positive conditional skewness.

To summarize, this section reveals that the negative idiosyncratic volatility effect documented by AHXZ (2006) exists intertemporally. Furthermore, two factors that previous studies have failed to take into consideration may help to explain the pricing anomaly: (1) the relationship between conditional idiosyncratic volatility and returns is nonlinear; and (2) the firm-level conditional skewness might be priced. In Section 4, we introduce a new concept that measures the firm-level conditional skewness, and investigate the impact of nonlinearity and conditional skewness on the contemporaneous relationship between idiosyncratic volatility and returns.

4. FURTHER CROSS-SECTIONAL INVESTIGATION ON STOCK RETURNS

The portfolio analysis described in Section 3 is a straightforward method in studying the relationship between idiosyncratic risk and returns, and has been used in previous literature. However, as we argued in the previous section, one cannot effectively control for other risk factors; in addition, the observed negative contemporaneous idiosyncratic volatility effect might be driven by the two extreme portfolios with information in other portfolios being completely discarded. Using Fama and MacBeth's (1973) cross-sectional regressions and taking into account the two additional factors, this section investigates the relationship between conditional idiosyncratic volatility and expected returns with a wide range of control variables and identifies a positive idiosyncratic volatility effect for stocks comprising over 99% of the total market capitalization.

The sample runs from July 1964 to December 2006, encompassing 510 months, and includes stocks traded on the NYSE, AMEX, and NASDAQ. The individual stock returns, outstanding number of shares, and average monthly trading volumes are from CRSP, and the annual book equity for individual firms are from the COMPUSTAT database. The systematic risk measures, including BETA, the market value of equity (size), and the book-to-market ratio (BE/ME), are constructed as described by Fama and French (1993), and later by Fu (2009). The momentum effect (Jegadeesh & Titman, 1993) in month t is captured by the geometric average return from month $(t-7)$ to month $(t-2)$.

The Fama–MacBeth regression test is conducted in two stages. In the first stage, for each month from July 1964 to December 2006, cross-sectional stock returns are regressed on potential determinants including conditional idiosyncratic volatility, the market beta, the log of firm size, the book-to-market ratio, lagged returns. The returns and explanatory variables are weighted by the square root of the firm's market capitalization at the end of the previous month. By forcing the model to better fit observations of large stocks, the idiosyncratic volatility effect examined here is less likely to be driven by small stocks. For each month t, where $t = 1,\ldots, 510$, the following least squares regression uses the square root of the firms' market capitalization in the previous month as weights,

$$r_{i,t}=\gamma_{0,t}+\gamma_{1,t}\sigma_{i,t}+\sum_{k=2}^{K}\gamma_{k,t}X_{i,k,t}+\nu_{i,t}, i=1,\ldots,N_t \tag{11}$$

where $r_{i,t}$ is the return on the ith stock in month t, $\sigma_{i,t}$ is the robust estimate of conditional idiosyncratic volatility, and $X_{i,k,t}$ are other explanatory variables including BETA, firm size, book-to-market ratio, etc. In the second stage, with the time-series of regression coefficients obtained from the first stage, we calculate the sample mean and the Newey and West (1987) t-statistic for each coefficient. The robust t-statistic is used to test whether the corresponding coefficient is statistically different from zero, and to determine whether the intended variable has significant explanatory power on cross-sectional expected returns holding other variables constant.

Table 4. Value-Weighted Fama–MacBeth Regression Results.

Model	Const.	σ	σ_2	$EW_{95\%}$	BETA	In (Size)	B/M	$ret_{-2:\,-7}$	RVol	ret_{-1}	$\bar{F}$
(1)	−0.007	0.022			0.172	0.012	0.002	0.73			–
	[−0.35]	[0.845]			[14.4]	[18.0]	[1.26]	[43.9]			
(2)	0.043	0.334	−1.798		0.168	0.013	0.002	0.712			50.33
	[2.33]	[7.63]	[−10.0]		[14.3]	[19.1]	[1.65]	[44.0]			
(3)	0.066	−0.687	−1.83	−0.1232	0.166	0.013	0.0024	0.707			24.59
	[3.50]	[9.60]	[−10.0]	[−9.58]	[14.3]	[19.8]	[2.0]	[44.7]			
(4)	0.058	0.698	−1.69	−0.126	0.164	0.013	0.002	0.712	−0.05		20.06
	[7.56]	[9.31]	[−9.82]	[−9.67]	[13.5]	[18.4]	[2.34]	[44.5]	[−1.61]		
(5)	0.081	0.684	−1.57	−0.124	0.14	0.011	0.002	0.679	−0.0597	0.0676	19.3
	[13.0]	[10.5]	[−10.1]	[−9.34]	[13.0]	[18.1]	[2.12]	[45.3]	[−1.87]	[2.31]	

For each month in the sample period, the raw returns are regressed on intended explanatory variables. The column labeled F reports the average *i*-statistic used to conduct the joint test on the coefficients before the first and second order of conditional idiosyncratic volatility. Robust Newey and West (1987) *t*-statistics are in square brackets under the coefficients.

We consider different models with different choices of potential explanatory variables for cross-sectional expected returns in our empirical analysis. Table 3 reports the results of the Fama–MacBeth regressions including regression coefficients and robust *t*-statistics in brackets. Each row of the table corresponds to a different model with different sets of explanatory variables.

4.1. Nonlinearity in Idiosyncratic Volatility Effect

The first model includes only conditional idiosyncratic volatility, market beta, firm size, book-to-market ratio, and lagged return. The estimation result in Table 4 suggests an ambiguous idiosyncratic volatility effect, as the mean of the coefficient on conditional idiosyncratic volatility estimates is 0.02 and statistically insignificant with a *t*-statistic of 0.085. While Fu (2009) reports a significant positive coefficient for EGARCH estimates of conditional idiosyncratic volatility, the result further suggests that the positive idiosyncratic effect of Fu (2009) might be driven by the estimation error in the Gaussian MLE.

Motivated by the nonlinearity of idiosyncratic volatility effect demonstrated in Table 3 and Fig. 2, we consider the following cross-sectional regression which includes high-order polynomials of the conditional idiosyncratic volatility:

$$r_{i,t} = \gamma_{0,t} + \sum_{l=1}^{L} \gamma_{l,t}\sigma_{i,t}^{l} + \sum_{k=L+1}^{K} \gamma_{k,t}X_{i,k,t} + \nu_{i,t}, i = 1,\ldots,N_t \tag{12}$$

Results of cross-sectional regression tests based on the above model confirm the existence of the nonlinear idiosyncratic volatility effect. As shown in Table 4 (row of Model (2)), the first two moments, idiosyncratic volatility and idiosyncratic variance, both have statistically significant predictive power on the cross-sectional expected returns and are jointly significant with an F-statistic of 50.3.[10]

Given the model $r_{i,t} = \gamma_{0,t} + \gamma_{1,t}\sigma_{i,t} + \gamma_{2,t}\sigma^2_{i,t} + \sum_{k=L+1}^{K} \gamma_{k,t} X_{i,k,t} + \nu_{i,t}$, the average effect of conditional idiosyncratic volatility on expected return is equal to

$$\frac{\partial \hat{r}_i}{\partial \sigma_i} = \hat{\gamma}_1 - 2\hat{\gamma}_2\sigma_i \tag{13}$$

where $\hat{\gamma}_1$ and $\hat{\gamma}_2$ are the average regression coefficients in front of conditional idiosyncratic volatility and variance estimates. For any stock i, as long as

$$\sigma_i < \frac{\hat{\gamma}_1}{2\hat{\gamma}_2} \tag{14}$$

then the value of the partial derivative of expected return with respect to conditional idiosyncratic volatility $\partial \hat{r}_i / \partial \sigma_i$ would be positive, indicating a positive idiosyncratic volatility effect. Substitute the regression coefficients and the effect of conditional idiosyncratic volatility on the expected return will be positive so long as conditional idiosyncratic volatility is less than 9.28% (annualized 32.15%). As stocks become more volatile with a level of monthly conditional idiosyncratic volatility higher than 9.28%, the idiosyncratic volatility effect is reversed as the value of the partial derivative $\partial \hat{r}_i / \partial \sigma_i$ becomes negative. Given the existence of the second-order term of idiosyncratic volatility, the cross-sectional expected return would drop precipitously as the level of volatility goes higher. This effect might help explain why there is a sharp drop in returns among the most volatile stocks, as shown in Fig. 2.

Only a small proportion of stocks (less than 15% of total market capitalization) have a level of conditional idiosyncratic volatility higher than 9.28%. Results in Table 4, Model (2) reveal a positive idiosyncratic volatility effect for stocks comprising over 85% of total market capitalization of stocks traded in the three major markets. This positive effect reverses among volatile stocks that have an average level of idiosyncratic volatility higher than 9.28%.

All other regression coefficients have meaningful magnitude and signs in the above regression test. The coefficient of BETA is positive and statistically significant. The coefficient of the firm (log) market capitalization is positive and significant, consistent with Merton's (1973) theoretical prediction that larger firms earn higher returns. In addition, the book-to-market ratio is positively related to the average cross-sectional returns, implying that value firms tend to have higher returns than growth firms. Moreover, the results confirm a positive momentum effect.

4.2. Individual Skewness: Expected Windfall

Our analysis in the previous section indicates that investors should expect a high return for bearing idiosyncratic risk, as long as the level of idiosyncratic volatility is less than 9.28% per monthly (annualized 32.15%). As shown in Table 3, this positive idiosyncratic volatility effect exists for stocks comprising over 85% of total market capitalization. The negative idiosyncratic volatility effect only concentrates among the most volatile, small-cap, low-price stocks. These stocks comprise less than 15% of total market capitalization.

As argued in the previous section, many volatile stocks tend to be small, and low-price stocks generally have more positively skewed returns than large-cap high-price stocks. As predicted by the theoretical model developed by Barberis and Huang (2008), lottery-like securities may be overpriced and are expected to yield low returns. Hence, if individual conditional skewness is also priced, it might help to explain why stocks with high idiosyncratic volatility have low returns.

In order to take this effect into account, an appropriate measurement for individual conditional skewness is needed. Empirically, it is difficult to construct an accurate measurement for firm-level conditional skewness that can be used to identify stocks having a small chance of "making it big." Zhang (2005) argues that past skewness is a poor candidate for such a measure due to data constraints and the time-varying property of individual skewness.[11] He then employs the realized intra-industry skewness as an alternative measure for firm level conditional skewness for all of the stocks within the same industry. Zhang (2005) also provides some evidence that stocks with high realized intra-industry skewness might be overpriced and expect low returns. However, by assuming companies within the same industry are equally likely to become successful, intra-group skewness has its limitations. The intra-group measure is particularly problematic since it assumes all firms within the same industry, regardless of size, have the same return skewness. On the other hand, Chen et al. (2001) and Duffee (2002a, 2002b) show that the firm size is the most important determinant for individual skewness. In addition, the intra-group skewness might not be appropriate for stocks in competitive industries where one company's breakthrough might be another's downfall. Moreover, as the intra-group measurement is calculated using raw returns, it might be contaminated by market or industry factors. For these reasons, a better measure for firm-level conditional skewness is needed.

We propose the "expected windfall" as an alternative measure for conditional skewness to quantify the upside potential of stock return distributions. The expected windfall (EW) measurement is an analogue to the expected shortfall (Artzner et al., 1997, 1999). It focuses exclusively on the upper tail of the stock return distribution, where the most profitable and most unlikely returns occur. For a random variable x with a distribution function $F_x(\cdot)$, the expected windfall, denoted as $\mathrm{EW}_x(\tau)$ is defined by Eq. (15) as the conditional expectation of x, given that the realized outcome is among the best $100(1-\tau)\%$ of all possible outcomes for any τ in the interval (0,1),

$$\mathrm{EW}_x(\tau) \equiv E[x|x > F_x^{-1}(\tau)] \tag{15}$$

where $F_x^{-1}(\tau)$ is the τth quantile of the distribution of x. For a value of τ of 0.95, EW(0.95) directly measures the expected value of x given that the outcome is among the best 5% of all possible outcomes. As a direct application of Theorem 2 in Bassett, Koenker, and Kordas (2006), Eq. (15) is equivalent to the following optimization problem that leads immediately to a linear quantile regression:

$$\mathrm{EW}_x(\tau) \equiv \frac{1}{1-\tau} \min_{\xi} E\rho_\tau(x-\xi) + E(x) \tag{16}$$

where $\rho_\tau(\cdot)$ is the check function such that $\rho_\tau(x) = x(\tau - I(x < 0))$ for $0 < \tau < 1$. Empirically, the value of the expected windfall for the ith stock in month $(t+1)$ can be estimated as follows:

$$\widehat{\mathrm{EW}}_{u_{i,t}}(\tau) = \frac{1}{t}\sum_{s=1}^{t}\left[\frac{1}{1-\tau}\rho_\tau(\hat{u}_{i,s} - \hat{\xi}_{i,\tau}) + \hat{u}_{i,s}\right] \tag{17}$$

where the time series of $\{\hat{u}_{i,s}\}_{s=1}^{t}$ contains all available idiosyncratic shocks for the *i*th stock at the end of month t and $\hat{\xi}_{i,\tau}$ is solved by the quantile regression $\arg\min_{\xi} \sum_{s=1}^{t} \rho_{\tau}(\hat{u}_{i,s} - \xi)$.

Expected windfall directly measures firm-level expected returns when "winning the lottery" and as such, the realization of the most profitable but uncommon idiosyncratic shocks. The expected windfall has computational advantages as the value of EW can be estimated by solving a quantile regression problem. Therefore, the expected windfall might serve as a more accurate alternative measurement for conditional skewness of individual stock returns.

We next look at the influence of individual skewness by including the "expected windfall" in the cross-sectional regression to control for individual stock conditional skewness. As shown in Table 4, Model (3), expected windfall has a significant predictive power on expected returns. The average regression coefficient for EW is −0.12 with a robust t-statistic of −9.58. This negative coefficient is consistent with the prediction of Barberis and Huang (2008), since a large value of EW would indicate a similarity of stock return distribution to that of a lottery. The stock may be overpriced and consequently earn low expected returns.

More importantly, after controlling for EW, the average value of the regression coefficient for conditional idiosyncratic volatility is almost doubled while that of conditional idiosyncratic variance stays roughly the same. As a result, there would be a positive idiosyncratic volatility effect ($\partial r_i/\partial \sigma_i > 0$) for any value of idiosyncratic volatility smaller than 18.77% (annualized 65%) while holding expected windfall and other variables constant. Only a very small proportion of stocks (comprising less than 1% of the total market capitalization) has an average level of conditional idiosyncratic volatility higher than 18.77%. The results presented in Table 4, Model (3) reveal a positive relationship between conditional idiosyncratic volatility and expected returns for stocks comprising over 99% of total market capitalization of major markets.

The rest of stocks are "penny-like" stocks, which are the most volatile, low-price, small stocks with an average monthly idiosyncratic volatility higher than 18.77%, an average price of $7.53 per share, and an average market capitalization of $93 million. Since these "penny-like" stocks are generally not in the main scope of financial studies, we conclude that there is a positive relationship between conditional idiosyncratic volatility and expected stock returns, which is consistent with the predictions of most finance theories.

As shown in Table 4, Models (4) and (5), the above results are robust after controlling for other known risk factors for cross-sectional stock returns including liquidity (measured as the relative volume defined as the ratio between share volume and share outstanding as in Malkiel and Xu (2004) and the most recent returns.

In summary, with the present robust estimates of conditional idiosyncratic volatility, controlling for the nonlinear idiosyncratic volatility effect and firm-level conditional skewness, we find a positive relationship between conditional idiosyncratic volatility and cross-sectional expected returns for stocks comprising over 99% of total market capitalization. This positive idiosyncratic volatility effect is consistent with predictions of financial theories.

5. CONCLUDING REMARKS

This paper analyzes the roles of idiosyncratic risk and individual stock conditional skewness in determining cross-sectional stock returns and makes two main contributions to the literature on idiosyncratic risk. For the first contribution, we show that the assumption of Gaussian innovations in EGARCH specification is firmly rejected for over 90% of stocks traded on major markets. Consequently, the EGARCH estimates of conditional idiosyncratic volatility may involve significant estimation errors that bias the empirical results of Fu (2009) and Spiegel and Wang (2005). We therefore develop a novel method to robustly estimate conditional idiosyncratic volatility in a quantile regression framework. Most importantly, in our setting, individual stocks are allowed to have firm-specific return distributions that can vary from stock to stock. Hence, the present model is more capable of better capturing distinctive features among different stock return processes. While the estimates of conditional idiosyncratic volatility are immune from estimation errors caused by unmodeled skewness and kurtosis, they are also robust to a potentially different return process across stocks.

In our second contribution, we show that both idiosyncratic variance (the nonlinear effect) and individual conditional skewness have significant predictive power on cross-sectional expected returns and help to explain the idiosyncratic volatility puzzle. In addition, "expected windfall" is introduced as an alternative measure for the conditional skewness of individual stock returns. After controlling for the nonlinear effect and individual conditional skewness, a major piece of the idiosyncratic volatility puzzle is solved. Specifically, the Fama–MacBeth regression tests identify a positive intertemporal idiosyncratic volatility effect on cross-sectional expected returns among stocks comprising about 99% of the total market capitalization of the NYSE, NASDAQ, and AMEX. Furthermore, our cross-sectional quantile regression test confirms that this positive relationship between conditional idiosyncratic volatility and expected returns is also statistically significant.

The puzzle of a negative intertemporal idiosyncratic volatility effect only remains among "penny-like" stocks that are the most volatile, micro-cap, low-price, underperforming stocks, and comprise only 1% of total market capitalization. Since these "penny-like" stocks may very likely be on the edge of bankruptcy and failure,[12] a promising topic for future research would be to control for distress risk while examining the negative intertemporal idiosyncratic volatility effect among these "penny-like" stocks.

NOTES

1. The same pattern also exists in AHXZ (2006). In AHXZ (2006, Table VIB), the average return increases from 1.04% for quintile 1 to 1.2% for quintile 3 and plunges to −0.02% for quintile 5. This leads to a large negative difference in average returns between quintile portfolios 5 and 1.
2. Not surprisingly, as reported in Section 3, the positive idiosyncratic volatility effect reported by Fu (2009), Spiegel and Wang (2006), and Eiling (2006) is reversed after relaxing the Gaussian innovations assumption on stock return.
3. Assuming a quadratic specification of conditional volatility will yield similar volatility estimates.
4. Other methods to combine information over different quantiles are possible. For example, it is possible to estimate volatility by solving a joint model across different quantiles. However, such an estimation method will almost certainly lead to an insurmountable computational burden given the large number of stocks in financial applications.
5. In this study, we estimate conditional idiosyncratic volatility using all the available return observations for individual stocks, instead of adopting a moving window to estimate the conditional idiosyncratic volatility as out-of-sample forecasts. Such practice might raise concerns about the looking-forward bias in my idiosyncratic volatility estimates. While Spiegel and Wang (2006) indeed fit EGARCH model with 60-month available data up to month t, and calculate idiosyncratic volatility for month $t + 1$ as out-of-sample forecasts, they present the same empirical findings regarding positive idiosyncratic volatility effect as in Fu (2009), where the in-sample estimates of conditional volatility are used as the measure for idiosyncratic volatility. So this looking-forward bias, if not negligible, are not big enough to change the relation between idiosyncratic risk and return.

6. A similar pattern for realized idiosyncratic volatility has been reported in Campebell et al. (2001) and Brandt, Brav, Graham, and Kumar (2010).

7. We also estimated the TGARCH model by the Maximum Likelihood method under the unified normality assumption on stock return innovations. The return difference between decile portfolio 10 and portfolio 1 in Table 2 becomes positive. (The results are available upon request.) This indicates that the estimation error caused by the unrealistic assumption on individual stock return process might indeed bias the empirical results reported by Fu (2009) and Spiegel and Wang (2006).

8. The same pattern also exists in AHXZ (2006). In AHXZ (2006, Table VIB), the average return increases from 1.04% for quintile 1 to 1.2% for quintile 3 and plunges to −0.02% for quintile 5. This leads to a large negative difference in average returns between quintile portfolios 5 and 1.

9. The similar fact between stock price and realized idiosyncratic volatility is also reported by Brandt et al. (2010). They show that high realized idiosyncratic volatility is concentrated in stocks with a stock price less than $10. They also confirm that such a distinctive feature of idiosyncratic volatility for high- and low-price stocks is robust after controlling for other explanatory factors, including firm size et al. However, the study of Brandt et al. (2010) aims mainly to explain the historical time variation in aggregated realized idiosyncratic volatility over 1998–2002.

10. The coefficients of third and higher-order terms are statistically insignificant.

11. Some conditional skewness models, e.g., Harvey and Siddique (1999), might not be a good alternative as they impose strong distribution assumption on the stock return process.

12. Campebell, Hilscher, and Szilagyi (2008) show that firms with lower profitability, lower market capitalization, lower past stock returns, more volatile past stock returns, and lower prices per share are more likely to file for bankruptcy, be delisted, or receive a D rating.

ACKNOWLEDGMENT

We thank Yoosoon Chang, Joon Park, Tom Fomby, participants of the 14th Advances in Econometrics Conference, and a referee for their very helpful comments on earlier versions of this paper.

REFERENCES

Ang, A., Hodrick, R., Xing, Y., & Zhang, X. (2006). The cross-section of volatility and expected returns. *Journal of Finance*, *61*, 259–299.

Artzner, P., Delbaen, F., Eber, J.-M., & Heath, D. (1997). Thinking coherently. *Risk*, *10, November*, 68–71.

Artzner, P., Delbaen, F., Eber, J.-M., & Heath, D. (1999). Coherent measures of risk. *Mathematical Finance*, *9*, 203–228.

Barberis, N., & Huang, M. (2001). Mental accounting, loss aversion, and individual stock returns. *Journal of Finance*, *56*(4), 1247–1292.

Barberis, N., & Huang, M. (2008). Stocks as lotteries: The implications of probability weighting for security prices. *American Economic Review*, *98*, 2066–2100.

Bassett, G. W., Koenker, R., & Kordas, G. (2006). Pessimistic portfolio allocation and Choquet expected utility. *Journal of Financial Econometrics*, *2*, 477–492.

Bekaert, G., & Wu, G. (2000). Asymmetric volatility and risk in equity markets. *Review of Financial Studies*, *13*, 1–42.

Bollerslev, T. (1986). Generalized autoregressive conditional heteroskedasticity. *Journal of Econometrics*, *31*, 307–328.

Bollerslev, T. (1987). A conditionally heteroskedastic time series model for speculative prices and rates of return. *Review of Economics and Statistics*, *69*, 542–547.

Brandt, M., Brav, A., Graham, J., & Kumar, A. (2010). The idiosyncratic volatility puzzle: Time trend or speculative episodes? *Review of Financial Studies*, *23*, 863–899.

Campbell, J. Y., Hilscher, J., & Szilagyi, J. (2008). In search of distress risk. *Journal of Finance*, *63*, 2899–2939.

Campbell, J. Y., Lettau, M., Malkiel, B. G., & Xu, Y. (2001). Have individual stocks become more volatile? An empirical exploration of idiosyncratic risk. *Journal of Finance*, *56*, 1–43.

Chen, J., Hong, H., & Stein, J. C. (2001). Forecasting crashes: Trading volume, past returns, and conditional skewness in stock prices. *Journal of Financial Economics*, *61*, 345–381.

D'Agostino, R. B., Belanger, A. J., & D'Agostino, R. B., Jr. (1990). A suggestion for using powerful and informative tests of normality. *American Statistician*, *44*, 316–321.

Duffee, G. R. (2002a). *Balance sheet explanations for asymmetric volatility*. Working paper, Berkeley, CA: University of California.

Duffee, G. R. (2002b). *The long-run behavior of firms' stock returns: Evidence and interpretations*. Working paper, Berkeley, CA: University of California.

Duffie, D., & Pan, J. (1997). An overview of value at risk. *Journal of Derivatives*, *4*(3), 7–49.

Eiling, E. (2006). *Can nontradable assets explain the apparent premium for idiosyncratic risk? The case of industry-specific human capital*. Unpublished working paper. Netherlands: Tilburg University.

Engle, R. F., & Ng, V. (1993, December). Measuring and testing the impact of news on volatility. *Journal of Finance*, *48*, 1749–1778.

Engle, R. (1982). Autorregressive conditional heteroskedasticity with estimates of United Kingdom inflation. *Econometrica*, *50*, 987–1008.

Fama, E., & French, K. (1993). Common risk factors in the returns on stocks and bonds. *Journal of Financial Economics*, *33*, 3–56.

Fama, E. F., & MacBeth, J. D. (1973). Risk, return, and equilibrium: Empirical tests. *Journal of Political Economics*, *81*, 607–636.

Fu, F. (2009). Idiosyncratic risk and the cross-section of expected stock returns. *Journal of Financial Economics*, *91*, 24–37.

Glosten, L. R., Jagannathan, R., & Runkle, D. E. (1993). On the relation between the expected value and the volatility of the nominal excess return on stocks. *Journal of Finance*, *48*, 1779–1801.

Harvey, C. R., & Siddique, A. (1999). Autoregressive conditional skewness. *Journal of Financial and Quantitative Analysis*, *34*, 465–487.

Harvey, C., & Siddique, A. (2000). Conditional skewness in asset pricing tests. *Journal of Finance*, *55*, 1263–1295.

Huber, P. J. (1967). The behavior of maximum likelihood estimates under nonstandard conditions. *Proceedings of the fifth Berkeley symposium on mathematical statistics and probability* (Vol. I, pp. 221–233).

Jegadeesh, N., & Titman, S. (1993). Returns to buying winners and selling losers: Implications for stock market efficiency. *Journal of Finance*, *48*, 65–92.

Koenker, R., & Zhao, Q. (1996). Conditional quantile estimation and inference for arch models. *Econometric Theory*, *12*(5), 793–813.

Malkiel, B. G., & Xu, Y. (2004). *Idiosyncratic risk and security returns*. Working Paper, Princeton University.

Merton, R. C. (1973). Theory of rational option pricing. *Bell Journal of Economics and Management Science*, *4*, 141–183.

Merton, R. (1987). A simple model of capital market equilibrium with incomplete information. *Journal of Finance*, *42*, 483–510.

Nelson, D. B. (1991, March). Conditional heteroskedasticity in asset return: A new approach. *Econometrica*, *59*, 347–370.

Newey, W. K., & West, K. D. (1987). A simple, positive semi-definite, heteroskedasticity and autocorrelation consistent covariance matrix. *Econometrica*, *55*, 703–708.

Spiegel, M., & Wang, X. (2005). *Cross-sectional variation in stock returns: Liquidity and idiosyncratic risk*. Working Paper. Yale University.

Spiegel, M., & Wang, X. (2006). *Cross-sectional variation in stock returns: Liquidity and idiosyncratic risk*. Unpublished working paper, Yale University.

Taylor, S. (1986). *Modelling financial time series*. Chichester: Wiley.

Tversky, A., & Kahneman, D. (1992). Advances in prospect theory: Cumulative representation of uncertainty. *Journal of Risk and Uncertainty*, *5*, 297–323.

Xiao, Z., & Koenker, R. (2009). Conditional quantile estimation and inference for GARCH models. *Journal of the American Statistical Association*, *104*, 1696–1712.

Zhang, Y. (2005). *Individual skewness and the cross-section of expected returns*. Working Paper. Yale University.

Zhang, Y. (2005). *Individual skewness and the cross-section of expected returns*. Working Paper, Yale University.

APPENDIX: PROPERTIES OF THE ESTIMATOR

Notice that the linear TGARCH model has the following variance structure:

$$u_{i,t} = \sigma_{i,t}\varepsilon_{i,t}, \text{ where } \varepsilon i, t \sim \text{i.i.d. } F_i(0,1)$$

where

$$\sigma_{i,t} = \sigma_{i,t}(\alpha_i) = \beta_{i,0} + \beta_{i,1}\sigma_{i,t-1} + \gamma_{i,1}|u_{i,t-1}| + \gamma_{i,2}|u_{i,t-1}|I(u_{i,t-1} < 0) = \alpha_i' x_{i,t}$$

and the τth conditional quantile function of $u_{i,t}$ is given by

$$Q_{u_{i,t}}(\tau|\mathcal{F}_{t-1}) = H(x_{it}, \theta_i(\tau))$$

For convenience of asymptotic analysis, we introduce the following regularity assumptions.

Assumptions

A1. Θ is a compact subset of the Euclidean space.
A2. Let $\dot{H}_\theta(x_{it}, \theta) = \partial H(x_{it}; \theta)/\partial\theta$, $\Omega_i(\tau)$ are nonsingular for any stock i, where

$$\Omega_i(\tau) = E[\dot{H}_\theta(x_{i,t}, \theta_i(\tau))\dot{H}_\theta(x_{i,t}, \theta_i(\tau))']$$

A3. For each i, $\varepsilon_{i,t}$ are iid with mean zero and unit variance. The density of ε_{it}, $f_i(\varepsilon)$ is continuous and bounded from above. There exist $\varepsilon_1 > 0$ and $p > 0$ such that

$$\mathrm{P}\left(\frac{1}{\sigma_t} f_i(F_i^{-1}(\tau)) \geq \epsilon_1)\right) \geq p$$

A4. $u_{i,t}(\theta) = \sigma_{i,t}\varepsilon_{i,t}$ are stationary β-mixing with mixing decay rate $\beta_t = O(b^{-t})$ for some $b > 1$.
A5. For each i, there exist a measurable function a_{it} such that for all θ and t,n, $|H(x_{it},\theta)| \leq a_{it}$, where $\mathrm{E}|a_{it}|^{r_0} \leq \Delta < \infty$ for some $r_0 > 1$.

We give the statistical property of the estimators in each step and a sketch of the proof in this appendix.

Step 1 estimates the linear TGARCH model of $u_{i,t}$ at quantile τ based on nonlinear quantile regression estimation. Theorem 1 below gives the asymptotic property of the quantile regression TGARCH estimator.

Theorem 1. Under Assumptions A1–A5, for any $\tau \in (0,1)$, (1) $\hat{\theta}_i(\tau) = \theta_i(\tau) + o_p(1)$; (2)

$$\sqrt{n}(\hat{\theta}_i(\tau) - \theta_i(\tau)) \Rightarrow N(0,\Sigma_i(\tau))$$

where

$$\Sigma_i(\tau) = \tau(1-\tau)V_i(\tau)^{-1}\Omega_i(\tau)V_i(\tau)^{-1}$$

$$V_i(\tau) \equiv \mathrm{E}\left[f_{u|x}\left(Q_{u_{i,t}}(\tau|x_{i,t})\right)\dot{H}_\theta(x_{i,t}, \theta_i(\tau))\dot{H}_\theta(x_{i,t}, \theta_i(\tau))^\tau\right]$$

$$\Omega_i(\tau) \equiv E[H_\theta(x_{i,t}, \theta_i(\tau))\dot{H}_\theta(x_{i,t}, \theta_i(\tau))^\tau]$$

Proof of Theorem 1: Minimization of the objective function is equivalent to minimizing

$$\frac{1}{n}\sum_t \rho_\tau(u_{i,t} - H(x_{it}, \theta)) - \frac{1}{n}\sum_t \rho_\tau(u_{it\tau})$$

where $u_{it\tau} \equiv u_{it} - H(x_{it},\theta_i(\tau))$, which satisfies

$$Q_{u_{it\tau}}(\tau|x_{it}) = 0 \quad \text{i.e.,} \quad \tau = \Pr[u_{it\tau} \leq 0|x_{it}]$$

Denote

$$\overline{H}_t = H(x_{it}, \theta) - H(x_{it}, \theta_i(\tau)), \text{ and } q_\tau(u_{it}, x_{it}, \theta) = \rho_\tau(u_{it\tau} - \overline{H}_t) - \rho_\tau(u_{it\tau})$$

then

$$\hat{\theta}(\tau) = \arg\min_{\theta \in \Theta} Q_n(\theta) \quad \text{with} \quad Q_n(\theta) = \frac{1}{n}\sum_t q_\tau(u_{it}, x_{it}, \theta)$$

We first establish consistency by verifying uniform convergence of $Q_n(\theta)$ and the identification condition of $E[Q_n(\theta)]$. Let $B(\theta,\eta)$ be a η – neighborhood around θ, and let

$$\Delta_{t\eta} = \sup_{\theta\in\Theta}\ \sup_{\theta'\in B(\theta,\eta)} |q_\tau(u_{it}, x_{it}, \theta) - q_\tau(u_{it}, x_{it}, \theta')|$$

then

$$\begin{aligned}
&\Pr\left(\sup_{\theta\in\Theta}\ \sup_{\theta'\in B(\theta,\eta)} |Q_n(\theta) - Q_n(\theta') - E(Q_n(\theta) - Q_n(\theta'))| > \varepsilon\right)\\
\leq\ &\Pr\left(\frac{1}{n}\sum_t [\Delta_{t\eta} + E\Delta_{t\eta}] > \varepsilon\right)\\
\leq\ &\frac{E\left(\frac{1}{n}\sum_t [\Delta_{t\eta} + E\Delta_{t\eta}]\right)}{\varepsilon} = \frac{2}{\varepsilon} E\Delta_{t\eta}
\end{aligned}$$

which converges to zero by the dominated convergence theorem.

Next, notice that,

$$\begin{aligned}
&\frac{1}{n}\sum_t E\{\rho_\tau(u_{it\tau} - \overline{H}_t) - \rho_\tau(u_{it\tau})|x_{it}\}\\
&= \frac{1}{n}\sum_{t=1}^{n} 1(\overline{H}_t > 0) \mathrm{E}\left\{\int_0^{\overline{H}_t} I(0 \leq u_{it\tau} \leq s) ds|x_{it}\right\} + \frac{1}{n}\sum_{t=1}^{n} 1(\overline{H}_t < 0) \mathrm{E}\left\{\int_{\overline{H}_t}^{0} I(s \leq u_{it\tau} \leq 0) ds|x_{it}\right\}
\end{aligned}$$

under Assumptions A3, we have

$$E[Q_n(\theta)] \geq \frac{\epsilon_1}{2} \mathrm{E}\left[\overline{H}_t^2 1\left(\frac{1}{\sigma_t} f_i(F_i^{-1}(\tau)) \geq \epsilon_1\right)\right]$$

which, under Assumption A4, is strictly positive. Thus for any $\varepsilon > 0$, $\overline{Q}_n(\theta)$ is bounded away from zero for $||\theta - \theta_i(\tau)|| \geq \varepsilon$.

We next derive the limiting distribution of $\hat{\theta}(\tau)$. Let

$$\varphi_{it\tau}(\theta) = [\tau - I(u_{it} < H(x_{it}, \theta))]\dot{H}_\theta(x_{it}, \theta)$$

and define $\lambda_\tau(\theta) = \mathrm{E}\varphi_{it\tau}(\theta)$. Under Assumptions A2 and A3, notice that $Q_{u_{it}}(\tau|x_{it}) = H(x_{it}, \theta_i(\tau))$, we can show that

$$||\lambda_\tau(\theta) - V_i(\tau)(\theta - \theta_i(\tau))|| = o(||\theta - \theta(\tau)||)$$

Next, notice that

$$\begin{aligned}\sum_t \varphi_{it\tau}(\hat{\theta}_i(\tau)) &= \left\{\sum_t [\varphi_{it\tau}(\hat{\theta}_i(\tau)) - \lambda_\tau(\hat{\theta}_i(\tau))] - \sum_t [\varphi_{it\tau}(\theta_i(\tau)) - \lambda_\tau(\theta_i(\tau))]\right\} \\ &\quad + \sum_t [\varphi_{it\tau}(\theta_i(\tau)) + \lambda_\tau(\hat{\theta}_i(\tau))]\end{aligned}$$

in addition, for θ that are close to $\hat{\theta}_i(\tau)$, we have

$$\begin{aligned}&\frac{\left\|\sum_t [\varphi_{it\tau}(\theta_i(\tau)) + \lambda_\tau(\hat{\theta}_i(\tau))]\right\|}{\sqrt{n} + n||\lambda_\tau(\hat{\theta}_i(\tau))||} \\ &\leq \sup_{\|\bar{\theta} - \theta\| \leq d} \frac{\left|\sum_t [\varphi_{it\tau}(\theta) - \lambda_\tau(\theta)] - \sum_t [\varphi_{it\tau}(\theta_i(\tau)) - \lambda_\tau(\theta(\tau))]\right|}{\sqrt{n} + n||\lambda_\tau(\theta)||} \\ &\quad + \left\|\frac{1}{\sqrt{n}} \sum_t \varphi_{it\tau}(\hat{\theta}_i(\tau))\right\|\end{aligned}$$

Using similar argument as Huber (1967), we show that the two terms on the right-hand side of the above inequality are $o_p(1)$. Thus under Assumption A5,

$$\sqrt{n}(\hat{\theta}_i(\tau) - \theta_i(\tau)) \Rightarrow N(0, \Sigma_i(\tau)).$$

■

Using the result of Theorem 1, we can obtain the limiting distribution for the vector $\hat{\pi}_i = [\hat{\theta}_i(\tau_1)^\top, \cdots, \hat{\theta}_i(\tau_K)^\top]^\top$.

Step 2 combines information over multiple quantiles to obtain a globally coherent estimate of the TGARCH parameters. Theorem 2 gives the asymptotic distribution of the minimum distance estimator.

Theorem 2. Under Assumptions A1–A5, let $A = \lim_{n\to\infty} A_n$, and $G_i = \partial\phi(\mathbf{a}_i)/\partial\mathbf{a}_i^{\top}$, then

$$\sqrt{n}(\hat{\mathbf{a}}_i - \mathbf{a}_i) \Rightarrow N(0,\Pi_i)$$

where $\Pi_i = [G_i^{\top} A G_i]^{-1} G_i^{\top} A \Sigma_i A G_i [G_i^{\top} A_n G_i]^{-1}$, and $\Sigma_i = diag[\Sigma_i(\tau_1), \cdots, \Sigma_i(\tau_K)]$.

Proof of Theorem 2: The result of Theorem 2 can be obtained similarly to Xiao and Koenker (2009). ■

The conditional idiosyncratic volatility is estimated in Step 3 using the estimates from the second step. The following theorem gives its limiting distribution.

Theorem 3. Under Assumptions A1–A5, let $\hat{\sigma}_{i,t} = \sigma_{i,t}(\hat{\beta}_i, \hat{\gamma}_i)$, $\underline{x}_{i,t} = A_i(L)x_{i,t}$, where $A_i(L)=1-\beta_{i,1}L$, denote the sub-matrix of Π_i corresponding to $(\hat{\beta}_i, \hat{\gamma}_i)$ as $\Pi_{i\alpha}$, and define $\omega_{i,t}^2 = \underline{x}'_t \Sigma_{i\alpha}(\tau)\ \underline{x}_t$, then

$$\sqrt{n}(\hat{\sigma}_t - \sigma_t) \Rightarrow N(0,\omega_{it}^2)$$

Proof of Theorem 3: Notice that $\hat{\sigma}_t\ \hat{\sigma}_{i,t} = \sigma_{i,t}(\hat{\beta}_i, \hat{\gamma}_i) = \hat{\alpha}'_i x_{it}(\hat{\alpha}_i)$, and

$$\begin{aligned} x_{it}(\hat{\alpha}_i) - x_{it}(\alpha_i) &\\ &= (1,\hat{\sigma}_{i,t-1}, |u_{i,t-1}|, |u_{i,t-1}| 1(u_{i,t-1} < 0))' \\ &\quad - (1,\sigma_{i,t-1}, |u_{i,t-1}|, |u_{i,t-1}| 1(u_{i,t-1} < 0))' \\ &= \ (0,\hat{\sigma}_{i,t-1} - \sigma_{i,t-1},, 0,\cdots, 0)' \end{aligned}$$

we can show that

$$\sqrt{n}(\hat{\sigma}_{it} - \sigma_{it}) = \underline{x}'_{it} \sqrt{n}(\hat{\alpha}_i - \alpha_i) + O_p(n^{-1/2})$$

Thus, by results of Theorem 2, let $\omega_{it}^2 = \underline{x}'_{it} \Sigma_{i\alpha\alpha} \underline{x}_{it}$,

$$\frac{\sqrt{n}(\hat{\sigma}_t - \sigma_t)}{\omega_{it}} \Rightarrow N(0, 1)$$

■